S0-AZY-252

A TREATISE ON LOVESICKNESS

Galen's diagnosis of *amor hereos*. From a woodcut in *Omnia Opera Galeni* (Venice, 1541). Courtesy of the National Library of Medicine, Bethesda.

A ❀ TREATISE ❀ ON LOVESICKNESS

Jacques Ferrand

Translated and Edited
and with a Critical Introduction and Notes by

DONALD A. BEECHER
and
MASSIMO CIAVOLELLA

SYRACUSE UNIVERSITY PRESS

Copyright © 1990 by Syracuse University Press
Syracuse, New York 13244–5160

ALL RIGHTS RESERVED

First Edition 1990
99 98 97 96 95 94 93 92 91 90   6 5 4 3 2 1

The paper used in this publication meets the minimum requirements of American National Standard for Information Sciences—Permanence of Paper for Printed Library Materials, ANSI Z39.48–1984. ∞

Library of Congress Cataloguing-in-Publication Data

Ferrand, Jacques, médicin.
    [Traité de l'essence et guérison de l'amour. English]
    A treatise on lovesickness / Jacques Ferrand : translated and
edited with a critical introduction and notes by Donald A.
Beecher and Massimo Ciavolella. — 1st ed.
        p.   cm.
    Translation of: Traité de l'essence et guérison de l'amour.
    Bibliography: p.
    Includes indexes.
    ISBN 0–8156–2467–8 (alk. paper)
    1. Psychosexual disorders—Early works to 1800. 2. Love—Early
works to 1800. 3. Melancholy—Early works to 1800. 4. Ferrand,
Jacques, médicin. Traité de l'essence et guérison de l'amour.
I. Beecher, Donald. II. Ciavolella, Massimo, 1942–   . III. Title.
RC556.F48   1989
616.85'83—dc20   89–31514
                                                                              CIP

MANUFACTURED IN THE UNITED STATES OF AMERICA

To
Marie Andrée and Hiroko
without whose love this book may have described our destiny;
without whose indulgence this book may have spelled our doom.

DONALD BEECHER is Professor, Department of English, Carleton University, long-time director of the Carleton Renaissance Centre for Renaissance Studies and Research, founder of the Barnabe Riche Society for the Diffusion of English Renaissance Prose, and co-editor with Massimo Ciavolella of the Carleton Renaissance Plays in Translation Series. His scholarly publications include articles on Renaissance theater, the trickster in literature, Spenser, medicine and the history of ideas, translations of plays by Turnèbe, Caro, Bernini, and Leone de'Sommi, and 22 editions of Renaissance and Baroque solo and ensemble music. (In his spare time he is interested in scholarly publishing and the viola da gamba.)

MASSIMO CIAVOLELLA is Professor, Department of Italian, University of Toronto. He has written numerous articles on medieval and Renaissance literature and has collaborated with Donald Beecher in editing and translating Annibal Caro's *The Scruffy Scoundrels* and Gian Lorenzo Bernini's *The Impresario*. He is also the author of *La malattia d'amore dall'antichità al Medioevo*. He was a founding editor of *Quaderni d'italianistica*, the official journal of the Canadian Society for Italian Studies, and serves as Associate Director of the University of Toronto's Italian Theatre Research Institute.

Contents

Preface

Jacques Ferrand's engagingly comprehensive treatise *Of Lovesickness, or Erotic Melancholy* is presented here in translation for the benefit of the many possible English readers who would otherwise have found his elaborate and sometimes ellyptical seventeenth-century French style something of an obstacle. We are convinced that while he meant primarily to instruct, he also meant to delight, and that his book can be read with pleasure and satisfaction both by the specialist and by the generalist unacquainted with the erudite medical and philosophical traditions upon which it is based. In that sense, Ferrand's text is self-contained and needs little editorial interference. Yet a learned treatise it remains, for its informing ideas have complex histories going back through the Latin and Arabic Middle Ages to the ancients; and much of the scope of that history is hinted at by Ferrand's nearly 2,000 marginal references—references that supply cryptic identification of his many sources. To deal with such a treatise in a fully annotated edition—given Ferrand's erudition and his encyclopedic purposes—is to deal by definition with the question of pathological love as an intellectual idea in Western culture, while the process of documentation involves a handling of all of the major and many of the minor sources of that medical-philosophical tradition deriving from a 2,000-year period of intellectual history. There was no satisfactory way of serving Ferrand's text critically and editorially without simultaneously creating an introductory essay and a critical apparatus that suggest by their scope a certain independence of purpose. Hence, the double focus of the book—as a critical edition of a seventeenth-century text, and as a resource book that begins with a lengthy examination of an idea in Western culture and that concludes with annotations that amount to a full compendium of research materials.

We were encouraged from the outset in the pursuit of this dual mission by our publishers and by their readers, who recognized the independent value of a full-length critical and historical treatment of Ferrand's subject, and of the extended annotations and commentaries on his sources, given that many of these materials are either little known or relatively inaccessible today. Thus, in addition to citing the references, we have also quoted selectively from these texts, we have sometimes traced their origins in prior texts, and we have elaborated upon the channels of transmission in brief interpretative commentaries. Ferrand's eclectic reading habits and the chapter subdivisions, divided as they are by topics and arranged according to definitions, symptoms, diagnosis, and cures, have provided the scope and structure of the materials that make up the annotations section—that is, Ferrand's own disposition of chapters has served as a frame for the grouping of these bibliographical materials, thereby giving topical coherence to each section. The preparation of a full research tool on love melancholy and its related subtopics corresponds perfectly with the purposes of an annotator of Ferrand's text. We have sought to serve both ends in performing our task. We could have detected a touch of irony in one reader's report, who found the annotations and commentaries not only to be the most valuable but also the most enjoyable part of the book, if we did not, ourselves, believe in their potential usefulness to scholars, and if we had not experienced firsthand the many truly curious and intriguing stories and observations they contain. We only regret that all these many contributing and parallel texts in Latin, Greek, Italian, and French—some of them admittedly rather difficult and demanding—could not also have been translated for the benefit of the general reader. But if by one decision we opted to serve the widest readership possible with the translation of Ferrand's text (and given that a facsimile of the French original is currently available), by another we decided to serve the specialist in preserving the source materials in their original languages (because many remain without the benefit of any modern consideration whatsoever). Yet even here, the surrounding commentaries will often serve to illuminate the ideas under examination in these quotations.

Hence, we have set out to serve multiple purposes and a multiple readership in the preparation of this edition. The first few pages in part 1 have been written as a brief self-contained introductory essay for those anxious to move on to Ferrand's treatise. Other readers, more interested in the idea of pathological love from a historical point of view, will linger over the chapters dealing with its origins in ancient and medieval medicine, while still others will pursue their interests in specific and related topics through the indexes and the bibliography. Undoubtedly, there will be readers who prefer the goldmine in the annotations to the treasures in the principal text; we have intended to serve them as readily as the others.

It was no easy task to sort out the often convoluted channels through which Ferrand's ideas made their ways through a host of sources down to his text, and to trace Ferrand's sometimes devious habits of scholarship required a degree of commentary beyond our initial expectations. Committed to the concept of preparing a fully annotated edition, however, there was no turning back from these problems concerning the transmission of materials. Yet, in exploring these byways, in citing generously from source texts, especially those from the sixteenth century, in adding our own commentaries, we have nevertheless tried to preserve a format that allows for a rapid identification of Ferrand's principal sources for those seeking only the quick overview or the brief account. Ferrand often worked with whole groups of authors and placed them together in his marginal references. We have honored this grouping in compound annotations, yet each author or item has been assigned a separate paragraph, so that by scaning for the paragraph identations, the identifications of all the sources should become readily apparent. Moreover, we have maintained a consistent pattern of citation and annotation within each note for purposes of quick orientation. Typically, an entry will begin with a transcription of Ferrand's marginal reference, followed by expanded versions of names and titles, then by his quotations in the languages he cites them in, and then by locations in modern or contemporary editions, a list of the variants, and our own commentary on the text, or, where no identification of Ferrand's source is given, followed by quotations from that source, where appropriate, and commentary. The translators' preface at the beginning of part 2 will provide a full account of our editorial procedures, our criteria for the selection of source editions and for the handling of quotations, principles of translation, conventions for proper names, and other related issues.

In sum, tracing an encyclopedic writer such as Ferrand to his intellectual roots has been tantamount, in itself, to researching the materials needed for a complete critical treatment of his informing ideas. We have allowed ourselves to go far in that second direction because, in the absence of any modern treatment of this continuum of intellectual history, such a study was needed to place Ferrand in complete perspective. Our purpose has thus been, in the first instance, to provide a fully annotated edition of the seventeenth-century text; but, at the same time, it has been a study on the transmission and representation of a medical-philosophical concept in Western culture down to the Renaissance, together with an extended dossier of research materials. It is hoped that the work, in its various dimensions, will lend itself to different kinds of employments in accordance with the needs and interests of the individual reader, and we venture at the same time a hope that much of the delightful and the suprising as well as the instructive in Ferrand will come through to the modern reader.

Acknowledgments

It is a pleasure for us to think back over the many stages passed through during the past four years or more in the preparation of this book, now that the work is done, and it is a pleasure to recall, as well, the many kindnesses that made our work easier, and to acknowledge with true appreciation the help and encouragement received from many of our associates and colleagues. First, our thanks to Tony Miller for her contribution to an initial research bibliography; to Joseph Dallett for his helpful perusal of our translation; to Thanos Fotiou for a hand with the Greek; to Yvonne David-Peyre for comments on sections of our introduction; to Douglas Campbell, Peter Clive, and Douglas Wurtele for the many hours of careful attention they devoted to a thorough scrutiny of our prose; to Patrick Rumble for his invaluable help with the subject index: we owe to them our thanks for many a happier turn of phrase.

Second, we acknowledge the help rendered by friends in various centers who checked out references and annotations for us: Jean-Jacques Jully in the Bibliothèque Nationale, Vivian Nutton in the Wellcome Institute for the History of Medicine in London, Yvonne David-Peyre in Nantes, Paolo Cerchi in Chicago. We owe thanks to Willard McCarty of the Centre for Computing in the Humanities at the University of Toronto, to Michael McVaugh of the University of North Carolina for leads on the works cited by Arnald of Villanova, and to Jean Céard of the University of Paris XII for his insights and encouragement.

Third, we want to remember with gratitude the many services cheerfully rendered by the library staffs at Carleton University's MacOdrum Library and at the University of Toronto's Fisher Rare Book Library. To Faith Wallis of McGill's Osler Medical Library a special thanks, as to Mesdames Nik and Tito of the Medical Faculty Library of the University of Montpellier, and to their venerable institution for its hospitality, to the staff of the Municipal Library of Toulouse, and to Mrs. Dorothy Hanks of the National Library of Medicine in Bethesda, Maryland, whose responsive processing of our microfilm requests was of inestimable value in the furthering of our work, a policy that has regrettably passed with her recent retirement; we hope our appreciation will be relayed to her. We wish also to thank our keyboard technician, Deborah Wills, and our TEXpert, Michael Dunleavy, for their patience when all these final adjustments had to be done.

Finally, we most gratefully acknowledge the financial assistance made available to us through the Social Sciences and Humanities Research Council of Canada, first in the form of a research grant for the initial stages of our work, and subsequently in the form of a leave fellowship without which a critical five-month research period in France in 1985 would have been an impossibility.

PART 1

Jacques Ferrand and the Tradition
of Erotic Melancholy in Western Culture

Introduction

Jacques Ferrand's treatise on the diseases caused by erotic love begins with the question that a reader from any era might pose: Is love a state of sickness, and if so must it then be cured?[1] For the Renaissance physician the answer lies in the definition of love itself, for by the same word was designated that form of desire that leads to reciprocal affection, to marriage, to the rearing of children, to loyalty in service, to noble devotion, as well as that form of desire that eroticizes the mind, perverts the judgment, and afflicts the body with all the symptoms of disease. Hence, Battista Fregoso could protest in his *Contramours* that he did not find "universal fault with all manner of love, but only with that which is driven by lechery and disordinate appetite outside of the limits of marriage." Yet, once the distinction is made, Fregoso is ready with his answer to the question. When the erotic appetite provokes a melancholy brooding, fires the passions, burns the humors, and wastes the strengths of the body, love "is not merely behavior resembling sickness, but it is a true disease, virulent and dangerous."[2] In that declaration, he spoke for the physicians of his age. Given the repercussions of the perturbations of the soul upon the body, there could be, for them, little doubt that those afflicted by erotomania were in need of the succor that only a trained physician could provide.

Coming to his subject as a medical practitioner, Ferrand was obliged to identify those two kinds of love; he had first to make it clear that he taught the curing only of obsessive and degrading passion, second to show that such love was an affliction of the soul, third to demonstrate that it was related to the diseases of melancholy, and that its treatment must therefore form a subgenre of that established area of medical theory and practice.

Ferrand resorted to a classification of love originating in Plato's *Symposium* that was handed down through a chain of Renaissance Neoplatonists: that there were two Venuses, the celestial and the earthly. The celestial is associated with the contemplations of the spirit; the earthly, with the preoccupations of the flesh. Plato, Christianized, led to a pervasive Renaissance classification of love as either "pudique" or "impudique," either chaste or unchaste: love that was moderate, sanctioned by religion and social custom leading to friendship or to marriage and children, or love that was recalcitrant to reason and a tyrannous expression of the concupiscent desires.[3] Again in the words of Battista Fregoso: "the love expressed by children, parents, or friends is in accordance with nature; the other, which is foreign to human clemency and benignity, though it is commonly called love, is merely a driving instinctual craving. Such is mistaken for love by those carnal lovers who take the whole man to be only what they see. Plato forbids that such perturbations of the spirit should be called friendship, which are neither mutual nor reciprocal, for often such love is one-sided and not returned. Furthermore, there is no constancy in it, and even less trust; such infatuations always end in grief and regret."[4] Such a bifurcation, with its moral overtones, was taken for granted by the medical writers on love and often precisely in those allegorical terms. It was the earthly Venus, according to Ferrand, who led both men and women into erotic fixations that offered no promise of joy or mutuality. That allegory was an elegant cover for the lack of a more penetrating analysis of the psyche and of the physiological mechanisms accounting for the erotic appetites in mankind; myth continued to serve its turn in intimating the structures and patterns of the subliminal and instinctual forces. The victims of the disease were those who were unable to quell their erotic 'desires through reason or distraction, those whose natures were inclined to succumb to the tyrannous demands created by the image of the beloved object engraved upon their imaginations. This fixation of the will, this exclusivity of devotion, led in turn to the burning of the blood and of the other humors in accordance with the constitution of the individual, thereby directing the victim toward chronic melancholy, mania, or suicide.

The Western physicians, following the Arab founders of the tradition of *amor hereos*, perpetuated the definition of love as a form of insanity arising from an inordinate desire to enjoy an object of beauty, an insanity accompanied by intense fear and sadness. Such a definition allowed for a complex interplay between physiological and psychological causes, between love as an endogenous disease conditioned by the complexions of the body and love as a passion of the soul that begins in an act of misguided volition. It was understood that the depraved judgments and imaginations of lovers came about as the result of the cloudy soots and vapors generated by the adustion of humors, for it was the burning by the passions that provoked the decline into states of depression or mania. Yet it was the fixing of the will upon the beloved object that first stamped the imagination, imprinting it with an image that displaced all other considerations, that dried and chilled the brain and brought on the illness. Any definition of love must involve both the mechanisms of perverted reason and the mechanisms of the body whereby the corruption is spread throughout the physical organism.

So defined, love is not yet an entirely somatogenetic disease, and therein lay the challenge of the matter for the physician seeking to exercise his professional control over the passions of the soul. Only through the demonstration of material causes could the physician assert his prerogative. One solution was to suggest that some individuals possess a hereditary predisposition toward the malady; that is, their inclination toward natural melancholy makes them more susceptible to the diseases of burnt melancholy. A second is to associate erotic love with other states of mania and melancholy that arise entirely from conditions within the body; namely, a surfeit of humors erupting from the hypochondries that is capable of emitting the noxious and offending fumes once they have been burned by the passions. A third is to explain love as a disease of the blood brought on by the reception of alien and thus poisonous spirits or subtle vapors of the blood taken in through the eyes that, in turn, spread their infection to all parts of the body through the veins. A fourth is to attribute the perverse longings to an overabundance of corrupt semen that is itself either the true cause or a contributing cause of venereal desire and all the accompanying erotic states of mind and body. For only when love is defined in material terms can it be effectively treated by altering the conditions within the body: drawing off the polluted blood, purging the black sludge of adustion, humidifying the dryness, and enforcing repose through narcotics and soporifics. In dealing with the diseases caused by the passions, physicians in the Galenic tradition equated deranged states of the psyche with the correspondingly unbalanced states of the humors. It was an essential doctrine for the medical practitioner, for only those conditions that were also diseases in the body could be treated in the conventional pharmaceutical and surgical ways.

The numerous spiritual and material causes recognized by the medical philosophers barely admitted of systematic arrangement given their conflicting claims, though every Renaissance observer made some effort to disguise that fact, often by attempting to weld these elements into a single sequence from definition to diagnosis and from diagnosis to cure. Fregoso dealt with his options in the form of a dialogue in which the interlocutors presented the various points of view—that love was a result of the repletion of seed, that it was a form of sin produced by Satan and his followers through the perversion of the will, that it was a form of fascination shot into the eyes and carried into the blood—without choosing categorically for or against any of these points of view. François Valleriola favored the Platonic view of love as a disease of the blood introduced through the sight. André Du Laurens preserved his fidelity to the Galenic system of the humors. Ferrand, in his encyclopedic way, is perhaps more vulnerable than the others for attempting to incorporate all of these views into a single coherent medical-philosophical system by subdividing his work into chapters wherein he treats the components serially.

Ferrand was a writer of mixed loyalties: he was committed first, though at times tenuously, to the order of discourse appropriate to the philosophical-medical treatise concerned with the descriptions and cures of diseases; secondly, he shared the humanist penchant for exhaustive examinations of historical and contemporary sources; thirdly, he was attracted to the styles and preoccupations of the Italian literary philosophers who wrote expository books on the dangers of love in the tradition of Ovid, a form of quasi-literary discourse that drew variously upon the love poets, the medical writers, the mythographers, and the Neoplatonists. In the appraisal of Ferrand that follows, it will be seen that inconsistencies arise not only from his analysis of causes and their effects, but also from the diversity of his modes of discourse. Yet Ferrand is important precisely because he allows an encyclopedic inclusiveness to win out over methodological or stylistic consistency, for it is his encyclopedic scope that allows this work to stand over all contenders as the medical *summa* in the Renaissance on the diseases of erotic love.

Ferrand's goals are, in their way, remarkable, for after a thorough sifting of nearly everything that had been written on the topic, he purports to do no less than furnish a complete account of the physiology of love—a perdurable topic as passionately pursued today as it was then. Everyday experience suggests that falling in love involves a combination of aesthetics and instincts, of occasion and fate, of gonads and ganglia driven by forces we are wont to call appetites that combine the influences of the will, the senses, and the endocrine system; we are still adjusting and readjusting those contributing elements to one another and are likely to continue the inquiry for years to come. Ferrand set about to do no less, according to the best principles of analysis of his age: arranging the causes of love according to the principles of logic; describing the channels of the body whereby the aesthetics of sight are converted into infections of the blood assessing the means whereby the fumes of combustion mount from liver to heart to brain, from the burning of the passions to the confusion of the judgment; examining the sequence whereby the memory imprints the desired image upon the imagination and thereby distracts the digestive processes, draws the blood, chills the mind, and brings on paleness and loss of appetite. The questions are indeed difficult, and we may smile today at solutions that made a furnace of the heart, a wax tablet of the brain, and, of the eyes, the recipients of poisoned darts composed of the airy vapors of the blood. But we pause before our own imperfect understanding of these same processes in demetaphorized form.

Ferrand was limited by the state of knowledge of his age concerning the endocrine system, the processes of digestion, the production of sperm, and the functioning of the central nervous system, so that while perceptions concerning human behavior could be acute and penetrating, the physiological and psychological explanations are, of necessity, framed according to a system suspended between the observations of a Vesalius or a Du Laurens and the "laws" of sympathy and the volitions of the parts that had more to do with metaphor than with physiological processes as we know them. Yet Ferrand's assessments, with all their limitations, are seldom without value and insight, whether as tributes to the thought of Galen or Plato or Avicenna, or as gestures of conciliation among conflicting theories, or as assertions guided by his own powers of logic and observation. A metaphorical order imposed upon corporeal behavior is enduringly seductive given our longings to see the body conform to a moral order. It is for this reason that the language of humoral analysis, the burning heart, the vapors, the volitions of the blood, and the obscuring mists have survived the destruction of the system that gave them birth.

Ferrand makes clear that erotic love is a compound disease, the product of causes efficient, real, internal, external, contributing, remote, and material, and that he can do no more than remain faithful to its complex nature. He asserts from the outset that love is a malaise of the body as well as of the soul, joined in their courses through a natural sympathy, and that therefore it is incumbent upon the physician to arm himself with the precepts of Plato and with the arts of Aesculapius in order to effect a cure. This double focus is an inherent part of his analysis. The awkward juxtaposition of an agitation of the soul that assaults the physical organism with a disease of the blood or of the hypochondries that redounds upon the psyche was entirely unavoidable. Ferrand defined melancholy diseases in terms of the body so that in that theater they could be treated and the disease purged. Such an approach should logically have rendered irrelevant all moral admonitions, all applications to the reason, all use of distractions and social therapy; yet Ferrand could not let them go. As with the definition, the cure would consider both components of the patient.

The received doctrines accounting for the behavior of the psyche could be refined and rationalized, but never granted freedom from the juggling implicit in the following credo by Levinus Lemnius: "For since all passions of the mind are quieted by reason, but the diseases of the body are cured by fit remedies, who can refer the causes of diseases better than to the quantity and quality of the humours? And if a man please to examine the humours of the body, and what force they have he shall find that they do not only constitute the habit of the body but the manners also of the mind."[5] What was of the spirit was of the spirit and of the body, the body. But by degrees what was of the spirit was also of the body, as Lemnius asserts, so that states of the psyche, conditioned by the complexions and humors, could also be coerced and altered by ministrations to the body. It was, with Ferrand's generation of physicians, an unbroken but challenged doctrine and still the most cogent and satisfactory explanation of the governing principles of the body.

There can be little doubt that Ferrand created his book out of other books, for above all he anatomizes a medical idea—one that had been current in Western medicine from at least the eleventh century onward. The concept of erotic melancholy, inherited from the Arab physicians principally through translations of Avicenna, can be said to have a history through the five hundred years of its currency before Ferrand, though Ferrand, himself, was entirely oblivious to the stages of its development. He knew most of the major texts, yet read them all as equal and authoritative, intent on working out a synoptic approach to his topic. Where there were differences of definition or application, he searched out grounds for conciliation by subdividing the circumstances in a way that allowed for both views. Such were his habits of scholarship. Yet if not a conscious historian of this "idea" he was nevertheless one of its principal curators in the Renaissance.

Ferrand prefaced his second treatise on love (1623), the basis of our edition, with a statement to the effect that it had been conceived as a clinical manual, urgently needed in light of the large numbers of the afflicted to be seen everywhere in society—love being one of the most common of complaints—and in light of the many who had been misdiagnosed and mistreated by physicians. A first caveat is that such had not been his declared purpose in writing his first treatise on love (1610), which was directed, rather, to the lovers themselves in the spirit of Ovid's poems on the self-curing of love. A second is that while it cannot be denied that love was sometimes treated clinically, as the case studies of Amatus Lusitanus and François Valleriola would appear to confirm, and that hence malpractice on the part of the misinformed was always possible, nevertheless one can find as far back as the chapter on love by Paul of Aegina statements against those who, out of ignorance, refused baths, humidifying foods, and appropriate recreations to lovers: such pleadings were part of the tradition.

If a clientele indeed there was, by all indications it would have been made up of members of the leisure classes—aristocrats, courtiers, and their bourgeois imitators, as well as young people, generally, in the warm and full-blooded phases of life—whether in psychopathic states of depression or mania, in various antisocial, rapturous or "poetic" moods, or simply coming down from a broken love affair, as was the case with the young student Ferrand treated in Agen in 1603. But though Ferrand creates an elaborate regime for the curing of love, for lack of a reasonable sampling of case studies, we can never be certain that medical treatment by the means prescribed by Ferrand becomes an established dimension of practical medicine. Certainly, that was Ferrand's purpose, but there are dangers in assuming automatically that his treatise led to widespread developments in the clinical analysis and treatment of erotic melancholy. To be sure, there is evidence of a certain number of individuals suffering from erotic passions actually treated by physicians—cases that would have encouraged theorists to think in terms of developing broader clinical applications. Yet the place of Ferrand's treatise in social and clinical history should be distinguished from its place in the history of ideas. *Amor hereos*, as Ferrand described it, must first be taken as one of the received ideas of his age. It may be viewed, in turn, as an *idée force*, an idea that by its popularity and persuasiveness had the power to reshape social reality in its own image. Hence, our introduction will be concerned principally with literary and medical sources, and with the development in Western medicine of the concept of erotic love as a disease of melancholy, a concept that came to its apogee in Ferrand. Only secondarily and tentatively can we turn to his work as a document in social history.

Physicians writing on insane love early in the sixteenth century traditionally placed their modest chapters in company with those on melancholy, mania, hysteria, and lycanthropy in a way that suggested close pathological relationships among them to later observers. These early physicians were, for the most part, content to record with minimal comment the views of Avicenna. He recommends baths and topicals, defamation of the desired object, and, with a view both to therapy and to evacuation, coitus; he has little to say about purges. By slow degrees the influence of Galenic analysis, with its emphasis on purges and internal alteratives, brought the Arabic approach to the curing of love under examination. Through a subtle redefinition of the disease, the purges and alteratives gained in status over the "methodical" cures such as moral counsel, travel, or social distractions, so that by the late sixteenth century those physicians who objected to coitus as a treatment on the grounds of Christian morality and the integrity of the profession had strong alternative cures to offer in the form of more direct pharmaceutical assaults upon the imbalanced humors and upon the surfeit of seed. The ascendancy of Galenic theories provided the first incentive to reexamine the methods for dealing with love, with such as Luis Mercado in the vanguard, later echoed by Rodrigo de Castro and André Du Laurens. A second incentive emerged with François Valleriola's *Observationum medicinalium libri sex* published in 1558. This writer looked, not to the Arabian physicians or to Galen for his etiological study of eros, but to Marsilio Ficino in his *Commentaries on Plato's Symposium on Love*. Valleriola devised an uncomfortable conflation of the Platonic theory of love as a form of fascination entering through the eyes and the Galenic theories of humoral physiopsychology. Yet so confirmed a Galenist as Du Laurens allowed himself to subscribe, some nine years later, to this theory favored by poets and Neoplatonists; it soon became a permanent aspect of the anatomization of erotic love. The infiltration of Ficino into French medicine was symptomatic of a general broadening of the analysis of the physiology of love that incorporated materials from a number of distinct medical and philosophical schools ancient and modern. The time had become ripe for eclectic, full-length studies that would attempt to absorb the parallel literary and mythological lore into the medical modes of discourse. That challenge was taken up by Jean Aubery in 1599, by Jean de Veyries in 1609, by Jacques Ferrand in 1610 (the date of the publication of his first treatise on love melancholy), and nearly simultaneously in England by Robert Burton, whose first edition of *The Anatomy of Melancholy* was published in Oxford in 1621.

Much that was needed for expanding the topic in these treatises came from a perusal of remote medical sources. Ferrand, alone among them, seems to have rediscovered Arnald of Villanova, as well as the Byzantine worthies who wrote of love and melancholy diseases. He likewise took careful note of the observations of the Spanish physicians, Francesco Valles, Cristóbal de Vega, Luis Mercado, and Rodrigo de Castro. Equally important was his appropriation of lore from the Italian expository books on love, notably those by Capretto, Platina, Fregoso, and Equicola, albeit all of them probably came to Ferrand through Equicola's digest of their works. They furnished him with a wealth of philosophical and medical speculations, the mythology of eros, and lore on the occult and supernatural forces that can influence the course of love. Ferrand was initially dazzled by these works and nearly foundered in his first treatise for not knowing precisely what manner of work he wanted to write, whether an imitation of these courtly essays or an imitation of the scholastic models of his medical training.

Such varied topics as philters, astrology, "tell-love" magic, the interpretation of dreams, physiognomy, and chiromancy, as well as cures for sterility, satyriasis, and the incubus were by no means new to sixteenth-century scholarship, but it was only in the final phases of the development of erotic love as a medical idea that these components were drawn into the discussion, whether as parallel diseases, as techniques of diagnosis, or as methods for winning or coercing love. Ferrand ventured to examine dreams and horoscopes, physiognomy, and chiromancy for their potential value as diagnostic tools. In the same spirit he considered whether love could be forced by charms, philters, and aphrodisiacs. He remarked the similarities between erotomania and uterine fury, and he extended his descriptions of the diseases of love to include hysteria and satyriasis, as well as the incubus or suffocating nightmare. Any sexual behavior perceived to be pathological in its origins was matter for his consideration. Inevitably, a certain degree of cogency is traded for such breadth and scope. Yet by these means his treatise was filled out, so that erotic melancholy became the organizing *topos* under which a host of diverse subjects relating to sexuality were brought into close proximity. Ferrand surpassed all others in his unwillingness to leave any relevant issues unsifted. The imprudence of some of his choices of *topoi*, together with his adventurous style, brought his first treatise under the scrutiny of the ecclesiastical censors, for many of these were forbidden subjects; in 1620 all known copies of that treatise were called in for burning. Ferrand's challenge in rewriting the work lay precisely in separating the inherently offensive content from that which was frank but necessary, or from that which was part of his medical world order and, for the sake of truth, could not be suppressed. That process depended, at the same time, on his construction of the new treatise on a rhetorical base more firmly fixed on scientific models.

If Ferrand in this second work on love appears to have abandoned his temptation to write a speculative courtly essay, nevertheless, his new eclectic medical treatise cannot escape comparison with the Ovidian, French—especially Andreas Capellanus's *De honeste amore*—and Neoplatonic attacks on earthly love that came together in the high Italian Renaissance and that gave rise to the "contramour" or "Eros and Anteros" tradition; he preserves a great deal of material in common with these works. What began among medical writers in the early sixteenth century as a specific treatment for *amor hereos* ended in a spate of eclectic and encyclopedic medical treatises. These treatises contributed simultaneously to the more general hue and cry against dishonest love that had inspired writers from Ficino and Fregoso to Leon Hebreo and Giordano Bruno. Borrowing and conflation had become the rule; and by such means Ferrand came to write his own "contramour," whatever else his intentions. Yet by just such cross-contamination of both manner and matter, the entire issue was revitalized, its literary centrality confirmed by science, its clinical reality urged by the necessities of theory. Just as the physicians had drawn upon the expository book writers, novelists and playwrights borrowed from the medical treatises the principles whereby the characters in their works could be motivated according to received scientific ideas—these authors vacillating in their thematic assumptions between the moral censure of the philosophers and theologians and the compassion of the physiological determinists. The specific contribution Ferrand's treatise made to the world of letters will likely remain beyond analysis, but that the foundational theories informing his work made themselves felt in the works of such as Cervantes, Camoëns, Tirso de Molina, Antonio Ferreira, Webster, Ford, and many others is beyond all doubt.

In 1484 Ficino published his *De amore*, or *Commentary on Plato's Symposium on Love*. Trained as a physician, he might very well write, "that the anxious care by which vulgar lovers are vexed day and night is a certain species of madness. As long as love lasts, they are afflicted first by the burning of the bile, then by the burning of the black bile, and they rush into frenzies and fire, and as if blind do not know where they are being precipitated."[6] These lines will stand as a credo for the medical tradition concerning erotic love. They summarize the course of love as a disease, confirming the reality of the sequence. The superimposition of diverse vocabularies is widely evident in Ficino, who wrote in Speech VII, ch. 2, how Socrates is like Cupid, and in ch. 7 how love is a perturbation of the blood. Aretino, the least likely of writers one might suppose to espouse sympathetic views concerning the tortures and anguish of love, wrote in a letter to the Count di San Secondo of the desire that is "poison at lunch and wormwood at dinner; your bed is a stone, friendship is hateful and your fancy is always fixed on one thing; until I am astonished that it is possible for the mind to be in so continuous a tempest without losing itself."[7] Behind his full and eloquent style are the symptoms endorsed by medical observers: sleeplessness and starvation, intense concentration upon the desired object, and mental turmoil that can lead to insanity. By contrast, André Du Laurens, in a medical treatise devoted to melancholy diseases, explains how the condition can take such hold that "everything is lost, the man is done for, his senses wander, his judgment is deranged, his imagination is depraved, his conversation goes awry, and the poor lover sees only his idol in his mind's eye."[8] He goes on to describe symptoms of love derived from both poets and physicians; his final proofs on the nature of love are drawn from Plautus. Just as Aretino knew the vocabulary of medicine, Du Laurens recognized the poet's flames and ice and quaking heart. In his turn, the bishop of Marseilles, F. N. Coëffeteau, engages in a condemnation of love on moral grounds, as the cause of "horrors, lecheries, adulteries, incests, sacrileges, quarrels, wars, treacheries, murders, parricides, cruelties, and violences" in a tone that would seem to have little in common with that of the poet or the physician; yet he too shares in the vocabulary of Du Laurens: "for inasmuch as the soul of the person who loves passionately is perpetually preoccupied by contemplation of the thing affected, thinking only of its merits, the heat leaves the other parts and retires to the brain, leaving in the rest of the body a chill that corrupts and consumes the purest blood, discolors and whitens the face, gives palpitations to the heart, elicits strange convulsions, strangles the spirits in a way that makes the lover appear before one's eyes more like an effigy of death than a living creature," and he shares the terminology of Aretino: "this miserable soul, thus tormented, follows no constant course, but drifts between hope and fear, giving now signs of joy, now signs of pain, it is one moment all ice, the next all fire."[9] So much interreferentiality between philosopher, physician, and theologian represents a complex heritage, and Ferrand was not equipped to deal with it either as a historian of ideas in the modern sense of the term, or as a literary critic. Writing as a physician, he found himself, nevertheless, the custodian of moral and philosophical premises, the curator of a rich mythological and allegorical tradition, and the connoisseur of ancient and contemporary poetry. Yet, by 1623, the publication date of his second and expanded treatise, he had managed to discipline all these materials in accordance with a pervasive Galenism to which his work ultimately conformed.

Within this frame, Ferrand the syncretist surveyed the multifarious views on erotic love from antiquity down to his own age. His purpose was neither historical nor moral, but an expression of faith in the capacities of the medical profession both to diagnose accurately the presence of erotic desire in patients—even those refusing to cooperate with the physician—and to cure such passions of the soul through the medical arts. Fundamental premises about the functions of the body were slow to change, but within that structure of beliefs based on humoral medicine there were innovations that fastened clinical practices more closely to theory, innovations that included observations of an empirical nature.

The physician, as a publishing scholar, sought his reputation either by codifying in ever greater and more comprehensive systems the general practices and theories of medicine or by conquering new territory for the profession in bringing "new" diseases or disputed diseases within the province of traditional medical definition and practice. Love had, for centuries, been a topic of medical concern, though its status as a melancholy disease was in doubt among certain of the Roman physicians. Interest in the *topos* was constant in Western medicine from the eleventh century onward, but after Arnald of Villanova there was little innovative commentary. It became clear to a number of sixteenth-century writers that love melancholy was due for more cogent and extensive medical analysis. Ferrand's bid for recognition resides exclusively in his campaign to conquer love for the medical profession by providing an indisputable anatomization of the erotic drives as pathogenetic forces that can lead to love melancholy or love mania, diseases that could also be made to respond to a precise regimen for their cures compounded of all the known treatments for love: methodical, surgical, and pharmaceutical.

I

Jacques Ferrand

The Man, His Treatise, and Ecclesiastical Censorship

Early Allusions and Recent Scholarship

We would be grateful today for information on the reception of Ferrand's treatise by his contemporaries, but to our knowledge no information of that nature has come down to us. This is not to suppose that he was without esteem in his day, or that no use was made of him in subsequent works, given that many another treatise of similar scope and erudition likewise failed to enter into the record of the age, or was plundered anonymously by successors. But there is irony in the fact that Ferrand had so liberally employed his margins to credit the work of others, and that only one writer would follow who would return that favor. The fact is, however, that Ferrand's kind of scholarship was going out of vogue. His treatise appears not only as a kind of final and ultimate statement in a cumulative scholarly tradition concerned with the diseases caused by amorous desire, but it also arrives at the end of an era of encyclopedic humanism in general. The antiquarian passion that gave rise to Ferrand's methodologies was, in the age of Bacon and Descartes, under intense review; it was in fact crumbling under the weight of its own agglomerative and incremental habits. The substance of Ferrand's fundamental ideas was still very much apparent in *Les passions de l'ame* (1644), but Descartes assumed a new freedom to expound according to his own analytical reasoning on this ancient topic without constant reference to past authorities.[1] Only one further writer on the diseases of love had the courage to bring forward the entire weight of the past represented in Ferrand's treatise, namely Robert Burton. By his time that sort of literary acquisitiveness had already taken on a somewhat eccentric look. Hence, it is not surprising that in his pages alone are to be found the only published references by a contemporary to Ferrand's *De la maladie d'amour ou melancholie erotique*.

During the period following the publication of Ferrand's treatise

14

there continued in the medical schools an active interest in psychosomatic diseases, with a special concentration on melancholy and hysteria.
Among the 1,100 medical dissertations of psychiatric interest printed before 1750, as cataloged by Oskar Diethelm, there are to be found some 42
dealing with excessive love and bearing such titles as *De malo aphrodiseo*
(Utrecht, 1697), or *De amore insano eiusque cure* (Tubingen, 1633), or *Aeger
melancholia amatoria variisque symptomatibus gravioribus macitatus* (Erfurt,
1701).[2] It is perhaps significant that nearly all of the medical writers influencing Ferrand were active in the Mediterranean countries, while in the
seventeenth century (judging by the trends in Diethelm's list) the subject
appears to have moved on to the northern schools. These treatises are
not easily found today, but in the ones we examined there were no traces
of Ferrand.

The absence of allusions in the contemporary record is by no means
proof that Ferrand did not make his mark, either with the medical specialist or with a general reading public. What Louis Wright states about
popularized scientific writing and the common Elizabethan reader will
undoubtedly hold for the common French reader of the period: "not
merely were a few great minds making investigations that were to become the foundations of modern science, but the rank and file of the
citizenry were displaying a curiosity about the natural world that was
to prove a seed ground favorable to the growth of a popular interest in
things scientific."[3] Ferrand's treatise is learned, yet accessible and full of
variety, and it deals with a topic of eternal interest. There is no reason to think he did not attract a readership among the book-purchasing
clientele of the early seventeenth century.[4]

Perhaps the strongest indication of this popular favor is that Ferrand
was chosen from a host of possible candidates for translation into English. It was the work of Edmund Chilmead, and appeared in Oxford in
1640—some seventeen years after the original publication in Paris.[5] By
implication, Ferrand possessed all the prerequisites in the eyes of this
professional translator (undoubtedly working in commercial collaboration with his printer) for success with an English readership. We cannot
imagine Chilmead otherwise engaging in so arduous a task, and at such
great risk in terms both of time and of money.

The English, following the French, had already demonstrated a substantial appetite for treatises dealing with melancholy, the derangements
of the humors, or the inner workings of the soul, an appetite that could
not be entirely satisfied by native writers. The French, in the second half
of the sixteenth century, had imported, through translation, the works
of Lemnius, Fregoso, Equicola, Aeneas Sylvius, Huarte, and others. In
England, the treatise on the humors by Lemnius had been translated as
The Touchstone of Complexions as early as 1576 (from the Latin original of
1561),[6] Juan Huarte's treatise appeared as *The Examination of Men's Wits*

in 1594 (from the Spanish of 1575),[7] André Du Laurens's as *A Discourse of the Preservation of the Sight; of Melancholike Diseases; of Rheumes and of Old Age* in 1599 (from the French of 1597),[8] Pierre Charron's as *Of Wisdome, Three Bookes* in 1606 (from the French of 1601),[9] F. N. Coëffeteau's as *A Table of Humane Passions* in 1621 (from the French of 1619).[10] There were, of course, others, some translated as soon as they could cross the channel, standing as witness to the presumed eagerness with which these works were sought, or at least as testimony of the hopes and aspirations of the printers to turn a dollar on these foreign imports that absorbed the skills of some of England's best scholars and translators. Ferrand's book takes its place in this commercial-scholarly channel of cultural transmission.[11]

Given Robert Burton's voracious reading habits and compulsive interest in all that had to do with melancholy, it is not surprising that allusions to Ferrand should begin to appear in his *Anatomy of Melancholy* in the fourth edition of 1632. Yet the references are slight. He mentions Ferrand in conjunction with "atomi in the seed" and singles him out for his contribution to the pharmaceutical cures of love.[12] It is not much, considering the degree to which the two treatises share a common subject. There is the possibility of greater debt buried below the ventriloquistic surface of voices and references that characterizes Burton's style, though given the long history of the idea with its many medical sources, there is no reason to think that Burton could not have produced what he did concerning love melancholy without the help of Ferrand. In effect, both writers belonged to a well-established and "anonymous" medical tradition concerning love insofar as it was beyond either of their powers or purposes to furnish a truly historical anatomization of the origins and critical moments of that movement of thought. After Ferrand, only Burton had the energy to peruse the vast documentation traditionally attached to the *topos*, but for reasons differing from Ferrand's. In the latter we have the efforts of a physician who firmly believed in the terms of his argument as pertaining to theoretical and practical medicine, a writer perhaps not unmindful of the popular dimensions of his subject, but for the most part disciplined by the standards of his profession. A similar case has been made for Burton, but one that is only partly convincing when one considers the stylistic procedures that associate the entire work with concerns more literary than scientific.[13] Burton is more interested in the symbolic dialogue between a melancholy self and a melancholy world, more interested in creating a work that teases the reader with its play of forms and realities than in creating a manual that defines a disease in a way leading to clinical cures. Burton's vision is so sweeping that melancholy itself becomes the *status quo* of human existence, whereas Ferrand continues to consider it an aberrant state that could be cured in the name of health and society by medical rather than by literary means.

Apart from these references by Burton, it would appear that Ferrand's name was kept alive over the intervening years down to the early nineteenth century only through brief biographical and bibliographical entries in medical and general dictionaries, such as in Pierre Bayle's great *Dictionnaire historique et critique* of 1697, translated into English as *The Dictionary Historical and Critical*, published in London in 1736. There we read of Ferrand's book that "the historians of the physicians have as yet made no mention of it," and that "it deserved however to be taken notice of better than many others which they have mentioned." Ferrand receives mention again in the *Dictionnaire historique de la médecine ancienne et moderne* of N. F. J. Eloy, published in Mons in 1778. We presume there were other such citations, but if they resemble the two cited here, they contain little that will shed true critical insight or historical perspective upon Ferrand's work and reputation. Bayle, for example, takes up his own interests immediately in speaking of erotic passion as a result of the Fall and as "a new spring very necessary to give motion to nature," a topic Ferrand had put behind him in the first pages of his work.

It is not until 1838, with the publication of Esquirol's *Des maladies mentales* (appearing in English seven years later as *Mental Maladies: A Treatise on Insanity*),[14] that Ferrand's name reappears in the context of a sustained analysis of erotic monomania as a chronic cerebral affection. Esquirol carefully describes the causes and symptoms, makes distinctions between those whose imaginations are fixed to a single identifiable object, and those who are suffering from generalized erotic delirium. It is significant, however, that he offers nothing essential to the description of the condition that is not fully anticipated by the Renaissance physicians, and that he does not go much beyond them in relating the disturbances affecting reason, memory, and imagination to the derangement of the total organism and personality. He, too, deals in isolated pathological systems without linking the multiple causal factors in individual cases. Of interest here is the fact that he knew much of the earlier medical tradition such as it was recorded by Ferrand; he relates as perfectly apt to the condition under examination the example of Sappho, whose leap from the Leucadian rock he considered a form of cure by "strong moral shock," the story of Antiochus and Stratonice, Galen's treatment of the wife of Justus, Valleriola's observation on the lovesick merchant of Arles, and the case study which concludes the fourteenth chapter of Ferrand's 1623 treatise. Equally significant is the fact that only two bibliographical references appear in this entire chapter, the first to an article on satyriasis in a modern dictionary and the second to Ferrand, thereby raising the prospect that much of what Esquirol knew about the medical tradition concerning the diseases of erotomania he had gleaned from the *Traicté de la maladie d'amour ou melancholie erotique*.

There can be little doubt that Esquirol, as an early nineteenth-century observer, was interested in the irrational and hidden forces of the mind that corresponded to the emergence of Romanticism and to the "romanticization" of the entire psyche that was in large part induced by the literary and cultural biases of his age. The affinity with Ferrand may well have been owing to an intuitive recognition that the Renaissance physicians wrote out of a sense of the cultural preconditions that encourage the psychic calamities peculiar to an age. Just as Ferrand recognized, two centuries earlier, that youth raised in leisure and nourished on courtly and poetic sentiments are vulnerable to certain erotic affectations and disorders, so Esquirol points out that erotic monomania is largely an affliction of the young "who lead a life of indolence, and exhalt the imagination by reading romances, and have received a voluptuous and effeminate education."[15] Just how much of this cultural scope of analysis, by comparison with the narrowness of the eighteenth-century treatises on erotic disorders, Esquirol learned through his contact with Ferrand is difficult to assess. Ferrand may have supplied only corroborating evidence, though given his literary as well as his Galenic orientation, he may have taught more than meets the eye concerning the usefulness of the cumulative literary record in demonstrating the generic and cultural nature of this psychic disorder.

In a series of examples not derived from Ferrand, Esquirol sets out to demonstrate that the condition has always been both social and literary as well as pathological, and that in certain cultural periods it is particularly widespread. "Tasso breathes forth his love and despair for fourteen years. Cervantes has given the most varied description of this disease, which prevailed almost as an epidemic in his time. . . . In the case of Héloïse and Abailard, the erotomania associates itself with the religious sentiments which prevail at this period during which they lived."[16] In justifying Ferrand's assertion that erotic disorders had reached epidemic proportions in the Renaissance, Esquirol establishes, at the same time, the correlation between the cultural biases of an age and the inclination to certain kinds of psychic disorders. That Ferrand anatomized the epidemic manifestations of erotic love apparent in the age of Cervantes must have contributed to Esquirol's own awareness that he spoke for an age equally disposed to the cultivation of supercharged romantic attachments. His task must then, in a sense, resemble Ferrand's, which was to broaden the definition of erotic monomania in order to form the medical counterpart to the aberrancies instigated by the romantic impulses of his own age. Such a purpose must entail a break with the eighteenth-century preoccupation with nymphomania and satyriasis in order to bring within clinical consideration those suffering from a misplaced committment of the soul to an impossible object of love.[17] To this end, Esquirol concentrated his case studies upon those who become depressed or distracted through frustrated devotion to another person or who experience illusions of requited love where they are, in fact, looked upon with indifference or scorn. Certainly in parallel with, and possibly through, the mediation of Ferrand, Esquirol distinguished between the eroticism generated by random instinctual cravings and the eroticism that is a product of sentiment and aesthetic ideals.

Esquirol, like Ferrand, could demonstrate only partially the relationship between this "chronic cerebral affection . . . characterized by excessive sexual passion"[18] and the physiological degeneration that leads to wasting, insomnia, and death, but he clearly recognized that therapy must include both psychological and physiological measures. The similarity between these two authors concerning regimens of cure is immediately apparent. There is, in effect, no category of treatment in Esquirol that is not included in Ferrand. Esquirol concedes that the most efficient cure is to grant to the patient the object of desire in marriage, but that where such a union is impossible, the physician should employ someone to weaken the impression of that object through dispraise. He, in turn, recommends isolation, diversion, travel, manual labor, and shock therapy. For the body he specifies prolonged bathing in tepid water, a diet without meat to calm the carnal appetites, and various sorts of tonics to build up the body. When the erethism of the sexual organs contributes to the condition, he prescribes cold sit baths and enemas.

There is, to be sure, the danger of overstating the case for Ferrand's influence on Esquirol, an influence that is acknowledged specifically only in a single brief reference. Esquirol, for the most part, bases his section on erotic monomania on contemporary case studies. He does not share with Ferrand the same language of the humors, and indeed confesses to his own ignorance of the exact physiological disfunctions that give rise to chronic erotic dementia. It is clear from his account that these are not remote studies, but that many such cases, especially of "women who had been affected primarily with chronic erotomania" had been assigned to his care.[19] Nevertheless, Ferrand's treatise remains the only early and comprehensive source mentioned in Esquirol's chapter, and there exists between the two writers a largely synonymous view of the *maladie d'amour* as interpreted in terms of their respective social contexts and medical vocabularies, thereby maintaining the probability that Ferrand, through Esquirol, had a far greater influence on psychological thought in the nineteenth century than can be formally documented.

A second and somewhat more surprising use of Ferrand's name appears in *Les mystères de Paris*, a novel published in 1843 by the celebrated Eugène Sue. There we find the portrait of a bizarre notary, a miser whose outward life was calm enough, but who suffered from a bitter and impure ferment in the blood and a devouring heat that rose up to the brain. "Rampant desire, brutal ardor, wild contempt—such were the different phases of love in the man."[20] Sue named his amorous neurotic

Jacques Ferrand, allowing for no mistake in the origins of the portrait. Nevertheless, the striking fact remains that Sue, who was trained as a doctor and who came from a family of physicians going back several generations, knew Jacques Ferrand, whether firsthand or through an intermediary source, and that he recognized in Ferrand's heritage of the composite medical description of the erotic lover, the basis of an engaging character type whose luxurious fixations would intrigue readers. He had, in effect, rediscovered in the pages of an early seventeenth-century physician what the Elizabethan dramatists, in particular, had discovered in the contemporary medical tradition: a form of character motivation based on a scientific analysis of this unique manifestation of the erotic passions. Insofar as Esquirol could subscribe to the entire diagnosis of erotic love proposed by Ferrand, there is no reason to believe that Sue did not believe in the reality of the psychic circumstances that generate erotic monomania or hysteria. It may well be that we need look no further than Esquirol's great work for Sue's source, and that, moreover, we may suppose that it was in the pages of *Des maladies mentales* that he found the name of Jacques Ferrand. That point could, perhaps, be demonstrated more forcefully through a close examination of Sue's character in light of details presented in Esquirol's case studies in order to evaluate his acquaintance with the work. But whatever Sue's exact sources, his treatment of the erotomaniac in the name of Ferrand is undeniable testimony of at least a certain kind of status which Ferrand maintained in the nineteenth century.

Later in the century, Ferrand became the object of bibliographers, archivists, and regional historians, and his name continues to appear in dictionaries and medical encyclopedias as a scholar whose work is recommended for perusal at least for antiquarian and philological purposes. Some of these will be mentioned when we come to deal with Ferrand's sketchy biography. A lengthy citation from Ferrand's twentieth chapter appears in the *Dictionnaire d'Ancien Français* (p. 109), published in Paris in 1875. It is not before the twentieth century, however, that scholars return to him as a fount of Renaissance ideas regarding culture, medicine, and melancholy.

To our knowledge, the first among recent scholars to note the importance of Ferrand was John Livingston Lowes in his now well-known article, published in 1914, that led the way to the rediscovery of *amor hereos* as a medical-literary idea.[21] But the first direct employment of Ferrand's materials appear in Lawrence Babb's *The Elizabethan Malady*, appearing in 1951, which includes a chapter largely documented from Ferrand and Du Laurens entitled "The Lover's Malady in Medical Theory." It is one of the first modern critical résumés of the general process whereby love enters the body and creates a diseased state. Thereafter, passing references begin to appear with greater frequency, as in Michael

McVaugh's Introduction to the *Tractatus de amore heroico* of Arnald of Villanova,[22] or in an article entitled "La folie amoureuse dans la roman pastoral espagnol" by Françoise Vigier.[23] But apart from the biographical and biblioqraphical notes on Ferrand by the nineteenth-century physician Desbarreaux-Bernard, only Yvonne David-Peyre has consecrated a series of articles specifically to Ferrand, articles that deal broadly with his career, with the Spanish sources cited in his work, and with the interventions of the Inquisition in Toulouse.[24] Such does not constitute a ground swell, but it is a significant renewal of interest. Ferrand is destined to find an important place for his contribution to early theories of psychology because he, more than anyone of his age, relates the received ideas concerning *amor heroes* to both *medica practica* and *medica theorica*. Michel Simonin singles him out as one of the most thorough and reliable of Renaissance sources on the disease. "For the person who wishes to study love melancholy, his book is recommended, particularly for its bibliographical qualities. He leafed through everything, which is to say that everything or nearly everything is there. . . . And if he took up pen, it was because his colleagues, failing to recognize that love was a disease unique unto itself, failed to treat it properly."[25] In identifying these two features of the treatise, Simonin points to the origins of Ferrand's *theorica* in the vast body of erudition that deals with erotic love as an idea going back to the foundations of Western medicine, and to his renewed sense of the *practica* in the fact that he was concerned for the patients who, for lack of accurate diagnoses and appropriate cures, were being mishandled by the profession. In brief, Ferrand is being consulted with increasing frequency by specialists as a point of reference, but only in a cursory way. Everything remains to be done in terms of evaluating his specific contribution to the history of this medical idea and its place in early psychology.

The Two Treatises on Love and Their Audiences

Just what kind of a treatise Ferrand wrote and just who it was destined for are complex issues. What follows is intended to help frame answers to these two questions, though the components are many and contradictory. Much of our uncertainty regarding the intended audience arises from the nature of the encyclopedic treatise itself, which, in a sense, has something for the specialist and the popular reader alike. Ferrand arranges to have his second and much expanded edition of 1623 (the basis of the present translation) dedicated to the students in the Faculty of Medicine in Paris, a procedure that signals specialized intentions for a professional readership. But the popularization of medicine through treatises on the more engaging topics, written in the vernacular instead of Latin, was also an important factor of that period of publication. It is difficult to believe, in spite of his dedication to specialists, that Ferrand, in choosing subject, style, and language as he did, was unmindful of that nonspecialist book-purchasing clientele.

Some of the ostensibly most scholarly elements of the work are precisely those with the widest appeal. Ferrand was a compulsive borrower from the works of others, at times assembling whole passages in pastiche. Those habits were characteristic of his age of scholarship and the basis for scholarly authority. Ferrand includes quotations, exempla, and allusions—barely a page in the treatise escapes—from just over three hundred authorities: physicians, theologians, historians, essayists, poets, and dramatists. This methodology gave rise to a reader's banquet of lore, anecdotes, passages of poetry, and vignettes illustrating all manner of practices, oddities, and anomalies concerning the relations between the sexes. The very same dichotomy of purposes and audiences pertains to Burton's *Anatomy*. One recent scholar pleads for the high seriousness of the work underneath its dazzling erudition, by treating it as a philosophical study of the human condition that "seeks not only to prescribe cure for disease, but to be cure for the melancholy that is life."[26] By contrast, however, the editors of a recent edition, no doubt seeking the patronage of a modern easy-reading clientele, state on the dust-jacket that the work is "full of Rabelaisian humor and malicious satire . . . an omnium gatherum of wayward fancies, oddities and curiosities, of fact, fiction and folklore from every field of knowledge—art and astrology to philosophy and medicine."[27] That dual perspective enters into the consideration of nearly every aspect of Ferrand's work.[28]

The very question "for whom?" haunted Ferrand's first edition of the treatise and may have contributed to its fate before the ecclesiastical tribunal of Toulouse. Ferrand could well have escaped had he dealt with his topic in the "privacy" of Latin, but to expose such sex-related matters to the general public was a matter of serious concern for certain sectors of the clergy in seventeenth-century France. The fact that Ferrand wrote two versions of this treatise, and that the second differs from the first in substantial ways, makes the question kaleidoscopic by bringing into consideration Ferrand's own predilections and second thoughts as a writer. He was an eclectic, trained as a physician, but motivated as a philosopher and attracted to literature. Love had been an issue with the physicians for centuries, but it had also been a subject with the poets, the essayists, the courtesy and expository book writers of Italy, many of whose works Ferrand knew intimately. The ambiguity of his treatise arises with the very breadth and scope of his erudition, and with all the heterogenous views of love he incorporated into his text.

Ferrand's first treatise on lovesickness was published in Toulouse in 1610, under the title *Traicté de l'essence et guerison de l'amour ou de la melancholie erotique,* the second in Paris in 1623. Given the paucity of information about Ferrand from external sources, the best insights we can gain into his career as a scholar are to be derived through a comparison of these two editions. They are separated by a period of thirteen years, the first the work of a provincial physician in his mid-thirties, the second the work of a man nearing fifty who had spent perhaps twenty years researching and writing on erotic love. In a sense, the latter is but an extension of the former, for the philosophical and rhetorical intent of each is the same: to define, diagnose, and cure erotic melancholy. Both evince the tripartite structure of the scholastic medical treatise in which the philosophical descriptions of the disease are separated from the prognostics and diagnostics, and from a final section on cures—again subdivided according to tradition between the methodical, surgical, and pharmaceutical practices. Both works contain chapters built around medical questions or *disputationes* in the style of the school treatise in which multiple aspects of a subtopic are debated in sequence with a view to resolution or compromise.[29] Yet the second treatise, while it manages to include nearly every argument, quotation, and exemplum of the first, contains major alterations: materials are employed differently; arguments change focus and new arguments appear. But more important, the tone and tenor of the work have undergone subtle metamorphosis in favor of a more circumspect, cautious, and professional attitude. In the first, Ferrand addresses the lovers themselves, captivated by the beauty of their ladies, whereas in the second he addresses the medical profession concerning these lovers. To the readers of the first he offers advice on how to avoid the pitfalls of love—a kind of handbook for courtiers for the preservation of their bodies and souls against the hazards of their social pastimes. He professes to them openly to have gleaned his lore not only from theologians, philosophers, and physicians but also from the fields of the poets, as he says, in order to please them by a "variety naturally agreeable to lovers."[30] Such a treatise, by definition, reveals a design calculated as much to delight as to instruct; it is a work of admonition embellished with literary distractions. Stylistically and structurally, it is both a medical treatise and an expository book. We are tempted to assert that Ferrand was doing more than popularizing medical precepts—that he was, in fact, exploiting his training to create a new literary pastime.[31] In the first treatise, the Ovidian tradition is in competition with the Galenic. The second treatise is more sober and vigilant, more disciplined by the procedures of the scholastic medical treatise. That metamorphosis may have come about for a number reasons, as the following pages will show.

A Life Sketch

Amorous melancholy was a unique disease requiring specific and accurate description in order that doctors should not only diagnose it correctly, but treat it with the remedies alone appropriate to it. That was Ferrand's declared intention in writing his second treatise. A second and related goal was equally profession-oriented. Therapeutic coitus as recommended by the Arab physicians, as well as by many of the physicians of the Christian West, nevertheless jarred with Christian morality. Ferrand undertook to exercise both moral censure and medical logic against this established but pernicious view. A number of other *disputationes* had become a traditional part of the discussion of the disease: whether there was a pulse peculiar to lovers, whether the heart or the head was the seat of the disease, whether love could enter by the eyes, whether the disease was hereditary, whether it was greater in men or in women, and several others. These were all matters of both philosophical and clinical concern requiring sensible readjustments in the light of more recent thought. Ferrand was intent not only upon capping the definition and description of love philosophically, but upon bringing all such materials into a rhetorical whole, in a common cause with clinical components of erotic melancholy. Ferrand's second treatise on love preserves all the pleasing variety of the first, but underscores from the outset a more forceful sense of purpose on the medical side. But purely professional criteria may not alone have been responsible for the contrasting tones of his two treatises, for there are several factors at play.

There is a strong temptation to explain the differences between the earlier and later editions in terms of biographical truisms: that the first is the work of a young libertine fond of literary recreations with a penchant for the Italian expository books on love, while the second is the work of a middle-aged Parisian physician and professor intent upon securing his professional status through publication. Yet in the former the medical argument is, in spite of all, intact, and in the latter the literary diversions and philosophical digressions, though disciplined, remain present. Moreover, it cannot be ventured with certainty just what portion of that presumed maturity as a writer was a matter of age and intellectual change, and what portion was thrust upon him by his brush with the church authorities in 1620. The fact that his first treatise was, indeed, called in for burning cannot have left Ferrand entirely indifferent. That assumption sends the reader to the second treatise in search of evidence of Ferrand's new strategies for the defense of his former theories or for signs of his capitulation to authority. Our conclusion from such a comparison of texts is that he followed both courses almost equally. Evidence suggests that the encounter with the church had made its mark on him, though it does not represent for Ferrand the watershed in his intellectual career that it would have been for a man of a more polemical turn of mind. Yet it must remain in the forefront of any analysis of the man and his work because it furnishes the only contemporary report on Ferrand that we have—albeit a highly biased and interested one. We will return to this matter in greater detail in the following pages.

Like so many biographical accounts of men of that age, ours too must plead ignorance on such basic matters as the dates of Ferrand's birth and death, his marital status, whether he had children, his material circumstances, his social and intellectual associations. He was born in Agen, as he himself declared; a reasonable guess at the year would be around 1575.[32] On the title page of his first work he is identified as a doctor of laws and a member of the faculty of medicine (Par M. Jacques Ferrand Agenois, Docteur en Droit, et en la faculté de médecine). We know the work was published by the Colomiez family, printer-in-ordinary to the university. All indications point to a close association with Toulouse. Quite probably he carried out his studies there and later became affiliated with the faculty. Indeed, Toulouse is almost assured by default, since there is no record of his presence in either Montpellier or Bordeaux. In confirmation, he states in ch. XIV of his second treatise that in 1603 he had just arrived in Agen from Toulouse to set up his first medical practice. The implications of these several clues appear self-evident enough, though it is to be remarked that his name does not appear in the history of the medical faculty of Toulouse.

It is striking that at this early moment in his career, Ferrand encountered a case of lovesickness in a young man from the region who had been misdiagnosed by local charlatans. Ferrand states that he was able to help his patient by first using the pulse ruse for determining the true cause of distress, and then by cajoling him into the use of proper medications. By implication, erotic melancholy had been a part of his clinical practice from the earliest days of his professional career. Mention of a second case history dated 1606 reveals that Ferrand had not remained long in Agen; he was by then practicing in Castelnaudary, a few miles to the east of Toulouse. By the same token, from the title page of the treatise of 1623, published in Paris by Denis Moreau and dedicated "A Messieurs les Estudians en Medecine à Paris," we may assume that Ferrand had, by that date, left the provinces and had made new affiliations with the faculty in Paris. In fact, the Parisian provenance encourages belief that Ferrand had at last found his way to the capital in keeping with the career ambitions we have already presumed for him.

Two details put the nineteenth-century archivist Dr. Desbarreaux-Bernard on the path to further discoveries about Ferrand's career: the mention of Castelnaudary and the fact that the first treatise was dedicated to the "Tres-Illustre Prince, Claude de Lorraine, Duc de Chevreuse, Prince de Joinville, Pair de France etc.," whom Ferrand thanks for the honor of being received as his doctor-in-ordinary. The text is, in fact, signed "De Castelnaudarry en Lauragois ce 9. Aoust, dedié à S. Amour 1610." Dr. Desbarreaux-Bernard was an active member of a group interested in medical history. No doubt his personal copy of Ferrand's early treatise (housed today in the Municipal Library in Toulouse, and still bearing his book plate) was an incentive to find out what he could about its author. His examination of the municipal records in Castelnaudary revealed that Ferrand had spent at least twelve and up to sixteen years in the city, not only as a practising physician and writer, but also as second consul in 1612 and as first consul in 1618.[33] We may conjecture that his first arrival in the city coincided with his appointment as physician-in-ordinary to Claude, duke of Lorraine, sometime between 1603 and 1606. (The duke himself had been named governor of Provence by Henry IV in 1595.) His relationship with the duke also invites speculation, though little can be assured. Was it in the duke's library that Ferrand gained access to the many unusual and exotic works he cites in his margins, many of which are not available in Toulouse or Montpellier today? Was the spirit of that first treatise in deference to the duke's interests as a scholar-courtier? Was it his influence and his powerful family connections that kept Ferrand free of censure during the ten years that elapsed between the publication and the recall of that first book? The possibilities suggested by these questions are of the greatest importance, even if they are beyond documentation today.

The man himself we can only describe in the most general of terms. His interest in the diseases of mania and melancholy associated with love can be thought of as a lifelong preoccupation. His encounters with the disease began as early as 1603, and it is likely that his knowledge of it goes back to his years in medical school, where such topics were formally debated.[34] The reading and gathering of materials must have absorbed a great deal of the leisure time of a man otherwise occupied with patients, a patron, and a municipal government. The treatises themselves testify to a range of interests from the literary to the scientific. His approach to medicine is generally Galenic and conservative. We sense him to be a man of the establishment, both professionally and in terms of his moral and social vision. He had a distrust of charlatans and quacks. He avows at a strategic point in his second treatise a rigorous loyalty to the Roman Catholic faith, and he manifests in general a humane and tolerant attitude toward those suffering from the diseases of the passions of the soul. Little more can be surmised about the man behind the book.

Ferrand and the Ecclesiastical Tribunal of Toulouse

While Ferrand's declaration of faith is not to be doubted, he did not have an easy time with the church in professional matters, for the one remaining aspect of his career awaiting comment is the condemnation of his first treatise by the church and by the Parliament of Toulouse in 1620. We are left to speculate whether Ferrand had intimations of the storm to come when writing the work, given the tendentious nature of his appeal to his patron for protection. What might otherwise pass as merely formulaic takes on a more urgent and aggressive look in light of the actual fate of the book, for Ferrand requests defense "against the assaults and impetuosities of slanderous tongues aroused to loud protestations and railing by a pack of vain and indolent backbiters, overseers, and censors of other men's works."[35] If this is more than rhetoric, who else but the clergy could qualify as a "pack of vain and indolent backbiters, overseers, and censors"? If Ferrand did publish in anticipation of being attacked, did not such pleading in the dedication act as a provocation? Why, too, given the nature of the book, would Ferrand add the name of the duke's pious sister, Jeanne de Lorraine, prioress of the Devout Monastery of Prouille, to his appeal for protection? What interest could she have had in speaking up for the contents of this book? The appeal alone may be Ferrand's clearest indication that he was potentially aware of antagonizing the church by writing on subjects they would not find suitable for popular reading and by publishing his book in a city as League-bound and as conservative as Toulouse.[36]

Ferrand's case is particularly apt for study, not only because the two editions remain available for comparison today but also because the documents issuing from the trial survive in the ecclesiastical archives of the Département of the Haute Garonne, and have been transcribed into the "Notice Biographique et Bibliographique sur Jacques Ferrand" by Desbarreaux-Bernard. The assault on the 1610 treatise is composed of several specific accusations, though they point in chorus to a more perva-sive issue of contention that can be dealt with here only in a cursory way, namely the professional rivalry between the church and the physicians concerning the care for those suffering from diseases of the soul. In a Latin document dated July 16, 1620, the ecclesiastical judges declared the work sacrilegious and pernicious in the extreme, and in full defiance of the church in its discussion of matters pertaining to judiciary astrology. In a more detailed document, in French, issued on the same date and signed by the same authority—Johannes de Rudèle, vicar general to the archbishop—the treatise was held to be an affront to public morality and decency. Ferrand was accused of making a profane and lascivious use of the words of sacred scripture, of defending judiciary astrologers, of fur-nishing recipes for compelling love from the ladies ("donne des remèdes damnable pour se faire aimer des dames"), of teaching the tools of abom-ination, of offering pharmaceutical preparations that could not be used without corrupting the individual, and of giving accounts of the most damnable books and inventions ever written concerning lechery and the sorceries of love. The third document to survive was addressed to the booksellers specifically forbidding the sale of Ferrand's treatise, together with all the works of Vanini. Order was given for recalling all known copies for burning under threat of heavy fines for noncompliance. This recall of the books seems to have been the extent of the action taken against Ferrand, though he must have felt a certain anxiety in seeing his book grouped with those of the notorious Vanini, for Vanini had been arraigned the preceding year, had stood his defense brilliantly, but had paid the supreme price for his academic freedom by being garrotted and publicly burned.

We could, in light of this association, project upon Ferrand more notoriety than he deserves, because it is possible that had Vanini never settled in Toulouse, history would have taken a different turn and Ferrand's treatise might have escaped notice altogether. Giulio Cesare Vanini arrived in the city in 1617, his reputation as a freethinker preceding him. Vanini thought himself safe under the protection of Le Mazuyer, the first president of the Parliament. He was an Averroist in the Paduan tradition, a follower of Pomponazzi and Cardano, and an avowed atheist.[37] Hence, as David-Peyre has pointed out, Vanini had offended more egregiously than had Ferrand, and had, moreover, brazenly defended himself. Not only had he upheld the judiciary astrologers in his *Amphitheatrum aeternae providentiae divino-magicum*, but he had abjured the faith and had openly attacked the fundamental doctrines of the church.[38] That he had also touched upon erotic melancholy, fates, divinations, love philters, and related topics could well have been the cause of the new repression that took Ferrand in its sweep.

The Catholic League was strong in Toulouse in those troubled years of the Counter-Reformation. The Inquisition was active, the surrounding countryside was under constant surveillance for witches and sorcerers, and authors were under the perpetual threat of the Index.[39] The well-intending Sieur de Lancre, the witch-hunter magistrate of Bordeaux, reveals this dimension of the spiritual climate of the Southwest in his *Tableau de l'inconstance des mauvais anges et démons, ou il est amplement traité des sorciers et de la sorcellerie* (1612).[40] Béarn had been the scene of a famous series of recent prosecutions, and the trial of Elisabeth Roussillon had caused considerable stir. A full profile is given in Robert Mandrou's *Magistrats et sorciers en France au XVIIᵉ siècle*.[41] One of the rhythms of civic life in Toulouse was the vacillation between periods of inquisitorial rigor and relaxation. Such facts have suggested to Professor David-Peyre that Ferrand was quite simply a victim of those repressive times, and that his work contained nothing more than a few indiscretions that had attracted the attention of humorless and illiberal churchmen.

Yet while that assessment is undoubtedly true, there remain certain facts that count against him. To come to the work two centuries later, as Desbarreaux-Bernard did, and to exonerate the author by the standards of a different era is to miss the point of the allegations entirely. Oddly enough, for Desbarreaux-Bernard only the passage describing the removal of obstructions to the vaginal tract struck him as being offensive and somewhat "Rabelaisian"—an odd matter for a physician to find offensive, and an odd use of the term "Rabelaisian." He goes on: "besides this peccadillo, we have looked in vain in Ferrand's treatise for the reasons that would call down on his head the severity of the church. The motive for his prosecution escapes us."[42] But the issues in the three reports were perfectly clear; the tribunal was not guided by whim or by matters of personal taste. Had Ferrand raised the issue of judiciary astrology, or had he not, for it was a subject formally and unequivocally forbidden by the bull of Pope Sixtus V, *Coeli et terrae*, issued in 1586? Had Ferrand discussed love philters and the pharmaceutical means for luring ladies into lovers' powers, or had he not? These are the essential questions.

The church of the Counter-Reformation had become completely intransigent on the matter of astrology. At stake for them was the freedom of the will. No determinist philosophies could be allowed to interfere with a man's full responsibility for his own moral choices, including those astral influences that threaten to impose destinies upon men through the channels causally relating the heavens to human behavior through the doctrine of sympathies. The age was alive with debate on the issue, for, as Gregory Hanlon writes, "the early seventeenth century gives witness to multiple efforts of reconciliation between astrology, which was part of the cultural baggage of each educated man, and the Catholic doctrine that favors the prevalence of free will over all forms of determinism."[43] Paradoxically, those physicians we might have taken for leaders in contemporary thought and thus potentially the most vocal in laying such humbuggery to rest were precisely those who came repeatedly to its defense, not actively, but philosophically, because so much in the theory of medicine depended on that same doctrine of the sympathies that accounts for the communication between the body and the soul, as well as between external causes and internal effects. The physicians found themselves at an impasse, yet they continued to defend the theory out of a reflex loyalty to Galen—most of them without any intention of making clinical use of astrological operations in their diagnoses.[44]

In the *De diebus decretoriis*, Galen dealt with critical days and the influence of the moon. Because his authorship of the work was not in dispute, its adverse theories had to be accepted yet explained away through sophistry and choplogic. Giovanni Manardo, who would accept nothing of the treatise, nevertheless had to defend his stance by claiming in his *Epistolae medicinales* that Galen had written that book not as a physician but as an astrologer. Leonhard Fuchs in his *Methodus seu ratio compendiaria cognoscendi veram solidamque medicinam* simply asserted that the authority of Hippocrates took precedence over Galen's.[45] But a more typical management of the issue can be found in Du Laurens's *Historia anatomica humani corporis*, bk. I. ch. 2, where he insists upon the distinction between theory and practice, that astrology can be credited, but never taught or employed. That was the best that could be done.

Ferrand went no further in his own assertions in his early treatise. He speculated cautiously on the ways in which the horoscope and other astrological techniques might be used to diagnose those inclined to erotic melancholy; he did not, however, advocate their employment. Evidence is insufficient to determine the degree to which Ferrand spoke out of rote loyalty to Galen or covert belief in the theories. Quite simply, for the church authorities, Ferrand had speculated on a forbidden topic, thereby at least passively endorsing its principles. That he had cautioned against its many abuses was clearly insufficient to placate the tribunal.

One looks in vain to the edition of 1623 for revisions clarifying Ferrand's position one way or the other. He expands his section on astrology into an entire chapter (XXI) and gives greater prominence to the organizing question, whether astrology can serve to determine a predisposition to erotic melancholy. By all indications, Ferrand would seem to be preparing a stout rebuttal predicated upon his professional convictions in the matter. But there was perhaps more honor than truth to be preserved in the exercise. He merely takes up the old philosophical arguments about astrology itself in a style characterized by qualifiers and disclaimers as well as by an excessive employment of citations and allusions that tend to distance Ferrand from the statements made. In fact, nearly the whole of the chapter is borrowed from Jean Taxil's *L' astrologie et physiognomie en leur splendeur,* in which Ferrand finds his references to Manardo, Del Rio, Tolet, Giuntini, Rodrigo de Castro, Thomas Aquinas and Cardano—all lumped into the debate that issues merely in the hackneyed compromise: that the stars may work upon the spirit, but only accidentally and indirectly through the sympathy that must exist between the body and the soul.[46] Ferrand found himself committed to beliefs concerning the six nonnatural things and the temperaments of the body, but as part of a philosophical cul-de-sac. He might stand his ground in this evasive way, never hoping to prove that a man's horoscope might indeed predict accurately that he was prone to erotic excesses. But Ferrand never attempts to assert that diagnostic technique, indeed, would not have dared to do so. Because there was no pragmatic reason for raising this dangerous topic in the first place, we can only assume that his interest was at the level of theoretical speculation.[47]

Adding to our uncertainty is the fact that Ferrand also assures the reader that Pope Sixtus V was perfectly justified in banning astrology given the many abuses and superstitions it engendered, and that he himself held to the doctrines of the Holy Catholic and Apostolic Church, to which he submitted all his writings! At best, the chapter is rhetorically inconclusive, a halting defense of the *status quo* among the conventional medical writers, and a declaration of submission. Ferrand's revisions suggest that he was determined to maintain his double allegiance to these two contending ideological systems despite the inherent contradictions and despite the accusations of the tribunal.

On the score of offending public decency, arguments in Ferrand's defense ring particularly hollow. There are passages in that first treatise that would raise eyebrows even today. The members of the tribunal undoubtedly had his ch. XXII in mind when they called him to account for encouraging the lecheries and sorceries of love, and for providing the recipes for aphrodisiacs. The chapter is entitled, "The means and recipes to make yourself lovable and to have the pleasure of the ladies, which is the chief cure for love and erotic melancholy." In this instance Ferrand could not cite the traditional authority of Avicenna in making coitus the principal cure, for the terms of his advice are entirely different. Ferrand's is a gossipy chapter that promises help to frustrated and ineffectual lovers by counseling them on how to dress the lover's part, how to chat up the ladies, how to show the bare breast to advantage, how to buy favors with money or with presents, how to make and use love philters. That Ferrand cautions at the same time against dangers, abuses, and superstitions would not have mollified the censors because he described things that, unknown, could not have been abused.

The following chapter bears a more innocent title, but delivers more forbidden information. It is entitled "The means for keeping married couples in love and for curing illicit affairs." It deals with problems of sexual incompatibility. The topic was not new, but it was customarily dealt with in treatises on sterility,[48] on procreation, and the diseases of women, and it is a topic that, in any case, bears little relationship to the curing of love melancholy, unless we are to understand that such incompatibility can also initiate the burning of the humors; Ferrand does not so specify. He dispenses with the usual theoretical and anatomical discussions that lead to consideration of the dysfunctions of the reproductory organs, moving straightway to the pharmaceutical concoctions to be applied to the genitals variously to stretch or constrict the vagina, to stimulate the male member, or to increase the pleasurable sensations. At the same time, he allows himself certain stylistic indulgences, such as calling the vagina "Venus's garden," "the vale of sighs and misery," or "Venus's pigsty." He attributes the loss of male pleasure to a "wicket that is too split and a tunnel that is too stretched, or the door to Alibec's inferno that is too wide, so that Rustic gets no thrill out of running his devil."[49] He concerns himself, likewise, with unguents for women that prevent "cobwebs" and membranes from forming during periods of sexual inactivity, and mentions the preparations used by Italian courtesans to enable them to sell themselves as virgins. On the matter of offending decency, Ferrand had exercised no caution at all.[50]

In the new treatise, Ferrand jettisons the entire chapter on how to make oneself attractive to the ladies, and his advice to married couples experiencing social and sexual difficulties he trims according to more rigorous bounds of decorum. He is more discreet and less detailed in his descriptions of aphrodisiacs, charms, potions, "tell-love" procedures and all that has to do with magic. He warns repeatedly against the spiritual dangers even in those silly rituals that girls learn from their mothers and nursemaids, for in using them they "paganize to their damnation." Even the rhetorical frame has been altered. Whereas in the first treatise Ferrand speaks of the means whereby love can be commanded by the lover through the employment of magic, in the second he asks whether the physician can or should use magic as a means for diagnosing lovers. The first treatise proposes concrete advice; the second asks theoretical questions about the place of these forbidden practices within the profession. All along, his revisions may have been guided by new theoretical criteria, by a clearer medical purpose, by the redeployment of his arguments for the purposes of the physician rather than for those of the courtier and lover. At the same time, it cannot be denied that this second work would have passed ecclesiastical inspection more easily than the first, especially in terms of offending public decency, and Ferrand may well have intended it that way.

Nevertheless, Ferrand's concessions on matters of decency would not alone have served to reconcile the clergy to his underlying assertion that the medical profession had just claims to the treatment of love as one of the passions of the soul. While the issue was not raised as such by the documents of the tribunal, it may very well have been the most contentious.[51] It is far easier to prosecute on the grounds of taste, morality, and interdicted topics, than on the grounds of professional rivalry. There is a statement in ch. III of the early edition, however, that may have been more threatening in its purport than all the violations of taste and interdiction combined, for there Ferrand makes a declaration of the territorial prerogatives of his discipline that poach directly on ecclesiastical preserves. The very tone of his statement indicates a baiting and adversarial stance that leaves little doubt of his tendentiousness in the matter. In effect, he asserts that it was God Himself who had furnished the natural world with all the materials requisite for the curing of amorous melancholy, and that the physician follows a commission from the divine in searching out those cures. Second, he proclaims that it should come as no surprise that medical science has made so much progress in that direction, since physicians have been at the task for several thousand years. Third, he argues that to define love as pertaining exclusively to the soul and thus as a matter reserved for philosophers and theologians would not stand up to scrutiny, for it is clearly a disease of the body and of the soul interacting with one another. This is why the doctrine of the sympathies, already mentioned in our discussion of astrology, is so entirely critical. Ferrand was intent on establishing a definition of the diseases of the soul that would attach them firmly to the temperaments, humors, and vapors that cause and condition them. As he states clearly at the beginning of ch. XXIX: "of primary importance for the prevention of all diseases is the removal of the [offending] disposition of the body, according to Galen, which is nothing other than the interior cause of the illness." Because, according to medical reasoning, no counseling, sermonizing, exorcising, or other religious practice could alone serve to alter the material causes affecting the soul, the physician becomes essential. In fact, because he is both a philosopher and a physician, he alone is equipped to deal with the disease by combining moral counseling with the alteratives, diminutives, and soporifics that promise healing through a restoration of the balances within the body. In this matter the physician could not capitulate.

Ferrand's antogonistic position is made clear by his refusal to compromise or to make gestures of conciliation; he cannot invite the clergy to share in the curing of these derangements of the soul because without medical knowledge they could only do more damage than good. It was as a philosopher that Galen wrote his book on the description and curing of the diseases of the soul, and it is as philosophers that physicians continue to deal with such diseases. Ferrand, then, turns on those who malign the authority of medicine by attributing their attacks to mere rancor and spite—in short, to professional jealousy and hostility. That retributive tone on Ferrand's part may well have contributed to the reception of his work in 1620. The same accusations appear in undiluted form in 1623; the polemic was critical to Ferrand and his claims. It was the basis for his imperialistic bid for medical control over spiritual diseases.

Ferrand's most egregious fault in the eyes of the ecclesiastical tribunal, according to its declaration, was that he wrote in the vernacular ("ce qui est d'autant plus perilleux qu'il escript en langage vulgaire").[52] This is a reminder to a specialist like Ferrand that the church is perhaps willing to make allowances for works intended for other specialists, kept from the untutored eye by the privacy of Latin, but that its stand must be firm and uncompromising with regard to the popularizing of delicate and forbidden topics by making them available in French. Ferrand's motives for writing in the vernacular can only be surmised. Presumably, he envisioned for himself a national rather than an international audience, and a popular as well as a professional readership. For the courtly audience apparently intended for his first edition, Latin clearly would not have served. That he persisted in his employment of French in the second edition is proof that he had a mixed readership in mind for his second treatise on love.

Ferrand's choice was by no means without precedent in the field of medicine. With increasing frequency throughout the last quarter of the sixteenth and the early seventeenth centuries, medical writers of serious intent catered to the interests of a wider book-buying public. As early as 1570, Laurent Joubert published his enormously successful *Traicté des erreurs populaires touchant la médecine et régime de la santé*,[53] and many other such works followed, some conceived in French, others translated from Latin, such as Jean Liébault's long and sometimes quite graphic *Trois livres des maladies et infirmites des femmes*. The Italian love treatise writers, to come closer to the topic, were translated one by one: Equicola, Fregoso, Aeneas Sylvius, Platina—all before 1600.[54] Jean Aubery published his *L'antidote d'amour* in 1599.[55] Ferrand's readership had already been established by these publications, and the hopes of capturing that market cannot have been a negligible factor.

A close comparison of the two treatises can leave little doubt of Ferrand's sustained interest in the topic of erotic love throughout the intervening years. The statistical record alone bears witness. The edition of 1610 is a text of 222 pages divided into 26 chapters. Ferrand's list of authors cited contains 165 names, several of whom play minor roles or are not even named in the text. The edition of 1623 grows to 270 pages and is divided into 39 chapters, though by word count (given the very different type sizes and number of lines per page) the second text is 60 percent longer. The list of authors cited has grown to 323. Of these, 58 do not appear in the text or in the margins, while another 37 who do appear in the text are omitted from the list. The final number of those actually mentioned in the text is 302. Some of the casualties from the first edition include Francis de Sales, bishop of Geneva; Jean Corve Chiromancien; Julien Oneiromancien; Leonicenus; Loxus; Nicholas Florentin; Solin; and Vopiscus. Far more important than these deletions are the additions to the second list that testify to the new directions in Ferrand's reading and the increased scope of his work.

In preparing his first treatise, Ferrand had been remiss in his examination of the Renaissance physicians: they are, in fact, conspicuous by their absence. In writing the second, Ferrand makes use of some of the leading medical writers of his age on the diseases of women, on medical controversies, and on melancholy: Annuce Foës, Jean de Gorris, Mathieu Gradi, Johann van Heurne, Jacques Houllier, Giovanni Marinello, Felix Platter, Ambroise Paré, Joseph Du Chesne, Girolamo Mercuriale, Luis Mercado, Cristóbal de Vega, Pedro Fonseca, Johann Schenck, Martin Ruland, Jean Taxil, Giovanni Battista Silvatico, Jourdain Guibelet, Jean de Veyries, André Du Laurens, François Valleriola, and Rodrigo de Castro. In his first treatise, Ferrand had also ignored two outstanding earlier writers on *amor hereos* in the Montpellier school: Bernard of Gordon and Arnald of Villanova. François Valleriola, in 1588, published a long "observation" on erotic love that, if it had not escaped Ferrand's notice, nevertheless escaped all mention in his early work. Several others, such as Mercado and Cristóbal de Vega, included chapters on erotic love in their medical treatises. That none of these were featured in Ferrand's first book is of self-evident importance; it is our guess that he attempted to exaggerate his own originality by deliberately overlooking many of them. Evidence lies in the fact that a few are quoted who receive no credit. On the other hand, his references to the ancients are generous, no doubt because the young scholar, in keeping with his training, intended to show the right kind of erudition by basing his treatise entirely upon the most venerable names: Hippocrates, Galen, Avicenna, Plato, and Aristotle. Hence, we cannot say which of the Renaissance authors of pertinent texts Ferrand had actually read by 1610, but we can assert that by 1623 he had read generously and that he had adopted a policy of acknowledgment that was fair to most, by Renaissance standards of scholarship, and that was patently unfair to only three or four.

The reorientation toward the moderns in the second treatise on love entailed a change in the aims and rationale of the entire work, for Ferrand had formerly included a chapter addressed to the very question, "Why so few physicians had taught the curing of love and of love melancholy." Given the number of works existing to contradict this thesis, Ferrand no doubt recognized that it would be prudent to acknowledge them in a second treatise addressed to medical specialists. What he lost in terms of presenting himself as an innovator he more than regained in contemporaneousness, scope—and honesty.

If Ferrand's first change was a general acknowledgment of the work of recent physicians on love, the second was the broadening of his definition of erotic love to include several of the traditional diseases involving behavioral aberrances attributed to the reproductive organs: prurient tickling in the genitals, satyriasis, and uterine fury or hysteria. The idea of including these among the diseases of melancholy relating to love may have come to him from his reading of Mercado.[56] A third major adjustment entailed a clear theoretical and organizational distinction between the prevention of the disease in those inclined to erotic love and the curing of the disease in those already afflicted. That is to say, Ferrand extends his discussion of diagnostic techniques to include not only the identification of melancholy lovers by their symptoms but also of the potentially amorous by their characteristics and temperaments. He likewise separates the methodical, dietary, surgical, and pharmaceutical treatments appropriate for the prevention of the disease from those appropriate for its cure. It is in the interests of preventive medicine that Ferrand speculates on the uses of physiognomy, astrology, magic, and the interpretation of dreams. A fourth reorientation was the particular emphasis he placed on the pharmaceutical cures. Their role had been implied in many of the earlier treatises; Ferrand makes their use not only explicit but crucial to his proposals concerning remedies and central to his entire purpose for writing.

In keeping with these new directions, Ferrand drops those sections of the earlier treatise dealing with manners and the social conventions regulating the relations between the sexes. He omits all comment on the false kisses of ladies and the strategies for making partners jealous, for such social maneuvers had nothing to do with altering adust humors or controlling diseased imaginations; in short, they are inappropriate to therapy under the direction of the medical profession. A clear perception of these profession-related criteria is, in fact, a distinguishing feature of the second treatise. In the formal topics selected there for debate, Ferrand favors the medical ones over the social. In his first treatise he was concerned with such issues as whether love could thrive in the absence of jealousy, whether love could continue after marriage, or whether women were more passionate than men, while in the second he sought out *disputationes* of a more philosophical bent: whether the head or the heart was the seat of the disease, whether love was a hereditary weakness, during what ages love melancholy can develop, whether uterine fury is a form of the disease, whether love can be diagnosed without the cooperation of the patient. Each of these formed the basis for a chapter unique to the treatise of 1623; each underscores the new emphasis placed on issues of a philosophical or clinical nature that characterize the new work.

Our approach to the study of Ferrand's treatise of 1623 in this section of our introduction has been based on four critical questions: who was Ferrand's audience, and did his perception of it change? what do we know of the man and his career? what was the influence of the church censors on the writing of this book? and what can be ascertained through a close comparison of this work with the former by Ferrand on the same general subject? The questions seem natural enough in themselves given that the two treatises are extant and that the documents of the tribunal have survived. But for the reasons expressed throughout this section, the trends and influences can be handled only in conjectural ways. Our sense of Ferrand's audience can only be derived from the clues within his own texts. There is the danger of making critical imperatives out of an interpretation of the contents and the rhetorical biases of the works themselves. In the same way, the influence of the ecclesiastical oppression is ambiguous. We are entirely clear about what the church objected to in his early work; we are less sure about what Ferrand thought of that harshest of all possible book reviews in examining the revisions represented by his second treatise. There are reasons both scholarly and personal that may account for those changes, including the new reading Ferrand had undertaken in the intervening years. Finally, while a close comparison of the two texts would seem to be a nearly infallible way of measuring at least his intellectual growth in those years, the evidence nevertheless lends itself to several interpretations. We detect a clear trend away from the cavalier courtly love treatise with a medical substructure in the favor of a fully constituted medical treatise with a vestige of interest in the nonmedical essayists on love. That is not to say that Ferrand, himself, had fundamentally changed his mind about his thesis or his audience, but only that he had changed strategies or that we detect as much in assessing his changes. The fact remains that these two treatises continue to have far more in common, both in terms of rhetorical intent and general content, than either does with any other book of the age on the topic. Yet if the conclusions must remain qualified, the questions nevertheless had to be raised for the hints they promise toward understanding the genesis of his second treatise on the diseases of love.

In addition to the apparent trends and directions in his work suggested by an assessment of his career ambitions, by the possible influence of the tribunal in Toulouse, by an identification of his readership, or by a comparison of his two treatises, there is the fact that Ferrand was a voracious reader and that he was often directly influenced by the dozen or more key works which he must have had frequently open before him as he wrote. We have already looked to some of these for parallel explanations to certain revisions that might otherwise have been attributed exclusively to the influence of the recall or to his own reflections or moral scruples. Ferrand's relationship to his many medical and literary sources is a complex matter that we will examine in the following section of our introduction. Given the paucity of materials that would allow us to evaluate this treatise more satisfactorily in the light of its author's career, we are compelled to turn, perhaps sooner than we would have liked, to a consideration of its ideas and its place in the context created by similar works of that era. But as we have argued at the outset, to examine Ferrand's place in the history of ideas is by no means an approach for lack of a better; it is the essential approach given the nature of the work. As Ferrand grappled for directions in his second thesis, he was also grappling for the directions inherent in his materials that had been created by the force within the ideas themselves. *Amor heroes* was a medical concept with a destiny for development that could only come about through a consolidation of the several trends within the medical tradition and through a collation of these materials with ideas to be found in the Renaissance philosophical treatises on love. That process had already been advanced by such writers as Ficino and Equicola, a process attempting to reproduce itself in France, but in versions more rigorously Galenic and medical in their rhetorical orientations. That was the intellectual current in the air that Ferrand had detected and had made his life's work. In that sense, while Jacques Ferrand researched the materials, his book was organized according to the principles of scholarship that were endemic to his training and second nature to his age.

II

Love Melancholy as a Medical Idea
in the Ancient World

For the reasons set out above, an examination of Ferrand's treatise must begin with an examination of the origins and development of the theories concerning the diseases of the passions and erotic love that inform his work, since the *De la maladie d'amour ou melancholie erotique* is above all a cumulative contribution to the history of erotic melancholy as a medical idea. The history of that idea or cluster of ideas has, in fact, never been written, though segments have been documented by scholars in dealing with individual writers who have touched upon the topic.[1] What follows cannot claim to be such a history, though it can serve as an initial overview. The comprehensiveness of Ferrand's work demands that all the principal moments in the formation of this specific body of thought be taken into account as prolegomena to his treatise. It is, of course, history only after the fact because the phenomenon owes its perpetuation to the incremental force in the ideas themselves, to the authority of those writers who propounded them, and to the persistent appeal they had for succeeding ages.

Quite paradoxical is the fact that, for the modern observer, the materials of that history are so full of bewildering recombinations of motifs as to render a linear narrative almost impossible, whereas for the Renaissance observer, the entire literature from a nearly two-thousand-year span of time was understood to offer but a single set of definitions, symptoms, and cures. Ferrand, among those observers, was inclined to consolidate all the medical sources before 1580 and to deal with their respective elements as having a nearly total complementarity. The discrepancies that do intrude he neutralizes through conciliation. Ferrand is forced to exercise a selective judgment only when dealing with the much longer and more differentiated treatises written during the 1580s and after—the period in which the medical treatise on love opens itself to the broader contexts of love poetry, mythology, philosophy, and the occult sciences.

39

Our consideration of the medical writers on love from 1580 to 1620 will appear in a subsequent section on Renaissance sources and analogues, a section that will concentrate on the very profound influence of his contemporaries and near contemporaries upon the treatise under consideration. Nevertheless, this section offering the materials for the history of the idea should be looked upon as a study in sources as well because Ferrand will call upon a large number of them for the documentation of his work. Moreover, it is to be understood that the consensus of views forming the scholastic tradition that explains the parts of the soul, the seats of the faculties, the processes of the imagination, and the roles of the spirits is pertinent in its entirety to Ferrand; for it is by these faculties and their operations that he understood the physiology of desire and the pathological behavior of the humors that lead to erotic diseases.

Love, Melancholy, and Madness

> Peer of gods he seemeth to me, the blissful
> Man who sits and gazes at thee before him,
> Close beside thee sits, and in silence hears thee
> Silvery speaking,
>
> Laughing Love's low laughter. Oh this, this only
> Stirs the troubled heart in my breast to tremble,
> For should I but see thee a little moment,
> Straight is my voice hushed.
>
> Yea, my tongue is broken, and through and through me
> 'Neath the flesh, impalpable fire runs tingling;
> Nothing see mine eyes, and a noise of roaring
> Waves in my ears sounds;
>
> Sweat runs down in rivers, a tremor seizes
> All my limbs, and paler than grass in autumn,
> Caught by pains of menacing death, I falter,
> Lost in the love trance.

Do you not marvel how she seeks to make her mind, body, ears, tongue, eyes, and complexion, as if they were scattered elements strange to her, join together in the same moment of experience? In contradictory phrases she describes herself as hot and cold at once, rational and irrational, at the same time terrified and almost dead, in order to appear afflicted not by one passion but by a swarm of passions. Lovers do have all those feelings, but it is, as I said, her selection of the most vital details and her working them into one whole which produce the outstanding quality of the poem.[2]

This poem by Sappho together with the comments by Longinus, to whom we owe the preservation of the poem, are representative of the way in which the ancient world viewed erotic passion. The poem itself becomes a touchstone for identifying the symptoms of love. Ferrand, in his ch. XIV, goes so far as to say that Sappho was "as experienced in this art as our Greek, Latin, and Arab physicians in light of the fact that they mentioned no indisputable signs that this lady did not already know."[3] Love was taken for a malaise capable of deranging both body and soul, accompanied by well-defined psychological and somatic symptoms. But before such love, in its most morbid manifestations, could acquire a pathological definition, its causes and symptoms had to be defined in the terms of the diseases of melancholy and madness—terms developed by the *physici* of the school of Hippocrates.

There was a certain reticence on the part of the early physicians to speak plainly of erotic melancholy, which is to say, a melancholy disease caused by love or a form of erotic passion that is, itself, a disease. On the one hand, the early medical theorists devised the foundations of humoral medicine and the nature of melancholy with its attendant pathological states, while on the other the moral philosophers speculated about the passions, the nature of love, the instincts of desire, and the derangements of the soul. But throughout the ancient period, those elements came together in a way that leaves little doubt about the general association of the diseases raised by black bile with the perturbations caused by inordinate passion.

Paradoxically, however, those who come closest to an explicit formulation of the thesis are precisely those who are most hesitant to endorse it. Aretaeus the Cappadocian, a first-century physician practicing in Rome, offers a perfect case in point, for in his chapter on melancholy he repeats a story from a remote source of a certain person "incurably affected" by love for a girl and therefore beyond the help of medicine. That the issue was raised in this context is proof that love and melancholy had become associated. Yet he goes on to explain that the defective state was owing to love itself, and that the young man merely "appeared to the common people to be melancholic."[4] For him, unrequited love does not produce melancholy, though the symptoms are similar. Presumably because melancholy arises within the body while love is a passion of the soul, they could not be causally related, though Aretaeus readily admits elsewhere that bile passes upwards and can attack the brain and that the derangements of the soul can have their effects upon the body. The same distinctions will prevail in Galen and in the Byzantine physicians down to Paul of Aegina.

The identification of that first moment when the medical profession refers formally to erotic melancholy is, in one sense, critical for the development of the idea. In another, it is but an academic detail since there was a groundswell acceptance of love as a condition of melancholy in the ancient world well before the physicians remaining on record endorsed that association of ideas. Sappho wrote of love in the terms of the symptoms of disease, the early humoral writers explained madness and all emotional disturbances in the brain in terms of the invasion of black bile, Plato spoke of sexual love as a disease of the soul, and Aristotle assigned the origins of eros not to the soul but to a boiling of blood around the heart. On the one hand, not all of the ancient world agreed that erotic love was of the soul, for some placed its origins in the reproductive organs, the heart, or the blood, while, on the other, not all in the ancient world agreed that melancholy was of the body only because some believed that thought and the operations of the faculties of the soul could, themselves, generate melancholy conditions within the brain which, in turn, attack the body. Even more to the point is the fact that Renaissance observers were entirely oblivious of the technicalities of medical history; they could return to the chapters on melancholy and mania by Aretaeus and Galen, and to those chapters on love in Oribasius and Paul of Aegina with full conviction that in speaking of melancholy, the two former included erotic love, and in speaking of such love the two latter meant melancholy diseases.

The Humors and the Hippocratic School

Health, for the physicians of the Hippocratic school, depends upon maintaining the four basic humors of the body in an isonomic state; the imbalance caused by the predominance of one humor over the others leads to disease.[5] They concentrate their professional interests upon the diagnostics of the melancholy humor (μέλαινα χόλη) because its pathological symptoms are more marked than those of the other temperaments, consisting mainly of psychological perturbations (fright, depression, folly) with strong somatic side effects.[6] The author of the treatise *The Sacred Disease* (probably a young contemporary of Socrates),[7] attributes the origins of that malady to an excess of black bile capable of affecting not only the organs of the body but the brain itself. His pathology is based on an axiomatic belief in the brain as the pilot of the entire organism and the seat of the affections and emotions. Hence, such disturbances must follow from abnormal states owing to material alterations within the brain itself caused by excessive coldness or heat, moisture or dryness. Madness is attributed to excessive moisture.[8] This mental condition is carried to the body by the heart, not that the heart consciously feels pain or anxiety itself, but because through the veins that congregate around it, the heart senses the pain or tension and is convulsed through sympathy.[9] In sum, madness and other emotional disturbances

are caused by an invasion of the brain by black bile while the entire
body is affected through the sympathetic convulsions of the heart, each
mental state producing its characteristic symptoms, such as palpitations,
trembling, blurred vision, stammering, or loss of speech.[10] Melancholy
became the favored explanation not only for depression but for madness and other forms of nervous breakdown to the point that the verb
μελαγχολᾶν (to be melancholy) became synonymous with μαίνεσθαι (to
be mad).[11]

Aphrodite Pandemia and Aphrodite Urania

The fusion of the concept of folly with that of melancholy prepared
the way for including erotic desire with states inclining toward insanity.
That association of ideas was sanctioned both by Euripidean tragedy and
by the philosophical speculations of Plato and Aristotle. Euripides wrote
his tragedies during the period in which the Sophists were revolutioniz-
ing Athenian life by placing a new emphasis upon the subjective nature
of experience, and by developing their theories concerning the process
of sensation and perception, the nature of understanding and feeling.
Euripides's conception of eros is strongly influenced by their thought.[12]
While for the tragedians who preceded him eros was a cosmic, ob-
jective force, for Euripides it becomes a passion, a subjective force that
takes hold of the entire human being almost as a sickness.[13] The vital
principle of man is no longer the supernatural, but his θυμός, his soul;
thus the reality of human experience is seen in relation to it, and the poet
lingers on the psychological motivations—the chief among them being
love—which drive man in his actions. A cursory reading of the Hyppolytus indicates that the poetic focus of the drama, the love of Phaedra
for her stepson Hippolytus, is a conflict of mythical dimensions, a battle between Aphrodite and Artemis. A more critical reading, however,
shows that the two goddesses are merely traditional figures that the poet
uses in order to crystallize the deepest emotions of the protagonists. At
the center of the tragedy there is, in fact, the struggle (ἀγών) of Phaedra,
the conflict between her passion and her rationality. Phaedra's love is
not unlike that of Pasiphae and of Ariadne: it is not a divine force, but
a tragic impulse (ἄτη), a pathos (πάθος) that springs from the soul and
leads to a complete mental and physical disintegration:

PHAEDRA: You likewise, give me pure advice. Today I shall be rid of
life, and so shall give pleasure to Aphrodite, who is my destroyer; and
I shall die defeated; love is merciless. Yet my death shall prove fatal
to another's life and teach him to ride roughshod on my misery. He

shall share equally in my sickness, and learn that chastity is humility and gentleness.[14]

For Plato, love is occasioned by the sensible perception of beauty; that is to say, love finds its external cause in the phenomenal world. Eros, we read in the *Cratylus*, is so called because (according to Plato's etymology) "it flows in from the outside."[15] Thus eros comes into being as sexual love, kindled by contact with the visible forms. Because that which pleases sight (the most perfect of the senses)[16] is beauty, eros is love of the beautiful, and the beautiful pleases because it is a reflection of the Idea within sensible things.[17] The human soul, which in its superior part (νοητικόν)[18] is in intimate contact with the Idea, feels its presence, and in the moment of contact with the sensible beauty it produces a mysterious shiver.[19] Eros begins its ascent toward the eternal with an irrational act, a kind of mania that, while estranging man from himself, announces to him a value beyond the world of appearances.[20] Thus love is conditioned, *a parte obiecti*, by the beauty of human forms, while the soul must be capable of recognizing ever more consciously the ideal value that appears through the appearances, because without the active intervention of the soul the message of the Idea could not be deciphered. Man is therefore in a position to choose one of two attitudes toward the form perceived by the senses: he can love the beautiful appearance because within it he recognizes the eternal, and therefore he can transcend the sensible beauty in order to possess, noetically, that which is eternal; or he can accept and love the object perceived as absolute reality and desire to possess it because he does not see anything outside of it. The first is the pure love that saves the soul, Aphrodite Urania; the second is Aphrodite Pandemia, sexual love, a disease (νόσημα) that destroys the soul.[21]

In the *Symposium* the distinction between positive and negative eros derives from the distinction between the state of health and that of sickness. The problem of eros is thus brought back to the traditional medical *techne* from which it originates: "Reverence for my profession— Eryximachus states—prompts me to begin with the witness of medicine. This double love (earthly and celestial) belongs to the nature of all bodies: for between bodily health and sickness there is an admitted difference of dissimilarity, and what is dissimilar craves and loves dissimilar things. And so the desire felt by a sound body is quite other than that of a sickly one."[22] Sexual love is thus "love of sickness," while celestial love is "love of health." The distinction between the two types of love is no longer based solely on a moralistic concept but on a scientific one.

It was Aristotle, however, who, through his natural philosophy, gave a systematic form to the concept of erotic passion as disease. The fundamental axiom of his psychophysiological approach is that sensation is a motion common to soul and body.[23] Passions in general are κινήσεις ψυχῆς, alterations of the senses through which the intellect moves the body,[24] and are divided into two groups: mental and somatic perturbations. To the first group belong all those passions which express tendencies, desires, appetites, and which Aristotle defines as λόγοι ἔνυλοι, that is to say, mental processes intimately connected to the bodily processes, so that in order to describe them, both aspects have to be taken into consideration.[25] To the second group belong the σωματικὰ πάθη, namely those passions that, like eros, originate in the body and also have a deep influence upon the mental constitution of the individual.[26] Aristotle defines eros as a desire for reproduction.[27] As for its physiological cause it consists, just like anger, in a boiling of the blood around the heart.[28]

Aristotle thereby places the causes of love more firmly in the body, assigning to the heart and reproductive organs more central roles in the generation of erotic appetites. According to a definition found in a fragment of the Aristotelian treatise *Eroticos* preserved in Abū 'l 'Alī ben Muhammed al-Daimali's *Al ma'tuf* (eleventh century), eros is born in the heart and from there flows throughout the body:

> Love is an impulse generated in the heart; once generated, it moves and grows, afterwards it matures. Once matured, whenever excitement, perseverance, desire, concentration, and wishful thinking grow within the heart of the lover, love is joined by affections and appetite. This brings the lover to disquieting grief, to continuous sleeplessness, hopeless passion, sadness, and destruction of mind.[29]

The differences between the physiology of love posited here and that of the Hippocratic school will result in endless polemics among medieval physicians as to whether the head or the heart is the seat of the disease. These differences, likewise, account for the elaborate and clumsy mechanisms in conflationist treatises whereby heart, brain, liver, genitals, blood, and blood vapors are joined in a complex sequence of causes and effects. Upon the authority of Aristotle, the functions of the heart are irrevocably drawn into the discussion and will find their way into many of the later treatises on erotic passion.

For affections to arise, there must be an appetite, an inclination, because "that which is moved is moved under the influence of appetite. Thus appetite is the mover, and appetite is a kind of movement."[30] Because "desire coincides with the initial movement of practical intellect,"[31] the first mover[32] is the object perceived by the subject, ἡ διὰ τῆς ὄψεος ἡδονή, the pleasure determined by the sight of something beautiful.[33] Once the affection has come into being, it irradiates from the heart as a moving force in the form of pneuma.[34] The pneuma, which Aristotle considers the vital principal of the organism, the source of the inner bodily heat and thus bound to the blood, determines the physical and mental constitution of man.[35] It is for this reason that he can compare love to drunkenness and madness, that is to say, to pathological moments when reason is almost totally darkened.[36] The sight of something beautiful gives rise to a desire which, by altering the inner temperature of the body through the heart, upsets its physiological and psychological balance; "it is in fact evident that rage, sexual desires, and the other passions of this type alter also the disposition of the body, and at times they also cause madness."[37]

Given the fact that love influences body and soul, we can summarize the psychophysiological process occasioned by the sight of a pleasing object in the following terms: for those beings having the capacity for feeling,[38] the form of the object is communicated by means of the intermediary bodies[39] to the five external senses, and principally to sight, being the most perfect among the senses.[40] In the *De anima* the process of sensation is summarized through a simile derived from Plato that will enjoy enormous popularity during the Middle Ages:

> In regard to sense generally we must understand that sense is that which is receptive of sensible forms apart from their matter, as wax receives the imprint of the signet ring apart from the iron or gold of which it is made . . . similarly sense as relative to each sensible is acted upon by that which possesses color, flavor or sound.[41]

In the *De memoria* the print produced by sensation is defined as a ζωγρά-φημα, a drawing: "The passion produced by sensation in the soul and in the part of the body which has sensation is something like a drawing. . . . In fact, the movement produces within the soul a kind of drawing of the perceived object, just like those who mark a seal with a ring."[42] It is worth noting at this point that Aristotle does not accept the widely held idea that sight involves a material flow of ether or of the airy vapors of the blood toward the object, a theory that will be granted new force in the Renaissance by Ficino. Rather, for him, sight is a passion, a modification within the eye itself where color and form are imprinted upon the watery element of the eye, and are, in turn, reflected as in a mirror.

The passion or movement produced by sensation is then handed over to the internal senses,[43] first to the imagination or fantasy, which is the mnemonic vision of modifications received even after the object of sensation is no longer present.[44] Although Aristotle does not define this part of the soul, he establishes it as the means "through which the phantasm is produced within us":

> If then, imagination possesses no other characteristics than the aforesaid [that of being different from sensation, and of not being identifiable with science and intellection] and if it is what it has been described to

be, imagination will be a motion generated by actual perception. And, since sight is the principle sense, imagination has derived even its name [φαντασία] from light [φάος], because without light one cannot see. Again, because imagined objects remain in us and resemble the corresponding sensations, animals perform many actions under their influence; some, that is, the brutes, through not having intellects, and others, that is, men, because intellect is sometimes obscured by passion or disease or sleep.[45]

The image produced by the fantasy is a potential intelligible[46] that becomes active through the mediation of the agent intellect.[47] In the *phantasma*, therefore, lies the form of the object of sensation, which is then "extracted" through a process of illumination, then purified of any residual materiality.[48]

Once the image is acted upon by the agent intellect, the form within the image regains its innate, dynamogenic power.[49] (The dynamic power proper to the form that is communicated to the possible intellect by the image under the influence of the agent intellect is that which later will be called *species intelligibilis*). Because this intelligible is produced in the intellect, which is thus activated, the intellect is now capable of understanding the immaterial form, which is kept in memory as the "possession of an image as icon of that of which it is image."[50] As we can see, the function of the *phantasm* both in memory and in the process of knowledge is fundamental. Aristotle states that the intellect is a φαντασία τις, a kind of fantasy, and he repeats several times a principle that medieval scholasticism will accept as basic to the whole cognitive process, namely that man can understand nothing without *phantasms*:

> But it would seem that without objects of sensation there is nothing independently existent, so that it is in the sensible forms alone that the intelligible forms exist. . . . And for this reason, given that without sensation a man could not learn or understand anything, we must understand that at the very time when man is actually thinking he must have an image before him.[51]

As soon as a person recognizes an object, the imagination presents the object as an appetitive end that can be reached by means of the practical intellect.[52] Yet because desire does not reside within the intellect, whose end is truth, but in the appetite, whose perfection is that toward which all love tends, the appetite in motion is not the rational but the sensible one.[53] Thus love, being caused by a visible form (*species*) that reaches the intellect, is subjected to reason, yet being ultimately a motion of the sensible appetite can, through the pneuma and the body's innate heat, darken man's reason and cause him to seek a particular good in lieu of the true, universal good. This theory of the imagination is central to the medical concept of erotic desire, for it is in the imagination that the image of the beloved is fixed in a state abstracted from actual perceptions of the senses, and altered into an exaggerated version that preoccupies the mind and provokes the state of disease.

Antiochus and Stratonice

Erotic passion was pursued as a *topos* after Aristotle by a number of other writers, including Heracleides Ponticus (ca. 390–310 B.C.),[54] Theophrastus (fl. 255 B.C.),[55] and Clearcus (a younger contemporary of Aristotle).[56] This tradition of thought was resumed by Galen, was passed on to the Byzantine physicians Oribasius and Paul of Aegina, and through them to the Syrians and finally to the Arabs, who in turn influenced the medical writers of the schools of Salerno, Bologna, and Montpellier. Such was the course of transmission to western Europe of this medical concept of erotic melancholy, a concept tracing its origins to a fusion of the Hippocratic and Aristotelian traditions concerning the passions and their courses in the body, developed under the influence of the early Greek love poets, Sappho in particular, but also Archilocus, and the influence of Greek tragedy. That fusion of components, literary and scientific, achieved its fullest development in the lyrics and romances of the Alexandrian age, and in the rhetorical *disputationes* popular in the Roman world. This period of integration and literary exemplification of the idea projected love as a form of disease in social contexts that hovered between fiction and history. Subsequent observers were led thereby into considering love in a clinical sense as a condition to be diagnosed in accordance with its symptoms as related by the poets and novelists, and treated in accordance with its nature.

The most conspicuous example of this amalgamation, and without any doubt the account that received the greatest attention by poets and physicians throughout the centuries to follow, was the story of Antiochus and Stratonice. The story was attributed to the physician Erasistratus (fl. end of the fourth century B.C.) as the record of a true event. It was, in turn, popularized by Valerius Maximus (fl. first century B.C.) in his *Factorum et dictorum memorabilium*, a book of anecdotes for orators, and by Plutarch (50 B.C.–A.D. 12) in his *Life of Demetrius*.

Valerius Maximus tells of how Antiochus, the young son of King Seleucus was:

> overwhelmed by an infinite love for his stepmother, Stratonice, and how, out of reverence for his father, he hid the merciless wound in his heart, though he knew of the danger in that fire that consumed him. His heart enclosed the different effects; his boundless desire and his deep

bashfulness reduced his body to a state of extreme sickness. He lay in his bed like a man at death's door, to the great grief of his kin. The father, prostrate with misery, anticipated the death of his only son and pondered the weight of so great a loss. The household appeared more funereal than regal. But the provident intervention of the mathematician Leptine or of Erasistratus dissipated the cloud of gloom. Sitting close to Antiochus, he [Erasistratus] noticed how the young man blushed and turned pale when Stratonice entered, and how his breathing became calm again when she went out of the room. Observing this with greater attention he unveiled the truth; taking as if by chance the young man's arm he recognized the disease he suffered by the throb of the arteries, now intense now languid as Stratonice came and went. Immediately he told Seleucus. Without hesitation the king gave his beloved wife to his son, attributing to fate the fact that he had fallen in love, but to his great modesty the fact that he had been ready to dissimulate his passion unto death.[57]

What interested Valerius Maximus in the tale is not the scientific method of diagnosis used by Erasistratus, nor the narrative possibilities offered by the episode, which he undoubtedly took from an earlier model, but the anecdote that, in its brevity, could serve the turn of a public orator. What concerns us is the way in which the story found its way into the medical world through subsequent accounts as an epitome of the treatment of unfulfilled passion as a true disease, a model for the diagnostic methods of the physician based on the variations in the intensity of the pulse, and as a precedent for advocating sexual gratification as a cure for this melancholy disease.

The version that had the most direct influence upon Western medicine was Plutarch's, for it was his account of the story, with its interest in medical symptoms, that caught the attention of Galen, the great Roman physician, whose enormous influence upon Arabic and Western medicine established the subsequent importance of the *topos*. Indeed, it could be said that Galen's interest in the tale gave birth to that medical tradition insofar as it was his commentary on this anecdote concerning the diagnosis of love by medical means that provided the paradigm for subsequent writers to follow. Plutarch takes into consideration the symptoms of the patient and the strategies of the attending physician. He tells how Antiochus, being desperately in love with Stratonice, "resorted to many means of fighting down his passion, but at last, condemning himself for his inordinate desires, for his incurable malady, and for the subjugation of his reason . . . determined to seek a way of escape from life and to destroy himself gradually by neglecting his person and abstaining from food, under pretense of having some disease." The physician Erasistratus, realizing the cause of the malady, decided to remain in the youth's bed chamber, "and if any of the beauties of the court came in, male or female, he would study the countenance of Antiochus, and watch those parts and movements of his person which nature has made to sympathize most with the inclinations of the soul." As soon as Stratonice enters, "lo, those tell-tale signs of which Sappho sings are all there in him: stammering speech, fiery flushes, darkened vision, sudden sweating, irregular palpitations of the heart, and finally, as his soul was taken by storm, helplessness, stupor, and pallor."[58] Plutarch, following Aristotle, considers erotic passion an ὄρεξις, which has its seat in the heart and which, as it grows, combines with ἐπιθυμία and becomes the cause of suffering, sleeplessness, and ultimately madness.[59] Unlike Valerius Maximus, however, Plutarch does not refer to the beating of the pulse (or of the heart) as the only means to diagnose the disease. By ascribing scientific value to the signs of the passion of love taken from the poetic tradition, he inaugurates a medical-poetic symptomatology that will remain fundamentally unchanged throughout the entire literature on the disease down to the end of the eighteenth century.

After Plutarch, the story of Antiochus divided into two main currents, each partaking of elements of the other: a literary one and a medical one. To the first group belong the versions of the historian Appian (Antiochus thinks of killing himself), and of Lucian (who treats the story in a brief humorous way in *De conscribenda historia* and the *Icaromenippus*, and at greater length in the *De dea Syra*). Also belonging to this group are the versions by Julian the Apostate, by Petrarch in the *Triumphus cupidinis*, and by Bandello. There are others, by Claudianus, Soranus, Dracontius, and Aristenetus that introduce such variants as a change of names for the protagonists. The story appears in the anonymous *Aegritudo Perdiccae*, in brief hints in the *Historia Apollonii Tyri* and in Suidas, in various stories in the *Thousand and One Nights*, in story XL of the *Gesta Romanorum*, in the opening pages of the *Mesnewi* by Shelaleddin Rumi, in the episode of Giachetto and Gianetta in Boccaccio's *Decameron*, and in the novels of Ascanio dei Mori, Parabosco, Leon Battista Alberti, down to Goethe's *Wilhelm Meister*, Charles Reade's *The Cloister and the Hearth*, and Giovanni Verga's "Drammi intimi." It was developed by Luís de Camoëns in his "El-Rei Seleuco" and was the subject of a whole iconographic tradition that includes a magnificent painting by Ingres. The list is far from complete.[60]

In the second group are the discussions of the story in Galen and Avicenna and the references either to the story of Antiochus or to the diagnostic method based upon the variation of the pulse found in practically every medical chapter on erotic melancholy down to the eighteenth century. Galen leaves a personal account of how he, by using the method ascribed to Erasistratus, was able to diagnose as erotic melancholy the disease that had befallen the wife of a certain Iustus. The many references to erotic melancholy and erotic obsession spread throughout his many works and in his brief treatise on the subject set the scientific perimeters for all later discussions:

> Therefore I shall tell you the rest of what I promised you after this [digression], for just now I must add this discussion, especially since a number of sophistic physicians—ignorant of the method by which Erasistratus recognized the love that a young man felt for a maid-servant of his father—write that he discovered a pulse peculiar to love by the increased pulsation in the arteries of the young man. However, he does not offer any further proofs that would allow one to substantiate the claim that [love] was discovered by the pulse. I cannot say in which way Erasistratus managed to discover it. However, I will reveal to you the way in which I came to know about it. I was called in to see a woman who was tormented by sleeplessness in the night, and who shifted herself from one position to another in her bed. Since I found this woman lacking in fever, I began asking in a very particular way about everything that had happened to her so that we could discover why the sleeplessness occurred. However, she answered almost nothing at all, which indicated to me that I was questioning her in vain. At last, she turned her face away, threw her clothes over her body and hid herself away completely. She bent her head like someone overcome by sleep and looking for some small pillow to lean it on. After my departure, I reasoned that she was suffering from one of two things: either she was tormented by melancholy, or she was grieving over some cause she did not want to confess. . . . I returned [a fourth time], and after discussing, alone with a maidservant, all sorts of things, I came to understand quite clearly that she was afflicted by sorrow, the cause of which I was able to discover by chance, just as I believe Erasistratus did. I was certain that her condition did not arise in the body, but rather in the soul—which was confirmed, as it happened, at the very moment I was visiting her. When someone came in from the theater and announced that he had seen Pylades dancing, both the expression on her face and her color changed. Seeing this, I placed my hand on her wrist and detected an uneven pulse, one that is suddenly irregular and agitated, a clear indication of a troubled spirit . . . thus I discovered that the woman was in love with Pylades, a fact confirmed by similar observations in the following days.[61]

The episode which Galen relates does not differ substantially from those in Valerius Maximus and Plutarch. What has changed is the ultimate significance of the episode, which no longer fulfills a moral, didactic, historical, or merely anecdotal function, but a rigorously scientific one: unfulfilled erotic passion can turn into a melancholy disease, and it is the task of the physician to examine its causes, symptoms, and the proper methods of cure. This scientific rigor was inherited by post-Galenic physicians, who considered love as a potential mental disease to be studied separately or together with melancholy and madness.[62]

Love and Its Illusions

Classical Roman literature and philosophy teem with accounts of unhappy lovers and with discourses on love. An exhaustive study of *aegritudo amoris* in the language, metaphors, and doctrines of the time would entail the examination of a vast literature and a consideration of the many correlations between the works involved.[63] For our purposes, two salient examples will suffice to represent the way in which such love was perceived in the last years of the pagan age: the fierce diatribe against the passion of love in the final section of bk. IV of Lucretius's *De rerum natura*, and the episode of Echo and Narcissus in Ovid's *Metamorphoses*.

In the universe of Lucretius, controlled by the laws of Epicurean materialism, love, like all human feelings, is reduced to a physical stimulus and is thus subject to a close physiological analysis. Love occurs when the *simulacra* or images of a body invade the mind of another person. Then "arises the desire to seek that body by which the mind has been smitten."[64] Lucretius continues, "he who receives the blow . . . inclines toward the one who strikes and desires union in order to cast fluid from body to body for his unspoken desire anticipates delight."[65] Lucretius separates love from erotic passion, and it is the latter which he condemns because it is the cause of profound perturbations that lead man to disease and madness, even once the object of desire is no longer present:

> For if what you love is absent, yet its images are there, and the sweet name sounds in your ears. But it is fitting to flee those images, to frighten away what feeds love, to turn the mind in other directions, to cast the collected liquid into any body, and not to retain it, being wrapped up once for all in the love of one person, and thereby to insure care and certain pain for yourself. For the sore quickens and becomes inveterate by feeding; daily the madness grows and the tribulation becomes heavier unless you overlay the first wounds with new blows, and cure them while they are still fresh by wandering with Venus light-o'-love, or can turn your thoughts in some other direction.[66]

Lucretius, following the well-established Epicurean tradition, considers erotic passion a disease of the soul that slowly pervades the entire body, just like madness,[67] and that must be eradicated before it completely upsets the physiopsychological balance of the man, namely that condition of *ataraxia* in which the ultimate pleasure, that is to say the ultimate good, consists.[68] It is worth noticing that Lucretius prescribes, as an effective cure for the disease, falling in love with other women and copulation, possibly within the boundaries of matrimony,[69] thus anticipating a therapeutic methodology that will enjoy great popularity among the fathers of the church (who derive it from the Scriptures) and afterwards among the medieval and Renaissance physicians. In the final analysis, Lucretius develops his concept of eros along traditional lines; the *topos* of melancholy madness and of erotic passion as disease reflects a way of thinking well-rooted in the culture of his time.

Ovid also follows this tradition (which was defined—at least in its literary dimensions—by the Hellenistic and neoteric poets).[70] In the episode of Echo and Narcissus in bk. III of the *Metamorphoses*, the nymph Echo, daughter of the Air and Earth, falls in love with Narcissus. Rejected by him, she runs away,

> spurned and hiding,
> Ashamed, in the leafy forests, in lonely caverns.
> But still her love clings to her and increases
> And grows on suffering; she cannot sleep,
> She frets and pines, becomes all gaunt and haggard,
> Her body dries and shrivels till voice only
> And bones remain, and then she is voice only
> For the bones are turned to stone.[71]

Cruel Narcissus, while hunting one day in the forest, having stopped at a spring to quench his thirst, and seeing in the water a reflection, not realizing that it is his own image he is seeing, falls in love with himself, and languishes, consumed by love, unable to touch food or drink until he brings on his own death:

> As yellow wax dissolves with warmth around it,
> As the white frost is gone in morning sunshine,
> Narcissus, in the hidden fire of passion,
> Wanes slowly, with the ruddy color going,
> The strength and hardihood and comeliness,
> Fading away, and even the very body
> Echo had loved. She was sorry for him now,
> Though angry still, remembering; you could hear her
> Answer "Alas:" in pity, when Narcissus
> Cried out "Alas:" You could hear her own hands beating
> Her breast when he beat his. "Farewell, dear boy,
> Beloved in vain!" were his last words, and Echo
> Called the same words to him. His weary head
> Sank to the greensward, and death closed the eyes
> That once had marveled at their owner's beauty.[72]

Certainly, it is an eccentric death if considered in relation to a tradition of narrative realism, yet an exemplary one if considered in terms of the tradition of erotic melancholy.

The passion of both Echo and Narcissus presents a clearly pathological symptomatology: the passion of unrequited love is a malady against which there is little defense, a malady whose end is death. The influence of Ovid is well known throughout the Middle Ages and the Renaissance. However, his importance in the development of the language of love does not rest exclusively with his narratives. Fundamental here is the discourse on love in the *Ars Amatoria* that will become almost a form of teaching by precept, and that will profoundly influence the culture of the Middle Ages because of its systematic and didactic character.

The Fathers of the Church

Christian thinkers in the first centuries accept, for the most part, the doctrine of the passions developed by Greek and Roman philosophers and physicians. The system of psychology employed by the church fathers is, in fact, built upon the foundations laid by Plato and especially by the Stoics, while their physiological beliefs derive mostly from the Hippocratic tradition systematized by Galen.[73] Love, within this tradition, is conceived as an impulse of the appetitive faculty, and its phenomenology is explained by the fact that its organic component includes a state of alteration which can reach a high degree of violence and permanence.

Because of this physicial coefficient and the degree of alteration it carries, the early fathers considered sexual love a harmful impulse, capable of deflecting man from the road of reason and virtue. Man, writes Clement of Alexandria, is made of soul and body, and the body is the seat and the vehicle of the soul. Being made of soul and body, man consists of a rational part (τὸ λογιστικόν) and of an irrational part (τὸ ἄλογον).[74] The rational soul vivifies the body, and by means of the vital spirit it becomes the principle of its animal constitution.

> We accordingly assert that the rational and ruling power is the cause of the constitution of the living creature, and also that the irrational part is animated by and is a part of it. Now the vital force (in which is comprehended the power of nutrition and growth, and generally of motion), is assigned to the carnal spirit, which has a great susceptibility to motion and which passes in all directions through the senses.
>
> Through the corporeal spirit, then, man perceives, desires, rejoices, is angry. . . . It is by it, too, that thoughts and conceptions advance to actions. And when it masters the desires, the ruling faculty reigns.[75]

Clement accepts the threefold division of the soul postulated by Plato;[76] the rational soul has to be in a position to rule over the irascible and the concupiscible parts, seats of all the passions. Because of original sin, however, it has lost its control, and the passions, through the work of the demons,[77] can disturb the soul unless they are subjected to a new force, that of the Christian Logos, the only force capable of reestablishing the order desired by God.

Consequently, Clement considers sexual love an *epithymia* (ἐπιθυμία) a desire that hinders reason: "They who are skilled in such matters distinguish it from lust, and assign the latter, as being irrational, to pleasure and licentiousness."[78] Love, in fact, is a kind of sickness of the spirit and of the body: "I agree with Antisthenes when he says: 'could I catch Aphrodite, I would shoot her; for she has destroyed many of our beautiful women.' And he says that 'love is a vice of nature, and the wretches who fall under its power call the disease a deity.'"[79] Therefore, love—together with the other passions—must be resisted by every means, so that man may find again that equilibrium of body and soul without which he cannot hope to regain the kingdom of heaven:

> As Aristo says, "against the whole tetrachord of pleasure, pain, fear, and lust, there is need of much exercise and struggle."
> "For it is these, it is these that go through our bowels, and throw into disorder men's hearts."[80]

The early Christian writers concurred in the opinion that love is a disease of the senses that also fatally corrupts the soul. It should not be forgotten that in the Greco-Roman world religion and healing were two notions intimately connected.[81] Both pre-Christians and early Christians did not distinguish, in a rigorous manner, the diseases of the body from those of the spirit. The physician was not the only one capable of healing the sick; the philosopher and the Christian teacher also had this power insofar as to heal the body meant also to heal the soul, and *vice versa*. Consequently, medical language could be used in moral teaching and in preaching, while religious language could be used in the medical arts; for the Platonic philosophers, for the Stoics, and for the Christians alike the passions, and especially lust, are true sicknesses.[82]

Tertullian, who was well versed in the medical sciences of his times,[83] writes in this context:

> the soul shares the pain of the body when the latter suffers from bruises, wounds, or sores, and the body will reflect the disabilities of the soul under the influence of anxiety, worry, or love by a parallel weakness, as when the body testifies to the presence of shame and fear in the soul by blushing or growing pale.[84]

St. Basil considers love a sickness inasmuch as it is a passion, and that Christ, the great Doctor of souls, is the only one capable of healing man.[85] He, too, recognizes the detrimental effects of love on the body:

are not wanton chamberings, impure embraces, and all such acts of maddened and frenzied mind manifestly and in every respect detrimental to nature and notoriously harmful? Do they not represent the loss or diminution of powers which are in a very real sense proper and personal to the individual, since by such unions the body is weakened and depleted of aliment that is in the highest degree congruent with it and preservative of its members?[86]

The treatise *De virginitate*, attributed to Basil of Ancyra,[87] is of considerable interest inasmuch as it reflects the psychological and physiological theories of both the philosophical schools (especially the Neoplatonists) and the medical schools. According to this author, human love is a *contagium* taken in through the eyes (although this passion involves all the senses), and is seated in the liver.[88] Following the psychology of Plato and of the early fathers, Basil considers man to be formed of a rational and an irrational part, comparable to a centaur, half man and half beast:

according to the account of our physiology, our Creator made man of a rational and an irrational part, just like a centaur. The superior part, from the head to the chest was endowed with human form. The rest of the body, from the navel to the loins, He shaped like that of the horse, which is inclined towards the pleasures of the belly and, like the brutes, is prone to unbridled lust.[89]

It is this ferine part that nourishes passions such as love and envy. If they are not checked in time, they grow until they overwhelm the rational part of man, and slowly but unrelentingly consume his soul and body:

he who loves and he who envies suffer alike. For just as love with its concupiscence consumes the soul and the body of the lover, envy decomposes the soul and body of the envious. For the same reason both lovers and the envious are defrauded, because love with its desire and envy with its concupiscence make them idle and cause them to waste away both in body and in soul.[90]

In fact, Basil continues, "those who, through vices and inordinate passions, mix the soul with the body destroy that good which exists in both and which is necessary to life. With the filth of the pleasures of the flesh they corrupt the shining and clear spirit, and, in a similar manner, taint the cleanliness and beauty of the body; in this manner, they show that this [mixing] is injurious to the business of life."[91]

In the final analysis, the bodies of lovers are attracted to one another like iron to the magnet so that the souls "attached by the amorous union of the bodies experience the passions through an infinity of forms."[92]

The most exhaustive and systematic study of the passions, the one

which sums up the speculations of the fathers and anticipates the solutions that will be offered by scholastic philosophy, is found in the
treatise *De natura hominis* by Nemesius of Emesa, written near the end
of the fourth century.[93] Nemesius, well-versed both in philosophy and
in the sciences of his times, and especially in medicine, tries to interpret
the conscious life of the soul through the study of the elements consti-
tuting the human body. Thus it is physiology that offers the key to the
unveiling of man's psyche: "As man is corporeal and the body is composed of the four elements, it follows that he is liable to all contingencies
to which those elements are liable, namely scission, mutation, and flux,
three things affecting the body only."[94] The harmonious mixing of these
elements and of the corresponding humors forms the temperament of
man which controls his state of health and of sickness:

> When change takes place in some quality, we need to restore the balance
> by introducing the opposite quality so as to bring the constitution of the
> body back to normal. The physician's art is not, as some think, just to
> cool a fevered body, but to restore it to an equable temperament.[95]

In order to refute the opinion of those who identify the soul with temperament Nemesius asks himself how it is possible that certain vices and
virtues arise naturally in man:

> It is true that it [the soul] proceeds from bodily temperament. For just
> as men are naturally healthy or sickly by temperament, so some are
> naturally choleric, some proud, some craven, some lecherous. Never-
> theless, some such persons master these tendencies and prevail. Now
> it is clear that they master temperament. And what masters and what
> is mastered are different things. So temperament is one thing and soul
> another. For the body is the soul's instrument. If it is well constituted,
> it helps the soul, and is, itself, in good condition. But if the body is not
> well constituted, it impedes the soul. . . . Moreover, unless the soul is
> watchful, it too is perverted, together with its instrument.[96]

The passion of love is caused by temperament,[97] and inasmuch as sexual
desire enters through the senses, which are common both to the soul and
to the body,[98] it has an effect on the entire being. Concupiscence, in fact,
is a passion of the soul, but it takes its seat in the liver: "concupiscence,
which is roused by things that we perceive, has the liver as its organ"[99]
and spreads throughout the rest of the body by means of the sensorial
nerves.[100] For Nemesius, sexual desire has strictly physiological causes,
although, because of the physical alteration it produces, it can also influence the psyche of man. Since it is a voluntary act, however, it can,
indeed it must, be subjected to reason:

Let no one suppose that because lascivious desires or anger have an inciting source outside the subject that these transgressions are involuntary. . . . Even though these motions had a first cause external to the subject, the subjects nevertheless did their deeds themselves with their own proper members.[101] When the soul, therefore, yields to physical temperament, and gives way to lust or anger . . . the evil so constituted is voluntary.[102]

We have already spoken of the fact that in the Greco-Roman world physical and spiritual diseases were considered as having strict correlations. Likewise, the Christian fathers considered soul and body an indissoluble binomial. It is evident that sexual desire—considered a pathological disease of melancholy natures whose symptoms are clearly perceived in the physical organism of those who suffer from it—was also considered as having a negative influence on man's spiritual sphere. Because passions, sexual love, and melancholy came into being through original sin, they are perceived as negative alterations that threaten man's journey to salvation; they can be confronted and overcome only through a profound act of faith, by means of meditation that mortifies the body to raise the spirit, or through the help of an apostolate capable of revealing man's blindness and the true path to heaven.

III

Erotic Melancholy
and Medieval Medicine

Before the fourth century A.D., discussions of sexual desire had been concerned principally with the psychological aspects of the problem. Through the influence of Galen, discussions from the fourth century onward concentrated more specifically on the medical categories and on the physiology of love. Because love could turn into a disease, it was no longer exclusively the interest of writers and philosophers but became part of the official medical *curriculum* as physicians began to study its causes, symptoms, and the methods for its cure. This new tendency is evident in the medical treatises of the Byzantine physicians Oribasius (325–403) and Paul of Aegina (fl. 650). It was through their works that classical medical culture was carried through to the Middle Ages. Their ideas would stand unchallenged and would be repeated for centuries to come.

The description offered by Oribasius of the malady of love (τὸν ἐρῶτον) in his *Synopsis* is brief and lacks any discussion of the etiology of the passion.[1] Those who are sick with love, he writes, are sad, cannot sleep or eat, and therefore waste away. When the physician realizes that love is the cause of his patient's disease he must immediately try to remove the lover's fixation upon the object of his desire, compel him to drink in the company of friends, to take baths, to hear stories. Because it is difficult to distract the lover's attention, the physician should make use of subterfuge: he must strike fear into the lover's heart, and with severe reproaches he must convince him to abandon his fixation. The *signa* of the disease listed by Oribasius were often repeated down to the eighteenth century: hollow eyes deprived of tears, continuous motion of the eyelids, and the weakening of the whole body.[2]

Paul of Aegina, a Byzantine surgeon writing in the seventh century, offers a very similar description in ch. 17 of his *De re medica libri septem*.[3] He considers unrequited love to be a disease of the mind, a passion of the soul caused by a state of violent emotion and the derangement of the reason. It is a form of the disease called *cura*. Mental activity and love are by now seen as being strictly connected, and because excessive thinking is also at the basis of melancholy, love and melancholy come to assume tacitly similar connotations. Because *cura* strikes both the psyche and the bodily constitution, the therapy must be designed to act upon both components. Baths, libations of wine, physical exercise, plays, and stories are all methods aimed at distracting the lover's mind to make him forget the object of his love. The symptoms of the malady are those described by Oribasius. Paul also mentions that the pulse of the lover undergoes a noticeable change in intensity when the beloved appears. He does not consider this variation of the pulse to be unique to lovers but typical of all those who suffer from *cura*, a point which was at the center of a polemic with other physicians. Worth noting also is the fact that both Oribasius and Paul of Aegina consider coitus to be an effective cure for both melancholy and for love, if properly prescribed.[4]

Even with Paul we cannot be certain that erotic passion is to be officially classified among the diseases of melancholy. The chapter on lovesick persons follows the chapter on lycanthropy, which was without question such a disease: Haly Abbas calls it *melancholia canina*.[5] Paul defends his placement of the section on love because love is an affection of the brain consisting of cares and sorrows, and "care is a passion of the soul occasioned by the reason's being in a state of laborious emotion."[6] It is an association by common effects. But Paul, like Oribasius, remarks that some physicians mistake the affection, presumably for a disease of melancholy, and treat the patient accordingly, which is extremely dangerous. For to deprive the lover of food when he is already weak from fasting, and of baths when his intense thought has dried out his brain is the wrong approach. Such is our interpretation of his comment that translates literally: "some persons, therefore, being desponding and sleepless, some physicians, mistaking their affection, have wasted them by prohibiting baths, and enjoining quietude, and a spare diet."[7]

A tradition following from Theocritus that love had no medicinal cures was countered by several of the ancient physicians who devised remedies for the treatment of desponding lovers as a disease-like condition in a category of its own. The question of starving lovers or regaling them with moist foods persisted as a *topos* down to the Renaissance. Ferrand accepts both therapies by arguing that fasting is appropriate as a preventive measure where the overfed and sanguine person is inclined to convert excess blood to seed, but that once the condition enters into pathological states, fasting is clearly harmful. For Ferrand, this polemic is cause for a conciliation of opposites through juxtaposition.[8] A forthright association of erotic passion and melancholy would have to wait another three centuries for the works of Rhazes, though ironically Rhazes looks back to several earlier writers for his authority in making that association.

One of the names he mentions is Alexander of Tralles, a physician of the Byzantine school practicing in Rome during the sixth century. In a section of his *Therapeutika* (bk. I, ch. 17) dealing specifically with melancholy, he relates the story of a woman who was afflicted with this disease during the long absence of her husband, and who was cured of her fears and inordinate sorrow by his return. Melancholy was traditionally classified as a state of depression without apparent cause. Yet Alexander allows this case, with its very real cause, to be a state of true melancholy—a cause, furthermore, that is associated with love.[9] The case parallels a similar one cited by Galen in the *De locis affectis* of a man who so lamented the death of his wife that he lost all appetite, could no longer digest what little he ate, and was seized by a sorrow that went beyond all reasonable cause in a way resembling melancholy. But again, Galen refuses to allow that a condition caused by the loss of a person loved can lead to a state of true melancholy. Rather, he concludes that because this man was accustomed to frequent intercourse, the absence of his partner produced a surfeit of seed that spread throughout the body like a poison, the semen itself serving as a form of infection. Galen associates this condition neither with erotic love, as in the case of Justus's wife, nor with melancholy, but rather with hysteria, with its purely somatic causes.[10] This explanation will also persist; among the Renaissance physicians retention of seed will become one of the recognized material causes of erotic melancholy. But Alexander of Tralles does not resort to these explanations; he allows the case he describes to stand, by all appearances, as a true example of melancholy. That fact invites us to consider him as perhaps the only pre-Arabic physician (of those whose works survive) who permits this association.

With the tantalizing hints in the life of Hippocrates attributed to Soranus of Ephesus about the curing of Perdicca, king of Macedonia, wasted for love of Phila, one of the concubines of his deceased father, Alexander (a narrative conspicuously similar to that of Antiochus and Stratonice), we have a traditional interpretation of erotic love in terms of the symptoms of disease.[11] Despite the reticence on technical grounds suggested in the medical treatises, the idea appears to have been generally received in antiquity, and is to be traced, whether by history or by hearsay, to the father of Western medicine himself. The descriptions of the symptoms in Sappho, Euripides, the Greek romances, Ovid, Plutarch, and others argue that the ancient world understood the nature of love melancholy in fact if not in name, and that for the physicians to deny such a condition in medical terms because love is a perturbation of the soul while melancholy is a product of black bile was for them to do battle with an idea already widely endorsed. Certainly, the evidence is strong from an early date on that the poets recognized the capacity for love to bring about pathological conditions affecting both the body and the soul. It only remained for the Arab physicians to reassess that material in terms of a modified and expanded application of the theories of humoral medicine to place love systematically among the diseases of melancholy.

The Arab Physicians

Abū Bakr Muḥammad ibn zakarīyā al-Rasi (ca. 850–923 or 924), known in the West as Rhazes, or Rasis, was the most illustrious and prolific physician of Islam. In his medical encyclopedia entitled *Al-awī* (*Liber continens*)—a vast compendium of quotations gathered from Greek, Arabic, Persian, and Indian sources—there is a statement on erotic melancholy, which he identifies with lycanthropy (*quṭrub*), a kind of madness that compels the sufferer to behave like a wolf.[12] Love is no longer perceived merely as a tragic force but as a horrifying form of mental derangement capable of destroying the very essence of man. Rhazes describes in detail the physical progression of the disease. At first the eyesight weakens; the eyes become hollow and dry. The tongue gradually dries up, and pustules grow on it. The body becomes progressively dehydrated, and the patient is constantly thirsty. If the disease is not stopped the symptoms of *usues* (Arabic *wiswas*, meaning incoherent speech) and of melancholy *birsem* (Arabic *birsam*, meaning death in the heart, or pleurisy) begin to appear (Caelius Aurelianus described similar symptoms).[13] Finally, blisters appear all over the body. Following Rufus of Ephesus, Rhazes states that the sick lover spends his days prostrate, face downward, a symptom that reappears in iconography and in literature.[14] On the face, back, and calves a kind of dust afterwards appears, together with marks similar to dog bites. At the height of the disease, the lover is seen wandering by night through cemeteries howling like a wolf. For this advanced state there is no other remedy but death.

Citing the authority of Rufus, Alexander of Tralles, Paul of Aegina, Isaac Judaeus, and Symeon Seth, Rhazes considers *quṭrub* to be a disease of the brain capable of overwhelming the whole organism. In prescribing the proper therapy, therefore, the physician must consider both components of the malady. Opiums are recommended to induce sleep, baths and topicals to humidify the brain. The patient should also be bled frequently to the point of fainting, and should be purged often.

These are traditional therapies for melancholy adapted for the treatment of love. Such adaptations will continue to provide the major source for new cures for erotic diseases throughout the Renaissance. In the *Taksimu-l-'ilal* (*Liber divisionum*), translated for the first time into Latin by Gerard of Cremona, Rhazes adds traditional cures such as frequent

coitus, walking, and drinking.[15] It is noteworthy that Gerard, in his translation of Rhazes's *Kitāb al-Mansuri* (*Liber regius*, a compendium in 10
books dedicated to the governor of Chorasan, al-Mansur Ibn Ishaq, concerning the most important medical doctrines then current), remarks that
Rhazes in his chapter on melancholy "did not mention gabod . . . nor did
he mention that type of derangement that occurs for love of a woman or
of some object, and whose cure consists in drinking, moving from place
to place, and coitus with a woman other than the one affected."[16] But
while Rhazes may have overlooked this occasion to present his thoughts
on erotic love as a disease, Gerard's comment reveals that the idea, as
discussed in his other treatise, had taken hold.

Following Rhazes, the malady caused by unfulfilled love was examined by the Persian physician ʿAlī al-Abbās al-Majūsī, who flourished in
the middle of the tenth century and who was known in the Latin West
as Haly Abbas. Ch. 7, treatise 9 of his great medical epitome *al-Kitāb al-
mālikī* (*Pantegni*) is entitled "De malincolia et canina et amore causisque
eorum et signis" and indicates that melancholy, lycanthropy, and the
derangements caused by love are considered as one disease and are thus
studied together.[17]

According to theory, melancholy is a disease of the body while love
is a disease of the soul; so it had been among the ancient physicians.
Haly Abbas recognizes love as a disease of the brain because it is a *sollicitudo* toward a person or an object, accompanied by an obsessive desire
for possession. Yet with him that distinction between melancholy and
love begins to lose its force, because his definition of love as a *sollicitudo*
is drawn from the definition of melancholy, which is also a disease that
befalls those who cannot obtain or who have already lost the object of
their desires. Thereafter, the interreferentiality continues until love becomes, essentially, yet another of the purely psychological causes capable
of bringing on a state of melancholy. The amalgamation was inevitable.
On the one hand, Haly Abbas recognizes how melancholy, as a somatic
illness, can still have injurious effects upon the mind: a "certain feeling
of dejection and isolation that forms in the soul because of something
which the patients think is real that is in fact unreal."[18] On the other
hand, he lists the conventional physical causes of melancholy: a person
can have a predisposition to melancholy because of his inherited temperament (including such causes in the parents as damaged sperm or a
poor uterus), or it can be acquired by immoderate eating or drinking,
or by insufficient cleanliness of the internal organism, or by disturbing
the balance required by the six basic conditions of life: movement and
rest, sleeping and waking, evacuation and retention (to which baths and
coitus belong), eating and drinking, inhalation and exhalation, joy and
sadness. He notes too how black bile can also be produced by the in-
terruption of a habit, such as regular exercise, or by eating heavy food

that engenders hot dry blood, or by drunkenness or asceticism. But he also admits, in accordance with tradition, that melancholy could have purely psychological causes such as fear, annoyance, anger, or the loss of something irreplaceable, such as a child or a library. In these cases it is sadness or rejection that produces the melancholy state.

Following Aristotle's "Problem XXX," Arab physicians also postulated a melancholy of genius that befalls doctors, mathematicians, and philosophers when they memorize and meditate too much. That form of melancholy was likewise a product of cogitative processes.[19] Thus by degrees, love was absorbed into the classification of melancholy diseases as a *sollicitudo* causing the fear and sorrow that provoke the melancholy state. At the same time, as Ferrand clearly reveals, all of the traditional somatic causes of melancholy, including inherited temperaments, indolence, an overly rich diet, and conditions of the blood will become an integral part of the etiology of the diseases of love, thereby accounting for the vexingly diverse categories of causes to be found in the Renaissance treatises on love. They are a heritage of this conflation of love as a disease of the soul with the traditional diseases of melancholy that began in Haly Abbas. By the time of Ferrand, indeed much earlier, it was understood that all that pertained to melancholic diseases going back to Hippocrates automatically pertained to the diseases of erotic love. That inevitability came about with the adoption of the definition of love as an obsessive desire that afflicted and tormented the psyche; with such a definition, one that remained constant over a period of six hundred years of medical history, the other elements were destined to fall into place.

Haly Abbas was also concerned with the three types of melancholy: of the head only, of the entire body, and of the hypochondries. This classification was doctrine for the physicians of the Latin West, and love, as a disease of melancholy, had to find its place in this scheme (Ferrand, following Du Laurens, was entirely orthodox in his endorsement of the tradition). They were summarized in the work of an important mediator between the now lost works of Rufus of Ephesus and the Latin West, Ish'ḥāq ibn-Imrān (d. before 909). This link with Rufus is critical because it was he who postulated the importance of mental activity in the generation of melancholic diseases. His theories opened the way for the Arab philosophers to show how a man could think himself into a state of illness; and hence how love, as such a mental disturbance, could produce a state of disease. Rufus, with his foundation in the Peripatetic philosophers, and with his categorization of the types of melancholy in accordance with the humors and their specific behaviors, may have been the instigating authority of this entire tradition.[20]

The first type, according to Ish'ḥāq originates in the brain and is an idiopathic melancholy. This type must be divided into two subspecies:

the one, accompanied by high fever and originating in yellow bile following adustion, is characterized by awkward movements and foolish actions; the other must, in turn, be divided into two more subspecies, the first called *al-waswās as-sabu'i*, signifying predatory behavior such as is implied by lycanthropy, which is determined by black bile in the brain, the second comes from the corruption of black bile. The symptoms of this type of "cerebral" melancholy are sleeplessness, headache, flickering eyes, a craving for food, or a loss of appetite.

The second type derives from black bile released into the entire body before moving eventually to the brain. The symptoms include those of the first, as well as depression, anxiety, and terror.

The third type is caused by the spread of black bile throughout the body, and by its discharge into the upper orifice of the stomach or epigastrium. This is the melancholy of the hypochondrium, though it too can affect the brain because the epigastrium was thought to be in a reciprocal relation to the brain. The symptoms of this type are excessive flatulence, heaviness of the head, acid vomit, and constant weeping owing to vapor in the brain. For as long as the body preserves an abundance of good blood, this condition may also be accompanied by laughter.

Haly Abbas, in discussing hypochondriacal melancholy, divides it also into three parts: the first, arising from the blood, causes mental confusion that expresses itself in euphoria and laughter; the second, generated by yellow bile burnt in the body, causes wavering gaze, mischievous behavior, angry outbursts, sleeplessness, and restlessness; the third, arising from the black bile causes broodings, anxiety, evil imaginations, and love of solitude.[21] Haly declares forthrightly that erotic desire can produce both melancholy and lycanthropy; that point is no longer in question. Moreover, with Haly Abbas, as we have noted, the concept that the passion of love can deceive the lover into believing that the object of his desire is an obtainable good—indeed the only true good for him—enters into the discussion of *hereos*. A profound depression follows when the lover comes to understand that the object is eternally lost. Haly Abbas insists on the importance of recognizing the specific symptoms of the malady, noting that one cannot trust general symptoms insofar as they are common to several diseases of the brain. Yet his list does not differ in substance from those already encountered: hollow eyes constantly in motion, lack of tears, arhythmicity of the pulse. The methods proposed for the cure are equally traditional. They are aimed at trying to convince the lover to forget the object of his desire. The lover is encouraged to have sexual relations with other women, to exercise with moderation, to bathe in tepid water, and to have a humidifying diet. He must also listen to harmonious music—a therapy suggested by Theophrastus for those suffering from melancholy and passed down by Asclepiades of Bithynia and Caelius Aurelianus.[22]

The most famous philosopher and physician of this period was 'Abū 'Alī Ḥusayn 'Abdullāh ibn Sīnā, known in the West as Avicenna (980–1037). It is in his vast medical epitome entitled *Al-qānūn fi't-ṭibb* (*Canon medicinae*) that we find the most complete disquisition on love among the Arab writers.[23] He referred to it as *al-'ishq* (*alhasch* in the Latin translation by Gerard of Cremona). Avicenna's definition of *al-'ishq* is very similar to Rufus of Ephesus's definition of melancholy: "multa cogitatio et tristitia faciunt accidere melancoliam." Avicenna defines love as a melancholy anguish similar to melancholy that is self-induced by thinking vehemently and continuously of a beautiful object, of its form, gestures, and manner, features that are fixed in the mind. Love is not inherently a disease, but it can take on a morbid disposition when it is not fulfilled. When the sexual appetite is not appeased, the memory continuously represents the object of beauty to the appetitive faculties, thereby increasing a desire that brings on a whole series of physical and mental complications. The disease has closely defined symptoms that the trained physician should be able to detect. To the traditional ones named above, he adds others: the respiration of the patient is irregular, the lover sometimes laughs, sometimes cries depending on the ethos of his thoughts, the entire body becomes dried out with the exception of the eyes with their lids heavy from the sighing and the sleepless nights. The irregularity of the pulse remains the decisive sign that reveals the true cause of the disease. Avicenna refines the techniques whereby the identity of the beloved can be determined by extending the questioning not only to the names of all the potential candidates in the entourage but also to "streets, dwellings, arts, crafts, families, and countries, joining each one with the name of the beloved, all the time feeling the pulse so that when it alters on the mention of any one thing several times, you will infer from this all the particulars about the beloved as regards name, appearance, and occupation." He attests to its efficacy from his own practice.

Finally he recommends union:

> If you can discover no cure except to unite the two in such wise as is sanctioned by religion and law, you will do so. We have seen cases where health and strength were completely restored and flesh regained in a very short time when the lover was accorded union with the beloved, even after the patient had become greatly attenuated and had suffered from severe chronic diseases and protracted accesses of fever . . . so that we were astonished thereat and realized the subordination of [human] nature to mental imaginations.[24]

Should this union not be possible, the physician must resort to traditional therapy. Avicenna insists on the fact that this melancholy disease, being caused by the obsessive permanence of the image of the beloved within the mind of the lover, must be treated first "psychologically," which is to say through a therapy capable of distracting the patient's mind from the object of his obsession. To this end the physician will prescribe baths, sleep, moderate physical exercise, and humectants. He should also hire an old woman to denigrate the beloved by saying horrible things about her to the lover. Old women, Avicenna adds, are much more expert than young women or men in these sorts of things. Often music constitutes a valid therapy, though he warns of potentially contrary effects. Should these methods prove insufficient, the physician has no choice but to resort to the therapy used for melancholy, mania, and *quṭrub*: bloodletting, and the evacuation of the humors through purges such as those made with aloes.

How far this concept of excessive sexual passion had pervaded the medieval Arabic world, and how seriously it was considered in the Latin West can be seen by the inclusion of a chapter on the disease in one of the most widely circulated books of the High Middle Ages, the small encyclopedia for travelers entitled *Viaticum*. The treatise, often erroneously attributed to Isaac Judaeus, Gerard of Cremona, or Gerard of Berry, is a translation by Constantinus Africanus[25] of the *Zād al-musāfir* by Abu Jafar Aḥmed Ibn Ibrāhīm Ibn ʾAlī Khālid, nicknamed Ibn Eddjezzar (the butcher's son: d. ca. 1004). A Greek translation of the work was also undertaken in the same years when Constantinus was active (the oldest MS Vatican N.CCC dates to the end of the tenth or the beginning of the eleventh century);[26] it is quite likely that both versions were prepared independently the one from the other, directly from the Arabic original.[27]

Ibn Eddjezzar's term for excessive love was translated as *hereos* by Constantinus, a term that will enjoy a long and widespread diffusion. He places his chapter on the subject in the section on mental illnesses, for he considers *hereos* a disease of the brain consisting of excessive desire accompanied by a severe state of anguish and the derangement of the cognitive powers.[28] His description is modeled on Avicenna's, whose medical text had already been invested with complete authority. Like Avicenna, and Rhazes before him, Ibn Eddjezzar considers *hereos* to be a melancholy disease, and that, as such, it can also be caused by the necessity of the organism to evacuate excessive humors: "at times the cause of this type of love is nature's necessity to expel a large superfluity of humors, whence Rufus said that sexual intercourse is a valid therapy for those who suffer from burnt yellow bile and melancholy." Because of their incessant thinking upon the object of desire, lovers have hollow eyes in constant motion and heavy eyelids. Because they suffer from insomnia, their inborn heat moves throughout their body in very irregular ways, and the color of their complexion turns yellowish green. Sleep, according to contemporaneous medicine, requires a moderately wet brain, that is to say, it occurs when good and moist vapors reach the brain. Sleep fulfills two functions: it tranquilizes the brain, the senses, and all mental functions; it allows the innate heat to permeate the entire body in order to digest the food and to mature the humors. The heat of passion, however, by drying up the brain, causes sleeplessness and draws the humors, not toward the interior where they are needed for digestion, but to the brain and to the outer layers of the body, causing the skin to acquire a dark yellow green color. This is the tint of melancholy, a sure sign that the health of the patient is gravely compromised.

The therapy suggested by Ibn Eddjezzar is, for the most part, already familiar and seems to have been derived from the remedies prescribed by Asclepiades of Bithynia for the healing of melancholy: the patient should be given wine in moderation, should listen to music and poetry, should walk through gardens full of light, perfumes, fruits, crossed by brooks with clear and soft-flowing water. He should also spend time with friends, walk with attractive men and women, bathe often, because bathing predisposes to joy, exercise in moderation, and travel. These remedies are clearly aimed at making the patient forget the object of his affection.

Almost every medical book of the time at least touched upon erotic melancholy, as in the case of the treatise *Takwīm al-abdān fī tadbīr al-insān* by Abū 'Alī Yahyā Ibn 'Isā Ibn Jazla (known in the West as Byngezla, Ben Gezla, or Buhahylayha: d. 1100), translated into Latin by Faraj Ibn Salim with the title *Tacuini aegritudinum*. The work consists of 44 tables (*canones*) describing 352 diseases and the relative therapies. The sixteenth canon discusses melancholy and mentions briefly *hereos*: "the love called hereos at its height causes the entire body to grow lean and sickly with the exception of the eyes. The eyelids will be very hot, the eyes will shed few tears, and the pulse of the lover is similar to that of one who suffers from distress."[29]

Of greater interest is the description by Abū al-Qāsim al-Zaharāwī Khalaf Ibn 'Abbās (called Albucasis or Alsaharavi by scholastic writers: d. after 1009–1010), the most famous among the Arabic writers on surgical procedures. In the second section of the first book of his best known medical compendium entitled *At-taṣrīf* (*Vade mecum*), Albucasis summarizes in a brief chapter what had been expounded previously concerning *hereos*.[30] He adds certain new concepts, however, that are the by-product of the gradual evolution of the problematic concerning sexual superexcitation. *Hereos*, Albucasis writes, is a disease that attacks the brain and damages the animal faculties. The definition is much more specific than those previously examined, given this implicit reference to a cellular division of the brain—a concept to be developed extensively by Western physicians. Given that such desire can be caused either by love for a person of the opposite sex or by an object, Albucasis divides the disease into two species: one occasioned by the necessity of the organism to expel an excessive quantity of humors (this is *amor hereos*, or excessive sexual appetite), the other by an affection of the soul arising from a deep craving for an object such as a plant, a garden, or a building. The dynamics of these two species of love are the same: a disease of the imagination accompanied by terrible symptoms arising from the incontrovertible conviction that the object can be obtained and that no efforts should be spared in achieving what all others take for a futile quest. Because melancholy destroys both the body and the mind, treatment should not be delayed. The first solution is the granting of the desired object or, failing that in the case of the first species, pressing the patient to have sexual intercourse with other women. The remaining therapy suggested by Albucasis is strictly traditional.[31]

While in the Arabic world the medical sciences had reached a position of great prominence owing to the protection and support of the Caliphs and as a result of the many translations and glosses of the ancient Greek and oriental texts, in the West medicine had been relegated to the monasteries. Until the end of the eighth century, the study of medicine was restricted to those very few people, mainly prelates, who could read Greek. There were no centers of medical education, nor were there academies where these texts could be translated into Latin.[32] We know that in the monastery founded by Cassiodorus (490–585) there was a collection of ancient manuscripts containing several medical works, and that Cassiodorus advised his disciples to study the medical arts. Isidor of Seville (560–639) includes many medical quotations in his monumental work, *Etimologiae*.[33] Some of the works of the Venerable Bede deal with medicine,[34] and some specific medical works have survived, such as the *Commentarium medicinale* by a deacon of the church of Milan named Crispo (first half of the eighth century)[35] and the *Dietetica* by Anthimus, personal physician to Theodoricus.[36] The nature of all these works, however, is basically therapeutic. They are concerned with herbal remedies confined, for the most part, to use in churches and monasteries, which also served, at the time, for hospitals.

The study of medicine entered into the regular curriculum of the schools of the Western Roman Empire only in 805, by decree of Charlemagne.[37] Around the same time there began, in the school of Tours founded by Alcuin (735–804), a systematic translation and transcription of classical Greek and Latin works, including several medical texts.[38] The most important centers of study were still the monasteries, and especially the Benedictine monasteries of Chartres, Fulda, Bobbio, and Montecassino. Between the ninth and the tenth centuries Montecassino became one of the most important medical centers in Western Europe. These schools were instrumental in the evolution of medical science because they constituted the link between ancient medicine and the lay schools of the Middle Ages, the first of which was the medical school founded in Salerno. The School of Salerno was the focal point toward which all the most important medical currents, both classical and contemporaneous, Greek, Latin, and Arabic, converged.[39] The first period of the school, from its foundation (traditionally placed at the end of the seventh century) to the arrival of Constantinus Africanus, was characterized by a study of Hippocratic medicine. The works compiled by the writers of the *Collegium Hippocraticum* consist mainly in summaries of Greek and Latin texts dealing with simple medicines. With Constantinus, the works of the great Arabic physicians were for the first time introduced into the West. This was the most important period of the School of Salerno, which reached its apogee with the rebirth of Latin medicine in the universities.[40]

The gradual decline of the school coincided with the growth of the universities, whose medical faculties prospered because of the translations of medical works from Arabic done by Constantinus and by the translators of the School of Toledo.[41] In the *Studium* of Bologna, the teaching of medicine was introduced in the twelfth century; the general *Studium* of Paris was founded in 1110, and in the years that followed were founded the universities of Montpellier (1181), Padova (1222), and Naples (1224).[42]

Love Melancholy in the Latin West

Around 1280, a friend of Arnald of Villanova, while practicing medicine in Sardinia, encountered the concept of *hereos* and was puzzled by its significance. He wrote to Arnald on the matter and thereby prompted the great Catalan physician to write a short treatise on "how it happens that such a strong and irrational emotion is generated in *heroical* love."[43] Though the doctrine of erotic melancholy had already become a part of the culture of the Latin West, Arnald's *Tractatus de amore heroico* indicates the doubts and confusion that still surrounded the nature of inordinate sexual desire. Physicians and natural philosophers were in agreement that it was a state of disease. Medical writers had provided a symptomatology and a range of cures for this condition, but they had nowhere discussed its etiology in any programmatic and scientific way. Even the identification of its chronic stages with other forms of mental aberrations, such as melancholia or mania, had been implied rather than stated. The Arabic texts had not attempted to rectify these ambiguities, and the early Western writers simply transcribed them without attempting to gloss the difficulties.

There is little doubt that the credit for introducing the concept of erotic melancholy into the West goes to Constantinus's translation of the

Zād al-musāfir. Very likely the translation also introduced the term *hereos* as well, though the problem of its etymological derivation, although extensively discussed by literary critics and historians of medicine, has eluded us.[44] Constantinus often took liberties with the content and arrangement of the parts of his sources, but in the case of the section dealing with *hereos* he was content to repeat the original text. Even in his own medical epitomes, such as the *De communibus medico cognitu locis* he deals with the disease in a few words; he states simply that "those who are distressed, sad and fearful, suspicious and enamoured, often fall prey to terrible diseases and to sudden death."[45]

This is also true of the others, such as Stephen of Antioch's translation of Haly Abbas's *al-Kitāb al-mālikī*, or the aforementioned translation of Rhazes's *Kitāb al-Mansuri* by Gerard of Cremona. Gerard informs the reader that Rhazes at that point of his exegesis should have mentioned erotic melancholy, but he does not attempt to fill in the gap.

Mary Wack and Michael R. McVaugh have repeatedly pointed out the importance of the commentaries on the *Viaticum* for the establishment of the etiology of erotic melancholy, with particular reference to a work written sometime before 1237 by Gerard of Berry.[46] Before glossing a number of phrases from the *Viaticum*, Gerard presents his own interpretation of *amor hereos*, drawn from the *Canon* of Avicenna. The central portion of his commentary attempts to explain the etiology of the disease:

What the cause of this malady is by which the virtues are affected is difficult to understand. The cause of the malady . . . is a defect in the estimative virtue, which is induced by sensed *intentiones* to apprehend insensible accidents that may perhaps not be real, so that it may believe some women to be better and more desirable than all others. This happens, then, when something highly acceptable and pleasing strikes the mind, which then judges other sense-objects to be similar, so that if it should encounter sensations that are not desirable they are hidden from the obsessive concentration of the mind.

As regards the sensitive soul, then, the estimative virtue (which is the noblest judge among the powers of the soul) commands the imaginative virtue to concentrate its attention on a particular person, and the imaginative virtue commands the concupiscible virtue; and thus the concupiscible virtue does not act alone, for just as it is obedient to the imaginative virtue, so too the imaginative is obedient to the estimative— by whose command all the virtues turn to the person whom the estimative virtue judges to be desirable, even though she may not be. Now the imaginative virtue fixes upon an object due to the unhealthy cold and dry complexion of its organ. As to the middle ventricle, where *estimatio* is located, the spirit and innate heat are drawn there, where *estimatio* is at work; thus the front ventricle is chilled and dried, so that a melancholy disposition, desire, and care (*sollicitudo*) persist. Where the concupiscible virtue is located, however, I will not try to decide.

Michael R. McVaugh, quoting this passage, finds its most provocative feature in "its attempt to fuse psychology, physiology, and physical causation in an account of *amor hereos*, one fully in the Galenic tradition of providing material explanations of mental states."[47] In fact, the fusion of psychology, physiology, and physical causation already belonged to the Aristotelian system of natural philosophy, as we have shown above, and it is through the revival of Aristotle that it enters into the Latin West. What Gerard of Berry understands quite well is the phantasmological nature of desire—that the *phantasma* plays a fundamental role in causing emotional and mental derangements.

It is very likely, as McVaugh suggests, that Gerard drew his characterization of the internal powers of the soul from Avicenna's *Canon*, and especially from the *De anima*. While Avicenna's classification of the "internal senses" is neither the first nor the most traditional, it remains, nevertheless, one of the most meticulous. His writings on natural philosophy and on physiology—that is to say, on the Aristotelian-Galenic system of the soul and of the passions, together with those of Averroes—profoundly influenced medieval and Renaissance culture. Gerard of Berry's text also shows the uncertainty surrounding the classification of the powers that were thought to make up the internal senses, even while it takes for granted the connection between the powers of the soul and the three-fold partition of the brain that was postulated by Greek philosophers and physicians as well as by Galen, and that was fully discussed and accepted by Avicenna. It is to this theory of the *virtutes* of the soul and of the phantasmological nature of sensation inherited from Aristotle and Galen through the mediation of Arabic natural philosophy and medicine that we must return in order to understand the medical and philosophical implications of excessive desire or erotic melancholy.

In order to present this system as it would have been understood throughout the fifteenth, sixteenth, and part of the seventeenth centuries, we will rely mainly on the texts by Avicenna, Averroes, and on the major disquisitions on *amor hereos* written before Du Laurens and Jacques Ferrand: Arnald of Villanova's *De amore heroico*; Bernard of Gordon's chapter on *hereos* in the vastly influential *Lilium medicinae*, written in Montpellier in 1305; and the Florentine physician Dino del Garbo's commentary on Guido Cavalcanti's "Donna me prega," the poem taken as the "erotic manifesto" by the *fedeli d'amore*—the poets in the circle of Dante Alighieri.

A few preliminary remarks are necessary on the medieval concept of love. It has often been said that medieval culture differentiated between two types of love: pure, disinterested love, always subordinate to Christian reason and therefore never excessive, never harmful either to man or to society; and natural love, which, having a component of original sin, namely that of sexual desire, is characterized by excess, turmoil, and transgression. According to this widely held view,[48] the former was called *amor caritatis* by the theologians (the *amor amicitiae* of Saint Thomas Aquinas), and *fin' amor* by the Provençal poets. Guilhelm Montanhagol tells how from this type of love chastity is born ("d'Amor moù castitatz"); the latter is called *amor concupiscentiae*, or carnal desire, according to Saint Thomas, and false friendship ("fals'amistat") according to the Provençal poet Marcabru.[49]

But any interpretation that postulates a dogmatic division between spiritual and natural love outside of the field of theological speculation is not only unhistorical but leaves more problems than it solves. One such problem is the fundamental ambiguity in the very concept of *amour courtois*, for courtly love vacillates continuously between pure love and erotic desire. Through this dualistic classification, we cannot explain Dante Alighieri's canto on Paolo and Francesca (*Inferno* V), where he systematically rejects the love exalted by courtly literature and by the *fedeli d'amore* or Saint Augustine's condemnation, in Petrarch's *Secretum*, of the poet's "pure" love for Laura, defined as a "love which has drawn your [Petrarch's] soul away from celestial things and has turned it from the Creator to the desire for the creature."[50] Such an interpretation confuses two quite different issues: the nature of love itself, and the nature of the object of love. As will be seen, in psychogenetic terms love is but one single phenomenon. It can vary in intensity, and it can direct itself toward a wide variety of objects in a way that leads to ethical considerations concerning the choice of that object. But even where that object is spiritual in nature, it activates the same physiological and psychological mechanisms. A consideration of the physiology of desire as it was generally understood by the Western physicians will make the distinctions clear between the medical and theological premises concerning love.

The medical tradition taught that excessive desire pours its deleterious effects on the mind and body by altering the very regimen that regulates man's existence. It contravenes the rules of balance and order that control such elements in the body as sleep, food and drink, exercise, and sexual relations. These rules were discussed by Hippocrates in bk. VI of the *Epidemics*, again by Aristotle in bk. III of the *Nichomachean Ethics*, and they were universally endorsed by the Arabic and Western physicians. Christianity incorporated the concept of regimen into its ethical view concerning the choice of objects by holding as axiomatic that the degree of immorality in an act of pleasure is equivalent to the intensity of the desire for the object of pleasure. While *amor amicitiae* is regulated by reason and is a totally selfless love, all other forms of love are always egocentric, excessive, contrary to the rules of morality and to the regimen of health. For the theologians, *amor amicitiae* attempts, in its way, to reproduce love as it must have existed before the Fall of Man;

amor concupiscentiae is the desire accompanying love after the Fall—a perversion of the original love. Yet the matrix and the psychophysiology of these two manifestations of love are the same, because both are born out of the same loss: that of the true object of desire. For the Christian, man's craving for love is a constant reminder of the loss of the earthly paradise. The true object of desire is not outside the self, no matter how beautiful or noble. It is only with the eyes of the mind that man can search out the half-forgotten traces of true Love that exist within. The guide is Christ, the Physician of the soul, who opened the way back to that paradise through the crucifixion.

We have, of course, been mixing two quite different things: the speculation of the theologians concerning the objects of desire pertaining to the hereafter, and the discourse of the poets and physicians concerning the objects of desire in the here and now. Both physicians and poets speak of the same absence, and analyze this absence within the subject of desire, the distraught lover. The difference consists in the fact that the physician examines the negative effects of the absence in terms of the human organism, and tries to find a cure, a method of restoring organic harmony through the precepts of traditional medicine. The poet describes the experience itself that is based on the irremediable absence of the beloved because that lack is the very *antefactum* of the poetic discourse. Within the conventions of poetry in which the Lady occupies a position loftier than the poet's own, he can never seek or expect favor. He can only love the Lady as a *phantasm* of his imagination, speak to her image inside himself, analyze the effects of that love on his entire being, and, within this solipsistic discourse, find his joy in loving from afar, in suffering, and in speaking of this constant suffering. The poet's sorrow and solace is his poetry, which somehow helps him exorcise the longing left by the unattainability of the object.

"If in fact you can love only what appears to sight," Staint Augustine reproaches Petrarch in the *Secretum*, "then you have loved the body."[51] Because human love, in all its manifestations, consists of speculation on bodily forms apprehended through the senses, it is *amor concupiscentiae*, including *fin' amor* or that of the *fedeli d'amore*, the *Roman de la rose* and the *Decameron*; it is the same as that described by the natural philosophers and the physicians. All are forms of the same love; they share a common causality and psychophysiological development. Both the poets and the *physici* were interested in erotic obsession; ultimately, they share a common vocabulary. The poet adopted a "scientific" symptomatology in order to enhance the verisimilitude of his wanton longing. The physician, in his pragmatic way, considered this poetic record to be like any other phenomenon verifiable in nature. The frequency of pathological manifestations of erotic melancholy in literature became, for them, not only a further demonstration of the universality of the syndrome, but this literature constituted a source of historical documentation—a corpus of case histories understood in clinical rather than in literary terms. This entire nucleus of ideas was based on the Aristotelian-Galenic system of the soul and of the passions as it was espoused generally by the medical writers in the scholastic tradition. There were, to be sure, variations in its interpretation that will be evident even in the writers we have selected for documentation. But in its global design, this system remained remarkably uniform throughout that period of intellectual history. It was the basis for the analysis of the diseases arising from desire in the writings of those who deal with *amor hereos* and forms the intellectual substructure for all that Ferrand believed, and professed, concerning the etiology of erotic love.

Because human love is fundamentally *amor concupiscentiae*, carnal desire, it is, by definition, capable of causing states of disease because, being a *passio*, it could alter the balance of elements within the body that constitutes health. Love can be deleterious if it includes a component of desire, if it involves the opposite sex—if it is occasioned by "the dispositions of the body inclining toward such a desire (*concupiscentia*) because of some compulsion of necessity, such as . . . a venereal complexion or moistness and tickling in the organs of generation."[52] Carnal desire arises where there is an excess of humors (especially blood) or of pneuma, that is, when the body is in a hot and humid condition.[53] Blood, in fact, produces semen, and an excessive quantity of blood will result in a state of repletion, a *complexio venerea*,[54] responsible for the attraction between the sexes.[55] Hence, those who possess a sanguine complexion are more prone to the stimuli of the flesh. Moreover, since a complexion can be acquired through a diet of rich, fatty foods, or through a sedentary life, it is the wealthy classes and the nobility who are more prone to the excesses of erotic desire.[56] Work and a lean diet are both preventive measures and figure among Ferrand's recommendations.

Gerard of Berry, in his commentary on the *Viaticum*, glosses the expression *amor hereos* as meaning "the noblemen who, because of their wealth and the softness of their life suffer this passion," and that for this reason they are called "heroic lovers." This sense of *amor hereos* as deriving from the Greek ἥρως, or hero, became a commonplace in subsequent treatises on erotic love and can also be verified in the alphabetical lexica of the thirteenth and fourteenth centuries. According to Danielle Jacquart and Claude Thomasset, in the lexica edited by Mario Roques, the following equivalences are given from Latin into French: MS Paris, Bibl. Nat., Lat. 13032, *heroicus* signifies baron, *heroys*, baronesse, *heronicus, id est heroicus heros, -ois,* baron; MS Paris, Bibl. Nat., Lat. 7692, *heroys* signifies dame; MS Vatican Lat. 2784, *hero* signifies dame.[57] Courtly love was the expression of a style of life chosen as a manifestation of the superiority of the ruling classes; that fact underscored the appropriateness of the association between hero and *hereos*. The *physici*, in their position of social subservience, also looked upon *hereos* as a sign of the corrupt, dissipated life of the *signori*. The disease is called *hereos*, remarks Bernard of Gordon, "because the 'hereois' and the nobles are more inclined to fall into this passion, given the abundance of delights," for as the *Viaticum* says, "just as happiness is the highest level of pleasure, so *hereos* is the highest stage of pleasure."[58] Today we would call these factors in a life style culturally or socially induced causes. Ferrand, too, will cite them among the remote causes of erotic love.

The main cause, however, is an extrinsic one that is in the form of the desired person or object itself, a form perceived by the external senses, especially by the sight, and judged to be overwhelmingly pleasing.[59] Erotic desire, according to Albucasis, is born of two causes: the necessity of the organism to eliminate superfluous and harmful elements, or an affection of the soul caused by the sight of something extraneous which the subject desires.[60] The Florentine physician, Dino del Garbo, commenting upon one of the most obscure yet influential of poems, "Donna me prega," by Guido Cavalcanti, develops the same concept, quite probably taken from the following gloss by Gerard of Berry: "the passion called love is caused by the apprehension of some visible form, which is apprehended by reason of its excessive pleasantness." And he adds, "for love is a passion of the appetite and the appetite follows the form of the apprehended object first through the organ of external sensation, then through the internal powers [*virtutes*] of the senses . . . therefore in love the two-fold sensitive passion happens at the same time, that is to say, the cognitive and the appetitive, since every appetite which is in us follows cognition."[61] The comment points clearly to the fusion of Aristotelian and Galenic thought that was the basis of scholastic medicine.

Arnald of Villanova specifies further that *hereos* is a "violent and obsessive cogitation upon the object of desire accompanied by the confidence of being able to obtain the pleasure perceived from it."[62] If the confidence is well placed, if the lover can satisfy his sexual appetites, the organism will be freed of the excess of semen, will be granted its pleasure, and will be returned to a state of normality. If that confidence is caused by a deranged reason, by an *idée fixe*, and the lover insists upon encouraging that passion, the increased state of sexual tension can be ruinous.[63] In medical terms, the solution is simple, or better simplistic: check the excess through a regimen capable of counteracting the cause of the excess. A surplus of semen requires evacuation, if possible through sexual intercourse within the bonds of marriage. The physician, however, is not concerned with the quality of the object of desire or with the social boundaries regulating the act itself. What counts is the quality of the act, which must be capable of reestablishing order out of disorder and which must, therefore, be conducted in accordance with medical practice.

When someone is *philocaptus in amore* by a woman, explains Bernard of Gordon, "he dotes on her form, figure, and manner so intensely because he believes her to be the best, the most beautiful and most respectable, the most handsome and most gifted, both in moral and natural qualities, a woman without peer. Hence, he covets her ardently, without limit or measure, wondering if he can reach his goal, for this is his happiness and blessedness. Meanwhile, his reason becomes corrupt, for he thinks of her continuously leaving aside all other considerations."[64] This corruption of the judgment is caused by the derangement of the power of estimation (*virtus aestimativa*), one of the animal faculties (*virtutes animales*) of the soul.[65] This concept has already been noted in a statement by Gerard of Berry. It takes us to the system of medieval and Renaissance psychology, one that was characterized by a compliance with the Aristotelian doctrine of cognition and sensation, and that remained remarkably uniform throughout the Middle Ages and the Renaissance.

Already mentioned is the three-fold partition of the soul: the rational part in the encephalic area; the emotional center in the heart; and the appetitive part in the liver. Each one of these parts of the soul carries out specific operations, and therefore each has specific powers and faculties that characterize its functions and activities. The three types of faculties corresponding to the three parts are: the animal faculty, seated in the encephalon; the vital faculty, located in the heart; the natural faculty, with its two parts seated respectively in the liver (power of nutrition) and in the testicles (power of generation).

The animal faculties are divided into two groups: the power of cognition and the power of movement. The power of cognition apprehends the object of sensation through the external senses and prepares it by abstracting the form from its materiality through a progressive *denudatio* or "unveiling," thereby rendering it manageable as an object of intellection, a *species intelligibilis*. This process is carried out by the internal senses, formed of a series of apprehensive powers (*vires apprehendi ab intus*) located in the three cavities of the brain, powers in the service of the animal faculty.[66]

Averroes gives one of the most comprehensive and exemplary syntheses of the process whereby the object of sensation is apprehended by the senses and is converted into a *phantasma* or image prepared for intellection. He first explains away one of the difficulties that had troubled medieval scientists, namely how the forms of large objects could be taken in by an organ so small as the eye, and how those forms could be so compressed. (Giacomo da Lentini, one of the poets at the court of Emperor Frederic II, wrote a poem on this very problem: "Or come pote sí gran donna entrare.")[67] Averroes denies the theories of reduction or compression; he points out that "the senses do not comprehend the intentions of the objects of sensation unless they have first been abstracted from matter." The explanation is essentially part of a paraphrase of Aristotle's *De sensu et sensibilibus* where he deals with the operations of the eye and its role in converting sensible objects into images that can be processed by the common sense, and in turn handed over to the imagination. The eye functions as a series of mirrors that causes the image, as it passes through, to become spiritualized through the lenses and the different media that make up the eye. "Forms, in fact, have three orders: the first is the corporeal one; the second, in the common sense is spiritual; the third in the imagination is even more spiritual. And because it is more spiritual than in the common sense, imagination has no need for the external object in order to make it present. The imagination, therefore, does not deal with corporeal forms."[68] This process has much to do with the way in which the imagination handles the image of the beloved object and with the possibilities for the corruption of that image through the influence of the burned humors.

Quite aptly Giorgio Agamben remarks that the cognitive process under consideration "is conceived as a speculation *sensu stricto*, a reflection of phantasms from mirror to mirror: mirror and water are the eyes and the sense that reflect the form of the object, while speculation is a form of fantasy that imagines the phantasms in the absence of the object. To know is to depend on a mirror wherein the world is reflected, to spy on images that reverberate from lens to lens. The medieval man is always in front of a mirror when he looks around himself, as well as when he abandons himself to his own imagination. Love is by necessity a speculation . . . because medieval psychology, with an invention that is among the most fruitful ever to have been transmitted to Western culture, conceives of love as an essentially phantasmatic process that involves imagination and memory in a state of continuous torment over an image painted or reflected in the depths of the mind."[69]

The nature of the lover's torment can be explained only in terms of the physiology of the brain itself. Very briefly, the frontal lobe of the anterior ventricle is occupied by the common sense; it receives from the eyes the form of the object of sensation. The dorsal lobe of the same ventricle hosts fantasy (the Greek *phantasia*, which corresponds to the Latin *imaginatio*, or retentive imagination) whose purpose is to retain the form once the object of sensation is no longer present. (We must pass over the debate then current regarding whether the *phantasia* and the *sensus communis* were a single power or separate powers.) The second is the imaginative power that is situated in the middle ventricle of the brain and serves to combine or separate impressions into *phantasia*. In relation to the rational soul of man, it is the power of cognition (*virtus cogitativa*). The dorsal part of the same ventricle is occupied by the power that perceives the nonsensitive intentions that exist in the single objects of sensation; it is called the power of estimation (*virtus aestimativa*). (It was not recognized by all physicians). The memory (*virtus conservativa et memorialis*) occupies the posterior ventricle of the brain; it preserves the nonsensitive impressions of the single objects of sensation perceived by the power of estimation, paralleling the fantasy that preserves the sense impressions received from the common sense. The last power, the *humana rationalis*, is recognized only by the philosophers.

According to the medical tradition dealing with love, the first stage of the torment of the obsessed lover is caused by the corruption of the faculty of the estimation, that power responsible for judging whether the nonsensitive intentions of the object of sensation are good or harmful. If the desire for the object is strong and persistent, this power can become confused, allowing the subject to believe that harmful things are good and unattainable things attainable. Arnald of Villanova sums up this state in the lover in the following way:

> Because of the violent desire, he retains the form imprinted upon his mind by the fantasy, and because of memory, he is constantly reminded of the object. From these two actions a third follows: from the violent desire and from the constant recollection arises compulsive cogitation. The lover dwells on how and through which methods he will be able to obtain this object for his own pleasure so that he may come to the enjoyment of this destructive delight that he has formulated in his psyche.[70]

The object of desire becomes an obsessive idea that polarizes all the cogitative activities, while the corruption of the power of estimation brings about the derangement of the remaining faculties of the soul, because all other powers are subject to the *aestimativa*.[71] In time, this obsession can darken and overpower reason itself, driving the lover to seek the gratification of his sexual impulses in opposition to all sense and good judgment. The faculties of the soul, however, cannot undergo change, and therefore they cannot be mistaken. The cause of error must lie with the instruments employed by the faculty in order to carry out its functions: the middle cavity of the brain and the *pneuma* or the spirits it contains.[72]

According to medieval and Renaissance psychology,[73] the well-being of man is controlled by the spirits, for they provide that essential link between matter (the body) and spirit (the soul) without which man could not exist. They are the instruments of the faculties and correspond to the natural, vital, and animal parts. The natural spirit is generated in the liver from pure blood, and from the liver it circulates to all parts of the body through the veins. The vital spirit comprises two elements: inhaled air and the exhalations of the blood. These two elements are blended in the heart as soon as the air has been transformed and purified in the lungs through a process quite similar to digestion. From the left ventricle of the heart, the vital spirit is passed to the arteries and to the retiform plexus at the base of the brain, where it undergoes a further transformation. Finally, it enters the lateral ventricles of the brain where it joins with the air inhaled through the nostrils; the result is the animal spirit that occupies the major ventricle of the brain, the parencephalon. This spirit performs all the operations required by the rational soul and controls, through the nerves, the sensory activities of man, as well as voluntary motion.

In brief, in every human being there are three vital centers: the liver, the heart, the brain. From these centers an interlacing network of vital currents branches out across the body by means of the veins, arteries, and nerves. They are critical to the efficiency and well-being of the organism. Being formed of air and blood, they are susceptible to changes in the internal balance of the humors as well as to external conditions such as atmospheric pressure. Accordingly, certain races were thought to possess characteristics in keeping with geographical regions: in the south the elements were more conducive to passion than in the north. Internally, the malignant humors were certain to take their toll upon the spirits by altering the temperature of the innate heat that regulates the function of the heart.

The psychological process must be understood to operate by means of this pneumatic circulation. Avicenna, in the De *anima*, explains in these terms the process through which the form of the object passes from the external senses to the internal powers of the soul:

> The similitude [of the object] is fused with the spirit that carries the power of vision . . . and it penetrates into the spirit that is located in the first ventricle of the brain. It is then imprinted upon this spirit, which is the one that carries the power of the common sense. . . . Then the common sense transmits the form to the neighboring spirit, imprinting it with the form, and thereby places the object in the imaginative power, that which creates forms. . . . Then the form that is in the imagination enters into the posterior ventricle of the brain and unites itself with the spirit that carries the power of estimation . . . and the form that was in the *imaginativa* imprints itself upon the spirit of the power of estimation.[74]

Now we are in a position to summarize the psychophysiological process that leads to erotic melancholy.

When a pleasing form reaches the internal powers of the soul, the sudden pleasure that accompanies it causes a rapid multiplication of the vital spirits which overheat and spread throughout the body, thereby overheating the entire organism:

> When something pleasing or enjoyable is presented to the soul, the

joy coming from the apprehended pleasure multiplies the spirits in the heart. Suddenly they heat up, and this heat . . . causes the spirits to be spread to all the members of the body.[75]

Because the vital spirits generate the animal spirits, these will also over-heat. The receptacle of the faculty of estimation, the dorsal portion of the middle ventricle of the brain, being in contact with the burning spirits coming from the heart, also becomes inflamed, and from this state of inflammation the permanence of the phantasms of perception occurs. The faculty of estimation controls the *imaginativa*, and the perma-nency of the *phantasmata* in the faculty of imagination depends upon its degree of dryness. The heating of the *aestimativa* through an overheat-ing of the encephalic area of the *imaginativa* causes a state of excessive dryness:

> Since dryness is necessary for the fixed retention of forms, it follows by necessity that the encephalic part of the power of imagination must suffer considerable dehydration. The anterior section in which the *imag-inativa* resides is abandoned by the warmth of the spirits as they flow toward the segment of the *estimativa* to accompany the strong and per-sistent thought and reflection. Because this intense heat consumes the humor in the anterior section, it necessarily becomes less humid than it previously was.[76]

Once the *imaginativa* becomes dry, the *phantasma* remains firmly im-printed in the organ of memory as a seal in wax polarizing the attention of thought itself; the image of the desired object remains the only datum present to the consciousness of the lover. It is this obsessive presence of the *phantasma* that causes the pathological condition known as *amor hereos*.

As we have observed in the Arabic chapters on *ilischi*, the physician is mainly concerned with this pathological stage of *hereos* because, as Arnald of Villanova states it, "from the intense force of this cogitation, 'heroical' lovers suffer many accidents." The first is insomnia, which wears the body out by producing an excessive evaporation of the vital humor. Because the health of the body depends upon the balanced com-bination of the four humors, the evaporation of the vital humor breaks this tenuous balance. The excessive dryness and the heating of the spirits prevent the instruments of the natural faculty, that is to say the natural spirit and the liver, from performing their functions. As a result, the lover becomes anorexic. The body becomes gradually thinner and drier, the eyes become hollow and tearless. The medieval and Renaissance medical treatises explain in detail the symptoms of this fearful disease: why lovers are pale, why they sigh, why the pulse slows down in mo-ments of desperation and races with the sudden remembrance of a joyful moment. They also explain, in great detail, the therapy: light diet, sleep, frequent baths (to nourish and humidify the body), blood-letting (given the close relationship between blood and semen), intercourse, and the more "psychological" cures such as listening to music, distracting conversation, exercise, and travel.

If these therapies do not succeed in returning the body to the required state of equilibrium, the continuous overheating and overdrying of the organism will produce an excessive quantity of melancholy humors (*melancholia adusta*), which will dry the body completely, will turn the skin dark, and will ultimately cause madness and death.[77]

Ferrand takes entirely for granted this system of perception, sensation, and the functions of the soul, as well as the conventional involvement of the heart and hypochondries in the diseases of melancholy. His sense of the etiology of erotic melancholy depends upon the interplay of these mechanisms of the psyche and the physiology of the humors. In that sense, what we have accounted for here as part of the history of a medical tradition on love will serve equally as a commentary upon Ferrand's medical premises and upon his assessment of the stages and symptoms of love in its diseased states. Much of his vocabulary of analysis and habits of thought coincide with those of his predecessors; it will be seen that few of the major developments within the medical tradition of *heroes* escaped some manner of incorporation into his treatise. This outline will serve to place in historical perspective those many elements that Ferrand treats in a completely contemporaneous way. In effect, Ferrand attempts to consolidate the salient features of a long history into a single authoritative synoptic statement. Some of these elements will require further elucidation in the pages to follow, but many, especially those of a more generic and widely received status require little further explication given Ferrand's entirely traditional employment of them in his work.

IV

Eros and the Occult
in Renaissance Medical Thought

With an interpretation of the *sollicitudo* that leads to the melancholy abyss in the terms of scholastic perception psychology, the psychophysiological mechanisms were finalized that formed the basis of Ferrand's central etiological analysis of love. Given a general faith among physicians in the sympathy that exists between the body and the soul, it was held self-evident that the perturbations of the psyche must redound upon the physiological organism, just as the corruption of the humors and the noxious vapors of adustion must assault and corrupt the imagination. But this symbiotic alignment of pathological systems, accounting in material terms for the diverse crises leading either to erotic melancholy or mania, was by no means invulnerable to further modification during the fourteenth, fifteenth, and sixteenth centuries.

These modifications were characterized, in general, by the infiltration of occult causes, some of them the legacy of folk medicine, others the result of an intensified interest among theologians in demonology and witchcraft. In one sense, such adaptations and mutations are irrelevant to a writer whose principal goal was to reconfirm the Aristotelian-Galenic theory of erotic love, with its emphasis on immediate and natural causes, but in another, the history of *amor hereos* as an intellectual idea during those intervening centuries can hardly be ignored, because Ferrand, though with considerable skepticism, nevertheless deals with a rich variety of remote causes and occult phenomena: astronomy and dreams, incantations and spells, incubi and succubi, philters and poisons, enchantments and fascinations, folk recipes, charms, and sorcery—some of them traceable in erudite ways to classical parallels, but most of them having direct origins in the superstitious beliefs and customs of the Middle Ages. Ferrand's treatise is predicated on a desire to preserve the integrity of the Arabic medical tradition concerning love, fortified by a thorough re-Galenization of its definitions and diagnostics, but he could not complete his encyclopedic treatise without simultaneously addressing the questions concerning love that had preoccupied the preceding age: whether love could be coerced by philters, or disrupted by liga- tures, whether demons could incite erotic desire, whether mortals could have carnal relations with incubi and succubi, or whether love could be cured by such occult means as incantations and charms. The debate over these issues dominated much that was written during those centuries on erotic love, and, without any question, they were the issues that gener- ated the greatest polemical energy. In the closing years of the sixteenth century, the wide gradation of compromise positions concerning natural and occult causes gave way to a direct confrontation between physicians and theologians on the matter of demonology and sorcery. Viewed in retrospect, Ferrand's treatise, despite its cautious speculation on such matters as magic, philters, and judiciary astrology, could barely hope, nevertheless, to avoid the risks of appearing in that polemical milieu.

The physicians who wrote on *amor hereos* in the twelfth and thirteenth centuries, essentially in the form of commentaries on the *Viaticum* of Con- stantinus and the *Canon* of Avicenna, scrupulously avoided making ref- erence to amatory magic, to supernatural causes and occult cures, as well as to folk customs and remedies. It was not that society did not abound with these beliefs and practices, but that the physicians viewed them- selves as part of an elite intellectual class; they were therefore disinclined to pollute their newly acquired corpus of Arabic medical writings with popular lore and ecclesiastical superstitions. As Mary Wack has pointed out, "the Arabic medical treatises that stimulated a renewed Western interest in love as a disease were informed by Galenic-Aristotelian ra- tionality. Magic had no place in this system because it could not be accounted for in rational causal terms; magic is magic because its work- ings are occult."[1]

The mutations and accretions that led to the polygenetic accounts of love in the Renaissance medical treatises began to appear in the four- teenth century. Amatory magic had been a part of the collective Euro- pean consciousness for centuries; but for reasons beyond the scope of our analysis, it was at this moment in intellectual history that it began to rec- ommend itself for closer scrutiny by both the theologians and the natural philosophers.[2] It had always been repressed by the church, but when the repression took exceptional prominence, the deviant patterns became au- tosuggestive, creating a wave of incidents of aberrant behavior that led to further speculation on occult causes and to further repression. For the demonologists, it stood to reason that the devil, who seeks to tempt man to his fall, must also be a persuasive agent in the corruption of carnal desires. That idea was not new. What followed, however, was a me- thodical anatomization of the means whereby devils and demons could play upon the sexual appetites and lure both men and women into the sin of lechery, or worse, into a state of heresy for having wilfully solicited the aid of demons in their erotic enterprises. The medical tradition of *hereos* provided the demonologists with the physiological mechanisms whereby demons, forbidden to assault the soul directly, might corrupt the will through the passions, the imagination, or the sexual instincts.

At the same time, physicians were confronted by the rising intellectual status of occult causes. The result was a cross-fertilization that created a new context, in the writings of the theologians, for the nucleus of ideas on erotic love drawn from the Arabic tradition, and a new context for amatory magic in the medical treatises on erotic melancholy. Paradoxically, it was the adaptability of Aristotelian perception psychology that allowed for the eventual breakdown of distinctions between the natural and the occult causes of love. As stated earlier, according to scholastic perception psychology, the object perceived was stripped of its material nature as it passed through the eye and was turned into a visual *species*. In that form it made its way to the *virtus estimativa*, where it was judged good or ill, desirable or undesirable, and from there it was passed to the imaginative faculty. The mind, following its own internal patterns of sensation, was able to deliver to the imagination a *species* so intense and captivating that it could, alone, confound the judgment, imprison the faculties of the soul in a cycle of desire and fear, and produce a state of chronic disease. The demonologists, reasoning differently concerning the nature of causes, were in need of a material mechanism that explained how malign spirits could influence sexual behavior without directly negating the free will of the soul. It was an easy step for them to account for demonic interference through these processes of perception. It was held that demons, as subtle essences, could infiltrate the faculties, corrupt the desired image, incite venereal longings, and, in general, expedite all the natural causes by which misplaced erotic desire could lead to a pathological crisis. At the same time, they accounted such a process as proof of capitulation to malign forces, as an act of moral turpitude, and, in cases of voluntary acquiescence to the devil, as an act of heresy as well.

One of the more comprehensive explorations of that nucleus of ideas was conducted by Heinrich Kramer and James Sprenger, the two Dominican inquisitors who, in 1486, wrote the *Malleus maleficarum*. Their work was a timely sequel to the papal bull, *Summis desiderantes affectibus* of Innocent VII, released in 1484, a document that dealt with possession by the devil, incubi and succubi, amatory charms, spells, and incantations—all preternatural agents and practices able to " 'hinder men from performing the sexual act and women from conceiving, when husbands cannot know their wives nor wives receive their husbands'."[3] Deviant sexuality and witchcraft had been drawn into such close association that the one was inseparable from the other. Where there was sorcery there was sexual perversion, and where there was inordinate desire, there the presence of the devil was presumed. Under analysis by Kramer and Sprenger, the vocabulary of medical causation was drawn in to abet their cause: "for fancy or imagination is as it were the treasury of ideas received through the senses. And through this it happens that devils so stir up the inner perceptions, that is the power of conserving images, that they appear to be a new impression at that moment received from exterior things."[4] In this way the devil deceives his victim, falsifies the *species* in the memory, and lures the person into sin. So defined, the involvement of the devil becomes one with the natural sequence of deranged perception, even though he is, himself, the cause of this deviancy—natural in the same sense that it is natural for apparitions to appear during sleep. So it is that "devils can stir up and excite inner perceptions and humors." This can be done in two ways: either with or without the help of witches. Devils, eager to betray mankind, automatically search out the longings to which men are most subject, and the chief of these is erotic passion. Moreover, "the devil invisibly lures a man to sin, not only by means of persuasion, as has been said, but also by the means of disposition."[5] By their temperaments, some men are disposed to anger, some to concupiscence, and the devil can play upon these susceptibilities. Of all the dispositions, melancholy was the most vulnerable to the wiles of the devil. That belief, going back to Saint Jerome and no doubt even further, completes the circle of reasoning, so that he who is melancholy is inclined both to erotic melancholy and to demonic temptation.[6] Where a person succumbs to love, the devil is almost certainly involved.

Clearly Sprenger and Kramer had read the medical literature carefully, for they cite Avicenna as readily as they cite Saint Thomas Aquinas. In their words, "*philocaption*, or inordinate love of one person for another, can be caused in three ways. Sometimes, it is due merely to a lack of control over the eyes; sometimes, to the temptations of devils; sometimes, to the spells of necromancers and witches, with the help of devils."[7] A small place was still reserved in the *Malleus maleficarum* for the simple allurements of the eye that could lead to a compulsive attachment to an object of beauty without involving demons or spells. Where such desire caused physical illness, they could still recommend, in deference to the medical tradition, the seven cures of Avicenna taken from the *Canon*. But their interests were primarily in the exorcisms needed to drive out malign spirits and in the arraignment of those who traffic in amorous philters and spells.

It was, in fact, only a matter of time before the *amor hereos* of the Arab physicians would lose its status among theologians in the age of the Inquisition. Indeed, Paolo Grillando, in his *Tractatus de sortilegiis*, makes love itself, together with divination and poisons (including philters), one of the three forms of magic spells.[8] Plato had associated love with enchantment in the *Symposium*, but only insofar as the force of attraction between individuals seemed to have extraordinary powers that could only be described in terms of magic. For Grillando, that force of love, likewise explained in occult terms, becomes a form of coercive magic, a Satanic snare, forbidden to all Christians. At the same time, there could be no tolerance for love's victims, for they are, by definition, morally responsible for their own despair. Vulgar love, as a human desire and a human passion, had itself become heresy. That mode of analysis, urged to its extremes (as in Jean Bodin's *De la démonomanie des sorciers*, 1580),[9] would attempt to eradicate the medical tradition entirely. In turn, that attack contributed to the growing bid on the part of the medical profession to reclaim, as part of their proper domain, the treatment of those suffering from melancholy and other illnesses falsely accused by the church as demoniacs.

If in the fifteenth century the demonologists extended and refined their definitions of erotic love by adopting the analytical vocabulary of the physicians, the medical writers responded, initially, by allowing for a broader description of causes, including, as one category, the interference of malign spirits. Perhaps the most that can be said of this movement is that in spite of continual opposition, the idea had considerable staying power in the writings of the medical establishment throughout the sixteenth century. Clearly, for many there was no distinction between demonic intervention and what was considered scientific, for it was precisely the purpose of the demonologists to demonstrate that such creatures were a part of the natural world order because they function through matter and natural causation. Hence, there were men of a scientific bent of mind, such as Agostino Nifo and Andrea Cesalpino, who saw no difficulty in dealing with the spirit world according to the standards of rational analysis. Stuart Clark lists Giovanni Battista Condronchi, Wilhelm Schreiber, Thomas Erastus, and John Cotta, as well as the many French doctors involved with cases of demon possession, such as Jacques Fontaine, Michel Marescot, and Pierre Yvelin, as some of "the many physicians who made special studies of demonic pathology."[10] In general, these works credit occult phenomena and seek to describe them in terms of scientific empiricism, without any sense of discrepancy between matter and method.

Mary Wack provides evidence of resistance from within the medical community to this "demonization of medicine" from as early as the middle of the fifteenth century. She cites Jacques Despars who, in his commentary on Avicenna's *Canon*, written in the early 1440s, goes on record as rejecting all occult and remote explanations of erotic love. He discredits entirely the folk tales about sorcery, the beliefs in spells, and the diabolical generation of insane eroticism, although, as Mary Wack points out, he may have been as much motivated by a desire to dissuade his professional colleagues from crediting this opinion of the *stolidum vulgus* in order to get rich by peddling folk cures, as by a desire to seek out the truth concerning the causes of occult phenomena.[11] In spite of his and like efforts, this association of ideas persisted in medical writing. Jason van der Velde (Jason Pratensis), a century later in his *De cerebri morbis*, opines that demons, given their subtle and elusive natures, are most assuredly capable of insinuating their way into the body.[12] There they may hide themselves in the vital organs, unbalance the humors, induce provocative dreams, stir up and madden the spirits. For van der Velde, a state of mania was entirely indecipherable from a state of possession by evil spirits. For him, the former was almost certain evidence of the latter.

Lynn Thorndike, in his monumental *History of Magic and Experimental Science* reports of Johann Bokel, author of a book on philters published in 1599, that although he denies the efficacy of love potions, he "still believes not only in the existence of the devil, but that the devil is a natural magician. He represents him as a foe of the divine order in nature, which he tries to upset and to induce men to abandon natural law and causes for his magical fallacies. Bokel thinks of the demon as an aerial spirit, more tenuous and subtle than the air itself, who mingles with human animal spirits and so disturbs them with false imaginations that men believe in magic."[13] Bokel's purpose was to disallow occult effects that did not conform to natural laws—at least where philters were concerned—but his confirmation of the power of malign spirits to disturb the imagination by infiltrating the animal spirits, albeit a subject attached to a different set of questions and problems, nevertheless reveals the paradoxical combinations of beliefs that were possible during that age.

A selection of statements from Ferrand's treatise will demonstrate that, in spite of his Aristotelian-Galenic orientation, he too was capable of making certain concessions to the occult. We receive signs of the growing antipathy evinced by his profession to the demonologists and their medical supporters in Ferrand's own opposition to those "several theologians and physicians, who believe, apparently, that the author of all evil, the devil, can extinguish sanctified love and enflame illicit love," pointing out that "care should be taken not to attribute to magic and sorcery out of ignorance, such effects as have natural causes." Unlike Bokel, Ferrand cannot credit the role of demons in human sexuality, but paradoxically he accepts that philters have the power to incite love, though not for a specific person, and he admits that "there are cases in which the mutual love of marriage is destroyed by charms and witchcraft, causing the partners to engage passionately in illicit affairs" (ch. XXXIV). Nowhere in his formal medical definitions does Ferrand suggest that occult forces could be responsible for amatory diseases, but in the chapters dealing specifically with questions of the occult, his susceptibilities become apparent.

Ferrand inherited from the sixteenth century both the naturalizing of occult phenomena, as exemplified in the writings of Pomponazzi, and the demonization of medicine, as exemplified in the treatises of the physician Francisco Valles. These movements of thought were to be reckoned with by anyone presuming to describe the mechanisms of the passions and the external forces that acted upon them. Pietro Pomponazzi, in his work on incantations, written in 1520, based his denial of the existence of demons on the authority of Aristotle.[14] His concern was to dismantle the occult world by tracing all such events to natural explanations. He could allow that the imagination was subject to remote influences, such as the fascination, but only when those influences were seen to function according to natural laws. The movement he espoused was fraught with dangers, but it persisted, nevertheless, in furnishing models of investigation based on the examination of immediate and efficient causes. Ferrand's elaborate stratification of causes—material, remote, efficient—is essentially classical in origin, though it reveals his sensitivity to the questions concerning cause, the clarification of which was one of his most pressing reasons for writing the treatise. Worth repeating here is the fact that it was one of Pomponazzi's students, Vanini, whose books were burned in Toulouse in 1620 by order of the same document in which Ferrand's first treatise on love was recalled. The inquisitors undoubtedly believed that both authors shared a common philosophy of investigation.

By contrast, the renowned Spanish physician Francisco Valles, in his book on sacred philosophy, endorsed the view of the theologians that the devil was, himself, a component of the natural world insofar as he could provoke melancholy through the channels of the body.[15] Demons, he reasoned, are capable of penetrating the body and of inflicting it with disease through the adustion of humors, through increasing the quantity of black bile, and through causing the black vapors to assault the brain. For Valles, the devil is a potential agent in the formation of each phase of the crisis leading to chronic melancholy induced by love. We are left to ponder whether Valles had relinquished all professional interest in the clinical treatment of love, or whether he had succeeded in medicalizing the role of demons. So conceived, the medical treatment for erotic melancholy with its bleedings, diets and purges must also be looked upon as a form of exorcism. Such works as Valles's could only quicken the debate concerning the relationship between the passions and the demonic world, particularly with regard to sexuality. The accommodation of amatory magic and demonic agents within the established medical tradition—Valles was an outstanding commentator on the writings of Hippocrates—would serve to keep a host of topics in the forefront of medical polemics: the demonic derangement of the sexual appetites and the corruption of the *species*, the power of charms, philters, and incantation, the nature of incubi and succubi, ligatures, the fascination with the role of witches and sorcerers in commanding and forcing love—a gamut of issues that Ferrand would include in his comprehensive treatise.

In effect, this bilateral exchange of systems allowed for a relatively peaceful coexistence of theologians and physicians down to the middle of the sixteenth century, each functioning in his respective sphere in an effort to repress excessive sexual behavior, the one by releasing the soul from the torments of the flesh and the devil through prayer and penitence, the other by treating the physiological causes of rampant erotic appetites according to the principles of medicine. But as Jean Céard has demonstrated, the attack on the practices of the church with regard to witchcraft by Johann Wier (Weyer) in his *De praestigiis daemonum*, a work that first appeared in 1563, and the equally celebrated counterattack by Jean Bodin in his *De la démonomanie des sorciers*, published in 1580, created a climate of confrontation between physicians and demonologists that would preclude all possibility of returning to former times of mutual tolerance.[16] Galenic skepticism, wielded by practitioners jealous of their professional interests, was ultimately bound to run into conflict with increasingly dogmatic theologians, intellectually conditioned as they were to see supernatural causes behind all irregular behavior. From the point of view of the inquisitors, not only are those persons heretics who have carnal relations with the devil or who engage his services in troubling others but also those who deny that such activities are possible. Under those circumstances, the danger of writing a treatise on love based on the principles of Arabic medicine becomes readily apparent.

There were still others in those centuries who were interested in the Aristotelian-Galenic doctrines on erotic love preserved in the writings of the physicians; namely, the humanist and social philosophers who wrote about the nature of love and its value to the human spirit, studied in light of the ideas and ideals of the classical poets and philosophers. Their essays on the qualities and consequences of divine and vulgar love offered a new spirit of inquiry that would also find its way into the more strictly medical treatises on the diseases of love in the late sixteenth and early seventeenth centuries. Though these essays are by no means free of the theological and medical polemics of the age, they are, nevertheless, written with greater scope and balance. These are works arising in the great humanist centers of learning in Italy—Genoa, Florence, Mantua, Venice—imbued not only with a tradition of learning based on a compulsive deference to the ancients, but also with the ideals concerning love that derive from the poets in the school of Petrarch. Ferrand adopted their habits of erudition in dotting his pages with quotations from classical sources. As we will argue in a subsequent section of this introduction, Ferrand knew the work of Pietro Capretto, Dino del Garbo, Pietro Bembo, and others, if not directly, then through an intimate knowledge of Mario Equicola's *Libro de natura de amore*.

Perhaps no work better characterizes the complex commingling of traditions concerning erotic love in the Renaissance than the *Anteros sive tractatus contra amorem* of Battista Fregoso, duke of Genoa, a work written before 1496, and hence within a very few years of the *Malleus maleficarum* in the north, and of Ficino's *Commentary on Plato's Symposium* in the south.[17] Fregoso was, above all, attracted to the rich new body of lore that had emerged from the sifting of Greek and Roman texts—texts abounding in stories and philosophies concerning love. Clearly a new subgenre of the expository book was in the making, generated by a philosophical inquiry into the moral nature of love with its social, psychological, and physiological causes. Through a series of questions dispersed among the three interlocutors who contribute to the dialogues, he achieves a balanced and variegated survey of the literary and medical traditions of love—copiously illustrated by allusions and anecdotes drawn from the ancient texts. The second book of the treatise deals with the causes of erotic desire, and especially the desire that generates melancholy. The leading etiological theories are advanced one by one, with the final word granted to the view that such love is a product of the temperament and of the humors through their influence on the imagination. In short, Fregoso endorses the official elite view of the Arabic medical tradition, but not without exploring three alternate explanations, each one describing a system whereby the pathological crisis caused by love can lead to chronic melancholy. The first reveals the considerable importance attached to the nature and behavior of semen by the writers in the Hippocratic tradition, for it was believed that the composition and movement of the seed accounted for the titillation that gave rise to venereal desire and pleasure. It was understood, at the same time, however, that seed retained overlong in the body was subject to corruption. Semen then became an irritant that required expulsion, failing which it produced vapors that could debilitate the faculties of the brain in a way paralleling the assault of the noxious vapors of adust biles. According to a second view, traceable to Plato, erotic love came about through fascination, though Fregoso's sense of the term vacillates between the enchantment that comes from seeing an object of beauty and dwelling upon it as a thing desired and the enchantment that follows when the beams emitted by the eyes of the beloved penetrate through the eyes of the beholder and thereby fire the concupiscent desires by magic, or through an infection of the blood, or through the transfer of alien vapors. This construction of the process of philocaption admits of several readings ranging from a metaphor for the compelling powers of beauty to a theory of poisoning akin to that which accounts for the powers of philters and charms. A third view begins with the "principalities and powers" of Saint Paul and proceeds though the writings of the church fathers concerning demons and devils. The question centers not on whether these creatures can actually influence erotic behavior but whether they serve as direct or as remote causes. Free will is essential to the Christian doctrine concerning sin and the moral responsibility of the individual. Hence, demons cannot be allowed to compel love by having the liberty to act directly upon the soul. The writers of the *Malleus maleficarum* insist on the point: "because this distinction is not sufficient to explain how the devil at times produces a frantic infatuation of love, it is further to be noted that though he cannot cause that inordinate love by directly compelling a man's will, yet he can do so by means of persuasion."[18] This can be carried out through demonic impersonations or through inciting the urges of the body and corrupting the phantasms in the imagination. Once Fregoso is past this difficulty, he cites at length the *Book on Divine Institutions* by Firmianus Lactantius in order to reveal how malign spirits operate upon emotions and yearnings, project false images of beauty before the mind's eye, manipulate natural sexual instincts, and inflame desires.

Fregoso's treatise embraces the Hippocratic view that erotic love is a function of the genitals and a by-product of sexual instincts, the Platonic view that love is an aesthetic fixation generated by sight and the imagination that can, at the same time, produce a state of disease in the body, the theological view that love is caused by the invasion of malign spirits, and the Aristotelian-Galenic view that it is a somatogenetic condition caused by an imbalance of the humors and by a corruption of the mental faculties.

Fregoso's legacy to subsequent writers on pathological love was not only his codification of its multiple causes but also an erudite repertoire of allusions to classical writers illustrating, by precept and anecdote, nearly every dimension of his analysis of love. In that sense, Fregoso showed the way not only for organizing a humanist inquiry into the nature of love around a series of essentially medical questions, as Dino del Garbo and others had done before, but also for embellishing the medical treatise with the lore of the ancients. From this quarter, whether directly or indirectly, Ferrand inherited both a model for eclecticism and a cumulative repository of topical tales and references.

Providing a final dimension to this necessarily brief summary of the principal trends of thought concerning erotic love in the Renaissance is Marsilio Ficino's highly influential *Commentary on Plato's Symposium*. It is well to remember that Ficino also received medical training, and that his seventh oration is taken up with many of the conventional cures for excessive sexual desire. But the idea transmitted by this work that had the greatest innovative influence on later theorists was his concept of vulgar or erotic love as a form of fascination. Because the blood of youth is warm, sweet, and clear, its spiritual humor must, he argues, send "out rays like itself through the eyes, which are like glass windows. . . . Therefore, what wonder is it if the eye, wide open and fixed

upon someone, shoots the darts of its own rays into the eyes of the bystander, and along with those darts, which are the vehicles of the spirits,
aims that sanguine vapor which we call spirit?"[19] This poisoned dart
seeks the heart of the beholder, wounds it, turns back into the blood and
infects it, causing a state of disease. To demonstrate the plausibility of
such a system, Ficino makes reference to the way in which menstruating
women can bewitch young boys, and he goes on to demonstrate how
dangerous those spirit vapors are for persons who are cold and melancholy by nature. In his own singular way, Ficino, too, is preoccupied
with an occult phenomenon which he labors to reduce to purely natural
physiological terms. By degrees, he elaborates a system that accounts
for love as a perturbation of the blood; he provides the causal mechanisms whereby the mystery of that sudden viewing of an object of desire
can alert and captivate the beholder; he explains how that exchange of
vapors leads both to intense venereal cravings, as well as to a pathological crisis. Ficino's system, in effect, has the virtue of forming a link
between quasi-medical principles of causation and the literary accounts
of the shock of sudden love and the psychophysiological trauma of unrequited love. If the physicians who endorsed demonic causes provided
the scientific basis for erotic love as a form of sinful demonic temptation or as a form of complete possession through the casting of spells,
the physicians who endorsed the physiological enchantment of Ficino
created the scientific basis for the love exchanges of the Petrarchan poets. These two systems, designed to account for the occult qualities of
love—compulsive, demonic, magical, enchanted—through all the range
of nuance in these terms, vied with one another throughout the sixteenth
century for confirmed status in the writings of the medical establishment.

Proof of the appeal of Ficino's theory of enchantment, even to some
of the most confirmed Galenists during the following one hundred fifty
years, is not difficult to demonstrate. An outstanding example is to be
found in the *Observationum medicinalium libri sex* (1588) of François Valleriola, about which a great deal more must be said in a subsequent section
of our introduction.[20] Valleriola wrote a long philosophical statement on
the origins of erotic love in the context of a case study of a lovesick merchant he treated in Arles. He described the origins of the disease not
only in the conventional terms of humoral medicine but also as a fascination that enters through the eye, and that, as an alien vapor, spreads
poisonous contagion throughout the body.

One of the most committed of Galenists of that age, André Du Laurens, conceded in his *Second discours au quel est traicté des maladies melancholiques et du moyen de les guarir* (1597), that love entered by the eyes
and moved in a material form through the channels of the body to the
liver, where it provoked the combustion of the humors. Kornmann, in
his *Linea amoris*, makes the *fascinatio* a basic component of his theory of

erotic love,[21] and Burton, in *The Anatomy of Melancholy*, was prepared to accept the entire pathological sequence derived from the invasion of blood spirits as one among equals: "the manner of the fascination, as Ficino declares it, is this: mortal men are then especially bewitched, when as by often gazing one on the other, they direct sight to sight, join eye to eye, and so drink and suck in Love between them; for the beginning of this desire is the Eye."[22]

The eye was at the center of the exchange, not as the Aristotelian organ of perception, but as the organ whereby the blood vapors were emitted and received. Ficino had theorized that a beautiful object caused the thinnest part of the blood to be drawn first toward the image in the brain, then to be drawn toward the object itself. There was, in fact, a double jeopardy involved; for just as the alien vapors received in at the eyes could variously attack the liver, heart, and blood, so the expenditure of vapors through the very act of gazing upon the beloved could deplete the blood, dry out the body, and deposit the lees of the blood in the form of a melancholy residue. In this way the causal system involving fascination and the blood vapors could be linked with the mechanisms of the diseases of melancholy. The adaptation of the modes familiar to conventional medical theory indicates the degree to which Ficino was influenced by his own medical training. Beauty itself, and the gaze of the lover, provoked an independent reaction that became a new cause in the production of common symptoms and a common disease. The dexterity with which the late Renaissance physicians juxtaposed this separate etiological account of the crisis leading to erotic dementia with the Arabic-Galenic system further demonstrates the relativity of the causes and effects within a circumscribing vocabulary of common analysis.

Ferrand'sresistance to the infiltration of occult causes into his etiological system contrasts with his otherwise eclectic inclination to accept any reasonable explanation for the rise of erotic passions and to superimpose theories of medical causation one on top of the other. That spirit is evinced by his declaration, following several pages in which he lists as many explanations of lovesickness as he could find, that "the efficient cause of this disease [is] anything that can provoke love and melancholy" (ch. VI). For him, it was one thing to incorporate occult causes, quite another to draw together several distinct pathological systems from within the recognized corpus of medical writing. Three such systems have already been seen juxtaposed in Fregoso's treatise, one relating to the humors, another to the sexual organs, and a third to the processes of the brain.

It was held that thought, alone, was capable of drying and chilling the brain, thereby bringing on a state of melancholy; the cognitive processes themselves, when deranged by fixations, were potentially pathogenic. At the same time, the seed could produce a chain of events equally capable of creating all the symptoms of mania or melancholy. The causal association of semen with erotomania can be traced back to such works as the *Vade mecum* of Albucasis (written before 1009), who attributed the rise of the disorder equally to the retention of superfluous sperm and to the sight of something extraneous that creates intense desire.[23] Bernard of Gordon, in the *Lilium medicinae*, argued that the genitals, rather than the hypochondries, heart or brain, were the true seat of the disease of *amor hereos*.[24] Thereafter, no comprehensive description of erotic dementia could be complete without reference to this center of the body. As Ferrand states at the opening of ch. XXXI, "the immediate cause of this disease is sperm" which "is nothing other than blood bleached by heat and an excrement of the third digestion. Depending on its quantity and quality, it irritates the body, thereby providing a natural expulsion. Otherwise it would remain in its reservoirs, turn corrupt, and from there, by means of the back bone and other secret channels, send a thousand noxious vapors to the brain, troubling the faculties and principal virtues." By contrast, in ch. VIII he gives a balanced resumé of the pathological events created by the penetration of blood vapors through the eyes. In this sense, Ferrand provides a treatise that is heterogeneous in nature, and that suggests, at first view, that he was unable to make choices or to rationalize the diverse components of his etiology. But, in his defense, it should be pointed out that he was not alone in his eclectic approach, and that the encyclopedic treatises of his contemporaries, Jean Aubery and Jean de Veyries, were far less integrated and schematic. Further in his defense, these pathological systems, though deriving from different centers of the body, share a common set of events and procedures, because the disruptions in each center set up repercussions by mechanical or sympathetic means in all the others. The corrupt seed mounts to the heart and brain, there confounding the faculties of imagination and judgment; the eye beams with their blood vapors, by contrast, descend to the liver and there initiate the burning of the humors. The effects from one center become causes in another, thereby creating a compound crisis that contributes to the general chronic malaise. Finally, what differentiates these centers is not the physiological processes so much as their symbolic and psychological significance to the medical philosopher. The crisis that originates in the putrefaction of the genital secretions responsible for exciting venereal desire conveys cultural connotations that contrast with those associated with the crisis that arises with the contemplation of a *phantasm* manipulated by the imagination and memory. It may be argued that each system corresponded to a perceived component of human sexuality.

It can be said that physicians in the late Renaissance refused to believe anything about the nature of erotic behavior that could not be documented in the ancients, or that they collected and juxtaposed these systems in deference to the authority of a diversified past. Yet it can also be said that the full measure of what they intuitively understood to be true about a phenomenon so complex as sexuality could only be expressed through an appropriation of established systems of physiological analysis. Through one of these systems, they recognized love as a commotion of the cognitive and imaginative faculties. Only then could they comprehend, in medical terms, the erotic fixations of the poets driven by a self-made world of images. Through another, they allowed for the intensifying role of the passions in an effort to account for the increase of feeling that comes with desire. Through yet another, they recognized the instinctual drives relating to the longing for union and reproduction, drives that were closely associated with erotic frenzy and madness. Through yet another, they brought into the sphere of medical causation the power residing in the object of beauty that can seize upon the psyche of the beholder. So perceived, the eclectic approaches of Ferrand and Burton should not be looked upon as evidence of methodological confusion but as means to an enrichment of the Renaissance understanding of sexuality in the only analytical terms at their disposal.

The innovative superimposition of these several traditional medical systems was also part of the history of *amor hereos* as an intellectual idea in the Renaissance. It represented a process of discovery and an arrangement of elements drawn from within the established body of medical documents that was as important to the history of this idea as the exchange of ideas with the occultists. Earlier physicians had extended their interests to include the amatory *maleficium* of the folk, and a few began to incorporate the cures and recipes belonging to that folk culture into their own treatises—such shock tactics as burning the excrement of the beloved in the presence of the lover. Ferrand lists a few and finds them offensive. These can be found as early as the middle of the thirteenth century in the *Thesaurus pauperum* attributed to Peter of Spain,[25] and they continue to appear three centuries later in the works of Giovanni di Vigo.[26] With the treatises accompanying the Inquisition, there appears a greater emphasis on the devil and his emissaries as agents in the provocation of erotic mania and melancholy. The complex debate that emerged between naturalists and theologians concerning the world of the occult raised the intellectual status of such *topoi* as amatory magic and all that had to do with philters, ligatures, incantations, and spells. Even the most orthodox medical writers in the late Renaissance were inclined to discuss these issues, if only to allow for a display of their superior skepticism. Jean Aubery's treatise on love is largely given over to these topics and to that rhetorical purpose. Ficino, alone, contributed a new etiology of love, based, to be sure, on classical concepts of the *fascinatio*, but a concept which he formalized into a complete analysis of eroticism. Ficino's erudition in both medical and philosophical matters enabled his theory to find favor within the Galenic medical establishment and a place beside the ideas derived from Galen, Aristotle, and Hippocrates. To this superimposition of pathological systems was added, in the late Renaissance, the rich lore of the ancient poets and philosophers disseminated by the love treatises of the Italian humanists. These were the dominant currents of thought concerning *amor hereos* in the centuries preceding Ferrand.

V

Ferrand's Renaissance Sources
and Analogues

A statistical appraisal of Ferrand's use of sources would be not only inconclusive but misleading. There are 126 references to Galen, followed by over 100 to Hippocrates, over 50 to Avicenna, some 20 to Valleriola, but only 8 to Ferrand's declared mentor Du Laurens, and none at all to Aubery, who is nevertheless echoed and paralleled in several passages. By the same token, Ficino is mentioned 20 times, by comparison with only 6 references to Rodrigo de Castro, whose work is of greater importance to Ferrand. Aristotle is the most frequently mentioned of the ancient philosophers with over 100 references, yet it would be erroneous to assume that Ferrand turned to him directly for more than corroborating words and phrases.

It is one of the anomalies of that age of scholarship that deference to the ancients was the first mark of a true scholar, even in such fields as clinical medicine. Ferrand had no choice but to go through the exercise of basing his book on the opinions of classical writers, even if that base was largely an illusory one, for such procedures would alone give to it the authority he sought. Insofar as Ferrand divides his treatise into shorter sections by topics that lend themselves to embellishment through quotations from the ancient writers, he is able to pay his debt to tradition. These references and allusions have been recorded in the annotations to the text. Yet given that erotic love as a medical concept had evolved slowly through the centuries and was to achieve its fullest development only in the late Renaissance, we would expect Ferrand to use the most recent treatises for his true principal sources. This is, in fact, the case. It was not in Aristotle, but in Valleriola, Du Laurens, and Aubery that he found his models for writing a full-length treatise on the diseases of love. Because the important pre-Renaissance contributors to Ferrand's thought have been covered in previous sections of the introduction, it remains for us here to examine the treatises of his immediate predecessors, to survey the uses Ferrand made of them, and to place Ferrand's work in the context which they together create. Moreover, in speaking of Ferrand's sources, we cannot confine our inquiry exclusively to medical sources, for equally important are the Italian expository book writers on love. It is Ferrand's conflation of these two currents of writing that accounts for the uniqueness of his approach.

A consideration of Ferrand's place among his contemporaries raises a question of perspective, for while his treatise is the continuation of a medical idea with a history belonging exclusively to medical writing, it is also a work in the spirit of humanist eclecticism that goes outside of the medical schools and into the world of letters and contemporary social philosophy. It becomes important, then, to distinguish between the sources that preserved that central medical idea and the highly diverse group that served to modify, explicate, and socialize that idea. To a degree, they can be divided into those that conform to the traditional medical treatise in both manner and matter in which erotic love is considered strictly as a disease relating to melancholy or mania, requiring specifically medical or methodical treatments traditionally sanctioned by physicians, and those that do not. Though it may appear difficult to apply criteria precisely and consistently given the presence of historical and literary allusions in the medical works, and the abundant use of medical terms in the expository books on love, nevertheless a distinction is necessary in order to measure the degree to which Ferrand superimposes humanist philosophical views and poetic observations upon his medical substructure.

Through the conflation of these different sources, Ferrand's work grew to its encyclopedic proportions. The medical tradition is to be identified with the works already described, works that contain a core of medical ideas on erotic love that is carried forward in the sixteenth century by Pereda, Cristóbal de Vega, Luis Mercado, Girolamo Mercuriale, Guillaume Rondelet, and Jean Liébault.[1] The expository books whose ideas infiltrated French medical writing on *heroes* after 1580 are difficult to classify both for the diversity of their contents and for the variety of their modes of discourse. These works are ultimately Italian in origin and can be traced back to the fourteenth-century medical-philosophical commentaries on Guido Cavalcanti's "Donna me prega" by Dino del Garbo and by an unknown author whose work was, until recently, attributed to Egidio Romano.[2] These formed an important subgenre of intellectual speculation upon the nature of love and the passions in which medical analysis was joined, on the one hand, with a reading of the ancient mythographers and philosophers (especially Plato, Plotinus, Proclus, and the Neoplatonists) and, on the other, with a reading of contemporary poets and essayists. It was principally through the mediation of Ficino that this material made its way north during the sixteenth century.[3] Without these writers, Ferrand could have written only another conventional medical treatise in the tradition of Arnald of Villanova or François Valle-riola. At the same time, as we shall discover, care must be taken not to overemphasize their philosophical importance to Ferrand because, given the rigidities within the Galenic system to which he subscribed, a syn-thesis between the medical approach to excessive eros and the ideal love of the Italian tradition was beyond his purposes.

By all appearances, Ferrand's knowledge of the Italian tradition and of the problems and controversies associated with it came to him sec-ond hand through his reading of Mario Equicola's *Libro de natura de amore*, a work published in 1525.[4] But before looking at Ferrand's use of Equicola, something should be said briefly about the Florentine human-ists, the Neoplatonic movement under Ficino, and the dissemination of those ideas through *Gli Asolani*, Pietro Bembo's all-important discourse on love, published some twenty years before Equicola. Before Bembo, Neoplatonic speculation on love had been confined mainly to Florentine aristocratic circles. These philosophers, with Ficino at their head, had taken a position in favor of love as a noble passion in opposition to the humanists who considered it fit only for the inferior language of the ver-nacular poets. The humanists preferred themes of classical derivation, such as "pleasure" or "virtue," upon which they expounded exclusively in Latin. The Neoplatonists offered a philosophy based on a fusion of classical Platonism and Neoplatonism with Christian Neoplatonism and the Italian lyric tradition, thereby promoting the reputations of the poets of the *dolce stil nuovo* and of Petrarch. Their treatises were also written in Latin, however, and were accessible only to a restricted group of Tuscan intellectuals who were members of the Neoplatonic Academy.

Pietro Bembo, a Venetian aristocrat, adapted the discourse on love to the needs, not of the academy, but of the court. He wrote in the vernac-ular, adopting for his purposes the florid language of the Tuscan love poets. Unlike Ficino, who considered love from a conceptual point of view, Bembo arrived at his understanding of love through an examina-tion of the finest pieces in the Tuscan lyric tradition. In Neoplatonism he saw a theoretical explanation of what he found in Petrarch's sonnets, and at the same time an ideological framework for his own "Petrarchism." Through constant reference to specific poems, to the themes and modes of expression, he avoided the disadvantages of abstract analysis. Bem-bo's *Asolani* was a complete work on love, for despite the honor of being chosen by Baldassar Castiglione as the spokesman for Neoplatonic love in *The Book of the Courtier*, Bembo deals with it only in the third of his three-book work. It was the comprehensiveness of his treatise, together with its innovations in style and content, that guaranteed its place in pos-terity. During the years that followed the publication of Bembo's work, there was a proliferation of treatises on love, most of them taking up the themes presented in the three books of the *Asolani*. Moreover, through the example set by Bembo, contemporary poetry became an integral part of the analysis of love in all of these new treatises. The same partiality of the age for *summas* and compendia that influenced Ferrand can be seen in Mario Equicola's encyclopedic discussion of love. Equicola prefaced his work with a series of analytical résumés arranged in historical order dealing with the opinions of the "modern" writers on love. Quite naturally he concentrated on authors in the Italian tradition: Guittone d'Arezzo; Guido Cavalcanti and Dino del Garbo's commentary on his "Donna me prega"; Dante Alighieri; Francesco Petrarca; Francesco da Barberino; Jean de Meung, author of *Le Roman de la Rose*, and other French writers; Giovanni Boccaccio; Marsilio Ficino; Giovanni and Giovan Francesco Pico della Mirandola. He gave brief accounts of Francesco Cattani da Diacceto's *I tre libri de amore con un panegirico all 'Amore,'* Battista Fregoso's *Anteros* (1496), Leon Battista Alberti's *Ecatomfila* and *Deifira*, Battista Platina's (Bartolomeo Secchi of Cremona) *Dialogus contra Amores* (1504), Pier Hedo's (Pietro Capretto) *Anterotica, sive de Amoris generibus* (1492), the love eclogues by Battista Carmelita, and the lost *Aura* by Jacopo Calandra. It is significant that his list contains the names of all the writers in the Italian tradition mentioned in Ferrand's pages, together with enough information to account for the content of most of Ferrand's references and allusions. Equally significant is the fact that the work was translated into French by Gabriel Chappuys in 1584, and that it immediately became one of the major sourcebooks for the history of love. There were others such as the dialogues by Platina and Fregoso, translated by Thomas Sibilet and published together in 1581 as *L'Antéros ou Contramour de Messire Baptiste Fulgose, jadis duc de Gennes.*[5] But Ferrand seems to have relied exclusively on Equicola, not only as his principal source for information on the Italian tradition, but perhaps the only one he trusted. In the edition of 1610, Ferrand mentions *La remède d'amour* by Aeneas Sylvius Piccolomini (Pope Pius II), a work translated into French as early as 1556.[6] That it does not reappear in the edition of 1623 is perhaps to be attributed to the fact that Ferrand decided to use only those authors included in Equicola's epitome.

In keeping with the approach to love exemplified in the *Asolani*, Ferrand likewise looked to the poets, both ancient and modern, for insights into the symptoms of love. The lyric tradition concerned with lovers who sigh and weep, who wander alone or sequester themselves, or who evince all the agitations of indecision and mental torment appropriate to the desiring and tortured soul was far too coherent and concentrated, too frequently iterated to ignore. The medical commentaries on the early Italian love poets had, in fact, created a powerful precedent for conflating the conventions of poetry with the observations of the physician. In that spirit, Ferrand refers to the flights of metaphor in praise of the lady's beauty, but ultimately as proof of the derangement of the imagination to be interpreted entirely within the frame of reference of humoral medicine.

It should be pointed out that for poetic manifestations of the deranged imagination caused by love or for poetic descriptions of the symptoms of love, Ferrand had only to look into the French literary tradition going back to the eleventh century, a tradition that was concerned above all with speculation on the nature and effects of natural love. In *Le Roman de la Rose, Le Roman de Tristan, Le Roman de Flamenca,* in the vast corpus of Provençal poetry, and in the *De honeste amore* of Andreas Capellanus—especially in the third book, the "De reprobatione amoris," the first and most influential statement on "anteros" written in the medieval West—Ferrand had at his disposal an incredible repertoire.[7] It is difficult to believe that he knew nothing of this literature, difficult to explain how Andreas Capellanus failed to merit a single reference in so purportedly encyclopedic a treatise as Ferrand's, difficult to explain why he should overlook the popular nonmedical texts from sixteenth-century France that dealt with the diseases of erotic love, such as Pierre Boaistuau's *Le théâtre du monde* (1558) with its lengthy and illustrated account of the miseries of pathological love. According to fashion, Ferrand does cite Ronsard, Héroët, and Remy Belleau, but that he ignores the whole of the French medieval tradition and many of the related texts from his own age is probably to be explained by the modishness of the Italian *trattati.*

Du Laurens provides an indication of the popularity of the *trattati* and of the growing tendency to accommodate their materials to French scholarship, in stating his own resistance to the temptation. "I don't wish to research here the etymology of love and why the name Eros was given to it: I don't propose to define it—too many great writers have tried, and none have managed it successfully. Moreover, I don't intend to examine all the different kinds of love, or their genealogies. You can read what has been written about it by Plato, Plotinus, Marsilio Ficino, Giovanni Pico della Mirandola, Mario Equicola, and Leon Hebreo. I am content to look at just one of its effects among the thousand it produces. I want everyone to recognize by the description of this melancholy [disease] just what such a violent love can do to the body and to the soul."[8] But though Du Laurens declares his independence from them, his statement was insufficient to stem the tide of interest among his followers. Ferrand, like Aubery and Jean de Veyries, takes the caveat as a commission and expounds at length upon these very topics. Ferrand turned to Equicola, not only as a model for studying the relationship between the love expressed by the poets and the love examined by the physicians (a matter to which we will return in the penultimate section of our introduction), but also as a source for dealing with the names of love, Cupid's wings, his nakedness, his bows and arrows, and much more which he used to embellish his thesis. Nevertheless, in looking at one kind of love, namely melancholy love defined according to the medical tradition, Ferrand was unable to go beyond the surfaces of the Italian tradition. Paradoxically, because he was led by his medical biases to see in Petrarch a victim of the erotic melancholy he was describing, he could not see in his poetry, at the same time, a manifestation of a love philosophy in the Neoplatonic tradition. Ferrand, in any case, probably knew little more of Ficino than what he had read of him in Equicola and Valleriola. More important, the fundamental incompatibility between his Galenic orientation and the Neoplatonic view was well beyond his powers of conciliation. Ferrand could have accepted Ficino's premises; he could have granted Ficino's association of the passions of excessive love with conditions of the body that lead to chronic incapacity, to a disease of the imagination and eventually to death. But that a man could, through powers of intellectual concentration and meditation, hold in the memory the object that incites the concupiscent appetites and control it in such a way that it leads him to the contemplation of perfect beauty was a proposition both outside of his medical frame of reference and irrelevant to him as a clinical practitioner. It is significant that Ferrand nowhere asks in his treatise whether the behavior of the imagination corrupted by the burned humors was not also an attempt to spiritualize the object and to enjoy it exclusively at the level of images as its chosen goal. Despite his desire to incorporate Italian matter into the French medical tradition on love, he too must choose between loyalties. In the final analysis, he follows Du Laurens, who admitted to those restrictions and who concentrated on that pathological form of love that can only do violence to the body and soul.

In the last two decades of the sixteenth century, there was a renewed interest in *amor hereos* as an issue in practical medicine. It came about strictly through an interest in the *topos* as it was discussed in the medical treatises. There were physicians before Du Laurens who expanded upon the subject of pathogenic love—Luis Mercado and François Valleriola, to whom we will return—but it is the treatise on melancholy by this one-time chancellor of the medical school in Montpellier, physician-in-ordinary to Henry IV, and one of the most remarkable of the Galenic apologists that most clearly epitomizes the renewal of medical interest in the topic of love melancholy. Ferrand, though greatly extending the topic, ventures nothing of a radical nature that goes beyond the theories of his mentor. Du Laurens's treatise was published in Paris in 1597, and dedicated to his patron, the Duchess of Uzés, who was allegedly suffering from the various illnesses described. That it is a concise work written in French in a relatively easy and accessible style may be attributed to the fact that it was conceived expressly for her. His study is illustrated by a few well-chosen anecdotes, but remains relatively unencumbered by critical references and scholarly apparatuses. Du Laurens arranges

his two chapters on love according to the conventional tripartite sectioning of definition, diagnosis, and cures. He tactfully omits the pedantic
disputations associated with the medical dissertation, preferring to write
with an air of balance and authority based on silent choices and private
reasoning. In this way he seems to sweep away the dialectics of past
treatises and to establish a new central and authoritative view of love
melancholy, a fact that may account for the work's success and influence.

Du Laurens's authority was the product of his sure hand as a writer,
his coherence as a thinker, and his clear rhetorical strategy. His ideas
reappear in Ferrand, not as grounds for debate and commentary, but as
matter entirely digested, memorized, and absorbed. The lack of references to him in Ferrand's margins is totally deceiving. Ferrand's debt
is in fact global in nature in a way that surpasses adequate acknowledgment through the occasional reference. It is our contention that even
such matters as the weight and proportion given to the principal parts,
the disposition and levels of intensity of the arguments, the techniques of
medical diagnosis, and the new emphasis placed upon pharmaceutical
cures owe much to Ferrand's reading of Du Laurens. Altogether there
is barely a concept or anecdote, barely a category of cause or cure mentioned in that part of Du Laurens's book relating to erotic melancholy
that does not have its counterpart in Ferrand. In a sense, he spoke with
the authority of the Montpellier tradition behind him, a medical faculty
where love as a disease had been under debate sporadically for several
centuries going back through Rondelet, Valleriola (born in Montpellier,
but physician in Arles and professor in Torino), Tornemire, Valescus of
Tarenta, Bernard of Gordon, Arnald of Villanova, and Gerard of Solo.[9]
Du Laurens gave to the topic a new status and a new clinical relevance
through a popular treatise backed up by his reputation as one of the
most renowned physicians of his age.

Du Laurens is brief but clear about the nature of the passions, and
Ferrand agrees with him in these matters entirely: that a man taken over
by his passions is capable of beastlike behavior; that man's first duty is
the exercise of reason as censor to the appetites; that failing this, the appetites themselves can generate states of disease. Just under the surface
of each treatise lies a shared bias that the passions can obscure man's innate nobility, that victims of desire are blameworthy in those cases where
reason is equal to the task of control, but to be pitied where the burned
humors assault and corrupt the reason. Each type of patient fails in his
responsibility to society and each requires a cure suited to his condition.
Given the Galenic orientation toward humoral causes and constitutional
weaknesses, lovers are more deserving of pity and care than of sermons
and beatings, as recommended by Bernard of Gordon.[10] Du Laurens accepts the notion that moral corruption can encourage desires that arise in
the soul alone, and that blasphemy and sin are matters pertaining more

to the church than to the physician. He is concerned only with those cases that involve physical causes. Ferrand, by contrast, is less disposed to the idea of desires arising in the soul alone and nowhere cedes professional territory in that way. Both Du Laurens and Ferrand underscore the involuntary nature of humoral diseases, including all manifestations of frenzy, madness, and melancholy. Both relate the course of events by which such conditions make their assault upon the judgment and imagination of the individual.

No writer of Ferrand's generation would go beyond Du Laurens in systematizing the established medical doctrines concerning the diseases of melancholy, and no one would improve upon his brief but concise outline of the definition, diagnosis, and curing of erotic love. But the age was far too interested in the topic to settle for so short an account. Several writers would take up the challenge of expanding philosophically and rhetorically upon the basic material. We can suggest, with the advantage of hindsight, that there were only a few general directions possible for its development. One lay in returning to the formal rhetorical disputations of the schools that originated in the scholastic treatises on medicine. A writer could subdivide his work into set pieces in which he debates the pros and cons of the many *topoi* relating to love, its nature, and diagnosis. Jean Aubery took this approach in a work published in 1599 that Ferrand knew well. The same techniques had been employed by Capretto in his treatise on love a hundred years earlier. Another lay in the extended case study in which the elements of the disease would receive analysis and exemplification in terms of the treatment of a particular patient. This procedure is followed by François Valleriola in a lengthy "observation" published in 1588 on a case of erotomania. A third lay in the conversion of the annotated case study into a fictive framing tale or romance narrative in which the patient and the literary protagonist are joined in a single portrait and which serves at the same time as the context for introducing a wide assortment of medical and nonmedical observations on erotic love. This is the format devised by Jean de Veyries in a work that appeared in 1609 under the title of *La généalogie de l'amour.*[11] A fourth lay in the encyclopedic compendium that employed much of the same material but which built upon a rhetorical structure drawn from the medical treatises. Such is the essential nature of Ferrand's treatise. These works, together with Du Laurens's, form the core of the extended treatment of love as a medical topic in France before Descartes. It can be argued, in fact, that after Ferrand erotic love as a medical topic could only be taken back to the schools for further refinement in terms of a richer sampling of case studies or elaborated upon in a treatise on the passions disciplined by more rigorous philosophical methodologies. The former direction is taken by the medical dissertations in the schools on psychiatric topics; the latter, by Descartes.

François Valleriola, in his *Observationum medicinalium libri VI* (1588), was the key formulator of the theories on melancholy love that antici- pated the encyclopedic approach, one in which metaphysical and mytho- logical speculations appear with the clinical. Valleriola presents his spec- ulations on the causes, symptoms, and cures of love in the context of a case study of a merchant of Arles who entered into a state of fury and madness because of unrequited love. This afflicted merchant was a true erotomaniac; the rebuff he had suffered incited him to anger and violence against those around him and would have led to violence against himself had his relatives not restrained him. He displayed the usual symptoms such as leanness, sleeplessness, incessant grieving; but he also suffered delusions of the mind, for in the middle of the night he would suddenly be seized by a powerful conviction that he was being caressed by his beloved. Valleriola boasted that he was able, by following the cures set out in the treatise, to restore this man to a perfect state of health.

Valleriola writes in a confident and magisterial Latin, as though con- scious of his own authority in these matters. He goes beyond the confines of Galenic analysis as epitomized by Du Laurens in joining to his medical theories the philosophical observations concerning love that stem from Plato and Plotinus, and that were renewed in the Renaissance by Ficino and his followers. He explains that only by following a long path of inquiry can one show just how it is that the passions are able to drive men to fury and madness. He takes up the tradition of the two Venuses, how they were born, and how they represent those forms of desire that are attached respectively to things divine and to things earthly. From this material, two ideas emerge that are fundamental to his thought: that love generated by the earthly Venus functions as a kind of charm, a "fas- cination" that enters through the eyes, manifests itself as a perturbation of the blood, and acts both as a poison and as an infection that spread throughout the body; and that love is a form of desire for that which is good, a desire that expresses itself as a longing to possess and enjoy an object of beauty.

Valleriola returns ultimately to the fundamental Galenic concept that melancholy diseases are caused by the adustion of humors. He also argues that the heart is the seat of the disease because it is there that the humors boil and overflow, giving off the black and sooty vapors that rise to the head and thereby create the restlessness and the fear. He explains how the lover is distracted by his continual brooding on the beloved and how such thought disrupts the natural faculties and obstructs the proper functioning of the rest of the body, for which reasons the digestion goes awry, matter spills over into the liver and then is diffused through the veins as yellowish waste material that causes the characteristic pallor of the skin. At the same time, Valleriola speculates on the ways in which contemplation, by corrupting the liver, can itself set up the causal chain that leads to the yellow tint. He allows for originating causes both in the head and in the hypochondries without any sense of contradiction. The issue is the same that arises in our discussion of Haly Abbas and Ish'ḥaq ībn-Imrān: the passion of the soul that becomes a disease of melancholy and the hypochondriacal melancholy that leaves its effects on the mind converge in Western medicine without entirely shedding the elements of their respective origins.

Valleriola goes on to discuss the madness caused by excessive blood and the madness caused by excessive bile, the former leading to laughter and giddiness, the latter to grief and sorrow. He distinguishes between the black bile in the brain, where true insanity occurs and the bile contained in the heart which produces only longing and grief. In all these distinctions he works out his own variations on the question of humors and adustion. Like Ferrand, he is unwilling to limit his options by fully rationalizing his system. He will not attempt to join into a single sequence of causation such diverse agents as the blood that carries pallid waste to the skin, the black vapors that rise to the brain, and the poisonous infection that spreads to the limbs. The several traditions involved are authoritative and are thus placed side by side. While both authors are willing to speak of love melancholy as a disease of the blood poisoned by the eyes of the beloved, Valleriola is more insistent on the matter. Likewise, both will follow Gàlen in attributing love madness to the vapors arising from the combustion of the biles, but Ferrand will do so with greater emphasis than Valleriola.

Valleriola's Neoplatonism is particularly evident in the several pages devoted to the eyes of the lover. It is the sight of a beautiful object and the power within that object to tyrannize over the beholder through the senses that brings on the malaise. Ferrand consecrates a chapter to the eyes, but he concentrates more on the effects of the disease: the sunken hollow appearance and the fluttering lids. Valleriola identifies the eyes as the initiating organs, the channels by which love is communicated by means of the clear and subtle beams, the vapors of the blood that can in turn charm as if by magic, penetrate as darts to the entrails, and infect the blood as a poison. These actions become material and pathogenic for Valleriola. In dwelling upon the eyes as nearly occult agents, he alludes to earlier theories concerning the eye as a system of mirrors through which the object beheld maintains a kind of reduced physical presence and a concentrated power to hurt. These issues have already been reviewed in our section on the history of the idea; Valleriola was an important mediator of these concepts in the late Renaissance. He found himself midway between Platonic and Galenic views of love. The bleeding that for Ferrand draws off the excess blood that produces semen for Valleriola draws off the blood that contains the venom of love that had been introduced through the eyes.

In his thirty-four quarto pages on love melancholy, Valleriola opens the way to a more omniphilosophical approach to erotic love within the context of the conventional medical treatise. His clinical frame attaches his speculations firmly to the matter of medicine; his detour into Plotinus and Ficino is justified by his definition and diagnosis of the disease. Ferrand will follow and enlarge upon that course, looking even further into the Italian tradition.

Valleriola provides a significant model for Ferrand: he writes a more open, more extended treatise than Du Laurens's, yet it is fully disciplined by the priorities of a physician and of a professor in a faculty of medicine. Ferrand read him closely and borrowed as much as he was able to harmonize with his own perception of the established medical tradition.

Jean Aubery's *L'antidote d'amour* (1599) is an important link between Du Laurens and Ferrand. Aubery, like Ferrand, set out to write in French (and thus for the benefit of a readership outside of the medical schools) a serious extended treatise on the subject of erotic love as a disease of melancholy. He alludes to the fame that should rightfully belong to the scholar who finds a cure for this universally acknowledged disease and offers his own book for consideration. His work is dedicated to the most esteemed Du Laurens whom he addresses as a personal associate (he probably first knew him as a student in Montpellier in 1590–91 when Du Laurens was chancellor).[12] Unfortunately, Aubery was fascinated by the art of formal debate for its own sake. His style is overwrought, copious, and full of refined reasonings. With regard to the content, he fails to pursue his topic to its inherent clinical conclusions, settling for the view that wisdom, continence, self-discipline, and a few right eating habits take precedence over purely medical procedures for the curing of the disease. In describing the distress caused by the burned humors he is given to metaphorical flights and literary indulgences of a decorative nature. Hence, as a thinker he is far less in Du Laurens's debt than is Ferrand because he abandons his mentor's clear analysis and loses himself in scholastic exercises.

Aubery does lay claim to the responsibility for the treatment of erotic love on behalf of the medical profession. He fails however to stress the somatogenesis of the disease and to develop the role of the humors as causal agents. In fact, the concept of melancholy is barely mentioned. Aubery emphasizes the importance of self-help and reserves his description of the physician's active role to the last twenty pages. His prescription of a good legal marriage provides the summit of his entire argument. Behind these sundry observations we detect a writer uncertain of his ultimate directions.

The balance of his treatise is taken up with a series of school points that are developed according to a rhetorical formula that at first baffles, then surprises, then cloys by its ultimate predictability. Invariably, he begins with the weaker or more outdated side of a set topic which he argues with a deceptive cogency before turning against that position with more modern and enlightened arguments. Having first tricked the reader into accepting the weaker argument, he then brings out a battery of examples to the contrary, all the while preening himself on his superior scepticism and his rhetorical cleverness, or so the reader is inclined to think. One by one he tackles the favored topics: that the concupiscible appetite resides in the liver as opposed to the other parts of the body; that given the condition of the blood, youth is the age most vulnerable to love; that there are two kinds of love, the celestial centered in the brain and the dishonest centered in the liver. He raises again the question of a pulse peculiar to lovers—a tiresome theme that goes back at least to Galen that was taken over by the Arab physicians and that had been long since dismissed by most of the Western physicians. He asks whether love is caused by sympathy as the pretext for a long sermon on the correspondences found in nature, a sermon based on the principle of the attraction of like objects and the philosophy of the magnet. Aubery's discussion of astral influences is completely innocuous and hardly worth mention except insofar as he shares the topic in common with Ferrand. He debates whether the eye has, in the manner of the basilisk, the power to enchant. He asks, too, whether love can be brought on forcefully by magic, numbers, figures, characters, or philters. His study takes a series of remote turns from the topic, dealing more with theories of numbers, magic, and astrology than with the nature and symptoms of love. Yet in this fact lies the work's greatest importance for Ferrand.

Ferrand knew Aubery's work, yet he refused to acknowledge it in his own treatise. We suspect that the omission was more than oversight and that, of all the books by his contemporaries, this was the one Ferrand would have most desired never to have been written because of the similarity of their declared purposes. Ironically, Aubery's rhetorical show of scepticism in dealing with the scholastic *topoi* fails to establish him as a progressive thinker so that, from this point of view, Ferrand had no cause for fear. Aubery's preoccupation with the occult properties of love distracted him from the more central matters concerning the etiology and cures of love as a disease of melancholy. Yet Ferrand's own sense of his debt to Aubery may have been far greater than we realize, for despite Ferrand's general adherence to the conventional approaches to love established by the medical writers in the Arabic-Galenic tradition, he was also greatly attracted to the possibility of integrating certain of the occult procedures alien to that tradition into his own diagnostics. Among the contemporary medical writers on love melancholy, only Aubery raises these issues in a systematic way, so that while in terms of actual materials the debt to Aubery may be slight, the credit for taking this new direction in his own research may, in itself, have been more than Ferrand wanted to share. The fact remains that neither Du Laurens nor Valleriola concerned themselves with such matters—matters that make up a significant portion of Ferrand's treatise—and that *L'antidote d'amour*, despite the radical differences separating it from Ferrand's treatise, comes closest to him in associating the occult sciences with love as a medical topic.

La Généalogie de l'amour (1609) was the work of a Montpellier-trained physician practicing in Bordeaux. It is mentioned here because it completes the survey of the methods employed by physicians of that age for expanding the medical treatise on love, in this case within a form that stands halfway between science and literature. Given his framing story of a lovesick marquis whose fiancée's mother calls in the family physician to effect a cure, de Veyries seems to view such manifestations of passion as pertaining most naturally to the aristocracy, who had both the time and the literary training necessary for the cultivation of the requisite sensibilities. He seems to have recognized, far more than his predecessors did, the social content and the conditioning in fantasized desire. Ferrand makes slight reference to de Veyries in his second treatise, and none in his first. But the question of influence here is of secondary importance. More to the point is that these two men were at work simultansously on eclectic developments of the same medical topic in the first decade of the seventeenth century. De Veyries, too, had read the Italian love books and the peripheral lore of the ancients pertaining to love, and had also seen fit to work the medical, mythological, and occult traditions concerning erotic love into a single fabric.

The physician in the tale is created principally as a vehicle for presenting de Veyries's vast erudition on love. This material, however, is presented in an entirely random fashion. In bk. I, ch. 1, sec. 4, he explains how love cannot be cured by herbs, while in ch. 15, sec. 3, he comes to the reasons why love belongs to the appetites; in bk. II, ch. 7, sec. 1, he addresses the question "What is love?" while in ch. 14, sec. 1, he examines the significance of beauty. Meanwhile, the tale of the lovers stands still and the romance element all but drops from sight. It is not the lack of organization or the imperfection of the narrative that quells interest, however, but the abstruse and impenetrable style, for the work is written in an inflated and tortured prose for which today's reader has no patience at all, and which may well have defied the interest of the seventeenth-century reader as well. The insights of the most promising passages are obscured by a compounding of qualifiers, negations, and counterturns.

De Veyries touches on a number of topics evident in Ferrand, drawn from a common repertoire. In piecemeal fashion he deals with the way in which love burns and blackens all it touches. He understands that love troubles the imagination, that blood in excess leads to the production of sperm, that love is hot and humid by nature. He deals with the influence of the senses and mentions the alluring and compelling nature of beauty. Toward the end of his seemingly interminable work he comes to a general statement on the subjection of the soul to the humors of the body. There are sections dealing with specific curiosities, several of which receive mention in Ferrand: that the remora is a fish that preserves love; that rocket is a very hot herb and thus dangerous to lovers; that love is betrayed by the countenance. Along with these items of medical lore he makes mention of occult properties, philters, the effects of flagellation, the nature and uses of hippomanes and other love potions. Two other now familiar components also appear: the scholastic topics and the mythological materials attached to love. De Veyries debates the difference between physicians and metaphysicians, whether a woman's love is stronger than a man's, whether old people are capable of love, whether love is the building force of the universe. Finally, he devotes a considerable portion of his work to just such issues as Du Laurens vowed to exclude: the names of love, whether the name of love is more dangerous than the thing itself, how Venus and Cupid are one, a description of the painting of Cupid stung by a bee, the sea as the chaos from which Venus and Cupid are born, and several others.

In brief, we see in *La Généalogie de l'amour* the book that Ferrand might have written had he allowed his literary and stylistic predilections to run uncurbed; had he devoted himself entirely to a readership among the genteel, the leisured, and the learned: and had he abandoned himself to the random collecting of materials without feeling bound to reorganize them according to the conventions of the medical treatise. Yet we are reminded at the same time of how much these two writers share in common in terms of the topic, the techniques for developing it through the accumulation of popular materials, and the sense of a wider reading audience. In the new synthesis the elements of diverse origins begin to shed their respective contexts. In de Veyries that process is virtually complete, so that pieces of the Galenic tradition appear intermingled with mythological lore, speculations on the occult, and fragments of philosophical thought concerning love. It is to Ferrand's credit in creating his own eclectic treatise that he built it up from the sources and that he documented his arguments far more scrupulously. Therein lies his claim to the attention of historians of Renaissance ideas.

In the final analysis it may be said that Valleriola and Du Laurens served Ferrand as mentors concerning both substance and rhetorical approach, but that Aubery and de Veyries served only as remote models for extending the range of his scholarship to cover areas not previously a part of the standard medical approaches to love. These four, together with Ferrand and Burton, represent the breadth of interest in erotic love as a medical topic and the various directions taken in an effort to combine the conventional medical ideas, outlined at the outset of our introduction, with the other traditional storehouses of materials concerning love. Ferrand's treatise takes its place in the context created by these works and distinguishes itself through a comparison with their methods and materials.

Ferrand's Definitions and Diagnostics of Erotic Melancholy and Erotic Mania

Ferrand's instincts as a scholar were those of the conciliator, to convert many voices of authority into a single voice. At the very center of his system, however, is a philosophical difficulty that could be molded, glossed, divided into more refined parts, ignored, but never fully conquered. Cicero, in the fourth book of his *Tusculan Disputations*, expresses his belief that ideal love or friendship is impossible, that even the most inspired relationship contains elements of interest or of lust, and that above all men "must be warned of the madness of the passion of love. For of all disturbances of the soul there is assuredly none more violent . . . the disorder of the mind in love is in itself abominable."[1] Ferrand could agree completely with this common premise. Cicero writes as a moralist concerned with the feebleness of the will, and so he states that "this characteristic, too, of all disorder must be made clear, namely, that there is no instance where it is not due to belief, due to an act of judgement, due to voluntary choice. For were love a matter of nature all men would love, as well as always love and love the same object, nor should we find one discouraged by shame, another by reflection, another by satiety."[2] In brief, while such love may produce states of disease, it is in itself a moral defect. Ferrand himself is seldom far from this conventional view; he closes his treatise in wishing "for all melancholy or maniacal lovers the ultimate cure . . . 'the honing and perfection of wisdom,' which is the true moly." He states this in apparent opposition to all the mechanistic and deterministic procedures by which love assaults the bodies of those who are temperamentally inclined to the diseases of melancholy.

Ferrand maneuvers through the difficulty by means of a constant refinement of categories through which certain of the moral and social factors may make their remote contributions without compromising the more immediate corporeal causes of melancholy diseases as dictated by medical tradition. Ferrand likewise divides erotic love into prepathological states and postpathological states in order to bridge the difficulty of moral versus material causes. He separates those chapters dealing with persons inclined to the disease from those concerned with persons already in advanced states of affliction. In ch. XXXVII, he reminds us that "it is easier to abolish love when it is new than after it has become diseased," and that there are, generally speaking, two kinds of cures, natural and artificial: the natural involves wise counsel, change of air, abstenance—recommended by Cicero as being more suitable to the prevention of the disease—while the artificial, namely the surgical and pharmaceutical treatments, are necessary once the disease has taken hold. If the amorist had not yet shown signs of affliction through adustion of the humors, the condition could be described in terms of the deficiency of the moral will, allowing for an effective employment of the methodical cures. This subdivision allows Ferrand to incorporate all of the considerations of the moralists while remaining faithful to the material determinism of the humors; it was his means for skirting a difficult issue without losing valuable material. Yet the underlying impasse remained, for to deny the will as liberal arbiter by subjecting it to the necessities of the diseased body is to render the argument vulnerable to attack by the theologians, while without the deterministic procedures of Galenic medicine the physician's claim to power over the disease had no substance. Despite Ferrand's traditionalism, there are many clues to suggest that he covertly sympathized with the Ciceronian view—that excessive love is a form of moral slackness. Up to a certain critical moment, the condition remains within the command of the reasoning faculties. Of necessity, however, that state passes with the inception of the pathological processes. Ferrand had no better solution to offer.

Anthony Levi states that "until 1637, the year of the *Discours de la méthode*, there was no sign of a coherent theory relating the passions to any physiological states which caused them,"[3] and to this it could be added that it was not until the publication of *Les passions de l'ame* in 1644 that a medical philosophy was systematically integrated with a system of ethics in such a way that the compulsive attractions and repulsions that move the soul were related to the conditions of the body—an approach that was then viewed as the only means for establishing ethics as an exact science. In this regard, no one would suggest that Ferrand or any of his sect was a true precursor to Descartes given the absence of a truly rigorous scientific methodology. Yet Ferrand's study was, in its philosophical dimensions, very much bent upon anatomizing the channels of sympathy and the means of physiological communication whereby the conditions of the soul were influenced by the physical constitution. Well before him, F. N. Coëffeteau, bishop of Marseilles, wrestled as best he could with the question and came close to the physicians when he credited to the influence of the stars, diet, climate, and heredity the shaping of the concupiscent appetites. If, as a good churchman, he was compelled to consider the somatic conditions to be effects of the passions rather than causes, he nevertheless went as far as he could in that direction. Huarte reasoned differently toward the same conclusions in his *Examen de ingenios para las ciencias*.[4] If the soul is the divine and immutable part, it must therefore also be identical in all men; if identical it cannot be the cause of intellectual and psychic differences. Those variations, he reasoned, must be owing to the body and to all the agents, accidents, and forces that play upon it. Sixty-two years before the *Discours*, Huarte was working toward a theory of the passions based on physiological causes.

By incessantly refining his categories of causation, Ferrand distracts his reader's attention away from his basic vacillation on these matters. The first several chapters are concerned with describing the causes of the disease—internal, external, efficient, material, contributing—then with describing the seats of the disease, and finally the seats of the causes of the disease. By such means he was able to incorporate into his argument all the divers elements that contribute to the malady: the stars, hot spicy food, the condition of the blood, the anatomy of the brain, the senses, the attraction to objects of beauty, the atoms entering and exiting by the eyes, idleness and leisure time, seasons and climates, the constitution of the humors, hereditary tendencies, and several others. His compound definition of love polarized these elements: a state of fear and sorrow, raised by intense desire for an object of beauty; a passion of the soul framed by complexions, humors, climate, food, excess sperm, burned bile, or blood. The brooding and depression associated with the former state corrupts the body; the corrupting influences of the latter pervert the imagination and the will. The reader grants him all these categories, not only because his debt to a variety of authorities must be conceded but because experience attests to the many factors and circumstances that contribute to the arousal of sensual desire.

As a physician, Ferrand subscribes unswervingly to a central doctrine: that the passions have the capacity through the heat they generate to burn the natural humors of the body, thereby changing them into adust states. This process of adustion, in turn, creates noxious vapors and fumes, like smoke from a furnace, that circulate throughout the body. Arriving in the brain, they have the capacity to obscure the mental vision, to corrupt the imagination, and to distort the judgment. Much that is endemic to the lover's perverse and antisocial behavior is to be credited directly to this process. A second and equally central doctrine holds that the brain itself produces its own condition of natural melancholy through intense fixation upon an object of desire, and that such brooding, by which means the image is etched and scored more deeply into the memory, is the same process as that by which the lover loses touch with other realities, taking the reconstructed, idealized, or otherwise falsified image of the beloved as the only true reality. The play of causes, both internal and external, had to be drawn up in uniform support of these two mechanisms: love as conditioned if not generated by the burned humors, and love as generated by an autonomous desire of the soul.

In this adjustment, Ferrand follows tradition. Du Laurens before him had explained how the symptoms of the disease, fear and sadness, are not causes but accidents that reveal the nature of the antecedent state; for fear and sadness are not the results of heat and adustion but of the cold, dry distemperature of the brain caused by sleeplessness and long hours of meditation. In keeping with the views of Aretaeus, if the drying and chilling sequence affects that part of the brain concerned with the actions of the soul, melancholy ensues; if it attacks the ventricles and the hollow passages, then epilepsy. Where intense thought produces a melancholy state tempered with a little blood, and where there are no excrements from combustion present to pollute the brain, this melancholy produces men with clear memories and deep thoughts, capable of the long reflections or the divine raptures we associate with poets, philosophers, and prophets.[5] Where those excrements of adustion are present, a feverless dotage is produced, accompanied by tendencies toward mania or depression, according to the bile that produces the vapors.

Ferrand is more brief on these distinctions than we would wish, undoubtedly assuming much of it to be common knowledge for his readers. In ch. IX, however, he states clearly that "the brain is the cause of the dotage when it is occupied by adust bile, burned blood or melancholy." We would interpret him as saying that love melancholy arises only where there are excrements of adustion present, that the burning not only of blood but of yellow and black biles can cause the disease, and that whichever preponderates will determine the nature of its expression. This would concur entirely with the general views set out by Du Laurens. Babb states that "frenzy is an inflammation of the brain due to an invasion of choler. . . . The symptoms of frenzy seem to be identical with those of wrathful and clamorous melancholy," citing Burton and Du Laurens as his sources.[6] Without close explanation, Ferrand preserves this essential difference throughout his treatise, that love may produce both erotic melancholy and erotic mania and that its expression runs the gamut from depressive suicide by starvation to lycanthropy. He underscores the point by noting in ch. III "that our ancient physicians often confound mania with melancholy, failing to note the varying degrees of difference between them."[7]

The description of the disease is further complicated by the traditional classification of melancholy into three kinds: that of the head, that of the entire body, and that of the hypochondries. Despite the fact that in love melancholy it is the head that is the diseased part and the fact that the burned vapors circulate through the veins and rise by their lightness to the brain, love is to be classified as a form of hypochondriacal melancholy originating in the liver, the spleen, and the mesentery because it is in the liver and the surrounding parts that the blackish vapors are generated. These same fumes, as Ferrand states at the end of ch. VII, are characteristic of hot, dry melancholiacs and "produce within a variety of flatulent vapors that tickle them, driving them to extremes of lasciviousness." In ch. IX, however, Ferrand finds himself speaking in agreement with Avicenna concerning "the vapors and humors produced by the heart" that are "sent up to the brain by means of vessels that interconnect them."[8] In a remote way the debate over causes, whether they lie in the actions of the soul or in the determining conditions of the body, perpetuates itself in the inevitable inconsistencies that arise over the respective roles of heart and liver and the perplexing relationship between a cold, dry melancholy of the head and a hot, dry melancholy of the hypochondries. The debate leads to ever-widening circles of definition and categorization that ultimately distract the reader from the issues under examination.

Our historical examination of *amor hereos* as a medical idea, while demonstrating the many phases of its complex development, also explains the origins of those many contradictory elements that vex Ferrand's treatise. His total lack of analysis or classification according to historical criteria produces an argument that continues to reveal unresolved vestiges of a complex history. Yet if Ferrand is to be accused of inconsistencies, he is also to be cherished as a representative of the general state of medical philosophy in his age regarding these matters. In his support, it is to be added that his views are in close agreement with those of Du Laurens, who may be read as a commentator upon the relationships, implicit and explicit, to be found in Ferrand. As Lawrence Babb has forewarned, "the physiological psychology of the Renaissance is a body of theory containing so many contradictions, semicontradictions, and disharmonies that any exposition of it is likely to misrepresent by introducing into it an orderliness which it does not really have."[9]

The traditional authority invested in these several theories concerning the behavior and origins of the diseases of melancholy contributed to this superimposition of etiological theories related to the various centers in the body. One means for drawing these centers into a single system was to elaborate upon the agents of communication within the body that would allow them all to work toward a common end. Ferrand takes up, in the wake of Du Laurens, the consideration of the role of the vital spirits in the generation of love melancholy. He understands these vapors of the blood to be the means whereby the image of the beloved was materially taken in through the eyes. As we explained earlier, the origin and behavior of this material was a topic of considerable controversy. It is significant that Du Laurens, as an anatomist, was among those who defended the existence of the vital spirits; he explained their origins in the choroid plexus and how they were boiled and distilled in the ventricles and perfected in the brain. The entire system depended on the operation of the *rete mirabile*, an extension of the carotid arteries. By means of these material agents, love enters the body and generates desire.[10]

Ferrand takes for granted a general knowledge of the spirits and their operations on the part of his readership and proceeds directly to an outline of the course of their travels in bringing on a state of depression or mania. He also adopts the overworked metaphors used to explain the independent volition of these agents insofar as they must attack and assault the parts of the body in a sequence leading by steps to the conquering of the citadel of Pallas. This is a manifestation of the teleological thinking that characterized even anatomical analysis: that the nature and behavior of each part is to be explained by its foreordained function. The description of such functions invited the use of military words and images: seat, citadel, fortress, imprisonment, or slavery. Because the reason is too strong to be attacked directly, the spirits carry the corrupting message first to the hypochondries. From the heated region of the liver the elements rise to make their assault upon the heart, which soon falls and joins in the conspiracy. Then the noble faculties of the soul can be overwhelmed and taken as slaves. By such a series of battles and victories, all the parts are joined and the metaphorical processes become synonymous with physiological processes. To be sure, Ferrand must momentarily disregard the reverse movement by which the passions of the mind, themselves, cause the condition of melancholy by changing the condition of the humors, though the view is equally fundamental to his thesis. Ferrand did well at this juncture to ignore the rival claim of the atomists that love was a kind of poison or charm conveyed from body to body, a venom that traveled straight to the entrails and from there spread throughout the body by means of the veins and arteries just as a contageous disease might do. This view had been championed by Ficino and by Valleriola.[11] Both explanations sought to account in physiological and material terms for the remarkable power of an object of beauty upon the body and imagination of a susceptible observer. Again, in these matters, Ferrand stays close to Du Laurens.

Once the disease has taken hold, its presence is revealed by a well-defined set of symptoms: a desire for solitariness, sighing, hollow eyes, sleeplessness, loss of appetite. As we have indicated in our historical survey, these indicators have been reckoned up in parallel traditions by both physicians and poets since ancient times. Physicians considered them crucial for identifying the disease—one not easily diagnosed because of the lover's reticence to reveal his devotion and because of the pleasure he takes from his own misery. In the words of Thomas Wright, "there is no Passion very vehement but that it alters extremely some of the four humours of the body. And all Physicians commonly agree that among divers other extrinsical causes of diseases one, and not the least, is the excess of some inordinate passion. . . . The Physicians therefore knowing by what Passion the malady was caused may well infer what humour aboundeth and consequently what ought to be purged, what remedy to be applied, and after, how it may be prevented."[12] Hence, Ferrand's long inquiry into the signs by which the offending passion and its causes can be identified. In addition to the internal causes deriving variously from the complexions and from the perturbations within the soul, there are the many external causes of love. They include diet, climate, astrological influences, and the stimulation of the senses. Lovers are sensitive to experience, vulnerable to disappointments and half-realized expectations; their imaginations are dominated by dreams and fantasies by night and by fixed ideas by day. Ferrand devotes chs. XIII to XIX of his treatise to training physicians in the symptomatology and diagnostics of erotic love.

Ferrand first declares that love can be diagnosed without the confession of the patient, whether by the tell-tale social behavior of the person, or by the changing of colors, the sighs, the condition of the eyes, the agitation of the lids, the pallor, the exact greenish yellow tint of the skin, the absence of fever, or the sudden tears. At the center of the debate on symptoms is the question of whether there is a pulse peculiar to lovers.[13] Avicenna, together with most of the Western physicians, holds that there is not, though all agree that the presence of the beloved can accelerate the pulse or make it uneven. Taking the pulse became a favored means for detecting lovers. Ferrand professes to have used this method with success in treating a lovesick student. The changing pulse revealed the young man's affection for a certain servant girl who appeared in the consulting room at the convenient moment.

It is in the chapters that follow (XX to XXV), that Ferrand made himself the most vulnerable to attack on nonmedical grounds. These chapters are, by rhetorical definition, merely an extension of the discussion of diagnostics, but the aims and operations change tenor. Where the symptoms are present and visible the trained eye of the physician will suffice to identify the cause. But where the symptoms are not yet in evidence, and the physician is concerned with identifying merely a constitutional weakness for the disease, he must rely upon a different genre of diagnostic techniques. Insofar as the diseases caused by the imbalance of the humors are present principally in those constitutionally predisposed to such diseases, an analysis of the temperament should serve to detect those inclinations. The aggressive Galenist was therefore easily lured into a consideration of the corporeal and extracorporeal signs related by sympathetic communication whereby such inclinations could be revealed. Their interest in occult semiotics was an extension of their interest in determining biological and constitutional signs that could lead to the development of a practice in preventive medicine for those in jeopardy of their own erotic passions.

He begins with the more obvious indicators: the temperature of the genitals; the quantity of body hair; the external signs attached to the internal imbalance of humors; the age, upbringing, and education of the individual; the climate; and national characteristics. By these several indicators the physician could work toward a classification according to types. This mixture of physiognomy and character typing is as close as Ferrand comes to an analysis of the individual in terms of his personal history and the stored-up experiences of the psyche. The idea that a man was born to his destiny emphasized the contrasting need simply to decode that inherited nature and to counteract its adverse qualities through an assault upon the humoral elements conditioning it. In order to identify the directions of that inner destiny, the physician, in due course, comes to horoscopes and astrology, to chiromancy, magic, divination, and the interpretation of dreams. Ferrand leaves his loyalties entirely obscure in these matters. He was apparently keen to take advantage of all that was permitted in order to advance his diagnostic insights yet concerned that an adequate warning be given against all things illegal, all things dangerous for the physician as well as for the patient. In the final analysis, he was compelled to disclaim the efficacy of most of these techniques, though he was clearly fascinated by them as philosophical *topoi* and more than willing to share the lore that he had accumulated about them.

If Ferrand extends his field of medicine by creating new divisions in his treatise between those actually afflicted and those merely showing amorous proclivities, between preventive treatments and cures, he also extends the scope of the disease itself by dividing love melancholy into three kinds: not only love melancholy and love mania, as described above, but also a third category comprising both satyriasis and uterine fury. This came to him presumably through his reading of Jean Liébault and Luis Mercado, in whose works he found descriptions of the symptoms and cures for uterine fury that he, in turn, conflated with those for *amor hereos*. He understood these diseases to differ from one another only by degrees. Liébault furnishes the essential details concerning the causes of hysteria and the means by which the vapors rise through the spinal column to attack the judgment and imagination, resulting in states of fury or melancholy so similar to those originating in the hypochondries as to be indistinguishable from them. Other characteristics common to the three states include the overabundance of blood and intense carnal desire, both of which Ferrand duly noted. In the domain of cures there was likewise a high degree of correlation, allowing Ferrand to condense the treatments into a single program.

In retrospect, if there is a fallacy, it is that he mistakes symptoms for causes. Uterine fury may produce intense venerean longings, but it is not caused by carnal desire or by the imagination. We are unable to say if Ferrand was the first to include hysteria with erotic melancholy and mania. The association was short lived in any case because the tendency in the medical dissertations later in the seventeenth century was to isolate such conditions as hysteria and nymphomania from one another as well as from melancholy and mania. The idea for this consolidation may have come to Ferrand from his reading of Mercado's chapter on uterine fury, which contains a classification of madness into five types: melancholy, fury, love, rabies, and lycanthropy. Because Ferrand finds melancholy and fury in this list as distinct from love, he reasons, according to his own paralleling of fury with love mania and melancholy with love melancholy, that this separate love must entail a third species, which he conveniently assigns to uterine fury and satyriasis. In doing so, Ferrand overlooks the fact that Mercado is describing madness and not the diseases of love and that if it were love he was concerned with, it would have had five and not three species.[14]

The issue of the diverse species of love melancholy is further complicated by the presence of Ferrand's ch. XXVII, in which he also associates the incubus or nightmare with love melancholy, though in this case perhaps only by juxtaposition rather than by formal classification. He raises the topic through references to an unspecified theologian interested in the question of whether supernatural creatures could suffer from erotic passions, and whether they could have intercourse with mortal women. Ferrand follows with a few tales in résumé concerning love between demons and humans. His purpose, however, is not to speculate on the psychic lives of supernatural beings, but to introduce a medical condition in which women believe they have been sexually assaulted by a supernatural being but are in fact merely suffering from a form of nightmare called incubus, characterized by a sensation of suffocation provoked by a heavy weight pressing down upon the entire body. This state has an established medical pedigree going back through Avicenna to Themison and ultimately back to episodes in Hippocrates. The delusions are produced by heavy vapors that affect the brain after the first hours of sleep. This condition is like love melancholy in that it is a disease of an imagination that is corrupted by vapors. Ferrand made the association, no doubt, on the basis of the venereal appetites common to both conditions. That the delusions of assault experienced by those suffering from the incubus do not result from the fixation of the imagination, or the sight of an object of beauty, or from a condition of the blood, or from the bile in the hypochondries apparently caused no difficulties for Ferrand. At this point he seems interested simply in gathering up all the medical conditions involving a component of sexuality in order to complete his encyclopedic survey of the diseases associated with love.[15]

It is significant, however, that by describing these conditions—uterine fury and the nightmare—Ferrand is able to relate love melancholy more closely to conditions that arise entirely from within the body, because neither of these states requires an initiating appetite of the soul nor an act of volition. To a degree, in approaching the section on cures, Ferrand had to reemphasize the somatogenesis of love. He had to concentrate on that concept of love as a passion of the mind that was a product of material causes in the body. As he states, "if the soul is afflicted by love, it is due to the mutual sympathy between it and the body," and a little later, the "diseases of the body amaze and baffle the soul and bind up the reason by sympathetic influence" (ch. XXVI). Ferrand had no choice but to favor a deterministic concept of disease and a material conception of the soul. That course was the only means whereby he could reduce moral counsel to a secondary status and raise the value of pharmaceutical cures to a level of nearly absolute efficacy—one of the main purposes of his treatise.

VII

The Cures for Erotic Mania
and Erotic Melancholy

Ferrand developed his section on cures in the same spirit of eclecticism that characterized the rest of his treatise. His purpose included the representation of nearly every recorded form of therapy for erotic love (including those for hysteria and satyriasis) that had turned up in his exhaustive reading on the subject. At the same time, however, if in no other way than in the rhetorical organization of these materials, Ferrand reveals a hierarchy of preferences ordered according to his professional perceptions and biases. These biases, in turn, imply a belief in the superior value of pharmaceutical remedies, a belief that was a product both of his training in Galenic medicine and of the developments in pharmacology during the previous century.[1] Faith in the pharmaceutical cures was predicated upon a belief in the purposeful correlation between the world of medical simples and the diseases of the body, a correlation based on the principle that the Creator had been mindful of his creation in furnishing herbal and mineral remedies for every ailment whether known or yet-to-be-discovered.[2] Ferrand's program of cures therefore progresses from the least esteemed remedies to those sanctioned by traditional medical authority and by experimentation, with a clear emphasis on the regimen of drugs, topicals, and opiates that were a conventional part of the treatment of melancholy diseases.

Once the disease had been defined and its clinical elements described, Ferrand could choose between two categories of cures: the methodical and the pharmaceutical. The problem for him was no doubt a problem of authorities and traditions. We have already noted that Roman and Byzantine physicians, with the possible exception of Alexander of Tralles, defined erotic love as a disease of the soul and thus without corporeal causes. They granted that love could produce all the symptoms of melancholy, but they insisted that the two conditions were not the same, nor would they respond to the same treatments. Heading the list of cures for erotic love in the ancient world was coitus. This was

123

the procedure sanctioned by the story of Antiochus and Stratonice, by the account of the frantic lover in Aretaeus, and by the case study of the lonely wife in Alexander of Tralles. Even after the Arab physicians had transformed the terms of analysis by treating the condition as a disease of melancholy, the cure by coitus continued to enjoy high prestige. It could be replaced by diversionary tactics, such as sending the lover on a trip, involving him in an active social life, terrifying or disgusting him, defaming the qualities of the beloved object, while baths, diet, and purges played subsidiary roles in their regimen of cures. This was equally so in the *Canon* of Avicenna largely upon whose authority the idea of *amor hereos*, with its symptoms and recommended cures, was introduced into the Latin West.

From the time of the earliest translations of the Arab physicians down to the sixteenth century, there was little change in the attitudes concerning cures, despite the fact that when love is taken to be a disease of melancholy it requires more refined and specific treatments. There were early hints in that direction, but the completion of the process was delayed for several centuries. It was, in fact, in this area that Ferrand's generation found room for innovation. His own treatise, without abandoning the diversionary and methodical cures, represents the ultimate transfer of emphasis from the ancients, who prescribed according to their perception of love as a passion of the soul, to a "modern" view of love as a condition subject to the physiological cures. Erasistratus was a clever analyst, but his solution was, in a sense, an admission of helplessness before the tyranny of love. Ferrand, by contrast, believed that he had in drug therapy the means to master the passions through a forceful manipulation of the bodily humors. In giving new prominence to these means, Ferrand makes explicit what had all along been implicit in the association of love with the diseases of melancholy: that as a disease of black bile, it could be reduced by purges and alteratives.

It is nevertheless important to note that Ferrand does not exclude old treatments in favor of new. His goal, at the most pragmatic level, was to reorganize all the accepted forms of treatment into a single paradigmatic regimen of therapy, giving prominence to the most effective. Because of his consideration of each kind of treatment in a separate chapter, Ferrand fails to render the sequence of the regimen as clearly as we would have preferred, though the scope and general design is clear enough. In this regard, André Du Laurens was altogether more schematic and François Valleriola slightly more linear. Given Ferrand's reliance on both, we may use them to supplement our interpretation. The generally accepted procedures would, in any case, have been self-evident to a contemporary physician consulting Ferrand's work. Furthermore, specific treatments would vary according to the constitution of the patient and the tenacity of the affliction. Ferrand concludes his ch. XXXVII, dealing with methodical, diversionary, and social cures, with the statement that "since all the remedies already mentioned are insufficient to heal those suffering from erotic melancholy . . . one must have recourse to the surgical and pharmaceutical cures." Only then does he create a hypothetical regimen applied to a hypothetical patient. The impression given is that his regimen consists entirely of drugs and topicals. He arranges the purges, baths, and opiates in a sequence that suggests an order of application. But he does not specify when the bleedings (prescribed in the previous chapter) should be carried out, how to integrate the diet with the purges, when to send for friends, or when to enforce sleep. Given the intransigent nature of the melancholy humors and the stubborn, secretive will of the confirmed erotomaniac, the treatment could be long and the time ample for experimenting with a variety of measures in a variety of sequences.

The first step in Ferrand's campaign to establish the paramount position of surgical and pharmaceutical cures was his attack, in ch. XXXIII, on the use of coitus as a form of therapy. To deny this practice on moral grounds was easy enough. How, indeed, could a Christian physician endorse therapeutic fornication? Yet on medical grounds Ferrand's point of view was, in a sense, heretical. The issue involved basic principles of Renaissance physiology. As we have seen, in earlier treatises the seed itself was considered at least a contributing, if not the principal, material cause of the amorous appetites. Only through the reduction of seed might there be hope for recovery from excessive erotic impulses. Fregoso in his *Contramours* gives the point a full hearing: "it is easy to believe that the cause of that biting and compelling appetite arises within the body by means of the sperm, which tickles the seminal vessels by means of the airy vapors and spirits of which it is composed. Its presence disturbs and harasses us, creating a desire for the friction that constitutes carnal union by which means this excremental humor is voided from the body."[3] This statement expresses a common medical postulate. In fact, nothing could be more Galenic than to locate the origins of the appetite in the organs and humors of the body itself. Seed was created of excess blood burned white by the heat of the passions, as well as being a by-product of the third coction and thus one of the normal excrements of the body. If venereal drives were the result of an overabundance of such seed, then its expenditure by whatever means, according to the laws of repletion and excretion, would diminish the undesirable agent. Hence, the theoretical conflict for the physician. Therapeutic coitus was endorsed not only by Avicenna, but by his many followers in the Latin West: Constantinus Africanus, Gerard of Cremona, and the other commentators on the *Viaticum*, as well as by his translator Villalobos, and by Arnald of Villanova, Bernard of Gordon, Marsilio Ficino, Pereda, Valesco de Taranta, to select only a few representative names.

Ferrand offers an argument in his first treatise against the impious recommendations of Ovid, Valesco de Tarenta, and Pereda—that a man attach himself to several women in order to avoid the inconveniences of being attached to only one—on the double grounds that a frequent indulgence of the sexual drives develops pernicious habits of the soul, and that excessive coitus swells the spermatic vessels and heightens the venerean appetites. He takes for his proof the passage from Galen where he argues that the more a woman gives suck, the more the breast is enlarged and the more it gives milk. These arguments reappear in the treatise of 1623. At the same time, however, Ferrand accepts the idea that marriage can cure erotic melancholy. Du Laurens had stated before him that "there are two means for curing this amorous melancholy: the first is the enjoyment of the thing desired, and the other depends on the artifice and industry of a good physician."[4] These points are only ostensibly self-evident. Ferrand complicates matters, as well, by interpreting "the enjoyment of the thing desired" in moral terms. He distinguishes between licit and illicit forms of coitus, declaring that a Christian physician should not tolerate therapeutic coitus, but that "no physician would refuse to someone suffering from erotic mania or melancholy the enjoyment of the object of desire in marriage in accordance with both divine and human laws" (ch. XXXIII). But if, as Ferrand argues, sexual activity will not quell but exacerbate the luxurious appetites and aggravate the disease, how can a legal wedding nullify that effect? Likewise, if voiding excess semen is beneficial, how can the body determine between the benefits of coitus in wedlock and the dangers of it outside of wedlock? Du Laurens had anticipated the problem, for he suggests that in marriage the cure is effected, not by reducing the material cause, but by satisfying the ardent desire that arises and resides in the soul.

The confusion here is part of a more general failure to recognize the qualitative differences between erotic desire produced by a corruption of the imagination, erotic appetite driven by sexual instincts, and a state of depression resulting from an inability to enjoy the company of a desired object. When Jean de Veyries insists upon a medical cure for the young marquis *before* he would be allowed to marry, he recognizes that marriage itself cannot undo the physiological and psychological damage caused by the burned humors, as distinct from passions of the soul, excess seed, or the victim of social obstacles.

Ferrand's logical fallacies must be attributed in part to the fact that the medical tradition itself had subscribed to these several contradictory views: that granting the object of desire was the first order of cure; that evacuation of seed would alleviate the material cause; and that indulgence in venery extends the vessels, incites further production of sperm, and weakens the body by dessication. If Ferrand is unable to reconcile these conflicting theories, nevertheless several points are clear. He would stand by his diplomatic and presumably personal arguments on moral grounds against therapeutic match-making, and he would attempt to extend the range of medical practice to include the pharmaceutical and surgical treatment of those suffering from the diseases caused by a surfeit of semen. Coitus as a form of therapy had to be disallowed at whatever cost on clinical grounds in order that the pharmaceutical remedies could gain in importance.

In his encyclopedic way, before he comes to the "true" cures in chs. XXXVII–XXXIX, Ferrand covers the magical and "Homeric" cures for love gleaned from a variety of sources. He mentions the magical rites, potions, incantations, philters, amulets, and spells that had entered into the literature and folklore of love. He poses academic questions about the power of philters to compel affection or of charms to ward off unwanted suitors. He explains the term *Homeric* as an allusion, not to actual practices that can be traced to the poet, but to the popular belief in the magical healing powers of the bard's words themselves. Clearly, such ritual magic was outside the sphere of the practicing physician.

The power of occult words to heal was a topic still fresh in Ferrand's time and one he would have been careful to shun. Pomponazzi had made claims of a man able to heal skin rashes and burns in children without the use of medications through the use of words alone.[5] Vanini had attempted to explain this practice as a natural rather than as an occult phenomenon. The Renaissance had become conscious of a distinction between the occult and the natural and had made it an intellectual battleground. Brian Vickers sums up that distinction as follows: "In the scientific tradition, I hold, a clear distinction is made between words and things and between literal and metaphorical language. The occult tradition does not recognize this distinction: Words are treated as if they are equivalent to things and can be substituted for them. Manipulate the one and you manipulate the other."[6] On the medical side, occult words challenged a philosophy of material causes and the mechanical operations used against them; on the side of the church, the explanation of the spiritual world in terms of natural forces and events was equally unacceptable.

The empirical remedies, those discussed in ch. XXXVI, are comprised of a number of curious customs and practices employed in antiquity: bathing in a certain lake above Athens, jumping from the Leucadian rock, calming tortured spirits with the affective powers of Dorian music, making sacrifices to certain gods, disgusting the lover by making him see the menstrual cloth or by having him smell the burned excrements of the beloved. Ferrand makes no comment, but passes on to the next chapter entitled "true and methodical remedies," true because condoned and recommended by recognized physicians and because they had become a part of the established practices for the treatment of melancholy, passed down from writer to writer.[7] All are variants on a few central principles: that melancholy is a drying and wasting disease and should be moistened; that the patient is suffering from a deranged reason that might respond to the admonitions of wise and respected persons; that the patient can become hectic, frenzied, or suicidal and should never be left alone; and, finally, that where no useful or permitted union with the desired object is possible, there is nothing to be gained by allowing continued sight of the object. Paul of Aegina recommended moral counseling, the drinking of wine, spectacles, and amusing stories. He also recommended frightening the patient so as to drive out his preoccupations with the beloved or thrusting the lover into the concerns of business. Rhazes adds to this list fasting, walking, much drinking, as well as frequent sexual intercourse. Avicenna and Haly Abbas add other sports, especially hunting. With the exception of coitus, Ferrand includes them all.

Foods that humidify the body and that build up the patient lean with sleeplessness and worry were a traditional component. Ferrand would have known these and similar prescriptions from a variety of sources. He noted the disagreements concerning fasting, for example, between Oribasius and Rondelet, a sixteenth-century chancellor of the medical faculty in Montpellier. Because both are reckoned authoritative, Ferrand works out a compromise so that both can be right—Rondelet referring to the early stages and to prevention, Oribasius to adust states and to cures. More frequently before his eyes, however, is the treatise by Valleriola with its detailed section on cures. Valleriola deals briefly with Paul of Aegina's recommendations concerning friends, music, and games; his own advice is that the lover be sent away from the place of his grief and beyond all possibility of contact with the beloved. Ferrand raises minor objections here and there largely as a way of demonstrating his own independence from a man to whom his debt is clear. He remonstrates that absenting oneself physically does not necessarily remove the *idée fixe* from the mind, that the injury to the imagination and memory will remain in spite of the distance; yet he will concede elsewhere that removal from the desired object is a first and essential step in any treatment.

At the basis of the pharmaceutical cures is the doctrine of opposites whereby the hot is cooled, the dry moistened, the overabundant drawn off, the toxic evacuated—operations carried out according to the physician's assessment of the state of the disease, the resistances of the constitution, and the parts affected. If melancholy becomes chronic, the black elements can lodge in the liver, the heart, the lungs, the blood, and the nerves, and can cause spasms, mania, or paralysis. Traditional measures for the evacuation of black bile included bleeding, cupping-glasses placed over the affected parts, vomits, and purges. Hellebore had been the favored emetic for melancholy diseases until the end of the sixteenth century.[8] So important was the concept of evacuation that Ferrand used it as a generic term for his clinical procedures: "of necessity love must be cured by discharge, of which there are two kinds, natural and artificial. The latter depends on evacuation . . . while the former includes remonstrations from pious, learned and virtuous people, a change of air, abstinence, a variety of attentions" (ch. XXXVII). This is the fundamental principle according to which Ferrand classifies his "true" cures. Defining the methods and ingredients necessary for the evacuation of the offending humors is the ultimate *raison d'être* of the treatise.

A regimen of phlebotomy and medicinal cures for the diseases of melancholy goes back to the foundations of Western medicine,[9] but these could not be adapted to the treatment of love before it was recognized as a disease of melancholy. As we have argued above, the protestations of such physicians as Galen and Paul of Aegina against those who did treat love as such a disease reveal, from their point of view, the ease with which the conditions of the two could be confused. They may have reasoned in any one of the following ways. Because melancholy was a disease involving sorrow without cause, love could not be such a disease because the cause was known. Love produces leanness and thus could not be the cause of mania, because leanness was not a symptom of mania. Feelings and emotions cannot cause a state of disease. Because there are no known cures for love, but many known cures for melancholy, love cannot be a disease of melancholy. Whatever the case, by the time of Rhazes the conflation of ideas had produced a program that contained all the rudiments of the regimen offered by Ferrand: bleeding the patient till he loses consciousness, a humidifying diet, baths, induced sleep, and where necessary, purgation. Rhazes concurs in urging the importance of narcotically induced sleep to relieve the patient from his long nocturnal cogitations, and of bleeding the patient as soon after the onset of the disease as possible.[10] Rhazes's pharmaceutical commentary is brief, but with his treatise the future treatment of love as a disease responding to the traditional regimen for the diseases of melancholy is made possible.

The early commentators on the sections dealing with *amor hereos* in the *Canon* and in the *Viaticum* of Constantinus were not particularly interested in developing a specific regimen of drugs for evacuating offending biles and the residues of their adustion, though it was clearly understood that an excess of black humor was the cause of the disease. Not even Arnald of Villanova, in his section on cures in the *Tractatus de amore heroico*, mentions either herbs or phlebotomy. Perhaps it was taken for granted among them that any purge suited for the treatment of melancholy in general would serve the purpose. Gerard of Paris (writing ca. 1235) in his commentary on the *Viaticum* considers how the soul, perceiving an object of beauty, can go mad with desire as the result of a cooling and drying of the front ventricle of the brain. Yet he accepted the theory of the black biles as well. The distinctions between causes suggested two sets of cures: those appropriate to the soul and those to the body. There was much discussion of wine and the usefulness of drunkenness, of baths, and of the evacuation of the seed. In keeping with the views of Avicenna, the place of prominence was reserved for this last form of treatment. Gerard of Berry, writing before 1237, in his commentary on the same work attempts the first complete synthesis between the *Viaticum* and the *Canon* of Avicenna, guided by a Galenism that seeks the explanation of mental states in their material causes. This continued emphasis upon somatogenetic principles could only encourage, in due course, a more specific regimen of drug cures adapted from the traditional recipes for the treatment of melancholy.

An early gesture in that direction was made by Bona Fortuna in the late thirteenth century. Despite the name, he was probably French and based in Montpellier; he wrote yet another commentary on the *Viaticum* in which he examines the causes and symptoms of erotic love. What is new is his interest in herbs and clinical procedures, emerging perhaps with the gradual Galenization of the Arabic tradition. As Mary Wack points out in her introduction to the treatise, a significant new weight is placed upon experimentation in the therapies advanced.[11] Given Bona Fortuna's empirical approach, she speculates that he must have been working with a "sizeable patient population" suffering from love; and that by inference, physicians in that period were equipped to diagnose *amor heroes* and to treat it using a number of therapies to be chosen in accordance with the patient's constitution.

Bona Fortuna maintains the distinction between spiritual and physical causes and therefore designates two separate sets of cures. For those causes related to the humors, he takes a new turn. The symptoms of an adust humor are exsiccation, a dryness of the mouth and tongue, and a bitter taste in the throat not unlike the effects of eating green prunes. Such conditions call for a purge that should be made of four herbs: wild endive, honeysuckle root, dandelion, and basil. Of these he made a decoction, to which he added epithyme. If this does not work, he counsels a stronger purge using hiera (this is the aloes purge of Avicenna). He also mentions fruit electuaries and recommends the bath after evacuation and a good diet.[12]

He follows with instructions for repose and sleep, and while inebriation is forbidden, he allows for alcohol in moderation to induce sleep. Thus, in the middle to late thirteenth century, the basic regimen for the curing of love was appearing in the West. Adust humors, including those which were a material cause of love, required purgation, followed by topical cures to moisten the dry humors, and by sleep, which not only gives repose to the body, but also builds moisture. That Bona Fortuna has been associated with Montpellier is indicative, for it was one of the leading centers for pharmaceutical research in Europe; it is tempting to speculate on how natural it would have been, in such an ambience, to include remedies of this kind for the treatment of *amor hereos*.

It is beyond our purposes here to attempt a complete history of the development of herbal remedies in the treatment of love; by all indications there was, before the sixteenth century, little substantive progress made in any case. Two centuries after Bona Fortuna, another physician in Montpellier would instruct the reader to make use of a purge if the humor was adust, and to refer to the chapter on melancholy for the particulars. This was the recommendation of Valesco de Taranta in his *Philonium pharmaceuticum et chirurgicum de medendis omnibus*.[13] Even Du Laurens uses the same approach as late as 1597. The disease was not given any special status among the diseases of melancholy on this score so that any purge devised to rid the body of black bile would serve, together with the topicals and opiates recommended for hypochondriacal melancholy. Du Laurens suggests that lovers should be cured by travel, music, the hunt, and other distractions, and that if none of these work "then lovers must be treated like the melancholiacs I described in the preceding chapter, and with nearly the same remedies."[14] He lists gentle purges, humectifying baths and diet, opiates to induce sleep, and cordials to refresh the heart and spirits, all of which were to be found elsewhere in the treatise. It is only with Valleriola in his *Observationum medicinalium libri sex* and with Jean Aubery in his *L'antidote d'amour* that specific treatments are described in the context of love, rendering more explicit, no doubt, what was already widely understood: that the traditional cures for melancholy will serve as cures for love melancholy.

Mercado's long chapter on melancholy in bk. I of the *De internorum morborum curatione* is filled with recipes for evacuants, emollients, opiates, and humectants. By the time he arrives at the topic of love melancholy he states merely that the crude biles should be purged, before going on to an exploration of musical therapy, games, visits, admonitions, baths, exercising, defaming the object, and finally prayer and fasting. By dint of his consideration of the topic within, rather than simply near, a chapter on melancholy, the association is all the more binding: the recipes in the surrounding paragraphs are components of his comprehensive analysis and equally applicable in the treatment of love melancholy.[15] Once that principle is confirmed, the possibilities for choice become staggering; by the end of the sixteenth century, the repertoire of recipes for the curing of melancholy in general had become truly vast.

Du Laurens summarizes the regimen that any selection of recipes must serve: "the humor must be purged gently and by intervals, for it has etched its dry nature upon the brain; it should be humidified by baths covering the entire body, and by a moistening diet such as good broths, almond milk, barley milk, porridge, and goat's milk. If there is sleeplessness, one should choose one of the remedies already described. The heart and mind should be comforted, too, with some opiat cordial."[16] This, in sum, is the program that Ferrand extends by assigning to love melancholy recipes drawn from Mercado, Houllier, Valleriola, Du Laurens, and others, and that he filled out from his reading of the ancients and from his own assessment of the nature of the disease and its special needs. Ferrand brought to fruition what was increasingly implicit, or indeed recommended by those who wrote on melancholy in the sixteenth century.

Just how much Ferrand owes to Valleriola can be indicated by a brief summary of the treatments Valleriola used in curing his lovesick merchant. There were two species of purges: that which corresponds to a definition of love as an enchantment or poisoning of the blood brought on by the bewitching eyes of the beloved, and that which corresponds to the concept of the burned humors that create a viscous residue, or sludge, in the stomach and intestines. For the former he recommends bleeding, for the latter dejectory purges, but now no longer just any purge, but those specially designed for the purpose. Three such recipes follow which he specifies for alternate use at the rate of one each month. For reticent patients, substitutions were allowed that included a supplementary extraction of 12 ounces of blood from the middle vein of the right arm. The third of the purgatives was designed for those cases where signs of black bile appeared in the urine. About six hours after the administration of such purges, the patient should be given a comfortative with a high sugar content in order to clean and refresh the stomach. Valleriola urged repeated use of these drugs given the heavy, cold nature of the residue to be evacuated, but in a measured way that avoids violent assault upon the body.

Valleriola also made use of lenitives or emollients to prepare the humor for further purges, and he prescribed stomach waters made with bugloss and white wine. He followed Hippocrates in opening the hemorrhoidal veins as a contributory cure. Sleep was not only a form of repose but was also classified officially among the humectants; it could be induced by a variety of opiums. He followed Aetius in shaving the head and in dripping specially prepared liquid medications upon the scalp; they were allegedly to soak through the sutures, without need of rubbing or friction, in order to moisten the dessicated brain. Valleriola also subscribed to the teachings concerning hellebore and prescribed a magistral syrup containing this ingredient to be taken twice a month.

He comes then to the baths, which were a highly authoritative remedy for melancholy in general, an activity he combines with scoldings and lectures, but also with music and the presence of friends and relatives. The baths should be taken every day for eight days, or every other day. The patient should not be allowed to perspire, and afterwards he should be wrapped to keep in the warmth, and sent to rest. The bath, taken two hours before dinner, not only served to humidify the body, but also aided in transporting the food to all parts of the body.

Finally, Valleriola concurs that a special fattening and moistening diet (not fasting) is needed to strengthen the patient lean from watching and worry. For this he recommends lotus bread, barley juice, almond milk, and rice mixed with soft flour and cooked in goat's milk with a good deal of sugar.

Valleriola deserves close examination because his regimen, though less detailed than Ferrand's, is more integrated. One can never be certain in Ferrand just how the bleeding, the diet, the purges, the exercise and the sleep, the baths, and the socializing are to be coordinated. Valleriola provides the outline of a regimen that begins straightway with the bleeding, and that continues with the purges and their preparative medications, which are in turn followed by comfortatives and opiates. The baths are given daily over a period of a week; the purges are given at longer intervals to avoid harm to the organism. Valleriola relates the baths to diet, entertainment, and repose in a way that suggests a full program of attentions and distractions that in itself could have therapeutic value. If the physician is required to be in attendance as master of ceremonies for such a heavy schedule of activities, one can understand why Valleriola spoke of the *rich* merchant of Arles. In this program we gain insights into the regimen implicit in Ferrand's various chapters on the true methodical, surgical, and pharmaceutical cures.

Ferrand prescribes according to the conventional tripartite classification of pharmaceutical actions. Du Laurens, who appears to have been his nearest source in these matters, describes them as diminutives, alteratives, and comfortatives. First the physician must effect an evacuation through the use of diminutives—those medications that diminish or evacuate the offending humors. He must then work upon the melancholy humors with alteratives in order to restore the desired isonomic state within the body. Finally, he must administer comfortatives, largely in the form of cordials and soporifics intended to strengthen the spirits and refresh the body. Both Du Laurens and Ferrand trust to the professional discriminations of practicing physicians to adjust these prescriptions to the age, condition, and temperament of the patient and to the state of the disease itself.

Ferrand prescribes first a light purge, then a preparative sirup for a second and more substantial purge to follow, a model supplied by Du Laurens. The second purge has a base of fruits and spices consisting of prunes, tamarinds, raisins, and currants, the whole flavored with cinnamon. The active ingredients added to the sirup are oriental senna, rhubarb, and Hamech's confection. The characteristically compound nature of the drugs of the sixteenth century is clearly in evidence, especially in those purges that also include a number of humidifying herbs in addition to spices or sweeteners to make the entire concoction more palatable. After these assaults upon the stomach and intestines, the patient is granted a period of repose, during which time he receives preserves of roses, borage flowers, and bugloss roots. These recipes for the diminutives are followed by the alteratives. Ferrand progresses by degrees in each category from the weakest to the strongest, arriving in due course at a cautious recommendation of such ingredients as Venetian turpentine, scammony, and the sap of annual mercury mixed with senna and fresh cassia. The inclusion of these elements in the sirups was a topic of great debate, for while the authority of tradition carried considerable weight, and while physicians were anxious to employ the drugs held for sovereign in these cases, they were also clinically experienced and could attest to the dangers of such drugs in actual practice.

Despite a stubborn adherence to the past, medicine had also made adjustments throughout the sixteenth century as the result of empirical investigations. In no field of endeavor was this more the case than in pharmacology, where the results of the administration of drugs could be scrutinized in a way that forced established doctrines to be challenged in the light of actual results.[17] Traditional purges that nevertheless poisoned and opiums that killed could no longer escape notice. The entire superstructure of metaphor that controlled the Galenic world order, with its balanced opposites, its classification of herbs into cold and hot, moist and dry, its categories of occult associations and effects, was intact but under threat, especially from the Paracelsians, and many of the sceptics such as Ambroise Paré were ready to expose hoaxes.[18] Ferrand was by no means of the Paracelsian sect, nor was he a methodical interrogator like Paré, but he joined in the spirit of scepticism in his cautious use of drugs. In the case of hellebore, scammony, and the metal antimony there was cause for suspicion, and Ferrand lent his voice to the rising opposition to them expressed by many of his contemporaries.[19] At the same time he remained open to new developments in pharmacology as witnessed in particular by his interest in the drugs made from plants recently brought back from the New World.

The alteratives were medically inert by modern standards and relatively inoffensive, however distasteful they must have been to the patient. At best they could have had but a placebo effect. Not all of Ferrand's preparations were bitter, however, for his comfortatives to the heart, liver, and brain—the three theaters of turbulence in this disease—were sweet as well as exotic. One in particular contained not only rose preserves, water lily flowers, and a variety of oriental fruits but also orient pearl and ivory powder. Seen from this perspective, the regimen of purges, comfortatives, and opiates followed by candies and other sweets to rebuild the body, appears as a scheme first to shock the patient with bitter herbs, then to reward and console him with agreeable confections. Ferrand is less concise than Du Laurens with regard to the separate characteristics of alteratives and comfortatives, though the latter are perhaps most easily recognized by the opiates they contain. Sleep inducement was a central part of the treatment. For this purpose, there were lozenges of roses and borage containing white poppy and hemp along with burned hartshorn and coral. There were, in addition, the external alteratives consisting principally of baths, but also of topical plasters, the narcotic rubefacients of Pliny, contra yerva powder, stone alum, and mineral waters. Ferrand includes rare and exotic ingredients, with the financially able patient in mind, when he prescribes nepanthe and ladunum, amber, red coral, mummy, pearl, and saffron, aware perhaps, of the therapeutic value of letting certain patients pay dearly for their cures.

Ferrand may be considered innovative insofar as he writes more extensively than any of his predecessors on the pharmaceutical treatments specifically intended for love melancholy; but in the design of his regimen and in the composition of his drugs, Ferrand remains entirely within the traditions of conventional medical practice. In another sense, by devising specific drugs and clinical practices corresponding to the unique nature of the disease, he was merely completing a process begun in ancillary works. Ferrand is casual in his acknowledgment of sources. He mentions Mercado, Haly Abbas, and Houllier, but overlooks Valleriola, who supplied him with four of his most important recipes. Though only one recipe comes from Du Laurens, his inspiration is easily detected in others where Ferrand has adjusted the ingredients according to personal preferences. To delve further into the mass of pharmacology associated with the treatment of melancholy would be supererogatory at this point, though we would suggest that those interested consult Wecker, van Heurne, and Ferrari da Grado for a preliminary sampling.[20] The structures of their recipes suggest many parallels that Ferrand could have adapted to his own ends. He twice states that there were hundreds of such recipes, and seems to be inclined to treat them as common property.

One of the leading theoretical apothecaries of that age, Joseph Du Chesne (Quercetanus), explains in his *Pharmacie des dogmatiques* how such recipes should be constructed according to Galenic dogmas. His models freely allow for individual variations once the principles of composition have been grasped. For the curing of atrabilious melancholy, he builds on a base that will first counteract the dryness of the condition; he was partial to fumatory, hops, bugloss, and a large number of the cool seeds and moist flowers. These preparations he aromatized to taste. To this base he added ingredients either for specific purgative actions or for touching certain parts of the body in accordance with inherent or occult traits in the plant itself that correspond to that part of the body. With such instructions to hand, one sees the futility in going in search of exact sources, because it would have been as easy for Ferrand to improvise with known materials as it would have been for him to borrow.[21]

A renascent faith in the power of herbs is one of Ferrand's underlying biases. In effect, Ferrand's treatise builds toward a psychopharmacology as the most forceful means for treating this recalcitrant passion of the soul. That rhetorical ordering, as suggested earlier, that grants the final word in the treatise to pharmacology for the treating of love coincides with an upsurge in pharmaceutical research and experimentation. An urgency to classify the plant world, with its myriad of simples designed by the Creator for man's use, was part of the medical *Zeitgeist*.

Friar Laurence, in *Romeo and Juliet* (II.iii.15–18), echoes the creed. Levinus Lemnius, in *The Secret Miracles of Nature*, claims that by an "astonishing force and efficacy, there are many herbs destined to many parts of the body with inbred qualities and virtues enabling them to help these parts."[22] Abetting this faith was the intensification of the Levantine trade, the Dutch and Portuguese rivalry with the Venetians, and the ransacking of the New World for more herbs and minerals, as recorded by Nicholas Monardes, physician of Seville.[23] Such a faith also motivated Mattioli, Dodoëns, Charles L'Ecluse, and many other indefatigable researchers of plants and their medicinal uses. Paré, in his "*De la faculté et vertu des medicamens simples*," studied and classified in a way that led from the field to the laboratory and to the compounding of new medications. Ferrand's purpose was to render his psychopharmacology of love complete and accurate in accordance both with tradition and with this new wave of research.

No approach to the treatment of the diseases of the soul could be more alluring and seductive. Whereas the patient might refuse to cooperate with counsel and therapy, such active agents as the opiates, senna, agaric, and the *solanaceae* derivatives were bound to have their effects; the patient had no powers to resist them. Insofar as the causes for the deranged behavior could be traced to conditions of the humors, and insofar as those humors could be reached by emetics, bleeding, and the like, the physician could assume a forceful mechanical control over the disease in ways that did not require the mental cooperation of the patient. When the somatic causes are reduced, the symptoms themselves must diminish; when the material base is altered, the disease can be controlled by force, if not cured altogether. Perhaps no age had a greater illusion of power over the diseases arising from the passions than Ferrand's. He had the satisfaction of believing that the material causes of love were within the reach of medications administered according to the principles of opposites. Nowhere in the medical tradition concerning erotic love is that belief more openly espoused. For Ferrand, the pharmaceuticals of his age promised the sovereign cure for love melancholy.

It would be easy to interject at this point that the cures attributed to such drugs could at best be credited to a placebo effect to which both patient and doctor were alike dupes, or to the distastefulness of the treatment itself, or to the passage of time, or to the techniques of distraction, or to the disgust of the patient with his regimen of laxatives and vomitives imposed upon a fantasy life revolving around an object of beauty. The contest of wills between the patient seeking his privacy and the physician seeking to cure him in the name of society promised to be long, because all the physicians agreed that melancholy was a sticky and viscous humor that could require many months to evacuate. One can hardly imagine a patient so resolute as to remain indifferent to so complete and varied a regimen. Thus, on the one hand, while the placebo effect is by no means a negligible one in the treatment of psychological disorders,[24] on the other, many of the ingredients were not without their striking results as vomits, emetics, and soporifics and therefore had to be credited by the patient as functioning according to their intended capacities, even against the patient's will. An intellectual conviction on the part of the patient that such treatments had power could, by the force of suggestion, trick the patient into a cure. Of greatest importance is the fact that the drugs themselves were incorporated into an all-encompassing rite of cure that involves patient, doctor, friends, and relatives, and that continues daily over a number of weeks and months. The physician creates not only a regimen of medications and diet, but a program of comfortatives, exercise, travel, baths, and entertainments that attest, implicitly, to an understanding of the disease as a social and psychological phenomenon that can in turn be treated by social means that have a psychotherapeutic content. In effect, the regimen of medications itself becomes a form of methodical cure, a therapy of distraction and preoccupation, quite apart from its claims to chemical coercion.[25]

When the patient himself becomes intellectually involved in the process of cure there are other effects to be derived from such a regimen of drugs. By the early seventeenth century the principles of the humoral system were widely disseminated and understood outside of medical circles. The fact is demonstrated not only by the circulation of popular treatises on medicine but by the abundant number of allusions to the system in the literary record. From this set of ideas emerged a vocabulary of the mechanisms of the body—the black sludge and the smoky vapors, the squeezing heart and the burning humors—that entered into common parlance. The concept of the body as an equilibrium of elements capable of a disharmony that could be rectified by mechanical operations upon the body, by heating and chilling, by the addition and removal of liquids and substances, and by drugs with occult properties that were capable of directing themselves to specific parts of the body, clearly appealed to the imagination.[26] There was, therefore, a psychological attractiveness in the operations performed by physicians and surgeons: the cleansing power of the purges, the rebuilding and rebalancing processes of the alteratives, and the soothing and condoling action of the comfortatives. Each answered to longings for a number of attentions to the mind as well as to the body. In the process, a kind of psychotherapy is created by projecting upon the body a variety of psychic states. Just as the causes of the diseases of the passions required physiological expression, so the contents of those passions could be thrown back upon the centers in the body where they were subject to "symbolic" manipulation that was understood to be real and material because of the effects upon those parts attributed to the medicinal simples and compounds in the physician's control. No other medical philosophy could grant a greater prerogative to the medical profession for the treatment of the passions of the soul.

VIII

Ferrand, Sexuality,
and Early Psychology

Given Ferrand's highly conventional approach to the diseases of the passions, to eroticism and to psychopathology, our claims for him as an innovator in the development of early psychology must remain modest. As we have stated earlier, the case for his importance rests principally on his value to the history of ideas as a formulator of the accumulated wisdom of his age concerning the maladies derived from love. His innovative dimensions reside in his encyclopedic and conciliatory instincts as a scholar and in his broadening of the terms of reference to include certain of the social and artistic factors affecting sexuality. The modern observer cannot help reading Ferrand with a double perspective, however. On one level he will seek instruction in the diseases of love in the terms employed by the author and his contemporaries. On another, he will employ his own critical insights in order to see the assumptions and prejudices of that age that underlie the arguments. Ferrand offers far more that he realizes, for example, about the role of the physician in society, about the relationship between the imaginative processes of the poet and of the melancholy lover, about the diverse customs and mores of mating, about the conflicting drives originating in cultural imperatives that contribute to the eroticization of the lover's mind. Reflections of this nature will suggest themselves repeatedly. They attest to the high value of his treatise, not only for the historian of ideas but for the cultural analyst, the social historian, and the literary critic.

In categorizing the many causes of erotic desire, Ferrand inevitably touches upon phenomena that we continue to investigate today: sexual instinct, erotic feeling, the hereditary and cultural factors of love, power principles, and pleasure principles in human sexuality to name but a few. In the terms of Renaissance psychology, Ferrand addresses the same kinds of questions that one finds in such modern works as the *Biologie des passions* by the neurophysiologist Jean-Didier Vincent: "What is desire, pleasure, and pain, the taste for power and domination? In brief, how do we explain our passions?"[1] Inevitably, we are cognizant of the distance between Ferrand and the twentieth century, but we are impressed not so much by his primitivism as by the cogency of his questioning even where a lack of methodology impedes him from pursuing his topics toward more innovative conclusions.[2] The paragraphs that follow seek to examine select features of Ferrand's psychology both from within and without the Galenic system that dictated his thoughts and to assess certain of his premises from a retrospective point of view.

In speaking of Ferrand we venture to use such words as *psychology* and *sexuality* because his purpose was none other than to anatomize the processes of the psyche in a prolonged state of erotic stimulation and to describe the sequence of those events that leads from a perception of the senses to a disease of the soul. He is concerned with the causes and the conditions accounting for states of dementia arising from sexual drives. To outline as he does the internal and external factors in the eroticization of the imaginative faculty is, itself, tantamount to presenting a philosophy of sexuality.

As we have already seen, however, Ferrand was dependent upon a vocabulary of sexual pathology derived from the operations of humoral medicine. All erotic disorders, whatever the contributing causes, were viewed as products of a single physiological process: the corruption of the brain by the vapors of burned humors. In fact, for Ferrand, all causes require somaticization before they acquire pathological capacities. According to this principle, all causes produce degrees of a single disease, love melancholy and love mania being but variants that are differentiated not by the nature of external provocations, but by the combinations and conditions of the humors. Hence, we are to understand that it is not the social circumstances themselves, not the reactions or behavior of the desired object, not the intellectual preoccupations of the lover, not his aesthetic ideals or his social expectations and conditioning that determine the characteristics of the disease and the forms of its expression, but the constitution of the body and the pathogenic inclinations of the humors.

Paradoxically, the fault with humoral medicine, in this context, is not so much with what it propounds in mechanical terms about the passions of the soul, but with what it simultaneously disallows in terms of the cultural analysis of this mental disorder. Ferrand sets out to define more precisely than before an important subgenre of melancholy by anatomizing that form of chronic depression caused by amorous appetites and thwarted desire. Yet while he contributes to the degeneralization of this generic term—melancholy—he continues to lump together the diverse manifestations of the disease. As Starobinski points out, whenever the ancients saw a condition of persistent sorrow and fear (conditions pertaining equally to love melancholy) they were certain of the diagnostic and were thus disinclined to make real distinctions between depressions brought about through internal causes and depressions brought on by an unhappy turn of external events.[3] The point holds true for Ferrand. Hence, throughout the period, the species of melancholy become increasingly specific, while the condition of dementia they produce remains generalized. The highly different cultural contents implicit in the diverse causes are obscured by the standardized pathological sequences that lead in turn to standardized effects.

We have argued that Ferrand's study is of a particular mental illness, that it is characterized by profound depression or mania brought on either by supercharged or by frustrated erotic impulses, and that it appears in persons whose entire organisms, following their temperaments, are susceptible to the corruptions of the natural instincts. But the fact remains that Ferrand, in spite of his partiality for somatogenetic analysis, alludes to numerous remote causes that together create a sense of the cultural contexts that shape and condition the eroticized psyche. Despite his radical Galenism, logic of a different sort intrudes with suggestions concerning the social origins of love and the cultural factors in aberrant behavior. Even within the terms proposed specifically by Ferrand, there is room to ask whether erotic melancholy is a disease of rebuffed instincts, a by-product of contrary social institutions, or a disease of the imagination evoked by the arts or by the idealizing of the object of beauty. Humoral analysis tends to overshadow an analysis of external stimuli. Yet literary and cultural elements find their way into his study of the etiology of love. This dual focus is, in fact, owing to aspects inherent in Ferrand's philosophical system that allow for a diversification of causes that goes back to the conflation of medical theories among the Arab physicians.

Ferrand formally favors endogenous causes for two essential reasons. In theoretical terms, only internal causes have pathological potential. In practical terms, only the physical components of the disease can be treated medically because they can be treated in the body. The concentration upon endogenous causes thus tends to remove the exogenous causes to a more remote and secondary status.[4] Ferrand himself attempts to minimize the role played by external agents or circumstances as he approaches his section on cures, even though they had taken up a significant portion of his discussion of causes.

Ferrand was, in fact, caught between two extremes: on the one hand, he did not wish to deal with love in terms of social causation; on the other, he did not wish to overemphasize the most obvious and direct of the internal causes, namely the surfeit of seed accumulated in the genitals. This latter approach risked to compromise the importance attributed to the head as the seat of the disease and to the heart as the seat of the cause of the disease. Moreover, the pharmaceutical means were limited for reducing this material cause, and coitus outside of marriage had been ruled out as immoral and potentially dangerous. Yet Ferrand could not deny that the influence of the reproductive organs was accounted one of the most important causes of the erotic instincts and thus of the entire system of amorous desire, while the corruption of seed was believed to be a principal cause of the corruption of the appetites and of the imaginative faculties.

According to the leading anatomists and the specialists on women's diseases—Venette, Liébault, Du Laurens—sexual desire begins with the pleasures associated with coitus, itself the product of the pleasing tickling sensations of the sperm and the friction created by its movement from several parts of the body toward the reproductive organs.[5] Such were the physiological foundations of the sexual instincts, and such were the mechanisms of nature for the preservation of the race. These physiological processes gave rise to the impetuosity of the appetites. The tyrannous demands of the seed alone were sufficient to provoke erotic ambitions exceeding social and moral tolerances. Unexpended seed was liable to corruption and to the production of noxious vapors that could bring on erotic dreams by night and sensual fantasies by day. Erotic melancholy could be accounted for entirely in these endogenous terms. Paré called the sexual appetite a "mad and raging lust," Du Laurens "an incredible desire for union" and "unbridled sensuality," and Liébault "a marvellous tickling urge."[6] Erotic melancholy began in the instinctual quest for sexual gratification. In that sense, the melancholy imagination is the mental counterpart to an incessant craving for coitus in order to release the tension created by the sexual drives.

Du Laurens described the womb in similar terms as "an animal full of concupiscent desires and thus lecherous and envious."[7] Not only was the uterus a passive ground that received fertilization, but it was an organ with a self-determined appetite for the male member, an organ that actively inclined toward intercourse and that craved the humidification of the superior male seed. The womb was insatiable; deprived of its pleasures, it created the vapors leading to hysteria. Conditions in the reproductive organs could hence drive a woman to frenzy or to suicide. Hippocrates described the condition in young girls and recommended hasty marriage. With the mechanisms of instinct located in the genitals and the seed, Ferrand anticipates a vocabulary based on models of tension and release, on surfeit and evacuation, and on the principle of anticipated pleasure and reward.

Ferrand is able to join sexual hyperexcitation to his definition of love melancholy largely by making love mania and love melancholy degrees of a common disease and then by failing to distinguish between love mania and uterine fury. The initial classification in ch. XII that promises to differentiate between prurient itching in the genitals, uterine fury, and satyriasis has the effect not only of grouping these even more closely with one another but also of grouping them with virtually unrelated conditions of hypersexuality such as philtromania and the incubus by virtue of their common symptoms: ardent erotic desire and unsatisfied sexual appetites. The taxonomical ambiguity involving hysteria and love melancholy can, in fact, be traced to Galen, whose melancholy widower was diagnosed as suffering from the former rather than from the latter because of the retention of seed.[8] This same ambiguity prevails in Valleriola's portrait of the frantic and suicidal merchant suffering from unrequited love, as it does in the case studies of Forestus and others of the period.[9]

The symptomatology of female hypersexuality includes the public exposure and frequent manipulation of the genitals, indiscriminate sexual assaults upon members of the household or institution (of either sex depending on the inclinations of the patient), and the singing of scatological songs as but one sign of the afflicted imagination.[10] Lochner, late in the seventeenth century, describes a case of nymphomania in which there is strong, acrid vaginal emission, a stinking breath, an enflamed face, a strong pulse, a dry tongue, and shiny eyes.[11] Du Laurens, in speaking of the uterus as a lecherous animal, indicates both subconscious drives and compulsive erotic behavior, while Liébault, in speaking of "a raging and furious frenzy due to the excessive ardor of the uterus" identifies the physiological force behind this category of mania.[12] For a modern observer the differences between nymphomania and a passion of the soul polarized by an object of desire would appear to be self-evident. *De facto*, even for Ferrand, a distinction is implicit given his general concentration upon a state of melancholy eroticization that begins variously with a condition of the humors or with a social encounter and that is consumated autistically in the imagination. In the final analysis, the principal determining factor, outside of the etiological variations pertaining to each state, is the quality of the relationship to the desired object in social and psychological terms; Ferrand, himself, spells out these terms in ways sufficient to reveal the underlying disparities.

Love melancholy, unlike hysteria, was not a product of a single center of the body. Even in terms of endogenous cause it was a phenomenon of the hypochondries, heart, and brain as well as of the genitals. The diversification of contributing centers, fully allowed for within the humoral system of medicine, was the most effective means for diversifying the range of causes. Just as the genitals represented instinct in an almost symbolic way, so the heart came to stand for the emotions, the hypochondries for the concupiscent appetites, and the brain for the intellectual component of love. The discussion of their respective contributions was carried out in the terms of a medical *disputatio* concerning the seats of the disease.

The head was the locale of the tormented imagination caught in its endless repetition of corrupted images and, by extension, of the cycle of morose thoughts that precluded all alleviating action. Following Aristotle, the heart was considered the locale of the burning passions and, for Ferrand, the seat of the cause of the disease. Nevertheless, Ferrand follows tradition in assigning love to hypochondriacal melancholy because the "essential faculties of the brain are corrupted by the blackish vapors that rise from the hypochondries." Ferrand does not attempt to reconcile the rival claims of the heart and the hypochondries as the site of the furnace of the passions. He gives the ultimate place of honor to the brain as the seat of the disease because of the role of the imagination, although he maintains the contributing roles of the other centers—centers that provide a figurative language for discussing diverse categories of cause: the instincts for sexual pleasure and for procreation; the intensification of feeling aroused by the contemplation of an object of beauty; the inherent excitability of the passions; the intense brooding arising from the corrupted faculties of the brain. Medical philosophers rarely confined themselves to a single choice in spite of the rhetorical demands of the *disputatio*, for if the primary cause was in the genitals, then erotomania must be viewed largely as a biodeterministic condition produced exclusively by a surfeit of seed, while if it was in the heart it must be seen as deriving from a disorder of the emotions only, and if in the head then a disease arising exclusively through a derangement of thought. Experience and common sense observations about the nature of erotic love would invalidate claims that any one of these alone could serve as an exclusive cause.

Ferrand is drawn further outside the order of strictly endogenous factors by the symptoms produced in the lover, for while they may be viewed as products of physiological malfunctions, they nevertheless encourage a degree of social analysis. Ferrand is concerned with a paralysis of the will that results from a sense of defeat, because the principal mark of the melancholy lover is his pensive demeanor and his withdrawal from society. Among the possible symptoms are torpor, confusion, preoccupation with the image of the beloved in the mind's eye, and endless deliberation over conflicting courses of action.

Yet Ferrand never concerns himself with the actual dynamics of the lover's thoughts. According to the definitions of melancholy cognition, the content of the tortured mind does not include strategies for action or retreat, does not provide for dialectics concerning hope and despair, or for self-affirmation through hatred of the scornful lady, or for self-loathing in light of her refusal (despite the medical interest in the experiences of the Petrarchan poets), but rather it is taken up with an image of the beloved. This interpretation of the content of the lover's imagination, based on Ferrand's use of the Aristotelian philosophy of perception and the faculties of the soul, militates against the psychological analysis of erotic desire in terms of social dynamics. Thus while Ferrand occasionally allows himself to be drawn into discussions of social causes and conditions, these discussions inevitably serve to incorporate the influences of external stimuli into a system of pathology traditional to melancholy diseases. Ferrand can name causes and symptoms charged with social significance, as the next few paragraphs will point out, but never in a way that encourages him to break with the analysis of desire in terms departing from established medical philosophy. In brief, Ferrand's psychophysiological approach to deranged eroticism obstructs any therapeutic approaches based on an analysis of the social content and psychic origins of the patient's thought. So many aspects of Ferrand's analysis of exterior causes point ostensibly to the concerns of psychotherapy in a quasi-modern sense, but the vocabulary of humoral medicine will always impede the development of analysis in such terms. Nevertheless, for the modern reader, his text is full of tantalizing hints, in anticipation of a more dynamic and comprehensive analysis of the eroticized psyche.

Ferrand's definition of erotic love is for these reasons potentially ambiguous for a modern observer: "a form of dotage, proceeding from an inordinate desire to enjoy the beloved object, accompanied by fear and sorrow" (ch. V). Of the three components of the dotage—desire, an object, fear and sorrow—only desire is conceivably a product of the instinctual or of the physiological processes. The "object" is an external stimulus and would seem to require identification and selection involving social and aesthetic criteria on the part of the beholder, while "fear and sorrow" would appear to be emotional responses that arise from the failure to negotiate the enjoyment of the object. Now, the object of desire, as a flesh and blood individual with an independent volition and a social identity, is not a part of the pathological process until it has been converted into an image that is subject to distortion by the lover's imagination. In the same fashion, that fear which would seem to be an expression of the lover's inability to act toward achieving his goal and that sorrow which would seem to be the lover's response to his sense of loss are, in fact, conventional components of the condition of melancholy; they are products of the blackness and coldness of the humor itself.

Ferrand places the emphasis in his definition of erotic love upon the intensity of desire and upon the role of the object. Both elements deserve closer examination for the ways in which they conform to a medical philosophy that sidesteps both social causation and, at the same time, a concomitant emphasis upon a whole range of methodical cures based on social or diversionary strategies as opposed to the favored surgical and pharmaceutical cures. Michel Foucault made a study of the dynamics of *aphrodisia* or the use of pleasure in the ancient world, dynamics which join into a circle the desire that leads to act, the act that is linked to pleasure, and the pleasure that leads to desire. This cyclic process he analyzed first quantitatively in terms of the degree of activity that is shown by the number and frequency of acts. "What differentiates men from one another, for medicine and for moral philosophy alike, is not so much the type of objects toward which they are oriented, nor the mode of sexual practice they prefer, but the intensity of that practice. The division is between lesser and greater, between moderation and excess."[13] This interpretation of the values of antiquity holds equally for Ferrand. His study is neither of the modes of sexual practice nor of the types of objects, but of the intensity of desire and of the inability to participate in that cycle of pleasure. Love as a disease is, by definition, a loss of society, a crisis of the ego in isolation fixed by an intense state of longing; erotic love is a condition of excess deprived of the opportunity or the ability to act. That is central to Ferrand's definition of pathological eroticism.

Desire as an anticipation of pleasure is thus an intense longing for that which is perceived to be lacking. Ferrand understands the sense of lack that creates sexual tension not only as a physical quest to expend seed, but also as a psychic deficiency—a deficiency he attempts to account for in the terms of the fable of the androgyne, that paradigmatic account of human sexual drives interpreted as a quest for the reintegration of the self through a sexual embrace that simultaneously fulfills deep psychological cravings. Desire is thus the anticipation of pleasure, but of a pleasure that joins ritual, consciousness, and memory to the significance of that embrace. This fable suggests a sexuality that includes psychic well-being produced through the mutuality of the bond and through the exclusivity of the miniature society that is formed both between self and other and between self and its own alter ego. Ferrand hints momentarily at the conditioning of desire not only by conscious social needs, but also by subliminal psychological forces. Plato's androgyne is but one instance of an intrusion of ideas from outside of the medical system that attempts to account for the psychic dimensions of desire and deprivation.

At the center of Ferrand's treatise, then, is not only a behavioral system determined by instincts and the humors, but also a behavioral system determined by desires of a higher order. Those desires are in turn influenced by the powers residing in the object, the existence of which is essential to any definition of desire itself. Willy nilly, Ferrand gets involved in a theory of the passions that attempts to account for the intensity of feeling—that perplexingly human component accompanying desire—now as a product of mental contemplation, now as a result of an abundance of semen, now as a force conveyed from the desired object. Insofar as Ferrand allows for the intensity of erotic desire to be a product of the powers residing in the object of beauty, or in the perception of the object held to be beautiful, he would seem to be escaping momentarily his somatogenetic system in order to consider the erotic condition as a relationship between the one who desires and the one who is desired. But by reducing the means of influence between them to the level of mechanisms of perception or the transfer of spirits, the object is completely depersonalized. That process, as we have already indicated, allows Ferrand to remain oblivious to the impact of the object as a social being upon the destiny of the patient. The object may generate an intensity of feeling, but once the passions are kindled they are alone sufficient to complete the pathological process. As the poets have often confessed, one fatal glance will serve. For Ferrand's system, passion in the abstract will also serve.

Pascal, in stating that "love arises in beauty" merely repeats a commonplace of that age, or indeed of any age, that desire is created by the sight of a person or object deemed beautiful. But there is a special dimension to the understanding of that concept in the Renaissance. It was held that such an object also possessed in itself a power to captivate in a physical sense, to fascinate and enslave by fixing the will of the beholder in a way that can lead to madness. In brief they subscribed to a theory of diseased love attributable to the capacity of the beautiful object to inject alien spirits into the body of the victim through the eyes. Ferrand shows signs of scepticism (ch. VIII), but these ideas were too well established to be ignored. Not only were the poets preoccupied with cataloging the traits of the lady of perfection capable of firing the poet's imagination but also the philosophers were concerned with explaining those psychophysiological means whereby beauty could stir up a sedition of the passions and produce a pathological derangement of the soul. Once again, the elements that seem most related to social and psychological conditions operating independently of the Galenic system are subordinated to the system of physiological causation.

Desire can perhaps exist without an object, but love cannot. Therefore, the medical philosopher had to incorporate this exogenous cause into the endogenous process. This could be done in several ways, all of which are mentioned by Ferrand. According to Ficino (later echoed by Valleriola), the eyes of the beautiful lady emit vapors. Entering the body of another, they function as a poison that is carried by the blood like a general infection. Similarly, Epicurus believed that the substance of sight turned to atoms that could join with the semen and thereby incite love. Valleriola espoused the idea of love as a form of enchantment or charm that held the lover in thrall and tormented him through a perturbation of the blood. Du Laurens stated that the vapors of the eyes first make their way to the liver and there create the ardent desires. In effect, these theories correspond to the various centers of the disease already mentioned. The force of the object of beauty is, through these ingenious explanations, made to support the pathogenic roles of the genitals, the liver, and the heart. Ferrand does not entirely deny these theories, though he dismisses Epicurus; he is sceptical of Valleriola's theories of fascination and the infection of the blood, and he paraphrases Du Laurens's theory involving the liver without further comment. Rather, Ferrand is partial to the Aristotelian theories concerning the psychology of perception that account for the means whereby the image that enters by the eye and is carried to the imagination engenders the disease. For Ferrand, desire is caused by images abstracted from the object, rather than by organic substances emitted by the object. The Aristotelian system emphasizes forms, esthetics, and the imagination, thereby making the captivated mind itself responsible for the passions that burn the humors.

Given this tyrannous force within the object itself, whatever the means for communicating it to the beholder, beauty takes on an awesome reality, a reality that exists outside of the physiological system of the beholder. It is a power that can be controlled only through a nearly superhuman exertion of the reasoning powers or through a spiritualization of the object in a way that terrifies the carnal appetites into retreat and replaces them with sacred adoration. We are reminded of the role assigned by Avicenna to the old lady who was to defame and discredit the object in the eyes of the *amoroso* so that what he once perceived to be beautiful he would find ugly. What Ferrand recognizes is an external causal force that had to be incorporated into his system of pathology. What he did not recognize is the cultural and social conditioning through which men learn to classify and select their objects of desire.

Thus far, Ferrand's psychology of love includes components of instinct and the passions with their various levels of intensity. It includes the internal causes associated with the humors and the external causes associated with the object of beauty and its power over the beholder. For Ferrand, the efficient cause of the disease is "anything that can provoke love and melancholy." He then divides causes between the internal and the external. But as we have seen, the external causes are largely limited to the roles played by the five senses as operations of the soul rather than as vehicles of social content. Ferrand goes on to list the dangers of dancing, kissing, and touching, of sensual music and poetry. But in returning to the more immediate question of love as the formation of a miniature society between two persons with its terms of manipulation and negotiation, Ferrand has little to say. Whether the frustration of desire is brought about through social conditions, as in the case of his student patient whose tender of marriage was refused by the girl's mother, or through an incapacity to express that desire, as in the case of Aretaeus of Cappadocia's patient, or as the result of a total loss of reality through the corruption of the imagination is immaterial to Ferrand. Insofar as all objects held in the mind are abstracted from the external object, and insofar as all such images are subject to the corruption of the vapors, all forms of erotic melancholy are a disease of the imagination.

Those social variables that affect the course of love belong to the world of the dramatists and novelists, rather than to the medical treatise. We nevertheless find it difficult to abandon that other perspective, namely that desire operates in a world of supply and demand, that it is relative to opportunity, and that melancholy pertains to the lack of opportunity.

For man, the economy of the appetites is regulated by adaptation and by strategies for the management of supply. Even in the search for sexual gratification there is the adaptive measure regarding both opportunity and failure. A melancholy depression ensuing from the quest signals either an inability to adapt to the obstacles posed, or an inability to initiate the quest in order to satisfy the desire. The pathological sequence initiated by the passions is the result of an incapacity, real or perceived, to possess the desired object. When that loss is absolute and irreversible, or is viewed to be so, the various measures of adaptation become irrelevant; despair sets in—despair being a state of the soul relative to the individual perception of the gravity of the loss. As we have seen, grief itself is sometimes sufficient to destroy the life of the organism. The temptation persists to evaluate such states of depression in terms of social variables and strategies—strategies of force, trickery, sublimation, or abandonment that might pertain to any case history proposed by the age. But these must remain, nevertheless, marginal to medical theory *per se*.

Ferrand would have accepted the following vignette as corroboration of all that he taught about the sensitivity of the soul to passion, the identity of the self with the beloved, and the madness of love. Pierre de L'Estoile, in his journal entry for Dec. 6, 1593, recounts briefly the story of his own niece, Marie de Baillon, who died for love. He described her case as proof of the "mad affections of young girls." At some twenty years of age she had developed a powerful love for a young man deemed unsuitable by her family. To prevent the marriage, they sent her to another household in Paris. But their efforts to quell her passions were in vain, for not only did she manage a rendezvous with her lover, but within twenty-four hours of that final exchange of affections she died of her grief.[14] Ferrand would have read into her case all of the conflicting passions, the riot of the imagination, the fixation upon the image of her beloved, and a temperament inclined to melancholy. Her case would stand, moreover, as a testimony to the reality of the disease he had set forth in his treatise. As a madness leading to a grief-inflicted suicide, itself the product of malign humors, questions of social strategy are irrelevant. Ferrand would not have asked, as a novelist might, why she did not temporize, cajole, elope, or carry on with her secret liasons. One fact alone is relevant: Marie de Baillon died of a broken heart resulting from a frustration of her erotic desires. Ferrand makes no distinctions between victims of erotic dementia and victims of adverse circumstances.

Likewise, Ferrand makes no distinction between the grief of mutual love thwarted and the grief of unrequited love. In the former, the loss is imposed upon those already enjoying the meeting of true minds, while in the latter, the injury is in the frustration of all that constitutes desire for the chosen object and the humiliation caused by refusal. We recognize the different social content of each state of mind. In the case of Ferrand's young patient in Agen, we see the self-tormenting behavior, resulting from his inability to marry the girl of his choice and, by implication, from his inability to find other means to his ends. It is true that Ferrand tries first to arrange the marriage for him, perhaps in imitation of Erasistratus, before turning to his medical cures. But he does not ask why the patient does not try other means—disguise, accomplices, bribery, secret liasons, elopement, or getting the girl pregnant—because they would be means alien to his philosophy and to the patient's nature. For the melancholy lover one could dispense with social options because the temperaments themselves make some persons lively and clever but others dull and despondent. Those who sink into depression do so because there is an ancillary weakness for moroseness waiting for provocation. The argument always comes full circle.

As stated earlier, the concept of love as a carnal desire based on sexual tension and the desire for the release of seed is placed in new perspective when that erotic desire is directed toward a unique object of beauty that engages the higher consciousness and that forces a reading of the anticipated pleasures in social and psychological terms. Desire arises from a variety of needs and expresses itself in multifaceted ways.

Ferrand's psychology allows for yet another manifestation of erotic love that stands in contrast both to the expenditure of seed and to the social pursuit of an object of beauty that has failed. That further manifestation is to be traced to the masochistic pleasures of the eroticized mind itself, for the erotic melancholiac, separated from society, enters into a realm of fantasies and fetishes in which the external object is reduced to a simulacrum. In this form of fetishism, the lover prefers the shadow to the thing itself. The distinction is important for our understanding of Ferrand, for it illustrates the compass of his psychology of eros, even though he makes no rhetorical distinction between the lover who seeks and fails to win an object of flesh and blood and the lover who intentionally creates an idealized image of the beloved beyond all possibility of possession in order to stimulate the delicious torture of grief and loss. For the modern observer such distinctions are critical, but for Ferrand they are completely obscured, in defiance of what would seem self-evident on the basis of social observation, by the premises of his medicophilosophical system. Perhaps the most perplexing factor of this conflation of erotic behaviors is that, while Ferrand concerns himself with men driven mad by their erotic impulses, by their corrupted spirits and perverted judgments, he also understands that their symptoms are synonymous with those described in the lyrics of the love poets. Perhaps the line may be drawn between the eroticized fanatic who loses touch with reality in a riot of mind and the erotic visionary who revels in the anxieties of verse, but in Ferrand's terms that demarcation is nearly invisible. The Italian love treatises had taught him to accept the witness of the poets concerning the sweet misery of an unattainable love as an accurate transcription of the melancholy mind. Again the explanation is to be found in Ferrand's psychology of the imagination.

The imagination, as we have seen, is a faculty that internalizes desires, including the concupiscent and erotic ones, as well as the form of the object that incites them. It is in the imagination that the critical falsification of both the anticipated pleasure and the desired object takes place. It is that falsification that removes, by degrees, the natural from the unnatural. Erotic love, in the final analysis, is a disease of the imagination, given the capacity of that faculty to create its own motions, its own principles of pleasure, and at the same time its own inferno of striving and loss, because in the imagination the object is always present to be enjoyed, yet always absent, unreal, and unattainable. The memory, the instincts, the passions all play their parts; but for the person of melancholy temper whose quest is lost in advance, they serve only to exacerbate the disease and to drive it into its chronic phases. Ferrand's psychology looks toward future developments in analysis, yet it returns inevitably to where it begins in the scholastic doctrines of the soul and in the lamentations expressed by the poets of the Petrarchan tradition— for to the diverse manifestations of erotic melancholy we may add that insanity unique to poets who believe that through their art they will be able to live forever with the objects of their desires. Without the intervention of the physician, the only destiny reserved for those so afflicted is madness or death, or so the terms of the medical analysis of erotic love would necessitate in the abstract.

Ferrand may have understood little about instincts and drives and nothing at all about natural selection and the endocrine system, but he understood in his own terms a great deal about sexuality, the origins of sexual stimulation, cerebral censorship, the psychic frustrations that paralyze the will, obsessions, and depression, if essentially through an adaptation of the terms of Galenic medicine. His treatise provides the received views of the Renaissance concerning the transition from the appetites and their anticipated pleasures to states of depression or mania. We could wish him to have been a more perceptive observer of the cultural contents of the deranged psyche, more acute in remarking the differences between unrequited desire and unrequitable desire, more rigorous in his classification of the diverse manifestations of neurotic and psychotic conditions caused by love. But our first line of responsibility must be to understand him fairly in his own terms and then to understand his importance to developing trends in Renaissance society. Our analytical critique of his thought and its implications is intended to place his system of thought in a broad perspective, but it is not intended to suggest that Ferrand should or could have drawn conclusions from his examination of sexuality in terms possible only for post-Freudian observers.

At the same time that Ferrand writes a treatise on the nature of a psychological disorder deriving from erotic desires, he writes a manual on the cures intended for clinical application. The pragmatic potential in his work is difficult for us to assess today; Ferrand assured his readers that there was a large clientele. In effect, he was attempting to create a new area of medical practice based on a recognized social malaise that also corresponded to traditional medical definitions and cures. His purpose involved a form of psychoanalysis insofar as the disease was easily misdiagnosed and could be identified only through a careful assessment of character types and through a correct reading of the specific symptoms unique to lovers. Ferrand may well have intended to popularize the topic, but he cannot have intended in the process to qualify every reader as a specialist in his science. Quite the contrary, the complex diagnostic procedures, the pharmaceutical recipes, and the surgical operations ensure that the treatment of love melancholy could be carried out only by trained members of the medical profession.

The apparent faith in the force of the pharmaceutical cures to eliminate the material conditions for the diseases of the soul anticipates a difficult problem in medical ethics. Ferrand goes well beyond any of his predecessors in his alarm over the danger of lovers to themselves and to society, to the extent that he proposes not only to treat those already afflicted but to identify at the earliest possible moment those merely prone to the disease and to impose treatment upon them. Were we to allow our imaginations a certain freedom, we could conceive of a utopia in which men and women with undesirable emotional characteristics are treated chemically and surgically in order to spare them the traumas of unhappy love and society the headache of their antisocial and unproductive behavior. All the facts are in place for seeing Ferrand as the mad scientist bent on improving the human condition through a medical regulation of personality. Ferrand's potential intrusion upon the psychic life of others is based on assumed norms of behavior drawn from an interpretation of collective values through which the physician also draws his authority to practice. It is an instance of science attempting to regulate the life of the individual in the name of the state. No doubt Ferrand would have been perplexed by the accusation. No doubt he would have considered his therapy to be in the best interests of a patient whose very corruption of the will and judgment by the conditions of the disease no longer allowed him to perceive the good. It is a classic dilemma. Should the physician have the power to legislate pharmaceutically and surgically against falling in love? An oath to preserve life and, by implication, to intercede where life and health are potentially in danger cannot be entirely separated from the implicit will of society concerning the handling of its marginal members. Convinced that reason and moderation are the ultimate arbiters of the civilized life and that love melancholy or mania is a serious, chronic, and potentially fatal condition, the debate comes its full circle. To read Ferrand as the unwitting founder of a brave-new-world therapy that could play into the hands of a police state is to pass beyond the vocabulary of the age or the authority, in actual practice, vested in the medical profession. Yet Ferrand sought just such an extension of control for the profession, and the circumstances of his clinical proposals, in their broadest contours, provide an uncanny forshadowing to a modern debate of considerable importance.

IX

Renaissance Literature
and the Diseases of Erotic Love

In his address to the reader Ferrand singles out the young courtiers who are seen every day in states of rapt devotion as epitomizing the disease of love melancholy. In that sense, he identifies a causal relationship between erotic mental disorders and a recognized set of social values and behavioral codes. The rites of aristocratic courtship come very close to being synonymous with the social causes of depression or mania. That is to say that certain of the causes of the disease are perceived by Ferrand to be outside of the organism and a function of the mores of the age governing the relations between the sexes. The romantic fervor espoused as a mark of the gentleman, fostered by literary as well as by social models, was but one of the contributing factors to a climate of psychological high risk in the fashions of love. Indeed, the degree to which the age endorsed such ideas of conduct as heroic fidelity and determination in love furnished models for adventures in the passions as essential adolescent rites of passage, raised the expectations in love in accordance with chivalric romances and Petrarchan lyrics, provided for the idealization of the lady as a chaste goddess or an amazon warrior, suggested a language of love drawn from Arcadia, to that very same degree it gave rise to a commensurate level of danger that the imagination could lose its way in a world of half-literary projections of the passions. In accordance with such a social milieu, Ferrand found justification for declaring the disease of love melancholy one of the most prominent of the age.

We can never be certain enough of the terrain to declare, in demographic terms, that his age was truly more prone to the diseases of love than another. There is, in fact, the autosuggestivity of the treatises themselves in serving, simultaneously, to popularize and hence to create the very condition of dementia they purported merely to describe. That is a phenomenon of another kind. The argument must finally end in a circle: that all ages have known the conditions for failure in love, that Ferrand's own examples are drawn more frequently from ancient writers than from those of his own times, and that the psyche has been capable of its own betrayal throughout history. Yet the argument remains that certain ages can institutionalize their own peculiar forms of neuroses and that certain sets of mores are more conducive to mental instability than others.

Surely, an effort to quantify the features of Renaissance society that could give rise to states of erotic despair would be not only a long but an inconclusive exercise. There is Ferrand's own evidence of a general kind that such lovers were seen every day, that cases were being regularly misdiagnosed, and that the profession was doing considerable harm to its patients. There is the record of marriage customs, forced unions, elopements and the maze of religious and civil codes that must have brought frustration to many. But the most compelling evidence remains at the level of culture and literature—evidence suggesting that Ferrand's age courted psychological disaster because of its romantic ideals concerning love. There is a conflict of behavioral codes behind the fiction created by Jean de Veyries concerning the lovelorn marquis whose treatment was a precondition for marriage to the object of his affections. Where did the young man learn his posture of suffering if not from the poetry and conventions of his class? Who taught Orlando in *As You Like It* to wander the forest carving Rosalind's name on trees, and by what contrasting standards does she understand that he must be cured? Ferrand, himself, cannot make his case against pathologically eroticized love without also indicting the courtier and the cultural manners of the aristocratic classes.

There is the sense in which Ferrand proposes to cure romantic love and the eroticized styles that accompany it, if not in the name of a repressive order based on bourgeois norms, at least in a way that favors such norms. Ferrand, in seeking to control impossible erotic desire through therapy, joins in the general movement toward a social regulation of love. It is his book, in fact, which is the tool of reform and not the clinic. As Michel Foucault sums it up, "the seventeenth century . . . will be the beginning of an age of repression pertaining to a society that we call bourgeois, one which we have not yet perhaps entirely passed through. To mention sex from that moment on becomes more difficult and more costly."[1] Unwittingly Ferrand, like Jean de Veyries and Rosalind, creates a case against the rightful place of rapture in seeing an object of sensual beauty.[2] In offering to cure erotic love as a form of psychic deviancy, Ferrand joins forces with those espousing a more desacramentalized view of human sexuality, if not a more philistine view of the utilitarian bond that contributes to social stability and productivity. Ferrand, in resisting the sentiments that were the by-products of the conditioning of *amour courtois*, must be viewed as a contributor to that change in social climate, marked during the age in so many ways: by the Counter-Reformation emphasis on obedience, by the rise of the Puritan family, and by a gradual change in literary ideals.[3] As Montaigne prophetically stated: "A good marriage (if any there be) refuseth the company and conditions of love; it endevoureth to present those of amity. It is a sweete society of life, full of constancy, of trust, and an infinite number of profitable and solid offices, and mutuall obligations."[4]

Ferrand's age is an age of transition in which expressions of love were either acts of conformity to a variety of codes of conduct, or acts of defiance whether against the self, against society, or against fortune. Eroticism turning to mental trauma is both an element of the human condition and an element of a specific milieu with its conflicting standards of behavior. Those diverse standards are implicit in Ferrand's treatise because, variously, the courtly affectations that become psychic realities are disciplined by the reality factor of medicine, while the well-intending victim of a circumstantial refusal is comforted by medicine and rescued from despair. If the hypereroticization of the mind is to be associated with courtly and literary ideals, the victim of adverse fortune is to be associated with the stringencies of immediate social and economic realities. Ferrand's brand of therapy, despite its purely theoretical basis in Galenic medicine, must also assume meaning in relation to the age for which it was conceived. Ferrand may take sides with the medical profession in protecting cases of depression attributed to social causes, protecting them from abusive treatment as sinners or as offenders at the hands of church or society. But at the same time he finds himself in company with Jean de Veyries and Montaigne in discouraging the psychic manifestations of courtly sentiment with its unrealistic aspirations and erotic raptures, with its narcissistic and fetishistic elements, presumably in favor of a concept of union based on contract, utilitarian mutuality, and a touch of friendship.

Persisting in this mode of analysis, one might turn to a well-balanced social history such as Robert Mandrou's *Introduction à la France moderne*, where he surveys the social conditions of the sixteenth and early seventeenth centuries from family life to religious persuasions to intellectual enthusiasms.[5] The only conclusions to be drawn are that it was an age of rigorous social codes and frustrating regulations but that it was at the same time an era of passions in which feeling was encouraged as a component of the religious and political life. The very word *renaissance* evokes a sense of the rebirth of the inner life in relationship to the world of learning, the arts, religion, and love. We are seeing two sets of criteria, both making their claims on the expression of love. It is one kind of argument to point out the cultural inducements to erotic longings. It is another to identify the social obstacles to love that could thwart the most practical of lovers and cast them into despair. Just as the two kinds of circumstances could not be entirely reconciled in the context of Ferrand's psychology, they cannot be reconciled here, for the one pertains to conditioning that stands as cause to the perverted imagination, while the other relates to psychological reactions to adverse circumstances. At best we must content ourselves with a declaration of a general nature, that the age was not only one of learning, of idealizing the past, of celebrating rarified beauty, of rendering the conduct of the courtier into a work of art, of refining the appetites for transcendental pleasures through the appreciation of mortal objects but it was also an age of regulation and controls, of dynastic and mercantile goals that limited personal freedoms, an age of religious censorship and repression, and of strict civil codes. Robert Mandrou concludes that "this century and a half of modern France is to be placed under the sign of the passions exasperated rather than under the sign of the pleasures refined."[6] The observation is well taken that romantic love had a myriad of hurdles to run despite the favoring of true love in the comedies of the age. But such declarations will never resolve the question of whether Ferrand's potential patient was more likely to be a victim of social obstacles or a victim of culturally eroticized appetites. The treatise campaigns openly against the excesses of courtly conduct in love and the cultivation of masochistic commitments to impossible erotic quests; thus, by implication, it is concerned with the kind of oversensitized behavior recounted in the romantic plays, novels, and love lyrics of the age.

Ferrand, by philosophical predilection, underscores the lover tormented by the folly of love, the victim whose imagination is depraved and whose judgment is corrupted, the lover who denies his need for a cure and who expends all his efforts in singing the praises of Cupid. All this follows from being struck by some mortal beauty, and sometimes even by an imaginary one. Confined to these terms, love melancholy is not only a disease of the imagination, but of the literary imagination; for it was above all in the love lyrics of the age that one finds the cult of induced suffering, the spiritualizing of the object of adoration in a way that allowed Ferrand to extract the symptoms of love from poetry as readily as from the observation of actual patients. That is to say, Ferrand found in the poets both a reflexion of and an advocation of the erotic attitudes that initiated chronic diseases or were symptoms of it.

Behind the Petrarchan cult lies a peculiar turn of mind that De Rougemont summarized in the following terms: "love is the privileged agent of the 'superior man's' spiritual progress—always on condition that he not be 'happy.' "[7] Suffering becomes the central feature and distinguishing mark of the man of refined spirits. Love is the context for testing the integrity of the soul, and is engaged upon as a quest of the spirit that passes through the dangers of psychic decomposition in an act of ultimate self-affirmation. It was a course of psychic submission to the exigencies of the passions in the name of the lady one serves. The mission of the vassal in feats of war is turned inward to a grappling with the warring elements of the mind. The heroic quest in the postchivalric age becomes a narcissistic preoccupation with the self in confrontation with a foreordained grief over the unattainability of the blessed object, a grief in turn celebrated in the eroticized deliberations of poetry. Such lovemaking is a calculated flirtation with the frontiers of the mind from which only the strongest return (it was a bizarre manifestation of social selection and survival that was not always clearly understood by all the participants: certainly not by Alison of "The Miller's Tale" or Rosalind of *As You Like It*). Because the physicians found the traditionally sanctioned symptoms of the lover in distress repeated in the lyrics, they could only assume that the makers were themselves victims of the passions they described. The authority of each kind of statement nourished the other in a relationship of symbiotic sources going back several centuries.

Why several generations of men of leisure and culturally heightened sensibilities should generate states of frustration and sorrow as an exercise of the spirit, an exercise that passes for insanity in the philistine views of the medical profession, is a question that goes beyond the scope of our study. It has been at the center of numerous inquiries into the foundations of the Petrarchan lyric, the rise of courtly love, the origins of the romantic spirit. Answers vary from projections of the virgin cult to the spiritual goals of the Cathars, from worship of the white goddess to the models furnished from the feudal system of vassalage, from ascetic and masochistic tendencies in the Western mind to courtly conditions during the Crusades. In this value system, desire for the object of beauty can be conflated with a longing for death; and for many of the poets the threat of death became the ultimate pledge of love and the ultimate bid for the surrender of the lady. We can never be certain whether the poet is in true fear of his life, or whether he is merely a rhetorical poseur. As we have stated in the preceding section, not only does Ferrand make little distinction between the victim of the muse and the victim of social obstacles to union with a woman of flesh and blood, but he makes no distinction between the poet lover of sweet contemplations whose solitary withdrawal is for the purpose of enjoying his poetic grief and the lover of demented imagination driven beyond all social reason by a riot of erotic fantasms. Ferrand's fundamental fallacy in equating the images of the depressed lover with the images of the Petrarchan poet, similar as they may appear, lies in his failure to appreciate the conventions of art, the poet's sense of an audience, the poet's contrived set of variations upon a common theme, the distance between the artist and his *persona*, the conscious play of language and image based on a common repertoire of tropes and figures, in short, the independent position of the artist who stands between his creation and his reader. Nor does Ferrand look into the variety of rhetorical postures that seek, through the images of art, the enjoyment of the absent lady or that seek to escape the anxieties raised by the deceptions of such illusive pleasure.

For the physician, the alternations between states of ecstasy and despair, between faith and apostasy, between meditation upon the object and meditation upon the self are simply self-evident witnesses of a psyche in distress. Yet an indictment of the physician's lack of skills in assessing the conventions of art will not resolve the issue because the formula that art itself is also an imitation of life will not be silenced—that behind the poetic voice there is a social and a psychological reality, one that marks and characterizes the age and one that preconditions at least certain men to indulge in an eroticism that could lead to melancholy depression. The case can still be made that the social realities reflected in art were the same that produced candidates for the clinic. In sum, Ferrand's treatise must inevitably assert its importance in relation not only to the social and legal conditions of the era that could obstruct love but also to the literary traditions that furnished the models for indulging the eroticized imagination and for exciting the passions as part of a dangerous quest that passes through a vale of self-torment and deprivation.

Quite paradoxically the disease that was conditioned by art could be reinforced by the treatises devoted to its cure. To a degree, the discovery of the condition in society was a product of the destiny created for it by the writings of the physicians themselves. In asserting the antiquity of the disease they were also re-creating it in a way entirely characteristic of the relationship between humanist scholarship and the evolution of Renaissance values. We have already demonstrated how such works as Ferrand's, written in the vernacular, must have served to spread the ideas concerning love as a potential cause of sickness to a general reading public. In a sense, where the concepts were understood, the disease could also exist. Literary writers in their turn relied upon the medical treatises for their representations of the disease and brought theory to example in the creation of characters possessed of the symptoms. Simonin points out the diffusion of ideas concerning love melancholy in the manuals appearing as far back as the beginning of the sixteenth century. He cites as examples of the literary exploitation of such ideas the *Tristan* of Pierre Sola, the novels of Juan de Flores, and the *Angoysses douloureuses* of Hélisenne de Crenne. He notes discussions of the *topos* in Mexía, DuVerdier, Guyon, and others.[8] In short, the evolution of the medical idea in the sixteenth century was paralleled and nourished by humanist and literary traditions, as we have amply demonstrated earlier. Simonin concludes that by midcentury the habit of medicalizing the presentation of love had become generalized and all the more so once it received the reinforcement of popularized Ficinism.

With the creation of literary characters in accordance with the dimensions set out by the physician, our study passes from the social sources of Ferrand to Ferrand as a literary source. To our knowledge, only the melancholy notary in the novel by Eugène Sue can be attributed directly to a reading of Ferrand. Yet whatever the sources, there can be no doubt that the dramatists and short fiction writers of the High Renaissance were increasingly interested in the erotic lover as a character study. The availability of specialized medical studies allowed for the creation of psychological characters based on recognized scientific authorities, possibly to the long-term detriment of the theater, but to the eventual gain of the psychological novel. Ferrand's importance, in this sense, again lies in the entirely representative nature of his treatise in terms of the received views of the age regarding the behavior of lovers. We suggest here the value of Ferrand in assessing the character portraits based on current concepts of desire, the humors, and the perverted imagination. These matters come to the foreground in such plays as John Ford's *Lover's Melancholy*, where the physician in attendance upon a court of youths variously afflicted by their passions lectures on love as a tyrant of the heart: "it darkens Reason, confounds discretion; deaf to counsel, It runs a headlong course to desperate madness" (III.iii.).[9] Ferrand's treatise stands to the emergence of the theater of psychopathic love as both a representative source and a philosophical guide.

To a degree, the evolution of the dramatic treatment of love can be understood in terms of the dynamics of desire. A love intrigue typically consists of the movement toward union of one or more sets of lovers— but a union delayed by obstacles that in turn necessitate adaptation and a deliberate course of action that will lead by degrees toward the desired dénouement. Adaptation in the course of seeking release from the tension of amorous desire is the quintessential ingredient of the comedy of love. Such comedy becomes, in its turn, a rite of passage in which love is earned by the capacity of the lovers to overcome the blocking characters or the circumstances of fortune. As in life, the theater demands attack through one of the infinite permutations of trickery, persuasion, or force. Love tragedy arises not only from the insuperable odds of opposing fortune but more tellingly from an incapacity on the part of the protagonists to adapt to the challenges confronting them, whether out of a defect of character, an encounter with insuperable odds, or both. Dramatists relished the recombinant properties of these elements of plot and character and were ever in search of novelty through their manipulation. One such trend was toward the development of the character of inward torment who reacted to the obstacles to desire by accusations of personal inadequacy, and by a morbid introspectiveness that ended in a paralysis of the will and defeat. Psychological love tragedy could emerge only in these terms and did so in all the major theaters of western Europe. The dramatists ran certain risks by exchanging action for philosophical speculation in these plays. But the risk was a measure of the degree to which they desired to make their plays serve new modes of inquiry into the passions played out in the theater of the mind, new modes undoubtedly influenced by the appearance of manu: the analysis of the psychic life—that inner life of the mind t all currents of will and action. The threat to the drama ar can be seen in such plays as Marlowe's *Dr. Faustus*, which highly praised for its insights into the psychic life and hig.... .... for its fragmented actions and episodes that appear so disproportionately trivial by comparison with the protagonist's tortured passions. The great love tragedies were variously studies in the obstruction of the erotic desires, in the failure to possess the object of beauty, in the incapacity of the lover to fix upon an efficacious course of action, or in the separation of lovers by social or political circumstances or by death. The full measure of such plays, many of them of extraordinary power and insight, can be had only through an understanding of the scientific principles that informed the process of characterization—scientific principles that became increasingly explicit as the "psychological" drama matured.

There is one final permutation to the relationship between love melancholy and art: the special use of love melancholy itself as a device of adaptation. It arises on two artistic fronts as well as in the clinic. Just as the poet may ultimately take hold of the manipulation of images that otherwise appear to dictate a state of disarray to the psyche in order to labor toward an integration of the soul, so the distraught lover may take secret command of his state and its symptoms as a means to the desired and not yet abandoned end. In keeping with the principle that psychosomatic diseases can themselves contain rhetorical significance in the form of a subliminal cry for help, so the symptoms of the wretched lover can be made to speak of the secluded desire. It is conceivable that a patient might persevere in his silence in anticipation that the determined physician would, in due course, discover the exact nature of the disorder. At that juncture, the disease itself becomes an element of trickery. Such a potential reversal of perspectives is already apparent in the earliest of paradigmatic accounts, the story of Antiochus and Stratonice. Given that Stratonice was his stepmother, Antiochus was bound to an eternal silence. Yet desire found a way in a show of sickness that allowed the celebrated physician to come to the truth without a word of indiscretion on the part of the lover. It was Antiochus's very determination to die in an act of self-sacrifice rather than to wound his father that disposed the latter to pity his son in the way he secretly desired— a subtle variation on the poetic cliché "have pity on me lest I die." It was the physician who took upon himself all the risk of opprobrium for playing the go-between. Troilus's relationship to Pandarus can be read in similar terms, for while Pandarus, of all people, must be held in ignorance because he was Criseyde's uncle, yet who better to perform the service Troilus required to come to his ends? It was Pandarus's curiosity to plumb the depths of Troilus's indisposition that coerced the lover to confession. Pandarus thereafter played his part as though the idea had come from his own generosity and not at all from Troilus's prompting. In Ferrand's own account of the young man treated in Agen, we note that the patient came to him voluntarily for treatment, yet refused to divulge the true source of his woe. As an acute diagnostician Ferrand, in a sense, played his part well; for in discovering the true cause, ostensibly against the patient's will, he too sought a solution in making every effort to win permission for the marriage to save the young man's life.

The line remains a fine one between the despairing lover as passive victim and as *animateur* of a last desperate ploy to possess the lady. It was the physician's serious and literal interpretation of the threat of madness or death that was carried to the attention of the person desired, or to those who might relent if they were convinced of the true gravity of the situation. The force of a literary figure was thereby renewed through the logic of psychosomatic diseases. We are never far from an Antiochus who, in collusion with a Stratonice anxious to get out of a bad marriage with the old king, plays out a charade, winking at her behind the doctor's back. Ferrand would be incredulous at the prospect of such an interpretation, no doubt, but gradations in literary models show how easily such patterns of conduct slip from mode to mode. (A variation on this arrangement, namely a collusion between two friends, one feigning lovesickness, the other assuming the role of the doctor, is the device employed to lure a rich lady into the bed of the "dying" lover in James Shirley's *Witty Fair One*.) The point is that in certain instances of frustrated desire, the best tactic of all is to succumb to the disease and to throw oneself upon the mercy of the medical profession for help. It may be a desperate and dubious form of trickery, but it may serve to turn the ultimate gesture of inadaptability into the ultimate form of adaptation.

Ferrand's employment of literary texts is largely literal. He sees only that which can be comprehended readily in the terms of his medical frame of reference. Yet despite his inadequacies as a literary and cultural critic, his implicit conflation of the literary and neurotic imaginations continually encourages an interpretation of the Petrarchan mode as a neurotic vein in Western thought that undoubtedly had a destructive autosuggestive power over courtly conduct and the relations between the sexes. Ferrand's treatise, in its unassuming way, lays the foundations for a critical analysis of one of the destabilizing subcurrents in Renaissance society insofar as it was conducive to a counterproductive eroticization of the mind.

From the opposite point of view, the artistic employment of Ferrand's treatise is apparently remote: no seventeenth-century literary writer has come to our attention who claims him as a direct source. Yet the affinity is strong between his doctrines and the characterizations of the erotic and melancholy lovers that abound with incremental frequency in the theaters especially of England and Spain in the first half of the century. It was an age fascinated by powerful manifestations of the passions and their sway over the psyche. Writers were concerned by the limits of human tolerance and endurance in the face of consuming appetites. They gave repeated representation to the darker side of the humanist quest for a passionate realization of the self, leading to a baroque turn toward the portrayal of the eccentric extremes of the passions as in the case of Webster's lycanthropic Duke Ferdinand or Ford's study of grief-inflicted death through a broken heart.

From clinic to salon to stage the melancholy lover as patient, poseur, or psychopath was a phenomenon of the age. The Renaissance found cause to re-create an ancient idea in its own image both philosophically and socially, and to coordinate its views of current conduct with the theories of conduct in the medical treatises. Whether such treatises as Ferrand's conditioned the perceptions of social reality more or less than that reality, under analysis, conditioned the treatises can be debated at considerable length. On the one hand is the treatise born of other treatises, written by a scholar who seeks an encyclopedic updating of ancient ideas concerning love. On the other is the treatise of the practicing physician who perceives his society as one particularly prone to disasters in love in a way that necessitates research into those ancient works and the remodeling and consolidation of definitions and cures in order to deal with current clinical and social realities. Ferrand's treatise, the product of two decades of research and writing, answers to both principles of genesis. Without question it is born of the impulses of a humanist medical scholar intent upon bringing forward the entire corpus of learning relating to erotic love, but equally without question the rhetorical thrust of that treatise is predicated upon a half-perceived, half-created medical reality that was confirmed for Ferrand by every instance, whether clinical or literary, of those who had suffered the ultimate pangs of erotic deprivation.

We must regret that the clinical record of that age concerning the victims of erotic melancholy is not more complete. If we include the literary record, as Ferrand himself did, however, we are confronted by a rich and complex body of portraits and views concerning the extremes of erotic behavior—portraits that come to us as "imitations of reality" with all of the qualifications inherent in that ancient critical concept. The dramatic portrayals and the poetic revelations of those suffering from love convey a composite account of the lover as a potential victim, a victim of circumstances, to be sure, but also of cultural preconditions and biases, as well as of individual physiopsychological constitutions. That is the essential point. Ferrand's treatise is a parallel witness to this human perplexity based upon its own vocabulary of causation and necessity. In Painter's story "The piteous death of an Amorouse Gentleman, for the slacke comfort geven him to late, by his beloved," the sixtieth novel in the *The Palace of Pleasure*, we see a representation of this vocabulary that allows the fictive narrative to function essentially as a case study. It is a subtle account of the pathological component that follows for some when rebuffed in love but that continues to sap an unwilling patient even after a reversal brings sure promise of the desired marriage. That death should follow from the sudden dilation of the heart upon the occasion of the parting kiss seals the dénoument in medical terms, with the final irony that he who was predestined to die of sorrow, in fact, expires from the physiological side-effects of an intolerable joy.[10]

It would stand to reason that the representations of erotic melancholy in the literature and art of the age demand analysis in the terms of the intellectual ideas then current because those were the only terms in which they could be understood by contemporary readers and viewers. By the same token, the invasion of literary considerations into the medical treatises on love suggests a conflation of medical and literary interests that further associates these two realms of endeavor. The associations are kaleidoscopic in nature and subject to such a great many conditions and conventions that uncertainties must always remain concerning the cross-fertilization between the matter of art and the matter of medicine. Yet the relationships and influences everywhere recommend themselves, given the representation of the melancholy lover as a common denominator. To be sure, we are constantly reminded of the conventions and biases that separate the order of art from the order of medical analysis. The passions that grip literary characters must seek resolution according to the nature and conventions of art: in comedy through the union of the lovers; in tragedy through death or madness; in the sonnet cycles through a complex encounter with the self in relationship to the erotic longing that concentrates creative energy or that leads to a disintegration of the psyche. Those same passions are troubling to society, and while the secretive and reclusive behavior of melancholy lovers may resemble poetic codes of conduct, true pathological conditions rarely admit of poetic solutions. It is at this juncture that the physician, in the name of compassion, duty, or the community, is called in to enjoin upon the victim an alternate course of behavior through the therapies derived from traditional medicine, therapies intended to rescue the patient from a psychopathic destiny that is related only remotely to the order of art and far more immediately to an irrevocable decline characteristic of chronic diseases.

Nevertheless, in the symptoms of the erotic melancholiac, we inevitably recognize the portrait of a generic type, and we cannot resist the belief that the medical and literary exponents relating to the type also stem from a common perception of the human condition. Hence, the relationship we are proposing between the scientific analysis of a disease and the portrait of the erotic recluse—the figure who, in the world of letters, stands opposite the Don Juan figure. If the inveterate seducer of women loses himself in hedonistic action, the morose lover loses himself in paralysis and thought, though both are driven by romantically supercharged appetites and expectations. The conduct associated with each type reveals a process leading to the disintegration of the psyche, Don Juan through a dulling pursuit of endless novelty, the melancholiac through a compulsive attachment to one sole object of desire he is powerless to claim or to abandon. Together, they complete a Renaissance essay on the dangers of excessive amorous passion, each a rejection of the position taken by the other. Clearly, Renaissance writers were fascinated by the erotic drives that become vocations and destinies, and for that reason they created a substantial body of literature to explore both the seducer and the melancholiac. Ferrand's treatise is the most complete account from that age of the medical ideas upon which the latter of these generic types was based.

NOTES TO PART 1

Introduction

1. Jacques Ferrand, *Traité de l'essence et guérison de l'Amour ou mélancolie érotique* (Toulouse: Chez la veuve de J. Colomiez, 1610). This work is often cited as being published in 1612 because, presumably, a certain number of unsold copies were updated by the addition of the Roman numeral "II"; *De la maladie d'Amour, ou mélancolie érotique, discours curieux qui enseigne à cognoistre l'essence, les causes, les signes, et les remedes de ce mal fantastique* (Paris: Chez Denis Moreau, 1623; rpt. Nendeln, Liechtenstein: Kraus-Thompson, 1978).
2. Battista Fregoso, *L'anteros ou contramours*, trans. Thomas Sibilet (Paris: Chez Martin le Jeune, 1581), pp. 60, 72.
3. A representative example may be found in the encyclopedia of Raphael Volaterranus (Raffaele Maffei), *Commentariorum urbanorum, libri XXXVIII* (Venundantur Parrhasii in via Jacobea ab Joanne Parvo et Jodoco Badio Ascenscio, [1511]): "Philologia," bk. XXXIII, pp. 337^{r-v}.
4. Battista Fregoso, *Contramour*, p. 57.
5. Levinus Lemnius, *The Secret Miracles of Nature: in Four Books* (London: J. Streater, 1658), p. 259 (a translation of *Occulta naturae miracula, ac varia rerum documenta* [Antverpiae apud Guilielmum Simonem: 1561]).
6. Marsilio Ficino, *Commentary on Plato's Symposium on Love*, trans. Sears Jayne (Dallas: Spring Publications, 1985), Speech VII, ch. 12, p. 168.
7. Pietro Aretino, *The Works*, trans. Samuel Putnam, 2 vols. (Chicago: Pascal Covici, 1926), vol. II, p. 132.
8. André Du Laurens, "Second discours, au quel est traicté des maladies melancholiques, et du moyen de les guarir," *Toutes les Oeuvres*, trans. Theophile Gelée (Paris: Chez P. Mettayer [1597], 1613), p. 34^v. This work was originally written in French, and hence is not part of Gelée's efforts as translator of the Latin works. The translations are our own, though this work was first rendered into English by Richard Surphlet as *A Discourse of the Preservation of the Sight: Of Melancholike Disease: Of Rheumes, and of Old Age* (London: Felix Kingston for Ralph Lacson, 1599).

9. F. N. Coëffeteau (bishop of Marseille), *Tableau des passions humaines, de leurs causes, et de leurs effects* (Lyon: Chez Jacques Carteron [1619], 1642), pp. 109–10 (our translation). The work was first translated by Edward Grimeston as *A Table of Humane Passions, with Their Causes and Effects* (London: N. Okes, 1621).

I. Jacques Ferrand:
The Man, His Treatise, and Ecclesiastical Censorship

1. A great deal has been written about the revolution in scientific method in the seventeenth century and the Baconian shift toward inductive and experimental methods. Few would deny the establishment of this new trend, though, as with all such movements, the exceptions are notable. That revolution had been in the making throughout the sixteenth century and one of the results was a parallel defense of scholastic learning and methods, of which Ferrand's book may be considered a part. As A. Rupert Hall states in his *The Revolution in Science 1500–1750* (London and New York: Longman, 1954, 1983), p. 39: when new criteria were established for applying nature's hidden powers "the cohesive strength of medieval science, and the extent of its consistency whereby one part reinforced another, became important in strengthening its resistance to criticism." But by Ferrand's time that resistance was running low. Ferrand, however, despite his innovative intentions, remains a scholar of the "time hallowed texts" that, throughout the seventeeth century, were to cede their place in academe to modern topics and texts. Hall makes a case for Descartes as the most influencial scholar in establishing a new methodology and in "claiming Aristotle's stolen mantle" (p. 176).

Still useful is the classic study by Richard Foster Jones, *Ancients and Moderns: A Study of the Rise of the Scientific Movement in Seventeenth-Century England* (New York: Dover Publications, 1936, 1982). See also N. W. Gilbert, *Renaissance Concepts of Method* (New York: Columbia University Press, 1960).

2. Oskar Diethelm, *Medical Dissertations of Psychiatric Interest Printed before 1750* (Basel: S. Karger, 1971).

3. Louis B. Wright, *Middle-Class Culture in Elizabethan England* (Ithaca, N.Y.: Cornell University Press, 1935, 1965), p. 549.

4. Studies of sixteenth- and seventeenth-century libraries and booksellers' stocks reveal the magnitude of the industry and indicate something of the voracious and diversified purchasing habits of a wide readership. As H. J. Martin argues, "the printed word . . . at that time was not simply restricted to small circles but reached the vast bulk of the population": "What Parisians Read in the Sixteenth Century," *French Humanism 1470–1600*, ed. Werner L. Gundersheimer (London: Macmillan and Co. , 1969), pp. 131–45. Gregory Hanlon reports on the library of Dr. Singlande of Agen who died in 1669, that his sixteenth- and seventeenth-century holdings included Leonhard Fuchs, Julius Caesar Scaliger, Pico

della Mirandola, Renou the apothecary, Jacques Ferrand, the surgeon Fabrice d'Aquapendente, the Paracelsan Fabre from Montpellier and Bienassis, who wrote a book on the plague. Here is at least one indication that Ferrand was known and purchased. "L'univers des Gens de bien: Culture et comportements des élites urbaines en Agenais-Condomois au 17e siècle" (Diss.: University of Bordeaux, 1985), p. 605.

5. Jacques Ferrand, *Erotomania or a Treatise Discoursing of the Essence, Causes, Symptoms, Prognosticks, and Cure of Love or Erotique Melancholy*, trans. Edmund Chilmead (Oxford: L. Lichfield, 1640).

6. Trans. Thomas Newton (London: Thomas Marsh, 1576).

7. Trans. Richard Carew, from the Italian translation by Camillo Camilli (London: Andrew Islip for Thomas Man, 1594).

8. Trans. Richard Surphlet (London: Felix Kingston for Ralph Lacson, 1599).

9. Trans. Samson Lennard (London: for Edward Blount and Will Aspley, ca. 1606).

10. Trans. Edward Grimeston (London: N. Okes, 1621).

11. See Louis B. Wright, "The Pathway to Foreign Learning and Languages," in *Middle-Class Culture in Elizabethan England*, pp. 339–72; Douglas Bush, *English Literature in the Early Seventeenth Century* (New York: Oxford University Press, 1945, 1952), pp. 56–75.

12. Robert Burton, *The Anatomy of Melancholy*, ed. Floyd Dell and Paul Jordan-Smith (New York: Tudor Publishing, 1927), pp. 661, 769. The question of Ferrand's influence upon Burton was debated early this century by Professors Maden and Bensly, the former claiming that, given the extraordinary similarity between their works, Burton must have borrowed extensively from Ferrand, the latter claiming that this could not be so because Burton himself denied it: ("which book came first to my hands after the third Edition" which is to say 1628). Record of this discussion is taken from J. L. Lowes, "The Loveres Maladye of Hereos," p. 536, whose references are as follows: "Madan (*Early Oxford Press*), p. 419; quoted by Professor Bensley in *Notes and Queries*, Ser. X, vol. XI, p. 286." Lowes goes on to explain that Burton must have seen the need to protest his independence from Ferrand when he, himself, recognized the remarkable similarity: "The Loveres Maladye of Hereos," p. 537. None of these scholars was aware of the work of Du Laurens, Jean Aubery, and Jean de Veyries, all of which detracts somewhat from the "amazing similarity between Ferrand's treatment of the subject—both in general and in detail—and that of Burton" simply because there was a great deal of momentum behind the formation of this kind of composite literary-medical treatise on love that came to its apogee more or less simultaneously in Burton and Ferrand.

13. For studies on Burton's strategies of art, see Bridget Gellert Lyons, *Voices of Melancholy: Studies in Literary Treatments of Melancholy in Renaissance England* (London: Routledge and Kegan Paul, 1971), pp. 113–48; Joan Webber, *The Eloquent "I": Style and Self in Seventeeth-Century Prose* (Madison: The University of Wisconsin Press, 1968), pp. 80–114.

14. Jean Etienne Dominique Esquirol, *Mental Maladies: A Treatise on Insanity*, Intro. Raymond de Saussure (1845; facs. New York and London:

Hafner Publishing Company, 1965), the English translation of *Des maladies mentales considérées sous les rapports médical, hygiénique et médico-légal*, 1838.

15. *Mental Maladies: A Treatise on Insanity*, p. 342.

16. Ibid., p. 341.

17. Ibid., p. 335: "Erotomania differs essentially from nymphomania, and satyriasis. In the latter, the evil originates in the organs of reproduction, whose irritation reacts upon the brain. In erotomania, the sentiment which characterizes it, is in the head. The nymphomaniac, as well as the victim of satyriasis, is the subject of a physical disorder. The erotomaniac is, on the contrary, the sport of his imagination. Erotomania is to nymphomania and satyriasis, what the ardent affections of the heart, when chaste and honorable are, in comparison with frightful libertinism; while proposals the most obscene, and actions the most shameful and humiliating, betray both nymphomania and satyriasis."

18. Ibid., p. 335.

19. Ibid., p. 341.

20. Eugène Sue, *Les Mystères de Paris*, 2 vols. (Paris: Editions Jean-Jacques Pauvert, 1963), vol. II, p. 75.

21. John Livingston Lowes, "The Loveres Maladye of Hereos," pp. 491–564.

22. *Opera medica omnia*, vol. III, p. 39.

23. Françoise Vigier, "La folie amoureuse dans le roman pastoral Espagnol," in *Visages de la folie (1500–1650)*, eds. Augustin Redondo and André Rochon (Paris: Publications de la Sorbonne, 1981), p. 120.

24. Yvonne David-Peyre, "Las Fuentes Ibéricas de Jacques Ferrand, médico de Agen," *Asclépio*, XXIII (Madrid, 1971), pp. 1–26; "Jacques Ferrand médicin agenais, ou les tracasseries d'un tribunal ecclésiastique," *Actes du Congrès National des Sociétés Savantes* (Nantes, 1972), pp. 561–72; "Jacques Ferrand médicin agenais 1575–16 . . . (?)," *Histoire des Sciences Médicales*, No. 5 (1973), pp. 1–11.

25. Michel Simonin, "*Aegritudo amoris* et *res literaria* à la Renaissance: Réflexions préliminaires," in *La folie et le corps*, pp. 87–88.

26. Ruth A. Fox, *The Tangled Chain: The Structure of Disorder in the "Anatomy of Melancholy"* (Berkeley: University of California Press, 1976), p. 267.

27. Robert Burton, *The Anatomy of Melancholy*, eds. Floyd Dell and Paul Jordan-Smith.

28. Burton himself states in a way perfectly apt for Ferrand: "But mine earnest intent is as much to profit as to please; and these my writings, I hope, shall take like gilded pills, which are so composed as well to tempt the appetite and deceive the palate, as to help and medicinally work upon the whole body; my lines shall not only recreate but rectify the mind": *The Anatomy of Melancholy*, p. 616; Jean Starobinski, "La mélancolie de l'anatomiste," *Tel Quel*, No. 10 (1962), p. 21, attributes this ambiguity of purpose to his baroque style, "où la démarche de *l'invention* est inséparable de celle de la *thésaurisation*. De là ce mélange de fraîcheur et de décrépitude qui, pour nous modernes, fait le charme hybride de ce livre." The attractions of that composite style were by no means lost on Ferrand's early readers, at least those who appended

their commendatory verses to the English edition (1640), for Richard West of Christ Church describes the book as a bitter medicine that is made sweet by its literary diversions, thereby making it appealing to a wide audience:

And least severer Druggs should fright, (as some
Will refuse Health, unlesse it neatly come.)
Poetry candies the Philosophy,
Like *Galen* mixt with *Sidnies* Arcadye.
    Which (like two Starres conjoyn'd) are so well laid,
That it will please Stoicke, and Chambermaid.
                                            (*Erotomania*, fol. c.)

29. Ferrand's work is a representative example of the "scholastic" treatise reflecting conventional rhetorical patterns of division and argumentation. Rhetorical methodology, of course, had a great deal to do with fundamental questions of investigation, evidence and proofs, and the revolution in scientific thinking that emerged during the sixteenth and seventeenth centuries had much to do with breaking the authority of former rhetorical models. These and related matters are discussed in a number of key works: generally, as in James Murphy, *Rhetoric in the Middle Ages: A History of Rhetorical Theory from St. Augustine to the Renaissance* (Berkeley: University of California Press, 1968); Paul Oskar Kristeller, *Renaissance Thought: The Classic, Scholastic and Humanistic Strains* (New York: Harper and Row, 1961); and more specifically in Barbara J. Shapiro, *Probability and Certainty in Seventeenth Century England* (Princeton: Princeton University Press, 1983); A. Rupert Hall, *The Revolution in Science 1500–1750*; Ruth A. Fox, *The Tangled Chain*..

30. *Traicté de l'essence et guérison de l'amour,* "Au lecteurs."

31. Ferrand's style is by no means overly studied in the first treatise, but there are moments when he was clearly trying his hand at the florid style. Consider the following example (our translation) of the kind of playful writing that is neutralized in a parallel passage in ch. IV of the second treatise: "Read in the *Toraxis* of Lucian, and there you will find that *Charyclea* for love of *Dinias* sent him withered nosegays and half-eaten apples. Some, instead of apples, send figs because theu are symbols of tenderness, and among the hieroglyphics, symbols of the softest part of the woman, in which it would seem nature has gathered up all the gentleness that should be scattered throughout the woman's body, for which reason her customs, habits, and conversation are difficult to abide—just as the bark of the fig tree, its sap and leaves are rude and bitter, while the fruit is entirely sweet": *Traicté de l'essence et guérison de l'amour,* pp. 169–70.

32. This was the date assigned by Jules Andrieu in the *Bibliographie Générale de l'Agenais* (Paris, 1886–91; Geneva: Slatkine Reprints, 1969), vol. I, pp. 297–98.

33. Dr. M. Desbarreaux-Bernard, "Notice biographique et bibliographique sur Jacques Ferrand," *Bulletin du bibliophile* (Toulouse: Douladoure, 1869), pp. 377–400.

34. We can only speculate about the curriculum in Toulouse. The number of

faculty members and students associated with the Faculty in Montpellier who wrote on love suggests that the *topos* was regularly considered. Diethelm's catalog of dissertations allows us to see centers of interest such as Giessen, where Gregor Horst's students produced a series of dissertations on the psychopathology and treatments of love. These were published in 1611, the same year that Horst himself published a lengthy treatise in which he defined love in poetic and philosophical as well as in medical terms. *Medical Dissertations of Psychiatric Interest*, p. 66.

35. *Traicté de l'essence et guerison de l'amour*, in the address to his patron.
36. Dr. Desbarreaux-Bernard emphasizes the point that of all the parliaments in France at that time, the parliament of Toulouse was the most rigid in observing the rulings of the Council of Trent. For the religious climate of southwestern France in the early seventeenth century, see also Y. David-Peyre, "La mélancolie érotique selon Jacques Ferrand l"Agenais ou les tracasseries d'un tribunal ecclésiastique," pp. 564–66.
37. There is a good review of Vanini's major ideas by William Hine in "Marin Marsenne: Renaissance Naturalism and Renaissance Magic," *Occult and Scientific Mentalities in the Renaissance*, ed. Brian Vickers (Cambridge: Cambridge University Press, 1984), pp. 166–70. Vanini was given to naturalist explanations of many events traditionally considered miraculous. He also denied the existence of angels. "For both naturalists and the magicians the stars played a significant role in influencing the terrestrial world. For the former, however, the influence of the stars amounted to a form of determinism, providing a source and guarantee of regularity and order in the universe. In such a world the difficulty was to explain how men can possess and exercise free will" (p. 168). This naturalist view of the world was taken for a form of atheism: "It was Vanini's misfortune . . . to carry these sophisticated Italian ideas into a provincial French town, which considered them far too radical" (p. 168).
38. Yvonne David-Peyre, "La mélancolie érotique selon Jacques Ferrand l'Agenais ou les tracasseries d'un tribunal eccésiastique," pp. 565–66. There is only the remotest possibility that Ferrand was influenced by Vanini, though clearly the tribunal in Toulouse saw common denominators in their works. The full title of Vanini's study is *Amphitheatrum aeternae providentiae divino-magicum, christiano-physicum, nec non astrologo-catholicum, adversus veteres philosophos, atheos, epicureos, peripateticos, et stoicos* (Lugduni: apud viduam Antonii de Marsy, 1615).
39. The works held in authority in that region were those that upheld the existence of supernatural and demonical forces and that licensed persecution for the good of the soul: Boquet, Bodin, Le Loyer, Le Sieur de Lancre, Martin Del Rio. The region had known a spate of trials in the 1570s that had claimed as many as four hundred prosecutions of witches and sorcerers, and it would enter into a similar period in the 1630s. See Emmanuel Le Roy Ladurie, *Histoire du Languedoc* (Paris: Presses Universitaires de France, 1962), p. 62.
40. Pierre de Lancre, king's counselor to the Parliament of Bordeaux, *Tableau*

de l'inconstance des mauvais anges et démons (Paris: Chez Nicolas Buon et Jean Berjon, 1612).

41. Robert Mandrou, *Magistrats et Sorciers en France au XVIIe siècle* (Paris: Librairie Plon, 1968).

42. Dr. Desbarreaux-Bernard, "Notice biographique et bibliographique sur Jacques Ferrand," p. 394.

43. Gregory Hanlon, *L'univers des gens de bien: Culture et comportements des élites urbaines en Agenais-Condomois au 17e siècle*, pp. 606–7.

44. See D. P. Walker, *Spiritual and Demonic Magic from Ficino to Campanella* (London: The Warburg Institute, 1958), pp. 205–6.

45. For these materials and references on Galen and astrology we are indebted to Andrew Wear, "Galen in the Renaissance," in *Galen: Problems and Prospects*, ed. Vivian Nutton (London: Wellcome Institute for the History of Medicine, 1981), pp. 229–56.

46. Jean Taxil, *L'astrologie et physiognomie en leur splendeur* (Tournon: par R. Reynaud Libraire juré d'Arles, 1614), passim.

47. The problem for Ferrand arises perhaps because he was out of touch with recent developments in the debate over astronomy. His loyalty may simply have been an extension of the interest shown in the topic by most medical practitioners and not as a participant in the war of ideas that began with the writing of Ficino and Pico della Mirandola. The physician was concerned with knowing the right moments for bleeding and administering purges and often little more. Even Jean Calvin in his *Traicté ou avertissement contre l'astrologie qu'on appelle judiciaire et autres curiosités qui règnent aujourd'hui au monde* (1549; rpt. Paris: Librairie Armand Colin, 1962), p. 6, agrees that physicians "use their knowledge of the heavens properly when they choose an opportune moment for bleeding or for dosing with pills and medicines, for we must confess that there is *quelque convenance* between the luminaries and our bodies": quoted from Wayne Shumaker, *The Occult Sciences in the Renaissance* (Berkeley and Los Angeles: University of California Press, 1972), p. 44. There are many general treatments of the subject, e. g. Christopher McIntosh, *The Astrologers and Their Creed: An Historical Outline* (London: Hutchinson, 1969); Don Cameron Allen, *The Star-Crossed Renaissance: The Quarrel about Astrology and Its Influence in England* (Durham, N.C.: Duke University Press, 1941).

48. Ferrand states in ch. XXXIV of the 1623 treatise that anyone desiring further information on preparations for making men virile and women fertile should read "our treatise on sterility." If Ferrand is referring to a work of his own on this topic, there is no record of its survival. Such a work is not unlikely, however, given his interest in the topic: the cases he claims to have treated in Castelnaudary and his recipes relating to impotency in the treatise of 1610. It should be added here that Ferrand was credited by N. F. J. Eloy in the eighteenth century, in his *Dictionnaire historique de la médecine ancienne et moderne* (Mons: Chez H. Hoyois, 1778), vol. II, p. 221, with the autorship of a work entitled *Lettres apologétiques*, published in Paris in 1685. The attribution, however, has been denied in later biographical entries on Ferrand, and the question is not mentioned

by Desbarreaux-Bernard. Of interest as well is the fact that Eloy knew the treatise on love and had the following remarks to make about it: "Il y considere moins l'amour comme passion, que comme infirmité corporelle; c'est-à-dire, qu'il regarde la propension à l'amour comme un effet du méchanisme des organes différemment constitués ou altérés."

49. The allusion is to Boccaccio's day three, novel 10, "Alibeck turns hermit, and a monk, Rustico, teaches her to put the Devil in Hell," *The Decameron*, trans. Edward Hutton (New York: The Heritage Press, 1940), pp. 177–81.

50. Ferrand was not alone in devising such names for the secret parts, however. Two examples worthy of comparison are recorded by Jacques Duval in his *Traicté des hermaphrodits, parties génitales, accouchemens des femmes* (Rouen, 1612; Paris: I. Liseux, 1880), the first by Le Sieur Veneur, bishop of Evreux, who called it the "vallée de Josaphat où se faict le viril combat" (p. 60), the second redolent of Ferrand's allusion to Alibec's inferno, "la porte d'enfer et l'entrée du Diable, par lequelle les sensuels gourmands de leurs plus ardens libidineus désirs descendent en enfer" (p. 60). St. Augustine and St. Thomas Aquinas both referred to it as the "porta inferni et janua diaboli."

51. French physicians in general had been uniting themselves against the church during the first decade of the seventeeth century with regard to its role in the witch trials. They declared that matters relating to mental health were beyond the competence of theologians. David-Peyre reminds us, in considering Ferrand's position before the tribunal, that many of his most distinguished contemporaries, Moreau, Riolan, Naudé and Guy Patin had circulated petitions concerning abusive ecclesiastical measures, and that Du Laurens was also among the signatories: "Jacques Ferrand, médicin agenais 1575–16 . . . (?)," p. 8.

52. M. Desbarreaux-Bernard, "Notice biographique et bibliographique sur Jacques Ferrand," p. 389.

53. Joubert's *Traicté* was published in Bordeaux in 1578, and republished, together with the treatise on laughter, as *Erreurs populaires touchant la médecine et régime de la santé* (Paris: Chez Claude Micard, 1587); the title of Liébault's work in its translated edition was *Trois livres appartenans aux infirmitez et maladies des femmes pris du Latin de M. Jean Liebaut* (Lyon: par Jean Veyrat, 1598).

54. These works will be documented in the section to follow on Renaissance sources and analogues.

55. This work appears to be the first treatise-length study uniquely devoted to the curing of love melancholy, and the second study written in French (after Du Laurens). The full title is: Jean Aubery, *L'antidote d'amour. Avec un ample discours, contenant la nature et les causes d'iceluy, ensemble les remedes les plus singuliers pour se preserver et guerir des passions amoureuses* (Paris: Chez Claude Chappelet, 1599).

56. The question here is one of formal classification. Uterine fury had long been associated with sexuality. Probably the most influencial source was Galen's *De locis affectis*, bk. VI. Galen remarks how this disease occurs particularly among young widows, and especially those who were fertile

and receptive to their husbands. The disease was the result of retension of semen or suppression of the menses. By analogy, Galen attributes a kind of love melancholy in men to retention of seed, but calls the disease not melancholy but hysteria. For a complete account, see Ilza Veith, *Hysteria: The History of a Disease* (Chicago: University of Chicago Press, 1965).

II. Love Melancholy as a Medical Idea in the Ancient World

1. Hjalmar Crohns, "Zur Geschichte der Liebe als 'Krankheit,'" *Archiv für Kulturgeschichte*, 3 (1905), pp. 66–86; John Livingston Lowes, "The Loveres Maladye of Hereos," *Modern Philology*, IX (1914), pp. 491–546; Bruno Nardi, "L'amore e i medici medievali," *Saggi e note di critica dantesca* (Milan-Naples: Ricciardi, 1964), pp. 238–67; Massimo Ciavolella, *La "malattia d'amore" dall'Antichità al Medio Evo* (Rome: Bulzoni, 1975); Giorgio Agamben, *Stanze. La parola e il fantasma nella cultura occidentale* (Turin: Einaudi, 1977); Mary Wack, "Memory and Love in Chaucer's 'Troilus and Criseyde'" (Diss.: Cornell University, 1982); Darrel W. Amundsen, "Romanticizing the Ancient Medical Profession," *Bulletin of the History of Medicine*, 48 (1974), pp. 328–37; Adelheid Giedke, *Die Liebeskrankheit in der Geschichte der Medizin* (Diss.: University of Düsseldorf, 1983); Michael R. McVaugh, introduction to his edition of Arnald of Villanova's *De amore heroico*, vol. III of his *Opera medica omnia* (Barcelona: Universitat de Barcelona, 1985); the collective volume *La folie et le corps*, ed. Jean Céard (Paris: Presses de l'École Normale Supérieure, 1985).
2. Longinus, *On the Sublime*, trans. G. M. A. Grube (New York: Bobbs-Merrill, 1957), pp. 17–18.
3. Ferrand was able to find several imitators among the ancients in Dionysius Longinus, Ovid, Statius, and Catullus in a way that suggests the importance of the poem. But that he finds a contemporary version by Remy Belleau is the more striking discovery in terms of the staying power of Sappho's lines.
4. Aretaeus the Cappadocian, *On the Causes and Symptoms of Chronic Diseases*, in *The Extant Works*, ed. Francis Adams (Boston: Longwood Press, 1978), p. 300.
5. Hippocrates, *De natura hominis*, in *Hippocrates*, ed. W. H. S. Jones (Loeb, 1962), vol. I, ch. 4. For the origin and the development of the humoral doctrine and of the concept of melancholy, see R. Klibansky, E. Panofsky, F. Saxl, *Saturn and Melancholy* (London: Nelson, 1964), especially pp. 3–15; W. H. S. Jones' introduction to his edition of Hippocrates, vol. I, pp. xlvi ff.; and J. Starobinski, *Histoire du traitement de la mélancolie des origines à 1900*, in *Acta psychosomatica*, no. 4 (Basel: J. R. Geigy, 1960).
6. Thus in *Epidemics*, bk. III, 17b, emotional disturbances are attributed to black bile, while the author of *Aphorisms*, bk. V, 23 writes: "fear and depression that is prolonged mean melancholia."
7. W. H. S. Jones in *Hippocrates*, vol. 2, p. 134, suggests that the work was

written by Polybius, brother-in-law of Hippocrates. The two following quotations are respectively from p. 174 and p. 180.

8. *The Sacred Disease*, trans. W. H. S. Jones, in *Hippocrates*, vol. II, p. 174.

9. *The Sacred Disease*, ed. W. H. S. Jones, in *Hippocrates*, vol. II, p. 180.

10. Cf. ΠΕΡΙ ΧΥΜΩΝ, ibid., vol. IV, p. 81.

11. See, for example, Plato, *Timaeus* 268d; Aristophanes, *Plutus*, ll. 10–14, 364–73, and *The Birds*, ll. 13–14. Cf. also R. Klibanski et al. , *Saturn and Melancholy*, p. 17; W. H. S. Jones, *Hippocrates*, vol. I, p. lviii; G. Rosen, *Madness in Society: Chapters in the Historical Sociology of Mental Illness* (New York: Harper and Row, 1969), p. 93.

12. An excellent examination of this problem is offered by F. Lasserre, *La figure d'Éros dans la poésie grecque* (Lausanne: Impr. réunies, 1946).

13. Sophocles, *Trachiniae*, trans. F. Storr (Loeb, 1961), l. 455. Sophocles, in this play, alludes to the "disease of love," but Euripides seems to have been the first writer to use this concept to describe the destructive effects of this passion upon the human organism.

14. Euripides, *Hyppolitus*, trans. Arthur S. Way (Loeb, 1964), ll. 337–39.

15. Plato, *Cratylus*, 420b. All the works of Plato have been consulted in *Platonis opera*, ed. Joannes Burnet (Oxford: Clarendon, 1900–1907), and in the Loeb Classical Library.

16. Plato, *Phaedrus*, 250d.

17. Plotinus in the *Enneades*, bk. V, ch. 3, pt. 3, calls it Αἴσθησις ἄγγελος: messenger of sensation.

18. In the *Republic*, 435b9, Plato enumerates three souls in man, or rather three parts of the soul. In the *Phaedrus*, 246a ff., this division is suggested by the myth of the chariot, of the charioteer, and of the horses: the charioteer symbolizes the rational soul; the noble horse is the courageous soul which, under the guide of the charioteer, pulls upwards; the least noble horse is the passionate soul, which leads man downwards. In the *Timaeus*, 69d-e, 70d, e, the division has become more scientific: the rational soul (νοητικόν) has its seat in the head and is separated from the other parts by the neck. The irascible soul (θυμός) is placed within the breast over the diaphragm, which separates it from the inferior soul. Being near the head, the θυμός can hear the voice of reason and repress the passionate soul (ἐπιθυμητικόν), which is located under the diaphragm and is there bound as a θρέμμα ἄγριον, a savage horse. This doctrine of the three parts of the soul will have wide currency in all Neoplatonic philosophies. For a detailed discussion of this problem, see T. M. Robinson, *Plato's Psychology* (Toronto: University of Toronto Press, 1970).

19. φρίκη: Plato, *Phaedrus*, 251a.

20. *Phaedrus*, 244a, 249d-e.

21. *Phaedrus*, 244a-b, 265a-b.

22. *The Banquet*, 186a-b. Plato also recognizes the influence of the body on the soul: see *Timaeus*, bk. I, 61e; 62a, 62b, 62c; 64b-d.

23. Aristotle, *On the Soul*, bk. I, ch. 4, 408b1–15. All the works by Aristotle have been consulted in the Latin edition *Aristotelis opera*, ed. Academia Regia Borusca, 5 vols. (Berolini: Koenigliche Akademie der Wissenschaf-

ten, 1831–70), as well as in the Loeb Classical Library.
24. *Politics*, bk. VIII, ch. 7, 1342a8; cf. *On Memory and Recollection*, bk. I, 450b1.
25. *On the Soul*, bk. I, ch. 1, 403a25–b8.
26. *The Art of Rhetoric*, bk. I, ch. 2, 1370a22 ff.
27. *On the Soul*, bk. II, ch. 4, 415a23 ff.
28. *On the Soul*, bk. I, ch. 1, 403a25–b8.
29. The original Arabic text can be found in R. Walzer, "Aristotle, Galen, and Palladius on Love," *Greek into Arabic* (Cambridge, Mass.: Harvard University Press, 1962), p. 42–43.
30. *On the Soul*, bk. III, ch. 10, 433b17–18; cf. 433a21 and also 433a31b.
31. *On the Soul*, bk. III, ch. 10, 433a15–16.
32. *On the Movement of Animals*, bk. 6, 700b23–24.
33. *Nichomachean Ethics*, bk. IX, ch. 5, 1166ae–1167ac.
34. *On the Parts of Animals*, bk. III, ch. 3, 665a10: cf. bk. III, ch. 4, 666b10, and also *On Sleep and Wakefulness*, ch. 2, 456a f. On the pneuma, see the fundamental study by G. Verbeke, *L'évolution de la doctrine du pneuma du Stoïcism à S. Augustine. Ètude philosophique* (Louvain: Academia Lovaniensis, 1945).
35. *On the Parts of Animals*, bk. II, ch. 4, 651a12, but see also 667a9. Aristotle does not clarify the role of pneuma and its characteristics. There is no doubt that for him it has a material nature, and is capable of contracting and expanding. Through contraction and expansion the heart receives an impulse that causes the pneuma to change in volume, thereby affecting the neighboring spirits.
36. *Nichomachean Ethics*, bk. VII, ch. 3, 1147a10 ff.
37. Ibid., bk. VII, ch. 3, 1147a7–8.
38. Ibid., bk. II, ch. 5, 1105b20–28.
39. *On the Soul*, bk. II, ch. 7, 419a19–21.
40. Ibid., bk. III, ch. 3, 429a3.
41. Ibid., 424a. See Plato, *Theaetetus*, 191d-e. We have evidence as early as Plutarch that the concept of the perverted imagination and the etching of the image of the beloved upon the lover's mind had been established as a received idea—one that would have a history as an explanation for the behavior of lovers and that would become central to the medieval and Renaissance analyses of love: *The Dialogue on Love* (759c) in *The Moralia*, ed. W. C. Helmbold, 15 vols. (Loeb, 1969), vol. IX, p. 367: "Someone has said that the images entertained by the poetic imagination, because they impose themselves so vividly, are dreams of those wide awake; but this is much more true of the images entertained by the imagination of lovers who speak to the beloved and embrace him or chide him as though he were present. For our sight seems to paint its other pictures on wet plaster: they fade away quickly and slip from mind; the images of the beloved, however, burned into the mind by sight, as if using encaustic technique, leave behind in the memory shapes that move and live and speak and remain forever and ever."
42. *On Memory and Recollection*, 450a. See also G. Agamben, *Stanze*, pp. 84–129.

43. Sensation in fact remains as sensation as long as the object of sensation is present: *On the Soul*, bk. II, ch. 5, 417a2–9; cf. *De sensu et sensibilibus*, ch. 2, 438b22–24, and also the *Nichomachean Ethics*, bk. X, ch. 4, 1174b14. For an excellent account of the Western tradition of sense perception, see Louise Vinge, *The Five Senses: Studies in a Literary Tradition* (Lund: University of Lund, 1975).

44. *On the Soul*, bk. III, ch. 3, 429a; cf. bk. III, ch. 3, 427b14.

45. Ibid., 429a.

46. Ibid., bk. III, ch. 7, 431–32; cf. bk. III, ch. 7, 432a3–6.

47. The agent intellect, Aristotle writes in *On the Soul*, bk. III, ch. 5, 430a15 ff., "is separable, impassive and unmixed, since it is essentially an activity; for the agent is always superior to the patient, and the originating cause to the matter." Then in *Generation of Animals*, bk. II, ch. 3, 736a28, he states that it comes from the outside and that it is immortal and eternal. Aristotle, however, does not make clear whether the agent intellect belongs to the human soul or whether it is part of a divinity in as much as it is incorruptible. After Aristotle this problem generated three philosophical positions:

a. The agent intellect is separated from the human soul. Alexander of Aphrodisias (second century A.D.) defended this thesis, and postulated the identity of the agent intellect with the divinity. The soul comprises the possible intellect, whose purpose is to apprehend forms, and the acquired intellect, whose purpose is to perfect those forms. Because the agent intellect is separated from the soul, this must be mortal, and therefore intellectual activity is strictly dependent upon the senses. This interpretation was accepted by the Neoplatonic Arabic philosophers, by Al Kindi (ninth century), Al Farabi (ninth century), and finally by Avicenna (Ibn Sina, eleventh century), who, in his treatise *On the Soul* (trans. from Arabic into Latin by Andrea Alpago [Venetiis: ap. Juntas, 1546; rpt. Westmead: Gregg International Publishers, 1969]), tried to demonstrate that the thesis proposed by Alexander does not deny the immortality of the soul. The human soul, he says, depends upon the agent intellect, and this dependence does not cease even after the separation of the soul from the body. This solution was later defended by Avempace (thirteenth century) and by Maimonides (thirteenth century).

b. The agent and the passive intellect are separated from the human soul. This solution was defended by Averroes (Ibn Rušyd, 1126–98). The passive intellect, Averroes states, is nothing but a "disposition" of the soul, which is communicated to mankind by the agent intellect whose purpose is to abstract the concepts and the universal truths from the images of sensation. Thus man possesses only the acquired intellect whose end is the knowledge of universal truths (see his *On the Soul* in the edition by F. Stuart Crawford [Cambridge, Mass.: Medieval Academy of America, 1953]).

c. The agent and passive intellects are part of the human soul. This thesis was defended by Aristotle's commentator Themistius in the fourth century in his treatise *On the Soul*, ed. Richard Heinze (Berlin: G. Reimer, 1989), 103, 6, in a polemic against Alexander of Aphrodisias. It was followed by Plato's commentator Symplicius (sixth century), and it was accepted in the thirteenth century by scholastic philosophers in order to rebutt Alexander's and especially Averroes's theses. The problem of Latin Averroism has been at the center of a long debate among critics, one which has also involved the interpretation of important aspects of the medieval theory of love, especially those relating to the Italian tradition and the poet Guido Cavalcanti (Dante Alighieri's "first friend" in the *Vita Nuova*). For a comprehensive study of this polemic and a brilliant redefinition of the problem of the influence of Averroism (or radical Aristotelism) on Cavalcanti and his literary circle, see Maria Corti, *La felicità mentale. Nuove prospettive per Cavalcanti e Dante* (Turin: Einaudi, 1983). Cf. Agamben, *Stanze*, p. 100 ff.

48. Agent intellect and imagination are two powers of the same soul, and since the agent intellect is always active the image is always under its influence.

49. *Metaphysics*, ch. 8, 1050b2.

50. *On Memory and Recollection*, 415a. See also Agamben, *Stanze*, p. 88.

51. *On the Soul*, 432a.

52. Ibid., 433a13–15. The cynetic power, therefore, requires on the one hand appetite and practical intellect, on the other hand, the object of appetition, the immobile mover, which presented by the imagination, attracts to itself (without being moved) the capacity of appetition (the moved mover), which realizes itself in the living being (the moved).

53. *Politics*, 1267b4. See also *On the Soul*, 433b17–18, and cf. 433a21 and 433a31.

54. See Diogenes Laertius, *Lives of Eminent Philosophers*, trans. R. D. Hicks (Loeb, 1925, 1966), bk. V, ch. 2.

55. Ibid., bk. V, ch. 2.

56. Fritz Robert Wehrli, ed., *Die Schule des Aristoteles*, 10 vols. (Basel: B. Schwabe, 1967), vol. III. See also E. Rohde, *Der Griechische Roman und seine Vorläufer* (Hildesheim: Olms, 1960), pp. 57–58.

57. Valerius Maximus, *Factorum et dictorum memorabilium libri novem*, ed. C. Kempf (Leipzig: Teubner, 1966), bk. V, ch. 7, ext. 1.

58. Plutarch, *Vita Demetri*, ed. K. Ziegler (Leipzig: Teubner, 1960), XXXVII, 2–3.

59. See Plutarch *apud* Johannes Stobaeus (John of Stobi), *Anthologion*, ed. Curtis Wachsmuth and Otto Hense (Berlin: n.p., 1884–1912), vol. IV, pp. 468–69.

60. Appian, "Liber de rebus syriacis," *Romanorum historiarum libri*," trans. H. White, 11 vols. (London: n.p., 1912), vol. II, pp. 217–23; Lucian, "On the Syrian Goddess," *Complete Works*, trans. Thomas Francklin (London, 1781), vol. IV, pp. 351–84; Julian the Apostate, *The Orations and Satires of the Emperor Julian*, trans. W. C. Wright (Loeb, 1913–23), vol. II, pp. 447–49. The tradition of the story has been studied by Rohde, *Der Griechische Roman*, pp. 55 ff., and by Q. Cataudella, *La novella greca* (Naples: Edizioni Scientifiche Italiane, 1958), pp. 83–87. For the iconographic tradition, see Wolfgang Stechow, "The Love of Antiochus with Faire Stratonica," *Art Bulletin*, 27 (1945), pp. 221–37. Marsilio Ficino, in *Platonicam theo-*

logiam de animorum immortalitatem, ed. Raymond Marcel, bk. XIII, ch. 1 (Paris: Societé d'Éditiones "Les Belles Lettres," 1964), vol. II, pp. 196–97, mentions the story of Antiochus while speaking about the pulse. This famous medical anecdote is aluded to by such Spanish authors as Juan de Pineda, Sabuco de Nantes, and Vicente Espinel: see Yvonne David-Peyre, *Le personnage du médecin et la relation médecin-malade dans la littérature ibérique XVIe et XVIIe siécle* (Paris: Ediciones Hispano-Americanas, 1971), pp. 358–60.

It is also mentioned in the *Celestina* of Fernando de Rojas. The first play on the theme of detecting a secret love through the pulse is the *Aquilana* by the Spaniard Torres Naharro, written in the first quarter of the sixteenth century. It was followed shortly thereafter by *El-Rei Seleuco* of Luís de Camoëns, an early work that considers the feelings of the father who must part with his wife, no doubt inspired by the account in the *Triumphs* of Petrarch. The story is also the central episode in a play by Augustin Moreto (1618–69), *Antíoco y Seleuco*. For a full treatment of this theme in the Spanish theater, see Ruth Lee Kennedy, "The Theme of 'Stratonice' in the Drama of the Spanish Peninsula," *PMLA*, LV (1940), pp. 1010–32.

The story in the English Renaissance is owing to William Painter's translation of Bandello. See Novel 27, "The Love of Antiochus with Faire Stratonica," *The Palace of Pleasure* (1575; London: David Nutt, 1890). The story *per se* does not appear on the English stage before the early eighteenth century, according to *The Companion to the Play-House*, 2 vols. (London: T. Becket, P. A. Dehondt, and others, 1764), vol. 1, p. B6[r] (which also mentions an Italian opera called *Antiochus*, both published and performed ca. 1712), but there were several playwrights in the Elizabethan-Jacobean period who made use of erotic melancholy as the psychological imperative for their plots, and of the pulse ruse for detection of the secretive lover. The motif appears in the subplot of Shakespeare and Fletcher's *The Two Noble Kinsmen.* Medical symptoms, detection through doctors, and the transfer of a fiancée from her betrothed to an ailing friend are major elements in Beaumont and Fletcher's *Monsieur Thomas.* In Massinger's *Virgin Martyr,* the object of desire of the detected lover is captured and compelled to offer her virginity to save the patient by order of the young man's father, but the patient prefers death to the prostitution of his love, whose virginity is her bid for Christian sainthood. The doctor becomes part of a seduction plot in which disease is feigned to convince a woman to take pity on the patient in Shirley's *Witty Fair One.* The English dramatists, in fact, rang a series of changes on the Antiochus and Stratonice theme, despite the absence of their names, by using the equivalent of the father, son, stepmother relationship or the patient, doctor, and medical detection strategy.

61. Galen, *De praenotione ad Posthumum,* ed. Kühn, vol. XIV, pp. 631–33. The edition of the works of Galen by C. G. Kühn takes up the first 20 vols. of the series *Medicorum Graecorum opera quae extant* (Leipzig, 1821–33). Subsequent references to Galen's works will be to this edition unless

otherwise stated.

62. See also Aretaeus the Cappadocian, *The Extant Works*, p. 58.

63. We should consider, in fact, not only comic and tragic theater and epic and lyric poetry but also Stoic philosophy, which was fundamentally concerned with the problem of the passions and with their influence on the soul. For the Stoics the passions, which they consider diseases of the soul, are four: happiness and affliction in relation to present situations; desire and fear in relation to the future. Their variations dispose the pneuma in different manners, causing it to undergo moments of tension and of relaxation. Concerning the problem of the location of the passions, two opinions were prevalent: some, following Zeno, placed them in the irrational part of the soul, located near the rational soul; others, following Chrysippus, placed them in the *logos* itself which in this case lacks *tonos*, tension. For a more comprehensive discussion, see Michel Spanneut, *Le stoïcisme des Pères de l'Église* (Paris: Éditions du Seuil, 1957), p. 231 ff.

64. T. Lucretius Caro, *On the Nature of Things*, ed. C. Bailey (Oxford: Clarendon, 1963), vol. I, bk. IV, l. 1048.

65. Ibid., bk. IV, ll. 1052–57.

66. Ibid., bk. IV, ll. 1061–72.

67. For Lucretius sensation, which he considers the fundamental criterion for Truth and Good, is a motion common to and inseparable from the soul (*animus* and *anima*, which he considers corporeal) and of the body: see bk. III, ll. 94–416.

Asclepiades, following Epicurean philosophy, like Lucretius also had postulated that mental diseases were caused by emotional disturbances, which he calls "passions in the senses" ("alienatio est passio in sensibus"): see G. Zilboorg and G. Henry, *A History of Medical Psychology* (New York: Norton, 1941), p. 62 f. It is worth noticing that Asclepiades, in order to cure patients suffering of emotional disturbances, prescribed harmonious music, a method which will be adopted by medicine up to modern times. On this topic, see R. Francheville, "Une thérapeutique musicale dans la vieille médecine," *Pro Medico*, 4 (1927), pp. 243–48.

68. *On the Nature of Things*, bk. IV, ll. 865–76. See also the introduction by C. Bailey.

69. See the closing section of bk. IV in *On the Nature of Things*.

70. Brooks Otis, *Ovid as an Epic Poet* (Cambridge: Cambridge University Press, 1966), p. 265 writes: "Euripides and, more directly, Euphorion and the New Poets, had fixed the symptoms, defined the status, of amatory passion. It comes in an instant without warning in full force and fury; it overmasters every other interest or emotion; balked of continued fulfillment, it leads only to death and catastrophe. . . . *Amor* is an external, impersonal force (a kind of disease) that prostrates its victims."

71. Trans. Rolfe Humphries (Bloomington and London: Indiana University Press, 1967), bk. III, ll. 329–99.

72. Ll. 486–503.

73. See M. Spanneut, *Le stoïcisme des Pères de l'Église*, p. 232 f.

74. Clement of Alexandria, *Stromata*, bk. IV, ch. 3 (*P. G.*, vol. VIII, 9). Unless otherwise stated, all the works of the fathers have been consulted in the *Patrologiae cursus completus*, ed. by J. P. Migne, and henceforth indicated with the abbreviations *P. G.* (*Patrologia Graeca*) and *P. L.* (*Patrologia Latina*).

75. Clement of Alexandria, *Stromata*, bk. IV, ch. 9, 4, *P. G.*, vol. VIII, 9.

76. See *Paedagogus*, trans. Simon P. Wood, bk. III, 1–2 (Washington D.C.: Catholic University of America Press, 1954), pp. 511–12: "three . . . are the faculties of the soul. That of understanding, which is called rational, which is the interior soul, and guides this visible man, and is, in its turn, guided by another, by God. The irascible, which is something ferine, and is close to madness. The appetitive, is multiform and is the third one, varied more that the sea-god Proteus, taking now one form now another, it lures to adultery, voluptuousness, weakness."

77. These spiritual powers carry the soul images which deceive and weaken it, thus darkening the light of reason: *Stromata*, bk. II, ch. 20, *P. G.*, vol. VIII, 9, p. 1051.

78. Ibid.

79. Ibid.

80. Ibid.

81. See S. Angus, *The Religious Quest of the Graeco-Roman World* (New York: Scribner, 1929), esp. p. 414, and also R. Simboli, *Disease-Spirits and Divine Cures among the Greeks and Romans* (Diss. , New York, 1921).

82. See, e.g., Origen, *Contra Celsum*, ed. H. Chadwick, bk. III, 54 (Cambridge: Cambridge University Press, 1953), pp. 165–66, and cf. S. Angus, *The Religious Quests of the Graeco-Roman World*, pp. 414–24.

83. See his *Liber de anima*, *P. L.*, vol. II, p. 650: "I have also studied that science which is sister to philosophy, that is to say medicine, which claims for itself a special competence concerning the doctrine of the soul because of its ability to heal the body." His medical doctrines, as he tells us in the same book (*P. L.*, vol. II, p. 655), are derived mainly from Soranus of Ephesus.

84. *Liber de anima*, *P. L.*, vol. II, p. 653.

85. St. Basil, *Epistola* XLVI, *P. G.*, vol. XXXII, 4, p. 370.

86. St. Basil, *Homilia* XXI, *P. G.*, vol. XXX, 3, p. 547. See also his *Constitutiones monasticae*, ch. 3, *P. G.*, vol. XXXI, 3, pp. 1344–45.

87. See F. Cavallera, "Le 'De Virginitate' de Basile d'Ancyre," *Revue d'Histoire Ecclesiastique*, VI (1905), pp. 5–14. See also R. Janin, *Dictionnaire d'histoire et de géographie ecclesiastique*, ed. Alfred Baudrillard (Paris: Letouzey et Ané, 1912 ff.), s.v. "Basile d'Ancyre"; J. Quasten, *Patrology* (Westminster, Md: Newman Press, 1950), vol. III, pp. 201–2.

88. *De virginitate* (falsely attributed to), St. Basil of Ceasarea, *Opera omnia* (Paris, 1547), vol. II, p. 133^V. For the original Greek text, see *P. G.*, vol. XXX, p. 696 ff.

89. *De virginitate*, p. 147^V: "hepar sive iecur concupiscentiae organum est."

90. Ibid., p. 131^V.

91. Ibid., p. 142^r.

92. Ibid., p. 141^V.

93. The treatise, written near the end of the fourth century and unaninously attributed to Gregory of Nyssa enjoyed great popularity during the Middle Ages. The first Latin translation, used by Albert the Great, was prepared by Alfanus of Salerno (d. 1085). A second version, prepared by Burgundione of Pisa (d. 1194) was used by Petrus Lombardus and St. Thomas Aquinas. The treatise has been edited in English translation by W. Telfer, *Cyril of Jerusalem and Nemesius of Emesa* (London: CCM Press, 1955), with an excellent introduction. See also J. Quasten, *Patrology*, vol. III, pp. 351–55.
94. *Cyril of Jerusalem and Nemesius of Emesa*, p. 240.
95. Ibid., p. 242. Cf. p. 1.
96. Ibid., pp. 273–74.
97. Passion, explains Nemesius, p. 349 "is a movement of the faculty of appetite upon perceiving an image or something good or bad." And, "temperament is not antagonistic to bodily lusts, but rather furthers them, for it is temperament itself that produces them. But the soul opposes them."
98. *Cyril of Jerusalem and Nemesius of Emesa*, p. 302: "Some things are proper to the body, some to the soul, and some are the property of both in common. Among the things common to both, and although they operate through organs, we placed the senses, while we said that the organs themselves belong to the body."
99. Ibid., p. 348.
100. Ibid., p. 373: "The soft nerves of sensation descend from the middle part and from the front lobes of the brain."
101. Ibid., p. 385.
102. Ibid., p. 416.

III.   Erotic Melancholy and Medieval Medicine

1. The text has been edited by I. Raeder, *Oribasii Synopsis ad Eustathium* (Leipzig: Teubner, 1926; rpt. Amsterdam: A. M. Hakkert, 1964).
2. Oribasius, *Synopsis*, bk. VIII, ch. 9, pp. 249–50. The treatise of Oribasius is extant in a tenth century Latin MS Laon no. 424, in which the Greek ἔρως is translated as *ton heroton*; John Livingston Lowes, "The Loveres Maladye of Hereos," p. 519, believes that the medieval word for erotic melancholy, *hereos*, derives from this barbarism (see also McVaugh, introduction to Arnald of Villanova's *De amore heroico*, pp. 14–15). The oldest Latin translation of Oribasius, Latin 10233, calls the disease *amor*, and other contemporary writers call it by its Greek name. For example Caelius Aurelianus (second century A.D.), in his *Chronion*, in *Medici antiqui omnes*, bk. I, ch. 5 (Venetiis, 1547), p. 267, writes: "De furore sive insania, quam Graeci manian vocant. Magna Graecorum vetustas manian appellabant, quae nunc mantice dicta est. Item alium, inquit, ex libero fieri patre; alium ex amore, et appellavit heroticon."
3. The first Latin translation of his medical epitome was printed in Venice

in 1553. The original Greek has been edited in the *Corpus medicorum Graecorum* (Leipzig: Teubner, 1921–24), vol. IX, i–ii. Frances Adam has translated into English the entire work, *The Seven Books of Paulus Aegineta*, 3 vols. (London, 1844). The discussion on love, "De amantibus," is in bk. III, ch. 17.

4. Oribasius, *Synopsis*, bk. I, ch. 6, ed. I. Raeder, p. 250. F. Adam, *The Seven Books of Paulus Aegineta*, p. 44.

5. The order of the first ten chapters of bk. III is the following: vertigo, epilepsy, melancholy, mania, incubi, lycanthropy, love, apoplexy, paralysis, spasm.

6. F. Adam, *The Seven Books of Paulus Aegineta*, p. 390.

7. Ibid., p. 391.

8. The debate is in ch. XXXVII. On the side of fasting were Rondelet and Mercado, while Paul of Aegina and Oribasius were against the practice. See the annotations to this chapter, nn. 27, 28.

9. Alexander of Tralles, *Therapeutika*, bk. I, ch. 17, *Oeuvres médicales*, ed. F. Brunet (Paris: Librairie Orientaliste Paul Geuthner, 1937).

10. Galen, *De locis affectis*, ed. Kühn, vol. VI, p. 418.

11. See ch. II, n. 60, above.

12. The work, comprising twenty-five books, was published posthumously by Rhazes's disciples. It was translated for the first time into Latin in 1280 by Faraj ibn Sālim, a Sicilian Jew known as Farraguth.

13. Caelius Aurelianus, *On Acute Diseases and on Chronic Diseases*, ed. I. E. Drabkin (Chicago: University of Chicago Press, 1950), p. 180.

14. *Continens Rasis ordinatus et correctus per clarissimum artium et medicinae doctorem magistrum Hieronymum Surianum* (Venetiis: per Bon. Locatellum, 1505), bk. I, tr. 20, p. 23^{r-v}. Rhazes' expression, "et maesti iacent supra eorum faciem," is a translation of Rufus's καταφῆς, meaning simply that lovers are depressed.

15. In *Opera*, trans. Gerard of Cremona (Lugduni: n.p., 1510), ch. 9.

16. *Liber ad Almansorem decem tractatus continens*, in *Opera*, trans. Gerard of Cremona (Lugduni: n.p., 1510), p. 149. John Livingston Lowes, "The Loveres Maladye of Hereos," pp. 509–10, quotes the comment upon the same chapter by Gerard of Solo, who categorically identifies *amor hereos* with sexual appetite: "Sequitur de tertia specie melancoliae quae amor-ereos dicitur, circa quam passionem quattuor sunt pernotanda. Primo, secundum philosophum vi Ethicorum amor triplex est, quidam est propter bonum domesticum et vocatur amor virtuosus procedens a virtute, ita quod non patiatur secum illicitum. . . . Alter est amor propter bonum utilem, ut inter dominum et servum et communiter non est talis amor; et tertius est amor propter bonum et delectabile, [et] diversificatus [est] secundum fiens: secundum Avicen. iij Canonis nam aliqui in auro, aliqui in divitijs, aliqui in mulieribus est consequens appetitum; et ille amor est triplex: quidam est non multum intensus, et ille vocatur ereos et ille non multum intrat in voluntate, sicut amor qui non intrat multum inter dentes, ut dicitur proverbijs. Alter est amor in mulieribus qui est multum intensus et assiduus circa mulierem principaliter propter actus coitus exercendos, et talis vocatur amorereos, id est amor nobilis a no-

bilitate dictus, quia multum fortis amor, quia milites magis convenerunt habere istam passionem quam alii. Ideo illi sunt coacti qui sunt in delitiis. Et potest sic diffinire: amorereos est amor multum fortis servens et assiduus circa mulierem propter actus coitus exercendos, et talis vocatur amorereos."

17. Haly Abbas, *Liber totius medicinae*, trans. Stephen of Antioch (Lugduni: typis J. Myt., 1523), tr. 9, chs. 7 and 25. The work was translated into Latin in 1080 by Constantinus Africanus and in 1127 by Stephen of Antioch. We have used this latter translation, published in Lyons in 1523.

18. Haly Abbas, *Liber totius medicinae*, tr. 9, ch. 7.

19. The thesis, first postulated by Theophrastus in a work on melancholy now lost, was incorporated in the *Problemata physica* attributed throughout antiquity and up to recent times to Aristotle, and translated into Arabic under the title *Kitāb Mā bāl*. See Manfred Ullmann, *Islamic Medicine* (Edinburgh: Edinburgh University Press, 1978), p. 78 f.

20. See M. Ullmann, *Islamic Medicine*, pp. 72–79, whose account we follow.

21. Ibid., pp. 77–78.

22. Theophrastus, frag. 87–88, *Opera quae supersunt*, ed. F. Wimmer (Paris: Firmin-Didot et Socii, 1931), p. 436. Caelius Aurelianus, *On Acute Diseases*, bk. I, ch. 5, p. 180: "Asclepiades secundo libro adhibendam praecepit cantilenam." See also n. 76, ch. 2, above.

23. The *Canon*, translated in its entirety by Gerard of Cremona between 1150 and 1187, was later translated eighty-seven more times. Avicenna also wrote a philosophical treatise on love, entitled *Risalah fi'l ishq*, probably unknown to the Latin West. The original Arabic, with an English translation, has been edited by Emil Fackenheim, "A Treatise on Love by IBN SINA," *Medieval Studies*, 7 (1945), pp. 208–28.

24. We are following the text by Gerard of Cremona, *Avicennae medicorum Arabum principis, Liber canonis . . . a Gerardo Carmonensi ex Arabico sermone in Latinum conversus* (Basileae, 1556), bk. I, fen 7, tr. 5, chs. 23–24. All following references, unless otherwise stated, derive from this edition.

25. Constantinus Africanus is unanimously considered to be the one who brought Arabic medicine to the Latin West. Petrus Diaconus, his earliest biographer, writes that Constantinus was born in Carthage, and that during his youth he traveled to Syria, India, Ethiopia, and Egypt, where he became versed in Hebrew, Syriac, Chaldean, Greek, Latin, Ethiopian, and Indian. At the age of forty he went to Salerno, where he became the secretary of Duke Guiscard, and soon after professor of medicine in the School of Salerno. He later converted to Christianity and joined the Monastery of Monte Cassino, dedicating his remaining years to the translation of Arabic medical works into Latin. He died in 1087. His translations include part of the *al-Kitāb al-Mālikī* of Haly Abbas under the title *Pantegni*, the *Liber de urina*, *Liber febrium*, and the *Aphorisms* of Hippocrates together with Galen's commentary. He also wrote medical treatises of his own.

26. The Greek translation has been edited by C. Daremberg and E. Ruelle, *Oeuvres de Rufus d'Ephèse* (Amsterdam: Adolf Hakkert, 1963), app., sec. IV, pp. 582–84.

27. Much has been written on this point. For a summary of the problem, see M. McVaugh's introduction to Arnald of Villanova's *De amore heroico*, pp. 14–15.

28. *Breviarium Constantini dictum Viaticum* (Lugduni: n.p., 1510), bk. I, ch. 20, p. 12^{r-v}.

29. *Tacuini aegritudinum* (Argenturati: apud Jo. Schottum, 1532), can. XVI, p. 23.

30. The section on surgery was translated into Latin by Gerard of Cremona, and it became the main source for the earliest Italian writers on surgery, Lanfranco and Guglielmo of Saliceto. Guglielmo of Saliceto also included a chapter on *hereos* in his *Cyrurgia* (ca. 1275), modeled on Avicenna and especially on Albucasis.

31. Albucasis suggests travel as a possible palliative, a cure already suggested by Asclepiades and by Plotinus. See Porphyrius, *Life of Plotinus*, in *The Ethical Treatises*, trans. Stephen MacKenna (London: P. L. Warner, 1917), ch. 11.

32. On medieval Christian medicine, see F. Wüstenfeld, *Die Übersetzungen Arabisher Werke in das Lateinische XI Jahrhundert* (Göttingen: Abhandlungen der Königlichen Gesellschaft der Wissanschaften 24 Göttingen, 1877); T. C. Allbutt, *Science and Medieval Thought* (London: C. J. Clay and Sons, 1901); Loren Carey MacKinney, *Early Medieval Medicine with Special Reference to France and Chartres* (Baltimore: Johns Hopkins University Press, 1937).

   Translations of medical works into Latin must have already existed because Cassiodorus in his *Institutiones divinarum et humanarum litterarum*, ed. R. A. B. Mynors (Oxford: Clarendon, 1937), Lect. I, ch. 3 writes: "Read Hippocrates and Galen in Latin translation."

33. Isidore of Seville, *The Medical Writings*, ed. W. D. Sharpe (Philadelphia: American Philosophical Society, 1964).

34. See A. Castiglioni, *A History of Medicine*, trans. E. B. Krumbhaar (New York: Knopf, 1941), p. 297.

35. St. Crispo, *Commentarium medicinale*, ed. Angelo Main in *Classici auctores e Vaticanis codicibus editi* (Rome: Tipografia Vaticana, 1833).

36. The *De observatione ciborum epistola* was ed. by V. Rose (Leipzig: Teubner, 1870).

37. See A. Castiglioni, *A History of Medicine*, p. 293.

38. On Alcuin and the Scholastic reform in the Carolingian period, see the brief Introduction by R. S. Hoyt, *Europe in the Middle Ages* (New York: Harcourt, Brace, 1954), pp. 145–50. See also A. Castiglioni, *A History of Medicine*, p. 295.

39. The fundamental work on the School of Salerno is by Salvatore De Renzi, *Collectio Salernitana*, 5 vols. (Naples: tipografia Filiatre-Sebezio, 1852–59), followed by those by P. Giacosa, *Magistri Salernitani nondum editi* (Turin: Fratelli Bocca, 1901), and P. Capparoni, "Magistri Salernitani nondum cogniti," in *A Contribution to the History of the Medical School of Salerno* (London: J. Bale & Co., 1923). On the problem of the origin of the school, see among others, G. W. Corner, "The Rise of Medicine at Salerno in the Twelfth Century," *Annals of the History of Medicine*, 3 (1931); C. and

D. Singer, "The Origin of the Medical School of Salerno," *Essays on the History of Medicine* (Zurich: Landschlacht K. Hönn, 1924); P. O. Kristeller, "The School of Salerno, Its Development and Its Contribution to the History of Learning," *Bulletin of the History of Medicine*, 17 (1945); A. Castiglioni, *A History of Medicine*, pp. 299–322.

40. Donald Campbell, *Arabian Medicine and Its Influence on the Middle Ages* (London: Kegan Paul, 1926), vol. I, p. 24, writes: "Even after the two Gerards [Gherardo of Cremona and Gherardo of Sabbionetta] who worked at Toledo had produced their more accurate and fully credited translations of the Arabic works, the versions of Constantine continued to be read as authoritative and standard works."

41. Toledo was reconquered by the Christian forces of King Alphonse of Castille in 1085, and the "Society of Translators" was founded there in ca. 1130.

42. On the *Studium* of Bologna, see A. Sorbelli, *Storia dell'Università di Bologna* (Bologna: Zanichelli, 1944). On the origin and development of the universities in Europe, consult H. Rashdal, *The Universities of Europe in the Middle Ages* (Oxford: Clarendon Press, 1895; new ed. 1936), and Stephen d'Irsay, *Histoire des universités françaises et étrangères des origines à nos jours* (Paris: A. Picard, 1933–35).

43. See Arnald of Villanova, *De amore heroico*, p. 43, and M. McVaugh's introduction, p. 12.

44. See M. McVaugh's introduction to Arnald of Villanova's *De amore heroico*.

45. *De communibus medico cognitu locis*, in *Opera* (Basileae: apud Henricum Petrum, 1539), ch. 38, p. 142.

46. See Mary Wack, *Memory and Love in Chaucer's "Troilus and Criseyde,"* and M. McVaugh, introduction to Arnald of Villanova's *De amore heroico*, p. 21 ff. The English translation of Gerard of Berry's commentary on the *Viaticum* is from M. McVaugh's Introduction, pp. 22–23.

47. M. McVaugh, introduction, p. 23.

48. See, e.g., D. W. Robertson, "The Concept of Courtly Love as an Impediment to the Understanding of Medieval Texts," in *The Meaning of Courtly Love*, ed. F. X. Newman (Albany: State University of New York Press, 1968), pp. 1–18.

49. John F. Benton, "Clio and Venus: An Historical View of Medieval Love" in *The Meaning of Courtly Love*, ed. F. X. Newman (Albany: State University of New York Press, 1968), p. 31.

50. In Francesco Petrarca, *Opere*, ed. G. Ponte (Milan: Mursia, 1968), p. 541 (our translation).

51. Petrarca, *Secretum*, p. 543 (our translation).

52. Arnald of Villanova, *Liber de parte operativa*, in *Opera omnia* (Basileae: Conrad Waldkirch, 1585), p. 272.

53. Galen in his *De usu partium*, ed. Kühn, vol. IV, pp. 181 f., writes: "quando igitur non modo ejusmodi humores serosi vacuari postulant eoque nos excitant ac pungunt ad se excernendum, verum etiam spiritus multus ac calidus expirari gliscit, incredibilem quendam existimare oportet voluptatis esse excessum."

54. Albert the Great, *De animalibus*, in *Opera omnia*, vol. 29 (Monasterii West-

falorum: in aedibus Aschendorff, 1972–82), XII, i, ch. 1: "complexio enim
... est qualitas compositione in particulis minimis et dividentibus et al-
ternantibus se ad invicem. Ex hoc enim accidit in eis una qualitas quae
complexio vocatur."

55. Galen, *De usu partium*, ed. Kühn, vol. IV, pp. 183–84, explains the generation of semen in the following terms: "causa vero etiam generationis
hujus haec est. Ex hiis vasis [arteriae et venae ovaricae], quae ad ma-
trices accedunt (quae ad latera ipsarum distribui diximus), quae pars
fertur deorsum, involvitur modo per simili iis vasis [arteriae et venae
spertaricae internae], quae in testiculos masculorum perveniunt. Vena
enim superjacet, subjacet autem arteria, utraque flexus multos numero
aequales efficient instar capreolorum quorundam varie implexorum; quo
implexu sanguis et spiritus, qui ad testes feruntur, dintissime coquun-
tur; clareque cervas humorem, qui in primis flexibus habetur, adhuc
sanguinem, in sequentibus deinceps magis magisque albescere, quoad
in omnium postremis totus albus omnino fuerit redditus; qui flexus
postremi in testes terminantur. Testes vero, quum sint laxi ac caver-
nosi, humorem, qui in vasis coeperat concoqui, excipientes et ipsi rur-
sum percoquunt, perfectius quidem ad foetus procreationem masculorum testes."

56. Blood, in fact, is a by-product of digestion and therefore of food. See
Galen, *De usu partium*, ed. Kühn, vol. III, p. 267 f. See also Bernard of
Gordon, *Lilium medicinae* (Lugduni: apud G. Rovillium, 1574), p. 217,
and L. Babb, *The Elizabethan Malady* (1951; rpt. East Lansing: Michigan
State University Press, 1965), p. 128 f.

57. Danielle Jacquart and Claude Thomasset, "L'amour 'héroïque' à travers
le traité d'Arnaud de Villeneuve," in *La folie et le corps*, ed. Jean Céard
(Paris: Presses de L'Ecole Normale Supérieure, 1985), p. 152.

58. Bernard of Gordon, *Lilium medicinae*, p. 217.

59. Ibid., p. 216. Thus there must be a certain *similitudo* between subject
and object: Albert the Great, *De anima*, in *Opera omnia*, I, ii, ch. 14:
"Adhuc autem nihil appetit et quaerit nisi quod est sibi simile: et nihil
movetur ad aliquid, ut dicit Boetius, nisi per quod est simile illi," and
St. Thomas Aquinas, *Summa theologica*, in *Opera Omnia*, ed. Stanislaus
Fretté (Paris: apud Lodovium Vivès, 1871–80), II, i, ques. 27, art. 1:
"amor importat quamdam connaturalitatem vel complacentiam amantis
ad amatum: unicuique autem est bonum id quod est sibi connaturale
et proportionatum." See also *Summa theologica*, II, i, ques. 32, art. 7
(*conclusio*) and J. E. Shaw, *G. Cavalcanti's Theory of Love, the Canzone
d'Amore and Other Related Problems* (Toronto: Toronto University Press,
1949), p. 48.

60. Albucasis, *Liber theoricae necnon practicae Alsaharavii* (Venetiis: Augustus
Vindicianus, 1519), tr. I, sec. ii, cap. 17.

61. Dino del Garbo, *Scriptum super cantilena Guidonis de Cavalcantibus*, ed.
G. Favati, in *Rime di Guido Cavalcanti* (Milan: Marzorati, 1957).

62. Arnald of Villanova, *De amore heroico*, ed. M. McVaugh, p. 46.

63. St. Thomas Aquinas in the *Summa theologica*, II, ques. 27, art. 1, writes:
"ad tertium dicendum, quod spes causat vel auget amorem, et hoc ra-

tione delectationis, quia delectationem causat; et etiam ratione desiderii, quia spes desiderium fortificat. Non enim ita intense desideramus quae non speramus; sed tamen ipsa spes est alicujus boni amati."

64. Bernard of Gordon, *Lilium medicinae*, p. 216.

65. See, e.g., Bernard of Gordon, *Lilium medicinae*, p. 216: "causa huius passionis est corruptio aestimativae," and cf. Arnald of Villanova, *De amore heroico*, p. 48.

66. The evolution of the doctrine of the internal senses has been carefully traced by H. A. Wolfson, "The Internal Senses in Latin, Arabic, and Hebrew Philosophic Texts," *Harvard Theological Review*, XXVII, 2 (April 1935), pp. 69–133. See also G. Agamben, *Stanze*, pp. 91–92.

67. Giacomo da Lentini, *Rime*, ed. C. Antonelli (Rome: Bulzoni, 1979), p. 288.

68. The text, from Averroes's commentary on Aristotle's *De sensu et sensibilibus*, is quoted by G. Agamben, *Stanze*, pp. 94–95.

69. G. Agamben, *Stanze*, p. 95.

70. Arnald of Villanova, *De amore heroico*, pp. 46–47 (our translation).

71. Ibid., pp. 48–49: "cum igitur quasi ad imperium estimative cetere inclinentur virtutes, patet quod . . . scilicet rationis imperium sensibilium virtutem delusionibus subiugatur erroneis, cum decretum estimationis sustineat nec informet."

72. Arnald of Villanova, *De amore heroico*, p. 49: "causa vero propter quam estimativa virtus in opere vel iudicio suo claudicat sic et errat necessario sumenda videtur ex parte instrumentorum quibus dicta virtus suas perficit actiones, medie scilicet concavitatis cerebri et spirituum receptorum in ea. Virtutes enim non senescunt nec vitium in operibus patiuntur sui ratione sed organi, receptis spiritis vel etiam apparentis."

73. We are presenting the account found in Vincent of Beauvais (ca. 1190–1264), *Speculum doctrinale* (Graz: Akademische Druck-U. Verlagsanstalt, 1964–65), bk. XIII, ch. 48, pp. 1200–1. Vincent of Beauvais's *Speculum maius*, of which the *doctrinale* constitutes the second of three parts, was one of the most circulated and most influencial encyclopedias of the later Middle Ages.

74. *Avicenna Latinus, Liber de anima seu sextus naturalibus, De anima*, ed. S. van Riet (Louvain-Leiden: E. J. Brill, 1968–72).

75. Arnald of Villanova, *De amore heroico*, pp. 49–50.

76. Ibid., p. 50.

77. See, e.g., Bernard of Gordon, *Lilium medicinae*, pp. 217–18; Arnald of Villanova, *De amore heroico*, pp. 51 ff.; Giovanni Michele Savonarola, *Practica major* (Venetiis: apud Juntas, 1549), tr. VI, ch. 1, rub. 14: "*De ilisci*," p. 66^V.

IV.   Eros and the Occult in Renaissance Medical Thought

1. "From Mental Faculties to Magical Philters: The Entry of Magic into Academic Medical Writing on Lovesickness, 13th–17th Centuries," in *Eros and Anteros: The Medical Traditions of Love in Renaissance Culture*,

eds. Donald Beecher and Massimo Ciavolella (Montreal: McGill-Queen's University Press, forthcoming).

2. For further information on the major treatises on demonology and their intellectual contexts, see *The Damned Art: Essays in the Literature of Witchcraft*, ed. Sydney Anglo (London: Routledge and Kegan Paul, 1977). See also Wayne Schumaker, *The Occult Sciences in the Renaissance: A Study in Intellectual Patterns* (Berkeley: University of California Press, 1972), esp. ch. 2.

3. G. Rattray Taylor, *Sex in History* (New York: The Vanguard Press, 1954), p. 109.

4. *The Malleus maleficarum*, trans. Montague Summers (London: John Rodker, 1928; New York: Dover Publications, 1971), p. 50.

5. *The Malleus maleficarum*, p. 51.

6. Hildegard of Bingen, in *Causae et curae*, ed. P. Kaiser (Leipzig: Teubner, 1903), bk. II, "De Adae casu et melancolia," p. 143, declares that the *humor melancolicus* is produced from the *flatu serpentis e suggestione diaboli*, inherited by man through Adam's sin.

7. *The Malleus maleficarum*, p. 170.

8. *Tractatus de hereticis, et sortilegiis* (Lugduni: apud Jacobum Giuncti, 1536).

9. For a balanced assessment of this work, see Christopher Baxter, "Jean Bodin's, De la démonomanie des sorciers: the Logic of Persecution," in *The Damned Art*, ed. Sydney Anglo, pp. 76–105.

10. Stuart Clark, "The Scientific Status of Demonology," in *Occult and Scientific Mentalities in the Renaissance*, ed. Brian Vickers (Cambridge: Cambridge University Press, 1984), p. 352. John Cotta was the author of the *Triall of Witch-Craft*, published in London in 1616.

11. Mary Wack, "From Mental Faculties to Magical Philters," in *Eros and Anteros* (forthcoming).

12. Jason Pratensis, *De cerebri morbis* (Basileae: per Henrichum Petri, 1549), p. 213.

13. Lynn Thorndike, *A History of Magic and Experimental Science* (New York: Columbia University Press, 1941), vol. V, p. 486. Another observer who attempted to credit demonism in empirical terms was Loys le Caron (Charondas), *Questions divers et discours* (Paris: n.p., 1579), esp. ques. 7, "Si par incantations, parolles ou autres semblables sortileges l'homme peult estre ensorcelé et offensé en ses actions et forces naturelles," pp. 31ᵛ–43ᵛ.

14. Pietro Pomponazzi, *De naturalium effectuum admirandorum causis, sive de incantationibus liber* in *Opera* (Basileae: ex officina Henricpetrina, 1567).

15. Francisco Valles, *De iis quae scripta sunt physice in libris sacris* (Lugduni: apud Franciscum Le Fevre, 1588), pp. 226–27. For another writer of this conviction, see Johann Georg Godelmann, *Tractatus de magis, veneficiis et lamiis recte cognoscendis et puniendis* (Francofurti: ex officina typographica Nicolai Bassaei, 1591), esp. bk. I, ch. 8, "De curatoribus morborum hyperphysicorum praestigiosis."

16. "The Devil and Lovesickness According to the Physicians and Demonologists of the Sixteenth Century," in *Eros and Anteros*, eds. Donald Beecher and Massimo Ciavolella (Montreal: McGill-Queens Uni-

versity Press, forthcoming). See also Sydney Anglo, "Melancholia and Witchcraft: the Debate Between Wier, Bodin and Scot," and Jean Céard, "Folie et démonologie au XVIe siècle," both in *Folie et déraison à la Renaissance*, ed. A. Gerlo (Brussels: Editions de l'université de Bruxelles, 1976), pp. 129–47, 209–22.

17. Battista Fregoso, *Anteros, sive tractatus contra amorem* (Milan: Leonardus Pachel, 1496). We consulted this work in the French translation published in 1581 as *L'Anteros ou contramour de Messire Baptiste Fulgoses*.

18. *The Malleus maleficarum*, p. 49.

19. *Commentary on Plato's Symposium on Love*, Speech VII, ch. 4, p. 159. See also Ioan Peter Couliano, *Eros et magie à la Renaissance* (Paris: Flammarion, 1984), pp. 164 ff.

20. (Lugduni: apud Antonium Candidum, 1588).

21. In *Opera Henrici Kornmanni* (Francofurti: apud haeredes Jac. Fischeri, 1629), p. 60.

22. *The Anatomy of Melancholy*, pt. 3, sec. 2, memb. 2, subs. 2, p. 681.

23. See n. 1, above.

24. *Lilium medicinae*, pp. 216–17.

25. Mary F. Wack, "The Measure of Pleasure: Peter of Spain on Men, Women, and Lovesickness," *Viator* 17 (1986), pp. 173–96.

26. Giovanni de Vigo, *La practique et cirurgie . . . nouvellement imprimee et racogneue diligentement sur le latin* (n.p., 1537), bk. IX, ch. 8, "de maleficiatis," p. 319.

V.   Ferrand's Renaissance Sources and Analogues

1. These are the sixteenth-century medical writers who appear in Ferrand's preliminary list in the edition of 1623 entitled "The names and places of those physicians who have dealt with the curing of love of which I have made use": Girolamo Mercuriale, *De morbis muliebribus* (Venetiis: apud Felicem Valgrisium, 1587), Mercuriale does not have a chapter on love, but in bk. IV he relates traditional views on furor uterinus and satyriasis which he calls "pruritus matricis"; Luis Mercado, "De mulierum affectionibus libri quatuor," bk. II, chs. 4 and 10, in *Opera*, vol. III; "De internorum morborum curatione," bk. I, ch. 17, in *Opera*, vol. III (Francofurti: sumptibus haeredum D. Zachoriae Palthenii, 1620); Cristóbal de Vega, *Liber de arte medendi*, bk. III, sec. 1, ch. 17, "De iis qui amore insaniunt," in *Opera* (Lugduni: apud Gulielmum Rovillium, 1576); Petrus Paulus Peredus, *Michaelis Ioannis Paschalis methodum curandi scholia* (Lugduni: sumptibus Iacobi Cardon, 1630; 9th ed.), bk. I, ch. 11, "De iis qui amore insaniunt," p. 44. The chapter in Pereda is closely related to that of Cristóbal de Vega. He mentions the story of Antiochus and Stratonice and the chapter by Paul of Aegina. He describes the symptoms, the hollow eyes, the weeping and generally agitated manner, and the irregular pulse. The principal cures are traditional: absenting oneself from the person causing the commotion, travel, music, games and pastimes; and

he quotes Ovid, as Ferrand will do. Guillaume Rondelet, *Methodus curandorum omnium morborum corporis humani, in tres libris distincta* (Francofurti: apud heredes Andreae Wecheli, 1592). For Liébault, see four notes above. There are several others during this period who mention love melancholy or love mania in their treatises whom we mention here in order to make the list more comprehensive, though by no means complete. Ferrand mentions in passing Amatus Lusitanus (João Rodriguez de Castello Branco, 1511–68), who offers some notable case studies of patients afflicted with "morbus amoris, in his *Curationum medicinalium centuriae quatuor* (Basel, 1556; Venice: apud Balthesarem Constantinum, 1557). Petrus Forestus (Pieter van Foreest, 1522–97) also studies the disease in his bk. X, Obs. 29, "De furore ex vesano amore," and provides three case studies, *Observationum et curationum medicinalium sive medicinae theoricae et practicae libri XXVIII* (Frankfurt: E. Palthenia, 1602). Felix Platter (1536–1614) provides several case studies that demonstrate in more clinically observed terms the behavior of those afflicted with vehement or secretive love in *Observationum in hominis affectibus . . . libri tres* (Basel: impensis Ludovici König, typis Conradi, 1614), esp. pp. 49–54. Ferrand twice cites this work, but in a superficial way. Daniel Sennert (1577–1637) writes a chapter entitled "De amore insano," bk. I, pt. 3, ch. 10, *Practicae medicinae liber primus [sextus]* (Wittenbergae: impensis haeredum Doct. T. Mevii et E. Schuemacheri, 1652–62, but written early in the century), pp. 360–65, in which he discusses the eyes as conductors of the object to the mind, deals with the question of the pulse, and offers a number of literary examples and a list of conventional cures. Johann Schenck von Graffenberg is cited briefly by Ferrand. He discusses erotic melancholy in ch. 25 of his *Observationum medicarum rarum, novarum, admirabilium et monstrosarum* (Friburgi Brisgoiae: ex calcographia Martini Beckleri, 1599). Ferrand seems not to have known the two following published dissertations. Joannes Lamandus, *Theses medicae de natura amoris et amantium amentium cura* (Basileae: typis J. J. Genathi, 1614), thirty-six theses covering conventional points but with certain variations such as recommending castration as the ultimate cure. Gregor Horst published, while a professor at Giessen, his *Dissertatio de natura amoris, additis resolutionibus quaestionum candidatorum de cura furoris amatorii, de philtris, atque de pulsu amantium* (Giessen: typis et sumptibus Casparis Chemlini, 1611).

Barthélemy Pardoux (Bartholomaeus Perdulcis, 1545–1611) wrote on uterine fury and *amor insanus* in his *De morbis animi liber*, a sixteenth-century work that, nevertheless, may not have been published during Pardoux's lifetime (Parisiis: L. Bollenger, 1639) and in *Universa medicina. Ed. postrema.* (Lugduni: sumptibus Jacobi Carteron, 1649). Pardoux is a Parisian Galenist who endorsed the view of love as a delirium caused by the drying of the brain and also as a condition having its seat simultaneously in the liver, the center of the animal appetites. He deals with theories of the imagination and allows that the disease is spread corporeally through the circulation of crude adust blood. His regimen of cures and methodic treatments is Galenic in orientation and resembles that of Ferrand.

Finally, it is instructive to compare the range of Ferrand's citation of professional contemporaries with the list of the "many grave and worthy men" who wrote on love that appears in the Preface to Burton's section on love melancholy in the *Anatomy*, pt. 3, sec. 1, memb. 1, subs. 1, p. 612. To be sure, he mentions many of Ferrand's declared sources, but adds certain others apparently unknown to Ferrand. Burton, it would seem, was able to build up his treatise from a number of independent sources, and the fact that his design, premises, and conclusions so much resemble Ferrand's is further testimony to the existence of a generic repertoire of literature that had grown up around the *topos* throughout the sixteenth century. Among the principal were Petrus Godefridus in his *Dialogus de amoribus, tribus libris distinctus* (Antverpiae: apud G. Ludium [1551]); Filoteo Eliano de Montalto, known to Burton as Aelianus Montaltus, in his *Archipathologia, in qua internarum capitis affectionum essentia, causae, signa, praesagia et curatio . . . edisseruntur* (Lutetiae: apud F. Jacquin, sumptibus Caldorianae societatis, 1614); Jason van der Velde, whom Burton calls Jason Pratensis, in his *De cerebri morbis* (Basileae: per Henrichum Petri, 1549); Ercole Sassonia or Hercules of Saxonia in his *De melancholia tractatus perfectissimus* (Venetiis: apud Alexandrum Polum, 1620) a work included in his *Opera practica* (Patavii: ex typographia Matthaei de Cardorinis, 1658); Giovanni Michele Savonarola in his "De cerebri et capitus morbis," in *Practica major* (Venetiis: apud Vicentium Valgrisium, 1560; princeps 1479); and Heinrich Kornmann in his *Linea amoris, sive commentarius in versiculum glossae visus* (Francofurti: typis M. Beckeri, 1610). These various works on love, melancholy diseases, and the diseases of the head were at the center of Burton's knowledge of the subject and, hence, fully complement Ferrand's extensive list.

2. For a more detailed examination of the commentaries on "Donna me prega" see Marie-Madeleine Fontaine, "La lignée des commentaires à la chanson de Guido Cavalcanti *Donna me prega*: Evolution des relations entre philosophie, médecine et littérature dans le débat sur la nature d'amour (de la fin du XIIIe siècle à celle du XVIe)," *La folie et le corps*, pp. 159–78.

3. The following statement is an indicator of an important movement in the history of ideas; namely, the popularization of Ficino's ideas on love in France in the sixteenth century. "L'oeuvre de Tyard représente, en résumé, une sorte de laboratoire idéal où s'opère devant nos yeux la transformation des néo-platonismes, et plus particulièrement de l'apport de Ficin et de celui Léon l'Hébreu, dans la vision d'un poete et philosophe du XVIe siècle français." Eva Kushner, "Pontus de Tyard entre Ficin et Léon l'Hébreu," *Ficino and Renaissance Neoplatonism*, ed. Konrad Eisenbichler and Olga Zorzi Pugliese (Ottawa: Dovehouse Editions, 1986), p. 50. Of the medical writers on love, the first who has come to our attention to use Ficino is François Valleriola in his *Observationum medicinalium libri VI*, bk. II, obs. 7 (Lugduni: apud Antonium Candidum, 1588), who will be considered in detail in subsequent pages of this chapter. This is not to suggest that Ficino's ideas on the physiology of erotic love were not known in France at an earlier date in texts other than those written

by Galenic physicians. Witness the following passage from Pierre Boaistuau's *Le théatre du monde* (1558), ed. Michel Simonin (Geneva: Librairie Droz, 1981), pp. 214–15, derived from Speech VII of Ficino's *Commentary on Plato's Symposium*: "Autres philosophes ont dit, que nous venons à jetter nostre veuë sur la chose que nous desirons, soudain quelques esprits, lesquels sont engendrez de la plus subtile et parfaicte partie du sang, partent du cueur de la chose que nous aymons, et montent jusques aux yeulx, et puis après s'eslancent en vapeurs invisibles, et entrent en noz yeulx, lesquels sont disposez à les recevoir, tout ainsi qu'il demeure quelque tache sur un miroir après y avoir regardé, et puis de là penetrent jusques au cueur, et petit à petit se dilatent par tout."

4. For a brief yet informative account of the Italian treatises on love, see Mario Pozzi's introduction to *Trattati d'amore del Cinquecento* (rpt. Roma-Bari: Laterza, 1975), pp. vi-lix. See also John Charles Nelson, *Renaissance Theory of Love: The Context of Giordano Bruno's "Eroici furori"* (New York and London: Columbia University Press, 1955, 1963). Pietro Bembo's *Asolani* has been edited by C. Dionisotti in *Prose e rime* (Turin: Einaudi, 2d. ed., 1966). Mario Equicola's *Libro de natura de Amore* has not seen a modern edition. It was written in 1495, and the first edition in Italian, the one cited here, was published in Mantua (name of the publisher not given) in 1525. The work was translated into French by Gabriel Chappuys and published in 1584 as *De la nature d'amour, tant humain que divin, et de toutes les differences d'iceluy*. For further information on his importance and his influence, see R. Renier, "Per la cronologia e la composizione del *Libro de natura de Amore*," *Giornale Storico della Letteratura Italiana*, XIV (1889), 402–13; Domenico Santoro, *Della vita e opera di Mario Equicola* (Chieti: Pei tipi di N. Jecco, 1906); S. C. Vial, "M. Equicola in the Opinion of his Contemporaries," *Italica*, XXXIV (1957), pp. 202–21; S. C. Vial, "Equicola and the School of Lyons," *Comparative Literature* (1960), pp. 19–23; Domenico de Robertis, "La composizione del *De natura de Amore* e i canzonieri antichi maneggiati da M. Equicola," *Studi di Filologia Italiana*, XVII (1959), pp. 182–220. On the relationship between Petrarchism and Renaissance love treatises, see G. Toffanin, "Petrarchismo e trattati d'amore," *Nuova Antologia* (March 1925), pp. 30–51, and L. Baldacci, *Il petrarchismo italiano nel Cinquecento* (Milan-Naples: Ricciardi, 1957).

5. Included in the edition of Fregoso cited above is the dialogue by Battista Platina (Bartolomeo Secchi of Cremona), *Dialogue contre les folles amours*, trans. Thomas Sibelet in *Contramours, L'antéros ou contramour de Messire Baptiste Fulgose, jadis duc de Gennes* (Paris: Chez Martin le Jeune, 1581). The work by Platina was first published in Venice in 1504, the second of four dialogues. See *Traicté de l'essence et guerison de l'amour*, p. 157.

6. Aneas Sylvius Piccolomini (Pius II), *Le remède d'amour, translaté de latin en françoys par maistre Albin des Avenelles, avec les additions de Baptiste Mantuan* (Paris, n.p., 1556).

7. For an excellent treatment of the medical component in Andreas Capellanus' treatise, see Mary F. Wack, "Imagination, Medicine, and Rhetoric in Andreas Capellanus' 'De amore'," *Robert Earl Kaske* (New York: Ford-

ham University Press, 1956), pp. 101–15.

8. André Du Laurens, "Des maladies melancholiques et du moyen de les guarir," p. 34^v.

9. For a résumé of the interest in this topic in Montpellier, see Michael R. McVaugh's introduction to the *De amore heroico*, p. 37. Proof of continuing interest in the topic after the era of Du Laurens is suggested by the title of a dissertation by Charles Delorme, *An amantes iisdem remediis curentur quibus amentes?* (Montpellier, 1608).

10. Bernard of Gordon, *Lilium medicinae*, p. 217 f.

11. Jean de Veyries, *La geneaogie de l'amour divisée en deux livres* (Paris: Chez Abel l'Angelier, 1609).

12. Aubery matriculated in March 1590 and received his doctorate in the spring of 1593. He became physician to the Duke de Montpensier and practiced in Paris. His last publication is dated 1605. One sees in his book a manifestation of interest in the topic arising either with his studies in Montpellier or his contacts with Du Laurens. Louis Dulieu, *La médecine à Montpellier*, vol. II, *La Renaissance* (Avignon: Les presses universelles, 1979), p. 361.

VI. Ferrand's Definitions and Diagnostics of Erotic Melancholy and Erotic Mania

1. Cicero, *Tusculan Disputations*, IV, xxxv, trans. J. E. King (Loeb, 1950), p. 413.

2. Ibid., p. 415.

3. Anthony Levi, S. J., *French Moralists: The Theory of the Passions 1585 to 1649* (Oxford: Clarendon Press, 1964), p. 236.

4. Juan Huarte, *Examen de ingenios para las ciencias* (Baeza: n.p., 1575).

5. Ferrand makes no mention of that form of melancholy that characterizes philosophers and poets. Incessant thinking was believed to have the ability to bring about material alterations within the brain. The natural condition conducive to creating men of deep thought was a form of mixed melancholy more dry than moist, but with a little blood, and without excrements in the brain. This combination produced men with clear memories and deep thoughts, men capable of long hours of meditation or of divine rapture befitting poets, philosophers, and prophets. One of the more interesting discussions from the period on the melancholy of genius is to be found in Jourdain Guibelet's, *Trois discours philosophiques*, Discourse III, "De l'humeur mélancholique" (Evereux: Chez A. Le Marié, 1603). The principal source on scholar's melancholy, however, is Marsilio Ficino's *De vita libri tres*, written ca. 1480.

6. Lawrence Babb, *The Elizabethan Malady*, p. 36.

7. The difference between mania and melancholy and the confusion of the two among the ancients remained a much debated topic in the Renaissance. Forestus points out the difficulty in Galen and Alexander of Tralles and attempts to establish a clear set of distinctions according to

symptoms: "Sed nos loquimur nunc de vera insania et proprie dicta; quae differt a melancholia, quod sine metu et tristitia accidat, sed cum audacia, multiloquio, saltu, agitatione corporis immoderata, oculorum frequenti motu, cum aspectu torvo, intrepido et inverecundo." He goes on to characterize melancholy and phrenitis. Pieter van Foreest, *Observationum et curationum medicinalium sive medicinae theoricae et practicae, libri XXVIII* (Francofurti: E. Palthenia, 1602), pp. 341–42.

8. Avicenna, *Canon* (*Liber Canonis*), fen I, bk. 3, tr. 4, ch. 18.

9. Lawrence Babb, *Elizabethan Malady*, p. 65.

10. For a summary of the Renaissance views on the vital spirits, their creation, and their roles in the body, see Andrew Wear, "Galen in the Renaissance," *Galen: Problems and Prospects*, pp. 229–56.

11. François Valleriola, *Observationum medicinalium libri, VI*, pp. 198–200.

12. Thomas Wright, *The Passions of the Mind in General*, ed. William Webster Newbold (London, 1601; New York and London: Garland Publishing, 1986), p. 91.

13. At the time of Ferrand the question of whether there existed an "amatory pulse" was much debated. A student of Gregorius Horstius, Cristophorus Bilitzer, graduated with a medical thesis on *De pulso amatorio* (Giessen, 1609). See Oskar Diethelm, *Medical Dissertations*, pp. 157–206, for a list of dissertations, including several on this topic, printed before 1750.

14. For the bibliographical information on this topic see our annotations to ch. XII.

15. Paracelsus (1493–1541) also employed the term *hereos*, but in an entirely idiosyncratic way. *Amor hereos*, for him, begins in the imagination where the image of the fantasized lover is created. That image is the product of a mental perversion that not only preoccupies the mind but leads to a fantasized union and the emission of semen. Hence, by the process of the corrupted imagination, sperm is released that is not only useless for the procreation of children but that attracts the incubi and succubi who carry it away in order to engender more of their race in snakes and toads. *Amor hereos* is that unnatural desire that furnishes the seed necessary for the propagation of these creatures. According to this bizarre theory, Paracelsus provides a common ground between the nightmare that is a function of the fantasy and the nightmare that involves sexual assault by supernatural creatures. Ferrand makes no mention of these ideas in his chapter on the incubus, ideas which would certainly have provoked a reaction had he known them. There is virtually no evidence to suggest that Ferrand was influenced by Paracelsus with regard to the topic of *heroes*; moreover, he expresses grave concerns over the use of metals popular with the chemists and disdain for the local Paracelsan charlatans. For the theory on *hereos*, see *De origine morborum invisibilium* in *Opera omnia* (Genevaei: sumptibus I. Antonii et Samuelis De Tournes, 1658), vol. I, *Opera medica complectens*, p. 126, and John Livingston Lowes, "The Loveres Maladye of Hereos," pp. 533–34.

VII. The Cures for Erotic Mania and Erotic Melancholy

1. For an engaging account of the major developments in the quest for new simples and the growth of experimentation with pharmaceutical preparations in the sixteenth and seventeenth centuries, see Walter H. Lewis and Memory P. F. Lewis, *Medical Botany* (New York: John Wiley & Sons, 1977). Ferrand would have been capable of designing some of his own recipes and he may have been aware of recommendations of the type made by Quercetanus in his *Preparation Spagyrique des Medicamens* and in his *Pharmacie des Dogmatiques* (Paris: Chez Charles F. de C. Morel, 1629, but both written earlier). That is not to say that Ferrand was interested in or influenced by the alchemical schools of pharmacology associated with the name of Paracelsus. He says nothing of the controversy that had already struck the Parisian faculty concerning the new chemistry and the clinical use of metals, though he urges against the use of antimony. For Ferrand, even in the area of pharmacology, Starobinski's truism remains in force, that "les ouvrages médicaux du moyen âge, de la renaissance et de l'âge baroque ne sont, dans leur grande majorité, qu'une studieuse paraphrase de Galien, diversement agrémentée de preuves nouvelles, et enrichie de quelques recettes inédites." *Histoires du traitement de la mélancolie des origines à 1900*, p. 25. For a summary of the fundamental principles of Galenism, see Lester S. King, *The Growth of Medical Thought* (Chicago: University of Chicago Press, 1963), pp. 43–85.

2. Ambroise Paré stated his zeal for the cause in his "De la faculté et vertu des medicamens simples," in which he parallels the nature of medicinal cures with miracles, because the world of simples is witness of the meaningfulness and goodwill toward men manifested in God's creation of nature. Paré marvels at the abundance of plants, animals, and minerals existing on the earth, "a quoy la bonté de ce grand Archetecte se manifeste infiniement de les avoir donnés à l'homme, tant pour son contentement et plaisir, que pour le nourir et medicamenter." *Oeuvres complètes*, ed. J. -F. Malgaigne (Paris: 1840–41; Geneva: Slatkine Reprints, 1970), vol. III, p. 520. Levinus Lemnius, in his *Secret Miracles of Nature*, p. 759, states: "that every man may be the more in love with God that made him, and by a singular way hath brought forth all things for the use and good of mankind, and may admire the skill of nature, that she hath received from God; I thought good to shew, how commodiously and fitly, and with what wholesome operation, all hearbs, whereof some are fit for meat, others for medicine, and some for both, are appointed severally for severall parts of mans body, wherefore this is natural to plants, and they are endued with such a force, that by their inbred faculty they should help some parts, and that leaving other parts they should repair thither, for which they are ordained, and the parts do not onely draw greedily their nutriment, but also such medicaments that are wholesome for them, and they enjoy that."

3. Battista Fregoso, *Contramours*, p. 140. Though the theories concerning sperm as a by-product of digestion and as a distillation of the blood dominated, there were rival theories brought forward from the ancients.

Pythagoras called it the "foam of our best blood," while Plato spoke of it as the marrow of the spinal column, and Alcman before him as the "purest and most delicate part of the brain." Democritus thought of it as being drawn from all parts of the body, while Epicurus taught that it was an elixir of both the body and the soul. Hippocrates believed that it came from the brain and was closely related to the vital spirits. By such definitions the idea of the material soul was encouraged because by means of the seed it could be transmitted at the moment of conception. These definitions also argued against onanism and the dangers of wasting seed; coitus itself becomes enervating by depriving the body of its purest substance. Pierre Darmon, *Le mythe de la procréation à l'âge baroque* (Paris: Editions du Seuil, 1981), p. 12.

4. André Du Laurens, "Des maladies melancholiques et du moyen de les guarirs," p. 35^V.

5. Pietro Pomponazzi, *Les Causes des merveilles de la nature ou les enchantements*, trans. Henri Busson (Paris: Rieder, 1930), pp. 131–35.

6. Brian Vickers, "Analogy versus identity: the rejection of occult symbolism, 1580–1680," *Occult and Scientific Mentalities in the Renaissance*, p. 95.

7. Ferrand does not mention Celsus in conjunction with the methodical remedies, but the views of this Roman encyclopedist in his eight books on medicine favoring such therapy, as opposed to the use of strong drugs, may have helped to maintain their place even in the Galenic milieu. His works were, after all, the first of the classical medical works to be printed: Florence, 1478. For those suffering of melancholy, he recommended travel, music, games, conversation, and exercise; he urged, too, that these persons be removed from the circumstances causing the condition. He advised coddling and praising them as a form of encouragement. At the same time he mentioned shock therapy, chains, punishments, and frights in order to recall them to right behavior. (This kind of therapy will return, for example, in the works of Jacques Dubois (Jacobus Sylvius) of Amiens, *Opera Medica*, Geneva: sumptibus J. Chouët, 1630.) Celsus also advised rubbing oils, mild soporifics, as opposed to opiates and harsh drugs. These methods are preserved in the therapies offered by the Byzantine physicians. Aulus Cornelius Celsus, *De arte medica* in the *Corpus medicorum latinorum, vol. I*, ed. F. Marx (Berlin: Teubner, 1915), esp. bk. III, sec. 18.

8. Hippocrates knew of hellebore and its special properties for the purging of black bile. The black feces which it produces, full of dark blood, gave the impression that black bile was being eliminated from the body. Pliny, bk. XXV, chs. 21, 22, indicates that hellebore was employed with religious care because, before agaric and senna became available, it was the only sovereign specific for purging the corrupting humors. Starobinski recounts the probable mythological and ritualistic practices associated with this plant. *Histoire du traitemtent de la mélancolie des origines à 1900*, pp. 16–17.

9. Starobinski remarks upon the antiquity of the association of pharmaceuticals with the treatment of melancholy. The ancient Greeks recognized in certain drugs the power to tranquilize and to appease anguish:

Homère nous offre une image mythique de la mélancolie où le malheur de l'homme résulte de sa disgrâce devant les dieux, il nous propose aussi l'exemple d'un apaisement pharmaceutique du chagrin, qui ne doit rien à l'intervention des dieux." *Histoire du traitement de la mélancolie des origines à 1900*, p. 12.

10. Ferrand rehearses the procedures for phlebotomy with a clinical interest, citing Galen, Avicenna, Rhazes, Paul of Aegina, Rondelet, Moschion, and Arnald of Villanova, and ends with a warning not to cut such veins as those behind the ears, as the ancient Scythians did, as reported by Herodotus and Hippocrates, because those procedures not only can sterilize the individual but also affect the memory and judgment. Practice held that removal of blood would reduce the production of the offending seed—done by opening the hepatic vein in the right arm, and afterwards the ham vein and the saphena or ankle vein. Jean Starobinski comments upon the psychology of bleeding in *Histoire du traitement de la mélancolie des origines à 1900*, pp. 19 ff.

11. Mary F. Wack, "New Medieval Medical Texts on *Amor Hereos*," *Kongressakten zum Ersten Symposium des Mediävistenverbandes in Tübingen*, 1984, ed. J. O. Fichte et al. (Berlin: Walter de Gruyter, 1984), p. 297.

12. Ibid., p. 296. We are indebted to Prof. Wack for sending her transcription of Rouen A 176 f, Bona Fortuna's *Tractatus super Viaticum*, from which this information was taken.

13. Valesco de Taranta, *Philonium pharmaceuticum et chirurgicum de medendis omnibus, cum internis, cum externis humani corporis affectibus* (Francofurti et Lipsiae: sumptibus Joannis Adami Kastneri, 1680), p. 68.

14. André Du Laurens, "Des maladies melancholiques et du moyen de les guarir," p. 36^r.

15. L. Mercado, *Morborum curatione*, bk. I, ch. 17, in *Opera*, vol. III, pp. 102–8.

16. André Du Laurens, "Des maladies melancholiques et du moyen de les guarir," p. 36^r.

17. A. Rupert Hall gives a brief account of this revolution in pharmaceutical medicine in his outline of the Paracelsian movement which was felt in France through the writings of Joseph Du Chesne (Quercetanus), among others, in *The Revolution of Science 1500–1750*, pp. 80 ff. For a comprehensive summary of the Renaissance debate over the occult properties of drugs, see Ambroise Paré, "De la faculté et vertu de medicamens simples," *Oeuvres Complètes*, ed. J. -F. Malgaigne (Paris, 1840–41; Geneva: Slatkine Reprints, 1970), vol. III, where he describes the four classes of actions and the strain upon the humoral system created by the logistics of drug behavior in empirical terms.

18. Franz G. Alexander, Sheldon T. Selesnick, *The History of Psychiatry* (New York: Harper and Row, 1966), p. 75.

19. During the seventeenth century, the medical profession was divided on the question of antimony. Its use was advocated by Paracelsus many years earlier, and "vin émétique" had become very popular with the apothecaries. But it was a powerful and dangerous drug that had been fatal to many as witnessed by such diverse voices as Molière's and Guy Patin's. Francis R. Packard, *Guy Patin and the Medical Profession in Paris*

in the XVIIth Century (New York, 1924; New York: Augustus M. Kelley, Publishers, 1970), pp. 204–11.

20. Jacques Wecker (Johann Jacob), *Le grande thresor, ou dispensaire et antidotaire*, trans. Ian du Val (Genève: D'Estienne Gamonet, 1616); Joannis Matthei de Gradi, *Praxis in nonum Almansoris: omnibus medicine studiosis apprime necessaria* (Vincentius de Portonariis, de Tridino, de Monteferrato, 1527); Johannes Heurnius, *Methodi ad Praxin*, in *Opera Omnia* (Lugduni: sumptibus Joannis Antonii Huguetan & Marci Antonii Rivaud, 1658).

21. Joseph Du Chesne, *Pharmacie des Dogmatiques*, "Electuaire purgeant la melancholie et bile noire," p. 316; Sirops, "Voicy à peu pres ceux qui digerent l'humeur melancholique," p. 249; "Sirop magistral menalogogue avec sucs," pp. 270, 307.

22. Levinus Lemnius, *The Secret Miracles of Nature: In Four Books* (London, 1658), p. 259.

23. Nicholas Monardes, *Joyfull Newes out of the Newe Found Worlde, Written in Spanish*, trans. John Frampton (London, 1557; New York: AMS Press, 1967), from *Primera y Segunda y Tercera Partes de la Historia Medicinal de los coses que traen de nuestras Indias occidentales que sirven en medicina.*

24. Howard Haggard, in *Devils, Drugs and Doctors: The Story of the Science of Healing from Medicine-man to Doctor* (New York: Halcyon House [1929]), discusses the psychology of healing in former times and the placebo effect in which both doctor and patient are duped by their habits of attributing cures arising from natural causes to useless medications. A. K. Shapiro states, "for thousands of years physicians prescribed what we now know were useless and often dangerous medications. This would not have been possible were it not for the fact that physicians did in some way help their patients. Today we know that the effectiveness of their procedures was due to psychological factors that are often referred to as the placebo effect." "Placebo effects in medicine, psychotherapy, and psychoanalysis," *Handbook of Psychotherapy and Behaviour Change*, ed. A. E. Bergin & S. L. Garfield (New York: John Wiley, 1971), p. 794. See also Donald A. Bakal, *Psychology and Medicine: Psychobiological Dimensions of Health and Illness* (New York: Springer Publishing, 1979), pp. 181–87.

25. There is also the disgust factor: the patient finds himself subjected to laxatives, vomitives, bitter herbs, and forced sleep because of a fixation of the mind upon an object of beauty. Ferrand's program of drugs could also be used in much the same way as Esquirol, in the nineteenth century, used "tartrite antimonie de potasse," namely to cause intestinal upset so that patients would be more convinced of their sickness and thus more willing to follow the cure. See Jean Starobinski, *Histoire du traitement de la mélancolie des origines à 1900*, p. 65.

26. Clearly, the purge had enormous psychological appeal, in keeping with a mechanized view of the body. In the purge there is the sensation of liberating the self from evil ingredients, what Starobinski calls the "rêverie de libération," *Histoire du traitement de la mélancolie des origines à 1900*, p. 44.

VIII.   Ferrand, Sexuality, and Early Psychology

1. Jean-Didier Vincent, *Biologie des Passions* (Paris: Editions Odile Jacob, Seuil, 1986).
2. It is of note that the seventeenth-century term *erotomania* still serves modern analysts. See François Perrier, "De l'érotomanie," *Le désir et la perversion* (Paris: Éditions du Seuil, 1967), pp. 129–62.
3. Jean Starobinski, *Histoire du traitement de la mélancolie des origines à 1900*, p. 9.
4. "In diagnosing depression, a distinction is frequently made between *exogenous* depression and *endogenous* depression. The term *exogenous* (coming from without) *depression* is used to describe depression that results from psychosocial causes, such as a death in the family or the loss of a job. When the onset of a depressive episode is not traceable to a precipitating life experience, it is assumed that the disorder is endogenous (coming from within) and hence biological in origin." Donald A. Bakal, *Psychology and Medicine*, p. 111. Bakal goes on to give parallel lists of symptoms in states of depression arising from these contrasting causes.
5. Pierre Darmon, *Le mythe de la procréation à l'âge baroque*, p. 20.
6. Ibid., pp. 19–20.
7. Ibid., p. 16. The idea of the uterus being like an animal, however, is at least as old as Soranus, who uses these terms in his *Gynecology*, bk. I, ch. 3, trans. Owsei Temkin (Baltimore: Johns Hopkins Press, 1956), p. 9.
8. Galen, ed. Kühn, vol. VIII, p. 418.
9. François Valleriola, *Observationum medicinalium libri VI*, bk. II, obs. 7; pp. 184–219.
10. Oskar Diethelm, "La surexcitation sexuelle," *L'evolution psychiatrique* (1966), pp. 233–45.
11. M. F. Lochner, *De nymphomania* (Altdorf: typis Henrici Meyri, 1684), cited in Diethelm, "La surexcitation sexuelle," pp. 239–40.
12. Jean Liébault, *Trois livres appartenant aux infirmités et maladies des femmes* (Lyon: par Jean Veyrat, 1598), p. 95.
13. Michel Foucault, *Histoire de la sexualité*, vol. II, *L'usage des plaisirs* (Paris: Éditions Gallimard, 1984), p. 53.
14. Pierre de L'Estoile, *Journal pour le règne de Henry IV*, ed. L. R. Lefèvre, 3 vols. (Paris: Éditions Gallimard, 1948–1958), c.f., Dec. 6, 1593.

IX.   Renaissance Literature and the Diseases of Erotic Love

1. Michel Foucault, *Histoire de la sexualité*, vol. I, *La volonté de savoir* (Paris: Éditions Gallimard, 1976), p. 25.
2. See Lawrence Babb, *Elizabethan Malady*, pp. 156 ff., concerning the passionate lover in Elizabethan literature and the popularity of the cult of the melancholy *amoroso*, especially in the pastoral and in the theater.
3. For a résumé of the transformations affecting family life, see René Pillorget, *La tige et le rameau: familles anglaise et française 16°–18° siècle* (Paris:

Calmann-Lévy, 1979), esp. pp. 43 ff., and also Robert Wheaton and Tamara Hareven, *The Family and Sexuality in French History* (Philadelphia: University of Pennsylvania Press, 1980). One example of the change in literary styles is the new morality in evidence in Giambattista Giraldi's *Gli Ecatomniti*, wherein Flamineo, on the first day, mocks the casuistry of Platonic love and insists on the virtues of marriage as the only form of love on earth capable of bringing peace and satisfaction. The entire fifth day of the collection is devoted to stories of marital fidelity.

4. Michel de Montaigne, *Essays*, trans. John Florio, ed. Desmond Mac-Carthy, 3 vols. (London: J. M. Dent and Sons, 1928), vol. III, p. 74. Montaigne takes the lines from Pierre Charron, *De la Sagesse*, bk. I, ch. 46, *Oeuvres* (Paris: Chez Jacques Villery, 1635), p. 163.

5. Robert Mandrou, *Introduction à la France moderne 1500–1640*, (Paris: Éditions Albin Michel, 1961, 1974),

6. Robert Mandrou, *Introduction à la France moderne 1500–1640*, p. 89.

7. Denis de Rougemont, *The Myths of Love* (London: Faber and Faber, 1963), p. 175.

8. Michel Simonin, *"Aegritudo amoris* et *res literaria* à la Renaissance: Réflexions préliminaires," *La folie et le corps*, p. 86.

9. John Ford, "The Lover's Melancholy," ed. Havelock Ellis (London: T. Fisher Unwin, n.d.), p. 58.

10. William Painter, *The Palace of Pleasure*, ed. Joseph Jacobs (1575; London: David Nutt, 1890; rpt. New York: Dover Publications, 1965), vol. II, pp. 107–12.

PART 2

Of Lovesickness

or

Erotic Melancholy

with

Text, Annotations, and Commentary

Translators' Preface

In retranslating Jacques Ferrand's *De la maladie d'amour ou melancholie erotique* we have undertaken to serve an English readership in the twentieth century with this text, just as Edmund Chilmead did in the seventeenth century with the *Erotomania or a Treatise Discoursing of the Essence, Causes, Symptomes, Prognosticks, and Cure of Love, or Erotique Melancholy*—his translation of *De la maladie d'amour* published in Oxford in 1640. A first decision to be made by a modern editor of Ferrand is whether to use the seventeenth-century translation as the basis of the edition. It is an inviting prospect because such an edition would simultaneously provide another example of seventeenth-century English prose. But whether to modernize Chilmead's spelling and punctuation, or whether to translate his Latin passages are only two of the obstacles that present themselves in dealing with his text. Since Chilmead's translation is also often inaccurate, the editor must ask how much editorial intervention can reasonably be tolerated to set these lapses aright. Early on, respect for a sampling of English prose comes into conflict with respect for Ferrand's thought; the problems begin to outweigh the advantages.

Chilmead was a professional translator whose French was remarkably good, yet he was, at the same time, a literary hack who undoubtedly worked quickly and thus not entirely reliably. It must be said in Chilmead's defense that Ferrand, because of his sometimes technical meanings and his sprawling syntax, was not an easy subject for translation. But Chilmead's offenses were not only sins of haste or incomprehension; he was also given to loose paraphrase, to interpolated commentary and to rendering certain passages into Latin because he found them too frank for his readership. These tendencies, together with his often inappropriately florid style, make him less than an ideal mediator of Ferrand's work viewed as a scientific treatise. At the same time, as a practitioner of the English language Chilmead is workmanlike at best; he is not a distinguished stylist. To adopt his text as the basis of a modern critical edition is to render service neither to the historian of ideas who seeks a faithful representation of Ferrand's thought nor to the literary scholar who seeks further examples of fine prose, for which that age of English literature is justly famous.

Finally, however, it is the handling of the marginal references in the Oxford edition that precludes its usefulness for purposes of a modern critical edition. Not only do many of those references differ from their counterparts in the French, but about half way through they break off altogether. If the Chilmead translation becomes the authoritative text, the editor is caught between loyalties and must either supply and correct several hundred marginal references or simply retreat to a transcription that denies all possibility for a meaningful critical edition. We have therefore provided an entirely new translation based on the French text of 1623. In the present version, we have sought to take its stylistic hints from the various levels detected in Ferrand's own writing and to reproduce them as faithfully as modern idiomatic English will allow. But above all, our intention has been to render his ideas as forthrightly and as accurately as possible.

Ferrand is an uneven stylist whose prose is often direct and disciplined by the force of his argument, but is just as often circuitous and digressive. Typically, he writes in long, compound sentences, themselves architectonic units that bind together widely disparate ideas and allusions. His style is, in that sense, related to his habits of erudition: he forages widely, then assembles his materials often through the detection of remote correspondences between the elements. We have by no means sought to improve upon his logic, but we have made every effort to search out the syntactical arrangements best suited to render these associations as clear as possible. Where he reaches after stylistic effects in order to express an attitude toward his materials, we have looked for modern equivalents. His text abounds with quotations which we have translated likewise into modern idiomatic English, again placing clarity of content ahead of fidelity to original styles. Because Ferrand uses these quotations not only to embellish but also to extend, develop, and sometimes even to replace his argument, they are too important to be left in untranslated form.

The scholarly and bibliographical practices Ferrand employs are common enough in humanist treatises—the ubiquitous name dropping, the overt and covert use of citations, the ventriloquistic style, the cryptically abbreviated marginal references—but for all their conventionality, they are not easily dealt with in modern critical editions. Because it has been our purpose to relate Ferrand to a well-established scholarly tradition, those hundreds of marginal references demand special attention. Nothing would have been gained by translating the text without, at the same time, translating the references, which are themselves an integral part of the text—translating them, that is, into expanded and documented forms. Such a policy entails a whole series of decisions concerning format, placement, authority of the edition cited, amount of supplementary quotation, and commentary. Simply to locate copies of all the works cited by Ferrand is an obstacle course in its own right. Given that fact, our inclination has been to quote liberally from his sources once they were found, especially from the elusive Renaissance medical texts. For the annotations to the text, we have worked out our own program of procedures to handle documentation and commentary. We have also adopted a policy of including parallel sources, with quotations in the original languages, in order to build upon the clues in Ferrand's margins toward the development of a complete scholarly apparatus concerning the sources of the *topos* under examination. Our editorial principles for both text and annotations are outlined in the following paragraphs.

In the text itself we have placed brackets around all editorial interpolations. These are essentially of three different natures: editorial translations of words in original languages preserved in the text because they were the subject of discussion; explanations of epithets and, on rare occasion, of obscure or specialized words or phrases; additions to the text of key words implicit but not present in the original that were essential to a clear understanding of the text. Parentheses signify only material that was designated parenthetic by Ferrand; they are a literal element of the translation.

Ferrand quotes extensively from both Greek and Latin. We have replaced these quotations with translations, transferring his originals to the corresponding notes. It is to be pointed out that many of Ferrand's quotations do not correspond either to the modern or to the contemporaneous texts consulted, not because he was employing variant sources but because he made adjustments of greater and lesser importance according to the needs of his text. Though eager to associate his every thought with the words of other writers, Ferrand was, nevertheless, not above altering what he found, to the extent of changing even the subject matter, keeping only the phrasing of the original. In the same spirit, he could create a passage out of individual lines or couplets drawn from several different areas of an author's work. Given this license on Ferrand's part, given the wide variety of styles in modern translations, and given the unavailability of such translations for many of his quotations, it became necessary that we also retranslate all of the quoted material in Ferrand's text. Chilmead had done as much before, producing some extraordinarily copious and flowery versions—especially of the classical poets. We hasten to add, however, that where good modern translations do exist we have not refused their inspiration; the Loeb translators, in particular, have served as guides in many of our renditions. We attest to having borrowed words and phrases from any source that helped us to arrive at clear, direct versions slanted where necessary to accommodate the contexts in which they appear. That is to say, Ferrand sometimes read the poets in special ways, most of them entirely possible in terms of the original words, though in ways oblivious of the spirit of the original works. We have thus attempted translations that do as much justice as possible to Ferrand's specialized interpretation of the lines, without doing total violence to the spirit of the original. The point to be underscored is that we have not translated with the poet's reputation in mind, but with the demands of this particular treatise in mind. It should perhaps be pointed out as well that our poetry translations are indented and organized according to poetic conventions with capitals beginning each line to signify the nature of the originals, but we do not pretend to have been able to reflect the quality of the original prosody or even the exact number of lines.

Quotation marks have been used sparingly. Where Ferrand paraphrases quoted material in his own words they have not been employed. All quotations set apart from the main body of the text likewise appear without quotation marks. They appear only where Greek and Latin quotations, integrated into the main text, have been replaced by our own translations. Anomaly arises only in those passages where Ferrand's own paraphrase is so close to the original that a supplementary translation would have been entirely redundant. In those few instances we have replaced the quotation with Ferrand's "translation," placed in quotation marks to indicate that it has replaced an original text that has been transferred to the notes.

Ferrand identifies a number of works, especially medical treatises, in the main text, some by their general content, others by abbreviated Latin titles, and still others by French translations of those titles. Our policy has been to render all such references, as nearly as possible, by the titles generally known to modern English scholars: Schenck in his *Observations* or Hippocrates in his *On Airs, Waters, and Places*. Those cases where works are known only by titles in other languages we have, for the sake of consistency, translated them into English.

With regard to the proper names in the text, Ferrand's inconsistencies tempt the correcting stroke of the editor. But rules of conformity here are far more difficult to establish. The names of Renaissance scholars and physicians were often Latinized, thereby enabling them, in a sense, to pass frontiers more easily. By all rights, the editor should choose according to an editorial standard to render them all into Latin, or else into their true native or their English naturalized forms. But the criteria for making choices are unclear. Ferrand is inclined to use the familiar French names for his fellow countrymen, for example André Du Laurens, and to adopt the French versions of the names of the ancients, for example Pol Aeginette, while maintaining the Latin names of those from surrounding countries, for example Clusius, Heurnius, Rodericus à Castro. But there are many exceptions in both directions. For the Frenchman Joseph Duchesne he keeps Quercetanus, and for the foreigners Mercatus and Sylvaticus we find Louys Mercat and Jean Baptiste Silvat, while for Cristóbal de Vega he uses, not Christophorus according to custom, but Christophle à Vega. In the list of authorities cited at the end of the edition of 1623 we find Andernacus, for so he was known in his time, but not in German catalogues where he is Johannes Winter or Gunther von Andernach, or in English where he is Johann Guinterium, or in French where he is Jean Gonthier. Because English catalogs are divided on such matters, there is no authority by which these names can be rendered consistently in the form best suited to assist the English researcher in gaining rapid access to them in other sources. The choice, in fact, must be between actual given names (barely known, in many cases, in Renaissance usage, but sometimes preferred by modern bibliographies and catalogues) and Latin names (though not all scholars and physicians had such names). Given the impasse, we granted authority to usage in Ferrand, largely respecting his not entirely reasoned habit of dividing between national French and international Latin names, but regularizing some of the anomalies that occur within this practice. We have eliminated French versions of the names of the classical writers, substituting the standard forms familiar to English readers. Where there was a choice to be made in the case of Renaissance names, our preference was for the non-Latinized forms. That is, we favored Ferrand's first choice for such as Blaise de Vigenère, though he once or twice used Vigenarius. In actual practice, the issue can be overemphasized because the notes convey the alternate forms, providing the options necessary for further research. We are aware that there are strong feelings about these matters among scholars and bibliographers. By following Ferrand we may be disappointing certain expectations, but the grounds are too unclear for adopting any other solution.

Ferrand's marginal references are an important part of his text, at one with his encyclopedic purposes, symbols of his erudition, and quick references to the range and location of his many sources. They pose difficulties for the editor, however, because to replicate them in the margins in the form they take in the original is to offer references that are sometimes cryptic, sometimes inaccurate (Ferrand's printer had a penchant for reversing book and chapter numbers). Only the specialist could decipher to immediate satisfaction "Pl.l.7. c.4 Auson. Epig.71.Agel l.9.c.4 Volater." and, in turn, assign them accurately to the relevant passages on the page. To expand and correct them would require considerable additional space and would obliterate all traces of Ferrand's original references. To place them inside the text has the virtue of interpreting their appropriate locations for the reader, but at the cost of imposing constant interruptions. Lamentably, something of value is lost in removing them from immediate inspection by placing them in the notes, yet the advantages are on that side. The note numbers placed in the text designate precise locations, while in the note itself there is room for a methodical approach that records original as well as expanded versions of the references.

The initial task of correlating the multiple references clustered together in the margins to corresponding areas in the text is not always easily accomplished. Ferrand's printer complicates the task, as well, by his casual grouping and placing of them on the page. In the second chapter, for example, Ferrand discusses sex changes, alluding to incidents in Smyrna, Argos, Naples, Auch, Vitry, Coimbra, and Salerno as mentioned by Fulgosius, Amatus Lusitanus, Paré, Pineus, and Schenckius, the entire section accompanied by marginal references to Pliny, Ausonius, Aulus Gellius, and Volateranus. The passage is a bibliographical puzzle, the solution to which can be had only by first researching all the possible combinations. Ferrand's marginal clusters can be respected only by regrouping them in the notes, where the parts can be dealt with serially, each in an indented section, the entire group sometimes forming a small essay on sources related to the given topic. These clusters are handled intact in the event that Ferrand saw them as units or indeed derived them from single sources, though we are the first to allow that the printer likewise could have had a hand in the grouping.

The logic of the notes, given the complexity and variety of the materials, has had to be largely of our own devising. Ferrand's marginal references or clusters of references appear first, punctuated as in the original. Where no textual quotations are involved, this material is followed by the author's name, an expansion of the reference given in the margin, and, in turn, by a full reference to an edition where the material can be found. The relevant quotations from that text are then cited, followed, where necessary, by a commentary on Ferrand's special employment of those materials. Where textual quotations are involved, the expanded name and references are followed by the quoted text as it appears in Ferrand's edition and, in turn, by references to a modern or contemporary edition, parallel quotations where variants occur, and commentary. The same general order applies to notes relating to names and allusions in the text not accompanied by marginal references.

All works are given full documentation when they first appear in the notes. In subsequent listings the author and a short title appear, followed by volume and page numbers. Often we have included book and chapter numbers as well as chapter titles, where appropriate, in order to facilitate location in other editions. This material sometimes precedes the parenthetic information concerning publication, and sometimes follows: precedes where it is part of the marginal reference, and follows where it is not. Thus for a first listing: Luis Mercado (Ludovicus Mercatus), *De internorum morborum curatione libri IV* in *Opera* (Francofurti: sumptibus haeredum D. Zachariae Palthenii, 1620), bk. II, ch. 6, "*De febre alba, et de virginum obstructionibus*," vol. III, p. 564. In subsequent references: Luis Mercado, *De internorum morborum curatione libri IV* in *Opera*, bk. II, ch. 6, Vol. III, p. 564.

Ferrand's quotations are given in the notes verbatim with all the errors of whatever origin preserved. Ferrand may at times have worked from memory, or from compendia (which we will discuss later), and there is little doubt that he made alterations to suit his ends; we have not wished to erase any of this evidence that could be of interest to scholars with bibliographical inclinations going beyond what was necessary for the preparation of this edition. We have, furthermore, made no effort to trace Ferrand's quotations to any specific edition of the text. Such a task would have been almost impossible in the case of the major classical poets, given the numerous editions of their works that appeared throughout the sixteenth century.

The matter of sources raises underlying questions about Ferrand's habits of scholarship. Given the frequency of quotation from minor and obscure classical writers as well as from the major writers, we are to assume that Ferrand spent a lifetime in reading Greek and Latin, and that he had a complex system for noting quotable lines by topic; or that these references had become a traditional part of the medical and philosophical writing on love and were taken over by successive writers; or, finally, that Ferrand made use of compendia of Greek and Latin quotations that had become popular throughout the preceding century. There is cause to think that Ferrand followed all three of these courses in assembling his materials. We know that he was not above copying both quotations and their references from intermediary sources and that certain of his materials had traveled before him from writer to writer as integral parts of the discussion of medical *topoi*.

Altogether certain is that Ferrand, on numerous occasions, lifted quotations found in other treatises—references and all—and incorporated them into his own text. He would have simply considered this material common property. The several examples we have traced have been noted in the annotations to the relevant chapters. Some of the most notable cases involve major authors such as Mario Equicola, André Du Laurens, and Jean Liébault. The two most flagrant examples to our knowledge are his use of Jean Taxil for the chapter on astrology (no. XXI) and Rodrigo de Castro for the chapter on philters (no. XXXV). In both cases the moiety or more of his references are derived from these single sources. Paradoxically, while Ferrand can borrow materials in this wholesale fashion, he can remain on the opposite side of the argument, as in the case of his use of Taxil's *L'astrologie et physiognomie en leur splendeur*.

To use another's scholarship in this way did not constitute a problem in professional ethics for that age as it would for our own. The important witnesses for Ferrand are Aquinas and Mizaldus, not Taxil himself; he simply cites them from Taxil as a matter of convenience. But there are other instances where Ferrand appears more devious. We have already alluded to his failure to cite Jean Aubery, quite probably out of a sense of professional rivalry. Where Ferrand employed such intermediary texts, whether he acknowledged them or not, we have specified the extent of the borrowing. We did not stop with references to the intermediary texts however but also documented these quotations in appropriate modern or contemporaneous editions.

There have been no tidy solutions to questions concerning the choice of editions to be cited in the notes. One set of scholarly criteria suggests that the latest editions should be employed in every case possible. This leaves out nearly all of the dozens of Renaissance physicians cited by Ferrand because very few of them are available in recent editions. A different set of criteria suggests that in all cases possible, we should cite those editions most likely to have been used by Ferrand. This procedure would refer the reader to rare and inaccessible sixteenth-century editions of standard authors widely available in modern editions. We have resolved the issue according to the following scheme: for the ancient Greek and Latin authors we cite modern editions, using wherever possible the Loeb classics because of their wide availability and general recognition; for the ancient physicians we have cited the most authoritative modern editions. These choices seemed clear. In contradistinction, the Renaissance physicians have been consulted in sixteenth- and seventeenth-century editions, with preference given to those published nearest to the time Ferrand was active. This same procedure has been followed for the essayists, chroniclers, theologians, and encyclopedists not available in modern editions. This group includes most of the writers from that age cited by Ferrand. The actual copies consulted have primarily been those in the medical and law faculties in Montpellier, in the municipal libraries of Montpellier and Toulouse, in the Bibliothèque Nationale in Paris, and in the National Library of Medicine in Bethesda, Maryland.

A word must be added concerning our handling of these texts. In quoting, we have retained original spelling and punctuation where they appear authoritative because to edit these texts was beyond our purposes. Nevertheless, we have silently corrected blatant errors in typesetting. We have also expanded all the conventional Latin abbreviations, and we have introduced, where necessary, a certain standardization in order to accommodate the reader unfamiliar with early typographical conventions. Every effort has been made to respect the originals, though the task was not facilitated by the fact that many of the sources consulted were set in miniscule typefaces or else were in faded or otherwise imperfect condition, necessitating a certain amount of guesswork and a degree of reconstruction.

Finally, we reiterate here that in the interests of furthering scholarship on this subject we have quoted generously from both sources and parallel works in the period—beyond the needs of a simple annotation of Ferrand's text. It has been our intention that the materials of the notes serve simultaneously as vehicles for further research, thereby contributing to the encyclopedic intent and scope of Ferrand's treatise.

Of Lovesickness
or
Erotic Melancholy

An Unusual Discourse That Teaches How to
Recognize the Essence, the Causes,
the Signs, and the Remedies of
This Disease of the Fantasy

By Jacques Ferrand of Agen
Doctor in the Faculty of Medicine

[Epistle from the Publisher]

To the Gentlemen Students of Medicine in Paris

Sirs:

Although I can boast to be out of love's jurisdiction myself, and can utter aloud with the poet, "I do not know what love is, nor do I love, nor am I loved, nor did I ever love," nevertheless, just in seeing this little discourse on love, which came to my hands through the offices of one of my friends, I let myself, by imperceptible degrees, fall enamored of it with an affection that caused me to bring it to light by publishing it. It is true that this name of Love has I can hardly tell what alluring charms, even for those who would have nothing to do with it—a power to create even in the most rude and barbarian a state of gentleness and civility—which force moved the ancients to call it *artium magistrum*, the master of the arts, the guardian and caretaker of the universe:

> . . . he is master of all,
> of the heavens, of the sea, of the land.
>
> (Orpheus in the *Hymns*)*

Having seen him decked out and furnished, not in the nude or as a child such as the poets describe him, but in the garments of a philosopher as Plato sets him forth, I could hardly deny him this favor and courtesy. It is not that the clothes make the philosopher, or that in using that argument I think to have arrived at a true and perfect understanding of love. I am aware that this subject preoccupied all of antiquity, and that it gave considerable trouble to all those who embarked upon this ocean of marvels. For even after some have called him the father and the master

---

*The marginal references in the *Epistle* appear in parentheses, each following the appropriate allusion in the text.

217

of the gods (Hesiod in the *Theogony*), the demon of nature (Orpheus in the *Hymns*), the author of all things (Orpheus), he who chastizes Jupiter (Nonnus in the *Dionysus*, bk. I), he who punishes Neptune and Bacchus (Nonnus, bk. XLII), he who threatens and triumphs over the gods (Cointus of Smyrna, bk. XIII), he who was born before time itself (Hesiod in the *Theogony*), the great one (Cyr. Theod.), the powerful one (Orpheus), the monarch of the world (Orpheus). Even after others have called him a child (Calistratus), impotent (*Theogony*), a little runt (Nonnus, *Dionysus*, bk. XIV), bastard (Lucian, *Dialogues*), thief (*Theogony*), effeminate (Nonnus, bk. XXXVI), and timid (Moschus). Even after the wisest men have searched out and found the mysteries and secrets of his name (Marsilio Ficino *In Plato* and *Mythology*). After having transformed him into a magpie, a flea, a fly, the sun, glass, a feather, a vulture, and an owl (Brizardi, *Metamophosis*), after the theologians have called him charity and altruism, the philosophers a passion and movement of the soul, the physicians concupiscence, a disease of the psyche, melancholy, thievery, and madness, even after men have bestowed these titles of honor, and of infamy upon him, have named him heat, fire, torch, ice, snow, gall, poison, venom, plague, beast, tiger, lion, physician, alchemist, musician, soldier, enchanter, laborer, shepherd, charlatan, still there is the complaint that not enough has been said, and that not enough progress has been made in fathoming his nature and his power. Those men have better credit who, to excuse themselves from all these difficulties, freely confessed that love is I don't know what, that comes from I don't know where, sent by I don't know whom, or by what means, whose age I cannot tell, whose growth I cannot measure, who wanes and dies I don't know when, nor by what disease—who can guess what it is? I was thus assured that the nature of this little devil was not so easily identified as his philosophical apparel trimmed and styled in the French manner would seem to allow. Even so, following the counsel of certain learned men to whom I showed the work, I willingly let myself be persuaded by my first resolution to let him see the light of day, seeing that he carried on his brow the antidote and preservative against that poison that he allows to glide insensibly into the hearts of men. I will not boast of the merits of him who so worthily and judiciously penned this treatise, nor do I wish to recommend this work for its innovativeness, nor for its scrupulous inquiry into a host of subtle materials drawn from the best authors, especially because such would surpass the capacities of my mind, but rather I await, like Apelles for his Venus, the judgment of those who pause to contemplate and to peruse this book. Moreover, gentlemen, knowing how in our time the power of Love has produced strange and wondrous motions in the minds of young men like you, I thought that a good way to set you on the right path would be to reveal to you the disgrace and the offenses of lovers who have fallen into this painful and deadly passion, and I thought by these same means to give you the cures and preventatives for treating persons so afflicted who will one day come into your care. It is not without its advantages for you to have remedies for yourselves as well as protective measures for others. I must laugh at those astrologers and soothsayers who promise empires and mountains of gold to those who consult them, but who cannot rescue themselves from beggary and, more often than not, from an ignominious death. Cassandra predicted nothing but disaster and misfortune; Midas, for his folly, labored only for his heirs and for his own death; many make their fortune and build their houses at the expense and ruin of others; the lawyer profits from the suits of his clients, the physician from disease; everything has its backwards and forwards, its good and bad, its defects and perfection; but this discourse, gentlemen, has no backwardness or defaults. It is concerned only with your instruction and profit; it aims at that virtue, learning, honor, and sincerity which should render you all more praiseworthy. Now having learned by experience that the curiosity of your excellent wits leads you to make inquiries into all things new and profitable, I made so bold as to dedicate to you this small yet rare and precious work, being assured that having read it, you will give hearty thanks to its author, and to me who has given it to the public, and to yourselves for whom I am, sirs, your humble and affectionate servant, D[enis] Moreau, Librairie de Paris. From Paris, this _____ day of _____ sixteen hundred twenty three.

To the Reader, Greetings

Posidonius the philosopher, being once afflicted by a disease so painful that it made him twist his arms and gnash his teeth, thought to show an ultimate defiance of pain by exclaiming against it: all your efforts are in vain if I do not grant that you have hurt me. Every day we see a number of those fine wits captured by some mortal beauty—and sometimes by an imaginary one—so stung and tormented by the folly of love as to have their imaginations depraved and their judgments awry, yet in imitation of this fool philosopher, rather than look for some wholesome remedy for their ill they deny that their folly is a disease and instead apply their best efforts to singing the praises of love—the very cause of their indisposition. In order to make clear the uselessness of that Stoic opinion—and in consideration of the fact that I am a lover of learning rather than a lover of words and judge that person sufficiently eloquent who knows how to explain his precepts properly—I offer to you this little discourse devoid of all eloquence, as a discourse prepared by one who claims that faculty called "mute" by the prince of the Latin poets, in which you will find all manner of remedies for curing the most frequent and most dangerous disease which threatens mortals of both sexes, collected from the copses of philosophers and the gardens of the physicians, and gleaned from the fields of poets and lay theologians in order to please you by its variety. Two principal reasons have prompted me to write about this malady in imitation of certain physicians I will mention hereafter. The first is that I have known several practitioners of medicine who, for failing to heed the cause of the disease or the seat of the ill, have given treatment to those suffering from erotic melancholy or erotic mania that does not differ from the treatment given to other melancholiacs and madmen. In doing this they jeopardize the health of their patients, causing them considerable harm and confusion, without ever seeing the results promised through their medications. The second is to combat the erroneous opinions of certain philosophers or physi-

221

cians to be named hereafter, who, though for the most part Christians, recommend lechery and fornication for the curing of this disease, which I propose to refute for several important reasons both physical and moral, leaving the rest to theologians.

Treatise on the Nature
and Cure of Love
or of Erotic Melancholy

I

Whether it is useful
to teach the remedies
of love or erotic melancholy

At first it would appear a vain and useless enterprise to give instruction: on how to cure love, since poets, philosophers, and theologians have acknowledged it to be the cause of all good: ("love is the cause of all good, strife the cause of all evil.")[1] It is a chart-in-brief of justice, of temperance, of strength and wisdom, the author of medicine, poetry, and music—of all the liberal arts. It is the most noble and powerful as well as the most ancient of all the gods forged in the pagan imagination.[2] Truly, if I spoke against such love, I would be afraid of incurring the same affliction that befell the poet Stesichorus who, for finding fault with the beautiful Helen, was sorely punished until he composed his recantation.[3] Moreover, as a physician, to write against the principle of love would be to criticize my own profession since, according to Plato in the person of the physician Erysimachus, medicine is the science by which we understand the "loves" of the body that govern repletion and evacuation. He who is able to discern the honest affections from the dishonest in the inclinations of the natural humors is to be accounted the wisest of physicians.[4]

Nevertheless, we must recognize, as Pausanias does, that just as there are two Venuses, the one called Urania or the celestial, [born] a daughter of the heavens without a mother, the other called Pandemia or earthly, the youngest daughter of Jupiter and Diana, so there are two loves, sons of these two goddesses: divine love and common or vulgar love.[5] Metaphysicians and theologians discourse of the essence and properties of the first, while physicians deal with ordinary physical love, which is either honest or dishonest. They teach the means for preserving the former in marriage, and they prescribe the sovereign remedies for healing and preserving men from that lascivious, unchaste love that so often carries away base and corrupted souls.

The Greeks recount that Apollo had two sons, Aesculapius and Plato, the latter for healing the diseases of the spirit, the former those of the body.[6] But because love is a malady of both the body and the soul, I will make use of Plato's precepts and Aesculapius's remedies for the healing of love melancholy[7]—remedies which I learned from his nephew Hippocrates—understanding such love to be nothing other than a passion or a violent and dishonorable perturbation of the mind, intractable to reason.

> It is a profitable aim to extinguish savage flames
> And to have a heart not enslaved to its own frailty.[8]

But principally I want to give instruction in the methods for preventing erotic melancholy, which often attacks those who do not know how to govern their desires by reason,[9] inasmuch as wanton love is the nursery of a million ills as counted up by Plautus:

> For in the wake of love come all these
> Ills—care, sorrow and excessive display
> . . . .
> Sleeplessness, yes, and stupidity and recklessness, and
> Senseless unreflexion, immodesty, wantoness and lust,
> Ill-will, inertia, inordinate desire, sloth, injustice,
> Contumely and extravagance, overtalking, undertalking.[10]

Our poet and consul from Bordeaux [Ausonius] wrote that Venus one day stopped whipping her son Cupid and afterwards bound him to a myrtle tree, showing us by this poetic fiction that pleasure often scourges lovers with leather thongs, signified by the purple wings which, according to Guittone d'Arezzo, are hieroglyphs of sorrow and mortal pain.[11] For the same reason, Petrarch lodges him in a palace of hopes wherein all persons of whatever condition or sex desire to dwell. But the higher they rise, the lower they fall, because the stairways of the palace are made of a slippery substance.[12] The first three steps are the flirtations of the eyes, the overflowing of words, and the subtlety or craftiness of the hand. The bedrooms are decked with idleness, dreams, vain desires, and inconstancy. The fireplace in the great hall is the lover's breast, that of the bedroom is his heart, and of the kitchen his liver. The chairs of those who are entertained there are false contentment, on which these guests are no sooner seated but they break into pieces. To repair them, they send at all hours for the engineers tediousness, torment, and guile. Uncertainty and fear are the most trustworthy guards of the palace; false opinion, each evening, shuts the gates; during the night distrust serves as sentinel, and so forth.

Apollonius Thyaneus, one day sent for by the King of Babylon to invent a new form of torture for an adulterer whom the King had discovered with his favorite mistress, having carefully considered the matter, answered that in letting him live and go on loving, his love, with the passage of time, would punish him bitterly enough, because its beginning is fear, its middle loss, and its ending pain[13]—which you will understand more clearly when I have depicted for you the conventional symptoms of erotic melancholy.

II

The symptoms of erotic melancholy

The many vexations and perturbations that torture the soul of the passionate lover bring about greater harms to men than all the other affections of the mind, for we read in our classical authors of many who have died of extreme joy, such as Polycrita of Naxos, Diagoras of Rhodes, Chilo the Lacedaemonian, the poet Sophocles and Dionysius, tyrant of Syracuse; or of sorrow, such as Publius Rutilius, Marcus Lepidus, and Ely the high priest of the Jews; others of shame such as Homer, for failing to resolve the riddle of the fishermen, and Macrina, the wife of Torquatus, from an ardent desire to see a one-eyed Egyptian or cyclops passing in front of her house during the absence of her husband, because at that time modesty would not allow married women to look out of the window or leave the house while their husbands were away.[1]

Nevertheless, such passions as these sometimes have their good uses and are, for this reason, included by the physicians among the six non-natural things.[2] Anger, though it inclines toward madness ("wrath is but a short madness"),[3] is of value to dullards, brooders, sluggards, the lazy, those of cold and pale complexions; fear is of service to the foolish, the cowardly, the phrenetic, and the maniacal.[4] Sorrow is useful to laughers, the silly-minded and the foolhardy, and shame to the impudent, the brazen, and to those with pale and wan colors.[5]

But love does not seem to be of value to anyone, resembling instead, according to Andreas Alpagus, the kind of passion that Avicenna calls *heā* in Arabic, in that more often than not it consists of several contrary motions: joy and sorrow, hope and desperation, friendship and hatred or jealousy.[6]

> I hate and I love, perhaps you ask for what reason I do this.
> I do not know, but I feel it happening and I am tormented by it.[7]
>
> Struggling over my fickle heart, love draws it

228

Now this way, and now hate that—but love, I think, is winning.[8]

I would repeat that love is the ground and origin of all our affections and the epitome of all the perturbations of the soul. We call it covetousness or concupiscence when we desire to enjoy that which pleases, whether it be beautiful in truth or only in appearance. It is suffering and hopelessness when such enjoyment is denied. Love takes on the name of pleasure and voluptuousness when one possesses the thing desired. Hope is the belief that the object will eventually be obtained; jealousy is the belief that it will be entirely or partially lost.

Because of these agitations of the soul, the blood becomes adust, earthy, and melancholy, as in the case of all other violent passions except joy, according to Galen,[9] for which reason many have fallen into terrible circumstances and corrupt states of health, becoming melancholy, foolish, misanthropic, maniacal, and lycanthropic according to the report given by the learned Avicenna in his chapter on love.[10] Aretaeus the physician makes mention of a young dandy of his day who became love-mad and could not be cured through the ministrations of this learned doctor of Cappadocia.[11] Because of love the famous poet Lucretius lost his reason. Iphis fell into despair over Anaxaretes. A young Athenian became insane for love of a marble statue.[12] The same would have happened to a rich merchant of Arles not long ago had it not been for the help of the learned Valleriola, as recounted in his *Observations*.[13] According to Strabo and Suidas, Sappho the poetess, forlorn for her love of Phaon hurled herself from the Leucadian rock into the sea,[14] for women are more frequently and more grievously troubled by these ills than are men.[15] Such love gives rise to a pale and wan complexion, joined by a slow fever that modern practitioners call amorous fever,[16] to palpitations of the heart, swelling of the face, depraved appetite, a sense of grief, sighing, causeless tears, insatiable hunger, raging thirst, fainting, oppressions, suffocations, insomnia, headaches, melancholy, epilepsy, madness, uterine fury, satyriasis, and other pernicious symptoms that are, for the most part, without mitigation or cure other than through the [established medical] remedies for love and erotic melancholy, based on the teachings of Hippocrates toward the end of his book on the diseases of young women and in his book on generation.[17]

These symptoms of disease have caused many to believe that love is a kind of poison that is generated within the body itself, that slips in through the eyes, or that is caused by medications called philters—such as are numbered among the poisons by the jurisconsult [Ulpian] who wrote the *Lex Cornelia de sicariis et de veneficiis*[18]—poisons that corrupt the reason and destroy good blood, which is the cause of paleness in lovers. In the words of Theocritus:

> Ah, torturing love, why hast thou clung to me
> Like some leech of the fen, and drained all the
> Dark blood from my body?[19]

Hippocrates seems to attribute to passionate love the power to transform men into women [sic: women into men] when he explains how in the city of Abdera, Phaëtusa, who loved Pytheus her husband dearly, but who was not able to enjoy him due to his long absence, therewith became a man (ἠνδρώθη) with body hair, a masculine voice, and a beard. In the following aphorism this notable ancient states that Namysia, wife of Gorgippus, was transformed in the same way and that no means were found to make her a woman again (γυναικωθίναι).[20] I venture to believe that this metamorphosis was one of behavior and complexion only and not of sex, for according to the same author, and according to the Prince of Philosophers [Aristotle], the male is more robust, massive, and solid, the female by contrast less robust and nervous, but more moist, delicate, and softer mannered.[21] Nevertheless, Galen, Fuchsius, Foesius, and several other physicians or commentators upon the divine Hippocrates[22] (who, in the words of Macrobius, has never deceived anyone)[23] take him quite literally, so that, according to them, we are compelled to believe those stories about Iphis, Caeneus, and all that writers have told us about Cossitius, Cassinus, and many another young girl who turned masculine at the time of puberty: in Smyrna, Argos, Naples, Auch, Vitry, Coimbra, Salerno, and elsewhere, which you may read about in Fulgosius, Amatus Lusitanus, Paré, Pineus, and Schenckius in his *Observations*, ch. 25.[24]

The Peripatetics find nothing miraculous in this transformation in that their Coryphaeus [Aristotle] states in several places that woman is an imperfect man, ἄρρην πεπηρομένος,[25] in no way different from a man except for the genitals which in the female, according to Galen, are kept and enclosed within the body for want of the natural heat that would force them to the exterior.[26] Such an arrangement reveals no error or weakness on the part of nature, as certain dull-witted philosophers have asserted, for such a design was necessary for the preservation of the species.[27] Thus, according to the doctrines of the Genius of Nature and of Galen, it is quite plausible that the genitals of a girl, overheated by the fury of love, would be pushed outside the body, because those parts are the same as the male parts reversed according to the same physician [Galen], though he is contradicted in this by our modern anatomists, as you may amply read in the *Anatomical Questions* of our good teacher André Du Laurens.[28]

The learned Louis Mercatus and his imitator Rodericus à Castro are inconsistent in their explanations of these two Hippocratic texts:[29] in one place they say that these matrons suffered from the protrusion or descent of the matrix that bore a certain resemblance to the male member, and in another they assert that these good women had that organ that Manard names *queue*, Albucasis *tentiginem*, Moschion and Mercatus *symptoma turpitudinis*, Aretaeus *nympham*, Fallopius *clitorida*, Columbus *amorem et dulcedinem veneris*, Avicenna, *albatram, id est virgam*, so enlarged that it resembled the male member.[30] It is a condition known to many other women who unhappily abuse that part, women called *fricatrices* by the Latins, *tribades* by the Greeks and *ribaudes* by the French,[31] among whom Suidas and Muret place the learned Sappho.[32] In the final analysis, the wise Mercatus concludes that he does not intend to hinder anyone from believing in this transmutation or metamorphosis, in the light of the many examples given by the historians and physicians cited above.

III

Of the name of love
and erotic melancholy

All maladies, according to our Galen, take their names from the diseased part,[1] such as pleurisy and peripneumonia, or from the symptoms as shivering, or from the two together as headache, or from its resemblance to something else as cancer, or finally from the efficient cause, as with our erotic or amorous melancholy—called by certain physicians ἐρωτομανίαν, which is to say love madness or amorous folly, for quite rightly one can say of these lovers what Demodocus said of the Milesians (as stated in Aristotle), that if they are not crazy, they behave at least as if they were.[2] The poet Euripides wanted to teach us the same thing, according to Aristotle, in deriving the name of Venus from folly: "rightly does the name of the goddess [Aphrodite] begin like the word *aphrodias*—folly."[3]

It is not granted to the gods themselves to be both wise and in love.[4]

On this point you will notice that our ancient physicians often confound mania with melancholy, failing to note the varying degrees of difference between them[5]—though such degrees do not alter the species, as we will more clearly demonstrate below.

Avicenna, along with the whole Arabian clan, calls this sickness in his language *alhasch* and *iliscus*,[6] Arnald of Villanova, Bernard of Gordon, and their contemporaries call it heroical or lordly love,[7] either because the ancient heroes or demi-gods were often afflicted with this ill according to the mythical recitations of the poets, or because the great lords and ladies were more inclined to this malady than the common people, or finally because love rules and dominates the hearts of lovers.

Love is called by the Greeks ἔρος with *o* when, in general, it signifies the desire for something (though Pindar borrowed it to designate Cupid), and with ω when it signifies love in the true sense.[8] Some say that when written with ω it signifies lust, and with *o* honest and praiseworthy friendship.[9] Whatever the case, ἔρος or ἔρως either derives from

παρὰ τὸ ἐλεῖν ἐλόντα, which is to say "by capturing the one who captures" by changing λ into ρ, or else from ἀπὸ τοῦ "Αρηος, the name of
his father Mars, or from ἀπὸ τῆς ῥώμης, which is to say force or strength,
since love is the strongest of all the gods, as Agathon demonstrates in
Plato's *Symposium*. According to Lucian, love, while still in his cradle,
won the victory in a wrestling match against Pan who here represents
nature[10]—unless we prefer to take it from εἴρω (which in Hesiod signifies
to dedicate) because the passionate lover consecrates all his desires, his
will, and actions to the merits of the beloved. Plotinus has it derive from
ὁρᾶν [sight], because ὁρᾶν τὸ ἐρᾶν: "through the sight love is born."[11]
Theocritus writes:

> I saw, and madness seized me.[12]
>
> At the first look I perished: thus a wicked
> deception stole my soul.[13]

Aristotle states in the *Ethics* that the principle behind all manner of love
and friendship seems to be the pleasure taken in by the eyes,[14] for which
reason the poet Propertius calls the eyes the conductors and guides of
love:

> If you don't know, in love the eyes are guides.[15]

The eyes are the windows by which love enters to attack the brain, the
citadel of Athena; they are the true conduits by which it flows and glides
into our bowels, a point eruditely and copiously proven by Marsilio
Ficino and François Valleriola in his *Medical Observations*,[16] which they,
in turn, seem to have learned from the ancient poet Musaeus who, in his
hymns, sings as follows of the famous lovers Hero and Leander:

> For the beauty of an irreproachable woman, if all praise her,
> Penetrates mortals more than a well-feathered arrow.
> The eye is a path; from the eye which is touched,
> The wounding force slides toward a man's heart. [17]

The lady of incontestably perfect beauty, says the poet, wounds the
heart through the eye more quickly than the feathered arrow, and from
the eye love darts and glides into the vital organs where it generates
malign ulcers and venomous bile. In keeping with this, Plutarch teaches
that the lover, in a sense, melts away as he looks upon and contemplates
the beauty of his lady, as though he would fuse himself with her.[18]
Reciprocally, the sparkling eye of the beloved pursues from every side
in order to surround, bind, and tightly squeeze the lover's heart. For
this reason, Hesiod calls beautiful eyes ἑλικοβλεφάρους [quick-glancing]

and Pindar calls them ἑλικῶπιδος [bright-eyed] metaphorically derived from ἕλικες, the tender shoots and twining sprigs of the vine, for just as these tendrils attach themselves to the first branch they meet and wrap themselves around it, in the same fashion the eye of a beautiful lady twists about and attaches itself to the heart of the one who attentively looks at her.[19]

   Plato in his *Cratylus* wants love to be called ἔρως ὅτι εἰσρεῖ, which is to say flowing from the eyes to the heart, or else ἵμερως from ῥώ signifying the fluxion that draws in the soul (although others claim that he said ἵμερος as if it were ἥμερος meaning having the power to tame and make tractable), or else πόθος, which also differs from ἵμερος in that it signifies the desire for that which is absent, while the latter signifies the desire for that which is present.[20] Our grammarians have it derive from ἐρωτῶ because lovers are always suppliants, begging their mistresses for favors.[21] It seems to me that the carnal love for which we are seeking the cure Plato more fittingly calls πιγμὸς [suffocation or strangulation],[22] since this love chokes and smothers true love; it is even better named by the Aeolians Ἄρπυς [thief], because παρὰ τὸ ἁρπάζειν τας φρένας [it ravishes and steals the heart away], together with the lover's freedom and judgment. Parthenius in Crinagoras writes:

Love the spoiler leaped upon both and plundered them.[23]

Certain others call it φιλογυνίαν, φιλανδρίαν, αἰδρομανίαν: "the desire to touch is not an element of love, but rather a kind of wantonness and an enslaving passion of man" in the words of Marsilio Ficino, following his master Plato.[24] Such names as φιλία [friendship], φιλότης [benevolence], and εὐμαθεία [docility] are also characteristic and can be assigned to love.

   The Hebrews, it is said, call love *hahaba*, the Chaldeans *hebeda*, the Italians *amore*, which according to Guittone d'Arezzo and Giovanni Giacomo Calandro means cruel death when the word is divided into *a* and *more*.[25] By the Latins it is aptly called *amor*, and the French *amour*; improperly it is called delectation, friendship, and goodwill.

IV

Of melancholy
and its several varieties

Melancholy, according to Galen, is a form of dotage without fever accompanied by fear and sorrow, for which reason the Greeks use the term μελαγχολᾶν, meaning to be out of one's mind.[1] Aristophanes in his *Plutus* takes the term in this sense: "by heaven the man's mad;"[2] and τὸ χολᾶν in the Attic dialect means to be a fool, according to the scholiast of this poet. What we call dotage the Greeks call more appropriately παραφροσύνην [wandering of the mind] when one of the powerful faculties of the soul, such as the imagination or the judgment, becomes depraved[3]—a condition to be found in all melancholiacs insofar as they fashion a thousand fantastical chimeras and imagine objects that neither exist nor ever will.[4] Fear and sorrow are the inseparable symptoms of this miserable passion that prevents the immortal soul from exercising its faculties and virtues.[5]

Because all the physicians are in common agreement that, as the shadow follows the body, so all symptoms follow some disease, it is necessary to pose as a true and basic principle that melancholy corresponds to a related state of disease which they assert to be the cold and dry intemperature of the brain. It therefore follows that the brain is the diseased part (being that which is, according to Aretaeus χῶρος αἰσθήσιος [the seat of sensation]),[6] not in its structure, because there are no unnatural tumors, no ventricles crowded or overfilled, as in the case of epilepsy or apoplexy, but rather in its substance and temperature, for these become too dried out and refrigerated. We can find this described in Hippocrates in bk. VI of the *Epidemics* where he says that epileptics often become melancholiacs and vice versa according to the extent to which the melancholy humor occupies the ventricles, or rather the substance of the brain: "melancholiacs usually become epileptics, and epileptics melancholiacs; of these two states, what determines one over the other is the direction that the disease takes: if it develops in the body, epilepsy, if in the intelligence, melancholy."[7] According to Hippocrates, if this humor alters the soul, that is to say the temperature by which the noblest actions of the soul function, it causes melancholy, but if it spreads into the ventricles and cavities of the brain, falling sickness or epilepsy will result.

In addition, it is essential to know that there are three kinds of melancholy:[8] the first arises from black choler engendered in the brain; the second is produced when the humor is spread over the entire body through the veins; and the last is the flatulent or hypochondriacal, because the disease is situated in the hypochondries, containing the liver, the spleen, the mesentery, the intestines, the pylorus, the vein of the womb, and other [adjoining] parts of the body, any of which may be the seat of hypochondriacal melancholy, and not the orifice of the stomach only (which was the view of the ancient physician Diocles), as Giovanni Battista Silvatico learnedly debates in his Controversy no. 34.[9]

We are justified in relegating love and erotic melancholy to this last category because it is the liver and the surrounding parts that are principally affected[10] and because the essential faculties of the brain are corrupted by the blackish vapors that rise from the hypochondries to the citadel of Pallas, that is to say the brain, as I will explain more thoroughly in the following chapter.

V

Of the definition of love and erotic melancholy

A true definition, according to the teachings of the philosophers [of the Lyceum], consists of genre and difference, but because we are often lacking the true differences we are allowed to substitute the properties, which are not the same in all sciences.[1] For this reason, the physician defines otherwise than the metaphysician, the doctor differently than the lawyer, and the orator does not give the same definition as the poet. Verification of this doctrine can be seen in the way in which the Peripatetics define love as an argument and sign of goodwill by apparent favor; the Stoics claim that it is a desire raised by the beautiful; the Academics have determined that love is the desire to enjoy something of beauty and to make of two, one; Avicenna teaches that it is a passion of the soul produced by the senses seeking the satisfaction of a desire.[2] Theophrastus demonstrates it to be a desire of the soul that enters quickly and leaves very slowly. Plutarch, Marsilio Ficino, François Valleriola, and many other scholars understand love to be an agitation of the blood, given impetus little by little through the aspirations of the will—almost a kind of bewitching or enchantment. Cicero believed it was a form of well-wishing; Seneca, a liveliness of the understanding and a heat that gently invades the spirit.[3] Galen at one time says it is a form of desire, at another, a judgment of a beautiful object.[4]

We come even closer to the truth with Galen when he says that definitions are superfluous and useless in such matters because everyone knows perfectly well on his own what love is. The most subtle logician is unable to explain love through the definition of essences—a procedure that cannot usefully be applied to this topic. Anyone who attempts it is but a mere sophist.[5]

You will find several other definitions among our physicians which, to a certain degree, explain the nature of the disease, as in Arnald of Villanova, Bernard of Gordon, Christophorus à Vega, Mercatus, Rodericus à Castro, Haly Abbas, Alsaravius, Avicenna, and Paul of Aegina which I will not relate to you for the moment.[6] Rather I would request you to accept one of my own that will be based on causes, because the definition of things that have their essences ἐν τῷ γίνεται, that is, *in fieri* or dependent on their causes brought about by their efficient causes, is the best and most apt for [explaining] accidents as the essential [definition] is for [explaining] the substance. Because substances are composed of matter and form, and the form pertains to the substance without intermediary, of necessity the form is the essence of the substance. In an accident, the form, by contrast, relates to the subject by means of the efficient cause. For example, the eclipse of the moon is in the moon because of the interposition of the earth, whereas when this planet is at the full, it is to be found at the head or tail of the dragon; of necessity this efficient cause must be included in the definition of the eclipse of the moon.[7] Moreover, in the definition of the substance, kind [genre] takes the place of matter, and the difference holds the place of the form, which gives essence to the cause; in contrast, for the accident, form is genre and the matter together with the efficient cause forms the difference, for seeing that the accident inheres and is attached to the subject, then of necessity it is by the subject that one accident differs from another. Hippocrates recognized this in his book on winds [breaths] where he states that diseases are different to the degree that the diseased parts differ one from another.[8] But seeing that the essence of the accident depends on the efficient cause, then this cause must occupy the place of the last difference. On this basis I would say, then, that love or erotic passion is a form of dotage, proceeding from an inordinate desire to enjoy the beloved object, accompanied by fear and sorrow.

Love is a thing ever filled with anxious fear.[9]

It cannot be denied that all lovers suffer from depraved imaginations and corrupted reasoning—the reasoning, I would clarify, that follows choice, but not always that which precedes it, considering that lovers are unable to judge sensibly the thing loved, the subject of their affections, for which reason love has always been painted blind.[10]

But above all, lovers have depraved imaginations as demonstrated by the stories of Menippus, who fell in love with a lamia or fairy, of Machates, who was enamored of a specter resembling Philinion, and of Alkidias who loved a marble statue.[11] But to what purpose are all these examples when every day we notice young spruce gallants, with their long curled hair, all forlorn and sighing over some crooked and sway-backed old hag with a craggy brow, thick tufted eyebrows, weepy eyes, pendulous ears, a squashed nose, big blubbery lips curled inwards, teeth black and stinking, a protuberant chin twisted into a hideous frown, who, nevertheless, they will swear to be a second Helen whose very beauty lies in those superlative wrinkles, whose arched forehead resembles the clarified heavens, white and polished like alabaster, whose eyebrows are of ebony, below which are found two brightly beaming stars emitting, with unequaled softness, a thousand amorous rays, upon whose powerful influences their very life and happiness depend.[12] They imagine for themselves a turned-up nose, cheeks white and vermilion, like lilies colored with roses, revealing on each side a set of dimples between which appear two rows of orient pearl, perfectly white and even, wherefrom wafts a vapor more agreeable than amber and musk.

> All beauty's charms in you combined
> That love my reason could deceive
> And what you were not, that believe.[13]

If they see a neck painted, whitewashed, and bedaubed with ceruse, a breast spotted like a leopard, the teats of a goat, the centers of which look like two huge lead-colored buttons, yet they will see them in their mind's eye as a throat of snow, a neck of milk, a breast full of carnations, two little apples of alabaster swelling in tiny surges and diminishing like the ebb and flow of the ocean, in the middle of which shine two buttons tender green and red. In a word, they dare shamelessly affirm that this old trot has the thirty-six conditions Plato requires for perfect beauty. I wouldn't be surprised if they praised her excrements, or if they fed on them too, as Lucius Vitellius did by eating the saliva mixed with honey of a debauchée he was madly in love with.[14] Concerning this misguided imagination, listen to the poet Lucretius:

> The black girl is a nut-brown maid, the dirty and rank
>   is a sweet disorder,
> The green-eyed is a little Pallas, the stringy and wooden is a gazelle,
> The squat little dwarf is one of the graces, a pinch of embodied wit;
> The huge virago is a miracle, and full of dignity;
> If she stutters and cannot speak, *elle zezaye*;
> The dumb is modest; the fiery spiteful chatterbox is a little squib;
> When she is too skinny to live, she is his *maigrelette*, his *chérie*;
> She is *svelte* when she is half dead of consumption.
> A swollen thing with great breasts is Ceres herself with Iacchus at the
>   breast,
> The pug-nosed is Silena or the she-satyr, the thick-lipped is *kime*.
> . . . .
> Thus women that are in many ways crooked and ugly
> We often see to be thought darlings and to be held in the highest honor.[15]

Plutarch teaches us that this imperfection is common to all those who are besotted with love: "we know, at any rate, that all persons in the bloom of youth do somehow or other act as a stimulus upon the man inclined to love; the fair ones he names children of the gods, the dark manly, while the hook-nosed he endearingly terms kingly, the snub-nosed fetching, the sallow honey-hued, and so he likes them all."[16] That is to say, he who loves calls his friend if he is white, son of the gods, the black virile, the flat-nosed gentle, the aquiline royal, the pale a redhead. It is enough to set before the eyes of the passionate lover an object of partial beauty—whether in reality or merely in appearance—for him to fasten himself like ivy, ozier, or the tendrils of the vine, winding himself about and attaching himself to the first person he meets; soon after he is so besotted by love that one can scarcely recognize him.

> Good lord, what a strange disease this is;
> Think of men changing so much
> Because of love that you wouldn't know they are the same men.[17]

For this reason the poets, hiding truth under the shadow of fable, wrote stories about the suitors of Theophane transformed into werewolves, and about the courtiers of the goddess Circe metamorphosed into swine.[18]

According to Galen and his followers, fear and sorrow—the characters and accidents inseparable from the state of melancholy—are traceable to the blackness of the humor; they believe that once the animal spirits have become darkened by the black vapors arising from the melancholy blood, all objects presented to the imagination become horrible and frightening,[19] just as the blackness of the night normally provokes a sense of dread and fright, especially in idiots and small children, according to the Coryphaeus of the physicians [Hippocrates]. In the same way, melancholiacs live in perpetual fear, as if they had this murky darkness continually in their brains—an opinion the subtle Averroes could not accept, and for which he mocks Galen, extracting several absurd consequences from the assertion.[20] Rather, he traces melancholy fear and sorrow to the property and idiosyncrasy of the humor, or better, to its cold temperature, responsible for the effects contrary to natural heat. Such heat renders a person robust, active, and lively in his actions; the cold, contrariwise, renders him timid, sluggish, and dull, for which reason we see that eunuchs, old people, and women are more timid or more sorrowful than the rest of mankind, for according to Galen the habits and affections of the spirit follow the temperament of the body.[21]

I agree with the learned André Du Laurens that we can bring the differing opinions of these two excellent physicians and philosophers into accord if we join the two causes together: the temperature of the humor as the principal cause, and the black color of the spirits as a contributing cause.[22] The melancholy humor, being cold, chills down not only the brain but also the heart—seat of that courageous strength called irascible—quelling its ardor and instilling fear. The same black humor thickens and obscures, as with smoke, the animal spirits which should be clear, pure, subtle, and luminous. Then the spirits, the first and principal element of the soul, blackened and chilled at the same time, begin to disturb the more noble faculties, and above all the imagination, presenting it always with black species and strange visions that can be perceived with the eye (though they arise from within), a phenomenon demonstrated by Du Laurens to take place in persons about to experience a suffusion of blood or a critical hemorrhage.

Concerning desire, which is the efficient cause of erotic melancholy, I will recount to you a pleasant fable drawn from Plato's *Symposium* where Diotima relates to Socrates how, when Venus was born, all the gods came to a banquet, among them Porus, god of plenty and son of Good Counsel.[23] After they had all dined, there arrived also, though quite late, Penia or Poverty, who remained at the gate begging a few scraps of the meat remaining from the abundant feast. Porus, drunk on nectar, went into Jupiter's garden where he was overtaken by a profound sleep. Penia lay down beside him and by this ruse conceived Love who, in keeping with his mother's nature, is always poor, lean, dirty, barefoot, wandering the earth without bed, house, or blanket, sleeping in doorways and in the streets. But taking also after his father, he pursues good and beautiful objects, he is manly, courageous, impetuous, and wily, ever contriving new tricks, a huntsman, prudent, ingenious, a philosopher and subtle enchanter, a sorcerer and sophist. I will pass over in silence the allegorical interpretations of this fable by Plutarch, Marsilio Ficino, Plotinus, Pico della Mirandola, and several other academic philosophers and say that Penia or poverty represents the lover (love is desire, and desire is a kind of beggary or poverty according to Aristotle).[24] Porus is he who is worthy to be loved, being naturally perfect; but for all that, he is indifferent to love. Notwithstanding, while he is asleep—the eyelids of his soul heavy with the poppy of carelessness, and without any regard to the imperfections of his partner—he takes his pleasure.

VI

The external causes
of love melancholy

I will not waste time reporting the myriad opinions of the ancient poets, philosophers, and physicians concerning the causes of this disease because most of them are based on false principles and pure fantasy.[1] Such is the view of Epicurus who, according to Plutarch, claims that the image and species of the beloved object incite and tittilate the entire body, gliding along and slipping into the seed by a certain ordering of the atoms, thereby causing love.[2] Plato believes that it is caused by a ravishment of the spirit or a divine rapture.[3]

Following the teachings of Galen, I would state the efficient cause of this disease to be anything that can provoke love and melancholy, though there are two sorts of efficient causes, those which are internal, and those which are external, evident, manifest, or *procatarctic*, and which sometimes arise from what Galen calls τινὶ πρόφασιν, which is to say, opportunity.[4] The evident causes of love according to the moral philosophers and Platonists are five in number, namely the five natural senses, represented by the poets as the five golden arrows of Cupid.[5] The first is sight, according to the Prince of Philosophers, for: "no one loves without first seeing."[6]

> Cynthia was the first woman who made me the poor captive
>   of her eyes,
> When hitherto no touch of disease had reached me.[7]

If we read in Philostratus that Paris and Helen are the first to fall in love without first seeing one another, the story is meant to show us how exceptional such love is. Moreover, it was for their own ends that the Fates granted this immortal union. Juvenal makes mention of a blind lover as something of wonder. At the same time, we read in Mario Equicola how Jaufré Rudel Count of Blaye in Guyenne fell in love with the Countess of Tripoli without ever seeing her on the basis of reports carried to the Bordeaux region. So passionately he loved her that he set sail toward her country to see and contemplate this lady's beauty. But his voyage was full of mishap: before reaching land and his lady's arms, he fell sick so that she was, instead, taken aboard his ship to visit and cheer him.[8] Certain Italian writers assure us that the excellent poet Petrarch loved his Laura passionately over the years without ever having seen her, and that ever since that time such love has been called Petrarchan (*Amor petrarchevole*). To these instances I would reply, without impugning the veracity of these stories, that one swallow does not make a summer, and that such events are unusual, indeed rare. They recognize fortune as their mother, while on the contrary, "what is invariable and occurs in every case cannot be a chance arrangement, but must be due to nature."[9]

With the sense of hearing must be associated the reading of lewd and immoral books as well as those works that discuss sperm, human reproduction, and several hidden diseases concerning male impotency and female infertility, which the physicians are inclined to treat in rather crude but necessary terms. In the opinion of our Latin Hippocrates [Celsus], it is impossible to express the precepts of the discipline using modest language,[10] in spite of everything the impertinent Aristarchuses[11] have to say. Far more provocative are poetic fables, dirty sonnets, and odes; lascivious verses, songs, and the like are much more to be feared.

What caressing and naughty voice does not excite?[12]

Just as dangerous are the letters and love notes crammed with enticing words that lovers use for pressing and cajoling their ladies and for insinuating themselves into their good graces—something that Nature taught not only to men but even to the tiny birds who, pricked by love, make great efforts to render their songs and chatter more charming and melodious than usual in order to excite their mates.[13] If we are prepared to lend faith to what the Genius of Nature has written, the partridge is both drawn into an excited state and made to conceive by the male voice alone.[14] The ancient Greeks employed such terms as "life and soul," "dear heart," "little duck," "little dove," and the Latins "my light," "my swallow," "my snatch," "my little cunt" and so on.

Then call me your swallow, your jackdaw,
Your little sparrow, your little bird.[15]

According to the commentators on Plautus the words *putae* and *putillae*, signifying the parts that distinguish the female sex, were used of courtesans, but also of the ladies by their lovers, a possible source of the word *putain*, used for our women who employ that part too liberally. Respectively, the men were called "cock" and "lusty dick" and in this country *potons* from πόθων, πόθιον, πόθη, which words according to Dioscorides, Aristophanes, and Suidas signify the foreskin.[16] Others (according to Plautus still), use the following terms: "my heart," "my bee-stings," "my soft little cheese," and so forth.

I also associate music with the sense of hearing, for according to Boethius the Phrygian mode has such powers for exciting the spirit that a young Tauromenian, frustrated in his love for a lady, upon hearing this music went out of his mind with rage and burned down the house where she was hiding.[17] Occasionally, however, an awkwardness in singing, a displeasing voice, and an ill manner in execution will serve as a ready cure for love. Pallas, according to the poets, one day wanted to play the flute before the company present, to the annoyance of Venus and Juno. But in filling the flute with her breath, she made such a contorted face that Juno and Venus began cracking jests about it, making Pallas smash her pipe on the ground in anger.[18] I will leave aside the formulas for greetings, supplications, and complaints set out by Aeneas Sylvius, Jacopo Caviceo and Boccaccio, and by the Abbot Tritheim in his *Stenographia* and similar trifles.[19]

Blaise de Vigenère, commenting on Philostratus, says that the ancients used a certain perfume made of aloe wood, red roses, oriental musk, a paste of red coral in a conserve of sparrow's brain, and the blood of a young pigeon. This is not preposterous given that physicians prescribe musk, civet, ambergris, powder of violets, cypress, sweet-scented waters, and similar odoriferous medications for those who are barren or of a cold constitution and unable to perform their marital obligations. Justin and Plutarch, writing on the topic, relate that the great Alexander was much sought after by the ladies because he had an appealing odorous sweat.[20]

But the most effective cause of all and the most dangerous is the use of hot, spicy, flatulent and melancholy meats, which I will discuss more fully hereafter, though I would place as an even greater threat familiarity and frequent conversation.[21]

> It is habit that breeds love:
> For that which is frequently struck by a blow, however light,
> Still yields in the long run and is ready to fall.[22]

That was what brought the beautiful Deidamia to her demise—the daughter of King Lycomedes of the Isle of Scyros whom Achilles debauched while disguised as a girl—and also the lovely Helen.[23] Such familiarity leads to balls, dances, games, masquerades, and other pastimes dangerous to those inclined to love. Just as pikes, according to Battista Mantuano, are the arms of the Macedonians, lances of the Amazons, javelins of the Romans, arrows of the Parthians, so laughter and play are the arms of Cupid, and notably that kind of laughter the Greeks call κικλισμὸν ἀπὸ τῆς κίκλης (which according to Vigenère means [the cry of a] quail, and to Aristotle and Pierre Belon [that of] a throstle, mavis, or fieldfare); the French call it a *calheter*.[24] For this reason Venus is called by the poets φιλομηδεῖς, which is to say laughter-loving, παρὰ το μηδεῖς meaning to laugh or smile, though the scholiasts of Hesiod derive her name from μηδέα: τὰ αἰδοῖα τοῦ Κρόνου that is "genitals: the privy parts of Saturn" by whom she was conceived according to Plato in his *Phaedrus*, and Cupid was represented smiling by the painter Praxiteles.[25]

> Food itself is no longer pleasant when the vinegar is stolen away,
> Nor is a face winning when there are no dimples.[26]

Kisses are even more dangerous than laughter, according to the Greek poet Moschus, and to Socrates in Plato:

> kisses are noxious;
> For they transport the poisons of the lip.[27]

It is true that there is less kissing in France than in Italy and in Spain where kissing is employed as a form of salutation, a practice injurious to the ladies according to Michel de Montaigne in his *Essays*, because they are compelled to present their lips to any courtier with a few lackeys at his heels, however unpleasant it may be.[28]

You will notice with regard to these external causes, as Galen points out, that they are without power except over those spirits and weak bodies predisposed to the disease, for which reason the physicians have not considered them infectious, but merely occasional causes.[29] Yet it is not wise to expose oneself to them, because to be exposed to a danger is to perish by it. They may be reduced methodically into six classes: air, food, activity or repose, waking or sleeping, elimination or retention, and passions of the mind.

As for the first, the divine Hippocrates says that those who live in the cold septentrional regions, such as the Scythians and Sarmatians, are little given to this illness.[30] The contrary must then be the case for those exposed to warm air such as the Egyptians, Arabians, Moors, and Spanish—a fact daily confirmed by experience.[31] The poet Hesiod's opinion differs little from that of our Coryphaeus when he says that women are sexually excited during the summer and men during the winter, for the reasons Aristotle offers in his *Problems*.[32] To this I want to add a general axiom from Hippocrates (from his book just mentioned in the margin [*On Airs, Waters and Places*]): "the bowels and principal parts of the body change in complexion and temperature in proportion to the changing of the seasons."[33] He concludes from this that astronomy is quite necessary for those who mean to practice medicine.[34] But Aristotle goes even further in assuring us that: "the right temperature, which depends very much upon the air, is important to mental functions."[35] This view gave occasion to our Galen to write his book entitled *That mental behaviour is determined by the temperament of the body*,[36] a work in which he philosophizes about the soul in a sacrilegious or at least misguided way, as he does in all his writings—placing him in company with many another pagan philosopher.

The grand majority of astrologers and mathematicians are not content, as the physicians are, to attribute these effects to the manifest qualities of the air, and only indirectly to the celestial bodies that control them. They also trace them directly to the planets, saying that our soul takes its reasoning powers from Saturn, its actions from Jupiter, its courage and generosity from Mars, the senses from the sun, life from the moon, and finally love from the planet Venus which is warm, moderately humid, and benevolent in her influence.

I do not wish to discuss here whether astral influences can affect the human mind and body, a question I will treat more amply in due course. It is sufficient for the moment to state that such is the view of the judiciary astrologers, who believe that the stars have a considerable influence on both the body and the mind "by indirect motion and by contingency, not directly or by necessity; in fact the opinions of the astrologers are half way between the necessary and the possible," as St. Thomas Aquinas reports from Ptolemy, for otherwise they would work against [the will] as a frank and liberal arbiter.[37] Even the pagans did not deny such freedom, and in that show themselves wiser than our modern religionists. For the most part, guided only by the light of nature, they realized that the wise man overrules the stars, and that our appetites and lusts are in our own power. For this reason, I number these influences among the external causes, which are never the necessary causes of disease except in cases where they are in forceful conjunction and meet with bodies disposed to respond to their powers.[38] The same must be said of the palpable qualities of the air, for otherwise all Egyptians, Italians, Spaniards, and Africans would be lascivious of necessity, though in truth these climes have produced saintly individuals surpassing the English, the Scythians, the Muscovites, and the Poles in chastity.

> [Democritus], in his wisdom,
> Relates how men of high distinction and destined to set great examples
> May be born in a dullard air or in the land of muttonheads.[39]

The air acts upon our bodies more continuously and quickly, while food and drink act more forcibly and pervasively. They are of two varieties: those that are hot, flatulent, and highly nutritious; or else those that are able to generate melancholy humor. More can be had on the point from Galen toward the end of the last book of *On diseased parts*[40]— to be explained at greater length in the chapter on prevention.[41] In sum, those who desire to escape this fury or madness should avoid eating such foods.

Idleness also ranks high among the exterior and manifest causes of melancholy, because in such states of leisure, the melancholiac has the time to entertain his thoughts and so render himself more melancholy, given that all actions of the mind dry out the blood and render it melancholy. Idleness is the mother of lust, because lust is born among the indolent. In imitation of their mother, they spend their time in combing and curling their hair and contemplating themselves in mirrors, the avowed enemies of all labor and serious occupation, just as the poet Menander states:

> Love is idle and comes to those who are idle;
> He is fond of mirrors and dyed hair, and avoids toil.[42]

Rather, the idle spend their time in dancing, going to farces and comedies:

> For the marrow within is tickled by the tripping measure[43]

and at various games and pastimes of which these effeminate courtiers are the designers and adepts. We read in Theocritus, Philodemus of Gadera, Aristophanes, and Virgil that the game of apples was often praised by the ancients:

> Galatea, frolicsome girl, pelts me with an apple.[44]

Sometimes lovers offered them to their ladies as gifts, as these verses of the lyric poet [Horace] would indicate:

> [some men] with bits of fruit and apples hunt miserly widows.[45]

And Lucian in his *Toxaris* tells how Chariclea, in wooing Dinias, sent to him withered bouquets and half-eaten apples.[46] There were others who substituted figs, because the fig tree is the symbol of the woman, according to Plutarch, with its rude bark, its rough and bitter leaves, and its fruit, by contrast, so soft and savory that it stands as a hieroglyphic of daintiness.[47]

Just as too much sleep in soft beds inclines a person to excess, so immoderate waking dries out the brain and renders the person melancholy, so much so that I would agree with the divine Hippocrates in his *Aphorisms*: "excessive sleep and excessive watching are equally harmful to the health."[48] By general agreement among doctors, sleeping on the back provokes concupiscence and should be numbered among the manifest causes of erotic melancholy.[49]

Our Galen, near the end of his book *On the Affected Parts* proves, through a number of reasons and examples, that the retention of seed causes erotic melancholy, especially in those persons who are inactive and overnourished, unless by frequent and vigorous exercise or hard labor they burn up the excess blood that would otherwise turn to sperm.[50] Galen reports, "I have known some that were so modest of nature that they were ashamed to engage in sexual intercourse, and for this reason became very lethargic and unresponsive. Some became extremely timorous and sad, as the melancholy are inclined to be, losing both their appetites and the power to digest what they did eat. One in particular lost a wife whom he dearly loved and, in his enduring grief, refused to enjoy those [sexual] pleasures with another that he had known with his wife; for this reason he lost all appetite and could digest nothing at all—or if he forced himself to eat, he would soon after regurgitate it all. His sorrow ruled him completely, without any manifest cause, as is often the case with the melancholy."[51] A little further in the same chapter he mentions someone who developed priapism for the same reason—from a failure to exercise sufficiently or perform enough labor to burn off the excess blood. The same principles apply to women, according to Galen, who derived this view from his master Hippocrates in his *On the Diseases of [Young] Women*, which I will enlarge upon in the chapter on uterine fury.

On the other hand, in the same passage discussed above, Galen states that similar effects are also brought about by an immoderate evacuation of semen: "those who in early puberty engage frequently in sexual relations thereby stretch the vessels that serve for reproduction, attracting increasing quantities of blood to the region, blood that in turn serves to augment sexual desire."[52]

Among the passions of the soul, it is joy that most inclines people to love, while fear and sorrow make them melancholy. The Father of Medicine in his *Aphorisms* said that "if fear and sorrow persist, they turn into melancholy,"[53] because these two passions of the soul dry out and chill the body—especially the heart—stifling and quenching the natural heat and the vital spirits, resulting in sleeplessness, indigestion, and a thickening of the blood, making it melancholy.[54] In my opinion, it is for these reasons that Diotima, the prophetess in Plato's *Phaedrus* [*Symposium*], calls love αὐχμηρός that is, squalid.[55]

But the poets maintain that money and fortune are the most powerful causes of love and erotic melancholy, understanding by fortune those chance encounters and accidental opportunities that the wise should avoid if they don't want to be caught.

As for me, fortune has destined me always to be in love.[56]

Pausanias tells how the Achaeans placed Love and Fortune under the same roof in the city of Aegira. For gold Danaë gave in to the love of Jupiter, and Atalanta let herself be conquered by Hippomenes because of the golden apples he threw in her way as she ran.[57]

He who has the means to say "accept this,"
Whenever he likes, has no need of my devices;
They will not please as much as his.[58]

VII

The internal causes
of love melancholy

By using several of Galen's texts, I have sufficiently demonstrated above
how the evident or external causes can take hold only upon those bodies
too weak to resist the efforts of Cupid. Knowing this, the learned Sappho
ascribed to the tenderness of her heart the principal cause of her ardor
in love.

> That my soft and yielding heart can be injured by the dart,
> Is the reason that I am always in love.[1]

A proneness in the bodily disposition is a prerequisite for the disease.
For lack of it, children under fourteen, girls under twelve or thereabouts,
the old and decrepit, eunuchs, the frigid and impotent are in little danger
of this malady. This disposition Galen called the antecedent or interior
cause, consisting of the humors, excrements, and spirits of the body,[2]
all of which Hippocrates included under the heading τῶν συγγεγόνοντων:
congenital causes.[3]

A copious amount of blood of a good temper and rich in spirits
through the constant influence of the heart is a true antecedent cause of
love as a passion of the soul because blood is the material cause of seed.[4]
But the melancholy humor, hot and dry through the adustion of yellow
bile, blood, or natural melancholy, is the principal cause of erotic melancholy or erotic mania, for which reason Aristotle in his *Problems* says
that "melancholiacs are subject to incessant sexual desire."[5] This would
appear absurd if you understand this text to mean melancholy from an
abundance of natural melancholy, that is by nature cold and dry and
therefore contradictory to this disease. Otherwise, the elderly, who have
melancholy humors in abundance, would be more often wounded by
love than adolescents, and their desire would increase with their declin-
ing years. But in reality it is just the contrary, for when they hear love
spoken of, they:

Grow nauseous, as if they would vomit up their former loves.[6]

But those who are melancholy from adust humors (including hypochon-driacal melancholiacs with whom we have placed the amorous) are hot and dry and produce within a variety of flatulent vapors that tickle them, driving them to extremes of lasciviousness,[7] as Galen shows us in his commentaries on bk. VI of Hippocrates's *Epidemics*.[8] Moreover, those who are melancholy through the adustion of pure blood also have overactive imaginations, which will quicken a man's immoderate ap-petites according to Aristotle in his *Problems*.[9] Such could never be said of cold, dry melancholy that makes men dull, stupid, and listless, as Giovanni Battista Sylvaticus learnedly and liberally demonstrates in his first controversy.[10]

VIII

Of the generation of love melancholy

Once love deceives the eyes, which are the true spies and gatekeepers of the soul, she slips through the passageways, traveling imperceptibly by way of the veins to the liver where she suddenly imprints an ardent desire for that object that is either truly lovable, or appears so. There love ignites concupiscence and with such lust the entire sedition begins.[1]

> From this Cupid first trickled into the heart
> Venus' dewdrop of sweetness, and
> Then came up freezing care.[2]

But fearing her own powers insufficient for overthrowing the reason— the sovereign part of the soul—love turns directly upon the citadel of the heart, and once that salient stronghold is made subject, she attacks the reason and all the noble forces of the brain so vigorously that she overwhelms them and makes them all her slaves. Then all is lost: the man is finished, his senses wander, his reason is deranged, his imagination becomes depraved, and his speech incoherent. The poor lover thinks of nothing but his idol. All the actions of his body are equally corrupted: he becomes pale, lean, distracted, without appetite, his eyes hollow and sunk into his head and (as the poet says) he can see the night neither with his eyes nor with his breast.[3] You will see him crying, sobbing, and sighing, gasp upon gasp, and in a state of perpetual inquietude, fleeing all company, preferring solitude and his own thoughts: on the one side his fear of the encounter, and on the other, his despair.

François Valleriola, the learned physician of Arles, speaking of the cure of a rich merchant from Provence who had been undone by love, and Marsilio Ficino, in his commentary on Plato's *Symposium*, claim that love is caused by means of an enchantment or charm, seeing that according to them, the animal spirits radiate from the lover toward the beloved and are returned again where, because of their great thinness and subtlety, they enter the lover's entrails and spread throughout the body by means of the veins and arteries, troubling the blood and thereby bringing on this disease. This state, for them, is nothing but a perturbation of the blood, and especially of the melancholy.[4] They give several reasons for proof, citing the example of murdered bodies that bleed when they are looked at attentively by the murderer within the first six or seven hours after the deed.[5] It follows, according to these learned writers, that persons possessing beautiful eyes, no matter how unattractive the rest, will enamor all those who look at them, unless their passions are controlled by reason. And contrariwise, no matter how beautiful a person may be, if the eyes are not beautiful, that person will be incapable of inciting passionate love, but only simple friendship or goodwill. It is as if by the beauty of the eyes (which the Greeks quite justifiably called ἑλικοβλεφάρους [quick-glancing]) they beckon those watching from a distance to approach, and so draw them into love. But I then ask you what explanation these gentlemen academics give for the loves of Sir Jaufré Rudel Count of Blaye, of Petrarch, and of the Scythian women who put out the eyes of the slaves and prisoners of war they fancied for themselves before taking them as their lovers.[6]

Holding to my first opinion, however, I say that the liver is the hearth of this fire and the seat of love:

> The heart moves wisdom, the lungs speech, the gall bladder
>   causes anger,
> The spleen makes laughter, the liver draws up love.[7]

Which would seem to be confirmed by the Prophet when he states in the *Book of Proverbs*:

> The foolish youth follows a prostitute until an arrow pierces his liver.[8]

It is reconfirmed by the poets who devised [the myth] of the vulture assiduously gnawing at the liver of Tityus in punishment for his attempted rape of the goddess Leto. Just as one cuts the tongue of babbling slaves, liars, and gossips, and as one burns the legs of fugitives, so in the case of Tityus, Jupiter wanted the member that was at the origin of this foul attack to bare the brunt of the punishment.[9] For this reason the Grammarians call those who are without love *evisceratos* or lack-livers, the fearful and pusillanimous *excordes* [without heart], and fools brainless.[10]

> Your empty head
> Has long been in need of the windy cupping glass.[11]

Bernard of Gordon does not deny that the liver is the seat of love and an antecedent cause, but he would have the genitals considered in conjunction as joint causes.[12]

It would not be reasonable to close this chapter without reporting the opinion of the divine Plato who, in the person of Aristophanes, tells how in bygone days there were three sorts of men: male, female, and androgyne (of which there remains today only the opprobrious name).[13] In build and stature they were round, their backs and ribs forming a circle. They had four hands and as many legs, two faces, four ears, and so on for the other members. But having rashly conspired against the gods, Jupiter divided them in two (like those who slice eggs to preserve them in salt, or those who cut them with hair) and immediately after commanded Apollo to turn their faces and half their neck to the side where the separation was made so that in seeing the cut they would humble themselves, and then Apollo was to cure the wound. Thereafter, each one tried to recover the lost half, running from one to the other, seeking to be reunited, until they died of starvation, incapable of doing anything without the other. And when one of the halves perished, the remaining half went in search of another, whether it was the half of a woman or of a man, and in this way they died. But Jupiter took compassion and invented a remedy for them by arranging the genital organs in front, inventing in this way a method of reproduction between them based on the male and female, because formerly they conceived and gave birth on the ground like cicadas. That was the beginning of natural love among men and the means for reconciling themselves with their past nature, wanting to make of two, one. It was a remedy for human frailty that seemed to be nothing other than a desire and search for the whole. Doesn't it seem to you that Aristotle or, to follow Julius Caesar Scaliger, Theophrastus in his bk. II, ch. 1 of the *History of Plants* approves this Platonic view when he says that the male is separated from the female so he could devote himself to learning and to other actions more noble than regeneration? This he could not do without separating himself from the female part.[14]

It may well be that Plato developed these far-fetched ideas from a perverse reading of the books of Moses that he leafed through during his trip to Egypt, since Moses appears to say in the *Book of Genesis* that our first progenitor Adam at the time of the creation was made both male and female, and that later the woman was separated from Adam's body so that he would no longer remain alone in the world.[15] Certain rabbis, notably Abraham, Jeremias, and Abraham ibn Esra, have interpreted Moses to mean that Adam was created as two persons joined together, the one part male, the other female, which were since separated by divine power. But this opinion has been so thoroughly refuted by several doctors well versed in Hebrew that it would be foolhardy to take it up again. Notice what Ludovicus Regius has assembled on this subject in his commentaries on Plato's *Phaedrus*.[16]

I am of the opinion that the ancient pagan theologians such as Plato often hide the secrets of their learning in figures, hieroglyphs, and fables, though following St. Augustine, Marsilio Ficino advises that "not everything that appears in figures contains something of significance; many have been added to those that are significant for the sake of order and coherence."[17] Without denigrating this statement by Ficino, I still hold that by this imaginative discourse Plato wanted to show us the power of love, which he had formerly identified as the most puissant of all the gods who, as the force of restoration and reconciliation, makes of two divided beings, one, through the bonds of marriage and through the conformity of the wills that unite them.[18]

Whether in erotic melancholy
the heart or the brain
is the seat of the disease

If you question our lovers concerning the part wherein they feel the greatest affliction, they will all tell you that it is the heart. Agreeing with Aristotle, we may believe the heart to be the true seat of passionate love.[1] The authority of Hippocrates further confirms the point where he says in his *On the Diseases of Young Women* that women are troubled by fear, sorrow, anxiety, and distraction when the superfluous blood that each month should be excreted through the canals destined by nature for that purpose is retained in the body because these canals become obstructed. Such blood overflows the womb and rises to the heart where it causes fear, sorrow, and madness, symptoms that accompany melancholy as the shadow does the body.[2] Moreover, there can be no doubt that the true marks of melancholy are sorrow and fear without manifest cause. These same two passions are likewise the signs of a cold heart, according to the teachings of Aristotle and of Galen, for which reason the fearful normally are called ἄθυμος, *excordes* [without heart].[3] In fact, each one of us experiences daily how the heart squeezes up when we are sad or afraid, and how, on the contrary, it opens up and dilates when there is joy and hope.

This opinion seems to have derived from the great Avicenna where he says in bk. III, fen 1, tract. 4, ch. 18, that in cases of melancholy, it is the heart that communicates the intemperature to the brain because of the sympathy that joins them, and becáuse the vapors and humors produced by the heart are sent up to the brain by means of the vessels that interconnect them.[4]

Marsilio Ficino and François Valleriola (in the place already cited) understand there to be two kinds of dotage called *desipientia*, in Gk. παραφροσύνης or folly: the one caused by a defect of the brain, the other by a defect of the heart. The brain is the cause of the dotage when it is occupied by adust bile, burned blood, or melancholy. But when the humors are retained in the heart, they give rise only to grief and sorrow and not to folly or madness as such, although the brain, through sympathy, joins in the suffering. These scholars believe, then, that lovers are afflicted with a dotage that is brought on by a defect of the heart—a view that Valleriola attempts to prove by argumentation.[5]

But to the contrary, Guido Cavalcanti, in one of his songs commented upon by the Italian physician Dino del Garbo, demonstrates that the brain is the seat of love as well as the memory, for in the memory is lodged the image and imprint of the cherished object.[6] So it is that lovers above all else enjoy reflecting upon their memories of the beloved.

Even more to the point, the physicians claim first that fear is a disturbance or perturbation of the spirit brought on by the imagination of a real or of an apparent threat. Second, according to Aristotle in the *Rhetoric*, sorrow does not differ from an inveterate and deep-rooted fear.[7] Third, according to Galen, fear and sorrow are pathognomonic signs of all sorts of melancholy, representing, of necessity, that particular disease—as we have already shown above.[8] Finally, since fear and sorrow are the effects of a troubled imagination and signs of erotic melancholy, it follows that the disease arises in the brain or, more precisely, the imagination.

The learned Mercuriale speaks to the point where he says that the diseased part is often the seat of the disease, but that at times it is the seat of the cause of the disease.[9] I hold as a salient point that in erotic melancholy the brain is the diseased part, while the heart is the seat of the cause of the disease, just as in the case of love, the liver and the natural parts [genitals] are the joint or contributing causes, according to Gordon in his chapter on love.[10]

Now let me answer [those objections] based on the authority of Hippocrates in saying first that it is doubtful the book *On the Diseases of Young Women* was written by him; secondly that the text proves only that the heart is the seat of the cause of fear, sorrow, and madness; and finally, responding to Galen, that there are two species of fear, natural and unnatural: the former accompanies a person from birth and is generated by the distemperature of the heart, about which Galen speaks in the passage cited; the latter, that which is "against the natural," is born of the disease of the brain following the corruption of the imagination, as we are clearly and learnedly taught by the Father of Medicine in his book *On the Sacred Disease* where he refutes the opinion of those who believe that the heart is the seat of wisdom, diligence, and sorrow,[11] although the brain often develops this illness through communication, not only with the heart, but also the stomach,[12] especially in small children, as Nemesius demonstrates in ch. 20 of his book *On the Nature of Man*.[13]

X

Whether love melancholy
is a hereditary disease

The Genius of Nature says that "he who does not resemble his parents is, in a certain sense, a monster,"[1] for in such cases nature has neglected her duty and therefore has begun to decline—sometimes by absolute necessity, as in creating the woman for the preservation of the species. At other times she is obstructed by the inherent imperfections of the materials, or by external causes. Among them the genethliac astrologers include astral influences and our Hippocrates "the changing and variety of the seasons, and the nature of the environment."[2] But the Arab physicians do not fail to assign the highest rank of importance in such matters to the imagination,[3] seeking to prove their opinions by clear reasoning and by examples given in Pliny, bk. VII, ch. 12, in Francisco Valles, Albertus Magnus, and several other authoritative authors.[4]

This likeness or resemblance to parents found in children is of three kinds, namely in the species, the sex, and the accidents.[5] The first depends on the specific variety of the formative faculty involved. The second depends on the complexion and temperature of the seed or the menstrual blood, and on the condition of the uterus, according to Galen. The third takes its strength from the diversity of the formative faculty, no longer specific as in the first category, but individual, a faculty that slips into the sperm and is retained by the matter on which it places its mark and imprint, thereby exercising its powers to reproduce individuals with properties, qualities, and other accidents resembling those of the progenitor.[6]

But the corporeal qualities that are passed from fathers to their children consist only of those that have been well-nigh fixed by custom, while those properties and virtues that depend on the higher faculties—those more noble than the formative faculties such as the sensitive, the imaginative, and the rational—cannot be hereditary. (Were such the case, a learned physician could produce a son automatically knowledgeable in medicine and needing no study.) Neither can one inherit diseases

258

that are not habitual, such as corrupted fevers, pleurisy, catarrh, and
nonchronic conditions. Only those are hereditary that are confirmed and
habitual, whether they affect the entire body or only its principal parts.
For this reason bilious parents engender bilious sons, the weak have
weak children, and contrariwise:

> Strong men create stout and courageous children.[7]

Those who have hot, dry regenerative organs generate children given to
the same distemperature, and in consequence, according to Galen, they
are inclined to lust.[8] Helen made impertinent use of the principle as an
excuse for her adultery.

> How is it possible, if the powers of love are contained in the seed,
> That a daughter of Leda and Jove could be chaste?[9]

Nevertheless, Fernel in bk. I, ch. 1, of his *Pathology* affirms that often
sons inherit not only habitual diseases, ἐν ἕξει [in habit], but others as
well in that one often sees children subject to quartan fever, pleurisy,
catarrh, and like diseases because their mother was afflicted with them
during pregnancy.[10]

From this discourse, we may conclude that those children born to
persons so besotted in love that they became chronic melancholiacs do
run the risk of inheriting the same disease, unless the seed of the other
parent has corrected the vice, or else a counteragent has been supplied
through good discipline, education, and a well-ordered life-style.[11] Indeed, it is to be feared that those inclined to love resulting from a distemperature of the entire body, or of the principal parts, and not from the
derangement of the imaginative faculty (as is the case with the majority
of lovers) will give birth to children subject to the same disease.

XI

Of the differences of love melancholy

My purpose here is not to spell out the differences between Love, Cupid, and Venus. Those curious about such matters can read about them in the *Elis* and *Boeotia* of Pausanias, in the *Moralia* of Plutarch, in Cicero's *On the Nature of the Gods*, and in other pagan writers.[1] My goal, rather, is to reveal the differences between passionate love and erotic melancholy, in which either the imagination alone is affected or the imagination together with the judgment and reflective powers. Speaking on these matters, Galen, in several places, says that the dotages of the melancholy vary according to the diverse ways in which the imagination has been affected, a diversity depending, in turn, upon the various temperaments of the body,[2] for which reason Aristotle in his *Problems* and Anacreon in his *Odes* compare lovers to drunkards.[3]

There are individuals so blinded by their lasciviousness that they can love a Hecuba as much as a Helen, or a Thersites as much as an Achilles. There are others who have attached their loves to mute inanimate objects such as those mentioned by Aelian and by Philostratus in his *Life of Apollonius* who were so enamored of marble statues that they slew themselves for grief when the Athenian Senate refused to sell them these beautiful idols of their soul. Xerxes fell in love with a tree, Alkidias of Rhodes with a statue of Cupid sculpted by Praxiteles, Charicles with a statue of the Cnidian Venus, Narcissus and Eutelidas with their own shadows.[4] But the Prince of the Peripatetics in his *Ethics* teaches that the affection felt for inanimate objects is not true love because there is no possibility of reciprocal affection, and that therefore the well-wishing that is the essential nature of love is pointless in such cases.[5]

I will likewise pass over in silence those base and brutish loves of Myrrha, Valeria, Tusculanaria, Canace, Aristonymus, Fulvius, Tellus, Pasiphaë, Phaedra, Phyllis, and others—found in Ovid, Plutarch, Aelian, and other poets or historians—who engaged in lewd and foul relationships with their fathers, mothers, brothers, or with dumb beasts. I would ask you to note that the symptoms arising from love bring on different species of love melancholy: there is love with jealousy and without; furious and nonfurious and so forth, as well as the various influences of differing regions and climates.[6] The orientals run slavishly after the thing desired without any moderation or discretion. Those who live in southerly countries love with impatience, rage, and fury. Those of the western countries are industrious in their courting, and those of the northern are slow to woo at all.

The cunning Italian, in pursuit of his love, dissimulates his passion in pleasing and imaginative ways such as in composing sonnets and verses in praise of his lady.[7] If he enjoys her, he becomes jealous and wants to keep her under lock and key as his prisoner. If he fails in his suit, he hates her and will try to do her any injury in his power. The Spaniard, made impatient by the ardor that goads him, throws himself furiously upon love, madly and without a moment's respite, and with pitiable lamentations complains of the fire that consumes him, invoking and worshiping his lady. But when he has won her by devious and illegal means, he kills her out of wild jealousy, or prostitutes her for money. If he cannot win her, he torments himself even to death.

The sensual toying Frenchman plays the valet to his ladylove, trying to win her grace by honest means, amusing her with songs and pleasant conversation. If he grows jealous, he feels vexed and weeps. If a rival takes his place, he affronts her with insults and promised vengeance, often including threats of force. If he enjoys his lady, he begins to distrust her a short while after and looks for a new friend. Contrary to the Spaniard, the cold German warms himself to love by slow degrees, and once taken, he employs skill and judgment in the pursuit, attempting to win the lady with gifts. If he becomes jealous, his generosity ceases. If he is disappointed in love, he makes little of it. If he wins her, his love grows cold.

The Frenchman in love is a flatterer, the German hides his love, the Spaniard convinces himself that he is loved, and the Italian is in perpetual jealousy. The Frenchman likes a merry, pleasant lady, even if she isn't very beautiful. The Spaniard doesn't care if his lady is sluggish and dull so long as she is somewhat beautiful. The Italian likes his timid and bashful. The German prefers her to be robust. In pursuing long and persistently their respective loves: the discreet Frenchman becomes crazy; the German, after waiting a good while, leaves his folly and becomes wise; the Spaniard ventures everything for his lady; and the Italian will have her, fearing nothing in his way.[8]

Finally, the most marked differences in love derive from the diversity of complexions of those afflicted by the disease. If the sanguine person fancies someone of the same constitution, a gracious, gentle, and praiseworthy love will follow. But if a bilious person loves a choleric one, it is slavery rather than love that emerges, subject always to anger and fighting, in spite of the resemblances of complexion. When the choleric and the sanguine unite, risk is diminished; they are sometimes content and sometimes unhappy. Love between the melancholy and the sanguine creates a healthy and gracious relationship because blood tempers the bad qualities of the melancholy.[9] But if a melancholy person is attached to a choleric one, there is rather a plague than love between them, and they end up, often, in despair, as did Lucretia, Dido, Phyllis, and others mentioned above.

XII

Whether uterine fury is a species of love melancholy

I note in the writers on gynecology that there are five very similar diseases that derive from love: the overheating of the matrix, prurient tickling of the matrix, the shameful symptom or distended clitoris, satyriasis and uterine fury [hysteria].[1] It would be appropriate here to speak of all five, but in order not to be prolix I will discuss only the last two, which are the same in all but certain details. According to Moschion in ch. 128 of his *On the Diseases of Women*, satyriasis in women (a view Aretaeus denies) is defined as "an itching or tickling of the private parts, accompanied by pain that is caused by an insatiable desire for intercourse: women so afflicted touch these areas with their hands without any sense of shame or bashfulness."[2] This they could not bring themselves to do unless the brain was also affected, because every person of good understanding and a healthy mind is ashamed of all dishonest acts according to the philosophers: "it follows that we are ashamed of all such misdeeds as seem to be disgraceful."[3] But if satyriasis in women affects the brain, in what way does this disease differ from uterine fury? The latter is a raging or madness that comes from an excessive burning desire in the womb, or from a hot intemperature communicated to the brain and to the rest of the body through the channels in the spine, or from the biting vapors arising from the corrupted seed lying stagnant around the uterus.[4] This is the reason such women chatter incessantly and speak about, or like to hear about, sexual matters. They experience strong prurient sensations in the genitals, but without pain, thereby differing from satyriasis, perhaps due to the damage done to the principal faculties of the brain, for as Hippocrates has said: "those persons who have a painful affliction anywhere in the body and are nevertheless insensible of that pain, must also suffer from an intellectual disorder."[5] Because such symptoms are produced by a surfeit of acrid seed and flatulency, they are found only in young girls, widows, or women of a warm temperature who delight in dishonest pastimes and pleasures, who dine on rich foods, socialize, and think of nothing but satisfying their sensuality.[6]

You may read about the nature of this condition in Hippocrates's tract *On the Diseases of Young Women* where he describes how young girls on the point of marrying fall into some melancholy madness with which they are no sooner afflicted but that

> the acute inflammation drives them out of their wits, the putrefaction makes them homicidal, the blackness of the condition causes frights and starts, and the pressure around the heart brings on a desire to strangle themselves. The most inward reason, troubled and anguished by the corruption of the blood, in turn, becomes perverted.

For an appropriate cure he recommends marriage, for otherwise there is the risk that the woman will, in her madness, hurl herself into a pit or strangle herself, believing, though in error, that by these means "being fool-proof and as sure as any" she will put an end to her misery.[7] This makes me think that the girls of Milesia were suffering from this malady who, according to Plutarch,[8] hung themselves in numbers until it was ordered that the bodies of those who had so strangled themselves would remain unburied and would be cast out naked on the dung heaps, seeing that no other threats and remonstrations would work to deter them from such suicide.[9] I would venture the same explanation in the case of the women of Lyons who threw themselves into wells hoping in that way to quell their burning lust, just as the pest-ridden of Athens during the great plague, according to Thucydides and Lucretius, pitched themselves into rivers or sewers in search of relief from their burning fevers.[10]

Clearly, then, there is as much justification for numbering these two diseases (which in general terms we may call φιλανδρίαν [love for men], in the terms of Euripides),[11] among the three kinds of love melancholy as the priapism or satyriasis in men, even though one of them carries the name *furor*, seeing that Hippocrates and Galen often use the word "mania" interchangeably with "melancholy." They differ from one another only by degrees, a point already made above, and one that can be confirmed in Avicenna where he says, in the chapter on melancholy, "that when melancholy consists of quarreling, brawling, bickering, and fighting, it changes its name to mania."[12] Modern writers subdivide this condition into five species: madness, rabies, *hydorolcos* or λυκάων [lycanthropic] melancholy, and love—understanding the last to include satyriasis and uterine fury.[13] Therefore, I will describe their symptoms and their cures in conjunction with those of love melancholy and love madness, referring you for additional information to bk. II, ch. 10, of Mercatus's book on the diseases of women; to bk. II and also ch. 10, of Rodericus à Castro who copied from him; to bk. I, ch. 33, of Jean Liébault, and finally to bk. IV, chs. 9 and 10, of *The Diseases of Women* by the learned Mercuriale.[14]

XIII

Whether love can be diagnosed by the physician without the confession of the patient

The enemies of medicine (that art referred to by the philosopher Democritus as the sister and housemate of wisdom)[1] claim that the physician cannot identify love in a person who hides it, although everyday experience reveals the contrary, and there are many worthy authors who support that view.[2] The first that I will mention to you is Soranus of Ephesus who, in his life of the divine Hippocrates, recounts the means by which this goodly ancient identified the love of King Perdiccas for Phyla his father's concubine—a love that had already made him hectical.[3] The physician Erasistratus, following Hippocrates's example, employed the subtleties of his art in order to discover the desperate love of Antiochus for his stepmother Stratonice, a discovery, once it was related to Seleucus, that provided a complete cure.[4] Indeed, one need not always be a physician to identify this illness: Jonadab recognized the impassioned love of Amnon, second son of David, for his sister Tamar,[5] and the nurse of Canace discovered that of her "daughter."[6]

> My experienced nanny understood this disease.[7]

Galen, in his book on the causes of diseases, prides himself in having diagnosed the love of a certain servant to a Roman cavalier who had employed the juice of thapsia [t. garganica or drias] to make his knee swell so that he could stay at home with his girl instead of going off to the fields with his master. Again, in the book *On Prognostics*, he tells how he discovered the love of Justus's wife for Pylades by touching her hand and watching her face.[8]

> How can love possibly be concealed?
> The fire is revealed by love's own darting flame.[9]

But listen how Remy Belleau celebrates Anacreon for his perfect understanding of the art:

So that we may better recognize them
Horses often bear on their right flanks
The mark of the branding iron.
The barbarian Parthian is known
By the style of his headdress.
And I, as soon as I see
A lover, I can guess it:
For he wears on his breast
A faintly visible mark.[10]

For as soon as the god Cupid lights the fire in our hearts, we are compelled to open the breast and cry for help. The ardor of those flames
often shows in the cheeks, making as many patterns as there are in a
rainbow.

for who could conceal a fire
That even betrays itself by its own light.
. . . .
In whatever ways I am allowed and have the power
I endeavor to conceal my shame, but none the less
The love I cover up appears.[11]

For this reason Diotima in Plato' s *Symposium* said that love was ἄστρωτος,
that is, without covering and painted nude by the poets—a trait inherited
from his mother Penia. Erasmus says in his *Adages* that love cannot be
concealed, for the eyes reveal it whether they will or not,[12] and the speech
declares it as well as the face with its ever changing colors, along with the
sighs, the ceaseless complaining, the earnest praises, the boasting, and
impudent demands. Lovers imagine those feelings hidden, says Pietro
Capretto in his *Anterotica*, that are nevertheless known to everybody.[13]

I agree that it is not easy to discover those who are only lightly
touched by passion, but those who are so afflicted by love that love
melancholy or erotomania has already set in I can recognize as easily as
any other person troubled by a violent passion of the spirit, provided
I can observe their behavior for a time, following the instructions in
Galen.[14]

I will indicate hereafter the signs by which this disease can be identified, not only in those already afflicted but also in those inclined to
passionate love.[15] One must employ all the faculties, including at times
pure conjecture, according to Galen, for it was by this means that he
discovered the dissimulation of a Roman cavalier who complained of
colic in order to avoid going to the public assembly: "this was not a
discovery uniquely medical in nature, however, but one made through
reasoning and common sense which, though anyone can use them, are
used with precision only by a few. Where medical experience is joined

to this outside or general faculty, anyone can make such discoveries as these."[16]

XIV

Diagnostic signs
of love melancholy

Just as this disease slips into the entrails of the body through the eyes, so the eyes are our first testimonial of its presence.[1] When a soul is afflicted with this malady, the eyes take on a certain soft cast which the Latins call *emissitios oculos* [protruding eyes], the Greeks ὀψεών ἀπόδειξιν [eyes showing] or ὀμμάτων ἔρριξιν [restlessness of the eyes]. Our modern anatomists call the muscle responsible for this kind of look "l'amoureux."[2] When the condition is more advanced, the eyes become deep-set, dry, without tears (unless a refusal or the absence of the beloved brings them on). The amorous have a look about them that suggests they see, as with the eyes of the body or of the spirit, something pleasing, or else they are hearing it, or longing for it.[3] If these lovers have agitated eyes, they have even less tranquil spirits: one moment they laugh, a moment later they turn sad and weep; now they jest, speaking pleasantly and amorously, and a short time later they are sorrowful, pensive, and solitary. Notice how Virgil paints for us the symptoms of the disease in Dido:

> Wretched Dido with burning passion wandered through
> The city in anguish. . . .
> Now she led Aeneas along the city walls
> And showed to him the advantages of the city and Sidonian power,
> She would begin to speak, then break her words abruptly.
> In the evening she was ready for more banqueting,
> Eager to hear again the adventures of the Trojans,
> Begging him to speak, hanging on his every word.[4]

These agitations derive from the variety of objects lovers imagine for themselves, and to the degree those objects are sad or happy they blush or turn pale.[5]

> Nor does the love he has imbibed lie hidden,

But the flame pulsating in his inmost being
Returns to his face and colors the glow upon his cheeks,
And he feels its power, run o'er his body with a light sweat.[6]

The babbling comes from the surfeit of the heart. According to Plutarch, love is a tattler about everything, and even more, it is given to praising what it loves; lovers try to convince everyone else of what they have first convinced themselves—namely that they love nothing that is not perfect in generosity, beauty, and advantage, hoping that others will tell them the same thing.[7] Such were the motives that induced Candaules to pull Giges all the way to his bedroom to show him the beauty of his wife in the nude. Otherwise, one would be inclined to say that the lover is loquacious simply because he wants to be more persuasive and more attractive.

Ulysses was not comely, but he was eloquent;
Yet he fired two goddesses of the sea with love.[8]

For this reason the ancients assigned a place to the image of Venus between those of Mercury and Pytho: the one the god of eloquence, the other the goddess of persuasion. Lucian found in this the subject of the poem in which he tells how Mercury, as soon as he was born, was able to overcome the god Cupid at wrestling, who before Mercury's birth had triumphed over all the gods and spirits.[9]

By these signs and by a languishing manner Jonadab discovered that King David's son Amnon was enamored of some princess,[10] for in love, says Cydippe in Ovid, languishment without apparent cause characterizes the amorous, together with a pale color and a weakness in the knees.[11] Through the symptoms mentioned above, Apuleius was able to point out a stepmother madly in love with her son-in-law by her "ugly pallor, drooping eyes, weak knees, restless sleep, and deep sighing arising from a slow inner turmoil." Apuleius seems to have learned these from Avicenna or some other more ancient physician.[12] There is no pattern to their movements, gestures, and actions.[13] They sigh at frequent intervals and complain without reason.[14] Sappho could no longer weave her cloth. Paris could not sleep. Canace became pale, lean, wanting in appetite, insomniac, complaining without cause; by these signs her nurse knew she was in love.

My color had fled from my face; wasting had shrunk my frame;
I scarce took food, and with unwilling mouth;
My sleep was never easy, the night was a year for me,
And I groaned, though stricken with no pain.
. . . .
The first to perceive my pain, in her old wife's way, was my nurse.[15]

In former times, the sovereign physician Erasistratus in a most subtle and artistic way recognized that Prince Antiochus was in love with his stepmother Stratonice by remarking how the color changed in his face when she entered the bedroom, how his voice faltered, how his eyes were smiling and soft (or better, according to Blaise de Vigenère, "fixed"). His face was inflamed, the sweat bitter, the pulse excited and beating unsteadily. Finally, his heart became feeble and he turned pale, confused, and baffled. He was discovered by these and other signs Sappho assigned to melancholy lovers: "his voice faltered, his face became full of color, he glanced about secretly, he quickly broke into a general sweat, his heartbeat became erratic and violent. The passions overwhelming him, he would collapse into a swoon, supine and colorless."[16] We find the verses of the learned and amorous poet Sappho again in Dionysius Longinus:

> Speechless I gaze: the flame within
> Runs swift o'er all my quivering skin;
> My eye balls swim; with dizzy din,
> My brain reels round.[17]

The same have been well-rendered into Latin by Ovid and Statius, and by Catullus as follows:

> My tongue falters, a subtle flame steals down
> Through my limbs, my ears ring with inward humming,
> My eyes are shrouded in two-fold night.[18]

The ideas appear in a more copious and eloquent version in these verses by Remy Belleau, which I present here for those who hate Greek and like Latin no better:

> I should think no one better equals the high gods,
> Than he who hears you speak, face to face, and
> Sees the charm of your gracious smile.
>
> These allurements invade me to the bottom of my soul,
> Ravishing my spirit away, for seeing your rare beauty,
> I feel my voice fail me.
>
> My tongue becomes heavy and a fire comes
> Over me spreading out under my tender skin—
> Such is the hold your beauty has on me.
>
> I see nothing else near me except your eye.
> There is a trumpeting in my ears, and a sweat,
> Cold and heavy, that flows inside of me.

I am driven on by the horror, by the fear.
I am more pale and wan than the tops
Of the grass withered by the heat.

It would take little for death to send me aboard
His boat and, so suddenly that no one will see me,
Waft away my half-dead spirit.[19]

Does it not appear that Sappho was as wise and as experienced in this art as our Greek, Latin, and Arab physicians in light of the fact that they mentioned no indisputable signs that this lady did not already know?[20]

Galen, along with Erasistratus and all our modern physicians, adds to these indicators the erratic and unequal pulse, and through the use of all these signs together, boasts of having discovered how Justus's wife was perishing in her love for Pylades. Galen explains (in his book *On the Diagnosis and Treatment of Diseases of the Soul*, and in ch. 6 of his *Prognostics to Posthumum*) that because this matron was without fever and other physical illnesses it was easy to determine that she was in love. He observed further that on hearing the name Pylades, she changed color, the pulse became erratic in several ways, resembling the pulse of those who undertake some momentous act or decision, and in this way he was able to determine that she was in love with Pylades.[21] This text has raised a very interesting question among our modern physicians, namely whether there is a particular kind of pulse peculiar to lovers, other than the unequalness that Galen called ἀνωμαλίαν [anomaly], and Plutarch θόρυβον καὶ ἀταξίαν [confusion of mind], which you can read about in the Spanish physician Franciscus Vallesius.[22] He held with Avicenna and most of our physicians that there was not, because reasonable love is an affection of the brain, while irrational and disorderly love derives from the liver and not from the heart (as we have already proven above), which in cases of love suffers only by sympathy. He does not deny, however, that through the pulse one can diagnose passionate love because of the agitation of the spirit. For this reason Avicenna says that if you want to know the name of the beloved lady in question you must take the pulse, and at the same time name the person suspected to be the cause, praise her beauty, her graces, her youth, her good parentage, her clothes, and her attractive qualities of mind, for from that moment [you will notice] "a great diversification and variation in the pulse, sometimes unequal, sometimes interrupted"—something he learned, possibly, from Galen in the previously cited work, or from Paul of Aegina, bk. III, ch. 17.[23]

Christophorus à Vega teaches another symptom, which in my view is not a very reliable one, namely that lovers refuse to eat grapes because this fruit swells the stomach and belly, which in turn puts pressure on the diaphragm and the heart, impedes breathing, and thereby prevents them from sighing freely.[24]

In May 1604, when I was just beginning my practice in Agen (where I was born), I diagnosed, by the presence of most of these symptoms, the love madness of a young scholar, a native of Le Mas d'Agenais. He complained to me of the medications prescribed to him by the doctors of that region, and by a Paracelsian charlatan. He was unable to sleep and was content with nothing in the world. He was in such a state of agitation that he was forced to leave Toulouse for Agen, hoping to find relief from his malady by the change in cities; but instead, he found himself worse off, disenchanted and in an emotive state. I saw before me a young man, sad without any reason who was jovial only a short time before; I saw his pale, lemon-yellow and wan face, his hollow-set eyes, noting that the rest of his body was in rather good condition.[25] I began to suspect some passion of the spirit vexed his soul, and in light of his age, his sanguine temperament, and his occupation, I concluded, for my own part, that he was lovesick. As I pressed him to reveal to me the external cause of his disease, an attractive girl of the house came in with a lamp as I was taking his pulse, which from that moment went through a series of changes. He went pale, then red, and he could scarcely speak. Seeing his secret half-revealed, he confessed to the rest, but would consent only to be cured by the one who had wounded him. He implored me to ask the girl's mother to let them marry, trusting in the fact that, though she was below him in social status, his father, nevertheless, would not refuse him this happiness on which his life depended. Often he repeated the line of Propertius:

Love knows no pedigrees, will cede to no old portraits.[26]

But this marriage was not possible, and so he despaired, was suddenly taken with a fever, and spat up a great deal of blood. That shocked him profoundly and convinced him to take my advice. Through medical remedies he regained his health. You can read an even better account by the Arlesian physician Valleriola about a merchant of that city who remained love-demented for six months, and who, without the intervention of his family, would have committed suicide.[27] But of what use are these examples—since there is hardly a disease more often before our eyes—if all we know is how to distinguish this from other forms of melancholy and mania, and from suffocation of the uterus, with which love has affinities?

XV

The cause of paleness in lovers

A certain pale color is so characteristic of passionate lovers that Diogenes, one day meeting a young man, by his color alone could guess that he was either jealous or in love:[1]

All lovers are pale, an apt color for lovers.[2]

But the word should not be understood as meaning white, or a simple discoloration, such as Aristotle associates with a rotting of the skin: "because pallor appears to be a kind of decay of the skin,"[3] but rather a color blended of white and yellow, or of white, yellow, and green, that our Hippocrates calls ὠχρόν [pale], ἔπωχρον [yellowish], ὕπωχρον and ἀρπίπωχρον, Plutarch and Lucretius, μελίχρον [honey-colored], the Greeks χλωρόν or ἀπόχλωρον [greenish-yellow or pale].[4] These terms not only signify green, but also pale and the color that appears in wheat when excessive heat and winds from the south cause it to mature too rapidly. Galen, speaking of the Asiatics, shows us clearly what that color is in the following way: "when the Asiatics see someone pale, they ask the cause that has made them χλωρούς [green], as if there was no difference at all between the words χλωρός and ὠχρός [pale]."[5] But he also says that this pale color is the same that one sees in fire, and in the medication we call ocher or orpiment [arsenic trisulfide]. This shade is produced within the body by a mixture of yellow bile and the watery parts of the blood—a point confirmed in Favorinus who believes, moreover, that the word ὠχρός derives from χλωρός by adding a λ after χ and transposing the ω.[6] We see then how wrong Ruellius was in his commentary on ch. 78 of Dioscorides where he denies that we have true myrrh because it is not green, believing that the word ἀπόχλωρος means only green and not yellowish, or better, the color of dried herbs, lentils, and the bark of dried pomegranates.[7] That is why Hippocrates often calls pallid individuals σιδιοειδεῖς and ὑποφακώδεις [pale yellow and lentil colored], Areteus τοὺς χροίη κλοηβάφους [dyed-green complexion] and the comic poet [Plautus] *oculos herbeos* [grass-green eyes].[8]

The poets knew that this color and not white belonged to lovers when they wrote that Clytia, dying of her love for the sun, was transformed into a pale and bloodless herb the Greeks call *heliotropion*,[9] the French *souci*, *oeillets d'Inde* [marigold], or suchlike names. This color is the most frequent sign of liver ailments, according to Galen: "a yellowish color is an indication of a diseased liver"[10] which secretes a quantity of yellow bile that mixes with undigested food and spreads according to the disposition of the body, tainting the skin with its color—the skin acting as a general emunctory. So it is that the skin denotes the corruption of the humors standing stagnant within the body. "Unless the humors retire into the center of the body, their colors will be manifest in the skin,"[11] and especially in the face, because there the skin is thinner and finer, receiving more readily the color of the stagnant humor. Then if a small quantity of melancholy bile mixes in with the bilious humor, the person becomes tawny or green-brown, or rather, in the words of Aretaeus and Plutarch, μελαγχλωρός [dark-olive].[12]

XVI

What kinds of eyes
melancholy lovers have

There is no part anywhere that better indicates the indispositions of the body than the eyes; according to Hippocrates: "discover the condition of the eyes and you will see the condition of the rest of the body."[1] This I have observed holds equally true for lovers whose eyes, according to Avicenna, Paul of Aegina, Oribasius, Haly Abbas, and Alsaravius (in the places already cited),[2] are hollow and deep-set, dry and without tears, yet at the same time continually blinking with a smiling look about them. Alexander of Aphrodisias in his *Problems* calls that hollowness χοιλοφθαλμίαν [sunken eyes], and Rufus of Ephesus χολιδιᾶν [hollowness].[3] According to Stephen of Athens it is caused by the feebleness of the natural heat and the dissipation of the spirits that abound in the eyes, or else from the malignity of the humors, or finally from atrophy.[4]

But I notice, too, a number of contradictions among these authors, for on the one hand Avicenna, Oribasius, and Alsaravius say that love melancholiacs have bodies entirely lean and extenuated, as much because they eat and drink little as because of a vitiation of the digestion arising from the withdrawal of the spirits and natural heat from the stomach to the brain. Thus they say that the eyes "are not the only parts that are afflicted." On the other hand, Paul of Aegina says that "all the other parts of the body remain in good health; only the eyes of lovers are affected."[5]

Christophorus à Vega, trying to excuse Paul, claims that he meant "by *collapsum*, a sluggish downcast movement of the eyes,"[6] but I find this explanation rather forced, seeing that the same author agrees with the others above that lovers have eyelids in a perpetual movement (*semper coniventes*), which Hippocrates called ἔρριξιν [restlessness of the eyes] in his *Epidemics*.[7] Galen, it seems to me, favors the opinion of Oribasius and Avicenna when he says in bk. II of his *Crises* that hollow eyes and pale colors are the signs and symptoms of those who are sick from sorrow and similar passions.[8]

I would like to express my agreement with the opinion of Oribasius and Avicenna, which conforms best to reason and to experience. Their view was anticipated by the Divine Philosopher [Plato] in the *Symposium* where he says that love, by his very nature, and by the vices inherited from his mother Penia or Poverty, is hard, dry, lean, and dirty, σκληρός καὶ αὐχμηρός[9] since, because of too much pensiveness and anxiety, the lover loses his physical health. If Paul of Aegina denies this, it is because he speaks only of those mildly in love and not heavily afflicted. If you cannot accept this explanation, I expect a better one from you.

XVII

Whether tears are symptoms of love

Tears are of two kinds, according to Hippocrates in his *Epidemics*, voluntary and involuntary: the latter are produced when the retaining faculty of the brain is weakened and debilitated by sickness, or when there is an abundance of humidity surpassing the cranial capacities, or else when the expelling faculty of the brain is irritated by the bitter humors of the brain or by the vapors exhaled by the lower organs—which is often the case with those given to fevers—or finally when there is some specific disease of the eye such as ulcers, fistula, ophthalmia, epiphore [a rheumatic wateriness of the eyes] and the like, without forgetting smoke, dust and other external causes.[1]

As for the voluntary tears, Empedocles said long ago that when a person is troubled by a powerful passion of the soul, the blood is disturbed and turns into tears, like whey from milk. Alexander of Aphrodisias believes that melancholy stifles the heat, forcing the humidity to rise to where it finds a freer exit from the body.[2] But I would claim that the material cause of tears is the same as for saliva, namely the abundance of serosity remaining in the brain after the third digestion. For this reason women and children and the elderly cry more easily, namely because they are more humid than the rest of mankind.

This humidity flows from the eyes because of the compression of the brain during times of sadness, or because of dilation when one is happy or laughs heartily. Because lovers are subject to all these passions, joy, laughter, and sorrow, it is obvious that involuntary tears do not pertain to lovers—who have dry eyes, without tears—but only the voluntary, as when the lover doubts or despairs of the favors of his lady.[3] Hence you see why the poets represent lovers weeping and tearful; it is because love takes pleasure in tears:

Love delights in someone shedding tears.[4]

I would not conclude, however, that tears are pathognomical, or even certain symptoms, particularly in women who, according to the poet:

> Weep when they wish to, at any time they please.[5]

XVIII

The cause of insomnia
and sighing in lovers

The insomnia that troubles lovers, making them more melancholy, sad, lean, and dry,[1]

> Night vigils make the bodies of lovers lean,[2]

is caused by the diverse fantasies that run through their brains, never leaving the soul in peace, thereby making the brain cold and dry. Besides, the melancholy humor, which by nature is cold and dry like ashes, is unable to raise any sweet vapors serving to moisten, loosen, and relax; rather it obstructs the nerves, bringing all feeling and movement to a stop. If at times they fall into a light sleep sent by nature to repair the animal spirits dissipated by the violence of the imagination and excessive waking, such sleep is accompanied by a thousand fantasms and horrible dreams from which they awake more miserable, sad, pensive, more fearful and sorrowful, indeed more grieved by sleep than by waking.[3]

Sighs come to melancholy lovers because they forget to breathe due to the absorbing fantasies they feed upon, whether in looking upon the beloved or in contemplating her absence, in meditating upon her winning qualities or in searching for the means to enjoy the desired object. Once the lack is realized, nature is constrained to draw in the quantity of air in a single gasp that is taken in normally in two or three breaths: that form of respiration is called a sigh, which is in fact a doubling of the breath.[4]

XIX

During what age one is
subject to love melancholy

Although Democritus, as the divine Hippocrates reports of him, said that every man from the time of his birth is inclined not only to disease, but he himself is the disease,[1] nevertheless, certain diseases apply to specific age groups and occur in specific seasons, according to Hippocrates in bk. III, aphorism 19.[2] But he also teaches in his *Coan Prognoses* that man is subject to all kinds of diseases from age fourteen onwards till he is forty-two: from the age of fourteen to forty-two the body is capable of developing all diseases.[3] We must now try to find out if men outside this age group are subject to this disease.

Since love is, according to Plato, a powerful desire in man to reproduce, then as long as he is able to procreate, he will also be subject to love and therefore to love melancholy—if his desire goes beyond the limits of reason. There are those who claim that a man is capable of engendering from the age of nine or ten, a view confirmed by the examples of King Solomon and King Ahaz who had children at ten or eleven years. St. Gregory, St. Jerome, and Albertus Rosarius have written of other examples they have seen.[4] And what seems incredible, Pliny assures us that among the Indians, the Mandri and Calingi have children at five and six years old.[5]

Others, on the contrary, deny this faculty to men under the age of twenty, for which reason the Germans prohibit their adolescents from engaging in sexual intercourse before that age.[6] But I follow the common opinion that men and women are subject to erotic melancholy from the time they come into puberty, which is signaled in boys by the changing of the voice and in girls by the swelling of the breasts—for the vast majority of them between twelve and fourteen—the inspection of which rightly serves as a general rule for determining puberty, as specified in the constitution of the Emperor Justinian:

stopping shameful practices by searching the body.[7]

281

I would reply to the stories reported above, assuming them to be true, that such examples are extremely rare, and that such persons were short lived (indeed, witness Solomon who lived only forty years), for which reason their puberty came on more quickly insofar as nature wills that creatures who perish early should come sooner to their maturity. Such is the case with women who, according to Aristotle, "because they mature younger than men, often die before them."[8]

Just as adolescence or puberty opens the door to love, so old age closes it. When Solon saw this to be true in his own case, he thanked God for his advanced years, feeling more the pleasure and contentment of being delivered from the pangs of love than the inconveniences of old age. Aristotle says that it is around seventy that the advanced in years no longer fear Cupid and make signs of scorn at Venus.[9] The Emperor Tiberius desired that all those over sixty who allowed themselves to get carried away by such passions should be punished, and to that end published the *lex Papia Poppaea*, to which the poet Gallus makes allusion when he writes:

How miserable, when pleasures are reckoned by their punishments.[10]

The goodly ancient Avenzoar refutes Aristotle with several well-turned arguments that I will not relate here in order to avoid tedium.[11] Rather I will support them with the examples of King Massanissa, who had a child at eighty years of age, and Cato the Censor, at eighty-five.[12] Our historians surpass these with assurances that Vladislaus King of Poland at around ninety-two years had two sons, and the physician Felix Platter in his *Observations* avows that his father had a daughter when he was eighty, and that his great-great-grandfather had a son after he was a hundred.[13]

I would readily agree that a large proportion of men over sixty, where cupidity is concerned, have pretty well lost their grip, as Plutarch says, except for money, of course. Nevertheless, I would not exempt them entirely from the danger of this disease. In addition to the examples already cited, there was Theseus who was over sixty when he lost his wits over his love for Helen and took her by force.[14] Everyday experience shows us why the Emperor Claudius, Tiberius's successor, had good reason to repeal the *lex Papia Poppaea*.[15]

XX

The signs of those who are inclined to love melancholy

Aristotle in his *Ethics* and Cicero in his *Tusculan Disputations* distinguish between the lover or ἐραστής and the amorist or ἐρωτικός, as we distinguish between being drunk and a drunkard, since the lover is one who is besotted by love, and the amorist is one who is inclined to the folly by his natural complexion, food, discipline, habits and the rest.[1] I have already gone over the diagnostic symptoms of the lover. I must now deal with those of the inveterate amorist, because my purpose is to teach the prevention of the disease as well as its cure. In the first place, the constitution and habits of the entire body should be considered in order to recognize just which diseases one is inclined toward,[2] for by such observation Helen saw that Paris was more apt for love than for war.

> There is no use in speaking such brave and boasting words,
> Your face belies them all and makes them inappropriate.
> You are right for Venus—not at all suited for Mars.
> Let others fight the wars; you devote yourself only to love.[3]

In the second place, the temperature of the principal and of the secret parts [is to be considered], which I will explain in greater detail in the chapter on physiognomy. I will allow myself to say here that those with hot, dry complexions, or simply hot temperatures, are the most inclined to love. After them come the temperate, among whom the sanguine and jovial are ordinarily the most amorous—though for all that, I would not recommend trusting in those with austere, sad, and frowning faces, for

> even the most sober lust after young boys.[4]

Next, I consider the age, for the young are more inclined to this ill than the old, especially when the voice becomes harsh: the Greeks say rustic sounding (τραγίζειν),[5] the Latins goatlike (*hircire*). It comes in girls when

283

the breasts swell: the Greeks call this κυαμίζειν,[6] the Latins *fratrare, soro-riare, catullire,* and in Lauragais we say *vertiller.* The Genius of Nature [Aristotle] recommends to fathers that when this moment arrives they should take care to prevent their daughters from speaking with courtiers insofar as, at that age, there is an extraordinary fit of passion felt through-out the entire body. Contrariwise, old men are not inclined to venery unless they are lecherous and rascally by nature, for Euripides says that Venus is angry with old men, which is the reason, according to Plutarch, why pagans consider marriages celebrated in May to be ominous and bound for disaster,[7] just as superstitious Christians do today, because Venus loathes the month consecrated to the honor of old age.

King Lacydes of the Argians was discovered for a lover by his hair, curiously crisped and curled, as was Pompey the Great by the effeminate way he scratched his head using only one finger.

> The great man, feared by everyone, scratches his head
> With one finger; who do you think he desires? A man.[8]

Our ladies are of the same opinion as Aristotle concerning the hairy: "an abundance of hair indicates an excess of excrements, for which reason hairy men have more sperm and are therefore more given to venery than smooth men."[9] Perhaps this opinion is due to the hare, a furry creature who alone among the animals has the paw hairy both above and below, and who is also considered to be one of the most voluptuous.[10] Never-theless, our ladies hate men with scant beards, not only because they are frequently cold and sexually feeble, but also because they, like eunuchs, are inclined to cruelty and cheating.[11] Melitus Pitheus was such a man according to Plato—the accuser and false witness against Socrates.[12] The observation has even greater veracity when such people are lank, with hollow, lean, and furrowed cheeks, for according to the physiognomists such signs indicate not only a lascivious man by dint of his deranged imagination[13] but also an envious one, deceitful and consequently nasty according to Aristotle: "cleverness if not praiseworthy is knavery."[14]

A man's race and extraction are very important, as much because the sons can have the same temperature of the principal and regenera-tive organs as their fathers as because of bad discipline and training. I would add here the milk of the nurse, which, according to Favorinus, has a great power to improve or deteriorate the complexion of the body and the habits of the soul—also depending, to be sure, on the body's constitution.[15] Virgil, subscribing to this, has Dido reproach Aeneas for his education, to which she attributes his cruelty:

> You had no goddess for a mother, nor was Dardanus the
> founder of your family,

You perfidious man, but on the hard rocks of the rough Caucasus
You were born and suckled by a hircanien tigress.[16]

Michael Scotus, on this subject, claims to have seen a child nursed by a sow who, even when grown, continued to eat gluttonously like a pig and to wallow and besmear himself in the mire. Yet another who was nursed by a goat gamboled as he walked, and took pleasure in chewing on tree bark.[17]

Hippocrates, Ptolemy, and Vegetius attribute great importance to the air, the climate, country, and place of birth or of residence: "and the region of the sky [under which one is born] serves to determine not only the strength of the body but also that of the soul."[18] On the whole, you will find the Germans to be great drinkers, the Spanish haughty, the English false, the French inconstant, the Athenians ruseful, the Thracians thick, the Sarmatians chaste, and contrariwise the Neapolitans, Egyptians, Asiatics, and Africans bawdy and inclined to lust. Ovid puts the Thracians in the same category in speaking of Tereus:

Her beauty indeed was worth it; but in his case
His own passionate nature pricked him on,
And, besides, the men of his clime are quick to love;
His own fire and his nation's burnt in him.[19]

But all these signs are uncertain, indeed pure conjecture, for as Apuleius says: "in dull, backward Scythia the wise Anacharsis was born, in Athens the fool Melecides."[20]

What shall we say of the little blind dog living in Italy during the reign of Justinian that, by certain signs, could single out those spurred by lust, or of the bird porphyrion who looked as though she were strangling herself whenever she smelled an adulterer in her master's house,[21] or of the probationary waters of the ancient Hebrews, used to find out if a married woman was harboring any illicit loves, which when tasted would immediately parch and wither the unclean, but would bring greater health to the falsely accused?[22]

Finally [what shall we say] of that fountain, the water of which burned adulterous and wanton women, but in no way injured the chaste? Long ago, Burgolfe—who was thought to be lying—in order to give assurances to her husband, a Burgundian and a man justifiably jealous, one day plunged her arm into that fountain and in a trice withdrew it all broiled and burned.[23] What shall we say, I ask—unless God has given to many things occult properties that even the most learned philosopher could not pertinently account for? "Indeed the power and majesty of the nature of the universe at every turn lacks credence":[24]

Nature conceals many things with her sacred cover, preventing mortals from knowing all her secrets. Man is invited to marvel and worship, but we must not attempt to search out those deepest mysteries; rather we must accept that we cannot know those things that belong only to the spirits.[25]

It is much easier to explain how it is that many can identify wanton lovers by the precious stones in their rings, which become obscure, smoky, and pale due to the vapors given off by the lecherous—something particularly noticeable in eranos or turquoise.[26]

The genethliacal astrologers have more subtle signs taken from the horoscope, though they are no more trustworthy. They say that someone born under the conjunction of Venus and Mars will indubitably lean toward love and erotic melancholy, but perhaps to his great harm, for if the sun rises under the conjunction of these two planets, he will not be

> more fortunate under the sign of Mars
> In avoiding the snares [of love].[27]

Aristotle in his *Politics* takes this to mean that martial and military types are easily snared and beguiled by love: "all these kinds of men are prone to venery."[28] The physicians say that the astrologers by Venus mean phlegm or rather the blood, and by Mars the choler, for Mars is hot and dry, Venus humid, which two complexions joined together incline such people to mutual love. They say the same of those born when Venus is in Leo, or when the moon looks at Venus, or again when Jupiter is in the trine or sextile aspect with the sun or Mercury, particularly if they encounter one another on the second or the fifteenth day of the moon.[29]

But there is no need to linger over the words of these people who are usually charlatans, as St. Augustine instructs us,[30] for the reasons amply deduced by Giovanni Pico della Mirandola in the twelve books he wrote against judiciary astrologers (whom he hated because one of them, Bulanus, showed him by his horoscope that he would live to be only thirty-four years old; which turned out to be the case).[31] His work contained, it would seem, everything that could be said against these smoke-sellers, a work seconded by his nephew Giovanni Francesco Pico della Mirandola in his *De rerum praenotione*[32] and by several other modern authors.[33]

Nevertheless Galen, the prince of the rational physicians, in his bk. III, chs. 5 and 6, of his *Critical Days*, attributes a great deal of power to the planets to influence sublunary matter, and he divides those influences, as the astrologers do, into the benign and the malign.[34] Many make an effort to prove that no one can be a good physician without a knowledge of genethliacal astrology, which they say is as grounded upon experience as medicine is, and which possesses aphorisms of its own as certain as those of our profession. On the other side, there are those overly superstitious persons who abhor even the name of astrologer, esteeming them all to be sorcerers or magicians. It is expedient, then, to write the following chapter in order to explain the truth of that science and its utility in the practice of medicine, since Hippocrates has said that medicine and astronomy are sisters and daughters of a common father, Apollo.[35]

XXI

Whether by astrology
those inclined to love melancholy
can be known

Astrology, according to the opinion of certain philosophers, is a part of
natural philosophy dealing with the stars, invented by a certain Actinus, thereafter surnamed son of the sun, or else by Mercury, or by
his grandfather Atlas whom the poets fabled as holding all the heavens on his mighty shoulders.[1] Servius, commenting on the sixth eclogue
of Virgil, gives the honor to Prometheus,[2] Pliny to the Phoenicians or
to Jupiter Belus, and Diodorus Siculus to the Egyptians who learned it
first from Abraham the patriarch[3]—according to Josephus in his *Jewish
Antiquities*[4]—who by his contemplation of the azure vaults so magnifi-
cently adorned, of the domed ceiling so artistically crafted, was incited
to meditate upon divine bountifulness, providence, and might, thereby
setting the example for the many philosophers who have imitated him.
For astrology, says Plato in the *Timaeus* and in the *Laws*,[5] calls back the
atheists and the impious spirits to religion and to a knowledge of a true
God, the first mover and creator of all things[6]—for which reason many
have called astrology natural theology, and Ptolemy the path for arriving
at a knowledge of God.[7]

It is commonly divided into theoretical astronomy and judiciary astrology, that is, prognostical, divinatory, or practical astrology, of which
there are three kinds. The first is that which predicts common changes
and vicissitudes of things, such as rain, floods, fair weather, drought,
plague, health, scarcity, peace, war, and similar circumstances; the second contains the method for casting nativities and horoscopes, and is
therefore called genethliacal; the last teaches how to make elections concerning what times are best to build, to travel, to initiate legal proceedings, to be bled or purged—an art too superstitiously observed and
taught by several physicians such as Pietro D'Abano, Paracelsus, Arnald
of Villanova, Dariot, and others.[8]

Nevertheless Hippocrates and Galen, together with several learned
philosophers and physicians, confuse judiciary astrology or divination

with [theoretical] astronomy because their predictions are based on the courses, movements, conjunctions, oppositions and related aspects of the stars taught by astronomy.[9]

Manardo,[10] however, along with several other learned physicians and philosophers, holds, in conformity with the teachings of the Prince of the Peripatetics [Aristotle], that the stars act upon the lower, sublunary world only through [the medium of] their heat and motion,[11] and that everything said by Hippocrates, Plato and Avicenna about astrology must be understood as being said about astronomy, just as Celsus, imitating the poets, says the sky when he means the air, and Avicenna, by the celestial faculties understands "a certain measure and proportion of the primary qualities produced by the movement of the heavenly bodies" that he calls occult,[12] given that we cannot have a perfect knowledge of it, any more than of the mixture of the components of the elemental world, as Averroes said.[13]

Jean Taxil, annoyed that a certain bigot had accused him of errors and of impiety in his *Cometologie*, has produced a learned treatise on astrology in all its splendor, dedicated to Monsieur Du Vair, where he proves out of St. Thomas Aquinas that just as the physician can judge of the goodness of the understanding by the complexion and disposition of the brain as its immediate cause, so the astrologer can make similar judgments by means of the celestial motions, evaluating that same disposition by a distant cause.[14] Following this, he concludes that the astrologers are often accurate in their predictions concerning men's conditions, though without imposing any degree of necessity on future events, since such conditions can be altered in a variety of ways.[15] This has been confirmed by Martin Del Rio in the following terms: "That type of astrology is not a superstitious one if it is used only for precautionary purposes. For example: to be suspicious that such and such a child is of a particular nature, that he will have an inclination to certain things, that the horoscope predicts for him this or that event, and so forth. We are allowed to fear or to be suspicious of similar things. Nor is there any sin in being cautious in this way, for it is a part of prudence, and therefore good in itself."[16] Cardinal Toleti says nearly the same thing in bk. IV, ch. 5, of his *Instructions for the Priesthood*.[17] But one must not therefore conclude that astrologers impugn the freedom of the will as agent and arbiter, seeing that the pagans themselves did not believe that the stars controlled our wills, but rather that the wise man controlled the stars.[18] Yet the astrologers do say that the stars can move our wills "by indirect motion, that is to say at a distance and by accident, directing it [the will] by the intervention of the organs of the body and by the powers residing within them."[19] "The stars cannot move us by force," says Junctinus in his *Mirror of Astrology*. "In making this distinction, it is clear how much the Neoterici were in error for not being able to distinguish between these qualities of astrology, for all the authorities writing in the Holy Scriptures, and almost all the laws, go against the opinions of the Stoics and of the followers of Priscianus, and not against this type of astrology celebrated by the Blessed Theologians, and which the Holy Canons allowed."[20]

I would agree with Roderigo à Castro that there are two sorts of judiciary astrology: the physical [or natural], and the imaginary [or artificial], which differ from each other in three ways.[21] In the first place, the natural or physical observes the natural influences and impressions of the stars, which can be verified by the senses and natural demonstration, but the artificial forges certain influences of the constellations and imaginary star formations that the astrologers attribute to occult properties insofar as they cannot be verified by demonstration or by experience, as when they say that once arrived at the age of puberty, those born under Venus will be amorous, under Mars choleric, under Mercury eloquent, under the moon lunatic, under Capricorn kings, and so forth.

In the second place, physical judiciary astrology [natural astrology] believes that the powers and influences of the stars can do nothing to the soul except by accident and indirectly, because of the sympathy that exists between the body and the soul that often causes the behavior to follow the temperament of the body.

Finally, natural astrology makes no profession of predicting with precision and certainty the nature of specific events, as imaginary or artificial astrology does: predicting for Julius Caesar that he would die on the Ides of March, or for the poet Aeschylus that he would end his days with a blow on the head, or for Nero that he would become emperor, but that he would also kill his mother Agrippina, that Ascletarion would be eaten by dogs, that Galba, Vitellius, and Tiberius would be emperors, events that depend either on pure chance, which is to say on no certain or determined cause, or rather on our will over which the stars have no power, no more than over the intellect on which our will depends.[22]

But what is worse, these judiciary astrologers often attribute to the stars the power of miracles and prophecies together with a thousand other superstitions. Unfortunately, they at times even meddle with black magic under the cover of judiciary astrology, which occasioned Pope Sixtus V to threaten excommunication for all such astrologers and mathematicians.[23]

I hold to the doctrines of the Roman Catholic and Apostolic Church by whose directives I submit all my writings, although Jerome Cardan asserts with conviction that by judiciary astrology one can better know human passions and affections than predict the winds, rain, and hail, since we know with more certainty the hour of one's birth than the hour of amassed vapors and their evaporation.[24] I say that by judiciary astrology one cannot determine whether a person is inclined to passionate love or erotic melancholy because, according to Ptolemy Corypheus, speaking of astrologers: "only those with divine inspiration can predict specific future events."[25] If this were not the case, they could foretell the illicit affairs of their own wives and daughters. It was on this very score that Thomas More reproached a certain astrologer:

> All the stars explain themselves to you, the prophet of the sky,
> And inform you of the destiny of everyone.
> But the fact that your wife gives herself to everyone—
> Of that fact the stars, though they see everything, have not informed you.[26]

And for an answer to all the examples brought to their defense, let us say with the poet Euripides, that these are fellows accustomed to frequent lying and who rarely tell the truth, sons of fear, and nurslings of folly.[27]

> Folly brought you to the birth, and Rashness was your mother,
> Ye poor wretches, who know not even your own disrepute.[28]

XXII

Whether those inclined
to love can be known
by physiognomy and chiromancy

On the authority of the divine Hippocrates, Galen teaches that those who meddle with medicine without having a perfect knowledge of physiognomy are in perpetual darkness and commit gross errors,[1] because physiognomy is a part of semiotic medicine that the naturalists subdivide into metoposcopy [metopomantia], chiromancy, and physiognomy specifically.[2]

The first is the most reliable, because the face is like a miniature of the soul, its index, its picture, its escutcheon representing many regions, the assembly of all the titles of its nobility placed on the door and in the frontispiece, so that one may know the nature of the soul's palace and estate:

> For delivery is wholly the concern of the feelings, and these are mirrored
> by the face and expressed by the eyes . . . and nature has given us eyes,
> as she has given the horse and the lion their mane and tail and ears, to
> indicate the feeling [of the mind.][3]

Such is the reason Alexander of Aphrodisias calls the eyes "the mirrors of the soul."[4] It seems, says Plotinus, that everything that is beautiful must also be good (there is only one word for both in Greek, τὸ καλὸν) as if the exterior beauty depended on the internal form.[5] The ancient Greeks, in considering this, believed only beautiful persons were worthy of the scepter and the crown:

> Above all it is beauty that is worthy of sovereignty.[6]

They prove their opinion by the examples of Priam, Achilles, Saul, Cyrus, Darius, Alexander, Augustus, Hecuba, Andromeda, Esther, and many others who possessed a physical beauty in conjunction with the beauty of their souls, inasmuch as corporeal beauty depends upon a good temperature and sound habits, according to Galen.[7] It is a principle in our schools that a good and praiseworthy complexion of the body is often the cause of commendable actions, and consequently the cause of those of the mind: "there are many things in the body that sharpen the mind, and many that make it dull."[8] Similarly, Hippocrates opines in his *Epidemics* that being lean has a certain importance for being wise.[9] For those who are too fat, in the words of his faithful disciple Galen, have their souls as though buried in muck, and for that reason they are often lazy and stupid like brute beasts.[10] Homer depicts the notorious buffoon Thersites as small and ugly with a φόξον or pointed head in order to teach us how wicked, envious, brazen, and gossipy such people are.[11] Sallust makes note of the knavery and the physical unattractiveness of Catiline; the deformity of Julian the Apostate was a manifest argument for his wicked life. However, daily experience gives reason to believe, in keeping with the teaching of Hippocrates, that those who stutter and who hesitate in speaking (φαῦλοι, ἰχνέφωνοι) are good by their nature,[12] contrary to those who have dry, beady, and deep-set eyes, the face lean, drawn, and wrinkled, the cheeks creased, emaciated, hollow, and often twitching, for they are vain, sly, railers, jealous and greedy, sacrilegious, traitors, and extortioners. This is especially so if they are accustomed to attentive staring, if they bite their lips while thinking of their business, and above all if they have scrawny beards.[13]

> A little beard and less color—
> There is no worse under the heavens.[14]

Nearly all these characteristics applied to the physiognomy of that cursed Melitus Pitheus, the accuser of Socrates, according to Plato.[15]

I would not want these signs to be accounted binding in any sense, however, for Alcibiades was the most handsome young man of his century, yet he was wanton and envious. In contradistinction, the wise Socrates was ugly, bald-headed, hairy elsewhere, and flat-nosed; notwithstanding he was adjudged the exemplar and prototype of virtue, wisdom, and continence by the oracle of Apollo,[16] though he was the topic of much speculation among the women according to Cicero: "When Socrates saw women discussing among themselves how filthy a man he was, with his nostrils like a monkey, his bald head, hairy shoulders and bowed legs, he mocked them for it."[17] It was not that he was not inclined to lust by his very nature, as Zopyrus the famous physiognomist declared and Socrates himself freely confessed, but that by moral philosophy he corrected his bad natural inclinations.[18]

Physiognomy is based entirely on the sympathy that exists between the body and the soul for, as Aristotle says, "when the character of the soul changes, it changes also the form of the body, and conversely, when the form of the body changes, it changes the character of the soul."[19] For if the habits of the soul in no way depend on the complexion of the body, Aristotle says, then the physician would never be able to heal love folly by his medications and "helleborisms"—not that I would claim these physiognomical signs always and necessarily indicate the passions and affections of the soul, but quite often and with high probability. Moreover, all the physiognomists teach that one must not make conclusive judgments based on the disposition and temperature of one part only, but rather one must consult many signs at once, without forcing the jurisdiction of this science beyond the domain of the natural passions such as anger and lust. At the same time, one must not trespass on the freedom of the will and its elections such as whether to become an astrologer, a physician, or a lawyer.[20]

I would conclude that through physiognomy, one can determine, not only those who are actually stricken with erotic melancholy, but also those who are amorists and inclined to this disease, for seeing a man who has a hot temperature and a great deal of body hair, who is red in the face, with thick, curly black hair, who has large veins and a strong voice, I would say that he has a liver that is hot and dry, along with the privy parts, and that in consequence he is inclined to disordinate love—a condition even more certain if he is bald like Socrates, Galba, Otho, Domitian, and Julius Caesar,[21] of whom it was said in Rome in former times:

> Citizens, look after your wives, for we have brought
> with us a bald adulterer.[22]

The same holds true if he has small ears, a large nose, weak and overlarge thighs, and falling eyebrows, or if he is flat-nosed like Socrates.[23] Valescus of Tarenta, a famous physician in his time, accuses women with chapped lips of having this vice, for chapping denotes an intemperate dryness of the womb "which desires" (such are his terms) "the seed like the earth the dew of the sky."[24] And Levinus Lemnius, following Athenaeus and the Scholiast of Theocritus, includes the lame, thereby supplying a reason why the Amazons crippled their own children,[25] although our Hippocrates, more worthy of trust, gives other more pertinent reasons.[26]

Aristotle in bk II, ch. 7, of *The Generation of Animals* recommends that we pay close attention to the eye in making such predictions, "for the region around the eyes, of all the parts of the head, is the most closely connected with the sperm."[27] An astute observer can recognize an adulteress woman better and with greater assurance by her eyes than by her hand,[28] for the hand, according to Averroes, is not particularly useful in identifying the disposition of the body,[29] certainly no more than any other member, and in consequence is also not very useful in signifying our passions and affections, unless it is by the pulse in the arteries of the upper palm or the wrist. By the shape of the hand we may somewhat recognize, though not very well, the temperature of the liver, in light of the fact that the great Avicenna and Rhazes speculate on the size of the liver by examining the size of the fingers,[30] claiming by both reason and experience that the veins coming from the liver, which is their center of origin and distribution point,[31] and which terminate in the hands, explain the mutual and reciprocal sympathy between the hands and the liver, and therefore the temperature of the liver is reflected more in these parts than in many others.[32] Moreover, the size of the fingers indicates the quantity of matter transmitted from the liver to the extremities, and by consequence, the size of the liver. Or it is that those with large livers are often given to gluttony, and gluttons to wantonness and lust?

But this art of chiromancy is so infected with superstition, cheating and, dare I say, magic that the Canonists and, a short while ago, Pope Sixtus V were compelled to condemn it.[33] No one makes public profession of this fallacious art, except the rogues, beggars, and vagabonds we call Bohemians, Egyptians, or Caramaras coming into Europe since the year 1417 according to Gabriel Dupréau, Albert Kranz, and Polydore Virgil.[34]

XXIII

Whether by magic
one can recognize lovers

Inasmuch as Plato in the *Symposium* calls love "a subtle enchanter and sorcerer,"[1] certain fools have impiously recommended the practice of magic as a means for knowing and treating this disease, a view to be fully refuted later. Suffice it to say here that just as there are ill-adjusted stomachs that corrupt rather than digest the best of foods, so there are wicked minds and ignorant wits that pervert the sense of the writings of the best authors.

It is true that there are two kinds of magic, the natural and the artificial. By the first we mean an exact and perfect knowledge of the secrets of nature that allows us to anticipate and prognosticate future things by their present and past, which our Hippocrates in his *Prognostics* and in his *Epistle to Philopemen* calls "sister or cousin to medicine, both of them daughters of the same father, Apollo."[2] But the artificial, whether operative [by exerting force and influence] or divinatory, is entirely abominable and forbidden by both human laws and divine.[3] Those who formerly professed the cursed goetic and theurgic arts [black and white magic] include Numa Pompilius, Zoroaster, Phythagoras, Hostanes Procones, Democritus, the Egyptian priests, the Persian Magi, the French druids, and today, according to some, the Jewish rabbis.[4] This condemned art contains a thousand varieties described in the writings of the Canonists as well as by Lelio Giraldi, Franciscus Venetus, Polydore Virgil, Wecker, Del Rio and others.[5]

The overactive curiosity of some of our young girls unfortunately has lured them into practicing a few of these arts they learned by tradition from their mothers or nurses.[6] But without intending to do any harm, they paganize to their damnation, for there is no doubt that botanomancy, which they do with the cracking sounds of butcherbroom, box, and bay tree leaves broken between the hands or tossed upon hot coals, was practiced formerly by the pagans who broke the poppy flower between their hands, for which reason Theocritus used the name τηλίφιλον, a word very close to δηλίφιλον, which means "tell-love."[7]

Oionoscopy is done by means of dismembering [and examining] crows, ravens, sparrows, owls, horned owls, great owls, screech owls, and other birds they calles *oscines*. Or I could report on the augurs and auspices so famous among the profane[8] and talk about these monster fowlers along with Pacuvius:

> I think we should merely hear rather than actually listen to those who extract wisdom from the liver of another creature and profess to know more from another's liver than from their own.[9]

Theocritus in his *Idyls* makes mention of coscinomancy, carried out with sives or sifters,[10] others mention cleromancy, employing the fate and chance of fortune which they call "prenestine."[11] The chance advice found by letting books fall open was called the Valentinian fate or the Virgilian fate, one often used by the Emperor Adrian.[12] I will leave aside astragalomancy done with huckle bones and such like foolishness to which one must never resort for the diagnosis and treatment of this disease, but rather to an expert and prudent physician.[13]

XXIV

Whether lovers can be known
by oneiromancy or
the interpretation of dreams

Macrobius (treating the dream of Scipio as related by Cicero)[1] and Hugh
of St. Victor[2] describe five kinds of dreams, but St. Gregory in his *Morals*,
bk. VIII, ch. 16, and in bk. XIV, ch. 48, of his *Dialogues* holds for six.[3] Tertullian is content with only three,[4] and our Corypheus, Hippocrates, in
his book on dreams recognizes only two: the divine and the natural.[5] If
we include the animal dreams with the natural, and the diabolical with
the divine, then perhaps we could reconcile these scholars, although the
Prince of the Peripatetics[6] and Petronius do not recognize the divine
at all:

> It is not the shrines of the gods nor the light coming from the heavens
> that send the dreams that mock the mind with flitting shadows: each
> man makes his own dreams. When the limbs repose in slumber and
> the mind without burdens is free to play, the harlot writes to her lover
> and the adulteress gives a piece of money.[7]

The reasons given by Aristotle on this subject are without grounds if one
regards them carefully. His authority, in any case, carries less weight and
value than that of Moses and Hippocrates. Homer, too, teaches that:

> Dreaming comes from the gods,[8]

which Ronsard expresses as follows:

> Dreams most certainly arrive here below from the gods,
> And god is no artisan of lies.[9]

Diabolical dreams are caused by evil spirits.[10] A cunning magician raised
such dreams in the Emperor Tiberius: seeking money, he made the Emperor dream he was the magician's debtor, but Tiberius, detecting the

fraud, had the dream-monger hanged.[11] The pagans induced dreams by
sleeping on skins in the temple of Aesculapius or of Castor and Pollux.[12]

> [The priest] reclining on the skins of slaughtered sheep, spread about,
> Looking for sleep, saw flitting visions marvelous in nature,
> And heard many voices, enjoying dialogue with the gods,
> And spoke to Acheron in the depths of Avernus.[13]

Our love-smitten ladies would rather go to the temple of the Goddess
Bona[14] than to that of Aesculapius, if one could be found—that is, those
ladies who go backwards to their beds without a thought of God, a God
who, because of this pernicious sin, will remember them, but only to
punish them. Once they have had a few perplexing dreams, they have
recourse to the charlatans to have them explained—such explanations as
these deceitful interpreters know in advance will please them.

> The Jew will promise you dreams of whatever kind you may wish,
> A tender lover or a huge bequest
> From some rich and childless man.[15]

The natural dreams are those that come from the disposition of the body,
for during sleep the soul seems to retire to the deepest and most secret room of her palace, and there, exempt from all disturbances, perceives more easily the dispositions of the body and enjoys everything
she desires, whether possible or impossible, as if it were present and
in her control.[16] A consideration of these dreams is greatly necessary
to the physician for recognizing the dominant humor and for knowing
the disposition of the body—a view held in common by all the authors
consulted.[17] Those who have a great quantity of humors dream they carry
some heavy load, and those who are exempt from all repletion dream
they are running, jumping, or flying. The bilious dream of getting angry, of beating and injuring; the melancholy see in their dreams funerals,
darkness, murders; the phlegmatic and the rheumatic dream of rivers,
fountains, rain storms, and snow; the starved dream of banquets; and
lovers dream of being in the company of the ladies and of going to balls,
comedies, and masquerades.[18] In all this, you will notice that everything
in dreams appears more grand, more agreeable or disagreeable to the
imagination than in reality, for reasons you may read in Thomas à Viega
writing on Galen.[19]

Animal dreams, by contrast, come from what one has done, seen, or
meditated upon during the day, as Herodotus teaches:

> Those visions that rove about us in dreams are for the most part the
> thoughts of the day.[20]

The good have good dreams, says Aristotle in his *Problems*,[21] because while awake they have good thoughts. Such were the dreams of the first Christians, according to Philo the Jew, because they meditated continually upon the power and providence of God.[22] The lawyer pleads in his sleep, the soldier fights, the mariner sails with a full wind on the high seas and the hunter returns laden with his prey.[23]

> The judge dreams of lawsuits, the charioteer of his chariot,
> The mighty steeds of which he guides past a shadowy turning point.
> The lover repeats love's mysteries.[24]

If our dreams do not conform to the actions and thoughts of the day, there is evidence of some distemper in the humors. It is thus possible to find out if a person is amorous through the natural and animal dreams, if such a person is willing to relate them while awake and without any regard to the stars and other nonsense one reads in Julianus Cervus, Artemidorus, Arnald of Villanova, and other such authors who have polluted our medicine with a thousand inanities.[25]

XXV

Whether jealousy is a diagnostic sign of love melancholy

Alessandro Piccolomini in his *Moral Institutions* strives to prove that true love is completely free of jealousy, for he who pursues something virtuous is in no way burdened by a few companions in his retinue, provided they let him shine forth and do justice to his merits. Only the weak and feeble fear competition, knowing that all comparisons with others would immediately reveal their imperfections.[1] Plutarch says, however, that virtue is undeserving of praise and will produce none of the desired ends unless it strikes the heart to the quick, stirring it with a zeal, not to envy, but to emulate good men and to do one's duty—by such a course we arrive at the height of perfection;[2] in the same way, love, if there is not a little jealousy, will never stir, will never be strong and effective. This was what inflamed the love of Achilles for his slave Briseis, of Menelaus for Helen, and of Orestes for Hermione:

> The more Hermione began to belong to another,
> The more Orestes loved her.
> Why are you sorrowful, Menelaus?
> You went to Crete without a mate
> And were able to endure a long absence from your bride.
> Only when Paris takes her away
> Are you no longer able to be without a wife.
> It is someone else's love that has kindled yours.[3]

I would say with Simonides that just as every lapwing has a crest on its head, so every true lover feels a little jealousy. Hence, that voluntary cuckold Phaulius who knavishly pandered his own wife to King Philip of Macedonia could not have loved her with true love,[4] no more than the infamous Galba who, one evening, having Maecenas in to supper, noticed he was playing eye-games with his wife and so pretended to sleep, thereby giving him the freedom to satisfy his desires. However, there was a servant who, thinking his master was truly asleep, approached the table in order to steal a pot of wine, whereupon Galba, not wanting to lose it, exclaimed: " 'can't you see, you little rogue, that I'm only sleeping for Maecenas?' "[5] Both of them had the nature of the billy goat, which is the only one of all the animals that is not jealous, according to the naturalists (although the violent death of Gratis killed by a billy goat testifies to the contrary), nor are the women of Tartary today, nor were the Lacedaemonians, Cypriots, Rhodians, and Assyrians in former times.[6]

But when jealousy insinuates its way into the mind, as soon as it reaches the soul, in the guise of friendship it pulls it down and tyrannizes over it, rendering the lover pale, dazed, lean, at times casting him into despair, as it did Lepidus and a thousand others. The very causes that served as the basis of love, serve afterwards as the grounds of mortal hate: the virtue, health, merit, and reputation of the beloved. If we could chose from all the ills the one we would most prefer to avoid, there is, to my way of thinking, none more worth escaping than jealousy, for with the others the sorrow lasts no longer than the cause, while jealousy takes shape not only from what is, but equally from what is not and from what perhaps never will be. O ingenious passion, that can often draw forth a true and living sorrow from an imaginary evil! This is what the painter Parrhasius did when he put his servants to the torture so that he could more readily represent [from their faces] the agonized and sorrowful expression of the fictive Prometheus.[7] Why are we so ambitious for our own misery as to run out to meet it by anticipating it in our own thoughts? We have seen many who have lost their mistresses for doubting their chastity, like the hypochondriacs who, from their fear of becoming sick, actually fall sick. Hence, we can say that jealousy is a double weight that makes us stumble even where we would flee as quickly as possible. For that reason a witty author once said that cuckoldry and jealousy share the same feast day. Examples confirm it for a truth, for when Danaë was at liberty she preserved her chastity, but as soon as she was imprisoned by her father Acrisius in the brass tower she lost it.[8] For there is no bedroom so well locked nor closet so secret that the cat and the lecher cannot get in:

> Some men had a craftsman make for them a door so strong
> That no cat or adulterer could get through it.[9]

XXVI

The prognostic signs of
love and erotic melancholy

Many have said that this disease is incurable because, in their view, it is entirely supernatural, a punishment, revenge, or troubling passion raised by a little demon bearing the same name and with whom the pagans associate love, just as they do fever with the goddess Febris, nightmares and nocturnal visitations with Hecate or the demigods, terrors and frights in the night with Pan, and the falling-sickness with Hercules.[1] They make Cupid the author of love, Venus of lechery, Mercury of theft, and Mars of wrath, the better to excuse the faults men commit while under the influence of these passions: "as if heaven were the inevitable cause of your deeds, and Venus did this, or Saturn, or Mars, allowing man to go blameless while the creator and ruler of the heavens and the stars is inculpated."[2] Hippocrates observed that it is the misleading habit of fools to call such diseases and their causes divine that have something new or unusual about them. If such were the case, all newly perceived diseases, such as whooping cough,[3] the sweating sickness, smallpox, the crystalline, and the like would be taken for divine and, hence, for incurable because they cannot be healed by the vain remedies of the empirics,[4] charlatans, and treacle makers, or by the charms and witchcraft of magicians and sorcerers. But since not all persons are afflicted by this disease, such as eunuchs, children, and the decrepitly aged, and since love is born through the sight, grows through conversation and familiarity, kissing, and touching, is made fierce or insane by the use of certain animals, plants, and minerals, or is extinguished by remedies containing counteractive ingredients, there is nothing about this disease that makes it more divine or supernatural than any other. For in all diseases, generally, Hippocrates recognized θεῖον, something divine.

I would agree with Galen, then, that neither love nor the falling-sickness is a divine disease: "for which reason we believe epilepsy and love not to be sacred diseases."[5]

> Love is not a god, as people maintain,
> But a bitter taste and an error.[6]

Certain others have judged the malady incurable because those afflicted do not want to be cured.

"Lay aside your loves," should some god say to me, "and live without them," I would pray him not ask it—even so sweet an evil is a young girl.[7]

They feed themselves on the vain hope of finding a cure without the help of our skills, as though they were suffering merely from itch mite.[8]

> Fond hope keeps the spark of the lover alive,
> Whispering ever that tomorrow things will mend.

> But because we like to pluck the blooms of Venus,
> We go on repeating to ourselves, "tomorrow will do as well."
> Meanwhile the secret flames spread into our inmost being.[9]

This hope incites with its soft wind the fond desires of lovers, kindling in their minds a fire full of thick smoke that dims their understanding and carries their thoughts away, holding them suspended among the clouds; it steals away their judgment, corrupts their reason, and makes them dream while awake. As long as their hopes last, they will never abandon their desires. One, in spite of his uncomeliness, thinks to soften the adamantine heart of his lady by his handsomeness, another by his graces, gentleness, and soft manner; this one takes pride in his stature and in the nobility of his ancestors, that one in his polished discourse, or finally he hopes to excite the compassion of his mistress by his plaints and frequent sighs, which are the lover's last refuge.

I freely agree with those sectaries who believe that it is extremely difficult to cure men sick with diseases they do not desire to have cured, because the healing of all diseases depends as much upon the patient as upon the doctor: "Treatment: thwart the disease, do not aid it."[10] But this is not an ultimate obstacle, since often one can invent the means for creating a desire in the patient to search for his health, as you will see in ch. XXXI of this treatise [i.e., XXIX].

Finally, certain learned persons have called love incurable, not through the fault of the patient, but of the agent, which is to say the remedy. The desperate Oenone, more knowledgeable in love than in medicine, is of this opinion when she exclaims:

> Ah, miserable me, that love resists all medications,
> For all my healing arts, yet I must remain unhealed.[11]

Indeed, even Apollo the father and inventor of medicine is taxed for his want of recipes for the curing of this disease, given that he was unable to cure his own case of it.

> Nor could he cure his trouble by health-giving herbs.
> Love had triumphed over all resources of the healer's art.[12]

Such writers do great harm to the science of medicine, the sister and companion of wisdom (using Democritus's terms), in claiming she has no efficacious remedies for this disease, for in so speaking they imprudently chastize divine bounty itself which, as the prototype of all good, according to Galen, has refused us nothing that is necessary.[13] And if God has granted us these healing agents, it is not too much to believe that we have also discovered them over the last six or seven thousand years through reason and experience—the means by which the treatments and cures for all diseases have been invented.[14]

There is no value in saying that it is a disease of the soul, the healing of which should be left to the moral philosophers and theologians because the god Aesculapius and Apollonius Thyaneus refused treatment to a rich Cilician lord, desperately in love with a lady from Tarsus, in spite of the lavish presents he offered them.[15] For our predecessors have considered the treatment for this disease not only as physicians but as philosophers as well—a quality inseparable from a good physician, as Galen demonstrates in a treatise devoted entirely to the subject, and inspired by his master Hippocrates.[16]

If the soul is afflicted by love, it is owing to the mutual sympathy between it and the body, as the Genius of Nature [Aristotle] has clearly taught us in his *Physiognomy*, and several other texts I won't mention here.[17] I will be satisfied for now in just relating to you an observation by the ever-laughing Democritus, "that the diseases of the body amaze and baffle the soul and bind up the reason by sympathetic influence."[18] When Cleomenes, Anaxandrides's son, was sick, his friends accused him of having new humors and new opinions not at all like him, to which he answered: "that doesn't surprise me since I'm not the same person I was when healthy, and now being somebody else means having different humors and different opinions."[19] If apoplexy can make drowsy or altogether put out the eye of our intelligence, then there can be no doubt that melancholy, love, indeed even catching cold, can make it dim, so that scarcely is there an hour in a lifetime when our judgment finds itself in its proper estate. A body can undergo so many transformations and be stifled in so many of its jurisdictions, indeed find itself in a state of such agitation—as if someone were pulling and thwarting it—that a man cannot afford to be perpetually cognizant of the condition for fear of being entirely subjected to its contrary passions.

These considerations brought that same philosopher to wish that everyone knew the arts of medicine so that by healing their bodies they could, by these means, keep their minds in perfect health. Galen confirms this principle in his *Prognostics*, where he boasts of having cured several physical diseases by assuaging the perturbations of the soul through the use of medications combined with subtle strategies and oral counsel, which are the medications of the mentally distressed.[20]

When the soul is diseased, words are the [best] physician.[21]

From this we may extract the message that those who deny that medicine has any good words and wise counsel to offer are simply motivated by resentment; the poet writes amiss in calling it a mute science:

He preferred to know the powers of herbs and the practice of healing,
And to follow mute arts without glory.[22]

Unless we argue that Virgil calls medicine mute to discourage the physician from being a babbler and gossip, according to our Hippocrates,[23] for as the ancient comic poet says:

A garrulous physician is an added disease to a sick man.[24]

Finally, then, love is not incurable, though it is not easily cured, for which reason the poets attribute to love the gryphon's feet, indicating how quickly it enters, but how slowly it departs.[25]

Love enters under the will of the soul, it is not imposed.[26]

This malady is even more difficult to cure if it is accompanied by the symptoms mentioned in chapter XXV, namely those of jealousy:

The man afraid of losing his love, of having her taken by another,
Will never be cured by Machaon's skills.[27]

For then the heart and the brain suffer through the sympathetic influence of the liver and the secret parts. Or as Hippocrates says: "those diseases arising from the principal organs and parts of the body are always the worst."[28]

The astrologers say that it takes a great deal of time, care, and diligence to cure melancholy lovers if they suffer under the influence of Saturn, but especially if at the time this scythe-bearing god is either retrograde, or in conjunction with Mars, or in opposition to the sun. And if Venus is met with in the house of Saturn or is in a trine or sextile aspect with the moon at the time of the patient's birth, it is to be feared that he will be a long time afflicted with this disease.[29] Such is the opinion of the astrologers. Mine is that old men suffering from erotic melancholy are more dangerously sick than the young.

> Old men captured by love are in the gravest danger.[30]

Thus it was that our Corypheus said in his *Aphorisms* that the diseases not corresponding to the seasons, nature, habits, and age of the patient are more threatening than those that do.[31] Such is love in old men, which any wise person will condemn in the same fashion as the comic poet:

> For a young man to love is a pleasure, for an old man a crime.[32]

Pindar says of those forms of love prohibited by both human and divine laws "that men therefore seek them all the more, even going mad for what they cannot have,"[33] which our Hippocrates claims to be the case with old men in love. Avicenna teaches that if this disease becomes habitual it is incurable and renders the victim hectical, sottish, dull, and sometimes so savage that he turns lycanthropic or takes his own life, as I demonstrated earlier with several examples.[34]

XXVII

Of incubi and succubi

Certain theologians have believed that unbridled and melancholy love can spread its powers and jurisdiction even to the angels and demons, and that for this reason the Apostle [Paul] ordered women to veil their heads in the churches [that is "because of the angels"],[1] though by this word angel several say that the Apostle meant the priests, who for the sanctity of their lives should resemble the angels, or else the good Christians who by the integrity of their lives and the purity of their consciences differ from the vulgar and profane as angels do from men. Still others seek aid from the book of *Genesis* where Moses says that the sons of God, recognizing the beauty of the daughters of men, wooed them. Josephus, Clement of Alexandria, Justin, and others, in glossing this text, have taken sons of God to mean the angels, although the Rabbi Abraham ibn Esra interprets the words to mean virtuous men, or else the sons of the righteous Seth, while the daughters of men he understands to be those of the wicked and earthly Cain. The Rabbi Kimhi takes the sons of God for men of great physical stature, using Hebrew speech habits as his basis, for they also say the mountains of God for tall men—which he demonstrates from the Mosaic text that follows, where it is said that from the relations between the sons of God and the daughters of men giants were born.[2] As for myself, I am prepared to believe whatever the ecclesiastics say about this or any other sacred text.

But I will never lend credence to those silly rabbis who say that the incubi and succubi were born of the seed of Adam during the 130 years or thereabouts that he abstained from relations with his wife after the cursed Cain's murder of his brother, the just and good Abel.[3] It is even less credible, if I am not mistaken, that certain women have been impregnated by demon incubi, even though it has been reported that from such unions Hercules, Romulus, Servius Tullius, Merlin, that apostate epicurean Luther, and several others were born.[4] Perhaps Satan deludes the senses and the imaginations of such godforsaken women

308

and makes their bellies swell as if they were really pregnant by some proper creature, and perhaps at the time of their labor and delivery he makes them think they have had a child that was abandoned outdoors and lost.

Jacques le Roux [Jakob Rueff] tells of a certain Magdalena living in the city of Constance who, having dismissed her demon incubus at the bidding of her confessor, gave birth with extreme pain to a thousand trifles such as pieces of broken glass, nails, pegs, bits of wood, hair, pitch, flax fiber, stones, and bones.[5]

Sometimes the evil spirit hides in a dead body in order to entice the lecherous to have dealings with him. Vincent [of Beauvais] tells of a young man who went out at vespers time to wash himself. While swimming in the river, he caught hold of a young woman by her hair and led her back to his house, though she had not uttered a word. He had a son by her, and this son he one day pretended he was about to kill in order to make her break that long silence by which she had raised so much suspicion in him, his kinsmen, and neighbors concerning her unknown condition and origins. At that moment she uttered a few words, then instantly disappeared.[6]

The physician Jacques le Roux, mentioned above, tells how a certain butcher was seduced in much the same way by a demon succubus, a story that is scarcely different from that of Machates and Philinion as reported by Aelian, Phlegon, Loyer, and the Sieur de Lancre, Counsellor of Bordeaux.[7] If you wish to know more, you should look at what Jourdain Guibelet, a physician of Evreux, took from Jacques le Roux and wrote about in his discourse on melancholy, where he makes clear that, according to St. Chrysostome, "whoever the devil overcomes, he overcomes by melancholy." Not without good reason is the melancholy humor called the devil's bath.[8]

Nevertheless, the fact remains that there have been many women who believed they were forced into carnal relations and raped either by the devil or by magicians, women who were, in reality, simply troubled by the nightmare,[9] a disease called by the Latins *incubum* and *succubum*, by the Greeks ἐφιάλτην ἀπὸ τοῦ ἐφάλλεσθαι that is, *insilire vel ascendere* [to leap up or to mount], or rather ἐπιβολή [a fixing of the attention], and by the physician Themison πνιγάλιον ἀπὸ τοῦ πνίγεσθαι [nightmare derived from the verb to suffocate or strangle]. The Arabs called it *alchabum*, *algiathum*, or *alneidalan*, according to Avicenna.[10]

This disease comes on normally during the first hours of sleep when the thick and heavy vapors are carried from the upper parts of the body to the brain, blocking the nerves that serve the voice and the respiration, causing the sufferer to believe there is the heavy weight of a demon or a magician pressing upon her body and seeking to violate her chastity.[11] Hippocrates concurs when he says that nubile young girls and widows troubled by erotic melancholy believe or "imagine they see demons," for he doesn't say that they actually see the evil spirits.[12] And although this disease is caused "by the surfeit of vapors arising from a state of repletion and imperfect concoction that attacks the brain,"[13] yet the physicians do not call it incubus or nightmare unless the imagination is also injured (just as in the case of melancholy), a condition that often presages either melancholy or else the falling-sickness.[14] I can attest to having seen in this city of Castelnaudary in Languedoc two young women who insisted that the devil or a magician went to bed with them every night, even with their husbands right there by their sides, whom God has now healed through our remedies, and who now recognize the corruptness of their imaginations and their folly.

XXVIII

Whether love in women is greater and therefore worse than in men

According to the teachings of Galen, there can be no doubt that the hot complexion, or the dry and hot, is more inclined to rampant love than all the other complexions and temperatures.[1] From that, I would also infer that these complexions must experience more violent loves, and that by consequence men must be more often and more grievously tormented by this madness than women—who are endowed with a temperature less warm and dry, because nature never creates the female except through a lack of heat,[2] for which reason the Philosopher [Aristotle] calls her the defect and imperfection of nature: "the female appears to be the product of nature's deficiency."[3]

But Galen relates to us a view contrary to that of the philosopher Chrysippus who, without going into his reasoning, teaches that love is a movement of the soul opposing the reason, a view approved by Aristotle and the entire school of medicine. We can conclude, then, that without doubt the woman is more passionate in love and more frantic and rash in her folly than man ("by nature the woman possesses weaker spirits and less courage than the man, and her reasoning is not as strong," says the Father of Medicine)[4] since the woman does not have the rational powers for resisting such strong passions, as Galen says,[5] and which the beautiful Hero confesses to her dear Leander:

> I love with an equal fire, but I am not your equal in strength.
> The natural constitution of men is stronger, I imagine.
> While women's bodies are more tender, their minds more slight.[6]

This opinion is confirmed by daily experience which reveals to us a greater number of women witless, maniacal, and frantic from love than men—for men are far less often reduced to such extremities, unless they are effeminate courtiers, nourished on a life of riot and excess and on the breast of courtesans.

In us desire is weaker and not so frantic:
The manly flame knows a lawful bound.[7]

This view can be further strengthened by reasons out of natural philosophy drawn from the teaching of Aristotle in his works on animals
where he shows that nature gave straight intestines without convolutions
to all gluttonous and voracious animals such as the wolf and birds of
prey, but that she has diversely folded around and artistically interlaced
the guts of those for whom it is expedient to be sober and temperate,
such as man.[8] From this example we would teach that the same nature
"that does nothing that is superfluous or pointless, that chooses what is
best for each class of animal"[9] has placed the spermatic vessels in the
woman very close together, joining the horns of the uterus—which can
be verified by autopsy and anatomical dissection—and that contrariwise
in the man she has pushed them a fair distance outside the abdomen, for
fear that the principal faculties of the soul, the imagination, the memory, and the judgment, would be too inconvenienced by the sympathy
and proximity of these genital parts[10] ("the organs adjoining and common to the affected regions are the first and most grievously affected").[11]
Therefore, it is to be judged that the woman experiences more violently
this brutal desire, and not unreasonably so, since nature owes her some
compensating pleasures for the suffering she endures during pregnancy
and childbirth.[12]

　　If men seem at first more given to incontinency, we should not exempt women from the same desires, who disguise them as much as they
can. Their outward features are like the alembic quietly sitting on its
tower-like support, covering up the fire. But if you look underneath the
alembic and place the hand over the heart of a woman, you will find
great charcoal burners in both places.[13]

XXIX

On the prevention
of love and love melancholy

Of primary importance for the prevention of all diseases is the removal of the [offending] disposition of the body, according to Galen, which is nothing other than the interior cause of the illness.[1] But it cannot be uprooted without first banishing the external causes that feed and preserve it. Therefore, he who would undertake to cure or prevent love melancholy must, as the Father of Medicine says, be very well acquainted with the natural constitution of his patient so that he can "employ those remedies proper to the disease, fitted to the nature and age of the patient and to the times and seasons of the year," for otherwise he combats the disease blindly in the manner of the andabatae.[2]

Because this carnal love makes its attack upon the brain (the divine fortress of Pallas) by the windows of the eyes, you must make sure that no inciting object happens to come into view. You should never make any mention whatever to the patient about when you intend to discharge him, for fear that the same thing will happen to him that Galen describes happening of yore to Menelaus who, deciding to slay his adulterous wife, no sooner saw her white breasts and her neck of snow but the sword fell from his hand, whereupon he kissed her and by such means saw his fury turned into love[3]—although the Scholiast of Stesichorus reports this rather of the soldiers that Menelaus sent to stone Helen.[4] How often it happens that the quarrels of lovers rekindle their love:

> The spats of lovers bring renewed affection.[5]

Just as a half-stifled torch flares up again more brightly when it is laid on its side and made to lean downwards however little, so a half stifled love, if it is inclined and bent ever so little toward the beloved, catches flame again.

> One word can easily placate a lover's anger.[6]

313

Our defenses will be less resistant if the lady is beautiful, for beautiful women are like woodcutters: their beauty is the wedge that splits the heart; the cry that witnesses and follows the heavy puffing of the splitter corresponds to our sighs; but giving blow upon blow, the wood breaks, though in consequence the wedge is also dulled and broken. So it is with beauties who strike and strike again; having opened hardened hearts, they often fracture their honors as well.

Certain celebrated authors, impressed by the power of beauty, have opined that there are particular spirits that flow from the body of the lover into that of the beloved, there inciting a reciprocal and mutual love, an idea that in former times brought the Roman ladies to wear little lewd figures around their necks called *fascina* [charms against enchantment]. Perhaps from their example the Spanish in our century wear a hand made of coral or jet with the fist closed and the thumb passing between the index and the middle finger which they call *higo per no ser oiadas* [fig sign to prevent harm]. The Greeks called these trinkets τὰ βυσκάνια [the evil eye] which they also used to protect themselves from the envious.[7]

The Arabs who spoke of love remedies recommended that the physician find out who the patient's mistress is in order to parade her vices and imperfections before the lover's eyes, making mountains out of molehills as we say, and coloring all her virtues as vices.[8]

> Imperfections resemble attractions all too closely.
> Talking that way, virtues can often be held as vices.
> Wherever possible, make the girl's graces appear
> in the worst light.[9]

Avicenna recommends giving this job to some old matron who will be better than the doctor at disguising the qualities of the beloved: provided, of course, that the lover himself is not naturally depraved, filthy, and base, for everyone likes his equal. If the beauty of the lady cannot be denied, she must at least be brought down as much as possible by comparison with the most beautiful women he knows.[10]

> You too should compare your girlfriends with the most beautiful;
> Each will end up ashamed of his own mistress.[11]

By probable-sounding arguments it must be proved that what he finds attractive is, in the judgment of those who see better, actually ugly and deformed.[12] For example, if the lady has an elegant nose of moderate size but sharp, then you should say that she is a scold and a squabbler with an infernal temper according to Aristotle, praising afterwards the little nose as Catullus does, or the aquiline preferred by the Persians, or the large nose celebrated by Albertus Magnus as a sign of generosity.

If she has light, sparkling eyes you should say that she is frivolous, wanton, capricious, flighty, and vain,[13] that those with black eyes—the kind praised by Hesiod, Pindar, Juvenal, and Catullus—are far finer and so on through the other traits and qualities, for the conditions required for beauty are so many in number, as the natural philosophers have pointed out, that there is no one so beautiful and so well-endowed that one cannot find several imperfections in each part.[14] The painter Zeuxis was cognizant of this difficulty, for when he was asked by the city of Croton to create a representation of the beauty of Helen, he made as his prerequisite an examination in the nude of the most beautiful girls of the region so that he could take from each of them the traits he judged the most beautiful.[15] Besides, this question of beauty depends very much on the preferences of the individual: Ovid liked his women small and fair; Hector preferred them brown and husky like Andromache.

Belgian rouge looks foul on Roman cheeks.[16]

The Italian likes them thick-set, stout, and plump, the German strong, the Spaniard lean, gaunt, emaciated, the Frenchman soft, delicate, pretty, and quaint, and the Indian tawny.[17] Our Hippocrates and Celsus his emulator like tallness in the young and they loathe it in the old.[18] Therefore, with good cause beauty has been described as the daughter of Iris and the granddaughter of Admiration, for just as the sun shining on the clouds tricks us by making us see an illusion of diverse colors, so beauty is but a false allurement scattering her beams in a way that dazzles and deceives our sight when she appears in that cloud filled with her myriad graces. We may conclude that the rarest beauties are merely taken to be so by those with defective judgments and visual weaknesses, those who usually declare such women beautiful as are white, soft, and delicate, quite contrary to the judgment of our Galen who states that such traits denote only a false, painted beauty, and that true native beauty consists of the agreeableness, proportion, or symmetry of the parts; a moderate quantity of flesh; and a plausible color of complexion.[19] Whoever wishes to know whether the body is well-proportioned should, according to the anatomists, place it on the ground and spread the feet and the arms equally. Then, taking the navel for the center, draw a circle around it: all parts which either excede the circle or do not reach it are misproportioned.[20] The face, according to Vitruvius, should be equal to one tenth of the body. If the body is square and robust it will be over seven times the length of the head—or eight or nine times if it is delicate.[21] The eyebrows joined together complete the two circles of the eyes, and so forth for the rest of the body, as you can read in the authors already named, as well as in Equicola and the Sieur de Veyries in his *Genealogy of Love*.[22] Nevertheless, the inhabitants of the Indies prefer thick and swollen lips, the nose flat and wide, the Peruvians find those with large ears the most beautiful, while the Mexicans favor those with low foreheads.

If you are unable to convince the lover or to force him to admit that his lady is devoid of the principal conditions required of absolute beauty, you must then try to denigrate her beauty of motion called good grace consisting in the movement of the limbs, or else belittle that beauty of the spirit without which, according to Plato, Plutarch, and Galen, physical beauty is worthless.[23] You must demonstrate to him through reasoning, examples, and the authority of good authors that often the beautiful ones are as common as the ugly ones are bad and capricious. Take it from the comic poet Anaxandrides:

> If a man marries an ugly woman, he will soon find her loathsome;
> He will find no delight in her company, and will not even want to go home.
> But if he takes a beautiful wife,
> His neighbors will have as much to do with her as himself.
> Marriage seems to bring with it one of these two inconveniences.[24]

> it is rare to find beauty and chastity in the same person.[25]

Beauty is a prey with a thousand dogs and hunters in pursuit,[26] or else it is a letter of self-recommendation:

> A shapely figure is a silent advertisement[27]

which usurps and preoccupies the judgment, gives a strong impression of itself, and urges with authority—a letter like the others written in sand that is soon blotted out:

> The flower of beauty withers day by day.[28]

But insofar as it is completely necessary, according to all the physicians who have dealt with the curing of this disease, to urge upon all such besotted persons the nature of their fault and to depict for them in vivid colors the enormity of their errors and sins, I prefer to leave this difficult commission to the theologians, who are more capable in these matters than physicians.[29]

I would note at the same time, however, that such admonitions are of no value at all, that, on the contrary, they render the lover more rash and determined than ever in his madness,[30] as the poet Euripides says in a quotation found in Galen:

> Venus, even if admonished, doesn't give up.
> In fact, the more you try to force her, the more she sets her snares:
> Love scolded is all the more insistent.[31]

Plautus states it even better:

> And he changes men's ways,
> Saps away their wits and makes 'em wayward:
> The more a thing's approved, the less they like it,
> They like what's disapproved: when something's scarce you want it,
>   when plentiful, you don't.[32]

It is for this reason that all lovers live according to their passions, says Aristotle on the subject, and hence close their ears to that reason which alone can put them back on the road to virtue from which they have strayed: "for he that lives by the dictates of passion will not hear nor understand the reasoning of one who tries to dissuade him: but if so, how can you change his mind by argument?"[33] Tibullus often vowed and promised his friends never to see his mistress again, yet he could not keep himself away:

> How often have I sworn never to come back to this doorstep,
> But whenever I swear, though I swear my best,
> My foot itself returns.[34]

Perhaps [such oaths were broken] in the false belief held by the pagans that the gods would pardon perjured lovers because they possessed no more powers of reason and good judgment than little children.[35] We must then look for occasions to admonish them gently according to the precepts of Paul of Aegina and of the great Avicenna (in the places already cited),[36] for in time, as Galen says, the passions are quelled, though perhaps not always when one might wish. The philosopher Chrysippus furnishes a parallel. There are those who run on the flatland, stopping whenever they wish because the weight of their bodies does not push them on ahead, and those who roll down a slope and cannot stop when they wish, forced as they are by gravity to continue: just so when the reason is the cause of the motions of the soul, it is easy to stop them, but when lust and anger, faculties recalcitrant to reason, are joined together they are like the weight of a body that cannot be suddenly stopped, but only little by little. One must search out the exact moment for using this treatment, as with all the others, since knowing the right time and place is at the heart of medicine: "recognizing the right moment to intervene is essential to the healing of the soul."[37]

There is also much to be gained by converting love into hate or jealousy. The lover should be persuaded that his love is not returned, that all the caresses, favors, kisses, delights, and dalliances are merely enticements and tricks to keep him in continual servitude, that otherwise the beloved would satisfy the lover's desires, since true love is the wishing of all good to the beloved for his contentment and advantage and not for the self, and contrariwise to be grieved and afflicted by the hurts and sufferings of the person loved, more than for one's own woes.[38] I would add here [speaking now to women] that dissimulation is as frequently found in men as inconstancy in women, together with the danger of losing one's honor. With an intent to warn women of this very danger, Phidias the painter was in the habit of painting their goddess, Venus, with her right foot placed on a tortoise, not so much to denote women's falsehood, as someone has said, or the care they should take with domestic duties, but to admonish them to take care, rather, of their honors, for the tortoise has fears upon receiving the male of being turned over to face the sky since the male, after taking his pleasure with her, leaves her a prey to the eagle because of the difficulty she has in recovering her normal position. The tortoise prefers her life above pleasure.[39] Likewise, the woman should apprehend the danger she is exposed to once the male has turned over her honor, exposing her not only to the eagle (who is the devil) but also to the crows—the gossips, and slanderers who publicize her fault. It is said that by these same tactics the Milesian girls were cured of their love madness, for the Senate, having forbidden them to slay themselves under threat of being hung up dead in the nude, they repented of their ways, ceased running in the streets transported by their madness, and abandoned their desire for suicide.[40]

I would likewise urge men to see in their mind's eye the disasters that have befallen even the wisest, richest, and strongest who have abandoned themselves to their lust, and if that is insufficient, then they should meditate upon the imperfections and impurity of women.[41]

> Love was stopped in its tracks
> When the lover saw the obscene parts exposed.[42]

Hypatia, daughter of Theon the geometrician, was so learned and accomplished that she surpassed in virtue and wisdom all those in the city of Alexandria where she publicly read philosophy during the reigns of Honorius and Arcadius. It happened that one of her students was so taken by her physical and spiritual beauties that he went mad for love. One day the young lad, looking to be cured, invited her to bed, but instead this sagacious girl, who knew well enough the precepts of medicine, pulled from under her petticoat a cloth stained with her menstrual blood, saying to him, look, young man, and you will see that what you love so much is nothing but vileness and filth—which served to cool his ardor and preserve him from falling into love melancholy.[43]

The good Bernard of Gordon places so much faith in the efficacy of that remedy or medical stratagem that even if the patient is thought to be incurable, he will be cured by that trick: "and if this does not diminish his love, he is no man but a devil incarnate: send him to perdition and his folly with him."[44] And though there is a common proverb to the effect that the physician who goes without his Gordon goes without his staff, yet I will not pause to reflect upon this teaching, but instead look for more sound and profitable remedies to be found in the three fountains of medicine: dietetics, surgery, and pharmaceutics.

XXX

Order of diet for the
prevention of love melancholy

Mercuriale recommends for the curing and prevention of this disease that the patient remain in a cool, moist environment.[1] He is therefore quite surprised that Moschion, an early Greek physician, should prescribe for the patient a room moderately warm and bright.[2] As for myself, I prefer to follow Avicenna who, for the prevention of this condition, prescribes warm air for men and cold for women, and as the venerable Rhazes teaches, I would prohibit such persons from wearing clothes lined with fur, ermine skins, or velvet because they heat the blood.[3] Likewise, highly scented musk perfumes, Cyprian powder, civet, amber, French moschatel and moschatel ointment, and the like must be banished from the patient's room and clothes, substituting in their place camphor because: "breathed in through the nostrils, camphor, by its smell, renders the male sterile."[4] He should drink water but no wine, because it is conducive to love; "wine also makes men affectionate," according to Aristotle,[5] which is the reason the poets make the knave Priapus son to Bacchus, and also the reason why the ancient legislators of the Twelve Tables decreed for women who drank wine the same punishment as for adultery.[6] Bernard of Gordon, however, wants the lover to drink wine, but not enough to get drunk on either.[7] Ovid to the contrary says:

> Wine prepares the heart for love, unless you take o'ermuch
> And your spirits are dulled and drowned by too much liquor.
> By wind is a fire fostered, and by wind extinguished:
> A gentle breeze fans the flames, a strong breeze kills it.
> Either no drunkenness, or so much as to banish care;
> Aught between these two is harmful.[8]

I can pardon a poet for holding freely to such an opinion, but not a Platonic philosopher of the stature of Marsilio Ficino who, commenting on Plato's *Symposium*, recommends for the curing of this disease occasional drunkenness in order to regenerate the blood and the spirits, thereby replacing the blood and spirits infected by the looks and glances sent from the beloved.[9] Such a teaching strikes me as immoral—to cure one vice with another, and at the expense of good health—a view exposed as a falsehood and a lie by Lot's incest.[10] The patient then will drink water in place of wine, getting used to it little by little so that "the habits and disposition of the body will be altered by degrees to the opposite state."[11] Or better, one should have him fast on bread and water, for as the poet Acheus chants:

There is no desire for beautiful things if the belly is empty.[12]

Love never lodges in an empty belly, but on the contrary "Venus delights in full stomachs and a variety of delicacies,"[13] especially if the patient is corpulent, well-fed, with a sanguine, well-tempered, or choleric complexion, in which case all his meats should be lightly nourishing but refrigerative. Therefore, for his broths and salads I would use purslane, garden sorrel, endives, chicory, and lettuce, which is so effective for this disease that Venus, wanting to forget her illicit loves, had her beloved Adonis buried under a bed of lettuce.[14] Certain physicians use the seeds rather than the leaves, or else a conserve of red roses or of province roses which have been said to be very effective for these purposes.[15] The same has been said for mint, but not because of its cooling properties, as Aristotle, Pliny, Magnimus, Arnald of Villanova, and many others have thought.[16] They all failed to take note of Hippocrates' teaching that mint takes away venereal desire by melting and liquifying the male seed. If a man eats it often enough: "it causes his seed to dissolve, hindering it from flowing and increasing,"[17] which makes me think that Aristotle's text is corrupt—that in the place of κατὰ ψύχειν which means to chill, we should read κατατήκειν, which means to melt. For this reason Oppian called mint κακὴν βοτανὴν, cursed herb.[18] But the poets assign the causes of this curative property in mint to mythological origins, namely that Mentha was formerly a beautiful nymph, the daughter of Cocytus, one of the rivers of Hades and beloved of Pluto who, when she was warned that this god passionately loved Proserpina, the daughter of Ceres goddess of the plants and vegetables, ventured to boast of her beauty as surpassing Proserpina's, and that she would make war if Pluto offered to lead the rival into his underworld kingdom. When Ceres heard of this, she gained permission from Jupiter to metamorphose Mentha into a herb of the same name, and to place the curse upon her that she be forever useless to the mysteries of love.[19] Nevertheless, Avicenna holds a contrasting view to that of Hippocrates and the Prince of Philosophers, assuring us that mint is contrary to the prevention and curing of this disease, in conformity with the teachings of Paul of Aegina, Aetius, Dioscorides, and several others.[20]

In my view these solemn authors can be reconciled without entering into the opinions of Hermolaus Barbarus,[21] by saying that in keeping with the teachings of the Father of Medicine and the Genius of Nature, mint is indeed a counteractive to love when that love is caused by humid repletion, for then all dry foods and medications are profitable, as can be seen in Avicenna's bk. III, fen 20, tr. 1, chs. 28 and 29.[22] But if the complexion of the patient is hot and serous, the humors bitter and salty, then mint is extremely harmful in keeping with the views of Paul, Aetius, and Avicenna. The patient may also often eat melons, fresh grapes, cherries, plums, apples, pears, and similar fruits. As for his meats, the Epigrammatist [Martial] strongly recommends stockdoves, or rather ringdoves and culvers:

> Ringdoves dull and obstruct the forces of the groin.
> A man is advised not to eat this bird if he needs his sexual prowess.[23]

I would want him also to eat brown bread or "syncomist," breads made of rye, barley, millet, or spelt (Quercetanus in his *Treasure of Health* erroneously takes it for a species of beardless wheat because spelt is unanimously called zea by all the herbalists) which is a light grain, more nourishing than barley and much less nourishing than wheat.[24] One may occasionally use hemp seed or the seeds of the agnus castus or chaste tree (since Galen numbers these two seeds among the foods), rue, cumin, or coriander. In his sauces, use vinegar, lemon juice, citrons, sorrel, verjuice, and similar liquids. But he should beware of spicy, salty and fricasseed foods, because salt induces sensual desire by virtue of its heat and acrimony if one uses too much of it, which is why the Egyptian priests abstained from all salty meats, having experienced the itching and tickling in the reproductive organs caused by them.[25] The Rhodians, according to Athenaeus, called the feast of Cupid, Alia,[26] just as Plato and the poets have surnamed Venus daughter of salt, or born of the sea, a fiction that conveys by implication the generative power of salt, which is indeed very great. It is for this reason that fish are the most fecond of animals and that ships carrying salt give rise to so many mice, because, according to Aristotle, the females conceive without intervention of the male simply by licking the salt.[27] To this end shepherds give it to their goats and sheep, and hunters, in order to wake up the generative instincts of drowsy and lazy dogs, feed them salted meats. All this makes me think that the grammarians derived the word *salacitas* [lecherousness] from *sal*, a word that also means beauty or good grace among the Latins.

> There is not a grain of salt in the whole compass of her height.[28]

The patient should also refrain from meats that are highly nourishing, hot, flatulent, and melancholy, such as soft eggs, partridge, pigeon, sparrow, quail, young hare, and especially goose, because of certain occult influences attributed to it by Magnimus and Arnald of Villanova.[29] I assume they are referring to the liver which is very rich and which the Romans prized over the other parts of the goose, according to Athenaeus.[30] There is no doubt, however, that the flesh of the goose is very difficult to digest and abounds in excrements, except the wings, as Galen explains in bk. III of *On Nutrition*.[31] He should also very infrequently eat pine nuts, pistachios, hazelnuts, chives, artichokes, cabbage, turnips, carrots, parsnips, ginger conserves, eringoes, satyrion, onions, truffles, and rocket.

> You should no less avoid salty rocket
> And whatever else prepares the body for love.[32]

Also to be avoided are oysters, chestnuts, chickpeas, which Pliny calls venerean,[33] and all other such meats.

The alterative medications endowed with similar qualities are more dangerous than the foods, such as the seeds of the Roman or red nettle, ash keys, honeysuckle leaves, true skinks (which according to Rondelet are land crocodiles),[34] diasatyrion, tryphera saracenica [heartwort or the compound electuary], diazinzibar, and similar powders and opiates that you can find in Avicenna, Nicolas, Serapion, Mesué, Andernacus, Arnald [of Villanova], Matheus Gradeus, Rhazes, and other authorities.[35]

If the use of the above-mentioned foods and medications is dangerous, I hold that idleness is even more so; thus the lover must be kept occupied with serious activities according to his profession and abilities.[36]

> Love gives way to business;
> If you're seeking an end to love, keep busy and you'll be safe,[37]

whether in soldiering, hunting, studying in the arts, or keeping house, for the poets state that Cupid could never conquer Vesta, Pallas, and Diana, though he triumphed over all the [other] gods and goddesses.[38] I would understand by that fable that those who take pleasure in the study of letters, in hunting and in managing a household are not subject to the treacheries of love. In short, in every way he should avoid idleness:[39]

> When you are ready to make use of my healing arts
> Then heed my counsel, and first of all avoid leisure:
> That keeps you in love, that looks after past deeds,
> That is the cause and sustainer of the delectable ill.[40]

Mercuriale recommends moderate exercise. I prefer it to be more vigorous to induce sweating in accordance with Galen and Marsilio Ficino, except in cases where the patient has already become frenzied.[41] Of all the exercises I most prefer hunting—the means by which Hyppolitus preserved his chastity—and horseback riding, though in moderation. At first, riding seems to excite sexual sensations in the body, according to the Philosopher in the fourth section of his *Problems*,[42] but if it is done frequently, its remedial effects will become evident according to the testimony of the divine Hippocrates: "those people who are the greatest riders are the least inclined to venery," an observation confirmed by the example of the Scythians, who were "the most impotent and celibate men in the world" because of the violent exercises they performed on horseback over long periods of time.[43] There are, nevertheless, certain activities that are extremely dangerous such as reading dirty books, listening to music, playing viols, lutes, and other instruments, and even more, going to plays and farces, balls and dances, for such exercises open up the pores of the heart no less than those of the skin.[44] And then if some serpent comes breathing into the ears a few tempting words, proposes some dalliance or other, with her coaxing and wheedlings, or some basilisk comes along casting lascivious looks, winking, and making sheep's eyes, those hearts very quickly allow themselves to be seized and poisoned—especially the hearts of those who have already been wounded. The leopard attracts all sorts of animals by his odor, but primarily monkeys. And since they can't be taken in a chase because they climb up to the tops of the trees, he trys to have them by craft by covering himself with branches. He then feigns his dying gasps in such a way that the monkeys think him truly dead. They surround him dancing and teasing on all sides and stamping their feet until the leopard senses they are weary from their leaping, whereupon in a sudden bound he jumps up, taking one in his teeth, another with his claws, tearing and devouring both.[45] In just this way the demon of love and lechery plays it at the beginning with those he means to take, luring them by the pleasures and pastimes enjoyed at balls and assemblies, pushing them first into regular attendance, then into an honest friendship and from that friendship into passionate love, and from love he invites them to the consummation, and just as he feels them close, he seizes them in their most noble faculties, corrupting the judgment of one, troubling the imagination of the other, and under the guise of a tranquilizing softness he envelops them with a thousand palpable miseries. Love's sweetness is like the honey of Heraclea that is sweeter at first than common honey because of the aconite it contains, but that at the time of digestion causes dizziness and troubles the sight, the savory taste turning to bitterness in the mouth.[46]

Our ladies say that dalliance and kisses are harmless and innocent, just as Theocritus does in his pastoral,

Kisses are empty things they say,[47]

but in this they are mistaken, for these are the most dangerous of all such activities. Rather, such dalliances are like the Egyptian thieves of bygone days called "philettes" or kissers, who deceived and robbed their victims while embracing them. I fear even more the close courting and fondling, which come within the jurisdiction not only of the eyes, but of the hands and breasts. The Greeks call this βλιμέζειν—a pretty metaphor, for the word means literally handling birds in the market to find out if they are firm and fat, suggesting at the same time that anyone who tolerates such groping is up for sale or loan.[48]

Avicenna and Paul of Aegina claim that for the prevention of this disease some weighty affair, a criminal trial for example, or some conflicting source of grief and sorrow can be very effective.[49] But I would prefer some learned theologian to strike the fear of death and hellfire into him, and by such means render him devout, fervent in prayer—since prayer and fasting are sovereign remedies against the demon of fleshly delight—and I would want him to spend time with pious and virtuous people so that in time he will adopt their qualities, just as the vine planted near olive trees, according to the naturalists, brings forth a more oily fruit than usual.[50]

Some physicians recommend locking lovers up in prison and administering frequent punishment if they are young adolescents, but Gordon goes too far, I think, when he says the lover should be spanked and whipped *donec totus incipiat foetere*, until he begins to smell bad all over.[51] More appropriately, the ancients used to stop young wenchers from their lusty ways by attaching a ring or clasp to the foreskin, according to the physician Celsus.[52] Martial seems to allude to the practice in the lines:

> But while he was exercising himself in the view
> Of the people in the middle of the exercise ground,
> The sheath unluckily fell off: so he was circumcised.[53]

In order to prevent the overheating of the kidneys, he should not sleep on his back. Nor should he lace up his loins too tightly, causing the veins to dilate.[54] The mattress he sleeps on should not be stuffed with wool or feathers, but rather with straw, or the leaves of willows, or of rue, roses, water lily, poppy, or agnus castus, the last of which was used in the beds of the women of Attica during the Thesmophoria to keep them in a state of chastity.[55] Avicenna, Prince of the Arab physicians, in his chapter on love, Bernard of Gordon, Arnald of Villanova, and several other modern physicians teach that in order to prevent erotic melancholy in someone who starts meddling with love, we should make him fall in love with some new friend, and that when he starts making soft eyes at her, work at making him hate her too, and to fall for a third, and so on several times over until he is tired of love altogether, thinking that, as Aristotle says, those who have a lot of friends do not really have any.[56] Those who have a liking for several women cannot go mad for one, a point Bernard of Gordon claims to have learned from the wanton poet [Ovid]:

> This is my advice: take on two mistresses at once.
> He who can take on more is even stronger.
> When the attention is so divided, shifting from one to the other,
> The passion here drives out the passion there.[57]

If I dare speak out against these authorities, I find this opinion of theirs as pointless as it is dangerous, because there is no possibility of making a lover change loves at our bidding (which Avicenna seems to admit when he says that if we can't effect the change we turn it over to some toothless old bawd), and should we succeed in severing the lover from his first mistress by having him fall in love with another, we risk having him run completely mad for this second as well. Besides, I have seen several people who, because of this degrading habit, love indifferently only those women who pretend to like them and who behave like a group of silly young girls, and not the other kinds of women they meet. The passions that preoccupy the soul are imprinted there by the bad habits that generate them. These habits, in time, become natural forces that are activated by the least occasion, habits that can be erased only with the greatest effort. You will see this to be so of cowards who fear even those who rescue them, and of the choleric who are often angry at their friends. Likewise, those who are inclined to carnal love are never happy with loving one person alone, but in an indifferent way, because custom, which is like a second nature developed through repeated practice, has an extraordinary power to direct the disposition toward the known and familiar.[58] Like the man who is inclined to stumble and trip on every bump, the man who has developed an amorous disposition makes love according to the particularity of his passion, and when he is excited, he no longer does what he would, but what he has been conditioned and disposed to do. He is no more no less free than a ball that, set in motion, must of necessity follow a round pattern, just as a roller in motion must follow that of a roller, each in accordance with its shape. St. Augustine states that "when one serves his libidinous desires, they become custom and habit, and if such habits are not resisted, they become a kind of necessity."[59]

XXXI

Surgical remedies for the prevention of love melancholy

The immediate cause of this disease is sperm. Galen offers a number of reasons and examples to prove this point toward the end of bk. VI of his *On the Diseased Parts.*[1] Sperm is nothing other than blood bleached by natural heat, an excrement of the third digestion. Depending on its quantity and quality, it can irritate the body, thereby provoking a natural expulsion. Otherwise it would remain in its reservoirs, turn corrupt, and from there, by means of the back bone and other secret channels, send a thousand noxious vapors to the brain, troubling the faculties and principle virtues. For this reason, there is great utility in drawing off any superfluous blood by bleeding the liver vein of the right arm.[2] If the person is temperate, sanguine, well built and not too lean, allowing the patient to tolerate a copious bleeding, then a little more blood may be taken. This operation should be repeated three or four times a year, whenever one suspects the onset of the disease, especially where one has observed this to be an effective remedy from the outset.[3] After bleeding the liver vein, I would advise drawing a certain quantity, depending on the patient's strength, age, and constitution, from the ham vein [the back of the knee], particularly if there is satyriasis, and if the surgeon is able to perform it. If not from this vein, then I would open the saphena in one of the feet, or else apply cupping glasses on the thighs near the genitals with the requisite scarification. But one should not make use of these particular evacuations without first opening the arm (those in danger of satyriasis or uterine fury should receive this treatment starting on the first day) because otherwise the blood is drawn toward the affected parts, the seat of the cause of the disease, where it can no longer be drained off.[4]

Some cauterize the legs, but I find this an ineffective remedy. The Scythians, according to Herodotus, cut the veins or arteries behind the ears and by this means rendered themselves ἀγόνες, ἐνάριας and ἀνανδριοῖς, which is to say effeminate and impotent. Reduced to this miserable condition, they wore women's clothes and lingered about in their company.[5] Hippocrates explains that severing the veins or arteries adjacent to the ears causes sterility,[6] although Vesalius and certain other anatomists attribute this defect to the sectioning of the nerves of the sixth conjugation that pass close to the ears and disappear into the genitals and spermatic vessels.[7] This remedy would appear easy and useful to those who have made a vow of chastity if there were no fear of debilitating the memory and the reason as Avicenna testifies[8]—which has been confirmed in the case of the Scythians already mentioned who, because of this surgery, became fools and simpletons.

XXXII

Pharmaceutical means for the prevention of love melancholy

The first pharmaceutical remedy is an enema containing cooling and moistening ingredients, to which I strongly recommend adding hemp seed, agnus castus, and the like. The next day you should give a bolus of cassia, catholicon, diaprun, or tryphera persica with a few grains of agnus castus,[1] or else a quite mild purgative, for one should never use violent cathartics and strong laxatives, according to Avicenna, Paul of Aegina, and Aetius who, for these purposes, give a decoction of beets, mallows, and [the herb] mercury.[2] Virulent medications heat the humors, disturb the blood, and cause the excrements to descend toward the lower organs and spermatic vessels, for which reason Arnald of Villanova in his chapter "Regimen for living a chaste life" prefers emetics over purgatives.[3] During several mornings after, the patient should be given whey or broth, or else a julep devised to refresh the blood, adding to it a medication that will arrest the generation of sperm. If the patient is of a moist humor, such medications are especially appropriate, a fact confirmed by Avicenna.[4] Here is one I often use.

R̲x̲.   Take 5 ounces each of the roots of bugloss, borage, and chicory. To these add one large handful [manipule] of each of the following: the leaves of endive, wood sorrel, golden purslane, hops, and lettuce. Follow with 1 dram of the four major cold seeds and the four minor cold seeds [cucumber, gourd, melon, citron; escarole, endive, lettuce, and purslane]. Then include an equal measure of 2 scruples of the seeds of the three-leaved chaste tree and of the white poppy, followed by 1 small handful [pugille] each of passula, currants [Corinthian grapes], pond lily flowers, and sweet violet flowers. Boil these ingredients down to one pound and pass through a strainer. Into this dissolve a fruit sirup scented with 1 ounce each of violet flowers and pond lily. Mix all these together with 3 drams of white saunders [santal]. This will make a very clear and aromatic julep which is to be administered three or four times in the mornings.[5]

Sometimes I add to it a few grains of camphor, or else I mix it with water of lettuce, purslane, or water lily, giving it each morning for several days. It is especially good for those with hot bilious complexions, for according to Dioscorides, these plants are very effective in the prevention of this disease.[6]

The priests of Athens used hemlock for this purpose, though it was the poison ordinarily employed by the Areopagites for killing criminals, as can be gathered from Plato. Saint Basil (who was both a learned physician and an eloquent theologian) certifies having seen women use hemlock to diminish their sexual desires.[7] One must, nevertheless, take care not to use any diuretic medications for the same reasons given above concerning purgatives. Normally, such drugs are hot and dry unless they are corrected by adding such cooling agents as whey or mineral water.[8] Mercuriale claims to have cured women of love madness using only these remedies.[9] Or here is another:

Rx. Take 5 small handfuls of water lentils and 3 drams each of wild lettuce, golden purslane, and white poppy. Add in an equal measure of 5 small handfuls each of sweetbriar and pond lily. Let them cook in water. Then, using any kind of sugar, make a sirup which is to be used every day.[10]

Some put black nightshade and hemlock into their broths and cook them, but I would not do it.

If there is a danger of flatulence, as is the case with melancholy persons, use apozemes, juleps, or oxymels made with coriander seed, rue, cummin, agnus castus, and related plants, rather than the exclusively cooling simples.

After taking these beverages, it would be useful to purge our lover again with the same medications mentioned above, or else with either rhubarb and rose sirup, or chicory sirup made up with rhubarb.

I am not able to take Arnald of Villanova seriously when he writes that there is no better means for protecting oneself from this ill than to carry a knife with a handle made of agnus castus.[11] It would make more sense to soak the secret parts in a potion of water and vinegar [oxycrat] and the juices of morel, plantain, hipwort [penniwort or lady's navel], houseleek [sengreen], or similar liquors, especially if the patient has no intentions to marry. There is far less danger in bathing in cold water, and the results may be just as satisfactory in light of the fact that the girls of Lyons, in former times, cured themselves of this malady by throwing themselves in the Rhone, as mentioned earlier.[12] You should repeat these baths often, using cold water in the summer and luke warm in the winter, anointing the lumbar region, buttocks, and groin with Galen's refrigerating ointment, Mesue's rosatum, or with camphoratum to which you can add the juice of the cold herbs mentioned above.[13] Paul of Aegina states that "care must be taken in cooling the loins and genitals that the kidneys are not injured."[14] There is an even greater danger that the menstrual flow will be arrested in girls and women who use such cooling topical remedies and narcotics either improperly or too frequently. But in avoiding this Scylla, one must not, at the same time, sally into the Charybdis of prescribing for women internal medications using vinegar: "it causes pain in the uterus and cramps" according to Hippocrates for the reasons given by the venerable Avenzoar.[15]

Aetius is not satisfied with such medications to the small of the back, groin, buttocks, and perineum alone, but advises the application of liniments to the head, or else the rubbing of the forehead with oxyrrhodin [vinegar and rose water], especially if the lover is in danger of falling into frenzy, mania, uterine fury, or melancholy.[16]

Where there is a reticence to use these extremely cold liniments, oils, and fomentations, the patient should be encircled with a thin plate of lead, which Galen, Avicenna, Paul of Aegina, Andernacus, and all our modern physicians highly recommend for such symptoms.[17] Nevertheless, care must be taken not to let it be worn too long since, according to Avicenna, it can do damage to the kidneys.[18] In addition to these remedies, the good Arnald of Villanova advised the white friars and all others who wish to live in chastity to go barefoot.[19]

There are a few other remedies expressly for women in danger of love madness—which happens all too often. These include the vaginal douches, usually made with refrigerating herbs mixed with camphor, castoreum, or rue.[20] Or else use a uterine douche like the following:

R℞.   Take 2 small handfuls of shelled lentils, 1 small handful each of willow flowers and sweetbriar, and 1 large handful of olive leaves. Make a decoction boiling it down to 1 pound, in which dissolve a small ball [trochisc] of camphor weighing 1 dram, and make a vaginal douche.

Or else use this other from Aetius:

R℞.   Take in equal measures 1 dram of saltpetre and cardamon and mix them with wax. Make a pessary and insert it into the vagina. Or employ a certain quantity of diacodion mixed with the juice of the black nightshade, and introduce into the cave of Venus.[21]

The women who wanted to write about what they knew of medicine, such as Cleopatra the sister of Arsinoës, have given us several treatments for this disease. And should it develop into mania or uterine fury, this good lady (who according to her own prologue wished to be called the Queen of Physicians) taught her daughter Theodota to "take a root, wrap it in a rag" and put it into the said place, and that wonder of wonders, when it is withdrawn from the pigsty of Venus, she would find in this clout, little worms.[22]

This is an appropriate moment for me to certify to my reader that I wish to speak as modestly as possible, but that I must also express certain medical concepts that are often in disaccord with polite discourse: "I love modesty, but more than this, I love freedom of speech," said Cicero, though beyond that, I am not in agreement with Zeno and his sect "who named things however it pleased them, claiming that nothing was obscene, nothing was foul or disgraceful."[23] The words themselves cannot be objectionable, however, because the parts [of the anatomy] they stand for are natural, useful, and necessary—parts, moreover, that are now dissected and demonstrated in public in order to understand their substance, number, figure, placement, connection, action, and function.

Our own Penot in Agen distils camphor a dozen times, assuring us that this preparation is more effective than all the others,[24] and Arnald of Villanova says that if you place the right testicle of a wolf underneath the right testicle of a lecherous man, that it would, in no time, take away his villainous urges—and this is not the only twaddle this learned doctor relates in his book on venoms.[25] If it actually does work, we would have to attribute the effect to some occult property, as with the virtues that he and several other physicians attribute to carbuncle, sapphire, emeralds, and jasper for the prevention of love melancholy when such precious stones are worn on the ring finger of the left hand.[26]

XXXIII

How to cure erotic melancholy and love madness

Diogenes one day consulted the oracle of Apollo at Delphi to discover the most sovereign, speedy, and direct means for curing his son's love frenzy. The reply came that it was the enjoyment of her who had caused it. Jonadab, unfortunately, recommended the same remedy to Prince Amnon, son of David, mad with love for his sister Tamar; Hippocrates prescribed likewise for the son of King Perdiccas, and Erasistratus for the son of King Seleucus.[1] Hippocrates states this view explicitly toward the end of his treatise *On the Diseases of Young Women*: "all young women taken by this disease should be forthwith married."[2] Galen made the same recommendation toward the end of his excellent work on the diseased parts, written in his later years, as well as the great Avicenna, Haly Abbas, Bernard of Gordon, Arnald, Valescus de Tarenta, Pereda, Lucretius, Ficino, Ovid, and many others.[3] But the actual enjoyment of the lady is not always necessary to cure this disease, for sometimes merely the liberty or permission to do so will suffice.[4]

> The very means and license to sin took away his eagerness for it,
> And removed from his mind the desire for such things.[5]

Occasionally, just dreaming of it will work, as in the case of the young Egyptian Plutarch wrote about, who was lost in his love folly for the courtesan Theognis. One night, as it turned out, this poor lover merely dreamed that he slept with his Theognis. But upon waking he realized that the ardor threatening to consume him had been allayed. When word of this came to the courtesan, she had the young Egyptian taken to court, alleging that because she had cured him she was entitled to payment. Bochor the judge commanded the young man to fill his purse with the amount he had promised and to bring it into the court, where it was poured into a basin. The courtesan was thereby paid with the sound and color of the ecus, just as the young Egyptian was contented with

an imaginary pleasure. This decision received the approbation of everyone, except one of the courtesan's friends who complained to Demetrius
that the dream had satisfied the Egyptian's desires, whereas the sound
and color of the gold had merely whetted Theognis' desires, and that
therefore the decision was unjust.[6]

Before approving or disapproving this remedy, I must make a clear
distinction between licit and illicit lovemaking. No physician would
refuse to someone suffering from erotic mania or melancholy the enjoyment of the object of desire in marriage in accordance with both divine
and human laws, because:

> The wounds of love are cured only by those who made them.[7]
> I am Telephus, O maiden; be thou my true Achilles;
> With thy beauty allay the longing as thou didst kindle it.[8]

Avicenna, in the place mentioned earlier says that often this is the
last and only cure to which one must have recourse: "If a cure cannot be
found, with the exception of letting them join together in ways permitted
by religion and law, so be it. We have been witness to a case where the
patient returned to a state of health and strength and regained his proper
weight, even though he had reached an advanced state of dehydration—
had even gone beyond that stage—and though he had suffered terrible
chronic diseases and long-lasting fevers brought on by the wasting of his
life forces caused by excessive *ilisci*, that is to say love."[9] But if for any
reason a marriage cannot be contracted, it is totally absurd and immoral
to prescribe, as Avicenna and Haly Abbas do, that our lover "purchase
young girls and sleep with them frequently, and that he change them
regularly and take his pleasure with the new ones."[10] I am not surprised
if Mohammedans and infidels hold such an accursed view, since the Ko-
ran allows them to have as many wives or concubines as they can feed,
according to the narratives of those who have written about the customs
of the Turks and Mohammedans.[11] I am even less surprised in the case of
the poets Lucretius and Ovid who made a virtue of villainy and immod-
esty. But this opinion is completely sacrilegious and misguided in the
mouths of Arnald of Villanova, Magnimus, Valescus de Taranta, Pereda,
Marsilio Ficino, and other Christian writers.[12] I will leave it to the theologians to prove that fornication is never permitted to a Christian, and
that he is not allowed to commit an ill deed to avoid another ill. I will
restrict myself to saying, along with the moral philosophers, that vice
cannot be driven out by vice, but only by its opposite, which is virtue:
"contraries are remedied by their contraries."[13] I can prove to you out
of Aristotle that such persons, rather than finding a cure in fornication,
will only find themselves more inclined to lust and wantonness: "for
the passages become dilated thereby allowing for a freer flow of semi-

nal fluids, and moreover, the remembrance of past pleasures creates a powerful longing to repeat them."[14] Aristotle seems to have learned this from Hippocrates who discussed the subject in the following terms: "If a man engages in frequent coitus, the veins become distended, thereby attracting a greater quantity of sperm."[15] Galen follows his good master in this opinion, demonstrating it with this true and apt maxim from the divine Plato in his *Theaetetus*: "idleness leads to undoing, while the performance of one's duties leads to strength," and further proves the point by an analogy with the breast which, the more it is employed in nursing, the greater its capacity to retain milk. Inversely, our Coryphaeus [Galen] says that "the singers and athletes who, from the outset of their lives, have not contaminated themselves with any of the enticements of Venus, who have obstructed all access even through sexual fantasies, possess, by consequence of their habits, enfeebled and shriveled sexual organs like those of old people, and are thus not tempted by sexual desire,"[16] a text to be made note of by all those who have taken vows of chastity. Finally, if the view of the authors named above [concerning coitus as a cure for erotic love] was true and their advice to the point, then it would follow that married people would never be troubled by unchaste desires, which we know from experience to be patently false—a fact that has occasioned certain good fathers of the church to say that it is more difficult to preserve chastity than virginity.[17]

XXXIV

Remedies to cure
love melancholy in married persons

We see that married persons—whether they were joined together by their own will and consent and without any constraints, or against the will of one or the other—sometimes develop a secret hatred for each other, creating such discord, such distrust and recrimination that they come to loathe and flee each other's company. Thereafter, they find themselves easily carried away by their passions, seduced by some alien love contrary to all laws, divine, human, and natural. There are diverse causes for this calamity: sometimes it is owing to a difference in manners and customs or to a secret antipathy, sometimes to the imperfections of the body or of the spirit, or at times to some charm or ligature, or else to the impression that one is not loved by the other. Often it can be traced to an inability to enjoy the pleasures that nature has concentrated in the genitals by means of the nerves spread throughout that region and by the sharp prickly sensations of the watery liquid contained in the prostate. You may read about the cures for this problem in Marinello, Giovanni di Vigo, Avicenna, and other famous authors, and notably in the work by Liébault on the diseases of women—the chapter on reuniting the newly married who hate and flee from one another.[1] You will note that just as there are men who are frigid and disinclined to sexual intercourse, so there are women who experience no sexual impulses or incitement. Platter in his *Observations* mentions two such who, because of this condition, were entirely sterile.[2] Long ago Amasis King of Egypt was another according to Herodotus. Theodoric King of France, in Paulus Aemilius's account, was impotent with his wife but not with his concubines. The Annals of Aragon and of Dupréau for the year 1196 give similar accounts of Pedro II King of Aragon whose queen, however, taking measure of the situation slipped into the bed of the king's concubine and that night became pregnant with the good King James, after which ruse the king abstained from further illicit affairs.[3]

In order to hinder her husband Jupiter from falling passionately in love with Latona, Io, Calixto, and others of his mistresses, as recounted by Homer, Juno borrowed the embroidered girdle of Venus in which all the *cupidons*, graces, persuasions, baits, and enticements that pass between husband and wife had been interwoven:

> love, desire and the sugared coaxing
> That deprives even the most prudent and judicious of their reason.[4]

Here is how Ronsard expressed these same thoughts:

> Woven into this fabric were the portraits of two cupids, as if alive. The one had a bow of yew and mossy arrows which shoot the imagination with fears, suspicions, anger, and jealousy. The other held in his hand an embellished bow with an arrow tipped in gold that goes gliding and pricking, burying itself in the soul, where it pours a gentle flame into the blood that tickles us and generates our desires—securing the preservation of our entire race. Here is the very portrait of youth, in long hair, strong and powerful, but with a weighty heart, the retreat of burning desires—youth that always provides for the company of lovers that linger like children at the breast: deceitful games, fraud, sleights, laughter and tears, war and peace, truces, disagreements, and imperfect reconciliations and the words that baffle our minds, indeed the minds of the most sagacious.[5]

If one of these marriage partners has certain defects of beauty that have quelled the love of the other, that person should try to correct these imperfections by the appropriate remedies,[6] or if that is impossible, to compensate with a beauty of spirit.

> If obstinate nature has denied one outward beauty
> Then take instead the beauty of my intellect.[7]

Maximus Tyrius the Platonic philosopher wrote that Achilles appeared beautiful to whoever saw him, not so much because of his long, golden hair, for Euforbus had equally beautiful hair, but because his beauty was embellished with virtue.[8] The learned Sappho, transported by a burning love, made herself attractive through the cultivation of such virtues as she explains in her epistle to Phaon.

> Beauty I lack for nature has been unkind,
> But take in the place of beauty the imaginative
> genius she has given me.[9]

Married persons should also try to render themselves compatible in matters of will, life-style, and manners:[10]

> Love of character is lasting; beauty will be ravaged by age,
>   And the face that charmed will be ploughed by wrinkles.
> [. . . . .]
> Goodness is lasting and will endure for years,
>   And love is firmly grounded upon it during that time.[11]

If a couple notes certain antipathies arising, they should continue to make a show of love for one another, so that in time the feigned can change into true love. Caelius the Roman pretended to have gout—he went so far as to have his legs anointed and bound up in order to avoid paying his court to certain of the high-ranking Romans, till in the end fortune played him the trick of giving him for real the ailment he feigned. Martial states:

> What power there is in imagining and cultivating a disease!
> Now Caelius no longer merely pretends to have the gout.[12]

Appian wrote of another who pretended to have only one eye, and for that found himself a few days later totally blind.[13] Love is committed by nature to making affection reciprocal: "I will show you how to win love without using philters or magical incantations; if you wish to be loved, love," in the words of Seneca.[14] On this point there is a pleasant apologue or moral fable in Themistius and Porphyry, namely that Venus noticing one day that her little Cupid was no longer thriving went to consult with the goddess Themis, who told her that Cupid needed a brother who should be called Anteros or reciprocal love, allowing for each to aid the other. Anteros was no sooner born but Cupid began to lift and spread his wings and feathers. When Anteros was present Cupid even appeared larger and more handsome, while in his absence love seemed to diminish.[15] It is for this reason that honest caresses, soft words, and gentle civility are always in order, which is the reason the ancients, according to Plutarch, gave a quince to the bride to eat on her wedding day:[16]

> For a woman sometimes so manages herself by her own conduct,
> By obliging manners and bodily neatness and cleanliness,
> That she easily accustoms you to live with her.[17]

Philostratus reports that the Romans held the flesh of hare in very high esteem for preserving mutual friendship between married persons and for keeping them from outside relationships, perhaps because, as Pliny explains, hare's meat makes people beautiful and gracious.[18] Martial alludes to this belief in writing to a certain Gellia:

> If, when you send me a hare, Gellia, you say

> "Marcus, you will be handsome for seven days,"
> If you are not just teasing and laughing at me,
> If you are telling me the truth, then you, my
> Dearest Gellia, have never eaten a hare.[19]

Aristotle recommends the "ship-stopping" fish remora or echeneis, "used as a charm for love-suits and love affairs," which Pliny has translated in these terms: "remora has a bad reputation as a beneficial love-philter, and for obstructing legal procedures and litigations." There was a fable in those days, though I do not know if it was credited, that this fish stopped the ship of the ambassador sent by Periander to castrate all the youth of noble extraction: "because, according to the judgement of nature, it is shameful to remove from mankind that which was consecrated for the preservation of the species."[20]

The same virtue has been assigned by certain other naturalists to a coral called charitoblepharon and to the herb called catanance. Philostratus grants it to the oil that drops from trees native to the banks of the Hydaspes [Jhelum] River in India with which the Indians traditionally anointed themselves on their wedding days.[21] But I believe that the strongest bond for keeping couples in mutual friendship and concord is children, for as Menander says:

> The procreation of children is the strongest bond of love.[22]

Children, as the Philosopher teaches us, are held in common and shared equally by the parents, and what is shared in common has power to reconcile and reunite.[23] If you would know the remedies necessary for restoring virility in men and fertility in women you should read my discourse on sterility.[24]

I know that the ladies of Rome attribute great powers to the herb *hippoglossum* or horse's tongue (called by them bonifacium), to reconcile husbands and wives and to preserve marriages.[25] Albertus Magnus and Lemnius grant the same virtues to a certain stone found in the stomachs of capons that have been castrated for at least four years—a stone that is clear and transparent resembling crystal, equal to a bean in size. To gain the desired effect it must be worn wrapped in hide.[26] Pliny recommends eringo roots. But I agree with the poet who says that:

> It is useless to seek out herbs.
> Only virtue and beauty unite people in love.[27]

There are cases in which the mutual love of marriage is destroyed by charms and witchcraft, causing the partners to engage passionately in illicit affairs. These charms are commonly called ligatures or "noeuds d'aiguillette," a subject treated by several of our physicians, and in particular by Arnald of Villanova in his *A Treatise on Physical Ligatures*.[28]

Suffice it to say here, there are several theologians and physicians who believe, apparently, that the author of all evil, the devil, can extinguish sanctified love and enflame illicit love: first by making the man impotent with his wife through the application of certain natural means that are removed when the man approaches another woman; second, by stirring up hostility and jealousy in the marriage; or else by some disease such as when Medea, using her magical powers, made the women of Lemnos hateful to their husbands by giving them stinking breaths; or else by troubling the imagination so that spouses are made to appear ugly and the alien partner beautiful; or by bringing on some hidden and secret antipathy.[29] We read in Battista Egnatius that a certain Valasca, a Bohemian chambermaid, used her magic charms to incite the women of Bohemia to kill all the men of the region in a single night.[30] Finally, by some mysterious process the devil can alter the genital parts in either men or women, making the men impotent and the women to resemble dogs, according to Saxo Grammaticus.[31]

Care should be taken not to attribute to magic and sorcery, out of ignorance, such effects as have natural causes. The Scythians in former times, according to our Hippocrates, attributed their impotence—caused by cutting or draining the veins, arteries, or nerves joining at the ear—to the revenge of the goddess Venus Urania because their ancestors had spoiled and robbed her temple in Ascalon, a famous city in Palestine.[32]

One should make certain, too, that the woman is not "unperforated" and "incapacitated" such as was Cornelia, the mother of the Gracchi. In such cases, the passage is opened with a razor according to instructions given by Albucasis, Aetius, Johann Wier, Paré, and other authoritative authors.[33] I performed the operation in the city of Castelnaudary on two young girls, although this condition can appear in widows or in married women whose husbands are away for long periods. Jean Liébault has certified this to be the case for two of his neighbors.[34] Although our divine ancient [Hippocrates] claimed that Namysia and Phaëtusa were changed into men,[35] I suspect, rather, that they suffered from this ailment—one more rarely seen in women than its counterpart [in men] which is often responsible for the breakdown in marital relations. I will not speak here about the treatments for these two diseases, because you can find them in Avicenna, Aetius, Paul of Aegina, and in all the moderns who have written about sterility and the diseases of women.[36]

Arnald of Villanova, in a treatise on recipes against the devil and his machinations, prescribes the wearing of a feather filled with quicksilver, or the wearing of coral, the herb mugwort, or else squills or sea onion.[37] Giovanni di Vigo has the house of the bewitched sprinkled with the blood of a black dog.[38] A few other old dreamers have the victim eat the flesh of magpie or green woodpecker, or else have his body greased with the gall of the raven mixed with the powder of hartwort [seseli]. But I believe that charms and sorceries are cured rather by prayer, fasting, and meditation, than by such natural remedies.

XXXV

Of philters and Homerical remedies

Before writing of the remedies of erotic melancholy, it is necessary to know if this disease can be caused by philters, and if it is curable by poetic or Homerical remedies or other antidotes.

Those who hold that philters and love potions exist argue that if sorcerers and magicians can provoke hatred, they can just as easily excite love by using characters, charms, poisons, foods, or medications to stir up the humors, heat the body, or otherwise generate lust,[1] an argument they try to confirm out of a text by the prophet Nahum:

> And all for the countless harlotries of the harlot, graceful and of deadly charms, who betrays nations with her harlotries, and peoples with her charms,[2]

which they say means philters, of the kind made by burning olive stones, according to the *Book of Baruch*.[3] For this reason, according to them, the philosopher Plato in the *Symposium* says that love is a cunning magician and sorcerer.[4] The ancients attribute such power to these philters that whoever drinks one must, in their view, become a slave to the one who administers it:

> another sells charms from Thessaly
> That a woman may use to drive her husband mad
> And beat him on the rump with a slipper.[5]

Plutarch in his discourse on marriage reveals his faith in the power of such potions, but he condemns and rejects them, comparing the victims to fish caught with poisoned bait, for such bait works quickly and well, but the fish are thereby rendered unfit and dangerous to eat.[6] In the same way, women who confect these love potions, these charms and sorceries, in order to subjugate their lovers find themselves in possession of a friend who is either raging or witless and unable to give any pleasure. Circe, he continues, was of that nature and species, yet she placed little value in those she had bestialized and enchanted with her philters. On the contrary, she turned her amorous attentions toward Ulysses who, in spite of Circe's charm, knew how to love with prudence. You will meet with a variety of these follies in Tibullus, Propertius, Horace, Theocritus, including the following in Virgil:

> As this wax liquefies and this mud solidifies
> In one and the same fire, so Daphnis in our love.[7]

Apuleius relates at the beginning of his *Metamorphoses* [*The Golden Ass*] an amusing incident that befell his hostess Pamphile. Fotis her chamber-maid had been sent to fetch some of the hair of her beloved, but instead she brought back some goat's hair. Pamphile no sooner had performed her charms upon it but the barrels, covered with the hide of this goat, came banging at Pamphile's door in response to her spells.[8]

Joubert and Liébault report that there are women in many places who order the matrons in attendance at the births of their daughters to keep for them the birth cords or navel strings to use later for getting them husbands—superstitiously believing that if it is given in powdered form to a man, he will instantly fall in love with the girl it was taken from.[9] You can read the explanation of this custom or popular error in the writings of the physicians. The sorceress Medea, following the advice of the goddess Venus, made the same use of the jinx[10] which is, according to Natalis Comitis in his *Mythologies* and Vigenère on Philostratus, the bird named *moticilla* by the Latins, *hochequeue*, *lavandiere*, and *battelessive* by the French [the water wagtail, genus motacilla], a bird with the ability to cause passionate love, wherefore Pindar calls it a mad or raging bird.[11] It seems to me, nevertheless, that these authors are in error, for the jinx is the bird that Aristotle describes as having two toes in front on each foot and two others behind, unlike all other birds.[12] Belon calls it *turcot* or *tercot*,[13] the Latins *torquillam* [wryneck, genus jynx], Gaza and Pacius, translators of Aristotle, *turbinem*. The wagtail, on the contrary, is called in Greek κνιπολόγος, that is *culvilega* and *susurada*.[14]

The greatest number of philters were made up of certain poisonous simples that often caused death. Such was the one given to Lucullus and to Leander the son-in-law of Aretaphile, according to Plutarch, to Lucretius according to Eusebius, to Frederick Duke of Bavaria, the Holy Roman Emperor according to Cuspinian.[15] Such was the nature of the philter for which the Athenian matron Temnia was quite justifiably con-demned to death by the Athenians, although only a short while before, according to Aristotle, they had granted pardon to a woman accused of the same crime, in the belief held by the Areopagites that the grief for having killed her dear husband would be a more cruel torment to this miserable creature than the death penalty dealt out to such persons according to the *Lex Cornelia de sicariis et de veneficiis*.[16] I can add to these the potion that was given to Lancelot King of Naples by one of his physicians, angry because the King had basely taken his pleasure with the physician's daughter, whereby the King and the innocent girl both met cruel and accursed deaths, as you may read in Nauclerus, M. de Montaigne, and G. Dupréau for the year 1414.[17]

Those philters that do not take away life, take away the reason: such was the one Circe gave to Ulysses' soldiers, and Caesonia gave to her husband, the Emperor Caligula.

> Yet even that can be endured,
> If only you don't go stark mad like Nero's uncle
> When Caesonia poured the whole forehead of a newborn colt
> Into his drink.[18]

According to the satirist [Juvenal], this philter was composed of a certain lump of flesh that appears on the brow of young foals—about the size of a dried fig, black, and almost round according to Aristotle and Pliny.[19] But the same philosopher elsewhere gives this name to a certain liquor that drips from mares in heat, very like the seed of the mare but more clear and watery: "it is this substance that is called hippomanes by some people and not the growth on the forehead of colts."[20] The poet Tibullus is in agreement:

> All the hippomane that drips from mares in heat
> When Venus inspires the invincible herds with passion.[21]

Notwithstanding, Aloysius Anguillara, Cratevas, Dodoneus, and Weckerus assert that Theocritus called the herb stramonia "hippomanes," the same as the Arab *nux methel* and the French "pomme du Pérou" [thorn apple or jimsonweed]. Rodericus à Castro wants it to be a little plant from Arcadia that we call fern.[22]

Porphyry in his book *On Sacrifices* (himself a notorious magician according to St. Augustine, bk. X, ch. 9, *The City of God*) recognized that demons are the authors of such philters as they are all fraud, cheating and lies.[23] Granting this, I cannot believe that Moses was responsible for the composition of the rings of love and of forgetfulness as several, following Josephus, have claimed.[24]

Whatever the case, I confess that there truly are medications, foods, and poisons capable of inciting sexual desire; you will find several catalogues of them, as in Avicenna, Aetius, Paul of Aegina, Oribasius, and in all our modern physicians who have dealt with sterility or impotence in men.[25] But I deny that any can be found that will make John love Jean rather than Jill, much less make anyone fall into passionate love.

> Medean herbs cannot rescue love
> Nor the charms of Marsa joined to magic sounds.
> If love could be kept alive by spells alone,
> The Phasian would still have Aeson's son
> And Circe would have won Ulysses.[26]

As the poet [Propertius] says, those who boasted of changing men into several and diverse shapes were yet unable to alter Ulysses' will, because:

> For such a case as mine avails no drugs, no Colchian
> Sorceress of the night, nor the herbs distilled by Medean hand.[27]

The truest and most effective philters are beauty, grace, and gentle civility, which the Greeks called τὰ θίλτρα, especially among persons living in mutual sympathy, and whose life-style is one of ease and delight.[28]

> It is useless to seek out herbs;
> Only virtue and beauty unite people in love.[29]

Olympias agreed. When someone told her that her husband Philip [of Macedonia] was charmed by a young girl, after she had contemplated the beauty of her husband's favorite, she exclaimed: "Cease these false accusations. You are, yourself, the only philter involved."[30]

> If man could be made to fall in love by enticements,
> Then every old woman would have lovers.
> Youth, a soft body, and compliance:
> These are the magical potions of attractive women.
> Old age finds no solace.[31]

The pagans used certain remedies of the same stamp against these philters which they called Homerical, not because the poet Homer was the inventor of them, as some have thought, but rather because they were, in the pagans' view, entirely admirable, like all the actions of the famous poet who, it is said, had power in his words alone to cure several diseases, and with certain verses could stop hemorrhages in imitation of the son of Autolycus who, on Mount Parnassus, stopped the flow of blood from Ulysses' wounded thigh:[32]

> stanched
> The black blood with a charm.[33]

These Homerical remedies consist of charms, characters, amulets, or medications hung on the body. They are forbidden to Christian physicians, although the common people superstitiously make use of many such pagan devices. Finally, I would conclude that the most sovereign remedies against philters are prayer, the reading of good books, and other serious activities.[34]

> Therefore, whoever you are that seek aid in the physician's skill,
> Place no faith in spells and witchcraft.[35]

XXXVI

Empirical remedies for
the curing of love
and erotic melancholy

The ancient Greeks recommended for this purpose bathing in Lake Co-
pais as Agamemnon did, according to Plutarch, in order to cure his love
for Chryseis.[1] Dexicreon, by certain ceremonies and expiatory sacrifices,
cured the Samian women who had been running through the streets with
this affliction. Others offered prayers at the sepulcher of Rhadina and
Leontina or else at that of Iole. But the most famous remedy was the
leap made by mad lovers from the Leucadian rock into the sea, whose
virtues Sappho was the first to try:

> and bold Sappho
> Feared not Chalcedon, but took the heroic leap.[2]

As she laments in her poems, she was smitten by love for the comely
Phaon whose refusal first incited her to leap from the Leucadian rock in
order to cure her love madness.[3] But those who have researched more
diligently into ancient history say that the first to jump was Phocas or
else Cephalus who was in love with Pterela.[4] In Ovid's version, Sappho
herself gives the credit to Deucalion, overcome with love for his wife
Pyrrha.

> From here Deucalion, burning with love for his Pyrrha,
> Threw himself down, and landed in the water without bodily harm.
> At once, passion left his breast
> And Deucalion was set free from the fire of love.[5]

The beautiful Calyce (praised by the poet Stesichorus), was so passionately enamored of Evanthlus that, seeing herself refused in marriage, she
risked the same leap, but came to a more funest end than Sappho.[6] That
remedy being too rigorous caused many to substitute for it the fountain
of Cupid in Cyzicus which, according to Mutianus, had the ability to

cool down love folly, as did the River Selemnus in Argire.[7] But if it were so, says Pausanias, "the water of this river would be more precious than gold."[8] Nevertheless, I do not find this an absurd proposition, since there is little doubt that cold water baths are sovereign for the curing of uterine fury (which is a form of erotic mania) and also the dropsy, especially if it is mineral water, which could have been the case with these fountains. On this matter, Mercuriale boasts of having cured several women of excessive love by making them drink great quantities of cold water, and by having them take cold baths.[9]

Dorian music has such a reputation for pacifying the perturbations of the spirit, according to Galen, that King Agamemnon, who led the Greek army against the Trojans, would leave no other guardian of his wife's chastity than an excellent Dorian musician, who by his harmonies prevented Clytemnestra from falling into base and immodest love. This lasted until the adulterous Aegisthus had him killed, seeing that without this murder he would never succeed in his love for the queen.[10] Pythagoras, being in company with some young men heated up with feasting and drinking, overheard their plot to assault a woman from a chaste household, whereupon he commanded the minstrels to change the tone and with a grave, solemn and spondaical music to softly enchant their rash lust and put them to sleep.[11]

Ovid makes mention of a certain forgetful or Lethean love to which, in former times, the Romans erected a temple adjoining the temple of Venus on the top of Mount Eryx. Lovers had themselves taken there to make sacrifices to this god in order to forget their amorous fury.[12]

> Lethean love is there, who heals hearts
> And pours cold water on the flaming torch.
> There young men and maidens, in the grip
> Of cruel tormenting love, seek to break their vows.[13]

In the place of this god, the Greeks knew and honored Venus ἀποστροφία [Apostrophia], who was, in my view, the celestial Venus or Urania. Herodotus tells us that she was worshipped in Ascalon by the Scythians who severed the veins and arteries joining near the ears, thereby making themselves cowardly, sterile, and effeminate.[14]

Athenaeus reports of Thersites that he gave wine in which someone had suffocated a mullet or a seabarbel.[15] Pliny, instead, adds to the wine chrysocolla, called *baurach* by the Arabs. Or else urine can be used in which a lizard has been drowned. Equally great claims have been made for the wax of the left ear, for pigeon dung steeped in ordinary oil, and for the urine of the billy goat mixed with Indian or Celtic spikenard.[16] Giovanni di Vigo, surgeon to Pope Julius II, has the excrements of the person loved collected which he then burns, giving assurances that such perfume has the singular virtue of breaking the ties of illicit love if the lover breathes the stinking odor.[17] But such prescriptions come from the shops of the physicians Aristophanes calls "urine drinkers and shit eaters."[18]

Others cut off the hair of a girl who persists in her love madness, in imitation of the horse dealers who cut off the manes of mares in heat.[19] In short, there is not a naturalist who hasn't excogitated some remedy for the treatment of this disease. Albertus Magnus and Cardanus celebrate the virtues of emeralds, rubies, and sapphires, this person diamonds, that person topaz and amethyst.[20] The author of the *Picatrix* recommends myrtle sap, swallows' brain, and the blood of the person loved[21]—which we read to have been used by the Emperor Marcus Aurelius to quell the unruly love of his wife Faustina for a certain gladiator. He was given the idea by the Chaldeans, who advised him to have the fighter killed secretly, and then to have the blood given to his wife in a drink the same night he intended to sleep with her. All this took place as planned, but from that coupling Antoninus Commodus was conceived, one of the most cruel and bloody of the emperors of Rome who spent his time among swordsmen and behaved more like a gladiator than like the good Marcus Aurelius[22] who as Ausonius says:

Never did harm to his country except in begetting this son.[23]

Deianira became jealous of her valiant husband Hercules because, according to the fallacious report of the centaur Nessus, he was making love to Iole. To extinguish this illicit love she sent to him a tunic dipped in oil and the blood of the centaur. But rather than healing the great Hercules' love folly, it brought him a furious and tormenting death.[24]

XXXVII

True and methodical
remedies for the treatment
of erotic melancholy: dietetics

Marsilio Ficino on the *Symposium* of Plato and François Valleriola, the
wise physician of Arles, say that all diseases are cured by their contraries,
for according to the true and familiar axiom of the Father of Medicine,
"contraries are the remedies for their opposites"; "moreover, let that
contrary action be a loosening," for of necessity love must be cured by
discharge, of which there are two kinds: natural and artificial.[1] The latter
depends on evacuation, as I will explain in the following chapter, while
the former includes remonstrations from pious, learned, and virtuous
people, a change of air, abstinence, a variety of attentions and treatments,
as well as the effects of the fears and sorrows themselves—remedies that
I find more suitable to the prevention of this disease than to its cure (as
I stated earlier), especially because it is easier to abolish love when it is
new than after it has become diseased.

> While it is new, love can be resisted.
> A little water will douse a small fire.
> Crush while yet they are new the baneful seeds of sudden disease.
> Delay gives strength.[2]

The order of diet for erotic melancholiacs is scarcely different from
that prescribed for the prevention of love. Nevertheless, it should be
more humectant and less refrigerant, without forgetting those foods that,
by their occult properties, are beneficial to erotic melancholiacs such as
turtledove, heart of wolf, baby horned owls or great owls boiled in marjoram juice, rat's meat, and the like. If the patient is very dry and emaciated
he should be fed in the same way as the hectical, according to Avicenna.[3]

In addition, there can be no doubt that all our theologians, philosophers, physicians, orators, and poets advise for the patient a change of
air and a change of place,[4] not so much as a wholesome remedy for
all chronic and long-term ailments—according to the teachings of Hip-

pocrates in his *Epidemics*: "in cases of chronic diseases it is beneficial to change location"[5]—but rather because such change and variety of place wakes up the melancholy lover's spirit, diverts his thoughts, and not least of all, deprives him of the chance of seeing and keeping company with the object of his affections:[6] "the lover must be led to other interests, responsibilities, preoccupations and business matters. Then he has to be cured by a change of place just like other convalescents."[7] But this change of clime and place in itself has no virtue at all to cure folly, or to make a man wise who does not wish to be: "change of place neither removes a man's folly nor teaches him wisdom," in the words of one of the Greek sages.[8] Indeed, it is no more profitable than for a feverish man to change beds, according to Plato, because the lover is habitually longing for his lady and meditating on her attractive graces in a way that is intensified by her absence:[9]

> our mind is eager for what is lost,
> And moves with all its force among the shadows of the past.[10]

What use is it for a soul to flee, an ancient Greek poet writes, because Cupid has two wings for promptly catching evaders, even though they gallop?

> It is a vain effort to run away from love
> For no man can escape him. How can I, on foot,
> Escape from a winged creature in hot pursuit?[11]

These two wings according to Pietro Hedo in his *Anterotica* signify the double hopes of the lovers—to be loved and to be able to enjoy what he loves—which are the principal obstacles to the cure of erotic melancholy.[12] This remedy is efficacious for the prevention of this disease, and is not useless to someone who has made a good and firm resolution to desist in his desires—profitable for a Ulysses, or for a pious Aeneas, so caressed and adored by the Queen of Carthage—but otherwise this remedy is harmful to melancholy lovers.

> For if what you love is absent, yet its images are there,
> And the sweet name is kept in your ears.[13]

In order to make such a remedy effective, he must leave himself and his burning desire before he leaves the country (as Diogenes long ago counseled a long-haired young lovesick wooer), and in coming back from his pilgrimage he must answer his lady in the manner of the young man mentioned by St. Augustine: while you may still be the same as before, I am not.[14]

> May the gods grant you to be able to pass by the threshold
> Of a deserted mistress, and may your feet avail for your purpose!
> Yes, you will be able; only let your will not fail.[15]

Solitude brought no better relief to such as Phyllis, Echo, Pan, and many others mentioned by the poets. Indeed, I would dare to disprove it as a cure for this disease, agreeing with Paul of Aegina who asserts that several ignorant physicians have lost their lovesick patients by solitary isolation and forced abstinence: "but wiser ones, recognizing the lover, direct his attention to baths, the drinking of wine, gestation, spectacles, and amusing stories."[16] Such people, in their solitariness, otherwise dote on their loves and their wounds. They are filled with desires, their mouths full of sighs and laments, their eyes flowing with tears, all of which increase the malady.

> Whoever you are that love, solitary places are dangerous,
>   beware of solitudes.
> Whither do you flee? You will be safer in a crowd.
> You have no need for secrecy (secrecy adds to passion);
> A crowd will give you succour.
> If alone, you will be sad, and the shape of your deserted mistress
> Will stand, as if herself, before your eyes.[17]

Lot was carried away by his incestuous lust in the desert and not while living among the base and infamous dwellers in Sodom and Gomorrah. The poets depict for us the loves of a thousand fauns, satyrs, cyclops, nymphs, and hamadryads. Society, on the contrary, diverts the mind of the frantic lover, cheers him, and brings him to a recognition of his error. François Valleriola states in his *Medical Observations* that he found such solitariness harmful in the curing of a rich merchant of Arles mad with love, and therefore had him visited continually by his friends, relatives, and associates.[18] Even more, I would say that if this disease is the result of atrabilious humors, there is reason to fear suicide if the patient is abandoned, since many have taken their own lives, or that he will become lycanthropic, as Avicenna warns us at the end of his chapter "On love."[19] Nevertheless, I greatly approve of solitude for the prevention of the disease, provided that fasting, watching, and prayer are added in imitation of the several holy men who have retired into the desert for these same reasons.

Hunting has been included with solitude by several, for in this pursuit Diana defied lord Cupid and Hippolytus lived chastely, avoiding the vile affections and base machinations of his aggressive mother-in-law.[20] This remedy seems practical not only for the distractions it provides, but because it whets the appetite of the gaunt, wasted melancholiac, while the weariness that follows brings on a gentle sleep that prevents our stricken lover from meditating on his wild desires.[21] Nevertheless, the hunt sparked Dido's passion and the loves of many a nymph. Those who take no pleasure in hunting may substitute several other exercises of body and spirit ("the best therapy for men's souls is walking"),[22] which are among the most wholesome remedies for this disease by common consent of all the physicians. They are able to divert the thoughts of the lover, erase the memory of past pleasures, burn off the excess seed, revive the patient, and build him up if he is too lean. They include long walks, conversation, legitimate games, banquets, music, and related recreations,[23] from which I would banish young men if the patient is a young lady or widow, and vice versa if the patient is a man—contrary to the opinion of the learned Valleriola.[24] You will take note, however, that in the view of the Prince of the Arabs [Avicenna] these remedies are at times harmful to many patients so that the practicing physician is advised to prescribe them with prudence and dexterity.

The poet Menander adds to these poverty and hunger, pointing out that disordinate love never attacks paupers and beggars:[25]

> Can a man love life who has been turned into a beggar?
> Why has no man taken Hecale, no woman Irus?
> Surely, because she was poor, and he a beggar.
> Poverty has no means to feed its passion.[26]

Rondelet in his *Method*, Mercatus, and several other modern physicians prescribe fasting and abstinence for melancholy lovers.[27] The same is prescribed by the gynecological writers for women suffering from uterine fury, which we have already demonstrated to be a true species of erotic melancholy. In this, however, they go against the opinions of Paul of Aegina and Oribasius who, in their chapters on love, fault the physicians who recommend such deprivations. Here are their words in the Latin version of the original Greek: "There are many who are unaware that those who are afflicted by the cares of love, and who are tortured by their sleeplessness, waste away from lack of baths and meals, and from too light a diet. When I came to realize that love was the cause of those ills, I directed their thoughts away from love, and toward bathing, drinking parties and other activities, towards games and plays."[28] Starvation was of little avail to Phaedra, suffering from her love for Hippolytus, as she herself explains in Euripides' play. In spite of the familiar proverb that without Ceres and Bacchus, Venus is without force, we read in the poets that Neptune and the gods and goddesses of the sea, the rivers, and fountains were often stung by this disease, just as our early ancestors were who lived on acorns and chestnuts.

> Our forefathers lived on acorns; they enjoyed love without
> restraints.[29]

These authors can be reconciled if we point out the truth of the matter, namely that if the lovesick person is so afflicted with melancholy
that he has become lean, dried out, and wan, by no means can fasting
and abstinence be recommended—rather he should be given a variety
of humectifying foods; but if the patient is still in good physical condition, fleshy and moist, abstinence would do him good "so that the seed
(which is the primary cause of love) would be consumed."[30] Hence, our
conclusion that this remedy is more useful in the prevention of erotic
melancholy than in its cure.

Galen recognized the importance of time and its passage in the healing of our passions, describing it as a remedy for erotic melancholy.
Time achieves the desired ends by allowing all manner of new thoughts
and activities to preoccupy our minds, unraveling and fading the formerly frenzied and enraged imagination, no matter how strong it was.[31]
Clement of Alexandria says that it is the final remedy for love, except
death: "Crates Thebanus wrote very succinctly that to soften and re-
strain venerian desire, one must have recourse to fasting or else allow
time to pass, and that if these two remedies are not strong enough, there
remains the noose." Such is the way I would interpret this passage [from
Clement]; the verses of Crates Thebanus are also incorporated into a text
by Diogenes Laertius and appear in the first book of the *Greek Anthology*
in the following way:

> Hunger stops love; if not hunger, then time;
> If these do not extinguish the fire,
> Then let the noose be chosen as the final therapy.

The learned Alciati has translated these lines into Latin in the following
way:

> Unsatisfied hunger calms and overcomes love.
> But if not, then time.
> If time, however, will not vanquish it,
> Then a knotted cord applied to the throat will cure it.[32]

Many have had recourse to scourging and rods in order to tame the
inner fires by subduing and mortifying the flesh even until it becomes
rotten, as Bernard of Gordon says in his ch. 15 concerning love.[33] But the
courtesan who aroused and excited her mate by beating him, according
to Seneca, would argue to the contrary if she were here, and not without
good reason, for it is indeed true that the blood is heated by whipping

and pounding the back and flanks, in turn stirring up flatulent vapors that can fill the fistular nerve and bring on the disease physicians call satyriasis.[34] We can see this in the girlfriend of Cornelius Gallus who threw herself the more passionately into love the more vigorously her father beat her.

> She cries out, yet she yields to her father's beating,
> While fire flares up in her breast,
> Just like flames grow once the pyre is lit.
> Terrified, she seeks me with gasping heart,
> Although she thinks I am heedless of her suffering.[35]

This remedy in our view therefore seems to be more prophylactic than therapeutic.

But because all the remedies already mentioned are insufficient to heal those suffering from erotic melancholy—including those listed in ch. XXI [XXX?] that I do not want to repeat here—one must have recourse to the surgical and pharmaceutical cures.

XXXVIII

Surgical cures
for erotic melancholy

If our lover is sufficiently corpulent, well-fed and plump, from the moment my help is called for, I have a certain quantity of blood drawn from the hepatic vein in the right arm, according to the state of his disease and the complexion of his body, and in keeping with his physical tolerances, as explained above in the chapter on prevention, because:

> Bleeding cheers the pensive and removes
> The raging fires bred by burning love.[1]

But if the patient's imagination is already deranged, I prefer to have the median vein opened—which Rhazes and Almansor call the *vena matrix* or *cardiaca*—in imitation of François Valleriola,[2] keeping in mind the observation that if the blood flows black, thick, and heavy, a good deal can be drawn, but that if it is clear, thin, and vermilion in color, the vein should be closed right away according to the teachings of Galen, Avicenna, and their followers.[3] After completing the general bleeding—now in order to correct the intemperature of the liver, and in order to draw off a portion of the melancholy blood—I continue by bleeding the ankle [saphena], particularly in women patients, some of whom suffer specifically from hysterical suffocation or uterine fury,[4] because this bleeding brings about a more forceful and speedy transfer of the offending humors.[5] Besides, those parts situated below the kidneys have a greater affinity and sympathy ἀδελφιξίαν [brotherhood] and closer connections with the veins of the buttocks and ankles than with those of the arms.[6] A few modern physicians have the veins in the forehead opened with a scalpel or with leeches, but I would prefer bleeding the *salvatella* in the left hand, which I have found by experience to be useful in the curing of all melancholy disorders.[7] Or even more to the purpose, I would provoke the flowing of the hemorrhoidal veins, one of the most certain and necessary remedies for the treatment of all types of hypochondriacal melancholy,[8] because by this fluxion the gall bladder and the mesentery empty themselves of the thick and earthy humors that obstruct these areas—a practice taught by the great Hippocrates in his *Aphorisms* as well as in the *Epidemics*, and by his faithful interpreter Galen in his *Treaty on Melancholy* and in his [*Commentary on Hippocrates' Aphorisms*] bk. IV, no. 25: "the opening of the hemorrhoids is the surest remedy both for the prevention and the curing of any melancholy disease."[9]

If the lovesick patient has varicose veins, they will do nearly as well, because these veins draw the vapors and flatulence away from the genitals toward the buttocks and other regions where the veins are distended, according to Aristotle in his *Problems* and the general opinion of our physicians.[10] But to tell you frankly, my experiences with this remedy have produced little or no results. Therefore, following the good Arnald of Villanova, I would instead use cupping glasses with scarification on the legs or thighs, or apply one or two caustic compounds to these same areas.[11] If the clitoris, by its excessive length, is the cause of this furious desire and raging disease, as is often the case, it should be cut in the manner taught by the Greek Moschion and the Arab Albucasis, to whom I refer you in order not to be prolix.[12] I will simply add here that if the condition grows worse in a way suggesting that the erotic melancholy could turn into lycanthropy, then the veins in the arms must be bled until the patient faints or until there is a total failure of the heart, and in spite of this one must continue by cauterizing the front of the head with a searing iron [actual cautery], or if he refuses or cannot bear it, with a caustic compound [potential cautery] applied to the same place, as we have been taught to do by Paul of Aegina, Oribasius, Avicenna, and other classical authors in their chapters on *lycanthropia, lycaone, lycano, alchatrab,* and *alcutubut,* into which erotic melancholy sometimes degenerates according to the great Avicenna in his chapter on love or *ilisco.*[13]

XXXIX

Pharmaceutical remedies for love and erotic melancholy

Gall, scurf, and itch cannot be completely cured without first purifying the blood and purging the salty and nitrous humors that are mixed into the mass of blood in the veins.[1] This must be done with the correct medications appropriately administered, not recklessly and in haste, but slowly, methodically, and as we are accustomed to say, by *epicrasis* [replacing bad humors with good by gradual purgation]: "all sudden and violent evacuation, filling, heating, or cooling of the body, or any such violent motion is dangerous. Nature abhors things in excess and prefers balance and moderation in all things."[2] Though this aphorism from Hippocrates has general application, it is particularly apt with regard to the scurf and the itch, which are made worse by ointments and evacuations unwisely and overhastily administered. The curing of melancholy or erotic mania must be conducted with the same care and circumspection, for these diseases require a considerable period of time for their treatment, not only for the reasons set out in ch. XXI [XXVI], but because the offending humor is extremely rebellious as a result of its great dryness:[3] ("that which is dry is very difficult to evacuate or alter");[4] as Hippocrates teaches in his book *On the Nature of Man*: "melancholy is the most viscous and sticky of the humors and is therefore the most difficult to purge and requires the longest period of time."[5] That it took Valleriola some six or seven months to cure the rich merchant of Provence is proof of that fact.[6]

Now in order to proceed with the cure of this disease in a more methodical and medical way, I will divide it into two principal categories, namely the humectation of the body or of the offending humor, and the purgation of the blackish bile. According to the teachings of the Prince of the Arabs: "the rule for curing melancholy is that you attain, in the end, a state of complete rehumectation. If this does not diminish the melancholy condition, then you must set about the evacuation of the black bile."[7] The humectation is done with food, alterative medications, baths, and other remedies. The evacuation should be accomplished quickly, gently, but by intervals for fear of overexasperating the humor, although often it does not respond at all to benign and gentle medications. For this reason a comparison can be made, as an ancient doctor once did, between this disease and a troublesome garrison of soldiers who live as they please in a city: if they are treated gently they have regrets to leave, and if on the other hand any displeasure is shown, they stay even longer to avenge themselves and give more offense.[8]

I start the purgation with a gentle enema in order to evacuate the excrements from the first region of the body, for which I make a mollescent and refreshing decoction, adding to it catholicon, diaprunum simple, or similar opiates. The following day I give my patient a mouthful [bolus] of cassia with a little powder of well-prepared oriental senna, or else a dram of Hamech's confection or diasenna. Or if the patient prefers, there is a more gentle potion made with catholicon, triphera persica, and sweetbrier sirup, to which one can quite appropriately add rhubarb and agaric.[9] After this minorative, I am at leisure to turn to the preparation of the humor with juleps or decoctions [apozemes] similar to this one:

> Rx.   Take one large handful each of viper's bugloss and borage, with the roots of chicory, endives, wood sorrel, scarlet pimpernel, and hart's tongue fern. Add to these one half large handful each of hops, fumatory and wood betony, and a half ounce of common polypody [oak fern]. Follow with 3 drams each of well-cleaned passul [raisins] and currants and 3 sweet prunes. Then add $1\frac{1}{2}$ drams each of well-cleaned musk melon seeds, pumpkin seeds, and cucumber seeds. Add 1 dram each of the seeds of agnus castus and anise, and a small handful [pugille] of thyme, epithyme, and the three flower cordial. Make two pounds of the entire decoction. Bring to this mixture, in equal measure, 3 ounces of chicory, common borage, hops, and [a confection of] clean scented fruits. Let the ingredients boil a second time, adding a half pound of high-grade sugar. Make a very clear julep. [At this time one should take—or mix in] an aromatic powder, either Rhazes' "comfort," Galen's "comfort," or diamargariton frigium. Take $1\frac{1}{2}$ drams each day for five or six days.[10]

If you find it necessary, you can repeat this drug for another two or three days because this atrabilious humor—owing to its cold, dry, thick, and earthy qualities in opposition to nature—needs a thorough preparation. The physician should devote himself to this during several days so that the humor can be easily evacuated by dejectory medications. I prefer laxatives to emetics on the authority of our Coryphaeus [Hippocrates]: "the melancholy are more freely and copiously purged by laxatives"[11] (although the good Arnald of Villanova claims the contrary)[12] unless the patient complains of indigestion or a bitter taste in the mouth, and then he should be made to vomit, because these are signs of vitiated food in the stomach as Avicenna and Rhazes have taught in the texts already cited.[13] Once the humor has been prepared, it should be purged—especially if there are signs in the urine of an overheating and boiling of the humor—by using the following dejectory and cathartic medication:

> ℞.   Take 3 sweet prunes and 3 small handfuls each of currants and flower cordial [the *quinque flores cordiales* contained roses, violets, bugloss, borage, and rosemary flowers]. Follow with 2 drams of fresh and choice tamarinds. Add 3 drams of clean oriental senna leaves. Then add $\frac{1}{2}$ dram of anise, agnus castus, and the inside of cinnamon bark. Follow with $\frac{1}{2}$ small handful of epithyme [lesser dodder] and make a decoction boiling it down to 4 ounces, into which dissolve 4 scruples of squeezed rhubarb infused overnight in goat's whey, together with 8 grains of red saunders, 2 drams of Hamech's confection, and $1\frac{1}{2}$ ounces of rose water sirup. Make a potion and administer it in the morning under doctor's supervision.[14]

The following day you should give him a little conserve of roses, borage flowers, or bugloss root.

If you choose instead to use a vomitive, take an ounce of horseradish, a dram of agaric, and a half dram of hazelwort [wild nard] and boil all these together in barley water. Take 10 ounces of this decoction, thin it with 2 ounces of oxymel of squill or sirup of vinegar and have the melancholy patient take this lukewarm.[15] If you add flower of broom to this the emetic will be more forceful, but beware of going on to hellebore or antimony, for such vomitives are extremely dangerous.[16]

The Paracelsians use a more gentle purge made with 7 or 8 grains of iron salts [sal vitriol] which they give with wine or broth, or else some *vomitivum pantagogum* or other such emetics that you can read about in Rulandus, Quercetanus, and other authors of that sect.[17]

After the purgation, you should give your patient a few days of repose without any medications at all, and then repeat the alterative medications for the offending humor: "for the bad humor must be purged slowly and intermittently,"[18] keeping in mind the observations of the learned Rondelet in his chapter on love where he warns against the use of any alterative medications for the melancholy humor that can increase the sperm[19]—"seed self-generated by the passions"[20]—and by this means increase the disordinate desire of our melancholy lover. These include eringo roots, the roots of sweet cullions of orchis, and others with similar properties.[21] As for the purgation, if the patient is angry about having to retake the same cathartic medication set out above, he can take diasenna or the following magistral sirup once or twice a month.

> ℞.   Take 1 ounce each of the roots of both types of bugloss, aspara-

gus, capers, and scorzonera humilis. Add 1 small handful each of the
leaves of endive, chicory, bugloss, borage, wood sorrel, hops, fumitory,
and hart's tongue fern. Now add ½ large handful of Roman wormwood,
mint, and sweet balm [melissa]. Add 6 drams each of licorice, raisins,
and currants washed in warm water. Add 2 grains each of the seeds
of lemon [citron], holy thistle, lettuce, white poppy, and agnus castus.
Add 1 small handful each of the three cardiac flowers [flor trium car-
diac], thyme, and epithyme. Add 4 ounces each of oak fern [common
polypody] and the washed leaves of oriental senna. Add ½ ounce of
freshly-made agaric pills; ½ dram of soapwort; ½ small handful each of
water lily flowers and rosemary. Boil down to a decoction of 2 pounds
in which dissolve 2 ounces of expressed rhubarb infused with a little
cinnamon and mixed with any kind of white sugar. Make a magistral
sirup, and flavor it with 2 drams of the powder called Galen's "comfort." The patient will take 2 ounces of this twice a week with chicken
broth or cardiac water.[22]

François Valleriola, the learned Arlesian physician, included a dram
of black hellebore in the magistral sirup with which he purged his wealthy
lovesick merchant, but I dare not imitate him is this matter,[23] even though
hellebore was a medication familiar to the great Hippocrates and was
used for curing such diseases according to his works,[24] and even though
Melampus used it to cure the lovesick daughter of Proetus, giving rise
to the surname melampodium for *veratre* or hellebore.[25] Nor dare I follow the renowned Avicenna in prescribing the use of hiera [aloe].[26] But
if the remedies already mentioned are insufficient for purging this rebel
humor, I dare, rather, to give to the patient 2 or 3 grains, and very little
more, of prepared antimony in imitation of our modern authors.[27] Certain others of the Paracelsian cabal use turpeth mineral and ladanum
Mercurial, which are little different.[28]

I do not dislike the powder of Haly Abbas that he describes and
praises in the following fashion: "though other medications may not
work, this one works by the will and mercy of God, and should be
guarded in the most secret way, for human intellect desperately lost in
love can be restored by its virtues."[29]

Rx.   Take ½ ounce of epithyme, 2 drams each of lapis lazuli (or to be
safer, Mercatus' preparation of salt of ammon) and agaric, 1 dram of
scammony and prepared soapwort. With these make a powder of which
the patient should take, once a week, 2 or 2 ½ scruples together with a
solution of rose sirup or violet and sweetbrier preserves.[30]

If the patient is unwilling to purge so often using liquid medications,
although they are more effective in the expulsion of the melancholy hu-

mor than the solid, you may accommodate him by prescribing a laxative opiate with virtues equal to this following:

> R̥.   Take 2 ounces of clear annual mercury juice in which infuse during 24 hours 2 ounces of washed oriental senna. With this extraction make a decoction with any type of sugar in order to form an electuary. Then add 2 ounces of cassia pulp freshly extracted from the canes [shoots from the roots], followed by ½ ounce of epithyme and 2 drams of crushed soapwort. Mix these ingredients and make an opiate of which 1½ ounces should be taken once or twice a month.[31]

However, you must not forget to comfort the heart, the liver, and the brain of the patient with a few good opiates such as these:

> R̥.   Take 1 ounce of sweetbrier preserves, and 6 drams each of pond lily flower preserves and borage. Then add ½ ounce each of citrus pulp and wild lettuce seasoned with sugar [lettuce in a preserve], followed by 2 drams of myrobalan emblic in a sugar preserve and Alkermis Confection no. 2. Add 1 dram of Galen's "comfort" pulverized, followed by 4 scruples of oriental pearl and 2 scruples of powdered ivory. Mix all these ingredients with a fruit sirup and make an opiate, which the patient will take in quantities the size of a chestnut, chased with a little white wine greatly diluted with bugloss water. This should be taken twice a day approximately two hours before each meal.[32]

Or else:

> R̥.   Take ½ ounce of Venetian turpentine washed with lettuce water. Add 8 grains of carrot seeds, agnus castus, and cinnamon, followed by 1 dram of a newly made lozenge of agaric. Make a bolus which is good for the evacuation of semen. This recipe is taken from Hollerius, Mercatus, and others.[33]

Seeking these same effects, Dioscorides has the patient drink the powder of asphodel and coltsfoot seeds;[34] Porphyrius, according to Stobaeus and Pliny, gave willow flowers with cold water.[35]

> Whose blossoms, taken in cold water, forcibly bring about
> A cooling down of all the sharp, stimulating instincts
>   of Venus.[36]

I use these tablets or others of like virtue:

> R̥.   Take ½ scruple each of agnus castus seeds, golden purslane, and rue. Then add 2 scruples of lettuce seeds and 2 scruples of white poppy. Add 8 grains of hemp granules [hashish resin] followed by 6 grains each of burned stag horn, coral, and rose anthers, and 3 drams of musk melon

seeds. Now add a suitable quantity of sugar, rose water, and shredded borage, and mix them together so as to make tablets or lozenges of one dram each. These should be taken just before bedtime or in the morning well before eating.[37]

There is also good to be had in giving the patient, from time to time, 4 grains of oriental bezoar steeped in the water of scorzonera or of lettuce which, for its particular virtues, the Pythagoreans called ἐννούχεον according to Athanaeus.[38]

I leave these now to deal with the external medications, among which fresh water baths hold the highest place in light of the fact that Paul of Aegina and Oribasius compliment themselves, in their chapters on love, for having cured several persons sick with erotic melancholy by these baths of fresh water. They were also approved by the Coryphaeus of the Arabs [Avicenna]—"make them take baths according to the usual recipes for moistening the body"—and by all our respectable practitioners.[39] I may add to the bath certain simples appropriate to this disease, as in the manner following:

R. Take 4 large handfuls each of marsh mallows using the entire herb, blue mallows, wild lettuce [green endive], borage, white pond lily, pumpkin seeds, fumatory, hops, and sharp-pointed dock. Add in 2 large handfuls each of glasswort and tendrils of the grapevine. Put in ½ large handful each of water lily, sweet violet, borage, sweetbrier [eglantine], and marigold. Add 2 ounces of chaste tree seeds, hemp seeds and the heads of two wethers [castrated rams]. Make a decoction using river water, in which the patient will sit for about one hour a day for four days.[40]

Several authors recommend that, while the patient bathes, people be called into the room to jest and make merry, sing to him, and tell pleasant tales and stories.[41]

Aetius prescribes the application of an oxyrrhodin to the head for repelling the vapors that rise from the seminal vessels to the head and, in women, from the womb.[42] Women may also use a pessary made from *diacodion* mixed with a little vinegar and the juice of the black nightshade,[43] or else with a little sodium nitrate and a bit of cardamom, or finally a nascal or pessary made with *castoreum* mixed with rue, to which Avicenna adds the root of garden lily and of water lily.[44] Or else she may use this uterine clyster described by Ludovicus Mercatus, principal physician to the kings of Spain:

R. Take 4 ounces of goat's milk or cow's milk, 2 ounces of sea water, and 1 ounce of honey. Mix them together to make a clyster and introduce into the vagina.[45]

But I prefer the following:

> ℞.   Take 2 small handfuls of water lentils, 1 large handful of the
> flowers and leaves of the European willow. Make a decoction, boiling
> down to 1 pound, into which dissolve 1 dram each of the white trochisc
> of Rhazes and the trochisc of camphor. Mix these ingredients, make a
> clyster and introduce into the vagina.[46]

Eros [Trotula] adds opium to this recipe.[47] Pliny in his *Natural History*
and our Doctor Rondelet in bk. XII, ch. 19, of his book on fish have the
genital area rubbed with the gall of crampfish [electric ray] which has a
narcotic effect.[48] Or else a pessary using the root of white pond lily can
be used.

In short, you will find a thousand such recipes in the works of all our
physicians, and thus I will stop in order not to grow tedious, adding here
only that Nicholas Monardes, physician of Seville, and Clusius, speaking
of medications discovered in North America praise, as a sovereign remedy and antidote against illicit love and against philters, the powder of
the *contrayerva* recently brought back from the province of Los Charcas
in Peru, resembling the gladiolus but with leaves like fig leaves.[49] If that
is indeed true, we can say of that plant what Pausanias said of the fountain of Selemnus, that it is worth more than all the gold in the world.[50]
I would say the very same of the moonstone mentioned by Dioscorides
that the Greeks called *selenites* or *aphroselenon* [transparent gypsum],[51]
as well as asbestos or Cyprus stone that Pliny calls *linum vivum*, Strabo
carystium, Zoroaster *bostrychitem*, Solin *carbasum*, others *corsoïdem*, *spo-
liam*, and *spartopoliam*, the common people powder of salamander and
erroneously feathery alum with which, in former times, tablecloths were
made that could be whitened in the fire without being burned.[52]

The learned Mercuriale in bk. IV of his *Diseases of Women* boasts of
having cured several girls or women of uterine fury or love madness by
using cold mineral waters, such as the waters of the virgin or *de villa*
in Italy.[53] This is difficult to believe, however, seeing that without any
doubt, as I have set out above, the cure for love melancholy consists in
humectation, which Galen requires as part of the treatment for all diseases of melancholy.[54] But all the authors who have written about mineral
waters agree that they are desiccative and therefore contrary to the healing of erotic melancholy. I would say in Mercuriale's favor that in spite
of the drying properties, these waters are salubrious in melancholy diseases insofar as they refresh the liver—the seat of the disease—remove
the obstructions in the hypochondries, comfort the stomach, and purify
the blood by removing the serosities through the urine and the stool, as
Giovanni Battista Sylvaticus has amply demonstrated.[55] Moreover, not
all the dry medications have been excluded from cures for the melan-

choly, because Alexander of Tralles, Paul of Aegina, Oribasius, Avicenna, and Rhazes often give epithyme, aloes, and aristolochia while Aetius gives vinegar,[56] which Hippocrates says excites and increases the melancholy humor: "black humors are inclined to ferment, to rise up and to multiply."[57] Physicians in France and Germany attribute the same virtues to spa waters and in Gascony to the waters of Encausse, for although they are hot and dry, they are often not useless to the melancholy diseases arising from the indisposition of the hypochondries. I can attest to this from experience. Heurnius in his *Practice* substitutes the following decoction if the waters of the virgin are not available for drinking:

R̥.   Take a quantity of fountain water as necessary, 3 rams' heads and the trotters; add 3 large handfuls each or red roses, laurel leaves, 5 large handfuls of fresh golden purslane, and 2 large handfuls each of belladonna and houseleek. Mix these ingredients and make a decoction which the patient will take lukewarm twice a day, two hours before eating.[58]

You should, at the same time, provide treatment for the symptoms accompanying this disease, for they follow as the shadow follows the body, as I mentioned in ch. II, in accordance with the teachings of our authors—especially Galen, Avicenna, and Aetius. I will restrict myself to the remedies needed for the mitigation of two of the most frequent and annoying symptoms: insomnia and anorexia.[59]

For the first, I use a sirup of poppy, almonds, poppy seed, and lettuce in broth. I often employ from 4 to 5 grains of this opiate, called nepenthe of ladanum:

R̥.   Take 1 ounce of the confection of Alkermes, 3 drams of specierum diambrae, and Galen's "comfort" [*laetificans falso Galeno abscriptum*]. Add ½ ounce each of Albigensian saffron and opium. Once mixed, let them macerate in aqua-vitae, extract a tincture, then let it be reduced by evaporation to the consistency of an opiate.

Or:

R̥.   Take 2 ounces of specierum diambrae and infuse it for 12 days in a large finger's worth of distilled wine, and add 6 drams of opium, ¼ dram of mummy, 1 ounce of common henbane, 2 scruples each of red coral and carob pods, 1 scruple of saffron, 16 grains of oriental pearl, and 12 grains of amber. Pour these ingredients a second time into a large finger's worth of wine spirits, keep it next to a stove or furnace for a month, shaking it daily, to be given in doses of ½ scruples or 8 grains according to the patient's disposition.[60]

You will find a thousand similar recipes in Rulandus, Quercetanus, Penot, and several other alchemists, that you should nevertheless make use of with great prudence and only out of necessity—a caution holding for *diacodion* and *requies Nicolai* as well.[61] I much prefer to have the patient sniff a posy made with the flowers of roses, violets, carnations, or sprigs of marjoram soaked in vinegar in which has been steeped a few grains of camphor and opium[62]—or else this pomander:

R͎. For this pomander take 1 dram each of common henbane and hemlock seeds, 4 scruples of the bark of mandrake root and 1 scruple of opium. Mix these with mandrake oil and the sap of the greater aizoi, add 1 grain of pearl and make a pomander.[63]

Certain others have applied horseleeches behind the ears with happy results. Immediately after they have them removed, they place a grain of opium in the wound.[64]

I strengthen and rebuild my patients with ass's or goat's milk, which must be taken with sugar for about a month—not forgetting marchpane cakes, made in the following manner:

R͎. Take a quantity of sweet almonds washed in hot water and blanched; infuse them with 1½ pounds of rosewater; add 3 ounces of fresh and well-mundified white poppy seed; add 2 pounds of fine sugar. Work all these ingredients into a paste and, using rosewater, make a marchpane. Take this before going to bed. This paste is excellent for bringing sleep and, at the same time, it refreshes and nourishes.[65]

This following is even more nourishing:

R͎. Take 1 pound of maiden's hair fern, an appropriate quantity of rosewater, and 3 ounces of sugar. 2 drams of cinnamon should be added toward the end of the decoction. Let them cook together and then shape them into hard chunks.[66]

Beside these remedies, I would wish for all melancholy or maniacal lovers the ultimate cure—that wished upon the philosopher Democritus by the Father of Medicine: "the easiest and most effective cure known to my profession is the honing and perfection of wisdom,"[67] which is the true moly that Mercury, the god of prudence, gave to Homer's wise Ulysses as a perfect antidote against the inveiglements, baits, and enticements by which the infamous Circe tried to subject the soul of this noble warrior to her lust.

Later thoughts are wiser.[68]

Annotations and Commentary

I. Whether It Is Useful to Teach the Remedies of Love or Erotic Melancholy

1. [*Arist. 1. Metaph. c. 4.*]: Aristotle, *Metaphysics*, bk. I, ch. 4 (984 a): "αἴτιον τῶν ἀγαθῶν φιλία; τὸ δὲ νεῖκος τῶν κακῶν"; the modern text differs from Ferrand's: "αἰτίαν οὖσαν τῶν ἀγαθῶν, τό δέ νεῖκος τῶν κακῶν," trans. H. Tredennick (Loeb, 1968), pp. 26–27.
2. [*Plato in Conv. Plut. 1. Symp.*]: Plato, *Symposium* (196A–198A), trans. W. R. M. Lamb (Loeb, 1977), pp. 154–61.

    Plutarch, *Table-talk*, bk. VIII, ques. 5, *Moralia*, ed. Paul A. Clement (Loeb, 1969), vol. VIII, pp. 63–69. For a further treatment of these concepts, see also Plutarch, "On Love," *Moralia*, vol. XIII, ed. E. L. Minar Jr., F. H. Sandbach, W. C. Helmbold (Loeb, 1961), vol. II, pp. 347–57. In the edition of 1623 Ferrand has abbreviated to a list—justice, temperance, strength, wisdom—the virtues attributed to love, presumably because he saw that it was not in his interests to elaborate on the positive aspects. Ferrand's source is an unspecified passage in St. Augustine, where he speaks of love as a composite of the four principal virtues: "car il est temperance, en ce que l'amant tempere ses volontez, et les conforme aux chastes desirs de l'ame; amour est force, pource qu'il peut souffrir toute diversité en faveur de sa dame, et toutes ses imperfections: il est justice, pource qu'il rend reciproque amour: et finalement il est prudence, pource qu'il est orné de toute sagesse, accort et advisé, et celuy seul qui peut eslire le bon et le beau." Jacques Ferrand, *Traicté de l'essence et guerison de l'amour ou de la melancholie erotique*, p. 2.
3. [*Plato in Phedr.*]: Plato, *Phaedrus* (243 A-B), trans. H. N. Fowler (Loeb, 1953), pp. 461–62: "If Love is, as indeed he is, a god of something divine, he can be nothing evil; but the two speeches just now said that he was evil. So then they sinned against Love; but their foolishness was really very funny besides, for while they were saying nothing sound or true, they put on airs as though they amounted to something, if they could cheat some mere manikins and gain honour among them. Now I, my

friend, must purify myself; and for those who have sinned in matter of mythology there is an ancient purification, unknown to Homer, but known to Stesichorus. For when he was stricken with blindness for speaking ill of Helen, he was not, like Homer, ignorant of the reason, but since he was educated, he knew it and straight-way he writes the poem:

> "That saying is not true; thou didst not go within the
> well-oared ships, nor didst thou come to the walls of Troy";

and when he had written all the poem, which is called the recantation, he saw again at once. Now I will be wiser than they in just this point: before suffering any punishment for speaking ill of Love, I will try to atone by my recantation, with my head bare this time, not, as before, covered through shame."

4. Plato, *Symposium* (186C–E), p. 124: "Now I agree with what Pausanias was just saying, that it is right to gratify good men, base to gratify the dissolute: similarly, in treating actual bodies it is right and necessary to gratify the good and healthy elements of each, and this is what we term the physician's skill; but it is a disgrace to do aught but disappoint the bad and sickly parts, if one aims at being an adept. For the art of medicine may be summarily described as a knowledge of the love-matters of the body in regard to repletion and evacuation; and the master-physician is he who can distinguish there between the nobler and baser Lover, and can effect such alteration that the one passion is replaced by the other; and he will be deemed a good practitioner who is expert in producing Love where it ought to flourish but exists not, and in removing it from where it should not be. Indeed he must be able to make friends and happy lovers of the keenest opponents in the body. Now the most contrary qualities are most hostile to each other— cold and hot, bitter and sweet, dry and moist, and the rest of them. It was by knowing how to foster love and unanimity in these that, as our two poets here relate, and as I myself believe, our forefather Asclepius composed this science of ours."

5. [*Plotin l. de Amore. Cic. l. 3. de nat. deor. Fulgent. in Mythol.*]: Plotinus, *Enneads*, bk. III, tract. 5 , trans. Stephen MacKenna (London: Faber and Faber, 1969), p. 193: "To us Aphrodite is twofold; there is the heavenly Aphrodite, daughter of Ouranos or Heaven: and there is the other the daughter of Zeus and Dione, this is the Aphrodite who presides over earthly unions; the higher was not born of a mother and has no part in marriages, for in Heaven there is no marrying." For this concept, see also Plato's *Symposium* (Loeb, 1977), pp. 107–8; Plutarch's treatise *On Love* in the *Moralia*, vol. XIII, p. 397.

Cicero, *De natura deorum*, III, 59 ff., trans. H. Rackham (Loeb, 1961), p. 343.

Fabius Planciades Fulgentius, *Mitologiarum libri tres*. See *Fulgentius the Mythographer*, trans. L. G. Whitbread (Columbus: Ohio State University Press, 1971). Fulgentius devotes two *fabulae* to Venus in bk. II: "Of Venus," p. 66, and "The Fable of the Adultery of Venus," p. 72. In bk. III. 6, he retells the tale of Eros and Psyche, p. 88; the brother of

Eros is Anteros, the son of Aphrodite and Ares, known as the god of unrequited love, and sometimes of mutual love.

Pausanias, "Boeotia," XVI, 4, *Description of Greece*, trans. W. H. S. Jones (Loeb, 1965), vol. IV, p. 241: "At Thebes are three wooden images of Aphrodite, so very ancient that they are actually said to be votive offerings of Harmonia. . . . They call the first Heavenly to signify a love pure and free from bodily lust: that of Common, to denote sexual intercourse; the third, that of Rejecter, that mankind might reject unlawful passion and sinful acts."

Ferrand illustrates this point in his argument with a more simple and direct division of types of love in the edition of 1610, namely of "amour pudique" and "impudique," modest, chaste, discrete love as opposed to lecherous, passionate, and illicit love. The classification figures in a number of encyclopedias of the period as a basic dichotomy in medical, philosophical, and moral terms. Ferrand's readers would have understood the commonplace idea in a sense broader than moral versus immoral, for it is also love that is affirmative and love that is destructive. Ferrand is concerned with the cure of immoderate and illicit love, not with the cure of modest and honest love.

The probable source for this section on the two Venuses is François Valleriola, *Observationum medicinalium libri VI*, pp. 190 ff.: "Ergo duo amorum genera Plato facit siquidem cupidinem veneris comitem esse; Pausanias, amorem laudans apud Platonem, asserit totidemque esse cupidines seu amores quot sint et veneres, necessarium omnino existimat. . . ." Valleriola gives a lengthy account of the births of the two goddesses, the celestial born without a mother because she is characterized by mind rather than matter, while the vulgar Venus was born to Jove and Dione. It is the earthly Venus that causes the madness of love. "Quotuplex esset amor, et quid in nobis coelestis atque vulgaris efficiant, diximus: quantum virium amor hic vulgaris in hominum animis corporibusque sibi vendicet, et ut ex eo in insaniam non raro homines deducantur, nobis nunc est tertio loco dicendum" (p. 193).

6. Apollo was Ἀλεξίκακος, the averter of ills. As a healer of physical diseases he was worshipped together with his son Aesculapius (alias Asclepius), but in a higher sense he was a god of mental and moral purity. Hence, his association with Plato. See Diogenes Laertius, *Lives of Eminent Philosophers*, bk. III, ch. 45, trans. R. D. Hicks, 2 vols. (Loeb, 1966), vol. I, p. 317: "There is also an epitaph of my own which runs thus: If Phoebus did not cause Plato to be born in Greece, how came it that he healed the minds of men by letters? As the god's son Asclepius is a healer of the body, so is Plato of the immortal soul. And another on the manner of his death: Phoebus gave to mortals Asclepius and Plato, the one to save their souls, the other to save their body." These two epigrams are to be found in the *Greek Anthology*, bk. VII, nos. 108 and 109, ed. W. R. Paton (Loeb, 1953), vol. II, p. 65.

The reference was common in the Renaissance. See, e.g., Marc-Antoine Muret (Marcus Antonius Muretus), "*Oratio V*," in *Opera omnia*, ed. C.-H. Frotscher (Genève: Slatkine Reprints, 1971), vol. I, pp. 332–33.

7. [*Soranio*]: Soranus of Ephesus. The work Ferrand intends is in doubt, though probably he means the Βίος Ἱπποκράτους (*The Life of Hippocrates*), ed. Ilberg, *Corpus medicorum Graecorum*, vol. IV. However, in this work the references to Asclepius and Plato are not as specific as Ferrand makes them out to be.

In the corresponding passage of the argument in the edition of 1610, Ferrand makes clear that love is not a state of melancholy *per se*, but rather, has a natural capacity to rejoice the lover. Only defeat or a state of violent passion leads to disease.

8. Ovid, *Remedia amoris*, ll. 53–54: "Utile propositum est saevas extinguere flammas, / Nec servum vitiis pectus habere tuum." See *The Art of Love, and Other Poems*, trans. J. H. Mozley (Loeb, 1962), p. 180: "Utile propositum est saevas extinguere flammas / Nec servum vitii pectus habere sui."

9. [*Cic. de senect.*]: Cicero, *De senectute*, bk. XII.42, trans. William Armistead Falconer (Loeb, 1964), p. 51: "Now, why did I quote Archytas? To make you realize that if reason and wisdom did not enable us to reject pleasure, we should be very grateful to old age for taking away the desire to do what we ought not to do. For carnal pleasure hinders deliberation, is at war with reason, blindfolds the eyes of the mind, so to speak, and has no fellowship with virtue."

See also bk. XI.36: "Just as waywardness and lust are more often found in the young man than in the old, yet not in all who are young, but only in those naturally base; so that senile debility, usually called dotage, is a characteristic, not of all old men, but only of those who are weak in mind and will."

10. [*Plaut. act. 1. sc. 1. mercat.*]: Plautus, *Mercator*, I. i. 18–19, 25–31:

Amorem cuncta vitia sectari solent,
Cura, aegritudo, dolor, nimiaque elegantia,
Insomnia, aerumna, error, et terror, et fuga,
Ineptia, stultitiaque adeo, et temeritas,
Incogitantia, excors, immodestia,
Petulantia, cupiditas, et malevolentia:
Inhaeret etiam aviditas, desidia, injuria,
Inopia, contumelia, et dispendium,
Multiloquium, pauciloquium.

For a modern edition, see *Plautus*, trans. P. Nixon (Loeb, 1963), pp. 6, 8.

11. Ausonius, "Cupid Crucified," ll. 54–62; 88–92, in *Ausonius*, trans. Hugh G. Evelyn White, 2 vols. (Loeb, 1951), vol. II, pp. 213–15: "A myrtle-tree is chosen well known in that sad grove and hateful from the vengeance of the gods. Thereon had Proserpine, once slighted, tormented Adonis, mindful of his Venus. On the tall trunk of this Love was hung up, his hands bound behind his back, his feet tied fast; and though he weeps, they lay on him no milder punishment." Sometime later Venus arrives, and rather than protect her son, she too joins in the general berating for what love had also done to her. "But words were not enough: with her rosy wreath golden Venus scourged the boy who wept and feared yet harsher punishment." Ferrand takes liberties with Ausonius' allegori-

cal tale and its significance in order to turn it to his own more cryptic purposes.

The allusion to the purple wings of Cupid comes from a MS containing the so-called "love treatise" by Guittone d'Arezzo, a collection of poems on the nature and effects of love crowned. It is quite unlikely that Ferrand knew this particular MS (today in the Escurial Library). Almost certainly the reference is drawn from Mario Equicola's *Libro de natura de amore* (Venice: n.p., 1575), p. 4, who seems to have had firsthand knowledge of Guittone's treatise. The parallel passage in Ferrand's edition of 1610 contains in the margin "I. Bocace en son Phileloce," an indication that between his first treatise and his second Ferrand read Equicola and decided to substitute the general reference to Boccaccio's story of the contrasting love between Florio and Biancifiore with the more specific reference to the iconography of Cupid.

12. [*Petr. ch. 4. du triomphe d'Amour*]: Petrarca, *Trionfo d'Amore*, bk. IV, ll. 137–53, *Opere*, ed. G. Ponte (Milano: Mursia, 1968), p. 283:

> E vidi a qual selvaggio, ed a qual morte,
> a quale strazio va chi s'innamora.
>   Errori e sogni ed imagini smorte
> eran d'intorno a l'arco triunfale
> e false opinioni in su le porte.
>   e lubrico sperar su per le scale
> e dannoso guadagno ed util danno
> e gradi ove piú scende chi piú sale;
>   Stanco riposo e riposato affanno
> chiaro disnore e gloria oscura e nigra,
> perfida lealtate e fido inganno,
>   Sollicito furor e ragion pigra;
> carcer ove si ven per strade aperte
> onde per strette a gran pena si migra;
>   ratte scese a l'entrar, a l'uscir erte;
> dentro confusion turbida e mischia
> di certe doglie e d'allegrezze incerte.

13. [*Philostr. l. 1. c. 20*]: Flavius Philostratus the Elder, bk. I, ch. 36, *Life of Apollonius of Tyana*, trans. F. C. Conybeare, 2 vols. (Loeb, 1960), vol. I, pp. 105–7. Ferrand probably took the story from André Du Laurens, *Des maladies melancholiques et du moyen de les guarir* in *Toutes les oeuvres*, p. 35ᵛ: "Le Philosophe Thiánée le sceut bien dire à ce roy de Babylone, qui le priait d'inventer quelque cruel tourment pour chastier un gentil homme qu'il avoit trouvé couché avec sa favorite: Donne luy la vie (dit-il) et ses amours le puniront assez avec le temps."

II. The Symptoms of Erotic Melancholy

1. [*Arist. l. 1. Eth. c. 21. Gal. 2. de sympt. caus. c. 5. Val. Max. l. 9. c. 12 Pline l. 7. c. 36. M. Aurele Fulgose.*]: Aristotle, *Great Ethics* (*Magna moralia*)

(1191a–b), ed. G. Cyril Armstrong (Loeb, 1962), pp. 518–21. The passage deals with temperance, profligacy and insensibility. Since temperance is, like all virtues, a "best state" of the soul, that is to say a state "which possesses what is best; and what is best is the mean betwixt excess and defect," temperance is the best mean between profligacy and insensibility. The reference therefore establishes from the start the norm to follow vis-à-vis the examples of those who died for excessive love and grief.

Galen, *De symptomatum causis*, bk. II, 5, ed. Kühn, vol. VII, pp. 175–96, establishes the medical reasons why the perturbations that follow excessive joy and grief can lead to death (see esp. Kühn, vol. VII, pp. 192–93). The story of Polycrita of Naxos, who died of joy in front of the walls of her own city on her return from captivity, is told by Plutarch in his *Bravery of Women*, 17, *Moralia*, bk. III, pp. 533–36 ; she is also mentioned by Aulus Gellius in *Attic Nights*, bk. III, ch. xv, trans. J. C. Rolfe, 3 vols. (Loeb, 1960), vol. III, pp. 284–86, attributing the story to Aristotle. Aulus Gellius in bk. III, ch. xv, pp. 16–23, also tells the story of Diagoras, who died upon seeing his three sons being crowned together as victors at the Olympic games. Chilo the Lacedaemonian was one of the seven wisemen of Greece who died of joy at an advanced age because one of his sons had won a prize at the Olympic games as recounted by Diogenes Laertius, *Lives of Eminent Philosophers*, trans. R. D. Hicks, 2 vols. (Loeb, 1925), vol. I, pp. 69–75.

Valerius Maximus, *Factorum et dictorum memorabilium libri novem*, bk. VIII, ch. 12, ed. C. Kempf (Leipzig: Teubner, 1966), p. 461, relates that Sophocles died of joy upon hearing that one of his tragedies had won a prize. Diodorus Siculus in his *Library of History*, bk. XV.74, trans. C. L. Sherman (Loeb, 1952), vol. VII, pp. 157–58, tells the same story about Dionysius I, tyrant of Sicily.

Pliny, *Natural History*, bk. VII, ch. 36, trans. H. Rackham (Loeb, 1961), vol. II, pp. 586–87, tells how Publius Rutilius died when he received news of his brother's defeat in his candidature for the consulship and how Marcus Lepidus died of love for his wife after divorcing her.

Eli was the priest in the house of the Lord at Shiloh (I Samuel 4). Upon hearing the news that the Jews were fleeing the Philistines, that his two sons had been killed, and that the ark of the covenant had been taken away, he fell over backwards, being frail with age, broke his neck and died. The tale of Homer's death caused by excessive sorrow for not being able to solve the riddle of a fisherman from the island of Io is told by Valerius Maximus, *Factorum et dictorum memorabilium libri novem*, bk. VIII, ch. 12, ed. C. Kempf, p. 461.

The M. Aurelius who writes on this subject remains unidentified.

Giovan Battista Fregoso, *Factorum dictorumque memorabilium libri IX* (Paris: Cavellat, 1589), bk. IX, ch. 12: "De Diagora rhodio et Chilone philosopho," "De seniore Dionysio syracusano tyranno," "De Policreta Naxia."

These stories circulated widely during the sixteenth century. See Charles Estienne (Carolus Stephanus), *Dictionarium historicum, geographicum, poeticum* (Paris, 1596; rpt. New York and London: Garland Publishing, 1976): Polycrita, p. 360^V; Diagoras, p. 183^V; Chilo, p. 148^V; Sophocles, p. 406^r, and Dionysius, p. 187^r. See also the following for a chapter on those who have died of excessive sadness and excessive joy: Giovan Battista della Porta, *De humana physiognomia libri IV* (Ursellis: typis Cornelii Sutorii, sumptibus Jonae Rosae Fr., 1551).

2. [*Gal. l. 6. de plac. Hipp. l. 3. de diff. respir.*]: Galen, *De placitis Hippocratis et Platonis*, bk. VI, ed. Kühn, vol. V, pp. 505–85, deals with the problem of the activities (ἐνεργεῖαι) and the affections (πάθη) of the parts of the soul and tries to prove that each of the three parts of the soul has its place in the body: the rational in the head, the spirited in the heart, the desiderative in the liver. *De difficultate respirationis*, bk. III, ed. Kühn, vol. VII, pp. 888–960, discusses at length the various types of breaths (*spiritus*) and their symptomatology indicating sickness or health in acute situations. The book deals mainly with Hippocrates' *Epidemics*, bk. II.

3. Horace, *Epistles*, I. 62, "ira furor brevis est." See trans. C. E. Passage, *The Complete Works of Horace* (New York: Frederick Ungar, 1983), p. 260.

4. [*Hipp. 2. Ep. sect. 4. l. 6. Ep. sect. 8. Aph. 46*]: Hippocrates, *Epidemics*, bk. II, sec. 4 and bk. VI, sec. 8, in *Oeuvres complètes d'Hippocrate*, trans. E. Littré (avec le texte Grec en regard), 10 vols. (Amsterdam: Adolf Hakkert, 1978), vol. V, p. 127, and vol. V, pp. 342–57. The first passage deals with the effect of the emotions in the establishing of a good complexion and the balancing of the humors; the second consists of thirty-two subsections, of which the last two are most closely related to the topic under discussion. In no. 31 Hippocrates explains that melancholiacs usually become hypochondriacs and viceversa. In no. 32 he gives the case study of two women, Phaëthusa in Abdera and Nanno in Thasos, who became masculine after they ceased to menstruate and who later died. For the Hippocratic texts, see n. 20 to this chapter. The relationship between these Hippocratic texts and Ferrand's discussion are somewhat remote. Ferrand was working far more closely to a passage like the one following from Jean Fernel's *Pathologie* (Paris: Chez Jean Guignard le pere et Jean Guignard le fils, 1655), p. 68: "Les passions de l'ame, quoy que moderées, ne sont presque d'aucun usage qui soit utile à la santé, sinon la joye, laquelle dilatant le coeur recrée les esprits; excite la chaleur naturelle, subtilie le sang et les humeurs, ce qui cause et conserve la santé. La tristesse n'est utile à personne, si ce n'est à ceux qui sont joyeux par excez; ny la cholere, sinon aux paresseux et endormis; ny la crainte, fors qu'aux temeraires et furieux; ny la honte, qu'à ceux qui sont impudents, ou qui ont le visage trop blesme." The correlation here is, in fact, relatively high.

5. [*Avic. 1 p. Cant. tr. 1*]: Avicenna, treatise I, pt. 1, of his *Poem on medicine* ('*Arjuzat fi't-ṭibb*), *Cantica Avicennae* in *Liber canonis, de medicinis cordialibus et Cantica iam olim quidem a Gerardo Carmonensi ex arabico sermone in latinum conversa* (Venetiis: apud Juntas, 1555), p. 567^{r-v}. In the place cited above he discusses the elements, temperaments, the natural components of the body, and the necessary elements which themselves deviate from the normal state but serve to maintain balances in the body.

6. Avicenna, *Liber canonis* (Venice, 1555), p. 10^r. The reference is to a sec-

tion prepared by Andrea Alpago of Belluno, where he says: "Hea apud Arabes est passio animae permista ex spe et timore, sicut quando aliquis timet aliquod damnum futurum cum spe tamen aliqua, que illud possit amoveri."

Jean Aubery, *L'antidote d'amour*, p. 45^r: "L'amour ne produit jamais une seule passion tousjours il accouche de deux qui sont contraires, la jumelle de la peur et la hardiesse autant éventee en ses legeres entreprises que la peur est retenuë par ses coüardises."

7. Catullus, LXXXV. "Odi, et amo: quare id faciam fortasse requiris / Nescio, sed fieri sentio et excrucior." Trans. F. W. Cornish in *Catullus, Tibullus and Pervirgilium Veneris* (Loeb, 1950), pp. 162–63.

8. Ovid, *Amores*, bk. III.xl, 33–34, "Luctantur pectusque leve in contraria ducunt: / Hac Amor, hac odium: sed puto vincet Amor." Trans. G. Showerman (Loeb, 1914), pp. 490–91.

9. [*Ch. 86. art. med.*]: Galen, *Ars medicinalis*, in *Operum Galeni libri isagogici artis medicae*, ch. 86, "*De venereis*" (Lugduni: apud Joannem Fellonium, 1550), pp. 223–24. Today this is considered a fragment of a lost work.

Ferrand provides in this chapter an overview of the symptoms characterizing the erotic melancholiac, symptoms that will be identified more closely in subsequent chapters. Lists of these traits had been previously collected and had even passed into popular literature. Perhaps unique to the literature on love melancholy, however, is Pierre Boaistuau's claim to have seen the dissection of a deceased lover. See *Le théâtre du monde* (1558), ed. Michel Simonin (Genève: librairie Droz, 1981): p. 214: "Quant à mon regard j'en ay veu faire anatomie de quelques uns qui estoient mors de ceste maladie, qui avoient leurs entrailles toutes retirées, leur pauvre cueur tout bruslé, leur foye tout enfumé, leurs poulmons rostis, les ventricules de leur cerveau tous endommagez, et croy que leur pauvre ame estoit toute cuicte et arse à petit feu, pour l'excessive chaleur et ardeur qu'ilz enduroient lorsque la fiebvre d'amour les avoit surprins."

10. Avicenna, *Liber canonis*, bk. III, fen 1, tr. 4, ch. 23, "*De alhash' id est amantibus*," pp. 206^r–7^r. Avicenna, however, states only that those suffering of lovesickness (*alhash*, from the Arabic *'isq*), if they cannot be cured by traditional methods, should be treated like those suffering from melancholy, madness, and *cuturub* (the Arabic *quṭrub*, a form of madness, that renders the sufferer lycanthropic).

11. [*L. 1 chron. Morb.*]: Aretaeus, *Of Chronic Diseases*, bk. I, *The Extant Works*, trans. Francis Adams (Boston: Longwood Press, 1978), p. 300: "A story is told, that a certain person, incurably affected, fell in love with a girl; and when the physicians could bring him no relief, love cured him. But I think that he was originally in love, and that he was dejected and spiritless from being unsuccessful with the girl, and appeared to the common people to be melancholic. He then did not know that it was love; but when he imparted the love to the girl, he ceased from his dejection, and dispelled his passion and sorrow; and with joy he awoke from his lowness of spirits, and he became restored to understanding, love being his physician."

Aretaeus does not necessarily advocate coitus as a general cure, but states that in the case of this young man it was the only possible cure given the failure of medicine to relieve him. The passage was nevertheless cited often as yet another recommendation for coitus as therapy for love among the ancients.

12. Rodrigo de Castro, *Medicus-politicus: sive de officiis medico-politicis tractatus, quatuor distinctus libris* (Hamburgi: ex Bibliopolio Frobeniano, 1614), pp. 224–25: "His Eusebius refert Lucretium poetam dementatum, deinde etiam interemptum: atque idipsum Lucullo accidisse in eius vita Plutarchus scribit."

But clearly the most direct source for the entire passage in Ferrand is André Du Laurens, *Des maladies melancholiques et du moyen de les guarir*, ch. 10, in *Toutes les oeuvres*, p. 35^r: "Le poëte Lucrece qui avoit escrit des remedes d'amour, en devint si enragé, qu'il se tua soy-mesme. Iphis desesperé pour l'amour d'Anaxarete, se pendit. Un noble jouvenceau d'Athenes devint si amoureux d'une statuë de marbre merveilleusement bien élaborée, que l'ayant demandée au Senat pour l'acheter à quelque prix que ce fust, et le refus luy estant fait, avec deffence expresse d'en approcher, pource que ses folastres amours scandalisoient tout le peuple, vaincu de desespoir se tua. Voila comme l'amour deprave l'imagination, et peut estre causée d'un melancholie ou d'une manie." For Iphis and Lucretius, see also Charles Estienne, *Dictionarium historicum, geographicum, poeticum*, pp. 254^r and 275^r.

The edition of 1623 follows the same order of stories as in Du Laurens: Lucretius, Iphis, and the Athenian youth. There is a corresponding passage in the former edition that nevertheless omits the allusion to Lucretius, but relates the story from Aretaeus, mentions Iphis and the youth of Athens, followed by Sappho and the references to Strabo and Giraldi. The point is critical, for it bears evidence to the possibility that Ferrand knew Du Laurens earlier but nowhere acknowledged him, an author who could not have been read without being highly influential, and who Ferrand calls his "precepteur" in the later edition. Compare "un jeune Athenien pour une statuë de marbre, que le Senat luy defendit acheter" with the same passage above in Du Laurens. Or can the juxtaposition of Iphis with the youth of Athens be merely coincidental, or evidence of a common source? For Iphis, Ferrand cites Aelian as his source in the first edition, but suppresses that reference in the revised edition.

13. François Valleriola, *Observationum medicinalium libri VI*, pp. 184–85. Valleriola presents his study of erotic melancholy in terms of a case study. The Observation opens with an account of how a certain merchant of Arles turned melancholy for love, how he imagined that his beloved caressed him in the middle of the night, and how he then suddenly became angry or completely mad because this woman had rejected his love. The patient spoke incessantly of her, spent his days in lamentation and his nights awake pining and grieving over her. He would have killed himself had relatives not intervened. Valleriola was called to the place where this man worked and took him into his care. The condition

lasted over six months, but by using the right treatments he was able to cure this man and restore him to a healthy state of mind. Such were the particulars of the case; it became paradigmatic for subsequent writers on the topic. Many allusions to Valleriola appear in Ferrand, including several that recall this particular case as the context for Valleriola's commentary.

14. [*Lib. Greg. Girald. l. 9. de Poet. Hist.*]: Lelio Gregorio Giraldi, "Dialogus IX," in *Historiae poetarum tam Graecorum quam Latinorum dialogi decem* (Basileae: sumptibus M. Isengrin, 1545), vol. II, pp. 974–75: "Et tres item ab eadem puellas amatas prodidit, Atthida, Telesillam, et Megaram verum ego plures comperi, quarum haec nomina, Pyrino, Mnais, Anactorie, Cydno, Cyrene, et post has Phaon Lesbius adolescens, quem Plinium amatum tradit propter herbae radicem, quam nostri centum capita vocant, quae alterutrius sexus similitudinem refert: unde si viris contigerit mas, amabiles fiunt, quo pacto, inquit, amatus fertur Phaon Lesbius a Sappho: quem Phaonem cum in Siciliam navagasset, lepidissimo carmine Sappho est prosecuta: quod Ovidius poëta in epistola eius nominis imitatus creditur: cuius inquam Phaonis amore impatiens Sappho, se ex Leucade in mare praecipitem dedit: quem ex Leucade saltum et alios subiisse legimus."

   Suidae Lexicon, vol. II, pt. 2, ed. G. Bernhardy (Halle et Brunsvigae: sumptibus Schwetschkiorum, 1853), s.v. Σαπφώ, p. 674; Strabo, *Geography* 10. 2, trans. Horace Leonard Jones (Loeb, 1944), vol. V, p. 33. The story is a common one and can be found in any dictionary of the era: see, e.g., Charles Estienne (Carolus Stephanus), *Dictionarium historicum, geographicum, poeticum*, p. 387ᵛ.

15. Hippocrates, *On the Diseases of Young Women, Oeuvres complètes*, ed. Littré, vol. VIII, pp. 466–71. Ferrand uses the same reference in his ch. XXVIII, citing the line in question in Greek, which he translates: "La femme est en ses Amours plus passionnee, et plus acariastre en ses folies que l'homme."

16. [*Langius, Mercatus*]: Johann Lange, *Medicinalium epistolarum miscellanea* (Basileae: apud I. Oporinum, 1544), no. 21, "De morbo virgineo," p. 75: "Nec hic morbus propriam habet nomenclaturam, quam cum sit virginibus peculiaribus, virgineus quoque indigitari poterit: quem Brabantinorum matronea, febrem albam, ob faciei pallorem, et amatoriam appellare solent: quum palleat omnis amans, et color hic sit aptus amanti, quamvis febris admodum raro concidat."

   Luis Mercado (Ludovicus Mercatus), *De internorum morborum curatione libri IV* in *Opera* (Francofurti: sumptibus haeredum D. Zachariae Palthenii, 1620), bk. II, ch. 6, "De febre alba, et de virginum obstructionibus," vol. III, p. 564: "Inter virginum affectiones nullam profecto frequentius aut vulgarius reperies, quam eam, quae (*eo quod proprio nomine careat*) morbus virgineus appellari iure optimo potest, quia frequenter virginibus accidere conspicimus. Appellant sane, *ut refert Ioannes Langius*, eum affectum Brabantinorum foeminae *febrem albam*, ob conspicuum faciei alborem: quam quoque *febrem amatoriam* nonnulli appellant, cum palleat omnis amans, et color hic sit aptus amanti."

17. Hippocrates, *On the Diseases of Young Women, Oeuvres complètes*, ed. Littré, vol. VIII, pp. 469–71: "Les jeunes filles, quand vient l'epoque du mariage, ne se mariant pas, éprouvent de préférence, à la première éruption des regles; ces accidents auxquels auparavant elles n'étaient guère exposées. Car, à ce moment, le sang se porte à la matrice, comme pour s'écouler au dehors. Ainsi donc, quand l'orifice de l'issue n'est pas ouvert, et que le sang arrive en plus grande abondance, tant par les aliments que par l'accroissement, alors le sang, n'ayant point de sortie, s'élance, vue la quantité, sur le coeur et le diaphragme. Ces parties étant remplis, le coeur devient torpide; à la torpeur succède l'engourdissement, et à l'engourdissement le délire. . . . Quand ces parties [i. e. the heart and the diaphragm] ont été remplis, le frisson avec la fièvre se manifeste; ces fièvres sont appelées erratiques. Les choses étant ainsi, la femme a le transport à cause de l'inflammation aiguë, l'envie de tuer à cause de la putridité, des craintes et des frayeurs à cause des ténèbres, le désir de s'étrangler à cause de la pression autour du coeur. Le sens intime, troublé et dans l'angoisse en raison de la perversion du sang, se pervertit à son tour. La malade dit des choses terribles. Les visions lui ordonnent de sauter, de se jeter dans les puits, de s'étrangler, comme étant meilleur et ayant toute sorte d'utilité. Quand il n'y a pas de visions, il y a un certain plaisir qui fait souhaiter la mort comme quelque chose de bon" (pp. 467–69).

Hippocrates suggests marriage as a cure because "si elles deviennent enceintes, elles guérissent; dans le cas contraire, à l'époque même de la puberté, ou peu après, elles seront prises de cette affection, sinon d'une autre." For a fuller discussion of the effects produced by the absence or loss of menstruation, see his treatise *On the Diseases of Women* (vol. V, pp. 14–25) and *On Generation* (vol. VII, pp. 470–85, 495–97). This is the beginning of an association of ideas in Ferrand that will extend the scope of his definition of love melancholy to include the traditional diseases involving the genitalia (satyriasis) and the uterus (hysteria). Ferrand opens his twelfth chapter with the assertion that there are five very similar diseases that derive from love. Those arising in the reproductive organs are joined with the causes and symptoms of love melancholy in the following three ways: they are caused by an abundance of seed in various states of corruption around the uterus, just as an excess of seed is a material cause of love melancholy; the vapors rising from the corruption or the repletion of seed or blood by the spinal column affect the brain, its imaginative and reasoning powers as in the case of melancholy adust; this disease in women, according to Hippocrates and his followers is related to sexual desire, for it can be cured by marriage, just as Avicenna and his followers argued that *amor hereos* can be cured by coitus. The association was not a new one in Ferrand: Fregoso some 140 years later, begins bk. II of his *Anteros* on the causes of lovesickness with an argument tracing the causes to the corruption of seed (pp. 140 ff.: "la racine de cest ardent et mouvant appetit, naist du corps, par le moyen du sperme" etc.), and Galen traces the cause of the apparent melancholy of his widower, not to the loss of his wife, but to a surfeit of seed caused by the lack of coitus. See *De locis affectis*, bk. VI, ed. Kühn, vol. VIII, p. 418.

18. [*L. 4. ff. ad l. Corn. de sic. & venef.*]: *Lex Cornelia de sicaris veneficis et paricidiis*, Title VIII, Marcianus, *Institutes*, bk. XIV, *The Civil Code*, ed. S. P. Scott, 17 vols. (Cincinnati: The Central Trust Co., 1932), vol. XI, p. 60: "Anyone who has prepared poison, or sells it, or keeps it for the purpose of killing human beings, is punished by the Fifth Section of the same Cornelian Law relating to Assassins and Poisoners. . . . There are also preparations called love philters. These, however, are only forbidden by this law where they are designed to kill people. A woman was ordered by a decree of the Senate to be banished, who, not with malicious intent, but offering a bad example, administered for the purpose of producing conception a drug which, having been taken, caused death.

"It is provided by another decree of the Senate that dealers in ointments who rashly sell hemlock, salamander, aconite, pine-cones, buprestis, mandragora, and give cantharides as a purgative, are liable to the penalty of this law."

The probable source for this passage is François Valleriola, *Observationum medicinalium libri VI*, p. 189: "Hi profecto sunt quorum ministerio in hominum animos amor influit, sensimque illabitur: quod quum multo igneo radiosoque spiritu oculi niteant (quae ipsorum natura est) efficitur, ut patefactus oculus, et in pulchritudinis amatae speciem vehementer intentus, radiorum suorum aculeos in adstantis oculos eiaculetur, atque etiam cum aculeis istis, qui spirituum vehicula sunt, sanguineum vaporem illum, quem spiritum nuncupamus, intendit: hic incensus, et iam amatae rei specie agitatus, cor exagitat, inflammat, uritque nimio motu atque caloris aestu dum vehementer potiri re amata amans desiderat, dum vicissim aculeos ab re amata suis ipse oculis suscipiens, quodam modo inficitur amoris veneno."

19. Theocritus, *Idyll* II. 55–56:

αἰαῖ Ἔρως ἀνιαρέ, τί μεν μέλαν ἐκ χροὸς αἷμα
ἐμφὺς ὡς λιμνᾶτις ἅπαν ἐκ βδέλλα πέπωκας.

See *Theocritus*, ed. A. S. F. Gow (Cambridge: At the University Press, 1950), vol. I, p. 20.

20. [*L. 6. Epid. sec. 8. Aph. penult. & ult.*]: Hippocrates, *Epidemics. Aphorisms*, nos. 31 and 32, *Oeuvres complètes*, ed. Littré, vol. V, pp. 354; 355–57:

"31. (*Rapport entre l'épilepsie et la mélancolie*). Les mélancoliques deviennent d'ordinaire épileptiques, et les épileptiques mélancoliques; de ces deux états, ce qui détermine l'un de préférence, c'est la direction que prend la maladie: si elle se porte sur le corps, épilepsie; si sur l'intelligence, mélancolie."

"32. (*Deux observations de femmes qui prirent l'apparence virile à la suite de la suppresion des règles.*) A Abdère, Phaétuse, la femme de charge de Pythéas, avait eu des enfants auparavant; mais, son mari s'étant enfui, les règles se supprimèrent pendant longtemps; à la suite, douleurs et rougeurs aux articulations; cela étant ainsi, le corps prit l'apparence virile, cette femme devint velue partout, il lui poussa de la barbe, la voix contracta de la rudesse; et, malgré tout ce que nous pûmes faire pour rappeler les règles, elles ne vinrent pas; cette femme mourut au bout d'un temps qui ne fut pas très-long. Il en arriva autant à Nanno, femme de Gorgippe, à Thasos; d'après tous les médicins que je rencontrai, la seule espérance de voir reparaître les attributs de la femme était dans le retour des règles; mais chez elle aussi, malgré tout ce qu'on fit, elles ne purent venir; cette femme ne tarda pas à succomber."

γυναικωθίναι should read γυναικωθῆναι. The origin of Ferrand's error for the name of Nanno, wife of Gorgippus, is Du Laurens, from whom he no doubt took this story second hand. See n. 24, below.

21. [*Hipp. l. de gland. l. 1. de Morb. mul. Arist. 1. Physiog. c. 4. l. 4 de hist. an. c. 11. & l. 9 c. 1.*]: Hippocrates, *On Glands* in *Oeuvres complètes*, ed. Littré, vol. V, pp. 571–75. The treatise *On the Diseases of Women* discusses the difference between male and female constitutions in the first chapter (Littré, vol. V, pp. 13–15): "the female has a looser and softer flesh than the male's . . . the female has a warmer blood, and that is why she is warmer than the male."

Aristotle, in *Physiognomics* II (806b), discusses the differences between males and females. See *The Minor Works*, trans. W. S. Hett (Loeb, 1963), p. 95: "The male is larger and stronger than the female." In the same work, bk. V, pp. 109–10: "of all the animals which attempt to breed the females are tamer and gentler in disposition than the males, but less powerful, and more susceptible to rearing and handling. This being their character, they have less spirit than the males."

Aristotle, *The History of Animals*, bk. IV, ch. 11 (537b–538b), deals with the difference in size between males and females in various species of animals. See the trans. by A. L. Peck, 3 vols. (Loeb, 1970), vol. II, pp. 89–95.

22. Ferrand is safe in asserting that those who wrote commentaries on Hippocrates were, for the most part, inclined to take him at his word that the cases of sex changes described in the *Aphorisms* were authentic. According to Ferrand, Leonard Fuchs endorses this view, whether in the *Paradoxorum medicinae libri tres* (Basileae: ex aedibus Jo. Bebelii, 1535) or in the *Methodus seu ratio compendiaria cognoscendi veram solidamque medicinam* (Parisiis: apud Jacobum Dupuys, 1550).

Anuce Foës likewise gave his support to this view, undoubtedly in his commentaries on the *Aphorisms* in his *Magni Hippocratis opera omnia quae extant* (Francofurdi: apud Andreae Wechli haeredes, 1595). Ferrand is merely dropping names here of those who were among the best known supporters of the Greek as opposed to the Arabic school of medicine in the sixteenth century.

23. Macrobius, *Commentary on Scipio's Dream*, bk. I, ch. 6. l. 64, trans. William Harris Stahl (New York & London: Columbia University Press, 1952), p. 112: "Hippocrates himself, who cannot deceive nor be deceived."

24. [*Pl. l. 7. c. 4. Auson. Epig. 72. Agell l. 9. c. 4 Volater.*]: Pliny, *Natural History*, bk. VII, ch. 4, pp. 36–37, trans. T. E. Page et al. (Loeb, 1961), vol. II, pp. 530–31, mentions a girl of Casinum who changed into a boy, a man of Argos named Arescon who took on womanly features, was called Arescusa and had married a man, who later returned to his masculine

nature and took a wife; and Lucius Constitius, a citizen of Thysdritum in Africa, who once was a woman.

The story of Iphis is about a Cretan girl brought up as a boy who, on being betrothed to Ianthé, was metamorphosed into a youth; it is related by Ovid, *Metamorphosis*, bk. IX. 665 ff., but see also Charles Estienne's *Dictionarium*, p. 254ʳ, for a contemporary account. The story of Caenis, a girl transformed into a man by her lover Poseidon and then called Caeneus, is also related by Ovid, *Metamorphosis*, bk. XII. 171 ff., but see also Virgil, *Aeneid*, bk. VI. 448, and Aulus Gellius, *Attic Nights*, bk. IX. iv. 14–15, vol. II, p. 167.

Ausonius, *Epigrams on Various Matters*, no. 76, in *Ausonius*, ed. Hugh G. Evelyn White, 2 vols. (Loeb, 1949), vol. II, p. 199: "At Vallebana (a thing strange and scarce credible in a poet, but which is taken from a truthful tale) a male bird changed into female form, and an erstwhile peacock stood a peahen before men's eyes. All marvelled at the portent; but a girl softer than any lamb spake thus with maiden voice: 'Fools, why so amazed to see a thing strange yet not unknown? Or do ye not read Naso's verse? Consus, old Saturn's son, changed Caenis to a boy and Tiresias was not always of one sex. The fount Salmacis saw Hermaphroditus the half-man; Pliny saw a man-woman in the act. Nor is the tale yet old that in Campanian Beneventum a certain lad suddenly became a maid. Yet I would not cite you instances of old report: lo, I was changed from boy to girl.' "

Cardinal Raffaele Maffei of Volterra wrote on melancholy in his *Commentariorum urbanorum . . . octo et triginta libri . . .* (Venundantur Parrhasiis in via Jacobea ab Joanne Parvo et Jodoco Badio Ascensio, 1511), sec. "*Philologia*," bk. XXIIII, pp. 259ᵛ–260ᵛ. There is little reason to believe that Ferrand consulted Volaterranus directly (in light of the quotation to follow from Du Laurens). In bk. XXIV, ch. 13, of the *Commentariorum urbanorum*, Volaterranus relates the story about the Roman girl who suddenly found herself with a male member on the day of her marriage.

There can be little doubt, in spite of the several new references Ferrand brings to his discussion of sex changes in women, that this entire passage was inspired by the following paragraph from André Du Laurens, whose voice is detected throughout this chapter. The origins of such names and places cited in the text as Cossitius, Cassinus, Naples, Salerno, Coimbra (in Portugal), Auch (Aux in Gascony), Argos and Smyrna, as well as the stories of Phaëtusa and Namysia, will become clear in his pages. *Controverses anatomiques*, bk. VII, ch. 8, in *Les Oeuvres*, pp. 224ʳ–25ʳ: "Nous lisons que durant le consulat de Licinius Crassus et Cassius Longinus, une fille de Cursula devint garçon et fust confinée en une isle inhabitée par arrest des Aruspices. Lucinius Mutianus dit avoir veu à Argos un nommé Arescon, qui avoit autrefois esté marié pour femme ayant a nom Arescusa, mais que par trait de temps la barbe et le membre viril luy vint et print depuis femme comme un homme naturel. Il dit aussi avoir cognu à Smyurne [*sic*] un garçon à qui il en estoit arrivé tout de mesme qu'à lautre. Pline afferme avoir veu en Afrique Lucius Cossitius bourgeois de Trisdita, lequel avoit esté

changé de femelle en masle le jour mesme de ses nopces . . . . Il raconte
le mesme d'Iphis, dont voicy les vers,

> Iphis pour avoir veu sa priere complette,
> Garson paye le voeux, qu'il fist estant fillette.

Volaterran Cardinal, soubs Alexandre sixiesme tesmoigne avoir veu à
Rome, une fille, à qui le membre viril sortit soudain, le propre jour de
ses nopces. L'autheur de l'Antimaeologe, raconte qu'il a veu à Aux en
Gascogne un homme âgé de plus de soixante ans tout chenu, robuste
et fort velu, qui avoit esté fille jusques à quinze ans, et que par une
cheute les petits ligaments s'estants rompu, le membre viril luy sortit,
et changea ainsi de sexe, n'ayant jamais eu ses fleurs auparavant. Nous
lisons dans Pontanus, qu'à Cajete la femme d'un pescheur, quatorze
ans apres estre mariée, fut soudain changée en homme. Il en arriva de
mesme, à Emilie femme d'Antoine Spense apres avoir esté douze ans
en mariage. Du regne de Ferdinand, premier de ce nom Roy de Naples,
Charlotte et Françoise, filles de Loys Quarne de Salerne âgées de quinze
ans devindrent masles. Et Aimé Portugais, certifie avoir veu le mesme
aupres de Conimbrice, ville de Portugal. Nous avons dans nostre Hippocrate, une fort belle histoire faisant à ce suject, de Phaetusa, laquelle
s'affliga en sorte pour le bannissement de son mary, qu'elle en perdit
ses purgations avant le temps, et lors le corps luy devint comme celuy
d'un homme, tout velu, la barbe luy sortit, et la voix luy vint plus grosse
and plus rude. Il escrit, qu'il en advint tout autant à Namysie femme de
Gorgippus. Doncques si la femme se change quelques-fois en homme,
et si ses parties genitales cachées au dedans peuvent sortir, et pendre
dehors comme aux masles; il s'ensuit fort bien qu'elles different seulement en situation. L'antiquité l'a tousjours creu ainsi, et les Medicins
sont presques encore aujourd'huy, tous de mesme advis. Quant à moy
j'ay tousjours beaucoup prisé les Anciens, et neantmoins n'estant point
obligé par serment aux opinions d'autruy, guidé par le sens et la raison,
qui sont les instrumens, dont les philosophes se servent, pour rechercher
les causes de toutes choses, je diray içy en peu de mots, quelle est mon
opinion touchant cette question." For his objections to the explanation
of sex changes as the descent of the female organs to form a yard resembling the male member, see n. 28, below.

One further citation must serve to show the extent to which questions of sex change engaged contemporary scientific interest. Jean Liébault in bk. III, ch. 12, of *Des maladies des femmes* (Lyon: par Jean Veyrat,
1598), pp. 632–33, deals with birth defects, monsters, and their causes,
attributing such sex changes to an overabundance of seed at the time of
conception. His list of authorities is more extensive than both Ferrand's
and Du Laurens'. "Pareillement de l'abondance de semence accompaignee de chaleur abondante peut advenir que les femmes degenerent en
hommes, ainse que recite Hipp au 6. des epid. partic. 8 aph. 45. du
corps de Phaetusa femme de Pithee qui devint velue par tout, mesme
que la barbe luy creust au menton, et parloit d'une voix viril: ce qu'il
dict estre aussi advenu en Thase en Namisie femme de Gorgippe. Amatus Lusitanus en la seconde centurie, curation trentenevsiesme, recite

d'un fille nommee Marie, à laquelle à la venue de ses fleurs luy sortist un member viril, qui estoit caché dedans au paravant, et ainsi la fille devint masle. Pline pareillement au livr. 7. d'une fille qui devint garçon: nous avons ouy parler de nostre temps d'une fille laquelle sautant avec grande escousse une fosse, sentist à l'instant sortir au bas du ventre deux genitoires accompaignez d'un membre viril, ains de fille devint garçon." Many of these same stories concerning sex changes and monsters are also to be found in Levinus Lemnius, *Occulta naturae miracula, ac varia rerum documenta* (Antverpiae: apud Guilielmum Simonem, 1561).

Giovan Battista Fregoso, *Factorum dictorumque memorabilium libri IX*, bk. I, ch. 5, "De L. Cossitio Tisdritano."

Joâo Rodriguez Amato (Amatus Lusitanus), discusses the transformation of women into men in his *Curationum medicinalium centuriae duae* (Parisiis: apud Sebastianum Nivellium, 1554), centuria II, curatio 39, pp. 78^r–79^r. The treatise was later expanded into seven *Centuriae* and published repeatedly in Venice, Lyon, Paris, Bordeaux, Barcelona, etc.

Ambroise Paré (Pareus) dealt with this topic in his *De monstres et prodiges*, ch. 7, in *Oeuvres complètes*, ed. J. -F. Malgaine (Genève: Slatkine Reprints, 1970), vol. III, pp. 18–20. See also *On Monsters and Marvels*, trans. Janis L. Pallister (Chicago: University of Chicago Press, 1982).

Severin Pineau (Pineus) wrote on this topic in his *Opusculum physiologum et anatomicum* (Parisiis: ex typographia Stephanus Prenosteau, 1597), bk. I, ch. 4, prob. 2.

Johann Theodor Schenck von Grafenberg (Schenckius), *Observationum medicarum rarum, novarum, admirabilium, et monstrosarum, volumen tomis septem de toto homine institutum* (Francofurti: E. Paltheniana, sumptibus Jonae Rhodii, 1600).

Johann Wier, *Cinq livres de l'imposture et tromperie des diables*, trans. Jacques Grévin (Paris: n.p., 1567), bk. IV, ch. 24, vol. I, pp. 598–604. Wier offers an important summary of the medical debate over the natural transmutation of the sexes in humans and declares himself with the literalists who make the case for a sex change in women only through an extension of the clitoris. As for the nomenclature, Wier gives the following account, paralleling Ferrand: "Avicenne l'a descrite sous le nom d'albathara ou albandar. Elle est aussi nommee par Ruffus Ephesien, clitore en Grec, et ce que les Latins apellent Nympha, est nommé par luy hypoderme. Or ceste partie charnue peu à peu s'augmente et s'estend si bien qu'en la fin elle se fait en tout et par tout semblable à un membre viril" (p. 601). Ferrand may have taken Wier as his guide for the examples cited in the preceding pages because Wier also includes the following references: "Pline, bk. VII, ch. 4; Aulus Gellius bk. IX, ch. 4; Lucinius Mutianus; Tite Live, seconde guerre Punique bk. IV; Hippocrate, bk. VI des epidemies, pt. 8; Baptiste Fulgose, bk. III, ch. 6; Amat le Portugois [Amatus Lusitanus] Cent. II de ses consol. cure 39." Lusitanus tells the story of Marie Pacheco, who at the time of puberty, produced a penis which before that time had been hidden inside her body. Considered a sex change, she was renamed Manuel. An account is given of how he traveled to the Indies, where he became rich and famous, and how, upon his return, he became once again a woman. It was well known, we are told, that Manuel never grew a beard, however, as many who experienced sex changes had done.

25. [*L. 1 de gen. an. c. 20. L. 2. c. 3*]: Aristotle, *Generation of Animals*, bk. I, sec. 20; bk. II, sec. 3 (737a): "ἄρρεν πεπηρωμένον" is from bk. II, sec. 3. See trans. A. L. Peck (Loeb, 1963), p. 174. Bk. I, sec. 20 (p. 103) states: "A woman is as it were an infertile male; the female, in fact, is female on account of an inability . . . to concoct semen out of the final state of the nourishment . . . because of the coldness of its nature."

In ancient Greek tragedy the head of the chorus was called coriphaeus (κορυφαῖος). Here it is used in the sense of leading philosopher. Galen was the coriphaeus of the Roman physicians as Avicenna was of the Arab physicians. Ferrand uses the term several times in subsequent chapters. But invariably when he speaks of the coriphaeus of philosophers, the genius of nature, and other such epithets he means Aristotle. Plato uses the word *coriphaeus* in *Theaetetus* (173A), and later it was commonly used in referring to Plato, as, e.g., in Eusebius, *P. G. XI*, α 3, vol. II, p. 54.

26. [*Gal. l. 1. de sem. l .14. de usu par.*]: Galen, *De semine (On Seminal Fluids)*, bk. I, ed. Kühn, vol. IV, pp. 512–93.

De usu partium bk. XIV (*On the Usefulness of the Parts*), ed. Kühn, vol. III, pp. 628–30; also trans. Margaret Tallmadge May, 2 vols. (Ithaca, N.Y.: Cornell University Press, 1968), vol. II, p. 630: "Now just as mankind is the most perfect of all animals, so within mankind the man is more perfect than the woman, and the reason for his perfection is his excess of heat, for heat is Nature's primary instrument. Hence in those animals that have less of it, her workmanship is necessarily more imperfect. . . . For the [generative] parts were formed within her when she was still a fetus, but could not because of the defect in the heat emerge and project on the outside, and this, though making the animal itself that was being formed less perfect than one that is complete in all respects, provided no small advantage . . . for the race; for there needs must be a female. Indeed, you ought not to think that our Creator would purposely make half the whole race imperfect and, as it were, mutilated, unless there was to be some great advantage in such a mutilation."

27. [*Arist. c. 3. l. 4. de gen. anim*]: Aristotle, *Generation of Animals*, bk. IV, ch. 3 (767b), p. 401: "The first beginning of this deviation is when a female is formed instead of a male, though (*a*) this indeed is a necessity required by Nature, since the race of creatures which are separated into male and female has got to be kept in being."

28. [*L. 7. q. 8. anat.*]: André Du Laurens, *Controverses anatomiques*, bk. VII, ch. 8, "A sçavoir, si les parties genitales des femmes ne different de celles des hommes, qu'en situation, et si la femme peut estre changée en homme," in *Les Oeuvres*, pp. 224^r–25^r: "L'opinion des Anciens, confirmée par l'authorité des hommes doctes, et les escrits de quasi tous les Anatomists, est, que les parties des femmes, qui servent à la generation ne different de celles des hommes qu'en situation, parce que les parties des femmes demeurent cachees au dedans, à cause de leur debilité

naturelle, et de leur temperature plus froide, la ou celles des hommes sortent, et pendent dehors. Car elles ont les vases spermatiques, tant preparans comme ejaculatoires, et les testicules, et la verge, laquelle ils veulent estre fort bien representée par la matrice renversée. Car le long col d'icelle resemble au membre viril; et le fonds separé par la ligne mediane, au scrotum." Du Laurens rehearses the arguments by the major ancient and Arab physicians and continues with a lengthy discussion of stories offered as evidence for sex changes, many of which Ferrand alludes to briefly in previous paragraphs. Du Laurens is skeptical, however, for anatomical reasons. "Les parties genitales des hommes, et des femmes, ne different point seulement en situation: mais aussi en nombre, en forme et en composition." He points out at length how the female sex organs cannot be considered the male organs reversed and held in the body. "Dechassons donc ces nuages de nos entendemens, et concluons, que les parties feminines different des masculines, non seulement en situation, mais aussi en nombre, en figure, et en composition: comme nous avons plus au long declaré en l'histoire Anatomique." He then returns to the question of sex changes, expresses a firm disbelief, and offers a number of explanations to account for the case studies handed down by earlier observers. "Mais que dirons nous des femmes, qui ont esté changées en hommes. Certes je tiens que c'est chose monstrueuse fort difficile à croire. Que si elle arrive quelques fois, il est vray-semblable, que telles gens ont les parties genitales des deux sexes, lesquelles en leur petit aage, demeurent cachées au dedans, à raison de la foiblesse de la chaleur naturelle, laquelle venant par l'aage à croistre, et à esclater, les chasses en fin dehors. Ou bien il faut penser, qu'il y a des femmes, de complexion fort chaudes, de leur premiere naissance, et formées de Nature, en sorte, que leur clitoris pende hors de la fente, en maniere de verge, et ainsi abuse ceux qui n'y regardent point de trop pres, à raison qu'il resemble fort à la verge de l'homme."

29. [*Mercat. l. 2. c. 10. & 11. de Virg. & Viduar. Morb.*]: Luis Mercado, *De internorum morborum curatione libri IV*, in *Opera* (Francofurti: sumptibus haeredum D. Zachariae Palthenii, 1620), bk. II, ch. 10, "De pruritu et furore uteri, ac de symptomate turpitudinis," and ch. 11, "De uteri procidentia," vol. III, pp. 582–89. In ch. 11 Mercado discusses the transformation of females into males using several of the examples cited in Ferrand's text and attributes these changes to the descent of the uterus in accordance with the ancients, although he also takes up Du Laurens' view concerning the enlarged clitoris as an explanation of these putative transformations.

Rodrigo de Castro refers back to Mercado, for which reason Ferrand calls him Mercado's "singe." The reference is to his *De universa mulierum medicina* (Hamburgi: ex officina Frobenianus, 1603): bk. II (*De affectibus qui viduis ac virginibus accidunt*), ch. 9: "De uteri prurito." See our n. 14 to ch. XII.

30. [*Albuc. 2. Meth. c. 72. Laurens c. 12. l. 7. Anat.*]: Albucasis, *Methodus medendi certa* (Basileae: per Henricum Petrum, 1541), bk. II, ch. 72, pp. 120 ff.

André Du Laurens, *Historia anatomica humani corporis*, bk. VII, ch. 12 (Parisiis: M. Orry, 1600), p. 356: "Tandem in superiore et anteriore vulvae apice particula quaedam apparet, quam primus inter recentiores descripsit eleganter Fallopius. Non fuit tamen veteribus incognita; hanc Avicenna Albatram vocat, id ist, virgam; Abulcasis Tentiginem; Fallopius κλειτορίδα, ab obscoeno verbo κλειτορίζειν. Columbus Amorem et dulcedinem Veneris; nos mentulam muliebrem et penem foemineum."

Girolamo Mercuriale, *De morbis muliebribus libri IV*, in *Gynaeciorum sive de mulierum affectibus commentarii* (Basileae: apud Conradum Waldkirch, 1596), bk. IV, ch. 13, "De nympha et cauda," vol. II, p. 159: "In utero etiam interdum generatur Caro quaedam, aut genita, a materia augetur, quae caro duos Morbos facit, prout scilicet in duobus locis haec caro augetur, aut generatur. Si enim supra alas Uteri, ubi pudenda committuntur in quo loco est urinarius meatus, augeatur, appellatur hic morbus a Graecis Nympha, quod vocabulum refert Suidas fuisse Samiorum: apud Ruffum Ephesium gravissimum Medicum et apud Pollucem dicitur hic morbus κλητορίς et ὑποδερίς. . . . Albuchasis Chirurgus inter Arabes illustrissimus, vocavit hunc morbum Tentiginem: Avicenna, appellat Virgam, Moschio, Symptoma turpitudinis." See also ch. XII, n. 1.

Jean Liébault, bk. II, ch. 63, *Des maladies des femmes*, p. 511, offers the following parallel: "En aucunes femmes est produicte au couronnement et tout au haut des parties honteuses participante et prenent son commencement d'un costé et d'autre de l'os pubis sus le conduict de l'urine, conjoingnant les bors et ailes d'icelle partie honteuse d'un substance partie charneuse partie nerveuse, semblable au membre viril, si petite toutesfois qu'elle ne se cognoist sinon en peu de femmes: en d'aucunes aussi elle se monstre si grande et prenent telle croissance qu'elle represente le membre viril, dont aucunes femmes en abusent malheureusement: Elle est si grande quelquesfois que tantost remplist la nature de la femme, tantost sort dehors en façon d'une queuë, à raison dequoy aucuns l'appellent rentigine, d'autres Cercosis, autres verge. Fallopius la nomme Clitoris."

Du Laurens is the source of the phrase attributed to Colombo, "amorem et dulcedinem Veneris," but it does not appear in his section describing the clitoris. Colombo sees the organ as serving to cool the overheated womb. Realdo Colombo, *De re anatomica libri XV* (Parisiis: apud Andream Wechelum, 1572), pp. 444–45: "In cervicis uteri finibus vulvam versus nonnullae carunculae prominent, a quibus voluptas, ac delectatio in coëundo non parum augetur: sub hisce vulvae labellis duae adsunt a lateribus late membranae: ut a pulvere, frigore, et aëre uterum tueantur."

31. Johann Wier, *Histoires, disputes et discours des illusions et impostures des diables* (Paris: Chez Bonnet, 1579; Paris: aux Bureaux de Progrès Médical, 1885), vol. I, pp. 427–28. Wier discusses sexual deviation in women in a chapter entitled "De la vilaine copulation des sorcieres," where he recounts, from Leon Africanus, the encounters between women possessed by devils. "Mais ceux qui ont quelque jugement appelent telles femmes *sahacat* que les Latins nomment *Fricatrices*: pource que une coustume

abominable ces vilaines se polluent charnellement ensemble."
See also Girolamo Mercuriale, *De morbis mulieribus,* p. 254: "Imo
vero sunt mulieres quaedam, quae solummodo hanc frictionem amant, et
quae mutuo se fricant; et istae mulieres dicuntur Tribades, id est, fricatrices: saepe enim legetis hoc nomen apud Scriptores." Such women were
thought to be suffering from *furor uterinus,* or *nymphotomania,* which is
an immoderate burning in the genital area of the female, caused by the
surging of hot vapor, bringing about an erection of the clitoris. Because
of this burning sensation, women were thought to be driven insane, even
dangerously violent. Some threw themselves into the water to cool the
fire, as Sappho is alleged to have done; some killed themselves to escape
the misery. Ferrand deals at greater length with the *topos* in his ch. XII.
32. Marc Antoine Muret, *Variarum lectionum libri XV* (Antverpiae: apud
Christophorum Platinum, 1587), cap. 21, pp. 221–22: "*Mulieres eruditas
plerumque libidinosas esse, duorum poëtarum testimoniis confirmatum, Juvenalis locus cum quodam Platonis collatus*":
"Vaferrimus poëta, quique omnia suae tempestatis hominum vitia
et noverat optime, et insectabatur liberrime, Juvenalis, in ea satyra, qua
mulierum improbitatem detexit, non obscure significavit, displicere sibi
mulieres eruditas, et disertas. . . . Euripides quoque, magnus et ipse
mulierum osor, etsi dictus est a quodam eas odisse in choro, amare in
thoro, eiusdem sententiae fuit. Putavit enim, id quod res est, catas et
ingeniosas feminas promptiores et acutiores esse ad struendas machinas,
quibus decipiant viros. Itaque apud eum ita Hippolytus loquitur:
Odi eruditam ne meae umquam sit domi,
Quae plus sciat, quam mulierem scire expedit.
Namque eruditis ipsa maiorem Cypris.
Astutiam indit.
et sane non nimis pudicas esse ingeniosas et eruditas mulieres, fidem
facere poterit Sappho, neque mirum, multas enim historias legunt, pec-
care, ut ait Flaccus, docentes."
The fact that Sappho, according to Suidas, threw herself into the sea
from the Leucadian rock is interpreted by Ferrand to mean that Suidas
thought of her as suffering from *furor uterinus.*

III.   Of the Name of Love and Erotic Melancholy

1. [*L. 2. Meth. med.*]: Galen, *De methodo medendi,* bk. I, ch. 2, ed. Kühn,
vol. X, pp. 81–85. Galen, however, gives melancholy as an example of
a disease whose name originates from the efficient cause, and not love
melancholy.
2. [*Lib. 6. Eth. Eud. cap. 8*]: Aristotle, *Eudemian Ethics,* bk. VI, ch. 8, is
bk. VII, ch. 8, of the *Nicomachean Ethics* (1151a), trans. H. Rackham (Loeb,
1962), p. 419. Aristotle offers the example of the Milesians in discussing
unrestraint. Such men are not unjust in intent, but they do unjust things
all the same.

3. [2 *Rhet. c. 3*]: Aristotle *Rhetoric*, bk. II, ch. 23. 29: "ἀφροδίτης ἀπὸ τῆς ἀφροδίας." See *The Art of Rhetoric* (1400b), trans. John Henry Freese (Loeb, 1967), pp. 322–23. The quotation from Euripides is from the *Troades*, l. 990.

4. [*P. Syrus*]: Publilius Syrus, *Sententiae*, A 22: "Amare et sapere vix diis conceditur," in *Minor Latin Poets*, trans. Arnold M. Duff (Loeb, 1934), p. 16.

5. [*Trallian l. 3. ca. 7. Altim. li. 1. Meth. 7. c. 3*]: Alexander of Tralles, *Oeuvres médicales*, ed. F. Brunet (Paris: Librairie Orientaliste Paul Geuthner, 1936), bk. I, ch. 17; vol. II, p. 226: "Aussi faut-il s'efforcer d'abattre la maladie à ses débuts, car une fois ancienne et devenue en quelque sorte une habitude naturelle, elle est à peu près incurable et on ne l'appelle plus seulement état atrabilaire, mais folie furieuse. En effet, la manie n'est pas autre chose qu'une exagération de l'état atrabilaire poussé à une extrême sauvagerie." Ferrand's error concerning book and chapter is perhaps because he doubled the reference following to Altomari, or because he had read only Altomari and had mistaken his reference to Galen's *De locis affectis*, bk. III, ch. 7 (where this same topic is discussed), as a reference to Alexander, who is also frequently mentioned.

Donato-Antonio Altomari, *De medendis humanis corporis malis*, bk. I, ch. 7, in *Opera omnia* (Lugduni: apud Gulielmum Rovillium, 1565), p. 189: "quarum una melancholia tum a Graecis, tum a Latinis dicitur, reliqua vero μανία Graece, Latine insania, seu furor nuncupatur, de his propterea non immerito pertractabimus, de melancholia prius verba facientes."

In the Greek world to be mad is often synonymous with to be melancholy. See George Rosen, *Madness in Society* (New York: Harper and Row, 1969).

6. *Iliscus* is a transliteration of the Arabic word *al-'isq* meaning amorous passion. This latinate form can be traced to Gerard of Cremona, who introduced it in his translation of Avicenna's *Canon*, bk. I. fen 1, tr. 5, ch. 23: "De alhash id est amantibus." The renowned physician Guglielmo da Saliceto in the eighteenth chapter of his *Cyrurgia* (Venetiis: ap. Octavianum Scotum, 1502), calls it *ylischi*. Giovanni Michele Savonarola in his *Practica major* (Venetiis: ap. Juntas, 1549), tr. VI, ch. 1, rub. 14 "*De ilisci*," p. 66, writes: "Ilisci est sollicitudo melancholica qua quis ob amorem fortem et intensum sollicitat habere rem quam nimia aviditate concupiscit, cuius causa secundum plurimum est animi forte accidens. Et ilisci est nomen arabicum; apud nos vero interpretatur amor. Unde haec passio a multis dicta est haereos, quia haerois sive nobilibus plus contingit." See also our introduction.

7. Arnald of Villanova, *Tractatus de amore heroico*, in *Opera medica omnia*, vol. III, pp. 50–51, explains *amor heroicus* in the following terms: "it is called heroical as if to say lordly, not only because it befalls the lords, but also because it rules by subjugating the soul and by ruling over the hearts of men, or because the acts of such lovers toward the objects of their desires are similar to the acts of the subjects toward their masters [our translation]." Bernard of Gordon, *Lilium medicinae* (Lugduni: apud

Gulielmum Rovillium, 1574), "*De passionis capitis*," pt. 2, ch. 20, "*De amore qui hereos dicitur*," explains that the name *hereos* derives from the fact that those who suffer of it are generally wealthy and noble, for they are the ones who, "because of the wealth of pleasures at their disposal, usually fall into this passion." For the views of Mario Equicola on this topic, see n. 20, below. Ferrand seems to be aware that the etymology of *hereos* from the Greek word for heros or lord (ἥρως) is a late derivation. The origins, however, are already in Plato's *Cratylus* (398C-E), trans. M. N. Fowler (Loeb, 1953), pp. 54–57. Mario Equicola, *Libro de natura de amore*, p. 57ᵛ, discusses the same passage in Plato. The origin of this term has been a matter of controversy among scholars. It was discussed by J. L. Lowes in "The Loveres Maladye of Hereos," by G. Agamben in *Stanze: La parola e il fantasma nella cultura occidentale*, and by Michael R. McVaugh in his introduction to Arnald of Villanova's *Tractatus de amore heroico*, pp. 5–17.

      Bernard of Gordon, *Lilium medicinae*, pp. 216 ff.

8. [*Cal. Rodig. l. 12. c. 37.*]: Ludovico Celio Riccliieri (Rhodiginus), *Lectionum antiquarum libri triginta* (Genevae: excudebat Philippus Albertus, 1620), pp. 1272–73: "*Cur amor hereos dicatur, item eros, necnon amoris commendatio. De amicitia quaepiam haud exculcata: item Cratero, et Hephestione*": "Verum ut a campi pulvere et a palo (quod dicitur) ad tabernacul umbracula, hoc est ad leviora multo reclinemus, scribit Plotinus: Amorem heroa dici forte, quoniam ἀπὸ ὁράσεως, hoc est a visione substantiam habet: quando et amor, qui affectio est, ab hoc habet instinctum. Amorem porro, Graeci ἔρωτα vocant: quia (ut Plato inquit) εἰσρεῖ hoc est influit extrinsecus per oculos. Quamvis etiam in Phaedro, ἀπὸ τῆς ῥώμης id est a robore ac vehementia, dici erota Socrates putet. In quo libro et illud invenias quosdam tradisse, Amorem dici a mortalibus ἔρωτα, volatilem: ab immortalibus autem, πλέρωτα, id est alatum quendam, propter volandi necessitatem. In Symposio Socrates asserit, se nihil praeter amatoria scire. Phaedrus vero maximorum bonorum causam esse amorem, pronuntiat: nec se invenire, quid melius accidere possit adolescenti, quam optimus amator: aut amatori, quam amatus optimus. Et esse quidem duo, quae a pueritia per omnem vitam ducere illum debeant: in rebus turpibus, verecundiam honestis, studium."

9. Ferrand takes most of the section on the meaning of the word for love from Mario Equicola's *Libro de natura de amore*, bk. II, ch. 2, pp. 56ʳ–60ʳ, choosing and rearranging examples and filling them out with more extensive quotations. See also the discussion of the same distinctions deriving from the long and short vowels in Agostino Nifo (Augustinus Niphus), *Medici libri duo, de Pulchro primus, de Amore secundus* (Lugduni: apud G. et M. Beringos fratres, 1549), p. 111.

10. Agathon's speech is in *Symposium* (196D), ed. W. R. M. Lamb (Loeb, 1961), p. 157: "And observe how in valour 'not even the God of War withstands' Love; for we hear, not of Love caught by Ares, but of Ares caught by Love—of Aphrodite. The captor is stronger than the caught; and as he controls what is braver than any other he must be bravest of all."

Lucian, *Dialogues of the Gods*, VII, "Hephaestus and Apollo," trans. M. D. MacLeod, 8 vols. (Loeb, 1961), vol. VII, p. 295.

11. Hesiod, *Phythian* V. 145, ed. M. Sommer (Paris: Hachette, 1847), p. 132: "Λεγόμενον ἐρέω." This appears to be the only instance in Hesiod where the word is used in a way related to Ferrand, who probably took it from a secondary source.

Plotinus, *Enneads*, bk. III, tract. 5, pp. 193–94: "Thus, there is a strenuous activity of contemplation in the Soul: there is an emanation towards it from the object contemplated; and Eros is born, the Love which is an eye filled with its vision, a seeing that bears its image with it; Eros taking its name probably, from the fact that its essential being is due to this ὅρασις, this seeing."

See also Hesiod, "To Aphrodite," *The Homeric Hymns and Homerica*, ed. H. G. Evelyn-White (Loeb, 1950), bk. V, pp. 428–29: "ἑλικοβλέφαρε," "coy-eyed."

12. Theocritus, *Eclogue* II. 82: "χὼς ἴδον ὡς ἐμάνην." See trans. A. S. F. Gow 2 vols. (Cambridge: At the University Press, 1950), vol. I, p. 22.

13. Virgil, *Eclogue* VIII. 41: "Ut vidi, ut perii, sic me malus abstulit error." See trans. H. Rushton Fairclough (Loeb, 1965), vol. I, p. 58.

14. [9. *Eth. ca. 5. & 12*]: Aristotle, *Nichomachean Ethics*, bk. IX, ch. 5 (1167a); bk. IX, ch. 12 (1171b), trans. H. Rackham (Loeb, 1962), pp. 539, 573: "Goodwill seems therefore to be the beginning of friendship, just as the pleasure of the eye is the beginning of love. No one falls in love without first being charmed by beauty, but one may delight in another's beauty without necessarily being in love: one is in love only if one longs for the beloved when absent, and eagerly desires his presence." "As then lovers find their greatest delight in seeing those they love, and prefer the gratification of the sense of sight to that of all the other senses, that sense being the chief seat and source of love."

15. Propertius, bk. II, *Elegy* XVI. 12: Si nescis, oculi, in Amore duces." See trans. H. E. Butler (Loeb, 1962), p. 105.

16. Marsilio Ficino, *Commentary on Plato's Symposium on Love*, trans. Sears Jayne (Dallas, Tex.: Spring Publications, 1985), Speech VII, chs. 4 and 5, pp. 159–63. Ficino was the main channel by which Plato's ideas on the role of sight in the generation of love were transmitted to the sixteenth-century medical philosophers. He was the declared source for François Valleriola's study, which in turn served Ferrand.

François Valleriola, *Observationum medicinalium libri VI*, pp. 189, 196. Valleriola states that love or desire is born by vision giving the words of Jesus in the Gospel of St. Matthew as a base, because "He who looketh upon a woman." Not only does the eye perceive and communicate beauty to the senses, but the eye perceives the beauty of the beloved in concentrated form. It is by means of the vapors of the blood called spirits that the radiant and fiery eye projects the image and the observer receives it. He employs the image of arrows and of sliding and gliding into the senses and into the soul. It is the blood itself that is tainted, blood that has already been agitated by the image (species); it becomes excited, inflamed, and begins to burn with excessive heat, producing in the lover a vehement desire to possess the object of beauty. Catching the arrows of love, the beholder is, in a sense, poisoned, for the power of love weaves its way into the deepest parts of the heart, just as it has gone through the most acute part of the body, the eye. Valleriola adopts the Neoplatonic view on the physiology of love as a disease of the blood making its way throughout the body as a form of fascination rather more thoroughly and literally than does Ferrand. Yet Ferrand adapts the mechanism of the spirits and their entry by the eye to his own description of the course of love, relating the spirits to the role of the humors and the localized adustion of the humors in the hypochondries. He was less explicit on the matter of love as a poison or fascination touching the entire body, though there are incidental references to the theory scattered throughout the treatise.

17. Musaeus, *The Loves of Hero and Leander*, bk. VII. 7–10:

    Κάλλος γὰρ περίπυστον ἀμωμήτοιο γυναικὸς
    ὀξύτερον μερόπεσσι πέλει πτερόεντος ὀιστοῦ.
    Ὀφθαλμὸς δ'ὁδός ἐστιν· ἀπ'ὀφθαλμοῖο βολάων
    ἕλκος ὀλισθαίνειν, καὶ ἐπὶ φρένας ἀνδρὸς ὀδεύει.

    Trans. Cedric Whitman (Loeb, 1975).

18. [*L. 5 Symp. q. 7*]: Plutarch, *Table talk*, bk. VIII of the *Moralia*, ques. 7, ed. Paul A. Clement (Loeb, 1969), vol. VIII, pp. 420–23: "Vision provides access to the first impulse of love, that most powerful and violent experience of the soul, and causes the lover to melt and be dissolved when he looks at those who are beautiful, as if he were pouring forth his whole being towards them. . . . The answering glances of the young and the beautiful and the stream of influence from their eyes . . . melt the lovers and destroy them. . . . The glances of the beautiful kindle fire, even when returned from a great distance, in the souls of the amorous."

19. [*Vigenere sur Philostrate*]: Philostratus, *De la vie d'Apollonius Thyaneen en VIII livres*. De la traduction de B[laise] de Vigenère, Bourbonnois (Paris: Chez la veufue Matthieu Guillemot, 1611). Hesiod, *Theogony* l. 16, trans. Hugh G. Evelyn-White (Loeb, 1950), p. 79: "καὶ Θέμιν αἰδοίην ἑλικοβλέφαρόν τ''Αφροδίτην." Pindar, *Pythian Odes*, VI. 1, trans. Sir John Sandys (Loeb, 1968), p. 249: "ἦ γὰρ ἑλικώπιδος 'Αφροδίτας."

20. The entire discussion derives from Plato and Mario Equicola. See *Cratylus*, ed. H. N. Fowler; (Loeb, 1953), pp. 123–24: "The name ἵμερος (longing) was given to the stream (ῥοῦς) which most draws the soul; for because it flows with a rush (ἱέμενος) and with a desire for things and thus draws the soul on through the impulse of its flowing, all this power gives it the name ἵμερος. And the word πόθος (yearning) signifies that it pertains not to that which is present, but to that which is elsewhere (ἄλλοθί που) or absent, and therefore the same feeling which is called ἵμερος when its object is present, is called πόθος when it is absent. And ἔρως (love) is so called because it flows in (ἐσρεῖ) from without, and this flowing is not inherent in him who has it, but is introduced through the eyes; for this reason it was in ancient times called ἔσρος, from ἐσρεῖν—for we used to employ omicron instead of omega—but now it is called ἔρως through the change of omicron to omega."

See also Equicola's *Libro de natura de amore*, p. 57^{r-v}: "Li Greci di tutti loro vocabuli si sforzano rendere ragione mutando lettere et syllabe a loro arbitrio, per far il loro parlare pieno di dolceza, soli sepper ben dir quel ch'egli volsero; quello che noi dicemo Amore loro EPΩΣ: la quale dictione scritta per o significa desiderio di qualunche cosa, benché Pindaro usò EPOΣ per il figliolo di Venere. EPΩΣ per omega come dice Platone ha origine da ἔλω et significa piglio, mutata λ in ρ, overo παρὰ τὸ ἑλεῖν ἕλοντα, che piglia il pigliante. . . . Et EPΩΣ dicese che figliol di Marte. Over da εἴρω, cioè dico sono dedicati li amanti; altri da ὁρῶ, che denota vedo, che precipuamente dal senso del viso nasce Amore nelli animi nostri . . . et Plotino scrive esser chiamato Heroa per la sua substantia del vedere, e la sua opinione è questa: lo amante vedendo l'amata resguardare, et si alegra como dil suo bene, et in quella non ha li occhi fixi con negligentia, ma con attentione, se exagita circa quel spectaculo, dal quale como da suo simulacro nasce Amore, quasi un certo vedere, donde forsi è dicto EPΩΣ, perché da ὁράσεως cioè visione et vedere ha sua substantia, perché amore il quale è passione ὁρᾶν cioè amare se dice. Platone nel Cratylo disputando che significa EPΩΣ scrive questo non esser difficile a trovare, per esser poco differente il nome de li Heroi, dal origine, demostra questo vocabulo sua genitura da EPΩTOΣ cioè amore esser venuta et li semidei heroi esser nominati, perché tutti li heroi furono generati da lo amore de Dei verso le femine mortali, over da li homini verso le dee. . . . Poco poi nel medesimo dialogo ἔρως cioè amore, perché ἐσρεῖ, cioè influisce extrinseco è stato dicto per non havere ῥοὴ alcuna propria influxione, ma intrare per li occhi. Per la qual cosa da ἐσρεῖν che significa influere ἔσρως, cioè influxione, Amore è stato chiamato da antiqui, li quali soleano usare o per ω. Li Hebrei hahaba . . . cioè Amore da ahab verbo . . . cioè amo. El Caldeo hebeda cioè amicitia, et ahab cioè amo dicono."

21. One such grammarian consulted on other occasions by Ferrand was Hesychius Varinus, *Lexicon cum variis doctorum virorum notis vel editis antehac, vel ineditis* (Lugduni Batavorum et Roter.: ex officina Hackiana, 1668). For a modern edition, ed. K. Latte (Huniae: Ejner Munksgaard Editore, 1953), vol. I, p. 251, s.v. "ἄρπυν": "ἔρωτα. Αἰολεῖς."

22. The correct Greek word is πνῖγος (πνῖγος), and it is used with this meaning by Plato, Aristotle, etc.

23. Parthenius of Nicea, elegaic poet of the Alexandrine circle, was taken to Rome as a prisoner after the defeat of Mithridates. He became the Greek tutor of Virgil and continued to write poems and romances. The quotation is from the *Etymologicum genuinum*, in *The Love Romances of Parthenius and other Fragments*, ed. J. M. Edmonds (Loeb, 1962), s.v. "'Ἄρπυς: Love. So used by Parthenius in his Crinagoras: *Love, the Spoiler, leaped upon both and plundered them*. So called from his *spoiling* the understanding." The poet Crinagoras lived in the latter part of the reign of Augustus.

24. [*C. 9.orat.* 2]: Marsilio Ficino, *Commentary on Plato's Symposium*, bk. II, Speech IX: "tangendi enim cupido non Amoris pars est, sed potius petulantiae species, et servilis hominis perturbatio." See ed. with trans. by

Sears Reynolds Jayne (Columbia, Mo., 1944), p. 52: "Tangendi vero cupido, non amoris pars est, nec amantis affectus, sed petulantiae species, et servilis hominis perturbatio." We have also consulted the work in *Divini Platonis opera omnia Marsilio Ficino interprete* (Lugduni: apud Antonium Vincentium, 1557), p. 262, col. 1.

25. [*M. Equicola*.]: Mario Equicola, *Libro de natura de amore*, bk. I, p. 4: "Etymologicamente dice amor poterse dire dogliosa morte, per esser il suo nome partito in A e more."

IV. Of Melancholy and Its Several Varieties

1. [*C. 7. 1. de loc. aff.*]: Galen, *De locis affectis*, bk. III, ch. 7, ed. Kühn, vol. VIII, p. 178. The evolution of the concept of melancholy has received considerable critical treatment. Among the notable studies are those by R. Klibansky, E. Panofsky, P. Saxl, *Saturn and Melancholy*; Jean Starobinski, *Histoire du traitement de la mélancholie*; Rudolph E. Siegel, "Melancholy and Black Bile in Galen and Later Writers," *Bulletin of the Cleveland Medical Library*, 18 (1971), pp. 10–12; Siegel, *Galen's System of Medicine and Physiology, an Analysis of His Doctrines on Bloodflow, Respiration, Humours, and Internal Diseases* (Basel: Karger, 1968), esp. pp. 258–322; Siegel, *Galen on Psychology, Psychopathology, and Functions and Diseases of the Nervous System* (Basel: Karger, 1973), esp. pp. 189–99. See also Galen, *On the Affected Parts*, trans. Rudolph E. Siegel (Basel: Karger, 1976), p. 183.

2. Aristophanes, *Plutus*, l. 366: "μελαγχολᾶς, ὦνθρωπε, νὴ τὸν οὐρανόν." See ed. B. B. Rogers (Loeb, 1961), vol. III, p. 403. See n. 5, below, for Ferrand's source in Guibelet.

3. *Paraphrosyne*, or wandering of the mind, was used in Greek medicine as a general term for various forms of mental derangement. It usually denoted faulty reasoning accompanied by loss of memory or hallucinations; it is without fever, however, as distinct from phrenitis, which exhibited similar symptoms, but was caused by an inflammation of the brain and was therefore accompanied by fever. See Galen, *Hippocratis Epidemiorum I et Galeni in illum commentarius*, bk. I, sec. 59, ed. Kühn, vol. XVII, p. 159. See also Siegel's sections: *Delirium without Fever* (Paraphrosyne), *Delirium with Fever* (Phrenitis), *Madness* (Mania), *and Melancholy*, *Dementia* (Morosis), in *Galen on Psychology*, pp. 264–75.

4. Galen, *De locis affectis*, bk. III, ch. 10, ed. Kühn, vol. VIII, p. 190: "When melancholic symptoms affect the judgement (*dianoia*), great fear is prevalent and erroneous impressions arise (*ton para physin phantasion*) which we diagnose as hallucinatory delusions. A patient might think that he is an earthen vessel which a passer-by could easily shatter; another, when seeing a rooster batting his wings before crowing, flapped his own arms at the sides and imitated the bird's cry. A third patient feared that Atlas, tired of carrying the weight of the world, might throw off his burden and he therefore was afraid to be crushed. The number of these false imag-

inations was countless." See *On the Affected Parts*, ed. R. E. Siegel, p. 93.
5. Galen, *De locis affectis*, bk. III, ch. 10, ed. Kühn, vol. VIII, pp. 191–92;
On the Affected Parts, ed. R. E. Siegel, p. 93: "Although each melancholic patient acts quite differently than the others, all of them exhibit fear or despondency. They find fault with life and hate people; but not all want to die. For some the fear of death is of principal concern during melancholy. Others again will appear to you quite bizarre because they dread death and desire to die at the same time.

"Therefore, it seems correct that *Hippocrates* classified all their symptoms into two groups: fear and despondency." See also ch. 7, n. 53, corresponding to the text where Ferrand cites the appropriate passage from the *Aphorisms*.

Ferrand takes several ideas for this chapter, and the preceding lines specifically, from Jourdain Guibelet, *Trois Discours philosophiques, discours troisiesme de l'humeur melancholique* (Evreux: Chez Antoine le Marié, 1603), ch. 4, pp. 237^{r-v}: "Mais tout cela est peu encore à comparaison des autres maux qui pervertissent les operations de l'ame, comme sont la melancholie, maladie qui porte le nom de sa cause, et la manie. Il est certain que la cholere noire a cete proprieté, de corrompre l'imaginative, et bien souvent de dépraver ce qui est du judgment et de la raison. C'est pourquoy les Grecs usoient de ce mot μελαγχολᾶν, pour dire estre hors du sens: comme nous pouvons voir par ce lieu d'Aristophane μελαγχολᾶς ὦ ἄνθρωπε νῆ τὸν οὐρανόν. Je jure par le Ciel que tu n'est pas en ton bon sens. Et simplement ce mot χολᾶν, signifioit en langue Attique μαίνεσθαι estre fol ou enragé, comme l'explique le Scholiaste. De verité c'est avoir une force extréme, que d'abaisser tant l'ame qui est immortelle, que de luy oster l'exercice de ses facultez."

6. Aretaeus the Cappadocian, *On the Causes and Symptoms of Chronic Diseases*, p. 299. In the section dealing with melancholy, Aretaeus does not speak of the brain as the seat of the disease but rather a region affected by sympathy because black bile originates in the hypochondries and makes its way either upwards or downwards. "If the cause remain in the hypochondriac regions, it collects about the diaphragm, and the bile passes upwards, or downwards in cases of melancholy. But if it also affects the head from sympathy, and the abnormal irritability of temper change to laughter and joy for the greater part of their life, these become mad rather from the increase of the disease than from change of the affection. Dryness is the cause of both." Aretaeus does not go on to explain the origins of that dryness, though it was, as Ferrand claims, associated with the brain, a product of the intense concentration upon a desired object because laborious thinking drys and chills the brain.

7. [*Sect. 8. Aph. 54.*]: Hippocrates, *Epidemics*, bk. VI, sec. 8, aph. 31: "ἤν μὲν ἐς τὸ σῶμα, ἐπίληπτοι, ἤν δὲ ἐπὶ τὴν διάνοιαν, μελαγχολικοί." *Oeuvres complètes*, ed. Littré, vol. V, pp. 355, 357.

Ferrand's text has γίνονται (they become) after ἐπίληπτοι.

8. Galen, *De locis affectis*, bk. III, ch. 9, ed. Kühn, vol. VIII, pp. 173–79 (*On the Affected Parts*, ed. R. E. Siegel, pp. 86–88). Galen's definition of melancholy was accepted with very few variations until the end of the seven-

teenth century. For a discussion of the Galenic distinction of three kinds of melancholy, see Starobinski, *Histoire du traitement de la mélancholie*, pp. 25–27, and for the development of Galen's concept of melancholy in the sixteenth and seventeenth centuries, see O. Diethelms, *Medical Dissertations of Psychiatric Interest Printed before 1750* (Basel: Karger, 1971), pp. 32–49.

9. Giovanni Battista Silvatico, *Controversiae medicae numero centum*, Controversy 34, "*An in vocata melancholia hypochondriaca, unus tantum locus afficiatur; et a quibus illa fiat causis*" (Francofurti: typis Wechelianis apud Claudium Marnium, et heredes Joannis Aubrii, 1601), pp. 164–67. In the form of a complex debate between the Greeks and the Arabs, Sylvaticus explains which organs can be inflamed and obstructed by hypochondriacal melancholy, concluding that not only the stomach or pylorus or liver or intestines, but all the surrounding regions can also be touched.

There are many early medical sources dealing with the various kinds of melancholy diseases in accordance with the places first affected. Aretaeus the Cappadocian, *On the Causes and Symptoms of Chronic Diseases*, p. 298, explains how melancholy bile can either rise or descend, and how the direction of movement causes diverse effects. If it goes downwards it terminates in the liver. "But if it be determined upwards to the stomach and diaphragm, it forms melancholy; for it produces flatulence and eructations of a fetid and fishy nature, and it sends rumbling wind downwards, and disturbs the understanding." This latter effect is produced from sympathy of the head. There is little cause here, however, for preparing a history in résumé of the division of melancholies, for Ferrand had clearly been reading André Du Laurens' classification of love melancholy as a condition of the hypochondriacal variety, and more particularly Jourdain Guibelet.

Jourdain Guibelet, *Discours troisiesme de l'humeur melancholique*, ch. 4, p. 238^r: "Nous avons plusieurs especes de cete folie melancholique: Une causée de cholere noire engendrée dans le cerveau. Une autre en laquelle cete humeur est generalement espandue par tout le corps. La troisiéme nommée hypochondriaque parce que le sujet du mal est seulement aux hypochondres, en la region du foye et de la rate: Ou selon Diocles en l'orifice superieur du ventricule. L'amour qui est une passion placée principalement au foye, cause quelquefois une maniere de melancholie, qui pervertit aussi l'imaginative, par ce qu'elle échauffe et brusle le sang, et le rend melancholique."

10. That concupiscence is seated in the liver is a notion that goes back to Greek medicine; it was widely accepted during the sixteenth and seventeenth centuries. See, e.g., Francisco Valles, *Controversiarum medicarum et philosophicarum libri X* (Hanoviae: typis Wechelianis apud Claudium Marnium, 1606), bk. III, ch. 14, p. 145: "amor non est cordis affectus, sed cerebri, si rationalis est; iecoris, si turpis."

Ferrand, according to traditional classifications, places erotic melancholy under the heading of hypochondriacal or windy melancholy. Having once designated the classification, however, he scarcely returns to it later in the treatise, perhaps because he was not convinced, in fact, of the association between wind and lust, or because he was not interested in, or persuaded by, the cures for the reduction of wind. Nevertheless, Burton assures us in *The Anatomy of Melancholy*, pt. 1, sec. 3, memb. 2, subs. 2, p. 352, that "these windy flatuous have, lucid intervals, their symptoms and pains not usually so continuate as the rest, but come by fits, fear and sorrow and the rest: yet in another they exceed all others; and this is, they are luxurious, incontinent, and prone to Venery, by reason of wind, and fall easily in love, and are generally not very particular who the woman is, (Jason Pratensis). Rhasis is of opinion, that Venus doth many of them much good; the other symptoms of the mind be common with the rest." In pt. 2, sec. 5, memb. 3, subs. 2, pp. 605–6, Burton offers the "Correctors to expel Wind," which include medications, a number of oils and ointments, and cupping glasses applied to the hypochondries. "Amatus Lusitanus for an Hypochondriacal person that was extremely tormented with wind, prescribes a strange remedy. Put a pair of bellows' end into a clyster pipe, and applying it to the fundament, open the bowels, so draw forth the wind; nature abhors a vacuum. He vaunts he was the first invented this remedy, and by means of it speedily eased a melancholy man."

V.   Of the Definition of Love and Erotic Melancholy

1. [*Arist. l. 2. post. anal. c. 10. l. 1. de anima l .7. Metaph. c. 12*]: Aristotle, *Posterior Analytics*, bk. II, ch. 13 (97a), trans. Hugh Tredennick (Loeb, 1966), p. 235: "In order to establish a definition by division, we must keep three things in mind: (1) to select attributes which describe the essence, (2) to arrange them in order of priority, and (3) to make sure that the selection is complete. (1) The first object can be achieved through the possibility of establishing the genus and differentia by the topic of genus, just as we can infer the inherence of an attribute by the topic of accident."

Aristotle, *On the Soul*, bk. I (402a–b), trans. W. S. Hett (Loeb, 1964), pp. 9, 11: "This inquiry, I mean that which treats of the essence or essential nature, is common to many other fields, and one might suppose that there is one method applicable to all the things whose real nature we wish to understand, just as logical demonstration applies to all their [essential] attributes. If so this method must be discovered; but if there is no common method of finding the essential nature, our handling of the subject becomes still more difficult." He conducts an inquiry into procedures of definition of the soul, whether to examine first the essences or the attributes, the parts or the whole, the elements or the functions, and what the affections of the soul are in relation to the body. Ferrand takes this discussion as a basis for creating definitions of subjects.

Aristotle, *Metaphysics*, bk. VII, ch. 12 (1037b–1038b), trans. Hugh Tredennick (Loeb, 1967), pp. 371–77. Another discussion on definition by division.

2. Avicenna, *Liber canonis*, bk. III, fen 20, tr. 1, ch. 25, p. 375^V f.: "*De multitudine desiderij.*" The source for this concept is Galen's *De locis affectis*, bk. VI, ch. 6, as the marginal note to Avicenna's text correctly identifies.

3. Ferrand summarizes Mario Equicola's definition of love, *Libro de natura de amore*, bk. II, pp. 77^V–78^r, rearranging his examples and adding the names of Ficino and Valleriola to that of Plutarch: "Stoici dicono esser una cupidità la quale advene per belleza; Peripatetici essere argumento di benivolentia per l'apparente venustà; li Academici furon di opinione che amor fosse un desio di goder et fruire quello compitamente che li par ornato di ogni somma belleza, onde lo amante desia tutto esser nel corpo de l'amato, perché sempre da li dardi di Venere ferito, subito desidera coniungerle, né altro desidera (come dice Aristophane) che di doi diventar uno. . . . Avicenna nel quarto tractato del terzo libro, dimostra esser passione di animo introducta da li sensi per satisfar al desiderio, li Physici esser una perturbatione proxima, overo simile al morbo malancolico: Dicemo quel furore il quale ne aliena dal nostro proprio essere, malancolia parola greca. . . . Theofrasto scrisse esser concupiscentia de l'animo la quale ha veloce ingresso et tardo exito; Plutarco credette esser commotione di sangue, ma non como la ira occupare tutto 'l corpo subito, perché a poco a poco piglia forza per la speranza de la voluptà. . . . Marco Tullio existimò esser ben volere; Seneca nelle tragedie dice che Amore è un vigor grande de la mente, et un caldo che suavemente bolle ne l'animo."

4. [*L. 4. deplat. Hipp. & Plat.*]: Galen, *De placitis Hippocratis et Platonis*, bk. IV, ch. 6, ed. Kühn, vol. V, p. 413: "Constat enim, quum concupiscibilis facultatis, non rationalis, amor sit affectus, totum animum educere, hominemque in contrarias actione rapere iis, quae initio statuerat." The chapter is important for the several polemical positions it offers against Chrysippus.

5. [*L. 4. de diff. puls.*]: Galen, *De differentia pulsuum*, bk. IV, ch. 2, ed. Kühn, vol. VIII, pp. 703–4. Galen, however, is not speaking about love, but rather he is criticizing all previous theories concerning the pulse.

6. Arnald of Villanova, *Opera medica omnia*, vol. III, *Tractatus de amore heroico*, p. 46: "Dico igitur, nullis aliorum prejudicando sententiis, quod amor talis (videlicet qui dicitur hereos) est vehemens et assidua cogitatio supra rem desideratam cum confidentia obtinendi delectabile apprehensum ex ea."

Bernard of Gordon, *Lilium medicinae*, pt. 2, ch. 20, p. 216: "Amor, qui hereos dicitur, est solicitudo melancholica propter mulieris amorem. Causa huius passionis est corruptio aestimativae, propter formam et figuram fortiter affixam; unde, cum aliquis philocaptus est in amore alicuius mulieris, ita fortiter concipit formam et figuram et modum, quoniam credit et opinatur hanc esse meliorem, pulchriorem et magis venerabilem, magis speciosam et melius dotatam in naturalibus et moralibus quam aliquam aliarum."

Christóbal de Vega, *Liber de arte medendi*, bk. III, ch. 17 (Lugduni: apud Gulielmum Rovillium, 1576), p. 414: "Amoris affectus, animi motus est et ipsius conflictatio, cuius naturam et generationem, nos in ora-tione de amore publice habita pateficimus late. Est enim amor animi solicitudo perpetua, et cura pertinax, spei, timoris, tristitiae, et laetitiae plena: haec vero cum diu perseverat, cerebrum exsiccat, et hominem evigilat, et delirare cogit."

Luis Mercado, *De internorum morborum curatione*, in *Opera*, vol. III, p. 102: "Est enim amor adeo vehemens animi affectio, ut in maniam et ferina deliramenta non raro commigrasse visum sit. Diffinit quidem amorem Plato, *perfruendae pulchritudinis desiderium:* ita ut ad eius procreationem satis sit, rem pulcram semel vidisse, et idolum pulchritudinis acceptum memoria collocare: verum propter egestatem amantis, et celerem fugam accepti simulachri, non cessant procaces oblectantis figurae praesentiam exigere."

Rodrigo de Castro, *Medicus-politicus* (Hamburgi: ex bibliopolio Frobeniano, 1614), p. 218: "Sciendum praeterea amorem esse desiderium pulchri: illum vero de quo agimus, esse affectum vehementissimum, et pene indomitum, visu vel notitia rei amatae per sensus excitatum, quo amantis voluntas libero mentis judicio impellitur, ut illud objectum prosequatur, ex quo plus commodi et voluptatis sperat."

Haly Abbas, *Liber medicinae dictus regius* (Venetiis: opera Bernardini Ricii de Novaria, 1492), "*Theoricae,*" bk. IX, ch. 7, pp. 60^V–61^r: "*De melancolia et canina et amore causisque eorum et signis,*" p. 61^r: "Amor autem est animae sollicitudo in id quod amatur et cogitationis in idipsum perseverantia. . . . Haec est passionum quae in cerebro sunt assignatio causaeque et signa singularium."

Albucasis (Abū al-Qāsim al-Zaharáwī Khalaf ibn ˙Abbās [Alsaharavi, Alsaravius]), *Liber theoricae necnon practicae* (Venetiis: Augustus Vindicianus, 1519), tr. 1, sec. 2, ch. 17.

Avicenna, *Liber canonis*, bk. III, fen 1, tr. 5, ch. 23, p. 206^V: "Hec aegritudo est solicitudo melancholica similis melancholiae, in qua homo sibi iam induxit incitationem seu applicationem cogitationis suae continuam super pulchritudine ipsius quarundam formarum, et gestuum, sue morum, quae insunt ei."

Paul of Aegina (Paulus Aegineta), *The Seven Books*, trans. Francis Adams, 3 vols. (London: The Sydenham Society, 1844–47), vol. I, p. 390: "It will not be out of place here to join love to the affections of the brain, since it consists of certain cares. For care is a passion of the soul occasioned by the reason's being in a state of laborious emotion."

7. [*Io. de Sacrobosco Cantuar. lib. 1. de Persp. c. 22*]: Christoph Clavius, *In Sphaeram Joannis de Sacro Bosco, Commentarius* (Lugduni: ex officina Q. Hug, A. Porta, sumptibus Jo. de Gabiano, 1607), p. 613: "Quilibet autem planeta, praeter solem, tres habet circulos, scilicet aequantem, deferentem, et epicyclum. Aequans lunae est circulus concentricus cum terra, et est in superficie eclipticae. Eius vero deferens est circulus eccentricus, nec est in superficie eclipticae, immo una eius medietas declinat versus septentrionem, altera versus austrum. Et deferens aequantem intersecat in duobus locis: Et figura intersectionis appellatur draco, quoniam lata est in medio, et augustior versus finem. Intersectio igitur illa, per quam luna movetur ab austro versus aquilonem, appellatur caput

draconis: reliqua vero intersectio, per quam movetur a septentrione in austrum dicitur cauda draconis." Also p. 288: "Unde eclipsis lunae nihil aliud est, quam interpositio terrae inter corpus solis, et lunae."

8. Hippocrates, *De flatibus*, ch. 2, ed. Littré, vol. VI, p. 93: "Morborum autem omnium cum idem modus sit, locus tamen diversus est." The nature of all maladies is the same. They differ only in relation to their seat.

9. Ovid, *Heroides* I, "Penelope Ulixi," l.12: "Res est solliciti plena timoris Amor." See *Epistulae Heroidum*, ed. Henricus Dörrie (Berlin: Walter de Gruyter, 1971), p. 47.

10. [*Gal. de cogn. & cur. animi morbis. Quinct. l. 6. de div. aff.*]: Galen, *De cognoscendis curandisque animi morbis*, bk. I, ch. 2, ed. Kühn, vol. V, pp. 1–57. See also P. W. Hankins's translation of Galen, *On the passions and errors of the soul* (Columbus: Ohio State University Press, 1963), pp. 31–32, 76–79.

Quintilian, *Institutio Oratoria*, bk. VI, ch. 2, sec. 6, trans. H. E. Butler (Loeb, 1966), vol. II, p. 419: "lovers are incapable of forming a reasoned judgement on the beauty of the object of their affections, because passion forestalls the sense of sight."

11. [*Philost in Apol. l. 4. cap 8. Aelian, Phlegon.*] Philostratus, *In Honour of Apollonius of Tyana*, bk. IV, ch. 25, trans. J. S. Phillimore, 2 vols. (Oxford: Clarendon, 1912), vol. II, pp. 24–26: "It was a matter of common report that Menippus had inspired a strange woman with a passion for him. She was beautiful to look at, in a particularly voluptuous style, and gave herself out for wealthy. But this was all show, and in reality she was no such thing: as presently appeared. . . . Apollonius perceived her fraud and alerted Menippus on the eve of the wedding, 'You, sir, with your good looks and the pretty women all running after you, you cherish a serpent and a serpent cherishes you.' . . . And to prove what I say, Madam the bride is an Empusa, such as are commonly called *Lamias* and *Mormolukias*. They have amorous appetites, but their chief appetite is for human flesh, and they snare their intended victims with the bait of love." Philostratus does not mention Alkidias, but he does tell the story of a man in love with a statue of Aphrodite in bk. VI, ch. 40 (vol. II, p. 146).

Claudius Aelianus, *Variae historiae libri XIV* (Argentorati: sumptibus Johannis Friderici Spoor et Reinhardi Waechtleri, 1685). This is a supplemental reference because a thorough perusal has produced nothing of the stories Ferrand mentions in the text. Aelian will be associated with Philostratus again later in the text in ch. XI where he again mentions Alkidias. Aelian's story in that context is of Xerxes. There is, however, a chapter on the lamia, bk. XIII, ch. 9, p. 666: "Lamia igitur seortum Atticum dixit, Leones Graeciae, Ephesi reddunter vulpes."

Phlegon of Tralles, *De mirabilibus liber deest principium in Antigoni Corystii historiarum mirabilium collectanea*, Joannes Meursius recensuit, et notas addidit (Lugduni Batavorum: apud Isaacum Elzevirium, 1619), p. 14. Phlegon is the source of the story of Machates and Philinion. The story is told in an expanded and commented version in the *Histoires prodigieuses et memorables, extraictes de plusieurs fameux autheurs, Grecs, et Latins, sacrez et prophanes, divisées en six livres* (Paris: par la vefue de Gabriel Buon, 1598), bk. VI, ch. 1, pp. 1127–45. This story, according to Boaistuau comes from Phlegon by way of Le Loyer: "les deux histoires rapportées par ledict Sieur Loyer de la boutique du mesme Phlegon. . . ." (p. 1146). Pierre Le Loyer, *Discours et histoires des spectres, visions et apparitions des esprits, anges, demons et ames, se monstrans visibles aux hommes, divisez en huict livres* (Paris: Chez Nicolas Buon, 1605), bk. III, ch. 11, pp. 245–49: "Ceste histoire est d'une Philinnion qui apparut à un Machates apres son decez, ayant emprunté ou plutost le Diable en la place de Philinnion deceddee, non un corps aërien, mais le corps mort et ensepulturé de Philinnion. Je tiens ce que j'en vay dire de Phlegon natif de Tralles affrachy de l'Empereur Adrian qui ne nous monstre point en quel lieu cecy arriva, d'autant que son livre est defectueux." The story, Le Loyer speculates, comes from the region of Thessaly, famous from Apuleius's report, for its sorcerers, a place where miraculous things happened nearly every day.

12. André Du Laurens, *Des maladies melancholiques et du moyen de les guarir* in *Toutes les oeuvres*, pp. 35^{r-v}. The entire passage on the corrupted imagination—seeing as in a vision the perfection of beauty and relating it to a person lacking such virtues, following the shadow as if it were real—is derived in its entirety, with modest additions—notably a quotation from Propertius—from Du Laurens, ch. 10. The list is conventionally ordered beginning with the golden hair, the forehead, the eyes, the eyebrows, cheeks, mouth, its shape and odor, the chin, neck, bosom, the excitement of her breathing, her skin, and blue veins. The spirit of this passage in both authors is in turn drawn from Lucretius, bk. IV. 1152–72. See n. 16, below. There are, however, many intermediary passages which were part of a protest against the blazon to the lady in the Petrarchan tradition. Pierre Boiastuau in bk. III of *Le théâtre du monde*, p. 217, proffers such a sequence: "Si l'amoureux est lettré, et qu'il ayt quelque peu l'esprit esveillé, vous le verrez feindre une mer de larmes, un lac de miseres, redoubler ses cris, accuser le ciel, faire une anatomie de son cueur. . . . Et s'il advient qu'il vueille exalter ce qu'il ayme, ce n'est plus qu'or traict de ses cheveux, ses sourcils arches et voultes d'Ebene, ses yeux astres jumeaux, ses regardz esclairs, sa bouche coral, ses dents perles d'Orient, son aleine basme, ambres, et musc, sa gorge de neige, son col de laict, ses montaignes qu'elle a sur l'estomac, pommes d'albastre." For further treatment of this subject, see J. Vianey, *Le pétrarquisme en France au XVIe siècle* (Montpellier: Coulet et fils, 1909), esp. pp. 165–78; and J. G. Fucilla, "Sources of du Bellay's *Contre les Pétrarquistes*" *Modern Philology*, 28 (1930–31), pp. 1–11.

Ferrand is still reading Du Laurens in the lines to follow dealing with Plato's qualifications for beauty, *Des maladies melancholiques et du moyen de les guarir*, p. 35^v: "Bref, ce pauvre melancholique s'en va tousjours imaginant les trente six beautez qui sont requises à la perfection, et la grace qui est par-dessus tout, resve tousjours à cét object, court apres son ombre, et n'est jamais en repos." See also Mario Equicola, *Libro de natura de amore*, bk. IV, ch. 3.

13. [*Propert. el. penul. lib. 3.*]: Propertius, bk. III, Elegy XXIV. 5–6: "Mixtam te varia laudati saepe figura, / Ut quod non esses, esse putaret Amor." *The Elegies of Propertius*, trans. H. E. Butler, p. 256.

14. [*Suet. in Vitel.*]: Suetonius, *The Lives of the Caesars*, trans. J. C. Rolfe, 2 vols. (Loeb, 1950), vol. II, p. 251: of Lucius Vitellius he reports that "he was an honest and active man, but of very ill repute because of his passion for a freedwoman, which went so far that he used her spittle mixed with honey to rub on his throat and jaws as a medicine, not secretly nor seldom, but openly and every day."

15. [*Lucr. l. 4*]: Lucretius, *De rerum natura*, bk. IV. 1160–69; 1155–56:

    nigra "melichrus" est, immunda et foetida "acosmos,"
    caesia "palladium," nervosa et lignea "dorcas,"
    parvula pumilio, "chariton mia," "tota merum sal,"
    magna atque immanis "cataplexis plenaque honoris."
    balba loqui non quit—"traulizi"; muta "pudens" est;
    at flagrans odiosa loquacula "Lampadium" fit;
    "ischnon eromenion" tum fit, cum vivere non quit
    prae macie; "rhadine" verost iam mortua tussi;
    at gemina et mammosa "Ceres" est "ipsa ab Iaccho,"
    simula "Silena ac satyrast;" labiosa "philema."
    .... multimodis igitur pravas turpisque videmus
    esse in deliciis summoque in honore vigere.

    See ed. W. H. D. Rouse, with the revisions of M. Ferguson Smith (Loeb, 1975), p. 366. In Ferrand's text the words *melichrus, acosmos, dorcas, chariton, cataplexis, traulizi, lampadium, ischnon eromenion, rhadine, Silena, philema* are in Greek.

16. [*De audit.*]: Plutarch, *De recta ratione audiendi* (*On Listening to Lectures*), *Moralia*, bk. I: "οἱ γοῦν ἐν ὥρᾳ πάντες, ὥς φησιν ὁ Πλάτων, ἀμηγέπη δάκνουσι τὸν ἐρωτικόν, καὶ λευκοὺς μὲν θεῶν παῖδας ἀνακαλῶν μέλανας δ'ἀνδρικούς, καὶ τὸν γρυπὸν βασιλικὸν καὶ τὸν σιμὸν ἐπίχαριν τὸν δ'ὠχρὸν μελίχρουν ὑποκοριζόμενος ἀσπάζεται καὶ ἀγαπᾷ." See trans. Frank Cole Babbitt, vol. I, p. 240. Ferrand leaves out the words "ὥς φησιν ὁ Πλάτων," "as Plato says." The passage, in fact, derives from Plato's *Republic* (474D).

17. [*Terent. in Eun. act. 1. sc. 2.*]: Terence, *The Eunuch*, II. i: "Dii boni! quid hoc morbi est? adeo homines immutarier / Ex Amore, ut non cognoscas eosdem esse." *Terence*, trans. John Sargeaunt (Loeb, 1964), vol. I, pp. 254–55.

18. [*Higin. c. 184. Home. Od. 1.*]: Hyginus, *Fables*, ch. 188, "Theophane." See *Hygini fabulae*, ed. H. I. Rose (Lugduni Batavorum: in aedibus A. W. Sijthoff, 1967), p. 132; for Circe, see ch. 125, "Odyssea," p. 90. See also *The Myths of Hyginus*, trans. Mary Grant (Lawrence: University of Kansas Publications, 1960), p. 145.

    Homer, *The Odyssey*, bk. X. 229–40.

    Ferrand will cite Du Laurens as his inspiration for reconciling the differences of opinion between Galen and Averroes concerning the physiological causes of fear and sorrow in the melancholy, but there is a likelihood that Ferrand became interested in the controversy from his reading of Jourdain Guibelet, *Discours troisiesme de l'humeur melancholique*, ch. 7, pp. 245^V–46^r: "Tous les medecins confessent que les melancholiques sont tousjours accompagnez de crainte et de tristesse, encores qu'ils n'en eussent aucune occasion. La cause de ce symptome est doctement deduicte par Galien, quoy qu'il soit contredit par Averroys. Il dit que la couleur noire de l'humeur melancholique est cause de cete crainte, et explique cela par une similitude. Tout ainsi, dit-il, que les tenebres épouventent les enfans, ainsi la noirceur de l'humeur melancholique semblable à une nuict, enveloppe la clarté de l'ame dans ses tenebres, qui est cause de la peur, si nous n'y opposons la clarté de la raison. Pour éclaircir cete doctrine de Galien, nous disons que comme Hippocrate n'entend pas que l'ame soit sujete à aucune maladie, encore qu'il dic que la maladie de l'ame soit cause que les phrenetiques ne sentent point de douleur, voulant signifier par là que les esprits, retenus par la nature, pour aider à la partie malade, ne sont point representez à l'imaginative, pour imprimer l'espece de la chose qui blesse: Galien aussi en ce lieu allegué n'entend pas que la peur des melancholiques provienne de ce que l'ame soit noire, ou qu'elle soit épouventée à la veüe de cete noirceur, comme pense Averroys. Mais à raison que les esprits, qui luy servent d'instrument en toutes ses actions, sont obscurcis. Les fonctions de l'ame sont entieres, quand cet instrument est naturellement disposé, c'est à dire pur et point defectueux en sa quantité, et au contraire corrompues lors qu'il manque, ou qu'il a de l'impurité. Quand donc il y a quelque vapeur ou matiere melancholique, portée ou élevée parmy les voyes de l'ame disoit Platon ταῖς τῆς ψυχῆς πρωριοδοῖς, c'est à dire au cerveau siege du jugement de l'imaginative et de la raison. Il ne faut point douter que les esprits estants obscurcis de cete impurité, ne corrompent les fonctions de ses facultez, et produisent des imaginations faulses, et par consequent la peur et la tristesse."

19. [*L. 2 de symp. caus. l. 3 de loc. aff.*]: Galen, *De symptomatum causis liber*. Ferrand's intended reference is to bk. I, ch. 10, ed. Kühn, vol. VII, pp. 189–93.

Galen, *De locis affectis*, bk. III, ed. Kühn, vol. VIII, pp. 189–90; *On the Affected Parts*, ed. R. E. Siegel, p. 93. Concerning *On the Affected Parts*, see ch. IV, nn. 4 and 5.

20. [*L. 3. Coll. c. ult.*]: Averroes, *Colliget*, bk. III, ch. 41. For this long polemic which Ferrand states in accurate résumé, see *Averrois Cordubensis Colliget libri VII* (Venetiis: apud Junctas, 1562; rpr. Frankfurt am Main: Minerva, 1962), p. 57^V.

21. [*L. quod animi mores corp. temp. seq.*]: Galen, *Quod animi mores corporis temperamenta sequantur* [*That the Faculties of the Soul Follow the Temperament of the Body*], ed. Kühn, vol. IV, pp. 767–822. This work has been translated into Italian, *Opere scelte di Galeno*, trans. Ivan Garofalo and Mario Vegeti (Turin: UTET, 1978), pp. 957–97.

22. [*Laur. tr de la Melanc. chap. 5*]: André Du Laurens, *Des maladies melancholiques et du moyen de les guarir*, p. 26^V: "Voila ces deux grands personnages bien differens en opinion, je pense qu'on les pourra accorder si on joinct ces deux causes ensemble, la temperature de l'humeur comme la principale, et la couleur noire des esprits comme celle qui peut beau-

coup aider. L'humeur melancholique estant froide, refroidit non seulement le cerveau, mais aussi le coeur, qui est le siege de ceste puissance
courageuse, qu'on nomme irascible, et abbat son ardeur: de la vient la
crainte: la mesme humeur estant noire, rend tous les esprits animaux qui
doivent estre purs, subtils, clairs et lumineux, les rend, dy je, grossiers,
obscure, et comme tous enfermez: or l'esprit estant le premier et principal instrument de l'ame, s'il est noircy et refroidy tout ensemble, trouble
ses plus nobles puissances, et sur tout l'imagination: luy representant
tousjours des especes noires, et des visions estranges qui peuvent estre
veuës de l'oeil encores qu'elles soient au dedans."

23. Plato, *Symposium* (201D–204E), trans. W. R. M. Lamb, pp. 179–81. The
story of Penia and Porus appears in the speech on love by Socrates
which he claims, in turn, to have learned from Diotima of Mantinea.
The story was much commented upon in the Renaissance and frequently
allegorized.

   The most important of all the commentaries on this story from the
Symposium is by Plotinus, *Ennead* III, tr. 5, where he develops his entire
theory of love on the dual nature of Aphrodite and the dual nature
of Eros, born to Penia and Porus. His tractatus on love became the
fountainhead for the neoplatonic theories enlarged upon by Ficino and
his many followers in the Renaissance. See trans. Stephen MacKenna,
pp. 191–201.

24. [*Prob. l. 7. sec. 3*]: Aristotle, *Problems*, bk. III, sec. 7 (872a): "ἔρως, ἐπιθυμία
τίς εστιν, ἐπιθυμία καὶ ἔνδειά τις εστιν." See trans. W. S. Hett (Loeb, 1953),
vol. I, p. 81. Aristotle is discussing wine, however, and not love; his
axiom concerns desire in a more general sense. Cf. *Problems*, bk. XXII,
sec. 3 (930a), vol. II, p. 5.

VI.   The External Causes of Love Melancholy

1. Ferrand says that he will not lose his time in giving the opinions of
ancient authorities, though in fact he often goes back on his word in
subsequent chapters. This chapter is a kind of introduction to much
that follows, touching as he does on several topics that he promises to
enlarge upon in other chapters, even to the extent of anticipating the
principal quotations.

2. [*In Erotico*]: Plutarch, *The Dialogue on Love*, sec. 19, in the *Moralia*, vol. IX,
p. 405: "This warmth [of love, as opposed to the fire of passion beyond
reason] does not, as someone has affirmed, set up a churning that leads
to the formation of seed through the gliding of atoms that are rubbed
off in the smooth, tickling contact; rather, it produces a marvellous and
fruitful circulation of sap, as in a plant that sprouts and grows, a circulation that opens the way to acquiescence and affection." Plutarch
is referring to Epicurus, frag. 311 (Usener). Parallel texts dealing with
similar ideas relating to love as the production of atoms passed between
the lovers are to be found in Plato's *Phaedrus* (241A, 250A–256E); and

Lucretius' *De rerum natura* bk. IV. 1121 ff. Plutarch is not concerned with the mechanisms of causation here. This idea was to remain popular down to the Renaissance, especially with the poets who wrote of the exchanges of ethereal beams through the eyes of lovers, and the imprinting of images upon their hearts and memories.

3. In Plato, ἐνθυσιασμός (from ἐνθουσιάξω, "I am filled by the divinity") is the emotional equivalent of the orgiastic (Dionysus), poetic (muses), amorous (Aphrodite), exhaltation (*mania*) characteristic of soothsayers, poets, and lovers. When they are "inspired and possessed by the divinity they are capable of saying many great things without knowing what they are saying," *Phaedrus* (265B). "There are two kinds of mania: one caused by human infirmities, the other by . . . the divinity," *Phaedrus* (265A–B), ed. H. N. Fowler (Loeb, 1953), pp. 529 ff.

4. [*L. de diff. morb. L. 1. therap. L. de caus. procat. L. de diff. Symp. L. de opt. secta.*]: Galen, *De morborum differentiis*, ed. Kühn, vol. VI, pp. 836–80.

   Galen, probably a reference to the opening of his *De methodo medendi libri*, bk. I, ch. 1, ed. Kühn, vol. X, pp. 1–6.

   Galen, *De causis procatarcticis liber*, bk. I, ch. 1, in *Galeni Opera* (Lugduni: apud Joannem Fellonium, 1550), vol. II, pp. 495–96.

   Galen, *De symptomatum differentiis liber*, ed. Kühn, vol. VII, pp. 42–53, esp. p. 47. Galen discusses at length the definition of *passio*.

   Galen, *De optima secta ad Thrasybulum liber*, ed. Kühn, vol. I, p. 168 ff. This is a passing reference.

5. [*Bēbe en ses Azolins*]: Pietro Bembo, *Asolani*. In Ferrand's *index nominorum* the name is spelled Bombe. Ferrand probably acquired this reference from Mario Equicola, *Libro de natura de Amore*, bk. I, "Pier Bembo," pp. 33ʳ–36ᵛ.

   Bembo was translated into French as *Les asolaines de Monseigneur Pierre Bembo, de la nature d'amour, traduits d'italien en français, par Jean Martin, secrétaire de M. le Cardinal de Lenoncourt* (Paris: M. de Vascosan, 1545).

6. [*L. 9 Eth. cap. 5*]: Aristotle, *Nicomachean Ethics*, bk. IX, ch. 5 (1167a). "μὴ γάρ προησθεὶς τῇ ἰδέα οὐθεὶς ἐρᾷ." See trans. H. Rackham (Loeb, 1962), pp. 538–39.

7. [*Propert. el. I. l. I.*]: Propertius, bk. I, Elegy I: "Cynthia prima suis miserum me cepit ocellis, / Contactum nullis antem cupidinibus." See trans. H. E. Butler, p. 2.

8. [*L. 5. ca c de Amore*]: Mario Equicola, *Libro de natura de amore*. As the following two quotations will reveal, Ferrand borrows freely from this source. Ferrand alters Equicola's account by supplying Paris in the place of Achilles: "Narra Philostrato ne li soi Heroi, che secundo li poeti, amore si causa dal vedere, et li primi essere stati Achille et Helena non avendosi mai veduti che se amarno; essendo Helena in Egypto et Achille in Troia, et como per solo udita se inamorarno insieme, da le Parche li fu concessa congiontione immortale. . . . Iuvenale como un prodigio scrive di un ceco inamorato" (p. 195ʳ). "Iamfres Rudels signore di Blaia se inamorò de la Contessa di Tripoli senza vederla, per lo ben che ne aveva odito dire da li peregrini che tornavano da Antiochia; fece di lei

molti versi et bon sons, per vederla navigò, et amandose in nave fu infermo conducto in Tripoli. La Contessa lo andò ad vedere, et egli ringratiò Dio che li avesse la vita sustenuta fin che avesse veduto quel che tanto desiava vedere, et cosí ne le braccia de l'amata donna finí sua vita" (pp. 194ᵛ–95ʳ). Equicola's story is about Jaufré Rudel, lord of Blaye, a Provençal troubadour who flourished in the middle of the twelfth century. He is known to have made a visit to the Holy Land in 1148. The story of his love for the Countess of Tripoli derives from his thirteenth-century *vida*: "Jaufres Rudels de Blaia, si fo mout gentils hom, princes de Blaia. Et enamoret se de la comtessa de Tripol, ses vezer per lo ben qu'el n'auzi dire als pelerins que venguen d'Antiocha; e fez de leis mains vers ab bons sons ab paubres motzs. E per voluntat de leis vezer, el se crozet e se mes en mar; e pres lo malautia en la nau, e fo condug a Tripol en un alberc, per mort. E fo fait saber a la comtessa, et ella nenc ad el, al son leit, e pres lo antre sos bratz; e saup qu'ella era la comtessa, e mantenent recobret l'auzir e· l flazar, e lauzet Dieu que l'avia la vida sostenguda tro qu'el l'agues vista. Et enaissi el mori entre sos bratz; et ella lo fez a gran honor sepellir en la maison del Temple, e pois en aquel dia ella se rendet morga, per la dolor qu'ella n'ac de la mort de lui." See J. Boutière and A. H. Schutz, *Biographies des troubadours: textes provençaux des XIIIe et XIVe siècles* (Paris: Éditions A. G. Nizet, 1964), p. 16 f. His poems deal with sensual and earthly love, but they contain a degree of Christian mysticism suggested by the adoration for someone who is far away and who is thus loved from afar. Equicola's most probable source is Petrarch's *Triumph of Desire*.

This story of Jaufré or Geoffroi Rudel of Blaye may well have been the inspiration for Margaret of Navarre's Novel IX of the First Day of the *Heptameron*, in which a young man dies in the arms of a lady who had come to realize her love for him only after he was too sick for love of her to recover. That Ferrand nowhere makes use of these tales of lovesick characters in the corpus of the French *nouvelle* is perhaps to be explained by the vogue of Italian expository books. Such a tale as this would have served his ends very well, for the young man evinces many of the symptoms in his languishing death that Ferrand sets out in subsequent chapters. The story combines melancholy, a wasting sickness, and death from a weakened heart, for "he clasped her again in his embrace with such vehemence, that his enfeebled heart, being unable to sustain the effort, was abandoned by all his spirits; for joy so dilated them, that the seat of the soul gave way and fled to its Creator." His joy was only that of a final embrace that had to serve in the stead of marriage and a long life together, for we are told earlier that "so entirely did he give himself up to despair, that he neither ate, drank, slept, nor rested; and became so lean and wan that he was no longer to be recognized." *The Heptameron of Margaret, Queen of Navarre*, trans. Walter K. Kelley (London, n.d.), pp. 49–51.

9. [*Arist. Prob. 3. sect. 15*]: Aristotle, *Problems*, bk. XV, sec. 3 (910b): "τὸ ἐιεὶ καὶ ἐπὶ πάντων οὐκ ἀπὸ τύχης, ἀλλὰ φυσικόν." See ed. W. S. Hett, p. 329: "το δὲ ἀεὶ καὶ ἐπὶ πάντων οὐκ ἀπὸ τύχης, ἀλλὰ φυσικόν."

10. [*Cels. l. 6. de re medica c. 18. Manard. l. 7. epi. med. epist. 2.*]: Celsus, *De medicina*, bk. VI, ch. 18, ed. W. G. Spencer, 3 vols. (Loeb, 1961), p. 269: "Not even the common use has commended our coarser words for those who would speak with modesty. Hence it is more difficult to set forth these matters and at the same time to observe both propriety and the precepts of the art. Nevertheless, this ought not to deter me from writing, firstly in order that I may include everything which I have heard of as salutary, secondly because their treatment ought above all things to be generally understood, since every one is most unwilling to show such a complaint to another person."

    Giovanni Manardi, *Epistolae medicinales diversorum authorum* (Lugduni: apud haeredes Jacobi Juntae, 1557), p. 43ª: "*De nominibus morborum in exterioribus corporis partibus evenientium.*"

11. Aristarchus, the celebrated Alexandrine critic (born in Samothrace, 160 B.C.), is best known for his scrupulous edition of Homer. His name came to represent any harsh and rigorous form of criticism, usually in the sense of severe but just and enlightened criticism, but here as crabbed and narrow-minded.

12. Juvenal, Satire VI. 196–97: "Quid enim non excitat inguen / Vox blanda et nequam?" See *Juvenal and Persius*, trans. G. G. Ramsay (Loeb, 1961), p. 98.

13. [*Arist. l. 4. de histor. anim. c 9.*]: Aristotle, *History of Animals*, bk. IV, ch. 9 (536a), ed. A. L. Peck, vol. II, p. 81: "The smaller birds are more vocal and chatter more than the larger ones, and every kind of bird is noisiest of all at the pairing season."

14. [*Arist. l. 4. de hist. ani. c. 5.*]: Aristotle, *History of Animals*, bk. IV, ch. 5 is in fact bk. V, ch. 5 (541a), trans. A. L. Peck, vol. II, p. 111: "When female partridges stand to leeward of the males, they become impregnated; they often do so too when they hear the voice of the male, if they are on heat, or when the male flies over them and breathes down on them." The note to this passage suggests that it is out of place and refers to an ancient concept of impregnation by the wind.

15. [*Plaut, in Asin.*]: Plautus, *Asinaria*, ll. 693–94: "dic me tuam / Hirundenem, menedulam, passerculam, putillam." See Plautus, *The Comedy of Asses*, trans. Paul Nixon, 4 vols. (London and New York: G. P. Putnam's Sons, 1916), vol. 1, pp. 198–99: "Dic igitur med aniticulam columbam vel catellum, / hirundinem, monerulam, passerculum putillum." The Greek words quoted in Ferrand's text: "ζωὴ καὶ ψυχή, ὦ φίλη κεφαλή, βάτιόν μου καὶ νιτάριον," and the Latin words: "lux mea, hirundo mea, puta mea, putilla mea," are probably derived from contemporary dictionaries.

16. [*Dios. c. 247 l. 4. Aristoph. in Neb.*]: Dioscorides, *Pharmacorum simplicium . . . Joanne Ruellio interprete* (Argentorato: apud Jo. Schottum, 1529), contains only 205 chapters in book four, and the *preputium* is not mentioned in any of the indexes. Pietro Andrea Mattioli, *Commentarii in libros sex Pedacii Dioscoridis Anazarbei de medica materia* (Venetiis: apud Vincentium Valgrisium, 1558), contains 182 chapters in book four, and the concept is not mentioned in any of the indexes to the six books.

    Aristophanes, *Clouds*. He does not, however, use the word "πόθων" in this play, though it appears in others of his comedies: e.g., *Birds*, l. 362 and *Frogs*, ll. 53, 55, 66, etc. The word means longing or desire.

17. Boethius (Anich Manlius Torquatus Severinus Boetius), *De institutione arithmetica libri duo, de institutione musica, libri quinque*, ed. Godofredus Friedlein (Lipsiae: in aedibus B. G. Teubneri, 1867), pp. 184–85: "Nam cum scortum in rivalis domo esset clausum atque ille furens domum vellet amburere, cumque Pythagoras stellarum cursus, ut ei mos, nocturnus inspiceret, ubi intellexit, sono phrygii modi incitatum multis amicorum monitionibus a facinore noluisse desistere, mutari modum praecepit atque ita furentis animum adulescentis ad statum mentis pacatissimae temperavit."

18. [*Higin. c. 165*]: Julius Hyginus, *Fabularum liber ad omnium poetarum lectionem mire necessarius et nunc denua excusus* (Lugduni: apud Joannem Degabiano, 1608), pp. 36^{r-v}. See also Hyginus, *Fabulae*, ch. 165, "Marsyas," ed. H. I. Rose (Lugduni Batarorum: in aedibus A. W. Sijthoff, 1967), pp. 115–16. The story is also found in Plutarch and Aulus Gellius.

Giovan Battista Fregoso relates a variant on the story in his *Contramours*, p. 106: "L'Athenien Alcibiade, mené chez un musicien joüeur d'instrumens, pour apprendre a sonner des flutes: quand il vid la difformité du visage des corneurs et flusteurs, qui faisoyent la moüe, ou enfloyent les joües en flustant et cornant: émeu de la lassivie de tel exercise, rompit les instruments qu'on luy presenta; et n'en voulu onques apprendre."

19. Henricus Cornelius Agrippa from Nettesheim, *De vanitate scientiarum*, ch. 64, "De lenonia," in *Operum pars posterior* (Lugduni: per Beringos Fratres, c. 1550), p. 129, is the likely source for Ferrand's list of names of those who wrote trifles concerning lovers' salutations: "multi etiam inter praeclaros scriptores istis operam navarunt: cuiusmodi ex recentioribus Aeneas Sylvius, Dantes, Petrarcha, Bocatius, Pontanus, Baptista de Campofragoso, et alter Baptista de Albertis Florentinus: item Petrus Hoe[d]ius, et Petrus Bembus, Jacobus Caviceus, et Jacobus Calandrus, Mantuanus, et multi alii, inter quos tamen Joannes Bocatius, superatis omnibus, lenonum palmam sibi lucratus est." On the previous page he mentions "Trithemius Abbas Spanheimen sis duo ingeniosa volumina, quorum unum nuncupavit Polygraphia alterum Steganographiae." More particularly, they are: Aeneas Sylvius Piccolomini (Pope Pius II), *Le remède d'amour, translaté de latin en françoys par maistre Albin des Avenelles, avec les additions de Baptiste Mantuan* (Paris: n.p., 1556); Giacomo Caviceo, *Le Peregrin. Dialogue treselegant intitulé le Peregrin traictant de l'honneste et pudique amour concisie par pure et sincere vertu traduict de vulgaire italien en langue francoyse par maistre Francoys Dassy* (Lyon: Claude Nourry, [1528]) containing many pages of words and phrases for making elegant and amorous speeches. Johann von Tritheim, *Steganographia: hoc est: ars per occultam scripturam animi sui voluntatem absentibus aperiendi certa* (Darmbstadii: ex officina typographica Balthasaris Aulaeandri; sumptibus vero Joannis Berni, 1621). Tritheim provides an elaborate defense of the practical and utilitarian values of secret writing in the Proemium to the *Clavis steganographie*, suggesting reasons of state. But essentially it was a form

of erudite game enabling lovers to pass secret messages based on a system of numerological equivalents for elements in various occult systems such as the ten angels, Gabriel, Raphael, etc. A sample (Liber secundus, p. 103) reads: "Quabriel, odiel, amear, cayn alco mean chyr pareas payr peray." Translated, they offer compliments, suggest trysting places, and urge secrecy on the part of the other.

20. Philostratus, *Les images*, trans. Blaise de Vigenère (Paris, 1614; rpt. New York: Garland Publishing, 1976), "Venus Elephantine," pp. 279–80.

Plutarch, *Life of Alexander*, in *Lives*, ed. B. Perrin (Loeb, 1919), vol. VII, p. 233.

21. Ferrand will elaborate on these and related topics in his ch. XXX on the prevention of love melancholy, though much of that material is anticipated in passing here, possibly as a result of an imperfect subdividing of references and allusions taken from the edition of 1610, which Ferrand disperses in this much expanded version.

22. Lucretius, *De rerum natura*, bk. IV. 1283–85: "Consuetudo concinnat amorem: / Nam leviter quamvis, quod crebro tunditur ictu, / Vincitur in longo spatio tamen, atque labascit." See trans. W. H. D. Rouse (Loeb, 1966), p. 338.

23. Achilles landed at Scyros and formally married Deidamia on his way to the Trojan War. See, e. g., Philostratus, *Heroica*, bk. III, ch. 35, and Apollodorus, *Epitome*, bk. III, ch. 18, trans. Sir J. G. Frazer, 2 vols. (Loeb, 1956).

24. Giovanni Battista Spagnuoli called Mantuano, *Opera omnia in quatuor tomos distincta, pluribus libris aucta* (Antwerpiae: apud J. Bellerum, 1576). We have not been able to examine this work.

The reference from Blaise de Vigenère will be found in his commentaries to *Philostrate de la vie d'Apollonius Thyaneen en VIII livres* (Paris: Chez la veufue Matthieu Guillemot, 1611).

Pierre Belon du Mans, *L'histoire de la nature des oyseaux, avec leurs descriptions; et naifs portraicts . . . en sept livres* (Paris: Chez Guillaume Cavellat, 1555), *sub voce*.

Aristotle, *History of Animals*, bk. IV, ch. 1 (559a), trans. A. L. Peck (Loeb, 1970), vol. II, p. 222, speaks of the thrushes (κίκλαι). There are several subsequent references. But for the relationship between laughter and the fieldfare, see Aristophanes, *The Clouds*, l. 1073, trans. Benjamin Bickley Rogers (Loeb, 1967), p. 362: "κιχλισμῶν."

25. [*Pausan. in Att. Cic. 2 de nat. deor.*]: Pausanias, *Description of Greece*, "Attica." He refers several times to shrines dedicated to the cult of Aphrodite, but he nowhere specifically mentions her relationship to the genitals of Kronus. The story originates in Hesiod, who claimed that she was born of the foam that gathered around the genitals of Uranus as they floated in the sea toward Cyprus, after his castration by Kronus. See Mircea Eliade, *A History of Religious Ideas*, 2 vols. (Chicago: University of Chicago Press, 1978), vol. I, pp. 282–83.

Cicero, *De natura deorum*, bk. II, 27, trans. H. Rackham (Loeb, 1961), p. 191: "Venus was so named by our countrymen as the goddess who 'comes' (*venire*) to all things; her name is not derived from the word *venustas* (beauty) but rather *venustas* from it."

Hesiod, *The Homeric Hymns and Homerica*, "To Aphrodite," trans. Hugh G. Evelyn-White (Loeb, 1982), bk. V, l. 17, p. 406: "φιλομμειδής," laughter-loving.

For an explanation of the relationship between μηδέα and the genitals of Kronus, see M. L. West's introduction to Hesiod's *Theogony* (Oxford: Clarendon Press, 1966), p. 86.

26. [*Martial*]: Martial, *Epigrams*, bk. VII, no. XXV. 5–6:

Nec cibus ipse iuvat morsu fraudatus aceti,
Nec facies grata est, cui gelasinus abest.

Ed. Walter C. A. Ker, 2 vols. (Loeb, 1919), vol. I, p. 438. Verse 6 in the modern edition reads: "Nec grata est facies."

27. [*L. I. Anthol.*]: Moschus, "Fugitive Love," in the *Greek Anthology*, bk. IX, epigram 440. Ferrand's quotation, "sunt oscula noxia, in ipsis / Sunt venena labris" is a direct translation into Latin of l. 27. For a modern edition of the *Anthology*, see trans. W. R. Paton, 5 vols. (Loeb, 1948), vol. III, p. 245.

28. [*L. 3. c. 4*]: Michel de Montaigne, *Essais*, ed. Maurice Rat (Paris: Garniers Frères, 1962), bk. III, ch. 5, vol. II, p. 310: "Voyer combien la forme des salutations, qui est particuliere à nostre nation, abastardit par sa facilité la grace des baisers, lesquels Socrates dit estre si puissans et dangereux à volet nos cueurs. C'est une desplaisante coustume, et injurieuse aux dames, d'avoir à prester leurs lévres à quiconque a trois valets à sa suitte, pour mal plaisant qu'il soit."

29. [*L. 1. de cau. procat. c. 1*]; Galen, *De causis procatarcticis liber*, bk. I, ch. 1, in *Galeni Opera*, vol. II, p. 495.

30. [*L. de aëre, loc. & ag.*]: Hippocrates, *Of Airs, Waters and Places*, in *Oeuvres complètes*, ed. Littré, vol. II, p. 75 ; see Ferrand's ch. XXXI, n. 6, for the text.

31. [*l. 3. fen 20. tr. 1. c. 25*]: Avicenna, *Liber canonis*, bk. III, fen 20, tr. 1, ch. 25, p. 375^V–76^r: "De multitudine desiderij."

32. [*Sect. 4 Probl. 26*]: Aristotle, *Problems*, bk. IV, no. 28, trans. W. S. Hett, vol. I, p. 131: "Why are men more inclined for sexual intercourse in winter and women in summer? Is it because men are naturally inclined to be hot and dry, but women are moist and chilled? In men the moisture and warmth lead to desire in the winter (the production of semen arises from these), but in women the heat is less and the moisture is congealed owing to lack of warmth; and this occurs in summer. In women the heat is balanced, but in men it is more than sufficient; and its excess weakens much of their power."

Hesiod, "Works and Days," *The Homeric Hymns and Homerica*, trans. Hugh G. Evelyn-White (Loeb, 1982), p. 47: "But when the artichoke flowers, and the chirping grass-hopper sits in a tree and pours down his shrill song continually from under his wings in the season of wearisome heat, then goats are plumpest and wine sweetest; women are most wanton, but men are feeblest, because Sirius parches head and knees and the skin is dry through heat."

Jean Aubery, *L'antidote d'amour*, p. 28^V argues out of the aphorisms of Hippocrates [aph. 20, sec. 3] that spring is the time most propitious for love, while elsewhere it is argued that winter is the more condusive time because the natural heat necessary to resist the cold also creates the conditions for love [aph. 15, sec. 1]. By sleeping longer, eating more meat that creates blood, the ticklings of desire are incited. But then the heat of summer would seem to produce exactly those same conditions, though Aubery goes to some length to explain away the difficulties: "concluons que l'amour se peut engendier en toutes natures, aages, habitudes, seize saisons et regions, la seule difference gardee de plus ou de moins" (p. 29^r).

33. Hippocrates, *Of Airs, Waters and Places*: "τῇσιν ὥρῃσι καὶ αἱ κοιλίαι μεταβάλλουσι, διότι οὐκ ἐλάχιστον μέρος ξυνβάλλεται ἀστρονομίη εἰς ἰητρικὴν." *Oeuvres complètes*, ed. Littré, vol. II, p. 15. The complete text of Hippocrates reads: "Εἰ δὲ δοκέοι τις ταῦτα μετεωρολόγα εἶναι, εἰ μετασταίη τῆς γνώμης, μάθοι ἂν ὅτι οὐκ ἐλάχιστον μέρος ξυμβάλλεται ἀστρονομίη ἐς ἰητρικήν, ἀλλὰ πάνυ πλεῖστον. Ἅμα γὰρ τῇσιν ὥρῃσι καὶ αἱ κοιλίαι μεταβάλλουσι τοῖσιν ἀνθρώποισιν." Ferrand rearranges and edits Hippocrates' text.

34. [*Valeriola l. 6. anar. c. 2 Mizald. in Plat. Aleman. in l. de aere, loc. & aq. D. Hieron. ep. ad Paul*]: François Valleriola, *Observationum medicinalium libri VI*, bk. VI, ana. ii, "probat astrologiam medico esse necessariam"; Antoine Mizauld, *L'explication, usage et practique de l'Ephemeride celeste* (Paris: Chez Jacques Kerver, 1556); Adrien Aleman, (L'Alemant), ed., *Hippocratis de aere, aquis et locis . . . liber commentariis illustratus* (Parisiis: apud Aegidium Gorbinum, 1557); St. Jerome, "Epistola 10 ad Paulum senem concordiae" in *Opera* (Parisiis: apud Claudium Rigaud, 1706). This list of scholars does not represent original research on Ferrand's part, for the names are taken together from the marginal citations of a work by Jean Taxil, *L'astrologie et physiognomie en leur splendeur* (Tournon: par R. Reynaud, Libraire juré d'Arles, 1614), pp. 31–33: "Ptolomaeus (inquit Mizaldus) testatur Aegyptos praedictionibus astronomicis ubique medicinam adjunxisse, ut, et futuri mali aversio, et praesentim curatio perspecta eis esse melius. Aleman, docte Medecin n'a donc pas moins de grace, que de raison, de dire commentant Hippocrate, que le medecin ignorant de l'astrologie est semblable au nautonnier, qui single en mer sans rames ny gouvernail. Sine clavo ac remis navigat naufragum tandem facturus, qui absque ulla temporum, et astrorum observatione medicinam factitat. Est enim astrologia (dit le mesme) medici oculus cuius si fuerit expers merito coecus appellabitur. Que dites vous, sainct Hierosme? estes vous d'opinion que la science du ciel soit du tout inutile, comme ce magot s'est indignement efforcé d'asseurer? Non de vray, vous n'estes pas de cest advis, car vous nous avez laissé par vos saincts escrits que l'astronomie, et l'astrologie sont utiles, et necessaires aux humains."

The *Ephemeride celeste* of Mizaldus was one of the most accessible books of its kind in the period, clearly declaring the techniques by which predictions can be made based on the planets. "Qui sera cause que je me contenterai d'escrire par quelz planetes sont excitez les ventz, et par quelz signes, et en quel temps ilz doibuent regner, avecques leurs dispositions et qualitez: chose certs tresutile: car d'elle dependent les principaulx jugementz de l'air, et predictions, je ne dirai des bonnes et mauvaises saisons de l'annee, mais aussi bien et seurement semer, naviger, planter, prevoir maladies, et autres secretz"(p. 42^r).

35. [*Probl. 1. Sect. 14*]: Aristotle, *Problems*, bk. XIV, no. 1 (909a): "ἀρίστη κρᾶσις καὶ τῇ διανοίᾳ συμφέρει." Trans. W. S. Hett, pp. 316–17: "Why are those who live in conditions of excessive cold or heat beast-like both in habits and in appearance? Are both results due to the same cause? For the best mixture benefits the mind but excesses disturb it, and just as they cause distortion to the body, so do they also affect the mental temperament."

36. Galen, *De temperamentis*, ed. Kühn, vol. I, pp. 509–694.

37. [*L. 3. contra. gent. c. 86*]: St. Thomas Aquinas, *Summa Theologica*, III, 83: "indirecta motione et contingenter, non directa et necessario: Judicia quippe Astrologorum sunt media inter necessarium et possibile." See *Somme de la foi catholique contre les Gentils*, (French and Latin texts), trans. M. L'Abbé P. -F. Ecalle (Paris: Louis Vivès, 1856), vol. III, pp. 43–44: "Ptolomaeus etiam in Quadripartito dicit: rursus nec aestimare debemus quod superiora procedunt inevitabiliter, ut ea quae divina dispositione contingunt et quae nullatenus sunt vitanda, nec non quae veraciter et ex necessitate proveniunt. In Centiloquio etiam dicit: 'Haec indicia quae tibi trado sunt media inter necessarium et possibile.' " See also St. Thomas Aquinas, *Summa contra Gentiles*, in *Opera omnia*, ed. Stanislaus Fretté (Paris: apud Ludovicum Vivès, 1872), vol. XII, pp. 366–68.

38. [*Gal. l. de caus. procat. c. 1. 1. Introd. in puls. & 1. l. de feb.*]: Galen, *De causis procatarcticis liber*, bk. I, ch. 1, in *Galeni opera*, vol. II, p. 495.

   Galen, *De febrium differentiis liber*, bk. I, ed. Kühn, vol. VII, pp. 273 ff. In both places Galen speaks of the excessive heat generated by the dog star and of its influence on fever.

   Galen, *De causis pulsuum*, ch. 1, ed. Kühn, vol. IX, p. 1 ff.

39. Juvenal, Satire X. 48–50: "Democriti sapientia monstrat / Summos posse viros, et magna exempla daturos, / Vervecum in patria, crassoque sub aere nasci." See trans. G. G. Ramsay (Loeb, 1961), p. 198. Ferrand adds "Democriti," in keeping with Juvenal's context.

40. Galen, *On the Affected Parts*, bk. VI, ch. 6, trans. Siegel, p. 197: "There are some foodstuffs which produce much sperm and, therefore, stimulate the desire for intercourse." See below, ch. XXX, esp. n. 29.

41. See esp. ch. XXX, nn. 35–41, below.

42. Menander (falsely att. to):

   ἔρως γὰρ ἀργὸν, κ'απὶ τοῖς ἀργοῖς ἔφυ,

   φιλεῖ κάτοπτρα καὶ κόμης ξανθίσματα,

   φεύγει δὲ μόχθους.

   The fragment is from Euripides' *Danaes*, in Stobaeus, *Anthologium*, bk. IV, ch. 20, sec. 40 (frag. 322 N.²). The confusion stems from the fact that the preceding fragment (no. 39), from Menander, also refers to ἔρως.

43. [*L. 7. Anthol.*]: This reference is set in the margin opposite a line in Latin, but in fact refers to Philodemus whose poem in the anthology inspired his comments about dancing, music and effeminate behaviour. *Greek*

Anthology, ed. W. R. Paton (Loeb, 1948), bk. VII, no. 222, p. 127. The unidentified Latin line is as follows: "Scalpuntur ubi intima versu."

44. Virgil, Eclogue III. 64: "Malo me Galataea petit lasciva puella." See trans. H. Rushton Fairclough (Loeb, 1965), vol. II, p. 22.

Theocritus, ed. A. S. F. Gow. Apples are mentioned as love gifts in Idyll III. 8–9, vol. I, p. 31; in Idyll VI. 6–7, vol. I, p. 53, he recounts how Galatea expresses her scorn for Polyphemus by calling him cursed in love, a goatherd, and by pelting his flocks with apples; Idyll XI. 10–11, vol. I, p. 87: "And he loved not with apples, or roses, or ringlets, but with downright frenzy, counting all else but trifles."

Philostratus, *Love Letters,* ed. Allen Rogers and Francis H. Forbes (Loeb, 1949), letter 63, p. 531. The apple was the traditional gift of love given to the fairest woman.

45. Horace, *Epistles* I. i. 78: "Frustis et pomis viduas venentur avaras." See *Satires, Epistles, and Ars Poetica,* trans. H. Rushton Fairclough (Loeb, 1961), p. 256.

In ch. 22 of the edition of 1610 Ferrand elaborates that "Aristophanes, speaking of the caresses with which a certain courtesan tried to lure a young wencher, tells how she oftentimes would strike him with half-eaten apples."

46. Lucian, *Toxaris or Friendship* in *Lucian,* trans. A. M. Harmon, 8 vols. (Loeb, 1962), vol. V, p. 125: "Notes from the woman kept coming into his house; also, half-faded wreaths, apples with a piece bitten out, and every other contrivance with which go-betweens lay siege to young men, gradually working up their love-affairs for them and inflaming them at the start with the thought that they are adored (for this is extremely seductive, especially to those who think themselves handsome), until they fall unawares into the net."

47. Giovanni Pierio Valeriano Bolzani [Jan-Pierre Valerian; Pierius], *Les hieroglyphiques nouvellement donnez aux François, par I. de Montlyart* (Lyon: par Paul Frellon, 1615), "La Douceur," ch. 29, pp. 713 ff.: "Or son principal hieroglyphique est de signifier la douceur; et ce tant pour exprimer l'agreable conversation et gracieusité des hommes, que les autres choses amiables et recreatifues," followed by several examples and quotations.

48. Hippocrates, *Aphorisms,* bk. II, no. 3: "somnus et vigilia, utraque si modum excesserint, malum." *Aphorismi Hippocratis Graecae et Latinae una cum Galeni commentariis, interprete Nicolao Leoniceno Vicentino* (Parisiis: ex officina Jacobi Bogardi, 1542), p. 30^r: "somnus atque vigilia, utrumque si modum excesserit malum." Ferrand read only the aphorisms of Hippocrates in Latin. We have also consulted the two following Renaissance editions in an attempt to find the exact wording used in the three he cites (see also n. 53 and ch. XII, n. 5, below): ed. Gulielmum Plautium Cenomanum (Lugduni: apud Guil. Rovilium , 1555) and ed. Jöannem Frerum (Londini: apud G. Seresium, 1567).

49. [*Avic. l. 3. fen 20 tr. 1 c. 25*]: Avicenna, *Liber canonis,* bk. III, fen 20, tr. 1, ch. 25, p. 376^r: "Et dormire super dorsum est de facientibus erectionem." This dictum was repeated by many of the Renaissance physicians.

50. [*L. 6. c. 6.*]: Galen, *On the Affected Parts,* bk. VI, ch. 6, trans. Siegel, p. 197:

"This occurs in persons who have much sperm but remain continent at the same time, contrary to their usual behavior. By lack of much exercise these patients fail to get rid of an excess of blood, particularly when they do not refrain from erotic ideas. Likewise do persons suffer who are chaste by nature and accustomed to self-control over a long time but who indulge in [erotic] imaginations in order to stimulate themselves by such spectacles and memories."

51. Galen, *On the Affected Parts*, bk. VI, ch. 6: "Equidem, novi quosdam, quibus huiusmodi erat natura, qui prae pudore a libidinis usu abhorrentes torpidi, pigrique facti sunt: nonnulli etiam melancholicorum instar, praeter modum moesti ac timidi, cibi etiam tum cupiditate, tum concoctione vitiata. Quidam uxoris mortem lugens, et a concubitu, quo antea creberrime fuerat usus, abstinens, cibi cipiditatem amisit, atque ne exiguum quidem cibum concoquere potuit. Ubi vero seipsum cogendo, plus cibi ingerebat, protinus ad vomitum excitabatur: moestus etiam apparebat, non solum has ob causas, sed etiam ut melancholici solent citra manifestam occasionem." See trans. Siegel, p. 184.

52. Galen, *On the Affected Parts*, bk. VI, ch. 6: "Qui protinus iuventute prima immodice sese permiserunt libidini, id etiam evenit, ut horum locorum vasa amplius patentia maiorem ad se sanguinis copiam alliciant, et coeundi cupiditas magis increscat." See trans. Siegel, p. 197. For the Latin texts, see *De locis affectis*, in *Opera*, ed. Kühn, vol. VIII, pp. 377–52.

53. Hippocrates, *Aphorisms*, bk. VI, no. 23: "si metus et moestitia perseveraverint melancholia fit." *Aphorismi Hippocratis Graecae et Latinae*, p. 147[r]: "si timor atque moestitia longo tempore perseverent, ex eo atro bilis significatur."

54. [*Gal. l. de praecogn ex puls. & l 4. de caus. puls.*]: Galen, *De praesagitione ex pulsu*, bk. IV, chs. 8–9, ed. Kühn, vol. IX, pp. 405–16.

 Galen, *De causis pulsuum*, bk. IV, ed. Kühn, vol. IX, pp.156–204. Book four raises general questions about the pulse in relation to diseases of the emotions, including those arising from fear and sorrow.

55. Plato, *Symposium* (203c), ed. W. R. M. Lamb, p. 180.

56. [*Propert.*]: Propertius, *The Elegies*, bk. II, XXII. 18: "Me fortuna aliquid semper amare dedit." See trans. H. E. Butler, p. 124.

57. Pausanias, *Description of Greece*, "Attica," bk. I, ch. 43; vol. III, p. 235: "Near the temple of Aphrodite is a sanctuary of Fortune, the image being one of the works of Praxiteles."

 Theocritus, ed. A. S. F. Gow, vol. I, p. 33; Idyll, III. 40–42: "Hippomenes, when he would wed the maid, took apples in his hand and ran his course; and Atalanta saw, and frenzy seized her and deep in love she plunged."

58. Ovid, *The Art of Love*, bk. II. 63–64: "Secum habet ingenium, qui cum licet, Accipe, dicit. / Cedimus, inventis plus valet ille meis." See *The Art of Love, and Other Poems*, trans. J. H. Mozley (Loeb, 1962), p. 76.

VII.   The Internal Causes of Love Melancholy

1. Ovid, *Heroides* XV. 79–80: "Molle meum livibus cor est violabile telis: / Haec semper causa est cur ego semper amem." See ed. Henricus Dörrie, p. 318.
2. [*Cap. 88. art. med.*]: Galen, *Ars medicinalis*, in *Operum Galeni libri isagogici artis medicae*, ch. 88, "*De solutione continuitatis*," p. 225 f.
3. Hippocrates, *On the Nature of Man*, ch. 5, ed. Littré, vol. VI, p. 42.
4. [*Valeriola obs. 7. l. 2.*]: François Valleriola, *Observationum medicinalium libri sex*, bk. II, obs. 7, p. 196.

Battista Fregoso, *Contramours*, p. 173. There was considerable discussion throughout the preceding century of the role played by the seed in causing love. The debate goes back in part to the implications of Avicenna's recommendation that intercourse was a form of cure because it reduced the quantity of sperm. Baptiste, the persona of Fregoso in the dialogue on love, argues that the presence of seed is the cause of love itself. Claude argues rather for spirits, diminishing the influence of Avicenna in the following way: "Semblablement, combien que Constantin et Avicenne (comme vous disiez) en la cure de la maladie d'Amour, mettent l'embrassement et copulation charnelle, pour le plus propre et le plus souverain reméde: toutesfois si de plus prés vous prenez garde a leur conclusion; ils résouldent, que la parfaite cure de ceste maladie, est l'embrassement; mais de la personne aymée. Au demourant, ils sont bien d'accord que l'embrassement des autres femmes donne quelque alégeance a ce mal; mais non que du tout il le guérisse; ains que seulement il diminue une partie de la nourriture, qui donne a ce feu son embrasement. Mais pource ne faut il conclure, comme de nécéssaire argument; combien qu'il soit maniféste, que la genitale semence nourrit le feu amoureux; qu'elle en soit la source, et principale origine" (p. 173). Here is a variant on the argument against Avicenna, largely on moral grounds despite the argument in other terms, for using coitus as a cure for love. Ferrand does not examine in detail the elements on the two sides of this argument, largely out of an inability to reconcile medical terms and conclusions with moral reticenses.

Fregoso explains the mechanism in the following terms: "Pourtant est il bien aisé a croire, que la racine de cest ardent et mouvant appetit, naist du corps, par le moyen du sperme: lequel chatoillant les vaisseaux seminaires, par les esprits, et ventositez, esquels il se resoult; émeut un desir de confriction, qui est la conjonction charnelle: et nous moleste et presse de jetter dehors cest humeur excrémenteux" (p. 140).

The other approach to the reduction of semen acceptable to Ferrand was the employment of foods and pharmaceutical preparations. Levinus Lemnius provides a representative statement on the means for controlling the superfluous production of seed in *Occulta naturae miracula* (Gandavi: ex officina Gisleni Manilii, 1572), bk. I, ch. 9, p. 43: "Inter ea autem quae Venerem excitant, ac seminis generationi sunt accommoda, cibi numerantur laudabilis succi, quique probe nutriunt, ac corpus vegetum reddunt, ac succulentum: cuius facultatis sunt calidae et humida. Conficitur enim, Galeno teste, seminis substantia ex syncera excoctaque sanguinis superfluitate, simul et flatuosa. Plerisque autem vis inest augendi cumulandique seminis. Nonnullis efficacia incitandae movendeque tentiginis, atque humoris propellendi." See also ch. XXXIX, nn. 19 and 21. N. 21 contains the list of foods given by Lemnius for increasing the production of semen, and therefore foods to be avoided by melancholy lovers whose condition is either caused by excess seed or is aggravated by its presence.

It is at this point in the argument that Ferrand departs in the present edition from the corresponding place in his edition of 1610. Here he develops the central theory of the adustion of yellow or black bile (natural melancholy) or of blood in the hypochondries. This medical explanation is weakly expressed in the former treatise, and in its place Ferrand states that at puberty men have bodies as though full and souls as if pregnant, and that they are visited by a powerful desire to engender children, to seek their immortality in fertility, and that two types of men emerge: those who address women directly to those ends and those who honor the image of the beloved, intending by that course to arrive at a possession of divine beauty. This reflection of the dual pattern of love, shaped no doubt by his reading of Ficino and Equicola, is entirely suppressed in the 1623 edition. He appears to have dismissed the more transcendental forms of erotic passion in favor of an entirely medical analysis that does not allow for aesthetic or sublimational dimensions. Ferrand thereby outlines an essentially bourgeois view of love that accepts only conventional marriage and marital friendship.

5. [*Probl. 31. Sect. 4.*]: Aristotle, *Problems*, bk. IV, sec. 30 (880a): "οἱ μελαγχολι-κοί ἀφροδισιαστικοί." See trans. W. S. Hett (Loeb, 1953), pp. 132–33: "Why are the melancholic inclined to sexual intercourse? Is it because they are full of breath and semen is an emission of breath? Those therefore who have a quantity of semen which is full of breath must often desire to be purged of it; for by this means they are relieved." Aristotle's text reads: "διὰ τί ἀφροδισιαστικοί οἱ μελαγχολικοί."

6. [*Corn. Gall.*]: Cornelius Gallus, Elegy II. 15: "Nauseat, et priscum vomitu ceu fundit amorem." *Catullus, Tibullus, Propertius cum Galli fragmentis* (Biponti: ex typographia societatis, 1783), p. 327. Read "fundat."

7. Jean Liébault, *Des maladies des femmes*, bk. I ch. 39, pp. 65–69. Liébault writes a chapter on young married couples who, even in marriage, become far too ardent in their passion and excessive in their desires, thereby risking the loss of their forces. In keeping with the medical logic of the age, he traces this condition to physiological origins, including the good health and sanguine complexions of youth: "Quelquesfois la semence retenue par trop long temps, laquelle est comme un venin mortel en nostre corps, principalement de ceux qui sont du naturel susdit, ésquels petite quantité de semence est assez suffisante pour conforter le coeur, et entretenir le corps en ses forces, mais trop long temps retenue se corrompt facilement, pour sa subtilité et delicatesse, ains gaste le bon teinct, debilite la memoire, et rend l'entendement tout hebeté et eslourdy: qui plus est, excite des accidens merveilleux, principalement és femmes

sanguines et succulentes; ainsi qu'avons discouru cy devant: Quelquesfois aussi, non seulement la trop grande abondance de la semence, mais
aussi l'acrimonie et chaleur d'icelle stimule la concupiscence charnelle:
aucunesfois l'excessive chaleur des lombes et vaisseaux spermatiques qui
attirent incessamment la matiere seminale: ou, la debilité d'iceux, qui
reçoivent plus grande quantité de sperme que n'est besoin; ou, quelque
prurit et demangeson provenante d'un humeur acre, salé et sereux qui
excite un desir insatiable és parties honteuse, ainsi que nous voyons advenir en la bouche de l'amarry: ou, abondance de ventositez retenues,
ainsi que nous observons le plus souvent és melancholiques atrabiliaires,
lesquels à raison des vents dont ils sont pleins, tombent souvent, ainsi
que dit Hippocrate en un priapisme ou satyriase: ou le dormir assidu
sur le dos en lict de plumes, ou plusieurs autres cause."

8. [*Part. 2. com. 12*]: In the text Ferrand refers specifically to Galen's second
commentary on Hippocrates' *Epidemics*, bk. VI, but the reference is, in
fact, to Galen's third commentary on Hippocrates' *Epidemics*, bk. VI,
ch. 12, ed. Kühn, vol. XVII/2, pp. 25 ff. The following reference to
Aristotle's *Problems* (see n. 9, below) comes from Galen.

9. [*Probl. 7. Sect. 29.*]: Aristotle, *Problems*, bk. XXX, sec. 1 (953b). See trans.
W. S. Hett (Loeb, 1957), vol. II, p. 159: "the melancholic are usually
lustful."

10. Giovanni Battista Silvatico, *Controversiae medicae numero centum*, pp. 1–3.
    Jean Aubery, *L'antidote d'amour*, pp. 27^r–28^v, is more explicit on the
subject of the natural temperaments inclined to love. He joins his discussion with speculations on the relative heats of men and women, a topic
Ferrand deals with in his ch. XXVIII. Aubery states that "les sanguins
qui sont chaults et humides, sont plus disposez à recevoir le caractere
de l'amour, ils ont une foye liberal à transmuer le chile en sang, comme
estant la fontaine de la gratieuse et moite vapeur cause materielle de
l'amour [Hippocr. li. de genit.]." The bilious with their hot, dry temperament are like dry kindling and very vulnerable to love and quick to
seek pleasure, "mais moins capables d'un amour dilayé." "Les phlegmatiques et melancholiques n'en sont exempts, mais il faut beaucoup de
flammes pour fondre les glaçons des uns, et beaucoup d'arres de faveurs
pour asseurer la crainte des autres, les poëtes nous feignent le Neptune
amoureux, et les nayades brusler dans le froid crystal de leurs eaux, et
le Pluton terrestre et melancholique avoir enlevé Proserpine dans les in-
fernales ombres, qui ont bruit de plus grand effroy que d'amour, mais
les phlegmatiques et melancholiques sçavent mieux prendre leur pair en
amour, que les autres, et le loisir de mieux recognoistre l'humeur du sujet
aymé pour s'y accommoder, toutes fois telles ames molles et terrestres,
son insensibles aux pointes des desdains, esquelles s'emoussent dans
leurs froides contenances." For such reasons as are implied here, Ferrand sees the need to distinguish melancholy temperament from adust
melancholy that arises from burning the other humors. Yet the theory
of causes does not remain entirely uncompromised because there is the
related question having to do with the natural melancholy in the brain
that is cold and dry, generated by the long meditation upon the object

of beauty. How is it that a single object can cause both cold deliberation in the brain breeding one kind of melancholy and a hot ferment in the blood that in turn rises to the brain in fumes to cause a second set of conditions? Ferrand simply treats these contributing mechanisms in their respective places in the general program of causes relating to erotic melancholy without mention of conflict. They were both too integral to the established traditions to raise particular notice.

VIII.   Of the Generation of Love Melancholy

1. [*Dulaurens c. 10 des mal Melanch.*]: André Du Laurens, *Des maladies melancholiques, et du moyen de les guarir*, ch. 10, p. 34ᵛ. "L'amour doncques ayant abusé les yeux, comme vrays espions et portiers de l'ame, se laisse tout doucement glisser par des canaux, et cheminant insensiblement par les veines jusques au foye, imprime soudain un desir ardent de la chose qui est, ou paroist aimable, allume ceste concupiscence, et commence par ce desir toute la sedition: mais craignant d'estre trop foible pour renverser la raison, partie souveraine de l'ame, s'en va droit gaigner le coeur, duquel s'estant une fois asseurée comme de la plus forte place, attaque apres si vivement la raison et toutes ses puissances nobles, qu'elle se les assubjettit, et rend du tout esclaves. Tout est perdu pour lors, c'est faict de l'homme, les sens sont esgarez, la raison est troublée, l'imagination depravée, les discours sont fols, le pauvre amoureux ne se represente plus rien que son idole: toutes les actions du corps sont pareillement perverties; il devient palle, maigre, transi, sans appetit, ayant les yeux caves et enfoncez, et ne peut (comme dit le Poëte) voir la nuict, ny des yeux, ny de la poictrine; Tu le verras pleurant, sanglottant et souspirant coup sur coup, et en une perpetuelle inquietude, fuyant toutes les compagnies, aymant la solitude pour entretenir ses pensées; la crainte la combat d'un costé, et le desespoir bien souvent de l'autre." There can be little doubt that Ferrand is working with Du Laurens' text in hand throughout this opening passage. Du Laurens, himself, is working in the spirit of another, namely Marsilio Ficino, to whom Ferrand turns next for his inspiration for much that follows in the chapter.

2. [*Lucret.*]: Lucretius, *De rerum natura*, bk. IV. 1059–60: "illae primae Veneris dulcedinis in cor stillavit gutta, et successit frigida cura." See ed. W. H. D. Rouse, p. 322. This quotation was suggested, no doubt, by its appearance in Ficino's *Commentary*, Speech VII, ch. 5. Ficino understands these verses to reveal how the spirit emitted by the eye travels through the eye of the beholder and penetrates the entrails, thereby initiating the disease of love, and how that spirit must by nature be light, clear, warm, and soft.

3. Ferrand does not identify the poet in question because he is still paraphrasing Du Laurens, who also leaves the poet unidentified. See n. 1, above, for the text.

4. [*C. 3. 9. & 10. orat. 7*]: Marsilio Ficino, *Commentary on Plato's Symposium*

on Love, Speech VII, chs. 4, 5, 10, pp. 159–63, 166–67. The following is from ch. 4, pp. 160–61: "Therefore, what wonder is it if the eye, wide open and fixed upon someone, shoots the darts of its own rays into the eyes of the bystander, and along with those darts, which are the vehicles of the spirits, aims that sanguine vapor which we call spirit? Hence, the poisoned dart pierces through the eyes, and because it is shot from the heart of the shooter, it seeks again the heart of the man being shot, as its proper home; it wounds the heart, but in the heart's hard back wall it is blunted and turns back into blood. This foreign blood, being somewhat foreign to the nature of the wounded man, infects his blood. The infected blood becomes sick. Hence follows a double bewitchment. The sight of a stinking old man or a woman suffering her period bewitches a boy. The sight of a young man bewitches an older man. But since the humor of an older man is cold and very slow, it hardly reaches the back of the heart in the boy, and ill-fitted for passing across, moves the heart entirely too little, unless on account of infancy it is very tender. Therefore this is a light bewitchment."

François Valleriola, *Observationum medicinalium libri VI*, pp. 196–205, draws on Ficino for his lengthy discussion of the role of the eyes in causing love, a passage Ferrand knew well. Ferrand was, nevertheless, not inclined to develop these theories as extensively as Valleriola in order to avoid conflict with the Galenic mechanisms explaining the causes of love in terms of the humors.

5. [*Mars. Ficin. c. 10*]: Marsilio Ficino, *Commentary on Plato's Symposium on Love*, Speech VII, ch. 10, p. 166: "How lovers are bewitched we seem to have explained sufficiently above, if only we may add that mortals are bewitched the most when, by very frequent gazing, directing their sight eye to eye, they join lights with lights and drink a long love together, poor wretches. As Musaeus says, the whole cause and origin of this illness is certainly the eye. For this reason anyone who is powerful in the shining of his eyes, even if he is less attractive in his other parts, drives people mad who look at him very often, for the reason we have given."

6. [*M. de Montagne*]: In citing Michel de Montaigne concerning the Scyths, Ferrand must have had in mind the passage in bk. I, ch. 20, of the *Essays* where he speaks of the women of Scythia who could kill by their look. For the origins of the reference to Jaufré Rudel and to Petrarch, see the passage from Mario Equicola set out in ch. VI, n. 8, above.

The original reference is to *Herodotus*, trans. A. D. Godley (Loeb, 1963), bk. IV, ch. 1, vol. II, pp. 199–201: "Now the Scythians blind all their slaves, by reason of the milk whereof they drink. . . . So it came about that a younger race grew up, born of these slaves and the women." The idea of blinding the slaves, however, seems to derive from the term used by the Scythians for slaves that was misunderstood by the Greeks.

7. Unidentified lines:
"Cor sapit, et pulmo loquitur, fel commovet iras,
Splen ridere facit, cogit amare iecur."

8. [*Cap. 7*]: Proverbs 7:22–23: "Sequitur meretricem vecors iuvenis donec

sagitta transfigat iecur eius."

9. Ferrand does not specify a source for the story of Tityus the giant who was punished in Hades for his attempted rape of Leto, one of Jove's mistresses. Not only was he shot by Apollo and Artemis for this deed but he was also staked to the ground where vultures and snakes ate his heart and liver—the organs responsible for inciting his crime—which, to prolong the torment, grew back again with each cycle of the moon. The story is told in a number of sources, including the following, all of which Ferrand cites elsewhere in the treatise: Homer, *The Odyssey*, bk. XI. 567–81; Pindar, *Pythian Odes*, bk. IV. 46; Apollodorus, *The Library*, bk. I, IV, 1, trans. Sir J. G. Frazer, 2 vols. (Loeb, 1961), vol. 1, p. 29; Ovid, *Metamorphosis*, bk. IV. 457–58; Hyginus, *Fabulae*, no. 55; Pausanias, *Description of Greece*, bk. X, IV, 5–6, trans. W. H. S. Jones, vol. IV, p. 387.

Jean Aubery, *L'antidote d'amour*, p. 122ᵛ: "Ce roy qui avoit decretté une loy, per laquelle on crevoit les yeux aux adulteres, avoit bien recogneu qu'il falloit punir les offences par les parties que premierement avoient offencé."

10. [*Gal. 3. de placitis Hippo. & Plat.*]: Galen, *De placitis Hippocratis et Platonis*, bk. III, ch. 4, ed. Kühn, vol. V, pp. 310–20. Galen refers to Euripides on this matter.

11. Juvenal, *Satire* XIV. 57: "Vacumque cerebro / Iamdudum caput hoc ventosa cucurbita quaerit." See G. G. Ramsay, p. 265: "vacumque cerebro / iam pridem caput."

12. [*Part. 2 c. de amore*]: Bernard of Gordon, *Lilium medicinae*, the chapter on love, p. 216 f.

13. [*In Phedr*]: Plato, *Phaedrus*. Aristophanes' speech about love is not in the *Phaedrus*, however, but in the *Symposium* (189D ff.), ed. W. R. M. Lamb, vol. V, pp. 134 ff.

14. [*L. 2. De gen. an. c. 1*]: Aristotle, *Generation of Animals*, bk. II, ch. 1 (732a), trans. A. L. Peck, pp. 131, 133: "And as the proximate motive cause to which belong the *logos* and the Form, is *better* and more divine in its nature than the Matter, it is *better* also that the superior one should be separate from the inferior one. That is why wherever possible and so far as possible the male is separate from the female, since it is something *better* and more divine in that it is the principle of movement for generated things, while the female serves as their matter."

For the observation by Scaliger, see *Theophrasti Eresii de historia plantarum libri decem Graece et Latine . . . Latinam Gazae versionem nova interpretatione . . . accesserunt Julii Caesaris Scaligeri in eosdem libros animadversiones* (Amstelodami: apud Henricum Laurentium, 1644).

15. [*Euseb. de prep. Evan. ca. 7*]: Eusebius of Cesarea was, in fact, trying to demonstrate Plato's adhesion to Hebrew doctrine. Eusebius does not mention Plato's voyage to Egypt, but he does compare the biblical account of God's creation of woman with Aristophane's fable of the androgyne in Plato's *Symposium*, stating that "Plato does not understand the intention of this [Moses'] text." See Eusebius, *La préparation évangélique*, bks. XII–XIII, ed. with a French trans. by Edouard des Places (Paris: Les éditions du Cerf, 1983), bk. XII, ch. 12, pp. 70–73.

16. Ferrand means the commentaries on the *Symposium* rather than on the *Phaedrus*. Louis Le Roy (Ludovicus Regius) *Le Sympose de Platon, ou de l'amour et de beauté, traduit de grec en françois, avec trois livres de commentaires* (Parisiis: Sertenas, 1559), p. 42^r ff. Ferrand made use of Le Roy's commentary for his views on the androgyne, and it is undoubtedly from this source that he took his knowledge of Eusebius of Cesarea's bk. XII of the *Evangelica praeparatio* (see the preceding note), as well as of the Hebrew authorities mentioned in his text. Certain fathers of the church wished to endorse Plato's standing by urging that his image of the souls divided and reunited through love reflected the Mosaic doctrine that Eve was created from a part of Adam's body, so that love of Eve was simultaneously a search for a reintegration and perfection of the self. The same idea appears in Arabic literature, notably in Ibn Ḥazm al-Andalusī, 'Ali Ben Abmed, *A Book Containing the Risala Known as the Dove's Neck-Ring about Love and Lovers*, trans. A. R. Nykl (Paris, 1931), p. 7: "There is a good deal of dispute among people about the nature of love, and there is much lengthy discussion. What I believe myself is that it is a reunion of parts of the soul, separated in this creation (world), within their original higher element, not according to what Muhammad b. Dawud, may God have mercy on him, said, basing himself upon (the views of) some philosophers, that: 'Spirits are divided spheres,' but along the line of the resemblance of their (motive) forces in the (firm) abode of their higher world and their mutual approximation to the form of their make-up."

17. Marsilio Ficino, *Commentarium in Convivium Platonis de amore*, oratio IV, ch. 2: "non omnia quae in figuris finguntur, aliquid significare putanda sunt: multa enim propter illa quae significant, ordinis et connexionis gratia sunt adjuncta." See ed. Sears Reynolds Jayne, (Columbia, Missouri: University of Missouri Press, 1944) pp. 72–73.

18. [*A. Heroet en l'Andr.*]: Antoine Héroët, "L'androgyne de Platon," *Oeuvres poëtiques*, ed. critique par Ferdinand Gohin (Paris: Société de textes Français modernes, Eduard Cornély et Cie., 1909), pp. 76–95. A poem accounting for our spiritual origins:

> Au premier temps que le monde vivoit
> D'herbe et de gland, troys sortes y avoit
> D'hommes; les deux telz qu'ilz sont maintenant,
> Et l'aultre double estoit, s'entretenant
> Ensemblément, tant masle que femelle. (ll. 141–45)

He recounts their nature, the single soul and the separation of the two by the gods, and the origins of love as the divine force that causes men to look for their self-completion in a spiritual-physical union. He does not speak formally of marriage and social institutions but rather of love as a spiritual force.

> Syre, il vous fault en memoire reduire,
> Ce que scavez myeulx qu'on ne le peult dire;
> C'est que l'amour est passion gentille,
> Nous esclayrant de flamme si subtile,
> Que du ciel semble en la terre demys,
> Pour esveiller les espirits endormys,

Et les lever jusques à la partie,
Dont la clairté de sa torche est sortie. (ll. 293–300)
In this fashion man comes to a remembrance of himself in light of divine love, "Comme voirrons en la descouverture / De nostre double estrange creature" (ll. 307–8), and for such reason man was separated in the first place, leading to faith "et intention, / Elle ayme Dieu et requiert sa moytié." (ll. 334–35).

IX. Whether in Erotic Melancholy the Heart or the Brain Is the Seat of the Disease

1. [*L. 3. de par. anim. ca. 4.*]: Aristotle, *Parts of Animals*, bk. III, ch. 4 (666a), trans. A. L. Peck (Loeb, 1961), p. 237: "Further, all motions of sensation, including those produced by what is pleasant and painful, undoubtedly begin in the heart and have their final ending there."
2. Hippocrates, *On the Diseases of Young Women*, in *Oeuvres complètes*, ed. Littré, vol. VIII, pp. 467–71. See ch. II, n. 17, and also *Aphorisms*, bk. VI, no. 23: "Fear or depression that is prolonged means melancholia."
3. [*2. de part. anim. ca. 4. 2. 3. de plac. c. 4. C. 3. art. med.*]: Aristotle, *Parts of Animals*, bk. II, sec. 4 (650b), trans. A. L. Peck, p. 139: "Those, however, that have excessively watery blood are somewhat timorous. This is because water is congealed by cold; and coldness also accompanies fear."
   Galen, *De placitis Hippocratis et Platonis*, bk. III, ch. 4, ed. Kühn, vol. V, p. 311.
   Galen, *Ars medicinalis*, in *Operum Galeni libri isagogici artis medicinae*, ch. 30, p. 210: "Signa cordis frigidi."
4. [*Fen 1. lib. 3. tract. 4. cap. 18*]: Avicenna, *Liber canonis*, bk. III, fen 1, tr. 4, ch. 18, pp. 204^r ff., "De melancholia."
5. Marsilio Ficino, *Commentary on Plato's Symposium*, Speech VII, ch. 3, p. 158: "There are two kinds of insanity. One rises from a defect of the brain, the other from a defect of the heart. The brain often becomes too much occupied with burned bile, burned blood, or sometimes black bile. Hence men are sometimes rendered insane. Those who are troubled by burned bile, though provoked by no one, are violently enraged, scream loudly, attack those they meet, and kill themselves and others. Those who suffer from burned blood break out too much into uncontrolled laughter, make themselves conspicuous beyond common custom, promise marvels about themselves, and revel in song, and riot in dancing. Those who are oppressed by black bile lament perpetually; they imagine dreams for themselves, which they fear in the present or dread in the future. And these three kinds of insanity certainly result from a defect of the brain. For when those humors are retained in the heart, they produce distress and anxiety, but not insanity; they cause insanity only when they oppress the head. Therefore these are said to occur through a defect of the brain. We think that the madness by which those who are desperately in love are afflicted is, strictly speaking, caused by

a disease of the heart, and that it is wrong to associate the most sacred name of love with these. But lest perhaps we seem to be too wise against the many, for the sake of this discussion let us too use the name love for these." The passage is worth extensive quotation because François Valleriola takes it nearly verbatim from Ficino for his analysis of the generation of love. His patient likewise manifests many of the symptoms described by Ficino as pertaining to those troubled by burned bile, notably screaming loudly, attacking others and threatening suicide. Moreover, he follows this passage closely in separating melancholy of the heart and of the head, and the symptoms of those with burned blood from those with burned bile.

François Valleriola, *Observationum medicinalium libri VI*, p. 196. This page contains what is essentially a paraphrase of the passage quoted from Ficino, above.

6. Ferrand's information on Dino del Garbo undoubtedly derives from Mario Equicola, *Libro de natura de amore*, bk. I, "Guido Cavalcante," p. 9^r, where Equicola summarizes Cavalcanti's poem "Donna me prega" and mentions the treatise by the Florentine physician Dino del Garbo, "Commentum supra cantilena Guidonis de Cavalcantibus." See also our introduction.

7. [2. *Rhet. c. 2.*]: Aristotle, *Rhetoric*, bk. II, ch. 5, trans. John Henry Freese, p. 201: "Let fear be defined as a painful or troubled feeling caused by the impression of an imminent evil that causes destruction or pain."

8. [4. *De caus pulsuum.*]: Galen, *De causis pulsuum*, bk. IV, chs. 4–5, ed. Kühn, vol. IX, p. 160.

9. [*L. I. Meth. cap. 10.*]: This marginal reference appears to correspond to the statement concerning the seats of the causes of diseases attributed to Girolamo Mercuriale, but no title containing the word "methodus" is assigned to him today, unless Ferrand intended by it the *Medicina practica . . . libri IV* (Francofurdi: in officina Joannis Schonwetteri, 1602). There is an equal chance, however, that Ferrand intended for the text the name of one of the several physicians who had written a *Methodus medendi*.

10. Bernard of Gordon *Lilium medicinae*, the chapter on love, p. 216 f.

11. Hippocrates, *On the Sacred Disease* (Loeb, 1952) vol. II, pp. 175 ff., sec. 17: "Men ought to know that from the brain, and from the brain only, arise our pleasures, joys, laughter and jests, as well as our sorrows, pains, griefs and tears." Sec. 20: "Wherefore I assert that the brain is the interpreter of consciousness." Hippocrates puts forward an innovative case for the brain as the center of consciousness, an idea endorsed by Plato, but not by Aristotle. See *Oeuvres complètes*, ed. Littré, vol. VI, pp. 357–91.

12. [*Ga. li. De demonst. 3. l. 2. de plac. c. 2.*]: The reference to Galen's *On demonstration*, bk. III is taken from Nemesius of Emesa's ch. 20, "Of fear" in *Of the Nature of Man*, pp. 360–61: "So Galen, in his work, *On demonstration*, bk. III, says something to this effect: 'People attacked by fear experience no slight inflow of yellow bile into the stomach, which makes them feel a gnawing sensation, and they do not cease feeling both

distress of mind and the gnawing until they have vomited up the bile.' "
Galen, *De placitis Hippocratis et Platonis*, bk. II, ch. 8, ed. Kühn, vol. V,
pp. 273–84.

13. *Cyril of Jerusalem and Nemesius of Emesa*, "*Of the Nature of Man*," ch. 20,
p. 361.

X. Whether Love Melancholy Is a Hereditary Disease

1. Aristotle, *Generation of Animals*, bk. IV, ch. 3 (767b): "ὁ μὴ ἐοικὼς τοῖς
γονεῦσιν ἤδη τρόπον τινὰ τέρας ἐστίν." Ed. A. L. Peck (Loeb, 1963), p. 400.
2. [*L. De aere. loc. et aqu*]: Hippocrates, *On Airs, Waters and Places*, ch. 13:
"ὁ μὴ ἐοικὼς τοῖς γονοῦσιν, ἤδη τόπον τινα τέρας ἐστί." Ed. Littré, vol. II,
p. 56.
3. [*Avicen l. 9. anim. Gal. l. de Theriaca ad Pison. cha. 14.*]: Avicenna, *Compendium de anima. Ab Andrea Alpago Bellunensi ex Arabico in Latinum versa*,
ch. 7, "On the internal senses of the soul" (Venetiis: apud Juntas, 1546;
rpt. Westmead: Gregg International Publishers, 1969), pp. 20ʳ–21ᵛ.

   Galen, *De theriaca ad Pisonem liber*, ch. 14, ed. Kühn, vol. XIV, pp. 267–
70. The chapter deals with the composition and the effects of theriaca,
and seems to have little to do with Ferrand's context.
4. [*Valles. l. 4. contr Med. & Phil. c. 6*]: Francisco Valles, *Controversiarum medicarum et philosophicarum . . . liber* (Compluti: excudebat Ioannes Iñiguez
à Lequerica, 1583), bk. IV, ch. 6, pp. 76ʳb–77ᵛ: "De sympathia, et idio-
pathia, protopathia, et antipathia et consensu."

   Pliny, *Natural History*, trans. T. E. Page, bk. VII, ch. 12, sec. 52,
vol. II, p. 541: "Cases of likeness are indeed an extremely wide subject,
and one which includes the belief that a great many accidental circumstances are influential—recollections of sights and sounds and actual
sense-impressions received at the time of conception. Also a thought
suddenly flitting across the mind of either parent is supposed to produce likeness or to cause a combination of features, and the reason why
there are more differences in man than in all the other animals is that
his swiftness of thought and quickness of mind and variety of mental
character impress a great diversity of patterns." This is but part of a
longer discussion of the topic.

   Ferrand indulges in an anachronism here in stating that the Arab
physicians looked to Valles and Albert the Great for proofs of their views,
though the reader is at liberty to read his sentence as meaning arguments
that also appear in these authors. On the whole, however, Ferrand does
not evince a very clear sense of chronology or of the historical development of ideas.
5. [*Tho. à Veiga in c. 49. ars. med.*]: Tomás Rodriguez da Viega, *Ars medica*, in *Opera omnia in Galeni libros edita, et commentariis in partes novem
distincta* (Lugduni: apud Petrum Landry, 1593), p. 77: "De altera vero
quaestione, de causa, inquam, similitudinis factum ad parentes, propo-
sitionibus quibusdam quesitum indagabitur. Prima, similitudo triplex

est, in specie, in sexu, in accidentibus. Prima nascitur ex specifica varietate informatricis: idea enim hominis semen hominem generat, quia vis eius seminis informatrix actus est sui generis, sicut semen gallinae gallinam. Secunda, similitudo sexus, causam habet seminum menstrui, et uteri temperamentum. Si enim calidum siccum est, mas gignitur; si frigidum humidum, foemina. Tertia causa est, varietas facultatis formatricis non specifica, sed individualis. Facultas enim informatrix plurima expanditur per continentem aërem a coelo, gignens innumera, plantas, animalia, metalla, lapides: in aëre, aqua, terra, sub terra: manens actus non contractus ad naturam individui per signatam materiam, sed unus species actus malvae genitor, alius lumbrici. Hic ergo cum non sit per proprietates certae materiae coërcitus, producit semper sibi simile specie, non tamen simile huic, vel illi individuo. Quae vero informatrix in animatorum semine continetur, cum sit per signatum materiam contracta, ab illa recipit, ut producat speciem similem respondentem tumen etiam certis definitisque affectibus et proprietatibus eius individui, unde decisa est: Cum enim si vis corporea informatrix residua in parentis membris, et sui similitudinem testibus inducat, necessario inducet similitudinem, non solum actus et formae, in qua species consistit, sed et materiae, et qualitatum corporalium in quibus similitudo haec tertia intelligitur."

Luis Mercado, De morbis haereditariis, in Opera, vol. II, p. 670: "Quippem triplex in nobis ad parentes elucet similitudo. Prima est in specie, (qua deficiente monstrosus efficitur conceptus) secunda in sexu, qua foemina sicut mater, vel mas, ut pater filius nascitur. Tertia vero et ultima in proprietatibus individualibus, quibus filius similis patri aut matri nascitur; quatenus pertinet ad particulares et individuas delineationes, temperici aut substantiae, coloris vel configutationis modos."

6. [Fernel. c. 11. l. 7. Phys.]: Jean Fernel, Les VII livres de la physiologie, composez en latin . . . traduits en françois par Charles de Saint-Germain (Paris: Chez Jean Gaignard le Jeune, 1655), pp. 758–63. Ferrand is influenced throughout his discussion of the topic by Fernel, whose chapter is too long to quote in its entirety. The following are the essential passages for understanding the origins of Ferrands ideas—from bk. VII, ch. 12, "Pour quelles causes les enfans sont faits semblables ou dissemblables à leurs peres et meres": "j'observeray premierement qu'il y a trois sortes de genre de ressemblance, l'un en l'espece, l'autre en sexe, et le troisiéme en l'image ou effigie. La ressemblance qui est en l'espece provient sur tout de la matiere sujette: delà vient que ce qui est engendré du meslange des animaux de divers genre, approche de plus prés a l'espece de la femelle que du male. . . .

"En apres la sexe provient de la temperature et de la moderation des agens et des principales qualitez qui sont dedans les semences. Car si la semence du pere et de la mere excelle beaucoup en chaleur et en secheresse, il sera engendré un masle; au contraire si le froid et l'humide predomine et surabbonde, une femelle.

"Galien raporte la ressemblance de la forme et de l'effigie, a la forme de la faculté formatrice qui est l'ouvrier dedans la semence. Mais afin que quelqu'un n'insere point qu'il faut toujours qu'il soit engendré un enfant semblable à son pere, dautant que la semence du pere est plus forte et robuste que celle de la mere, il dit que la semence feminine prevaut et excelle quelquesfois, par ce qu'il reçoit pendant l'espace de neuf mois beaucoup de vertus de sang menstruel, et delà il dit que quelquesfois les enfans ressemblent à leur mere, ou quelquesfois qu'ils ressemblent en une partie à leur mere, et en une autre partie à leur pere, quand l'une n'y l'autre semence n'a point du tout surmonté le reste."

He goes on with a long series of objections occasioned by the wide variety of variances in the offspring yet unaccounted for. "Il est donc bien probable que cette vertu et faculté qui forme le foetus est conduite et gouvernée par la forte apprehension et la ferme imagination des femmes grasse. Car de celle, sur tout qui est donnee aux hommes, la vertu et la puissance est si grand et si forte, que comme pour l'ordinaire elle change le corps de celuy qui s'imagine quelque chose, ainsi de mesme elle communique sa force et sa vertu en la semence qui est conceuë."

Citing Pliny, he reports: "L'image . . . apprehendée à l'heure de la conception est reputée estre la cause de la ressemblance. Car l'imagination de l'un ou de l'autre des parens passant et volant promptement dedans l'esprit, est estimée graver la ressemblance . . . je me persuade du tout que la vertu et la faculté formatrice de la forme est conduite par l'imagination, et qu'elle est gouvernée par elle seule."

Fernel is but one of the many physicians of the age concerned with the topic of heredity, and it is conceivable that Ferrand consulted others in order to shape and consolidate his views. One such work with a high degree of corroboration with Fernel on these points is Levinus Lemnius, *Occulta naturae miracula, ac varia rerum documenta, probabili ratione atque artifici conjectura duobus libris explicata* (Antverpiae: apud Guiliel-mum Simonem, 1561). This work is extraordinary for the way in which it presents the received views of the age concerning the strange and wonderful in slightly sensationalist ways for the satisfaction of the curious without challenging the medical and philosophical foundations on which they were based. What Lemnius has to say about the transmission of traits from parent to child is both extraordinary, yet received doctrine. In bk. I, ch. 4, Lemnius concurs that if the woman provides the most seed the child will be like her, and the contrary if it is the father. If the provisions are equal, the child will resemble both. He believed strongly in the role of the mother's imagination, that if she fixes on certain objects and ideas during the pregnancy, the child will bear marks of those objects in its physical makeup. If during the embrace she thinks of her husband, the child will resemble him, a technique she can use if the child is the product of an adulterous relationship in order to hide the fact from him as well. Concerning wit, manners, and propensities of the mind, he claims that the resemblances between parents and children must be in part owing to heredity, those qualities transmitted by the force and vital spirits inherent in the faculty of the seed. The real challenge was in accounting for children who do not resemble their parents, and this is explained in terms of the influences of erratic imaginations in the parents, that unique quality with human beings that allows for such variety in the species. Lemnius remarks that the vices of parents are replicated in the offspring as well, but whether from hereditary influences or example he leaves moot. But he will stand firm on the principle that because the seed flows from all parts of the bodies of the parents, as was currently believed by most physicians (providing the general pleasure produced by the friction of the seed as it gathered from all parts for the climactic emission), by such means the diseases as well as the traits of any part could be transmitted to the child. Even the habitual practices of the parents are communicated, though only to the lower faculties, and not to such higher faculties as memory, for then the child would be born with all the knowledge of the parents as well. The moralist in Lemnius appears in his belief that an immoral mother can do more damage to the child than an immoral father, for vices in woman affect the humors and spirits that are communicated directly to the womb.

Johann Wier in bk. III, ch. 8, of *Histoires, disputes et discours des illusions et impostures des diables,* bk. I, p. 310, explains how such credulity was necessitated by their theories concerning the imagination: "Qu'est-ce que l'imagination de la femme grosse n'imprime au petit enfant, estant encore au ventre de la mere, par un subit trepercement des esprits qui se partent aux nerfs par lequels l'amarry est conjoint avec le cerveau?" This imagination was in turn closely related to the humors and temperatures of the body. Ferrand remains somewhat ambiguous on the topic in that while parents besotted by love leave tendencies for it in their children, it is not a question of their perverted imaginations but of the temperature of the whole body or its principal parts that is communicated to the child, that is, the temperature that brought the parents into the condition of love melancholy or erotic mania in the first place. Such a discussion, if pursued to its premises, would return the inquirer to questions of cause related to the presence of natural melancholy humors and to acts of volition, will, and desire. Both are fundamental to Ferrand's definition of erotomania. Ferrand avoids here a discussion of free will and moral responsibility versus physiological and humoral determinism. That which was habitual could be hereditary, including both moral and humoral propensities, as in the case of such habitual diseases as asthma, but not in the case of fevers. It stood to reason, then, that angry men should beget angry children, and that parents with hot, dry temperatures in the generative parts should beget children inclined to lust. Likewise, parents besotted with love and inclined to melancholy will pass on this tendency, unless the seed of one parent cancels that of the other.

For a parallel treatment, see Jean Liébault, *Des maladies des femmes,* bk. III, esp. ch. 7: "Les causes de la conception des masles et femelles," pp. 563–84, and ch. 9: "Si les vices, indispositions et maladies des peres et meres sont imparties à la conception," pp. 602–4. He concludes that the seed carries in itself the "idea" of the temperaments and all other dispositions of the two parents. According to Hippocrates, healthy parents engender healthy children, and the unhealthy, unhealthy children. Thus they do inherit the diseases, indispositions, good habits, and virtues of their progenitors. Liébault goes so far as to say that "le pere boiteux ou bigle, ou borgne, ou bossu, engendrera un enfant ayant telles imperfections" (p. 604), a view in a highly serious work as curious as anything in Lemnius. He concludes that where children escape the patent imperfections of their parents, it is owing to the beneficent action of the matrix itself, which often exhibits the power to correct seed of bad quality (p. 602). Likewise, the male seed, if it is of good quality, also has the power to counteract the corrupt seed of the mother to the benefit of the offspring. Liébault, bk. III, ch. 12, p. 638, also gives a thorough account of the ways in which the imagination of the mother affects the nature of the unborn child. These influences have to do with fixed ideas, or even with pictures attached to the bed and frequently viewed, and many like instances of ideas and objects that shape the imagination, usually to the detriment of the child.

The origin of the ideas concerning the hereditary influences upon diseases of the psyche through the seed can be traced back to Hippocrates, *The Sacred Disease*: the origin of this disease "like that of other diseases, lies in heredity. For if a phlegmatic parent has a phlegmatic child, a bilious parent a bilious child, a consumptive parent a consumptive child, and a splenetic parent a splenetic child, there is nothing to prevent some of the children suffering from this disease when one or the other of the parents suffered from it; for the seed comes from every part of the body, healthy seed from the healthy parts, diseased seed from the diseased parts." Trans. W. H. S. Jones (Loeb, 1952), vol. II. p. 151; *Oeuvres complètes*, ed. Littré, vol. VI, pp. 365–67.

7. [*Hor. Od. 4 l.* 4]: Horace, bk. IV, *Ode IV*: "fortes creantur fortibus et bonis." See trans. C. E. Bennett (Loeb, 1968), p. 296.

8. [*C. 46. art. med.*]: Galen, *Ars medicinalis*, in *Operum Galeni libri isagogici artis medicae*, ch. 46, p. 212: "Signa calidae, et siccae temperaturae testiculorum": "Calidor vero, ac siccior, et crassissimum semen habet, et foecundissima est, ac celeriter ab initio protinus ad coitum excitat animal. Sed et his genitales partes citissime hispide fiunt, atque omnes, quae circumstant, supra quidem usque ad umbilicum, infra vero usque ad media femora. Petulca igitur est, et ad libidinem prona huiuscemodi temperatura, statim vero satiatur, et si cogatur, offenditur."

9. Ovid, *Heroides* XVI. 293–94: "Qui fieri, si sint vires in semine amorum, / Et Iovis et Ledae filia casta potes?" See ed. Henricus Dörrie, p. 208. The modern text reads: "Vix fieri" and is not a question as in Ferrand.

10. Jean Fernel, bk. I, ch. 9, "Les genres et differences des maladies," *La pathologie de Jean Fernel . . . mis en françois par A. D. M. docteur en medecine* (Paris: Jean Guignard le pere et Jean Guignard le fils, 1655), pp. 36–37: "Les causes qui sont en nous autre l'order naturel sont celles, lesquelles estans, provenuës du vice de la semence, ou du sang maternel, produisent en nous finalement certaines maladies. Telle qu'est la semence des parens, et principalement celle du pere, telles deviennent les parties similaires et spermatique. La semence bien temperée cause une bonne temperature en ses parties-là, celle qui est chaude et seche, ou froide et humide, leur communique une semblable temperature na-

turelle. Pareillement de quelque mal que le pere soit attaint quand il engendre, il le transfere à l'enfant par l'entremise de la semence. . . . C'est
pourquoy les vieillards, et les valetudinaires, font des enfans imbecilles;
les graveleux, goutteux, epiléptiques, laissent à leur race une constitution vicieuse, par laquelle ils encourent enfin semblables maladies, que
pour se sujet en appelle hereditaires. . . . Le sang maternel lequel sert
de premier aliment à l'enfant pendant qu'il est encor au ventre de la
mere, est aussi cause du temperament et de la constitution, et imprime
pareillement ses vices au corps de l'enfant, mais non si fort comme fait
la semence. . . celles qu sont addonnees ou vin, font des enfans qui ai-
ment bien à en boire, et celles qui se medicamentent souvent pendant
leur grossesse, laissent à leurs enfans une inclination aux remedes. Le
mesme se remarque des maladies, car si une femme enceinte vient à
estre surprise de fièvre quarte, vers le milieu de son terme, l'enfant dont
elle accouchera sera en suitte longtemps travaillé de semblable maladie."
Fernel continues with many similar examples.

11. [*Mercat. de mor. haered.*]: Luis Mercado, *De morbis haereditariis*, in *Opera*,
vol. II, pp. 678–79: "Sic enim a generatione in generationem delitescet
magis sigillum haereditarium vincens inculpatum semen, ac praevelens
supra vitiosum et prave affectum: siquidem, ut dictum est, causae, quae
necessario conveniunt in generatione animalis, non sunt ita necessariae
et prorsus rebelles et indomitae, quod non possint a multis externis et
internis caussis impediri mutarique."

XI.   Of the Differences of Love Melancholy

1. [*M. Equic. l. 3. de la nat. d'Amour.*]: Mario Equicola, *Libro de natura de
amore*, a generic reference to bk. III, which contains chapters on the praise
of love, love of God, angelic love, man's love for God, and man's love
for man.
    Pausanias, *Description of Greece*, trans. W. H. S. Jones (Loeb, 1965),
"Beotia," bk. IX, generally, and bk. XVI.4, vol. IV, p. 241; "Ellis," bk. V,
and bk. II.25, vol. III, pp. 152–53. Cicero, *De natura deorum*, bk. III,
sec. 57, trans. H. Rackham (Loeb, 1961), p. 343. Plutarch, *The Dialogue on
Love* in the *Moralia*, trans. W. C. Helmbold. Plutarch creates a dialogue
in which many conflicting aspects of love are discussed in terms of the
different elements and manifestations of Eros and Aphrodite, Apollo,
Dionysus, and the Muses, e.g., pp. 361 ff.

2. [*2. de Symp. caus. 3. de loc. aff. c. 7.*]: Galen, *De symptomatum causis liber*.
As in ch. V (see n. 18, below) where this same set of references appears,
Ferrand means bk. I, ch. 10. See ed. Kühn, vol. VII, pp. 189–93.
    Galen, *De locis affectis*, bk. III, ed. Kühn, vol. VIII, pp. 189–90; *On the
Affected Parts*, bk. III, ch. 7, ed. Siegel, pp. 82–84; bk. III, ch. 10, pp. 89–94;
bk. VI, ch. 6, pp. 192–97.

3. Aristotle, *Problems*, XXX.1 (953a), trans. W. S. Hett, 2 vols. (Loeb, 1957),
vol. II, p. 157: "For wine in large quantities seems to produce the char-

acteristics which we ascribe to the melancholic, and when it is drunk produces a variety of qualities, making men ill-tempered, kindly, merciful or reckless." The parallel between inebriation and melancholy is maintained throughout the problem.

Anacreon, with trans. by Thomas Stanley, ed. A. H. Bullen (London: 1983), no. XIII, pp. 32–33, compares lovers to drunken fellows:

> Atis through deserted groves,
> Cybele invoking roves;
> And like madness them befell
> Who were drunk at Phoebus' well;
> But I willingly will prove
> Both these furies, Wine and Love.

4. [L. 6. c. 17]: Philostratus, Life of Apollonius of Tyana, bk. VI, ch. 50, trans. F. C. Conybeare (Loeb, 1960), vol. II, pp. 136–39: A story is related of a young man "in love with a nude statue of Aphrodite which is erected in the island of Cnidus; and he was making offerings to it, and said that he would make yet others with a view to marrying the statue." This is not the same tale related by Ferrand of the man who died with grief because the statue he sought for purchase was refused him. Apollonius reasons with the man described above and cures him of his folly by relating to him the destiny of Ixion.

Claudius Aelianus, Variae historiae libri XIV (Argentorati: sumptibus Johannes Friderici Spoor, et Reinhardi Waechtleri, 1685), bk. IX, ch. 39, pp. 484–85: "Quis neget hoc amores et ridiculos esse, et absurdos? Primum Xerxis, quod platani amore capiebatur. Deinde cuiusdam adolescentis Atheniensis, honesto loco nati, qui statuam bonae Fortunae, ad Pyrtaneum stantem, deperibat: et saepe in complexus eius se insinuans, oscula dabat: atque inde raptus in furorem, oestroque percitus, propter cupiditatem, in senatum venit, et enixe rogavit, ut sibi eam liceret utcunque magno emere. At quum nihil proficere, multis redimita taenis et coronis imagine coronata, oblato sacrificio ipsaque precioso vestitu exornata, profusis innumerabilibus lacrymis ipse sibi mortem conscrivit. Glaucam citharistriam alii serunt, canem, alii arietem, alii anserem admasse. Solis etiam, quae Cilicia urbs est, Xenophontem, puerum, ajunt canem deperiisse. Item deformem puerum Spartae graculum in deliciis habuisse." For a critical edition, see Varia Historia, ed. Mervin R. Dilts (Leipzig: B. G. Teubner, 1974), pp. 112–13.

The probable intermediary source for these two tales, however, is one derived from Pedro Mexía, Les diverse leçons (Lyon: par Claude Michel, 1526), bk. III, ch. 14: " De l'estrange et furieuse amour, d'un jeune Athenlen et du ridicule amour du Roy Xerxes, et comme les bestes ont maintesfois aimé les hommes et les femmes," p. 511.

Plutarch, Moralia (682B), "Table-talk," bk. V, ch. 7, trans. Paul A. Clement, vol. VIII, p. 429:

> "Fair once were, fair indeed the tresses of Eutelidas;
> But he cast an evil spell on himself, that baneful man,
> Beholding self in river's eddy; and straight the fell disease.

The legend is that Eutelidas, beautiful in his own estimation, being affected by what he saw, fell sick and lost his beauty with his health. See if you have the ingenuity to account for extraordinary phenomena like that."

5. [*L. 8 Eth. c. 2. L. 2 mag. mor. c. 21.*]: Aristotle, *Nicomachean Ethics* VIII, 2 (1155b 25), trans. H. Rackham (Loeb, 1962), p. 457: "the term friendship is not applied to love for inanimate objects, since here there is no return of affection, and also no wish for the good of the object."

Aristotle, *Magna moralia*, II, xi, 7 (1208b 30), trans. G. Cyril Armstrong (Loeb, 1962), p. 651: "Equally impossible is the return of affection by things that are lifeless."

6. [*Hipp. l. De aire, loc. & aq.*]: Hippocrates, *Of Airs, Waters and Places*, *Oeuvres complètes*, ed. Littré, vol. II, pp. 30–85.

7. [*Aequic. l. 4. de l'amour cha. 7.*]. Probably a reference to the very end of the chapter devoted to the "Causes of Sighs, Paleness, and Tears of Lovers," Mario Equicola, *Libro de natura de amore*, p. 158: "Se possono le lacrime fingere, ma in breve spazio. Quelle sono precipue de amanti, che rare e grosse cadeno. Quelle de femine vengono facilmente, ma non sempre se li deve prestar fede, che presto se seccano e hanno qualche similitudine con quelle del cocredillo."

8. [*Agrip. l. des Paradox.*]: Cornelius Agrippa of Nettesheim, *Paradoxe sur l'incertitude, vanité et abus des sciencés, traduicte en françois du latin* (n.p., 1603), pp. 72–74: "L'amour des hommes est plus ardant, celuy des femmes plus perseverant et obstiné: l'amour des jeunes gents est plaisant et follastre, celuy des vieils ridicule; le povre s'essaye d'estre aymé en faisant service, le riche par dons et presents: le menu peuple entretient ses amours par banquets et bonnes cheres, les grands par pompes, jeux, et spectacles; l'Italien rusé poursuit celle dont il veut jouïr en dissimulant son ardeur avec façons plaisantes, mais belles et proprement inventees, et se met à composer des sonnets et autres vers en loüange d'icelle, la faisant la premiere du monde. S'il parvient où il pretend, il est jaloux incontinent d'elle, et la voudra tenir toujours enfermee et garder comme prisonniere. S'il est frustré de son amour, et hors d'esperance d'en pouvoir jouïr, il n'y a mal qu'il n'en dise, et l'a en tres grande detestation. L'Espagnol prompt et soudain, impatient, de l'ardeur qui l'esquillonne se ruë furieusement sur l'amour, folastrant, mais sans se donner repos aucun, et par pytoyables lamentations se plaint du feu qui le consomme, invoque et adore son amoureuse; mais quand il l'a gaignee, ou il la tue par jalousie, où il en devient ruffien, et la prostitue pour le gain et profit. S'il n'en peut jouïr, il se tormente, jusques à se resoudre à mourir.

"Le follastre et lascif François fait le serviteur envers celle qu'il ayme, essaye d'acquerir sa bonne grace par honesteté, l'entretient, de chants et plaisans devis: s'il devient jaloux, il s'afflige et pleure: si on luy donne congé, et qu'il voye ne pouvoir venir à son attente, il brave avec injures, menasse de se venger, et mesmes veut user de force. S'il vient à son désseing, il mesprise tost apres et cherche une nouvelle amie. L'Allemand froid s'eschauffe d'amour peu à peu, estant enflammé il poursuit avec art et jugement, et cherche d'attirer la dame par dons: s'il entre en jalousie, il retire sa liberalité; est il deceu, il en fait peu de compte: jouït il, son amour se refroidit. Le François est dissimulateur à aymer, l'Allemand cache son amour, l'Espagnol se persuade d'estre aymé, l'Italien est en perpetuelle jalousie. Le François ayme celle qui est plaisante et de bonne grace, encor qu'elle soit laide: il ne chaut à l'Espagnol si elle est un peu endormie, pourveu qu'elle soit belle; l'Italien la veut craintive et honteuse; l'Allemand ayme celle qui est un peu hardie. En poursuyvant obstinement ses amours le François de sage devient fol: l'Allemand apres avoir tout despendu ce qu'il a en faisant l'amour sur le tard de fol devient sage: l'Espagnol pour acquerir la bonne grace de sa dame se hazarde a grandes entreprinses. Il n'y a chose pour grande qu'elle soit que l'Italien ne mesprise pour jouir de sa mie."

9. [*Marsil. Ficin. c. 9. orat. 7. in Com. Plat. Fr. Valer. Observ. 7. l. 2.*]: Marsilio Ficino, *Commentary on Plato's Symposium*, Speech VII, ch. 9, p. 166: "When a sanguine captures a sanguine, it is a light yoke, an agreeable bond, for a like complexion creates mutual love. Moreover, the amiability of this humor offers faith and hope to the lover. When a choleric captures a choleric, the bondage is more intolerable. Certainly, their likeness of complexion affords some interchange of goodwill between them, but that fiery humor of bile disturbs them with frequent irascibility. When a sanguine captures a choleric, or vice versa, on account of a pleasant humor and a painful one together, a certain alternation of irascibility and affability, pleasure and pain results. When a sanguine harnesses a melancholic, the knot is permanent, but not unpleasant. Certainly the sweetness of the sanguine tempers the bitterness of the melancholy. But when a choleric traps a melancholic, the disease is the most destructive of all. The very painful humor of the younger glides throughout the viscera of the older. The soft flame eats his marrow. The unfortunate lover is consumed. Choler provokes to wrath and killings. Melancholy provokes to sulking and perpetual complaining; for these the issue of love is often the same as it was for Phyllis, Dido, and Lucretius. But a phlegmatic or melancholy young man, on account of the thickness of his blood and spirits catches no one."

François Valleriola, *Observationum medicinalium libri VI*, bk. II, obs. 7, p. 206, takes his ideas directly from Ficino in the passage quoted above. Both writers testify to the importance of the temperaments and complexions as antecedent conditions for the development of states of the passions and their concomitant diseases.

See also Mario Equicola, *Libro de natura de amore*, bk. IV, ch. 7.

XII.   Whether Uterine Fury Is a Species of Love Melancholy

1. There were many writers on gynecology in the sixteenth century, many of whom were anthologized—notably in the four volume *Gynaeciorum* published in 1586 in Basel by Conrad Waldkirch. Ferrand was inclined to disguise his debts to major sources by crediting them only with details.

Girolamo Mercuriale enjoys brief mention at the end of this chapter, though here and in ch. XXXII Ferrand relies upon him heavily for his views on uterine fury. In the *De morbis muliebribus libri IV*, bk. IV, ch. 8, Mercuriale deals with the classification of the related conditions: "De pruritu matricis": "Huic congener est alter affectus, qui dicitur pruritus matricis, ab Arabibus dicitur priapismus: Aetius lib. 16. cap. 82. vocabit satyriasim. Et nihil est aliud hic affectus, nisi ardens desiderium scalpendi et ardens cupiditas coitus, cum dolore: qui a coitu potius efferatur, quam mitigetur, ea quod, ex contrectatione, humores magis decurrunt ad locum affectum." In ch. 9, "De mala uteri temperie" he speaks of the following signs: "Ad haec, in intemperie calida, menstrua sunt pauca, crassa, flava, adusta, mordicantia: pili in pectine cito nascuntur, multus adest coitus appetitus, velox seminis effusio frigidus vero uterus, similiter cognoscitur ex intemperie totius, menses pituitosi sunt, crassi, pauci, tardi, albi, interdum aquosi. Veneris abominatio est, aut exiguus appetitus, nulla in coitu delectatio." Hence, Ferrand's prurient tickling and overheating of the matrix. In ch. 10, "De furore uterino," Mercuriale writes at length on the origins, signs, prognostics, and cures of this condition, a section Ferrand has read closely and has used in several other contexts. Finally, ch. 13, "De nympha et cauda," deals with the clitoris and the condition called by Moschion "Symptoma turpitudinis: eo quod (ut Aetius scripsit) saepe haec caruncula ad tantam magnitudinem augetur, ut non solum deformitatem inducat, verum etiam pudorem aliquem immittat mulieribus." This section corresponds to the fifth "disease," the "shameful symptom or distended clitoris." For further information, see ch. II, nn. 29 and 30.

This chapter, in which Ferrand proposes that certain traditional diseases associated with the genitals and reproductive organs, notably satyriasis and uterine fury, is new to the edition of 1623. Presumably, as a result of his more extensive reading on the subject after 1610, Ferrand came to consider these conditions as belonging to amorous melancholy.

His sources were Luis Mercado, Jean Liébault, and Mercuriale in the places cited at the end of the chapter. In a sense, Ferrand was attempting to extend the range of his thesis by subsuming as many related conditions as possible. Under his general diagnosis, Ferrand reasons that the womb also sent vapors to the brain by the spinal column and caused disorders of the mind that resulted in hysterical behavior. Moreover, excess blood around the uterus or an overabundance of seed were potential sources of corruption and could serve as the somatic or material causes for afflictions of the mind and soul. But Ferrand must rely for his success, in part, on the collaboration of the reader, for such diseases have little to do with passions of the soul provoked by powerful erotic desires fixed upon an object of beauty. Insofar as love is such a passion, while satyriasis and uterine fury are conditions entirely somatic in origin, the similarities in the symptoms produced are parallel rather than identical. Yet Ferrand was attracted by the prospect that where excess seed could be understood to produce both love melancholy and satyriasis, the cures could be combined.

Galen, himself, in the *De locis affectis*, ed. Kühn, vol. VI, p. 418, deals with hysteria as related to sexual behavior. He describes those who, out of overmodesty, refrain from all venerean pleasures, and relates how certain of them, in a manner resembling those suffering from melancholy, are stricken by a sense of irrational sorrow and despair, accompanied by bad digestion and a loss of appetite. Another example is of the man who lost his wife, ceased all sexual activity, and therefore became morose in a way resembling melancholy. But Galen refused to see either condition as a form of amorous melancholy because such diseases derived entirely from somatic causes that, on the one hand, merely resembled melancholy, and on the other, were unrelated to love, which was, for him, a passion of the soul. In ch. III of the 1610 edition Ferrand had tried to use other passages in Galen to prove in error those who looked upon love as a condition exclusively of the soul. Such is to ignore Galen's clear declarations on the matter in the *De praenotione ad Posthumum*, ed. Kühn, vol. XIV, p. 630, concerning the story of Erasistratus and Antiochus where he denies that the condition of the young lover is a disease of melancholy with somatic origins. Ferrand avoids the problem of somatic vs. psychic causes in dropping his chapters on why earlier physicians had failed to teach the cure of love as a somatopsychic disease but raises the problem again here. Ferrand will make occasional references in subsequent chapters to uterine fury and satyriasis, but he will not urge the matter.

2. Moschion, *On the Diseases of Women*, ch. 128: "κνησμονή τῶν αἰδοίων μερῶν σὺν ὀδύνη, οὕτως αἰνυπρωφέροντως τὰς ἰδίας χαίρας, ἐκεῖσε βάλλουσι σὺν ἀκορέζω ἀνδρῶν ἐφέσει, ἀποβαλλοῦσαι δηλονότι πάσης αἰδοῦς εὐλάβειαν." See *De morbis muliebribus liber, Graece cum scholiis et emendationibus Conradi Gesneri* (Basileae: Th. Guarin, 1566), p. 28.

"*De satyriasi*," ch. III ex Moschione, from Félix Platter, *De mulierum partibus generationi dicatis*, in *Gynaeciorum sive de mulierum affectibus* (Basileae: per Conradum Waldkirch, 1586), p. 51: "Satyriasis est commune vitium viris et mulieribus, sed frequentius viris occurrit. Inde a Satyris nomen accepti, quod fabulosa antiquitas proclives in Venerem scripsit. Mulierum autem satyriasis est, partium pudendarum prurigo cum dolore, ita ut impatienter manus suas illuc mittant, cum insatiabili virorum desiderio, amissa scilicet omnis pudoris verecundia. Siquidem enim res quae matricis con sensum habeat, et verecundiam eis condundat et tollat, et aliquantulum eas delirare faciat. Curam autem earum eandem adhibemus, quam in strictura matricis et in fervore posuimus." Ferrand includes prurient tickling with satyriasis, but does not explain the symptoms or physiology of these conditions. Jean Aubery in *L'antidote d'amour*, p. 139ᵛ, attaches these conditions to the spirits in the blood, stating that bleeding is the only evacuation for this material cause of erotic love: "Souvent l'amour luy mesme se pert comme le prurit, duquel il semble estre une espece: car le prurit est une exclusion d'une humeur spiritueuse renfermee contre nature, la semence est de mesme en l'acte venerien, de sorte que tout ainsi qu'en ceste volupté de mesme en la demangeaison tout le corps est chatouïllé de plaisir laissant une cuisante ardeur, qui ne cesse de molester jusques a tant que le sang eschauffé qui cause ce prurit, soit vuidé, par la section des veines." This passage serves to explain the link between the heated blood and the sensation of sexual excitation felt throughout the body, and further explains the use of phlebotomy in the cure.

3. [*L. 2. rhetor. c. 6. L. 4. Ethic. c. 15*]: Aristotle, *Rhetoric*, bk. II, ch. 6 (1383b 22): "ὅσα ἀπὸ κακίας ἔργα ἐστίν, οἷον τὸ ἀχολασίας." For ἀχολασίας read ἀποβαλεῖν." See trans. John Henry Freese (Loeb, 1967), p. 211. The entire passage reads: "if this definition of shame is correct [a kind of pain of uneasiness in respect of misdeeds which brings dishonour] it follows that we are ashamed of all such misdeeds as seem to be disgraceful, either for ourselves or for those whom we care for. Such are all those that are due to vice, such as throwing away one's shield or taking to flight, for this is due to cowardice; or withholding a deposit, for this is due to injustice; and illicit relations with any persons, at forbidden places or times, for this is due to licentiousness."

Aristotle, *Nichomachean Ethics*, bk. IV, ch. 9 (1128b 1–8), deals with shame, as does bk. II, ch. 14. See trans. H. Rackham, p. 251.

4. [*Aëce tetrab. 4. ser. 4. c. 82*]: Aetius of Amida, *Tetrabiblos . . . per Ianum Cornarium . . . Latine conscripti* (Basileae: Froben, 1542), bk. IV, sermo 4, ch. 82, p. 909: "De Satyriasi. Eiusdem [i.e. from Soranus] mulieribus quoque satyriasis et tentigo accidit, qualem viris fieri supra retulimus. Consequitur ad hanc ingens pudendorum pruritus cum dolore, ita ut mulier locis assidue manus admoveat. Atque ideo intole abili veneris desiderio contabescit salsi humoris effluentis acrimoniam ac mordacitatem percipit. Et loci utero vicini inflammantur. Illud vero ardens coëundi desiderium saeviorem reddit affectionem. Quum enim partes affectae distensae sint, et semen excerni non possit, quoniam meatus per inflammationem obturantur, maior materiae copia frustra ad locum attrahitur. Statim igitur a principio vena secanda est, et alimentum contrahendum, et pubi ac lumbis illinenda quae leniter regrigerant ac contrahunt. Caput aceto et rosaceo irrigetur. Et in potu aqua tepida exhibeatur. Cibi vero sint sorbiles, omnis prorsus flatus ac veneree concitationis exortes. Duobus vero a vene sectione diebus, cucurbitae cum scarnificatione affigantur. Reliqua vero curatio eadem sit cum ea quam ad inflammationem uteri mox referemus."

5. Hippocrates, *Aphorisms*, bk. II, aph. 6: "dolentes aliqua parte corporis, si dolorem non sentiunt, his mens aegrotat." *Aphorismi Hippocratis Graecae et Latinae*, p. 30^v: "quicunque dolentes parte aliqua corporis, omnino dolorem non sentiunt, iis mens aegrotat."

6. Jean Liébault, *Des maladies des femmes*, bk. I, ch. 33: "Fureur de l'amarry," p. 95: "Ce mal est beaucoup plus grief aux femmes que la satyriase, d'autant qu'il est accompagné de rage et phrenesie furieuse, à raison d'un ardeur excessive de l'amarry, qui est communiqué au cerveau et au reste du corps par la conduicte de l'espine du doz ou par les vapeurs acres qui montent au cerveau de la matrice embrasee. En ce mal les femmes transportees de leur bonne raison ne font que babiller incessamment et parler des choses veneriennes: sentent incroyables prurits

et demangesons les parties honteuses, à l'attractation desquelles prennent plaisir esmerveillable: tel accident procede la plus grand part de l'abondance du sperme acre et flatulent, et ne se trouve qu'és femmes chaudes de nature, qui sont jeunes, se plaisent à tous delices et voluptez, se nourrissent beaucoup, et ne pensent qu'à contenter leurs charnalitez: les remedes susdites serviront à la guarison de ce mal, si outre iceux lon fait des bains foies actuellement et refreschissans avec fueilles de laictues, nenuphar, morelle, cigue, iombarde, insquiame, pavot, concombre, citrouilles: mesme injections dedans la matrice, de la decoction de toutes ces herbes: qui plus est, pessairez de just de mercuire, iombarde, plantain et morelle: et pour assoupir la phrenesie lon frotte le front et toute la teste d'oxyrhodinon ou autre tel liniment: voyez encore cy apres de la fureur uterine."

The entire chapter by Liébault has been cited, not only as further clarification of the subject but as an indication of Ferrand's methods of scholarship, and of the encyclopedic method in general: Ferrand incorporates more than half of the above into his own text, the ideas and the phrasing treated, more or less, as common property. The fundamental argument of Ferrand's chapter is thus heavily based on Liébault, to which Ferrand adds his own references to parallel literatures. Ferrand's innovativeness is in extending the range and definition of love mania and melancholy to include these traditional diseases involving the regenerative organs and sexual desire. This association allows Ferrand to consolidate the cures for melancholy with those for fury and madness, stating that he will set out the symptoms of these diseases when he comes to speak of the cure of love melancholy. Ferrand also returns to this plan of treatment in ch. XXXII on the prevention of erotic melancholy by pharmaceutical means, mentioning the baths, the topicals to the head and the vaginal pessaries, further testifying to the borrowing and consolidation.

On the whole, however, Ferrand's contemporaries were inclined to make a clear distinction, despite the similarities of both the causes and the effects, between insane love and uterine fury, or nymphomania. The latter was described as an ardent desire for sexual intercourse that effects the brain and can drive the patient insane, while the former was seen as a condition simultaneously of the body and of the soul generated by a desire for an object, the loss or inaccessibility of which could cause melancholy; the mechanisms were different. Yet Ferrand was right in seeing how these traditional distinctions were easily threatened by rigorous examination. He maintains a middle course. The Parisian physician Barthélemy Pardoux (active in the second half of the sixteenth century) in his De morbis animi liber, pp. 49–51, maintains the distinction, though by juxtaposing his chapter on uterine fury with the following on insane love, he too allows for the association of the two. He states that the itch or ardent longing is communicated to the brain by way of the diaphragm, though he adds that the serous, salty humor that troubles the sexual organs—especially the neck and mouth of the uterus—mounts to the brain by way of the nerves in the spinal column and troubles the brain with its vapors. These humors are associated with the retention and corruption of seed.

He deals with external causes that are closely related to those cited by Ferrand with regard to love melancholy: hot climates, spicy and aromatic foods such as artichokes and onions, strong wine, overstuffed beds, and idle lifestyle, erotic books, and entertainments. Internal causes include a hot, moist mixture of humors and a bilious constitution. The recommended cures function by the principle of opposites—hence, the prescription of refrigerating foods such as cucumbers, prunes, apples, chicken soup, lettuce, chicory, and purslane, cold water, beer, and barley water, cold baths and narrow, lightly covered beds. Predictably, the patient should be kept active, forthwith married where possible, in accordance with the precepts of Hippocrates, or else threatened in terms of her honor. Pardoux then moves on to purges and enemas, phlebotomy, especially from the ankle veins, scarification of the thighs and cupping, the application of leeches, and the opening of the hemorrhoids. Finally, he mentions vaginal pessaries containing purslane, rue, and coriander. Certain ingredients may differ from those recommended by Ferrand, but it is instructive that Ferrand drew upon the same general repertoire of definitions and cures that informs the pages of Pardoux. This is not to say that Ferrand knew or did not know this work—the association with Liébault seems, in any case, the more direct—but rather to point up the currency of this material in sixteenth-century medical circles, and the existence of the generic associations that gave rise to Ferrand's chapter.

7. Hippocrates, *On the Diseases of Young Women*: "ὑπὸ τῆς ὀξυφλεγμασίης μαίνεται, ὑπὸ δὲ τῆς σηπεδόνος φονᾷ, ὑπὸ δὲ τοῦ ζοφεροῦ φοβέεται καὶ δέδοικεν, ὑπὸ δὲ τῆς περὶ τὴν καρδίην πιέξιος ἀγχόνας κραίνουσιν, ὑπὸ δὲ τῆς κακίης τοῦ αἵματος ἀλύων καὶ ἀδημονέων ὁ θυμὸς κακὸν ἐφέλκεται." *Oeuvres complètes*, ed. Littré, vol. VIII, pp. 468–69. Ferrand continues with the line: "ὅτε ἀμείνονά τε ἐόντα καὶ χρείην . . . ἐξέχοντα παντοί," while the Hippocratic text reads: ἄτε ἀμείνονά ἐόντα καὶ χρείην ἔχοντα παντοίην."

8. Plutarch, "Bravery of Women," *Moralia*, ed. Frank Cole Babbitt (Loeb, 1961), vol. III, p. 509.

9. Girolamo Mercuriale, *De morbis muliebribus libri IV* (Venetiis: apud Felicem Valgrisium, 1587), bk. IV, ch. 10, pp. 153–54: "Posset quis eruditus dubitare, an morbus quo virgines Milesiae laborarunt et mulieres Lugdunenses, fuerit hic morbus, quoniam refert Plutarchus lib. de virtut. mulierum, interdum virgines Milesias sese catervatim suspendisse, nec potuisse ulla vi, aut precibus impediri: quod refert a nonnullis a-scriptum fuisse a aeris vitio. Relatum etiam est, Lugdunenses mulieres catervatim sese in fluvios praecipitasse, atque hoc attributum fuisse defluvio stellarum. Ego vero puto nullum aliud morbi genus extitisse, quam hunc morbum: primo, quia mulieres Milesiae virgines erant. Hippocrates vero, Soranus et alij, scribunt hunc morbum peculiarem esse virginibus et castis. De Lugdunensibus idem dico, quae se ipsas praecipitabant in aquam, non ob aliud, quam ob ardorem, qui cum in nulla alia parte appareret, et puderet manifestare, ideo ruebant in aquam, tan-

quam remedium. Nam relatum est a Lucretio 6. de natura, in peste illa Atheniensi, aegros prae ardore in fluvios se praecipitasse, ita ut verisimile sit mulieres eam ob causam eo devenisse. Est hic affectus, symptoma in genere actionum naturalium et animalium laesarum: nam cum coitus appetitus depravatur, clarum est naturalem operationem offendi, similiter cum laedatur cogitatio et imaginatio, perspectum est animalem functionem offendi. Morbus quem sequitur hoc symptoma, nullus alius est quam intemperies calida uteri. Locus affectus primo est uterus, deinde diaphragma et cerebrum: si quidem, ut docet Soranus, uterus, dum fervet, immotus manens, vapores fervidos et pravos in cerebrum et diaphragma mittit, vel per spinalem medullam, vel per alia vasa, qui fervor communicatus cerebro, omnia hec mala facit."

10. Thucydides, *The Peloponnesian War*, bk. II, ch. 49, trans. Charles Forster Smith (Loeb, 1962), vol. I, p. 345.

Lucretius, *On the Nature of Things*, bk. VI, 1172–79, trans. W. H. D. Rouse (Loeb, 1966), p. 526.

11. Euripides, *Andromache*, l. 229: "φιλανδρίᾳ," in *Euripides*, trans. A. S. Way in 4 vols. (Loeb, 1968), vol. II, p. 432. Ferrand uses the accusative, "φιλανδρίαν."

12. [*L. 3 fen. I. tract. 4. c. 18*]: Avicenna, *Liber canonis*, bk. III, fen 1, tr. 4, ch. 9, p. 149ᵛ.

13. [*Mercat. c. de mania*]: Luis Mercado, *De internorum morborum curatione libri IV*, bk. I, ch. 18, "De mania et reliquis furoris generibus," in *Opera* (Francofurti: sumptibus haeredum D. Zachariae Palthenii, 1620), vol. III, p. 109: "Ut certum est, melancholiae amnera speciem cum timore et tristitia esse, ita proculdubio maniam cum furore et contentione conjungi arbitramur: et hoc est, quod dixerat Avicenna I. 3. tract. 4. cap. 18. *Cumque melancholia componitur cum rixa et saltu et contentione seu pugna, mutatur eius nomen, diciturque mania, quae nil aliud est, quam princeps functio depravata, propter servidam cerebri sine tumore caliditatem.* At species huius mali, licet sint numerosae, quae conspicuae magis exsistunt, sunt quinque, *melancholia* nimirum, *furor, amor, rabies, hydorolcos*, quam Avicenna vocavit *curbut* [*cuturub*], et Greci *Lycaonem*, id est, lupinam insaniam, *ut mox latius sum expositurus*, si prius dixero, unde maniam Graeci dixerint." The quotation from Avicenna in this chapter reveals the order and origins of Ferrand's text in relation to the preceding note.

14. Luis Mercado, *De internorum morborum curatione libri IV*, in *Opera*, bk. II, ch. 10, pp. 582–86. This work was a major vehicle of ideas and furnished materials and recipes that were copied throughout the latter half of the sixteenth century. The following chapter was derived from Mercado and will serve for both authors: Rodrigo de Castro, *De universa mulierum medicina*, bk. II, ch. 10, "De furore uterino," p. 152: "Uterinus furor est immodica et effrenis coëundi appetentia, adeo inextinguibilis, ut in furorem et diliramentum migrare foemina videatur, ardore, et fervore uteri ad cerebrum et universum corpus distributo. Symptoma censetur in genere actionum laesarum tam naturalium, quam animalium, nam immoderata libido ad naturalem, depravata veneris imaginatio ad animalem seu rectricem spectat, sitque iam malignae, ac foedissimae mentis

passio. Provenit ex vitiato uteri temperamento, unde locus primario affectus uterus est, ac eius partes, in quibus veneris viget appetitus, ut sunt testes, et processus ille, quem delectationis sedem in quibusdam statuimus, ac praesertim colum uteri, et eius osculum, sicuti canina fames, et immodica sitis in ore ventriculi fiunt; per consensum autem communicato fervore, diaphragma, et cerebrum etiam compatiuntur, utrolibet enim vitiato delirium sequitur. Ex dictis liquet, differre a pruritu uteri, quia hic in sui consensum cerebrum non trahit, neque rabiosum delirium ad illum sequitur, ex quo foeminae deposita omni pudoris verecundia insatiabili desiderio viros palam insectantur, aut sese suspendio, flammae, et in puteos praecipites dant, majoris dedecoris fugiendi gratia; ad haec uti pruritus satyriasi virorum, ita furor priapismo videtur correspondere, ac in pruritu quia humor turget, partes cum delectatione dolent, in furore non dolent; tandem quia pruritus annosis, furor virginibus magis contingit; nec aliter differt a fervore matricis, nisi quod in hoc uteri substantia, et universum eius corpus, eisdem afficitur symptomatibus, quibus partes pudendae in pruritu, et furore." For Jean Liébault, see n. 6, above.

Girolamo Mercuriale, *De morbis muliebribus libri IV*, bk. IV, ch. 9, "De mala uteri temperie," pp. 152–53; ch. 10, "De furore uterino," pp. 153–57. See n. 1, above, for an explanation of the probable use made of Mercuriale in this section of the treatise.

XIII.   Whether Love Can Be Diagnosed by the Physician Without the Confession of the Patient

1. [*Epist. ad Hippocr.*]: Hippocrates, "Letter from Democritus," *Oeuvres complètes*, ed. Littré, vol. IX, p. 395; see also Ferrand, ch. XXVI, n. 13.
2. [*Avic. l. 3. fen. 1 tetrab. 4. c. de amore*]: Avicenna, *Liber canonis*, bk. III, fen 1, tr. 5, chs. 23–24. The chapter on love is the "de alhash, id est amantibus" to which Ferrand so often makes allusion; "tetrab. " should in fact read "tract."
3. Soranus of Ephesus, *Life of Hippocrates*, Βίος Ἱπποκράτους. This work, dubiously attributed to Soranus, recounts the curing of Perdiccas, son of Alexander, who became king of Macedonia after his father's death. Finding himself in a wasted and languishing state, he called in the two most renowned physicians of the age, Hippocrates and Euryphon. Hippocrates saw that he was aging prematurely, thereby showing signs of a psychic disease. Noting the total transformation of the king's appearance when Phila, his father's concubine, was present, he made his diagnosis and was thereby able to propose a cure. No account is given of how that diagnosis was made or what kind of cure was proposed. Because his father was dead, a match would have been the easiest solution. In such a case, we are unclear as to what the real obstacle was in the first place. The authority of the anecdote is made suspect by the absence of all comment by Galen in his commentary on the second chapter of Hip-

pocrates' *Prognostics*, in which he deals with Erasistratus. Indeed, the story suggests origins in the story of Antiochus and Stratonice. Marie-Paul Duminil explains, in "La mélancolie amoureuse dans l'Antiquité," that the *Life* could not go back much beyond the first century A.D. and that it was derived from the account of Erasistratus: *La folie et le corps*, p. 106. A point of interest is that the mother of Stratonice in Plutarch's account (see the following note) was also called Phila.

Ferrand employs the word *hetique*, which signifies both a hectic or continual fever and consumption characterized by leanness and dryness. The leanness and dryness would tend to serve his purposes more easily because the question of amatory fever was a highly controversial one concerning which Ferrand remains rather ambiguous, though he tends to favor the definition of erotic love as a disease lacking fever. The popular sense of the term in English as meaning wild, exciting, or impassioned presumably does not apply.

4. [*Plutarq in Demetr. Val. Max. l. 5. c. 7*]: *Plutarch's Lives*, "Demetrius," XXXVIII, trans. Bernadotte Perrin, 11 vols. (Loeb, 1959), vol. IX, pp. 93–97. Plutarch's account of this story became the basis of a medical tradition concerning the physician and the diagnosis of lovesickness. The importance of the narrative cannot be overemphasized, for it became a central account that helped define both the symptoms of the disease and the role of the physician. "Accordingly, when any one else came, Antiochus showed no change; but whenever Stratonicé came to see him, as she often did, either alone, or with Seleucus, lo, those tell-tale signs of which Sappho sings were all there in him,—stammering speech, fiery flushes, darkened vision, sudden sweats, irregular palpitations of the heart, and finally, as his soul was taken by storm, helplessness, stupor, and pallor." These symptoms became the basis for speculation on the pulse of lovers and the signs by which the disease could be recognized. Moreover, this story established a precedent for curing love with love rather than by medications, insofar as Antiochus was cured by marriage to his stepmother after Erasistratus gained the king's consent. Important, too, is the tyranny of the disease: "Antiochus was distressed, and resorted to many means of fighting down his passion, but at last, condemning himself for his inordinate desires, for his incurable malady, and for the subjugation of his reason, he determined to seek a way of escape from life, and to destroy himself gradually by neglecting his person and abstaining from food, under pretence of having some disease." The story was repeated in a variety of contexts by later physicians dealing with the disease of love, as does Ferrand.

Valerius Maximus, bk. V, ch. 7, *Factorum et dictorum memorabilium libri novem*, pp. 261–63, retells in résumé the story of Antiochus and Stratonice. His version predates Plutarch's by 75–100 years insofar as Valerius was writing before A.D. 31. There is the possibility that Plutarch knew both this account and a similar story in the works of Aretaeus the Cappadocian, which, though it lacks the names of Antiochus and Stratonice, preserves elements of the Greek romance tradition evident in Plutarch. The dual dimensions of the story appear to have existed even before Valerius: a literary one concerned with the loves of princes and the sensibilities of the refined and delicate soul; a medical one concerned with the symptoms of melancholy. For further treatment of this problem, see the article by Marie-Paule Duminil, "La mélancolie amoureuse dans l'Antiquité," *La folie et le corps*, pp. 91–109.

5. [*L. 2 Reg. c. 13.*]: The reference is to the Vulgate for II Samuel 13. Amnon was King David's son by Ahinoam of Jezreel; Tamar was his half sister by Māacah, the daughter of King Talmai of Geshur. The story is concerned with love passion, for "Amnon was so tormented that he made himself ill because of his sister Tamar, for she was a virgin, and it seemed impossible to Amnon to do anything to her." Amnon found a cure for his torment through a ruse that led to Tamar's seduction, but his actions also led to his murder by her full brother Absolom.

Long before Ferrand, the story had entered into the literature on *philocaption* and was subject to a variety of interpretations. Kramer and Sprenger, in the *Malleus maleficarum*, ed. Montague Summers (New York: Dover Publications, 1971), pt. 2, ques. 2, ch. 3, p. 170, are persuaded that Amnon was the victim of "the temptation of devils," for he "loved his beautiful sister Tamar, and was so vexed that he fell sick for love of her (II. *Samuel* xiii). For he could not have been so totally corrupt in his mind as to fall into so great a crime of incest unless he had been grievously tempted by the devil." This form of temptation is the second cause of erotic love, in contrast to the first which is owing to "a lack of control over the eyes," and to a third that involves, "the spells of necromancers and witches, with the help of devils."

6. Ferrand mentions the story of Canace as another example of love discovered by one who was not a physician. In fact, the story resembles the preceding one in that Canace's love was for her brother, Macareus, with whom she committed incest, for which deed she then either killed herself or was destroyed by her father, Aeolus. The sequence suggests that Ferrand was consulting a list of moral tales concerning incest and its devastating results. Confusion is added by calling her the daughter of the nurse, presumably a figurative use of the term. The story can be found in Apollodorus bk. VII, 3–4; and in Hyginus, *Fabulae*, nos. 238 and 242. See also ch. XIV, n. 14, where the story is traced to Cristóbal de Vega, bk. III, ch. 17, of his *Liber de arte medendi*. See also Ovid, *Heroides*, no. XI, "Canace to Macareus." The origin of this story may have been Euripides' lost play *Aeolus*.

7. Ovid, *Heroides* XI. 33: "Prima malum nutrix animo praesensit anili." Ed. Henricus Dörrie, p. 143. We have also consulted the edition ed. by A. Palmer (Hildesheim: George Olms, 1967), p. 67. The line is from Canace's letter to her brother Macareus.

8. Galen, *Quomodo morbum simulantes sint deprehendendi libellus*, ed. Kühn, vol. XIX, pp. 4–5.

Galen, *De praenotione ad Posthumum*, ed. Kühn, vol. XIV, pp. 630–35.

9. Ovid, *Heroides* XII. 39–40: "Quis enim bene celat amorem? / Emicat inditio prodita flamma suo." See ed. Henricus Dörrie, p. 160. His edition reads "Eminet indicio."

10. Remy Belleau, "Qu'on cognoist les amoureux," *Les odes d'Anacreon*:

> Les chevaux pour les mieux cognoistre
> Bien souvent à la cuisse dextre
> Portent une marque de feu:
> On cognoist la Parthe Barbare
> A la façon de sa tiare:
> Et moy, aussi tost que j'ay veu
> Un amoureux, je le devine:
> Car il porte en sa poictrine
> Un signal, qui paroist peu.

   See *Oeuvres poetiques de Remy Belleau*, ed. Ch. Marty-Laveaux (Paris: Alphonse Lemerre, 1878), vol. I, p. 45. The last line reads "Un signal, qui paroist un peu."

11. [*Ovid ep. 25*]: Ovid, *Heroides* XVI. 7–8, 237–38:

> bene quis celaverit ignem?
> Lumine nam semper proditur ipse suo.
> Quod licet, et possum conor celare pudorem,
> Attamen apparet dissimulatus amor.

   See ed. A. Palmer, pp. 101, 109. These lines are from "Paris to Helen," the last two reading:

> Qua licet et possum, luctor celare furorem,
> Sed tamen apparet dissimulatus amor.

12. Erasmus, *Chiliadis* IV, centuria 8, "In ore atque oculis," 23, in *Adagiorum Chiliades quatuor* (Lugduni: apud haeredes Sebast. Gryphii, 1592), p. 1142: "Quae propalam fiunt, in ore atque; oculis omnium fieri dicuntur . . . rursus in divinatione; in mentem tibi non venit, quid negotii sit causam publicam sustinere; vitam alterius totam explicare? atque, eam non modo in animis judicum, sed etiam in oculis conspectuque omnium exponere?"

13. Pietro Capretto (Petrus Haedo), *Anterotica* (Treviso: Gerardus Lisa, 1492), bk. I, "*Primo autem libro tractatur de cupidinis natura*," ch. 27: "*De amantum dolore et cruciatu*," p. 21^r.

14. [*L. de cogn. & cur animi morb. L. de praecogn. ex puls.*]: Galen, *De cognoscendis curandisque animi morbis*, ed. Kühn, vol. V, pp. 1–570. Galen refers to this work in the most general way. In ch. VI, pp. 26–34, he discusses the excessiveness of concupiscence and compares those who fall prey to it to brutes.

   Galen, *De praesagitione ex pulsu*, ed. Kühn, vol. IX, pp. 205 ff. This is a very general reference.

15. [*Heurn. l. 3. meth. c. 30*]: Johann van Heurne (Ioanne Heurnio), *Praxis medicinae nova ratio qua libris tribus methodi ad praxin medicam*, bk. III, ch. 30 (Lugduni Batavorum: ex officina Plantiniana, 1590), p. 496. Ferrand is concerned with the use of conjecture in detecting love. The passage in van Heurne is not so specific, though he mentions the stories of Perdiccas and of Antiochus and Stratonice, two instances in which the physician was obliged to make guesses concerning the true cause of the disease. "Saepe ab amore haec scabies et tabes invadit, ac eam tegunt aegri, et medicos ludunt et se laedunt. Quare stratagemate hinc

opus est astuto, et caute omnia perlustranda."
16. [*L. quom. morb. simul. sint arguendi*]: Galen, *Quomodo morbum simulantes sint deprehendendi libellus*: "quod medicinae proprium non fuerat, sed captus eius et rationis, quae communis dicitur: quam licet amnibus sit communis, pauci tamen exactam habent. Experientia igitur medicae si conjungatur haec externa facultas, alia quoque similia fingentes deprehendere licet." See ed. Kühn, vol. XIX, pp. 3–4.

XIV. Diagnostic Signs of Love Melancholy

1. [*Avic. l. 3. fen. I. tract. 4. c. 23*]: Avicenna, *Liber canonis*, bk. III, fen 1, tr. 5, chs. 23–24. Avicenna does not, however, dwell on sight as Ferrand implies.
2. [*A. Dulaurens*]: *Questiones anatomiques*, bk. V, ch. 12, in *Toutes les oeuvres*, p. 119ʳ. "Doncques les muscles de l'oeil sont seulement six, ausquels les anatomistes ont donné des noms particuliers, appellants le premier *hausser* et *superbe*, le second *abbaisseur* et *humble*, le troisiesme *ameneur* et *beuveur*, le quatriesme *emmeneur* et *dedaigneux*, et les deux obliques *tournoyeurs, circulaires*, et *amoureux*; d'autant qu'ils sont comme les guides et messagers de l'amour."
3. [*Gordon c. de Amore part 2 de ulspe capit. Mercat l. 1 meth med. l. 17*]: Bernard of Gordon, *Lilium medicinae*, "De passionibus capitis," particula 2, ch. 20: "De amore, qui hereos dicitur," pp. 216–19.

   Luis Mercado, *De internorum morborum curatione*, bk. I, ch. 17, in *Opera*, vol. III, p. 103: "Unum quidem, qui rationi adesset, et alterum, qui sensui assisteret: illum ad divinae lucis contemplationem, ad puram castamque vitam semper adspirantem; hunc vero Veneris esse stimulum, qui ubi procax petulansque projectis habenis ac devorato pudore exorbitat, infra hominis speciem ipsum hominem deiicit, et ad ferinas damnatasque cupiditates impellit: cui profecto congruere magis furoris et insaniae nomen, quam amoris multi ex philosophis consuerunt."
4. [*4. Aeneid.*]: Virgil, bk. IV. 68–69, 74–78:
   > Uritur infelix Dido, totaque vagatur
   > Urbe furens . . .
   > Nunc media Aeneam secum per moenia ducit,
   > Sidoniasque ostentat opes, urbemque paratam.
   > Incipit effari, mediaque in voce resistit:
   > Nunc eadem labente dic convivia quaerit,
   > Iliacosque iterum demens audire labores
   > Exposcit, pendetque iterum narrantis ab ore.

   See trans. H. Rushton Fairclough (Loeb, 1965), p. 400.
5. [*Gal. com. 1. progn.*]: Galen, *In Hippocratis prognostica commentarius*, bk. 1, ch. 4, ed. Kühn, vol. XVIII/2, p. 19: "Sunt autem et qui propter amorem moerore afficiuntur."
6. [*Stat. l. 2. Achill.*]: Statius, *Achilleid* I. 304–306:
   > Nec latet haustus amour, sed fax vibrata medullis

> Un vultus, atque ora redit, lucemque genarum
> Fingit, et impulsam tenui sudore pererrat.

See trans. J. H. Mozley, 2 vols. (Loeb, 1961), vol. II, pp. 530–31. Read, "tingit et impulsum tenui sudore perrerrat."

7. [*Quest. 5. l. 1. sympos.*]: Plutarch, *Table Talk*, bk. I, no. 5, *Moralia*, vol. VIII, p. 65, "For inasmuch as lovers have persuaded themselves that the objects of their affections are fair and noble, they want everybody to be persuaded. This desire incited the Lydian Candaules to drag his servant into his own wife's bedroom to gaze upon her: for lovers want others to bear them witness." The story of Candaules comes originally from Herodotus, *The Histories*, bk. I, 8–12.

8. Ovid, *The Art of Love* II. 123:

> Non formosus erat, sed erat facundus Ulysses:
> Attamen aequoreas torsit amore deas.

See ed. J. H. Mozley, pp. 74–75.

9. [*Pausan. in Eliac. Plut. tract. de praecept. matrim*]: Pausanias, *Description of Greece*, bk. V, "*Elis*," trans. W. H. S. Jones, vol. II, p. 443.

Plutarch, *Advice to Bride and Groom* (*Conjugalia praecepta*), in *Moralia*, vol. II, p. 301: "Indeed, the ancients gave Hermes a place at the side of Aphrodite, in the conviction that the pleasure in marriage stands especially in need of reason; and they also assigned a place there to Persuasion and the Graces, so that married people should succeed in attaining their mutual desires by persuasion and not by fighting and quarrelling."

Lucian, *Dialogues of the Gods* VII, vol. VII, p. 295.

10. II Samuel 13:4: The topic is diagnostic signs of love melancholy, illustrated here by the story of Amnon and Tamar mentioned in the previous chapter (see n. 5, above): "And he [Jonadab] said to him, 'O son of the king, why are you so haggard morning after morning?' Amnon said to him 'I love Tâmar, my brother Absolom's sister.'" Then Jonadab taught him the ruse for luring her to his bed to seduce her. The languishing countenance was the sign of love that Jonadab had noticed.

11. Ovid, *Heroides* XXI, "Cydippe to Acontius," ll. 215–20.

12. Lucius Apuleius, *Metamorphoses*, bk. X: "Pallor deformis, marcentes oculi, lassa genua, quies turbida et spiritus cruciatus tarditate vehementior": See trans. W. Adlington, 1566, rev. S. Gaselee (Loeb, 1947), pp. 474–75: "Every man knoweth well the signs and tokens of love, and how that sickness is convenient to the same, working upon health and countenance; her knees weak, her rest disturbed, and she would sigh deeply by reason of her slow torment; there was no comfort in her, but continual weeping and sobbing, in so much you would have thought that she had some spice of an ague, saving that she wept unreasonably." Ferrand argues that by these symptoms the lady was discovered to her son-in-law, though in Apuleius' tale no one was able to find out, and in desperation she was forced to tell him herself. Ferrand believes that Apuleius must have learned these symptoms from one of the ancient doctors such as Avicenna, an anacronism the English translator noted and sets right in a marginal note: "Apuleius could not learn any thing of Avicenna,

before whose time he lived above 800 years. But this Chronologicall errour the Reader may be pleas'd to passe by: since it cannot argue any want of judgement in the Author, but meere incogitancy only." In point of fact, the probable origin of this reference to Apuleius is Giovan Battista della Porta, *De humana physiognomonia libri IV*, bk. I, ch. 1, p. 2: "Apulei noverca privigni sui amore aestuans, ita describitur: *Pallor deformis, marcentes oculi, lassa genua, quies turbida, et spiritus cruciatus tarditate vehementior.*" It is also probable that Ferrand took his reference to Dido's love symptoms from the same source, given its proximity in both works to this reference to Apuleius.

13. [*Arnal. de Villan. cap. de Amore.*]: Arnald of Villanova, *De amore heroico*, p. 51: This section deals with the "accidentia" of the disease.

14. [*Chr. Avega l. 3. met. med. c. 17.*]: Cristóbal de Vega, *Liber de arte medendi*, bk. III, ch. 17, p. 414: "Est enim amor animi solicitudo perpetua, et cura pertinax, spei, timoris, tristitiae, et laetitiae plena: haec vero cum diu perseverat, cerebrum exsiccat, et hominem evigilat, et delirare cogit, et omnia praeter unum amatum odio prosequi, oculi excavantur, nec tamen lachrymas fundunt, voluptate pleni apparent, et palpebras continenter movent, pallet etiam facies: fiunt enim (ut Galenus inquit in comme. praefationis in lib. progno.) decolorati, et insomnes, graciles quoque fieri testatur, cui sententiae experimentum subscribit."

15. Ovid, *Heroides* XI. 29–32, 35:

> Fugerat ore color, maciesque obduxerat artus.
> Sumebant minimos ora coacta cibos:
> Nec somni faciles, et non erat annua nobis,
> Et gemitum nullo pressa dolore dabant,
> Prima malum nutrix animo praesensit anili.

See ed. Henricus Dörrie, p. 151: "Fugerat ore color, macies adduxerat artus"; "Nec somni facile et nox erat annua nobis"; "laesa" for "pressa."

16. [*Val Max. l. 5. c. 7. Plut. in Demetr.*]: Valerius Maximus, *Factorum et dictorum memorabilium libri novem*, bk. V, ch. 7, pp. 261–63.

Plutarch's *Lives*, "Demetrius," XXXVIII: "stammering speech, fiery flushes, darkened vision, sudden sweats, irregular palpitations of the heart, and finally, as his soul was taken by storm, helplessness, stupor, and pallor." See trans. Bernadotte Perrin, vol. IX, pp. 92–94. See n. 4 of the previous chapter.

This passage invites confusion insofar as Ferrand's list concludes with a reference to Sappho, followed by an unidentified Greek text that is, in fact, from Plutarch's *Life of Demetrius*, then by a second reference to Sappho and a Greek text from Longinus attributed to her, and finally by a translation of the line by Catullus that is simultaneously attributed to both Ovid and Statius. Subsequent annotations will clarify origins and attributions.

17. [*L. de subl. gen. dicend.*]: Longinus, *A Treatise Concerning Sublimity*: "ἀλλὰ καμμὲν γλῶος'ἔαν ἄν δὲ λεπτὸν / ἀντίκα χρῶ πῦρ λώοδεδρόμακεν. / ομμάτεσσιν δ'οὐδὲν δ'ὅρηνυ. βομβεῦσιν δ'ἀχοαὶ μοι." Ed. D. A. Russell (Oxford: Clarendon, 1967), p. 15: "ἀλλὰ κὰμ μὲν γλῶσσα †έαγε. λέπτον δ' / ἄυτικα χπῶ πῦρ ὑπαδεδρόμακεν· / ὀππάτεσσι δ'οὐδὲν ὄπημμ', ἐπιρρόμβεισι δ'ἄκουαι."

18. Catullus, L. 9–11:

> Lingua sed torpet, tenues sub artus
> Flamma demanat, sonitu suopte
> Tinniunt aures, gemina et teguntur
> Lumina nocte.

See trans. F. W. Cornish (Loeb, 1962), pp. 60–61. This text reads *tenuis* for *tenues* and *tintinant* for *tinniunt*.

19. Remy Belleau, "Traduction d'une Ode de Sapphon":

> Nul ne me semble egaler mieux
> Les hauts Dieux
> Que celuy qui face à face
> T'oit parler, et voit la grace
> De ton soubs-ris gracieux.
>
> Ce qui va jusqu'au dedans
> De mes sens
> Piller l'esprit qui s'esgare,
> Car voyant ta beauté rare,
> Le voir fallir je me sens.
>
> Ma langue morne devient,
> Et me vient
> Un feu qui furette
> Desoubs ma peau tendrelette:
> Tant ta beauté me retient!
>
> Rien plus de l'oeil je ne voy
> Prez de moy:
> Tousjours l'oreille me corne,
> Une sueur froide, et morne
> Soudain coule dedans moy.
>
> Je suis en chasse, à l'horreur
> A la peur,
> Je suis plus palle, et blesmie,
> Que n'est la teste flestrie
> De l'herbe par la chaleur.
>
> La peu s'en faut que la mort,
> Sur le bord
> De sa barque ne m'envoye,
> Et soudain que l'on me voye
> Souffler l'esprit demy-mort.

See *Oeuvres poetiques de Remy Belleau*, vol. I, p. 46, l. 10: "Le voix faillir"; l. 13: "Un petit feu"; l. 17: "Prez de toi."

20. [*Oribas. l. 8. synops. c. 9. de amore. Paul Aegineta. l. 3. c. 17. de amore. Haly*

Abb. 9. Theo. c. 7 Alsar. lib. pract. sec. 2 c. 17]: Oribasius, *Synopsis*, in *Oeuvres*, ed. U. C. Bussemaker and C. Daremberg, 7 vols. (Paris: Imprimerie National, 1873), vol. V, p. 413 f. Vols. 5 and 6 of this edition contain a transcription of early Latin translations of Oribasius' text. For a modern critical edition, see the bibliography.

Paul of Aegina, *The Seven Books*, bk. III, ch. 17: "De amantibus," p. 254.

Haly Abbas, *Liber medicinae dictus Regius*, bk. VIII, ch. 7: "De amore," pp. 60ᵛ–61ʳ.

Albucasis (Alsaharavi or Alsaravius), *Liber theoricae necnon practicae* (Venetiis: Augustus Vindicianus, 1519), tr. 1, sec. 2, ch. 17.

21. Galen, *De cognoscendis curandisque animi morbis*, ed. Kühn, vol. V, pp. 1–570. This is a passing reference. The story of Justus' wife and Pylades is from the following.

Galen, *De praenotione ad Posthumum*, ch. 6, ed. Kühn, vol. XIV, pp. 630–35. Galen mocks those who believe in the existence of a pulse peculiar to love: "Nugae igitur sunt pulsus amatorie moti eorum qui ignorant nullum quidem pulsum amoris esse indicem, sed anima turbata ob quamcunque rem pulsus alterari, neque naturalem aequalitatem neque ordinem conservantes" (p. 635). The issue was much debated in the medical schools of the Renaissance, together with that of amatory fever (which Galen postulated); many dissertations were written on these topics.

22. [*L. 3 contr. Philos. et medic c. 14 Christ à Vega. ca de amore.*]: Francisco Valles, *Controversiarum medicarum et philosophicarum*, bk. III, ch. 14: "Utrum sit aliquis pulsus amatorius," pp. 51ᵛ–52ᵛ.

Cristóbal de Vega, *Liber de arte medendi*, bk. III, ch. 17, p. 414: "Pulsus autem eorum qui amore correpti sunt, nullus est peculiaris, sed qualis in animi conturbationibus et conflictationibus, verum amato praesenti, inaequalis sit, aut ubi eius mentio fiat, subito praesertim. Erasistratus namque filium regis novercae Stratonicae, amore correptum intellexit, quoniam ipsa praesente mirum in modum pulsus fuit immutatus. Et Galen foeminam Pyladis amore captam agnovit, ut lib. de praenotione testatur, quoniam cum Pyladis mentio habita fuisset, pulsum variis modis agitatum invenit. Ipso vero absente pulsus peruus fit et imbecillus, et temporis processu durus."

Plutarch, "Demetrius," in *Lives*, vol. IX, p. 95: "ἀταξία καὶ θόρυβος."

Avicenna does not discuss the problem of an amatory pulse in his chapter on love. He simply states that the pulse of the lover is irregular ("diversus absque ordine"). See n. 23, below.

23. [*L. 3. Fen I. tract. 4. ca. 23 de Amore*]: Avicenna, *Liber canonis*, bk. III, fen 1, tr. 4, ch. 23, p. 206ᵛ: "Et pulsus ipsius est pulsus diversus absque ordine omnino: sicut est pulsus habentium moestitiam seu fastidium vel timorem.

Cumque propter illud diversificatur diversitate magna et fit similis interfecto."

Avicenna continues: "deinde iteratur et experitur illud multotiens, scitur quod illud est nomen eius, quod diligitur; deinde similiter rememorentur figura, et mansio, et illud in quo valet, et artes, et genus, et regiones, et comparetur ad nomen eius, quod diligitur unumquodque eorum, et servetur pulsus, ita ut cum alteratur apud rememorationem unius rei multotiens; aggregentur inde proprietates eius, quod diligitur ex nomine et habitu et statura, et ex eo in quo praevalet, et ex his, quae inducunt, in cognitionem illius." The method suggested by Avicenna is simply an extension of that first developed by Erasistratus in the story of Antiochus and Stratonice.

Galen, *De praenotione ad Posthumum*, ch. 6, ed. Kühn, vol. XIV, pp. 630–35.

Paul of Aegina, *The Seven Books*, bk. III, ch. 17: "De amantibus," p. 254.

Jean Aubery, *L'antidote d'amour*, pp. 56^V–63^r, asks if there is a special pulse belonging to lovers, for were that the case, then the pulse could be used to determine those inclined to love, and not only as an indication of love when the beloved was present. There was the belief that certain conditions and general temperaments should be reflected in the pulse. Aubery cites Galen's book *De differentia pulsuum* as the model for his lengthy discourse on the pulse and the factors leading to its variations. Aubery concludes, however, that there is not a pulse characteristic to lovers after playing advocate to the theory over several pages. In the cases of the consul's wife's love for Pylades, and of Antiochus' love for Stratonice, the pulse merely indicated an agitation of the soul, produced only when the beloved is evoked or brought into the room. Yet Aubery seems to endorse the principle that there are pulses peculiar to the different passions and that because love is based on such other passions its pulse is mixed and thus disguised by the others. This solution leaves the medical controversy underlying the discussion entirely unresolved. He argues that by the pulse alone it is impossible to identify love, but only because it is so similar to other pulses that it escapes exact analysis. Aubery thereby rescues the concept of the distinct pulse on a theoretical level, but removes the possibility of empirical demonstration for lack of refinement in the monitoring.

24. [*l. 2. arth. Medic. sec. 3. cap. 6.*]: Cristóbal de Vega, *Liber de arte medendi*, bk. II, sec. 3, ch. 6, p. 200: "Quod si uvae praedictae in ventre remorentur, improbe coquentur, et in venis pravum succum generabunt. Capitis dolores afferunt, ventrem distendunt quapropter respirationem impediunt, et suspiria adhuc magis. Ea de causa qui amore conflictantur uvas edere nolunt, quoniam cordis compressionem patiuntur, ex uvarum esu, distento ore ventriculi, compresso tamen corde, nec probe ventilantur: nec suspirare vacat, ob loci angustiam."

25. In ch. XVI Ferrand will take the side of Oribasius and Alsaravius against Paul of Aegina in a discussion he raises from their views concerning the eyes of lovers, whether only the eyes are affected as Paul asserts, or the entire body as Oribasius and Alsaravius hold. Yet in this case study, based on his own practice and therefore a statement central to the entire treatise, he remarks that hollow-set eyes, with the rest of the body in good condition, are indicative of an affliction of the soul. Ferrand

finds himself between two traditions, the one holding that love as a psychological derangement is minimally reflected in the body, and the other, that love, in particular, produces a number of physical symptoms brought about by the burned humors, the sleeplessness, and the self-imposed starvation. In this case study, Ferrand may, in fact, be more faithful to what he actually observed than to the traditional medical and poetic accounts with their conventionalized symptoms. In brief, despite his long analysis of the physiological signs of love, in his one case study, Ferrand sees a young man in good physical condition, but showing signs of grief through his sunken eyes—an analysis perfectly in keeping with that of Paul of Aegina.

The case study of the young man from the Mas d'Agen in love with the hostess' daughter has been altered slightly from the earlier edition. It is not clear in either version whether the girl with the lamp is the girl beloved or merely a catalyst to the changing of the pulse. Ferrand states specifically in the 1610 edition that the young man came from Toulouse to Agen to escape his misery, that Ferrand had known the patient happy and jovial in Toulouse only a short time before, and that the young man was in love with the daughter of his hostess, presumably also in Toulouse. Whether this vagueness was an accident of Ferrand's desire to play Erasistratus with the pulse that caused him to invent the beautiful girl who walks through his consulting room, or whether they had a hostess in common whom the young man had come from Toulouse to be near is difficult to say. Such would stand in contradiction to the tradition that one flees the place where the beloved is in order to find relief.

26. [*Eleg. 5. l. 1.*]: Propertius, bk. I, *Elegy* V. 24: "Nescit amor priscis cedere imaginibus." See trans. H. E. Butler, p. 14.

27. François Valleriola, *Observationum medicinalium libri VI*, p. 185. See also ch. II above, n. 13.

For another contemporary medical case study, see João Rodriguez de Castello Branco (Amatus Lusitanus), *Curationum medicinalium centuriae septem* (Burdigalae: ex typographia Gilberii Vernoi, 1620), "Medicinalium centuria tertia, curatio LVI, in qua agitur de iuvene Hebraeo, puellae Hebreae capto," p. 309: "Iuvenis Thessalonicensis Hebraeus puellae Hebreae amore captus, ita eam deperibat, ut brevi in insaniam devenerit. Huius igitur nos curam suscipientes, optimo victus ordine pro ut atra bile affectis convenit constituto *illi ex elleboro syrupum a nobis compositum saepe ad humoris praeparationem dabamus.* At quum nocte quadam ex lapide cyaneo stellato dicto, catapotiis eum purgare decreveramus, hic puellae domum pervenit, quam chordis dispositis per fenestram intravit, ubi puellae parentes inveniens, eos pugnis pessime affecit. Sed illico convocato principe satellitum, in carcerem fuit ductus, ubi obstrusus per aliquot dies resipuit, et mente constans factus est." A scholia follows in which he deals with the meanings of the word *hereos*, showing how the word came to mean lord, or herren, for the Germans because of the strength of love. He describes love as a form of insanity and cites the texts on love by Avicenna, Paul of Aegina, and Galen on the woman in love with Pylades: "Caeterum memini me in agro Eborensi apud Lusitanos, puellam iuvenem nobilem amantem deperisse, et in insania devenisse: non minus superioribus diebus filia Benaheni mercatoris, cum ab eius patre eam esse nuptam expositum esset, ac postea eius loco soror locata esset in insaniam devenit, quae hodie quoque insana perseverat. Nata autem puella haec est, semibrachio dextro tantum, caetera omnia membra perfecta habens."

XV. The Cause of Paleness in Lovers

1. Ferrand's probable source is Levinus Lemnius, *Occulta naturae miracula*, bk. 1, ch. 12, p. 64: "Diogenes aliquando conspicatus exangui gilvoque color iuvenem, aut amare illum, aut invidere pronunciatis. Invidi enim cum aliena virtute discruciantur, contabescunt, ac medullarum, ossiumque putredinem concipiunt. Alium quendam cum ex amore pallescere videret, in proprio quidem corpore mortuum illum dictitabat, vivet autem in alieno."

2. Ovid, *The Art of Love* I. 729: "Palleat omnis amans, color hic est aptus amanti." Ed. J. H. Mozley, p. 6ء. This line from Ovid is the first of a number of quotations and paraphraᴢᵉs in this chapter taken directly from Giovan Battista della Porta's *De humana physiognomonia libri IV*, bk. III, pp. 200–202.

3. [*Problem 4. sec. 38*]: Aristotle, *Problems*, bk. IV, no. 35, is bk. XXXVIII, no. 4 (967a): "ἄχροια ἔοικεν εἶναι οἷον σῆψίς τις χρωτός." Ed. W. S. Hett, p. 251.

4. Ferrand finds this discussion of color in Giovan Battista della Porta, *De humana physiognomonia libri IV*, p. 201: "Sed oriri posset difficultas ex nominis χλωροῦς significatione, cum apud Graecos χλωρόν *viride* significet, et nulla facies hominibus viridis sit, sed flava, vel pallida aut livida, ut nos vertimus." Ferrand adds further examples derived from Plutarch and Lucretius.

5. [*Com. 3. in l. 6. epid. Com. 47. l. 2. Proch.*]: "ὠχροὺς τινας ἰδόντες, ἐρωτῶσι τινι αἰτίαν, δια ἣν οὕτω γεγόνασι χλωροί: μηδὲν διαφέρειν ἡγούμενοι χλωρὸν εἰπεῖν καὶ ὠχρόν." The quotation comes from Galen's *In Hippocratis de victu acutorum commentarii quatuor*, ed. G. Helmereich, in *Corpus medicorum Graecorum*, vol. V. 9. 1 (Leipzig: Teubner, 1914), p. 182. The critical text reads: "ὠχροὺς γάρ τινας ἰδόντες ἐρωτῶσι τὴν αἰτίαν, δι'ἣν οὕτω γεγόνασι χλωροί, μηδὲν διαφέρειν ἡγούμενοι χλωρὸν εἰπεῖν ἢ ὠχρόν."

   Galen, *Commentarium in Hippocratis prognostica*, ed. Kühn, vol. XVIII. 2, pp. 70–71: "Siccum quidem omnino erit ulcus ob imbecillitatem corpus alentis facultatis. Color autem nunquam semper unus erit, sed eum partim quod plurimum corpora humoribus a se invicem differant, partim ob noxae magnitudinem immutari necesse est. Si namque humores biliosi exsuperent, color erit pallidus; si vero melancholici aut lividus aut altero τοῦ χλωροῦ significatur aeruginosus. Diximus vero antea idem nonnunquam τὸ χλωρὸν significare quod pallidum, aliquando vero colorem fere aerugini similem, quo quidem significatu etiam brassicam homines Graeci χλωρὰν dicere solent. Ad eundem modum ipsa quoque noxa major quidem colorem lividum, accedit enim is ad nigrum, minor vero rubrum atque pallidum generat. Eamque ob rem plerique extremum sententiae scribunt hoc modo ἢ ὠχρόν τε καὶ ξηρόν, id est aut pallidum et siccum, alii vero illo ἢ χλωρόν τε καὶ ξηρόν."

6. This entire discussion, including the references to Favorinus, Dioscorides, and Aristotle (documented in n. 7, below), is derived from Giovan Battista della Porta, p. 202: "Et Dioscorides optimum myrrhae colorem describens, ὑπόχλωρον vocat, id est, subflavum, nos subviridem, cum laudatissimae myrrhae color non sit subviris. Facit ad rem nostram Favorinus, qui docet, eosdem esse χλωρούς, qui ὠχροὶ, id est pallidi; et dictione ὠχρὸς, ex dictione χλωρὸς deduci, transposita litera ω, et sublata λ." Ferrand alters the order somewhat and adds the elusive reference to Jean Ruel [Ruellius]. In the edition we examined of Dioscorides' *De medica materia libri sex, Joanne Ruellio Successionensi interprete* (Lugduni: apud Joan. Francis de Gabiano, 1555), there was no commentary on myrrhe (see bk. III, ch. 39). We note the following however: Ruellius, *De natura stirpium libri tres* (Paris: ex officina Simonis Colinaei, 1536), bk. I, ch. 98, pp. 256–57: "Dioscoridi pinguitudo est reventis myrrhae, tunditur haec cum pauxillo aquae, dein prelo vel machinis aqua, stracten vocatum, commendatissima quae impromiscua, et oleo libera sit. Stacte Graecis nominatur, quoniam e stillatitia myrrha fiat, colore pallido suavitate mira."

For the reference to Guarino of Favora [Varinus Favorinus], see his *Dictionarium . . . multis variisque ex autoribus collectum totius linguae Graecae commentarius* (Basileae: R. Chimerinus, 1538), p. 1868.

7. [*Arist l. de color.*]: Aristotle, *On Colours*, in *Minor Works*, (797a) trans. W. S. Hett (Loeb, 1963), p. 35: "For the moisture in them being no longer blackened by drying causes the change of colour. For when growing black and mixed with green it becomes, as has been said, greenish [τῷ χλωρῷ]: but as the black grows steadily weaker, the colour changes back again gradually to green, and at last becomes yellow." The reference comes from Della Porta; see the preceding note.

8. [*L. de in ter. aff. Aret. l. 1. de caus. l. sig. morb. chr. c. 13.*]: Hippocrates, *On Internal Infections*: "οιδιοειδὴς" "ὑπωφακώδης." *Oeuvres complètes*, ed. Littré, vol. VII, p. 249.

Aretaeus the Cappadocian, *On the Causes and Symptoms of Chronic Diseases*, ch. 13: "*On the Liver*": "χροιὴ χλοήβαφος," See *The Extant Works of Aretaeus, the Cappadocian*, ed. F. Adam, p. 76. The quotation is to be found in bk. I, ch. 13, of the *editio princeps* of the Greek, *De acutorum et diuturnorum morborum causis et signis*, ed. J. Goupyl (Paris: A. Turnebus, 1554). For a modern edition, see Aretaeus, ed. C. Hude in the *Corpus medicorum Graecorum*, (Berlin: Teubner, 1958), vol. II, p. 54.

Plautus, *Curculio*, l. 231. See *Plautus*, trans. P. Nixon, 5 vols. (Loeb, 1963), vol. II, p. 214.

9. [*Ovid. 4. Metam.*]: *Metamorphoses* IV. 264–70, trans. Frank Justus Miller (Loeb, 1944), vol. I, pp. 196–97: "They say that her limbs grew fast to

the soil and her deathly pallor changed in part to a bloodless plant; but in part 'twas red, and a flower, much like a violet, came where her face had been. Still, though roots hold her fast, she turns ever towards the sun and, though changed herself, preserves her love unchanged."

10. [3. De diff. resp.]: Galen, De difficultate respirationis, bk. III, ch. 12: "τὸ γὰρ ὦχρωδες χρῶμα κακοπραγοῦντος ἥπατον γνώρισμα," ed. Kühn, vol. VII, p. 952.

11. [Hipp. l. de humor.]: Hippocrates, On the Humors: "τὸ χρῶμα τῶν χυμῶν ὅκου μὴ ἄμπωτις ἐστιν· ὥσπερ ἀνθέων." Oeuvres complètes, ed. Littré, vol. V, p. 477. The original reads: "Τὸ μὲν χρῶμα τῶν χυμῶν, ὅκου μὴ ἄμπωτις ἐστι τῶν χυμῶν, ὥσπερ ἀνθέων."

12. Aretaeus the Cappadocian, On the Causes and Symptoms of Chronic Diseases, p. 300: "The habit of the body also becomes perverted: colour, a darkish-green, unless the bile do not pass downward, but is diffused with the blood over the whole system."

XVI.   What Kinds of Eyes Melancholy Lovers Have

1. [L. 6. Epid. sec. 4. aph. 26.]: Hippocrates, Epidemics: "ὀφθαλμοὶ ὡς ἂν ἰσκύωσν, οὕτω καὶ γῆον." This aphorism is generally not credited to Hippocrates.

   Of note is the fact that Ferrand, in treating this topic, does not refer to the text in Aristotle's On the Generation of Animals, which deals with the relationship between the eyes and the regenerative parts. See n. 3, below.

2. Avicenna, Liber canonis, bk. III, fen 1, tr. 4, ch. 23, p. 206[V]. For further references see ch. XIV, n. 20, and n. 5, below.

3. [L. de corp. part.]: Rufus of Ephesus, a reference either to the Names of the Parts of the Body or to the Anatomy of the Parts of the Body. In both treatises Rufus describes the eye; in neither does he speak of the hollowness specifically caused by a general dehumidification of that region. Ferrand's "χοιλιδιᾶν" is approximated only by Rufus' "κοῖλα" describing the depression at the corner of the eye near the nose. See Oeuvres de Rufus d'Ephèse, ed. Charles Daremberg and Emile Ruelle (Amsterdam: Adolf Hakkert, 1963), p. 136.

   Alexander of Aphrodisias, Problemata, bk. I, no. 98, in Physici et medici Graeci minores, ed. I. L. Ideler (Amsterdam: Adolf Hakkert, 1963), p. 34.

4. [Gorraus. Merc. in progn. Hip. Foesius in Hippocr.]: Jean de Gorris [Gorraeus], Definitionem medicarum libri XXIV literis Graecis distincti (Francofurdi: apud Claudium Marnium, et heredes Joannis Aubrii, 1601), p. 233.

   Girolamo Mercuriale, Commentarii eruditissimi in Hippocratis . . . prognostica, prorrhetica, de victus ratione in morbis acutis, et epidemicas historias (Francofurti: typis Joannis Saurii, 1602), p. 735.

   Hippocratis, Opera omnia, ed. Anuce Foës (Francofurdi: apud Andreae Wechli heredes, 1595), p. 277: "κοῖλα dicuntur partes oculorum concavae quae genis inferioribus subiacent, et plurimum in pravo cor-

poris habitu, et insignem oruditamem ex crapula ac ingurgitatione coacervantibus, aut longum morbum trahentibus, sanguine defectis, hydrope ac lienis tumore laborantibus intumescunt. Isagoges author et si eas cavitates quae ex utraque nasi parte insunt κοῖλα vocari scribit."
Stephan of Athens, *Alphabetum empiricum, sive Dioscorides et Stephani Atheniensis philosophorum et medicorum, de remediis expertis liber, justa alphabeti ordinem digestus* (n. p. , 1581), pp. 18^r –51^v.
Of course, Ferrand could make no use here of the passage in Aristotle's *On the Generation of Animals*, bk. II, ch. 7, where he states that "of all the regions in the head the eyes are the most seminal, as is proved by the fact that this is the only region which unmistakenly changes its appearance during sexual intercourse, and those who overfrequently indulge in it have noticeably sunken eyes," because the same condition of the eyes is here attributed to those who are wanton and lustful as opposed to the frustrated lover who may, in fact, be suffering from a surfeit of unexpended seed. Aristotle theorized that copious expenditures of semen draw vital corresponding fluids from the eyes, thereby bringing on the hollow appearance. Ferrand does not enter into the controversy that is potentially here. See below, ch. XXII, n. 27.
5. Avicenna, *Liber canonis*, bk. III, fen 1, tr. 5, ch. 23.
   Oribasius, *Synopsis*, bk. VIII, ch. 9, p. 414: "Voici quels sont les symptômes qu'on observe chez les amoureux: les yeux sont creux, quoiqu'ils ne pleurent pas; ils semblent être remplis de volupté; les paupières sont continuellement agitées; et, tandis que toutes les autres parties du corps sont affaissées, les paupières seules ne le sont pas chez les amoureux."
   Albucasis, *Liber theoricae necnon practicae*, tr. 1, sec. 2, ch. 17.
   Paul of Aegina, *The Seven Books*, bk. III, sec. 17: "caeteris partibus corporis illaesis, nullaque calamitate collabentibus soli illi amatoribus concidunt." See ed. Francis Adams, vol. I, p. 391.
6. [*L. 3. de arte Medica ca. de Amore*]: Cristóbal de Vega, *Liber de arte medendi*, bk. III, ch. 17, p. 414: "Paulus dixerit, nulla ex corporis partibus collabente, solos oculos collabi. Nisi dixeris, collapsum intellexisse segnem motum, et decidentiam."
7. Hippocrates, *Epidemics*, bk. VI, sec. 1, aph. 15: "ἔρριψιν." *Oeuvres complètes*, ed. Littré, vol. V, pp. 276–77.
8. Galen, *De crisibus*, bk. II, ch. 13, ed. Kühn, vol. IX, pp. 695 ff. Discussing ephemeral fevers, which he considers affections of the spirit, Galen analyzes those symptoms which will later be applied to erotic melancholy: "Sunt autem hae [febres ephemerae] tantummodo spiritus affectiones, absque humorum putredine aut partis inflammatione, nisi inflammatis inguinibus accidant. Earum autem generationis causae sunt vigiliae ac cruditas et tristitia et timor et ira et curae deustioque ac refrigeratio, lassitudo et ebrietas et quaecunque similia sunt. . . . Adest autem iis quidem qui ob tristitiam febricitant, acrimonia potius quam multitudo caloris, sicuti iis qui ob iram contrario modo. Sed et tenuitas corporis in iis qui tristitia quam in iis qui cogitationibus vexati sunt manifestius apparet et oculorum cavitas et quaedam insolita decoloratio. . . . Eos

autem qui nimium vigilarunt, distinguit et decolorationis modus, nam subtumida ipsis facies inest et oculorum motus manifesti, vix enim attollunt palpebras; et humiditas oculorum, sicci enim contristati fiunt et cogitantibus. Cavitas vero commune omnium symptoma est, tristitia, vigiliae, curarum, non tamen et irae." Avicenna, *Liber canonis*, bk. III, fen 1, tr. 4, ch. 23, p. 206^V.

9. Plato, *Symposium* (203D), ed. W. R. M. Lamb, p. 181.

XVII.   Whether Tears Are Symptoms of Love

1. [*Aphor. 17. sec. 1. l. 6*]: Hippocrates, *Epidemics*, bk. VI, sec. 1, aph. 13, *Oeuvres complètes*, ed. Littré, vol. V, p. 273.
2. Alexander of Aphrodisias, *Problemata*, bk. I. no. 21, in *Physici et medici Graeci minores*, ed. I. L. Ideler, vol. 1, p. 10.
3. [*Avicen. Arnald.*]: Avicenna, *Liber canonis*, bk. III, fen 1, tr. 4, ch. 23, p. 206^V.
   Arnald of Villanova, *De amore heroico*, p. 52.
4. [*Propert. l. 1. eleg. 11.*]: Propertius, bk. I, Elegy XII. 16: "Non nihil aspersis gaudet Amor lachrymis," See trans. H. E. Butler, p. 32.
5. Ovid, *The Art of Love*, bk. III. 292: "quoque volunt plorant tempore, quoque modo," See ed. J. H. Mozley, pp. 138–39.

XVIII.   The Cause of Insomnia and Sighing in Lovers

1. [*Arnal. c de Amore. Gord. de Amore.*]: Arnald of Villanova, *Tractatus de amore heroico*, in *Opera medica omnia*, vol. III, p. 51.
   Bernard of Gordon, *Lilium medicinae*, "*De passionibus capitis*," pt. 2, ch. 20: "De amore, qui hereos dicitur," pp. 216–19.
2. Ovid, *The Art of Love*, bk. I. 735: "Attenuant iuvenum vigilata corpora noctes," See trans. J. H. Mozley, pp. 62–63: "Attenuant invenum vigitatae corpora noctes."
3. André Du Laurens, *Des maladies melancholiques, et du moyen de les guarir*, in *Toutes les oeuvres*, pp. 27^V–28^r: "Aux melancholiques la matiere defaut, l'ame n'est point en repos, le cerveau est mal disposé, la matiere est une humeur melancholique, seiche comme la cendre, de laquelle ne se peut eslever aucune vapeur douce, le cerveau est intemperé et du tout desseiche, l'ame est en perpetuelle inquietude: car la peur qu'ils ont leur represente tousjours des fascheux objects qui les rongent et les empeschent de dormir. Que si par fois il arrive qu'ils soient surpris de quelque sommeil, c'est un dormir fascheux, accompagné de mille phantosmes hideux, et de songes si effroyables, que les veilles leur sont plus agreables."
4. André Du Laurens, *Des maladies melancholiques, et du moyen de les guarir*, in *Toutes les oeuvres*, p. 27^V: "Les melancholiques souspirent ordinairement, pource que l'ame estant occupée à la varieté de phantosmes, ne

se ressouviennent pas de respirer, de façon que la Nature est contraincte de tirer en un coup autant d'air qu'elle faisoit en deux, ou trois; et ceste grande respiration s'apelle souspir, qui est comme un redoublement d'haleine. Autant en arrive-il aux amoureux, et à tous ceux qui sont attentifs à quelque profonde contemplation." See also Jean Aubery, *L'antidote d'amour*, p. 31ᵛ. Aubery's discussion not only parallels Ferrand's quite closely but is even more elaborately argued. There is some reason to think that in this instance Aubery serves as a source for Ferrand because a discussion on waking and sleep follows in Aubery (essentially a résumé of Aristotle's *On Sleep and Sleeplessness*). Du Laurens could, of course, have served both independently as a common source.

Cristóbal de Vega, *Liber de arte medendi*, bk. II, ch. 6, p. 200: "Quapropter respirationem impediunt, et suspiria adhuc magis. Ea de causa qui amore conflictantur uvas edere nolunt, quoniam cordis compressionem patiuntur ex uvarum esu, distento ore ventriculi, compresso tamen corde, nec probe ventilantur: nec suspirare vacat, ob loci angustiam."

Whatever Ferrand's sources, however, the entire tradition on the physiology of sighs derives from Alexander of Aphrodisias in the *Problemata*, bk. I, no. 21 (Venetiis: apud Aldum, 1497). See ed. I. L. Ideler, in *Physici et medici Graeci minores*, vol. I, p. 10. Moreover, the entire section from Alexander is cited in Battista Fregoso, *Contramours*, pp. 11–12. In essence, the intense concentration upon the object of the beloved causes the animal spirits to leave the muscles, including those in the chest responsible for breathing. The lack of oxygen causes the heart to load up with excrements, in turn alerting the soul, which responds by causing the lungs to draw in and release air in an effort to catch up and to expel the waste materials, in brief, to sigh.

XIX. During What Age One Is Subject to Love Melancholy

1. [*Epist. ad Damag.*]: Hippocrates, *Epistle to Damagete*: "ὅλος ὁ ἄνθρωπος ἐκ γενετῆς νοῦσος ἐστι," *Oeuvres complètes*, ed. Littré, vol. IX, p. 372.
2. Hippocrates, *Aphorisms*, sec. 3, no. 19; *Oeuvres complètes*, ed. Littré, vol. IV, p. 495.
3. [*Sent. 571*]: Hippocrates, *Coan Prognoses*: "ἀπὸ ιδ' ἐτέων μέχρι β καὶ μ. πάμφορος ἡ φύσις νοσημάτων ἤδη τοῦ σώματος γίνεται." *Oeuvres complètes*, ed. Littré, vol. IV, p. 487; in the original the years are spelled out and "ἐτέων" follows 42 instead of 14.
4. [*Rosar. in Ind. l. I. ver. matrim.*]: Alberico da Rosate (Rosciate), *Vocabularius utriusque iuris* (Lugduni: apud Jacobum Wyt, 1535), also called *Lexicon* as in the edition of 1498, and later *Dictionarium iuris tam civilis, quam canonici*, ed. Giovanni Francesco Deciani (Venetiis: apud Guerreos fratres et socios, 1573). We have been unable to examine this work, though we believe that it is the one intended by Ferrand, that it was

also referred to as "Index," and that Ferrand's reference will be found in bk. I, "verbo matrimonii." Given Ferrand's habits of scholarship, we suspect, moveover, that the passing references to St. Gregory and St. Jerome will also be found in this source.

5. [*Pli. l. 7. c. 2.*]: Pliny, *Natural History*, bk. VII, sec. 29, vol. II, p. 525: "Clitarchus gave them the name of Mandi; and Megasthenes also assigns them three hundred villages, and says that the women bear children at the age of seven and old age comes at forty." Ferrand advanced the figure to age five or six. Of note is that next to the Mandi was the Paudae tribe, in which men and women lived to be over two hundred years old.

6. [*Caesar l. 6. de bello Gall.*]: Julius Caesar, *The Gallic War*, bk. VI, 22, trans. H. J. Edwards (Loeb, 1946), p. 347: "Those who remain longest in chastity win greatest praise among their kindred; some think that stature, some that strength and sinew are fortified thereby. Further, they deem it a most disgraceful thing to have had knowledge of a woman before the twentieth year; and there is no secrecy in the matter, for both sexes bathe in the rivers and wear skins or small cloaks of reindeer hide, leaving a great part of the body bare." This observation is no argument, however, that German men are infertile before the age of twenty.

7. [*Lib. 1. Instit. tit. 22. l. ult. C. quando tut. esse desin.*]: Justinian, *Institutes of Law*, title xxii, "Quibus modis tutela finitur," "indagatione corporis inhonesta cessante." See *Justiniani, Institutionum juris, libri IV, compositi per Tribonianum v. magnificum et exquaestorem sacri palatii, et Theophilum et Dorotheum VV. illustres et antecessores* (Genevae: apud Eustathium Vignon, 1580), pp. 13–14: "Pupilli pupillaeque, cum puberes esse coeperint, [a] tutela liberantur. Pubertatem autem veteres quidem non solum ex annis, sed etiam ex habitu corporis in maculis aestimari volebant. Nostra autem majestas dignum este castitate nostrorum temporum existimans, bene putavit; quod in foeminis etiam antiquis impudicum esse visum est, id est, inspectionem habitudinis corporis, hoc etiam in masculos extendere. Et ideo nostra sancta constitutione promulgata, pubertatem in masculis post decimum quartum annum completum illico initium accipere disposuimus: antiquitatis normam in foeminis bene positam in suo ordine relinquentes ut post duodecim annos completos viri potentes esse credantur. Item finitur tutela, si adrogati sint adhuc impuberes, vel deportati: item si in servitutem pupillus redigatur, vel si ab hostibus captus fuerit."

8. Aristotle, *On the Generation of Animals*, IV, vi: "θᾶττων νεότητα ἀκμὴν, καὶ γῆρας λαμβάνει τῶν ἀρρένων." See trans. A. L. Peck (Loeb, 1963), pp. 459–61: "though once birth has taken place everything reaches its perfection sooner in females than in males—e.g., puberty, maturity, old age—because females are weaker and colder in their nature."

The idea was commonplace in Renaissance thought. See Levinus Lemnius , *Occulta naturae miracula*, bk. II, ch. 39, p. 251: "Quaecunque propere ac festinanter maturescunt, vel iustam longitudinem assequuntur, celerius intercidunt, nec diutinam aetatem perferunt, quod infantes ac stirpium aliquot genera commonstrant."

The topic was also considered under the subject of sterility, including the ages in which men and women are unable to enjoy Venus or to engender offspring. Medicine was as concerned with the curing of sterility in married couples as in preventing erotic excess in those of childbearing ages. Jean Liébault goes back to Aristotle as his authority in the treatment of the *topos* in *Des maladies des femmes*, bk. II, p. 167: "pareillement l'homme plus jeune que douze ans, et plus vieil que soixante, ne peut engendrer pour la plus grand part, je dis pour la plus grand part, parce qu'Aristote en ses polit. livre 7. chapitre seziesme, estime que l'homme peut engendrer jusques à soixante et dix ans: et la femme concevoir jusques à cinquante: semblablement on a veu des hommes qui à septante cinq ans et plus tard, ont eu des enfans sans aucun soubçon qu'ils leur fussent attribuez. Et de fait, il y a des hommes plus verds et vigoureux à septante cinq, que plusieurs autres à cinquante ans: d'autant que la force de l'homme ne depend de l'aage: ny la foiblesse doit estre limitee des annees passees: mais toutes les deux doivent estre mesurees selon la complexion et habitude bonne ou mauvaise, tant naturelle que acquise du corps."

9. [*4. polit. c. 16. 5. de histor. an. c. 14. et l. 7. c. 6.*]: Aristotle, *Politics*, bk. VII, ch. xiv. 3 (1335a 5), trans. H. Rackham (Loeb, 1967), p. 619: "For since the period of parentage terminates, speaking generally, with men at the age of seventy at the outside, and with women at fifty."

Aristotle, *The History of Animals*, bk. V, ch. 14 (544b), trans. A. L. Peck (Loeb, 1970), vol. II, pp. 135, 141: "Man first produces semen about the age of fourteen, and becomes able to generate at about twenty-one. . . . Among human beings, a man can, at the longest, generate up to the age of seventy, a woman up to fifty; but both occur infrequently. Few people at these ages produce children. Generally the limit for men is sixty-five, for women forty-five."

Aristotle, *The History of Animals*, bk. VII, ch. 6 (585b), ed. Jonathan Barnes in *The Complete Works of Aristotle* (Princeton: Princeton University Press, 1984), vol. I, p. 917: "Men in most cases continue to be fertile until they are sixty years old, and if that limit be overpassed then until seventy years; and men have been actually known to procreate children at seventy years of age."

10. Cornelius Gallus, Elegy I. 180: "A miseri, quorum gaudia crimen habent." *Catullus, Tibullus, Propertius cum Galli fragmentis*, p. 323.

11. [*L. 2. tr. 3. c. 1*]: Avenzoar (Ibn Zuhr), *Liber Theizir*, printed with Averroes' *Colliget* (Venetiis: Otinus de Luna, 1497), bk. II, tr. 3, ch. 1: "Quod est de testiculis et de sterilitate que ex mala complexione ipsorum procedit," p. CII^V b: "Et dicunt similiter medici quod habentes talem complexionem caldam et humidam generant multos filios, et generant quasi usque ad finem senectutis. . . . Aristoteles vero dicit quod a septuaginta annis supra nullus potest masculum generare; sed experimentum nobis certificat, et manifestat quod non sic est, quia multos vidimus octogenarios et supra masculos generasse."

12. [*Pl. l. 7. c. 14*]: Pliny, *Natural History*, bk. VII, ch. 14, pp. 547–49: "A woman does not bear children after the age of 50, and with the majority

menstruation ceases at 40. As for the case of men, it is well known that King Masinissa begot a son when over 86, whom he called Methimannus, and Cato the ex-censor had a son by the daughter of his client Salanicus when he was 81."

13. Felix Platter, *Observationes et curationes aliquot affectuum partibus mulieris generationi dicatis accidentium*, in Israel Spachius, *Gynaeciorum sive de mulierum tum communibus, tum gravidarum, parientium, et puerperarum affectibus et morbis* (Argentinae: sumptibus Lazari Zetneri, 1593) (unnumbered pages at beginning of collection): "Quod ut multa exempla demonstrant: sic parentis et proavi, tanquam propinquiora, adducere satis erit. E quibus genitor meus, post septuagesimum secundum aetatis annum novas nuptias contrahens, liberos sex, et postremam filiam anno aetatis octogesimo procreavit cuius avum, post centesimum vitae annum, filium adhuc genuisse, et donec ille nuptias celebraret vixisse, non solum illum narrantem, verum et ab aliis plurimis, qui illum noverant, saepe audivi. Caeterum causam huius Divinae ordinationis, viro nullum terminum, mulieri vero certum definiente, idque a mundi primordio, (cum et tunc mulieres senes, procreare miraculosum, non naturale fuerit: sicuti exemplo Sarae, uxoris Abrahae demonstratur) esse existimamus, ne humanum genus nimium excresceret, providentia Dei, quae certum numerum eorum qui nasci debuerunt praedestinavit, haecque etiam per naturales causas dirigit, factum esse, cum, si mulier ad extremam aetatem usque procrearet, in infinitum, quod nec terrae totius amplitudo alere posset, humanum genus excresceret."

The topic was pursued in literature as well. See Fletcher and Shakespeare, *The Two Noble Kinsmen*, ed. G. R. Proudfoot (London: Edward Arnold Ltd., 1970), pp. 108–9. Palamon, in his prayer to Venus, celebrates her powers in the following terms:

> I knew a man
> Of eighty winters, . . . who
> A lass of fourteen brided. 'Twas thy power
> To put life into dust: the aged cramp
> Had screw'd his square foot round
> The gout had knit his fingers into knots,
> Torturing convulsions from his globy eyes
> Had almost drawn their spheres, that what was life
> In him seem'd torture; this anatomy
> Had by his fair young fere a boy, and I
> Believ'd it was his, for she sware it was,
> And who would not believe her? (V. i. 109–18)

14. Plutarch in the *Parallel Lives* gives an account of Theseus that suggests Ferrand was exaggerating somewhat about his age because Plutarch says he was somewhat above 50 when he pursued Helen.

15. For information on the *Lex Papia Poppaea*, see Ronald Syme, *The Roman Revolution* (Oxford: Oxford University Press, 1939, 1960), pp. 443 ff., and H. B. Scullard, *From the Gracchi to Nero* (London, Methuen, 1959, 1968), p. 239.

XX. The Signs of Those Who Are Inclined to Love Melancholy

1. [2. ad. Eud. 2]: Aristotle *Eudemian Ethics*, bk. II, ch. 2, 1–5 (1220b), trans. H. Rackham (Loeb, 1961), pp. 247–49: "Let moral character then be defined as a quality of the spirit in accordance with governing reason that is capable of following the reason. We have then to say what is the part of the spirit in respect of which our moral characters are of a certain quality. And it will be in respect of our faculties for emotions according to which people receive certain designations in respect of the emotions, because of their experiencing or being exempt from some form of emotion. . . . But quality corresponds to the faculties: by faculties I mean the properties acting by which persons are designated by the names of the various emotions, for instance choleric, insensitive, erotic, bashful, shameless." The habitual conditions that give rise to emotion and thus to moral temperament lead the inquirer from ethical considerations to the humors, physiognomy, popular theories of trait inheritance and other quasi-medical approaches to behavior. This statement allows Ferrand to anatomize the amorist as one destined to the disease not only by habit, but by "natural constitution and temper of body."

   Cicero, *Tusculan Disputations*, bk. IV. xii. 27, trans. J. E. King (Loeb, 1968), p. 355: "just as for instance there is a difference between intoxication and habitual drunkenness, and it is one thing to be a gallant and another thing to be in love."

   There is an intriguing entry in the *Dictionnaire d'ancien Français* (Paris: 1875), p. 109: "L'amant est celuy qui est jà embabouiné de l'amour ; et l'amoureux celuy qui est enclin à cette folie, de sa complexion naturelle, nourriture, dèscipline, habitude ou autrement," attributed to a work entitled *Maladie d'amour*. It is, in fact, a direct quotation from the opening of Ferrand's chapter, and proof that the work was at least occasionally consulted in the nineteenth century. There remains the possibility, as well, that this passage in Ferrand contains a word echo from Boiastuau in the *Théâtre du monde*, p. 214, where he says "que ceste furie d'amour qui presse si fort, et qui *embabouyne* ainsi le monde, procede de la correspondante qualité du sang."

2. [*Hipp. l. de steril. L. de mor. mul. Gal. l. 1. ad Glauc. c. 1.*]: Hippocrates, *On Sterility in Women*, bk. III of *On the Diseases of Women*. This is a passing reference. See his *Oeuvres complètes*, ed. Littré, vol. VIII.

   Hippocrates, *On the Diseases of Young Women*, *Oeuvres complètes*, ed. Littré, vol. VIII, pp. 467–71.

   Galen, *Ad Glauconem de methodo medendi*, bk. I, ch. 1, ed. Kühn, vol. XI, pp. 1–6.

3. Ovid, *Heroides* XVII. 253–56:

   > Quod bene te iactas, et fortia facta recenses,
   > A verbis facies dissidet ista tuis.
   > Apta magis Veneri, quam sunt tua corpora Marti.
   > Bella gerant fortes, tu Pari semper ama.

   See ed. Henricus Dörrie, p. 229. Read "suis" for "tuis," and "Quod bene te iactes et fortia facta loquaris."

4. [*Martial l. 7. ep. 57*]: Martial, *Epigrams*, bk. VII, no. lviii. 9: "habet tristis quoque turba cynaedos." See trans. Walter C. A. Ker (Loeb, 1961), vol. I, pp. 462–63: "but even the grim tribe [of so-called philosophers] has its paederasts" is his rendering of the line. Martial has been talking about false appearances, about the philosophical man "with a savage look of stubborn rusticity" and his attraction to boys in particular. Ferrand generalizes the argument and drops the reference to the philosophers and to pederasty in favor of a sense of general lasciviousness. The point is that sad or serious men can also be lustful.

5. [*Arist. l. 7. de hist an. c. 1. et l. 5. de gen. an. c. 7.*]: Aristotle, *The History of Animals*, bk. VII, ch. 1 (581 a), ed. Jonathan Barnes in *Works*, vol. I, p. 911. This entire chapter deals with puberty and the signs of its arrival. The changing voice Aristotle describes as "an instrument whose strings are frayed and out of tune," but while the word in Aristotle is translated in the Barnes edition as "breaking," it is rendered in the Oxford translation, ed. by W. D. Ross (of which this is a revision) as "the bleat of the billy-goat," which is the allusion Ferrand is after. Aristotle specifically refers to this breaking as "τραγίζειν."

Aristotle, *Generation of Animals*, bk. V, ch. vii (787b–788a), trans. A. L. Peck (Loeb, 1963), p. 551: "This is the way in which the testes are attached to the seminal passages, which in their turn are attached to the blood-vessel which has its starting-point at the heart near the part which sets the voice in movement. And so, as the seminal passages undergo a change at the approach of the age when they can secrete semen, this part undergoes a simultaneous change. And as this changes, so too does the voice."

6. [*Alex. Aphrod. l 1. probl. 123. Cal. l. 13. c. 24. Alb. Botton. c. 15. de morb. mul.*]: Alexander of Aphrodisias, *Problemata*, bk. I, no. 123, in *Physici et medici Graeci minores*, ed. I. L. Ideler (Amsterdam: Adolf M. Hakkert, 1963), p. 42.

Nicephorus Callistus, *L'histoire ecclésiastique* . . . (Paris: Antoine le Blanc, 1587), bk. II, p. 941.

Albertino Bottoni, *De morbis muliebribus*, ch. 15: "Quo tempore menstrua fluere incipiant," in Israel Spachius, *Gynaeciorum sive de mulierum affectibus*, vol. II, p. 291: "Quo autem tempore, quave aetate fluxio menstruorum in mulieribus incipiat, non est ita certum cum in aliquibus citius, in quibusdam tardius, id contingat. Commune autem omnibus videtur, ut ante duodecimum annum non appareat, et si in aliquibus anno aetatis suae undecimo, vel paulo ante conspecta fuerit, ut in sanguineis et latiores venas habentibus, evenire potest, sciendum hoc raro contingere, et propterea, hanc fluxionem non omnino naturae modum servare, quod testari potest vitae earum brevitas: contra vero, in illis longior judicatur, in quibus haec menstrua purgatio tardius conspicitur: communiter autem et ut in pluribus, ac secundum naturam consuevit haec purgatio incipere circiter annum decimum quartum, quo tempore incipiunt etiam mammillae intumescere, et vox paulo minus acuta auditur quam antea, gravior tamen redditur."

The term *vertiller*, according to Cotgrave in his French-English dictionary of 1611, means "to swell, or increase, as womens breasts doe when the matricall veins are stretched by the menstruall bloud."

The term κυαμίζειν comes from Aristophanes, frag. 500 (*Pollux* II. 18), in *Comoediae*, ex recensione C. Dindorfii, vol. II: "Perditarum fabularum fragmenta" (Oxonii: ex Typographeo Academico, 1835), p. 672.

7. Plutarch, *The Roman Questions*, in *Moralia*, vol. IV, p. 133: "Why do men not marry during the month of May. . . . Or is May, as some relate, named after the older (*maior*) and June after the younger generation (*iunior*)? For youth is better fitted for marriage, as Euripides also says:

Old age bids Love to take her leave for aye
And Aphrodite wearies of the old.

They do not, therefore, marry in May, but wait for June which comes next after May."

8. Gaius Licinius Calvus, frag. 18: "Magnus, quem metuunt omnes, digito caput uno / Scalpit, quid credas hund sibi velle? virum." In *Fragmenta poetarum Latinorum epicorum et liricorum*, ed. W. Morel (Lipsiae: B. G. Teubner, 1927), p. 18.

9. Aristotle, *Generation of Animals*, bk. IV, ch. 5 (774b): "ἡ διασύτης . . . σημεῖον πλήθους περιττώματός ἐστι, διὸ καὶ τῶν ἀνθρώπων οἱ δασεῖς ἀφροδισιαστικοὶ καὶ πολύσπερμοι μᾶλλόν εἰσι τῶν λείων." See trans. A. L. Peck, pp. 453–55. "This hairiness is a sign that it [the hare] has a large amount of residue; and for this same reason, too, men that are hairy are more prone to sexual intercourse and have more semen than men that are smooth."

10. [*Io. Bapt. Porta.*]: Giovan Battista della Porta, *De humana physiognomonia libri IV*, bk. II, ch. 24, p. 262. Della Porta is also Ferrand's source for the following references to works on physiognomy by Polemon, Aristotle, and Adamantius.

11. [*Polemon*]: Antonius Polemo, *Polemonis physionomia*, in Claudius Aelianus, *Variae historiae libri XIV* (Romae: [A. Blado], 1545); Antonius Polemo, *Physiognomica*, in *Aristotle varia opuscula* (Francofurdi, 1587).

12. [*In Eutyph*]: Plato, *Eutyphro* (16A), in *Plato*, trans. H. N. Fowler (Loeb, 1966), p. 59.

13. [*Adamant Porta.*]: Adamantius, *Physiognomonicon, id est de naturae indiciis cognoscendis libri duo*, per Janum Cornarium medicum physicum Latine conscripti (Basileae: per Robertum Winter, 1543), ch. 20: "De genis et faciebus," p. 60: "Genis carnosis secordiam ac ebrietatem adesse dicito, tenuibus vero valde, malignitatem ac versutiam. Invidi vero sunt et hi, quibus crasse naxillae procul ab oculis distant. Rotundae, dolosorum; valde longae, nugatorum ac uniloquorum. Facies hominis tota, si quidem carnosa est, delilicati est ac viri vigescentis. Se vero excarnis, soliciti ac insidiatoris. Exiguae facies, exiguos etiam mores indicant, magnae vero valde, stultitiam et indocilitatem."

Giovan Battista della Porta, *De humana physiognomonia libri IV*, bk. II, ch. 10, p. 176. Ferrand's reference to Adamantius is derived from this passage.

14. [*In physiog.*]: Aristotle, *Physiognomics*, but the words are, in fact, from *Nicomachean Ethics*, bk. VI, ch. 12 (1144a): "πανουργία δεινότης οὐκ ἐπαινετὴ

ἐστι." See trans. H. Rackham, p. 368. Ferrand has rearranged these words according to his own ends; they are only remotely associated in the original text.

15. [*Agell. l. 12. Noct. Att. c. 2.*]: Aulus Gellius, *The Attic Nights*, bk. XII, ch. 1, trans. John C. Rolfe (Loeb, 1960), vol. II, pp. 352–61. The argument is complex, but based on the principle that "just as the power and nature of the seed are able to form likenesses of body and mind, so the qualities and properties of the milk have the same effect." Therefore it is of great importance to the development of the child that the milk be of high quality. By analogy he argues that it is as important that the mother nurse the child as to have carried it in her own body. "What the mischief, then, is the reason for corrupting the nobility of body and mind of a newly born being, formed from gifted seeds, by the alien and degenerate nourishment of another's milk? Especially if she whom you employ to furnish the milk is either a slave or of servile origin and, as usually happens, of a foreign and barbarous nation, if she is dishonest, ugly, unchaste and a wine-bibber." If one must have a nurse, she should be a person of quality. He underscores the principle that the milk is related to seed and therefore contributes to the physical form and constitution of the child. "And there is no doubt that in forming character, the disposition of the nurse and the quality of the milk play a great part."

Ferrand draws upon an intermediary source as well, the *Dictionarium multis variisque ex autoribus collectum totius linguae Graecae commentarius* of Guarino of Favora [Varinus Favorinus], who takes his materials from Aulus Gellius.

The issue also made its appearance in popularized form in the Renaissance: E.g., William Painter, *The Palace of Pleasure*, Novel 23, "A pretie disputation of the philosopher Phauorinus, to perswade a woman not to put forth her child to nursse, but to nourishe it herselfe with her owne milke," ed. Joseph Jacobs, 3 vols. (New York: Dover Publications, 1966), vol. I, p. 91. Painter published his first volume in London in 1556.

16. [*4. Aen.*]: Virgil, *The Aeneid*, bk. IV. 365–67:
> Non tibi diva parens, generis nec Dardanus author,
> Perfide, sed duris genuit te cautibus horrens
> Caucasus, hircanaeque admorunt ubera Tygres.

See trans. H. Rushton Fairclough, pp. 420–21.

17. Michael Scot, *De secretis naturae opusculum* in Albertus Magnus, *De secretis mulierum libellus* (Amstelodami, n. p., 1740).

18. [*Veget. l. 1. c. 2.*]: Flavius Vegetius, *De re militari libri quatuor*, bk. I, ch. 2: "Ex quibus regionibus tyro eligendus": "et plaga coeli non solum ad robura corporum, sed etiam animorum facit" (Parisiis: apud Carolum Perier, 1553), p. 2. The following is the original context of the words Ferrand arranges to his own purposes: "Rerum ordo deposcit, ut ex quibus provinciis vel regionibus tyrones legendi sint prima parte tractetur. Constat enim in omnibus locis et ignavos et strenuos nasci. Sed tamen, quia gens gentem precedit in bello, et plaga coeli non ad robur corporum tantum, sed etiam animorum plurimum valet, quo loco ea

quae a doctissimis hominibus comprobata sunt, non omittam. Omnes nationes, quae vicinae sunt soli, nimio calore siccitas, amplius quidem sapere, sed minus habere sanguinis dicunt, ac propterea constantiam ac fiduciam cominus non habere pugnandi, quia metuunt vulnera, qui se exiguum sanguinem habere noverint. Contra, septentrionales populi, remoti a solis ardoribus, inconsultiores quidem, sed tamen largo sanguine redundantes, sunt ad bella promptissimi. Tyrones igitur de temperatioribus legendi sunt plagis, quibus et copia sanguinis suppetat ad vulnerum mortisque contemptum, et non posit deesse prudentia que ad modestiam servat in castris, et non parum prodest in dimicatione, consiliis."

19. Ovid, *Metamorphosis* bk. VI. 458–60:

   Digna quidem facies, ast hunc innata libido
   Exstimulat, pronumque genus regionibus illis
   In Venerem, et flagrat vitio gentisque suoque.

   See trans. Frank Justus Miller, vol. I, pp. 320–21. Read, "sed et hunc" for "ast hunc" and "In Venerem est: flagrat." The text is concerned with the enflamed passion of Tereus for Philomela, who has just entered wearing an elegant gown. Ovid explains the components of the fatal attraction. Tereus designs his strategy, either to woo her by corrupting her attendants, or to ravish her away and defend his act by war. "There was nothing which he would not do or dare, smitten by this mad passion."

20. Apuleius, *Apologia sive pro se de magia liber*, ch. 24: "apuc socordissimos Scythas Anacharsis sapiens natus est, et apud Athenienses Melecides fatuus." Eds. H. E. Butler and A. S. Owen (Hildesheim: Georg Olms, 1967), ch. 25. 18–19: "apud Athenienses catos Melicides fatuus."

21. [*Niceph. Cal. l. 17. c. 32. Dupreau en l'an 563.*]: Nicephorus Callistus Xenthopoulos, *L'histoire ecclesiastique*, vol. II, p. 941: "Aussi un petit chien aveugle faisoit merveilles: il declaroit à chacun le naturel qu'on avoit, et demonstroit les complections de chacun, et reveloit par certains signes les choses les plus secrettes et cachees."

   Gabriel Dupréau, *Histoire de l'estat et succès de l' Eglise, dressée en forme de chronique géneralle et universelle . . . depuis la nativité de Jésus Christ jusques en l'an 1580* (Paris: J. Kerver, 1583), year 563.

   Athenaeus, *Deipnosophistarum libri quindecim* (Lugduni: apud viduam Antonii de Harsy, 1612), bk. IX, ch. 10, p. 388: "Polemon quinto suorum commentariorum ad Antigonum et Adaeum, indocilem nec unquam mansuescentem Porphyrionem quem tradit, cum domi alitur, foeminas virorum conjuges, tanta severitate custodire, tantumque stupri sensum habere, ut cum id deprehenderit, prae monstrer antea domino, et vitam laqueo finiat."

22. [*P. Belon*]; [*Fulgos. l. 8*]: Pierre Belon, *Les observations de plusieurs singularitez et choses memorables, trouvées en Grece, Asie, Judée, Eqypte, Arabie, et autres pays estranges, redigées en trois livres* (Paris: Gilles Corrozet, 1553), p. 142ᵛ: "Un peu plus bas à costé nous veismes la piscine probatique, qui arrouse la vallée de Josaphat."

   Giovan Battista Fregoso, *Factorum dictorumque memorabilium libri IX* (Paris: Cavellat, 1589), bk. II, ch. 1, p. 59ᵛ: "De veteribus Hebraeis zelotypis." Such trials were of very ancient practice among the Hebrews. We note the following example from Josephus, *Antiquities of the Jews*, bk. III, ch. 11, trans. William Whiston (New York: Worthington, 1890), p. 98. An accused woman was taken to the temple and made to swear her innocence before a parchment on which the name of God was written. "Now when these oaths were over, the priest wiped the name of God out of the parchment, and wrung the water into a vial. He also took some dust out of the temple . . . and put a little of it into the vial, and gave it her to drink; whereupon the woman, if she were unjustly accused, conceived with child, and brought it to perfection in her womb; but if she had broken her faith of wedlock to her husband, and had sworn falsely before God, she died in a reproachful manner: her thigh fell off from her, and her belly swelled with a dropsy."

23. [*Ebor. tit. de absol. reor*]: Andreas Rodrigues da Viega (Andreas Eborensis), *Exemplorum memorabilium . . . per Andream Eborensem Lusitanum selectorum* (Paris: Nicolas Nivelle, 1590), vol. II, sec. "De reorum quorumdam absolutione," p. 207: "Gandolphi autem Burgondionis uxor adulterio commaculata, cum probare vellet innoxiam se esse, in frigido fonte demersa manu adiuravit, ne eam sine prodigii specie si culpam ferret, inde posset elevare. Mira et a Deo res facta fuit, cum a fonte manum tolleret, desiccatam extraxit, non aliter, quam si in mediis eam ignibus tenuisset. Itaque ob prodigium in vivo separata fuit. Saepe igitur ignis, et aqua ad eruendum verum plusquam consuetus naturae cursus efficiunt, cum ut veri vis inveniatur, affectus adeo naturae suae contrarios parturiant." This example is taken from bk. VIII of the work by Battista Fregoso, mentioned in the preceding note.

24. [*Pl. l. 7. c. 1.*]: Pliny, *Natural History*, bk. VII, sec. 7: "Naturae rerum vis, atque majestas in omnibus momentis fide caret." See trans. H. Rackham, vol. II, pp. 510–11. The context for this statement is as follows: "For whoever believed in the Ethiopians before actually seeing them? or what is not deemed miraculous when first it comes into knowledge? how many things are judged impossible before they actually occur? Indeed the power and majesty of the nature of the universe at every turn lacks credence if one's mind embraces parts of it only and not the whole." Pliny is rendering in a prose paraphrase Lucretius, *De rerum natura*, ll. 1022 ff.

25. [*Lucret.*]: unidentified lines attributed to Lucretius. Ferrand's source is Jean Fernel, *De abditis rerum causis* (Paris: A. Wechel, 1567), bk. II, ch. 18, pt. 2, p. 130: "Est quippe ea verissima praestantissimaque cognitio, quae nos una scientissimos reddat: difficiles tamen salebrososque aditus habens, quasi deserta praetermittitur:

> Multa tegit sacro involucro natura: neque ullis
> Fas est scire quidem mortalibus omnia: multa
> Admirare modo, nec non venerare: necque illa
> Inquires quae sunt arcanis proxima, namque
> In manibus quae sunt, haec nos vix scire putandum:
> Est procul a nobis adeo praesentia veri.

Una proprietatum cognitio res ipsas exercet, reliquae omnes vix aliud

quam verba. Quae quum ipse mihi ante oculos propono, iam fere an-
teactorum laborum me taedet vehementerque poenitet: idemque opto
quod Euripides ut res ipsae cum hominibus colloquantur, et se quales
sint explicent, ut procul amandentur artificiosi sermones." Fernel gives
no reference for these lines and thus it was perhaps Ferrand himself who
ventured to assign them to Lucretius. The only variant in Ferrand's text
is the addition of "est" after "putandum" in the next last line.

26. [*Lemn. de occ. nat. mirac. c. 30*]: Levinus Lemnius, *Occulta naturae miracula*, bk. II, ch. 30, pp. 224–25: "Eranon siquidem gemmam, quae vulgo
turcosa dicitur, saepius mutari conspexi, atque expallescere, nativoque
colore destitui, ubi qui hanc gestat, languescit, aut valetudinarius existit,
eandem rursus cum corpore reviviscere, ac colorem amabilem, nempe
qualis est serenissime caeli, caeruleum exhibere, ex nativi caloris temperamento; nec est ulla propemodum gemma, quae non mutationem
sustineat, si homo vel intemperans est, vel non satis pro dignitate con-
tinentiam servet ac tuetur. Deperit enim illi vis insita, omnisque nitor
sordescit, atque obscuratur. Quo fit, ut qui se adulterio contaminant,
thorumque legitimum ac genialem commaculant, cum qui vago sordi-
doque concubitu se polluunt, nunquam speciosas nitidasque gemmas
circumferant, sed fuliginosas et nubilas."

See also Johann Jacob Wecker, *Les secrets et merveilles de nature, recueilles de divers autheurs, et divisez en XVII livres* (Lyon: Chez Louys Odin,
1652), [a late edition] bk. XVII, p. 902: "Pour scavoir si une femme est
adultere": "On dit que si quelqu'un met un diamant sur la teste d'une
femme qui dort, il manifestera si elle est adultere pource que si elle l'est,
elle se levera du lict espouventée; mais si elle ne l'est pas, elle embrassera
son mary avec un grand amour." In the margin: *Albert*.

Albert the Great, *De secretis mulierum libellus* (Amstelodami: n.p.,
1740), p. 142. Reporting on Galerites, following Avicenna he says, "quod
se iste lapis teratur et lavetur, sine lavandus detur alicui mulieri, si virgo
non fit, statim urinabit: si virgo est, non."

27. [*Ptolem. in Cent. prop. 51. Jul. Firmicus*]: Ptolemy, *Centiloquium, sive centum sententiae, Jo. Joviano Pontano interprete* (Basileae: per Joannem Hervagium, 1551), Proposition LI, p. 76: "In quo signo luna est geniture
tempore, illud in conceptu fac ascendens. Et in quo signo inventa fuit in
conceptu, illud, aut eius oppositum fac ascendens in partu." The application to Ferrand's passage is remote; there is reason to believe Ferrand
was using these sources generally and indirectly, given the lack of specific references. However, see p. 139: Venus "In ══ ♀ si fuerit inventa,
qui sic eam habuerint, homines erunt aucupiis tantum et venationibus
dediti: in caeteris vero pigri, inertes, ociosi, melancholici, et qui nullis
sciunt se bonarum rerum operibus applicare."

Julius Firmicus Maternus, *Lollianum, Astronomicon libri VIII, per Nicolaum Prucknerum astrologum nuper ab innumeris mendis vindicati* (Basileae:
per Joannem Hervagium, 1551), esp. ch. 38, p. 191: "Veneris decreta cum
temporum domina fuerit." This work is a manual of occult signs and
symbols with instructions for the casting of horoscopes; it is without
benefit of an index. Ferrand's use of it is as an erudite reference.

Juvenal, Satire X. 313–14: "—felicior astro / Martis, ut in laqueos non incidat—" See trans. G. G. Ramsay (Loeb, 1961), p. 216. Read, "laqueos numquam incidat."

28. [*3. Polit. c. 9.*]: Aristotle, *Politics*, bk. II, ch. 6 (1269b): "φαίνονται κατακώχιμοι πάντες οἱ τοιοῦτοι εἰς ὁμιλίαν." Ed. H. Rackham, p. 135; Ferrand adds "εἰς ὁμιλίαν."

We note that the Rackham translation plays down the sexual connotations: "for all men of martial spirit appear to be attracted to the companionship either of male associates or of women."

29. [*Ficin. c. 9. orat. 7. in conv. Plat. Fr. Valer. Obs. 7. l. 2. Aequic. c. 2. l. 4. de nat. anim.*]: Marsilio Ficino, *Commentary on Plato's Symposium*, Speech VII, ch. 9, pp. 165–66: "In addition they are quickly ensnared at whose birth Venus was in Leo, or Luna looked vehemently on Venus, and those who are endowed with the same complexion. Phlegmatics, in whom phlegm dominates, are never caught. Melancholics, in whom black bile dominates, are rarely caught, but once caught are never afterward freed."

François Valleriola, *Observationum medicinalium libri VI*, bk. II, obs. 7, pp. 205–6: "Et si ex astris petendum judicium sit (quanquam parum ego astrorum in his influxui ac viribus tribuo, quum magis hoc quicquid est mali, affectui corporeo amantium, et depravato eorum iudicio, quam astris merito tribuendum sit) aiunt astrorum periti, irretiri cito amantes, si in eorum genesi Venus in Leone fuerit, vel Luna vehementer Venerem aspexerit." Valleriola continues to follow Ficino in this passage. Ferrand records material of this nature, but keeps his distance from it.

Mario Equicola, *Libro de natura de amore*, bk. IV, "Causes why one is inclined to love one person more than another," p. 130ʳ.

30. [*L. 7. Conf. c. 6 l. 2. de doctr. Chr. c. 21.*]: St. Augustine, *Confessions*, bk.VII, ch. 6, trans. William Watts, 2 vols. (Loeb, 1931), vol. I, p. 350: "Iam etiam mathematicorum fallaces divinationes et inpia deliramenta reieceram." St. Augustine gives examples of experiments in astrology carried out on two children born at the same moment, and reveals how their divergent fortunes disprove the divinations of astrologers. Men's conjectures sometimes merely have the help of fortune so "that by talking many things, something to come was oft-times perchance forespoken of; the parties that spoke little knowing of it, but stumbling now and then upon the right by their not saying nothing."

St. Augustine, *De doctrina* (*On Christian Doctrine*), bk. II, ch. 21, "Superstition of Astrologers," trans. D. W. Robertson Jr. (New York: Bobbs-Merrill, 1958), pp. 56–57.

31. Giovanni Pico della Mirandola, *Disputationes adversus astrologiam*, ed. Eugenio Garin (Latin and Italian texts), 3 vols. (Florence: Vallecchi Editore, 1946), vol. I, p. 47. Ferrand's reference is a general one, but the following is a partial statement of Pico's purposes in writing. "Voglio innanzi tutto che il lettore sappia che questo mio proposito de confutare l'astrologia non è un audace ritrovato poiché, fino dalla piú remota antichità, a chi ben giudicava, essa parve sempre un'arte arrecante da ogni parte all'uomo disturbi e follie sotto il pretesto della scienza e dell'utilità. La eliminano perciò dalle città, come nociva, le leggi dei Cesari e dei saggi;

perció gli oracoli dei profeti, le sanzioni dei pontefici, le parole e le dottrine degli uomini piú santi la condannano come esiziale per i costumi e per la religione; perció filosofi ed i matematici, quanti nei libri appresero sapienza e non eloquenza, la disprezzano e la combattono come falsa, inutile, impossibile, nemica della filosofia." Ferrand took his reference, however, from Christopher Clavius, *In Sphaeram Joannis de Sacro Bosco. Commentarius.* See n. 33, below.

32. [*Cardan. Aph 63. segm. 1 Aph. Astr.*]: Girolamo Cardano, *Aphorismorum astronomicorum segmenta VII*, in *Opera omnia in decem tomos digesta* (Lugduni: sumptibus I. A. Huguetan & M. A. Ravard, 1663), vol. V, p. 37b: "Cum Iupiter et Venus Soli, nec iuncti, in eadem domo fuerint, in Scorpione, Virgine, Tauro, vel Capricorno, item in Geminis, natus potius vitam ducet amoenam, quam quod sit foelix."

The reference to the *Praenotione* of Francesco Pico della Mirandola was taken from the commentaries of Christopher Clavius on the *Sphaeram Joannis de Sacro Bosco.* We note, however, in the edition of Cardano's *Aphorismorum astronomicorum liber* (Nuremberg: J. Petreius, 1547) the following note in the margin at fol. 211^V: "Ioanni Pico Mirandulae Lucius Bellanius Senensis, qui contra eum scripsit, annum 34. illi ultimum ac fatalem praedixit ex revolutione, nec deceptus est." Giovanni Francesco Pico della Mirandola, *De rerum praenotione libri novem* (Argentorati: Joannes Knoblochus, 1507).

See also Mario Equicola, *Libro de natura de amore*, bk. IV, ch. 2, on the relationship between astrology and love.

33. [*Jul. Syren. l. de fato. A. Bernard. Mirand. l. 22. 23. & 24. monom. Michael Medina l. de rect. in Deum fide. c. 1. Vultur. l. 3 de art. mil. chap 1*]: Christopher Clavius is not mentioned in this chapter, but this lengthy marginal note of parallel references, taken verbatim from him, is proof that Ferrand was relying on him for the preparation of this chapter. The procedure is typical of Ferrand; it is to Clavius that we can look for the structures of the arguments advanced here against the astrologers. For this reason too, it would be supererogation on our part to look for materials in the works cited in the margin, because Ferrand was using them so remotely, though their works will be listed for purposes of further consultation. Christopher Clavius, *In Sphaeram Joannis de Sacro Bosco. Commentarius* (Lugduni: ex officina Q. Hug, A. Porta, sumpt. Jo. de Gabiano, 1607), from the introduction: "Verum quoniam huic astronomia parti multi multa temerarie, ac perperam ausi sunt adicere, adeoque hanc partem prognosticam amplificara voluerunt, ut sit iam res omnio superstitiosa, exosaque et merito ab Ecclesia suspecta habeatur, mirumque in modum a B. Augustino damnata in libris de Doctrina Christiana, propterea nihil omnio de ea nobis dicendum existimo, nisi quod illam funditus evertunt Joan Picus Mirandulanus libris 12. adversus Astrologos conscriptis: Franciscus Picus eius nepos in libris de Praenotione: Antonius Bernardus Mirandalanus episcopus Casertanus lib. 22. 23. et 24. Monomachiae. Michael Medina li 2. de recta in Deum fide, c. 1. et Julius Syrenus in libris de Fato."

Julius Sirenius, *De fato libri novem in quibus inter alia: de contigen-*

tia, de necessitate, de providentia divina, de praescentia divina, de prophetia, et de divinatione tam secundum philosophorum opinionem, quam secundum catholicorum theologorum sententiam (Venetiis: ex officina Jordani Zileti, 1563), esp. bk. IX, ch. 18, pp. 153 ff. Sirenius writes in the form of a Scholastic dialogue between the philosopher and the theologian in the name of theology in order to refute divination.

Antonio de Bernardi della Mirandola, presumably in *Disputationes . . . accessit locuples rerum et verborum toto opere memorabilium* (Basileae: H. Petri et N. Bryling, 1562). We have not examined this work.

P. Miguel Medina, O. F. M., *Christianae paraenesis, sive de recta in Deum fide libri septem. . .* (Venetiis: ex officina Jordani Zileti, 1564), esp. ch. 1.

"*Vultur*" is Roberto Valturio (Robertus Valturius), *De re militari libris XII* (Paris: apud Christianum Wechelum, 1535). We note, as well, the French translation, *Les douze livres de Robert Valtrin touchant la discipline militaire*, trans. Loys Meigret (Paris: Chez Charles Perier, 1555).

34. Galen, *De diebus decretoriis liber*, bk. III, chs. 5–6, ed. Kühn, vol. IX, pp. 908–13.

35. Hippocrates, *Hippocrates to Philopemen,*" *Oeuvres complètes*, ed. Littré, vol. IX, p. 343. See also ch. XXIII, n. 2.

XXI.   Whether by Astrology Those Inclined to Love Melancholy Can Be Known

1. [*1 Aristot. l. Phys. c. 2. Fonseca 2. Metaph. c. 3. q. 3. Polyd.Ver. l. 17 de Invent. rer. c. 17. S. August. l. 18. de Civ. Dei.*]: The sources for this chapter are particularly complex. There is little to suggest that Ferrand consulted many of these works directly because they appear exactly as cited in a few key works he used closely for the preparation of this chapter. The most important of these is Jean Taxil, *L'astrologie et physiognomie en leur splendeur* (Tournon: par R. Reynaud, Libraire juré d'Arles, 1614). Corresponding places in this work will be signaled by "Taxil" and the page number. Nevertheless, where the work cited contains in itself pertinent information to the material under discussion, we will also treat it as an independent source, giving modern editions for the classics and contemporary editions for the Renaissance authors.

Aristotle, *Physics*, bk. II, ch. 2 (193b), trans. Philip H. Wickstead and Francis M. Cornford (Loeb, 1857), vol. I, p. 119. Taxil, p. 119.

Pedro da Fonseca, *Commentarium . . . in libros metaphysicorum Aristotelis Stagiritae*, ch. 3 (Lugduni: sumptibus Aratii Cardon, 1601), pp. 165–73. Taxil, p. 119.

Taxil, in turn, owes many of his facts and materials to Polidoro Virgilio of Urbino as the following sample will reveal, including several of his references: *Des inventeurs des choses, traduict de Latin en François, et de nouveau reveuz et corrigez* (Lyon: par Benoist Rigaud, 1576), pp. 81–82: "Mon injure [referring to a line by Ovid] disoit elle, pourquoy à elle faict

les corps celestes mauvais et iniques, pour la cause l'observation des estoilles et corps celestes fut, par les hommes faicte et inventee l'astrologie:
laquelle les Egyptiens se glorifient avoir trouvee comme dit Diodore, les
autres disent que c'est Mercure, mais ledit Diodore sur son cinquiesme
livre dit Actinus fils du soleil avoir baillé la notice de cette science jadis
aux Egyptiens, mais Josephus au premier des antiquities demonstre que
le patriarche sainct Abraham bailla premierement l'astrologie qu'il avoit
euë de ses maieurs et anciens aux peuples d'Egypt: comme nous disons:
quand il s'en alla futif en Egypte. Dit aussi que les Egyptiens et Caldees
la baillerent aux Grecs, disant ainsi, tous ceux qui ont philosophé en
Grece, c'est assavoir Pherecides, Pithagoras, et Thales qui parlerent des
choses divines et celestes concordantement confessent tous avoir esté
disciples des Egyptiens et Caldees. En outre Pline dit en son septieme
que le grand Athlos fils de Libie jadis inventa l'astrologie. Parquoy les
poetes l'ont chanté soustenir le ciel sur les espaules: comme dit Vergile
sur son 6. des Eneid. *Ubi coelifer Athlas axem humero torquet stellio arden-
tibus aptum.* C'est à dire le grand Athlas portant le ciel, tourne la mobilité
du ciel, et la nuict illuminé des estoilles ardantes. Mais Pline mesmement assigne l'invention de l'astrologie venir et tomber sur l'honneur
de Jupiter Belus disant, que le temple de Jupiter Belus est encor la ou il
trouva l'invention. Aucuns disent que ce furent les Assiriens, pourtant
Servius sur l'Eglegue 6 des Bucoliques Vergilianes dit que Prometheus
la demonstra premierement." Polidoro is cited in Taxil, p. 81.

St. Augustine, *The City of God*, bk. XVIII, trans. Marcus Dods (New
York: Modern Library, 1950), p. 615: "Some have thought that Prometheus lived during the reign of the Kings now named (Saphrus of
Assyria, Orthopolis of Sicyon, Criasus of Argos). He is reported to have
formed men out of clay, because he was esteemed the best teacher of
wisdom; yet it does not appear what wise men there were in his days.
His brother Atlas is said to have been a great astrologer; and this gave
occasion for the fable that he held up the sky, although the vulgar opinion about his holding up the sky appears rather to have been suggested
by a high mountain named after him." Taxil, p. 162. But the reference
seems to have come originally from Clavius, *In Sphaeram Joannis de Sacro
Bosco. Commentarius*, p. 4. See n. 7, below.

2. The reference to Servius on Virgil's Sixth Eclogue is derived from Polidoro Virgilio [n. 1], p. 81.

Virgil, *Eclogue* VI. 42, trans. H. Rushton Fairclough, p. 45; only this
line deals with Prometheus, mentioning his act of theft on behalf of
mankind.

3. [*Pl. 1. l. c. 15 & 16. Diod. sic. l. 4.*]: Pliny, *Natural History*, bk. V, chs. 15
and 16, ed. H. Rackham, vol. II, p. 271: "The Phoenician race itself has
the great distinction of having invented the alphabet and the sciences of
astronomy, navigation and strategy."

Diodorus of Sicily (Diodorus Siculus), trans. C. H. Oldfather, 12 vols.
(Loeb, 1952), vol. II, p. 359. He nowhere speaks of the origins of astrology
in Egypt in bk. IV, though in sec. 6 he traces to Egypt the origins of
Priapus and his cult.

Both references are from Taxil, p. 118, and Polidoro Virgilio cites the Pliny reference on p. 82.

4. Josephus, *Antiquities of the Jews*, bk. I, ch. 7, trans. William Whiston (New York: Worthington Co. , 1890), p. 38. Abraham observed that the irregular motion of the heavenly bodies meant they were in need of regulation by God, a view that angered the Chaldeans and Mesopotamians and led to his departure. Ferrand came by his reference through Polidoro Virgilio, p. 81. See this chapter, n. 1.

5. [*Procl. in Plat.*]: Taxil, p. 119. The reference to whichever work was intended by Proclus appears to be remote both in Taxil and in Ferrand. "*In Plat.*" could refer to any of his several commentaries on the various books of Plato, including the *In Platonis theologiam libri sex*, in which, for example, he consecrates bk. I, ch. 14, to the hierarchical structures of the universe and the communication between the parts (we are aware that chs. 14 and 15 are reported missing according to the numeration of the edition of 1618, ed. Aemilium Portum et al. [Frankfurt am Main: Minerva, 1960]). See Proclus, *Théologie Platonicienne*, ed. H. O. Saffrey and L. C. Westerink (Paris: Les Belles Lettres, 1968), pp. 60–69. Both Taxil and Ferrand might better have consulted *Procli hypotyposis astronomicarum positionum*—this work has been edited by C. Manitius (Leipzig: 1909)—and his commentary on the *Timaeus*, the relevant passage being the following from Plato.

Plato, *Timaeus* (71E–72A), trans. R. G. Bury (Loeb, 1966), p. 187. *Laws*, bk. XII (967D–968B), ed. R. G. Bury (Loeb, 1971), pp. 563–65: "It is impossible for any mortal man to become permanently god-fearing if he does not grasp the two truths now stated,—namely, how that the soul is oldest of all things that partake of generation, and is immortal, and rules over all bodies,—and in addition to this, as we have often affirmed, he must also grasp that reason which controls what exists among the stars." Ferrand's references are from Taxil, p. 119.

6. [*Cic. 2. de nat. deor. Sen l. de vita beat. c. 32.*]: Jean Taxil, pp. 4–5: "In media sui parte natura nos constituit, et circumspectum omnium nobis dedit: nec erexit tantummodo hominem, sed etiam ad contemplationem factum, ut ab ortu sidera in occasum labentia prosequi posset, et vultum suum circumferre, cum toto sublime fecit illi caput, et collo flexibili imposuit [in margin: *Senec. lib. de vita beat. cap. 32.*]. Quid potest esse tam apertum tamque perspicuum cum coelum suspexerimus, coelestiaque contemplati sumus, quam esse aliquod numen praestantissimae mentis quo haec regantur? (disoit ce grand orateur Romain) [in margin: *Cicer. 2. de nat. Deor.*]."

Cicero, *On the Nature of the Gods*, bk. II, trans. H. Rackham (Loeb, 1961), p. 141, opens with a long discussion of the necessity of god based essentially on the principle that where a thing exists, something superior to it must also exist in order to account for that thing's existence and comportment; e.g.: "Yet ever man's intelligence must lead us to infer the existence of a mind [in the universe], and that a mind of surpassing ability, and in fact divine."

Seneca, *On the Happy Life*. Ferrand alludes to this work in the context of a discussion on astrology as a teacher of true religion, a topic not treated in Seneca's essay. Because modern editors agree that the essay is incomplete and breaks off in the middle of ch. 28, perhaps the reference to a ch. 32 indicates a Renaissance edition which has been completed by another hand. See *Moral Essays*, trans. John W. Basore (Loeb, 1951), pp. 99–179.

7. [*Clavius praef. in Jo. de Sacrob. P. de Alliaco in conc. Theol. & Astrol.*]: Clavius, *In Sphaeram Joannis de Sacro Bosco. Commentarius*, p. 7, "Introduction": "Quanto sit huius praestantissimae scientiae utilitas, immo vero necessitas, vix explicari potest. Ad omnes siquidem disciplinas videtur Astronomia viam quommodo parare, et aditum monstrare securum. Conducit enim in primus plurimum sacrae Theologiae. . . . Ut non immerito Ptolemaeus in principio Almagesti, secundum traditionem Arabam asserverit, hanc unam scientiam esse viam ac semitam ad sciendum Deum altissimum. . . . Ex quo factum est, ut Astronomia, quae de praestantissimis istis corporibus disputat, a plerisque theologia naturalis vocetur."

Pierre d'Ailly (Petrus de Alliaco), *Concordia Astronomiae cum Theologia et concordantia Astronomiae cum Hystorica narratione* (Vienna, 1594). From Taxil, pp. 165–66: "Je ne veux pas taire icy ce grand docteur, Pierre de Alliaco, la doctrine duquel luy fit obtenir une des plus grandes dignitez en l'Eglise de Dieu, lequel estant bien versé en toutes les especes de l'Astrologie, exhorte les Chrestiens de s'en servir, asseurant que, *Astrologia est altera Theologia Naturalis, quia sicut superior Theologia per supernaturalem fidem ad Dei cognitionem ducit, sic ista inferior Theologia velut ancilla, eidem subserviens, ad divinae cognitionis introductionem per naturalem rationem manu ducit.* [in margin: *Lege Petrum de Alliaco Cardinalem in concordantia Theologiae, et Astrologiae.*]"

8. Ferrand paraphrases Taxil throughout the paragraph from pp. 8–9, bringing forward the supplementary references to Apono, Paracelsus, and Dario from p. 120: "L'Astrologie Divinatrice ou Judiciare, est celle qui predit les evenemens non necessaires, mais contingens, aussi est elle appuyée sur des principes communs et variables. Elle est distinguée par nous en trois partes.

"La premiere, est celle qui consiste en revolutions, et predit les changemens et vicissitudes des choses, comme les brouillards, la serénité, les pluyes, les debordemens, la salubrité, ou l'infection de l'air, la santé, ou maladie des animaux, l'abondance ou cherté des fruicts, la paix, ou la guerre, et choses semblables.

"La seconde, contient en soy la façon de dresser les Nativitez, et les Horoscopes, les Professeurs de laquelle sont appellez Astrologues Genethliaques.

"La troisiesme enseigne les elections, c'est à dire ce qu'il faut utilement observer en plusieurs choses, ce qu'il faut eviter, en quel temps bastir, fonder villes, saigner, ou donner medecines, entreprendre à voyager par mer, et par terre."

Pietro D'Abano (Petrus Aponensis), *Conciliator controversiarum, quae inter philosophos et medicos versantur* (Venetiis: apud Juntas, 1548). The book is a medical encyclopedia dealing with the philosophy and the cure of diseases, yet there are several passages containing information about astronomy and the forecasting of future events; e.g., "Differentia LX, propter tertium," (p. 93) on the correspondences between incorporeal intelligences and matter.

Pietro D'Abano's career was complex and invited a conflation of fact with fanciful lore. He had the reputation of being a magician, and it may be that such a reputation followed him down to Ferrand's time. Witness in his *Heptameron seu elementa magica*, pp. 455–77, bound with *Henrici Cornelii Agrippae ab Nettesheym . . . Opera* (Lugduni: per Beringos Fratres, ca. 1550), a sample befitting Ferrand's interests: "Spiritus aeris diei Veneris subiiciuntur Zephyro. Eorum natura est dare argentum, homines excitare, et procliviores reddere ad luxuriam, inimicos per luxuriam concordare, et matrimonia facere, homines in amorem mulierum allicere, infirmitates dare vel auferre, et omnia quae habent motum, facere."

Paracelsus, *Operum medico-chimicorum sive paradoxorum tomus genuinus sextus*, 4 vols. (Francofurti: a collegio Musarum Palthenianarum, 1603–05), esp. "De generatione rerum. Liber nonus de signatura rerum naturalium," e.g., p. 248: "Astrorum signa dant prophetias, praesagia, etc. rerumque supernaturales vires indicant, et vera judicia ac indicia promunt in Geomantia, Chiromantia, Physionomia, Hydromantia, Pyromantia, Necromantia, Astromonia, Berilistica, etc. et aliis scientiis Astralibus."

Claude Dariot (Dariotus) *Ad astrorum judicia facilis introductio [et] tractatus de electionibus principiorum idoneorum rebus inchoandis* (Lugduni: apud Mauricium Roy & Ludovicum Pesnot, 1557). Dariot explains the division of the heavens according to the signs of the zodiac, the planets, their motions and natures, and the significances of the twelve houses. He is concerned, not with omens and disasters, but with conditions of life and health, and in a subsequent tract he assigns all the parts of the body to the various figures and signs in order to diagnose diseases according to a complex chart of correspondences with Galenic categories of the humors.

Antoine Mizauld (Mizaldus), *L'explication usage et practique de l'Ephemeride celeste* (Paris: Chez Jacques Kerver, 1556). Mizauld provided a manual for calculating when to plant, write, court the ladies, begin construction, and many like activities, systematically explicated through pages of charts progressing through the planets, their several conjunctions and aspects, e.g., ch. VI, "Saturne estant avec la lune en Sextile aspect" (p. 61^V): "Il fait bon avoir affaire avec gens vieulx, et de conseil, fonder chasteaulx, et bastir edifices, eriger les choses ruinees, labourer la terre, planter vignes et jardins et maulvais traicter amour de femme."

See also Jean Aubery, *L'antidote d'amour*, pp. 81^V–89^r. Aubery begins as a full defender of natural astrology, urging that the stars harbor the constant principles of order, reflect the Creator, and rule over the world of change and extension. "Et en ceste façon, la force de ce grand Univers suit le mouvement des corps celestes, et par consequent preside sur nos actions, mouvemens et evenemens de nostre vie" (p. 82^V). He agrees that the heavens should be studied by physicians for practicing their arts, citing Mercurius Trismegistus, believing that each individual is attached to his particular astral formation. He claims that they control "tous les evenemens de la vie, et mesmes l'election d'amour en despandront" (p. 84^V). Yet he qualifies by saying that the specific agent is also required and that its own disposition and nature have causal force. Thus in love our nature will determine more than the stars. Aubery then goes through a long list of forces and agents that compromise the powers of the stars until he can conclude that it is a vanity to make a case for necessity out of the stars, denying all sinners the right to blame the heavens for their crimes.

Almanacs were in wide circulation during that age that identified according to their tables and charts the lucky and unlucky days—and even hours of the day—for carrying out elective activities: weaning children, watering crops, bleeding, purging, taking pills and other forms of medication, moving house, taking journeys, even cutting nails and hair. Thomas Erastus provides a full account of the use of these manuals and the difficulties he had with his superstitious patients when he, as a physician, refused to use them. It was the medical use of astronomy throughout the sixteenth century in determining the auspicious moments for elective treatments that had kept the subject central to intellectual debate: Thomas Erastus, *De astrologie divinatrice epistolae . . . iam olim ab eodem ad diversos scriptae, et in duos libros digestae* (Basiliae: per Petrum Pernam, 1580), passim.

9. [*L. de aere, loc. & aqu. Gal. l. 3. de dieb. decr. Delrio l. 4. cap 3. qu 1. disq mag.*]: Hippocrates, *Of Airs, Waters and Places,* in *Oeuvres complètes,* ed. Littré, vol. II, p. 15.

Galen, *De diebus decretoriis liber,* bk. III, ed. Kühn, vol. IX, pp. 901 ff. See esp. ch. 2, where Galen states in precise terms that the planets influence the constitution and the well-being of man. Taxil, p. 121.

Martin Del Rio, *Disquisitionum magicarum libri sex* (Lugduni: apud Joannem Phillehotte, 1612), bk. IV. ch. 3, ques. 1, p. 259: "Merito suspecta sunt haec omnia, quia stellarum non est tanta vis in haec inferiora; et qua talis vis foret, ea posset et soleret aliarum particularium causarum concursu plane impediri. Imo et sola materiae indispositio, lunae et astrorum omnium actiones evariare facit, teste Galeno; cui Avicenna consentit, quare observationes et effectus huiusmodi dierum indicum[i], provocantium, vel criticorum, longe magis dependet ex materiae dispositione, concoctione, et statis morbi temporibus ac symptomatibus, quam ex syderibus, quae est vera sententia Hippocratis et Celsi" [in margin: *Galen li. 2 de dieb. criticis. Avicenna li. 4. Fen 2, tracta. 2 ca. 1. Hippocr. passim et Cels. lib. 4. cap. 4.*]. Ref. Taxil, p. 64.

10. [*L 2. Epist. 1 & l 15 Ep. 5*]: Taxil, p. 121, Giovanni Manardo, *Epistolae medicinales diversorum authorum,* bk. I, ep. 2; bk. XV, ep. 5; pp. 8, 156–57: "Qualis vero esset vis ista, merito cuius coelum universalis causa

dici mereatur, libro primo mostraverat, ubi influxus declarans qui ex multarum stellarum coitu in nos proveniunt, non alterius influentiae commeminit quam caloris, quem vertici nostro propinquantes, et frigoris, quod ab eodem discendentes, ex accidenti, atque non agendo (ut ita dixerim) in nostra hac agunt regione" (p. 8).

Bk. XV, ep. 5, deals with the falseness of judiciary astrology and includes references to many who appear in Ferrand's discussion of the topic.

11. [*8. Phys l. 2. de gen & corrupt. & l. 2. de coelo.*]: These references to works by Aristotle were taken from Taxil, p. 121; *Physics*, bk. VIII, ch. 6 (260a), ed. Philip H. Wickstead and Francis M. Cornford (Loeb, 1968), vol. II, pp. 351–53, is one of the few passages in this work that speaks specifically of the movement of the heavens and of the relationship of this movement to earthly events. He argues that the heavenly bodies that influence events on earth have compound and therefore variable motions in contrast to those things that are eternal because they are moved directly by the prime mover.

On Generation and Corruption, bk. IV, offers a discussion of the four basic elements and how, through their mixing and transformation, they combine to create all things. Aristotle then discusses the material, formal and final causes of "coming-to-be" and "passing-away," and concludes that the cause of these processes is the sun's annual movement.

In *On the Heavens*, ed. W. K. Guthrie (Loeb, 1960), bk. I, ch. 3 (270b), pp. 23–27, Aristotle maintains that the heavens move themselves by virtue of an inherent vital principle which he finds in a fifth substance he calls *aither*, an element more subtle and divine than the four known elements. In bk. II, ch. 7 (289a), pp. 279–81, he states that the stars are not made of fire as one could think by the fact that they seem to emit heat and light, but that instead the "heat and light which they emit are engendered as the air is chafed by their movement." The line quoted in the text, "coelum, in haec inferiora agit mediante lumine et motu" has not been traced to a Renaissance Latin text of one of these works.

12. "Certam et praefinitam qualitatum primarum mensuram, et coelestium siderum accessu, et recessu progenitam"; Ferrand's quotation, attributed to Avicenna, has not been located in a Latin edition of his works, but the concept expressed corresponds to a passage in *The Metaphysica*, sec. 57. See the translation by Parviz Morewedge (New York: Columbia University Press, 1973), p. 107, and commentary, pp. 252, 255. Manardo in the *Epistolae medicinales diversorum authorum*, bk. II, ep. 1, and bk. XV, ep. 5, carried out a concerted opposition to the use of astrology in medicine and set out to diminish the stature of the received passages in the standard medical treatises. He claimed that where the texts read sky, one should understand air, and quoted Galen's commentaries on the *Epidemics* for proof. Where Galen himself wrote on astrology, Manardo argues that he was writing as an astrologer and not as a physician. See Andrew Wear, "Galen in the Renaissance," in *Galen: Problems and Prospects*, ed. Vivian Nutton (London: The Wellcome Institute for the History of Medicine, 1981), pp. 247–48. See n. 10, above.

13. A quotation to follow from Averroes was omitted by the printer; there is no corresponding passage in the 1610 edition.

14. [*L. 3. contr. gent. ca. 54 84 & 86 L. de gener. sub finem.*]: Taxil, p. 69, St. Thomas Aquinas, *Summa contra Gentiles*, bk. III; see *Somme de la foi Catholique contre les Gentils*, "De la Providence divine," bk. III, ch. 54, vol. II, pp. 519–25; ch. 84, vol. III, pp. 19–28; ch. 86, vol. III, pp. 37–44. Aquinas argues at length about cause and effect, and sides generally with the notion that causes belong to the natures and behaviors of objects and organisms and not to extraneous influences upon them. Thus "les effets physiques, dans les êtres inferiers, ne résultent pas nécessairement de l'action des corps célestes." Nevertheless, Taxil will read him to his own ends as follows: "Ce grand docteur de l'Eglise, ce glorieux sainct Thomas d'Aquin, qui pour son rare sçavoir s'est acquis le surnom d'Angelique, dit que Dieu gouverne les choses de ça bas par le moyen des corps superieurs, qui sont les cieux, alleguant sainct Damascene, qui dit que, *alii atque alii Planetae diversas complexiones habitus, et dispositiones in nobis constituunt* [in margin: *Lege D. Th. lib. 2 contra Gent. c. 54 84 86. & D. Dionysic. 4 caelest. hierarch. D. Damase lib. 2. de orthodoxa fide.*], et par ainsi, dit il, comme le Medecin peut juger de la bonté de l'entendement par la complexion du corps, comme par une prochaine cause, semblable jugement en pourra faire l'astrologue par le moyen des mouvemens celestes, comme par cause esloignée de la mesme disposition; et de la on peut conclurre veritable (dit ce docteur) ce que Ptalomee dit en l'Aphorisme [in margin: *D. Th. lib. 3. contra gentes c. 84*] trente huictiesme de son Centiloque, que lors que Mercure se treuve à la nativité de quelqu'un l'une des maisons de Saturne, que telles planetes le font de bel entendement. Et de plus, le mesme docteur [in margin: *D. Thom. l. part. q. 115. art. 4. & l. 2. q. 9. art. 5.*], proteste que les Astrologues sont le plus souvent veritables en ce qui concerne les moeurs des hommes, et qu'il faut croire au sens, et à l'experience. Et dit encor sur la fin du livre *de generatione*, qu'a mesure que les planetes se treuvent plus fortes en vertu, et en certains periodes, et cercles, qu'elles donnent davantage d'années; et estans qu contraire, qu'elles en donnent moins. Que si quelqu'un pouvoit bien scavoir la vertu des signes, et des estoiles qui sont posées en iceux, il pourroit prognostiquer de toute la vie de celuy qui vient de naistre, veu que telle vertu n'apporte aucune necessité [in margin: *Lege Ptol. aph. 5. & 8.*] aux choses qui sont à venir, lesquelles peuvent estre empeschées en beaucoup de façons."

The corresponding passages in the *Summa contra Gentiles* in *Opera omnia*, ed. Stanislaus Fretté (Paris: apud Ludovicum Vivès, 1872), are in vol. XII: ch. 54, pp. 168–69; ch. 84, pp. 361–63; ch. 86, pp. 366–68 (Latin only).

Thomas Aquinas, *In Aristotelis stagiritae libros nonnullos commentaria*, in *Opera omnia*, ed. S. Fretté, *De generatione et corruptione*, bk. I, lect. 24, vol. II, p. 337.

15. [*I. part qu 115 ar. 4 l. 2 q 9 art. 5. sta de Iud. astror*]: Thomas Aquinas, *Summa theologica*, in *Opera omnia*, ed. S. Fretté (Paris: apud Ludovicum Vivès, 1872), pt. 1, ques. 115, art. 4, "Utrum corpora caelestis sint causa

humanorum," vol. II, pp. 53–54; pt. 2, ques. 9, art. 5, "Utrum voluntas moveatur a corpore caelesti," vol. II, p. 137.

16. [*L 6. c. 3. q 1. disq magi.*], Taxil, p. 64; Martin Del Rio, *Disquisitionum magicarum libri sex*, bk. VI, ch. 3, ques. 1: "Astrologiae illa species non est superstitiosa, si tantum profitetur opinionem seu suspicionem oppositi. V. G. suspicio est, hunc puerum fore talem, inclinabitur ad hac, horoscopus illi talia portendit, etc. Licet enim nobis metuere aut suspicari similia, neque ullum peccatum in hac observationis cautione versatur, quae est portio quaedam prudentiae, et idea secundum se bona." The quotation is found in Taxil as follows: "Le mesme en dit le docte, et subtil Del Rio en ces termes. *Astrologiae illa species non est superstitiosa si tantum profitetur opinionem, seu suspicionem cum formidine oppositi: verbi gratia minantur Astra annonae caritatem, suspicio est hunc puerum fore talem, inclinabitur ad hoc, horoscopus illi talia portendit, etc. Licet enim nobis suspicari, aut metuere similia, neque ullum peccatum in hac observationis cautione versatur, quae est portio quaedam prudentiae, et idea secundum se bona est.* Ce n'est pas la condamner (ô docte Del Rio) que de l'appeller partie, et portion de la prudence, vray naucher de nos actions; au contraire c'est d'advoüer, et affirmer soubs vostre authorité pour l'affranchir des injures de l'Anticometiste; moins injures toutesfois que lourdes ignorances, puis qu'elles l'obligent au repenter de les avoir publiées."

17. Taxil, p. 66: "Le Cardinal Tolet [in margin: *Tolet. lib. 4. c. 15 instruc. Sacerdot.*] tant haut loué par les doctes, dit que, *non est peccatum ex Astrologia inquirere naturales effectus, ut futuras eclipses pluviasque imo, et complexiones hominum, ac naturales inclinationes unde permittitur huius scientiae speculatio, imo*, dit il, *si quis vellet per Astrologiam cognoscere futurum aliquod contingens, etiam liberum non peccaret mortaliter.*"

Franciscus Tolet, *Instructio sacerdotum ac de septem peccatis mortalibus*, 2 vols. (Lugduni: apud Horatium Cardon, 1604), bk. IV, ch. 15; vol. I, p. 241^V. Taxil gathers these points from several areas in Tolet's text and underscores the innocence rather more that Tolet does, whose point in writing is to warn of all the dangers of divination. On the page following (242^r) he states: "Circa Astrologiam notandum est, quod non negamus, posse naturales effectus sciri, ut eclipses, pluvias futuras, et alia huiusmodi, et similiter complexiones, et inclinationes hominum, nam coeli influunt in humana corpora: tamen triplici casu uti Astrologia est peccatum mortale."

18. [*Ptolem. in Centil. l. 1. quadr. c 3*]: Taxil, p. 123, Ptolemy, *Tetrabiblos*, trans. F. E. Robbins (Loeb, 1956), p. 23: "We should not believe that separate events attend mankind as the result of the heavenly cause as if they had been originally ordained for each person by some irrevocable divine command and destined to take place by necessity without the possibility of any other cause whatever interfering."

The reference is paralleled in Jean Aubery, *L'antidote d'amour*, p. 88^V: "Parquoy les astres indifferemment par leurs influences, ne nous peuvent forcer: car le Sage commande aux astres: que bien est vray que nostre volonté disposee, peut recevoir l'impression de leur charactere, et que fortuitement sans aucune specialité balançans, sur l'amour nous y pouvons estre portez et incitez d'avantage par l'inclination des estoiles."

19. [*D. Th contr. gent. ca 85. 86. & 92*]: Taxil, p. 69, St. Thomas Aquinas, *Summa contra Gentiles*, ed. Abbé P. -F. Ecalle (1856), bk. III, ch. 85: "indirecta motione, id est remote et ex accidente, eam inclinando interventu organorum corporis, et potentiarum ei inhaerentium." The direct source is from Taxil as follows: "Je voy bien que quelqu'un pourroit dire, s'il est vray, que par les Astres qui preside a la naissance des hommes on puisse predire ce qui sera de leur vie ou moeurs, qu'il s'ensuivra que les mesmes Astres peuvent mouvoir nostre volonté en quelque façon, ce que est, toutesfois, contraire à nostre liberal arbitre; à celà on respond, avec sainct Thomas, et les autres docteurs, estre veritable que les Astres ont pouvoir de mouvoir nostre volonté, mais c'est *indirecta motione, id est remote, et ex accidente eam inclinando interventu organorum corporis, et potentiarum eis inhaerentium.*" Taxil gives no reference for this quotation; Ferrand, however, places beside it in his margin the three chapters above taken from three different notes on subsequent pages in Taxil.

Aquinas says in the *Summa contra Gentiles*, ed. Abbé P.-F. Ecalle, bk. III, ch. 85, vol. III, pp. 35–36: "Sciendum tamen est quod, licet corpora coelestia non sint directe causa electionum nostrarum, quasi directe in voluntates nostras imprementia, indirecte tamen ex his aliqua occasio nostris electionibus praestatur, secundum quod habent impressionem super corpora. Et hoc dupliciter: uno quidem modo, secundum quod impressiones corporum coelestium in exteriora corpora sunt nobis causa alicuius electionis, sicut, quum per corpora coelestia disponitur aer ad frigus intensum, eligimus calefieri ad ignem vel aliqua huiusmodi facere quae congruunt tempori: alio modo, secundum quod imprimunt in corpora nostra, ad quorum immutationem insurgunt nobis aliqui motus passionum, vel per eorum impressionem efficimur habiles ad aliquas passiones, sicut cholerici sunt proni ad iram, vel secundum quod ex eorum impressione causatur in nobis aliqua dispositio corporalis quae est occasio alicuius electionis, sicut quum, nobis infirmantibus, eligimus accipere medicinam; interdum etiam ex corporibus coelestibus humani causantur, in quantum ex indispositione corporis aliqui amentes efficiuntur, usu rationis privati, in quibus proprie electio non est, sed moventur aliquo naturali instinctu, sicut et bruta.

"Manifestum est autem et experimento cognitum quod tales occasiones, sive sint exteriores sive interiores, non sunt causa necessaria electionis quum homo per rationem possit eis resistere vel obedire." The corresponding passages in the *Summa contra Gentiles*, in *Opera omnia*, ed. Stanislaus Fretté are as follows: ch. 85, "Quod corpora coelestia non sunt causae voluntatum et electionum nostrarum," vol. XII, pp. 363–66; ch. 86, "Quod corporales effectus, in istis inferioribus, non sequuntur ex necessitate a corporibus coelestibus," vol. XII, pp. 366–68; ch. 92, "Quomodo dicitur aliquis bene fortunatus, et quomodo adjuratur homo ex superioribus causis," vol. XII, pp. 373–76.

20. [*Can. non licet 26. q. 5. glos in verb. propt. seget*]: This reference appears in Taxil, pp. 71–72, as part of the discussion taken nearly verbatim from Francesco Giuntini that includes the balance of the quotation in Ferrand,

obviating any need to quote Taxil as an intermediary, with the exception of his version of the actual reference. Ferrand's original: "Astra non cogunt, dict Junctin in Spec. Astrol. Hac distinctione manifestum est, quantum errarint Neoterici nescientes distinguere hoc nomen Astrologiae: omnes enim sacrae Scripturae authoritates, et omnes fere leges adversantur opinioni Stoicae et Priscianistae, et non huic Astrologiae a SS. Theologis decantatae, et quam SS. Canones concessere." Taxil's reference: "In canon nonlicit causa 26. q. 5. gl. in verbis propter segetes non reprobatur illa Astrologia quae à corporibus coelestibus necessitatem non imponit, lege Archidicconum in decreto."

Francesco Giuntini (Junctinus), *Speculum Astrologiae universam mathematicum scientiam, in certas classes digestam complectens* (Lugduni: in officina Q. Phil. Tinghi, Florentini: apud Simphorianum Beraud, 1583), vol. I, p. 2: "Hac distinctione manifestum est, quantum errarint neoterici calumniatores, nescientes distinguere hoc nomen Astrologia. Omnes enim sacrae scripturae autoritates, et omnes fere leges adversantur primae opinioni Stoice et Priscillianisticae, et non huic Astrologiae a S. Theologis declaratae, et quam S. Canones confessere, ut in causis 26. q. 5. ca. Non licet Christianis. Glossa dicit in sententia, non reprobatur illa Astrologia, quae a corporibus superioribus necessitatem non imponit. Propterea dicimus cum glossa ibidem."

21. [*L 2 Medicopo. c. 2*]: Rodrigo de Castro, *Medicus-politicus*, bk. II, ch. 2, pp. 58–59: "Porro huius adhec duplex est genus, physicum unum, alterium fictitium et imaginarium, quae tripliciter inter se differunt: primum enim physicas tantum stellarum. . . ." Ferrand paraphrases him closely throughout the following three paragraphs. Ref. Taxil, p. 31.

22. [*Sueton. in Caes. et Neron & Domit. Val. Max. l. 8 ca. 11. Volat. l. 13. Pl. l. 10. c. 3. Tac. l. 14. ann.*]: All appear in Taxil, pp. 78–79. Ferrand condenses the two separate entries on Suetonius and the placement of the references in the margins is badly coordinated with the text. Taxil's text clarifies: "Quelle merveille nous à lessé de son sçavoir ce grand Astrologue Spurina [in margin: *Sueton. in Julio Caesar c. 81. & Valer. Max. lib. 8. c. 11.*] pour avoir predit à Caesar que les Ides de Mars luy estoient funestes, estant lors menacé d'estre tué? auquel jour Caesar trouvant Spurina, se mocqua de luy, disant que les Ides estoient venue, à quoy Spurina repondit, qu'elles estoient venues, mais non pas passees; et fut Caesar, ce mesme jour, tué dans le senat.

"Quelques Astrologues Chaldeens ne predirent-il pas à Agripine, mere de Neron, que son fils seroit un jour Empereur, mais qu'il la feroit mourir? ausquels elle respondit en ces termes, *occidat modo imperet* [in margin: *Cornel. Tacit. annal. li. 14.*].

"Volateran nous raconte que le Philosophe Aeschile estant adverty des Astrologues qui avoient dressé son horoscope, qu'il couroit fortune de mourir d'un coup sur la teste, qui luy arriveroit d'en haut, pour gauchir ce desastre, se resolut d'eviter les couverts, en demeurant aux champs, mais un jour comme il estoit assis, teste nuë, une aigle luy laissa tomber sur la teste une Tortue, qui le tua [in margin: *Volateran. li. 13. & Plin. lib. 10. c. 3.*].

"La prognostication d'Ascletarion, mathematicien tant estimé, ne fut-elle pas veritable? lequel asseura à Domitian, que les astres luy predisoient en bref sa mort; contra lequel, Domitian, enflé de despit, et enflammé de caurroux parla ainsi.

"Tu dis que je dois tost mourir? et toy, de qu'elle mort te menacent les Astres? de bien tost estre mangé des chiens, respond le Mathematicien; lors Domitian, pour faire mentir telle prediction, commanda qu'il fut bruslé: et comme il l'estoit desia à demy, une grosse pluye, faisant retirer les assistans, permit aux chiens de la devorer, et rendre sa prediction veritable, ce qui donna de l'apprehension à Domitian, lequel tost apres fut tué [in margin: *Sueton. in Domit. c. 15.*]."

Suetonius, *The Lives of the Caesars*, trans. J. C. Rolfe, 2 vols. (Loeb, 1950) "The Deified Julius," ch. 81, vol. I, p. 109; "Domitian," ch. 15, vol. II, p. 373–75: "When this man [Ascletarion the astrologer] was accused before the emperor and did not deny that he had spoken of certain things which he had foreseen through his art, he was asked what his own end would be. When he replied that he would shortly be rent by dogs, Domitian ordered him killed at once; but to prove the fallibility of his art, he ordered besides that his funeral be attended to with the greatest care. While this was being done, it chanced that the pyre was overset by a sudden storm and that the dogs mangled the corpse, which was only partly consumed."

Valerius Maximus, *Factorum et dictorum memorabilium libri novem*, bk. VIII, ch. 11, p. 401, gives a brief account of Julius Caesar's encounter with Spurina on the Ides of March.

Raffaele Maffei (Volaterranus), *Commentariorum urbanorum*, bk. XIII.

Pliny, *Natural History*, bk. X, sec. 3; vol. III, p. 297. In speaking of the "morphnos," or dusky eagle, he explains that "it has a clever device for breaking tortoise-shells that it has carried off, by dropping them from a height; this accident caused the death of the poet Aeschylus, who was trying to avoid a disaster of this nature that had been foretold by the fates, as the story goes, by trustfully relying on the open sky."

Tacitus, *The Annals*, bk. XIV, ch. 9, ed. John Jackson (Loeb, 1956), vol. IV, p. 123: "This was that ending to which, years before, Agrippina had given her credence, and her contempt. For to her inquiries as to the destiny of Nero the astrologers answered that he should reign, and slay his mother; and 'Let him slay,' she had said, 'so that he reign.' "

Ferrand makes an error here in saying "physique, ou artificielle, et imaginaire" when he means the physical or natural and the imaginary or artificial.

23. Pope Sixtus V, from Taxil, p. 68: "Que si le Pape Sixte V à fait une Bulle contre les Astrologues, et Chiromanciens, ce n'est que contre ceux qui en abusent qu'il à fulminé."

24. [*Aph. 27. segm. 5. Aph. Astr.*]: Girolamo Cardano, *Aphorismorum astronomicorum liber*, segm. V, aph. 26: "Facilius ac certius de genitura quam de tempore iudicamus, quoniam scimus horam nativitatis, non congregationis vaporum." We have confirmed Ferrand's quotation in the Nuremberg edition of 1547, though his source is Taxil, p. 129, where he also

found the above marginal reference and numbering of the aphorism.
25. Ptolemy, *Centiloquium*, prop. I: "soli divino numine afflati praedicunt futura particularia." See Taxil, p. 126.
26. St. Thomas More, *Epigrams*, no. 61:

Astra tibi aethereo pandunt sese omnia vati,
Omnibus et quae sunt fata futura monent.
Omnibus ast uxor quod se tua publicat, id te
Astra, licet videant omnia, nulla monent.

The Complete Works of St. Thomas More, ed. Clarence H. Miller et al. (New Haven: Yale University Press, 1984), vol. III, pt. 2, p. 135. For *sint* read *sunt*.
27. [*In Iphig.*]: Taxil, p. 126, Euripides, *Iphigeneia at Aulis*, ll. 520–21, trans. Arthur S. Way (Loeb, 1959), vol. I, p. 49: "Agamemnon: The whole seer-tribe is an ambitious curse. Menelaus: Abominable and useless."
28. [*Leonid in Anthol.*]: Leonidas of Alexandria, in the *Greek Anthology*, bk. IX, no. 80:

Ὑμέας ἀφροσύνη μαιώσατο, τόλμα δ'ἔτικτεν,
τλήμονας, οὐδ' ἰδίην εἰδότας ἀκλεΐην.

See trans. W. R. Paton (Loeb, 1948), vol. III, p. 43.

XXII.   Whether Those Inclined to Love Can Be Known by Physiognomy and Chiromancy

1. [*Libr. de decub. agr.*]: Galen, *Prognostica de decubitu ex mathematica scientia*, ch. 1, ed. Kühn, vol. XIX, p. 530.
2. Jean Taxil, *L'astrologie et physiognomie en leur splendeur*, ch. 1, p. 2: "La physiognomie est divisee en trois parties, sçavoir, en metoposcopie, physiognomique, et chiromantie."

The correlation of materials suggests Ferrand was also reading Levinus Lemnius, *Occulta naturae miracula*, bk. II, ch. 26, pp. 212–15. Concerning physiognomy, Lemnius posits that the body has no parts, no matter how small or ignoble, that are incapable of reflecting certain aspects of the inner nature and the inclinations of the mind. The most sensative and revealing area is the face, and particularly the eyes. Therefore, as Ferrand will argue, love can be identified in the features in the same way that wicked men show their guilt. The science of physiognomy grew out of an attempt to catalog the correspondences between conditions of the soul and gestures, traits, and features. In reverse direction, it was believed that imperfections of the body also, of necessity, tainted the soul and moral nature, so that hunchbacks had to have vicious natures just as the beautiful had to have a beauty of spirit as well. Yet Ferrand, aware of the difficulties, will point out that some handsome men have been deceitful, and that some less endowed have made efforts to correct their natures through moral training. Ferrand steers a middle course, attempting only to give a convincing profile of the lustful man.
3. [*L. 3. de ora. Cael. Rodig. l. 2. c. 27.*]: Cicero, *De Oratore*, bk. III, ch. 59: "an-

imi est omnis actio, et imago animi vultus est. Indices oculi, dit Cicer. quos natura dedit nobis, ut equo, et leoni setas, caudam, aures ad motus declarandos." See trans. H. Rackham (Loeb, 1968), vol. II, pp. 178–79: "Est enim actio quasi sermo corporis, quo magis menti congruens esse debet; oculos autem natura nobis, ut equo et leoni iubas, caudam, aures, ad motus animorum declarandos dedit, quare in hac nostra actione secundum vocem vultus valet; is autem oculis gubernatur."

Lodovico Ricchieri (Rhodoginus), *Lectionum antiquarum libri triginta*, cols. 96–97. The reference is, however, from Taxil, p. 8: "Ac ut imago animi vultus est ita indices oculi."

4. "τὰ τῆς ψυχῆς κάτοπτα." Ferrand attributes these words to Alexander of Aphrodisias; the *Problems* is their most likely source, though our word search suggests that they may not be by Alexander.

5. Plotinus, *Enneads*, bk. I, tr. 6, p. 61: "We may even say that Beauty *is* the Authentic-Existents [*sic*] and Ugliness is the Principle contrary to Existence: and the Ugly is also the primal evil; therefore its contrary is at once good and beautiful, or is Good and Beauty: and hence the one method will discover to us the Beauty-Good and the Ugliness-Evil."

6. πρῶτον μὲν εἶδος ἄξιον τυραννίδος," Euripides, *Fragmenta*, ed. A. Nauch, in *Tragicorum Graecorum fragmenta* (Leipzig: Teubner, 1889; rpt. Hildesheim: Olms, 1964), no. 15, l. 2, p. 367.

7. [*L. 1. de san. tu.*]: Galen, *De sanitate tuenda*, bk. I, ed. Kühn, vol. VI, pp. 6–7.

8. [*Cic. Tusc. 1*]: Cicero, *Tusculan Disputations*, bk. I, ch. 33, sec. 80: "multa enim in corpore existunt, quae acuant mentem, multa quae obtundant." See trans. J. E. King (Loeb, 1966), pp. 94–95.

9. [*L. 6. Ep. sect. 5.*]: Hippocrates, the reference to bk. VI of the *Epidemics* is in error for *Regimen*, bk. I: "συμφέρει καὶ ἀσαρκέειν πρὸς τὸ φρονίμους εἶναι," *Oeuvres complètes*, ed. Littré, vol. VI, p. 521; the original reads: "Συμφέρει δὲ καὶ ἀσαρκέειν τοῖσι τοιούτοισι πρὸς τὸ φρονίμους εἶναι."

10. [*Exhort. ad bon. discip. l. I. de san. tu. L. 5 de plat.*]: Galen, *Adhortatio ad artes addiscendas*, ed. Kühn, vol. I, p. 24.

Galen, *De sanitate tuenda*, ed. Kühn, vol. VI, p. 28.

Galen, *De placitis Hippocratis et Platonis*, bk. VI, ch. 6, ed. Kühn, vol. V, pp. 472–73.

11. [*L. De mutua corp & an. mor. consec.*]: Galen, *Quod animi mores corporis temperamenta sequantur*, ed. Kühn, vol. IV, chs. 9–10, pp. 807 ff.

12. [*2. Epidem. sect. 5.*]: Hippocrates, *Epidemics*, bk. II, sec. 5: "τραυλοὶ, ἰσχνόφωνοι." *Oeuvres complètes*, ed. Littré, vol. V, p. 128.

13. [*Arist. Polem. Porta*]: Aristotle and Polemo are repeatedly referred to by Giovan Battista della Porta, *De humana physiognomonia libri IV*, which Ferrand is using for this chapter. For information on Polemo, see n. 11 to ch. XX, above.

Physiognomy as a technique for identifying erotic appetites appeared in medical treatises later in the seventeenth century. See, for example, Giovanni Benedetto Sinibaldi, *Geneanthropeiae, sive de hominis generatione decateuchon* (Romae: ex typo. Fran. Caballi, 1642), which was also translated into English in 1657 and entitled *Rare Verities*. In this work the writer addresses the question "what are the physiological signs of lust," and provides a series of observations paralleling those of Ferrand: that a small, straight forehead indicates uncontrolled erotic desires; that small ears indicate strong venal tendencies; that a young bald man is inclined to lust; and that an old and hairy one has lost one or both of his testicles.

14. Giovan Battista della Porta, *De humana physiognomonia libri IV*, bk. II, ch. 24, p. 261: "Poco barba, et men colore / Sotto 'l ciel non è pegiore."

15. [*In Eutyph*]: Plato, *Eutyphro* (16A), in *Plato*, trans. H. N. Fowler, p. 59.

16. [*Pl. in The. Xenoph. Ammon. Hieron. ad Jovin.*]: Plato, *Theaetetus* (143–44), trans. H. N. Fowler (Loeb, 1961), p. 13: "But the fact is—now don't be angry with me—he [a young man met by Theodorus] is not handsome, but is like you in his snub nose and protruding eyes, only those features are less marked in him than in you [Socrates]."

Xenophon, *Symposium*, IV. 9 ff., in *Xenophon*, trans. O. J. Todd (Loeb, 1968), vol. II, p. 570 ff.: " 'How now' exclaimed Socrates. 'You boast as though you actually thought yourself a handsomer man than me.'

'Of course,' was Critobolus' reply; 'otherwise I should be the ugliest of all the Satyrs ever on the stage.'

Now Socrates, as fortune would have it, really resembled these creatures."

Ammon is probably a reference to the Greek philosopher Ammonius, author of a series of philosophical works and of a *Life of Aristotle*, published several times during the sixteenth and seventeenth centuries.

St. Jerome, *Adversus Jovinianum libri duo*, in *Oeuvres complètes de Saint Jerome*, trans. L'Abbé Bareille, 18 vols. (Paris: Louis Vivès, 1877–85), vol. II, pp. 500–633. Ferrand's reference is to Jovinianus himself, who had earned the name of the epicure of the Christians for his luxurious style of living.

See also Jean Taxil, *L'astrologie et physiognomie en leur splendeur*, ch. 1, p. 14: "Il ne faut pourtant croire comme article de foy, que tousjours le visage represente la verité des qualitez interieures: car on void quelquefois des ames bonnes, et vertueuses soubs des images laids, et contrefaicts, tesmoin celle de Socrate: on en void aussi de mauvaises, et vicieuses, couvertes d'une beauté de visage, comme celle de Saul, et d'Absalon."

17. [*L. de fato*]: Cicero, *De fato*: "Cum Socrates videret uxores inter se jurgantes, et ille eas deridebat, quod propter se foedissimum hominem, simis naribus, recalva fronte, pilosis humeris, repandis cruribus disceptarent." See *De Oratore*, trans. H. Rackham (Loeb, 1960), pp. 203–5. But the citation is, in fact, from Taxil, p. 87, the transcription faithful to the intermediary text.

18. André Du Laurens, *Des maladies melancholique et du moyen de les guarir*, in *Toutes les oeuvres*, p. 24^V. Du Laurens tells the story of Zopyrus and Sophocles to demonstrate that man is not entirely fated by his physiological heritage in light of the discussion of Galen, who argued that the brain was conditioned by its temperature. Du Laurens was careful not to make the soul entirely victim to a biological heritage lest men should

abandon their spiritual responsibilities. "Zopyre grand Philosophe, qui se mesloit de juger et cognoistre à la simple veuë, les moeurs d'un chacun, comme il eust un jour contemplé Socrate lisant, estant fort importuné de tous les assistans de dire ce qu'il luy en sembloit, respondit en fin qu'il l'avoit recogneu pour le plus corrompu et vicieux homme du monde. Le rapport en fut soudain fait à Socrate par l'un de ses disciples, qui se moquoit de Zopyre. Lors Socrate par admiration s'escria, ô le grand Philosophe! il a du tout recogneu mes humeurs; j'estois de mon naturel enclin à tous ces vices, mais la philosophie morale m'en a destourné. Et à la verité Socrate avoit une teste fort longue, et mal figurée, le visage difforme, le nez retroussé. Ces moeurs donc naturelles qui viennent de la temperature et conformation du corps, pourveu que ces deux vices ne soient excessifs, comme aux melancholiques, peuvent estre domptées et corrigées par les moeurs que nous acquerons par la philosophie morale, par la lecture des beaux livres, et par la frequentation des hommes vertueux." Ferrand does his best to reconcile two conflicting theoretical claims: one, that the manners of the mind depend on the temperature of the body in a way that enables the practicing physician to attack derangements of the spirit by treating physiological causes; the other that the mind is not entirely predetermined by those bodily conditions. Hence, his qualification that physiognomical signs do not always reveal the passions and affections of the mind, though often they do, with a certain degree of probability. Ferrand is concerned with this diagnostic dimension of medicine insofar as it can help in the identification of disease. This moralizing anecdote about Socrates circulated widely and was put to various uses according to the rhetorical purposes of the writer. Liébault, in discussing the ways in which congenital imperfections can be overcome in children, speaks of astral influences, climate, and environment as well as industry and education, citing how some "par le moyen de la bonne education et de leur industrie deviennent grands personnages, sages, vertueux et bien advisez, et lesquels s'adonnent à toutes louables et honnestes actions: ainsi que nous lisons de Socrates qui de son naturel estoit lourdaut et vicieux sur tous les hommes de son temps: mais par son industrie fut rendu le plus sage et le plus vertueux philosophe de son aage." *Des maladies des femmes*, (Lyon, 1598), bk. III, ch. 19, p. 709.

19. [*L. Physion. c. I. & 4.*]: Aristotle, *Physiognomics*, ch. IV (1808b 10): "ἡ τῆς ψυχῆς ἕξις ἀλλοιουμέη συναλλοιοῖ τὴν τοῦ σώματος μορφήν, πάλιν τε ἡ τοῦ σώματος μορφὴ ἀλλοιουμένη συναλλοιοῖ τὴν τῆς ψυχῆς ἕξιν." In *Minor Works*, trans. W. S. Hett, p. 104. Both chs. 1 and 4 discuss the relationship between the body and the soul.

20. [*Innoc. V. l. 2. comp. Theol. c. 32*]: Pope Innocent V, *In IV libros sententiarum commentaria* (Tolosae: apud Arnaldum Colomerium, 1652), bk. II, "Distinctio 32," vol. I, p. 273. We believe that Ferrand is referring to the passage as cited, although Innocent V is speaking about the traits inherited as original sin that may be cleansed by baptism. The relationship to Ferrand's context is, in fact, rather remote, and it is probable that he derived this reference through an intermediary source.

21. [*Gal. in Microtegn. Arist. 3 de gen. ca. 1. Problem. 2. sec. 4. et 26 sec. 10*]: Galen, *Ars medica*, ed. Kühn, vol. I, p. 324. This work was referred to throughout the Middle Ages and the Renaissance as *Microtechni* or *Tegni Galieni*; it was a standard text in the medical schools.

Aristotle, *On the Generation of Animals*. The reference intended is to bk. III, ch. 3 (783b) rather than ch. 1 (which deals with birds), p. 523: "For human beings, however, it is the seasons of life which play the part of summer and winter; and that is why no one goes bald before the time of sexual intercourse, and also why that is the time when those who are naturally prone to intercourse go bald."

Aristotle, *Problems*, bk. IV (876a–877a), "Problems concerning Sexual Intercourse," vol. I, pp. 109–13. Ferrand mentions sec. 2, but summarizes ideas from various parts, esp. 2, 4, and 31. See also bk. X, no. 34, p. 219: "Why are hairy men and thick-feathered birds lustful? Is it because they are naturally hot and moist, and both these qualities are necessary to intercourse?"

22. [*Sueton.*]: Suetonius, *The Lives of the Caesars*, "The Deified Julius," ch. 51: "Urbani servate uxores, nam moechum calvum adducimus." See trans. J. C. Rolfe, 2 vols. (Loeb, 1951), vol. I, p. 71: "Urbani, servate uxores: moechum calvom adducimus."

23. [*Arist. ca. 6. Physiog. Proble. 19. sec. 4.*]: Aristotle, *Physiognomics*, ch. VI. Extrapolating from this work, Ferrand concludes that the lover will have little ears, a great nose, etc., though the lover is not so specified by Aristotle. Rather he offers a series of maxims such as the following: "Those with small ears are ape-like" (p. 125); "Those that have a circular nose tip, but a flat one are magnanimous; witness the lions" (p. 121); "Those that have full legs as if they were bursting are foul-minded and shameless; this is appropriate" (p. 115); "Those with an overhanging brow are over bold" (p. 125); "But the snub-nosed are salacious" (p. 123); "But those who have gleaming eyes are sensual" (p. 129); "Creatures with hairy legs are sensual; witness goats" (p. 129); "The knock-kneed are lustful" (p. 117); "Those that have light sinewy legs are salacious" (p. 115).

Aristotle, *Problems*, bk. IV, ch. 18 (878b), vol. I, p. 123, deals with sexuality and baldness. His observations include the following:. "Why are those lustful whose eyelashes fall out? Is it for the same reason as that for which the bald are also lustful?"

24. [*C. ult. l. 2. Meth. med.*]: Valescus de Taranta, *Epitome morbis curandis in septem congesta libros* (Lugduni: apud Joan. Tornaesium, et Gulielmum Gazeium, 1560), bk. II, last sec., "De affectibus labiorum," p. 208: "Labiorum fixurae in mulieribus uteri arguunt siccitatem, qui saepe rorari appetit: propterea tales mulieres ut plurimum coitum prae caeteris amant."

25. [*L. 2. de occult. nat. mira. c. 26*]: Levinus Lemnius, *Occulta naturae miracula*, bk. II, ch. 26, p. 213. Lemnius reasons that the blood and nutriments that would otherwise nourish the lower limbs are retained in the generative parts causing an increase in the seed, prurient itching, and erection of the parts in lame persons.

Lemnius claims *The Deipnosophists* of Athenaeus as his source, but this aspect of Amazon behavior does not appear to be recorded in that work.

26. [*L. de Artic*]: Hippocrates, *Des articulations* (On the Joints), in *Oeuvres complètes*, ed. Littré, vol. IV, p. 233: "Quelques-uns racontent que les Amazones font subir à leurs enfants de sexe masculin, dès le bas âge, une luxation soit aux hanches, afin sans doute de les rendre boîteux, et d'empêcher les hommes de rien tramer contre les femmes; puis, elles se servent de ces infirmes, comme ouvriers, pour les métiers de cordonnier, de forgeron, et autres métiers sédentaires. Je ne sais pas si ce récit est véritable; mais ce que je sais, c'est que les choses se passeraient de la sorte si on estropiait ainsi les enfants en bas âge."

27. Aristotle, *On the Generation of Animals*, bk. II, sec. 7: "ὅ τε γὰρ περὶ τοὺς ὀφθαλμοὺς τόπος τῶν περὶ τὴν κεφαλὴν σπερματικώτατός ἐστιν." See trans. A. L. Peck, pp. 247–49: The entire passage reads, "for of all the regions in the head the eyes are the most seminal, as is proved by the fact that this is the only region which unmistakably changes its appearance during sexual intercourse, and those who overfrequently indulge in it have noticeably sunken eyes."

28. There is the possibility that Ferrand intends here a reference to Solomon, for he says literally: "And even the wise man [le sage] recognized." But while such texts as Proverbs 6:25 caution against the allurements of the harlot's eyes, no passage has been traced in which the hands and the eyes are compared.

29. [*L. 4. Coll. c. 5. & 6.*]: Averroes, *Colliget*, bk. IV, ch. 4, p.62ᵛ: "Et homo, quem tu scis dicit quod brevitas digitorum significat parvitatem hepatis, et hic apparet quod nescivit bene, et non consyderavit nisi in materiebus, et dimittamus istum cum aliis." In chs. 5 and 6 he says nothing about the value of touch or the hand, though in chs. 15 and 16 he speaks of the role of the pulse in terms reminiscent of this reference.

30. [*Fen 2. l. 1. doctr. 3. c. 1. Fen 14. l. 3. tr. 1*]: Avicenna, *Liber canonis*, bk. I, fen 2, tr. 3, ch. 1, p. 42ᵛ ff, "De accidentibus et significationibus."

Liber canonis, bk. I, fen 14, tr. 1: "De universalibus dispositionibus hepatis."

31. Hippocrates, *On Food*, sec. 31: "ῥίζωσιν φλεβῶν ἧπαρ," *Oeuvres complètes*, ed. Littré, vol. IX, p. 111.

32. [*Th à Vega in c. 8. art. med.*]: Thomas à Viega (Tomás Rodriguez da Viega), *Ars medica*, in *Opera omnia in Galeni libros edita*, pp. 16b ff. In this chapter he speaks of temperaments and temperature, but nowhere speaks of the liver or its relationship to the hands. For his discussion of the liver see sec. 5, chs. 37 and 38, pp. 65a ff.

33. [*C. illud 26. q. 2. Tol. Sacer. Instr. c. 15. l. 4.*]: See ch. XXI nn. 17, 20, and 23. These passing references to the Canonists, Cardinal Tolet, and Pope Sixtus V are derived from Taxil.

Franciscus Tolet, *Instructio sacerdotum ac de septem peccatis mortalibus*, 2 vols. (Lugduni: apud Horatium Cardon, 1604), bk. IV, ch. 15, vol. I, p. 242ʳ: "Chiromantiam, quae fit per signa, et figuras corporis humani . . . tamen triplici casu uti Astrologia est peccatum mortale."

In the edition of 1610 Ferrand elaborates on the topic of palmistry in the following way: "the man who has the figure D on his second finger, or an E on any other is inclined to love, or else he is compelled to be amorous if the muscle under the thumb (which is called the mount of Venus) is fleshy and crossed with wrinkles. Likewise, if a woman has a deep black line on the middle finger, according to these charlatans, she will fall in love with all manner of men, unless the black line is broken and interrupted by several others that are strongly detached. The same judgment is given of those who have a large triangle of Mars or who have three stars above the mount of Jupiter and Saturn. Corvé [whom we have identified as Jan Cornario] in his book of Chirom. [which we take to be his translation of Artemidorus, see ch. XXIV, n. 25] and Mario Equicola of Alveto in his book on the nature of love, bk. IV, ch. 3."

34. [*Krants l. 11. ca. 2. Verg. l. 7. c. de rer. invent.*]: Albert Krantz, *Rerum Germanicarum liber* (Francofurti: ad Moenum apud A. Wechelum, 1580), bk. II, ch. 2, year 1417: "primum apparvere his nostris maritimis locis ad mare Germanicum homines nigredine informes, excocti sole, immundi veste, et usu rerum omnium foedi, furtis imprimis acres, praesertim foeminae eius gentis: nam viris ex furto foeminarum victus est. Tartaros vulgus appellat: in Italia vocant Cianos . . . hominem genus, quod usu compertum est in peregrinatione natum, ocio deditum, nullam agnoscens patriam. Ita circuit provincias, furto (ut diximus) foeminarum victitans, canino ritu degit, nulla religionis illi cura, in diem vivit. Ex provincia demigrat in provinciam."

Polidoro Virgilio, *Des inventeurs des choses*, bk. VII, ch. 23, pp. 108–9. The reference is specific and should, from the context, have to do with the Bohemians or Egyptians in Europe who practiced magic. Rather, the reference is to magic in general as a dangerous art: "Ces choses nous faut eviter comme toutes supersticieuses et malefiques, qui toutes bonnes choses corrompent et font perir, et ensuyvons les sectes de vraye religion et saincte foy Catholique, pour honnestement vivre."

Gabriel Dupréau, *Histoire de l'estat et succès de l'Eglise, dressée en forme de chronique géneralle et universelle*, year 1417.

XXIII.   Whether by Magic One Can Recognize Lovers

1. "δεινὸν γόητα καὶ φαρμακέα." The sentence comes from Plato's *Symposium*, 203D, ed. J. B. Bury, p. 180: "δεινὸς γόης καὶ φαρμακεύς."

In the present edition, Ferrand makes new rhetorical use of his materials on magic and dreams. Whereas he was concerned in the edition of 1610 with the magic rites and superstitions of lovers themselves for predicting and controlling their futures, he is here concerned with clinical matters, namely whether the physician can or should use magic and dreams in the diagnosing of love. He begins ch. XIII of the earlier edition with the declaration that "unfortunate and indiscrete lovers, unable to win the hearts of the ladies through their own merits, turn to magic, whether in order to win their good graces or to see if there is any hope of possessing and enjoying them." He makes certain to declare such arts as abominations before God, but goes on to explain precisely what they are and how they are practiced. Here much of the specifics of that folkloric use of magic is suppressed. Possibly, his change in perspective is the result of the charges made by the tribunal, perhaps of his more clinically and professionally oriented approach to the subject.

2. Hippocrates, *Prognostics*, in *Oeuvres complètes*, ed. Littré, vol. II, pp. 111, 113; *Hippocrates to Philopemen*, vol. IX, p. 343. The paraphrase in Ferrand is from the latter text.

3. [*C. 18. Deut. C. 13. Paral. Can. sort. 26. q. 1. Aug. ep. ad Jan et c. 3. l. 4. confes.*]: *The Fifth Book of Moses commonly called Deuteronomy* 18:10–14, RSV: "There shall not be found among you any one who burns his son or his daughter as an offering, any one who practices divination, a soothsayer, or an augur, or a sorcerer, or a charmer, or a medium, or a wizard, or a necromancer. For whoever does these things is an abomination to the Lord; and because of these abominable practices the Lord your God is driving them out before you. You shall be blameless before the Lord your God. For these nations, which you are about to dispossess, give heed to soothsayers and to diviners; but as for you, the Lord your God has not allowed you so to do."

Corpus Juris Canonici, pt. 2, causa 26, Gratianus, ques. 1–4, ed. A. L. Richter, 2 vols. (Graz: Akademische Druck-U. Verlagsanstalt, 1959), vol. I, pp. 1019–26.

St. Augustine, *Ad inquisitiones Januarii liber II, seu epistola LV*, pt. 8, in *Opera*, vol. XXXVIII of *Collectio selecta SS. Ecclesiae Patrum*, ed. D. A. B. Caillan (Parisiis: ap. Parent-Desbarres, 1840), sec. 7, p. 499.

St. Augustine, *Confessions*, trans. William Watts, bk. IV, ch. 3, vol. I, p. 153.

4. This passage bears a certain resemblance to the following in Johann van Heurne, *Praxis medicinae nova ratio qua libris tribus methodi ad praxin medicam*, bk. III, ch. 28, p. 481: "Ethnicorum autem Magia orta est ex medicina, astrologia, et daemonum cultu. A Persis Magi dicebantur Sophi: ab Indis, Brachmani: Gallis, Druides: Graecis et Aegyptiis mystae et prophetae, sacrorum antistites. Huius Magiae documenta auctoribus nocumenta esse Nero Cesar etiam didicit, qui maximas effudit opes ut hanc disceret artem: sed falsam expertus, postremo repudiavit. Si quid veritatis et utilitatis haec res haberet, profecto libri Numae Pompilii non fuissent prudentissimi Senatus Romani decreto in foro combusti: extarent scripta Democriti, Pythagorae, Aegyptiorum sacerdotum, Zoroastri, Hostanis, Proconesii, Dardani, et Druidum."

5. [*Giral. de diis gent. synt. 7. Venet. in praef. sacr. Scrip. tom. 2. prob. 275 276 277 & 286*]: Lilio Gregorio Giraldi, *De deis gentium libri sive syntagmata XVII. Quibus varia ac multiplex deorum gentium historia, imagines ac cognomina, plurimaque simul multis hactenus ignota explicantur* (Lugduni: apud haeredes Jacobi Junctae, 1565), "Syntagma VII," p. 201: "Mithrae meminit Strabo et Suidas, item Maritianus ad Solem: Memphis, inquit, veneratur Osirin, Dissona sacra Mithran. In Persidis montibus Zoroaster

primus antrum floridum Mithrae dicasse fertur, propre frontes. Ex quo postea mansit religio, ut ubicunque coleratur, antrum vel specus similiter eius templi loco statueretur."

Francesco Giorgio (Francescus Venetus), *In scripturam sacram problemata* (Venice: 1536), vol. II, probs. 275, 276, 277 and 289.

Polidoro Virgilio, *Des inventeurs des choses*, pp. 81 ff. See ch. XXI, n. 1.

Johann Jakob Wecker, *Les secrets et merveilles de nature, recueilles de divers autheurs, et divisez en XVII livres*, bk. XV, ch. 8: "De la goetie, et necromantie," p. 694: "On dit que S. Heros en a fait mention escrivant à Paulin, où il dit que Appollinus Thianaeus a esté magicien, ou philosophe, comme les Pythagoriciens. Et que tels ont esté les magiciens qui ont visité Jesus-Christ né, luy ont porté presens, et l'ont adoré, que les expositeurs des Evangiles interpretent Philosophes des Chaldeens. Comme ont esté Hiarchas entre les Bragmes, Thespion entre les Gimnosophistes, Budda entre les Babyloniens, Numa Pompilius entre les Romains, Zamolxides entre les Scythes, Abbaris entre les Hyperborées, Hermes entre les Egyptiens, Zoroastres fils de Oramasus entre les Perses. Car les Indes, Ethopiens, et Chaldeens, et les Perses ont excellé par dessus tous autres l'art de magie."

Martin Del Rio, *Disquisitionum magicarum libri sex*, deals with magic, its origins and practices throughout this work. See ch. XXI, nn. 9, 16.

Corpus Juris Canonici, pt. 2, causa 26, ques. 3, ch. 1, "De multiplici genera divinationis," vol. I, pp. 1024–25.

6. Johann Jakob Wecker opens a paragraph in much the same way, but follows a different course, in *Les secrets et merveilles de nature*, pp. 701–2: "Et pource que les femmes sont plus curieuses des secrets, moins advisées, enclinées à superstition, elles sont plus aisément deceuës et se presentent à elles faciles, et font de grands prodiges: comme les Poëtes, chantent de Circé, Medée et autres: Pline, Ciceron, Seneque, Augustin, et plusieurs autres tant Philosophes que Catholiques Docteurs et Historiens, et mesmes les lettres sainctes le certifient. Car nous lisons au livre des Roys que la femme Pythonisse qui estoit en Endor, fit venir l'ame du Prophete Samuël, qui n'estoit pas toutesfois l'ame du vray Samuël, mais un esprit malin qui avoit pris la forme de Samuël. Ce neantmoins les maistres des Hebrieux, qu'ils appellent Rabians, disent (ce que Augustin escrivant à Simplician, ne nie pas le pouvoir faire) que c'estoit le vray esprit de Samuël."

In the 1610 edition (p. 96) Ferrand states cleary why these girls carry out such rituals, namely because "our ladies smitten by love want to know who their servant in love will be." He also makes several allusions to the occasions upon which these rites are carried out, allusions suppressed in the 1623 edition: "Botonomancy is the first in importance: on the eve of the Kings [Epiphany] or of Saint John the Baptist [June 23] they throw the leaves of butcherbroom, box or bay into the fire." See ch. XXIV, n. 14. In the 1610 edition (p. 97) Ferrand also relates that "some [girls] collected on the night of St. John the seeds of the 'faugere' with certain words and gestures that they learn from their mothers."

7. Theocritus, *Idyll* III. 29: "δηλέφιλον," the poppy called "tell-love" or love-in-absence. See trans. A. S. F. Gow, vol. I, pp. 32–33: "I learnt the truth of late when I bethought me dost thou love me, and the smack caused not the love-in-absence to cling, but idly it shrivelled on my smooth forearm.

"And Agroeo too, that divines with her sieve—she that was lately cutting grass by my side, told me truth, how that my heart was wholly thine while thou madest no account of me."

This passage refers to a rustic form of divination which may entail crushing the leaves of a poppy over a circle of the left hand made by joining the ends of the thumb and index, or to a kind of noise made by slapping the right hand over the flower, or finally by observing whether the flower sticks there or falls when it is smacked. The exact meanings of the words are debated by specialists. A résumé of the possible meanings is given by Gow in vol. II, pp. 70–71. One authority asserts that the plant "was laid on various parts of the arm and struck with the other hand, omens being either from the sound produced or from the mark left upon the skin." Ferrand reports that they were bruised, taking his clue no doubt from the word "προσμάσσειν," meaning to press one thing upon another—a smack or blow.

Ferrand makes mention thirty lines later of coscinomancy, a form of divination employing a sieve, derived from this same idyll. The methods, according to Gow (vol. II, p. 71), "are not recorded, but its practitioners are spoken of with some contempt both by Lucian (Alex. 9) and by Artemidorus (2. 69)."

8. [*Varro 5. de ling. lat. Horat 4. Carmin.*]: Marcus Terentius Varro, *In libro de lingua Latina conjectanea Josephi Scaligeri*, in *Opera quae supersunt* (no place or publisher, 1581), p. 59: "Oro ab ore, et Perorat, et Exorat, et Oratio, et Orator, et Osculum dictum. Inde Omen, et Ornamentum. Alterum quod ex ore primum elatum est, Osmen dictum; alterum cum praepositione dicitur nunc ornamentum, olim ornamenta scaenici plerique dicunt. Hinc Oscines dicuntur apud augures, quod ore faciunt auspicium." For a modern edition of Varro, see *On the Latin Language*, trans. Roland G. Kent, 2 vols. (Loeb, 1958), vol. I, pp. 242–45.

Horace, *Carmina*, bk. III, Ode xxvii. 11 ff, ed. E. C. Wickham (Oxford: Clarendon, 1896), vol. I, p. 266.

9. Pacuvius, *Plays*, "Chryses," ll. 104–6:

istis qui ex alieno iecore intelligunt
Plusque ex alieno iecore sapiunt, quam ex suo,
Magis audiendum, quam auscultandum censeo.

See *Remains of Old Latin*, trans. E. H. Warmington, 4 vols. (Loeb, 1961), vol. II, p. 200. The quotation is also to be found in Cicero, *De divinatione*, bk. I, ch. 57, p. 131. Ferrand removes the first line and replaces it with another, perhaps his own. It reads, "nam isti qui linguam avium intellegunt."

10. Theocritus, *Idyll* III. 31–34. See n. 7, above, for text and commentary.

11. [*Val. Max. l. I. c. 4*]: Valerius Maximus, *Factorum et dictorum memorabilium libri novem*, bk. I, ch. 4, pp. 18–21. The chapter deals with auspices

generally but not with the specific concepts mentioned by Ferrand such as coscinomantia or cleromantia. Ferrand, in the edition of 1610, is more specifically concerned with such practices as hydromancy, "which is done by making a ring that is perched or suspended in the air strike against a tumbler filled with water, but without pushing it," a practice which he says is particularly forbidden according to "C. Nec. mirum 20 q. 5."

12. [*Cael. Rodi. l. 15. c. 5.*]: Luigi Ricchieri (Rhodoginus), *Lectionum antiquarum libri triginta*, bk. XV, ch. 5, is an error because Ferrand's references elsewhere to this work correspond. In bk. VIII, ch. 8, vol. II, p. 720, Ricchieri records Vigenarius as saying of the Emperor Adrian that he was an "homme fort adonné à la Magie, aussi bien qu'à l'Astrologie, et si plein de vanité, que voulant qu'on creust qu'il excelloit les hommes en toutes choses."

Virgil's Works, "Introduction," ed. William C. McDermott (New York: 1950), p. xxiv: "In later classical times two uses of Virgil show the wide influence of the poet. Half-lines and lines of his poems were artificially welded into patchwork poems (centos) such as the fourth-century poems of Valeria Falconia Proba on creation, the origin of sin, and the birth of Christ. Again in the practice of Virgilian lots (sortes vergilianae) the poems were opened at random and the chosen verse was used as a guide for conduct and a prophecy of the future."

Ferrand explains in the edition of 1610 (p. 98) that it is also called the Valentinian fate because it is practiced on the eve of St. Valentine's Day. Again, he points to traditional magical practices employed by girls on saints' days associated with love in order to know the future.

13. The sixteenth century proffers a rich variety of writings on the subject and practice of magic, concentrating often on the names and origins of the types practiced. Of note are the two following: Raffaele Maffei (Volaterranus), *Commentariorum urbanorum octo et triginta libri*, bk. XXX, "De Divinatione," p. 326: "Hincquoque et illa dependere videntur Hydromantia ex aqua; Geomantia ex terra; Necromantia ex mortuis; Coschinomantia ex cribro; Cleromantia ex sortibus; Lecanomantia ex pelui. Strabo Lecanomantas et Hydromantas in Perside frequentes esse ait. Physiognomia ex natura membrorum; Chiromantia ex manibus sicut ab uxiorum genere de quibus in geographia dixi; Astrognomia ex astris ut a Babyloniis et Chaldeis; Botanomantia ex herbis, ut a Thessalis foeminis, quae Latinis sage dicuntur. Gastromantia ex amphora ventrosa quae a puero solet inspici, etiam apud veteres. Hoc Cicero forte intelligit in libro de divinatione quum dicit auspicia militum per acumina, nisi de lapide siderite intelligat, cuius est ea virtus teste Orpheo de lapidibus ut noctu velatus ad lucernam expiatis mente introspicientibus moreti, responsaque dare videatur."

Lilio Gregorio Giraldi, *De deis gentium libri sive syntagmata XVII*, pp. 198–99. In discussing the history of Mithraeism, Giraldi provides a list of the forms of magic and augury practiced in that age: "Geomantia, Catoptromantia, Astrogolomantia, Tyromantia, Auguria, Auspicia, Alectryomantia, Haruspicina, Extispicia, Coscinomantia, Axinoman-

tia, Lecanomantia, Βοτανομαντία [a plant sacred to women] Necromantia, Necyomantia, Sciomantia, Astronomia, Asteroscopia, Aëromantia,
Nephelmantia, Metoscopia, Metopomantia, Physiognomia, Prosoposco-
pia, Chiromantia, Arithmantia, Ichthyomantia, Palmicum Augurium,
Oniromantia, Onirocrises, Pyromantia, Ignispicina, (Hirpini), Hydromantia, Aleuromantia, Alphitomantia." The various origins are implicit in
the text, as in Pythius or in Delphos, etc., according to sources.

Ferrand's discussion of magic was more extensive in the edition
of 1610, and more openly informative concerning popular customs and
rituals, for which reason among others the work was condemned in
Toulouse in 1620 by the church authorities. We may assume by the
omissions in the 1623 edition that Ferrand interpreted such passages
as the following as part of the offending material: "chrystalomancy, to
which the naturalists have given a certain credence, for Albertus Magnus, Cardano, and others assert that whoever holds an emerald under
his tongue, or an amethyst, or the stone which is found in the nest of
the horned owl, will easily be able to guess if the love of the person in
mind will succeed. The pagans place equal confidence for knowing such
things in the noise and squeals of mice thrown against the threshold of
the door, in sobbing and sighs, the pulse of the artery, in appositions,
retrogradations, and conjunctions of the moon, the calends, Egyptian
days, and endless others that you can read about in Polidoro Vergilio
[in margin: *Lib. de invent. rer. cap. 23 & 24*; see ch. XXI, n. 1] that I won't
explain to you, for fear that the misguided lover will employ them,
and that this treatise will run the risk of censure and be condemned to
the flames according to the laws of the Emperor." It is of interest that
Ferrand should have so accurately predicted the very fate of his book
some ten years after its publication, almost as if this passage served the
inquisitors as a guide and sanction.

XXIV.   Whether Lovers Can be Known by Oneiromancy or the Interpretation of Dreams

1. Macrobius, *Commentary on the Dream of Scipio*, trans. William Harris Stahl
(New York: Columbia University Press, 1952), pp. 87–89: "All dreams
may be classified under five main types: there is the enigmatic dream,
in Greek *oneiros*, in Latin *somnium*; second, there is the prophetic vision,
in Greek *horama*, in Latin *visio*; third, there is the oracular dream, in
Greek *chrematismos*, in Latin *oraculum*; fourth, there is the nightmare, in
Greek *enypnion*, in Latin *insomnium*; and last, the apparition, in Greek
phantasma, which Cicero, when he has occasion to use the word, calls
visum." Although Ferrand rehearses the old dispute concerning spiritual and natural dreams and argues in favor of the existence of divine
visions and prophecy, his own topic is concerned only with the natural
dreams, those that reflect, in exaggerated states, the preoccupations of
the patient's mind. Macrobius is concerned with visions and prophecy

and dismisses the natural dream as an inferior experience in a few paragraphs. Those paragraphs, nevertheless, became a major component in the dream lore of the Middle Ages and justify selective quotation. Ferrand goes on to discuss precisely the mechanism set out by Macrobius, but with an emphasis on the state of the humors that condition dream contents as well as thought because the love melancholiac not only dotes upon the beloved but is possessed by a condition of humors that taints both the reason and the imagination.

"The last two, the nightmare and the apparition, are not worth interpreting because they have no prophetic significance. Nightmares may be caused by mental or physical distress or anxiety about the future: the patient experiences in dreams vexations similar to those that disturb him during the day. As examples of the mental variety, we might mention the lover who dreams of possessing his sweetheart or of losing her, or the man who fears the plots or might of an enemy and is confronted with him in his dream or seems to be fleeing him. The physical variety might be illustrated by one who has overindulged in eating or drinking and dreams that he is either choking with food or unburdening himself, or by one who has been suffering from hunger or thirst and dreams that he is craving and searching for food or drink or has found it. Anxiety about the future would cause a man to dream that he is gaining a prominent position or office as he hoped or that he is being deprived of it as he feared."

These ideas are not original to Macrobius, though his writings were responsible for transporting them to subsequent ages; rather the foundational treatise seems to be the *Oneirocriticon* of Artemidorus upon which Macrobius relied, though through which intermediary sources, whether Porphyry or another, is a complex question, concerning which consult Stahl's introduction.

2. [*Hugo, l. de Spir. & an. c. 25*]: Hugh of St. Victor, *De anima libri quatuor*, in *Opera omnia tribus tomis digesta* . . . (Rothomagi: sumptibus Ioannis Berthelin, 1648), bk. II, ch. 16, vol. II, p. 157: "De oraculo, visione somnio, insomnio, et phantasmate, et quibusdam aliis dormientibus accidere solitis apparitionibus": "Omnium, quae sibi videre videntur dormientes, quinque sunt genera, videlicet oraculum, visio, somnium, insomnium, phantasma." See also vol. 177 of the *Patrologiae cursus completus seria latina*, ed. J. P. Migne, cols. 165–90. The *De anima* cited here was included in sixteenth- and seventeenth-century editions of his works. For its place in the Hugh canon, see B. Heurtebize, s.v. "Hugues de Saint-Victor," *Dictionnaire* (Paris: Librairie Letouzey et Avé, 1909–1972), vol. VII (1922), cols. 240–308.

3. Pope Gregory I, *Dialogorum libri*, in *Opera omnia* (Parisiis: sumptibus Claudii Rigaud, 1705), vol. II, pp. 456–57. For an English translation, see St. Gregory, *Dialogues*, trans. Odo John Zimmerman (New York: Fathers of the Church, Inc., 1959), bk. IV, ch. 50, p. 261: "It is important to realize, Peter, that dreams come to the soul in six ways." St. Gregory's discussion forms part of an important debate during that period on the use and origins of dreams. Clearly, a Christian could not reject

revelation, but the danger of demonic dreams meant, likewise, that he should not cultivate them to his destruction. In a sense, St. Gregory also speaks only of two kinds of dreams, natural and divine, though he recognizes dreams by causes and circumstances as well as by quality.

4. [*Tertul. l. de anim. c. 47.*]: Tertullian, *De anima*, ch. 47, ed. J. H. Waszink (Amsterdam: J. M. Meulenhoff, 1947), pp. 65–66.

5. *Hippocrates, Regimen IV or Dreams*, trans. W. H. S. Jones (Loeb, 1967), vol. IV, pp. 420–47: "Now such dreams as are divine, and foretell to cities or to private persons things evil or things good, have interpreters in those who possess the art of dealing with such things" (IV. lxxxvii). "Such dreams as repeat in the night a man's actions or thoughts in the day-time, representing them as occurring naturally, just as they were done or planned during the day in a normal act" (IV. lxxxviii). Hippocrates nowhere states explicitly that he classifies dreams into two categories, but this is implied in the structure of his discussion of dreams. His distinctions correspond to *somnium coeleste* and *somnium animale*, with the natural dreams (*somnium naturale*) grouped with the latter; at least that is how we must assume Ferrand understood Hippocrates. See also *Oeuvres complètes*, ed. Littré, vol. VI, pp. 641–63. One of the most consulted sources of information on the interpretation of dreams during the Middle Ages was the *Speculum naturale* of Vincent of Beauvais, especially bk. 26, chs. 1–41. Dreams were traditionally classified by their causes: *somnium naturale, animale* and *coeleste*. Natural dreams originate in bodily complexions and humors. Animal dreams come from the anxieties and perturbations of the waking mind. Celestial dreams derive from impressions made by the celestial mind or intelligences which imprint their influences upon the imagination according to their natures and to the fitness of the mind for receiving them. Such dreams can, in fact, be cultivated, leading to considerable speculation upon fasting, forced watching, and other techniques employed to induce spiritual dreams. Such practices were used by mystery cult priests throughout the Mediterranean area during Roman times and before. Ferrand alludes to them later in the chapter. A similar classification of dreams can be found in the writings of the pseudo-Augustine, John of Salisbury, and Albertus Magnus. For the passages in Vincent, see *Speculum quadruplex, naturale, doctrinale, morale, historiale* (Dauci: Baltazaris Belleri, 1624). The *Speculum quadruplex* was also published in Graz (Akademische Druck-U. Verlagsanstalt, 1964–65).

6. Aristotle, *On Prophecy in Sleep*, trans. W. S. Hett (Loeb, 1964), p. 375: "It is absurd to hold that it is God who sends such dreams, and yet that He sends them not to the best and wisest, but to any chance person. But, if we dismiss the theory of causation by God, none of the other causes seems probable; for it seems beyond our understanding to find any reason why anyone should foresee things occurring at the Pillars of Heracles or on the Borystheses." Aristotle attributes them neither to divine influences nor to physiological and humoral conditions of the body. Dreams are merely reflections of the thoughts of the day when the mind is relaxed in sleep, and those that seem to come true as predictions of

future events are merely coincidences. See n. 16 for further commentary on Ferrand's use of Aristotle concerning dreams.

7. Petronius, no. 31:

> Somnia quae mentes ludunt volitantibus umbris,
> Non delubra deum, nec ab aethere lumina mittunt:
> Sed sibi quisque facit: nam cum prostrata sopore
> Languent membra, quies et mens sine pondere ludit,
> Scribit amatori meretrix, dat adultera numos.

The poem survives in an imperfect form with lines and parts of lines missing: thus the variations between editions. The central point remains clear: the gods have no part in dreams; men dream what they experience by day. See *Petronius*, trans. Michael Heseltine (Loeb, 1939), pp. 358–61. We have translated Ferrand's text as it is with phrases from Heseltine where they correspond; we have rendered *numos* as "a piece of money," though it is likely a corruption of *munus*, "the adulteress yields herself."

8. [Ἰλ. *a*]: Homer, *The Iliad*, bk. I. 64: "ὄναρ ἐκ Διός ἐστιν."

9. [*4. Franc.*]: Ronsard, "La Franciade," bk. IV. 181–82:

> Des dieus çà bas certains viennent les songes,
> Et Dieu n'est pas artisan des mensonges.

For a modern edition, see *Les oeuvres de Pierre de Ronsard*, texte de 1587, ed. Isadore Silver (Chicago: University of Chicago Press, 1967), p. 178:

> (De Dieu certain çà bas viennent les songes,
> Et Dieu n'est pas artizan de monsonges.)

10. [*Tertul. in Apol.*]: Tertullian, *Apologeticus [adversus Gentes]*, XXIII. 1. See trans. T. R. Glover (Cambridge, Mass.: Harvard University Press, 1960), p. 123. Ferrand's reference to Tertullian is undoubtedly indirect. There are few specific pronouncements on dreams in the *Apology*, though there is a substantial section dealing with demons. Of magicians he says, "if they send dreams to people; assisted by the power of the angels and demons invoked, those same beings by whose aid she-goats and tables have acquired the habit of divining; how much more, think you? would that power [of demons], acting on its own behalf and in its own business, take pains to use its full strength to achieve what it does in the affairs of others."

11. [*Dio*]: Dio Cassius, *Dio's Roman History*, trans. E. Cary (Loeb, 1965), vol. VII, p. 153: "Tiberius, moreover, was forever in the company of Thrasyllus and made some use of the art of divination every day, becoming so proficient in the subject himself, that when he was once bidden in a dream to give money to a certain man, he realized that a spirit had been called up before him by deceit, and so put the man to death."

12. [*Philostr. in vita Apoll. l. 4. c. 3.*]: Philostratus, *Life of Apollonius of Tyana*, bk. IV, ch. 11 (Loeb, 1960), vol. I, pp. 366–67: "Having made his way then to Pergamum, and being pleased with the temple of Asclepius, he gave hints to the supplicants of the god, what to do in order to obtain favourable dreams."

Ferrand alludes here to the practice of "incubation" or sleeping in temples in order to achieve a desired effect during sleep through dreams, through union with a supernatural being or through a combination of the two. Ernest Jones in *On the Nightmare* (1931; New York: Grove Press, 1954), p. 92, points out that the practice involving dream cults, healing, and divination has been found in Central America, North Africa, Australia, Borneo, China, India, and Persia. The form of healing employed by Asclepius in his incubation cult is closely related to the incubus or suffocation nightmare in which women believe themselves to be sexually assaulted by supernatural beings. The association is clear when one remembers how Andromache of Epirus visited Epicauros, the center of the Asclepian cult, in order to cure her sterility, and how the god lifted up her dress and touched her womb in a dream and made her fertile. See Mary Hamilton, *Incubation, or the Cure of Diseases in Pagan Temples and Christian Churches* (London: Simpkin, Marshall, Hamilton, Kent. & Co. , 1906), p. 25.

These associations were at least generally understood by Ferrand, given the juxtaposition in this chapter of the interpretation of dreams relating to eroticism as a means of diagnosis, the use of dreams for purposes of ritual cures among the ancients, and oneiromancy or divination through means of dreams. These would at first appear to be unrelated dimensions of the dream phenomenon, but the common denominator lies in the fact that all these forms are related to erotic projections. Dreams cultivated by following a prescribed ritual, or by sleeping in places consecrated to a cult under the administration of a physician with the intent of finding a cure have equally to do with medicine and healing, with engaging sexually with a supernatural being during sleep, and with gaining knowledge of the future. Oneiromancy has to do with divination because dreams come from the gods, and hence the word means for Ferrand diagnosis through dreams as well. Yet Ernest Jones, p. 95, states: "This cure of disease by Incubation—known as oneiromancy—was practiced in Scotland and Ireland to an even later date, and it is interesting to note that here the person slept in the skin of a sacrificed sheep, just as the worshippers of Ammon did in Thebes [Herodotus, bk. II, par. 42], or those of Amphiarus in Attica [Pausanias, bk. I, ch. 34]." Under the heading of oneiromancy, as in Ferrand, we find definitions that range from divination as in the temple of the Bona Dea to healing in the temple of Asclepius. We are dealing here with a complex idea cluster that Ferrand could assess only in its parts. In another chapter he will deal with incubation as suffocation or the nightmare, and in yet another with the magic techniques employed by girls to know the identity of their future lovers, such as on St. Agnes' Eve when young girls, by following certain preparatory rites before going to bed, could expect to dream of their future mates. Anxiety, fears of illness or sterility, unfulfilled erotic longings are all subject to expression through dreams—dreams conditioned through autosuggestion during previous waking states. Such dreams vacillate between nightmares that frighten and perplex and erotic dreams that excite and bring pleasure. There is, hence, a paradoxical relationship between the therapeutic dreams of the temple cults entailing a meeting with a supernatural creature and the nightmare involving an assault by such a creature. Oneiromancy becomes for Ferrand the generic term for both dream therapy and diagnosis by dreams. That the later is closely related to divination provides obstacles to the cultivation of dreams through magic, something he could not propose, while the simple analysis of the dreams of a cooperative patient promised to reveal nothing more than the common actions of the day which they reflect according to conventional theories of the dream. Ferrand had to arrive at an impasse on this topic.

13. [*Vergil 7. Aen.*]: Virgil, *Aeneid*, bk. VII. 88–91:

> Pellibus incubuit stratis, somnosque petivit,
> Multa modis simulacra videt volitantia miris;
> Et varias audit voces, fruiturque deorum
> Colloquio, atque imis Acheronta affatur avernis.

See trans. H. Rushton Fairclough (Loeb, 1965), vol. II, pp. 8–9.

14. The sick who went into the temples of Asclepius were directed according to the rules of the sanctuary, administered by the priests of the cult. Usually, they had to spend several nights as though in a kind of hospital. The remedies for their various diseases came to them in the form of dreams from the god. It was for this reason that many of the temples contained statues to sleep and dreams. Aristophanes tells of taking the blind Plutus to the temple of Asclepius and of the merry capers in the night and of the treatment by which he was cured of blindness. *Plutus*, ll. 662 ff.

The ancient origins of the goddess Bona as a fertility goddess, with her parallels in Ops, Maia, and Faunus, may be passed over quickly here because Ferrand is referring to the orgiastic tradition that developed as part of her cult, principally in Rome under the Empire. Though the Bona Dea had temples in many locations, the principal ceremonies (strictly reserved for women), the sacrifices, and orgies were carried out in the homes of consuls or preators in the month of December. They became frankly erotic and involved practices employing Priapus, possibly accounting for Ferrand's allusion to the women going backwards to their beds, or simply to their general lesbian indulgences. Ferrand's account serves as a rhetorical bridge from the dreams in the temple of Asclepius to the employment of opportunist dream interpreters. The reference to the orgies suggests dreams were involved, when, in fact, the associations joining the passages have to do with "temple" and with "women as opposed to men," providing an opportunity to moralize in passing. The reference to "our ladies bitten by love" who prefer this temple implies that they seek the temple for a cure, while in reality it was a place of indulgence. The best source of information on the orgiastic practices of the cult is Juvenal, Satire VI. 315–32, in *Juvenal and Persius*, trans. G. G. Ramsay (Loeb, 1961), p. 109. There he speaks of the flute music, the wine, the howling and frenzy, the "foul longings," the dancing, the rites with Priapus, the love-drenched thighs, the slave girls, and the rest.

Consultation of the edition of 1610 can only add confusion to the interpretation of the line "se mettent au lict de reculons," for there Ferrand describes this practice as part of a ritual for inducing dreams undoubtedly of a prognostic nature on the eve of the feast of St. John (June 23), a far more innocent kind of activity than the orgies associated with the festival of the goddess Bona. (See John Keats, "The Eve of St. Agnes," *The Poetical Works*, ed. Lord Houghton [London, 1897], st. 26, p. 320: "Pensive awhile she dreams awake, and sees / In fancy, fair St. Agnes in her bed / But dares not look behind, or all the charm is fled.") The section was clearly lifted from the first edition and placed in the second as a bridge in a way that obscures the intention of the first. In the 1610 edition Ferrand is offering examples of the ways young girls practice magic (in that edition magic and dreams are dealt with in a single chapter) in order to know the course of future love. This point is made clear by the fact that the quotation from Juvenal anticipates rather than follows the passage in question. Ferrand was presumably thinking of some tradition similar to the one practiced on the eve of the feast of St. Agnes (Jan. 20) at which time, according to legend, if a young girl goes to bed without her supper, she will dream of the man she is to marry—that is, gain knowledge of the future through dreams following certain ritual preparations.

How the two traditions, that of the goddess Bona and that of the eve of St. Agnes or the eve of St. John were conflated, or whether Ferrand makes an error in his juxtaposing of passages, is unclear. But whether as a relatively innocent ritual upon going to bed in order to bring dreams of future love or as an indication of orgiastic indulgence, Ferrand follows with identical words in each edition, that such a practice is a threat to one's well-being for it signifies abandoning one's duty to God, a sin that merits oblivion in the eyes of God. Ferrand had implied as much in ch. XXI of the 1623 edition concerning young girls who innocently practice botomancy to know who their future lovers would be, for "without intending to do any harm, they paganize to their damnation."

15. [*Iuuen.*]: Juvenal, *Satire VI*. ll. 547–49:

> Qualiacumque voles Iudaeus somnia vendit,
> Spondet amatorem tenerum, vel divitis orbi
> Testamentum ingens. . . .

See *Juvenal and Persius*, trans. G. G. Ramsay, p. 126:

> qualiacumque voles Iudaei somnia vendunt.
> Splendet amatorem tenerum vel divitis orbi
> testamentum ingens.

16. [*Hipp. de Insomn. Aris. de divin. per insomn. Gal. eod. ti.*]: Hippocrates, *Regimen IV or Dreams*; Aristotle, *On prophesying by Dreams*; Galen, (*eodem titulo*, that is, a work with the same title as the preceding), *De dignotione ex insomniis*.

Hippocrates, trans. W. H. S. Jones (Loeb, 1967), vol. IV, pp. 420–47. His statement on dreams is fundamental to the medical tradition of which Ferrand is a part. According to Hippocrates, dreams are diagnostic by definition. Without so stating, he makes the traditional distinction between animal dreams and natural dreams, the former produced by the soul in a healthy body, replicating in the imagination certain activities "just as they were done or planned during the day in a normal act." Natural dreams occur when disturbed conditions in the body cause dreams to go contrary to the acts of the day, indicating struggle and conflict within the physiological systems. (Hippocrates does not dwell on the role of the emotions, which could equally disturb sleep, though such emotions derange the humors and thereby have their effect). He asserts that disturbances of whatever kind are caused or accompanied by physiological change—vapors, secretions, fluxes, repletions—and that the body should be treated accordingly. He then proceeds to his various regimens fitted to the conditions of each kind of dream. The soul alone, during sleep, is left in charge of the body and is, according to Hippocrates (IV. lxxxvi), the cause of senselike sensations in dreaming that imitate the office of the senses, the soul herself performing all the acts of the body. By dint of the soul assuming such a role in sleep, the products of the soul's activities become monitors of the conditions of the body, allowing for the diagnosing of physical complications insofar as Hippocrates considers all dreams as potential prologues to disease. If there is a weakness in his system, it is that he provides no explanation for the causes whereby the dream, in its particular structure and design, must by definition reveal the exact nature of the bodily distress. Yet his faith that the dream does so, as revealed through the cataloging of correspondences and symbols based on resemblances, became gospel for generations of physicians. A few examples of this system of correspondences must serve. "Fruitless trees signify corruption of the human seed. Now if the trees are shedding their leaves, the harm is caused by moist, cold influences; if leaves abound without any fruit, the ailment is caused by hot, dry influences. In the former case regimen must be directed towards warming and drying; in the latter towards cooling and moistening. When rivers are abnormal they indicate a circulation of the blood; high water excess of blood, low water defect of blood. Regimen should be made to increase the latter and lessen the former" (IV. xc). See *Oeuvres complètes*, ed. Littré, vol. VI, pp. 641–63.

Aristotle, *On Prophesying by Dreams*, trans. W. S. Hett (Loeb, 1957), pp. 374–85. The reference to this work is *pro forma* because Aristotle was skeptical about the interpretation of dreams whether natural or divine in origin, and therefore Ferrand manifests an inclination to pass over his work quickly. Aristotle's view was incompatible with the established medical tradition as well as with the theological. He conformed neither to Galen nor to Macrobius. The citation is cursory, moreover, in that the role of the soul in sleep and the physiological origins of dreams is not discussed in this work, but rather in *On Sleep and Sleeplessness* and *On Dreams*. The problem for Aristotle was causation. In *On Prophesying by Dreams*, he states that dreams may very well be exaggerated versions in the imagination of concurrent bodily functions. A ringing in the ears may produce dreams of thunder, a drop of phlegm swallowed may produce sensations of honey or sweets, or a warmth in the body may appear as fire or intense heat (sec. 1). But beyond this, he could concede no general law that what is dreamed is a picture of its cause or, in the other direction, that it predicts what must come to pass. In fact,

Aristotle works against Ferrand's beliefs and the medical tradition in his statement that dreams are like reflections in water, in that the greater the motion of the dream, the less it resembles the original, and the less the forms in dreams resemble real objects (sec. 2). Thus, while the dream may indeed reveal an intense state of emotion, the dream need not reveal in itself the causes because he denies that in a mechanical way the lover will dream of love, but will say only that melancholy lovers are more inclined to dream because of the vapors produced by the disease. In contrast to Hippocrates, Aristotle is ready to assign more of the cause of dreams to emotions, fear, desire, anger, than to the "disposition and temper of the body" as Ferrand states it. By day, the reason acts as a censor which is relaxed in sleep. It is then that persons subject to illusions, each according to the different emotions he is feeling, will have dreams which, though the images resemble little the external reality, will nevertheless appear real and immediate to the dreamer (sec. 3). Thus Aristotle supports the basic mechanism, but allows for no specific diagnoses of causes through dream interpretation.

Galen, *De dignotione ex in somniis*, ed. Kühn, vol. VI, pp. 832–35. This work is one of the key treatises in the medical tradition relating to dreams. Galen explains how dreams are indicators of the condition of the body: any disturbance in the natural balance of the humors is reflected in dreams—corresponding to *somnium naturale*. Because the imagination also records all mental conditions, its impressions can be reproduced in sleep in the form of the *somnium animale*. There is little in Ferrand's chapter to suggest that he wished to go further into the debate on dreams than Galen himself.

Avicenna in the *Liber canonis*, bk. III, fen 1, tr. 1, ch. 7, provides an account of the psychology of sleep that predominated in medieval thought. Sleep was thought to be a withdrawal of the *virtus animalis* from the senses and the muscles leaving the *virtus naturalis* in charge of the body. In this way the essential processes of retention, expulsion, and digestion are carried out in order to restore the natural heat that is lost while the body is awake. In short, the *spiritus animalis*, governing mobility and the senses, is withdrawn, thereby allowing the *spiritus naturalis* to rehabilitate the *spiritus vitalis*. The natural spirits retreat into the body to aid digestion. Sleep itself is brought on by humid vapors from the digestive processes that, in turn, mount to the brain where chilling and humidity produce sleep. A close relationship exists between the vital and the animal spirits so that dreams reflect the conditions of the humors. Avicenna's mechanism is similar to the one set out by Aristotle in *On Sleep and Sleeplessness*.

17. André Du Laurens, *Des maladies melancholiques, et du moyen de les guarir*, in *Toutes les Oeuvres*, p. 28[r]: The similarity between Ferrand's text and the following suggests a borrowing. "La cause de tous ces songes se rapporte à la proprieté de l'humeur: car comme le phlegmatique songe ordinairement un ravage d'eaux, le cholerique un embrasement; ainsi le melancholique ne songe que de morts, sepulchres, et toutes choses funestes, pource qu'il se presente à l'imagination une espece semblable

à l'humeur qui domine, de laquelle la memoire vient à s'esveiller, ou pource que les esprits estans comme sauvages, et tous noircis, voltigeans par tout le cerveau, et se pourmenans jusques à l'oeil, representent à l'imagination toutes choses obscures."

Levinus Lemnius, *Occulta naturae miracula*, bk. II, ch. 31, p. 229: Lemnius advises doctors to inform themselves of the dreams of their patients, for dreams reveal the diseases of the body. He repeats here one of the received ideas of the age concerning the usefulness of dreams in making diagnoses. Ferrand's views follow the tradition. Lemnius goes on to outline the dreams characteristic of the four different humors.

18. [*Plu. de san: Pl. l. 7. c. 50. Alex. ab Alex. l. 1. genial dior c.11. & l. 3. c. 26*]: Plutarch, *De tuenda sanitate praecepta*, in *Moralia*, ed. Frank Cole Babbitt (Loeb, 1966), vol. II, pp. 249–50: "also, in the matter of sleep, we need to beware of lack of continuity and of evenness, marked by irregularities and sharp interruptions, and to beware also of the abnormal in dreams, which, if so be that our visions are improper or unwonted, argues an over-abundance or concretion of humours, or a disturbance of spirit within us."

Pliny, *Natural History*, bk. VII, ch. 36, (Loeb, 1961), pp. 586–87.

Alessandro Alessandri (Alexander ab Alexandro), *Genialium deorum libri sex* (Paris: apud Joannem Roigny, 1550). Ferrand cites as an adjunct commentary on the relationship between dreams and the influence of the humors the following two chapters, bk. I, ch. 11, pp. 16–17, and bk. III, ch. 26, pp. 164–65, dealing with the dreams reported of notorious Romans, their origins, and powers of prognostication. This work was first published in 1522 and again with a learned commentary by André Tiraqueau in Lyons in 1586 entitled *Semestria*. It is based in form and inspiration on the *Attic Nights* of Aulus Gellius and the *Saturnales* of Macrobius—an erudite work credulous of the popular beliefs of the day concerning dreams, sorcery, magic, and apparitions.

Avicenna, *Liber canonis*, bk. I, fen 2, tr. 3, ch. 7, discusses the phlegmatic and rheumatic who dream of rivers, snow, rain, and cold weather. This system of correspondences in dream interpretation goes back to antiquity and is at the center of the Hippocratic-Galenic tradition on dreams.

Pietro D'Abano (Aponensis), *Conciliator controversiarum, quae inter philosophos et medicos versantur*, dif. CLVII, p. 202, provides a parallel account of the dark imaginings of melancholy men who dream of frightful black apparitions, catastrophes, funerals, and cemetaries. This work was first published in Mantua in 1472. His goal was to reconcile the views of medicine with those of philosophy, astrology, and alchemy, and especially with the views of Averroes.

See Jean Aubery, *L'antidote d'amour*, pp. 34ʳ–35ᵛ for a parallel discussion of lovers and natural dreams. Similarities suggest a common source, though Ferrand does not use the same examples.

A concern with the dreams of melancholiacs is of ancient standing, as the references to Hipppocrates attest. Aretaeus the Cappadocian, *On the Causes and Symptoms of Chronic Diseases*, pp. 299–300 states: "unreasonable fear also seizes them, if the disease tend to increase, when their dreams are true, terrifying, and clear: for whatever, when awake, they have an aversion to, as being an evil, rushes upon their visions in sleep." That view remains a constant in dream theory down to the Renaissance.

19. [*In c. 84. art. med.*]: Thomas à Viega (Tomás Rodrigues da Viega), *Ars medica*, ch. 84, in *Opera omnia in Galeni libros edita*, pp. 107 ff.

20. [*In Polyhymn.*]: Herodotus, bk. VII, entitled "Polymnia," sec. 16: "αὗται μάλιστα ἐώθασι αἱ ὄψιες τῶν ὀνειράτων, τά τις ἡμέρης φροντίζει." See *History of Greece*, trans. A. D. Godley (Loeb, 1963), vol. III, p. 329. Xerxes, dreaming nightly that he should wage war on the Greeks, is initially dissuaded by his minister Artabanus with this understanding of such visions: that they were not divine in origin but merely reflections of what a man had been thinking during the day. He reversed his views when he was prevailed upon to wear the king's clothes and sleep in his bed, for there Artabanus had the same vision as the king. Ferrand uses this text in a selective way that proves precisely the contrary of what we must conclude from a reading of his entire chapter.

21. [*Sect. 30. Probl ult.*]: Aristotle, *Problems*, bk. XXX, no. 14 (957a), vol. II, p. 181: "Now, a dream comes when sleep overtakes men while they are thinking and have something before their eyes. This is why we most often see what we are doing or intending to do or wishing to do; for it is in connexion with these things that calculations and fantasies most often occur. Better men have better dreams for this reason, that they think of better things when they are awake, but those who are inferior either in mind or in body think of inferior things. For the condition of the body does contribute to the appearance of dreams; the projections of a sick man's thought are inferior, and also his soul cannot rest because of the disturbance which exists in his body. This is why the melancholic start in their sleep, because, as the heat is excessive, the soul has more movement than the normal, and as the movement is more violent they cannot sleep."

Jean Aubery, *L'antidote d'amour*, pp. 35^V–37^r, writes about animal dreams in terms similar to Ferrand's, giving considerably more information about the physiological origins of dreams that are an extension, in sleep, of the fantasies of the lover's imagination. He speculates that the lover believes in the reality of the dream and that the enjoyment of forbidden acts in that form produces moments of respite and satisfaction. In this context Aubery recounts the story of Theognis the courtesan and her frustrated lover who enjoyed her in a dream and thus freed himself from his longings for her. Ferrand relates the story in ch. XXXIII on cures. It comes from Plutarch through Du Laurens.

22. The reference is to Philo of Alexandria's treatise *Quod a Deo mittantur somnia*, which we have consulted in the Greek edition with a French trans. by Pierre Savinel, *Les oeuvres de Philon D'Alexandrie: De somniis*, bks. I-II (Paris: Éditions du Cerf, 1962). His works have also been translated into English by F. H. Colson, G. H. Whitaker, G. and R. Marcus (London-New York: 1929–53). The allusion to Christian dreams condi-

tioned by their pious meditations is apocryphal. Writing in the early
decades of the first century, he could have had little knowledge of the
early Christians and no mention is made of them in the work cited above.

23. Lucretius, *On the Nature of Things*, bk. IV. pp. 961 ff. See trans. by Cyril
Bailey (Oxford: Clarendon, 1910), p. 176: "And for the most part to
whatever pursuit each man clings and cleaves, or on whatever things
we have before spent much time, so that the mind was more strained
in the task than is its wont, in our sleep we seem mostly to traffic in
the same things; lawyers think that they plead their cases and confront
law with law, generals that they fight and engage in battles, sailors that
they pass a life of conflict waged with winds, and we that we pursue
our task and seek for the nature of things for ever, and set it forth,
when it is found, in writings in our country's tongue." While there is
no evidence that Ferrand used Lucretius directly for this passage, there
can be little doubt that the poet was one of the sources of this sequence
of observations concerning natural dreams.

24. Claudian, *Sextum consulatum Honorii Augusti praefatio*, ll. 5–7:

> Iudicibus lites, aurigae somnia currus,
> Vanaque nocturnis meta cavetur equis:
> Gaudet amans furto.

See *Claudian*, trans. H. Platnauer (Loeb, 1956), vol. II, p. 70. The passage
became traditional in discussions of dreams in the Middle Ages and the
Renaissance. Chaucer cites it near the beginning of his "Parlement of
Foulys," ed. D. S. Brewer (London: Thomas Nelson and Sons Ltd. 1960),
p. 74:

> The wery huntere, slepynge in his bed,
> To wode ayen his mynde goth anon;
> The iuge dremyth how hise pleis been sped;
> The cartere dremyth how his carte is gon;
> The riche of gold; the knyght fygt with his fon:
> The syke met he drynkyth of the tunne,
> The louere met he hath his lady wonne.

These lines may well have been made commonplace to the medieval
reader through their appearance in the *Liber Catonianus*, used for many
years as a textbook. The passage appeared as a preface to bk. III of Claudian's "De raptu Proserpinae." But the original inspiration for these lines
seems to be Lucretius or a tradition older than both poets. Another version appears in Levinus Lemnius, *The Secret Miracles of Nature* (London,
1658), p. 141, in his discussion on dreams, again testifying to the popularity of the passage during the Renaissance:

> On what by day our senses chance to light,
> When that we sleep, we see the same by night,
> The Hunts-man when he rests, his mind then roves
> Of Hills and Dales, of shady woods and Groves.
> Lawyers plead causes, Coach-men Coaches drive,
> And the night Horses seem to be alive.
> The Sea-man loads his wares, the Lover comes by stelth.
> And as by day the miser hunts for wealth,

>And he that thirsts as standing on the brink
>Of Rivers, then believes that he doth drink.
>And I in silent night am wont to muse,
>Of divers Arts that in the day I use.

25. [*Arnal. tr. de vision. per insomn.*]: Arnald of Villanova, *Expositiones visionum quae fiunt in somnia*, pt. I, chs. 1–2, in *Opera omnia* (Basileae: Conrad Waldkirch, 1585), pp. 625 ff. Arnald of Villanova classifies all dreams under two headings: natural and doctrinal. Natural dreams are caused by the *sensibilia* of the body upon the imagination, including the complexions of the humors, indigestion, fatigue, hunger, fear, or other distractions. He groups together physiological and emotional causes. He notes as contributors the way in which the body adjusts to environments and to the different seasons. Dreams arising from these sources have no prophetic value; in this he follows Macrobius. Doctrinal dreams arise not only from supernatural but also from astral sources. Ferrand objects, not to divine dreams, but to Arnald's idea that the occult powers of the planets, the signs of the Zodiac, and the twelve houses of the horoscope have the power to influence dreams. By the horoscope, according to Arnald, dreams can be interpreted. In accordance, he sets out a complex plan for relating dreams to given subjects corresponding to parts of the body: gold and blood correspond to the liver and to the second house, for example.

This system is, in effect, a further refinement upon the correspondences by which any natural or animal dream can be interpreted, all of them by definition predicated on the belief that the dream symbol, if properly read, is diagnostic in physiological terms. The correlation between dream symbol and bodily conditions was taken for granted in both systems. The vehemence with which Ferrand rejects Arnald's system as "fopperies" is largely the protest of a "modern" man signaling his recognition of the disrepute into which the astrological sciences had fallen among the greater part of the intelligentsia by 1623.

The references to Artemidorus and to Julianus Cervus, or Jean Corvé, as Ferrand calls him in the edition of 1610 are, in fact, to the same work, one which was well known in the Renaissance but passingly used here, namely Artemidorus Daldianus, *De somniorum interpretatione libri quinque*, trans. into Latin by Jan Hagenbut (Julianus Cervus, but more frequently Janus Cornarius) (Lugduni: apud S. Gryphium, 1546).

For information on the Arabic tradition of the astral interpretation of dreams, consult Albohazen Haly Filius Abenragel, *De judiciis astrorum* (Basileae: n.p., 1551), pt. III, esp. ch. 12.

Ferrand does not continue, as Jean Aubery does in *L'antidote d'amour*, pp. 37^V–39^V, with diabolical dreams that surprise the lover as a temptation to sin by reveling in lascivious pleasures. This takes Aubery, by another route, to the dream that becomes reality, that is nothing other than the pleasure lovers take in their realistic visions, in taking statues for animate objects, or in otherwise failing to distinguish between the real and the fantastic. Such a dream life causes the lover to be removed from society and hence useless to it: "notre imagination corrompuë par l'amour d'une infinité de veines illusions, nous fait embrasser des phantasmes pour nous desrober la jouyssance du vray bien, qui gist en nostre salut" (p. 38^r). The ensuing stage is total distraction in which the lover goes out of himself, entering by thought into the other—a state of ecstasy, melting and remelting in the delectations of love (p. 40^v). The dream becomes indistinguishable from a neurotic condition that confuses reality with states of trance or enthusiasm. John Donne examines such conditions in lovers in his poems, defending them against accusations of antisocial and unproductive behavior.

XXV.   Whether Jealousy Is a Diagnostic Sign of Love Melancholy

1. Alessandro Piccolomini, *Della institution morale* (Venetia: apresso Giordano Ziletti, 1579), bk. X, ch. 7, "Quante specie se trovino di timore amoroso; et di quella specie, che si chiama gelosia," pp. 447–52.

   For a general introduction to the subject of jealousy as a Renaissance *topos* there is perhaps no more comprehensive a treatment than that by Robert Burton in *The Anatomy of Melancholy*, where he deals with the definition, causes, symptoms, and cures of jealousy, pt. 3, sec. 2, subs. 1–memb. 4, subs. 2, pp. 821–66; among the key writers he mentions are Benedetto Varchi, Torquato Tasso, Girolamo Cardano, and Juan Luis Vives. See also Paolo Cherchi, "A Dossier for the Study of Jealousy," *Eros and Anteros: The Medical Traditions of Love in Renaissance Culture,* eds. Donald A. Beecher and Massimo Ciavolella (Montreal: McGill-Queen's University Press, forthcoming).

   This *topos* was one of a group of three in the edition of 1610 entitled respectively "Whether love lasts after marriage," "Whether love in women is greater than it is in men, and who is most inclined to love," "Whether true love is without jealousy." In the later edition they are reduced to two (see ch. XXVIII, below) and are reduced in length as well. No doubt Ferrand realized that all three were more or less peripheral to his central topic and that it was perhaps not wise to debate at length the prospect that the satisfaction of love quells desire and that hence love cannot continue in marriage. There were those who pointed out that love was not possible in marriage because the latter is a state of possession of the object, while love is a state of desire for that which is not possessed. Others argued from popular evidence that men who served their ladies before marriage dominated and abused them after marriage. The argument in favor of coitus as a cure for erotic love is proof that the very act of intercourse destroys the desire, and thus the passion itself. After a woman is enjoyed, she is liked and respected less; often she will come to be despised—as in the case of Aeneas for Dido, Paris for Oenone, Theseus for Ariadne, and Agamemnon for Clytemnestra. This is followed by a distinction between love and friendship, between affection and sexual enjoyment. Those of contrary opinion cite Cicero, who makes love and desire twins, so that where desire continues, love also continues. Others point to cycles of excitation, satisfaction, satiation, and renewed longing in marriage, making conjugal love eternally renewing and rejuvenating. Others simply see failure in marriage as a problem of practical mismanagement. It is contended that those for whom love dies in marriage never truly loved, but married only for utility or duty: Theseus took Ariadne merely to escape the labyrinth, Aeneas, Dido merely to repose his army. Typically, the arguments are uneven, taken in order of con and pro, and are uncritically juxtaposed with each other. If a preference is shown, it is signaled only by giving the position favoring love in marriage the last and slightly longer word.

If there is love after marriage, then less defense can be put forward for courtly or adulterous love as the only mode for expressing the desires that generate erotic love, and marriage can be looked upon as the approved form of "amour pudique" that Ferrand accepts as right and appropriate, not as a cure for diseased eroticism that requires the attention of a physician, but for the expression of amorous desires associated with affection and the desire for children.

2. Plutarch, *Moralia* (84F), "Progress in Virtue," ed. Frank Cole Babbitt, vol. I, p. 451: "Whenever, therefore, we begin so to love good men, that . . . through our admiration and affection for his habit, gait, look, and smile, we are eager to join, as it were, and cement ourselves to him, then we must believe that we are truly making progress." This treatise was written in polemic against the Stoic philosophers who held that men were only moved by jealousy. As Plutarch argues, "if any man is imbued with a spirit of contentiousness and envy towards his betters, let him understand that he is merely chafing with jealousy at another's repute or power, but not honouring or even admiring virtue."

3. Ovid, *The Remedies of Love*, ll. 771–76:

> Acrius Hermionen ideo dilexit Orestes,
> > Esse quod alterius coeperat illa viri.
> Quid Menelae doles? ibas sine conjuge Creten,
> > Et poteras nupta laetus abesse tua.
> Ut Paris hanc rapuit, tum demum vxore carere
> > Non potes, alterius crevit amore tuus.

See *The Art of Love, and Other Poems*, trans. J. H. Mozley, p. 230: read *lentus* for *laetus* and *nunc* for *tum*.

4. Plutarch, *Moralia* (760B), trans. W. C. Helmbold, vol. IX, p. 373: "When King Philip came to town, everyone thought that Phaÿllus, who had a wife of great beauty, would obtain a dominant position for himself if his wife should become intimate with Philip. Nocostratus' party got wind of this and patrolled the street before Phaÿllus' door. The latter, however, put soldiers' boots on his wife and a cape and a Macedonian hat and got her undetected to Philip, since she passed for one of the royal pages."

5. Plutarch, *Moralia* (760A), "The Dialogue on Love," trans. W. C. Helmbold, vol. IX, p. 371. Galba (Gabbas) was a jester at the court of Augustus who was, in fact, reciting a joke from Lucilius (v. frag. 251), echoed in Juvenal's Satire I. 57.

6. [*Bellef. l. 2. c. 2. Boem. Auban. l. 2. c. 3.*]: François de Belleforest, bk. II,
ch. 2, of *L'histoire universelle du monde, contenant l'entière description et
situation des quatres parties de la terre* . . . *ensemble l'origine et particulières
moeurs, loix, coustumes, religion et ceremonies de toutes les nations, et peoples
par qui elles sont habitées* (Paris: Chez G. Mallot, 1570).

    Johann Boemus (Aubanus Bohemus), *Discours des Païs selon leur sit-
uation, avec les moeurs, loix, et ceremonies d'iceux. Reveu et corrigé* (Lyon:
par Jean de Tournes, 1552), bk. III, ch. 3, "De Laconie, et moeurs des
Laconiens, autrement dit Lacedemoniens," p. 110: "Et a ces hommes
si dignes davoir enfans et lignee, estoit encores une autre chose per-
mise, car toutefois et quantes que un dentre eux estoit par son ancien
aage indispost à engendrer, il lui estoit loisible de prendre quelque beau
jeune personnage et bien conditionné, et le substituer en son lieu envers
sa femme, pour plus facilement avoir lignee, tellement quil vendiquoit
lenfant que sa femme apportoit, apres avoir eu la compagnie du jeune
homme: et ne tournoit cest requeste à infamie, si quelcun prioit autrui
de lui vouloir prester sa femme, encores quelle fut chaste et pudique,
comme se il leust requis de labourer en bonne et fertile terre, et propre
à porter enfans."

7. This anecdote about Parrhasius of Ephesus, the Greek painter famous
for his faithful portraiture (fl. 400 B.C.), comes from Pliny, *Natural History*,
bk. L, ch. 100.

    Ferrand cites no reference for this story, which suggests a secondary
source. One of the most probable is Jean Aubery, *L'antidote d'amour*,
p. 48[V]: "Veritablement Parrhasius qui mettoit ses serfs aux tourmens
pour exprimer les cris, peines et grimaces du damné Promethee devait
peindre un amoureux comme pour son patron et exemplaire." because
the lover is the most tormented of all creatures who knows in himself
all the torments invented by antiquity.

8. Danaë was the daughter of Acrisius King of Argos, who, to protect
her virginity, had her imprisoned in a tower. Nevertheless, she bore
a son, Perseus, to Zeus. Ferrand's most probable source is Hyginus,
Fables, no. 63. See *Hygini fabulae*, ed. H. I. Rose (Lugduni Batavorum: in
aedibus A. W. Sijthoff, 1967), p. 48.

9. [*Apollodor. comic.*]:

      ἀλλ'οὐδὲ εἶς τέκνον ὀχυρὰν οὕτως ἐποίησεν θύραν

      δι'ῆς γαλῆ καὶ μοιχὸς οὐκ εἰσερπύσει.

See Apollodorus of Carystus, *The Slanderer*, ed. John Maxwell Edmonds,
The Fragments of Attic Comedy, new edition with trans. , vol. III–A (Leiden:
E. J. Brill, n.d.), p. 188 f. Ferrand leaves out the first half of the first line
of the fragment:

      κεκλείοεθ'ή θύρα μοχλοῖς.

See also Stobaeus, *Anthology*, VI. 28, "On Licentiousness."

XXVI.   The Prognostic Signs of Love and Erotic Melancholy

1. [*Hipp. l. de Epil. l. de morb. virg. Gal. l. prognost. com. 5. Val. Max. l. 2. c. 1.*]: Hippocrates, *The Sacred Disease*: "Now while men continue to be-lieve in its divine origin because they are at a loss to understand it, they really disprove its divinity by the facile method of healing which they adopt. . . . But if it is to be considered divine just because it is won-derful, there will be not one sacred disease but many, for I will show that other diseases are no less wonderful and portentous. . . . My own view is that those who first attributed a sacred character to this malady were like the magicians, purifiers, charlatans, and quacks of our own day, men who claim great piety and superior knowledge. Being at a loss, and having no treatment which would help, they concealed and sheltered themselves behind superstition, and called this illness sacred." *Hippocrates*, trans. W. H. S. Jones (Loeb, 1952), vol. II, pp. 139, 141; see also *Oeuvres complètes*, ed. Littré, vol. VI, pp. 353, 355.

Hippocrates, *On the Diseases of Young Women*, ed. Littré, vol. VIII, p. 467.

Galen, *In Hippocratis prognostica commentaris*. The reference is to bk. V but is, in fact, to bk. I, ch. 4, ed. Kühn, vol. XVIII/2, p. 18.

Valerius Maximus, *Factorum et dictorum memorabilium libri novem*, bk. II, ch. 1, pp. 57 ff. The reference is related in a general way only, for Valerius speaks of ancient institutions and of certain of the gods who exemplify particular traits.

Ferrand conducts an important discussion in ch. III of the edition of 1610 concerning the justification for his own treatise and why so few physicians have taught the curing of love and erotic melancholy. He alters his strategy in the later edition, however, perhaps because after reading further in the works of contemporary physicians he realized the claim was no longer true, or at the least that it would be imprudent to go on claiming as much, especially if his reading included Valleriola, Rodrigo de Castro, Jean de Veyries, and Jean Aubery.

In fact, Ferrand does not stay long with the question: why indeed love was often discussed as a great plague but seldom as a disease to be cured. The question was potentially troubling because Ferrand was likely unwilling to admit in print, if he recognized the point, that the ancients who were his guides for the most part did not recognize love as a disease and that Galen even wrote to resist the idea. In dropping the heading of the chapter in the second edition, he may have indicated awareness of his own vulnerability. Nevertheless, he transferred much of his material to the new ch. XXVI concerning prognostic signs of love and erotic melancholy. In fact, the chapter heading does not fit and sug-gests some fumbling of the rhetorical cogency of the section. The new chapter leads, not to a discussion of why that topic was overlooked, but to an attack upon those outside of the profession who claim that love cannot be cured because it is either not a disease or is a disease of the soul and therefore falls outside of the physician's range of authority. The materials of the earlier chapter are now marshaled as an outright assault upon those who defame the powers and prerogatives of the medical profession. There is cause to think that while the Inquisition of 1620 did not single out this matter for objection directly, that nevertheless the general territory claimed for medicine by the treatise was a source of irritation. The grounds of the analysis of love as a disease rest squarely on the Galenic doctrine of sympathies whereby all psychic states are explained in somatic terms, the doctrine whereby certain passions and movements of the soul are brought into the sphere of medical practice. Ferrand in the edition of 1610 spells out the implications of this theory: that no person is evil by nature, but is made so only by poor habits, by the disposition of the body, bad education, and bad discipline, by the influence of the stars, and by bad nutrition. He proves this principally out of Plato's *Timaeus* and Galen, in turn illustrated by cases of disturbances of the soul cured by ministrations to the body. He insists, ironically, that those who defame physicians as philosophers commit blasphemy against God, because God has granted to physicians the means and skills for healing such diseases as love. The same arguments are maintained in the present chapter.

The other side of the argument has to do with the intervention of the devil or of demons in the creation of supernatural diseases. The issue had come to a head in the late sixteenth century and Ferrand, though briefly here, was nevertheless compelled to take a stand. The noted physician Francisco Valles had argued that the devil is among the external causes of diseases, because he can transport the prerequisite conditions for diseases into the body. He can also alter matter within the body, increase melancholy bile, for example, and carry the black vapors from one part of the body to another. He is also able to deregulate bodily functions such as evacuation and to provoke the adustion of humors, thereby bringing on such conditions as epilepsy, apoplexy, and paralysis. Erotic love, of course, falls under these same influences: *De iis quae scripta sunt physice in libris sacris, sive de sacra philosophia* (Lugduni: apud Franciscum Le Fevre, 1588), pp. 226–27. Martin Del Rio countered, making direct reference to Valles, in asserting that diseases could arise only from natural causes and that demons could have no part in their generation: *Les controverses et recherches magiques*, trans. André du Chesne (Paris: n.p., 1611, first publ. 1608), pp. 399 ff. Among the best of the modern investigations into this issue is the article by Jean Céard, "Folie et démonologie au XVIe siècle," in *Folie et déraison à la Renaissance*, ed. A. Gerlo (Bruxelles: Editions de l'université, 1976), pp. 129–47. Céard explains the medical tradition whereby such leading physicians as Fernel, in the *De abditis rerum causis*, and Paré could believe that the devil could simulate natural causes relating to diseases. He summarizes the dilemma for the practicing physician as follows: "Mais, dira-t-on, si le démon procède comme les maladies naturelles, comment distinguer les cas où il intervient de ceux où la nature agit seule? Tel est bien le débat auquel le XVIe siècle nous fait assister. Remarquons d'abord que les uns concèdent que le démon peut intervenir, mais demandent qu'on fasse la part des troubles naturels, pendant que les autres concèdent que ces troubles peuvent être naturels, mais demandent qu'on fasse la part de l'intervention du démon!" (p. 139). In the face of ecclesiastical threats Ferrand seems steadfast and no doubt would have subscribed generally to the idea, as expressed in Céard's words, that "il y a peut-être certaines maladies démoniaques, mais elles sont exceptionnelles et ont des caractères exceptionnels, et il est de la compétence du médecin d'en décider" (p. 142). The attitudes of Marescot in the Marthe Brossier affair gave rise to the *Traicté des energumenes* (Troyes, 1599) by Pierre de Bérulle (Léon d'Alexis), that contained a stout reproach against the meddling of physicians in church matters. That work signals for Céard the end of an unsteady collaboration among doctors and theologians during the sixteenth century, and the declaration of more open hostilities of the kind encountered by Ferrand's first treaty on love in Toulouse in 1620.

2. [*S. August. 4. Confess. c. 3.*]: St. Augustine, *Confessions*, bk. IV, ch. 3: "Quasi de caelo tibi sit inevitabilis causa peccandi, et Venus hoc fecerit, aut Saturnus, aut Mars: scilicet ut homo sine culpa sit, culpandus autem coeli ac siderum creator et ordinator." See trans. William Watts (Loeb, 1931), pp. 152–53. The modern text reads: " 'de caelo tibi est inevitabilis causa peccandi' et 'Venus hoc fecit aut Saturnus aut Mars,' scilicet ut homo sine culpa sit, caro et sanguis et superba putredo, culpandus sit autem caeli ac siderum creator et ordinator."

For the references to Mercury and Mars the edition of 1610 directs the reader to Galen, *Prognostics*, bk. I, ch. 5, and to the *Hippolytus* and *Octavia* traditionally attributed to Seneca.

3. *Coqueluche* in the original, for which there was no name in English at the time of the first translation of Ferrand's text in 1640, because this was a new disease; it was there translated as "a disease that the French not many years since were infected with" (p. 193). The word does not appear in Randle Cotgrave, *A Dictionarie of the French and English Tongues* (London, 1611).

4. Cotgrave, *A Dictionarie of the French and English Tongues*, describes an *empiric* as "a Physitian which without regard either of the cause of a disease, or of the constitution of the patient, applies those medicines whereof he hath had experience in others, worke they how they will."

5. [*L. I. progn. part. 2*]: Galen, *In Hippocratis prognostica commentarius*, bk. I, pt. 1: "μήτ᾽ οὖν οἰόμεθα τὴν ἐπιληψίαν θεῖον εἶναι νόσημα μηδὲ τὸν ἔρωτα," ed. Kühn, vol. XVIII/2, p. 18. The quotation indicates that love was already considered a disease in Galen's time and was treated as such by physicians. The symptomatology associated with love in the Renaissance is also in evidence.

6. "Non Deus, ut perhibent, Amor est, sed amaror et error." Unidentified line.

7. Ovid, *Amorum libri tres*, bk. II, ix. 26: "Vive, Deus, posito, si quis mihi dicat, Amore: / Deprecor, usque adeo dulce puella malum est." See ed. P. Brandt (Hildesheim: Georg Olms, 1963), p. 111. The lines are given as follows:

'Vice' deus 'posito' signis mihi dicat 'amore,'
Deprecer: usque adeo dulce puella malum est.

8. "des Playes Chironiennes"; the chiron or ciron is defined variously as the handworm (Cotgrave), a very small spider found in cheese (Robert), the mite (Robert and Collins); Chilmead in the edition of 1640 translates it as "flea-biting." Cotgrave mentions that the ciron or handworm was a popular pretext for making obscene gestures with the fingers while pretending to scratch between them.

9. [*Tibul. el. 7. l. 2. Ovid.*]: Tibullus, bk. II, Elegy VI. 19–20: "Amantis credula vitam / Spes fovet et melius cras fore semper ait." *The Elegies*, ed. Kirby Flower Smith (Darmstadt: Wissenschaftliche Buchgesellschaft, 1964), p. 147. Ferrand adds "Amantis," and reverses the words "fore cras." For a recent translation, see Tibullus, *Elegies*, trans. Guy Lee (Cambridge: St. John's College, 1975).

   Ovid, *The Remedies of Love*, ll. 103–5:
   Sed quia delectat Veneris decerpere fructus,
   Decimus assidue, cras quoque fiet idem.
   Interea tacitae serpunt in viscera flammae.
   See *The Art of Love, and Other Poems*, trans. J. H. Mozley, p. 184.

10. [*Aph 7 sec. 8. l. 6. Epid.*]: Hippocrates, *Epidemics*, bk. VI, sec. 5, aph. 4: "Ἵησις ἀντίνοον μὴ δμονοεῖν τῷ πάθει," *Oeuvres complètes*, ed. Littré, vol. V, p. 316. Chilmead, in his translation of Ferrand's text, expands the meaning of this cryptic aphorism to suit the text as follows: "for the curing of a disease, it is required of the Patient also, as well as of the Physitian, that he make what resistance he can against it, and by no meanes yield to it in the least degree" (p. 197).

11. Ovid, *Heroides* V. 149–50: "Me miseram: quod non est medicabilis herbis, / Destituor prudens artis ab arte mea." See ed. Henricus Dörrie, p. 90.

12. Tibullus, bk. II, Elegy III. 13–14: "Ne potuit curas sanare salubribus herbis, / Quicquid erat medicae vicerat artis amor." *The Elegies*, ed. Kirby Flower Smith, p. 138. Read *nec* for *ne*, and *quidquid* for *quicquid*. See also Ovid, *The Metamorphoses*, I. 521–26, where Apollo makes the same lament.

13. [*de usu part.*]: Galen, *On the Usefulness of the Parts*, bk. III, ed. Kühn, vol. III, p. 200; trans. M. T. May, vol. I, p. 189: "I regard it as proof of perfect goodness that one should will to order everything in the best possible way, not grudging benefits to any creature, and therefore we must praise him as good. But to have discovered how everything should best be ordered is the height of wisdom, and to have accomplished his will in all things is proof of his invincible power."

   Hippocrates, "Letter from Democritus," *Oeuvres complètes*, ed. Littré, vol. IX, p. 395: "Je pense que la connaissance de la philosophie est soeur de la médecine et vit sous le même toit; en effet, la philosophie délivre l'âme des passions, et la médecine enlève au corps les maladies."

14. [*Arist. I. Meta. I.*]: Aristotle, *Metaphysics*, bk. I, sec. 1 (981a), p. 5. Aristotle discusses the healing arts in the context of the importance of experience in the application of those arts. Ferrand draws Aristotle to his defense only in this general way.

15. [*Philostr. l. 1. c. 2. in vita Apoll.*]: Philostratus, *Life of Apollonius of Tyana*,

trans. F. C. Conybeare (Loeb, 1960), bk. I, chs. 10 or 12; vol. I. pp. 22–27, 28–31. There are two stories relating to citizens of Cilicia seeking cures from the temple of Asclepius and from Apollonius, and who are rejected: the first is a rich criminal who made such lavish sacrifices that he was suspected of expiating guilt rather than of seeking the restoration of his eye. Apollonius had inquiries made through the priest, whereupon it was discovered that the ruffian's wife had stabbed him in the eye with a bodkin for seducing her daughter by a former marriage; the second was of the Governor of Cilicia who was addicted to infamous forms of passion. His ploy was to feign sickness in order to gain access to Apollonius, whom he loved for his beauty. In a prayer, the governor asked him to share his beauty and charms. "This he said with a vile leer and voluptuous air and all the usual wriggles of such infamous debauchees; but Apollonius with a stern fierce glance at him, said: 'You are mad, you scum.' " Apollonius was saved from beheading only because the governor, himself, was three days later executed for plotting against the Romans.

16. [*L. de dec. hab.*]: Galen, *De bono habitu liber*, ed. Kühn, vol. IV, pp. 750–56. This work, which Ferrand knew as *De decoroso habitu*, though it mentions Hippocrates and Plato, is principally concerned with the definition of good and bad habits and is not the work Ferrand intended. His point is that physicians are also natural philosophers, a point insisted upon by Galen in his *Quod optimus medicus sit quoque philosophus*, and one much debated during the Renaissance.

See also Hippocrates, *De la bienséance*, (On the Proper Behavior), sec. 5, "Il faut transporter la philosophie dans la médecine, et la médecine dans la philosophie," in *Oeuvres complètes*, ed. Littré, vol. IX, pp. 233–35.

17. [*Probl. 1. Sect 14. L 1. Eth. c. 6. L. de anima c. 1. c.14.*]: Aristotle, *Problems*, bk. I, sec. 14 is, in fact, bk. XIV, sec. 1 (909a); vol. I, p. 317. This and the following two references are of a passing nature only. The concept is more directly expressed in the *Physiognomics*.

Aristotle, *Nicomachean Ethics*, bk. I, ch. 6, trans. H. Rackham, deals with the idea of the "good" but does not mention sympathy within the body. A more apt reference would have been to bk. VIII, ch. 11 (1161b), p. 497.

Aristotle, *On the Soul*, trans. W. S. Hett (Loeb, 1964). Many sections in this work deal with the relationship between the body and the soul. See esp. bk. I, ch. 3 (p. 41) and bk. II, ch. 1 (p. 71 f).

The "several other texts" alluded to by Ferrand are mentioned specifically in the text of 1610: Plutarch, *Table Talk*, bk. V, ques. 7; Galen, *On the Substance of the Natural Faculties*, ch. 3, drawn from Hippocrates' *Epidemics*, bk. VI, sec. 2, aph. 29; Hippocrates, *On Flatulence* (*Winds; Breaths*).

18. [*Democr. epist. 1. ad Hipp.*]: Hippocrates, "Letter from Democritus": "νοῦσος παρεοῦσα ψυχὴν δεινῶς ἀμαυροῖ, τὴν φρόνησιν ἐς συμπαθείην ἄγουσα." *Oeuvres complètes*, ed. Littré, vol. IX, p. 395: "νοῦσος γὰρ παρεοῦσα δεινῶς ψυχὴν ἀμαυροῖ, φρόνησιν ἐς συμπαθείην ἄγουσα."

19. The life of Cleomenes, son of Anaxandridas and king of the Spartans, is recounted by Herodotus in *The History*, bk. V, sec. 40 to bk. VI, sec. 85,

ed. A. D. Godley, vol. III, pp. 43–235.

20. Galen, *De praenotione ad Posthumum* is presumably the work alluded to; it contains the paradigmatic story of Justus's wife and her love for Pylades, ed. Kühn, vol. XIV, pp. 599–673.

21. "ψυχῆς νοσούσης οἶσιν ἰατροὶ λόγοι." The verse is derived from Aeschylus, *Prometheus Bound*, l. 380. See *Aeschylus*, trans. H. W. Smyth (Loeb, 1953), p. 117: "ὀργῆς νοσούσης εἰσὶν ἰατροὶ λόγοι."

22. Virgil, *Aeneid*, bk. XII. 396–97: "Scire potestates herbarum, usumque medendi / Malvit, et mutas agitare inglorius artes." See trans. H. Rushton Fairclough, pp. 326–27. For *artes* read *artis*.

23. [*De dec. hab.*]: Hippocrates, *On the proper behavior*, in *Oeuvres complètes*, ed. Littré, vol. IX, p. 237.

24. "Ἰατρὸς ἀδόλεσχος νοσοῦντι πάλιν νόσος." From a senario of uncertain origin. See *Theasaurus Graecae Linguae*, vol. II (Graz: Akademische Druck-U. Verlagsanstalt, 1954), s.v. "Ἀδόλεσχος."

25. [*Boccace*]: Giovanni Boccaccio, *Genealogie deorum gentilium libri*, ed. Vincenzo Romano, 2 vols. (Bari: Laterza, 1951), vol. II, p. 451: "Franciscus autem de Barbarino non postponendus homo, in quibusdam suis poematibus vulgaribus, huic [i. e. Cupid] oculos fascea velat, et gryphis pedes attribuit, atque cingulo cordium pleno circundat." Ferrand's intermediary source, however, is Mario Equicola, *Libro de natura de amore*, p. 19ᵛ.

26. Publilius Syrus, *Sententiae*, A 31: "Amor animi arbitrio sumitur, non ponitur." In *Minor Latin Poets*, ed. A. M. Duff (Loeb, 1934), p. 18.

27. Ovid, *The Remedies of Love*, ll. 545–46: "Qui timet ut sua sit, ne quis sibi subtrahat illam, / Ille Machaonia vix ope tutus erit." See trans. J. H. Mozley, p. 214. Machaon was the brother of Podalirius, son of Asclepius; Podalirius was the healer of the Greeks in Homer.

28. Hippocrates, *On the Nature of Man*: "Ὁκόσα δὲ τῶν νουσημάτων γίνεται ἀπὸ τοῦ σώματος τῶν μελέων τοῦ ἰσχυροτάτου, ταῦτα δεινότατα ἐστιν." *Oeuvres complètes*, ed. Littré, vol. VI, p. 56.

29. [*Mar. Ficin. orat. 7. c. 11 in conv. Plat.*]: Marsilio Ficino, *Commentary on Plato's Symposium*, Speech VII, ch. 11, p. 167: "However, a deliberate care in evacuation contributes most. A precipitous evacuation or ointment is judged very dangerous. Also the disquiet of lovers necessarily lasts as long as that infection of the blood, injected into the viscera through bewitchment, lasts; it presses the heart with heavy care, feeds the wound through the veins, and burns the members with unseen flames. For its passage is made from the heart into the veins, and from the veins into the members. When this infection is finally purged away, the disquiet of the erotics (or rather erratics) ceases. This purging requires a long space of time in all, but longest in melancholics, especially if they were snared under the influence of Saturn. And also very bitter if they were subjugated when Saturn was retrograde or in conjunction with Mars, or in opposition to the Sun. Also they are ill the longest at whose birth Venus was in the house of Saturn, or was looking vehemently on Saturn and the Moon." This key passage is paraphrased in Valleriola, *Observationum medicinalium libri VI*, pp. 206, 211. See ch. XX, n. 29, for

collateral references to these works, and to Equicola.
30. [*Menander*]: "Senex amore captus ultimum malum": We have been un-
    able to find the original Greek verse in the works by Menander.
31. Hippocrates, *Aphorisms*, sec. 3, aph. 3: "Certaines maladies et certains
    âges sont bien ou mal disposés pour telle ou telle saison, tel ou tel lieu,
    tel ou tel genre de vie." *Oeuvres complètes*, ed. Littré, vol. IV, p. 487. This
    is but one of several possible aphorisms that expresses this concept.

    This view concerning the danger of love to old men has to do with
    medical theories stating that those who are cold and dry by nature
    are in far greater danger from fevers and hot afflictions than younger
    people, characterized by their heat and moisture. See Jean Aubery,
    L'antidote d'amour, p. 26ᵛ: "Et tout ainsi que les medecins prennent pour
    mauvais augure quand un viellard est embrasé par une fievre ardante,
    soupçonnans la grandeur et violence de la cause, qui a peu ainsi eschauf-
    fer ses humeurs glacees, ainsi nous prenons à tres-mauvais jugement les
    vieillards amoureux et r'avalons beaucoup de leurs merites."
32. Publilius Syrus, *Sententiae*, A. 29: "Amare iuveni fructus est, crimen
    seni." See trans. A. M. Duff, p. 16.
33. Pindar, *Nemean Odes*, Ode I, l. 48: "ἀπρόσικτων ἐρώτων ὀξύτεραι μανίαι":
    see *The Odes of Pindar*, trans. Sir J. Sandys (Loeb, 1924), p. 432.
34. [*L. 3. Fen. I. tr 4. c. 23.*]: Avicenna, *Liber canonis*, bk. III, fen 1, tr. 4, ch. 23,
    p. 207ʳ. Avicenna says that perhaps it will be necessary to treat lovers
    with the same regimen as those suffering of "melancoliam, et maniam,
    et alcutubut [cuturub, qutrub]."

    Ferrand agrees with the general opinion regarding the prognostics
    for the cure of love that it is difficult to effect, but he rarely speaks
    of the incurable. Jean Aubery, *L'antidote d'amour*, pp. 111ᵛ–112ʳ, gives
    a long lesson on prognostics and describes the conditions of love that
    are beyond help: "Ces choses ainsi considerees si quelqu'un est malade
    d'une espece d'amour qui soit nourry dans un humeur bruslé et melan-
    cholique, qui soit revesche, inveteré par longue suitte de jour, de sorte
    qu'il se soit acquis une egale immoderation, tant en ses esprits, facultez
    nobles qu'aux humeurs, auquel soit survenu quelque delire, ou manie,
    une extenuation de tout le corps, une couleur plombee, son esprit imbe-
    cille et extravagant, s'il recuse ou desdaigne le secours que l'on luy veut
    donner, s'il ne dort nuit ne jour, si son poux est petit, rare et desistant,
    une respiration entrecoupee, une chaleur excessive au dedans, et dehors
    un froid aux extrémes, bref toutes les choses observees qui dependent de
    l'espece de l'amour, de sa grandeur movement et moeurs, de la qualité
    et actions du malade amoureux, si elles sousignent et conspirent à ce que
    dessus, cest amour est incurable de toute son essence, et le faut laisser
    occire à la seule immisericorde des prognostiques."

XXVII. Of Incubi and Succubi

1. [*L. ad Cor. 11.*]: *I Corinthians* 11:10: "That is why a woman ought to

have a veil on her head, because of the angels." Ferrand rehearses the commonplace explanations of this arcane statement that because of the angels women should wear a veil of authority. The veil appears not to have been understood by medieval and Renaissance commentators as a symbolic covering, and thus their glosses turned toward women as the tempter of fallen angels. Rossell Hope Robbins discusses the verse as seen in this context, "And there was evidence that the demons must have felt some physical pleasure in that they were strongly attracted to women with beautiful hair (compare I Corinthians XI:10, where *angelos* was equated with *incubos*)." *The Encyclopedia of Witchcraft and Demonology* (New York: Crown Publishers Inc. , 1963), p. 257. The larger question, with regard to incubi and succubi is, indeed, whether spirits of the underworld are or can be sexually attracted to humans. It is somewhat fetched to think that women could ward off devils by covering their hair. Ferrand sees the difficulty and thus attempts to gloss the word with a more figurative meaning: ministers of the church or all Christians. Ferrand, however, is by no means prepared to rule out the existence of demons and their sexual attraction to humans, whether for their own pleasure or in order to degrade humans. The Old Testament, read literally, becomes the major authority. Ferrand rejects the wild claims about strange offspring being born from the union of women and devils, but typically, after his disclaimer, he is prepared to repeat the stories from other sources.

One contemporary believer in the literal interpretation of the text was Pierre de Lancre, *Tableau de l'inconstance des mauvais anges et demons, ou il est amplement traicté des sorciers et de la sorcelerie, livre tres-utile et necessaire, non seulement aux Juges, mais à tous ceux qui vivent soubs les loix chrestiennes* (Paris: Chez Nicolas Buon, 1612), p. 131: "Bouguet dict que c'est donc â cause des mauvais Anges et Demons qui ayment les cheveux de la femme, qui faict qu'on voit tant de femmes voilees."

Robert Burton raises the same question concerning sexual relations with supernatural creatures in his comments on the passage in Genesis where it is suggested that relations between mortals and demons or fallen angels afterwards resulted in the birth of giants. He reports that Justin Martyr, Clement of Alexandria, Sulpicius Severus, and Eusebius all dealt with the topic. Skeptical in the matter, he goes on to interpret demon seduction as the pranks of "juggling Priests" and urges that more be read on this topic in Johann Wier, Giraldus Cambrensis, Jacques le Roux, Godelman, Erastus, Valles, John Nider, Del Rio, Lipsius, Bodin, Pererius, and King James: *The Anatomy of Melancholy*, pp. 649–50. Clearly, the entire issue had become a set *topos* with materials ready-to-hand in abundance and with a tradition of imitation and amplification.

Ferrand largely dismisses the idea that there were supernatural creatures capable of seducing both men and women, and who were able to beget offspring upon mortal women, favoring instead the medical tradition of the nightmare as a delusion in which the patient experiences the sensation of intercourse owing to vapors and suffocation. He is unable to deal with the underlying denominators that join the several ostensibly remote ideas into a single cluster of ancient associations involving belief in the possibility of intercourse with supernatural beings. Ernest Jones in *On the Nightmare*, p. 97, develops a Freudian analysis in stating that the group of ideas associated with the incubus not only acquired its patterns of experience and sensation from the nightmare but also its latent content: "That is to say, it consists of an imaginary fulfilment of certain repressed wishes for sexual intercourse, especially with parents." Nevertheless, his survey of the central idea takes in a much broader spectrum of cultural and occult phenomena, including the classical myths involving union between Olympians and mortals. His basic claim is that throughout history human nature has sought to avoid responsibility for nocturnal erotic wishes by projecting their causes upon other beings or circumstances. In the first instance, these erotic experiences were blamed upon demons, incubi, and succubi. Throughout the Middle Ages this form of projection was stimulated by the autosuggestive teachings of the church, and by such books as the *Malleus maleficarum*, which provided a complete anatomy of the nature and quality of the diverse forms of encounter with these creatures, including degrees of pleasure and pain. See, e.g., pt. 2, ques. 2, ch. 1, p. 164: "With regard to the bewitchment of human beings by means of Incubus and Succubus devils, it is to be noted that this can happen in three ways. First as in the case of witches themselves, when women voluntarily prostitute themselves to Incubus devils. Secondly, when men have connexion with Succubus devils; yet it does not appear that men thus devilishly fornicate with the same degree of culpability; for men, being by nature intellectually stronger than women, are more apt to abhor such practices. Thirdly, it may happen that men or women are by witchcraft entangled with Incubi or Succubi against their will." In the second instance, one promoted generally by the physicians, such nocturnal hallucinations were attributed to physicial origins—those subscribed to by Ferrand. Ernest Jones in *On the Nightmare*, p. 89, cites Gervasius of Tilburg in his *Otia imperialia* for the year 1214 as an early observer who endorsed the medical view, even though he continues to believe in succubi as supernatural creatures. Paradoxically, at the same time that the ancient medical explanation was being reestablished, the theological views fortified the belief in the presence of an actual partner in the erotic encounter. Ferrand inherited both forms of projection, those upon a supernatural being and those upon the physiological conditions in the body that stimulate the hallucination. He favored the explanation in terms of physiological causes, even while finding himself attracted to the stories involving demons and magic.

2. For a criticism of these theories in Ferrand's own time, see Jean Riolan, *Gigantologie, histoire de la grandeur des giants, ou il est demonstré que, de toute ancienneté, les plus grands hommes et giants n'ont esté plus hauts que ceux de ce temps* (Paris: Adrian Perier, 1618).

Martin Del Rio, *Disquisitionum magicarum libri VI*, bk. II, ques. 15, p. 76: "Haec ille doctus simul physicus et philosophus, de eo quod fieri potuit, preclare, sed erronee, quantenus gigantes illos sacra Scriptura putat ex daemonibus incubis et succubis ita procreatos; quod iam a theologis improbatum docui. Nos inde sumamus tantum, non repugnare hoc daemonis potentiae et industria. Nam gigantes fuisse, impudentis proterve sit negare, cum sacra Scriptura testetur, et omnium gentium annales similia multa proferant."

This entire discussion was generated by Ferrand's reading of Jourdain Guibelet, *Trois discours philosophiques: Discours second du principe de la generation de l'homme*, ch. 18, "Sçavoir si les Demons ont semence de laquelle puisse estre engendré un homme" (Evreux: Chez Antoine la Marié, 1603), pp. 215–16: "Deux choses à mon advis, ont donné entrée à ceste opinion de la generation par les Demons. La premiere un passage de Moyse mal entendu, quand il dit que les fils de Dieu ayants recogneu la beauté des filles des hommes, prindrent à femmes celles qu'ils choysirent entre toutes. Tertullian, Josephe, Justin Martyr ont entendu par les fils de Dieu, les Anges contre toute apparence. Aben Esra interprete, les hommes vertueux. Raby Kimhy explique, les hommes de grand stature, selon la maniere de parler des Hebrieux, qui nomment les haultes montagnes, les montagnes de Dieu. Et semble que cete intelligence soit conforme à la verité, eu égard que l'écriture adjouste puis apres, que de cete conjonction des fils de Dieu avec les filles des hommes nasquirent les geans."

3. [*Fernel li. 1. de abd. rer. causis. Hollerius l. 1. Meth. med. c. 14*]: Jean Fernel, *De abditis rerum causis* (Paris: apud Jacobum Dupuys, 1551), bk. I, p. 69: "In his quidem, maxime vero in Aristotelicis, audire mihi videor Mosem, qui innumeris ante seculis conditi mundi historiam perfectus, Aeternum Deum condita coelo omnique ornatus genere instructo, ait vim illi naturalem impartiisse, quae nobis in signa esset et tempora. Deinde animantium omni genere mundum iam genitum implesse, quorum quidem mortalium ne continuatio ac genus aliquando intercideret, illi rei pro sua sapientia prospicientem, seminibus eorum vim divinam indidisse, que se in omne evum gignende propagarent."

Jacques Houllier, *De morbis internis libri II* (Parisiis: apud Carolum Macaeum, 1577), pp. 50^{r-v}: "Non omnino certe contemnenda est veterum theologorum authoritas, omniumque gentium communis ille consensus de incubo et succubo, cui etiam attestatur experientia. Memini enim me in primitivae Ecclesiae historiis legisse Cathecumenon huiusmodi daemonum ludibus vexari solitos, qui deinde caenae sumptione liberabantur. Multa quoque sunt apud D. Augustinum de incubis et succubis lib. 15. de Civitate Dei, ut hinc fere cogamur fateri incubum alium demonis arte induci, alium corporis morbum esse. Nisi quod summa Christi luce nobis affulgente, ab his tenebris nunc non est metuendum. In Gentilitiis illis ceremoniis multa huius modi deliramenta reperiuntur de Sympythis, et Pythone, spiritu divinatore occupatis, sed multo lepidiora in Hebraeorum Rabbinis. Scribunt enim huiusmodi phantasmata ex semine Adam procreata fuisse centum illis et triginta annis, quibus ab uxore abstinuit, postquam Cain fratrem interfecit. Pro singulari remedio iubent circulos septem circum sepulchrum fieri, ne cadaver intromittendum subeant, eoque ad nocendum utantur. Alcinous in dogmate Platonis retulit ad vaticinia, oracula, somnia, etc. Sed et in veterum medicorum libris multa remedia reperiuntur ad Sympythos, et daemone occupatos, et incubos, ut apud Actuarium et Alexandrum. Qualis est illa Hippocrat. antidotus territis lemuribus et demonia occupatis, lunaticis cum spuma tauri, quae in codice manuscripto sic legitur."

Ferrand places these learned references in the margin beside his refutation of the idea that the incubi and succubi were born to Adam. But in spite of these, the passage continues to take its inspiration from Jourdain Guibelet, *Trois discours philosophiques: Discours second du principe de la generation de l'homme*, ch. 18, p. 215: "Nous concluons donc avec Ulricus Molitor, Pererius et autres, que les demons ne peuvent engendrer, encore qu'ils ayent affaire avec les hommes. Nous rejettons les opinions premieres pour estre du tout banies, avec les sornettes des Rabins, qui disent que les demons incubes et succubes prindrent naissance de la semence d'Adam, en cent trente ans qu'ils s'abstint de la compagnie de sa femme, apres le meurtre commis par Cain, en la personne d'Abel son frere. Si les uns croyent que les hommes peuvent estre engendrez de demons, et les autres que les demons soient produits de semence d'homme, comment en cete sorte contrarieté pourrons-nous asseoir quelque jugement? Les demons ont esté crées au commencement du monde en mesme nombre qu'ils font aujourd'huy; ils son perpetuels, incorruptibles, et sans aucun corps s'il n'est emprunté, et par consequent sans aucune semence, si elle n'est pareillement empruntée. Resulte donc qu'ils sont inhabiles au fait de la generation."

4. [*Vinc. Hist. spec. l. 21. c. 30 Delrio l. 2. contr. mag. De Raemond de l'Heres.*]: The work indicated by the marginal note is Vincent of Beauvais, *Speculum Quadruplex, naturale, doctrinale, morale, historiale* (Dauci: Baltazaris Belleri, 1624), but the names cited in Ferrand's text are not to be found in the places indicated.

The source of this list of famous men who were the offspring of unions between demons and humans is, rather, Jourdain Guibelet, *Trois discours philosophiques: Discours second du principe de la generation de l'homme*, ch. 18: "Sçavoir si les demons ont semence de laquelle puisse estre engendré un homme," pp. 201–11: "Qu'un demon incubes non Jupiter fut pere d'Hercules. Qu'Aeneas fut engendré d'Anchise et d'un succube. Romulus d'un incube et de Rhea Silvia. Que le serpent qui coucha avec Olympias femme de Philippes, estoit un demon incube qui fut pere d'Alexandre. Que Merlin en Angleterre fut ainsi engendré. Balderus entre les Gots. Que les Huns tirent leur origine de quelques demons incubes, qui engrosserent certaines femmes de la Gothie. Que Mellusine estoit un demon succube, et que Servius Tullius roy des Romains fut fils d'un demon incube *laris familiaris filius*, comme dit Pline. L'histoire en est assez notable. . . . Et que l'on a attesté le semblable de Martin Luther, qui a esté un des monstres de nostre siecle. Mais pour plus grande foy, ils produisent outre cela les histoires qui ensuivent."

Martin Del Rio, *Disquisitionum magicarum libri VI*, bk. II, ques. 15: "An sint unquam daemones incubi et succubae, et an ex tali congressu proles nasci queat?" pp. 74–77: "His consentaneum est, *posse daemones efficere ut virgo mente et corpore permanens, non tamen sine virili semine, con-*

cipiat probatur quia potest virgini dormienti et ignarae aliunde sumptum verum et foecundum semen, sine congressu carnali, hymene aliisque claustris virginitas conservetur, hoc daemon nequit. Cum enim ad hoc vera corporum penetratio requiratur, quae virtuti divinae reservatur, id, sine speciali miraculo, fieri non potest. . . . Daemon sic nobili huic imposuit, et aliunde subtractos furto liberos sibi supposuit. Ad posterius genus fraudis refero parvulos; quos, non ex incubis, sed per fraudem, quasi ex succubis daemonibus natos."

Florimond de Raemond, *L'histoire de la naissance, progrez et decadence de l'heresie de ce siecle divisee en huit livres* . . . (Paris: Chez la Vefue Guillaume de la Nore, 1610), bk. I, ch. 5: "La naissance de Martin Luther, autheur du schisme qui afflige la Chrétienté," p. 26: "Or le pere de cet homme dont nous parlons, se nommoit Ian Ludder, et sa mere Marguerite, laquelle gagnoit sa vie, dit-on, à décrasser ceux qui alloient laisser leurs ordures aux étuves publique. On raconte de choses étranges de l'acouplement d'un demon avec céte femme, lors que le diable en forme de marchant lapidaire, vint loger chez son pere. Je suis content passer sous silence ce qu'on en a écrit: car encor que la privée communication que Luther a eu avec le diable, comme il raconte en divers lieux, et ce qui fut veu par l'Empereur Maximillian sus les épaules de Luther, les corbeaus croassans la nuit qu'il quitta le monde, les demoniacles delivree le jour de sa sepulture, dont je parleray ailleurs, semblent donner credit au conte qu'ils font: si est-ce que je ne veux entrer caution de la verité de céte Histoire, que sa mere se fût joüée avec un demon. Erasme pourtant en parle à mots couverts, dans une de ses epîtres. Et Vier l'a recité comme chose fabuleuse: Coclée et Simon Fontaines comme histoire veritable."

That Merlin was born of an unnatural union between a demon and a woman is related, though with total incredulity, by Johann Wier, *Histoires, disputes et discours des illusions et impostures des diables*, vol. I, p. 444: "Item que le gendarme estoit aussi incube, et que Merlin estoit un Daemon supposé à la mere trompee par l'artifice du diable."

Pierre de Lancre, *Tableau de l'inconstance des mauvais anges et demons*, p. 230: "C'est ce qu'on raconte de Merlin, qu'on dict estre né d'un Incube et d'une religieuse."

Ferrand is only momentarily delayed here by another of the medical-theological polemics of his age, and again sides with medical skepticism. Perhaps the clearest supporting voice to be cited is that of Ambroise Paré, who denies that demons could have carnal relations with women and thereby produce monsters or devils. Yet he is not as assertive as Ferrand on the matter of demonic intervention in the production of melancholy diseases, a point rather more complex and one that augmented the standing dispute over cures, whether by medicine or through exorcism. See Ambroise Paré, *On Monsters and Marvels*, trans. Janis L. Pallister (Chicago: University of Chicago Press, 1982), ch. 28, p. 93.

5. Jakob Rueff (Jacques le Roux), *De conceptu et generatione hominis* (1558; Francfort: ad Moenum, 1580), bk. I, ch. 6, p. 59b, is the originator of

the story of Magdalena of Constance. Ferrand's source is, however, either Jourdain Guibelet, *Trois discours philosophiques: Discours second du principe de la generation de l'homme*, ch. 18, pp. 214–15, or more likely, Johann Wier, *Histoires, disputes et discours des illusions et impostures des diables*, bk. III, ch. 32, vol. I, pp. 444–45: "Jacques le Roux escrit que de nostre temps il y a eu à Constance la chambriere d'un bourgeois, nommee Magdeleine, qui a esté souventesfois embrassee par un daemon, auquel en fin elle donna congé par le conseil et penitence que luy enjoignirent les ministres de l'eglise. Il escrit aussi que depuis ce temps là, presque d'heure en heure elle sentit tant de douleurs en son ventre qu'il luy sembloit qu'elle deust accoucher: dont en fin il luy sortit de l'amary des cloux de fer, du bois, des verres rompus, des cheveux, des estoupes, des pierres, des os, du fer, et une infinité d'autres telles choses."

The story was popular and is to be found in Pierre Boaistuau, *Histoires prodigieuses*, ch. 7, in Ambroise Paré, *On Monsters and Marvels*, p. 92, as well as in the English translation of Rueff, *The Expert Midwife, or an Excellent and most necessary Treatise of the generation and birth of men* (London: by E. G. for S. E., sold by Thomas Alehorn, 1637).

6. [*L. 3. ca. 26. & 27*]: The reference is to Vincent of Beauvais, as cited in Johann Wier, *Histoires, disputes et discours des illusions et impostures des diables*, vol. I, p. 443: "Le mesme Vincent, escrit au troisieme livre, chap. 26, un miracle autant veritable que le precedent . . . d'un jeune homme puissant, et fort bon nageur, lequel se baignant sur le commencement de la nuict, au clair de lune, print une femme par les cheveux pensant que ce fust quelqu'un de ses compagnons qui le voulust tirer au fond de l'eau: et apres l'avoir interroguee, et qu'il n'en peut avoit responce, il l'envelopa d'un manteau, et la mena en sa maison, où peu de temps apres il la prit pour femme en grande solennité. Mais estant avenu quelque fois qu'un sien compagnon luy reprocha qu'il embrassoit un fantosme, il s'espouvanta, et ayant tiré son espee, manaça sa femme de tuer l'enfant qu'il avoit eu d'elle, si presentement elle ne parloit et confessoit son origine. Alors elle luy dit, malheur sur toy, miserable, qui pour m'avoit contrainte de parler, fais perte d'une femme qui t'est utile. J'eusse tousjours demeuré avec toy et pour ton proufit, si tu m'eusses permis le silence, lequel m'a esté enjoint, mais tu ne me verras plus desormais, et en disant cela, elle disparut."

The story is also told by Jourdain Guibelet, *Trois discours philosophiques: Discours second du principe de la generation de l'homme*, ch. 18, pp. 211^v–212^r. He attributes it to Godefroy d'Authun and states that the young man was from Sicily, suggesting that Guibelet had the narrative from a source differing from Wier's.

The story has a structure in common with others current in the period. Robert Burton provides several analogues in *The Anatomy of Melancholy*, pp. 648–49, one of which he traces to Philostratus, *Life of Apollonius*, bk. IV, and another to a certain Sabine who, in a commentary on the tenth book of Ovid's *Metamorphoses*, tells the anecdote of a man of Bavaria whose grief over the loss of his wife brought forth a demon in disguise who promised her return if the man would remarry her and vow never to swear again. She brought him children in the new marriage, but was always pale and sad. One day they entered into an argument, and when he "fell a swearing; she vanished therupon, and was never after seen." Burton is also aware of the paradigmatic story of Philinion and Machates in Phlegon of Tralles' *De mirabilibus liber*.

7. Ferrand continues to relate anecdotes from Jakob Rueff found in an intermediary source, but originating in *De conceptu et generatione hominis*, bk. V, ch. 6, p. 59a: "Erat et cuiusdam lanii servus, qui iter faciens et de libidine cogitans, mox obvium daemonem egregia mulieris forma habuit, cum qua, ignarus se cum daemone rem habere, concubuit. Sed mox pudenda eius inflammata, cita tabe exulcerata sunt." That intermediary source was undoubtedly Jourdain Guibelet, *Trois discours philosophiques: Discours second du principe de la generation de l'homme*, ch. 18, p. 215: "ainsi fut traicté le serviteur d'un boucher qui allant par pays, rencontra un demon en habit d'une jeune femme belle et agreable, avec laquelle il eut affaire, ignorant qu'elle fust un demon. Peu apres il eut une telle inflammation aux parties secrettes, qu'elles luy devindrent totalement ulcerées. D'ou nous pouvons conjecturer, qu'ils se servent de corps morts pour se joindre avec les hommes, et que de là previent cete corruption: ce qui n'advient toutefois quand ils trompent l'imaginative."

Phlegon of Tralles, *De mirabilibus liber*, ch. 7, bound with *Apollonii Dyscoli, Historiae commentitiae liber* (Lugduni Batavorum: apud Isaacum Elzevirium, 1620), pp. 1–14. See also ch. V, n. 11, above.

Pierre le Loyer, *Discours et histoires des spectres, visions et apparitions des esprits, anges, demons, et ames, se monstrans visibles aux hommes* (Paris: Chez Nicholas Buon, 1605), bk. III, ch. 11: "L'histoire de Philinnion qui apparut à Machates en son propre corps et cadaver mort," pp. 245–49: "Ceste histoire est d'une Philinnion qui apparut à un Machates apres son decez, ayant emprunté ou plustost le diable en la place de Philinnion deceddee, non un corps aerien, mais le corps mort et ensepulturé de Philinnion. Je tiens ce que j'en vay dire de Phlegon natif de Tralles affranchy de l'Empereur Adrian qui ne nous monstre point en quel lieu cecy arriva, d'autant que son livre est defectueux." Le Loyer speculates that the story comes from the region of Thessaly, famous from Apuleius' report for its sorcerers, a place where miraculous things happened nearly every day. Phillinion was a young girl who died and was buried by her parents. Machates came to the city on business after the event and was lodged with Phillinion's parents. The girl came to him in the night, proposed her love and was accepted. They exchanged tokens, rings and a cup for a necklace, and enjoyed themselves physically before Phillinion retired. All was seen secretly by the nurse, and by degrees the news of Phillinion's return came to her parents. In the end, the entire household surprised the lovers and Phillinion pronounced her three days of joy and the unfortunate curiosity of her parents before "dying" a second time. The tomb was opened and her place found empty save for the tokens given her by Machates. The point of the story is to illustrate how demons can inhabit dead bodies and therein circulate among the living. Machates enjoyed his carnal desires with a demon.

The story is told in an expanded version in the popular collection of tales and lore by Belleforest and Boaistuau, *Histoires prodigieuses et memorables, extraictes de plusieurs fameux autheurs Grecs, et Latins, sacrez et profanes, divisées en six livres* (Paris: par la vefue de Gabriel Buon, 1598), bk. VI, ch. 1: "merveilleuse histoire d'un cadaver d'une fille duquelle diable se servit pour exercer luxure avec un jeune homme." Boaistuau used Le Loyer as his source (p. 1146). Ferrand also mentions Le Sieur de Lancre, *Tableau de l'inconstance des mauvais anges et demons*, but presumably in a more general sense because the story of Machates does not appear in this work. There are, nevertheless, numerous accounts of couplings with incubi and succubi in his chapter "De l'accouplement de Satan avec les sorciers, et sorcieres, et si d'iceluy se peut engendrer quelque fruict." There is little indication that Ferrand used de Lancre extensively, though certainly his work was well-known and popular. Ferrand passes no judgment on a man who was no doubt sincere, but entirely credulous concerning matters of magic, sorcery, and demons. De Lancre had read widely, but more often in Del Rio and Bodin than in Wier and Agrippa. He relates without critical insight many of the testimonies of those apprehended for witchcraft and related offenses in the region of Bordeaux, and describes every aspect of the pact, the sabbat, transformations and ligatures, poisons, hexes, the participation of the clergy, and related topics.

8. [*C. 18. Chr. l. de Provid.*]: St. John Chrysostome, *De providentia Dei ad Stagirium monachum obrepitium* [*On the Providence of God*], ch. 9: "Quos cumque diabolus superat, per melancholiam superat," in *Opera omnia, tomus quintus* (Parisiis: apud Robertum Pipic, 1687). The quotation, however, cannot be found in this work in the present form because it is ·a corruption of a quotation taken from Jourdain Guibelet, *Discours troisiesme de l'humeur melancholique*, ch. 10, pp. 284–84: "le desespoir, qui est une des portes principales, pour donner entrée au Diable. *Daemon quoscunque superat per maerorem superat*." [in margin: *Johannes Chrysost. lib. 9. de provid.*].

Chrysostome speaks at length on the ways in which the devil works in insidious ways to corrupt the reason and the will: "Videbis nullam vim restare daemoni, non solum ad persuadendum ista, verum ne ad suggerendum quidem. Nam quamadmodum hi qui parietes suffodiunt, noctis tempore, extincto lumine, et furari opes, et earum dominos cum omni facultate jugulare possunt: ita et hic per caecae noctis horrorem ac tenebras moererem effundens cogitationes omnes, quae ad munimen nostrum esse possunt, subducere prias ac furori nititur, ut defertam et sine adjutorio animam invadens, plagis eam innumeris confodiat. At vero cum quis summa et intentissima in Deum spe assurgens, has tenebras disjecerit, atque ad Solem justitiae confugiens, darissimum illius jubat totis animae viribus haurire et recondere studuerit, protinus cogitationum suarum tumultum in latronem illum impurum transfundet. Nam et qui furta noctu aucupentur, cum qui illos deprehenderit, ac lumen ostenderit, tremunt, fluctuant atque perturbantur. Et quomodo, inquies, possit quis hoc dolore liberati, nisi prius eripiatur a daemone agitatore, eiusque doloris incensore? Non daemon est qui maerorem movet, sed moeror potius vires daemoni administrat, cogitationesque malas suscitat" (p. 249).

The probable source of Ferrand's conclusion that the melancholy humor is the devil's bath is Rodrigo de Castro, *Medicus-politicus*, pp. 172–73. Nevertheless, the originator of this saying appears to be St. Jerome, according to Johann Wier, *Histoires, disputes et discours des illusions et impostures des diables . . . ,*" bk. IV, ch. 25, vol. I, p. 603: "car le diable, comme j'ay dit ci devant, se mesle tres volontiers avec l'humeur melancholique, comme le trouvant apte et fort commode pour executer ses impostures: a raison dequoy S. Jerosme a dit fort à propos que la melancholie est le bain du diable."

9. For the other definition of *incubus* Ferrand continues to employ Jourdain Guibelet before turning to other writers. *Trois discours philosophiques: Discours second du principe de la generation de l'homme*, ch. 18, p. 216ᵛ: "L'autre est une maladie nommée ἐφιάλτης *incubus* coquemare, qui à la verité est tellement estrange, que celuy qui en est saisi, pense estre suffoqué par un demon. Ce mal prend principalement au commencement du dormir, quand quelques vapeurs épesse et grossieres portées des parties inferieures, principalement de l'estomach au cerveau, bouchent les nerfs qui servent à la voix et à la respiration. Au moyen dequoy le malade a opinion d'un pesant fardeau sur sa poictrine, ou d'un demon qui veut faire force à sa pudicité. De verité ce mal peut estre causé par un demon. Toutefois le vulgaire qui ignore les causes des choses, et qui ne s'arreste qu'à l'apparence exterieure, croit que ce sont tousjours esprits qui apportent telles maladies. Pline a suivy l'erreur du vulgaire en ce qu'il nomme ceste indisposition *faunorum ludibrium*, le passetemps des fées. Nous lison de ce subject une histoire assez plaisante, d'un faict que raconte un medecin de ce temps estre nagueres advenue en un convent du pays d'Auvergne. Ce medecin ayant esté appellé pour visiter en ce lieu quelque malade, l'apotiquaire qu'il avoit mené avec luy, voulut un matin, apres avoir esté tourmenté de la coquemare, quereller ceux qui avoient couché en la mesme chambre, de ce qu'ils luy avoient tellement serré et pressé le col, qu'ils l'avoient, disoit-il, presque suffoqué. Ses compagnons au contraire nyoient hardiment, et le blasmant rejectoient sur luy toute la faute, de ce qu'il avoit passé toute la nuict sans dormir, comme s'il eust esté oultré de folie. Le jour ensuivant apres avoir soupé largement, et pris des viandes flatueuses, qu'on luy avoit presentées de propos delibereé, on le fit coucher seul en une chambre, bien close et fermée de toutes parts, où l'accez l'ayant repris comme en la nuict precedente, il jura que c'estoit un demon, duquel mesme il dépeignoit fort naivement les gestes et le visage. Ce que depuis on ne luy peut oster de la phantasie, sinon apres avoir consulté les medecins, et par leur moyen receu la guerison de son mal."

10. [*Gorraeus.*]; [*Aurel. c. 3. l. 1. Chron. Avic. l. 3. Fen. 1. tr. 5. c. 5.*]: Jean de Gorris, *Definitionem medicarum libri XXIV literis Graecis distincti* (Francofurti: typis Wechelianis apud Claudium Marnium, et heredes Joannis Aubrii, 1601), p. 162: "Ἐφθότης: incubus. Est nocturna corporis op-

pressio et suffocatio. Quidam daemonem esse putaverunt, aut externam quandam vim quae quiescentes invaderet. . . . At daemon non est, nec vis ulla externa, sed tota mali causa intra corpus est. Ea autem est non humor, sed crassus et frigidus vapor, ut scripsit Posidonius, ventriculos cerebri implens et prohibens spiritus animales per nervos ferri. Per somnum tantum fit, coque laborantes per ipsam accessionem eadem patiuntur quae et apoplexia correpti, sed tamen mitiora. Quia enim vapor in causa est, non in totum opplentur ventriculi cerebri, nectam difficulter excitantur qui ea laborant. Manent tamen aliquandia immobiles: deinde vero multo labore et conatu tenuato discussoque spiritu, et meatibus obstructione solutis, derepente e somno excitantur. Laeditur illis potissimum imaginatio: ex quo verisimile est in priori potissimum ventriculo morbum consistere. . . . Themison vero a suffocatione πνιγαλιωνα appellavit."

Caelius Aurelianus, *De morbis acutis et chronicis libri VIII* (Amstelaedami: Wetsteniana, 1755), bk. I, ch. 3: "De Incubone," pp. 288–89: "Incubonem aliqui ab hominis forma vel similitudine nomen ducere dixerunt: aliqui a phantasia qua patientes afficiuntur: siquidem veluti ascendere atque insidere suo pectori sentiunt quicquam. *Themison* secundo epistolarum libro Πνιγαλιωνα vocavit, siquidem praefocat aegrotantes. Quidam veteres ἐφιάλτην vocaverunt, alii ἐπιβολὴν quod utilis patientibus perhibeatur. Afficit *crapula* vel *indigestione* jugi vexatos. Accidens igitur semel, ita ut nullam vigilantibus querelam, aut displicentem sanitatem faciat, sed solius somni turbatio noscatur, minime passio dici potest, sicut neque semel effectus per somnum *seminis lapsus*, quem Graeci ὀνειρόγονον appellant, passio nuncupatur, nisi jugiter, atque cum corporis incommoditate fuerit effectus. Est autem supradicta passio epilepsiae tentatio. Nam quod neque *deus*, neque *semideus*, neque *cupido* sit, libris causarum quos αἰτιολογουμένους appellavit, plenissime *Soranus* explicavit. Ista igitur *passione* possessos sequitur corporis tardissimus motus, atque torpor, et magis per *somnium gravedo*, atque pressura, et veluti *praefocatio*, qua sibi quenquam irruisse repente existimant, qui sensibus oppressis, corpus exanimet, neque clamare permittat. Quo fit ut saepe erumpentes non articulata, sed confusa voce exclament. Quidam denique ita inanibus adficiuntur visis, ut et se videre credant irruentem sibi, et usum *turpissimae libidinis* persuadentem, cujus si digitos apprehendere nixi fuerint fugatum existiment. Tunc autem cum *somno* surrexerint, faciem atque transforationis partes uvidas et humectas sentiunt, attestante gravedine *cervicis*, cum *tussicula* levi, molli stimulatione commota. Plurimum autem possessis accidit *pallor*, et corporis *tenuitas*, quippe cum somnum, timendo, non capiant. Apparet igitur *stricturae* passio ex gravedine, *tarda* autem ex temporis tractu, et non semper sine periculo salutis. Cum enim vehementer impresserit *praefocatio*, quosdam interficit."

Avicenna, *Liber canonis*, bk. III, fen 1, tr. 5, p. 208[r]: "De alchabus, et nominatur strangulator, et quandoque nominatur arabice algiathum, et alneidalan seu albeidalan id est Incubo, sive ephialte": "Incubus autem est aegritudo, in qua homo sentit, cum in somno ingreditur phantasma grave super se cadens, et conprimens ipsum, et angustiatur eius spiritus, et intersecatur vox ipsius, et motus eius, et existimat praefocari propter oppilationes pororum; et cum ab ipso separatur, excitat eum subito. Et est antecessor unius trium aegritudinum, aut apoplexiae, aut epilepsiae, aut maniae; et illud quidem cum fuerit ex materiebus comprimentibus, et non fuerit ex causi; aljis non materialibus. Eius vero causa secundum plurimum est vapor materierum grossarum sanguinearum, aut phlegmaticarum, aut melancholicarum, elevatus ad cerebrum subito in dispositione quietis motus vigiliarum resolventis vapores, et unusquisque humor causat phantasma cum colore suo."

Johann Wier, *Histoires, disputes et discours*, bk. III, ch. 19, vol. I, pp. 387–89, gives an account of the nightmare called incubus: "Ce que je feray apres que j'auray remonstré que nous avons en l'art de medecine une maladie nommee incube par les Latins, pour autant que ceux que en sont tourmentez, pensent en dormant qu'ils ayent un fardeau, appuyé sur eux, lequel empesche le respirer, et par consequent la voix et la parole." Wier also gives the various names as follows: Pliny, *suppression* or *estoufement*; Avicenna, *albealilon et alcranum*; Averroes *elgadum*; Alsaravius, *alcaiq*; the Germans *diemarydetuns*; the Greeks, *ephialte*.

Jacques Houllier, *De morbis internis libri II*, ch. 14, p. 48^V: "Incubus, qui εφιάλτης, ἐπιβολή, à Themisone πνιγαλίον dicitur, neque deus, neque semideus, neque Cupido, quod veteres crediderunt, neque daemon, quod theologi existimant, neque incubans vetula, sed vapor quidam crassus, qui partim vias spiritus animalis intercipit, unde et loquendi, et respirandi difficultas: partim animae offunditur, quale frequens est in somniis."

Despite these many marginal references suggesting themselves as sources for the section on incubo or the nightmare, the most probable general source is Rondelet. His ch. XLIV, "De incubo," follows the chapters on mania and hypochondriacal melancholy and precedes the chapter on love, "De amantibus" which Ferrand had read carefully. Ferrand's order and wording most closely resemble the following passage from Guillaume Rondelet, *Methodus curandorum omnium morborum corporis humani in tres libros distincta*, p. 237: "Ἐφιάλτης Graecis, incubus Latinis dicitur, et incubo ab incubando. Ob summam enim venarum plenitudinem, thoracis scilicet, quiddam nobis incumbere, et supra nos stare putamus, respirationem opprimens, et impediens ac vocem simul, ita ut suffocari in eo aegrotantes videantur. Quare a Themisione, ut Paulus testatur, κρίγαμων a suffocando vocatur. Solet etiam post primum somnum, et non nisi in somno evenire, vel sentiri, ob id incubonem dici existimo. Cum enim dormimus, non tam libere respiramus, quam cum vigilamus. Atque inter dormiendum, vel in inchoata actione, fumi et flatus elevati pulmones, et septum premunt. Quare cum suspirio, et suffocationis timore, et motu difficili thoracis expergiscuntur. Oritur id vitii ex crapula, pessima victus ratione, et a multitudine crassi sanguinis."

11. [*Aegin. l. 3 c. 15. Aet. tetr. 2 ser. 2. c. 12 Haly Abbas 9. theor c. 6*]: Paul of Aegina, *Opera*, bk. III, ch. 15, pp. 252 ff.

Aetius of Amida, *Tetrabiblos*, bk. II, ser. 2, ch. 12, p. 281.
Haly Abbas, *Liber medicinae dictus regius*, "Theoricae," bk. 9, ch. 6, p. 60.
12. [*L. de Virg. morb.*]: Hippocrates, *On the Diseases of Young Women*: "ὀρῆν δοκεοῦσι δαίμονας,"*Oeuvres complètes*, ed. Littré, vol. VIII, p. 467: "ὀρῆν δοκέειν δαίμονας."
13. "διὰ τίνι εἰς κεφαλὴν ἀναζζούχουσαν ἀναθυμίασιν ἐξ ἀδδηφάγας καὶ ἀποψίας." We have been unable to trace the author of the passage.
14. Hugh of St. Victor, *Opera omnia tribus tomis digesta* (Rothomagi: sumptibus Joannis Berthelin, 1648), bk. II, ch. 16, vol. II, p. 157: "Phantasma est, quando qui dormire vix coepit, et adhuc vigilare se existimat, aspicere videtur irruentes in se, vel passim vagantes formas, discrepantes, et varias, laetas vel turbulentas. In hoc genere est ephialtes, quem publica persuasio quiescentes opinatur invadere, et pondere suo pressos, ac sentientes gravare: quod non est aliud, nisi quaedam fumositas a stomacho, vel a corde ad cerebrum ascendens, et ibi vim animalem comprimens. Dicit etiam humana opinio, quod quadam arte mulierum, et potestate daemonum homines converti possint in lupos et jumenta, et quaeque necessaria portare: postque peracta opera iterum ad se redire, nec fieri in eis mentem bestialem, sed rationalem humanam que servare. Hoc sic intelligendum est, quoniam daemones naturas non creant, sed aliquid tale facere possunt, ut videantur esse quod non sunt. Nulla enim arte, vel potestate animus, sed nec corpus quidem aliqua ratione in membra et lineamenta bestialia veraciter converti potest. Sed phantasticum hominis, quod etiam cogitando sive somniando per rerum innumerabilium genera variatur, et cum corpus non sit, corporum similes formas mira celeritate capit, sopitis aut oppressis corporeis hominis sensibus, ad aliorum sensum figura corporea perduci potest: ita tamen quod corpora ipsa hominum alicubi iaceant viventia quidem, sed multo gravius atque expressius quam somno suis sensibus obseratis."

XXVIII.   Whether Love in Women Is Greater and Therefore Worse Than in Men

1. [*C. 46. art. med.*]: Galen, *Ars medicinalis*, in *Operum Galeni libri isagogici artis medicae*, ch. 46, p. 212.
2. [*Arist. 4. de gen. an. c. 5. Hipp l 1. de diaeta. Gal. ca. 6 l. 14 de usu part.*]: Aristotle, *Generation of Animals*, bk. IV, ch. 5 (774a), p. 451. This chapter deals with superfetation and only a few sentences approach the topic in Ferrand: "Hence, too, those women who are incontinent in the matter of sexual intercourse, cease from their passionate excitement when they have bourne several children, because once the seminal residue has been expelled from the body it no longer produces the desire for this intercourse."
Hippocrates, *Regimen*, bk. I: "En général, les mâles sont plus chauds et plus secs; les femelles plus humides et plus froides; en voici la raison:

à la vérité, dans l'origine, les uns et les autres sont formés semblablement et croissent semblablement; mais une fois nés, les mâles usent d'un régime plus laborieux, de manière à s'échaffer et à se dessécher, les femmes usent d'un régime plus humide et plus oisif et éprouvent tous les mois une purgation qui emporte le chaud hors du corps." *Oeuvres complètes*, ed. Littré, Vol. VI, p. 513.

Galen, *On the Usefulness of the Parts*, bk. XIV, ch. 6, ed. Kühn. vol. II, pp. 628–30; trans. M. T. May, vol. II, p. 630. See ch. II, n. 26.

One of the physicians of the age to defend this point of view, that the male was more inclined to *amor insanus* than the female, was Bartholomy Pardoux in his *De morbis animi*, pp. 51–52, on the grounds that men have warmer temperaments and are thus more ardent and volatile in love. This perspective came about, perhaps, because he separated his chapter on erotic love from his consideration of uterine fury, and thereby established a structure for assigning erotic excess in the two sexes to distinct categories of causation. Those distinctions are clouded in Ferrand, who speaks in practical terms of rapt courtiers as being most in danger, and confirms his views with only one case study involving a male student, yet claims in theory that women are the more vulnerable. It is to be pointed out that much of the evidence presented in the debate is drawn from the literature on uterine fury rather than from the literature on melancholy, as in the case of Jean Aubery cited below in n. 5, in the case of Jean Liébault cited in n. 12, as well as in Ferrand's own text.

3. [*L. I: de gen. an. c. 20. & l. 4. c. 6.*]: Aristotle, *Generation of Animals*, bk. I, ch. 20 (728a), p. 103: "A woman is as it were an infertile male; the female, in fact, is female on account of an inability of a sort, viz., it lacks the power to concoct semen out of the final state of the nourishment (this is either blood, or its counterpart in bloodless animals) because of the coldness of its nature."

Generation of Animals, bk. IV, ch. 6 (775a), pp. 459–61: "Because females are weaker and colder in their nature; and we should look upon the female state as being as it were a deformity, though one which occurs in the ordinary course of nature." Ferrand derives his Greek quotation from this passage: "ἀναπηρίαν φυσικήν, ἀδυναμία γάρ τινι τὸ θῆλύ ἐστι."

4. [*L. de morb. virg.*]: Hippocrates, *On the Diseases of Young Women*: "ἀθυμοτέρη γὰρ καὶ ὀλιγωτέρη ἡ φύσις ἡ γυναικείη." Ferrand substitutes the word "γυναικείη" with "τῶν θηλειῶν," "of females." *Oeuvres complètes*, ed. Littré, vol. VIII, p. 466.

5. [*5. de plac.*]: Galen, *De placitis Hippocratis et Platonis*, ed. Kühn, vol. V, p. 429.

Jean Aubery, *L'antidote d'amour*, pp. 26^V–27^r, devises a theory similar to Ferrand's concerning the passions relative to the two sexes. The woman is more amorous because, contrary to Aristotle, she possesses greater heat than the male "ce qui se voit par l'eminance jumelle qui bosse leur sein, et autres indices de chaleur que l'honesteté reserve plus en la chaste pensee, qu'au discours." This additional heat also accounts for the brevity of their lives, for things that mature quickly do not last as long (a commonplace also stated by Ferrand, see ch. XIX, n. 8; the idea derives essentially from Aristotle). Because of their faster maturity, their love is more intense, while the stronger reason in men allows them greater control over their desires, in compensation for their natural proclivities to love. Aubery hints at the controversy inherent in the theories of heat and propensity vs. reason and self-control, but avoids the problem by altering the theories on the defect of heat in females.

6. Ovid, *Heroides* XIX. 5–7:

> Urimur igne pari, sed sum tibi viribus impar,
> Fortius ingenium suspicor esse viris
> Ut corpus teneris, sic mens infirma puellis.

See Henricus Dörrie, p. 245.

7. Ovid, *The Art of Love* I. 281:

> Parcior in nobis, nec tam furiosa libido:
> Legitimum finem flamma virilis habet.

See ed. J. H. Mozley, pp. 32–33.

8. [*L. 3. de par. an. c. 4. L. 1. de gen. an. c. 4.*]: Aristotle, *Parts of Animals*, bk. III, ch. 14, trans. A. L. Peck, p. 295: "Of all, those which have a straight intestine are especially gluttonous, since the food passes through quickly, which means that their enjoyment of it is brief, and therefore in its turn the desire for food must come on again very quickly."

Aristotle, *Generation of Animals*, bk. I, ch. 4 (717a), p. 19: "Animals which have straight intestines are more violent in their desire for food."

9. [*Arist. 2. de gen. c. 4. l. 3 de ani. c. 9 t. 45*]: "οὐδὲν ποιεῖ περίεργον οὔτε μάτην, ἀλλ'ἀεὶ ἐκ τῶν ἐνδεχομένον τῇ οὐσίᾳ περὶ ἕχαστον γένος ζῴου το ἄριστον." The part preceding the comma comes from *Generation of Animals* (744a), see trans. A. L. Peck, p. 228; the remaining derives from *Progression of Animals* (2. 704b 16), see trans. E. S. Forster (Loeb, 1945), p. 486. Ferrand changes "οὐθέν" for "οὐδέν."

10. [*Gal. l. de Dissect. uteri & l. 4. de usu par.*]: Galen, *De uteri dissectione liber*, ed. Kühn, vol. II, pp. 900–901. Galen mentions only that the spermatic vases of females are farther apart than those of males.

Galen, *On the Usefulness of the Parts*, bk. XIV, ed. Kühn, vol. III, pp. 628 ff.; trans. M. T. May, vol. II, pp. 628–32.

11. [*Hipp. l. de humor.*]: Hippocrates, *On the Humors*: "τὰ γὰρ ἐγγῆ καὶ τὰ κοινὰ πρῶτα καὶ μάλιστα κακοῦται." *Oeuvres complètes*, ed. Littré, vol. V, pp. 482–83: "Τὰ ἐγγὺς καὶ τὰ κοινὰ τοῖσι παθήμασι πρῶτα καὶ μάλιστα κακοῦται."

12. Ferrand's chapter on the relative strengths of male and female sexual desire is remotely based upon a serious medical literature concerned with the mechanisms of sexual desire, the relative body heat and moisture in each of the sexes, and the comparative degrees of carnal pleasure each derives from intercourse. Because women are considered to be cold and moist by comparison with men, they are therefore less perfect, and because of this imperfection, they must by extension be morally inferior and therefore given to lustful behavior. This leads back to medical considerations and to the conclusion that women must take greater pleasure in the venerian act. The debate over the question goes back to the very foundations of Western medicine. Hippocrates, himself, was

of two opinions on the matter: Ferrand cites his work on the diseases of women to prove that women are more passionate in love because of their physical natures, while Jean Liébault in *Des maladies des femmes*, bk. III, ch. 2, p. 528, cites his book on generation to show that the male has a greater and more sustained pleasure in the sexual act because the seed itself is warmer and "spirituous," more biting and in larger quantity. Moreover, the more active male with his larger body heats up the seed even more and engenders a large quantity of spirits, so that seed and spirits passing through the genitals excite and tickle to a greater extent. In addition, the male genitalia seem to have an innate sensitivity with sharper and more delicate feelings than the female. Macrobius and Plutarch, however, attribute to women greater heat than to men, and thus greater voluptuousness, looking to Hippocrates' book on the diseases of women to show that women have more blood as well. She is of a temperament far more inclined to reproduce and to take pleasure in rendering her seed. When one considers the forces, faculties, and marvelous movements of the matrix, one can see easily that it is necessary that the woman receives the greatest satisfaction in love making. Nature has placed in the womb itself an extraordinary craving to conceive and to procreate, driven by a greediness for the male seed which she extracts from him with force and efficiency, and in turn preserves and nurtures toward achieving fertility. The woman is, in fact, a veritable victim of her uterus which, driven by the urges of nature, exercises a tyrannical control over her. By this fact is to be explained all the erratic and frenzied aspects of her behavior. Liébault writes in *Des maladies des femmes*, in a chapter entitled, "On la semence tant virile que foeminine," p. 513: "Considerez je vous prie combien de troubles, de seditions, de commandemens petulans et imperieux la matrice suscite au corps de la femme, s'il advient quelquefois qu'elle soit provee de ses voluptueux desirs, et retranchee de son service accoustumé. Qu'ainsi soit vous voyez plusieurs femmes pour ce defaut, quasi prestes à rendre l'ame. Autres estre destituees de voix, parolle, sentiment et respiration totale. Aucunes devenir phrenetiques, epileptiques, maniaques, melancholiques. Plusieurs rire, plorer, saulter, danser, sans occasion manifeste. Autres estre tourmentees de convulsions et d'une infinité de semblables accidens, tant de corps que d'esprit: de façon que le philosophe Platon non sans bonne raison a estimé la matrice devoir estre appellee non quelque chose d'animé au corps de la femme, mais un animal imperieux, petulant, n'obeissant aucunement à raison, impatient de toute attente, et transporté de certaine rage et furieuse cupidité. Ne faut donc douter que les femmes ne reçoivent plus de plaisir au combat venerien que les hommes: encores qu'elles n'ayent tant de chaleur, ny se grande quantité de semence que les hommes: principalement celles qui sont sanguines, charneuses, doüees d'une tres bonne habitude de corps, pleines de suc, oysives, addonnees aux delices et danses, nourries liberalement et de viandes delicates, se delectans et plaisans fort aux compaignies, conversation et colloques familiers des jeunes hommes. Sur tout si elles sont mariees à jeunes maris, voluptueux, libidineux et vaillans combattans."

13. Ferrand is disappointing in his treatment of this popular topic in that he ignores the polemics of the Montpellier school writers who dealt at length with the subject in their commentaries on Arnald of Villanova and Avicenna. To an extent Ferrand extracts, by a process of force and association, certain of the positions in the debate from the ancients: Galen, Aristotle, Chrysippus (cited in Galen), Hippocrates, and Ovid. But he makes no mention of Arnald's view that women were less disposed to amorous passion than men. When the ancients spoke of melancholy they were not making references to love as a melancholy disease. It is the physicians following Arnald who, in dealing with love, were inclined to consult former treatises on melancholy and to make parallel judgments: that women were less inclined to passion and lovesickness for the same reasons they were less inclined to melancholy diseases in general. The source of this complex of ideas is in the *Canon* of Avicenna, bk. III, fen 1, tr. 4, chs. 18–22, where he discusses the nature of melancholy. "Et hec quidem egritudo plus accidit in viris, sed in mulieribus est deterior." This view that women were less often melancholy than men, but more seriously attacked by it, was easily translated into terms that included love, that women once taken by fits of amorous passion became grave and desperate cases. Bernard of Gordon expressed this concept in terms closer to the humors, that men are by nature hotter, but that coitus could generate even more heat in women.

Ferrand employed the same techniques of reasoning: that what was true of melancholy behavior was also true of love. That Ferrand ignores the recent literature on the question and terminates his statement with an appeal to everyday experience is evasive, though his assertion that it is common knowledge that women are ever ready to run mad for love, but men seldom, could have significance for determining who Ferrand's clientele was, marking the difference between the courtly conventions of Arnald's day in which men engaged in the passionate pursuit, and the bourgeois conditions of Ferrand's, characterized by the ambience of the salon and the reading of romances in which women had far freer parts to play.

Underlying the entire discussion is a conflicting definition of love. If love is stronger in creatures that are hot and dry, then men by their natural heat must have the stronger inclinations. But if love is contrary to reason, and cannot rule where reason is in control, then it must be stronger in women. Thus women are also more obstinate and irrational in their loves. Proofs then appear from literary sources on all sides. Hero was thus, Clytemnestra so, Dido thus, Medea so. If men are irrational in love it is because they are weak spirited from being raised in the company of the ladies. Those with the genitals closer to the liver are more inclined to luxury than those whose genitals are exterior to the body, though paradoxically it is the heat in males that has forced the genitals outside of the body. The discussion ends in a draw, that men pursue more openly, but that women are more ruseful, and that once they are in love they can be more tenacious than men.

XXIX.   On the Prevention of Love and Love Melancholy

1. [*C. 88 art. med l. 4. Meth. med.*]: Galen, *Ars medicinalis*, in *Operum Galeni libri isagogici artis medicae*, ch. 88, p. 225 f: "De solutione continuitatis."
   Galen, *De methodo medendi*, bk. IV, ed. Kühn, vol. X, pp. 232–304.
   Ferrand's reference is to the entire treatise.
2. [*L. de nat. hom.*]: Hippocrates, *On the Nature of Man*: "ἐναντίον ἵστασθαι τοῖσι καθεστεῶσι καὶ νουσήμασι καὶ εἴδεσι καὶ ὥρῃσι καὶ ἡλικίῃσι." *Oeuvres complètes*, ed. Littré, vol. VI, pp. 52–53.
3. [*L. 4. de plat. Hipp. & Plat.*]: Galen, *De placitis Hippocratis et Platonis*, bk. IV, ch. 6, ed. Kühn, vol. V, p. 405 f. Galen refers to Helen's beauty, but not specifically to her neck and breasts, as Ferrand suggests.
4. Ovid depicts a parallel episode in *The Remedies of Love*, ll. 661–70, see *The Art of Love, and Other Poems*, ed. J. H. Mozley, p. 223: "I happened to be in the company of a youth; his lady was in her litter: all his speech bristled with savage threats. On the point of summoning her on bail, 'Let her come forth from the litter,' he cried; forth she came: when he saw his wife, he was dumb. His hands dropped, and from his hands the double tablet; he rushed into her arms, and cried, 'Thus thou dost conquer.' "
5. [*Terent. in Andr. act. 3 sc. 3.*]: Terence, *Andros*, act III, sc. iii., l. 555: "amantium irae amoris redintegratio est." See trans. John Sargeaunt, 2 vols. (Loeb, 1912), vol. I, pp. 60–61.
6. [*Proper. l. 2. el. 4.*]: Propertius, bk. II, Elegy IV. 13: "Quam facile irati verbo placantur amantes." See trans. H. E. Butler, p. 76. Read "mutantur" for "placantur."
7. [*Pollux l. 7.*]: Julius Pollux, *Onomasticum Graece et Latine*, bk. VII, ch. 24 (Amstelaedami: ex officina Wetsteniana, 1706), vol. II, pp. 764–65: "Ante carmina vero, fabri solebant ridicula quaedam suspendere, aut formare, ad invidiae eversionem: quae Bascania (βασκανια) appellabantur, ut et Aristophanes inquit: Praeterquam quis emat indigens bascano fabri. Plumbum vero operari, plumbum fundere vocatur. His etiam conveniunt fortassis, statuas formare, et statuaria ars, et imagines effingere, et sculptoria. Aurifabrorum vero, et sculptorum anulorum nomina, apud Critiam extant, et Platonem: Philyllius vero Urbibus, anularium vocavit."
   We have translated as "trinket" Ferrand's "brouillerie" that Cotgrave renders as things in disorder, a "tumbling of things together" and the *Robert* as a kind of trivial argument based on gossip. The sense of the passage suggests toys, trifles, charms, or ornaments.
   "Higo per no ser oiados" (from the verb *hollar*, to make a hole in, as well as to trample down or humiliate) means literally "a withered fig for lack of intercourse." Ferrand is right in tracing it to the Romans, the thumb representing the phallus as inserted into the fist as fig, a symbol of the female. That this lewd symbol should be used as a fascinum to ward off the evil eye can only be explained by seeing it as a shocking object that would draw the attention of the evil eye, thereby diverting it from the wearer, a gesture not unlike the custom of lifting the skirts

to show the genital regions in order to frighten the devil or to ward off demons. For this interpretation, see Desmond Morris, *Manwatching: A Field Guide to Human Behaviour* (St. Albans: n.p., 1978), p. 202.

8. [*Avic. l. 3. Fen 20. t. [?]. c. 24. Alsarav l pract. sec. 2. c. 17*]: Avicenna, *Liber canonis*, bk III, fen 1, tr. 4, ch. 23. The theme of using an old woman who, by badmouthing the loved girl in front of the lover, and by showing him her menstrual towels, draws the lover away from the object of his desire, is found in almost all the chapters on love written by the Arab physicians, and will enjoy great fortune also in the literary tradition. For an account of its use by Dante Alighieri, see Paolo Cherchi, "Per la femmina 'balba,'" *Quaderni d'italianistica*, vol. VI, no. 2 (1985), pp. 228–32.

Abū al-Qūasim, *Liber theoricae necnon practicae*, tr. 1, sec. 2, ch. 17, only mentions, among the cures for excessive love, "uti frequenter coitu cum quacumque poterit et cum non dilecta, et assidue ieunare et itinerare ei inebriari."

9. Ovid, *The Remedies of Love*, ll. 323–25:
> Et mala sunt vicina bonis, errore sub illo:
> Pro vitio virtus crimina saepe tulit.
> Quam potes in peius dotes deflecte puellae.

See *The Art of Love, and Other Poems*, trans. J. H. Mozley, p. 200.

10. [*Gordon c. de amore part. 2. Chr. à Vega c de amore. l. 3. Meth. med.*]: Bernard of Gordon, *Lilium medicinae*, pt. 2, ch. 20, pp. 218–19: "Finaliter autem cum aliud consilium non habemus, imploremus auxilium et consilium vetularum, ut ipsam dehonestent et diffament quantum possunt."

Cristóbal de Vega, *De Arte medendi*, bk. III, ch. 17, pp. 414–15: "Sunt quidem admonendi virtutis, religionis, et sanctimoniae, et distrahendi, et in diversa revocandi, et quandoque increpandi acerbius, et flagellis caedendi. . . . Praeterea pro pulchra amata, pulchrior alia ob oculos offeratur, et pro viro alter elegantior, quibus nubere posint. Vitia quoque et turpitudines amatorum, coram amante referri debent, nisi amantes valde abiecto animo fuerint: qui enim tales sunt, similes concupiscunt: quamobrem eis praestantia, dignitas, et personarum disparitas opponenda."

11. Ovid, *The Remedies of Love*, ll. 709–10: "Vos quoque formosis vestras conferte puellae. / Incipiet dominae quemque pudere suae." See *The Art of Love, and Other Poems*, trans. J. H. Mozley, p. 224.

12. [*Alex Picolom. l. 10 Inst mor c. 6.*]: Alessandro Piccolomini, *Della institution morale . . . libri XII*, bk. X, ch. 6: "Del disoglimento dell'amore," p. 443.

Cicero, *Tusculan Disputations*, bk. IV, ch. 35, sec. 74, trans. J. E. King, p. 413. Cicero also urges the technique of convincing the lover that what he sees as attractive is a false impression: "The treatment applicable to a man so victimized is to make it plain how trivial, contemptible and absolutely insignificant is the object of his desire, how easily it can either be secured from elsewhere or in another way, or else wholly put out of mind." Cicero goes on to caution against love's greatest threat: that it leads to madness.

Ovid, *The Remedies of Love*, ll. 325–35, trans. J. H. Mozley, p. 201, also suggests this strategem for misrepresenting the lady's qualities and traits to the lover by casting them all in an unattractive light through Sophistic arguments.

13. [*Bapt. Porta cap. 9. l. 3. physion. Aristot. c. 6. physion*]: Giovan Battista della Porta, *De humana physiognomonia libri IV*, bk. III, ch. 11: "Splendidi oculi," p. 422. He discusses the eyes of those who are prone to sexual desire, but he does not refer specifically to women. The following reference to Aristotle comes from this same passage.

Aristotle, *Physiognomics*, VI, in *Minor Works*, trans. W. S. Hett, p. 121: "Those that have a sharp nose-tip are prone to anger."

See also della Porta, p. 110: "Magnus naso: nasus praegrandis probi viri indicium affert; Polemon: Praegransi nasus melior; Adamantius: Magnus nasus semper minori melior; ex his Albertus"; Catullus, no. XLIII, trans. F. W. Cornish (Loeb, 1962), p. 51: "I greet you, lady, you who neither have a tiny nose, nor a pretty foot, nor black eyes, nor long fingers."

14. [*Vitruvius. Aequicola l 2. c. 8. de nat. am*]: Pollio Vitruvius, *The Ten Books on Architecture*, trans. M. H. Morgan (New York; Dover Publications [Harvard, 1914], 1960), bk. III, ch.1, pt. 3, pp. 72–73. Vitruvius, speaking of beauty in general, sees natural beauty in the proportions and relationships between the parts of the body. These he describes mathematically, and by implication these must be in harmony in order to produce the desired effect. The Latin text is available in the Loeb series, 1955–56, ed. Frank Granger.

Mario Equicola, *Libro de natura de amore*, bk. II, "What is beauty," pp. 81^V–88^V.

15. Zeuxis was a painter from Heraclea in southern Italy who flourished in the latter part of the fifth century B.C. He was one of the most celebrated of ancient Greece, especially for his rendering of women. One of his best known was the picture of Helen commissioned for the temple of Hera on the Lacinian promontory in Magna Graecia, the colonial region including Tarentum and Croton. This is most probably the same representation of Helen as the one mentioned by Ferrand.

16. [*Propert. l. 2 el. 13.*]: Propertius, bk. II, Elegy xviiiB. 26: "Turpis Romano Belgicus ore color." See trans. H. E. Butler, p. 114.

17. [*De Lancre l. 4. disc. 4. de l'inconst.*]: Pierre de Lancre, *Tableau de l'inconstance et instabilité de toutes choses, où il est montré qu'en Dieu seul gît la vraie constance, à laquelle l'homme sage doit viser* (Paris: Chez A. L'Angelier, 1607), republished in 1610 with a *Livre nouveau de l'inconstance de toutes les nations*. This latter work is presumed to be Ferrand's source; the text is not easily found today. For further information on De Lancre's publications, see the "Introduction critique" by Nicole Jacques-Chaquin in *Tableau de l'inconstance des mauvais anges et démons* (abridged edition) (Paris: Éditions Aubier Montaigne, 1982).

18. [*Aph. ult. l. 2. Cels. l. 3. c. 1.*]: Hippocrates, *Aphorisms*, sec. 2, no. 54, *Oeuvres complètes*, ed. Littré, vol. V, p. 487: "Une haute taille, dans la

jeunesse, est noble et non sans grâce; mais, dans la vieillesse, elle est plus embarrassante et moins avantageuse qu'une taille moindre."

Celsus, *De medicina*, ed. W. G. Spencer, bk. II, ch. 1, vol. I, p. 89: "The square-built frame, neither thin nor fat, is the fittest; for tallness, as it is graceful in youth, shrinks in the fulness of age; a thin frame is weak, a fat one sluggish."

19. [*L. de san. ad Thras. 5. De plac. Hipp. l. 1. & 11. de usu part.*]: Galen, *Ad Thrasybulum liber, utium medicinae sit an gymnastices hygiene*, ch. 14, ed. Kühn, vol. V, pp. 828 ff.

　Galen, *De placitis Hippocratis et Platonis*, bk. V, ch. 3, Kühn, vol. V, p. 449.

　Galen, *On the Usefulness of the Parts*, bk. I, trans. M. T. May, vol. I, p. 79: "In fact, this is your standard, measure, and criterion of proper form and true beauty, since true beauty is nothing but excellence of construction, and in obedience to Hippocrates you will judge that excellence from actions, not from whiteness, softness, or other such qualities, which are indications of a beauty meretricious and false, not natural and true." Bk. 11 deals with the usefulness of the features of the face.

20. [*A. Laurent. l. 1. anat. c. 2.*]: André Du Laurens, *Questiones anatomiques*, in *Toutes les oeuvres*, pp. 2–3: "Or la symmetrie et proportion des parties du corps humain est admirable. Les artisans se la proposent comme un modele tres-parfait. . . . Mais on remarque aussi en ceste proportion des parties du corps humain, la figure circulaire qui est la plus parfaite de toutes, et la quarrée; chose qui ne se void point aux autres animaux: Car ayant mis le nombril pour le centre, si on le couche à l'envers et qu'on luy face estendre les pieds et les mains de plus qu'il pourra, et puis qu'on mette l'un des pieds du compas sur le nombril, et qu'en tournant l'autre on face un circle entier, on touchera les gros orteils des deux pieds et les doigts du mitan de la main: que s'il manque en quelque endroit, il faut croire qu'il y a du defaut et du vice. Que si apres avoir fait le circle, tu viens à tuer une ligne entre les deux pieds estendus, et une autre entre la main et le pied de costé et d'autre; tu auras un quarré parfaict desirit dans un circle. Ces choses que nous venons de desduire touchant la figure, temperature, et proportion du corps humain sont tres-belles; mais ceste derniere icy surpasse toute admiration. C'est qu'il contient dans soy toutes les choses que tout ce grand monde comprend en sa cavité tres-ample: tellement que ce n'a point esté sans bonne raison que les anciens l'ont nommé *petit monde, et patron ou abbregé de l'Univers.*" Du Laurens continues to elaborate on the microcosm-macrocosm idea that established the system of correspondences between the body and the astral world to name but one level of application of the theory.

21. Vitruvius, *The Ten Books on Architecture*, trans. M. H. Morgan, bk. III, ch. 1, pt. 3, p. 72: "For the human body is so designed by nature that the face, from the chin to the top of the forehead and the lowest roots of the hair, is a tenth part of the whole height; the open hand from the wrist to the tip of the middle finger is just the same; the head from the chin to the crown is an eighth, and with the neck and shoulder from the top of the breast to the lowest roots of the hair is a sixth; from the

middle of the breast to the summit of the crown is a fourth."

Pietro Bembo, *Les Azolains*, bk. III, in *De la nature d'amour*, traduictz d'italien en françoys par Jan Martin (Paris: M. de Vascosan, 1545), p. 163: "Qu'il soit vray, c'est une maxime toute certaine, et à nous parvenue des escoles plus aprouvées des antiques difinisseurs, que bon amour n'est autre chose fors desir de beaulté. Si donc vous eussiez mis autant de peine par le passé à cognoistre quelle est ceste beaulté, comme vous en princtes hier pour nous paindre subtillement les perfections exterieures de vostre dame, à la vérité vous n'eussiez pas aymé comme avez fait, ny conseillé aux autres de poursuivre ce que vous cherchez en amours, car beaulté . . . n'est sinon une grace qui provient de proportion, convenance, et armonie des choses, et tant plus est parfaicte en ses subjectz, plus les rend elle gracieux et desirables, pour estre non moins accidentalle aux espritz des hommes, qu'elle est à leurs parties corporelles."

22. Ferrand is referring to Mario Equicola, *Libro de natura de amore*, bk. IV, "Segni da cognoscere li inclinati ad amare il presente amatore," p. 134^r. Equicola reviews all the signs by which a libidinous person can be known and illustrates them with examples from ancient literature.

Jean de Veyries, *La Genealogie de l'amour* (Paris: Chez Abel L'Angelier, 1609), bk. II, ch. 15, p. 327.

23. [*Plut in qu. Plat. Gal. l. de usu part. l. 5. de Placit. Hip.*]: Plutarch, *Platonic Questions*, no. 6, in *Moralia*, vol. XIII, pt. 1, p. 63.

Galen, *On the Usefulness of the Parts*, bk. I, trans. M. T. May, vol. I, p. 79; this is a general reference to a passage he cites more explicitly above. See n. 19.

Galen, *De placitis Hippocratis et Platonis*, bk. V, ch. 3, ed. Kühn, vol. V, p. 450 f.

24. The following lines by Anaxandrides (fr. 52 K.) are to be found in Joannes Stobaeus, *Anthologium*:

ἀλλ'ἔλαβεν αἰσχράν· οὐ βιωτόν ἐστ'ἔτι,
οὐδ'εἴσοδος τὸ παραπάν εἰς τὴν οἰχίαν.
ἀλλ'ἔλαβεν ὡραίαν τις· οὐδὲν γίνεται
μᾶλλόν τι τοῦ γήμαντος ἢ τῶν γειτόνων·
ὥστ'οὐδαμῶς χαχοῦ γ'ἁμαρτεῖν γίνεται.

ed. C. Wachsmuth and Otto Hense (Berolini: apud Weidmannos, 1958), vol. IV, p. 512.

25. The line comes from Juvenal, Satire X. 298: "—rara est concordia formae / Atque pudicitiae—." See trans. G. G. Ramsay, p. 214.

26. [*Stobaeus*]: Joannes Stobaeus, *Anthologium*, vol. IV, "Eclogues," ch. 22, pt. 2, p. 512.

27. [*P. Syrus*]: Publilius Syrus, in *Minor Latin Poems*: "Formosa facies muta commendation est." ed. A. M. Duff (Loeb, 1961), p. 40.

28. [*Seneca in Octa. act. 2.*]: Seneca, *Octavia*, II. 550: "florem decoris singuli carpunt dies." See trans. Frank Justus Miller, 2 vols. (Loeb, 1968), p. 452.

29. [*Oribas. c. 9. l. 8. synop. Gordon. c. de Amore. Plato l 8. de leg. Valer. Obs. 7. l 2.*]: Oribasius, *Synopsis*, bk. VIII, ch. 9, in *Oeuvres*, vol. V, p. 413 f.

Bernard of Gordon, *Lilium medicinae*, pt. 2, ch. 20, pp. 218–19: "Finaliter autem cum aliud consilium non habemus, imploremus auxilium et consilium vetularum, ut ipsam dehonestent et diffament quantum possunt." See n. 10, above.

Plato, *Laws*, bk. VIII (841A-E), vol. II, pp. 165–67.

François Valleriola, *Observationum medicinalium libri VI*, p. 209: "Itaque adhortationibus et blanda correctione deducendi sunt a proposito, qui perdite amant, ut et Avicenna consuluit, et docuit Paulus. Quod et ipse in hoc meo laborante, summo profecto conatu, et multis ad id suasionibus effeci: difficulter namque ab concepto amore dimoveri poterat."

Battista Fregoso, *Contramours*, p. 215. Such advice for the curing of love had become traditional, finding its base in Lucretius and Ovid. The lover must avoid anything that may incite love folly. The following from Fregoso is typical of the advice concerning the senses and sensual stimulation: "Et pource que la flamme d'amour ne s'esprend pas seulement par le fuzil des yeux, et s'esmeut l'esprit par les trais diceux: mais encores bien souvent il en vient des allumettes par les aureilles: faut fuir, (comme serpens) les lassifs sons, et les impudiques chansons; tous devis et propos d'amour; et tous livres qui en parlent, ou en traitent: et au contraire s'efforcer d'avoir avéques soy des personnes, qui par tous moyens possibles généralement blasment toute amour: et spéciallement l'amour de celle, a laquelle desia s'encline l'affection. Cestuy dit Avicenne (en la cure de la maladie, qu'en langue Arabique il appelle ylisci; cestadire amoureuse rage) estre le souverain reméde, pour convertir cest amour en haine; ou vrayement pour le modérer et moindrir; plus qu'aucune autre médecine."

30. [*Ficin. orat. 7. c. 11*]: Marsilio Ficino, *Commentary on Plato's Symposium*, Speech VII, ch. 11, pp. 167–68: "We must watch out in the first place lest we try to pull up or cut off things not yet mature, and lest we tear apart with the greatest danger things which we can more safely unstitch. A breaking off of habitual relations must be achieved. One must be especially careful lest the lights of the eyes be joined with the lights. If there is any defect in the soul or body of the beloved, it is to be diligently revolved by the soul. The soul is to be kept busy with many, varied, and demanding matters." Ferrand's reference to this passage in Ficino does not correspond to the context. Ficino seems to be recommending a touch of counsel and admonition, but in any event does not speak against the value of such an approach as Ferrand suggests. The error lies more likely with the printer, however, who placed this marginal reference too far down the page. Because Ferrand is in the habit of quoting Ficino and Valleriola together, more probably this reference is intended to accompany the previous paragraph and the previous note.

31. [*Gal. 4. de Plat.*]: Galen, *De placitis Hippocratis et Platonis*, bk. V, ch. 3:

    —Venus admonita laxat nihil,
    Si namque cogas, amplius intendere appetit:
    Admonitus antem Amor magis premit.

ed. Kühn, vol. V, p. 411.

32. [*In Trinum. act. 3. sc. 2.*]: Plautus, *Trinummus*, III. ii. 669–72:

    Amor mores hominum moros et morosos efficit,
    Minus placet quod suadetur; quod dissuadetur, placet.

Cum inopia est, cupias: quando copia est, tum non velis:
Ille qui aspellit, is compellit; ille qui non suadet vetat.
Insanum est malum divuorti ad cupidinem.
See trans. Paul Nixon, 5 vols. (Loeb, 1952), vol. 5, pp. 162–63. The original reads:

ita est amor, ballista ut iacitur: nihil sic celere est
    neque volat;
atque is mores hominum moros et morosos efficit;
minus placet magis quod suadetur, quod dissuadetur placet;
quom inopiast, cupias, quando eius copiast, tum non velis;
[*ille qui aspellit is compellit, ille qui consuadet vetat*]
insanum malumst in hospitium devorti ad Cupidinem.

33. [*L. 10. Eth. c. 10.*]: Aristotle, *Nicomachean Ethics*, bk. X, ch. 9 (1179b): "ὁ κατὰ πάθος ζῶν οὐχ ἂν ἀχούσειε λόγου ἀποτρέποντος οὐδ'ἂν συνείη." See trans. H. Rackham, pp. 630–31. Ferrand preserves the words, but reverses the order of the original.

34. Tibullus, bk. II, Elegy VI. 13–14: "Iuravi quoties rediturum ad limina numquam, / Cum bene iuravi, pes tamen ipse redit." *The Elegies*, ed. Kirby Flower Smith, p. 147. Read "quotiens" for "quoties."

35. [*Plato in Philebo*]: Plato, *Philebus* (65D), ed. Harold N. Fowler (Loeb, 1962), pp. 91–93.

36. Avicenna, *Liber canonis*, bk. III, fen 1, tr. 4, ch. 24.

37. [*Galien 4. de Plac. Hipp. & Plat.*]: Galen, *De placitis Hippocratis et Platonis*, bk. IV, ch. 2, ed. Kühn, vol. V, pp. 368 ff: "Ψυχαὶ τῶν θεραπειῶν οἱ καιροί, ὦν ἡ παραφυλακὴ τὸ τέλος."

38. [*Arist. 2. Rhet. c. 4. l. 8. Eth c. 3. & 4.*]: Aristotle, *Rhetoric*, bk. II, ch. 4 (1380b–1381a), trans. John Henry Freese, p. 193: "Let loving, then, be defined as wishing for anyone the things which we believe to be good, for his sake but not for our own, and procuring them for him as far as lies in our power."

Aristotle, *Nicomachean Ethics*, bk. VIII, ch. 13 (1162b), trans. H. Rackham, p. 505: "In a friendship based on virtue each party is eager to benefit the other, for this is characteristic of virtue and of friendship; and as they vie with each other in giving and not in getting benefit, no complaints nor quarrels can arise, since nobody is angry with one who loves him and benefits him."

But the question of jealousy as a strategem for effecting a cure is entirely ambivalent in Ferrand, as it is in the literature on the question at large, simply because two different criteria are so easily brought to bear on the question. We are to assume that Ferrand has changed contexts and has forgotten what he states in ch. XXVI, where he says that the disease is more difficult to cure where the lover is also jealous.

39. Pausanias, *Description of Greece, Elis*, bk. II, ch. 25, trans. W. H. S. Jones, vol. III, pp. 152–53: "The goddess in the temple they call Heavenly; she is of ivory and gold, the work of Pheidias, and she stands with one foot upon a tortoise. The precinct of the other Aphrodite is surrounded by a wall, and within the precinct has been made a basement, upon which sits a bronze he-goat. It is a work of Scopas, and the Aphrodite is named

Common. The meaning of the tortoise and of the he-goat I leave to those who care to guess."

40. [*Mercur. l. 4 de morb. mul. c. 10*]: Girolamo Mercuriale, *De morbis muliebribus*, bk. IV, ch. 10, p. 154: "Posset quis eruditus dubitare, an morbus quo virgines Milesiae laborarunt et mulieres Lugdunenses, fuerit hic morbus, quoniam recitat Plutarchus lib. de virtut. mulierum, interdum virgines Milesias sese catervatim suspendisse, nec potuisse ulla vi, aut precibus impedire: quod refert a nonnullis ascriptum fuisse aeris vitio. Relatum etiam est, Lugdunenses mulieres catervatim sese in fluvios praecipitasse, atque hoc attributum fuisse, defluvio stellarum. Ego vero puto nullum aliud morbi genus extitisse, quam hunc morbum: primo, quia mulieres Milesiae virgines erant. Hippocrates vero, Soranus et alii, scribunt hunc morbum peculiarem esse virginibus et castis. De Lugdunensibus idem dico, quod cum amarent se praecipitasse in aquam, non ob aliud factum est quam ob ardorem, qui cum in nulla alia parte appareret et puderet manifestare, ideo ruebant in aquam, tanquam remedium. Nam relatum est a Lucretio 6. de natura, in peste illa Atheniensi, agros prae ardore in fluvios se praecipitasse, ita ut verisimile sit mulieres eam ob causam eo devenisse." See also ch. XII, n. 9, above.

It is probable that this anecdote concerning the virgins of Miletus running naked through the marketplace had become, by Ferrand's time, an established medical *topos*. It appears in Barthélemy Pardoux, *De morbis animi*, p. 50, as an example of uterine fury or nymphomania.

41. Arnald of Villanova, *De amore heroico*, p. 53: "Hec vero perficient competenter quecumque per representationem suarum formarum in virtute fantastica distrahunt in diversam a predicta cogitationem, in toto vel in aliqua parte—saltim veluti forme rerum ducentium rem desideratam in odium, sicut rei turpitudines oculo monstrare vel enarrare sermonibus et cetera."

42. Ovid, *The Remedies of Love*, ll. 429–30: "Ille quod obscoenas in aperto corpore partes / Viderit in cursu qui fuit haesit Amor." See ed. J. H. Mozley, pp. 206–7.

43. [*Niceph. Cal. l. 14. c. 16. Dupreau Suydas.*]: Nicephorus Callistus, *L'histoire ecclesiastique*, bk. XIV, ch. 16, pp. 764–65. Nicephorus tells a story entirely different from the one suggested in Ferrand's text, though the book and chapter are accurately cited. Nicephorus says that Hypatia died in the sixth year of the reign of Theodosius, but makes no mention of Honorius or Arcadius. Rather than describe her graphic cure for erotic melancholy, he tells the story of her death. "Tous l'honneroyent et reveroyent pour son excellente pudicité, de sorte que tous parloyent d'elle avec admiration. Or l'envie pour lors s'arma et enflamba contre elle. Car pource que souvent elle hantoit Oreste, le clergé en conceut quelque reproche, comme si elle empeschoit que Cyrille et Oreste ne retournassent en grace et amitié l'un avec l'autre. Parquoy aucuns d'iceux qui de grand amour poursuyvoyent Cyrille, s'assemblerent, desquels le chef fut un nommé Pierre, de l'ordre des lecteurs, et l'observerent insideusement lors qu'elle revenoit de quelque part, et la tirerent de son chariot, et la trainerent hastivement en l'Eglise de Cesar: puis l'ayant despouillee de ses ha-

billements, la mirent à mort avec des tets de pots: et non contens de ce, la mirent en pieces, et dechirerent membre a membre et l'apporterent au lieu dict Cineron, ou ils la bruslerent. Ce forfait fut grandement reprins en Cyrille et son Eglise, consideré que les envies, dissensions, effors de contention, bateries, meurtres et autres pareils actes sont du tout alienes des sectateurs de Jesus-Christ. Ces choses furent faictes l'an quatriesme de l'Episcopat de Cyrille d'Alexandrin, et l'an sixiesme de l'Empire de Theodose."

Gabriel Dupréau, *Histoire de l'estat et succès de l'Eglise, dressée en forme de chronique générale et universelle*, vol. I, p. 141^r: "Avec le manière et le méthode d'enseigner qu'elle avoit, elle parvint au comble de vertu, estant juste, tempérante et sobre, et garda tousjours sa chasteté, estant douée d'une si excellente beauté, et d'un si parfaict et beau traict de visage, qu'un de ses auditeurs en devint amoureux, lequel toutes fois n'en peut jamais jouyr, nonobstant qu'il luy eust declaré son mal et passion. Laquelle luy fit passer et l'en destourna par la monstre qu'elle luy fit d'un drap teinct de ses fleurs—luy voulant par cela donner à entendre et prouver combien nostre origine et naissance estoit infectée et corrompue, luy tenant tels propos—Voila, jeune adolescent, ce que tu aymes tant, là où il n'y a rien de beau. Dès ceste heure là, de honte que ce jeune homme eut, s'ermerveillant de la turpitude qui estoit en le chose à luy monstrée, changea de passion et de vouloir, et devint plus chaste et tempérant, voyla quelle estoit Ypatia." Dupréau gives this account of her for the year 398 with the information about the reigns of Arcadius and Honorius, together with the story of her death and the references to Nicephorus Callistus.

Suydas, *Lexicon*, ed. Ada Adler (Stuttgart: Teubner, 1961), vol. I, pt. iv, pp. 644–66: "Ὑπατία."

44. Bernard of Gordon, *Lilium medicinae*, "De passionis capitis," partic. 2, ch. 20: "De amore, qui hereos dicitur," p. 218: "Et si ex his non dimiserit, non est homo seu diabolus incarnatus. Fatuitas igitur sua ulterius secum fit in perditione."

XXX.   Order of Diet for the Prevention of Love Melancholy

1. Girolamo Mercuriale, *De morbis muliebribus*, bk. IV, ch. 10, p. 156: "Qua propter satagendum est, circa curationem huius affectus, quae tota posita est, in uteri refrigeratione, quare aer eligendus est frigidus et humidus: et miror qua ratione motus Moschio, voluerit in hac curatione, aerem esse calidum. Exercitationes moderate conveniunt, omnes animi motus sive ad iram, sive ad letitiam vitandi: vitandae etiam lectiones rerum venerearum, semper loquendum est ipsis de rebus pertinentibus ad honestatem et pudorem."

2. [*C. 128*]: Moschion, *De morbis muliebribus liber*, pp. 27–29.

3. [*L. 3. fen 20. tr. 1. c. 25*]: Ferrand is referring to *Liber canonis*, bk. III, fen 20, tr. 1, ch. 27, p. 376^r, in which Avicenna offers the cures for overwhelming

desire discussed previously in his ch. 25.

4. "Camphora per nares castrat odore mares." Ferrand lists both "gallia moschata," and "alipta moschata," making a distinction between the musks of France and those associated with ancient Rome; the *alipta* was the anointer for the Roman wrestlers and in the Roman baths.

5. [*Arist. probl. 1. Sect. 30. Hieron. ep. ad Eustoch.*]: Aristotle, *Problems*, bk. I, no. 30, is, in fact, bk. XXX, no. 1: "ποιεῖ τοὺς φιλητικοὺς οἶνος." Ed. W. S. Hett (Loeb, 1957), vol. II, p. 159 (953b): "ποιεῖ δὲ καὶ φιλητικοὺς ὁ οἶνος."

St. Jerome, "Epistola XVIII ad Eustochium, de custodia virginitatis," in *Opera*, vol. IV, p. 30: "Si quid itaque in me potest esse consilii, si experto creditur, hoc primum moneo, hoc obtestor, ut sponsa Christi vinum fugiat pro veneno. Haec adversus adolescentiam, prima arma sunt daemonum. Non sic avaritia quatit, inflat superbia, delectat ambitio. Facile aliis caremus vitiis; hic hostis nobis inclusus est. Quoquumque pergimus, nobiscum portamus inimicum. Vinum et adolescentia, duplex incendium voluptatis est."

6. [*Halycarn. l. 2: Pl. l. 14. c. 19. Agel. l. I. c. 23.*]: Dionysius of Halicarnassus, bk. II, *Roman Antiquities*, trans. E. Cary (Loeb, 1937), vol. I, pp. 382–85: "But if she did wrong, the injured party was her judge and determined the degree of her punishment. Other offences, however, were judged by her relations together with her husband: among them was adultery, or where it was found she had drunk wine—a thing which the Greeks would look upon as the least of all faults. For Romulus permitted them to punish both these acts with death, as being the gravest offences women could be guilty of, since he looked upon adultery as the source of reckless folly, and drunkenness as the source of adultery."

Pliny, *Natural History*, bk. XIV, ch. 19, trans. H. Rackham (Loeb, 1960), vol. IV, p. 257. This book deals with wine generally, and sec. 19 with "artificial wines" and those made of cereals, exotic fruits, herbs and vegetables. The presence of the reference must be accounted for in terms of the list of perfumes banished from the lover's room produced from the same ingredients used for making wines. "I also find that aromatic wine is constantly made from almost exactly the same ingredients as perfumes—first from myrrh, as we have said, next also from Celtic nard, reed and aspalathus." He mentions here Gallic and wild nard, as well as wines made from hellebore, scammony and Pontic wormwood.

Aulus Gellius, *Attic Nights*, bk. X, ch. 23., sec. 1, ed. John C. Rolfe, 3 vols. (Loeb, 1960), vol. II, p. 279: "And these things are indeed made known in those books which I have mentioned, but Marcus Cato declares that women were not only censured but also punished by a judge no less severely if they had drunk wine than if they had disgraced themselves by adultery."

Rabelais cites the adage and gives its pedigree: "Et estoit l'opinion des anciens, scelon le recit de Diodore Sicilien, mesmement des Lampsaciens, comme atteste Pausanias, que messer Priapus feut filz de Bacchus et Venus." *Le Tiers Livre*, ed. Pierre Michel (Paris: Éditions Gallimard,

1966), p. 345.

7. Bernard of Gordon, *Lilium medicinae*, pt. 2, ch. 20, "De amore, qui hereos dicitur," p. 219: "Secondo notandum quod vinum, quia laetificat et humectat, si cum temperamento sumitur, quia digestionem confortat, ideo bene competit. Opus igitur quod vinum non sumatur in pauca quantitatae nec in tanta quod inebriet seu in tali quod letificat et curas tollat vinum: ubi ebrietas nulla vel tanta fit ut sibi curas eripiat si qua est inter utriumque nocet. Et ideo dicebat Viaticus: 'qui primo vinum de vite ducere mollitus est inter sapientissimos debet reputari.'"

8. Ovid, *The Remedies of Love*, ll. 805–10:

> Vina parant animos Veneri, nisi plurima sumas,
> Et stupeant multos corda sepulta mero.
> Nutritur vento, vento restinguitur ignis:
> Lenis alit flammas, grandior aura necat.
> Aut nulla ebrietas, aut tanta sit, ut tibi curas.
> Eripiat, si qua est inter utrumque, nocet.

See *The Art of Love, and Other Poems*, trans. J. H. Mozley, pp. 232–33.

9. [*c. 11. orat. 7*]: Marsilio Ficino, *Commentary on Plato's Symposium*, Speech VII, ch. 11, p. 168: "A clear wine is to be used, sometimes even with intoxication, in order that when the old blood has been evacuated, new blood may approach and new spirit." Ficino had a number of authorities on his side concerning the drinking of wine for curing love, including Paul of Aegina, Haly Abbas, and Guglielmo da Saliceto in his *Cyrurgia*, ch. 18 (Venetiis, 1520): "Et ebrietas valde utilis est in hoc casu." Bernard of Gordon raised the question to the level of a formal *topos*, in his *Lilium medicinae*, p. 219: see n. 7, above.

In times closer to Ferrand, certain physicians were categorically against the use of wine, however, such as Luis Mercado, who states simply in his *De internorum morborum curatione*, in *Opera*, vol. III, p. 103: "vinum fugiat." As one last example, Jean Aubery joins those who counsel against the use of wine, now on moral grounds that an evil cannot be employed to produce a good. *L'antidote de l'amour*, p. 135[V]. He was speaking of drunkenness, as was Ferrand, who followed Aubery in objecting on moral grounds.

As a final point of view on the topic, among many possible, there is the advice given by Rondibilis in Rabelais' *Le Tiers Livre*, ch. 31, p. 343, that wine was an effective retardant of carnal desire if taken in sufficient quantities "car par l'intemperance du vin advient au corps humain refroidissement de sang, resolution des nerfs, dissipation de semence generative, hebetation des sens, perversion des mouvemens, qui sont toutes impertinences à l'acte de generation."

10. Genesis 19:30–38. The story is used loosely since Lot was not, in fact, looking to wine as a cure for love. He was not conscious of the schemes of his two daughters. Nevertheless, Ferrand has the narrative stand as both a rejoinder to Ficino's view that drunkenness is a cure for love and as proof that one vice should not be used to drive out another.

11. [*Hipp. Aph. 18. sec. 7. l. 6. Epid.*]: Hippocrates, *Epidemics*, bk. VI, sec. 2, no. 12: "ἐκ προσαγωγῆς τ'ἀναντια αἳ προσάγειν, καὶ διαναπαύειν." *Oeuvres*

complètes, ed. Littré, vol. V, p. 284: " Ἐκ προσαγωγῆς τἀναντία προσάγειν, καὶ διαναπαύειν."

12. Achaeus, Αισθων (frag. from a lost satiric play):

ἐν ᾗ κενῇ γὰρ γασρὶ τῶν καλῶν ἔρως.

ἐκ ἔζι.

See *Achaei Eretriensis quae supersunt,* collecta et illustrata a C. L. Urlichs (Bonnae: ap. A. Marcum, 1834): " Ἐν κενῇ γαρ γαστρὶ τῶν καλῶν ἔρως." The following Greek quotation in Ferrand's text, "ἐν πλησμονῇ κύπρις," comes from Athenaeus VI, 270C, and is found in Achaeus, p. 43: " Ἐν πλασμονῇ τοι Κύπρις, ἐν πεινῶντι δ'οὔ."

13. [*Arist. Prob. 9. Sect. 4.*]: Aristotle, *Problems,* bk. IV, ch. 9 (877b); bk IV, ch. 17 (878b). This citation is another instance of reversed numbers in the margin, though even in this section of bk. IV dealing with sexual intercourse, Aristotle does not speak expressly of love on a full stomach. He says intercourse is more rapid when men are fasting (sec. 9), and that intercourse chills and drys the stomach (sec. 17); trans. W. S. Hett (Loeb, 1953), vol. I, pp. 115, 123.

The topic of wine, food, and fasting in relation to love was complex and full of contradictions. Melancholy is a dry disease and requires humidification for its treatment. But Paul of Aegina in *The Seven Books,* bk. I, ch. 35, "On Venery," pp. 44–45, states that "the diet . . . ought to be moistening and heating" to induce venereal desire. Paul agrees that love-making dries and cools and that he thus greatly approves "of grapes, which supply the body with moisture, and fill the blood with flatus, which rouses to venery." No doubt by reasoning in these terms, Rondelet came to recommend fasting as a cure for erotic melancholy. Ferrand takes up the subject again in ch. XXXVII; see nn. 27 and 28 of that chapter for further documentation.

14. [*Lev Lemnius de occult. nat. mirac. c. 43*]: Levinus Lemnius, *Occulta naturae miracula,* bk. II, ch. 42, pp. 264–65: "ex immoderata Venere contingat siccescere, verum calorificis herbis retundi debet eius frigiditas, ne semen genitale plussatis diluatur, atque ad progignendos liberos fiat inefficax, parumque idoneum."

15. Luis Mercado, *De internorum morborum curatione libri IV,* in *Opera,* bk. II, ch. 10, vol. III, p. 585: "Inter quae ad geniturae effluvia et adversus Veneris ludibria in somnis et vigilia, *semen lactucae* plurimum valere scribunt multi: sicut *de rosa hortensi rubra saccharo* condita etiam fertur: cui malo non minus portulaca mansa et comesta remedio esse solet, sicut *melonum* frequentior usus."

16. [*Sect. 10 prob. 1.*]: Aristotle, *Problems,* bk. XX, no. 1 (923a, 9–13), p. 417: "What is the meaning of the saying 'Neither eat nor plant mint in war time?' Is it because it has a chilling effect on the body? Its corruption of semen proves this. . . . And this being similar in nature is contrary to courage and high temper."

Pliny, *Natural History,* bk. XX, ch. 53, vol. VI, p. 87: "Through the same property it is believed to be a hindrance to generation by not allowing the genital fluids to thicken." This was interpreted by later writers to mean dissolving the seed, and therefore it is to be debated whether Pliny is to be grouped with Aristotle or Hippocrates. Pliny neither discusses the chilling effects of mint nor the danger of taking it too often as was claimed for him in the French translation of the *Regimen* of the School of Salerno: *Le Regime de Santé de l'eschole de Salerne, traduit et commente par Maistre Michel le Long, Provinois, Docteur en Medecine* (Paris, 1637), ch. 64, p. 373: "Pline lib. 20. cap. 14 tient pour suspect son usage trop frequent, d'autant qu'a a son dire elle dissout la semence de l'homme, et empesche la generation."

Magnimus is a pseudonym for Arnald of Villanova, *Medicina Salernitana id est conservandae bonae valetudinis praecepta, cum luculenta et succincta Arnoldi Villanovani in singula capita exegesi* (Excudebat Jacobus Stoer, 1599), ch. 61: "De mentha," pp. 259–61: "Est enim ut si qua alia herba, tenuium partium gustu acri, et facultate calida, ex tertio nimirum ordine excalfacientium et secundo siccantium. . . . Hepar enim frigidum et ventriculum iuvat, corroborat et stomachum et concoctionem facit, sedat quoque singulatum, et vomitum phlegmaticum atque sanguineum. . . . Mediocriter item ad Venerem excitat: id quod omnibus accidit, quae humiditatem semicoctam et flatuosam continent . . . et crassus ac melancholicus relinquatur: atque ideirco oportet biliosos ab ea abstinere. . . . Arida vero trita et post cibum sumpta ad concoctionem facit, et lienosos iuvat . . . quodque eius decoctum obsorptum confestim sanguinem e faucibus eiicientes sanet. . . . Huius semen ventrem purgat, et pulmonem laedit."

The foundation for this opposing view, that mint is hot rather than cold and conducive to love, is Dioscorides. Pietro Andrea Mattioli, *Commentarii . . . in libros sex Pedacii Dioscoridis Anazarbei de medica materia* (Venetiis: in officina Erasmiana apud Vincentium Valgrisium, 1558), bk. III, ch. 35, p. 379: "Mentha congita herba est. Calefaciendi, adstringendi, atque exiccandi vim habet. Sistit sanguinem, poto ex aceto succo: tineas in ventre teretes enecat; venerem stimulat." Mattioli comments: "Veneris voluptatibus mentha commendata est: etsi Plinius sine errore lib. XX. cap. xiv. plane contrarium scriptis tradiderit. Huius menthae facultatis causam scite reddidit Galenus libro VI simplicium medicamentorum, ubi de ea iis disserit verbis."

17. [2. *De dieta*.]: Hippocrates, *Regimen*, bk. II: "ἢν πολλάκις ἐσθίῃ τις, τὸν πρόσογον αἰτιῶν τήχει ὥστε ῥέειν, καὶ ἐντείνειν χωλύει." *Oeuvres complètes*, ed. Littré, vol. VI, p. 560: "ἢν πολλάχις ἐσθίῃ τις, τὴν γονὴν τήχει ὥστε ῥέειν, καὶ ἐντείνειν χωλύει."

The principle of dissolving excess seed through the use of herbs and drugs is clearly set out by Rabelais in *Le Tiers Livre*, ch. 31, p. 345, in the advice given by Rondibilis for reducing carnal desire: "Secondement, par certaines drogues et plantes, les quelles rendent l'homme refroidy, maleficié et impotent à generation. L'experience y est en nymphoea heraclia, amerine, saule, chenevé, periclymenos, tamarix, vitex, mandragore, cigüe, orchis le petit, la peau d'un hippopotame, et aultres, les quelles, dedans les corps humains tant par leurs vertus elementaires que par leurs proprietez specificques, glassent et mortifient le germe prolificque, ou dissipent les espritz qui le doibvoient conduire aux lieux destinez par nature, ou oppilent les voyes et conduictz par les quelz povoit estre expulsé, comme, au contraire, nous en avons qui eschauffent, excitent et habilitent l'homme à l'acte venerien." He speaks here not only of the need to reduce sperm, but to dissipate the animal spirits that conduct the sperm to the testicles (see *Le tiers livre*, ch. 4, near the end, p. 107).

18. Oppian of Cilicia, *Halieutica*, trans. A. W. Mair (Loeb, 1928), p. 386. In bk. III, p. 485, he mentions mint, but not in the terms used by Ferrand. There he calls it "weak herb" in relating the myth of the nymph of Cocytus, who was turned into mint by Demeter.

That Ferrand should record this view of mint as a cursed herb is a *non sequitur* in a sequence that has otherwise been entirely favorable because Aristotle implies that mint melts away excess sperm. Ferrand is surely working from an encyclopedia or topicon at this point and presumably forgets himself. The 1640 translator, baffled by the entry, leaves it out entirely.

Likewise, in the passage to follow where Ferrand introduces an argument from Ermanolao Barbaro, then continues with one of his own, Chilmead detects the clumsiness and leaves the reference to Barbaro out as well.

19. *P. Dioscoridae pharmacorum simplicium . . . libri VIII. Io. Ruellio interprete una cum Hermolai Barbari corollariis, et Marci Vergilii, in singula capita censuris sive annotationibus* (Argentorato: apud Jo. Schottum, 1529), p. 165ᵛ: "Theophrastus enim non alio que minthes nomine, pluribus locis mentham indicavit, et ante cum tota Graecia, praesertimque Arcadia: in qua non procul a Pylo nobilis minthes cognomine monsuit: quam Plutonis pellicam poetarum fabulae, et a Proserpina, ut solent pellices semper odisse uxores, in hortemsem mentham transformatam fuisse narrant, aeterno in aeterna planta hominis monumento. Quam vocem Romani magis amantes, quia in ea male habitae ob amorem puellae memoria servaretur, una tantum et altera mutatis literis Graecorum, minthen, menthum et suam fecerunt."

20. [*L. 2. tr. 2. c. 495 L. 3. fen. 20 tr. 1 c. 32 Paul. l. 7 Aet. tetr. 1 Diosc. l. 3. c. 37*]: Avicenna, *Liber canonis*, bk. II, tr. 2, ch. 495, p. 148ʳ, discusses the curative powers of mint, while in bk. II, fen 20, tr. 1, ch. 32, p. 376ᵛ, he presents the cures for the condition discussed in ch. 30: "De multitudine exuberationis spermatis, et humoris, qui praecedit coitum, et humoris, qui praecedit urinam vel qui egreditur post ipsam."

Paul of Aegina discusses mint in several places in bk. VII of his *Opera*.

Aetius of Amida, *Tetrabiblos*, bk. I, sermo 1, p. 31: "Edyosmon, menta, minthe."

Dioscorides, *Pharmacorum simplicium libri VIII*, p. 165, and the passage cited in n. 19, above.

21. [*Herm. Barb. c. 363*]: Ermanolao Barbaro, C. *Plinii naturalis historiae libros castigationes* (Basileae: apud Joannem Valderum, 1534), bk. XIX, ch. 8, p. 285. Ermanolao Barbaro deals at length with questions of nomenclature, whether the plant known to the Greeks as mint was the same known to the Romans by that name, concluding that it was not. The reference is merely an erudite allusion to a dissenting view concerning

botanical classification. The insertion struck the English translator of the Oxford, 1640, edition as irrelevant: he omitted it altogether, especially because Ferrand does not explain Barbaro's reasons. Ferrand's reference to ch. 363 suggests a printer's error, or that he did not consult the 1534 edition, which is divided according to Pliny's book and chapter designations.

22. The reference is to Avicenna, *Liber canonis*, bk. II, fen 20, tr. 1, ch. 28, p. 376^r. Ch. 28 deals with "De exiccativis frigidis spermatis," while ch. 29, p. 376^{r-v}, is entitled "De exiccativis spermatis calidis."

23. Martial, *Epigrams*, XIII, 67: " Inguina torquati tardant hebetaneque palumbi, / Non edat hanc volucrem qui cupit esse salax." See trans. Walter C. A. Ker (Loeb, 1920), pp. 414–15. Martial counsels those who would be sexually vigorous to avoid eating the flesh of this bird. Therefore, Ferrand reasons that it must be a cure for love. Burton confirms Ferrand's recommendation of melons, apples, and grapes, but strictly forbids eating marsh birds, peacock, and pigeons. See J. R. Simon, *Robert Burton (1577–1640) et "L'Anatomie de la Mélancolie"* (Paris: Didier, 1964), p. 276. In Theocritus the ringdove was given as a gift but also seems to cool love, as with Alcippa, in idyll V. 131–32, ed. A. S. F. Gow, 2 vols. (Cambridge: At the University Press, 1950), vol. I, p. 51.

24. [*Theophr. l. 8. de hist. plant. Dioscor. l. 2. Mathiol.*]: *Theophrasti Eresii Graece et Latine opera omnia* (Lugduni Batavorum: ex typographio Henrici ab Plaestens, 1613), p. 173.

Pietro Andrea Mattioli, *Commentarii in libros sex Pedacii Dioscoridis Anazarbei de medica materia*, bk. II, ch. 82, pp. 251–52: "Zea duorum generum est: una simplex, altera in geminis putaminibus grana bina juncta gerit, ob id dicoccos appellatur. Plus quam hordeum alit, ori grata; digeritur in panificia, minus quam triticum alens."

Mattioli comments: " Zeae meminit Galenus lib. VI. simplicium medicamentorum sic inquiens: Zea universa sua facultate quadammodo in medio est tritici, et hordei. Itaque ex illis cognoscatur."

25. Jean Aubery, *L'antidote d'amour*, pp. 135^v–36^v: "Il usera d'herbes tant en salades, qu'en ses bouïllons, comme de l'oseille, laictuë, endive, cychoree, pourpil, cuittes en eau ferree: ses sauces seront le vinaigre, le suc d'orenges aigres, de lymons, ou de citrons: que ses reins soient peu chaude couverts, sur lesquels il portera nuict et jour, une platine de plomb, avec la pudique estrainte du ceston de Venus, ou mesmes en lieu de chemise qu'il endosse la haire, se couchant sur feuilles de nymphee, d'agnus castus, de soules, de roses, tousjours sur l'un de ses costez, de peur d'eshauffer le tronc de la veine cave couchee sur les lombes, d'où ruisselle et bouïllonne la semence: qu'il s'abstienne de la roquette, et de feves comme faisoient les sacrificateurs d'Egypte, qu'il n'use de sel, et toutes autres choses qui enfluent les veines de vents, et que esmeuvent le sang, que si son habitude est plethorique, on luy poura tirer du sang par intervalles, de la basilique droicte, comme de la fontaine ou cause antecedente, et puis de la gauche à raison de la partie enflammer, et que le coeur et le cerveau se secourent mutuellement: que si nostre malade est bilieux la seignee sera interdite, d'autant que le sang sert de bride

à la bile. Toutesfois on pourra un peu esventer la veine pour donner passage aux vapeurs qui groüent dans les veines."

26. Athenaeus, *The Deipnosophists*, trans. Charles Burton Gulick, 7 vols. (Loeb, 1950), vol. VI, p. 35: "And the Athenians were so far removed from apprehending Eros as a god presiding over sexual intercourse, that right in the Academy, which was quite obviously consecrated to Athena, they enshrined Eros and joined his sacrifices with hers. Further, the people of Thespiae celebrate the Erotidia as religiously as Athenians the Athenaea or Elians the Olympia or Rhodians their Halieia. And speaking generally, Eros is honoured at all public sacrifices."

27. [*L. 6. de His. anim. c. 19. & 37.*]: Aristotle, *History of Animals*, bk. IV, ch. 19 (574a); bk. VI, ch. 37 (580b), trans. A. L. Peck (Loeb, 1970), vol. II, p. 309; p. 349: "salt must be supplied before and after lambing, and again in spring." "Some people say, indeed stoutly maintain, that, if they merely lick salt, mice become pregnant, without any copulation." *Salacitas* is the key word here, for Ferrand is assuming that his readers know the common meaning of *salax*: lecherousness or lustfulness. His main point is quickly taken for granted, while the secondary one about beauty is simply a clause introducing the following lines by Catullus.

This entire sequence, however, no doubt derives from Plutarch, *Moralia* (685 D-E), "*Table-Talk*," bk. V, ch. 10, vol. VIII, p. 447: "Well, people hold that salt contributes not a little to generation. . . . Dog-fanciers, at any rate, whenever their dogs are sluggish towards copulation stimulate and intensify the seminal power dormant in the animals by feeding them salty meat and other briny food. Ships carrying salt breed an infinite number of rats, because, according to some authorities, the females conceive without coition by licking salt. But it is more likely that the saltiness imparts a sting to the sexual members and serves to stimulate copulation. . . . I imagine that the poets called Aphroditê 'born of the brine' and have spread the fiction of her origin in the sea by way of alluding to the generative property of salt."

28. [*Catul.*]: Catullus, Poem LXXXVI. 4: "Neque est in tanto corpore mica salis." See *Catullus*, ed. F. W. Cornish, Loeb, p. 162.

29. [*Gal. 6. de loc. aff. c. 6. Arnal. tr. de coitu c. 4. Plut. in qu. Rom.*] [*Parr. 2. c. 6. de reg. san.*]: Galen, *On the Affected Parts*, bk. VI, ch. 6, trans. Siegel, p. 196. In bk. III, ch. 10, p. 90, Galen gives a list of foods that cause melancholy.

Plutarch, *The Roman Questions*, in *Moralia*, vol. IV, p. 143: "Why is it the customary rule that those who are practising holy living must abstain from legumes? [. . .] is it because the windy and flatulent quality of the food stimulates desire?"

Arnald of Villanova, *De coitu*, ch. 4: "De his, quae multiplicant semen, et augmentum faciunt in coitu," in *Opera omnia*, pp. 846–48.

Magnimus and Arnald of Villanova were, as we have explained in n. 16, above, one and the same person. See *Medicina Salernitana id est conservandae valetudinis praecepta*.

For an alternate source recommending against the use of hot spicy foods by those inclined to venery, see Aristotle, *Generation of Animals*, bk. I, ch. 20 (728a), p. 103, where he speaks of the production of semen: "Furthermore, differences of food cause a great difference in the amount of this discharge which is produced: e.g., some pungent foods cause a noticeable increase in the amount."

30. [*L. 9. dipnos.*]: Athenaeus, *The Deipnosophists*, trans. C. B. Gulick, bk. IX, vol. IV, p. 237: "As for goose-livers, which are excessively sought after in Rome, Eubulus mentions them in *The Wreath-sellers*, saying: 'Unless you have the liver or mind of a goose.'"

There is a clear relationship understood between the lists of foods prescribed for the cure of infertility and those forbidden to sufferers of erotic meiancholy. Compare the following list from the English translation of Levinus Lemnius' *Occulta naturae miracula, ac varia rerum documenta, The Secret Miracles of Nature* (London: 1658), p. 26. Ferrand's list has half its elements in common with Lemnius. According to Lemnius, speaking of infertility, the foods that "drive forth the humour" include "Hen-eggs, Pheasants, Thrushes, Blackbirds, Gnat-snappers, Woodcocks, young Pigeons, Sparrows, Partridges, Capons, Pullets, Almonds, Pine-Nuts, Raisins, Currans, all strong Wines, that are sweet and pleasant, especially made of grapes of Italy, which they call Muscadel. But the genitals are erected and provoked by Satyrium, Eryngos, Cresses, Erysimum, Parsnips, Hartichokes, Onions, Turneps, Rapes, Asparagus, candid Ginger, Galanga, Acorns, Scallions, Sea shelfish."

31. Galen, *De alimentorum facultatibus liber*, ed. Kühn, vol. VI, pp. 703–6.

32. Ovid, *The Remedies of Love*, ll. 799–800: "Nec minus erucas aptum est vitare salaces, / Et quicquid Veneri corcora nostra parat." See ed. J. H. Mozley, p. 232.

33. [*L. 18. c. 12*]: The reference is to Pliny, *Natural History*, but undoubtedly from an inaccurate intermediary source. Bk. XVIII, ch. 12, deals with wheat; the appropriate chapters dealing with the chestnut and the chick-pea do not suggest that either was considered "venerian." There are multiple references to oysters, none of them in bk. XVIII. We cannot account for this allusion to Pliny. For the medicinal uses of the wild chick-pea, see bk. XXII, ch. 72, and for the chestnut, see bk. XXIII, ch. 78.

34. [*L. de Amphib. c. 4.*]: Guillaume Rondelet, *L'Histoire entiere des poissons, composée premierement en Latin . . . traduite en françois* (Lyon: par Mace Bonhome, 1558), p. 173: "Davantage le scince est le crocodile terrestre, comme dit Pline, ce qui ne se peut dire du susdit animal, qui n'est semblable ou crocodile, ne de figure de corps, ne de vie: car il vit plus en l'eau qu'en la terre."

35. It would be supererogation to list the works of all the authorities mentioned in Ferrand's text; his list is partially an erudite decoration because none of the names he mentions was within eighty years of his writing, and so rarely were the Arab pharmacologists quoted as from their own works that we would be right to suspect that he has an intermediary source in hand. Given the list, that source could be Gradius in which the recipes of Rhazes, Serapion, and Mesué are found in quantity. Giovanni Matteo Ferrari da Grado's *Praxis in nonum Almansoris* (Vincentius de Portonariis de Tridino de Monte Ferrato, 1527). ch. IX: "De melanco-

lia," pp. lviii^r–lxvii^r, offers several pages of recipes from many Arabic sources and in many different formats frequently employing hellebore.

Andernacus was Johann Winter of Andernach (alias Johannes Guinterius and Jean Gonthier), a prolific writer whose works are, nevertheless, rare today. His best known work in France was *Le Régime de vivre et de prendre médecine que l'on doibt observer en tout temps et principallement en temps de peste* (Poitiers: J. et E. de Marnef, 1544). In this passage Ferrand was more likely referring to his commentary on Hippocrates' *Medicamentis purgatoriis libri*, in *Anatomicorum institutionum libri IV* (Lugduni: Seb. Gryphius, 1541), but we have not been able to examine this work. We have examined without success with regard to recipes of diazinzibar and diasatyrion, Andernacus' *De medicina veteri et nova tum cognoscenda, tum faciunda commentarii duo* (Basileae: ex officina Henricpetrina, 1571), which is an immense work in dialogue form without benefit of index or of chapter headings, discussing all manner of diseases, their conditions, natures and remedies. We note the section, pp. 730–31, on hypochondriacal melancholy, as well as the section on the same beginning, pp. 582 ff., and his division between *melancholia obnoxia* and *insania seu furor*.

Because he is nowhere else mentioned in the treatise, we record here that Serapion was known in the Renaissance in a separate publication: *Serapionis medici Arabis celeberrimi practica studiosis medicinae utilissima: quam postremo Andreas Alpagus . . . translatio nunc primum exit in lucem* (Venetiis: apud Juntas, 1550). The section in question is the "Tractatus septimus . . . continent capitula 37, De antidotis," wherein there are many recipes of the type alluded to by Ferrand.

36. [*P. Aeginet c. 17. l. 3.*]: Paul of Aegina, *The Seven Books*, bk. III, ch. 17, p. 391: "Wherefore, they ought also to be roused to emulation with regard to the objects of their peculiar interest in life; and, upon the whole, their understanding should be diverted to other concerns."

37. Ovid, *The Remedies of Love*, ll. 143–44: "finem qui quaeris Amori, / Cedit Amor rebus, res age, tutus eris." See *The Art of Love, and other Poems*, trans. J. H. Mozley, pp. 188–89.

38. [*Plut. in Erot.*]: The reference suggests a source for this fable in Plutarch's *Dialogue on Love* in the *Moralia*, but while many stories are told illustrating Cupid's attributes, this one is not among them. Rather the source is André Du Laurens, *Des maladies melancholiques et du moyen de les guarir*, p. 36^r. "Les Poëtes chantent par tout que Venus n'a jamais peu attraper avec toutes ses ruses ces trois Deesses, Pallas, Diane et Vesta. Pallas represente le guerre, Diane la chasse, Vesta le jeusne et austerité de vie."

Jean Aubery, *L'antidote d'amour*, p. 131^r, tells the same anecdote giving Homer as his source, namely that these three goddesses were never vanquished by love because of their love of great learning, of the hunt, and of piety.

39. [*Rondel. c. de Amant.*]: Guillaume Rondelet, *Methodus curandorum omnium morborum corporis humani, in tres libros distincta* (Francofurti: apud heredes Andreae Wecheli, 1592), bk. II, ch. 45, p. 239: "Seminis redundantia et otium sunt caussae amoris insani, unde Ovidius: otia si tollas, periere cupidinis arres." The line is from Ovid's *Remedia Amoris*, l. 139, and

should read "Otia si tolles periere cupidinis arcus."

Rabelais in *Le tiers livre*, ch. 31, pp. 345–46, offers as the third treatment of carnal longings "labeur assidu" in order to avoid idleness. He speaks of the hunt, for "ainsi est dicte Diane chaste, laquelle continuellement travaille à la chasse." He speaks of the chastity of warriors and athletes and cites the same example cited by Ferrand from Hippocrates concerning the horseback riding of the Scythians who were impotent "parce que continuellement ilz estoient à cheval et au travail, comme au contraire disent les philosophes, oysiveté estre mere de luxure." He cites further examples from Ovid, Theophrastus, and Diogenes Laertius.

40. Ovid, *The Remedies of Love*, ll. 135–38:

> Ergo ubi visus eris nostra medicabilis arte,
> Fac monitis fugias otia prima meis:
> Haec ut ames, faciunt; haec quae fecere, tuentur;
> Haec sunt iucundi causa, cibusque mali.

See *The Art of Love, and other Poems*, trans. J. H. Mozley, p. 186.

41. [*L. 4 de mor. mul. c. 10. l. 6. de loc. affect. c. 6. Avic. l. 3. en 20. tr. 1. c. 35.*]: Girolamo Mercuriale, *De morbis muliebribus*, bk. IV, ch. 10, p. 156: "Exercitationes moderate conveniunt, omnes animi motus, sive ad iram, sive ad laetitiam vitandi."

Galen, *On the Affected Parts*, bk. VI, trans. Siegel, p. 197.

Plato, in *Laws*, bk. VIII (841A), vol. II, p. 165, discusses means for controlling "lawless Love" and proposes that "One ought to put the force of pleasures as far as possible out of gear, by diverting its increase and nutriment to another part of the body by means of exercise."

Avicenna, *Liber canonis*, bk. III, fen 20, tr. 1, ch. 35, p. 377^r: "De regimine eius quem laedit coitus, et dimissio eius." In discussing various sexual diseases, such as satyriasis and nocturnal emission, Avicenna invariably prescribes rest and sleep.

Marsilio Ficino, *Commentary on Plato's Symposium*, Speech VII, ch. 11, p. 168: "It is important to use exercise, often to the point of perspiration, by which the pores of the body may be opened, for expurgation to be achieved."

42. Aristotle, *Problems*, bk. IV, ch. 11 (877b), trans. W. S. Hett, vol. I, p. 117: "Why are men who continually ride more inclined to sexual intercourse? Is it because owing to the heat and movement their condition is the same as during that of intercourse? So owing to the growth of the private parts in increasing age these parts grow larger. So owing to the continual movement caused by riding their bodies develop large pores, and so are inclined to sexual intercourse."

43. Hippocrates, *Of Airs, Waters and Places*: "῝Οκου ἱππάζονται μάλιστα καὶ πυκνότατα, ἐχεῖ λαγνεύειν κάκιστοί εἰσι," and "εὐνουχοειδέστατοι τῶν ἀνθρώπων." *Oeuvres complètes*, ed. Littré, vol. II, pp. 80–81. The original texts read: "῝Ακου γὰρ ἱππάζονται μάλιστα καὶ πυκνότατα, ἐχεῖ πλεῖστοι ὑπὸ κεδμάτων καὶ ἰσχιάδων καὶ ποδαγριῶν ἁλίσκονται, καὶ λαγνεύειν κάκιστοί εἰσιν," and "εὐνουχοειδέστατοί εἰσιν ἀνθρώπων."

44. [*Tertul. l de spectat. Cyprian. l .2 epist.*]: Tertullian, *De spectaculis*, trans. T. R. Glover (Loeb, 1960), pp. 257, 259: "The theatre is, properly speak-

ing, the shrine of Venus; and that was how this kind of structure came to exist in the world. For often the censors would destroy the theatres at their very birth; they did it in the interests of morals, for they foresaw that great danger to morals must arise from the theatre's licentiousness."
"So the theatre of Venus is also the house of Liber (Bacchus). For there were other stage plays to which they suitably gave the name Liberalia (Dionysia among the Greeks), not only dedicated to Liber, but instituted by Liber. And quite obviously Liber and Venus are the patrons of the arts of the stage. Those features of the stage peculiarly and especially its own, that effeminacy of gesture and posture, they dedicate to Venus and Liber, wanton gods, the one in her sex, the other in his dress; while all that is done with voice and song, instrument and book, is the affair of the Apollos and the Muses, the Minervas and Mercuries."

St. Cyprian, *Letters*, trans. Sister Rose Bernard Donna (Washington D.C., Catholic University of America Press, 1964), pp. 5–6: "I think that it is fitting neither to the Divine Majesty nor to evangelical discipline that the respect and honor of the Church should be defiled by such base and infamous contamination. For since in the law men are forbidden to wear women's clothing and are judged accursed if they do so, how much greater is the offense not only to wear the garments of women, but also by gesture to imitate the unseemly, the unmanly, and the effeminate, in the office of an instructor of a shameless art.

"Let no one excuse himself that he himself has withdrawn from the theater when he is still teaching this to others. For he cannot be considered to have withdrawn who has substituted others and who supplies many proxies for himself alone, instructing them contrary to the plan of God and teaching how a man may be weakened into a woman, and sex may be changed by art, and the divine image may be pleasing to the devil, who stains it through the sin of the corrupt and effeminate body."

These two texts are of particular interest for their attitudes concerning theater. St. Cyprian is counseling members of the religious community of his time to avoid acting in plays, even out of material necessity. On the whole, however, they are rather remote in spirit from Ferrand's context.

45. T. H. White, *The Bestiary: A Book of Beasts* (New York: G. P. Putnam's Sons, 1960), pp. 53–54: "Vulpis the fox . . . is a fraudulent and ingenious animal. When he is hungry and nothing turns up for him to devour, he rolls himself in red mud so that he looks as if he were stained with blood. Then he throws himself on the ground and holds his breath, so that he positively does not seem to breathe. The birds, seeing that he is not breathing and that he looks as if he were covered with blood with his tongue hanging out, think he is dead and come down to sit on him. Well, thus he grabs them and gobbles them up." White mentions that cats and rats played the parts in certain medieval versions and that it was told of leopards and monkeys by Francis Meres in *Palladis Tamia* (London: P. Short for Cuthbert Burbie, 1598).

46. [*Albert. Arnal. de Vallan. tr. de venef.*]: Albert the Great, *De mirabilibus mundi*, in *De secretis mulierum libellus*, p. 188: "Ut mulier cum aliquo

adulterare non possit, incide de capillis eius, et pulverem illorum ibi super feretrum sparge, ante tamen unge feretrum cum melle, et mox coëas cum muliere, et cum volueris solvere, ex tuis capillis fac similiter." This work, however, is no longer attributed to Albert the Great.

Arnald of Villanova, *De venenis*, in *Opera omnia*, pp. 1531–62.

Dioscorides, *De medica materia libri sex, Joanne Ruellio . . . interprete* (Lugduni: apud Joan. Francis de Gabiano, 1555), bk. VI, ch. 8: "De venenato Heracliae melle."

47. Theocritus, Idyll XXVII. 3: "κενὸν τὸ φίλομα λέγουσιν." ed. A. S. F. Gow, vol. I, p. 3.

48. [*Hesichius Varinus. Aristoph. in Avib. Foes. in l. 5. Epid. sec. 1*]: Hesychius of Alexandria, *Lexicon*, s.v. "βλιμάζειν," ed. M. Schmidt (Amsterdam: Adolf M. Hakkert, n.d.), vol. I, p. 381.

Aristophanes, *The Birds*, l. 530: "βλιμάζοντες," in *Aristophanes*, trans. B. B. Rogers (Loeb, 1961), vol. II, p. 180.

Hippocrates, *Epidemics*, bk. V, ch. 1: "ἐβλιμάσθη," ed. Littré, vol. V, p. 204.

Hippocrates, *Opera omnia*, ed. Anuce Foës, p. 234.

49. Avicenna, *Liber canonis*, bk. III, fen 1, tr. 5, ch. 23, p. 206^V: "Et sit casus eorum in disceptationibus ipsorum, et occupationibus, et controversiis, et universaliter in rebus negociosis. Illud nam facit eos fortasse oblivisci illius, quod est causam macrefactionis eorum, aut ingenietur ut ipsi diligant aliud ab eo, quod diligunt, ex eis quae lex permittit."

Paul of Aegina, *The Seven Books*, bk. III, sec. 17, p. 391: "Some must also be attacked with fear; for, while they think of nothing but love, the affection is difficult to remove. Wherefore, they ought also to be roused to emulation with regard to the objects of their peculiar interest in life; and, upon the whole, their understanding should be diverted to other concerns."

50. [*Mercat. l. 2 de morb. mul. Roder. à Castro l. 4. medicopol. c. 2.*]: Luis Mercado, *De internorum morborum curatione libri IV*, in *Opera*, bk. II, offers merely hints to this effect in the various chapters on the tickling of the private parts and uterine fury. More apt is the following from *De internorum morborum*, bk. I, ch. 17, vol. III, p. 103: "atque hi salutaria suggerant, et recta admoneant, subinde objurgent, increpent, absterreant, et rem amatam indecoris verbis notent." Such recommendations were commonplace in earlier treatises concerned with the treatment of melancholy diseases.

Rodrigo de Castro, *Medicus-politicus*, bk. IV, ch. 2, p. 223: "Sed quodnam erit remedium contra philtrum sive oculorum veneficium? Occupatio mentis in rebus gravioribus, lectio bonorum librorum, preces ad Deum ut nos liberet a pravis cogitationibus, saepiusque in mentem revocare ea, quae indignam faciunt foeminam, ut ametur, fugacitas nimirum pulchritudinis, menstrua, et quod tandem futura sit vermium esca, ex cuius putri cadaveris medulla spinae, ut plerique scribunt, serpens terribilis enascetur. His accedat quod dum forma diligitur, negligitur fama, abbreviatur vita, bona et honor amittuntur, ac in iram divinam incurritur."

51. [*Avic. c. de coitu inhonesto.*]: Ferrand is probably referring to Avicenna, *Liber canonis*, bk. III, fen 20, tr. 1, "*De universalibus appetitu coeundi,*" and esp. to ch. 2, p. 373^{r-v}: "De nocumento coitus, et dispositionibus eius, et malitia figurarum," and to ch. 15: "De diminutione coitus."

Bernard of Gordon, *Lilium medicinae*, pt. 2, ch. 20: "De amore, qui hereos dicitur," p. 218: "Et si rationi non est obediens, et si esset iuvenis, quod esset sub ferula, tunc frequenter et fortiter flagelletur, donec totus incipiat foetere; deinde nuntientur sibi valde tristabilia, ut maior tristitia minorem habeat obfuscare."

For an additional treatment, see Valesco de Taranta, who recommends similar severity in *Epitome operis perquam utilis morbis curandis in septem congesta libros* (Lugduni: apud Joan. Tornaesium, et Gulielmum Gazeium, 1560), p. 36: "Si videatur adesse humor adustus, purgentur, ut in cap. de melancholia dicetur. Si sit in adolescentia prima, cedatur virgis, et incarceretur, atque illic nutriatur pane et aqua donec veniam petat."

52. [*Mercur. l. I. de var. lect. c. 19*]: Girolamo Mercuriale, *Variarum lectionum libri IV* (Venetiis: sumptibus Pauli et Antonii Meieti fratres librarii Patavini, 1571), bk. I, ch. 19, pp. 22–23: "Neque vero adolescentes tantum (ut ait Celsus) infibulatos, verum etiam adultos, et quod maiori admiratione dignum verpos ac recutitos credo."

Laurent Joubert, *La premiere et seconde partie des erreurs populaires touchant la médecine et le régime de santé* (Paris: Chez Claude Micard, 1587), bk. V, ch. 4, p. 215: "Ainsi pourroit bien faire une folle à son cas, duquel les bors sont de mesme substance, que le bout des aureilles, ou que le prepuce de l'homme. Ainsi faisoit on anciennement l'infibulation ou boucleure, comme Celse le recite, afin que lés garçons n'abusassent des femmes, avant l'aage competant. On tire avant le prepuce, dit il, ou bout duquel on passe une esguille enfilee. Le fil demeure, qu'on remue tous les jours pour frayer les trous, jusques à tant qu'il s'y face une legiere cicatrice à l'entour. Puis on y met une boucle que l'on peut oster et remettre sans douleur."

For further information on the practice, see Eric John Dingwall, *Male Infibulation* (London: J. Bale and Sons Ltd., 1925).

53. Martial, *Epigrams*, bk. VII, Epigram 82. 5–6: "Dum ludit media popula spectante palaestra: / Heu! cecidit misero fibula, verpus erat." See trans. Walter C. A. Ker (Loeb, 1919), pp. 478–79. Martial refers here to the great sheath worn by comic actors to exaggerate the phallus, or to a phallic sheath worn by comic actors and singers designed to prevent them from sexual activities in order to save their voices. The fibula was also apparently worn by slaves. See XI. 75: "Your slave bathes with you, Caelia, covered with a sheath of brass; to what end, I pray, seeing he is no harper or flutist in the chorus?" XIV. 215, entitled "Fibula" (a singer's clasp), speaks of harpers and comedians undoing the clasp for money. See also Juvenal, *Satire* VI. 379 ff.

54. [*Gal. l. 6. de loc. aff c. 6. Avic. l. 3. Fen. 20. tr. 1. ca. 25. 32. 47*]: Galen, *On the Affected Parts*, trans. Siegel, p. 192: "Priapism is, however, an increase in length and circumference of the male genitalia without sexual desire

and without the acquired increase in heat which some people experience in recumbent position."

Avicenna, *Liber canonis*, bk. III, fen 1, tr. 5, ch. 24, p. 207^r. This is his chapter on the cures for melancholy.

For ch. 25 of Avicenna, see Ferrand ch. V, n. 2, above, where it is extensively quoted.

Bk. II, fen 20, tr. 1, ch. 32, p. 376^v, deals with the cures relating to "De multitudine exuberationis spermatis, et humoris, qui praecedit coitum, et humoris, qui praecedit urinam vel qui egreditur post ipsam." Ch. 37, p. 377^r, is concerned with "De multitudine erectionis absque desiderio, et de priapismo."

55. [*Rhazis 24 cont.*]: Rhazes, *Liber continens*, bk. XXIV. Ferrand's reference is, in fact, from the margins of the edition of Avicenna as cited in the preceding note.

The Thesmophoria was a festival celebrated in ancient Greece; it was held in October and attended only by women, a festival in honor of Demeter with the purpose of assuring the fertility of the fields. Agnus castus was employed during the event, being placed under matresses and pillows, in order to quell sexual desire. See ch. XXXII, n. 1 below.

56. For references to the relevant passages in Bernard of Gordon and Avicenna, see ch. XXXIII, n. 3, below.

57. Ovid, *The Remedies of Love*, ll. 441–44:

> Hortor et ut pariter binas habeatis amicas:
> Fortior est, plures si quis habere potest.
> Secta bipartito cum mens discurrit utroque,
> Alterius vires subtrahit alter Amor.

See trans. J. H. Mozley (Loeb, 1962), pp. 230–31.

Jean Aubery, *L'antidote d'amour*, pp. 127^r–28^r, mentions this same passage in Ovid and gives his own approbation to the idea that loving another woman, perhaps of less beauty and spirit, is an effective way to drive out the memories of a hopeless former love.

58. [*Gal. 2 de motu muscul. Plutarq.*]: Galen, *De motu musculorum*, bk. II, ed. Kühn, vol. IV, pp. 440 ff. Galen discusses voluntary and involuntary motion. The comparison is a remote one; Ferrand seeks to demonstrate the formation of moral and behavioral habits through a description of the involuntary movement of the eye muscles. Ironically, he would here seem to be criticizing those lovers who lack sincerity and constancy to one person by drifting compulsively from partner to partner—unsuitable behavior even as a cure for erotic love simply because it is yet another form of deviant eroticization. His specifications circumscribe, in implicit moral terms, a sense of moderation in sexual matters that serves him throughout the treatise as a moral norm.

59. [*L. 7. Confes.*]: St. Augustine, *Confessions*, bk. VIII, ch. 5: "Dum servitur libidini facta est consuetudo, et dum consuetudini non resistitur, facta est necessitas." See trans. W. Watts (Loeb, 1977), vol. I, p. 424.

XXXI. Surgical Remedies for the Prevention of Love Melancholy

1. Galen, *On the Affected Parts*, bk. VI, trans. Siegel, pp. 196–97.
2. [*Avic. l. 3. Fen. 20. tr. I. c. 27. & 39. Rhaz. l. divi. c. 80*]: Avicenna, *Liber canonis*, bk. III, fen 20, tr. 1, ch. 27, p. 376^V, deals with the cures of overwhelming desire (see ch. 25, p. 375^V), and establishes phlebotomy as one of the cures: "Illius quae est a repletione calida curatio est phlebotomia, et alleviatio cibi, et assumptio infrigidantium."

Ch. 39, p. 377^{r-V}, recommends bloodletting as a cure for priapism.

Rhazes, *Divisionum liber* (Basileae: in officina Henrichi Petri, 1594: rpt. Bruxelles, 1973), ch. 80, p. 403: "De nocumento quod fit ex multitudine desiderij coitus et spermatis": "Fit illud propter multitudinem sanguinis, cuius signa sunt, virtus corporis, et rubedo coloris, et paucitas debilitatis super multitudinem coitus, et pollutionis. Et cura eius est, phlebotomia, et solutio ventris, et minoratio cibi." Avicenna and Rhazes, however, do not direct the physician to specific areas of the body as Ferrand seems to imply.

Rabelais, in *Le tiers livre*, ch. 31, p. 345, provides a close parallel to this passage suggesting that by intensive labor, rather than by phlebotomy, carnal desire can be reduced, "car en icelluy est faicte si grande dissolution du corps, que le sang, qui est par icelluy espars pour l'alimentation d'un chascun membre, n'a temps ne loisir ne faculté de rendre celle resudation seminale et superfluité de la tierce concoction." Sperm was considered by Aristotle, and presumably by Rabelais, to be a by-product of digestion and the assimilation of food, a view differing radically from the ancient idea that sperm was a spiritual substance drawn from the brain or from all parts of the body and that possessed the capacity to transport the characteristics of the parent to the offspring. For a summary of ancient and Renaissance views concerning the nature of the seed, see Pierre Darmon, *Le mythe de la procréation à l'âge baroque* (Paris: Editions du Seuil, 1981), p. 12. Galen, following Hippocrates, believed it was derived from the brain and mixed with the most subtle humors of the body. It was on this basis that fears arose concerning the loss of this vital body fluid, while it was on the basis of sperm as a form of corrupting excrement that coitus was recommended as a cure for love melancholy. Ferrand does not deal with the problem, either because it did not occur to him, or because he had no solution for it. Here he is concerned with sperm as a waste product of digestion insofar as it produces noxious vapors that rise through the spine and corrupt the faculties of the brain in a way that parallels the vapors of adust biles. That sperm could be reduced through operations resembling those employed to eliminate the offending black bile had obvious appeal to physicians concerned with attacking the material causes of this disease of the soul.
3. [*Mars. Ficin. c. 11. orat. 7. in symp. Plat.*]: Marsilio Ficino, *Commentary on Plato's Symposium*, Speech VII, ch. 11, p. 168: "The blood is to be drawn often."

Jean Aubery, in *L'antidote d'amour*, p. 136^{r-V}, states, however, that if the patient is not sanguine certain precautions are in order: "que si son habitude est plethorique, on luy pourra tirer du sang par intervalles, de la basilique droicte . . . que si nostre malade est bilieux, la seignee sera interdite, d'autant que le sang sert de bride à la bile."

4. [*Paul. l. 3. c. 56 Aet. tetr. 3. ser. 4. c. 32 Rondel. c. 56. l. 3 Meth. Moschio c. 128. Arnal. de regim. san. c. 28*]: Paul of Aegina, *Opera*, bk. III, ch. 56: "De satyriasi," p. 386: "sanguinem igitur protinus dimittere convenit, victu uti tenui, et abstemio." Paul of Aegina is discussing female superexcitation, in the tradition of Soranus and Aetius of Amida.

Aetius of Amida, *Tetrabiblos*, bk. III, sermo 4, ch. 32, p. 657 f.: "Pharmaca et edulia eorum, qui flavae bilis influxu infestantur."

Guillaume Rondelet, *Methodus curandorum omnium morborum corporis humani*, in *Opera omnia medica* (Genevae: apud Petrum et Jacobum Chouët, 1620), bk. III, ch. 56, p. 548: "De priapismo."

Moschion, *De morbis muliebribus liber*, pp. 27–29. See also ch. XXX, n. 2.

Arnald of Villanova, *Commentum super regimen Salernitanum*, in *Medicina Salernitana, id est conservanda bonae valetudinis praecepta, cum . . . Arnaldi Villanovani in singula capita exegesi* (Roterodami: ex officina Arnoldi Leert, 1599).

5. *Herodotus*, trans. A. D. Godley, vol. I, pp. 136–37: "So they turned back, and when they came on their way to the city of Ascalon in Syria, most of the Scythians passed by and did no harm, but a few remained behind and plundered the temple of Heavenly Aphrodite. This temple, as I learn from what I hear, is the oldest of all the temples of the goddess. . . . But the Scythians who pillaged the temple, and all their descendants after them, were afflicted by the goddess with the 'female' sickness: insomuch that the Scythians say that this is the cause of their disease, and that those who come to Scythia can see there the plight of the men whom they call 'Enareis.' "

The first of the three Greek words in Ferrand's text is not from Herodotus. They signify a lack of manly courage, to be hermaphrodite, to lack virility. The word *enareis* is of unknown origin, presumably a Scythian word describing priests of the cult of Aphrodite, a word that took on, in the context of their virile culture, pejorative connotations. Herodotus states in bk. IV of the *Histories*, vol. II, p. 265: "The Enareis, who are epicene, say that Aphrodite gave them the art of divination, which they practise by means of lime-tree bark." The explanation of their epicene condition by the cutting of the vessels behind the ears is not from Herodotus, but from Hippocrates.

6. [*L. de aere, loc & ac. L. de genit.*]: Hippocrates, *Of Airs, Waters and Places*, See *Oeuvres complètes*, ed. Littré, vol. II, pp. 79, 81; *Hippocrates*, trans. W. H. S. Jones (Loeb, 1972), vol. I, pp. 127, 129: "At the beginning of the disease [impotence] they cut the vein behind each ear. When the blood has ceased to flow faintness comes over them and they sleep. Afterwards they get up, some cured and some not. Now, in my opinion, by this treatment the seed is destroyed. For by the side of the ear are veins, to cut which causes impotence, and I believe that these are the veins which they cut. After this treatment, when the Scythians approach

a woman but cannot have intercourse, at first they take no notice and think no more about it. But when two, three or even more attempts are attended with no better success, thinking that they have sinned against Heaven they attribute thereto the cause, and put on women's clothes, holding that they have lost their manhood. So they play the woman, and with the women do the same work as women do."

Hippocrates, *On Generation*. See *Oeuvres complètes*, ed. Littré, vol. VII, p. 473.

7. Andreas Vesalius, *Opera omnia anatomica et chirurgica, cura Hermanni Boer-haave . . . et Bernhard Sidgfried Albini* (Lugduni Batavorum: apud Joannem du Vivie, et Joan. et Herm. Verbeck, 1725), vol. I, pp. 372, 449: "A propaginibus in mesenterium sparsis, interdum cum y seminalibus venis et arteriis surculos ad testes usque deductos me animadvertisse arbitror. Huiusmodi itaque sexti paris nervorum cerebri est series."

Battista Fregoso, *Contramours*, bk. II, p. 158: "Et pource qu'avec la semence est meslée la grande quantité de spiritueuse substance, qui procede du coeur comme de sa propre source, et en partie aussi du cerveau: la personne qui a les veines de derriere l'aureille, couppées, ou autrement viciées (lesquelles partans de la teste viennent aboutir aux rongnons) le plussouvent (ce dit Hippocras) demeure brehaigne et stérile."

8. [*L. 3. Fen 20 tr. 1. c. 25*]: Avicenna, *Liber canonis*, bk. III, fen 20, tr. 1, ch. 25. This is the chapter on excessive desire previously cited.

XXXII. Pharmaceutical Means for the Prevention of Love Melancholy

1. Agnus castus is the chaste tree, the seeds of which were believed to have the power to preserve chastity. Robert Burton, in *The Anatomy of Melancholy*, pt. III, sec. 2, memb. 5, subs. 1, ed. Floyd Dell and Paul Jordan-Smith, p. 768, resorts to Aelian for an explanation of how the Athenian women, during the solemn feast of the Thesmophoria, placed agnus castus in their beds to quell venal desires during the nine-day period of abstention. Cassia from the orient was popular in Renaissance Europe as a purgative. The black pulp is used and is classified as hot and moist in the first degree. Catholicons, as the name implies, are general tonics and good for nearly all maladies of the body. Several recipes survive from the period, most of them involving a large number of simples. The Diacatholicon Nicolai is in the *London Pharmacopoeia*, p. 83. We have chosen this work as our standard reference for the established pharmaceutical simples and compounds used in Ferrand because it is a complete and accurate work, because it is the most familiar to English readers, and because it is readily available in facsimile. It will be cited as *L. P.* with a page reference. *Pharmacopoeia Londinensis 1618*, Intro. by George Urdang, Hollister Pharmaceutical Library Number Two (Madison: State Historical Society of Wisconsin, 1944). Diaprum is Diaprunum simplex, rectius lenitivum Nicolai with a base of 100 ripe damascene plums mixed with a number of flowers and other fruit pulps; it is an

electuary: *L. P.*, p. 82. Tryphere Persica is a syrup with a peach flower base to which medicinal powders can be added. The recipe for "Syrupus ex floribus persicorum" is in *L. P.*, p. 27.

2. [*Paul. Aegi. l. 3. c. 36 Aet. tetr. 3. ser. 4. c. 32*]: Paul of Aegina, *Opera*, bk. III, ch. 36.

    Aetius of Amida, *Tetrabiblos*, bk. III, sermo 4, ch. 32; see ch. 31, n. 4.

    Avicenna treats this topic in the *Liber canonis*, bk. III, fen 1, tr. 4, ch. 20, p. 205^{r-v}.

3. Arnald of Villanova, "De regimine caste viventium," ch. 28 of *De regimine sanitatis*, in *Opera omnia*, p. 749. The same passage from Arnald is cited again in ch. XXXIX, stating his preference for emetics over dejectory purges.

4. [*L. 3. fen 20. tr. 1. c. 27, 33*]: Avicenna, *Liber canonis*, bk. III, fen 20, tr. 1, p. 376^{r-v}. Ch. 27 gives a list of medications for the cure of excessive desire; ch. 28 offers recipes for the drying of cold sperm; ch. 29, for the drying of warm sperm. Ferrand deals with the point at greater length in ch. XXXIX and cautions against the use of any foods or medications that are hot in nature, that feed the blood, and thereby increase the quantity of seed.

5. ℞.   Rad. buglos. borrag. & cichor. ana ℥. 5. fol. endiv. acetos. portul. lupul. & lactue. ana m. 1. semin. 4. frigid. major & minor. ana ℈. 1. semin. viticis & papav. albi ana ℈. ii. passul. corinth. flor. nenufar. & viol. an. p. i. decoq. ad lib. i. In colat. dissol. syrupi de pomis redolent. viol. & nenuf. ana ℥. i. & ½ misce fiat julep. clarif. & aromat. ℈. i. santal. albi pro tribus aut 4. dosibus matutinis.

6. [*C. 117. 115 l. 2.*]: Dioscorides *De medica materia libri sex*, bk. II, ch. 128, p. 180: "Lactucae: Epotum semen, assiduas libidinum imaginationes in somno, compescit, et veneri refregatur."

    The point is corroborated by Levinus Lemnius in *The Secret Miracles of Nature*, pp.163–64: "Also lettice is good, for that it be carried into the veins before all other meat, it cools the heat of the blood, and abates the hot distemper of the liver and of the Heart, so that the immoderate use of it will bridle venerous actions, and extinguish the desire of lust, as Cucumber, Pompions, Purslane, and Camphor do." Such was the power of lettuce, cucumber, and camphor that Lemnius warns further on: "But the coldnesse of it must be corrected with heating hearbs, least it weaken the generative seed too much, and make it uneffectual to beget children, and altogether unfit for it."

7. [*Homil. 5. sup. hexam.*]: St. Basil, *Exegetic Homilies*, "On the Hexaemeron," trans. Agnes Clare Way (Washington, D.C.: The Catholic University of America Press, 1963), pp. 71–72: "Some also have already dulled even their mad appetites with hemlock, and with hellebore have banished many of the long continued sufferings." For an edition contemporary with Ferrand, see *Opera omnia . . . Graece et Latine* (Parisiis: sumptibus Claudii Morelli, 1618), *Hexameron, homilia quinta*: "*De germinatione terrae*," pp. 58–59.

    Ferrand's intermediary source, however, is Girolamo Mercuriale, *De morbis muliebrium libri IV*, bk. IV, ch. 10, p. 157: "Usus herbarum refrigerantium convenit, lactucae, endivie, nympheae, agni casti et usus cicutae hac in re probatur. Nam Basilius, qui fuit et insignis medicus et theologus, 5. homilia supra Hexameron, scribit se vidisse quosdam quae potione cicutae extinxerunt rabiosas cupiditates. Quod, tametsi intelligi potest, de appetitu ciborum, tamen magis placet, ut intelligatur de appetitu venereo, nam relatum est, sacerdotes Athenienses cicutae usu, libidinis incendia extinguere consuevisse."

8. The possibility of rendering hot and dry elements suitable for treating a hot and dry disease by tempering them with buttermilk or other cool, moist elements led to complex philosophical discussions concerning the occult natures of herbs. Could purges, that were for the most part made up of spicy and dry elements, produce only the purgative effect without affecting the quality and condition of the humors as well? Such possibilities had to be explored in contradiction to the theory of treatment by opposites. One recourse was to play ingredients against one another in the compounds so that hot, dry purgatives could work absolutely as purges, yet be counteracted in other theatres by the cool, moist hosting compound; this principle was at work in the formulation of many of the purgative electuaries. Quercetanus built up many of his compounds on a buttermilk base, for example.

9. Girolamo Mercuriale, *De morbis muliebribus libri IV*, bk. IV, ch. 10, p. 157: "Praeter victum, sunt et alia quae in usu sunt remedia, et quia in his mulieribus, saepe abundant humores calidi et fervidi, propterea expurgandi sunt ante caetera, illi humores." See also n. 7, above.

10. ℞. lent. palust. p. 5. sem. lact. port. & papau. albi ana ℈. i. rosar. & nenuf. ana p. 5. coquant. in qua & cum q. s. sacchari fiat syrup. quo utatur singul. diebus.

11. [*C. 26. l. 2. pract. med.*]: Arnald of Villanova, *Breviarium practicae*, bk. II, ch. 26. In the edition we have consulted the reference is to ch. 40: "De extinguenda libidini, et voluntate coeundi removenda," in *Opera omnia* (1585), p. 1283, but in other editions, e.g., 1520, the chapter number is correct.

12. Jean Fernel, *La pathologie*, p. 72. There are many elements that have an influence upon the body for regulating states too cold, dry, or hot, including those caused by passions of the soul: "Les bains, dont les uns rafraischissent et humectent, les autres échauffent et humectent, et d'autres échauffent et desseichent, telles sont les eaux saulpherics, nitreuses, alumineuse, et marines, lesquelles impriment au corps les qualitez dont elles sont doüées. Semblablement les onguents et les emplastres appliquez par dehors, nous communiquent leurs vertus, qu'ils vont influans, et enfonçans par les pores de la peau, quand notre chaleur les excites."

13. [*Gal. 6. de loc. aff c. 6. L. de san. tu. L. 9. sec. loc. L. 14. Meth. med.*]: Galen, *On the Affected Parts*, bk. VI, ch. 6, contains no specific discussion of medications.

Galen, *De sanitate tuenda*, ed. Kühn, vol. VI, pp. 390 ff. See esp. bk. VI, chs. 3 and 14.

Galen, *De methodo medendi*, ed. Kühn, vol. X, pp. 951 ff. This is the source of the following recipe.

For Galen's refrigerating ointment, see *L. P.*, p. 128: "Unguentum infrigidans, Galeni. ℞. Cerae albae uncias quatuor. Olei Rosati Omphacini libram unam. Liquentur in duplici vase et transfusa in vas aliud, sensim effusa aqua fregidissima ac subinde mutata diù subigantur, postremo adde Aceti clari et tenuis parum."

One camphoreum recipe by Mesué is his "Trochisci de camphora," *L. P.*, p. 101. It calls for 2 scruples of camphor as well as for licorice, the four major cold seeds, manna, and rose water, and other ingredients. The "unguentum rosatum Mesué" is also in the *L. P.*, p. 130.

Jean Aubery, *L'antidote d'amour*, pp. 137ᵛ–138ʳ: "pendant l'usage des bains, on luy oindra les reins et tout le bas du ventre d'huile de ranes de pavot, de semence de ioschiame, ou on les reduira en onguent en ceste façon. Prenez huiles de nymphee, de ranes, de pavot de chacun deux onces, de la pierre de jaspe une dragme, des semences de laictues et de ioschiame blanc de chacun une demy dragme avec la cire blanche, on incorporera le tout, et reduira-on en consistance d'onguent, duquel on usera comme dessus jay dit."

André Du Laurens, *Des maladies melancholiquies, et du moyen de les guarir*, in *Toutes les oeuvres*, p. 32ᵛ: "Les remedes externes sont ou universels, ou particuliers; les universels sont les bains. Galien se vente d'avoir guary plusieurs melancholiques par le seul usage du bain d'eau tiede: ou bien on pourra, si tout le corps est extremement sec, et que la peau soit fort rude, en faire un artificiel avec les racines de guimauve, fueilles de mauve, violettes, laictues, cichorées, semences de melon, de courges, d'orge, fleurs de violes: on se baignera bien souvent, et doit-on demeurer long-temps dans le bain sans provoquer les sueurs. Estant dans le bain on pourra avoir deux sachets remplis d'amandes douces et ameres pilées grossierement, et de semence de melon, et s'en frotter toute la peau. Si tu veux bien faire ton bain il faut jetter le soir l'eau chaude dans la cuve, et la laisser fumer toute la nuict, puis le matin tu t'y mettras dedans. Il y a plusieurs praticiens qui font des bains du seul laict, comme on fait souvent aux ectiques."

For further information on the use of refrigerating ointments in the lumbar region, see Luis Mercado, *De internorum morborum curatione libri IV*, in *Opera*, bk. II, ch. 10, vol. III, p. 586. See also ch. XXXVI, n. 20, below.

14. Paul of Aegina, *The Seven Books*, bk. I, sec. 37: "On redundance of semen," p. 48: "Observare tamen convenit, ne dum tanto certatim studio lumbos refrigerare molimur, renes iacturam faciant." Aegineta discusses the cooling herbs such as house-leek, nightshade, the navelwort or fleawort, lettuce juice, linseed boiled in water, rue, and the chaste tree used variously in rubbing lotions.

15. [*L. 2. tr. 5. c. 1.*]: Avenzoar (Ibn Zuhr), *Liber Theizir*, bk. II, tr. 5, ch. 1: "De sterilitate propter malam complexionem," esp. p. civʳb, where the negative effects of vinegar are discussed at length.

Hippocrates, *On Regimen in Acute Diseases*: "ὑστεραλγὲς γάρ ἐστιν." *Oeuvres complètes*, ed. Littré, vol. II, pp. 358–59.

In the discussion to follow concerning vinegar, a distinction should be made between internal and external uses. Ferrand cautions here against the use of vinegar in the vaginal douche, but in ch. XXXIX he allows, without special notice, a pessary made with "diacodion mixed with a little vinegar and the juice of the black nightshade." Luis Mercado contributes the following to the debate on the use of vinegar, *De internorum morborum curatione*, in *Opera*, bk. I, ch. 17, vol. III, p. 98: "[in margin: *Acetum an melancholicis humoribus conterendis aliquo modo prosit*]."

Jourdain Guibelet, "*Discours troisiesme de l'humeur melancholique*," ch. 4, pp. 233^r–234^r: "Ce n'est sans cause donc que la cholere noire est comparée au vinaigre, veu qu'il y a une telle affinité entre l'un et l'autre. Le vinaigre qui n'est que moderement fort, ne monstre avec son aigreur qu'une acrimonie moderée, mais estant distillé il consomme les perles et les metaux. [. . .] [Black bile] quand d'un feu violent elle a esté consommée et peut estre bruslée plusieurs fois, principalement si elle a la bile pour matiere, elle ronge et mange les parties comme il appert aux chancres ulcerez. Le grand Hippocrate a donné fondement a cete doctrine, car il dit que le vinaigre enfle la melancholie et luy sert de levain. Et partant qu'il est contraire aux melancholiques."

His reasoning is not specific, but Aubery's long discussion suggests that bitter, acidic vomit also seems to loosen and purge the earthy qualities of melancholy. In effect, the corrosive and dissolving properties of vinegar, rather than contribute to the acrid bile, aid in the thinning and flushing out of the thick, viscous melancholy residue and sludge. Hippocrates was therefore subject to two interpretations according to two different mechanical operations affecting the offending humor.

Guibelet speaks of burned humors as agents in a cancerlike reaction that eats away the body and that, therefore, there are certain diseases of melancholy "qui n'obeit qu'à grande peine à la purgation . . . que toutes ulceres causées de melancholie ne reçoivent point guarison." Ferrand cites Guibelet at length in his ch. XXXIX, beginning only two sentences later to illustrate how difficult it is to purge such melancholy. But Ferrand nowhere subscribes to the cancer theory of black humors or to the analogy with vinegar in which the acidic bile becomes a dissolving agent, nor does he consign his patients to such bleak prospects. "Que cete humeur se mocque ordinairement de noz remedes," Guibelet continues, because gentle ones cannot touch it and harsh ones merely irritate and offend it making it more bitter. Time may indeed, then, be the only cure. "Aëtius dit fort bien que les maladies melancholiques cessent quand les medecins quittent et n'en peuvent plus." There is perhaps a hint here of a kind of contest between the physicians and the moral-theological writers for the curing of this disease. Ferrand's purpose is in part to secure the claims of medicine as the appropriate course for curing love, especially through pharmaceutical preparations.

Vinegar was the subject of considerable inquiry in the sixteenth century; the following item is indicative—a full-length study of its values and properties: Giovanni Battista Cavigioli, *Livres des proprietes du vinaigre* (Poictiers, n.p., 1541).

16. Ferrand is probably referring to Aetius' *Tetrabiblos*, bk. IV, sermo 4, ch. 74: "De furore uterino," p. 903. Aetius, however, does not mention *oxyrrhodinon*.

We have translated Ferrand's "embrocations" as *linements*, though we note at the same time the definition of this term by Cotgrave in his French-English dictionary of 1611 as a "besprinkling, or gentle bathing of the head, or any other part, with a liquor falling from aloft upon it in the manner of raine." The *oxyrrhodinon*, variously spelled *oxyrhodeum* and *oxyrrhodinum*, is a liquid medicine with a vinegar and rose water base that is applied to the head of victims of frenzy and hysteria. Du Laurens discusses similar epithemes for the head as lotions or embrocations variously containing the oils of the seeds of gourds, sweet almonds, and violets, or else of milk: *Les maladies melancholiques, et du moyen de les guarir* in *Toutes les Oeuvres*, p. 33^r. On the following page he states, "La forme de l'onguent sera telle. Prenez du populeum demy once, de l'onguent de Galien, que se nomme refrigerant, autant, une once d'huile rosat, meslez le tout ensemble avec un peu de vin-aigre, et en oignez la teste, le front et le nez."

João Rodriguez de Castello Branco (Amatus Lusitanus), *Curationum medicinalium centuriae duae* (Parisiis: apud Sebastianum Nivellium, 1554), p. 123: "Capiti porro oxyrhodinum applicare fecimus, quod habet. Reci. aquarum rosarum libram mediam, plantaginis uncias tres, aceti rosati, uncias duas, olei rosacei unam et mediam, pulveris santalorum rubeorum drachmam unam et mediam, misce, et sincipiti et temporibus cum panno lineo applicetur et saepe innovetur."

17. [*L. 6. de san. c. 14*]: Galen, *De sanitate tuenda*, bk. VI, ch. 14, ed. Kühn, vol. VI, p. 446: " Porro gymnastarum quempiam vidimus exiis, qui athletis praesuerant, qui athletae cujusdam renibus plumbi laminam superposuit, quo nocturnis veneris imaginibus careret." This recommendation became the basis for a traditional therapy in Renaissance medical treatises. See, among others, Jean Liébault, *Des maladies des femmes*, bk. I, ch. 30, p. 74, who provides a description of the lead leaves and their use for preventing nocturnal emission owing to an overabundance of seed and related conditions including melancholy from venerean causes. "Semblablement faictes deux lames de plomb fort tenues, subtiles et deliees, troueës par tout: qu'elles trempent trois ou quatre jours dans vinaigre rouge bouillant faict de vin debile, auquel ayent bouillies semences d'agnus castus de laictues et de pourpier, puis avant que de les appliquer si vous les frottez de vif argent elles en rafreschiront d'avantage; par ce que le vif argent voire à son premier contact rafreschist bien fort: mais par ce que l'argent vif à longue, consume la lame faudra en avoir tousjours d'apprestees: appliquez en une avec une ceincture tout le long de l'espine du dos, l'autre un doigt plus bas sur les lombes: ce remede ne vous rafreschira pas trop, lequel cependant n'a son pareil pour appaiser la pollution nocturne et toute autre sorte de flux de semence."

Jean Aubery, *L'antidote d'amour*, p. 136^r, explains that the back and kidneys should be kept cool and that a lead sheath (platine) can be worn, and that the groin can be bound up with a girdle of Venus as follows: "que ses reins soient peu chaudement couverts, sur lesquels il portera nuict et jour, une platine de plomb, avec la pudique estrainte du ceston de Venus, ou mesmes en lieu de chemise qu'il endosse la haire, se couchant sur feuilles de nymphee, d'agnus castus, de saules, de roses, tousjours sur l'un de ses costez, de peur d'échauffer le tronc de la veine cave couchee sur les lombes, d'où ruisselle et bouïllonne la semence."

Luis Mercado, *De internorum morborum curatione libri IV*, in *Opera*, bk. II, ch. 10, vol. III, p. 585: "Lumbos item foeminae cinges plumbea lamina."

See also ch. XXXVI, n. 20, below.

18. [*L. 3. fen 20. tr. 1 c. 27, 33*]: Avicenna, *Liber canonis*, bk. III, fen 20, tr. 1, ch. 27, p. 376^r: "et administratio lamina plumbi super dorsum" for the cure of excessive desire.

Ch. 33, p. 376^v: "De multitudine pollutionis": "Et stricturae laminae plumbi super dorsum est impressio magna: verum quandoque nocet renibus: quare oportet ut attendatur hoc in eo iterum."

19. [*L. 2. pract. c .26.*]: Arnald of Villanova, *Breviarium practicae*, bk. II, ch. 26: "De provocantibus et stringendibus haemorrhoides ," pp. 1241–44.

Aristotle, *Problems*, bk. IV, no. 5 (877a), trans. W. S. Hett, vol. I, p. 113, could have served to establish this idea: "Why is it that bare feet are not good for sexual intercourse? Is it because the body intending sexual intercourse should be warm and moist within?"

The white friars were the monks of Cisteaux, founded in 1090, "who under their (upmost) white habit weare a black one, and red shoes." Cotgrave, *A Dictionarie of the French and English Tongues* (1611).

20. [*Tetrab. 4. ser. 4. c. 74*]: Aetius of Amida, *Tetrabiblos*, bk. IV, sermo 4, ch. 74, p. 903. See also n. 16, above.

21. ℞. lent. excortic. p. ii. flor. salec. & rosar. ana. p. i. fol. olivae m. i. fiat decoct. ad lib. i. in qua dissol. trochisc. de camphor. Ə i. misce, fiat clyster, iniiciatur in sinum pudoris. Vel ex Aëtio:

℞. nitri & cardamomi ana. Ə. i. cum ceratis excipito, fiat pessus quem pudendis subdito, vel certam quantitatem diacodii cum solani succo mixtum in sinum Veneris indito.

See ch. XXXIX, n. 42, below.

22. [*Harm. gynac. part. 2. c. 3.*]: Cleopatra, "De fervore matricis," in *Harmonia gynaeciorum, sive de morbis muliebribus liber*, in Spach, *Gynaeciorum libri IV*, vol. I, p. 23: "Althea decocta, et adeps anserinus, et vitu linus, resina et terebinthina modice addantur, quod appositum, plurimum prodest, etiam uteri praefocatione valde utile. *Item.* Altheam coque, exinde supersedere mulierem facito ad vaporem. *Item.* tolle radices, quas homines in usu habent, et diligenter panno inducens, naturae impone, et sanabitur. Invenies vero in ea panniculo vermes, et miraberis."

See also Girolamo Mercuriale, *De morbis muliebribus libri IV*, in Spach, *Gynaeciorum libri IV*, bk. IV, ch. 10, p. 157: "Laudat Moschio radiculam, panno involutam et immissam, de qua narrant quod vermes in ipsa generentur, tanquam miraculo quodam."

23. [*Cels. l. 6 de re med. c. 18. Manard. l. 7. epist. 2. Cic. l. 9 ep. fam ep. 2*]:

Celsus, *De medicina*, trans. W. G. Spencer, bk. VI, ch. 18, vol. II, p. 269.
See ch. VI, n. 10, above, for the text.

Giovanni Manardo, *Epistolae medicinales diversorum authorum*, bk. VII,
ep. 2, pp. 43a–54a.

Cicero, *The Letters to his Friends* (*Epistulae ad familiares*), IX. 22. 1,
trans. W. G. Williams (Loeb, 1959), p. 264: "Amo verecundiam, alii
potius libertatem loquendi. Atqui hoc Zenoni placuit, homini mehercule
acuto, etsi Academiae nostrae cum eo magna rixa est. Sed, ut dico, placet
Stoicis, suo quamque rem nomine appellare. Sic enim disserunt, nihil
esse obscenum, nihil turpe dictu." The beginning of Ferrand's translation, "I like modesty, but much more freedom in speech," is quite the
opposite of Cicero's words.

24. Bernard Penot, *Tractatus varii, de vera praeparatione, et usu medicamentorum chymicorum* (Basileae: impensis Ludovico Regis, 1616), p. 59: "De
medicamentis chymicis oleum camphorae etiam ita fit: ℞. camphoram,
pinguedinem gallinarum, aut oleum nucis, distilla simul. *Additio*: camphora oleo amygdalarum incorporata omnem calorem renum tollit illita.
Camphoram cum succaro in calore balnei distilla et habebis pulcherri-
mum oleum in doloribus calidis. Camphora cruda gonorrheam curat.
Camphora duodecies sublimata per se igne lenissimo saepius voluendo
vas. tandem vertetur in oleum, quod bubones cum ficu resoluendo
consumit et gonorrhaeam vertustissimam curat. Camphora accensa in
mediis undis ardet."

25. [*Tract. de Venen.*]: Arnald of Villanova, *De venenis*, in *Opera omnia*, p. 1531.

26. [*Lemnius c. 11. l. 2. de occult. nat. mirac. Paracelse l. vexat. Cardan. Albert.*]: Levinus Lemnius, *Occulta naturae miracula, ac varia rerum documenta*, p. 179: "Hinc itaque mos inolevit apud veteres, ut is digitus auro
insigneretur, talique gestamine decorus esset, potius quam caeteri: quod
tenuis quidam arteriae ductus, non nervi, ut Gellius existimavit, a corde
ad hanc digitum porrigatur, cuius motum in parturientibus ac delas-
satis, omnibusque cordis affectibus indicis attactu manifeste percipis. . . .
Huius quoque dignitas, quam a corde consequitur, hoc effecit, ut veteres medici, a quibus etiam nomen obtinuit, medicamenta ac potiones
illo commiscerent. Nihil enim venenati vel extremis eius radicibus ad-
haerere potest, quin homini infestum sit, virusque cordi communicetur."
Paracelsus, *Operum medico-chimicorum sive paradoxorum, coelum philosophorum sive liber vexationum*, p. 292: "Sapphrus, lapis est coelestis coloris, et pulcri, coelieaeque naturae. Carbunculus. Solaris lapis lucet
ex propria natura sicut sol." No other information is given on these
stones or their medical applications. But see *De mineralibus liber*, tr. I,
pp. 242–43: "Sic et nonullae gemmae sunt homini utiles, non sub forma
metallica, sed ut gestentur, et hominis sanitati praesint, quales sunt
saphyrus, magnes, carniolus. etc. Hae iam alia specie conditae sunt, ut
jure eas homo secum circumferre possit. Porro et genus aliud lapidum
est, quibus homo non indiget, ut metallo aut gemma, sed ad extruendas
domos et reservacula alia humanae vitae necessaria."
Girolamo Cardano, *Somniorum synesiorum omnis generis insomnia explicantes libri IV*, including *Actio in Thessalicum medicum, de secretis, de*

gemmis et coloribus (Basileae: ex officina Henrici Petri, 1562). See also *Les livres . . . intitulés de la subtilité et subtiles inventions, ensemble les causes occultes et raisons d'icelles*, trad. Richard Le Blanc (Paris: G. Le Noir, 1556).

For references to Albert on precious stones, see ch. XX, n. 26, above, and ch. XXXVI, n. 20, below.

XXXIII.   How to Cure Erotic Melancholy and Love Madness

1. [*Soran. in vita Hippoc.*]: Soranus of Ephesus, *Life of Hippocrates*. This reference goes with the story of the healing of Perdiccas, for which see ch. XIII, n. 3, above.

   The principal source for the opening of this chapter is André Du Laurens, *Des maladies melancholiques, et du moyen de les guarir*, p. 35^V: "Ainsi Erasistrate ayant descouvert à Seleuque la passion d'Antioque, qui mouroit pour l'amour de sa belle mere, sauva la vie à ce jouvenceau: car le pere ayant compassion de son fils, et le voyant en extréme danger de sa vie, luy permit, comme payen, de jouyr de sa femme propre. Diogene ayant un fils forcené et enragé d'amour, fut contrainct apres avoit consulté l'oracle d'Apollon, de luy permettre la jouyssance de ses amours, et la guarir par ce moyen."

   For the story of Tamar, see ch. XIII, n. 5, above.

2. Hippocrates *On the Diseases of Young Women*: "κελεύω δ'ἔγωγε τὰς ὁκόταν τὸ τοιοῦτον πάσχωσιν, ὡς τάχιστα ξυνοικῆσαι ἀνδράσιν." *Oeuvres complètes*, ed. Littré, vol. VIII, pp. 468–69. Ferrand leaves out "παρθένους" after "τὰς."

3. Galen, *On the Affected Parts*, bk. VI, ch. 6, trans. Siegel, p. 197. In response to a friend of his who had refrained from intercourse and who in turn developed a swelling of the male organ, Galen advised him "to excrete the accumulated semen but afterwards to refrain completely from [erotic] spectacles, nor to tell stories or recall memories which could stimulate his sexual desire." On the basis of this evidence, Ferrand places Galen at the head of his list of those who recommended coitus as a cure for erotic diseases.

   Ferrand directs the reader to the familiar and oft cited texts dealing with the curing of amorous melancholy:

   Haly Abbas, *Liber medicinae dictus Regius*, tr. 9, ch. 7, "de amore."

   Avicenna, *Liber canonis*, bk. III, fen 1, tr. 5, ch. 23, sect, "de cura."

   Bernard of Gordon, *Lilium medicinae*, pt. 2 , ch. 20: "De amore, qui hereos dicitur," p. 218: "Deinde hortetur ad diligendum multas, ut distrahatur amor unius propter amorem alterius."

   Arnald of Villanova, *De amore heroico*, in *Opera medica omnia*, III, ed. M. McVaugh, p. 53: "et etiam quantum est ex arte coitus—precipue si cum iuvenibus et magis delectationi congruis exerceatur."

   Valesco de Taranta, *Epitome operis perquam utilis morbis curandis in septem congesta libros* (Lugduni: apud Joan. Tornaesium, et Gulielmum Gazeium, 1560), p. 36: "Item distrahetur confabulatione cum amicis, admonitione parentum et gravium virorum, mutatione patriae, ad plures amicas animi applicatione, et historiarum lectione, poterit etiam distrahi alteram sibi matrimonia conjungendo, vetularum vituperia audiendo vino indulgendo, et cum alia honesta venerem saepe exercendo."

Pedro Pablo Pereda, *Michaelis Joannis Paschalis methodum curandi scholia* (Lugduni: sumptibus Jacobi Cardon, 1630, editio novissima), bk. I, ch. 11: "De iis qui amore insaniunt," p. 44: "Aliquando curatur haec insania ebrietate, et coitu non immodicis." He says no more on the matter than this. His chapter is brief, mentions Paul of Aegina, and repeats the story of Antiochus and Stratonice. He briefly describes the symptoms, such as hollow eyes, the irregularity of the pulse, and suggests such cures as absenting oneself from the beloved object, travel, music, games, and pastimes with friends. He also cites two passages from Ovid, perhaps accounting for the name in Ferrand.

Marsilio Ficino, *Commentary on Plato's Symposium*, p. 168: "Lucretius also prescribes frequent coitus:

> But it is fitting to avoid images and remove from himself
> the foods of love, and turn his mind elsewhere, and cast
> the accumulated humor into various bodies and not retain
> it, once it has been infected by love for a certain person."

Ficino's quotation is from *De rerum natura*, bk. IV. 1063–66. See trans. W. H. D. Rouse (Loeb, 1966), p. 323.

Battista Fregoso, *Contramours*, p. 218: "Et si par fortune il advenoit; que pour toutes ces médecines, on ne reconnust au passionné patient aucun signe d'amendement: ains que peu a peu deséchant il monstrat apparence de prochaine mort: pour mettre toute pierre en besongne, plus tost que le laisser mourir; il seroit bon de prendre peine, par quelques secondes et nouvelles amours, luy oster les prémiéres de la phantasie: se donnant toutesfois garde, que par trop il ne s'y acharnast: comme a ce propos a bien dit Lucréce, en ces vers:

> De jour en jour ceste fureur glissante,
> Son mal rengrége en l'Ame languissante:
> Si par un coup second, on ne s'essaye
> Couper chemin a la prémiére playe:
> [Lucréce, au 4. livre de la nature des choses.]"

4. [*L. 3. fen. 1. tr. 4. c. 23*]: Avicenna, *Liber canonis*, bk. III, fen 1, tr. 4, ch. 23.
5. [*Corn. Gallus*]: Cornelius Gallus, Elegy III. 91–92: "Illi peccandi studium permisso potestas / Abstulit, atque ipsum talia velle subit." *Catullus, Tibullus, Propertius cum Galli fragmentis*, p. 332: "Si tibi peccandi . . . velle sugit."
6. Plutarch, "Demetrius," *Lives*, vol. IX, p. 67. Ferrand illustrates the concept of enjoyment of the desired object as cure, or a substitute of the same, with the story of Theognis.

The same story is told by André Du Laurens, Ferrand's probable source, *Des maladies melancholiques et du moyen de les guarir*, p. 35^V: "pour faire voir que ceste rage et furie erotique se pouvoit moderer par la jouyssance de ce qu'on ayme: Mais ce moyen ne se devant ny pouvant tousjours executer, comme contraire aux loix divines et humaines, il faut recourir à l'autre, qui depend de l'industrie d'un bon medecin."

Jean Aubery, *L'antidote d'amour*, p. 36[V], uses this story to illustrate the power of animal dreams to reproduce in sleep the desires that are pondered in the imagination by day. The seeming reality of dreams can serve to satisfy lascivious desires in lovers: "ainsi beaucoup d'amoreux durant leurs songes, jouyssent quelquefois des delices qui ne sont permises qu'à la pensee, et ou esveillees ils n'oseroient attenter." This suggested to Ferrand that dreams, on occasion, can serve as cures, though they are hardly within the command of the physician.

7. "Amoris vulnus idem qui facit, sanat": Publilius Syrus, in *Minor Latin Poets*, ed. J. W. Duff, p. 18: "Amoris vulnus idem sanat qui facit."

8. [*Maced. 7. Anth.*]: Macedonius the consul, in *Greek Anthology*, bk. V, no. 225. 5–6, vol. I, p. 223:

Τήλεφος εἰμὶ κόρη, σὺ δὲ γίνεο πιστὸς Ἀχιλλεύς:
κάλλει σου παῦσος τὸν πόθον, ὡς ἔβαλες.

9. [*C. de amore*]: Avicenna, *Liber canonis*, bk. III, fen 1, tr. 4, ch. 23, p. 206[V].

10. [*Avic. l. 3. fen. I. tr. 4. c. 24. Haly. l. 5. pract c. 25.*]: Avicenna, *Liber canonis*, bk. III, fen 1, tr. 4, ch. 24, deals with the cures of love, p. 207[r]: "Et ex occupationibus praedictis est emptio puellarum, et plurimum concubitus ipsarum, et renovatio ipsarum, et delectatio cum ipsis."

Haly Abbas, *Liber medicinae dictus Regius, Practicae*, bk. 5, ch. 25: "De hereos et amoris medela," p. 128[V]: "Coitus quoque cum ea quae non amatur cogitationem flectit ab amata et extenuat ac amata removet."

Ferrand mentions here a list of Arab and Christian physicians who recommend coitus as a cure for erotic melancholy and he takes up a polemical course against them as recommending not only an immoral form of treatment but one that would be, in any case, entirely ineffective on clinical grounds. Ferrand does not report of any actual use of this therapy by Christian doctors, though, in fact, the medical treatises of the age suggest that it was, indeed, employed. Pierre le Loyer, in his *Discours et histoires des spectres, visions et apparitions des esprits, anges, demons, et ames se monstrans visibles aux hommes*, bk. I, ch. 11, relates the story of the man from Toulouse who falls passionately in love with a Venetian woman while visiting in the city and who becomes enraged and maniacal by her rejection. Arrested while trying to assault the Doge in the Basilica of St. Mark, he is taken for treatment to the famous physician Girolamo Fracastoro. The doctor instructed a courtesan to offer her services to this man and to allow him to stay with her until he was entirely satiated and exhausted and then to cover him well to make him perspire. Le Loyer comments that he will not find fault with this cure because there were many physicians at the time of Fracastoro and before who made use of this treatment to their great credit. Moreover, the books of the most recent physicians are full of such information which he will not enlarge upon because lovesickness is not his topic. He concludes: "et me suffira de dire que c'est une espece de melancholie pour laquelle guerir beaucoup de medecins doctes et experts enseignent le remede de la copulation charnelle avecques la femme, car par ce moyen, disent-ils, on se descharge des fumeuses vapeurs de la semence lesquelles troublent et corrompent le cerveau et principalement offensent les personnes amoureuses, en ce que tant plus elles demeurent dans le corps, plus elle engendrent et accumulent de soucis et de pensers qui se tournent en rage." Le Loyer suggests that therapeutic coitus was not only possible in such cities as Venice but that it was practiced widely as a form of medical treatment for erotic melancholy and mania.

Rabelais, in *Le tiers livre*, ch. 31, p. 351, offers a variation on this cure. In the name of Rondibilis he suggests that the final cure for carnal desire is repeated carnal indulgence, ironically as a form of mortification of the flesh: "Fray Scyllino [Roscelino], prieur de Sainct Victor lez Marseille . . . suys en ceste opinion (aussi estoit l'hermite de Saincte Radegonde au dessus de Chinon) que plus aptement ne porroient les hermites de Thebaïde macerer leurs corps, dompter ceste paillarde sensualité, deprimer la rebellion de la chair, que le feisant vingt et cinq ou trente foys par jour." One senses the high probability of Rabelaisian irony in this fifth and final recommendation, however.

11. [*G. Postel. P. Jovius. Chalcondyl.*]: Guillaume Postel, *De la republique des Turcs: et là ou l'occasion s'offrera, des meurs et loys de tous muhamedistes* (Poitiers: de l'imprimerie d'Enguilbert de Marnes, n.d.), pp. 4–5: "Mais pource que du nombre des femmes il y en a grosse difference non entr'eus, car par la loy il est arbitraire, mais entre les escrivains de deça: pour monstrer la verité, et oster d'erreur ceus qui sont en fausse opinion, premierement je diray: Lapluspart des escrivains dit que les populaires et riches peuvent espouser ou avoir douze femmes, et tant d'esclaves ou captives qu'ils veulent, ou peuvent entretenir et nourrir: et les princes des, femmes septente, des serves tant qu'ils veulent: les autres quatre ou six femmes: ce qui est en partie faus, pource que tous escrivent nombre certain pour incertain. . . . Quant est au nombre des esclaves et femmes, Muhamed dit en l'Alcoran, qu'on en achette et prenne tant qu'on veut et peut nourir, et que c'est la possission de l'homme, achettée de son argent, et qu'il en peut faire a son plaisir."

Paolo Giovio, *Turcicorum rerum commentarius . . . ex Italico Latinus factus* (D. Petrus Abbas Cluniansis, 1550), 2 vols. in 1, second set of pagination, 107–40. This is a brief political and military history that has little about the customs and mores of the Turks and Mohammedans. Ferrand probably knew the title only by reputation or secondary citation.

Laonicus Chalcondylas, *L'histoire de la decadence de l'empire Grec et establissement de celuy des Turcs de la traduction de B. de Vigenere* (Paris: Chez Sebastien Cramoisy, 1650), vol. I, p. 59. This is essentially a military and political history in the form of a chronicle completed to the year 1465, and continued thereafter by Artus Thomas. He was little concerned with domestic matters and marriage customs, but in bk. III concerning Tamerlan he cites: "Car chacun espouse plusieurs femmes, et tient encore (si bon lui semble) autant d'esclaves pour concubines, comme il en peut nourrir: Neantmoins pour le regard de leurs femmes legitimes, ils ont de coustume de les prendre vierges: surquoy ne leur est donné aucun empeschement jusques au nombre de cinq, et si pour cela les enfans qu'ils ont de leurs esclaves ne sont pas tenus pour bastarde."

Pierre Belon, *Les observations de plusieurs singularitez et choses memorables, trouvées en Grece, Asie, Judée, Egypte, Arabie, et autres pays estranges, redigées en trois livres* (Paris: Gilles Corrozet, 1553). The question of marriage customs and multiple wives is discussed in ch. 10: "Du mariage des Turcs et dont viet qu'ils ont le congé de se marier à quatre femmes," p. 178.

12. See n. 3, above. See also Auger Ferrier, *Vera medendi methodus, duobus libris comprehensa, eiusdem castigationes practicae medicinae* (Tolosae: apud Petrum du Puys, 1557), pp. 271–72: "Venus moderata plenitudinem vacuat, corpus vegetius, et alacrius reddit. Itaque ad universi corporus vacuationem confert. Sed particulariter vasa spermatica exonerat, et renum fervorem extinguit. Immoderata corpus ad tabem ducit. In omnibus autem particularibus vacuationibus tria praecipue attendenda sunt. Primo ne corpori non vacuato adhibeantur. Praemittenda enim semper universalis purgatio. Deinde ne influentibus, aut fluere paratis adhuc humoribus ad moveantur: sed quiescentibus quando inquam malum firmatum, aut inveteratum fuerit, ipsaque restiterit humorum fluxio. Quod revulsiones, ac derivationes prius factas supponit. Nam si fluente adhuc humore adhibeantur, ad partem affectam attrahent, et moribum geminabunt."

Arnald of Villanova, *De amore heroico*, p. 53, says, in fact, that pleasures are good cures for *hereos* including "quantum est ex arte coitus precipue vi cum iuvenibus et magis delectationi congruis exerceatur." The only difference between the Christian writers and the Moslems seems to be the fact that the Cristians do not exercise slavery.

13. Hippocrates, *De flatibus*, ch. 1: "τὰ ἐωαντία τῶν ἐναντίων ἐστὶν ἰήματα," see ed. Littré, vol. VI, p. 92.

14. [*Arist. l. 7. de hist. an. c. 1*]: Aristotle, *The History of Animals*, bk. VII, ch. 6, ed. Jonathan Barnes, in *Works* (Princeton: Princeton University Press, 1984), vol. I, p. 911.

15. [*Hipp. l. de nat. pueri.*]: Hippocrates, *On Generation: Of the Nature of the Child*: "ὁ ἀνὴρ ἦν λαγνεύῃ πολλὰ, εὐρωότερα γινόμενα τὰ φλέβια μᾶλλον ἐπάγει τὴν λαγνείην." *Oeuvres complètes*, ed. Littré, vol. VII, pp. 514–15.

16. [*Gal. 6. de loc. aff. c. ult.*]: Galen, *On the Affected Parts*, bk. VI, ch. 6. Ferrand draws the following materials from Galen, reversing the order. The Latin version of the quotation of Plato's *Theaetetus* in Galen: "ignavia quidem exsolvit, proprii autem officii exercitatio robur auget." The example of the breasts, trans. Siegel, p. 197: "Equally the breasts of women who never become pregnant remain atrophic; but the breasts of those who are feeding their children after delivery become large and continue producing milk as long as they nurse their children; but soon after they stop feeding, the production of milk in the breast ceases." The concepts concerning trained singers and athletes who have underdeveloped sexual organs in consequence of their early training: "cantoribus et athletis, qui iam inde ab initio nullam vita partem veneris illecebris contaminaverunt, nullam admittentes venereorum cogitationem vel imagi-

nationem, iis pudenda exilia et rugosa veluti senibus fieri consueverunt, nullaque abidine tentantur."

17. [*D. Hieron. ad Gerunt. Tertul. l. I. ad uxor*]: St. Jerome, *Opera*, 5 vols., "*Ad Geruntii Filias de contemnenda haereditate*," vol. V, pp. 33–36.

Tertullian, *Ad uxorem*, bk. I, in *Treatises on Marriage and Remarriage*, trans. William P. le Saint (Westminster, Md.: Newman Press, 1951), p. 18. For an early edition, see *Ad uxorem*, in *Opera* (Pariis: apud Audoënum Parvum, 1566), p. 115.

The probable intermediary source for this material, however, is Girolamo Mercuriale, *De morbis muliebribus libri IV*, bk. IV, ch. 10, in *Gynaeciorum libri IV*, vol. II, pp. 155–56: "Nam D. Hieronymus in Epistola ad Geruntiam et Tertul. lib. 1. ad uxorem, probavit facilius esse servare virginitatem quam castitatem, eo quod facilius est non optare quod nunquam est habitum, quam quod aliquando est habitur."

XXXIV. Remedies to Cure Love Melancholy in Married Persons

1. [*Io. de Vigo l. 9 de addit. c. de his qua delecti fac. in coitu Avic. l. 3. fen. 10 tr. 1. c. 44. & 45. Rhaz. 14. contin.*]: Giovanni da Vigo, *La practique et cirurgie* . . . (n.p., n.p., 1537), bk. IX: "Sensuit le chapi. V. lequel traicte de his que augmentant sperma, et delectationem prebent in coitu," pp. 317–18: "Sperma et delectatio in coitu sont necessaires a la propagation humaine ainsi que tesmoignent les philosophes. Et pource voulons en bref reciter les choses qui le augmentent et donnent delectation in coitu. Et premier les raves les naveaux pastenades feves chiches augmentent le sperme, et principalement quand ilz sont appareilles avec un petit de poivre ou de cinamome ou de zinziber. En apres les amandes les avellanes les grains de pommes de pins et fistici cum zuccaro confecti. Et dit Mesue que oleum amigdalinum spermam auget. Et Avicenne dit avellane cum melle comeste coitum vigorant. Pareillement eruca prinse en petite quantite incite ad coitum. Et pource dit Ovide en son livre de remedia amoris. Nec minus est aptum erucas vitare salaces. Et aulcuns disent que se on en usoit en grande quantite elle destruiroit et consummeroit le sperme, et la volunte de venus. Diascorides dit que se on usoit quelque temps de la pouldre faicte de feuilles de matrissilva a chascune foys la quantite de vii. ʒ. avec vin ou avec oximel elle multiplieroit le sperme, et le nourriroir. Et le avons esprouve, et le avons trouve vray. Les oeufz molz menges avec un petit de poivre et de cinamome sont de mesme effect, et apres que on a menge les oeufz ainsi appare. Iles on doibt boire de vin doulx. Sensuit une confection fort utile pour ceulx qui ont perdu la volunte de venus, et est multiplicative de la geniture. ℞. pulpe caponum decocte. ℥. iii. pulpe perdicum pulpe pulli columbini silvestris, ana. ℥. ii. radicis satirionis. ℥. i. et ½ radicum enule. ʒ. ii. piperis. ʒ. i. cinamomi nucis muscate: ana. ʒ. i. zinzinberis galange cubebe assari: ana. Ɔ. iiii. amigdalarum dulcium pineorum: ana. ℥. ii. et ½ fisticore. ʒ. ii. passularum. ℥. v. omnia decoquantur simul et cum

zuccaro sufficienti secundum artem fiat confectio solida vel mollis, de qua patiens sumat mane et sero quantitatem nucis vel parum plus. Les chiches rouges cuittes avec brouet de gellines blanches: ou avec laict augmente le sperme, et pource Galien in libro de elementis dit cicera excitant voluntatem ad libidinem." "Le chap. VI. traicte de his que faciunt ad erectionem virge." "Pource que aulcuns sont ineptes ad coitum quand ilz sont en eage suffisante et maries, nous declarerons aulcunes choses qui faciunt ad erectionem virge. Et premier les poreaux menges avec miel et cinam. galanga tenue en la bouche. Et a ce est tresutile ceste confection. ℞. seis eruce. ʒ. ii. et ½ semis rape. ʒ. i. et. ½ cinamo. cubebe zinziberis galange piperis: ana. ʒ. i. elmini. ʒ. ii. omnia conficiantur cum melle et zuccaro, et de ea sumat patiens mane et fero coclear unum. La decoction de chiches et de semence de baucia meslees avec un petit de miel de poivre et de cinamome est de mesme operation. Rasis dit que oleii sambucinum dedens lequel sont boullies des formis q'ont des elles: et apres mise au soleil sont de mesme vertu quand virga illita est ex eo. Et pareillement ledict huile avec un petit de musc est de mesme vertu quand on en met sus les cuisses ou dessus les parties genitales. Les remedes escriptz au chapitre precedant sont en ce cas convenables."

Avicenna, *Liber canonis*, bk. III, fen 10, tr. 1, ch. 44: "De excusatione medici in illis quae docet de delectatione, et magnificatione virgae, et coangustatione receptricis, et calefactione eius"; ch. 45: "De delectando viros et mulieres," p. 377ᵛ. Both chapters deal with ways to enhance sexual pleasure.

Rhazes, *Liber continens*, bk. XIV. Ferrand's reference is taken from the margins of the edition of Avicenna cited above.

Giovanni Marinello, *Le medicine partenenti alle infermità delle donne* (Venetia: apresso Giovanni Valgrisio, 1574), ch. 9: "Come quegli, i quali per la continua erettione de' membri genitali diconsi incordati, siano guariti," pp. 17ʳ ff.; ch. 10: "Le cagioni, i segni, et la cura di quegli, che sono debili, et impotenti al generare," pp. 19ᵛ ff.; ch. 11: "Il marito, o la moglie che odia la compagnia e fugga, come naturalmente, e senza offendere la divina legge, tornano santamente ad unirsi," pp. 36 ff. These chapters contain many recipes and remedies too extensive to quote here.

Jean Liébault, *Des maladies des femmes*, bk. I, ch. 35: "Rejoindre et reunit les nouveaux mariez qui hayent et fuyent la compaignie de l'un l'autre," pp. 130–34: "Nous voyons advenir bien souvent que les nouveaux mariez, soit qu'ils ayent esté conjoins ensemble de leur bon gre, consentement, et sans aucune contraincte: ou contre la volonté et souhait de l'un ou de l'autre, conçoivent l'un contre l'autre une hayne secrette qui engendre en eux tel discord, contemnement, et mespris qu'ils fuyent et abhorrent du tout la compaignie de l'un l'autre: chose certes entierement contraire aux loix divines, humaines, et naturelles, pour l'empeschement qui survient à la generation qui est la fin et but du mariage. L'occasion de ce divorce est diverse: aucunesfois la dissimilitude des meurs: quelquesfois l'imperfection corporelle de l'un l'autre: le plus souvent le peu de plaisir que l'un ou l'autre prend au combat

venerien: car ce qui plus incite à ce combat cest le plaisir tres-grand que
les deux combatans y sentent, à raison dequoy aussi nature a donné aux
parties genitales un merveilleux sentiment plus aigu et vif qu'à nulle
autre partie, par le moyen des nerfs qui y sont dispersez: outre cela a
inseré dedans les prostates une certaine humidité sereuse semblable à la
semence, mais plus liquide et subtile, laquelle a une acrimonie picquante
et aiguillonnante avec un petit prurit et demangeson, qui irrite lesdites
parties genitales à faire leur action, en donnant volupté et plaisir, parce
qu'elle est accompaignee de grande quantité d'esprits qui s'eschauffent
et sont stimulez à sortir hors. Nous laisserons toutes les autres occasions
et parlerons seulement de ceste derniere: pour la curation de laquelle
descrirons quelques remedes faciles et utiles: outre lesquels toutesfois
nous conseillons que l'une et l'autre partie prie Dieu ad ce que luy, qui
est autheur de toute union et paix, les vueille reduire en bonne concorde
et amitié.

"Donc pour esguillonner les parties genitales à quelque chatoüilleuse
volupté. Ayez pirethre et asse douce de chacun une dracme: pulverisez
les, mesles avec dix dracmes d'huyle de suzeau en forme d'onguent:
duquel l'homme frottera sa verge trois jours durans: et la femme, sa
nature: cela les allechera à prendre plaisir, ains à s'aimer infiniment:
autrement, prenez poyvre long, poyvre noir, pirethre et galangue, tous
pulverisez de chacun une dracme: meslez ceste poudre avec miel: et
quand voudrez habiter ensemble frottez en les parties genitales.

"Et si la damoiselle desire une plus belle et gentille maniere, qu'elle
mette dedans sa nature comme un pessaire assez long fait de demie once
de gallia moschata, et une once de ladanum, le tout incorporé et malaxé
ensemble.

"D'autre part si quelque homme souhaitte d'estre aymé et caressé
de sa damoiselle, doit mascher des grains de cubebes et s'en estuver
avec sa salive, c'est un remede singulier pour engendrer: le pirethre
faict le semblable. Ce remede aussi serait fort excellent pour la damoiselle s'il ne luy apportoit une ardeur et mordication appliqué sur les
lieux. Semblablement le liniment fait de dix dracmes d'huyle de liz, ou
de spiquenard en lequelle ait trempé trois ou quatre fois un drachme
d'assa fetida pulverisee. Mais d'autant que l'assa est fort puante, vau-
droit meiux mettre parmy l'huyle au lieu d'icelle, quelques grains de
cubebes pulverisez.

"Pulverisez aussi pirethre, zingembre, canelle de chacun une dracme:
malaxez ceste poudre avec eau en laquelle aurez dissoult un peu de
gomme arabique: de ceste paste faites trocisques aussi gros que lupins:
si tost que seront seichez, maschez en un ou deux, et vous estuvez de
vostre salive.

"Aucuns maschent grains de cubebes avec demy grain de musch
ou d'ambre, et se fomentent les lieux de leur salive: mais cependant
faut tenir pour asseuré que le musch, ambre, et civette sont les meilleurs
entre tous: si leur cherté n'estoit si grande.

"Autres font poudre de pirethre et de poyvre en egale portion, la
meslent avec miel, et s'en oindent le membre genital non sans grand

fruit.

"Certains personnages dissoudent dedans un peu d'huyle chaude fiels de bouc et de loup deseichez au paravant, et s'en frottent le membre lors du coyt, ils afferment que cest le moyen plus assuré pour remettre en grande union le mary avec la femme: ne manquent aussi d'autres qui se frottent avec suif de bouc jeune, et dient que rien n'est plus excellent en cest endroit.

"Plusieurs autheurs dignes de croire afferment que si le mary desire que sa femme n'ait la cognoissance d'autre que de luy, et la femme d'autre que d'elle, doit recuillir les cheveux qui tombent quand elle se peigne, les brusler et en faire poudre, mesler ceste poudre evec graisse de bouc et fiel de poulle, et s'en oindre. Aucuns cerchent d'avoir une corneille toute vive laquelle ils font mourir et tirent hors la cervelle, et l'incorporent avec miel, et s'en oindent. Autres font casser oeufs de corneilles, et s'en frottent et fomentent les testicules: ils afferment que rien n'est plus excellent pour garder la vraye amitié et loyauté. Les oeufs d'arondelles mis en usage de ceste façon font le pareil.

"Si quelqu'un frotte avec huyle tiede où sera meslee fiente de dain, tienne pour certain que la femme n'aymera autre que son mary. L'on voit par experience le semblable advenir par le liniment faict de fiel de sanglier, nous pouvons juger que cela provient de la part de celuy qui est le plus amoureux plus que de l'autre, toutefois les simples medicamens ont certaines proprietez occultes, desquelles nous ne pourrions avoir asseuree cognoissance, ny rendre certaine raison sinon par experience."

Many of these preparations are derived from Liébault's principal source, Marinello, and in turn Ferrand, in the edition of 1610, draws heavily upon Liébault for the several recipes he offers in his ch. XXIII: "Les moyens pour conserver les mariez en amitié, et les guerir des amours illicites." That these recipes are suppressed in the later edition is an indication that they were among the elements of the first edition that raised the anger of the ecclesiastical censors in Toulouse.

The irony in this section of Ferrand's study is that what must be cured in the unmarried must be enhanced in the married, namely the pleasures of Venus. Both Ferrand and Liébault deal with the topic of sexual failure and give their advice on how to cure the conditions that impede the regenerative process. But while Ferrand eliminates the frank discussion of how to stimulate the male member and tighten the vagina in his later and expanded edition, he does refer the reader to these authorities cited above for solutions to such problems, indicating that he continued to believe that there was a kind of love melancholy belonging specifically to married couples deriving from the various incompatibilities that can threaten the union.

2. Felix Platter, *Observationes et curationes aliquot affectuum partibus mulieris generationi dicatis accidentium*, in *Gyneciorum libri IV* (pp. before pagination begins), sec. "Congressus sine voluptatis sensu": "Nobilis quidam uxoris suae hunc casum mihi aliquando patefecit, quod cum eam puellam juvenem, iam ante multos annos duxisset, et cum ea venereum actum decenter, toto matrimonii tempore peregisset, ab eo tempore illam

ad cum actum ne tantillum quidem commoveri, faterique; se inde nihil penitus voluptatis aut titillationis unquam percepisse, nec magis sentire, quam alioquin ab externo cutis contactu alibi sentire soleat: et quod illum admittat, in ipsius saltem gratiam fieri. In eodem statu adhuc eam permanere, licet frustra multa tentarit remedia, et sterilem esse, denuo mihi ipsius amita retulit.

"Eodem et simili penitus accidente generosam dominam labore, multis quoque iam annis, conquestus est mihi ipsius dominus ad maritus. Quod a primo concubitus actu ad hunc asque diem ex congressu nihil penitus afficiatur, aut lucunditatem aliquam sentiat, cum tamen ipsae viduus non minus quam in primo matrimonio actum hunc perfecte exerceat: ipsamque fateri, quod cum virgo ad quadregesimum usque annum permansisset (tunc enim primum illi nupserat) nunquam ullum stimulum, aut per nocturnas imaginationes, aut alio modo, senserit, aut toto virginitatis tempore, appetitu aliquo foemineo affecta fuerit. Sed et mirum, utramque foeminam, si modo tales nominandae sunt, maritum suum, supra modum diligere et maritis quoque in se danda libidine aliquo modo, hoc concubitu imperfecto satisfieri."

Ferrand restricts his discussion to natural causes for sterility and incompatibility between spouses, no doubt, because he wishes to avoid the description of supernatural causes that suggest exorcism and other spiritual cures. Nevertheless, there was a well-established tradition that considered marital breakdown in terms of the influence of the devil or of demons. Johann Nieder in his *De maleficis et eorum deceptionibus*, in the *Malleus maleficarum ex plurimis auctoribus coacervatus* (Lugduni: apud P. Landry, 1615), vol. I, pp. 470 ff., relates how witches can excite women's love for men other than their husbands and how no amount of words or threats or blows can correct them. He explains how the devil creates hatred, not by attacking the soul, but by working on the body, the senses, the imagination, and the memory. The cure for malific love was closely related to the cures for *inordinatus amor* caused by intense sensual desire. Nieder identified three causes: the lure of the eye alone; the temptation caused by demons; the spells of witches and necromancers. That position was confirmed in the *Malleus maleficarum* of Jakob Sprenger and Heinrich Kramer, first published in 1486 or 1487, trans. Montague Summers (1928; New York: Dover Publications, 1971), a work that resulted from a commission by Pope Innocent VIII. See Sydney Anglo, "Evident Authority and Authoritative Evidence: The Malleus Maleficarum," in *The Damned Art: Essays in the Literature of Witchcraft* (London: Routledge and Kegan Paul, 1977, 1985), pp. 14 ff. The two chapters in question in the *Malleus* are those that question whether sorcerers can change the disposition of the spirits in order to cause love or hate and whether there are remedies suitable for those suffering from inordinate love or hate caused by malefice. Among the physicians of the sixteenth century who espoused the doctrine of the interference of the devil through the body in a way that provokes the diseases of melancholy are Jason van de Meersche, or van der Velde (Jason Pratensis), *De cerebri morbis* (Basileae: per Henrichum Petri, 1549), pp. 213–14: "Ac-

cidit profecto daemones, ut sunt tenues, et incompraehensibiles spiritus, sese insinuare corporibus hominum, qui occulte in visceribus operti
valetudinem vitiant, morbos citant, somniis animos exterrent, mentes
furoribus quatiunt, ut omnino morbos citant, somniis animos exterrent,
mentes furoribus quatiunt, ut omnino alienum non fuerit de mania cor-
reptis ambigere, huiusmodo ne spiritu pulsentur," and Francisco Valles,
De iis quae scripta sunt physice in libris sacris, sive de sacra philosophia (Lugduni: Fr. Le Fevre, 1587), pp. 226–27. The most forceful defendant of
demonological causes, closer to Ferrand's own age, was Jean Bodin in
his *De la démonomanie des sorciers* (Paris: Chez Jacques du Puys, 1580).
For further information on this topic, see Wayne Shumaker, *The Occult
Sciences in the Renaissance* (Berkeley: University of California Press, 1979),
pp. 60–107, and Jean Céard, "Folie et démonologie au XVIe siècle," in
Folie et déraison à la renaissance (Bruxelles: Editions de l'université de
Bruxelles, 1976), pp. 129–47.

3. *Herodotus*, trans. A. D. Godley, bk. II, sec. 181, vol. I, pp. 494–97: "But it
so fell out that Ladice was the only woman with whom Amasis could
not have intercourse; and this continuing, Amasis said to this Ladice,
'Woman, you have cast a spell on me, and most assuredly you shall
come to the most terrible end of all women.' So, the king's anger not
abating for all her denial, Ladice vowed in her heart to Aphrodite that
she would send the goddess a statue to Cyrene if Amasis had intercourse
with her that night; for that would remedy the evil; and thereafter all
went well, and Amasis loved his wife much."

[*L. 1*]: Paulo Emilio, *De rebus gestis francorum libri X* (Lutetiae: Parisiorum ex officina Vascosani, 1576), pp. 23^r–24^v. A separate marginal
reference vis-à-vis Dupréau is indecipherable.

Gabriel Dupréau, *Histoire de l'estat et succès de l'Eglise dressée en
forme de chronique généralle et universelle . . . depuis la nativité de Jésus-
Christ jusques en l'an 1580*, "l'an 1196," pp. 508^v–509^r. Ferrand cites
Dupréau's source in his own margin, but takes the story from Dupréau:
"Les chroniques des Roys d'Aragon les mesmes chroniques récitent une
fort plaisante histoire de ce Roy Pierre, touchant une tromperie que sa
femme luy fit. Ce Roy estoit fort adonné aux autres femmes et n'aymoit
guères la Royne ny ne luy faisoit telle compaignie qu'il estoit tenu luy
faire, quoy qu'elle fust assez belle et honneste, dont elle se contristoit
fort, pource que le Roy n'avoit aucun enfant à luy succeder du Royaume.
Parquoy avec l'ayde d'un sien chambellan, trouva moyen que soubz le
nom d'une des favorites du Roy, il l'introduisit a coucher une nuict avec
luy: où estant secretement conjuncte, et sentant le Roy que le jour ap-
procheoit, il voulu pour son honneur le faire retirer. Mais elle luy dit,
monseyneur et mary, je ne suis pas celle que vous pensez, ains sçachez
que vous avez en ceste nuict vostre femme auprès de vous. Faictes moi
endurer tel mal qu'il vous plaira, si est-ce que je ne bougeray d'icy, ny
de vostre presence, jusques à ce que quelque homme digne de foy sort
temoing que ceste nuict j'aye couché avec vous, afin que Dieu me faict la
grâce, que j'aye de vous le fruict que je désire, le monde sçache qu'il est
vostre. . . . Le Roy voyant l'honneste tromperie de sa femme, fut content,

et fit venir deux de ses gentils-hommes pour tesmoings de ceste vérité or pleut-il a Dieu qu'à temps convenable la Royne se sentit grosse, et au bout du terme enfanta un fils."

4. Aristotle, *Nicomachean Ethics*, bk. VII, ch. 6 (1149b), p. 409: "Now the hot-tempered man is not crafty, nor is anger, but open; whereas desire is crafty, as they say of Aphrodite: 'Weaver of wiles in Cyprus born' and Homer writes of her 'broidered girdle' 'Cajolery that cheats the wisest wits.'" The allusion to Venus' girdle comes from the *Iliad*, bk. XIV, ll. 214–17.

5. [*Livre 3. de la Franc.*]: Pierre Ronsard, *La Franciade*, bk. III. 627–46:

En la tissure estoient pourtraicts au vif
Deux Cupidons, l'un avoit un arc d'If
Au traict moussu, qui tire aux fantaisies,
Craintes, soubçons, rancueurs et jalousies:
L'autre de palme avoit l'arc decoré,
Son traict estoit à la pointe doré,
Poignant, glissant, dont il cache dans l'ame
Et verse au sang une gentille flamme
Qui nous chatoüille, et nous faict desirer,
Que nostre genre entier puisse durer.
Là fut jeunesse en long cheveux pourtraite,
Forte, puissante, au gros coeur, la retraicte
Des chauds desirs: jeunesse, qui tousjours
Pour compagnie ameine les amours
Comme un enfant pendoit à sa mammele
Le jeu trompeur, la fraude, et la cautele,
Les ris, les pleurs, les guerres et la paix,
Treves, discords et accords imparfaits,
Et le devis, qui deçoit nos courages,
Voire l'esprit des hommes les plus sages.

See *Oeuvres complètes*, ed. Paul Laumonier (Paris: Librairie Marcel Didier, 1952), vol. XVI, p. 302.

6. [*Vice Rondel. tr. de fucis.*]: Guillaume Rondelet, *Tractatus de fucis*, following the *Methodus curandorum omnium morborum corporis humani*, pp. 1256–77. In this little treatise Rondelet gives the formulae, ingredients, and preparations for beautifying baths, face washes, recipes for coloring the teeth, beard, eyelashes and skin, rubefacients, and stimulants for the face and hands. It is an extraordinary treatise by the great doctor of Montpellier, a little best seller on how to repair the defects of nature.

7. Ovid, *The Art of Love*, II. 111: "Ut teneas dominam, nec te mirere relictum, / Ingenii dotes corporis adde bonis." See trans. J. H. Mozley, p. 72. In the modern edition "teneas dominam" is reversed.

8. Maximus of Tyre, *Dissertationes XLI Graece* (Lugduni Batavorum: apud I. Patium, 1607). Ferrand may have known this work in the following edition, *Traitez de Maxime de Tyr autheur grec, qui sont quarante et un discours mis en françois* [by Guillebert] (Rouen: J. Osmont, 1617). See also *The Dissertations of M. Tyrius*, trans. Thomas Taylor, 2 vols. (London: C. Whittingham, 1804).

9. Ovid, *Heroides*, XV. 31–32: "Si mihi difficilis formam natura negavit, / Ingenio formae damnare pendo meae." See ed. Henricus Dörrie, p. 315. Read "damna repende meae."

10. [*Arist. 8. Eth. c. 20. l. 9. ca. 5.*]: Aristotle, *Nicomachean Ethics*, bk. VIII, ch. 5 (1162a), trans. H. Rackham, p. 503. Aristotle speaks in general terms of conjugal affection as a friendship built on utility and pleasure, but also on virtue if the partners are of high moral character. The rules of conduct governing the relations between man and wife are questions of justice. In bk. IX, ch. 5 (1167a), pp. 539–41, he speaks of goodwill as the basis of friendship. In neither passage does Aristotle discuss the topic as intently as Ferrand's text would suggest.

11. Ovid, *On Painting the Face (De medicamine faciei liber)*:
> Certus amor morum est, formam populabatur aetas,
> Et placitus rugis vultus aratus erit.
> [2 lines removed]
> Sufficit, et longum probitas perdurat in aevum,
> Perque suos annos hinc bene pendet Amor.

In *The Art of Love, and Other Poems*, ed. J. H. Mozley, p. 4.

12. [*L. 1. epigr. 28.*]: Martial, *Epigrams*, bk. VII. xxxix. 8–9: "Tantum cura potest et ars doloris, / Desiit fingere Coelius podagram." See trans. Walter C. A. Ker, vol. I, p. 450: "(quantum cura potest et ars doloris!) / desit fingere Caelius podagram."

13. The lack of specific references here suggests Ferrand was using an intermediary source for this anecdote deriving from Appian's *Roman History*.

14. [*L. 1. ep. 9*]: Seneca, *Moral Epistles*, bk. I, no. 9: "monstrabo tibi amatorium sine medicamento sine ullius veneficae carmine; Si vis amari, ama." *Ad Lucilium epistulae morales*, ed. L. D. Reynolds (Oxford: Clarendon, 1965), vol. I, p. 18: "monstrabo amatorium sine medicamento, sine herba, sine ullius veneficae carmine: si vis amari, ama."

15. Themistius, *Orationes*, ed. Wilhelm Dindorf (Hildesheim: Georg Olms Verlagsbuchhandlung, 1961), orat. 24, pp. 367 ff. Ferrand employs the story of the birth of Anteros to Venus as an exemplum emblematic of the mutuality and reciprocity required for a successful marriage. To make use of this myth in any other context of a treatise concerned with love that is either entirely hopeless, or that is perverted in its erotic intensity and by its pathological origins, is to presuppose one of a number of different meanings for Anteros, meanings that were current in Renaissance thought, but which Ferrand did not know, or more likely, had rejected on historical and linguistic grounds. For in contrast to those who understood Anteros to signify wholeness in love and the avenger of love spurned, there were those who understood Anteros to mean opposition to Eros, or sexual desire, either as a moral force against lust in Scholastic-Christian terms, or as the principle of virtuous love that transcends and conquors sensuality in Neoplatonic terms, or as a Lethean force, oblivion, to which Venus' temple on Mt. Eryx was dedicated (Ovid, *Remedies of Love*, ll. 551–54). These currents of thought kept the anecdote alive in the Renaissance and provoked a variety of interpretations according to the philosophical biases of the various contributors. Because Ferrand

sides with those who subscribe to the essentially classical view that Anteros is desire fulfilled and the power who punishes those who reject
the tender of love, he cannot use the myth as a central metaphor for the
countering of erotic desire, such as Battista Fregoso does in his *Anteros
ou contramours*, but the need for mutuality in marriage provides him
with the occasion for at least this brief revisiting of one of the popular
myths of his age.

Ferrand cites both the fourth-century rhetorician Themistius and the
third-century Neoplatonist Porphyry as sources, but again he was undoubtedly relying upon more recent authorities. The question of sources
leads, in fact, to the heart of the question of interpretation of the figure.
Like the seminal story of Antiochus and Stratonice, this tale has a complex history revealing multiple applications according to the needs of
the borrower. It can be traced at least as far back as Pausanias, who
in his *Description of Greece, Attica*, ch. 30, vol. I, p. 165, tells of an altar
to Eros and Anteros in conjunction with the story of Meles (or Meletus)
and Timagoras. It was a story of one man's love for another, but one
who, nevertheless, scorned and taunted the lover, provoking his suicide,
and who then slew himself in remorse at the prompting, as it were, of
the god who avenges those refused in love. Some believe Virgil had
this god in mind when he has Dido (*Aeneid*, bk. IV. 520) pray to the
power who deals justly with unequal love. It is an Athenian story that
Pausanias tells, and that is retold by Aelian and Suidas in his *Lexicon*,
under " Ἀντέρος." In addition to the many ancient sources, it was often
treated by Renaissance writers: Battista Fregoso, Celio Calcagnini, Lelio
Gregorio Giraldi, Agostino Nifo, and Mario Equicola, to name the principal ones.

The last named would seem to be the most probable source for Ferrand, given the number of occasions both credited and noncredited that
he drew from Equicola. In the *Libro de natura de amore*, pp. 69^V–70^V,
Equicola not only translates the passage in question from Themistius,
but he summarizes the controversy over meanings, mentions Pausanias
and the story of Meles and Timagoras, and defends the view that Anteros is the completion of love, or Eros, and not its opposition. The
only hint that Ferrand must have looked further into the matter is the
absence of any reference in Equicola to Porphyry. The originator of that
attribution seems to have been Celio Calcagnini of Ferrara in his *Anteros sive de mutuo amore* (Basileae: Froben, 1544), pp. 436 ff., who claims
Porphyry for his source despite the fact that the version he presents is
accurately transcribed from Themistius. Calcagnini deals at length with
the confusion over the interpretations of the allegory, and traces much
of the trouble to Servius the Grammarian who took "ἀντι" only in the
sense of opposition, and not in the sense of equality or complementarity to Eros. See his *In Vergilii carmina commentarii*, ed. Thilo and Hagen
(Leipzig: Teubner, 1881–84), vol. I, p. 559. Calcagnini argues that Anteros is not anti-Eros, but his completion and the avenger of those who
fail to reciprocate love; likewise, he is not the oblivion of Lethean love
(see ch. XXXVI, n. 12, below), but the god of reciprocity. He retraces

the entire tradition back to the stories of Meletus and Timagoras, and of Chariton and Melanippus in Suidas.

Calcagnini is doubly suggested as Ferrand's source, not only because his name appears at the end of the treatise in the list of authors cited, but also because he is nowhere else referred to in the treatise, so that this passage alone redeems his appearance in the list. There can be no certainties, however, because Calcagnini's friend Lelio Gregorio Giraldi offers a nearly identical version in a book known to Ferrand, the *De deis gentium libri sive syntagmata XVII*, where the material appears in syntagma XII (see ch. XXIII, n. 5, above). Renaissance variants include the version by Alciat in his *Emblemata*, no. CX: "'Aντέρος, amor virtutis alium Cupidinem superans," that returns to a moralizing tradition in which Anteros is taken for the force that restrains and binds lust or erotic desire. It is not clear whether his approach is strictly moral or whether it takes up the Neoplatonic tendency to identify Anteros with virtuous love, beauty, and transcendence. Agostino Nifo treats the material in his *Medici libri duo, de Pulchro primus, de Amore secundus* (Lugduni: apud G. et M. Beringos fratres, 1549), pp. 111–13. His source may have been Equicola, and that he attributes the story to Themistius would further confirm the point. He agrees that Anteros is the completion of desire, but he is troubled by the dichotomy between the lower and higher forms of love. To avoid assigning Eros to lust and Anteros to virtuous love, he creates an Eros-Anteros pair for each kind of love.

The motif made its way into the poetry of the century, as well, and is perhaps most notably developed in a poem by Antoine Héroët. In the "Autre invention extraicte de Platon de n'aymer point sans estre aymé" (*Oeuvres poetiques*, p. 96), he gives an account of the birth of Anteros in order to persuade the lady to return his love. The anecdote is turned into a conceit of the *carpe diem* variety on the basis that just as Anteros may be the god who avenges the hard-hearted, so too, as the one who represents Eros completed, that is, requited love, he is a force that works toward the completion of that union. Eros and Anteros in mutual relation appears to represent for Héroët, not only the reciprocal union of a man and a woman, but also the androgyne and hence, perhaps, the false attribution to Plato of a story the author must have known to belong to other writers. Ferrand knew the poem on the androgyne but seems not to have taken into account here this related work (see ch. VIII, n. 18, above).

16. Plutarch, *Advice to Bride and Groom*, in *Moralia*, trans. Frank Cole Babbitt, vol. II, p. 301: "Solon directed that the bride should nibble a quince before getting into bed, intimating, presumably, that the delight from lips and speech should be harmonius and pleasant at the outset."

17. [*Lucret.*]: Lucretius, *De rerum natura*, bk. IV. 1280–82:

>Nam facit ipsa suis interdum foemina fastis,
>Morigerisque modis, et mundo corpori cultu,
>Ut facile insuescat, secum vir degere vitam.

See trans. W. H. D. Rouse, p. 338. Read *factis* for *fastis* and "ut facile insuescat te secum degere vitam."

18. [*L. 28. c. 10.*]: Pliny, *Natural History*, bk. XXVIII, ch. 79, ed. W. H. S. Jones, vol. III, p. 175: "Cato thought that to take hare as food is soporific, and a popular belief is that it also adds charm to the person for nine days, a flippant pun, but so strong a belief must have some justification." As the editor explains, "the pun is on *lepus* 'hare' and *lepos* 'charm.'"

19. Martial, *Epigrams*, bk. V. xxix:

> Si quando leporem mittis mihi, Gellia, mandas,
> Formosus septem, Marce, diebus eris.
> Si non derides, si verum, Gellia, mandas,
> Edisti numquam, Gellia, tu leporem.

See trans. Walter C. A. Ker, vol. I, p. 318. In line 1 read *dicis* for *mandas*; in line 3 read *lux mea* for *Gellia*.

20. [*Cap. 14. l. 2. de hist. anim.*]: Aristotle, *History of Animals*, bk. II, ch. 14 (505b): "χρῶντοί τινες αὐτῷ πρὸς δίκας καὶ φίλτρα." See trans. A. L. Peck, vol. I, p. 122.

Pliny, *Natural History*, bk. IX. xli: "Echeneis amatoriis beneficiis infamis, judiciorum et litium mora." See trans. H. Rackham, vol. III, p. 214: "quam ob causam amatoriis quoque veneficiis infamis est et iudiciorum ac litium mora." Ferrand attempts to adapt Pliny's words to his own ends by substituting *beneficiis* for *veneficiis*, a beneficial rather than poisonous potion (presuming it is not a misprint), and thereby creates an ambiguous or contadictory statement.

The lore of the remora was often repeated in the Renaissance. See Raffaele Maffei (Volaterranus), *Commentariorum urbanorum libri XXXVIII*, "*Philologia*," p. 277[V]: "Echeneis latine remora."

Rondelet, *L'histoire entiere des poissons*, bk. XII, ch. 18, p. 286, and bk. XVI, ch. 18, p. 334.

François Belleforest and Pierre Boaistuau, *Histoires prodigieuses et memorables*, bk. I, ch. 18, pp. 133–34.

Jean de Veyries, *La genealogie de l'amour*, bk. II, ch. 26, p. 418.

Remora comes from *remorari*, to slow or to stop, and this came, in turn, to mean any delay or impediment. The remora genus of fish belongs to the family *Echeneididae* and bears on its head an oval suction dish by which means it can attach itself to sharks or other large fish or floating objects and thereby travel many miles. Whether the story of Periander gave the name, or the name gave rise to the story, the fish has been credited with an ability to stop ships simply by attaching themselves in great numbers to the hull. That the men in the ship were destined to commit a crime against love, sexuality, and virility suggested, by analogy, that the flesh of the fish that could stop such an attack must also have occult properties in philters for protecting and prolonging love. Periander was a famous tyrant of Corinth who ruled from ca. 625 to ca. 585 B.C.

Pliny, *Natural History*, bk. IX, ch. 41, vol. III, p. 217: "Mucianus states that the murex is broader than the purple, and has a mouth that is not rough nor round and a beak that does not stick out into corners but shuts together in either side like a bivalve shell: and that owing to murexes clinging to the sides a ship was brought to a standstill when in full sail before the wind, carrying despatches from Periander ordering some noble youths to be castrated, and that the shell-fish that rendered this service are worshipped in the shrine of Venus at Cnidus."

21. [*In vita Apoll. l. 1. c. 3.*]: Philostratus, *The Life of Apollonius of Tyana*, bk. III, ch. 1, trans. F. C. Conybeare, p. 233: "Now the woods along the bank closely resemble those of the river in question, and a balm also is distilled from the trees, out of which the Indians make a nuptial ointment; and unless the people attending the wedding have besprinkled the young couple with this balm, the union is not considered complete nor compatible with Aphrodite bestowing her grace upon it."

   Jean de Veyries, *La genealogie de l'amour*, bk. II, ch. 26, p. 418: "Ils tenoient encores qu'il y avoit une espece de coral qu'ils appelloient charitoblepharon, qui advançoit fort les affaires de ce petit Dieu, mais je ne sçay pas comme ilz le preparoient, s'ils le pulverisoient et calcinoient du tout pour le potionner, ou s'ilz se contentoient de l'appliquer tout entier sur le corps."

   Bk. II, ch. 26, p. 419: "Je me souvins que la Thessalie nourrist une herbe nommée catanance, qui n'a autre usage qu'à servir à ce metier [worn by women as an allurement, in the sense both of a cosmetic and as a charm] . . . en se portant sur soy, pensants qu'elle eust quelque vertu attractive des femmes en son amour: or ces fumées magiques n'evaporoient que d'une fort fresle conjecture, tirée du naturel de ceste herbe, lors qu'elle se fanist et se seche, elle se ramasse et se reserre en guise de griffe d'un Milan qui se meurt, si qu'ilz pensoient qu'en l'ayant sur soy, elle leur influeroit une vertu rapace, laquelle leur agrapheroit celles qu'ils aymoient, voire contre leur propre gré. C'est un plaisir de lire chez les anciens les sottises de leurs magiciennes fort occupées à violenter les personnes à l'amour, elles n'y espargnent ny grué, ny rouë pour les bander et guinder au point de leurs intentions."

22. Menander, *Sententiae ex codicibus Byzantinis*, ed. S. Jaekel (Leipzig: Teubner, 1964), 33–83: "φιλίας μέγιστος δεσμὸς αἱ τέκνων γοναί." The modern text has "μέγιστον" in lieu of "μέγιστος."

23. [*L. 8. Eth. c. 14.*]: Aristotle, *Nicomachean Ethics*, bk. VIII, ch. 12. 7 (1162a): "τὰ γὰρ τέκνα κοινὸν ἀγαθὸν, συνέχει δὲ τὸ κοινόν." See trans. H. Rackham, p. 503. The entire passage translates: "Children, too, seem to be a bond of union, and therefore childless marriages are more easily dissolved; for children are a good possessed by both parents in common, and common property holds people together." Ferrand replaces the word "ἀμφοῖν" with a comma.

24. Ferrand's discourse on sterility and its cures has not been located; it is not mentioned in the bibliographical articles on him, and is likely not extant. Nevertheless, we have a sampling of his materials relating to this subject in ch. XXIII of his *Traicte* on love of 1610. In this chapter he mentions the remora, the coral charitoblepharon and the herb catanance, paralleling the present chapter. Afterward, he continues with a series of recipes, most of which are applied to the genitals in order to stimulate sexual appetite and performance. Whether he extrapolated this material and added to it to make another treatise, or whether he is merely

referring to this chapter as a "discourse" is open to debate. It is probable, however, that this was one of the offending passages that brought
the book under censure in Toulouse in 1619. Ferrand was undoubtedly
interested in the topic, for otherwise the discussion of philters and love
stimulants for use by married couples bears an oblique relationship to
the rest of the treatise with its campaign against all such preparations.
There was a considerable literature on the subject that ranged from seriously medical to folkloric. We have evidence that Ferrand had consulted Guglielmo da Varignana, Giovanni de Vigo, Laurent Joubert, Jean
Liébault, Hippocrates, Levinus Lemnius, and several others on sterility.
See n. 1, above.

25. [*Rondelet l. 1 de piscib. c. 1.*]: Guillaume Rondelet, *L'histoire entiere des
   poissons*, bk. IX, ch. 15, "Hippoglossum" is described as "ceste espece de
   sole, qu'en France on nomme Flettan."
      Albert the Great, *De virtutibus herbarum quinta herba . . . amorem in-
   ducit inter virum et uxorem si utatur illa in cibariis*, in *De secretis mulierum
   libellus*, p. 129: "Septima herba Veneris dicitur pisteriona, quibusdam hi-
   erobota dicitur, id est, herbae columbaria et verbena. . . . Valet etiam multum in aphrodisia, id est, coïtu, qui succus eius auget multum sperma,
   cum quis vult coïre addit ad desiderium eius, et major virtus ipsius
   herbae est, quia si quis eam portaverit, erit multum potens in coïtu."

26. [*Lemn. l 4. de occult. nat. mir. c. 12.*]: Levinus Lemnius, *Occulta naturae
   miracula*, bk. IV, ch. 12, pp. 433–35: "Caeterum cum monstruosus hic galli
   partus, ex cuius ovo basiliscum emergere vulgus opinatur, nullos non
   terret, ac formidine concutit, tum lapis alectorius, hoc est, gallinaceus
   omnes afficit, atque a nullo non expetitur: si quidem hoc gestamen virile
   robur adauget, ac cum fortitudinem, tum in rebus aggrediendis confi-
   dentiam adfert, eximitur autem ex castrati galli, hoc est, capi, cui testes
   ex"ecti sunt, ventriculo, tenui membrana aut pellicula inclusus, quarto
   a quo in spadonem et enuchum descivit, anno: gemma haec colore est
   pellucido cristalli specie, magnitudine fabae. Credo autem hanc ex semi-
   nali excremento concrescere ac conglobari coloris naturalis ad umento."
      Albert the Great, *De secretis mulierum libellus . . . de virtutibus herbarum,
   lapidum, et animalium*, pp. 135–36: "Si vis impetrare aliquid ab aliquo.
   Accipe lapidem, qui alectorius dicitur, et est lapis gallinacei vel galli, et
   est albus ut chrystallus, et extrahitur de ventriculo gallinacei, post quam
   fuerit castratus ultra annum quartum. Et ut quidam dicunt, post annum
   extrahitur de gallo decrepito. Et ad quantitatem fabae extat, ventrem
   gratum reddit et constantem: et sub lingua acceptum sitim extinguit: et
   hoc ultimum tempore nostro expertum est, et subtiliter percepi."

27. "male quaeritur herbis: / Moribus et forma conciliandus amor": Ovid,
   Heroides VI: "Hypsipyle Iasone, ll. 93–94. See *Epistolae Heroidum*, ed.
   Henricus Dörrie, p. 98.

28. [*Bodin, Delrio.*]: Jean Bodin, *De la demonomanie des sorciers* (Paris: Chez
   Jacques du Puys, 1587), pp. 61^V–64^r: "Mais de toutes ces ordures il n'y
   en a point de plus frequente par tout, ny de gueres plus pernicieuse,
   que l'empeschement qu'on donne a ceux qui se marient, qu'on appelle
   lier l'esguillette, les anciens Latins disoient *vaecordiam iniicere*, jusques

aux enfans qui en font mestier, avec telle impunité et licence, qu'on ne
s'en cache point et plusieurs s'en vantent, qui n'est pas chose nouvelle:
car nous lisons en Herodote [1 Lib. 2.] que le Roy d'Aegypte Amasis,
fut leé et empesché de cognoistre Laodice sa femme, jusques à ce qu'il
fut delié par charmes et precautions solennelles. Et en cas semblable les
concubines de Theodoric userent de mesmes ligatures envers Herman-
berge, comme nous lisons en Paul Aemil, en la vie de Clotaire 2. Les
philosophes epicuriens se mocquent de ces merveilles, si sont-ils eston-
nez de ces nouëurs d'esguillettes, qui se trouvent par tout, et n'y peuvent
jamais donner aucun remede naturel. C'est pourquoy au Canon, il est dit
[2. 33. q. 8. 1] ainsi: *Si per sortiarias, et maleficas artes, occulto, sed nunquam
injusto Dei judicio permittente, et diabolo praeparante, concubitus non sequitur,
ad Deum per humilem confessionem est recurrendum.* De ce passage on peut
retirer quatre ou cinq choses notables: Premierement, que la copulation
se peut empescher par art malefique, en quoy s'accordent les theolo-
giens, et mesmes Thomas d'Aquin, sur le quatriesme livre des Sentences,
distinctione XXIIII. où il est escrit, qu'on peut estre lié pour le regard
d'une femme, et non pour les autres, et au dernier chapitre *de frigidis*: En
second lieu que cela se faict par un secret, et toutesfois juste jugement
de Dieu, qui le permet: En troisiesme lieu, que le diable prepare tout
cela: En quatriesme lieu, qu'il faut avoir recours à Dieu, par jeusnes et
oraisons . . . qu'il y avoit plus de cinquante sortes de nouër l'esguillette:
l'une pour empescher l'homme marié seulement: l'autre pour empescher
la femme mariée seulement, à fin que l'un ennuyé de l'impuissance de sa
partie commette adultere avec d'autres. D'avantage elle disoit [his hostess in Poitiers] qu'il n'y avoit gueres quel'homme qu'on liast: Puis elle
disoit qu'on pouvoit lier pour un jour, pour un an, pour jamais, ou du
mois d'autant que l'esguillette dureroit, s'ils n'estoient desliez, et qu'il y
avoit une telle liaison, que l'un aimoit l'autre et neantmoins estoit hay
à mort: l'autre moyen qu'ils s'aymoient ardemment, et quand c'estoit
à s'approcher, ils s'egratignoient, et battoient outrageusement, comme
de faict estant à Thoulouze on me dist qu'il y avoit eu un homme et
une femme, qui estoient ainsi liez, et neantmoins trois ans apres ils se
rállurent, et eurent de beaux enfans. . . . Et ne se faut esmerveiller, si
le Diable se sert fort de telles liasons, car premierement il empesche la
procreation du genre humain, qu'il s'efforce tant qu'il peut d'exterminer:
En second lieu il oste le sacré lien d'amitié d'entre le mary et la femme:
En troisiesme lieu, ceux qui sont liez vont paillarder ou adulterer. C'est
donc une impieté detestable, et qui merite la mort."

Martin Del Rio, *Disquisitiones magicarum libri VI*, bk. III, p. 1, ques. 4,
sec. 8: "De maleficio ligaminis," pp. 60 ff.: "A viris doctioribus septem
traditas invenio causas proximas huius impotentiae, quibus causis daemon abutitur: *prima* est quando coniugem alterum alteri reddit odiosum; vel invicem sane odioso facit, per calumniam suspicionemque, aut
morbi alicuius immissionem, sicut cum vel Venus, iuxta Stesichorum, vel
Medea, iniecto pharmaco fecit, ut omnes feminae Lemni graviter oreole-
rent, sicque illas mariti sunt aspernati. Medeae facinus vult esse Myrtilus
lib. rerum Lesbicar. I.[b], [in margin: [b] *Natalis Mytholog. l. 6. c. 7.*] aut id

faciunt phantasia turbata, sic ut aliquid in compare vehementer odiosum vel formidabile inesse credant. Sic Valazca[c] [in margin: [c] *Aeneas Silvius in histor. Bohem. & Bap. Egna li. 3. c. 2*] Libussae Boëmae famula, mulieres a virorum amore per veneficium adeo avertit: *ut coniuratione inita, suos quaeque maritos, fratres, patres, filios una nocte interfecerint, mox arce Vissegradensi obsessa, Primislai regis exercitum ad internecionem fere ceciderint*. Aliquando faciunt, ut invicem quidem ament ardentissime, sed quando ad copulam ventum, subito accensi odio, alter alterum caedat, vel unguibus laceret, quod genus et theologi[d], [in margin: [d] *P. Henerique de Sacrament. lib. 12. c. 8. n. 2. Sot. in 4. d. 34. a. 3. Iaquer. flag. c. 12*] et Iurisconsulti[e] [in margin: [e] *auctor daemonoma. et auctor. li. de Lamiis. l. 2.*] noverunt, tunc daemon primo accendit ardorem libidinis proposita forma coniugis ut concupiscibili, et quando venitur ad amplexus, tunc proponit ut odiosam et exitialem, faciens ut membra generationis appareant vel magnitudinis prorsus incongruae, vel formae horribilis aut supra modum faedae. *Secunda* causa est, quando corpora impedit, ne queant ad se mutuo appropinquare, et sic ea dividit, vel detinens ea in locis diversis, vel cum conatur iungi, phantasma aut quid aliud iniiciens intermedium, ad prius videtur pertinere illud Propertii[f]: [in margin: [f] *l. 1. eleg. 12.*]

> *Invidiae fuimus, quis me Deus obruit? aut quae*
> *Lecta Prometheis dividit herba iugis?*

Pertinet ad posterius, quaedam narratio, plena admirandae novitatis, cuius fides penes auctores sit.   Narrat ex Vincentio Belluacensi D. Antoninus[g], [in margin: [g] *Vincent. lib. 26 histor. Antonin. p. 2. sum hist. ti. 16. c. 7. &. 4.*] Romae temporibus Henrici tertii Imp. fuisse iuvenem quendam locuplentem et nobilem, qui recens uxorem duxerat, et sodales suos opiparo convivio nuptiali excerperat. Exivere in campum a prandio lusuti pila. Sponsus, ludi dux, pilam poscit, et ne excideret anulus sponsalitius, inserit eum digito statuae Veneris aereae, quae in proximo erat: omnes unum petebant, sic cito defatigatus ipse a ludo secessit, et ad statuam rediens, anulum recepturus, ecce, videt digitum statuae usque ad volam manus recurvatum, et quantumvis conatus anulum recuperare, nec digitum inflectere, nec anulum valuit extrahere. Redit ad sodales, nec illis ea de re quicquam indicavit. Nocte intempesta cum famulo ad statuam revertitur, et extensum ut initio digitum repperit, sed sine anulo; iactura dissimulata, domum se confert ad novam nuptiam. Cumque thorum nebulosum ac densum intersuum coniugisque corpus volutari, sentiebat id tactu, videre tamen nequibat, hoc abitacul ab amplexu prohibebatur; audiebat etiam vocem dicentem: *Mecum concumbe, quia hodie me desponsasti. Ego sum Venus, cui digito anulum inseruisti, nec reddam.* . . .

"*Tertia* causa est, si spiritus vitales prohibeantur transire ad membra generationis, et sic seminis decisio impediatur, de quo impedimento, recte Ioan. Maior disseruit.[a] [in margin: [a] *in 4 d. 34. a.3.*]

"*Quarta* est, si semen prolificum exciccetur et subtrahatur.

"*Quinta*, si virga viri flaccida fiat, saltem quando quis vult actum matrimonii exercere.

"*Sexta*, si qua naturalia alia pharmaca applecentur, quibus vis patrandi quonvis modo tollatur. . . .

"*Septima* causa est rarior nemque muliebrium locorum observatio, vel nimia coarctatio, aut viri genitalium retractio, absconsio, vel vera ademptio."

Arnald of Villanova, *De physicis ligaturis*, in *Opera omnia*, pp. 619 ff. Ferrand does not seem to be aware that the treatise is not by Arnald but by Costa ben Lucas, a fact known to Del Rio, who identifies the author correctly in bk. I, ch. 4, ques. 4, pp. 45–46: "De amuletis et periaptis." See also Ambroise Paré, *On Monsters and Marvels*, ch. 34, pp. 105–6: "Knotting the point; and the words have no effect, but it is the devil's craft; and those who knot it cannot do it without having convened with the devil, which is a damnable wickedness. For the one who practices this cannot deny that he is a violator of the law of God and of nature, to [thus] prevent the law of marriage, ordained of God. By this [spell] it happens that they cause marriages to be broken, or at the least they keep them in sterility, which is a sacrilege. Moreover, they remove the mutual friendship from marriage, as well as human society, and they put a capital hate between the two spouses; likewise they are the cause of the adultery and lechery which result from it, for those who are tied [in matrimony] burn with cupidity for one another."

Michel Baudier, *Histoire du serrail, et de la cour du Grand Seigneur* (Paris: Chez Sebastien Cramoisy, 1650), bk. I, p. 25. Such charms were used by young girls in the seraglio to attract the attention of the grand master: "Les autres du serrail qui sont encores filles, ou qui n'ont eu qu'une seule fois la compagnie du Prince, employent tous leurs attraits pour lui plaire, et trouvons leurs artifices trop faibles, y adjoustent l'aide des charmes, et sorcelleries, qu'elles acheptent à quel prix que se soit."

Nicholas Venette, *Tableau de l'amour conjugal, ou histoire complete de la generation de l'homme* (Paris: Chez L. Duprat-Duverger, 1810; orig. 1687), vol. II, pp. 95–96: "Si un homme aime avec trop de passion, si la pudeur ou la timidité ne peuvent souffrir les amorces de l'amour, si les courtisanes ou la débauche ont épuisé ses forces, et qu'a cause de cela il ne puisse jouir des plaisirs du mariage, on dira aussitôt qu'il est ensorcelé, ainsi que le disoit autrefois l'empereur Néron de lui-même, et que l'aiguillette lui avoit été nouée, comme s'il n'avoit pas assez de causes naturelles qui le rendissent froid et languissant."

29. [*Paluda. in 4. sent. d. 34 q. 2. art. 3. Rod. à Castro l. 4. medico pol. c. 1.*]: Pierre de la Palud, *In quartum sententiarum* (Venetiis: impressum per B. Locatellum, 1493), p. 171^{r-v}. In all probability Ferrand took this reference from Martin Del Rio, *Disquisitiones magicarum libri sex*, bk. III, p. 1, ques. 3, p. 18, in margin.

Rodrigo de Castro, *Medicus-politicus*, bk. IV, ch. 1, pp. 212–13.

It is at this point in his treatise that Ferrand comes closest to the point of view concerning *philocaption* held by the late medieval theologians. Kramer and Springer in the *Malleus maleficarum*, pt. II, ques. 2, ch. 3, pp. 170–71, argue that "inordinate love of one person for another, can be caused in three ways. Sometimes it is due merely to a lack of control over the eyes; sometimes to the temptation of devils; sometimes to the spells of necromancers and witches, with the help of devils." They follow with a résumé of the cures recommended by Avicenna for those suffering from the desire created by the eyes, though these remedies are hardly relevant to their purposes except insofar as they relate to the diseases of the soul. Their concern was with the methods and exorcisms of the church used to discover witches and to drive out the devils that cause such inordinate desire. There are passages strikingly similar to Ferrand's which emphasize the truth of what Ferrand is intent on denying, namely "that it can be by the work of the devil that hatred is stirred up between married people so as to cause the crime of adultery. But when a man is so bound in the meshes of carnal lust and desire that he can be made to desist from it by no shame, words, blows or action; and when a man often puts away his beautiful wife to cleave to the most hideous of women . . . I say, of what use is it to speak of remedies to those who desire no remedy?" Though Ferrand does not discount the force of aphrodisiacs and of ligatures, he is generally skeptical concerning the belief that erotic passions can be generated by ritual magic or witchcraft. Rather, in the Hippocratic tradition, he insists upon the somatogenesis of the diseases of melancholy and the necessity for assigning the origins of such diseases to the humors and temperaments of the body. By dint of that commitment he must urge that what is to be owed to natural causes not be assigned to supernatural. Hence, one of the achievements of Ferrand's work, in historical terms, is his complete break with the theological traditions that had dwelt upon psychopathic desire in terms of sin, temptation, demon possession, and witchcraft; Ferrand's interest in these ideas remained marginal, anecdotal, and skeptical. Hubertus Tellenbach, in *Melancholy: History of the Problem, Endogeneity, Typology, Pathogenesis, Clinical Considerations*, trans. Erling Eng (Pittsburgh: Duquesne University Press, 1980), p. 2: "views the psychiatry of antiquity in the perspective of vacillation between initiatives toward a pathological anatomy and unbridled speculation." Ferrand is important as a perpetuator of that medical point of view in opposition to the "unbridled speculation" of the theologians. See also Giordano Bruno, *De magia et theses de magia* in *Opera latine conscripta publicis sumptibus edita*, ed. H. Vitelli (Neapoli: D. Morano, 1879–91), vol. III, and *De vinculis in genera*, in *Opera*, vol. III, for a point of view opposed to that of the theologians and physicians, and Ioan Couliano, *Eros et magie à la Renaissance* (Paris: Flammarion, 1984).

30. Ferrand's source, as he declares, is Giovanni Battista Cipelli (Egnazio) whom we consulted in the French translation by Geofroy Tory of Bourges, *Sommaire de chroniques . . . de tous les empereurs d'europe depuis Iules César, iusques à Maximilian dernier décédé* (Paris: G. Tory, 1529), whose version provided Ferrand with an exemplum of feminine wiles and sorcery. By other accounts Valasca was a legendary fifth-century queen of Bohemia who, according to the customs and practices of her era and nation, led the women troops into battle. That she employed magic in achieving her victories is recorded by Enea Silvio Piccolomini (Pope Pius II) in his

Historia Bohemica (1745; Basileae: Michael Furter, ca. 1489), chs. 7–8. He records that she was a valiant fighter and ruthless with her captives. The men whom she spared, she had blinded in one eye and had their thumbs cut off in order to render them unfit for further military service. After she had reigned as queen for seven years, she was killed by Primislaus. That she was also the liberator of her sex from the tyranny of men through the power of her magic spells is a dimension that appears in the *Commentariorum urbanorum libri XXXVIII* of Raffaele Maffei of Volterra (1506; 1511) in the "Geographia," bk. VII, where he tells how she incited the women to rise up during the night to slaughter the men, to take all their horses and treasure, and to establish a realm where they would live and rule for many years thereafter like Amazons. By degrees, her use of magic is overshadowed by her stature as a woman of martial valor and her reputation as a founder of an ideal matriarchy freed from masculine tyranny. That dimension was underscored by Ortensio Landi (Philalethe Polytopiensi) in his *Forcianae quaestiones, in quibus varia Italorum ingenia explicantur*, ed. Antiochus Lavintus (Neapoli: excudebat Martinus de Ragusia, 1536) where she is named in company with Berenice, Penthesilea, Thomyris, Zenobia, Hypsicratea, and other martial women of history and legend. The version of Raffaele Maffei is recapulated in Robert Estienne's *Dictionarium nominum propriorum virorum, mulierum, populorum*, 1546 (Coloniae Agrippinae: apud I. Gymnicum, 1576): "Valasca Bohemorum regina fuit, quae facta cum caeteris mulieribus coniuratione de excutiendo virorum principatu, copiarum ductrix bellum movit, interfectisque viris foemines omnes asservit in libertatem, ita ut instar Amazonum multos annos imperarint sine viris." In taking the story from Egnazio, Ferrand understood Valasca to be a diabolical chambermaid, rather than a queen, who used her black arts to cause the women of her city to join in an unnatural slaughter of their husbands. That she had also become a model for feminine valor and virtue had presumably escaped Ferrand's notice.

31. [*L. 14 de Histor. Dano.*]: Saxo Grammaticus, *Danorum historiae libri XVI . . . des Erasmi Roterdami de Saxone censura* (Basileae: apud Jo. Bebëlium, 1534), bk. XIV, p.162^{r-v}: "Siquidem mares in ea urbe cum foeminis in concubitum adictis, canum exemplo cohaerere solebant. Nec ab ipsis morando divelli poterant. Interdum utrisque perticis ediverso appensi, inusitato nexu ridiculum populo spectaculum praebuere. Ea miraculi foeditate solennis ignobilibus statuis cultus accessit, creditum est earum viribus effectum, quod daemonum erat praestigiis adumbratum. Sueno vero quo magis simulacra aspernenda docerent, super ea cum a Karentinis eiicererentur sublimis consistere voluit. Quo facto pondus contumelia auxit. Nec minus trahentes rubore quam onere vexavit, domestica numina alienigenae pontificis pedibus subjecta cernentes. . . . Ibidem quoque nuper clarum inaudita generis miraculum incidit. Matrona quaedam a viro immerens adulterii insimulata, cum purgandae infamiae gratia candenti lamine dexteram obtulisset, subito ferrum quod exceptura erat perinde atque innoxiae manus contactum fugiens, neglecto pondere sublime se extulit, penduloque motu gradientis foeminae incessum

comitans, cum ante aram iactandum erat, inter religiosam astantium admirationem proprio impulsu humi decidit. Ea res et mulieris infamiam levarit, et visentium animos religioni proniores effecit. Nec temere quidem pudicitiam suam tam ancipitis argumenti judicio credidit, cui corporis animisque fiduciam certae synceritatis conscientia ministravit." Ferrand almost certainly takes this reference, however, from a parallel context in Martin Del Rio's *Disquisitionum magicarum libri VI*, bk. III, pt. 1, ques. 4, sec. 8: "De maleficiis ligaminis," vol. I, p. 63.

32. [*L de aere loc. & aq. Herod. in Clio.*]: Hippocrates, "*Of Airs, Waters and Places*," See *Oeuvres complètes*, ed. Littré, vol. II, pp. 79, 81; see above ch. XXXI, n. 6.

   Herodotus, trans. A. D. Godley, bk. I, entitled *Clio*, vol. I, pp. 136–37. For the text, see ch. XXXI, n. 5, above.

33. [*Albuc. li. 2. c. 72. Cels. ca. 28. l. 7. Aegin. l. 6. c. 72.*]: *De chirurgia Arabice et Latine, cura Johannis Channing* (Oxonii: Clarendoniano, 1778), "Sectio septuagesima secunda: *De perforatione pudendi muliebris non perforati*," pp. 317–19: "Imperforatio est quando mulieris pudendum non est perforatum, vel foramine parvo. Est autem vel naturalis cum illa nata; vel accidentalis. Accidentalis porro ex morbo praecendenti: erit autem vel ex carne superflua germinata, vel membrana, tenui vel densa. Est etiam vel in fundo matricis, vel in lateribus eius, vel in parte eius superiori, vel inferiori: prohibetque et coitum, et conceptum, et partum; saepe etiam menstrua prohibit. Huius cognito, est per inspectionem ab obstetrice, si obstructio sit manifesta et propinqua.

   "Quodsi manifesta non fuerit, equidem digitis suis vel radio illam investiget. Et in obstructio est ex membrana tenui et sit labiis vicina, equidem ietius disrumpet illam. Id fiat, si applicet labiis pulvillorum similitudinem; dein ponat simul duos pollices manuum suarum. Et foemina sit super dorsum suum cruribus suis divaricatis, tum labia fortiter distendat, donec laceretur membrana tenuis, et obstructio aperiatur. Tum sumat lanam, quam in vino et olco submergat, et loco opponat. Et mulier coeat quotidie, ne alia vice locus consolidetur.

   "Quodsi crassa et densa membrana fuerit, oportet ut seces illam scalpello lato, quod est simile folio myrti.

   "Quodsi ex carne germinata fiat obstructio, hamo adhaereat, et abscinde illam: et tibi praesto sint remedia, quae haemorrhagiam sine stimulo sedant, sicat acacia, et sanguis draconis, et thus, ovi albumine subacta. Dein utitor cannula ex plumbo ampla, ne vulnus cito nimis consolidetur; illam teneat dies aliquot, et utitor penicillo ex lino sicco: dein curato cum reliqua curatione incarnativa. Donec sanetur.

   "Quandoque etiam accidit in matrice alias carnes germinare. Oportet igitur ut abscindas ad hunc modum omnes quae non sint tumor canserosus. Tumor etenim cancerosus qui in matrice oritur, non est omnio ferro tractandus."

   The operation as described above will stand as the foundation of the practice as set out in a number of treatises by Renaissance physicians. Liébault is, in fact, the probable source of Ferrand's information on Albucasis because Ferrand otherwise refers to him as Alsaravius and is possibly unaware that they were the same person. See n. 34, below. Celsus, *De medicina*, trans. W. G. Spencer, bk. VII, ch. 28, vol. III, pp. 453–55. Celsus describes both congenital blockage and blockage due to ulceration, the kinds of procedures for opening the passage and the packing and ointments needed for healing the wound.

The marginal reference to Paul of Aegina is of a general nature; the chapter deals with "De non perforatis et phymo."

Johann Wier, *Medicarum observationum rararum liber I*, sec. "De curatione meatum naturalium clausorum et quibusdam aliis" (Basileae: par Joannem Oporinum, 1567), p. 98: "Existit autem in aliis membrana haec tenuior, fragiliorsque: in plerisque tam solida, crassa et firma, ut sectione opus sit. Ea tamen a interdum a mariti validi insulta frequenti, etiam post menses aliquot pertum ditur: qui si quandoque segnior aut impotentior fuerit, chirurgi adminiculo erit iuvandus. Dum vero ea tenacior seduli initius violentia impeditur, fatigatur, quia intumescit plerunque usqueadeo cum annexis particulis, ut penem amplius non admittat, praecludaque viro accessum omnem, nisi incisa. Haec exemplis mihi notissimis facile demonstravero."

Wier provides a brief history, both medical and literary, of the hymen, the customs, and ideas related to it, citing among others, Avicenna lib. III, fen 21, tr. 1, cap. 1, Almanzoar, Celsus, Vesalius, bk. V, ch. 15 *Anatomicorum liber*, Fallopius, Soranus, Carpi, Moses, Cyprian epistle 2, Africanus, Barbaro, Bembo, Lusitano and Paracelsus.

34. [*Liebault l. 2 des mal. des femmes, ca. 61*]: Jean Liébault, *Des maladies des femmes*, bk. II, ch. 61. Ferrand probably consulted this work exclusively. Liébault writes a detailed chapter on the surgical techniques and procedures for removing obstructions, growths, and membranes blocking the vaginal tract. "Qu'ainsi soit je cognois des femmes autresfois miennes voisines et qui vivent encores, ésquelles pour la continence de leur mary, s'estoit engendree une membrane dans la partie honteuse, trois jours apres l'incision faicte de ceste membrane n'ont laisse d'exercer l'acte venerien" (p. 501). "Voyez paulus Aegineta chapitre septante deux du livre sixiesme, et Aëce chapitre 95. sermon quatriesme de la quatriesme Tetrabile. Celse chapitre vingt huict livre septiesme, Albucasis chapitre septante deux, livre second" (p. 503). Ferrand claims to have followed the instructions of Albucasis, Aëtius, Johann Wier, and Paré in performing this operation in Castelnaudary, but we note that in the parallel passage in the edition of 1610, ch. 23, p. 195, Ferrand cites as his own marginal references precisely those cited in Liébault, whereas in the later edition he includes Wier and Paré.

35. [*L. 6. epid. sec. 8.*]: Hippocrates, *Epidemics*, bk. V, sec. 8; *Oeuvres complètes*, ed. Littré, vol. V, p. 357; for the text see ch. II, n. 20, above.

36. For the modern physicians, see ch. XXXIV, n. 1, and ch. XXXV, n. 26, below. For the ancient physicians, see, e.g., Aëtius of Amida, *Tetrabiblos*, bk. IV, sermo 4, ch. 74, "De furore uterino."

37. Arnald of Villanova, *Remedia contra maleficia*, in *Opera omnia*, p. 1532.

38. [*C. de malefic. l. 9.*]: Giovanni de Vigo, *Le practique et cirurgie*, bk. IX, ch. 8: "De maleficiatis," p. 319: "Il ya aulcuns remplis de art diabolique

et contre la loy de dieu et de charite, substraient lamour naturel qui doibt estre entre lhomme et la femme, tellement quilz ne peuvent avoir copulation charnelle lun avec laultre, et pource les antiens et modernes docteurs ont volu escripre aulcuns remedes pour oster ceste mauvaise disposition. Et disent les anciens que le malefice peult advenir seullement a lhomme. Pour venir en bref a la cure dicelluy nous declarerons aulcuns remedes declarez par les docteurs. Et premier Diascorides dit que coral pendu en la chambre empesche tout melefice, et quand on le porte au col il le oste facilement. Aulcuns disent que artemisia pandue dessus lhuys de la maison ou de la chambre est le mesme vertu. Aulcuns disent que squilla est de mesme effect. Arsi dit de lauctorite de fidelis que se celluy qui est tenu in malefice mengeoit de un oiseau nomme picus martius, lequel demeure dedens les arbres et les cave de son bec, lequel fust rosti ou boulli il osteroit le malefice. Aulcuns disent que celluy qui est contrainct de aymer aulcun ou aulcune il fault quil prenne de stercore illius quam diligit inficiatus et le mettre dedens son soulier dextre, et incontinent quil sentira lodeur le malefice sera oste, et fault quil soit brusle devant que le mettre dedens le soulier, et avons veu aulcuns lesquelz ont experimente estre vray. Aulcuns disent que si on linissoit les parois de la maison ex stercore canis nigri, il osteroit le malefice des habitans en ladicte chambre."

XXXV.   Of Philters and Homerical Remedies

1. [*Rod à Castro l. 4 medicopol. c. 2.*]: Rodrigo de Castro, *Medicus-politicus*, bk. IV, ch. 2, p. 223: "Sed quodnam erit remedium contra philtrum, sive oculorum veneficium?   Occupatio mentis in rebus gravioribus, lectio bonorum librorum, preces ad Deum ut not siberet à pravis cogitationibus, saepiusque in mentem revocare ea, quae indignam faciunt foeminam, ut ametur, fugacitas nimirum pulchritudinis, menstrua, et quod tandem futura sit vermium.   Esca, ex cujus putri cadaveris medulla spinae, ut plerique scribunt, serpens terribilis enascetur.   His accedat quod dum forma diligitur, negligitur fama, abbreviatur vita, bona et honor amittuntur, ac in iram divinam incurritur." There can be no doubt that Ferrand relied heavily on De Castro for the writing and documentation of this chapter.   More than half of his references correspond to materials found in the *Medicus-politicus* with no attempts whatsoever to disguise the borrowings.   These will be identified in subsequent notes by "De Castro," and a page number.   All are from his bk. IV, ch. 2, on philters.   Nevertheless, we have treated them as original to Ferrand for purposes of annotating the text insofar as the material belongs to a common corpus of texts and citations found generally in discussions of the topic during the sixteenth century.   Ferrand cites De Castro as only one of the many in his age who believed that philters can cause love, but whether directly as a form of magical spell or only indirectly by heating the humors was the central point of contention.   Ferrand,

by his style, seems to dissociate himself from those who attribute magical powers to such potions, by implication citing De Castro as a subscriber to that school. Ferrand will deny that philters have the virtue of making the recipient fall in love with a prescribed person. He attests to their powers only as dangerous drugs that cause either madness or death, drugs that should never be used by Christian physicians. Insofar as potions could cause love, it might be argued that they could also be used to drive out love. Ferrand scrupulously avoids pushing his discussion toward this logical impasse, however, because he could not risk associating his pharmaceutical cures with philters treated as nonmagical potions, or risk proposing that such potions should be incorporated into the pharmaceutical treatment of love. One further contributor to the literature on philters should be mentioned here. Johann Wier, in his *Histoires, disputes et discours des illusions et impostures des diables*, offers two chapters of special interest: "De philtres, de l'hippomanes, et autres drogues amatoires"; and bk. III, ch. 40: "Que les boissons amoureuses, l'hippomanes, et toutes telles choses rendent plustost personnes furieuses, qu'amoureuses." Wier corroborates several of Ferrand's sources: Juvenal, "Satire 6"; Aristotle, *On the Nature of Animals*, bk. VI, chs. 18 and 22; bk. VIII, ch. 42; Virgil's *Aeneid*, bk. IV; Tibullus, bk. II, Elegy IV; Pliny, bk. VIII, ch. 22; as well as references to Apuleius, Propertius, Circe, and Medea. Wier's commentary is both more extended and more copiously illustrated than Ferrand's. Both writers agree that philters should be treated as poisons because they often had that effect on the victim. Both look to Aristotle for the foundational lore and beliefs on the topic. Clearly, there are suggestions of a relationship between Wier's chapters and De Castro's treatment, but these relationships are beyond our present study.

There is the prospect of another voice behind this chapter besides that of Rodrigo de Castro, namely that of Jean Aubery who, in *L'antidote d'amour*, pp. 92^v–96^r, deals with the powers of potions to make a specific person conform to the will of the person administering the philter. He likewise deals with the power of figures, characters, and numbers and whether they can force love. He states (p. 95^r) that "les philtres peuvent agiter et eschauffer les humeurs, et corrompre les facultez nobles de l'ame; mais qu'un tel amour ne peut estre agreable, et venir à contentement, à raison de sa violence; adjoustons que la volonté est libre, et qu'estant un principe indefini elle ne peut estre forcee par l'amour, s'il ne nous plaist." Aubery also warns against the power of philters to make men mad and maniacal. He mentions the deaths of Lucullus, Caligula, and Lucretius the poet, and he concludes with the story of Olympias, Queen of Macedonia, and the charms of her rival.

For another contemporary point of view on the efficacy of love philters, see Heinrich Kornmann, *De linea amoris commentarius*, ch. 3, pp. 59 ff.

A parallel passage occurs in the *Malleus maleficarum*, pt. 2, ques. 2, ch. 3, p. 172. Kramer and Springer make the point coming from the opposite direction, that just as witchcraft can be employed to stir up

inordinate desire, it can also be made to stir up hatred, especially between husbands and wives, driving them into adulterous relationships
with others: "It must be understood that what we have said concerning
inordinate love applies also to inordinate hatred, since the same discipline is of benefit for the two opposite extremes. But though the degree
of witchcraft is equal in each, yet there is this difference in the case of
hatred; the person who is hated must seek another remedy. For the man
who hates his wife and puts her out of his heart will not easily, if he
is an adulterer, be turned back again to his wife, even though he go on
many a pilgrimage."

For further information on the relationship between the uses of amatory philters and melancholy, see Ercole Sassonia, *De melancholia tractatus
perfectissimus* (Venetiis: apud Alexandrum Polum, 1620), ch. 12, p. 26.

2. [C. 3.]: Nahum, 3:4: "Propter multitudinem fornicationum meretricis
speciosae et gratae, et habentis maleficia." De Castro, pp. 215–16.

3. Rodrigo de Castro, *Medicus-politicus*, p. 216: "et in libro Baruch mentio
fit maleficii amatorii sub his verbis: mulieres circumdatae funibus in
viis sedent, succendentes offa olivarum, cum autem aliqua ipsis attracta
a transcunte dormierit cum eo, proximae suae exprobrat, quod digna
non sit habua sicut ipsa, neque funis eius disruptus."

4. Plato, *Symposium*, "δεινὸς γοής καὶ φαρμακεύς": "a master of jugglery and
of witchcraft." See trans. W. R. L. Lamb, pp. 180–81.

5. [*Iuuen. sat. 6*]: Juvenal, "Sixth Satire," ll. 610–12: "—hic Thessala vendit /
Philtra, quibus valeant mentem vexare mariti, / Et solea pulsare nates."
For a modern edition, see *Juvenal and Persius*, trans. G. G. Ramsay, p. 132.
The modern edition reads *valeat* for *valeant*, and *natis* for *nates*.

6. Plutarch, "*Advice to Bride and Groom*" in the *Moralia*, (139.5), trans. Frank
Cole Babbitt, vol. II p. 303: "Fishing with poison is a quick way to catch
fish and an easy method for taking them, but it makes the fish inedible
and bad. In the same way women who artfully employ love-potions
and magic spells upon their husbands, and gain the mastery over them
through pleasure, find themselves consorts of dull-witted, degenerate
fools. The men bewitched by Circe were of no service to her, nor did
she make the least use of them after they had been changed into swine
and asses, while for Odysseus, who had sense and showed discretion in
her company, she had an exceeding great love." Ferrand likely came to
this touchstone anecdote from Plutarch through such a work as Wier's
Histoires, disputes et discours des illusions et impostures des diables, cited
above, bk. I, p. 482. This moralizing construction of the Circe episode
goes back at least as far as Ovid's *Remedies of Love*, ll. 285–90. See *The Art
of Love, and Other Poems*, p 197: "She was yet speaking: Ulysses loosed
his ship; with the sails the winds bore away her unavailing words. Circe
aflame has recourse to her wonted arts, yet not by them is her passion
calmed. Therefore, whoever you are that seek aid in my skill, have no
faith in spells and witchcraft."

7. Virgil, *Eclogue* VIII. 80–81: "Limus ut hic durescit, et haec ut cera lique-
scit: / Uno et eodem igni, sic nostro Daphnis amore." See trans. Guy
Lee (Harmondsworth: Penguin Books, 1984), pp. 90–91. See De Castro,

p. 217.

8. Lucius Apuleius, *Metamorphoses*, trans. W. Adlington, 1566, rev. S. Gaselee (Loeb, 1947), pp. 123–29. Pamphile wanted to force a young Boeotian to her will by sorcery. According to Fotis her nurse even the powers of hell obeyed Pamphile's will; she made the planets tremble, she weakened the gods and subdued the elements. To win her way with the man, she commanded her maid to bring some of his clipped hair, but the maid was rebuked by the barber, knowing her intent, so Fotis took hair from "blown goat-skins." Pamphile tied up this hair and, after elaborate rites involving the bones, flesh and entrails of dead men, bound it up with perfumes and threw it into the fire. "Then by the strong force of this sorcery, and the invisible violence of the gods so compelled, those bodies, whose hair was burning in the fire, received human breath, and felt, heard, and walked, and, smelling the scent of their own hair, came and rapped at our doors." These bladders did not "come leaping into her chamber," as Ferrand has it, but were rather the bladders at the outside door run through by Lucian's sword, having taken them for robbers come to attack the house of his host. Clearly, the magic proposed by Pamphile is based on ritual spell casting and not on philters. Ferrand allows himself this detour no doubt because he associates such magic with the magical powers attributed to philters to compel love. The variations between this and Ferrand's version are doubtless to be traced to some intermediary version. Writers in his age were given to collecting and anthologizing such tales both from ancient and modern sources. One of the best known was the work of Pierre Boaistuau and François de Belleforest, the *Histoires prodigieuses et memorable*, which includes the following (bk. III, ch. 5, p. 607) of the young man of Freiburg in the time of St. Louis who, "amoureux d'une jeune fille sa voisine se laissa se miserablement gaigner à la folie de sa concupiscence, que ayant perdu tout moyen et espoir de jouyr de celle que tant il aymoit, pour le dernier remede il s'adressa à un magicien, luy declarant, à son affection, et le desespoir il estoit pour se voir hors d'attente de l'effect de ses desirs." For a fee he led the young man into a remote place promising there to conjure his sweetheart. The devil who came in her place tendered his hand, and when the young man took it, he was hurled against a wall and slain, and again with the body the devil struck the magician with such force that he was taken for dead as well.

9. [*Liebaut l. 3 des malad. des femm. c. 47.*]: Jean Liébault, *Des maladies des femmes*, bk. III. ch. 47, p. 892: "Les bonnes femmes, apres que le nombril est couppé, et le bout de la portion couppee ist tombé, gardent soigneusement ce bout de leurs filles qui est tombé, pour leur faire des amoureux quand il les faudra marier, la font secher, puis pulveriser: et pensent que ceste poudre beüe de l'homme le rend extremement amoureux: Je tiens cela pour une sotte opinion et abus trop evident."

Laurent Joubert, *La premiere et seconde partie des erreurs populaires, touchant la medecine et le regime de santé* (Paris: Chez Claude Micard, 1587), pp. 156–57: "En quelques pays les bonnes femmes gardent soigneusement celle [la vedille] de leurs filles, pour leur faire des amoureux quand il les faudra marier. C'est qu'elles ont opinion, que si on donne à manger ou à boire de ceste vedille mise en poudre, à l'homme qui leur est agreable, il devient extremement amoureux de la fille: et ne faut plus, sinon faire les pactes de mariage. Je tiens cela pour un erreur et abus trop evident: comme la plus part de ce qu'on dit des autres breuvages amoureux, en Grec dits *philtres*, que l'on attribue aux sorciers et vieilles putains, pour coiffer les hommes de leur amour. Mais je pense qu'il y a quelque secrette allegorie en telle opinion, et c'est (paraventure) que si les hommes viennent à si grand familiarité des filles trop faciles et ploy-ables, qu'ils puissent faire toucher et joindre leurs nombrilz, qu'elles les attirent par là, et font la conjonction de l'androgine Platonique par telle reunion. En quoy plusieurs sont attrapez, quelquefois à leur dam. Et voila comment le nombril des filles, non pas le mort, ains le vivant, duquel on donne gout aux hommes, en les affriandant les rend eschauf-fez et abetiz, si la raison ne les domine et regit."

10. [*Pindar. ode 4. Pyth.*]: Pindar, *Pythian Odes* IV. 214–19: "μαινάδ'ὄρνιν." *The Odes of Pindar*, trans. Sir John Sandys (Loeb, 1968), p. 223: "Then, for the first time, did the Queen of swiftest darts, in Cyprus born, bind the dappled wryneck to the four spokes of a wheel indissoluble, and brought from Olympus unto men that maddening bird; and she taught the son of Aeson the lore of suppliant incantations, that so he might rob Medea of her reverence for her parents, and that a longing for Hellas might lash her with the whip of suasion, while her heart was all aflame." The wryneck or "cuckoo's mate" was used as a love charm. "It was tied by the legs and wings to the four spokes of a wheel, which was made to revolve continuously in one direction . . . while the words of incantation were repeated" (p. 223, n. 1). See also Horace, *Epode* XVII. 7, and the refrain of Theocritus' *Idyll* II, the "Pharmaceutria," ed. A. S. F. Gow, vol. I, pp. 16 ff. See the note following on the jynx.

11. Natale Conti (Natalis Comitis), *Mythologiae sive explicationis fabularum, libri decem: in quibus omnia prope naturalis et moralis philosophiae dogmata fuisse demonstratur* (Francofurti: apud Andreae Wecheli, 1588), p. 571: "Utebatur et motacille carne in veneficiis, sed in amatoriis precipue, quam fabulantur fuisse Suadelae filiam: quae cum Iovem pharmacis in sui desiderium attrahere conaretur, a Junone in quem sui nominis mutata est: nam iynx vocata est a Graecis. Haec homines in varia brutorum genera vertere solita dicitur per vires collectarum herbarum."

Philostratus, *De la vie d'Apollonius Tyaneen en VIII livres*, trans. Blaise de Vigenère, pp. 255–56: "Il y a plusieurs especes de moticilles ou bransle queuë, au rapport de Gesner en ses recherches des oyseaux liv. 3. il les nomme, *cinclum, sisopygida* et *lyngem*, les une ayans la queuë tachetee de blanc, les autres la gorge, doree et tous branlans la queuë, mais sur tout le σισόπογις, qu'il dit estre, *un passeteau* qui se trouve proche de la rive, des eaux et les torrens, la queuë tousjours mouvante." Vigenère does not mention the properties attributed to the bird, whether to cause love or whether it is a mad or raging bird. The movement of the tail was the salient feature and was easily allegorized or turned into a symbol of nearly anything in continual motion.

Ferrand is correct in saying that the bird in question is the wryneck, or jinx, a bird used in witchcraft by the ancients, and from which we derive the word meaning "to bring bad luck." Theocritus builds his second idyll around a refrain that refers to the spinning of the jynx-wheel: "My magic wheel draw to my house the man I love." Pindar attributes its invention to Aphrodite. For purposes of ritual magic, the bird was splayed upon the disk, which was then spun in order to force another to the will of the person spinning it. In Theocritus the lovesick forlorn Simaetha spins the wheel to bring back her wayward lover. The bird may have been chosen for such purposes originally because of the odd twisting movements of its neck during mating seasons. *Theocritus*, ed. A. S. F. Gow, vol. II, p. 41. The bird seems to have passed out of use with the Greeks, for the Latin writers barely mention it. In the Renaissance its association with magic continues to come from Pindar. Hesychius mentions the jinx in his *Lexicon*. Ferrand writes at length on the subject because the magic associated with the bird deriving from Pindar seems clouded by the fact that the bird's identity was unsure. His goal was to relate this lore to the bird known as the turcot to such ornithologists as Belon and to the commentators on Aristotle such as Gaza and Pace.

12. [*L. 4 de par. an. cap. 12*]: Aristotle, *On the Parts of Animals*, bk. IV, ch. 12, trans. A. L. Peck, pp. 414–15: "This arrangement of the toes holds good generally, but the wryneck is an exception, for it has only two toes in front and two in the back. This is because the weight of its body tends forward less than that of other birds."

13. Pierre Belon, *L'histoire de la nature des oyseaux, avec leurs descriptions; et naifs portraicts . . . en sept livres*, sec. XVIII, "Du tercou, torcou ou turcot" (Paris: Chez Guillaume Cavellat, 1555), pp. 306–7: "Et tout ainsi que nature luy à baillé ses doigts differens aux autres, aussi à voulu qu'il luy fust facile de se percher en diverses manières. Et estant perché, il se tient plus en arriere que les autres, qui ont trois doigts es pieds."

14. Theodorus Gaza of Thessalonica, *Aristotelis de natura animalium; eiusdem de partibus animalium; eiusdem de generatione animalium; Theophrasti historia plantarum; eiusdem de causis plantarum; Aristotelis problemata: Alexandri Aphrodisiensis problemata* (Venetiis: apud Aldum, 1504; end of book Venetiis: In aedibus Aldi, et Andrea Asulani Soceri, Mense Februario, 1513). "ἰυγξ" Gaza translates *turbo*. Iynx appears in his index, but not by name in the interpretation of the text of *De partibus animalium*, bk. IV, ch. 12, pp. 70ᵛ–71ᵛ.

Ferrand also refers to Giulio Pace (Julius Pacius de Berigo), another of the early editors of the works of Aristotle, *Opera omnia quae extant, Graece et Latine* (Lutetiae Parisiorum: 1619).

Culvilega should read *culicilegam*, a term Ferrand could have found in Gaza. See Henri Estienne, *Thesaurus Graecae linguae* (rpt. with additions and indexes, Graz: Akademische Druck– U. Verlagsanstalt, 1954), s.v. "κνιπολόγος": "culicilegam vocat Gaza." He is also the probable source of the term *susurada*, meaning to whisper or to coo. This is a kind of woodpecker that feeds on insects: "κνῖπες."

15. The illustrative tales from Plutarch, Eusebius and Cuspinian, derive from De Castro, *Medicus-politicus*, p. 217: "His Eusebius refert Lucretium Poetam dementatum, deinde etiam interemptum: atque idipsum Lucullo accidisse in eius vita Plutarchus scribit: idemque fuit Caligulae interitus, cui Cesonia Hippomanes potandum porrexit, ut narrant Josephus et Suetonius, de quo Juvenalis:

> Ut avunculus ille Neronis
> Cui totam tremuli frontem
> Cesonia pulli
> Infudit.

Idem refert Cuspinianus de Friderico duce Bavariae electo Romanorum rege, exemplaque plurime passim in historiis leguntur.   Quare cum tam noxia sint philtra, merito Athenienses Temniam sagam morte mulctarunt, et immerito Areopagitae ulteri ignoverunt, [Leges de philtris] mortuo eo, qui acceperat: prudentissimeque jura civilia in eos, qui talia philtra seu pocula amatoria exhibuerunt, poenas constituunt capitales: fugiendaque semper sunt, etiamsi non in malum sed bonum finem exhiberentur, utpote ad conciliandum mutuum inter conjuges amorem."

Plutarch's Lives, "Lucullus," trans. B. Perrin, vol. II, p. 609: "Even before his death, it is said that his understanding was affected and gradually faded away. But Cornelius Nepos says that Lucullus lost his mind not from old age, nor yet from disease, but that he was disabled by drugs administered to him by one of his freedmen, Callisthenes; that the drugs were given him by Callisthenes in order to win more of his love, in the belief that they had such a power, but they drove him from his senses and overwhelmed his reason."

Cuspinianus is Johann Speisshammer, and the story of the Duke of Bavaria is to be found in *De Caesaribus atque Imperatoribus Romanis opus insigne . . . à Julio Caesare ad Maximilianum primum commentaris* (Strasbourg: Crato Mylius, 1540).

16. "l. etiam ff. ad 1. Corn. de sic. & venef." *Lex Cornelia de sicaris veneficis et paracidiis*, title VIII, Marcianus, *Institutes*, bk. XIV, *The Civil Law*, ed. S. P. Scott, vol. XI, p. 60: "Anyone who has prepared poison, or sells it or keeps it for the purpose of killing human beings, is punished by the Fifth Section of the same Cornelian Law relating to Assassins and Poisoners." The section mentions love philters specifically, but holds them to be illegal only where it can be shown they were intended to kill. They are classed with poisons, and poisoners were subject to the death penalty. Thus the exceptional nature of the ruling of the Areopagites.

17. Johann Vergen (Johannes Nauclerus), *Cronicon*, vol. II (Coloniae: apud Haeredes Johannes Quentel et Gervinum Calenium, 1564) covers the years in question, but this work barely mentions the Kingdom of Naples. The closest entry is for 1442 concerning unrelated matters. The source is rather Michel de Montaigne, *Essais*, bk. II, ch. 33, ed. Maurice Rat (Paris: Garnier Frères, 1962), vol. II, pp. 136–37: "Ayant range par un siege bien poursuivy la ville de Florence si à destroit que les habitans estoient après à composer de sa victoire, il la leur quitta pour veu qu'ils luy livrassent une fille de leur ville, dequoy il avoit ouy parler, de beauté

excellente. Force fut de la luy accorder et garantir la publique ruine par une injure privée. Elle estoit fille d'un medecin fameux de son temps, lequel, se trouvant engagé en si villaine necessité, se resolut à une haute entreprinse. Comme chacun paroit sa fille et l'attournoit d'ornements et joyaux qui la peussent rendre agreable à ce nouvel amant, luy aussi luy donna un mouchoir exquis en senteur et en ouvrage, duquel elle eust à se servir en leurs premieres approches, meuble qu'elles n'y oublient guere en ces quartiers là. Ce mouchoir, empoisonné selon la capacité de son art, venant à se frotter à ces chairs esmeues et pores ouverts, inspira son venin si promptement, qu'ayant soudain changé leur sueur chaude en froide, ils expirerent entre les bras l'un de l'autre."

The story is also told by Gabriel Dupréau, *Histoire de l'estat et succès de l'eglise*, for the year 1414.

For other versions, see Laon Chalcondylas, *Histoire de la décadence de l'empire Grec*, bk. V, ch. 2, and Paolo Giovio, *Turcicorum rerum commentarius*.

18. [*Iuuel sat. 6*]: Juvenal "Sixth Satire," ll. 614–17: "tamen hoc tolerabile, si non / Et furore incipias, ut avunculur ille Neronis / Cui totam tremuli frontem Caesonia pulli / Infudit." Expanded from De Castro, p. 224. For a modern edition, see *Juvenal and Persius*, trans. G. G. Ramsey, p. 132. This text alludes to hippomanes, as Ferrand rightly explains, an excrescence on the head of a young foal which was used in love potions. Johann Wier, whom Ferrand had most certainly been reading, cites, in addition to this passage from Juvenal, both Josephus and Suetonius, whose works also contain accounts of this story: *Histoires, disputes et discours des illusions et impostures des diables*, vol. I, p. 478.

19. [*Arist l. 6. de hist. an. c 22. Pl. l. 8. c. 42*]: Aristotle, *History of Animals*, bk. VI, ch. 22 (577a), vol. II, p. 327: "a mare will . . . also eat off the growth on the foal's forehead known as *hippomanés*: the size of this is slightly smaller than a dried fig, and to look at it is flat and round, and black in colour. If anyone gets hold of it before [the mare does] and she gets scent of it, the scent drives her mad and frantic. That is why it is in demand by sorceresses, who collect it for their purposes."

Pliny, *Natural History*, bk. VIII, ch. 46: "In the equine genus the pregnant female is delivered standing up; and she loves her offspring more than all other female animals. And in fact a love-poison called hippomanes is found in the forehead of horses at birth, the size of a dried fig, black in color, which a brood mare as soon as she had dropped her foal eats up, or else she refuses to suckle the foal. If anybody takes it before she gets it, and keeps it, the scent drives him into madness of the kind specified." See trans. H. Rackham, p. 115.

20. [*Ar. l. 6. c. 18*]: Aristotle, *History of Animals*, bk. VI, ch. 18 (572a): "καὶ καλοῦσι τοῦτο τινες Ἱππομανές, ἄλλοι δὲ τὸ πώλοις ἐμφύομενον." Trans. A. L. Peck, vol. II, p. 301: "A fluid also flows out of their sexual organs, similar to semen, but much thinner than the male's; and some people apply the name *hippomanés* to this instead of to the substance that grows on foals."

For hippomanes see also Pausanias, *Description of Greece*, trans. W.

H. S. Jones (Loeb, 1965), "Elis," vol. II, bk. V, ch. 27, p. 545, who tells of the bronze statue of a horse that maddens male horses, causing them to go into a frenzy trying to mount it, until they are driven off by whips. This account creates another link between horses and erotic excitation.

21. [*Eleg. 4 l. 2.*]: Tibullus, bk. II, Elegy IV. 56–57: "Ubi indomitis gregibus Venus afflat amores / Hippomanes rabidae stillat ab inguine equae." *The Elegies*, ed. Kirby Flower Smith, p. 142.

The modern edition reads *adflat* for *afflat* and *cupidae* for *rabidae*. That Tibullus speaks of a love potion is confirmed in the lines that follow where the speaker offers to drink this liquor mixed with a thousand other herbs if only Nemesis would look upon him with a kindly eye.

22. That hippomanes was also classified as a plant by the herbalists both ancient and modern, Ferrand mentions in an erudite aside. It is here in the margin that he again cites De Castro, the inspiration for the entire discussion on hippomanes: [*L 4. Medicop. c. de philtris.*]: *Medicus-politicus*, bk. IV, ch. "de philtris," p. 226: "Ut nos ab hac difficultate explicemus, sciendum primo, plurima philtra nobis veteres commemorasse, menstruum nimirum muliebre, sperma viri, cerebrum felis, vel pulli asinini, uterus hyaenae, virga lupi, remora, ossa rubetae, scinci, et potissimum hippomanes, quod triplex est, *unum* plantula quaedam Arcadiae, quae vulgo filix esse existimutur: *alterum* spuma genita in equae inguine, de quo Propertius: Viris cupida stillat ab inguine equa / Hippomanes. *Tertium* pellicula, quae avellitur a fronte pulli equini recens editi, cuius adore equos in furorem redigi creditur, de quibus Aristotles, Plinius, Columella et alii scripserunt. [in margin: *Aris. lib. 6 de hist. an. cap. 18. Pli. 8. c. 12. Col. lib. 6*]." Ferrand does his own research on the subject adding, though without benefit of reference, the names of Giovanni Andrea Anguillara (Aloysius Anguillara), Cratevas, Rembert Dodoëns (Dodonaeus), and Johann Jacob Wecker. For the curious, these references will be found in Anguillara's *De simplicibus liber primus, cum notis Gaspari Bauhini* (Basileae: apud Henricum Petrum, 1593). But the references to both Anguillara and to Cratevas were taken from Dodoëns, *Stirpium historiae pemptades sex sive libri XXX* (Antverpiae: ex officina Plantaniana, apud B. et J. Moretos, 1616), pp. 449–60: "Stramoniam nuncupant, et pomum sive malum spinosum: nonulli coronam regiam: alii melospinum: Graeci nostri temporis παορκόκκαλον aut potius βαρνοκόκαλον, quasi nucem gravantam et torporem ac molestiorem somnum inducentem: Itali hinc, ut quidem apparet, *paracoculi*: Germani *stechöpfel* vocant: Belgae *dozen* appelant, Galli *pomme de Peru*: Valerio Cordo hyoscayamus Peruvianus; Matthiole vero atque aliis nux methel Arabum esse videtur. Nucem autem methel Serapio cap CCCLXXV fructum esse scribit similem nuci vomicae, cuius semen sit veluti mandragorae: cortex asper, sapore gratus ac virtuosus: qualitus quatro ordine frigida. Aloysius Anguillara stramoniam hippomanes illud Theocriti esse suspicatur, quo in pharmaceutria equos in furorem agi refert. Cratevas siquidem, quem Theocriti citat interpres, hippomanis plantam fructum habere scribit, ut Cucumeris silvestris spinosum.

"Facultate autem stramonia soporifera ac narcotica, frigida etiam quarto ordine, mandragora non inferior." Dodoëns' famous *Pemptades,* first published in 1583, was the unacknowledged source for Gerard's *Herbal,* 1597, the standard reference work in English before the *Paradisi in sole paradisus terrestris* of John Parkinson, 1629, though it remained current for many years after with a much extended and corrected version appearing in 1633.

Johann Jacob Wecker, *Le grand thresor, ou dispensaire, et antidotaire special ou particulier des remedes servans a la santé du corps humain* (Geneve: de l'imprimerie D'Estienne Gamonet, 1616), p. 296: "[in margin: *Hyoscamus Peruvianus, Cordi nux methel Mathioli*] Valeri Cordus l'appele iusqutame du Perou, mais Mathiole, et quelques autres la prennens pour la noix methel des Arabes, et se fondant sur la description qu'en fait Serapion, au chap. 375, ou il escrit que la noix methel est semblable à la noix vomique, que sa semence ressemble à celle de la mandragore, que son excorce est rude, qu'elle est assez plaisante au goust, et froide au quatriesme degré. Aloysius Anguillara estime que ceste plante est l'hipomanes dont Theocrite fait mention en sa Pharmaceutria, et qui rend les chevuaux forcenez et furieux. La stramonia ou pomme du Perou est somnifere, narcotique, et froide en mesme degré que la mandragore. Le mesme."

Cratevas was a Greek rhizomist who flourished in the age of Mithridates. Dioscorides praised him for his exactitude and precision, while at the same time faulting him for not characterizing sufficiently a goodly number of plants. In fact, Sprengel, who has held in his hands a copy of a manuscript of Cratevas' work entitled Τὰ ῥιζοτομούμενα, the one cited by Pliny and Dioscorides, preserved in the Marciana Library in Venice, and from which Anguillara cited a few fragments in his history of simples, asserted that it contained only the names of the plants with indication of their properties. Pliny tells us that Cratevas included illustrations in his book to make it more intelligible.

23. Porphyry, *De regressu animae* is known to us only through fragments preserved by St. Augustine in *De civitate Dei,* bk. X, in the context of a polemic carried out against him for endorsing the theurgic arts as a means for attaining a purgation of the soul. Porphyry does not rule out the usefulness of cultivating some demon to aid the soul to heaven in the afterlife, but warns man to avoid the society of demons and the worship of them. As St. Augustine points out, the danger is in treating with powers that envy the soul its purity, powers that will seek to trick or betray even the good man. Hence, the danger of magic and spells: the jealousies and passions of demons can destroy men. See bk. X, ch. 9, "Of unlawful arts concerning the devil's worship, whereof Porphyry approves some, and disallows others," ed. Sir Ernest Barker (London: J. M. Dent, 1953), pp. 282–83.

24. [*Loys d'Orleans. Vigenere.*]: Philostratus, *De la vie d'Apolonius Thyaneen en VIII livres,* trans. Blaise de Vigenère, bk. I, p. 565: "Il se presente cyapres un subject particulier pour parler des anneaux, de sorte que cela m'empechera d'en faire icy une autre remarque, si ce n'est pour faire voir comment Philostrate veut esgaler ces sages a ce grand serviteur de

Dieu et conducteur de son peuple, Moyse, lequel avec sa verge a fait tant de miracles parmy les Egyptiens, et quant aux anneaux, bien qu'il n'y ait gueres d'apparence à ce qu'en dit Josephé et autres, qui malicieusement et non sans impieté, luy imposent la composition de certains livres de magie, toutesfois nostre autheur est qui n'a peu faire la discernement du vray et du faux soubs un ouy dire. Les livres qu'on dit qu'il a composez, disent qu'il fabriqua un anneau d'oubly pour amortir les flames impudiques de Thaïbi qui brusloit pour luy, l'autre anneau que ce fut celui de memoire qu'il donna à sa femme Sephora lors qu'il se separa d'avec elle pour venir en la cour de Pharaon; tous contes à plaisir aussi bien que celuy de Salomon."

Louis d'Orléans, despite his name a Parisian, published in 1622 the *Novae cogitationes in libros annalium C. Cornelii Taciti quae extant* (Parisiis: sumptibus T. Blasii, 1622), in which Moses is mentioned only once (p. 619) in a passing reference. He was a radical Catholic and supporter of the League who left many polemical tracts, extremely rare today, none bearing titles that suggest the source of Ferrand's reference.

25. Ferrand includes a number of recipes to cure sterility and to improve sexual performance and enjoyment in his ch. 23 of the 1610 edition of the treatise on love melancholy, a section suppressed in the second edition. As Ferrand states, there are many sources of such material in the medical writings of the age. Ferrand, in other contexts, indicates having read the following—all of whom include sections on sterility in their works: Fredericus à Fonseca, *Consultationes medicae singularibus remediis referte* (Venetiis: apud Joannem Guerilium, 1619): "*Consultatio LXXI*": "Pro sterilitate seu impedita conceptione atque abortu," pp. 209 ff.; Giovanni de Vigo, *La practique et cirurgie*; Guglielmo da Varignana, [*Secreta medicine], ne secreta sublunia ad varios curandos morbos verissimis autoritatibus illustrata* (Vicentius de Portonariis de Tridino de Monte Ferrato, 1553), pp. 54^v–46^r for the pharmaceutical preparations.

For the ancient physicians, see, e.g., Oribasius, *Synopsis*, bk. I, ch. 6, in *Oeuvres*, p. 10; Paul of Aegina, *Opera*, bk. III, ch. 66, p. 386; Aëtius of Amida, *Tetrabiblos*, bk. IV, sermo 4, ch. 74, p. 903.

26. Ovid, *The Art of Love*, II. 101–4: "Non facient ut vivat Amor, Medeides herbae, / Mixtaque cum magicis marsa venena sonis. / Phasias Aesonidem, Circe tenuisset Ulissem, / Si modo servari carmine posset Amor." For a modern edition, see *The Art of Love, and other Poems*, trans. J. H. Mozley, p. 72. In the modern edition the second line reads: "Mixtaque cum magicis naenia Marsa sonis." This quotation was cited by Wier in his ch. 11 on potions and was alluded to by De Castro, p. 222.

27. Propertius, *Elegies*, bk. II, LV, 7: "Non hic herbae valet, non hic nocturna Citaeis, / Non per Medeae graeminae cocta manus." See trans. H. E. Butler, pp. 74, 75.

28. [*Valeriol. obser. 7 l. 2. R. à Castro c. de Philtris, et c de fur. uteri.*]: Though found together in the margin these references are to be assigned to different parts of the text. The reference to Valleriola can only refer to the story of Ulysses and Circe, while the Rodrigo de Castro reference can apply only to the concept of sympathy and beauty as functioning like

philters.

François Valleriola, *Observationum medicinalium libri VI*, p. 219: "ut inde, ceu a Circes et Calypsus diro veneno tinctis poculis, cavere sciamus, et Ulyssis exemplo, virtutis et pulchri summique."

Rodrigo de Castro, *Medicus-politicus*, bk. IV, ch. 2, p. 222: "elegans forma, morum venustas, blanditiae, et illecebrae ex parte amatae maximo movent animos amantium, quibus si accedant occulta quaedam sympathia, et ex parte amantis otium, crapula, et sedentaria vita, habebis praecipuam vitiosi amoris causam, atque adea ut vulgo dicitur, amore captus animus non eget philtris."

Jean Aubery in *L'antidote d'amour*, pp. 71^{r}v–80^r, discusses sympathy as the cause of love, stating that objects attract their counterparts in society and in the natural world according to occult principles or ideas of symmetry. He observes that women have received, by divine will, more of this amorous power to attract by "la douceur de ses yeux, et les appas de ses graces, afin que par ces ravissemens attirant l'homme." But sympathy was something other than the attracting powers of beauty: "parquoy la sympathie qui vient d'un principe celeste et d'une proprieté cachee qui a quelque analogie à la chose attiree peut beaucoup en l'Amour, duquel nous l'asseurons l'une des causes principales" (pp. 79^v–80^r). Ferrand treats such categories of cause with philters and other forms of coersion of the will, placing them all in disreputable light.

Rodrigo de Castro, *De universa mulierum medicina*, bk. II, "De furore uteri" (Hamburgi: in officina Frobeniana, 1603), pp. 153 ff.

Finally, there are direct or indirect echoes in this part of Ferrand's chapter on philters from Jean Riolan, *Ad libros Fernelii de abditis rerum causis* (Parisiis: apud H. Perier, in officina Plantiniana, 1598), pp. 112–13. Riolan, in his two page treatment of the subject, declares that love cannot be forced and that while philters can make a person amorous, they cannot cause love for a specific person. He too, like Ferrand, concludes that the only truly effective philters are money, charm, and an affinity between persons based on personality, manners, and conversation.

29. Ovid, *Heroides* VI: "Hypsipyle Iasone," ll. 93–94: "Male quaeritur herbis: / Moribus et forma conciliandus Amor." See *Epistolae Heroidum*, ed. Henricus Dörrie, p. 98.

30. The verse, quoted by Ferrand in Latin: "Valeant calumniae, tu in te philtra habes," comes from Plutarch's "*Advice to Bride and Groom,*" sec. 23 in the *Moralia*, see trans. Frank Cole Babbit, vol. II, p. 315: "King Philip was enamoured of a Thessalian woman who was accused of using magic charms upon him. Olympias accordingly made haste to get the woman into her power. But when the latter had come into the queen's presence and was seen to be beautiful in appearance, and her conversation with the queen was not lacking in good-breeding or cleverness, Olympias exclaimed: 'Away with these slanders! You have magic charms in yourself.' " The story is also related by De Castro in his chapter "De philtris," p. 222, who in turn, may have taken it from Johann Wier, *Histoires, disputes et discours des illusions et impostures des diables*, bk. III, ch. 40, vol. I, pp. 481–82.

31. The verses come from a lost comedy by Lucius Afranius, *Vopisco*, and are preserved in Nonius Marcellus' *De compendiosa doctrina*, ed. W. M. Lindsay (Hildesheim: Georg Olms, 1964), I, 4:

> Si possent homines delinimentis capi,
> Omnes haberent nunc amatores anus.
> Aetas, et corpus tenerum et morigeratio,
> Haec sunt venena formosarum mulierum:
> Mala aetas nulla delinimenta invenit.

Ferrand takes these lines from De Castro, chapter "de philtris," p. 222. Afranius' fragment can also be found in O. Ribbeck, *Comicorum Romanorum poesis fragmenta* (Hildesheim: Georg Olms, 1962), vol. II, p. 213.

32. [*Alex. Tral. l. 9. c. 4. Heurn. l. 3. Meth. c. 28. Silvat. cont. 43.*]: Alexander of Tralles, *Affections génito-urinaires*, bk. XI, ch. 1, in *Oeuvres médicales*, ed. F. Brunet (Paris: Librairie Orientaliste Paul Geuthner, 1937), vol. IV, p. 169. In speaking of conjurations, he says that for the sake of healing, no possible means should be overlooked, and though he is sceptical he notes that, "le tout divin Galien lui-méme qui ne croyait cependant pas aux conjurations, reconnut après un temps d'observation très long et à la suite d'une grande expérience qu'elles peuvent avoir une puissante action. Ecoutons ce qu'il dit à propos d'une formule magique indiquée dans une étude médicale sur Homère." This medical study of Homer may supply yet another source for the term Homeric remedies.

Johann van Heurne, *Praxis medicinae nova ratio qua libris tribus methodi ad praxin medicam*, bk. III, ch. 28, pp. 481–82: "Homerus decimonono Odyssearum, dixit, cum Ulysses comitatus Autolyci filiis in Parnasso monte venationem exerceret, ab apro vulnerato foemore, ita ut magna pars carnis obliquo dente extraxisset illi aper, profluvium sanguinis carmine Autolyci filii inhibuere: ἐπ'ἀοιδῇ δ'αἷμα κελαινὸν ἔσχετον; hoc est, carmine atrum sanguinem inhibuerunt, unde haec curatio quae carmine et verbis fieret, Homerica olim dicta fuit." Ferrand may have taken his quotation from this passage rather than from Homer.

The principal source for Ferrand's passage on these remedies (including the reference to Trallianus as bk. 9, ch. 4), is Silvatico, "*controversia*" 34, in *Controversiae medicae numero centum*, p. 206: "Auxilia autem eiuscemodi omnia a medicis homerica appellari scripsit Alexander Trallianus libro 9. cap. 4. non certe, quod eorum inventor fuerit Homerus, sed quia forte simile quidpiam habent rebus admirandis, quae Homerum fecisse nonulli scribunt; quem nucis verbis fluentem sanguinem retinuisse aiunt, ingeniisque quibusdam obscuris multos affectus sanasse. At in quadruplici differentia esse cum dicentur homerica auxilia; ideo et id, de quo nostra fertur controversia, sub una earum contineri necesse est. Aut amuletis constat auxilium homericum, aut characteribus, aut carmine, aut stratagemate. Hi autem qui salvatellam in putridis febribus secant, cum nec characteres inscribant, nec cantiones adhibeant, neque etiam stratagema aliquod faciant; ex sufficienti partium enumeratione eo deducimur, ut amuletum an sit consideremus."

Jean Aubery, *L'antidote d'amour*, pp. 104ʳ–110ʳ, has an entire section devoted to the power of words and charms and their capacity to force, cure, or influence human health through occult means. He does not use the word *Homeric*, but cites the story of Autolycus and the boar wound. He proves out of a book by Jean Fernel on occult matters that there are many words in current use to cure toothache, colic fever, and other diseases (p. 105^r). In due course he makes his rhetorical counterturn against this superstitious use of magic words; "nous dirons donc premierement, que par paroles on ne peut contraindre et conjurer les esprits de nous rendre quelque service" (p. 106^r). Yet he does not deny that words have the ability to move and agitate the spirit and thereby produce their effects, as when people see blood they faint by some power the sight has over the spirits, or as when the words of a physician soothe a patient. But the virtue is not in the number or figure itself, but in its suggestive powers.

Several examples of such cures are given by Ambroise Paré, *On Monsters and Marvels*, ch. 32, p. 102, such as the following: "I saw someone stop blood from any part of the body whatsoever, [just] by humming some words or other. There are some [persons] who say these words: *De latere eius exivit sanguis et aqua.*"

33. [*od. 19*]: Homer, *The Odyssey*, bk. XIX. 457–58: ἐπαοιδῇ δ'αἷμα κελαινὸν ἔσχεθον." ed. A. T. Murray (Loeb, 1966), vol. II, pp. 260–61.

34. [*à Castro l. 4. medico. pol. c. 2.*]: Rodrigo de Castro, *Medicus-politicus*, bk. IV, ch. 2, p. 223, after so many unacknowledged borrowings, is here cited as dealing with a topic he barely mentions, for De Castro does not speak of Homerical remedies as such, and he offers no cautions concerning their employment. He does, however, recommend prayer, serious reading, and sober activities. Rather, the discussion derives from Wier, who devotes an entire chapter to charms and characters employed by doctors in *Histoires, disputes et discours des illusions et impostures des diables*, bk. II, pp. 102 ff. Wier includes la "guerison Homerique" attributing its origins to the use of certain magic words in Homer to stanch the flow of blood from a wound. He cites a *Traité de la guerison homerique* by Galen and another by Auger Ferrier. Wier also mentions the extensive use of charms for treating bleeding and fevers recommended by Bernard of Gordon. He considers them all superstitious and beneath a modern doctor's dignity.

It is nevertheless to be noted that a kind of magic antidotal power had been assigned to the sacred words of scripture and that Kramer and Springer in the *Malleus maleficarum*, pt. 2, ques. 2, ch. 3, pp. 172–73, encouraged those incited to carnal desire by bewitchment to wear these words as charms: "And when it is said that bewitched men can exorcise themselves, it is to be understood that they can wear the sacred words or benedictions or incantations round their necks, if they are unable to read or pronounce the benedictions; but it will be shown later in what way this should be done" (see pt. 2, ques. 2, ch. 6, p. 181).

35. Ovid, *The Remedies of Love*, ll. 289–90: "Ergo quisquis opem medica tibi poscis ab arte, / Deme veneficiis, carminibusque fidem." This is Ovid's final advice, and Ferrand's, after recounting the failure of Circe to woo Ulysses, a story serving almost as a *leit motif* to Ferrand's chapter. See

The Art of Love, and other Poems, trans. J. H. Mozley, p. 196. Ferrand substitutes Ovid's words *nostra . . . ab arte* with *medica . . . ab arte* to suit his own purposes.

XXXVI. Empirical Remedies for the Curing of Love and Erotic Melancholy

1. Plutarch, *Moralia*, "*Beasts are Rational,*" vol. XII, p. 521. Much of the material for this chapter was taken from a chapter in the edition of 1610 devoted to ancient cures. Ferrand here calls them empirical remedies in order to distinguish them from true and methodical cures. Ferrand's encyclopedic interest in the curing of the diseases of love would not allow him to leave out such remedies, even though they are of merely historical significance.

2. [*Stat. in Epic.*]: Statius, *Silvae* V, iii. 154–55: "—saltusque ingressa viriles / Non formidata temeraria Chalcide Sapho." See trans. J. H. Mozley (Loeb, 1967), vol. I, pp. 316–17. Read *Leucade* for *Chalcide*.

3. [*Auson. Suydas.*]: Ausonius, *Cupid Crucified*, trans. H. G. Evelyn White (Loeb, 1949–51), vol. I, p. 209: "And man-like Sappho, doomed to be slain by the shafts of love for Lesbian Phaon, threatens to leap from cloud-wrapped Leucas."

   Suidas, *Lexicon*, vol. II, pt. 2 (s.v. ΣΑΠΦΩ).

   See also Menander, *The Principal Fragments*, trans. Francis G. Allinson (Loeb, 1964), "The Lady of Leucas," p. 403: "Where you know, as the first—so the legend records—it was Sappho, in quest of her Phaon the proud, who was stung by desire and ventures the leap. From the headland far-seen."

   See also ch. II, n. 14, above, and the sources in Lelio Gregorio Giraldi, *De deis gentium libri*, bk. II.

4. [*Strabo l. 10 geogr.*]: Strabo, *Geography* 10. 2, vol. V, p. 33: "Now although Menander says that Sappho was the first to take the leap, yet those who are better versed than he in antiquities say that it was Cephalus, who was in love with Pterelas the son of Deioneus."

   Jean Aubery, *L'antidote d'amour*, p. 139^r, repeats the observation saying that Cephale was the first to leap, "estant forcé de l'amour de Ptarole fille de Degenetus."

5. Ovid, *Heroides* XV. 167–70:

   > Hinc se Deucalion Pyrrhae succensus amore
   >   Misit, et illaeso corpore pressit aquas:
   > Nec non versus Amor, fugit lentissima mersi
   >   Pectora, Deucalion igne levatus erat.

   See ed. Henricus Dörrie, p. 323. For line 3 read "Nec mora, versus amor fugit lentissima mersi."

6. Stesichorus, "ΚΑΛΥΚΗ," in *Poetae melici Graeci*, ed. D. L. Page (Oxford: Clarendon Press, 1962) pp. 136–37. But Ferrand's source was more probably Athenaeus, *The Deipnosophists*, trans. C. B. Gulick, bk. XIV, 619,

vol. VI, pp. 337–39: "The women of old sang a song called *Calycê*. It was composed by Stesichorus, and in it a maiden named Calycê, in love with a young man, Euathlus, modestly prays to Aphroditê that she may be married to him. But when the young man treated her with despite, she flung herself over a cliff. The tragedy occurred at Leucas."

7. The reference to Mutianus is derived *verbatim* from Mario Equicola, *Libro de natura de amore*, bk. IV, "*Force and Power of Love*," p. 153ʳ: "Se tutto il fonte in Cycyze, dicto di Cupidine, bevessemo, il quale fa (secondo scrive Mutiano) deponere amore, non scioglieria da gli amorosi lacci uno."

8. Pausanias, *Description of Greece*, "*Achaia*," ch. 23: "τιμιώτερον χρημάτων πολλῶν ἔστιν ἀνθρώποις τὸ ὕδωρ τοῦ Σελέμνου," trans. W. H. S. Jones, vol. III, p. 306.

9. Girolamo Mercuriale, *De morbis muliebribus praelectiones*, bk. IV, ch. 10, p. 157: "Sed efficacissima omnium habentur balnea refrigerantia, aquae thermarum refrigerantes: et nondum agitur annus, ex quo curavimus mulierem hoc solo remedio."

10. [*L. 5. de pla. Hipp. & Pl.*]: is clearly a reference to Galen, *De placitis Hippocratis et Platonis*, bk. V, though Galen nowhere speaks of Dorian music or of the story of Agamemnon and Clytemnestra in this work. One possible source is the following: Philostratus, *De la vie d'Apollonius Thyaneen en VIII livres*, bk. I, ch. 16, p. 281: "Aussi dict-on que Clytemnestre fut conservée en sa pudicité par le moyen du chant d'un musicien qu'Agamemnon allant au siege de Troye avoit laissé aupres d'elle, de sorte qu'elle resista vertueusement aux lascives poursuittes d'Egisiste, jusques à ce qu'aiant recogneu cest effect admirable de la musique, il trouva le moyen de la priver de ce parfaict musicien."

11. [*M. de Montagne l. 1. c. 46.*]: Michel de Montaigne, *Essais*, bk. I, ch. 46, ed. Maurice Rat, vol. I, p. 308: "Pythagoras, estant en companie de jeunes hommes, lesquels il sentit complotter, eschauffez de la feste, d'aller violer une maison pudique, commanda à la menestriere de changer de ton, et, par une musique poisante, severe et spondaïque, enchanta tout doucement leur ardeur et l'endormit."

Boethius, *De institutione arithmetica libri duo, de institutione musica libri quinque*, ed. Godofredus Friedlein (Lipsiae: in aedibus B. G. Teubneri, 1867), pp 184–85: "Tanta igitur apud eos fuit, musicae diligentia, ut eam animos quoque obtinere arbitrarentur. Vulgatum quippe est, quam saepe iracundias cantilena represserit, quam multa vel in corporum vel in animorum affectionibus miranda perfecerit. Cui enim est illud ignotum, quod Pythagoras ebrium adulescentem Tauromenitanum subphrygii modi sono incitatum spondeo succinente reddiderit mitiorem et sui compotem? . . . . Nam cum scortum in rivalis domo esset clausum atque ille furens domum vellet amburere, cumque Pythagoras stellarum cursus, ut ei mos, nocturnus inspiceret, ubi intellexit, sono phrygii modi incitatum multis amicorum monitionibus a facinore noluisse desistere, mutari modum praecepit atque ita furentis animum adulescentis ad statum mentis pacatissimae temperavit."

See also Jean Aubery, *L'antidote d'amour*, p. 132, for further discussion and examples of music therapy and love.

12. [*T. Livius. Cael. Rodigin.*]: *Livy*, trans. B. O. Foster (Loeb, 1963), bk. XXII, ch. 9, vol. V, p. 231.

Ludovico Celio Ricchieri (Rhodiginus), *Lectionum antiquarum libri triginta*, p. 338: "Ab iisdem quoque in Eryce populis religiose cultam legimus Venerem, cuius honori dicabantur anagogae." Bk. XIV, ch. 6, p. 741, also contains parallel material, and bk. XXIX, ch. 18, is devoted to Venus, her temples, emanations, and manifestations, but no mention is made of Lethean love in any of these sections.

See also *Diodorus of Sicily*, trans. C. H. Oldfather (Loeb, 1952), bk. IV. 83, vol. IV, pp. 79–81.

13. Ovid, *The Remedies of Love*, ll. 551–54:

Est illic lethaeus amor, qui pectora sanat,
    Inque suas gelidam lampadas addit aquam.
Illic et juvenes votis oblivia poscunt,
    Et siqua est duro capta marita viro.

See *The Art of Love, and Other Poems*, trans. J. H. Mozley, p. 214.

14. For Herodotus on the Scythians, see ch. XXXI, n. 5, above.

15. [*L. 7.*]: Athenaeus, *The Deipnosophists*, trans. C. B. Gulick, bk. VII, vol. III, p. 463: "If a triglê be smothered alive in wine and a man-drinks this, he will not be able to have sexual intercourse, as Terpsicles narrates in his book *On Sexual Pleasure*."

16. *Plin. l. 32. c. 15. l. 28. c. 30. 32.*]: Pliny, *Natural History*, bk. XXVIII, chs. 30 and 32; bk. XXXII, ch. 25, ed. W. H. S. Jones, vol. VIII, pp. 85, 87, 511: "the broth of a scincos taken with honey is anaphrodisiac." "They say that these ashes [of the nails and hide of the lynx] taken in drink by men check shameful conduct, and sprinkled on women lustful desire." "Most beneficial to the ears is the fresh gall of the skate, but also when preserved in wine, the gall of grey mullet, which some call mizyene, and also that of the star-gazer with rose-oil poured into the ears." The references would appear correct given their subject matter, though by what process their contents become transformed into the versions given by Ferrand is beyond our explanation. The third entry above is under the category of cures for diseases of the ears, linking the fish cures prescribed for ear ailments to the ear wax cures for love Ferrand proposes. This may be entirely coincidental. Also anaphrodisiac, according Pliny, bk. XXXII, ch. 50, p. 549, is the "echeneis, hide from the left side of the forehead of a hippopotemus attached as an amulet in lamb skin, or the gall of the torpedo, while it is still alive, applied to the genitals."

17. [*C. de Malef. l. 9. de addit.*]: Giovanni de Vigo, *Le practique et cirurgie*, bk. IX, ch. 18, p. 319: "De maleficiatis." For the text, see ch. XXXIV, n. 38, above.

18. Aristophanes, *Plutus*, l. 706, in *Aristophanes*, ed. B. B. Rogers, vol. III, p. 426. Cario uses the term "σκατόφαγον," "ordure-taster," in referring to Asclepius.

19. [*Arist. 6. de hist. an. c. 12.*]: Aristotle, *History of Animals*, bk. VI, ch. 18 (572a), vol. II, p. 301: "When mares have their manes shorn, their eagerness tends to slacken off and they take on a somewhat hangdog

appearance."

20. [*Arnauld de Regim. castor. c. 28*]: Arnald of Villanova, "De regimine caste viventium," ch. 28 of *De regimine sanitatis* in *Opera omnia*, p. 749: "qui ex coitus dimissione incurrere solet in stomachi et cordis debilitatem, portetur smaragdus, et sapphyrus, fiant unguenta frigida circa renes, et lamina plumbea ibidem portetur."

Albert the Great, *De virtutibus herbarum, lapidum, et animalium quorundam libellus*, in *De secretis mulierum libellus*, pp. 144–45. Of emerald, ruby, and sapphire, Albert speaks only of the last, that it "pacem creat et concordiam: parum et devotum ad Deum animum essuit, animum confirmat in bonis, et hominem refrigescere facit interiore ardore." In spite of his references, we have not traced the exact origins of Ferrand's comments on precious stones.

21. Abul-Casim Maslama Ben Ahmad, *Picatrix*, tratado III, ch. 10, ed. Marcelino Villegas (Madrid: Editora Nacional, 1982), pp. 293–94. The three ingredients mentioned by Ferrand do not, in fact, appear together, but in three separate recipes in consecutive order, the first a philter, the second and third antidotes for the preceding philter. The *Picatrix* does not say the blood of the loved person, but simply "media onza de sangre humana." Ferrand's wording is to be accounted for by the fact that he takes his reference from Mario Equicola, *Libro de natura de amore*, bk. IV: "*Force and Power of Love*," p. 153^r: "Ne Piccatrice ne Plines removeranno una minima particella di tal passione col sangue de homo, cerebro de rondina, lacte e succo do myrto."

22. [*Jul. Capitolin. Crinit. l 2. de hon discipl. c. 1.*]: Julius Capitolinus, "M. Antoninus philosophus ad Diocletianum Augustum," in *Scriptores Historiae Augustae*, ed. H. Iordan and F. Eyssenhardt (Berolini: apud Weidmannos, 1864), vol. I, p. 57 f. The story of Faustina gained great popularity and was often repeated.

Pietro Crinito (Piero Riccio), *De honesta disciplina libri XXV* (Basileae: excudebat Henricus Petrus, 1532): "Remedium de solvendis amoribus, cum mirifico exemplo Faustinae, ac de natali Commodi imperatoris qui omnium crudelissimus fuit," pp. 24–25: "Relatum est in Graecorum commentariis, qua nam ratione, ac remedio, uti homines oporteat, in solvendis amoribus. Necque Magi tantum in suis libris hoc tradiderunt, sed etiam Cadmus Milesius, qui inter alia historiae monumenta libros aliquot composuit, de abolendo amore, sicuti scriptum est in Suidae collectaneis. Nos vero exemplum nunc apponemus, de Faustina illustri foemina. Quae cum Antonii Pii imperatoris filia esset, et Marci philosophi uxor, cum gladiatoris amore nimio, ac supra fidem tabesceret, mirifico prorsus commento excogitatum est, ut a tanto amoris contagio eam redimerent. Nam cum Marcius imperator ex ea rem percepisset, Caldaeis hoc et mathematicis exposuit, a quibus decretum est pro Faustinae salute, ut occiso gladiatore (quem illa maxime deperibat) eiusdem crurore epoto, se sublevaret, ac statim cum viro suo concumberet. Quo facto (ut traditur) ipsa quidem Faustina amoris contagio liberata est, ac ex eo quidem concubitu, natus mox Antonius Commodus, qui Romanum imperium gladiatoriis pugnis, ac saevissimus caedibus, ut homo sanguinarius, adeo attrivit, ut gladiatoris nomen, non imperatoris meruerit. Quod et Julius Capitolinus ad Caesarem Diocletianum refert." Crinitus is the probable source for the reference to Julius Capitolinus, or André Du Laurens, for which see the note following.

23. Ausonius, *The Twelve Emperors*, XVII: "Hoc solum patriae, quod genuit, nocuit." See trans. Hugh G. Evelyn White (Loeb, 1951), pp. 342–43.

Ferrand's closest source for this story is André Du Laurens, *Des maladies melancholiques, et du moyen de les guarir*, p. 36^{r-v}: "J'ay leu dans Jule Capitolin, que Faustine femme de Marc Aurele, fut tellement esprise de l'amour d'un jeune gladiateur, qu'elle s'en alloit mourant; Marc Aurele recognoissaut sa passion, fit assembler tous les Chaldeens, magiciens et philosophes du pays, pour avoir un remede prompt et asseuré pour ceste maladie; ils luy conseillerent en fin de faire tuer secrettement l'escrimeur, de faire boire à sa femme de ce sang, et de coucher le soir mesmes avec elle. Cela fut executé, l'ardeur de Faustine fut estainte, mais de cest embrassement fut engendré Antonin Commode, qui fut un des plus sanguinaires et cruels Empereurs de Rome, qui ressembloit plus au gladiateur qu'à son pere, et ne bougeoit jamais d'avec les escrimeurs."

Other intermediary references for this story include Pierre Boaistuau, *Le théâtre du monde*, bk. III, p. 218 (ed. of 1558, p. 97^r) and Pedro Mexía (Pierre Messie), *Les diverses leçons* (Lyon: par Claude Michel, 1526), bk. III, ch. 13: "D'un medecine estrange, avec lequelle Faustine fut guerie de l'infirmitie d'amour deshonneste, et de plusieurs autres remedes contre ceste passion," pp. 208–11.

24. For the origins of the story of Deianira, see Apollodorus bk. II, ch. 7, secs. 5–8. Deianira is also a major character in Sophocles' *Women of Trachis*. Ferrand's relation differs in certain details from the general account. The Centaur Nessus had attempted to rape Deianira after she was Hercules' wife. The hero slew the Centaur there and then, but as he was dying he gave a potion to Deianira containing his blood and semen which he said would keep Hercules faithful to her. Thus when—not from the Centaur but from other sources—she learned of Hercules' unfaithfulness, she spread the potion on the tunic without knowing that it also contained the deadly venom of the Hydra. In this way the Centaur had his revenge, resulting in Hercules' death by poisoning and Deianira's by suicide. The story could have served Ferrand equally well in his sections on love potions and on jealousy. It is offered here as an example of an empirical remedy for love, rather than as a philter, for while philters are employed primarily to cause love for this or that person, they were also used as curses.

XXXVII.   True and Methodical Remedies for the Treatment of Erotic Melancholy: Dietetics

1. [*Val. Obser. 7. l. 2.*]: François Valleriola, *Observationum medicinalium libri*

VI, bk. II, obs. 7, pp. 208, 210: "Solutionis vero duplex est differentia: altera quidem naturae, diligentiae et artis altera est. Naturalis porro, ab interno principio provenit, quum seria et intenta in seipsum revocatione, redit ad se male compositus animus, mala quae in amore sunt cogitans, illaque perosus ab sese abdicans." The division was characteristic of later treatises combining medical traditions: on the one hand the methodical treatments stemming from Paul of Aegina, Avicenna, and others concerned with distracting the lover, and on the other the recognized cures for diseases of melancholy consisting of purges and phlebotomy for the evacuating of the offending humors.

Marsilio Ficino, *Commentary on Plato's Symposium*, Speech VII, ch. 11, p. 167, is the source of Valleriola's ideas concerning the natural and artificial cures for love.

2. Ovid, *Heroides*, XVII. 191–92: "Dum nonus est coepto potius medeamur Amori, / Flamma recens sparsa parva resedit aqua." See ed. Henricus Dörrie, p. 226. This edition reads "potius coepto pugnemus amore" and "parva sparsa."

Ovid, *The Remedies of Love*, ll. 81, 83: "Opprime dum nova sunt, subita mala semina morbi," "Nam mora dat vires." See *The Art of Love, and Other Poems*, trans. J. H. Mozley, p. 184.

3. Avicenna, *Liber canonis*, bk. III, fen 1, tr. 5, ch. 23, on the cure of melancholy; ch. 25, on the cure of love.

4. [*S. Ambrois. l. de poenit.*]: Saint Ambrose, *De poenitentia*, esp. bk. II, chs. 6 and 11, in *Opera*, 2 vols. (Paris: Johannis Baptistae Coignard, 1686), vol. II, pp. 425, 437. Ferrand's application is remote insofar as St. Ambrose speaks only of penitence for sins of the spirit and lapsing faith. He who is removed from the place of his sinning is better in a position to reform his faith, just as Ferrand urges the lover to remove himself from the object of his desires.

A more probable source for this idea is St. Francis de Sales, *The Introduction to the Devout Life*, trans. Michael Day (London: Burns and Oates, 1956; orig. publ. 1608), ch. 21, p. 145, which we know Ferrand was familiar with through references in his treatise of 1610: "I would strongly recommend you to separate if possible; two people stung by the dart of love, like two people bitten by the serpent, are more easily cured apart, while a change of scene greatly helps to alleviate the distressing pangs of sorrow or of love."

There is further reason to think Ferrand is reading Francis de Sales insofar as he gives below the story of the young man changed in his affections during his journey, a story attributed to St. Augustine, but which is, in fact, from St. Ambrose, bk. II of the *De poenitentia*, perhaps erroneously cited here instead of for the passage corresponding to our n. 14, below.

5. [*L. 6. Epist. Sect. 5. Aph. 19*]: Hippocrates, *Epidemics*, bk. VI, sec. 5, aph. 13: "Γῆν μεταμείβειν ξύμφορον ἐπὶ τοῖσι μακροῖσι νουσήμασιν." *Oeuvres complètes*, ed. Littré, vol. V, pp. 318–19; Ferrand inverts the position of the first three words, placing them at the end.

6. [*Gord. c. de Amore Arnauld. tr de Amo. Heroico c. 4.*]: Bernard of Gordon,

Lilium medicinae, ch. "De amore," pp. 216 ff.
Arnald of Villanova, *De amore heroico*, in *Opera medica omnia*, vol. III, p. 53 f.

7. Cicero, *Tusculan Disputations*, bk. IV, xxxv, 74: "Adducendus amator ad alia studia, curas, sollicitudines, negotia: loci denique mutatione, tanquam aegri convalescentes, curandus." See trans. J. E. King, pp. 412–13: "Abducendus etiam est non numquam ad alia studia, sollicitudines, curas, negotia: loci denique mutatione tamquam aegroti non convalescentes saepe curandus est."

8. [*Arist. c. 5 l 8. Eth.*]: Aristotle, *Nicomachean Ethics*, bk. VIII, ch. 5 (1157b), trans. H. Rackham, p. 469: "For separation does not destroy friendship absolutely, though it prevents its active exercise. If however the absence be prolonged, it seems to cause the friendly feeling itself to be forgotten: hence the poet's remark: Full many a man finds friendship end / For lack of converse with his friend."

Ferrand attributes the Greek quotation, "τύπων μεταβολαὶ οὔ τε ἀφρο-σύνην ἀφαιροῦνται, οὔτε φρόνησιν διδάσκυσι," to one of the seven sages. It comes in fact from Euripides, fr. 322 of A. Nauck's *Euripides tragoediae superstites* (Lipsiae: in aedibus B. G. Teubneri, 1854): "Τόπων μεταβολαὶ οὔτε φρόνησιν διδάσκουσιν οὔτε 'αφροσύνεν βέβαιον."

9. [*Arist. 9. Eth. c. 5. Plut. in Erot.*]: Aristotle, *Nicomachean Ethics*, bk. IX, ch. 5 (1167a), trans. H. Rackham, p. 539: "one is in love only if one longs for the beloved when absent, and eagerly desires his presence."

Plutarch, "The Dialogue on Love," in the *Moralia*, vol. IX. Only a phrase or two from this work can serve Ferrand's context, such as the following (p. 367): "In erotic madness, however, when once it has really seized upon a man and set him on fire, there is no reading of literature, no 'magic incantation,' no change of environment that restores him to calm. He loves when present and longs when absent, pursues by day and haunts the door by night." Ferrand's marginal reference indicates a remote allusion to this work.

10. [*Petron. Arbiter.*]: Petronius, *Satyricon*, 128 LO: "—animus quod perdidit optat: / Atque in praeterita se totus imagine versat." See trans. Michael Heseltine (Loeb, 1939), pp. 284–85.
For a parallel passage, see Ovid, *The Remedies of Love*, ll. 214–20.

11. [*L. 7. Anth.*]: Archias, in the *Greek Anthology*, bk. V, no. 59: "'Φεύγειν δεῖ τὸν "Ερωτα' κενὸς πόνος· οὐ γὰρ ἀλύξω / πεζὸς ὑπὸ πτηνοῦ πυκνὰ διωκόμενος." See trans. W. R. Paton, vol. II, p. 157. Ferrand's assignment to bk. VII is accounted for by the order of the *Planudean Anthology*, which he employed and in which the amatory epigrams appeared in bk. VII.

12. Pietro Capretto (Petrus Haedo), *Anterotica*, bk. I, ch. 19, p. 21^r: "Cur alae cupidini tribuantur: et quantae qualesque."

13. Lucretius, *De rerum natura*, bk. IV. 1061–62:
Namque si abest quod amas, praesto simulacra tamen sunt
Illius, et nomen dulce observatur ad aures.
See trans. W. M. D. Rouse, p. 328. Read "ames" and "obversatur."

14. The anecdote of the young man whose affections were altered by his

travel, attributed by Ferrand to St. Augustine, in fact derives from St. Ambrose, *De poenitentia*, bk. II, vaguely cited above in the place corresponding to our n. 4, but not derived directly because it was taken from St. Francis de Sales, *The Introduction to the Devout Life*, ch. 21, p. 146: "St. Ambrose, in his book on penance, speaks of a young man who returned from a long voyage completely cured of a foolish infatuation and so changed that, when his mistress met him with these words, 'Don't you know me? I am still the same,' he replied, 'Yes, but I am not' . . . a happy change brought about by their separation." The false ascription to St. Augustine is no doubt owing to the fact that the following lines in Francis de Sales read: "St Augustine tells us that to alleviate his sorrow at the death of his friend in Tagaste, he left there and went to Carthage."

Robert Burton relates a parallel version in *The Anatomy of Melancholy*, pt. 3, sec. 2, memb. 5, subs. 2, ed. Floyd Dell and Paul Jordan Smith, p. 774: "Peter Godefridus, in the last chapter of his third book, hath a story out of St. Ambrose, of a young man, that meeting his old love, after long absence, on whom he had extremely doted, would scarce take notice of her; she wondered at it, that he should so lightly esteem her, called him again, spoke persuasively, and told him who she was, I am so-and-so, she said: but he replied, he was not the same man: tore himself away, as Aeneas fled from Dido, not vouchsafing her any farther parley, loathing his folly, and ashamed of that which formerly he had done." Peter Godefridus, *Dialogus de amoribus, tribus libris distinctus* (Antverpiae: apud Gerardum Ludium, [1551]), bk. III, ch. 9, p. 374.

15. Ovid, *The Remedies of Love*, ll. 785–87:
> Di faciant, possis dominae transire relictae
> Limina, proposito sufficiantur pedes.
> Et poteris; modo velle tene. . . .

See *The Art of Love, and other Poems*, ed. J. H. Mozley, pp. 230–31.

16. [*Paul l. 3. c. de Amore; Mercat. l. 1. Meth. c. 17*]: Paul of Aegina, *The Seven Books*, bk. III, ch. 17: "Hos igitur moestos et pervigiles cum quidam dispositionem non satis pernossent, illotos in silenti solitudine, tenuique victus ratione collique facerent, ex quibus cordattores depresso amante, in lanacra et comessatum, et gestationes, et spectacula, et modulationes, fabulasque animum abducunt." See *The Seven Books*, vol. I, p. 391.

Luis Mercado, *De internorum morborum curatione*, bk. I, ch. 17, in *Opera*, vol. III, p. 103: "Quod enim in hoc potissimum est praesidium, fuga a re amata proculdubio exsistit: item exemplaris et sancta variarum rerum lectio, amicorum et familiarum mutatio, ludus, musica omnis generis, et omnis tandem distractionis modus."

17. Ovid, *The Remedies of Love*, ll. 579–84:
> Quisquis amas, loca sola cave, loca sola caveto:
> Quo fugis? in populo tutior esse potes.
> Nam tibi secretos augent secreta furores:
> Est opus auxilio, turba futura tibi est.
> Tristis eris si solus eris, dominaeque relictae.
> Ante oculos facies stabit ut ipsa tuos.

See trans. J. H. Mozley, p. 216. The first line reads, "Quisquis amas, loca sola cave nocent."

18. François Valleriola, *Observationum medicinalium libri VI*, p. 209; 210: "Item ad ludos, convivia, hilares compotationes, ad iocos et amoena virentibus in locis cum novis mulieribus et amicis colloquia traducendus aeger, ut ab amatorio cogitatu revoretur animus."

"magna puellarum, matronarumque caterva, tum et amicorum in id deindustria comparatorum copia: aderant et varii generis musica instrumenta ad exhilarandum hominem, et a summo quem conceperat amore moeroreque revocandum, ut iis intentus, amorum obliviisceretur."

19. Avicenna's chapter on love is *Liber canonis*, bk. III, fen 1, tr. 5, ch. 23. He simply says that "fortasse necessarium erit, ut isti regantur regimine habentium melancholiam, et maniam, et alcutubut [lycanthropy]."

20. [*Alex. Picolom. Seneca in Hipp.*]: Alessandro Piccolomini, *Della institution morale* (Venetia: appresso Giordano Ziletti, 1569). If Ferrand is referring to a passage in which the chase as a cure for love is mentioned, it has not been located. The reference is likely a general one to bk. X, ch. 6: "Del disciogimento dell'amore," pp. 443–47. In this chapter Piccolomini objects to those who believe that true love (*amore onesto*) can be chased away by traditional methods, such as slandering the loved one or by traveling to distant places, concluding that "per liberarsi d'amore, non si può trovare alcun certo rimedio, che dall'amante dipende" (p. 445). As for the treatment of the lower kind of love he states "due cose ancora il [i. e. amore] disciolgono: l'una è l'apparente brutezza, e l'altra il mancamento della speranza" (pp. 446–47).

Seneca, *Hippolytus or Phaedra*, in *Tragedies*, trans. Frank Justus Miller, 2 vols. (Loeb, 1967), vol. I, pp. 320–423. See esp. ll. 718 ff.

21. A passage from Ovid, *The Remedies of Love*, ll. 199–213, in *The Art of Love, and Other Poems*, ed. J. H. Mozley, pp. 191–93, would appear to be the founding text for recommendation of the hunt for the curing of love: "Or cultivate the pleasures of the chase; ofttimes has Venus, vanquished by Phoebus' sister, beaten a base retreat. Now pursue with cunning hound the forward-straining hare, now stretch your nets on leafy ridges; either with varied panic alarm the timid deer, or meet the boar and fell him with your spear-thrust. Tired out, at night-fall sleep, not thoughts of a girl, will await you, and refresh your limbs with healthy repose."

The Arab physicians Haly Abbas, Alsaravius, and Avicenna likewise recommended the hunt as a cure, though without mention of their sources for this idea.

22. [*Aph. 16. Sect. 4. l. 6. Epid.*]: Hippocrates, *Epidemics*, bk. VI, sec. 5, aph. 5: "Ψυχῆς περίπατος, φροντὶς ἀνθρώποισιν." *Oeuvres complètes*, ed. Littré, vol. V, p. 517. Ferrand appears to have taken the word for walking literally, though Hippocrates' meaning is figurative, "the soul walking is its exercise" that is "reflection is the exercise of the soul," which Ferrand could not have meant because erotic melancholy is a condition produced by too much reflection. His context is concerned with the distractions of physical exercise. Rhazes specifically recommended walking as a form of therapy.

23. André Du Laurens, *Des maladies melancholiques et du moyen de les guarir*, p. 36ʳ: "La fuite, c'est à dire, le changement d'air, est un des plus singuliers remedes, il le faut eslongner et depaïser du tout: car la veuë de sa maistresse luy r'alume tousjours son desir, et le recit du nom seulement sert comme d'amorce à ses ardeurs: il le faudra loger aux champs, ou en quelque maison plaisante, le pourmener souvent, l'occuper à toute heure à quelque jeu plaisant, luy proposer cent et cent differents objects, afin qu'il n'aye loisir de penser à ses amours, le mener à la chasse, à l'escrime, l'entretenir par fois de belles histoires et graves, par fois de fables plaisantes, avoir de la musique joyeuse: il ne faut le nourrir trop grassement, de peur que le sang venant à s'eschauffer, ne resveille la chair, et renouvelle ses flammes."

24. François Valleriola, *Observationum medicinalium libri VI*, p. 210. Valleriola does not deal specifically with the issue; Ferrand simply notices that in the case of the merchant, women were permitted in his company as part of the group of friends and relatives brought in to distract and amuse the patient.

25. "οὐδεὶς προσαιτῶν ἡράϑη βροτῶν," a line attributed to Menander, which, however, comes from Libanius, fr. 88 in *Opera*, ed. R. Foerster (Lipsiae: in aedibus G. B. Teubneri, 1922), vol. XI, p. 666: "οὐδεὶς προσαιτῶν βίοτον ἡράσϑη."

26. Ovid, *The Remedies of Love*, ll. 747–49:
Cur nemo est Hecalem, nulla est quae ceperit Irum?
Nempe quod alter egens, altera pauper erat.
Non habet unde suum paupertas pascat amorem.
See *The Art of Love, and Other Poems*, trans. J. H. Mozley, pp. 228–29.

27. [*L. 1. Meth. c. de amant. Merc. l. 1. Meth. c. 17*]: Guillaume Rondelet, *Methodus curandorum omnium morborum corporis humani*, bk. II, ch. 45, p. 239: "De amantibus nihil nobis est dicendum, quia illi nullam curam sibi adhibere volunt. Tamen si sanguine abundant, vena secetur. Imperandus victus tenuis et alicuius rei studium. Qui enim amori semper indulgent, his difficile potest abigi affectio."
Luis Mercado, *De internorum morborum curatione*, in *Opera*, bk. I, ch. 17, vol. III, p. 103: "Item si adhuc corpulentus fuerit amans, balneis et exercitiis utatur, vinum fugiat, et ciborum utatur parsimonia."

28. [*Paul. l. 3 c. 17. Orib. l. 8. synops. c. 9.*]: Paul of Aegina, *The Seven Books*, bk. III, sec. xvii, vol. I, p. 391: "Such persons, therefore, being desponding and sleepless, some physicians, mistaking their affection, have wasted them by prohibiting baths, and enjoining quietude, and a spare diet; but wiser ones, recognizing the lover, direct his attention to baths, the drinking of wine, gestation, spectacles, and amusing stories."
But the quotation in Ferrand's text comes from Oribasius, *Synopsis*, bk. VIII, ch. 9: "De amantibus," in *Oeuvres*, p. 413: "Certains médecins, voyant des amoureux en proie à la tristesse et à l'insomnie, méconnaissent leur maladie, et les épuisent en leur défendant de manger et de prendre des bains et en leur prescrivant un régime; mais, ayant reconnu, dans des cas analogues, qu'il s'agissait d'amour, nous avons tourné notre pensée vers les bains, l'usage du vin."

We note the parallel wording to Ferrand's passage to follow relating to Venus, Ceres, and Bacchus in Jean Aubery, *L'antidote d'amour*, pp. 135^{r-v}: "Il s'abstiendra du tout du vin, et en son lieu usera d'eau ferree: l'ancien proverbe chante que Venus est languide et refroidée sans l'assistance de Ceres, et de Bacchus."

The proverb originates in Terence, *The Eunuch*, IV.v: "Sine Cerere et Baccho, friget Venus." See trans. J. Sargeaunt (Loeb, 1964), p. 310. It reappears in the *Adages* of Erasmus and in Rabelais, *Le tiers livre*, ch. 31, p. 345: "L'antique proverbe nous le designe, on quel est dict: Que Venus se morfond sans la compaignie de Ceres et Bacchus."

29. [*Tibul. el. 3. l. 2.*]: Tibullus, bk. II, Elegy III. 69: "glans aluit vetares, et passim semper amarunt." *The Elegies*, ed. Kirby Flower Smith, p. 140.

Ferrand's sense of Tibullus wanders rather far from the text. Tibullus harkens to the days of his forefathers when love was theirs in abundance and not a curse to them. The simple primitive fare of acorns was their diet before agriculture, attractive to the poet because his love has been wooed away to the countryside. Tibullus says he can do without a variety of foods for the sake of keeping his girl; i. e., he would live on acorns to be near her. Ferrand, however, is discussing whether fasting is an aid to curing love melancholy; he uses Tibullus's ancients as examples of those who, living on a simple diet, still suffered all the trials of love. If the disease itself causes starvation, then dieting can only exacerbate the condition of the melancholy lover. Thus he comes to agree with those who favor nourishing the languishing lover. Restricted diet works only for the lover in full health whose surplus of flesh and blood contributes to the manufacture of seed. Thus Ferrand solves the argument between the opposed authorities.

The acorn diet of an idealized aboriginal society alluded to by Tibullus had, in fact, become one of the touchstone subjects in the debate between the ancients and the moderns. After another disastrous skirmish in the modern world as the representative of the ancient order of knight errantry, Don Quixote finds himself the guest of rustic goatherders. As they finish their simple meal, the Don takes up a handful of acorns and begins a discourse on the golden age when men were not concerned with property. Immediately following is the dolorous tale of Grisóstomo, whose passionate infatuation for Marcela leads him to a melancholy death. Miguel de Cervantes, *Don Quixote de La Mancha*, trans. John Ormsby, ed. Joseph Jones and Kenneth Douglas (New York: W. W. Norton, 1981), pt. 1, ch. 11; p. 74. Among the inevitable resonances of this sequence is the sense in which the world of acorn diets and unrestrained passion is a cruel deception, that neither the pastoral world nor the golden age world were apt descriptions of existing social realities. Polemicists later in the seventeenth century took up the cause against the nostalgia for a lost golden age even to the point of rejecting the notion that acorns could have been the diet of men in those early times. See, e.g., Secondo Lancellotti, *L'Hoggidi, overo il mondo peggiore ne piú calamitoso del passato* (Venezia: appresso gli G. Guerigli, 1636–37), pp. 171–79.

30. "ad seminis (utpote causae primariae Amoris) consumptionem." Unidentified line.

31. [*L. 4 de pla. Hipp. & Platon.*]: Galen, *De placitis Hippocratis et Platonis*, bk. IV, ed. Kühn, vol. V, p. 426. The book is important for what Galen says about love, and for the fact that he recognizes the existence of an amatory fever. The topic was much debated in the Renaissance. See also his *De crisibus*, bk. II, ch. 13, documented in n. 8 to Ferrand's ch. XVI.

32. "θηβαῖος κράτης ἄλλοις ἐν εὐηηρρη μόνιος γράφοι, τῆς εἰς τὰ ἀφροδίσια ἀκατασχούτου ὁρμῆς κατάπαυσμα εἶναι λιμὸν, εἰ δὲ μὴ χρόνον, εἰ δὲ μὴ βρόχον." We have been unable to locate this quotation in the works of Clement of Alexandria. The reference to the Cynic philosopher Crates of Thebes derives from Diogenes Laertius, *Lives of Eminent Philosophers*, bk. VI, p. 86 f., trans. R. D. Hicks (Loeb, 1966), vol. II, p. 90, where Crates's poem, from which Clement's quotation also derives, is quoted:

> Ἔρωτα παύει λιμός· εἰ δὲ μή, χρόνος.
> Ἐὰν δὲ μηδὲ ταῦτα τὴν φλόγα σβέσῃ,
> θεραπεία σοι τὸ λοιπὸν ἠρτήσθω βρόχος.

The poem is also in the *Greek Anthology*, no. 497, ed. W. R. Paton, vol. III, p. 274.

The story is also related by Mario Equicola, *Libro de natura de amore*, p. 152^V.

The quotation became commonplace in works on love. Ferrand may have gotten the idea for quoting it from Luis Mercado, *De internorum morborum curatione*, bk. I, ch. 17, vol. IV, p. 103.

33. [*Arnald. de Villan. tra. de Amore c. 4.*]: Arnald of Villanova, *De amore heroico*. Arnald does not suggest in this treatise the remedies mentioned by Ferrand.

Bernard of Gordon, *Lilium medicinae*, pt. 2, ch. 20: "De amore, qui hereos dicitur," p. 218. See ch. XXX, n. 51, above.

34. [*Gal. l 6. de loc. aff. ult.*]: Galen, *On the Affected Parts*, bk. VI, ch. 6, trans. Siegel, p. 196: "Medicine which increases the tension in the penis, whether taken [orally] as a fluid preparation or directly applied to the perineum or to the lumbar area, is always hot and causes flatulence, whereas opposite drugs do not develop gas and are cooling rather than warming."

35. Cornelius Gallus, Elegy III. 31–32, 35–36:

> Increpitat, ceditque, ignes in pectore crescunt:
> Ut solet accenso crescere flamma rogo:
> . . . .
> Tunc me visceribus perterrita quaerit anhelis,
> Emptum suppliciis quem putat esse suis.

Catullus, Tibullus, Propertius cum Galli fragmentis, p. 330: read *adjecto* for *accenso*.

XXXVIII.   Surgical Cures for Erotic Melancholy

1. [*Schola Salern.*]: Arnald of Villanova, Commentary on *Medicina saler-nitana, id est conservanda bonae valetudinis praecepta* (Excudebat Jacobus Stoer, 1599), ch. 97: "De quibusdam phlebotomiae effectibus," pp. 169–70.

   The lines quoted in Ferrand's text vis-à-vis the marginal designation are of uncertain origin, though they may well be in the School of Salerno tradition:

   > Exhilarat tristes, tratos placat, amantes,
   > Ne sint amentes phlebotomia facit.

2. François Valleriola, *Observationum medicinalium libri VI*, p. 212: "In crastinum etiam nolenti ac reluctanti sanguinem detrahi iubeo ex media dextri brachii, detrahoque ad ℥. xii. quod et viribus et aetate floreret aeger: prodiit autem sanguis teterrimus, et atra bili multa perfusus, crassus, faeculentus, niger." For Valleriola bleeding becomes particularly important because the blood itself contains the disease as a kind of poison. According to other theorists the principal purpose in drawing off blood was to reduce the excess blood that could otherwise be converted to sperm. For Valleriola, the agitation will persist as long as the blood remains that has been infected by the fascination: ("quandiu infectio illa sanguinis per fascinationem"). This infection in the entrails produces great pain and, once spread to the limbs, causes a burning with invisible flames. If the venom passes from the veins to the members and can be drawn off by bleeding and purging, then the symptoms of the tortured lover will abate. Ferrand makes passing references to the venom and infection model, but in general, he identifies the residual sludge of the burned humors as the object of his purges. Ferrand neither raises the issue as a controversy nor specifies a division.

3. [*Gal. l. 3 de loc aff c 6. Avic. l. 3. fen 1. tr. c. 10*]: Galen, *On the Affected Parts*, bk. III, ch. 6, trans. Siegel, pp. 80–82.

   Avicenna, *Liber canonis*, bk. III, fen 1, tr. 3, ch. 20, pp. 205^r–206^r, esp. p. 205^v. In this chapter Avicenna relates methods to cure melancholy.

4. [*Aret. li. 1. chr. morb. c 5. Arnal. tr. de amore*]: Aretaeus the Cappadocian, *On the Cure of Chronic Diseases*, pp. 473–74; 475. A great deal of what Ferrand says about bleeding in cases of melancholy is to be found nearly verbatim in this treatise by a Greek physician practicing in Rome in the second century of our era, a manifestation of the highly conservative approach to these subjects and practices that survived nearly unchanged over several centuries. "In cases of melancholy, there is need of consideration in regard to the abstraction of blood, from which the disease arises, but it also springs from cacochymy in no small amount thereof. When, therefore, the disease seizes a person in early life, and during the season of spring we are to open the median vein at the right elbow, so that there may be a seasonable flow from the liver; for this viscus is the fountain of the blood, and the source of the formation of the bile, both which are the pabulum of melancholy. We must open a vein even if the patients be spare and have deficient blood, but abstract little, so that

the strength may feel the evacuation but may not be shaken thereby; for even though the blood be thick, bilious, coagulated, and black as the lees of oil, yet still it is the seat and the pabulum of Nature. If, then, you abstract more than enough, Nature, by the loss of nourishment, is ejected from her seat. But if the patient has much blood, for the most part in such cases it is not much vitiated, but still we must open a vein, and not abstract all the blood required the same day, but after an interval, or, if the whole is taken the same day, the strength will indicate the amount." "Let there, then be no procrastination of time, but if the disease appear after suppression of the catamenial discharge in women, or the hemorrhoidal flux in men, we must stimulate the parts to throw off their accustomed evacuation. But if it is delayed and does not come, the blood having taken another direction, and if the disease progress rapidly, we must make evacuations, beginning from the ankles. And if you cannot get away from this place so much blood as you require, you must also open the vein at the elbow." For further commentary by Aretaeus see *De causis et notis diuturnorum affectuum*, bk. I, ch. 4: "De melancholia," in *Medicae artis principes post Hippocratem et Galenum* ([Geneva]: Henricus Stephanus, 1567), vol. I, p. 22.

Ferrand's second reference is to Arnald of Villanova, *Tractatus de amore heroico*, but Arnald does not mention phlebotomy in this work.

Guillaume Rondelet, *Methodus curandorum omnium morborum corporis humani*, ch. 42: "De melancholia hypochondriaca," pp. 223–29. There is general agreement concerning bleeding: "Quare solvenda primum plethora, basilicae sectione, postmodum veniendum ad saphenam."

5. [*Hipp. aph. 21. sec. 2. l. 6. Ep.*]: Hippocrates, *Epidemics*, bk. VI, sec. 2, aph. 14: " Ἀντισπᾶν, ἢν μὴ, ᾗ δεῖ, ῥέπῃ." *Oeuvres complètes*, ed. Littré, vol. V, p. 285.

Galen, *De atra bile liber*, ed. Kühn, vol. V, p. 121.

Galen, *In Hippocratis aphorismos commentarius*, bk. IV, aph. 25: "τῷ γὰρ ὄντι μελαγχολίας ἤδη γεγενημένης ἴαμα μέγιστόν ἐστιν αἱμορροῖς, μελλούσης ἔσεσθαί γε κώλυμα." Ferrand drops the γάρ. Ed. Kühn, vol. XVII, p. 652.

The pattern for the curing of love melancholy is closely paralleled by the treatments recommended for uterine fury. It is for this reason that Ferrand associates the two conditions and borrows freely from the literature on the diseases of women for his own purposes. Girolamo Mercuriale, in his chapter on uterine fury in *De morbis muliebribus libri IV*, bk. IV, ch. 10, p. 157, outlines the following treatment: "Praeter victum, sunt et alia quae in usu sunt remedia, et quia in his mulieribus, saepe abundant humores calidi et fervidi, propterea expurgandi sunt ante caetera, illi humores. Expurgantur autem faciliter, si prius praeparentur: ideo necesse est prius corpus praeparare. Quomodo vero praeparentur et evacuentur humores in huiusmodi affectibus calidis, pluries docui, non est ut hic repetam. Postquam praeparati erunt humores, vel dum praeparantur, est habenda cogitatio de sanguinis missione, quia nisi quid impediat, ab Hippocrate, nullum praestantius remedium, pro hoc morbo vincendo, judicatum est. Erit igitur sanguis mittendus a vena communi, et saphena, modo vires permittant et nihil impediat. Praeter evacuationem universalem et humorem peculiarem, est maxime vigilandum, et uteri calida intemperies, mitigetur: ad quod agendum, sunt medicamenta intrinseca et extrinseca. Intrinseca sunt brodia, in quibus solanum vel cicuta sunt cocta, quibus debetis semper commiscere quae peculiarem habent facultatem petendi uterum." For the section on baths see ch. XXXIX, n. 53, below.

6. [*Tract. de Mania. Gal. l. 13. Meth med.*]: Galen speaks of bloodletting in cases of inflammation (*phlegmone*) throughout bk. XIII of his *De methodo medendi*, ed. Kühn, vol. X, pp. 874–944. Galen, however, deals with bloodletting in much more detail in three separate works. See *Galen on Bloodletting: A Study of the Origins, Development and Validity of his Opinions, with a Translation of the Three Works*, trans. Peters Brain (Cambridge: Cambridge University Press, 1986).

7. [*Manard. l. 4. ep. 5 Mercat. l. 2. de morb. mul. c. 10*]: Giovanni Manardo, *Epistolae medicinales diversorum authorum*, bk. IV, ep. 5: "Ad amicum atra bile agitatum," p. 21b: "Humana tamen remedia, et quae Deus ipse de terra creavit, non sunt negligenda: inter quae id mihi praecipuum videtur, ut vena quae annularem minimunque digitum interiacet, secetur, sanguinisque sex unciae hauriantur."

Luis Mercado, *De internorum morborum curatione libri IV*, in *Opera*, bk. II, ch. 10, vol. III, p. 585: "item sanguine pauco per intervalla ex talo vel dextra salvatella extracto."

8. François Valleriola, *Observationum medicinalium libri VI*, p. 214, makes the same recommendation: "Nam memor illius Hippocratis sententiae, melancholicis haemorrhoides innatae bonum, inanitionem sanguinis e mariscis provocavi, ex foliis ficus fricato ano, et unguento ex aloë, pulpa colocynthidis, et suillo felle parato, et liciniis immissis sanguinem evocavi, magno aegri commodo."

9. Hippocrates, *On Joints*, ch. 57: "ἀδελφίξιας." See *Oeuvres complètes*, ed. Littré, vol. IV, p. 246: "Πολλὰ δέ καὶ ἄλλα κατὰ τὸ σῶμα τοιαύτας ἀδελφίξιας ἔχει" ("in the body there are many other similar connections").

See also Robert Burton, *The Anatomy of Melancholy*, pt. 1, sec. 4, memb. 1, p. 366, who not only traces the idea of evacuating the hemorrhoids to Hippocrates, but who also lists Montaltus, Hercules of Saxonia, Mercurialis, Vittorius, and Faventinus: "Sckenkius illustrates this Aphorism with an example of one Daniel Federer, a Coppersmith, that was long melancholy, and in the end mad about the 27th year of his age; these *varices* or water began to arise in his thighs, and he was freed from his madness. Marius the Roman was so cured, some say, though with great pain." Burton indicated that it was the melancholy state itself that produced water between the layers of skin forming blisters and scabs. Yet in contradistinction, he too states that "the opening of the haemrods" will aid greatly, but also that it should be done by consent and not by force.

See also Luis Mercado, *De internorum morborum curatione libri*, in *Opera*, vol. III, p. 105.

10. [*Prob. 21. sec. 4.*]: Aristotle, *Problems*, bk. VI, sec. 1 (885b), trans. W. S. Hett, vol. I, p. 167.

11. [*L. 2. c. 36*]: the reference is to Arnald of Villanova, *Breviarium practicae*, bk. II, ch. 40: "De extinguenda libidine, et voluntate coeundi removenda," in *Opera omnia*, pp. 1282–84. See also the commentary by Taurelli, pp. 1284–85. It is noteworthy that Arnald addresses the problem with reference specifically to the clergy.

12. [*Mosch. c. 18 Albuc. l 2. Method. c. 71*]: Moschion, *De morbis muliebribus liber*, ch. 18, p. 2.

   Albucasis, *Methodus medendi certa* (Basileae: per Henricum Petrum, c. 1541): "De incisione tetiginis et carnis eminentis ex vulvis mulierum," pp. 118–19: "Tetigo saepe augetur et excedit modum naturalem. Donec foedus et turpis aspectus eius fiat, et quandoque ad eam magnitudinem pervenit in quibusdam mulieribus ut expandatur sicut in viris, et pervenit usque ad coitum. Oportet ergo ut teneas superfluitatem tetiginis manu, aut uncino, et incidas, sed ne altius seces praecipue in profundo radicis, ut non accidat fluxus sanguinis. Deinde cura ipsum curatione vulnerum, donec sanetur. Caro autem saepe nascitur in orificio matris, donec impleat ipsum. Et nonnunquam egreditur ad exteriora secundum similitudi nem caudae. Et propter illud nominant quidam aegritudinem caudatam, oportet ergo ut incidemus eam sicut incidimus tetiginem, et curemus eam donec sanetur."

13. Oribasius, *Synopsis*, bk. VIII, ch. 10, in *Oeuvres*, p. 414 f. Paul of Aegina, *The Seven Books*, bk. III, sec. 16, pp. 389–90. Avicenna, *Liber canonis*, bk. III, fen 1, tr. 5, ch. 22. For a full list of the texts by ancient authorities treating this topic, see the commentary in Paul of Aegina, *The Seven Books*, p. 390, that traces the idea to works by Aëtius, Actuarius, Psellus, Haly Abbas, Albucasis, and Rhazes in addition to those sources cited above; also see our introduction.

   See Charlotte F. Otten, ed., *A Lycanthropy Reader: Werewolves in Western Culture* (Syracuse: Syracuse University Press, 1986).

XXXIX.   Pharmaceutical Remedies for Love and Erotic Melancholy

1. [*Marsil. Ficin. in Conviv. Plat. Valeriol. obs. 7. l. 2*]: Marsilio Ficino, *Commentary on Plato's Symposium*, Speech VII, ch. 11, p. 167: "For an itch in the skin remains only so long as the residue of decaying blood remains in the veins, or the saltiness of the phlegm is strong in the parts. When the blood has been purged and the phlegm deadened, the itch ceases and the foul stains of the skin are cleared up. However, a deliberate care in evacuation contributes most. A precipitous evacuation or ointment is judged very dangerous. Also the disquiet of lovers necessarily lasts as long as that infection of the blood, injected into the viscera through bewitchment, lasts; it presses the heart with heavy care, feeds the wound through the veins, and burns the members with unseen flames. For its passage is made from the heart into the veins, and from the veins into the members. When this infection is finally purged away, the disquiet of the erotics (or rather erratics) ceases. This purging requires a long

space of time in all, but longest in melancholics."

François Valleriola, *Observationum medicinalium libri VI*, bk. II, obs. 7, pp. 210–11: "Siquidem in cute eatenus affectus ii permanent, quatenus vitiosi et marcessentis sanguinis faex in venis, aut salsedo humorum viget in membris. Defaecato sanguine, et salsugine emollita congruis medicamentis, pruritus desinit, et foedae cutis maculae ulcusculaque abolentur. Evacuationum itaque matura diligentia, et in tempore adhibitae medelae, non praecipites, non incautae, huic morbo plurimum conferunt. Repentina evacuatio et unctio ut in scabie periculosissima habenda sunt, sic et in hoc affectu repentina omnia maxime noxia. Atque prout in scabie atque pruritu praesens in venis et membris vitium noxam parit, et exagitationem infert corpori molestam: sic et amantium quoque inquietudo tandiu necessario perstat, quandiu infectio illa sanguinis per fascinationem iniecta visceribus permanens, gravi cor premit cura, vulnus alit venis, caecis membra flammis aduritur a corde siquidem in venas, a venis in membra transitus fit; hac denique expurgata, amantium, aut verius amentium, cessat inquietudo." Valleriola's debt to Ficino is patently clear in this passage, and in turn Ferrand's debt to both. The association between the scurf and love melancholy had been well established by the time it reaches Ferrand, the analogy serving to illustrate the relationship between the condition of the blood and the external symptoms in both cases, and the need for a great deal of patience in the treating of both maladies. Significant, however, is the fact that Ferrand does not develop the concept of love as a form of fascination attacking the blood as a kind of poison, and thus he cannot continue with this line of reasoning. Nevertheless, of all the preceding writers on love, Valleriola is the most important as a guide for Ferrand in developing an extended pharmaceutical regimen specifically designed for the curing of love, including the recipes for two of his purgatives and the principal recipe for the bath. To a large extent, Ferrand works out a scheme of his own based on an amalgamation of Valleriola and Du Laurens.

2. [*Aph. 51. l. 2*]: Hippocrates, *Aphorisms*, sec. 2, no. 51: "Τὸ κατὰ πολὺ καὶ ἐξαπίνης κονοῦν, ἢ πληροῦν, ἢ θερμαίνειν, ἢ ψύχειν, ἢ ἄλλως ὀκωσοῦν τὸ σῶμα κινέειν, σφαλερὸν, καὶ πᾶν τὸ πολὺ τῇ φύσει πολέμιον· τὸ δὲ κατ'ὀλίγον, ἀσφαλὲς." *Oeuvres complètes*, ed. Littré, vol. IV, p. 485; Ferrand's text has γὰρ as the second word.

3. André Du Laurens, *Des maladies melancholiques et du moyen de les guarir*, ch. 9, p. 31[V]: "L'experience nous fait tous les jours paroistre que toutes les maladies melancholiques sont rebelles, longues, et tres-dificiles à guarir, la raison y est assez apparent; car l'humeur melancholique est terrestre et grossiere, ennemie de la lumiere, contraire aux deux principes de nostre vie, qui sont chaleur et humidité; opiniastre aux remedes, qui ne veut ouyr conseil, ne obeir aux preceptes de medecine, c'est en somme un vray fleau et tourment des Medecins."

Ficino sees love functioning as an infection that runs throughout the body (see note 1), Du Laurens sees it as a heavy thick sludge, a viscuous residue almost impossible to remove, while Jourdain Guibelet compares it to a cancer that eats away the body as strong vinegar dissolves pearls and metals and is therefore beyond cure once it has gone to such concentrated states (see ch. XXXII, n. 5, above). These three views of the action of black bile are by no means exclusive of each other. Ferrand is inclined to conflate them and to calculate his preparations to act upon the offending humor in all three theaters, though generally he follows Du Laurens in considering melancholy adust as the cause of a residue that must be purged by all appropriate means and in accordance with the complexion and constitution of the patient.

4. [*Alex. q. 21*]: Alexander of Aphrodisias, *Problemata*, bk. I, no. 84: "τό δὲ ξηρὸν δυσαλλοίωτον καὶ δυσμετάβλητον." See ed. I. L. Ideler, p. 27: "τὸ δὲ ψυχρὸν δυσαλλοίωτον καὶ δυσμετάβλητον."

5. Hippocrates, *On the Nature of Man*: "[μέλαινα χολὴ] τῶν ἐν τῷ σώματι ἐνεόντων χυμῶν γλιχρότατον, καὶ τὰς ἵδρας χρονιωτάτος πεποίηται." *Oeuvres complètes*, ed. Littré, vol. VI, p. 47; the original reads: "[μέλαινα χολῆ] ἐν τῷ σώματι ἐνεόντωον γλισχρότατον, καὶ τὰς ἕδρας χρονιωτάτος ποιεῖται."

Hippocrates, writing of phlegm, states that "elle a beaucoup de viscosité, et après la bile noire c'est l'humeur dont l'expulsion exige le plus de force."

6. François Valleriola, *Observationum medicinalium libri VI*, p. 213. Valleriola does not state precisely how much time was required for him to cure the merchant, but only that he was afflicted with the disease for over six months. Nevertheless, there are many statements in the section on cures to the effect that much time is required to cure such a disease. The purges must be given in measured doses and at intervals because nature cannot support sudden changes. The program of baths lasted a month. Because of the thickness and rebelliousness of the humor—the burned black bile infecting the patient—and because of the coldness that goes against nature, a long period is required for the evacuation. If we are to understand that the physician was called in soon after the onset of the disease, then the period of the cure can be read as being nearly synonymous with the length of the disease itself.

7. [*Avic. 3. 1 fen 1 tr. 4. c. 20 Rhaz. 7. cont. c. 3*]: Avicenna, *Liber canonis*, bk. III, fen 1, tr. 4, ch. 20, on the cures of melancholy, pp. 205^r–206^r, esp. p. 205^v.

Rhazes, *Liber continens*, bk. VII, ch. 3. As in the two former instances in which Ferrand cites this work, he places it in conjunction with Avicenna, from whose margins, in the same edition we have cited, he has taken all his references to Rhazes.

8. Jourdain Guibelet, *Trois discours philosophiques: Discours troisiesme de l'humeur melancholique*, ch. 4: "Que les maladies causées de cete humeur sont pour la pluspart estranges et incurables," pp. 234^r–v: "Nous la pouvons comparer à une fascheuse garnison, qui vit à discretion dans une ville. Si elle est traictée doucement, elle ne peut déloger qu'avec regret. Si elle reçoit de mécontentement, elle voudra tarder encore pour se venger, et donner davantage d'affliction."

9. Both of these preparations are electuaries consisting of a fruit syrup base to which medicinal powders are added. Diaprunum solutivum Nicolai (*London Pharmacopoeia*, p. 83) has as its active ingredient scammony pow-

der, confirmed by Joseph Du Chesne (Quercetanus) in his diaprunum compound. There are a number of recipes for Catholicon from the period. For representative examples, see Diacatholicon Nicolai (*L. P.* p. 83) and the Catholicon of Quercetanus from the *Pharmacie des Dogmatiques*, pp. 311–12, which has for active ingredients Calabrian manna, oriental senna powder, rhubarb, and cold diatragacanth. See also ch. XXXII, n. 1 above.

Cassia and oriental senna are among the most common simples used as purgatives, usually mixed, as specified here, with a refreshing syrup. Confectio Hamech Mesué (*L. P.* p. 85) is a complex electuary with some twenty-six different ingredients. It contained a mixed fruit and herb base and a number of spices, to which were added, as active powders, agaric, senna, rhubarb, epithyme, and ginger, as well as additional spices such as cinnamon, anise, and spikenard. Diasenna is not given in the *L. P.*, though recipes of the period often call for it. It is a powder used as a purgative containing either senna or trifolium. It is discussed by Quercetanus in the *Pharmacie des Dogmatiques*, p. 307.

Triphera Persicum is an electuary, the words derived from the Greek meaning "sumptuous" and "peach." Quercetanus uses it frequently as a purgative compound. The "Tryphere Persique de Jean Damascene" is good for all inflammations, fevers and agues, and for all ill conditions of the liver and ventricle, and brings comfort to all diseases caused by adust humors: *Pharmacie des Dogmatiques*, p. 448; see also p. 308. Quercetanus claims the word *tryphera* signifies "delicate" because the compound brings warm and attractive colors back to the complexions of women (p. 447). The recipe for triphera is in the *L. P.* "Syrupus ex floribus Persicorum," p. 27. Every apothecary had his own recipe for rose syrup, which was, for the most part, but a mixture of rose water and sugar boiled together. See, e.g., "Julepum rosatum Mesué," *L. P.* p. 24. Agaric is a mushroom that contains hydrocyanic acid and was among the more violent purgatives. It was usually made into pill form and these in turn were added to the base recipe. See the *L. P.* for "Agaricus Trochiscatus" and "Trochisci de agarica Mesué," p. 110.

Johann Winter (Andernacus), *Le regime de vivre et de prendre medecine . . . traduict de latin en francoys par Anthoine Pierre de Rieux* (Poitiers: J. et E. de Marnef, 1544), without page or chapter headings: "A ceulx qui sont de nature fort delicate, ou qui ont la chair tendre comme les enfans, les femmes, et les vieilles gens, il ist tresbon de user la casse, dequoy nous usons aujoudhuy, pour evacuer le cole, et en prendre la quantité d'une once seulle, ou y adjouster une drachme de Rhabarbe: et la peut on prendre tout ainsi que lon vouldra."

10. "℞. Buglossi & borrag. cum radic. cichor. endiv. acetosae, pimpinellae, & caeterach ana m. i. summit. lupuli, fumar, bethon, ana m. ½ polypod. querni ʒ. ½ passul. mundat. & corinth. ana ʒ . iii. prunorum dulc. par. iii. semin. melon. cucurb. & cucumer. mundat. ana ʒ . ii. semin: lactuc. & papav. albi ana ʒ . i. &. ½ semin. agni casti & anisi ana ʒ . i. flor. trium cordial. thymi & epithymi ana p. i. fiat omnium decoctio ad lb. ii. Colaturae adde sucor. borrag. lupuli & pomor. redolent. depuratorum ana ʒ. iii.

iterum leviter bulliant, addendo sacchari electi lib. ½ fiat julep. claris. & aromat. pulver. laetific. Rhazis, aut laetitiae Gal. vel diamarg. frigidi ʒ . i. & ½ pro quinque aut sex dosibus."

This recipe is taken, with minor variations, from François Valleriola, *Observationum medicinalium libri VI*, pp. 212–13. The dosage in the original is four times, with an explanation in Ferrand based on Valleriola's. In the case of Valleriola's rich merchant, because the burned bile was in a thick and rebellious state and because of the coldness of the disease going entirely contrary to nature, a long period of time would be required to effect its evacuation; hence, he was prepared to use this purge on several occasions.

In the edition of 1610, with regard to the alterative Ferrand states, "before the entire purgation and eradication of the melancholy humor, one must rather prepare it, together with the conduits of the body by the remedies possessing by nature the ability to cut and soften this thick and gluelike humor, and to moisten the dryness: such are march violets, bugloss, borage, lettuce, melissa, water lily, hops, fumitory, fern, the fruit and flowers of the apple tree with a thousand similar types."

11. [*Aph.* 9 l 4. *Gal. l. quos. quib. & quando.*]: Hippocrates, *Aphorisms*, sec. 4, no. 9: "τοὺς μελαγχολικοὺς, ἁδροτέρως τὰς κάτω." *Oeuvres complètes*, ed. Littré, vol. IV, p. 505; the Littré ed. has "δὲ" after "τοὺς."

Galen, *Quos, quibus catharticis medicamentis et quando purgare oporteat*, ed. Kühn, vol. XI, p. 347: "At melancholicus perpetuo per inferiora educendus."

12. Arnald of Villanova, *De regimine caste viventium*, ch. 28 of *De regimine sanitatis*, in *Opera omnia*, p. 749; see also ch. XXXII, n. 3, above.

13. See n. 7, above.

14. "℞. prunor. dulc. par. iii. passul. corinth. & flor. cordial. ana p. i. tamarind. recent. & select. ʒ . ii. fol. senae orient. mundat. ʒ . iii. anisi. agni casti & conam. interioris ana ʒ . ½ epithy. p. ½ fiat decoctio ad ℥. iiii. in quibus colatis dissol. espress. ℈. iiii. rhabarb. per nostem in sero caprillo infusi cum sex granis santali rubri, confection. hamech ʒ . ii. syrupi rosate solut. ℥ . i. & ½ fiat potio, detur mane cum regimine artis."

Ferrand continues to follow Valleriola from his *Observationum medicinalium libri VI*, p. 213, for this recipe and the surrounding comments. Valleriola states that this recipe should be given if there are signs of burned bile in the urine as opposed to the preceding recipe (the same used by Ferrand), whereas Ferrand offers it as the first purge. Valleriola states that by having his patient take this medication various things are evacuated, either yellow or black bile. Afterwards he gives a potion to comfort the patient made with a large quantity of sugar—about 6 hours after the purge. Ferrand probably extracts his own recommendations for a conserve of roses, borrage flowers, or bugloss root from Valleriola's: "In crastinum bolum paravi ex saccharo rosaceo et buglossato ad ℥ iii. quem in aurora sumere iussi." Here Valleriola states again the principle that such medications must be used many times, because it is dangerous to give massive doses all at once, for as Galen teaches, nature does not endure sudden changes.

15. "Asarum" is hazlewort, or wild nard, and gives both a volatile oil and a powder made of the rhizomes. It has been prescribed as a carminative and stimulant also suitable for treating hepatic and splenitic obstructions and rheumatic conditions. "Mel scyllitic" was made with honey and vinegar of the sea squill or scilla maritima. The plant is poisonous if taken in quantity, but has been employed medicinally as a diuretic, expectorant, and cardiac tonic. It was widely used by the Arab physicians whose recipes made it popular during the Renaissance. Quercetanus, in the *Pharmacie des Dogmatiques*, pp. 220–21, gives a recipe. See also the *L. P.* for "Oxymel Scylliticum simplex Nicolai," and "Oxymel Scylliticum Democriti Mesué," p. 42, and esp. "Acetum Scilliticum Mesué," p. 15.

16. [*Celsi.*]: Celsus, *De medicina*. No caution is mentioned in this work concerning hellebore as a vomitive. In every instance, Celsus recommends it without qualification as an appropriate treatment for melancholy. This is especially true where no fever is involved. See bk. III, ch. 18: "For depression black hellebore should be given as a purge, for hilarity white hellebore as an emetic; and if the patient will not take the hellebore in a draught, it should be put into his bread to deceive him the more easily; for if he has well purged himself, he will in great measure relieve himself of his malady." See trans. W. G. Spencer, vol. I, p. 301. That Ferrand came by this opinion indirectly is suggested not only by its inaccuracy but also by the fact that Ferrand offers no book and chapter numbers as he does in all other references to Celsus.

Both antimony and hellebore were at the center of a medical controversy concerning the use of dangerous and powerful drugs. Antimony is a silver-white metalic element ($Sb_2 O_3$ with small amounts of $Sb_2 S_3$ make up the compound "antimonii vitrum"); it is closely related to tin and to arsenic. The *L. P.*, p. 160, under the heading "Olea ex minera libus" gives the recipe for "Oleum antimonii." Hellebore is veratrum (Helleborus niger, Linn.), and is a native of Greece and Asia Minor. Although its usage medicinally goes back to the ancients, observation and experience indicated its dangers. It is a powerful poison which, though it functions as a strong purge, simultaneously has malign effects on the heart. Ferrand took the conservative and skeptical view. His contemporary Du Laurens was likewise cautious. He states in *Des maladies melancholiques, et du moyen de les guarir*, pp. 32^{r-v}: "Tous les medecins Grecs et Arabes ordonnent aux melancholies inveterées et opiniastres l'hellebore: il est vray qu'il y faut aller avec discretion, et ne le donner pas en substance, il le faut prendre en decoction ou en infusion, et faut qu'il soit du noir bien choisi, car les apothicaires vendent bien souvent de l'hellebore noir, qui est un espece d'aconit tres pernicieuse, le blanc ne vaut rien icy; il faut aussi se garder de ne mesler rien avec l'hellebore, qui ait astriction, comme les mirabolans, de peur que cela ne le retiene trop long-temps à l'estomach. Les anciens poëtes ont recogneu ceste proprieté de l'hellebore pour les melancholiques, car ils les renvoyent ordinairement in Anticyre où croist le bon hellebore; et dans Homere à la seconde Odyssée, Melampus grand medecin guarit avec l'hellebore les quatre filles du roy Proetus qui s'estoient voulu esgaler à Juno en beauté, et pour punition estoient devenuës foles. Il y en a qui usent de l'antimoine preparée; mais tous ces violens remedes doiuent estre ordonnez bien à propos et avec discretion."

Quercetanus, on the other hand, mindful of the controversy, declares himself in favor of the use of hellebore and uses it liberally in his recipes. In an "Advertisement" he remarks upon its special powers to penetrate and to purge where other preparations cannot reach. He insists that it be well prepared and, in its general defense, remarks that even Hippocrates used hellebore and praised it highly: *Pharmacie des Dogmatiques*, p. 318.

17. [*M Rulandi in Centur. Quercet. Pharm. rest. l. 1. c. 16.*]: Martin Ruland, *Curationum empiricarum et historicarum, centuria VII* (Basileae: Sebast. Henricpetri, 1595), centuria V, ch. 13, "Panchymagogum." But Ferrand's source is, in fact, Quercetanus, as follows.

Joseph Du Chesne (Quercetanus), *Pharmacie des Dogmatiques*, p. 370: "[Vomitif Pantagoge de Roland.]": "En fin se trouve encores un autre vomitif dans le mesme Roland, qui est son crocus de metaux, dont il prend seulement la grosseur d'un pois qu'il fait macerer par 24. heurs, en quatre ou 5. onces de vin blanc: le coule tout, et en fait prendre. Il l'appelle purgatif vomitoire pantagogue, il s'en sert contre la degoust, l'indigestion et le spasme."

A "crocus" is principally an iron oxide, but complex "crocus" recipes appear in the *L. P.*, p. 163, for "crocus Martis" and "crocus metallorum."

18. [*Aphor. 18. sec. 7. l. 6. epid. & l. de flat.*]: Hippocrates, *Epidemics*, bk. VI, sec. 2, aph. 12: " Ἐκ προσαγωγῆς τ'ἀναντία αἰ προσάγειν, καὶ διαναπαύειν." *Oeuvres complètes*, ed. Littré, vol. V, pp. 284–85. The Littré edition drops the "αἰ." See also *Winds* or *Breaths*, ed. Littré, vol. VI, pp. 91 ff.

19. Guillaume Rondelet, *Methodus curandorum omnium morborum corporis humani*, bk. II, ch. 45, p. 239: "A melancholicis autem medicamenta auferantur, quae venerem excitate nata sunt, ut satyrium, et conserva eryngii, quibus utimur in affectu melancholico."

Jean Aubery, *L'antidote d'amour*, pp. 136^v–137^r, is more explicit than Ferrand about the importance of pharmaceutical preparations that consume seed, though this action is implicit, given the ingredients, in many of Ferrand's recipes: "Pour les remedes qui consomment ou empeschent la naissance de la semence sont la semence de ruë et chanure, d'agnus castus, les lentilles. . . .

"La ruë mangee particulierement caillonne et consomme la semence par sa chaleur: de mesme la calaminthe: la pierre de jaspe portee sur les reins est fort recommandee. . . . Prenez de ruë, et agnus castus de chacun une dragme, semence de pavot blanc, de laictuë, de nymphee de chacun deux dragmes, le tout meslé ensemble sera reduit en poudre, de laquelle on prendra tous les jours une dragme avec un bouillon de lentilles, et de la mesme poudre avec miel escumé, on fera une opiate, de laquelle on pourra user trois dragmes, et aussi de la mesme pouldre avec mucilage de semence de coings tiree avec eau de nenufar on fabriquera des trochisques, desquels on destrempera la pesanteur de deux dragmes avec eau de pourpil ou de laictuë: ce pendant on pourra temperer les humeurs par juleps qui s'ensuivent."

There is no shortage of commentary among the ancient and medieval physicians concerning the reduction of semen and, inversely, the means for encouraging venery and fertility through pharmaceutical preparations. The various chapters on these matters by Paul of Aegina serve to summarize this series of related ideas and prescriptions. For inciting sexual enjoyment he recommends "mollusca; of pot-herbs, the allgood (horminum), hedge-mustard (crysimum), rocket (irio), and turnip. And the following are as medicines: of pulse, beans, chic-peas, Sicilian peas, kidney-beans and peas, which fill the body with vapours and abundance of food. Rue, as it concocts and dispels flatulence, blunts the venereal appetite." *The Seven Books*, bk. I, sec. 35, p. 45. On the question of the reduction of semen he gives the following account: "'Some persons collect much semen of a warm nature, and then proceeding to coition and discharging it, render the body weak, and the stomach languid, and so become emaciated and dried: or, if they abstain from venery, they are seized with heaviness of the head, and become feverish; after which they have libidinous dreams, and the same thing takes place. They must therefore avoid those things which engender semen, and take such kinds of food and medicines as consume it. After the bath they ought to have their loins rubbed with the oil of roses, or that of apples, or of unripe olives; and it is better to make them thick by mixing a little wax with them, and the juice of some cooling herb, such as the house-leek, nightshade, the navelwort, or fleawort. In summer these may be used, but at other seasons, salt and the juice of the lettuce and linseed boiled in water, for it also furnishes a cooling juice." *The Seven Books*, bk. I, sec. 38, p. 48. This advice derives essentially from Galen, *De sanitate tuenda*, bk. VI, sec. 14.

Ferrand includes the treatment, but does not place much emphasis upon it, perhaps because, in pragmatic terms, the expenditure of semen does not necessarily quell appetite or desire on a long-term basis, and that therefore the inhibition of the production of semen may do little more to prevent desire. Surgical and pharmaceutical means for the reduction of sperm were nevertheless frequently discussed in the previous centuries. There was an emphasis placed upon such means by Battista Fregoso in the *Contramours*, pp. 212 ff.

20. [*Nonnus in Dionys.*]: Nonnus of Panopolis, *Dyonisiaca*, bk. V, l. 613: "αὐτόσσυτον ἄφρον ἐρώτων," see trans. W. H. D. Rouse, 3 vols. (Loeb, 1940), vol. I, p. 210.

21. Levinus Lemnius, *Occulta naturae miracula*, bk. I, ch. 9, pp. 43–44, gives a list of foods that encourage the production of semen; by the logic of opposites, these same foods must be forbidden to melancholy lovers whose condition is caused, in part, by the overabundance of seed: "Edulia quae materiam suppeditant, ova sunt gallinacea, phasiani, turdi, merulae, sicedulae, gallinagines, pipiones, passerculi, perdices, capi pullastri, amygdala, nuclei pini, uvae passae et Corynthiacae, vina omnia generosa, dulcia ac meraca potissimum quae ex uva Apiana (quam muscatulam vocant) exprimuntur: Partes vero genitales erigunt, ac prurigine

afficiunt satyrion, iringium, nasturtium, erysimum, pastinaca, cinara, cepae, napi, rapae, asparagi, zinziber conditum, galanga, acorus, bulbi, cochleae marinae." See also ch. VII, n. 4, above.

See also Giovanni de Vigo, *La practique et cirurgie*, bk. IX, ch. 5, "lequel traicte de his que augmentant sperma, et delectationem prebent in coitu," pp. 317^V–318^r: "Et premier les raves les naveaux pastenades feves chiches augmentent le sperme, et principalement quand ilz sont appareilles avec un petit de poivre ou de cinamome ou de zinziber. En apres les amandes les avellanes les grains de pommes de pins et fistici cum zuccaro confecti. Et dit Mesue que oleum amigdalinum spermam auget. Et Avicenne dit avellane cum melle comeste coitum vigorant. Pareillement eruca prinse en petite quantite incite ad coitum, et pource dit Ovide en son livre de remedio amoris. Nec minus est aptum erucas vitare salaces. Et aulcuns disent que se on en usoit en grande quantite elle destruiroit et consummeroit le sperme, et la volunte de venus."

The same medications that produce cures for erotomania, deriving from an overstimulation of sexual desires, are closely related to those that, in different medical contexts, produce sterility. Ferrand works within a system of pharmaceutical principles that circumscribes, through its relationship of opposites, the entire process of generation and the mechanisms of pleasure, desire, and titillation that lead to procreation on the one hand and the processes that lead to sterility on the other. The following quotation from Jacques Dubois (Sylvius), treating the matter of fertility and sterility, illustrates the common denominators between the two issues: *Livre de le generation de l'homme* (Paris: Chez Guillaume Morel, 1559), pp. 44–47: "Laquelle vertu des puissances generatives, je n'attribue point à une occulte proprieté de l'air, (comme font aucuns) ou à l'influence des corps celestes sur l'air et sur les animaux, mais plus tost à ceste mutation evidente des qualitez, comme la sterilité faicte par opium, hyoscyame, cigue, mandragore, et autres semblables narcotiques, lesquelz estants appliquez par quelque temps aux genitoires de l'homme, ou en pessaire inserez dans la nature de la femme, et à meilleure raison le camphre, l'escaille de fer, les vers qui reluysent de nuict prins par dedans, sont estimez faire sterilité de toute leur substance, comme faict la fascination, incantation, sortilege, par le malefique ayde de quelque esperit, si ceux qui sont nais soubs certains horoscopes commandent aux demons et esperits, comme Ptolemée à esté d'advis en la quarte partie de son quadripartit, chapitre troisiesme. Neantmoins que le camphre aussi par sa frigidité, et l'escaille de fer par sa chaleur et siccité, peuvent faire les steriles, comme font toutes choses qui consument et dissipent la matiere de la semence: ou bien ils l'empeschent d'estre ejaculée et separée comme concrete et glacée. Et si elle est ainsi ejaculée et separée, elle ne sera jamais prolifique et generative: pource que l'esperit, et la chaleur y estants esteincts, il est exanimé et sans vie."

Eringo is the sea holly (eryngium maritinum), the roots of which are said to have aphrodisiac virtues. Colchester in East Anglia was famous for its "conditing" of the roots. Satyrion is known variously as orchis, cullians, and dog-stones. It is a hot and very moist plant with a root that has long been used medicinally and as an aphrodisiac. There is a recipe in the *L. P.*, p. 70, for "Diasatyrion Nicolae." Both plants have the power to produce seed and to restore fertility according to the lore of the sixteenth century. Levinus Lemnius states in *Occulta naturae miracula*, bk. I, ch. 9, p. 44, that the genitals are erected and provoked by satyrion and eryngoes. Throughout the period they were usually listed together for having these properties in common.

22. "℞. Rad. bugl. utriusque, aspar. capar. scorzon. ana ℥. i. endiviae, cichor. bugloss. borrag. acetos. lupuli, fumar, caeterach ana m. i. absynthii pont. menthae & melissae ana m. ½ glycirrh. & passul. corinth. aqua tepida lotar. ana ʒ . vi i. semen. citri. cardui bened. lactuc. papav. albi & agni casti ana ʒ . ii. flor. trium cardiac. thymi & epith. ana p. i. polyp. querni & fol. senae orient. mundat. ana ℥. iiii. agar. rec. trochisc. ℥. ½ caryophyll. ʒ . ½ florum nymphaeae, & anthos ana p. ½ fiat decoctio ad lib. ii. in quib. dissol. express. ℥.½ rhabarb. in parte dosis cum pauco cinnamomo infusi, & sacchari albi q. s. misce fiat syrupus perfecte coctus, & aromat. ʒ . ii. pulver. laetitiae Galen. de quo capiat aeger ℥ .ii. bis in Hebdomade cum iusculo pulli, vel aqua cardiaca."

23. François Valleriola, *Observationum medicinalium libri VI*, pp. 215–16. Valleriola's long recipe for the magistral syrup Ferrand passed by because it contained hellebore, though there is a great deal otherwise for comparison between this recipe and the one presented by Ferrand.

24. [*Hipp. epist. ad Crat. tr. de Mania, tr. de Helleb.*]: Hippocrates, "Letter to Cratevas": "Aussi les purgations par les ellébores sont-elles plus sûres, celles dont on raconte que Mélampe se servit pour les filles de Proëtus, et Anticyrée pour Hercule." *Oeuvres complètes*, ed. Littré, vol. IX, p. 347. This is the only reference to Melampus in the works of Hippocrates. No treatises on mania or hellebore are ascribed to Hippocrates, though the use of hellebore, particularly as a purge, figures prominently throughout the Hippocratic writings.

Hippocrates, *Discourse on Madness*, in *Oeuvres complètes*, ed. Littré, vol. IX, p. 387.

The authority of the ancients was difficult to ignore with regard to the use of hellebore because there was considerable agreement among them that it was the most efficacious purge for black bile. Aretaeus the Cappadocian, *On the Cure of Chronic Diseases*, p. 474, states: "Wherefore, having kept the patient on a restricted diet for one day previously, we must give hellebore to the amount of two drams with honeyed-water, for it evacuates black bile." But physicians in succeeding ages could not ignore the dangers associated with the use of this potent drug. On the nature and uses of this plant, Ferrand adopts the cautious approach of his mentor, Du Laurens. See n. 16, above.

25. Melampus was one of the most famous of the Greek seers. King Proëtus called him to cure his three daughters of madness. The fee demanded was one-third of the kingdom, which the king at first refused. But when the women turned wild and roamed through the hills as cows, their hair falling out, their skin turning leperous, and leading with them the other women of Tiryns, King Proëtus was forced to consent, even to two-thirds

of his kingdom. Melampus drove them down from the mountains with a band of youths from Argive and cured them through the use of herbs and through rites of purification. Homer does not relate this story in the *Odyssey*, bk. II, as Du Laurens suggests (see n. 16, above); the sources are, rather, Apollodorus, *The Library*, trans. Sir James George Frazer (Loeb, 1961), bk. I, ch. 9; bk. II, ch. 5, and Diodorus Siculus, [*Library of History*], trans. C. H. Oldfather (Loeb, 1957), bk. IV, ch. 12.

Ferrand gives considerably more lore about the use of hellebore in the edition of 1610: that it was often the final resort when other medicines failed; that Anticyreus administered it to Hercules with success; that when a person was in need of it the ancient Greeks would say that such a person should be sent to the isle of Anticyre (where the best hellebore grows) which was a way of saying that person was crazy: "In our own century, we dare not make use of it, either because people nowadays are more feeble and effeminate, or because the plant itself has taken on worse qualities due to the revolution of the stars, or else because finally we have lost the right techniques for preparing it."

26. Avicenna, *Liber canonis*, bk. IV, fen 1, tr. 5, ch. 24, p. 207^r: "et evacuentur humores eorum praedicti cum hieris magnis." Aloes was an emetic made from the juice of the aloe; its properties had been known for centuries. Aretaeus of Cappadocia, *On the Causes and Symptoms of Chronic Diseases*, p. 476, states that: "the hiera from aloe is to be given again and again; for this is the important medicine in melancholy, being the remedy for the stomach, the liver, and the purging of bile." Ferrand's objection to this traditional treatment undoubtedly stems from André Du Laurens, who states in *Des maladies melancholiques, et du moyen de les guarir*, p. 32^r: "Le Roy Ptolomée usoit aux melancholiques rebelles du hieralogadium, mais le hiere deseiche trop."

27. [*Mercat. l. I Meth. c. 17 et c. 6. l. 2. de morb. mul.*]: Luis Mercado, *De internorum morborum curatione libri IV*, bk. I, ch. 17, in *Opera*, vol. III, pp. 108 ff.

Luis Mercado, *De mulierum affectionibus libri IV*, bk. II, ch. 6, in *Opera*, vol. III, pp. 571–74. We find no information on the preparation of antimony in either of these sections; the page numbers given correspond to Mercado's lengthy explanations for the preparation of chalybs, or metal filings, which he favored for the curing of this complex of diseases, and which Ferrand may have associated with the metalic cures in general.

André Du Laurens, *Des maladies melancholiques et du moyen de les guarir*, p. 32^v, confirms the use of antimony in the treatment of melancholy diseases, but counsels against its use: "Il y en a qui usent de l'antimoine preparée; mais tous ces violens remedes doivent estre ordonnez bien a propos et avec discretion."

28. [*R a Castro l. 2. de mor. mul. c. 5.*]: Rodrigo de Castro, *De morbis mulierum*, bk. II, ch. 5, esp. pp. 136–38. In this chapter dealing with obstructions of the uterus, there is a section on cures concluding with a number of recipes based on iron filings (chalybs), mercury or sulphur, ingredients then studied—given their controversial natures—in a Scholium. Because Ferrand is wary of them and unwilling to recommend them, Rodrigo de

Castro's study goes beyond our purposes. Like Mercado, whom he follows closely in his study of the diseases of women, he makes no mention of antimony in this chapter, which corresponds to the same chapter cited above in Mercado. The *London Pharmacopoeia*, however, contains recipes for all of these under the names following: "Chalybs praeparatus per insolationem" (p. 162), "Chalybs praeparatus per ustionem" (p. 162), "Mercurius dulcis" (p. 165), "Mercurius vitae" (p. 165), "Turbith minerale" (p. 166), "Vitrum antimonii" (pp. 166–67).

29. The words ascribed to Haly Abbas appear to be spurious; we cannot account for Ferrand's source: "posito quod aliae medicinae non valeant, ista valet nutu Dei misericordis, et est medicina coronata, quae secretissime teneatur, ut humanus intellectus quasi deperditus cum hac medicina restauretur." Likewise, we have not succeeded in locating this recipe in the works of Haly Abbas; more likely it was among those ascribed to him at a later date in order to gain the authority vested in his name.

30. "℞. Epith. ℥.½ lapidis lazuli (aut securius cum Mercato, armeni) & agar. ana ʒ. ii. scammon. ʒ. i. caryoph. No. x. fiat pulvis, de quo aeger capiat semel in Hebdomade Э. ii. aut Э. ii.½ cum syrupo rosato solut, aut conserv. rosar. & viol."

Luis Mercado, *De mulierum affectionibus libri IV*, in *Opera*, bk. II, ch. 4, vol. III, pp. 555–56, mentions the use of lapis lazuli in the curing of melancholy in women. Mercado's treatise contains many dozens of pages of pharmaceutical preparations for the treatment of women's diseases, esp. in chapters 4, 6, and 10, where there is to be found an ordering and disposition of recipes that resemble Ferrand's. Mercado should be considered as one of Ferrand's mentors in pharmaceutical matters.

31. ℞. Succi Mercur. depurati ℥. ii. in quibus infunde per xxiiii. horas fol. senae mund. ℥. ii. expresio decoquantur cum s. q. sacchari in formam Electuarii, postea adde pulpae cassiae recenter e canna extractae ℥. 2. epith. ℥.½ caryophyllor. conquassat. ʒ. ii. misce fiat opiata, de qua capiat semel aut bis in mense ℥. i. & ½.

32. "℞. Conserv. rosar. ℥. i. conser. flor. nenufar. & borrag. ana ʒ. vi. carnis citri & lactucae saccharo conditae ana ℥.½ myrobal. emblic. saccharo condit. numii. confect. Alkermes ʒ. ii. pulveris laetit. Gal. ʒ. i. margar. Orient. Э. iiii. rasurae eboris Э. ii. misce cum syrupo de pomis fiat opiata, de qua capiat ad quantitatem unius castancae superhausto tantillo vino albo aqua buglossi multum diluto, alternis diebus horis circiter duabus ante cibum."

Ferrand takes this medication from François Valleriola, *Observationem medicinalium libri VI*, p. 214. Valleriola has his patient take it during the month in which the purges are administered, twice each day, as a comfortative. The regimen for both physicians during this period of treatment calls for a series of lenitive or preparative agents such as diasenna followed by the purges, differing from time to time, and frequent doses of these comforting opiates.

33. "℞. Terebinth. Venetae aqua lactucae lotae ℥.½ semin. dauci, agni casti & connam. ana gr. viii. agar. rec. troch. ʒ. i. fiat bolus purgando semini corrupto idoneus, ex Hollerio, Mercato, etc."

An original for this recipe has not come to view in Mercado; Ferrand does not specify context. Likely it is from the lengthy chapters on melancholia or mania in his *De internorum morborum curatione*, bk. I, chs. 17 and 18, in *Opera*, vol. III, pp. 87–120, or his *De mulierum affectionibus libri IV*, bk. II, chs. 6–11, vol. III, pp. 564–89, dealing with the diseases of the uterus. These are the sections of Mercato Ferrand has relied upon in previous passages. This passing reference to Mercado's pharmacology is an indication of the origins of Ferrand's inspiration for many of his preparations. The program of cures for both cerebral and hypochondiacal melancholy in Mercado anticipates Ferrand in many ways; there is a high degree of correlation between the ingredients used in their various parallel preparations. Both subscribed to the same doctrines concerning the humors and the pharmaceutical means for rectifying them, and Mercado offers a rich treasury of remedies for these specific conditions that could not have escaped Ferrand's attention while studying these chapters. It is to be noted that Mercado has an entire section devoted exclusively to "Melancholia ex amore qualiter curetur."

34. [*L. 2. c. 187 & 149*]: Dioscorides, *Commentarii secundo aucti in libros sex Pedacii Dioscoridis* (Venetiis: in officina Erasmiana, apud Vincentium Valgrisium, 1558), bk. II, p. 164: "*Hastula regia*" (Aphrodiles): "Ea vero vomitiones adiuvat, ludicri tali magnitudine communducata: a serpente demorsis datur aptissime, trium drachmarum pondere, verum foliis, floribus, et radice ex vino morsus illinire oportet." bk. III, ch. 109: "*Tussilago*" (Colt's foot): "Folia ex melle trita igni sacro, et omnibus inflammationis illitu medentur. Arida suffitu, ita ut sumus per infunbibilum hianti ore rapiatur, hos sanant, qui sicca tussi, atque orthopnoea infestantur: pectoris vomicas rumpunt. Eundem effectum praebet suffita radix. decocta in hydromelite, et pota, emortuos partus eiicit." A comfortative recipe combining these two simples has not been located in Dioscorides.

35. [*Stob ser. 98 Pl l 24. c. 9*]: Joannes Stobaeus, *Anthologium libri*, vol. IV, ch. 26, p. 873.

Pliny, *Natural History*, bk. XXIV. 38 (62), vol. VII, p. 48. Speaking of the agnus castus (vitex) he says that this plant "ad venerem impetus inhibent."

36. "Cuius flos in aqua sumptus frigescere cogit / Instinctus veneris cunctos acres stimulantes." We have been unable to identify the author of this quotation.

37. ℞. Semin. agni casti, portul. & rutae ana ℈. ½ semin. lactucae & papau. albi ana ℈. ii. granor. cannabis gr. viii. cornu cervi ustis corall. & anther. ana gr. vi. semin. melon. ℥. iii. sacch. aqua rosar. & borrag. dissoluti q. s. misce fiant tabellae vel lozengae ponder. ℥. i. vapiat unam hora somni, vel mane longe ante cibum.

38. Athenaeus, *The Deipnosophists*, trans. C. B. Gulick, bk. II, vol. I, p. 303: "Callimachus, too, says that Aphrodite hid Adonis in a lettuce-bed, since the poets mean by this allegory that constant eating of lettuce produces impotence. . . . Cratinus says that Aphrodite, when she fell in love with Phaon, hid him away in 'fair lettuce-beds,' while the younger Marsyas

declares that it was in a field of unripe barley. According to Pamphilus, in the *Dialect Lexicon*, Hipponax uses the form *tetrakine* for *thridax* ('lettuce'), and Cleitarchus says that this is the Phrygian term. Lycus the Pythagorean says that the naturally flat-leaved lettuce, smooth and stalkless, is called 'eunuch' by Pythagoreans, but 'impotent' by women; for it causes urination and relaxes desire; but it is the best to eat."

Charles L'Ecluse (Carolus Clusius), *Rariorum plantarum historia* (Antverpiae: ex officina Plantiniana, apud Joannem Moretum, n. d.), bk. V, sec. 137: "Scorsonera major Hispanica 1. " "Priori, angusta sunt folia, Hispanicae angustifoliae, quae odorata flore est, proxima, sive Bohemicae adeo vicina, ut ab illa differre non putem: Caulis, flores, radices lacteo succo turgentes, foris nigriconte cortice tectae, intus candidae admodum, conveniunt. Huic iconem latifoliae Hispanicae praeposuimus, ut quae sit inter utramque differentia, facilius observari possit."

Scorzonera was highly reputed in the sixteenth century for its antivenemous properties, particularly against the bite of the snake called "escuercos" in Spanish, according to Nicholas Monardes, who wrote a treatise on the subject translated into English by John Frampton and published in London in 1577 together with *Joyfull Newes out of the Newe Founde Worlde* (rpt. AMS Press, New York, 1967) as "Of the Bezar Stone and the Hearbe Escuerconera," vol. II, p. 93: "This roote is made in Conserva, and it is of a good taste and daintie, and being given with the water of the Hearbe distilled, it is a very good remedie for the sayde Fevers, and for soundinges, and Melancholies of the hearte."

The bezoar stone was equally famous and much sought after for its alleged occult properties against venoms, variously called "Bezaar" by the Persians, and "Alexipharmacum" by the Greeks. The stone can be found in a variety of animals from the mountain goat to birds, fishes, and field rats (Monardes, vol. II, p. 69). The literature written on the stone is impressive and includes treatises specifically on the bezoar by Pietro D'Abano and Valescus de Taranta.

Joseph Du Chesne uses both scorzonera and the stone in his "Eau theriacale, cordiale et bezoardique, bonne pour toutes passions de coeur, et affections pestiferes, et mousvant les sueurs," in *Pharmacie des Dogmatiques*, pp. 64–65.

39. [*Avic. l. 3. fen I tr. 4. c. 24. Haly Abbas c. 25. l. 5. pract.*]: Avicenna, *Liber canonis*, bk. III, fen 1, tr. 5, ch. 23: "fac ipsos balneari secundum conditionem humectationis notam."

Haly Abbas, *Liber totius medicinae*, bk. V, ch. 25: "Amorem patiens regimine disponendus est humectanti ut balneo suavis aqua."

Paul of Aegina, *The Seven Books*, bk. III, ch. 17, p. 391: "Such persons, therefore, being desponding and sleepless, some physicians, mistaking their affection, have wasted them by prohibiting baths, and enjoining quietude, and a spare diet; but wiser ones, recognizing the lover, direct his attention to baths."

Oribasius, *Synopsis*, bk. VIII, ch. 9: "de amantibus," p. 413: "In quibus quum nos amorem in causa eorum esse deprehenderimus, eorum animos ab amore ad balnea."

The use of baths goes back to the earliest records on the treatment of melancholy diseases. Aretaeus the Cappadocian, *On the Causes and Symptoms of Chronic Diseases*, p. 477: "Let the patient, then, proceed to the process of restoration by frequenting the natural hot baths; for the medicinal substances in them are beneficial, such as bitumen, or sulphur, or alum, and many others besides these which are possessed of remedial powers."

40. "℞. Althaeae cum toto, malvae, lactuc. borrag. nymphaeae, cucurb. fumar. lupul. lapathi acut. ana m. 4. summit. salic. & pampinor. vitis ana m. ii. flor. nenuf. viol. borrag. rosar. calend. ana p. 4. semin. viticis & cannab. ana ℥. ii. capit. vervec. num. ii. fiat decoctio in aqua fluvia-tili pro balneo 4. dierum, in quo sedeat hora una circiter."

This recipe for the bath was taken from François Valleriola, *Observationum medicinalium libri VI*, pp. 216–17. Valleriola, in treating his merchant, was more effusive than Ferrand concerning the uses of the bath and the place it had in the general regimen. He states Paul of Aegina as his authority for such baths. He used them with great success for bringing tranquility to both the body and the soul of the patient. Baths were for the entire body and not just parts of the body. In the same context he recommends having the patient admonished and scolded by a wise person, combined with such distractions as drinking parties, theatre performances, games, and story telling. The bath itself should be of tepid water and the patient should spend about 1½ hours for each session daily over a period of 8 days. He did not allow the patient to perspire. Once out of the bath the patient was covered and made to rest for as long as the heat of the bath remained. Then the patient was sent to a good and nourishing dinner. Sometimes the bath was given 2 hours before supper in order to humidify the body and to encourage the circulation of the food to all parts of the body.

Ferrand suggests that the bath was endorsed by all physicians concerned with erotomania, a view largely confirmed by our reading of his contemporaries. See ch. XXXII, nn. 13 and 14, above.

Jean Aubery, *L'antidote d'amour*, p.137[v]: "Les bains seront utiles pour l'humectation et rafraichissement faicts d'eau de riviere, avec orge, violes, mauves, coucourdes, saules, nymphee, comomille, melilot, des testes de mouton, de semence de psillium. Apres le bain où il aura sejourné selon ses forces, et reiteré matin et soir, avec toutes les cautions qui s'observent avant, et pendant l'usage des bains, on luy oindra les reins et tout le bas du ventre d'huile de ranes de pavot, de semence de ioschiame, ou on les reduira en onguent."

Aubery treats the bath as a serious component of the cure to be supervised and regularly repeated.

41. Paul of Aegina, *The Seven Books*, bk. III, sec. 17, p. 391, recommended "baths, the drinking of wine, gestation, spectacles, and amusing stories." By a process of association these separate but related items became part of combined treatment incorporating the bath with social distraction. Hence François Valleriola, *Observationum medicinalium libri VI*, bk. II, obs. 74, p. 217: "multo tempore attemperato balneo, in quo moram agebat

sesquihoram, quo in tempore musicis instrumentis et suorum praesentia amicorum, aegri animum delinire fomento salutari iusseram, cantilenis, fabulis ridiculis, et id genus blanditiis, quae a tetrico moerore revocare misere amantis animu possent."

42. [*Tetrab. 4. ser. 4. c. 74.*]: Aëtius of Amida, *Tetrabiblos*, bk. IV, sermo 4, ch. 74: "De furore uterino," p. 903: "Irrigationes autem capitis." The reader is directed to sermo 6 for the recipes.

Du Laurens also recommends the use of such epithemes and gives a number of recipes. See chap. XXXII, n. 16, above.

Ambroise Paré treats oxyrrhodin as a kind of electuary: *Oeuvres complètes*, vol. III, p. 637.

Luis Mercado, *De internorum morborum curatione libri IV*, bk. I, ch. 17, in *Opera*, vol. III, p. 96: "quod si primum curandum est, quidquid in caput influit repellere, non quidem his, qui vulgus *oxyrrhodinae* appellat, ni eis addideris ex his, quae humectandi et fraenandi humoris siccitatem et inclementiam vires obtineant, aliquid cui sane muneri oxyrrhodinis addes oleum amygdalarum dulcium, violarum, de semine curcurbitae aut melorum: ac si humoris fervorem cognoveris praeesse hordei decocto aut tremore vel lacte caprillo caput fovebis."

43. Diacodion is the powder of the opium poppy made into pill form (*L. P.*, p. 51). Nitre is saltpetre, potassium nitrate. Castoreum is the oily and odorous secretion expressed from the two glands found in the beaver under the tail. It was widely used medicinally and for making perfumes. Du Laurens calls for it in the preparation of a plaster for the temples, *Des maladies melancholiques, et du moyen de les guarir*, p. 116. The pessary described here using diacodion and the black nightshade is a recipe Ferrand takes from Aëtius, presumably from *Tetrabiblos* IV, sermo 4, ch. 74, which also discusses camphor, castoreum, and rue.

44. [*L. 3. fen. 20. tr. 2. c. 5*]: Avicenna, *Liber canonis*, bk. III, fen 20, tract. 2, ch. 5, p. 378^V: "Et radix quidem nenufaris, et radix lilij sunt convenientes ad hanc aegritudinem."

45. Luis Mercado is credited with the authorship of this recipe though it has not been located in his works in those sections dealing with melancholy or uterine fury.

"℞. Lactis caprilli vel bubuli ℈. iiii. aquae marinae ℥. ii. mellis ℥. i. misce fiat clyster, iniiciatur in sinum pudoris."

46. "℞. Lentium p. ii. fol. & flor. salicis ana m. i. fiat decoctio ad lib. i. m qua dissol. trochisc. albor. Rhazis & trochisc. de camphora ana. ʒ . i. misce, fiat clyster, infundatur in delta muliebre."

47. [*Eros c. 7. de morb. mul.*]: Trotula (Eros), *Curandorum aegritudinum muliebrium* (Lugduni: apud Sebastianum de Honoratis, 1558), ch. 7; "De nimia caliditate matricis," pp. 681–82: "Contingit quandaque matricem distemperari in caliditate, ita quod maximus ardor et calor ibi sentiatur. Cura hoc modo Recipe opii ℈ i. adipis anseris. ℈ i. cerae, mellis, ana ℈ iiii. oleo ℥. i. albumina duorum ovorum, & lac mulieris: commisceantur, & iniiciantur per pessarium."

48. [*Pl. l. 32. ca 10. & l. 26. c. 10.*]: Pliny, *Natural History*, bk. XXXII, ch. 50, trans. W. H. S. Jones, vol. VIII, p. 519: Antaphrodisiac is "the gall of the

torpedo, while it is still alive, applied to the genitals."

Guillaume Rondelet, *L'Histoire entiere des poissons*, bk. XII, ch. 18, p. 286: "De quatre sortes de torpille." Rondelet does not discuss the medical uses of the poison of this fish, but he does confirm its power to render other fish "endormis, estourdis, e immobiles, qu'elle les prend, e en jouit aisement. Non seulement ha ceste vertu contra les poissons, mais aussi contre les homes, car si un home lui touche d'une verge, elle lui endormira le bras. Elle use de ceste ruse quand elle se sent prise, car ell'embrasse la ligne de ses aeles, é par le long d'icelle endort le bras du peschur."

Pliny, *Natural History*, bk. XXV, ch. 37, trans. W. H. S. Jones, vol. VII, p. 191. Given the reputation of white water lily in Pliny, it is not surprising that it was used so widely in later centuries for curbing sexual appetites: "According to tradition nymphaea was born of a nymph who died of jealousy about Hercules—for this reason some call it heracleon, others rhopalon because its root is like a club—and therefore those who have taken it in drink for twelve days are incapable of intercourse and procreation." This plant, like lettuce, was capable of producing sterility. Dioscorides, according to the note by Jones, said its force lasted only twelve days, but Pliny, bk. XXVI, ch. 61, p. 335, repeats: "nymphaea heraclia . . . takes away altogether sexual desire; a single draught of it does so for forty days; sexual dreams too are prevented if it is taken in drink on an empty stomach and eaten with food. Applied to the genitals the root also checks not only desire but also excessive accumulation of semen."

49. The reference is to Nicholas Monardes, *Primera y segunda y tercera partes de la historia medicinal de las cosas que se traen de nuestras Indias Occidentales que sirven in medicina* (Sevilla: 1574). Monardes does not mention antidotes against philters using contra-yerva powders. The term is, in fact, a generic one: See "Contrahierba," in *Diccionario de autoridades, Real Academia Español*, vol.II, p. 563: "medicina especifica contra tota suerte de venenos, menos contra el del Soliman: y tambien es remedio especifico para mover el sudor en todas las enfermedades malignas, y perticularmente en la de las veruélas."

Ferrand is, in fact, once again multiplying references. The source is Charles L'Ecluse, *Atrebatis exoticoraum liber decimus, sive simplicium medicamentorum ex nove orbe delatorum, quorum in medicina usus est historia, Hispanico sermone tribus libris descripta à Nicolao Monardo*, (n.p.: ex officina Plantiniana, Raphelengii, 1605), ch.17: "Radices venenis adversantes," p. 311: "Ex Charcis provincia Perüana, radices quaedam advehuntur iridis radicibus valde similes, sed minores, et siculnei folii odore.

"Hispani Indias inhabitantes *contrayerva* appellant, quasi dicas alexipharmacum, quoniam earam pulvis ex albo vino sumptus, adversus omne venenum, cuiuscunque tandem sit generis, praesentissimum est remedium, (uno sublimato excepto, quod sola lactis potione extinguitur) vomitione illud reiicere faciens, aut per sudores evacuens. Sed et amatoria pocula, eo pulvere hausto, educi ferunt. Ventris etiam animalia pellit.

"Gustata radix, aromaticum quiddam sapit cum acrimonia conjunctum: quare calida videtur secundo gradu."

50. Pausanias, *Description of Greece*, "Achaia," ch. 23, vol. III, p. 307: "If there is any truth in the story the water of the Selemnus is of more value to mankind than great wealth." Jean Aubery, *L'anidote d'amour*, p. 114[r], mentions bathing in the fountain of Silenne in order to forget love, but does not mention his sources.

51. Dioscorides, *Commentarii secundo aucti, in libros sex Pedacii Dioscoridis Anazarbei de medica materia*, bk. V, ch. 116: "Lapis selenites," p. 704: "Selenites lapis, quem aliqui aphroselenon appellarunt quoniam noctu invenitur lunae imaginem reddere, quae cum ea quidem augetur, et decrescit. Nascitur in Arabia, candidus, transluscens, levis. Huius ramenta comitialibus in potu deri iubent. Eo ceu gestamine ad amuleta mulieres utuntur. Arbores ad alligato eodem frugiferae redduntur."

52. [*Mercur. l. 2. var. lect. c. 27. Apol. 1. mirab. hist.*]: Girolamo Mercuriale, *Variarum lectionum libri IV*, bk. II, ch. 27, pp. 67[v]–68[r]. This is Ferrand's source for all the various names for Pliny's "linum vivum"— "carpasium linum" (Pausanias), "carystium" (Strabo), "carbasum" (Solinas), "bostrychitem" (Zoroaster) "quidam corsoydem, alii poliam, alii spartopoliam, vulga res pulveres salamandrae aut alumen scissile falso dixere"—as well as for the reference to Apollonius.

Apollonius Dyscolus, *Historiae commentitiae liber. Joannes Meursius recensuit* (Lugduni Batavorum: apud Isaacum Elzevirium, 1620), pp. 33–35: "Tacus in libro De lapidibus: Lapis, inquit, is qui Carystius dicitur, annata sibi habet lanea quaedam, et colorata, ex qua materia nentur, ac texuntur, mantilia. Sed et fila pro lucernis inde torquentur, quae, dum uruntur, splendent, neque cremantur. Porro sordes mantilium non aqua elentur; sed clematis uritur, impositoque mantili sordes evanescunt, ipsumque album igni purumque redditur, ac prioribus commodum usibus. Lucernarii aulem funes usti cum oleo, nullo unquum tempore comburuntur. Atque odure harum lucernarum deprehenduntur, qui morbo laborunt caduco. Lapis iste nascitur sane Carysti, unde et nomen gerit: frequens tamen etiam in Cypro extat, qua a Gerandro solos versus iter deorsum ducit, ad laevam Elmaei infra rupes. Augescit circa plenilunium, rursumque, luna decrescente, minuitur."

Levinus Lemnius, *Occulta naturae miracula*, bk. II, ch. 12, p. 181: impossible to quote because of words lost in the binding, but in essence Lemnius reports on flax napkins that do not burn, and that need not be cleaned in conventional ways, but rather are simply cast in the fire. He goes on to discuss "asbestinum," which is woven into the linen resembling "lapis alumini scissili," commonly called feathery allum. Dioscorides explained how Indian artisans made sheets of this material which they cast into the fire.

53. Girolamo Mercuriale, *De morbis muliebribus*, bk. IV, ch. 10, p. 157: "Sed efficacissima omnium habentur balnea refrigerantia, aquae thermarum refrigerantes: et nondum agitur annus, ex quo curavimus mulierem hoc solo remedio. Igitur facta purgatione, praestantissimae erunt aquae refrigerantes, aquae virginis. Praeter haec, sunt extrinseca, quae applican-

tur partim capiti, partim utero: capiti conveniunt irrigationes ex aqua rosarum, solani, lactucae, nympheae et tandem ex omnibus alijs quae caput refrigerare possunt. Utero adhibetur pessulus, veluti est succus solani mixtus cum ruta et adhibitus. Ceratum etiam myrthinum, ruta et castorium commixta, quae licet sint calida, tamen cum adest multitudo seminis, nihil praestantius ruta, quia propria quadam facultate et etiam manifesta, absumit genituram."

54. [*L. 3. de loc. af. c. 7.*]: Galen, *On the Affected Parts*, bk. III, ch. 7, ed. Siegel, pp. 85–86. He remarks that "it is simply shameful that [certain physicians] pour water on the heads of all the sleepless and weakened [patients] and of those who are delirious, phrenetic and lethargic" (p. 83).

55. [*Controv. 64.*]: Giovanni Battista Silvatico, *Controversae medicae numero centum*, controversy 64, pp. 289–90: "Etenim si ex calidore iecinore sanguinem adurente, melancholiam effici contingat, ut saepe certe contingit, thermales aquas illas, in quibus ferri facultas praevalet, quales sunt in Italia Lucenses a villa dictae, eam iecinoris intemperiem posse maxime attemperare, adustique sanguinis generationem e vestigio impedire, satis est illis verisimile. Has vero easdem aquas ventriculum, qui in melancholicis fere semper infirmus est magnopere confirmare posse, ut certum supponunt. Si vero propter frigidam, simulque siccam naturalium membrorum intemperiem, terrestris, ac melancholicus succus in corpore coacervetur, aquas, metallorum ferro calidiorum virtutes continentes, quales sunt aquarienses dicte in Italia, magno usui esse posse, potuerunt persuaderi."

56. Alexander of Tralles, *Oeuvres médicales*, bk. I, ch. 17, pp. 232–33: "Quant à la purgation, provoquez-la avec de l'épithym et un peu de petit-lait. . . . Quelques jours après, prescrivez de nouveau de l'épithym." Paul of Aegina does not recommend it specifically in his chapter on love, though he prescribes it elsewhere; it was a favorite purge among the Byzantine physicians, and especially with Oribasius. For Avicenna, see n. 26, above. Epithyme is lesser dodder (cuscuta epithymum), which is a parasite on true thyme and resembles it in appearance. The plant is recorded by Dioscorides and thus has had a long history as a medical simple. Despite its classification among the dry plants, it has powers to drive out the atrabilious humors. Hiera is aloes (aloe vera, Linn.). It was known to Dioscorides, Pliny, and Celsus and was widely employed by the Arab physicians. Hartwort is aristolochia longa, or rotunda, called hertworte and hertworth by Turner in 1538. It is a snakeroot plant which produces an oil used medicinally since ancient times. Turner classifies it as hot and dry about the third degree, a plant closely related to eringo. Because erotic melancholy is a hot, dry humor, the advisability of using these desiccating plants was under much discussion. Because they functioned by their general natures and not by occult temperaments appointed to specific regions of the body, they could hardly be justified. Yet, as Ferrand points out, tradition held them in repute for the treatment of melancholy diseases.

Oribasius, *Synopsis*, bk. VIII, ch. 7, in *Oeuvres*, p. 411.

57. [*Hipp. l. de victu acut.*]: Hippocrates, *Of Regimen for Acute Diseases*: "τὰ

δὲ μέλανα ζυμοῦται καὶ μετεωρίζεται καὶ πολλαπλασιοῦται." *Oeuvres complètes*, ed. Littré, vol. II, pp. 358–59. On vinegar, see also ch. XXXII, n. 15, above. For the controversy on the use of acedic simples in the treatment of melancholy, see Giovanni Battista Silvatico, *Controversiae medicae numero centum*, no. 64, p. 290.

58. Johann van Heurne, *Praxis medicinae nova ratio qua libris tribus methodi ad praxin medicam*, p. 40: "Cum in Italia viverem, mirandosque balneorum vires animadverterem, quibus ad omnem morborum varietatem ibi utuntur medici doctissimi: diligenter ex illis indagabam, num imitatione effingere liceret easdem vires, ac aliis regionibus importare balneis fraudatis. Quare didici ab illis, ac apud aegros observavi ibi cum essem, illos et sua ἀνταλλάγματα succedaneaque habere, quibus et ipsi loco balneorum eodem fere successu uterentur. Hoc modo:

Succedaneum balnei D. Virginis Patavii.

℞. aquae fontis q. s. Capitum arietum numero tria; pedum eorundem quatuor; contundantur, quatianturque capita et pedes; rosarum rubrarum, foliorum lauri, ana manipulos tres: portulacae recentis, manipulos quinque; solatri, sempervivi, cuiusque manip. duos: misce, bulliant; hinc fiat colatura, eaque repente bis die utatur, duabus horis ante cibum."

Ferrand's version of this recipe from Heurnius is as follows:

"℞. Aquae font. q. s. capit. arietum n. iii. pedes vervecis n. 4. contusis capitibus & pedibus adde rosar, rubr. fol. lauri ana m. iii. portul. recent. m. v. solani, sempervivi ana m. ii. misce fiat decoctio, eaque tepente bis die utatur aeger, horis duabus ante cibum."

59. Ferrand accepts the well-established poetic tradition that lovers were thin and wasted by starvation, whether because the mind was too preoccupied with its ideas and fantasies of the beloved, or because the lover willed such privation in self-punishment. Traditionally, the glutted imagination, in its distraction, simply failed to attend to the needs of the body. Thus Ferrand chooses to ignore the conflicting view that melancholy persons, attacked by the bitter humor that dominates the body, develop a voracious appetite. Black bile produces not only extreme dryness, but also acridness, once the humor is burned, and it was believed that this extreme acidity created extreme hunger. Jourdain Guibelet, *Trois discours philosophiques: Discours troisiesme de l'humeur melancholique*, ch. 7, p. 248^V, develops the grounds for the controversy: "Nous observons davantage que tous melancholiques de temperament, ont un grand appetit, mangent et devorent beaucoup. . . . Les raison est que l'humeur melancholique a une certaine pointe d'aigreur, comme le vinaigre, qui donne l'appetit à l'estomach, quand elle est portée en cete partie. Quand donc la melancholie est naturelle, c'est à dire qu'elle obeit au gouvernment de la nature, et qu'elle est portée naturellement au ventricule, elle ne produit qu'un appetit naturel. Mais quand elle passe les bornes que nature luy a prescrites, et qu'elle est aigre exactement, elle apporte un faim ou appetit outre mesure." He attributes this "faim canine" to the bitterness of the humors corrupted in the stomach, to sleeplessness that drys the brain, and to the coldness of the humor,

because coldness excites the appetite.

Levinus Lemnius, *Occulta naturae miracula ac varia rerum documenta*, translated as *The Secret Miracles of Nature* (London: 1658), p. 342, states the conventional view concerning melancholy lovers: "Wherefore if by immoderate watchings, fastings, or night lucubrations, or too much labour or immoderate venery, our forces and spirits are exhausted and worn away, and we grow lean, the vital moysture being consumed, we must renew our strength with moistening diet and sleeping drinks, such are Lettice, Spinach, like Mallows in effect, Orach, Buglosse, and Burrage, the fresh seed of Poppy, Water-Lilly-flowers, called commonly Nenuphar, or water and Marsh-Lillies; the Hollanders call them Plompen, or Waterlelien: to these add Violet flowers, Pine-kernels, sweet Almonds, Pistaches, or fistick nuts, creme of Barley, Raysins and Currans that have small kernels but no stones, Dates, Oranges, or Citron-pills Candied with Sugar or Honey, for the vital or innate humour is refreshed by them, and the Brain, which is the seat of the mind, is moistened with a moist dew, and sweet vapour, from whence ariseth sweet sleep and rest, without trouble or tossing up and down."

This issue relates to that discussed earlier, whether the entire body is affected by melancholy or only the eyes. Ferrand remarks that the young man he treated in Agen was pale and had deep-set eyes, but that the rest of his body was in good condition, a sign that he was suffering from a passion of the soul. Ferrand is not entirely consistent on this matter, though as stated at the outset, it does not seem to have been a conscious issue with him.

Ercole Sassonia in his section on love melancholy in *De melancholia tractatus perfectissimus*, ch. 14, p. 31, remarks upon the inclination to insomnia and offers the following advice: "ad soporem inducendum aptus, nam amantes fere semper vigilant, idcirco humectantibus balneis, ac soporiferis sunt tractandi in quibus incoxerit lactuca, nymphea, viola, malva, hyosciamus, papaver, mandragora, folia vitis, salicis, et alia."

60. "℞. Confect. Alkermes ℥ i. specierum diambrae & laetitiae Gal. ana iii. croci Albigensis & opiiana ℥. ½ mista macerentur in aqua vitae, extrahatur tinctura, postea fiat consumptio evaporatione ad consistent. opiatae. Vel,

℞. Specier. diambr. ℥ ii. in fundantur per xii. dies in vino distill. ut latum digitum superemineat, & adde opii ʒ . vi. mumiae ʒ . ½ succi hioscyami ℥. i. coralli rubri & carabes ana Ɇ. ii. croci. Ɇ. i. moschi orient. gr. xvi. ambrae gr. xii. affuso rursus spiritu vini ut superemineat latum digitum, digeratur post fornacem per mensem quotidie agitando dosis Ɇ. ½ aut gr. viii. pro aegri constitutione."

"Alkermes confection" can be found in the *L. P.* (p. 68), "Specierum diambrae Mesué" (p. 59) and "Laetificans falso Galeno abscriptum" (p. 62).

61. Ferrand refers here in a general way to physicians whose writings were particularly rich in pharmaceutical recipes; all of them have been cited in previous notes: Martin Ruland, *Curationum empiricarum et historicarum centuria VII*; Joseph Du Chesne, *Pharmacie des Dogmatiques*; Bernard Penot, *Tractatus rarii, de vera praeparatione, et usu medicamentorum chymi-*

corum. This last work, however, contains no special preparations for insomnia or for leanness. In fact, Penot's recipes do not resemble the compound preparations in Ferrand's text. He is concerned essentially with the confectioning of oils, liquors, hydromels, and salts—operations having to do with chemistry and distillation. Ferrand may have known Penot personally, speaking of him as "our Penot." They were contemporaries, and both were natives of Agen.

For diacodion, see "Diacodium Galeni" (*L. P.*, p. 38), a recipe calling for the heads of the white poppy mixed with spring water and honey and cooked to a smooth consistency. "Requies Nicolai" (*L. P.* p. 78) is an electuary that contains for its active ingredients white henbane seeds, black and white poppy seeds, and powdered mandrake root, making the name of the concoction most fitting.

62. The nosegay suggested by Ferrand is similar to the one by Du Laurens, *Des maladies melancholiques, et du moyen de les guarir*, p. 34^r: "On fera des bouquets des fleurs de violes, roses, du saule avec un peu de marjolaine, et les faudra tremper dans le vin-aigre rosat, et dans le jus de laictuë et de pavot, avec un peu d'opium, et de camphre: oubien prenez deux testes de pavot concassées et enfermées dans trois nouëts, puis ayez de storax trois dragmes, et six onces d'eau rose avec un peu d'opium, trempez ces nouëts dans ceste liqueur, et les approchez du nez."

Fernel, *Pathologie*, p. 72: "Finalement les fleurs, les odeurs des aromates, et toutes sortes de fumées ou de vapeurs, qui ont quelque virtu, ou manifeste, ou occulte, alterent tout le dedans du corps, s'insinuans en icely parmy l'air que l'on respire."

63. Rx. Semin. hioscyami & cicutae ana ʒ . i. cortic. rad. mandrag. ϶. iiii. opii ϶. i. misce cum oleo mandragorae & succo aizoi maior. addendo moschi gr. i. fiat pomum.

64. André Du Laurens, *Des maladies melancholiques, et du moyen de les guarir*, p. 34^r: "Il y en a qui appliquent avec un heureux succez des sangsuës derriere les aureilles, et ayant osté les sangsuës, mettent quant et quant sur la playe un grain d'opium." Ferrand probably had Du Laurens in mind in making his observation on the use of leeches, but his is a contrasting view in that he did not find them useful or effective, though Du Laurens also distances himself somewhat because he is merely reporting that they were used by some with success.

65. Rx. Amygd. dulc. excortic. & lot. primo aqua tepida, postea aqua rosar. lib. i. quatuor semin. frigid. maior. mundat. & lotor. ana ʒ . vi. semin. papav. albi rec. & mundati ℥. iiii. sacchari albi lib. ii. fiat pasta, & cum aqua rosar. Martius panis, de quo capiat aeger certam quantit. ante somnum.

The source of this recipe is Johann van Heurne and is closely associated with the recipe to follow.

66. [*Heurn. l. I. Meth.*]: Johann van Heurne, *Praxis medicinae nova ratio qua libris tribus methodi ad praxin medicam*, p. 28. This recipe and the previous recipe come from a complex sequence in the section entitled "Pasta, regia et morselli": "Ut Rx amygdalarum dulcium excorticatarum ℥ ii. pinearum, pistaciorum. non rancidorum ana ℥ i. pulpae dactylorum, passu-

larum, jujubarum ana ℥ i. ſ. gummi tragacanthi, et arabici ana ℥ i. amyli ℥ ii. pulpae capi elixi ℥ iiii. fructus macerati aqua rosata, cum reliquis tundantur, et succharo paulatim asperso fi. massa, indeq. cuiusque figurae panes, sensim siccandi, ac auro obducantur.

"Addere licet sem, frigida, et papaveris ana ʒ ii. ne in bilem vertantur, et cinnamomi ℥ ſ. et ambrae vel musci gm. 6. vel 8. ad flatus.

"Ita fiunt et ex amygdalis cum sacchara et aqua rosata massae panis, quae dicuntur *marsepain*."

From this recipe, Ferrand takes the following: ℞. Pulpae capi lib i. aquae rosar. q. s. sacchari ℥ iii. cinnam. sub finem decoct. additi ʒ . ii. coquant. & fingantur frusta dura.

67. [*Epist. ad Crat.*]: Hippocrates, "Letter to Cratevas": "δραστικωτάτων καὶ ἰητρικωτάτων φαρμάκων σοφίη τέλος." *Oeuvres complètes*, ed. Littré, vol. IX, pp. 348–49.

68. The following line from Jean Aubery, *L'antidote d'amour*, p. 109ʳ, bears quotation for its possible relation to Ferrand's final line: "car il [Jesus] nous delivra par son sang, comme par un celeste moly des enchantemens de ceste infernalle Circe, et nous remit à nostre premiere forme." Aubery is speaking of ancient superstitious practices involving the use of magic words, enchantments, and Homeric remedies. Ferrand is speaking about reason as man's best means for resisting the temptations to lust. Both are moralizing. The loose parallel reveals either how Ferrand could catch a phrase from his reading and adapt it to his own purposes or how a reservoir of commonplaces and analogies served writers generally.

Perhaps the custom of closing such treatises with references to Circe is to be traced, however, to François Valleriola, *Observationum medicinalium libri VI*, p. 219: "Cuius exemplo discere omnes recte amantes possunt, in quas tenebras caecus amor incautos homines coniiciat: ut inde, ceu a Circes et Calypsus diro veneno tinctis poculis, cavere sciamus, et Ulyssis exemplo, virtutis et pulchri summique boni studiosi, ipsum unum colere, revereri, totisque animi viribus et integra mente amare Deum Optimum Maximum per omne vitae spatium consuescamus, illique firmiter adhaereamus: ut hoc terreno carcere liberati, frui nectare et ambrosia deorum in coelis, ductore ipsomet Deo fonte amoris, valeamus."

Bibliography

Name Index

Subject Index

Bibliography

Abravanel, Judah (Leon Hebraeus; 1460–1525). *The Philosophy of Love* (*Dialoghi dell'amore*). Trans. F. Friedeberg-Seely and J. Barnes. London: Soncino Press, 1937.

Abul-Casim Maslama Ben Ahmad. *Picatrix*. Ed. Marcelino Villegas. Madrid: Editora Nacional, 1982.

Achaeus. *Achaei Eretriensis quae supersunt*. Ed. C. L. Urlichs. Bonnae: apud A. Marcum, 1834.

Adamantius. *Physiognomonicon, id est de naturae judiciis cognoscendis libri duo, per Janum Cornarium (1500–1558) medicum physicum Latine conscripti*. Basileae: per Robertum Winter, 1543.

Aelianus, Claudius (Praenestinus; fl. 200). *Variae historiae libri XIV. Polemonis physionomia. Adamantii physionomia. Melampodis ex palpationibus divinato*. Ed. Camillus Peruseus. Romae: [A. Blado], 1545.

――――― . *Variae historiae libri XIV*. Argentorati: sumptibus Johannis Friderici Spoor et Reinhardi Waechtleri, 1685.

――――― . *Varia historia*. Ed. Mervin R. Dilts. Leipzig: B. G. Teubner, 1974.

Aelianus Montaltus. *See* Montalto, Filoteo Elião de.

Aemilius, Paulus. *See* Emilio of Verona, Paolo.

Aeschylus (525–456 B.C.). *Prometheus Bound*. Trans. H. W. Smyth. Loeb Classics, 1953.

Aëtius of Amida (502–75). *Tetrabiblos . . . per Ianum Cornarium . . . Latine conscripti*. Basileae: Froben, 1542.

Afranius, Lucius (b. ca. 150 B.C.). Fragment of *Vopiscus*. In *Comicorum romanorum poesis fragmenta*. Ed. O. Ribbeck. Hildesheim: Georg Olms, 1962.

――――― . *Vopiscus*. In Nonius Marcellus, *De compendiosa doctrina*. Ed. W. M. Lindsay. Hildesheim: George Olms, 1964.

Agamben, Georgio. *Stanze. La parola e il fantasma nella cultura occidentale*. Turin: Einaudi, 1977.

Agrippa of Nettesheim, Henricus Cornelius (1486–1533). *De vanitate scientiarum*. In *Operum pars posterior*. Lugduni: per Beringos Fratres, ca. 1550.

――――― . *Paradoxe sur l'incertitude, vanité et abus des sciences, traduicte en françois du latin*. N.p., n.p., 1603.

Ailly, Pierre d' (Petrus de Alliaco; 1350–1420). *Concordia astronomiae cum theologia concordantia astronomiae cum hystorica narratione.* Erhardi Ratdolt, Auguste Vindelicorum, 1490; Vienna, 1594.

Alberico da Rosate (Rosciate; d. 1354). *Dictionarium iuris tam civilis, quam canonici (Lexicon).* Ed. Giovanni Francesco Deciani. Venetiis: apud Guerreos fratres et socios, 1573.

————. *Vocabularius utriusque iuris.* Lugduni: apud Jacobum Wyt, 1535.

Albert the Great (Albertus Magnus; 1193–1280). *De animalibus.* In *Opera omnia,* vol. 29. Monasterii Westfalorum: in aedibus Aschendorff, 1972–82.

————. *De secretis mulierum libellus.* Amstelodami, n.p., 1740.

————. *De virtutibus herbarum, lapidum et animalium quorundam libellus.* In *De secretis mulierum libellus.* Amstelodami, n.p., 1740.

Alberti, Leone Battista (1404–72). *Deifira, che ne mostra fuggire il mal principiato amore. Mescolanze d'amore.* Ed. Carlo Téoli (Eugenio Camerini). Milano: G. Daelli, 1803.

————. *Ecatonphila de Messer Leon Battista Alberto Fiorentino ne la quale insegna a le fanciulle la bella arte de Amore.* Ed. Guiseppe Talamo Atenolfi. *Il Quattrocento: collezione di Storia e Arte.* Rome: G. Garzoni Provenzani, 1915.

————. *Hecatonphila: The arte of love.* London: by P. S. for William Leake, 1598.

Albohazen Haly Filius Abenragel. *De judiciis astrorum.* Basileae: n.p., 1551.

Albucasis (Alsaharavi; Abū al-Qāsim al-Zaharáwī Khalaf ibn 'Abbās; ca. 936–1013). *Liber theoricae necnon practicae Alsaharavii.* Venetiis: Augustus Vindicianus, 1519.

————. *Methodus medendi certa.* Basileae: per Henricum Petrum, 1541.

————. *Vade mecum (At-Taśrif).* Augustae Vindelicorum: Impensis Sigismundi Gritu et Marci Vuirsung, 1519.

————. *Albucasis.* In *De chirurgia Arabice et Latine.* Ed. John Channing. Oxonii: Clarendoniano, 1778.

Alciati, Andrea (1492–1550). *Emblemata cum commentariis* [by Claude Mignault]. Padua, 1621; rpt. New York and London: Garland Publishing, 1976.

Aleman. *See* L'Alemant, Adrien.

Alexander, Franz G., and Sheldon T. Selesnick. *The History of Psychiatry.* New York: Harper and Row, 1966.

Alexander Benedictus, Paeantius. *See* Benedetti, Alessandro.

Alexander of Aphrodisias (fl. 200). *Problemata.* Venezia: apud Aldum, 1497.

————. *Problemata.* Ed. I. L. Ideler. 2 vols. *Physici et medici graeci minores.* Berlin, 1841–42; Amsterdam: Adolf Hakkert, 1963.

Alexander of Tralles (Trallianus; 525–605). *Affections génito-urinaires.* In *Oeuvres médicales.* Ed. F. Brunet. Paris: Librairie Orientaliste Paul Geuthner, 1937.

————. *Therapeutika.* In *Oeuvres médicales.* Ed. F. Brunet. Paris: Librarie Orientaliste Paul Geuthner, 1937.

Alessandri, Alessandro (Alexander ab Alexandro; 1461–1523). *Genialium deorum libri sex.* Paris: apud Joannem Roigny, 1550.

Allbutt, Thomas Clifford. *Science and Medieval Thought.* London: C. J. Clay & Sons, 1901.

Allen, Don Cameron. *The Star-Crossed Renaissance: The Quarrel about Astrology and Its Influence in England.* Durham, N.C.: Duke University Press, 1941.

Alliaco, Petrus de. *See* Ailly, Pierre d'.

Alpago of Belluno, Andrea, commentator (fl. 16th c.). Avicenna. *Liber canonis de medicinis cordialibus et Cantica iam olim quidem a Gerardo Carmonensi ex arabico sermone in Latinum conversa.* Venetiis: apud Juntas, 1555.

Alsaharavi. *See* Albucasis.

Altomari, Donato-Antonio (1520–56). *De medendis humanis corporis malis.* In *Opera omnia.* Lugduni: apud Gulielmum Rovillium, 1565.

Amatus Lusitanus. *See* Rodrigues, João.

Ambrose, St. (339–97). *Libros de poenitentia.* In *Opera, duobus tomis comprehense, ad manuscriptos codices Vaticanos.* Paris: Johannis Baptistae Coignard, 1686.

Amundsen, Darrel W. "Romanticizing the Ancient Medical Profession." *Bulletin of the History of Medicine,* 48 (1974), pp. 328–37.

Anacreon (fl. 6th c. B.C.). [*Works*]. Trans. Thomas Stanley. Ed. A. H. Bullen. London: Lawrence & Bullen, 1893.

Andernacus. *See* Winter, Johann.

Anderson, Ruth Leila. *Elizabethan Psychology and Shakespeare's Plays.* 1927; rpt. New York: Haskell House, 1964.

Andreas Eborensis. *See* Rodrigues da Viega, Andreas.

André le Chapelain (fl. 1180). *Andreas Capellanus on Love.* Trans. P. G. Wash. London: Duckworth, 1982.

Andrieu, Jules. *Bibliographie Générale de l'Agenais.* Paris, 1886–91; rpt. Genève: Slatkine Reprints, 1969.

Anglo, Sydney, ed. *The Damned Art: Essays in the Literature of Witchcraft.* London: Routledge and Kegan Paul, 1977.

————— . "Melancholia and Witchcraft: the Debate between Wier, Bodin and Scot." *Folie et déraison à la Renaissance.* Ed. A. Gerlo. Bruxelles: Editions de l'université de Bruxelles, 1976.

Anguillara, Giovanni Andrea (Aloysius Anguillara; ca. 1500–1570). *De simplicibus liber primus, cum notis Gaspari Bauhini.* Basileae: apud Henricum Petrum, 1593.

Angus, S. *The Religious Quests of the Graeco-Roman World.* New York: Scribner, 1929.

Anthimus (fl. 500). *De observatione ciborum epistola.* Ed. V. Rose. Leipzig: Teubner, 1870.

Aphrodisias, Alexander of. *See* Alexander of Aphrodisias.

Apollodorus of Carystus (ca. 140 B.C.). *The Slanderer.* In *The Fragments of Attic Comedy,* vol. 3A. Ed. John Maxwell Edmonds. Leiden: E. J. Brill, n.d.

————— . *Epitome.* In *Apollodorus,* vol. 2. Trans. Sir James George Frazer. 2 vols. Loeb Classics, 1956.

————— . *The Library.* In *Apollodorus,* vol. 1. Trans. Sir James George Frazer. 2 vols. Loeb Classics, 1961.

Apollonius Dyscolus (2d c.). *Historiae commentitiae liber.* Joannes Meursius recensuit. Lugduni Batavorum: apud Isaacum Elzevirium, 1620.

Aponensis. *See* D'Abano, Pietro.

Appian (fl. 160). "Liber de rebus syriacis" in *Appian's Roman History.* Ed. H. White. 4 vols. Loeb Classics, 1912.

Apuleius, Lucius (fl. 155). *Apologia sive pro se de magia liber.* Ed. H. E. Butler and A. S. Owen. Hildesheim: Georg Olms, 1967.

————— . *Metamorphoses (Golden Ass).* Trans. W. Adlington, 1566. Revised by

S. Gaselee. Loeb Classics, 1947.

Aquinas, Thomas. *See* Thomas Aquinas, St.

Archias (fl. 62 B.C.). In the *Greek Anthology,* vol. 2. Trans. W. R. Paton. Loeb Classics, 1948.

Aretaeus the Cappadocian (81–ca. 138). *De acutorum et diuturnorum morborum causis et signis.* Ed. J. Goupyl. Paris: A. Turnebus, 1554.

──────. *De acutorum et diuturnorum morborum causis et signis.* Ed. C. Hude. *Corpus medicorum graecorum,* vol. 2. Berlin: Teubner, 1958.

──────. *De causis et notis diuturnorum affectum.* In *Medicae artis principes post Hippocratem et Galenum.* [Geneva]: Henricus Stephanus, 1567.

──────. *On the Causes and Symptoms of Chronic Diseases.* In *The Extant Works.* Ed. Francis Adams. Boston: Longwood Press, 1978.

Aretino, Pietro (1492–1556). *The Works of Aretino.* Trans. Samuel Putnam. 2 vols. Chicago: Pascal Covici, 1926.

Aristophanes (ca. 448–380 B.C.). *Birds.* Trans. B. B. Rogers. Loeb Classics, 1961.

──────. *Clouds.* Trans. B. B. Rogers. Loeb Classics, 1967.

──────. *Comoediae* (including frags.). Ed. G. Dindorfii. Oxonii: ex Typographeo Academico, 1835.

──────. *Frogs.* Trans. B. B. Rogers. Loeb Classics, 1961.

──────. *Plutus.* Trans. B. B. Rogers. Loeb Classics, 1961.

Aristotle (384–22 B.C.). *The Art of Rhetoric.* Trans. John Henry Freese. Loeb Classics, 1967.

──────. *De generatione et corruptione.* In *Aristotles Latinus.* Ed. Joanna Judycka. Leiden: E. J. Brill, 1986.

──────. *Eudemian Ethics* of the *Nicomachean Ethics.* Trans. H. Rackham. Loeb Classics, 1962.

──────. *Great Ethics* (*Magna moralia*). Trans. G. Cyril Armstrong. Loeb Classics, 1962.

──────. *The History of Animals.* Trans. A. L. Peck. 3 vols. Loeb Classics, 1970.

──────. *The History of Animals.* In *The Complete Works of Aristotle.* Ed. Jonathan Barnes. Princeton: Princeton University Press, 1984.

──────. *The Metaphysica.* Trans. Parviz Morewedge. New York: Columbia University Press, 1973.

──────. *Metaphysics.* Trans. H. Tredennick. Loeb Classics, 1968.

──────. *Nicomachean Ethics.* Trans. H. Rackham. Loeb Classics, 1962.

──────. *On Colours.* In *Minor Works.* Trans. W. S. Hett. Loeb Classics, 1963.

──────. *On Prophecy in Sleep.* Trans. W. S. Hett. Loeb Classics, 1964.

──────. "On Sleep and Sleeplessness." In *Parva naturalia.* Trans. W. S. Hett. Loeb Classics, 1964.

──────. *On the Generation of Animals.* Trans. A. L. Peck. Loeb Classics, 1963.

──────. *On the Heavens.* Trans. W. K. Guthrie. Loeb Classics, 1960.

──────. *On the Soul.* Trans. W. S. Hett. Loeb Classics, 1964.

──────. *Opera.* Editit Academia Regia Borusica. 5 vols. Berlin: Koenigliche Akademie der Wissenschaften, 1831–70.

──────. *Parts of Animals.* Trans. A. L. Peck. Loeb Classics, 1961.

──────. *Physics.* Trans. Philip H. Wickstead and Francis M. Cornford. Loeb Classics, 1968.

──────. *Physiognomics.* In *The Minor Works.* Trans. W. S. Hett. Loeb Classics,

1963.

———— . *Politics*. Trans. H. Rackham. Loeb Classics, 1967.

———— . *Posterior Analytics*. Trans. Hugh Tredennick. Loeb Classics, 1966.

———— . *Problems*. Trans. W. S. Hett. Loeb Classics, 1953.

———— . *Progression of Animals*. Trans. E. S. Forster. Loeb Classics, 1945.

Arnald of Villanova (d. ca. 1313). *Breviarium practicae* in *Opera omnia*. Basileae: Conrad Waldkirch, 1585.

———— . Commentary on *Medicina salernitana, id est conservandae bonae valetudinis praecepta*. Excudebat Jacobus Stoer, 1599.

———— . *Commentum super regimen Salernitanum*. In *Medicina Salernitana, id est conservanda bonae valetudinis praecepta*. Roterodami: ex officina Arnoldi Leert, 1599.

———— . *De coitu*. In *Opera omnia*. Basileae: Conrad Waldkirch, 1585.

———— . *De physicis ligaturis*. In *Opera omnia*. Basileae: Conrad Waldkirch, 1585.

———— . *De regimine caste viventium* of *De regimine sanitatis*. In *Opera omnia*. Basileae: Conrad Waldkirch, 1585.

———— . *De regime sanitatis*. In *Opera omnia*. Basileae: Conrad Waldkirch, 1585.

———— . *De venenis*. In *Opera omnia*. Basileae: Conrad Waldkirch, 1585.

———— . *Expositiones visionum quae fiunt in somnia*. In *Opera omnia*. Basileae: Conrad Waldkirch, 1585.

———— . *Liber de parte operativa*. In *Opera Omnia*. Basileae: Conrad Waldkirch, 1585.

———— . *Remedia contra maleficia*. In *Opera omnia*. Basileae: Conrad Waldkirch, 1585.

———— . *Tractatus de amore heroico*. In *Opera medica omnia*, vol. 3. Ed. Michael R. McVaugh. Barcelona: Universitat de Barcelona, 1985.

Artemidorus Daldianus (fl. 2d c.). *De somniorum interpretatione libri quinque*. Trans. Jan Hagenbut (Janus Cornarius; Julianus Cervus; Jean Corvé). Lugduni: apud S. Gryphium, 1546.

———— . *The Interpretation of Dreams* (*Oneirocritica*). Trans. Robert J. White. Park Ridge, N. J. : Noyes Press, 1975.

Athenaeus of Naucratis (fl. ca. 200). *Deipnosophistarum libri quindecim*. Lugduni: apud viduam Antonii de Harsy, 1612.

———— . *The Deipnosophists*. Trans. Charles Burton Gulick. 7 vols. Loeb Classics, 1950.

Aubanus Bohemus. *See* Boemus, Johann.

Aubery, Jean (1569–1622). *L'antidote d'amour. Avec un ample discours, contenant la nature et les causes d'iceluy, ensemble les remedes les plus singuliers pour se preserver et guerir des passions amoureuses*. Paris: Chez Claude Chappelet, 1599.

Augustine of Hippo, St. (354–430). *Ad inquisitiones Januarii liber II, seu epistola LV*. In *Opera*, vol. 38. Ed. D. A. B. Caillan. *Collectio selecta SS. ecclesiae patrum*. Parisiis: apud Parent-Desbarres, 1840.

———— . *The City of God*. Trans. Marcus Dods. New York: Modern Library, 1950.

———— . *Confessions*. Trans. William Watts. 2 vols. Loeb Classics, 1931, 1977.

———— . *De civitate dei*. Ed. Sir Ernest Barker. London: J. M. Dent, 1953.

———— . *De doctrina*. Trans. D. W. Robertson, Jr. New York: Bobbs-Merrill, 1958.

Aulus Gellius. *See* Gellius, Aulus.

Aurelianus, Caelius (fl. 5th c.). *Chronion.* In *Medici antiqui omnes.* Venetiis, 1547.

———. *De morbis acutis et chronicis libri VIII.* Amstelaedami: Wetsteniana, 1755.

———. *On Acute Diseases and on Chronic Diseases.* Ed. I. E. Drabkin. Chicago: University of Chicago Press, 1950.

Ausonius, Decimus Magnus (ca. 310–ca. 395). *Ausonius.* Trans. Hugh G. Evelyn White. 2 vols. Loeb Classics, 1949–51.

Avenzoar (Ibn Zuhr; 1113–62). *Liber Theizir* (publ. with Averroes, *Colliget*). Venetiis: Otinus de Luna, 1497.

Averroes of Cordoba (Ibn Roshd, Abū al-Walīd Muḥammad; 1126–98). *Colliget libri VII* (*Kitab-al-Kullyyat*). Venetiis: apud Junctas, 1562; rpt. Frankfurt am Main: Minerva, 1962.

———. *De anima.* Ed. F. Stuart Crawford. Cambridge, Mass.: Medieval Acadamy of America, 1953.

Avicenna ('Abū 'Alī Ḥusayn 'Abdullāh ibn Sīnā; 980–1037). *Canon.* (*liber III*) *cum Jacobus de Partibus.* Lugduni: Trechsel, 1498.

———. *De anima. Ab Andrea Alpago Bellunensi ex arabico in Latinum versa.* Venetiis: apud Juntas, 1546; rpt. Westmead: Gregg International Publishers, 1969.

———. *Liber canonis* (*Al-qānūn fi't-tibb*). Trans. Gerard of Cremona. Venetiis: apud Juntas, 1555.

———. *Liber de anima seu sextus de naturalibus.* Ed. S. Van Reit. *Avicenna Latinus.* Louvain and Leiden: E. J. Brill, 1968–72.

———. *Poem on medicine* ('*Arjuzat fi't-tibb*) or *Cantica Avicennae.* In *Liber canonis de medicinis cordialibus et cantica iam olim quidem a Gerardo Carmonensi ex arabico sermone in Latinum conversa.* Venetiis: apud Juntas, 1555.

———. *A Treatise on Love by IBN SINA* (*Rislah fi'l ishq*). Ed. E. L. Fackenheim. *Medieval Studies,* 7 (1945), pp. 208–28.

Babb, Lawrence. *The Elizabethan Malady. A Study of Melancholy in English Literature from 1580 to 1642.* 1951; rpt. East Lansing: Michigan State University Press, 1965.

Bakal, Donald A. *Psychology and Medicine: Psychobiological Dimensions of Health and Illness.* New York: Springer Publishing, 1979.

Baldacci, L. *Il petrarchismo italiano nel Cinquecento.* Milan-Naples: Ricciardi, 1957.

Bandello, Matteo (1485–1561). "The Love of Antioclus with Faire Stratonica," *The Palace of Pleasure,* 1575. Trans. William Painter. London: David Nutt, 1890.

Barbaro, Ermanolao (1454–93). *C. Plinii naturalis historiae libros castigationes.* Basileae: apud Joannem Valderum, 1534. *See also* Dioscorides.

Barraud, G. *L'humanisme et la médecine du XVIe siècle.* Paris: Vigot Frères, 1942.

Basil, Bishop of Ancyra (Ankara). *De virginitate.* In *Opera omnia.* Paris, 1547.

———. *De virginitate* (falsely attributed to Basil of Caesarea). Vol. 30 of the *Patrologiae cursus completus, series Graeca.* Ed. J. P. Migne. Paris: J. P. Migne, 1857–87.

———. *De virginitate.* Texte vieux-slave et traduction française par A. Vaillant. Paris: Institut d'Études Slaves, 1943.

Basil of Caesarea, St. (ca. 330–79). *Constitutiones monasticae.* Vol. 31 of the *Patrologiae cursus completus, series Graeca.* Ed. J. P. Migne. Paris: J. P. Migne, 1857–87.

———. *Epistolae.* Vol. 32 of the *Patrologiae cursus completus, series Graeca.* Ed.

J. P. Migne. Paris: J. P. Migne, 1857–87.

————. *Exegetic Homilies.* Trans. Agnes Clare Way. Washington, D.C.: Catholic University of America Press, 1963.

————. *Homiliae.* Vol. 30 of the *Patrologiae cursus completus, series Graeca.* Ed. J. P. Migne. Paris: J. P. Migne, 1857–87.

————. *Opera omnia . . . Graece et Latine.* Parisiis: sumptibus Claudii Morelli, 1618.

Battista, Giuseppe (1610–1675). *Delle poesie meliche de Giuseppe Battista.* In Venetia: per Francesco Baba, 1653.

Baudier, Michel (1589–1645). *Histoire du serrail, et de la cour du Grand Seigneur.* Paris: Chez Sebastien Cramoisy, 1650.

Baudrillart, Alfred, Cardinal, ed. *Dictionnaire d'Histoire et de Geographie Ecclesiastique.* Paris: Letouzey et Ané, 1912.

Baxter, Christopher. "Jean Bodin's *De la démonomanie des sorciers*: the Logic of Persecution." *The Damned Art: Essays in the Literature of Witchcraft.* Ed. Sydney Anglo. London: Routledge and Kegan Paul, 1977.

Bayle, Pierre. *The Dictionary Historical and Critical.* 1710; rpt. London: J. J. and P. Knapton, 1734–38.

Beaumont, Francis (1584–1616), and John Fletcher (1579–1625). *Monsieur Thomas.* In *Works.* Ed. A. R. Waller. 10 vols. Cambridge: Cambridge University Press, 1906; rpt. New York: Octagon Books, 1969.

Beauvois de Chauvincourt, Le Sieur de (fl. 16th c.). *Discours de la lycanthropie ou de la transmutation des hommes en loups.* Paris: J. Rezé, 1599.

Belleau, Remy (1528–77). *Oeuvres poétiques.* Ed. Ch. Marty-Laveaux. Paris: Alphonse Lemerre, 1878.

Belleforest, François de (1530–83). *L'histoire universelle du monde, contenant l'entière description et situation des quatres parties de la terre.* Paris: Chez G. Mallot, 1570.

Belon du Mons, Pierre (ca. 1517–64). *L'histoire de la nature des oyseaux, avec leurs descriptions et naifs portraicts . . . en sept livres.* Paris: Chez Guillaume Cavellat, 1555.

————. *Les observations de plusieurs singularitez et choses memorables, trouvées en Grece, Asie, Judée, Egypte, Arabie, et autres pays estranges, redigées en trois livres.* Paris: Gilles Corrozet, 1553.

Bembo, Pietro (1470–1547). *Gli Asolani.* In *Prose e rime.* Ed. C. Dionisotti. Turin: Einaudi, 1966.

————. *Les Azolains de Monsigneur Bembo, de la nature d'amour.* Trans. Jean Martin. Paris: M. de Vascosan, 1545; Paris: N. Chrestien, 1555.

Benedetti, Alessandro (Alexander Benedictus; ca. 1450–1525). *Opera.* Basileae: per Henricum Petrum [1539].

————. *Singulis corporum morbis a capite ad pedes.* Venetiis: in officina Lucaeantonii Juntae, 1533.

Benton, John F. "Clio and Venus: An Historical View of Medieval Love." In *The Meaning of Courtly Love.* Ed. F. X. Newman. Albany: State University of New York Press, 1973.

Bernardi della Mirandola, Antonio de (1573–1648). *Disputationes . . . accessit locuples rerum et verborum toto opere memorabilium.* Basileae: H. Petri et N. Bryling, 1562.

Bernard of Gordon (Gordonius; d. ca. 1310). *Opus lilium medicinae inscriptum.*

Lugduni: apud. G. Rovillium, 1574.

Berulle, Pierre de, Cardinal (Léon d'Alexis; 1575–1629). *Traicté des énergumènes.* Troyes: n. p., 1599.

Bilitzer, Christophorus. *De pulso amatorio.* Diss.: Giessen, 1609.

Bird, Otto. "The Canzone d'Amore of Cavalcanti According to the Commentary of Dino del Garbo." *Mediaeval Studies* 2 (1940), pp. 150–203.

Boaistuau, Pierre (d. 1566), and François de Belleforest (1530–1583). *Histoires prodigieuses et memorables, extraictes de plusieurs fameux autheurs grecs, et latins, sacrez et prophanes, divisées en six livres.* Paris: par la vefue de Gabriel Buon, 1598.

——— . *Le théâtre du monde,* 1588. Ed. Michel Simonin. Genève: Librairie Droz, 1981.

Boccaccio, Giovanni (1313–75). *The Decameron.* Trans. Edward Hutton. New York: Heritage Press, 1940.

——— . *Genealogie deorum gentilium libri.* Ed. Vincenzo Romano. 2 vols. Bari: Laterza, 1951.

Bodin, Jean (1530–96). *De la démonomanie des sorciers.* Paris: Chez Jacques du Puys, 1587.

Boemus, Johann (Aubanus Bohemus; fl. 1500–1520). *Discours des païs selon leur situation, avec les moeurs, loix, et ceremonies d'iceux.* 1520 (in Latin); Lyon: par Jean de Tournes, 1552.

Boethius, Anicius Manlius (480–524). *De institutione arithmetica libri duo; De institutione musica libri quinque.* Ed. Godofredus Friedlein. Lipsiae: in aedibus B. G. Teubneri, 1867.

Bona Fortuna (fl. early 14th c.). "Tractatus super Viaticum." MS Rouen A 176 f. Transcription by Mary F. Wack.

Bottoni, Albertino (d. ca. 1596). *De morbus muliebribus.* In *Gynaeciorum sive de mulierum affectibus.* Ed. Israel Spachius. Basileae: per Conradum Waldkirch, 1586.

Boutière, Jean and A.-H. Schutz. *Biographies des troubadours: textes provencaux des XIIIe et XIVe siècles.* Paris: Éditions A. G. Nizet, 1964.

Brabant, H. *Médicins, malades et maladies de la Renaissance.* Bruxelles: La Renaissance du Livre, 1966.

Brain, Peters. *Galen on Bloodletting: A Study of the Origins, Development and Validity of his Opinions, with a Translation of the Three Works.* Cambridge: Cambridge University Press, 1986.

Brett, George Sidney. *Psychology Ancient and Modern.* New York: Cooper Square Publishers, 1963.

Browne, E. G. *Arabian Medicine.* Cambridge: Cambridge University Press, 1962.

Bruno, Giordano (1548–1600). *The Heroic Frenzies. (De gli eroici furori).* Trans. Paul Eugene Memmo, Jr. New York: Columbia University Press, 1959.

——— . *De magia et theses de magia.* In *Opera Latine conscripta publicis sumptibus edita,* vol. III. Ed. H. Vitelli et al. Neapoli: D. Morano, 1879–91.

——— . *De vincula in genere.* In *Opera Latine conscripta publicis sumptibus edita,* vol. III. Ed. H. Vitelli et al. Neapoli: D. Morano, 1879–91.

Buhahylya. *See* Byngezla.

Bullough, Vern L. "Postscript: Heresy, Witchcraft, and Sexuality" in *Sexual Practices and the Medieval Church.* Eds. Vern L. Bullough and James Brundage.

Buffalo, N.Y.: Prometheus Books, 1982.

Burton, Robert (1577–1640). *The Anatomy of Melancholy*. Eds. Floyd Dell and Paul Jordan-Smith. New York: Tudor Publishing, 1927.

Bush, Douglas. *English Literature in the Early Seventeenth Century*. New York: Oxford University Press, 1952.

Byngezla, Buhahaylya (Yaḥyā ibn 'Isā ibn Jozlah; b. 1074). *Tacuini aegritudinum (Takwīm al-abdān fī tadbīr al-insān)*. Trans. Faraj ibn Salim (Farragut; fl. 1280). Argentorati: apud Jo. Schottum, 1532.

Caesar, Gaius Julius (102–44 B.C.). *The Gallic War*. Trans. H. J. Edwards. Loeb Classics, 1946.

Calcagnini of Ferrara, Celio (1479–1541). *Anteros sive de mutuo amore*. In *Opera aliquot*. Basileae: Froben, 1544.

Calvin, Jean (1509–64). *Traicté ou Avertissement contre l'astrologie qu'on appelle judiciaire et autres curiosités qui règnent aujourd'hui au monde*, 1549. Paris: Librairie Armand Colin, 1962.

Calvus, Gaius Licinius (82–47 B.C.). *Fragmenta poetarum Latinorum epicorum et liricorum*. Ed. W. Morel. Lipsiae: B. G. Teubner, 1927.

Campbell, Donald. *Arabian Medicine and its Influence on the Middle Ages*. London: Kegan Paul, 1926.

Camporesi, Piero. *I balsami di Venere*. Milan: Garzanti, 1989.

Capitolinus, Julius (fl. 300). *Scriptores historiae augustae*. Ed. H. Iordan and F. Eyssenhardt. Berolini: apud Weidmannos, 1864.

Capparoni, Pietro. "Magistri salernitani nondum cogniti." *A Contribution to the History of the Medical School of Salerno*. London: J. Bale, 1923.

Capretto (Cavretto), Pietro (Petrus Haedo, Pier Hedo; b. 1424). *Anterotica, sive de amoris generibus*. Treviso: Gerardus de Lisa de Flandria, 1492.

Cardano, Girolamo (1501–76). *Aphorismorum astronomicorum liber*. Nuremburg: J. Petreius, 1547.

——— . *Aphorismorum astronomicorum segmenta VII*. In *Opera omnia in decem tomos digesta*. Lugduni: sumptibus I. A. Huguetan & M. A. Ravard, 1663.

——— . *Les libres . . . intitulés de la subtilité et subtiles inventions, ensemble les causes occultes et raisons d'icelles*. Trans. Richard Le Blanc. Paris: G. Le Noir, 1556.

——— . *Somniorum synesiorum omnis generis insomnia explicantes libri IV; Actio in Thessalicum medicum, de secretis, de gemmis et coloribus*. Basileae: ex officina Henrici Petri, 1562.

Cassiodorus, Flavius (ca. 480–575). *Institutiones divinarum et humanarum litterarum*. Ed. R. A. B. Mynors. Oxford: Clarendon, 1937.

Castiglione, Baldassare (1478–1529). *The Book of the Courtier* (1528). Trans. Charles S. Singleton. Garden City, N.Y.: Doubleday, 1959.

Castiglioni, A. *A History of Medicine*. Trans. E. B. Krumbhaar. New York: Knopf, 1941.

Castro, Rodrigo de (Rodericus à Castro Lusitanus; 1546–1627). *De universa mulierum medicina*. Hamburgi: in officina Frobeniano, 1603.

——— . *Medicus-politicus: sive de officiis medico-politicis tractatus, quatuor distinctus libris*. Hamburgi: ex Bibliopolio Frobeniano, 1614.

Cataudella, Quintino. *La novella greca*. Napoli: Edizione Scientifiche Italiane, 1958.

Cattani da Diacceto, Francesco (1466–1522). *I tre libri de amore con un panegirico all' amore*. Vinegia: appresso G. Giolito de' Ferrari, 1561.

Catullus, Gaius Valerius (ca. 84–ca. 54 B.C.). *Catullus, Tibullus and Pervigilium Veneris*. Trans. F. W. Cornish. Loeb Classics, 1950, 1962.

Cavallera, F. "Le 'De Virginitate' de Basile D'Ancyre." *Revue d'Histoire Ecclesiastique*, 6 (1905), pp. 5–14.

Caviceo, Jacopo (1443–1511). *Le Peregrin. Dialogue treselegant intitulé le Peregrin traictant de l'honneste et pudique amour concisie par pure et sincere vertu*. Trad. François Dassy. Lyon: Claude Nourry, [1528].

Cavigioli, Giovanni Battista (fl. 16th c.). *Livres des proprietes du vinaigre*. Poictiers, 1541.

Céard, Jean. "Folie et démonologie au XVIe siècle." *Folie et déraison à la Renaissance*. Ed. A. Gerlo. Bruxelles: Editions de l'université de Bruxelles, 1976.

————. "The Devil and Lovesickness According to the Physicians and Demonologists of the Sixteenth Century." *Eros and Anteros: The Medical Traditions of Love in Renaissance Culture*. Ed. Donald Beecher and Massimo Ciavolella. Montreal: McGill-Queen's University Press, forthcoming.

Celsus, Aulus Cornelius (fl. 20–30). *De arte medica*. In *Corpus medicorum Latinorum*, vol. 1. Ed. F. Marx. Berlin: Teubner, 1915.

————. *De medicina*. Trans. W. G. Spencer. 3 vols. Loeb Classics, 1961.

Cherchi, Paolo. "Andreas' *De amore*: Its Unity and Polemical Origin." *Andrea Cappelano i trovatori e altri temi romanzi*. Rome: Bulzoni, 1979.

————. "A Dossier for the Study of Jealousy." *Eros and Anteros: The Medical Traditions of Love in Renaissance Culture*, ed. Donald Beecher and Massimo Ciavolella. Montreal: McGill-Queen's University Press, forthcoming.

————. "Per la femmina 'balba'," *Quaderni d'italianistica*, VI, 2 (1985), pp. 228–32.

Cervantes, Miguel de (1547–1616). *Don Quixote of La Mancha*. Trans. John Ormsby (1829–95). Eds. Joseph Jones and Kenneth Douglas. New York: W. W. Norton, 1981.

Chalcondylas, Laon (ca. 1430–ca. 1490). *L'histoire de la decadence de l'empire Grec et establissement de celuy des Turcs*. Trans. Blaise de Vigenère. Paris: Chez Sebastien Cramoisy, 1650.

Charondas. *See* Le Caron, Loys.

Charron, Pierre (1541–1603). *Of Wisdome, Three Bookes*. Trans. Samson Lennard. London: for Edward Blount and Will Aspley, ca. 1606.

Chaucer, Geoffrey (1340–1400). *Parlement of Foulys*. Ed. D. S. Brewer. London: Thomas Nelson and Sons, 1960.

Cheverny, Julien. *Sexologie de l'Occident*. Paris: Librairie Hachette, 1976.

Chrysostome, John, St. (d. 407). *De providentia Dei ad Stagirium monachum obrepitium*. In *Opera omnia tomus quintus*. Parisiis: apud Robertum Pipic, 1687.

Ciavolella, Massimo. *La "malattia d'amore" dall'Antichità al Medio Evo*. Rome: Bulzoni, 1975.

Cicero, Marcus Tullius (106–43 B.C.). *De fato* bound with *De oratore*, vol 2. Trans. H. Rackham. 2 vols. Loeb Classics, 1960.

————. *De natura deorum*. Trans. H. Rackham. 2 vols. Loeb Classics, 1961.

————. *De oratore*. Trans. H. Rackham. Loeb Classics, 1968.

————. *De senectute*. Trans. William Armistead Falconer. Loeb Classics, 1964.

————. *The Letters to his Friends (Epistulae ad familiares)*. Trans. W. G. Williams.

Loeb Classics, 1959.

————. *Tusculan Disputations*. Trans. J. E. King. Loeb Classics, 1950, 1968.

Cipelli, Giovanni Battista (Egnazio; ca. 1478–1553). *Sommaire de chroniques . . . de tous les empereurs d'europe depuis Iules César, iusques à Maximilian dernier décédé*. Trans. Geofroy Tory de Bourges. Paris: G. Tory, 1529.

Clark, Stuart. "The Scientific Status of Demonology." *Occult and Scientific Mentalities in the Renaissance*. Ed. Brian Vickers. Cambridge: Cambridge University Press, 1984.

Claudian (Claudius Claudianus; fl. 400). *[Works]*. Trans. H. Platnauer. Loeb Classics, 1956.

Clavius, Christoph (1538–1612). *In sphaeram Joannis de Sacro Bosco. Commentarius*. Lugduni: ex officina Q. Hug, A. Porta, sumptibus Jo. de Gabiano, 1607.

Clement of Alexandria (ca. 150–215). *Paedagogus*. Trans. Simon P. Wood. Washington D.C.: Catholic University of America Press, 1954.

————. *Stromata*. Vol. 8 of the *Patrologiae cursus completus, series Graeca*. Ed. J. P. Migne. Paris: J. P. Migne, 1859–87.

Cleopatra (Medica). *Harmonia gynaeciorum, sive de morbis muliebribus liber*. In *Gynaeciorum libri IV*. Ed. Israel Spachius. Basileae: per Conradum Waldkirch, 1586.

Clusius, Carolus. *See* L'Ecluse, Charles.

Coëffeteau, F. Nicolas, Bishop of Marseille (1574–1623). *A Table of Humane Passions with their causes and effects*. Trans. Edward Grimeston. London: N. Okes, 1621.

————. *Tableau de passions humaines, de leurs causes, et de leurs effects*. Lyon: Chez Jacques Carteron, 1619; rpt., 1642.

————. *Tableau des passions humaines, de leurs causes et de leurs effects*. Paris: S. Cramoisy, 1620.

Colombo, Realdo (1494–ca. 1559). *De re anatomica libri XV*. Parisiis: apud Andream Wechelum, 1572.

Companion to the Play-House, The. 2 vols. London: T. Becket and P. A. Dehondt et al., 1764.

Constantinus Africanus (fl. 1075). *Breviarium Constantini dictum Viaticum* (a trans. of the *Zād al-musāfir* of Ibn Eddjezzar). Lugduni: n.p., 1510–11.

————. *De communibus medico cognitu locis*. In *Opera*. Basileae: apud Henricum Petrum, 1539.

————. *Della melancolia*. Trans. M. T. Malato and U. de Martini. Rome: tipografia E. Cossidente, 1959.

————. *Viaticum*. In *Omnia opera Ysaac*. Lugduni: n.p., 1515.

Conti, Natale (Natalis Comitis; ca. 1520–ca.1580). *Mythologiae sive explicationis fabularum libri decem: in quibus omnia prope naturalis et moralis philosophiae dogmata fuisse demonstratur*. Francofurti: apud Andreae Wecheli, 1588.

Cornarius, Janus (Jan Hagenbut). *See* Artemidorus Daldianus.

Corner, G. W. "The Rise of Medicine at Salerno in the Twelfth Century." *Annals of the History of Medicine*, 3 (1931).

Corpus Juris Canonici. Ed. A. L. Richter. 2 vols. Graz: Akademische Druck-U. Verlagsanstalt, 1959.

Corti, Maria. *La felicità mentale. Nuove prospettive per Cavalcanti e Dante*. Turin: Einaudi, 1983.

Cotgrave, Randle. *A Dictionarie of the French and English Tongues.* London, 1611; rpt. Columbia: University of South Carolina Press, 1950, 1968.

Cotta, John (ca. 1575–ca. 1650). *Triall of Witch-Craft.* London: Printed by George Purslowe, 1616.

Couliano, Ioan Peter. *Eros et magie à la Rennaissance.* Paris: Flammarion, 1984.

Crinito, Pietro: see Riccio, Pieri.

Crispo, Benedetto (Benedictus Crispus), Archbishop of Milan. *Commentarium medicinale.* Romae: Angelo Mai, 1833; and in *Scripta varia.* Vol. 89 of the *Patrologiae cursus completus.* Ed. J. P. Migne. Paris: J. P. Migne, 1850.

Crohns, Hjalmar. "Zur Geschichte der Liebe als 'Krankheit'." *Archiv für Kulturgeschichte,* 3 (1905), pp. 66–86.

Cuspinianus, Johannes (Speisshammer; 1473–1529). *De Caesaribus atque Imperatoribus Romanis opus insigne.* Strasbourg: Crato Mylius, 1540.

Cyprian, St., Bishop of Carthage (Thascius Caecilius Cypridnus; 200–258). *Letters.* Trans. Sister Rose Bernard Donna. Washington D.C.: Catholic University of America Press, 1964.

D'Abano, Pietro (Petrus Aponensis; 1250–ca. 1315). *Conciliator controversiarum, quae inter philosophos et medicos versantur.* Venetiis: apud Juntas, 1548.

————. *Heptameron seu elementa magica.* Bound with H. C. Agrippa. *Opera.* Lugduni: per Beringos Fratres, ca. 1550.

D'Alexis, Léon. *See* Berulle, Pierre de, Cardinal.

Dariot, Claude (Dariotus; 1533–94). *Ad astrorum judicia facilis introductio [et] tractatus de electionibus principiorum idoneorum rebus inchoandis.* Lugduni: apud Mauricium Roy & Ludovicum Pesnot, 1557.

Darmon, Pierre. *Le mythe de la procréation à l'âge baroque.* Paris: Éditions du Seuil, 1981.

David-Peyre, Yvonne. "Jacques Ferrand médicin aganais 1575–16 . . . (?)" *Histoire des Sciences Médicales,* 4 (1973), pp. 1–11.

————. "Jacques Ferrand médecin agenais, ou les tracasseries d'un tribunal ecclésiastique." *Actes du Congrès National des Société Savantes.* Nantes, 1972, pp. 561–72.

————. "Las Fuentes Ibéricas de Jacques Ferrand, Médico de Agen." *Asclépio,* 23 (1971), pp. 1–26.

————. *Le personnage du médecin et la relation médecin-malade dans la littérature ibérique XVIe et XVIIe siècle.* Paris: Ediciones Hispano-Americanas, 1971.

De Castro, Rodrigo. *See* Castro, Rodrigo de.

De Lancre, Pierre. *See* Lancre, Pierre de.

De la Ruelle, Jean. *See* Ruelle, Jean de la.

Della Porta, Giovanni Battista (Giambattista; ca. 1535–1615). *De humana physiognomonia libri IV.* Ursellis: typis Cornelii Sutorii, sumptibus Jonae Rosae Fr., 1551.

Delorme, Carolus. *An amantes iisdem remediis curentur quibus amentes?* Diss.: Montpellier, 1608.

Del Rio, Martin Anton (1551–1608). *Disquisitionum magicarum libri sex.* Lugduni: apud Joannem Phillehotte, 1612. Lugduni: apud H. Cardon, 1612.

————. *Les controverses et recherches magiques.* Trans. André du Chesne. Paris: 1608; 1611.

De Renzi, Salvatore. *Collectio Salernitana.* 5 vols. Naples, 1852–59.

De Sales, Francis. *See* Francis de Sales.

Desbarreaux-Bernard, M. "Notice biographique et bibliographique sur Jacques Ferrand." *Bulletin du Bibliophile.* Toulouse: Douladoure, 1869.

Descartes, René (1596–1650). *Les passions de l'ame.* Ed. Geneviève Rodis-Lewis. Paris: Librairie Philosophique J. Vrin, 1970.

————. *Les passions de l'ame* (1649). Préface de Samuel Sylvestre de Sacy. Paris: Gallimard, 1969.

De Vega, Cristóbal. *See* Vega, Cristóbal de.

De Veyries, Jean. *See* Veyries, Jean de.

Dictionnaire d'Ancien Français. Paris, 1875.

Dictionnaire d'Histoire et de Geographie Ecclesiastique. See Baudrillart, Alfred.

Diethelm, Oskar. "La surexcitation sexuelle." *L'évolution psychiatrique,* 2 (1966), pp. 233–45.

————. *Medical Dissertations of Psychiatric Interest Printed before 1750.* Basel: S. Karger, 1971.

Dingwall, Eric John. *Male Infibulation.* London: J. Bale and Sons, 1925.

Dino del Garbo. *Scriptum super cantilena Guidonis de Cavalcantibus.* In *Rime di Guido Cavalcanti.* Ed. G. Favati. Milan: Marzorati, 1957.

Dio Cassius (Cocceianus; ca. 150–235). *Dio's Roman History.* Trans. E. Cary. Loeb Classics, 1965.

Diodorus Siculus (fl. 40 B.C.) [*Library of History*]. Trans. C. H. Oldfather et al. 12 vols. Loeb Classics, 1952.

Diogenes Laertius (ca. 200–250). *Lives of Eminent Philosophers.* Ed. R. D. Hicks. Loeb Classics, 1925, 1966.

Dionysius Halicarnassus (fl. ca. 25 B.C.) *Scripta quae extant, omnia, et historica, et rhetorica.* Ed. Frideric Sylburg. Francofurdi: apud heredes Andreae Wecheli, 1586.

Dioscorides, Pedanius of Anazarbos (fl. 50–60). *De medica materia libri sex, Joanne Ruellio Successionensi interprete.* Lugduni: apud Joan. Francis de Gabiano, 1555.

————. *Pharmacorum simplicium reique medicae libri viii. Jo[anne] Ruellio interprete una cum Hermolai Barbari corollariis, et Marci Vergilii, in singula capita censuris sive annotationibus.* Argentorato: apud Jo. Schottum, 1529.

————. *Pietro Andrea Mattiole commentarii in libros sex Pedacii Dioscoridis Anazarbei de medica materia.* Venetiis: in officina Erasmiana, apud Vincentium Valgrisium, 1558.

Dodoëns, Rembert (1517–85). *Stirpium historiae pemptades sex sive libri XXX.* Antverpiae: ex officina Plantiniana, apud B. et J. Moretos, 1616.

Dorléans, Ludovico. *See* Orléans, Louis d'.

Dubois, Jacques (Jacobus Sylvius of Amiens; 1478–1555). *Livre de la generation de l'homme.* Paris: Chez Guillaume Morel, 1559.

————. *Opera medica.* Genevae: sumptibus J. Chouët, 1630.

Du Chesne, Joseph (Quercetanus; ca. 1544–1609). *Pharmacie des Dogmatiques.* Paris: Chez Charles F. de C. Morel, 1629.

————. *Preparation Spagyrique des Medicamens.* Paris: Chez Charles F. de C. Morel, 1629.

Du Laurens, André (1558–1609). *A Discourse of the Preservation of the Sight; of Melancholike Diseases; of Rheumes, and of Old Age.* Trans. Richard Surphlet.

London: Felix Kingston for Ralph Lacson, 1599.

————. *Controverses anatomiques.* In *Toutes les oeuvres.* Trans. Theophile Gelée. Paris: Chez P. Mettayer, 1613.

————. *Historia anatomica humani corporus.* Parisiis: M. Orry, 1600.

————. *Second discours, au quel est traicté des maladies melancholiques, et du moyen de les guarir.* In *Toutes les oeuvres.* Trans. Theophile Gelée. Paris: Chez P. Mettayer, 1613.

Dulieu, Louis. *La médicine à Montpellier. Tome II, La Renaissance.* Avignon: Les presses universelles, 1979.

Duminil, Marie-Paul. "La mélancolie amoureuse dans l'Antiquité." *La folie et le corps.* Ed. Jean Céard. Paris: Presses de l'école normale supérieure, 1985.

Dupréau, Gabriel (1511–88). *Histoire de l'estat et succès de l'Eglise, dressée en forme de chronique géneralle et universelle . . . depuis la nativité de Jésus-Christ jusques en l'an 1580.* Paris: J. Kerver, 1583.

Duval, Jacques (ca. 1555–ca. 1615). *Traité des hermaphrodits, parties génitales, accouchemens des femmes.* Rouen, 1612; rpt. Paris: I. Liseux, 1880.

Egnazio. *See* Cipelli, Giovanni Battista.

Eliade, Mircea. *A History of Religious Ideas.* 2 vols. Chicago: University of Chicago Press, 1978.

Eloy, Nicolas François Joseph (1714–88). *Dictionnaire historique de la médecine ancienne et moderne.* Mons: H. Hoyois, 1778.

Emilio of Verona, Paulo (d. 1529). *De rebus gestis francorum libri X.* Lutetiae: Parisiorum ex officina Vascosani, 1576.

Equicola, Mario (1470–1525). *De la nature d'amour, tant humain que divin, et de toutes les differences d'iceluy.* Trans. Gabriel Chappuys. Paris: pour I. Housé, 1584.

————. *Libro de natura de amore* (*Libro di natura d'amore*). Venetia: per L. Lorio da Portes, 1525.

Erasmus of Rotterdam, Desiderius (1466–1536). *Adagiorum chiliades quatuor.* Lugduni: apud haered. Sebast. Gryphii, 1592.

Erastus, Thomas (1524–83). *De astrologie divinatrice epistolae . . . iam olim ab eodem ad diversos scriptae, et in duos libros digestae.* Basileae: par Petrum Pernam, 1580.

Esquirol, Jean Etienne Dominique (1772–1840). *Mental Maladies: A Treatise on Insanity.* Intro. Raymond de Saussure. 1845; facs. New York and London: Hafner Publishing, 1965. The English translation of *Des maladies mentales considérées sous les rapports médical, hygiénique et médico-légal,* 1838.

Estienne, Charles (Carolus Stephanus; ca. 1504–64). *Dictionarium historicum, geographicum, poeticum.* Paris, 1596; rpt. New York and London: Garland Publishing, 1976.

Estienne, Henri (1528–59). *Thesaurus Graecae linguae.* Graz: Academische Druck– U. Verlagsanstalt, 1954.

Estienne, Robert (1503–59). *Dictionarium nominum propriorum virorum, mulierum, populorum.* Coloniae Agrippinae: apud I. Gymnicum, 1576.

Euripides (ca. 480–406 B.C.). *Andromache.* In *Euripides,* vol. 2. Trans. Arthur S. Way. 4 vols. Loeb Classics, 1968.

————. *Fragmenta.* In *Tragicorum Graecorum fragmenta.* Ed. A. Nauch. Leipzig: Teubner, 1889; rpt. Hildesheim: Georg Olms, 1964.

———— . *Hyppolytus.*. In *Eupirides*, vol 4. Trans. Arthur S. Way. 4 vols. Loeb Classics, 1964.

———— . *Iphigeneia at Aulis.* In *Euripides*, vol. 1. Trans. Arthur S. Way. 4 vols. Loeb Classics, 1959.

Eusebius of Caesarea (265–340). *La préparation évangélique.* Trans. Edouard des Places. Paris: Les éditions du Cerf, 1983.

———— . *Opera omnia quae exstant curis variorum.* Vols. 19–24 in the *Patrologiae cursus completus, series Graeca.* Ed. J. P. Migne. Paris: J. P. Migne, 1857.

Evans, Bergen. *The Psychiatry of Robert Burton.* New York: Columbia University Press, 1944.

Fackenheim, Emil L. "A Treatise on Love by *Ibn Sina.*" *Medieval Studies,* 7 (1945), pp. 208–28.

Fattori, Marta. "Sogni e temperamenti." In Gregory Tullio, ed. *I sogni nel Medioevo.* Rome: Edizioni dell'Ateneo, 1983.

Fattori, Marta, and M. Bianchi, eds. *Phantasia-Imaginatio.* Rome: Edizioni dell'Ateneo, 1988.

Favati, G. "La glossa latina di Dino Del Garbo a *Donna me prega* del Cavalcanti." *Annali della r. scuola normale superiore de Pisa, lettere, storia e filosofia,* ser. 2, 21 (1952), pp. 70–103.

Faventius, Victorius Benedictus (1481–1561). *Practicae magni . . . de morbis curandis . . . tomi duo. Quorum alter agit de morbis curandis capitis, et membrorum ei attinentium: alter de morbis curandis membrorum spirationi observientium.* 2 vols. Venetiis, 1562.

Fernel, Jean (1497–1558). *De abditis rerum causis.* Paris: A. Wechel, 1567.

———— . *Les VII livres de la physiologie.* Trans. Charles de Saint-Germain. Paris: Chez Jean Guignard le Jeune, 1655.

———— . *Pathologie.* Trans. A. D. M. Paris: Chez Jean Guignard le pere et Jean Guignard le fils, 1655.

Ferrand, Jacques (ca. 1575–after 1623). *De la maladie d'amour ou melancholie erotique.* Paris: Chez Denis Moreau, 1623.

———— . *Erotomania or a Treatise Discoursing of the Essence, Causes, Symptomes, Prognosticks, and Cure of Love or Erotique Melancholy.* Trans. Edmund Chilmead. Oxford: L. Lichfield, 1640.

———— . *Traité de l'essence et guérison de l'amour ou mélancholie erotique.* Toulouse: Chez la veuve de J. Colomiez, 1610.

Ferrari da Grado, Giovanni Matteo (Joannis Mattei Gradius; d. 1472). *Praxis in nonum Almansoris: omnibus medicine studiosis apprime necessaria.* Vincentius de Portonariis, de Tridino, de Monteferrato, 1527.

Ferrier, Auger (1513–88). *Vera medendi methodus, duobus libris comprehensa, eiusdem castigationes practicae medicinae.* Tolosae: apud Petrum de Puys, 1557.

Ficino, Marsilio (1433–99). *Commentarium in Convivium Platonis de amore.* In *Divini Platonis Opera omnia.* Lugduni: apud Antonium Vincentium, 1557.

———— . *Commentarium in Convivium Platonis de amore.* Ed. Sears Reynolds Jayne. Columbia, Mo.: University of Missouri Press, 1944.

———— . *Commentary on Plato's Symposium on Love.* Trans. Sears Jayne. Dallas: Spring Publications, 1985.

———— . *Platonicam theologiam de animorum immortalitatem.* Ed. Raymond Marcel. Paris: Societé d'Editiones "Les Belles Lettres," 1964.

_____ . *Three Books on Life*. Ed. and trans. Carol V. Kaske and John R. Clark. Binghampton, N.Y.: Medieval and Renaissance Texts and Studies, 1988.

Firmian Lactantius. *See* Lactantius.

Firmicus Maternus, Julius (Firmin de Belleval?; fl. 14th c.). *Lollianum, Astronomicon libri VIII, per Nicolaum Prucknerum astrologum nuper ab innumeris mendis vindicati*. Basileae: per Joannem Hervagium, 1551.

Fletcher, John (1579–1625), and William Shakespeare (1564–1616). *The Two Noble Kinsmen*. Ed. G. R. Proudfoot. London: Edward Arnold, 1970.

Foës, Anuce (Foesius; 1528–95). *Magni Hippocratis opera omnia quae extant*. Francofurdi: apud Andreae Wechli haeredes, 1595.

_____ . *Oeconomia Hippocratis alphabeti serie distincta, in qua dictionum apud Hippocratem omnium, praesertim obscuriorum, usus explicatur, ita ut lexicon Hippocrateum merito dici possit*. Francofurdi: apud A. Wechli haeredes, 1588.

Fonseca, Cristóbal de (1550?–1621). *Tratado del amor de Dios*. Valladolid: por los herederos de Bernardino de Santodomingo, 1595.

_____ . *Theion enōtikon, a discourse of holy love, by which the soul is united unto God*. Trans. Sir George Strode. London: printed for J. Flesher for Richard Royston, 1652.

Fonseca, Fredericus à (fl. 16th c.). *Consultationes medicae singularibus remediis referte*. Venetiis: apud Joannem Guerilium, 1619.

Fonseca, Pedro da (1528–99). *Commentarium . . . in libros metaphysicorum Aristotelis Stagiritae*. Lugduni: sumptibus Aratii Cardon, 1601.

Fontaine, Marie-Madeleine. "La lignée des commentaires à la chanson de Guido Cavalcanti *Donna me prega*: Evolution des relations entre philosophie, médecine et littérature dans le débat sur la nature d'amour (de la fin du XIIIe siècle á celle du XVIe)." *La folie et le corps*. Ed. Jean Céard. Paris: Presses de l'école normale supérieure, 1985.

Fontanono, Dionysius. *De morborum internorum curatione libri quatuor*. Lugduni: apud Ioannem Frellonium, 1550.

Ford, John (1586–1638). *The Lover's Melancholy*. Ed. Havelock Ellis. London: T. Fisher Unwin, n.d.

Foreest, Pieter van (Petrus Forestus; 1522–97). *Observationum et curationum medicinalium sive medicinae theoricae et practicae libri XXVIII*. Francofurti: E. Palthenia, 1602.

Foucault, Michel. *L'usage des plaisirs. Histoire de la sexualité.*, vol. II. Paris: Éditions Gallimard, 1984.

_____ . *La volonté de savoir. Histoire de la sexualité*, vol. I. Paris: Éditions Gallimard, 1976.

Fox, Ruth A. *The Tangled Chain: The Structure of Disorder in the Anatomy of Melancholy*. Berkeley: University of California Press, 1976.

Francescus Venetus. *See* Giorgio, Francesco.

Francheville, R. "Une thérapeutique musicale dans la vieille médecine." *Pro Medico*, 4 (1927), pp. 243–48.

Francis de Sales, St. (1567–1622). *The Introduction to the Devout Life*. Trans. Michael Day. London: Burns and Oates, 1956; princeps, 1608.

Fregoso, Giovan Battista, Duke of Genoa (Fulgosius; 1453–1504). *Anteros, sive tractatus contra amorem*. Milan: Leonardus Pachel, 1496.

_____ . *L'anteros ou contramour de Messire Baptiste Fulgoses*. Trans. Thomas Sibilet.

Paris: Chez Martin le Jeune, 1581.

————. *Factorum dictorumque memorabilium libri IX*. Paris: Cavellat, 1589.

Freitag of Halberstadt, Johann Heinrich (1573–1643). *Medicina animae, quae moriandi ars est: ex Hetrusco idiomate in Latinam translata*. Eds. J[oannes] H[enricus] and G[alenus] A[rnaldus] F[reitag]. Bremae, [1614].

Fuchs, Leonhard (Fuchsius; 1501–66). *L'histoire des plantes reduicte en tres bon ordre*. Lyon: Charles Pesnot, 1575.

————. *Methodus seu ratio compendiaria cognoscendi veram solidamque medicinam*. Parisiis: apud Jacobum Dupuys, 1550.

————. *Paradoxorum medicinae libri tres*. Basileae: ex aedibus Jo. Bebelii, 1535.

Fucilla, J. G. "Sources of du Bellay's *Contre les Pétrarquistes*," *Modern Philology*, 28 (1930–31), pp. 1–11.

Fulgentius, Fabius Planciades (fl. ca. 500). *Mitologiarum libri tres*. Trans. L. G. Whitbread as *Fulgentius the Mythographer*. Columbus: Ohio State University Press, 1971.

Fulgosius. *See* Fregoso, Giovan Battista.

Galen of Pergamon (ca. 129–199). *Ad Glauconem de methodo medendi*. In *Opera quae extant*, vol. 11. Ed. C. G. Kühn. Vols. 1–20 of the *Medicorum Graecorum*. Leipzig: Teubner, 1821–33.

————. *Adhortatio ad artes addiscendas*. In *Opera quae extant*, vol. 1. Ed. C. G. Kühn, 1821–33.

————. *Ad Thrasybulum liber, utrum medicinae sit an gymnastices hygiene*. In *Opera quae extant*, vol. 5. Ed. C. G. Kühn. Leipzig, 1821–33.

————. *Ars medica* (*Microtechni* or *Tegni Galieni*). In *Opera quae extant*, vol. 1. Ed. C. G. Kühn. Leipzig, 1821–33.

————. *Ars medicinalis*. In *Operum Galeni libri isagogici artis medicae*. Lugduni: apud Joannem Fellonium, 1550.

————. *Commentarium in Hippocratis prognostica*. In *Opera quae extant*, vol. 18/2. Ed. C. G. Kühn. Leipzig, 1821–33.

————. *De alimentorum facultatibus liber*. In *Opera quae extant*, vol. 6. Ed. C. G. Kühn. Leipzig, 1821–33.

————. *De atra bile liber*. In *Opera quae extant*, vol. 5. Ed. C. G. Kühn. Leipzig, 1821–33.

————. *De bono habitu liber*. In *Opera quae extant*, vol. 4. Ed. C. G. Kühn. Leipzig, 1821–33.

————. *De causis procatarcticis liber*. In *Galeni Opera*. Lugduni: apud Joannem Fellonium, 1550.

————. *De causis pulsuum*. In *Opera quae extant*, vol. 9. Ed. C. G. Kühn. Leipzig, 1821–33.

————. *De cognoscendis curandisque animi morbis*. In *Opera quae extant*, vol. 5. Ed. C. G. Kühn. Leipzig, 1821–33.

————. *De crisibus*. In *Opera quae extant*, vol. 9. Ed. C. G. Kühn. Leipzig, 1821–33.

————. *De diebus decretoriis liber*. In *Opera quae extant*, vol. 9. Ed. C. G. Kühn. Leipzig, 1821–33.

————. *De differentia pulsuum*. In *Opera quae extant*, vol. 8. Ed. C. G. Kühn. Leipzig, 1821–33.

————. *De difficultate respirationis*. In *Opera quae extant*, vol. 7. Ed. C. G. Kühn.

Leipzig, 1821–33.

————. *De dignotione ex in somniis.* In *Opera quae extant*, vol. 6. Ed. C. G. Kühn. Leipzig, 1821–33.

————. *De febrium differentiis liber.* In *Opera quae extant*, vol. 7. Ed. C. G. Kühn. Leipzig, 1821–33.

————. *De locis affectis.* In *Opera quae extant*, vol. 6. Ed. C. G. Kühn. Leipzig, 1821–33.

————. *De methodo medendi libri XIV.* In *Opera quae extant*, vol. 10. Ed. C. G. Kühn. Leipzig, 1821–33.

————. *De morborum differentiis.* In *Opera quae extant*, vol. 6. Ed. C. G. Kühn. Leipzig, 1821–33.

————. *De motu musculorum.* In *Opera quae extant*, vol. 4. Ed. C. G. Kühn. Leipzig, 1821–33.

————. *De optima secta ad Thrasybulum liber.* In *Opera quae extant*, vol. 1. Ed. C. G. Kühn. Leipzig, 1821–33.

————. *De placitis Hippocratis et Platonis.* In *Opera quae extant*, vol. 5. Ed. C. G. Kühn. Leipzig, 1821–33.

————. *De praenotione ad Posthumum.* In *Opera quae extant*, vol. 14. Ed. C. G. Kühn. Leipzig, 1821–33.

————. *De praesagitione ex pulsu.* In *Opera quae extant*, vol. 9. Ed. C. G. Kühn. Leipzig, 1821–33.

————. *De sanitate tuenda.* In *Opera quae extant*, vol. 6. Ed. C. G. Kühn. Leipzig, 1821–33.

————. *De symptomatum causis liber.* In *Opera quae extant*, vol. 7. Ed. C. G. Kühn. Leipzig, 1821–33.

————. *De temperamentis.* In *Opera quae extant*, vol. 1. Ed. C. G. Kühn. Leipzig, 1821–33.

————. *De theriaca ad Pisonem liber.* In *Opera quae extant*, vol. 14. Ed C. G. Kühn. Leipzig, 1821–33.

————. *De usu partium.* In *Opera quae extant*, vols. 3–4. Ed. C. G. Kühn. Leipzig, 1821–33.

————. *De uteri dissectione liber.* In *Opera quae extant*, vol. 2. Ed. C. G. Kühn. Leipzig, 1821–33.

————. *Hippocratis epidemiorum I et Galeni in illum commentarius.* In *Opera quae extant*, vol. 17. Ed. C. G. Kühn. Leipzig, 1821–33.

————. *In Hippocratis aphorismos commentarius.* In *Opera quae extant*, vol 17. Ed. C. G. Kühn. Leipzig, 1821–33.

————. *In Hippocratis de victu acutorum commentatia IV.* Ed. G. Helmereich. *Corpus medicorum Graecorum*, vol. 5. Leipzig: Teubner, 1914.

————. *In Hippocratis prognostica commentarius.* In *Opera quae extant*, vol. 17/2. Ed. C. G. Kühn. Leipzig, 1821–33.

————. *On Seminal Fluids.* In *Opera quae extant*, vol. 4. Ed. C. G. Kühn. Leipzig, 1821–33.

————. *On the Affected Parts.* Trans. Rudolph E. Siegel. Basel: S. Karger, 1976.

————. *On the Passions and Errors of the Soul.* Trans. P. W. Hankins. Columbus: Ohio State University Press, 1963.

————. *On the Usefulness of the Parts.* Trans. Margaret Tallmadge May. 2 vols. Ithaca, N.Y.: Cornell University Press, 1968.

————. *Opere scelte de Galeno*. Trans. Ivan Garofalo and Mario Vegeti. Turin: UTET, 1978.

————. *Prognostica de decubitu ex mathematica scientia*. In *Opera quae extant*, vol. 19. Ed. C. G. Kühn. Leipzig, 1821–33.

————. *Quod animi mores corporis temperamenta sequantur* (*That the faculties of the soul follow the temperament of the body*). In *Opera quae extant*, vol. 4. Ed. C. G. Kühn. Leipzig, 1821–33.

————. *Quomodo morbum simulantes sint deprehendendi libellus*. In *Opera quae extant*, vol. 19. Ed. C. G. Kühn. Leipzig, 1821–33.

————. *Quos, quibus catharticis medicamentis et quando purgare oporteat*. In *Opera quae extant*, vol. 11. Ed. C. G. Kühn. Leipzig, 1821–33.

Gallus, Gaius Cornelius (69–26 B.C.) *Catullus, Tibullus, Propertius cum Galli fragmentis*. Biponti: ex typographia societatis, 1783.

Garbers, Karl. *Isḥāq ibn 'Imrān, Maqālā fī l-mālīhūliyā und Constantini Africani libri duo de melancholia*. Hamburg: Buske, 1977.

Gaza of Thessalonica, Theodorus interpreter (ca. 1400–ca. 1475). *Aristotelis de natura animalium; eius dem de partibus animalium; —eiusdem de generatione animalium; Theophrasti historia plantarum; eiusdem de causis plantarum; Aritotelis problemata; Alexandri Aphrodisiensis problemata*. Venetiis: apud Aldum, 1504.

Gellius, Aulus (fl. 143). *Attic Nights*. Trans. John C. Rolfe. 3 vols. Loeb Classics, 1960.

Gerard of Berry (Gerardus Bituricensis; fl. 1230). *Commentary on the Viaticum*. Ed. Mary Francis Wack (from MS Basel D.III.6). In *Memory and Love in Chaucer's "Troilus and Criseyde."* Diss.: Cornell University, 1982, pp. 244–66.

Gerard of Solo (fl. 1335–50). *Determinationes de situ spiritus et amore hereos*. MS. Erfurt Ampl., F. 270, ff. 76v–78v.

————. *Introductiorium Juvenum . . . et regimine corporis humani in morbis. . . . Libellus de febribus. . . . Commentum super nono Almansoris cum textu. Commentum . . . super viatico cum textu*. Venetiis: per Bonetum Locatellum, 1505.

————. *Practica Almansoris liber nonus cum expositione*. Lugduni: per Franciscum Fradin, 1504.

Gervais of Tilbury (Gervasius; fl. 11th c.). *Otia imperialia*. Ed. Joachimo Joanne Madero. Helmaestadii: typis N. D. Mulleri, 1673.

Gesner, Konrad. *See* Moschion.

Giacomo da Lentini (fl. 13th c.). *Rime*. Ed. C. Antonelli. Rome: Bulzoni, 1979.

Giacosa, Piero. *Magistri salernitani nondum editi*. Turin: Fratelli Bocca, 1901.

Giedke, Adelheid. *Die Liebeskrankheit in der Geschichte der Medizin*. Diss.: University of Düsseldorf, 1983.

Gilbert, N. W. *Renaissance Concepts of Method*. New York: Columbia University Press, 1960.

Giorgio, Francesco (Francescus Venetus; 1460–1540). *In scripturam sacram problemata*. Venice, 1536.

Giovanni de Vigo. *See* Vigo, Giovanni de.

Giovio, Paolo (Paulus Jovius; 1483–1552). *Turcicorum rerum commentarius . . . ex Italico Latinus factus. Francisco Nigro Bassianate interprete*. In *Machumetis Saracenorum principis*. D. Petrus Abbas Cluniansis, 1550. (Orig. *Commentari delle cose de' Turchi*. Venice, 1541).

Giraldi, Lilio Gregorio (Gyraldus; 1479–1552). *De deis gentium libri sive syntagmata*

XVII. Lugduni: apud haeredes Jacobi Junctae, 1565.

————. *Historiae poetarum tam Graecorum quam Latinorum dialogi decem.* Basileae: sumptibus M. Isengrin, 1545.

Giuntini, Francesco (Junctinus; ca. 1523–90). *Speculum astrologiae universam mathematicum scientiam, in certas classes digestam complectens.* Lugduni: in officina Q. Phil. Tinghi, Florentini: apud Simphorianum Beraud, 1583.

Givry, Grillot de. *Witchcraft, Magic and Alchemy.* Trans. J. Courtney Locke, 1931; New York: Dover Publications, 1971.

Godefridus, Petrus (d. 1558). *Dialogus de amoribus, tribus libris distinctus.* Antverpiae: apud Gerardum Ludium, 1551 [?].

Godelmann, Johann Georg (1559–1611). *Tractatus de magis, veneficis et lamiis deque his recte cognoscendis et puniendis.* Francofurti: ex officina typographica Nicolai Bassaei, 1591.

Gorceix, Bernard. "La mélancolie au XVIe et XVIIe siècles: Paracelse et Jacob Bohme." *Recherches Germaniques*, 9 (1979), pp. 18–29.

Gorris, Jean de (Gorraeus; 1505–77). *Definitionen medicarum libri XXIV literis Graecis distincti.* Francofurdi: typis Wechelianis apud Claudium Marnium et heredes Joannis Aubrii, 1601.

Gradius, Joannis Mattei. *See* Ferrari da Grado, Giovanni Matteo.

Grasset, J. *Le médicin de l'Amour aux temps de Marivaux: Etude sur Boissier de Sauvages d'apres de documents inedits.* Montpellier: C. Coulet, 1896; Paris: G. Masson, 1896.

Greek Anthology. Trans. W. R. Paton. Loeb Classics, 1953.

Gregory I, Pope (540–604). *Dialogorum libri.* In *Opera omnia . . . studio et labore monachorum ordinis sancti Benedicti e congregatione sancti Mauri.* Parisiis: sumptibus Claudii Rigaud, 1705.

————. *Dialogues.* Trans. Odo John Zimmerman. New York: Fathers of the Church, 1959.

Grieve, Maud. *A Modern Herbal.* Ed. C. Hilda Leyel. London: Jonathan Cape, 1931; Harmondsworth: Penguin, 1982.

Grillando, Paolo. *Tractatus de hereticis, et sortilegiis.* Lugduni: apud Jacobum Giuncti, 1536.

Guainerio, Antonio (d. 1440). *Practica.* Ed. Hieronymus Faventinus (Girolamo Salio de Faenza?). Lugduni: in bibliotheca Constantini Fradin [1517].

Guarino of Favora (Varinus Favorinus; d. 1537). *Dictionarium multis variisque ex autoribus collectum totius linguae Graecae commentarius.* Basileae: R. Chimerinus, 1538.

Guastavini, Giulio (d. 1633). *Commentarii in priores decem Aristotelis Problematum sectiones.* Lugduni: sumptibus Horatii Cardon, 1608.

————. *Locorum de medicina selectorum liber.* 2 vols. Lugduni: sumptibus H. Cardon: Florentiae: ex typographia Sermartelliana, 1616–25.

Guglielmo da Saliceto (ca. 1210–ca. 1280). *Cyrurgia.* Venetiis: apud Octavianum Scotum, 1502.

Guglielmo da Varignana (ca. 1270–1339). [*Secreta medicine*], *ne secreta sublunia ad varios curandos morbos verissimis autoritatibus illustrata.* Vicentius de Portonariis de Tridino de Monte Ferrato, 1553.

Guibelet, Jourdain. *Trois discours philosophiques.* Evereux: Chez Antoine Le Marié, 1603.

Guinterius, Johannes. *See* Winter, Johann.

Haggard, Howard Wilcox. *Devils, Drugs and Doctors. The Story of the Science of Healing from Medicine-man to Doctor.* New York: Halcyon House, [1929].

Hall, A. Rupert. *The Revolution in Science 1500–1750.* London and New York: Longman, 1983.

Haly Abbas (Albohazen; Alī ibn al-'ábbās; d. 994). . . . *liber regalis dispositio nominatus i arte medicine completus (Liber medicinae dictus regius).* Venetiis: opera Bernardini Ricii de Novaria, 1492.

————. *Liber totius medicinae (al-Kitāb al-mālikī).* Trans. Stephen of Antioch. Lugduni: typis J. Myt, 1523.

————. *Pantegni (al-Kitāb al-mālikī)* in *Omnia Opera Ysaac.* A free Latin trans. by Constantinus Africanus. Lugduni: in officina Johannis de Platea, 1515.

Hamilton, Mary. *Incubation, or the Cure of Diseases in Pagan Temples and Christian Churches.* London: Simpkin, Marshall, Hamilton, Kent, 1906.

Hanlon, Gregory. *L'univers des gens de bien: Culture et comportements des élites urbaines en Agenais-Condomois au 17e siècle.* Diss., University of Bordeaux, 1985.

Harvey, Ruth E. *The Inward Wits: Psychological Theory in the Middle Ages and the Renaissance.* London: Warburg Institute, 1975.

Hedo (Haedo), Petrus. *See* Capretto, Pietro.

Herodotus (ca. 480–ca. 425 B.C.). [*History of Greece*]. Trans. A. D. Godley. Loeb Classics, 1963.

Héroët, Antoine (d. 1568). *Oeuvres poétiques.* Ed. Ferdinand Gohin. Paris: Société de textes Français modernes, Edouard Cornély et Cie, 1909.

Hesiod (8th c. B.C.). *The Homeric Hymns and Homerica.* Ed. Hugh G. Evelyn-White. Loeb Classics, 1950, 1982.

————. *Phythian.* Ed. M. Sommer. Paris: Hachette, 1847.

————. *Theogony.* Trans. Hugh G. Evelyn-White. Loeb Classics, 1950.

————. *Theogony.* Ed. and Intro. M. L. West. Oxford: Clarendon Press, 1966.

Hesychius Varinus of Alexandria (5th–6th cc.). *Lexicon.* Ed. K. Latte. Huniae: Ejner Munksgaard Editore, 1953.

————. *Lexicon.* Ed. M. Schmidt. Amsterdam: Adolf Hakkert, n.d.

————. *Lexicon cum variis doctorum virorum notis vel editis antehac, vel ineditis.* Lugduni Batavorum et Roter[dam]: ex officina Hackiana, 1668.

Heurne, Johann van (Johannes Heurnius; 1543–1601). *Methodi ad praxin.* In *Opera omnia.* Lugduni: sumptibus Joannis Antonii Hugetan & Marci Antonii Rivaud, 1658.

————. *De morbis in singulis partibus humani capitis.* Lugduni Batavorum: in officina Plantiniana, 1594.

————. *Praxis medicinae nova ratio qua libris tribus methodi ad praxin medicam, aditus facillimus aperitur ad omnes morbos curandos.* Lugduni Batavorum: ex officina Plantiniana, apud Franciscum Raphelengium, 1590.

Heurtebize, B. "Hugues de Saint-Victor." *Dictionnaire.* Paris: Librairie Letouzey et Avé, 1909–72.

Higinus, Gaius Julius. *See* Hyginus, Gaius Julius.

Hildegard of Bingen (1098–1179). *Causae et curae.* Ed. P. Kaiser. Leipzig: Teubner, 1903.

Hildesheim, Franz (1551–1614). *De cerebri et capitis morbis internis spicilegia.* Francofurti: sumptibus Egonolphi Emmelli, 1612.

Hine, William. "Marin Mersenne: Renaissance Naturalism and Renaissance Magic." *Occult and Scientific Mentalities in the Renaissance.* Ed. Brian Vickers. Cambridge: Cambridge University Press, 1984.

Hippocrates (b. ca. 460 B.C.). *Aphorismi Hippocratis Graecae et Latinae una cum Galeni commentariis, interprete Nicolao Leoniceno Vincentino.* Parisiis: ex officina Jacobi Bogardi, 1542.

————. *Aphorisms.* In *Oeuvres complètes,* vol. 4. Ed. E. Littré. Amsterdam: Adolf Hakkert, 1978.

————. *Coan Prognoses.* In *Oeuvres complètes,* vol. 4. Ed. E. Littré. Amsterdam: Adolf Hakkert, 1978.

————. *De natura hominis.* In *Hippocrates,* vol. 1. Ed. W. H. S. Jones. Loeb Classics, 1962.

————. *Discourse on Madness.* In *Oeuvres complètes,* vol. 9. Ed. E. Littré. Amsterdam: Adolf Hakkert, 1821–33.

————. *Epidemics.* In *Oeuvres complètes,* vol. 5. Ed. E. Littré. 10 vols. Amsterdam: Adolf Hakkert, 1978.

————. *Epistle to Damagete.* In *Oeuvres complètes,* vol. 9. Ed. E. Littré. Amsterdam: Adolf Hakkert, 1978.

————. "Hippocrates to Philopemen." In *Oeuvres complètes,* vol. 9. Ed. E. Littré. Amsterdam: Adolf Hakkert, 1978.

————. "Letter from Democritus." In *Oeuvres complètes,* vol. 9. Ed. E. Littré. Amsterdam: Adolf Hakkert, 1978.

————. "Letter to Cratevas." In *Oeuvres complètes,* vol. 9. Ed. E. Littré. Amsterdam: Adolf Hakkert, 1978.

————. *Of Airs, Waters and Places.* In *Oeuvres complètes,* vol. 2. Ed. E. Littré. Amsterdam: Adolf Hakkert, 1978.

————. *On the Diseases of Women.* In *Oeuvres complètes,* vol. 5. Ed. E. Littré. Amsterdam: Adolf Hakkert, 1978.

————. *On the Diseases of Young Women.* In *Oeuvres complètes,* vol. 8. Ed. E. Littré. Amsterdam: Adolf Hakkert, 1978.

————. *On Food.* In *Oeuvres complètes,* vol. 9. Ed. E. Littré. Amsterdam: Adolf Hakkert, 1978.

————. *On Generation.* In *Oeuvres complètes,* vol. 7. Ed. E. Littré. Amsterdam: Adolf Hakkert, 1978.

————. *On Glands.* In *Oeuvres complètes,* vol. 5. Ed. E. Littré. Amsterdam: Adolf Hakkert, 1978.

————. *On Internal Infections.* In *Oeuvres complètes,* vol. 7. Ed. E. Littré. Amsterdam: Adolf Hakkert, 1978.

————. *On Regimen in Acute Diseases.* In *Oeuvres complètes,* vol. 2. Ed. E. Littré. Amsterdam: Adolf Hakkert, 1978.

————. *On the Humors.* In *Oeuvres complètes,* vol. 5. Ed. E. Littré. Amsterdam: Adolf Hakkert, 1978.

————. *On the Joints.* In *Oeuvres complètes,* vol. 4. Ed. E. Littré. Amsterdam: Adolf Hakkert, 1978.

————. *On the Nature of Man.* In *Oeuvres complètes,* vol. 6. Ed. E. Littré. Amsterdam: Adolf Hakkert, 1978.

————. *On the Proper Behavior.* In *Oeuvres complètes,* vol. 9. Ed. E. Littré. Amsterdam: Adolf Hakkert, 1978.

———. *On the Sacred Disease*. In *Oeuvres complètes*, vol. 6. Ed. E. Littré. Amsterdam: Adolf Hakkert, 1978.

———. *On Wind (De flatibus)*. In *Oeuvres complètes*, vol. 6. Ed. E. Littré. Amsterdam: Adolf Hakkert, 1978.

———. *Opera omnia*. Ed. Anuce Foës. Francofurdi: apud Andreae Wechli heredes, 1595.

———. ΠΕΡΙ ΧΥΜΩΝ. In *Hippocrates*, vol. 4. Trans. W. H. S. Jones. Loeb Classics, 1962.

———. *Prognostics*. In *Oeuvres complètes*, vol. 2. Ed. E. Littré. Amsterdam: Adolf Hakkert, 1978.

———. *Regimen*. In *Oeuvres complètes*, vol. 6. Ed. E. Littré. Amsterdam: Adolf Hakkert, 1978.

———. *Regimen IV or Dreams*. In *Oeuvres complètes* vol. 6. Ed. E. Littré. Amsterdam: Adolf Hakkert, 1978.

———. *Regimen IV or Dreams*. Trans. W. H. S. Jones. Loeb Classics, 1967.

———. *The Sacred Disease*. In *Hippocrates*, vol. 2. Trans. W. H. S. Jones. Loeb Classics, 1952.

Hollerius, Jacobus. *See* Houllier, Jacques.

Homer (ca. 9th c. B.C.). *The Iliad*. Trans. A. T. Murray. 2 vols. Loeb Classics, 1967.

———. *The Odyssey*. Trans. A. T. Murray. Loeb Classics, 1966.

Horace (Quintus Horatius Flaccus; 65–8 B.C.). *Carmina*. Ed. E. C. Wickham. Oxford: Clarendon Press, 1898.

———. *Epistles*. In *The Complete Works of Horace*. Trans. C. E. Passage. New York: Frederick Ungar, 1983.

———. *Odes*. Trans. C. E. Bennett. Loeb Classics, 1968.

———. *Satires, Epistles and Ars Poetica*. Trans. H. Rushton Fairclough. Loeb Classics, 1961.

Horst, Gregor (Horstius; 1578–1638). *Dissertatio de natura amoris, additis resolutionibus quaestionum candidatorum de cura furoris amatorii, de philtris, atque de pulsu amantium*. Giessae: typis et sumptibus Casparis Chemlini, 1611.

———. *Observationum medicinalium singularum libri IV*. Ulmae: typis Saurianis, 1628.

Houllier, Jacques (Jacobus Hollerius; 1509–62). *De morbis internis libri II*. Parisiis: apud Carolum Macaeum, 1577.

Hoyt, R. S. *Europe in the Middle Ages*. New York: Harcourt, Brace, 1954.

Huarte de San Juan, Juan (fl. 16th c.). *Examen de ingenios para las ciencias*. Baeza: n.p., 1575; rpt. 1593, 1603.

———. *The Examination of Men's Wits*. Trans. Richard Carew. London: Adam Islip for Thomas Man, 1594.

Hugh of Saint Victor (1096–1141). *De anima libri quatuor*. In *Opera omnia tribus tomis digesta*. Rothomagi: sumptibus Joannis Berthelin, 1648.

Hyginus, Gaius Julius (ca. 64 B.C.–A.D. 17). *Fabularum liber ad omnium poetarum lectionem mire necessarius et nunc denua excusus*. Lugduni: apud Joannem Degabiano, 1608.

———. *Fabulae*. Ed. H. I. Rose. Lugduni Batavorum: in aedibus A. W. Sijthoff, 1967.

————. *The Myths of Hyginus*. Trans. Mary Grant. Lawrence: University of Kansas Publications, 1960.

Ibn Eddjezzar (Abu Jafar Aḥmed ibn Ibrāhīm ibn 'Alī Khālid). *Zād al-musāfir*. *See* Constantinus Africanus. *Viaticum*.

Ibn Ḥazm al-Andalusī, 'Ali Ben Abmed. *A Book Containing the Risala Known as the Dove's Neck-Ring about Love and Lovers*. Trans. A. R. Nykl. Paris, 1931.

————. *Halsband der Taube. Uber die Liebe und die Liebenden (Tauq al-hamāma)*. Trans. M. Weisweiler. Leiden, 1941.

Innocent V, Pope (Peter of Tarentaise; 1225–76). *In IV libros sententiarum commentaria*. Tolosae: apud Arnaldum Colomerium, 1652.

Irsay, Stephen d'. *Histoire des universités françaises et étrangères des origines à nos jours*. Paris: A. Picard, 1933–35.

Isidore of Seville (ca. 560–636). *The Medical Writings*. Ed. W. D. Sharpe. Philadelphia: American Philosophical Society, 1964.

Jackson, Stanley W. *Melancholia and Depression from Hippocratic Times to Modern Times*. New Haven and London: Yale University Press, 1986.

Jacquart, Danielle. *Le milieu médical en France du XIIe au XVe siècles*. Genève: Droz, 1981.

————. "Le regard d'un médecin sur son temps: Jacques Despars (1380?–1458)." *Bibliothèque de l'Ecole des Chartes*, 138 (1980), pp. 35–86.

————, and Claude Thomasset. "L'amour 'heroique' à travers le traité d'Arnaud de Villeneuve." In *La folie et le corps*. Ed. Jean Céard. Paris: Presses de l'école normale supérieure, 1985.

Jalāl al-Dīn Rūmī, Mawlānā (1207–1273). *The Mathnawī of Jalālu'ddīn Rūmī*. Trans. Reynold A. Nicholson. London: Luzac, 1925–40.

Jason Pratensis. *See* van der Velde, Jason.

Jerome, St. (Hieronymus; ca. 342–420). *Ad Geruntii Filias de contemnenda haereditate*. In *Opera*, vol. 5. Parisiis: apud Claudium Rigaud, 1706.

————. *Adversus Jovinianum libri duo*. In *Oeuvres complètes*. Trans. L'Abbé Bareille. 18 vols. Paris: Louis Vivès, 1877–85.

————. "Epistola XVIII ad Eustochium, de custodia virginitatis." In *Opera*, vol. 4. Parisiis: apud Claudium Rigaud, 1706.

————. "Epistola X ad Paulum senem concordiae." In *Opera*, vol. 4. Parisiis: apud Claudium Rigaud, 1706.

Johann von Tritheim (1462–1516). *Steganographia. Hoc est ars per occultam scripturam animi sui voluntatem absentibus aperiendi certa*. Darmbstadii: ex officina typographica Balthasaris Aulaeandri; sumptibus vero Joannis Berni, 1621.

Jones, Ernest. *On the Nightmare*. 1931; New York: Grove Press, 1954.

Jones, Richard Foster. *Ancients and Moderns: A Study of the Rise of the Scientific Movement in Seventeenth-Century England*. 1936; rpt. New York: Dover Publications, 1982.

Josephus, Flavius (37–ca. 100). *Antiquities of the Jews*. Trans. William Whiston. New York: Worthington, 1890.

Joubert, Laurent (1529–83). *Erreurs populaires au fait de la médecine et régime de santé*. Paris: Chez Claude Micard, 1578.

————. *Le premier et seconde partie des Erreurs populaires touchant la médecine et régime de la santé*. Paris: Chez Claude Micard, 1587.

Jovius, Paulus. *See* Giovio, Paolo.

Julian the Apostate (Flavius Claudius Julianus; fl. 360). *The Orations and Satires of the Emperor Julian.* Trans. W. C. Wright. Loeb Classics, 1913–23.

Junctinus. *See* Giuntini, Francesco.

Justinian I (483–565). *Corpus juris civilis. The Institutions of Justinian.* Trans. J. B. Moyle. 5th ed. Oxford: Clarendon Press, 1955.

————. *Institutionum juris, libri IV.* Genevae: apud Eustathium Vignon, 1580.

Juvenal (Decimus Junius Juvenalis; fl. 98–128). *Satires.* In *Juvenal and Persius.* Trans. G. G. Ramsay. Loeb Classics, 1961.

Keats, John. *The Poetical Works.* Ed. Lord Houghton. London: George Bell and Sons, 1897.

Kennedy, Ruth Lee. "The Theme of 'Stratonice' in the Drama of the Spanish Peninsula." *PMLA*, 55 (1940), pp. 1010–32.

King, Lester S. *The Growth of Medical Thought.* Chicago: University of Chicago Press, 1963.

Kinsman, Robert S. "Folly, Melancholy, and Madness: A Study in Shifting Styles of Medical Analysis and Treatment 1450–1675." *The Darker Vision of the Renaissance.* Berkeley and Los Angeles: University of California Press, 1974.

Klibansky, Raymond, Erwin Panofsky and Fritz Saxl. *Saturn and Melancholy.* London: Nelson, 1964.

Kornmann, Heinrich (fl. 1607). *Linea amoris, sive commentarius in versiculum gl[ossae] visus.* Francofurti: typis M. Beckeri, 1610.

————. *Sibylla trygandriana seu de virginitate, virginum statu et iure tractatus.* Francofurti: apud haeredes Jac. Fischeri, 1629.

Kramer, Heinrich (d. 1505), and James Sprenger (ca. 1436–95). *The Malleus Maleficarum.* Trans. Montague Summers. London: John Rodker, 1928; rpt. New York: Dover Publications, 1977.

Krantz, Albert (d. 1517). *Rerum germanicarum liber.* Francofurti: ad Moenum apud A. Wechelum, 1580.

Kristeller, Paul Oskar. *Renaissance Thought: The Classic, Scholastic and Humanist Strains.* New York: Harper and Row, 1961.

————. "The School of Salerno, Its Development and Its Contribution to the History of Learning." *Bulletin of the History of Medicine*, 17 (1945).

Kushner, Eva. "Pontus de Tyard entre Ficin et Léon l'Hébreu." *Ficino and Renaissance Neoplatonism.* Ed. Konrad Eisenbichler and Olga Zorzi Pugliese. Ottawa: Dovehouse Editions, 1986.

Lactantius Firmianus (Lucius Caecilius Firmianus; b. ca. 250). *The Divine Institutes.* Trans. Sister Mary Francis McDonald. Washington: D.C.: The Catholic University of America Press, 1964.

L'Alemant, Adrien (1527–1559). *Hippocratis de aere, aquis et locis . . . ab Adriano Alemano liber commentariis quatuor illustratus.* Parisiis: apud Aegidium Gorbinum, 1557.

Lamandus, Joannes (fl. early 17th c.). *Theses medicae de natura amoris et amantium amentium cura.* Basileae: typis Ioh. Iacobi Genathi, 1614.

Lancelloti, Secondo (1575–1643). *L'Hoggidí, overo il mondo non peggiore ne più calamitoso del passato.* Venezia: appresso gli G. Guerigli, 1636–37.

Lancre, Pierre de (1553–1631). *Tableau de l'inconstance des mauvais anges et démons.* Paris: Chez Nicolas Buon, 1612.

————. *Tableau de l'inconstance des mauvais anges et démons* (abridged). "Introduction critique," Nicole Jacques-Chaquin. Paris: Editions Aubier Montaigne, 1982.

Landi, Ortensio (Philalethe Polytopiensi; ca. 1512–ca. 53). *Forcianae quaestiones, in quibus veria Italorum ingenia explicantur.* Ed. Antiochus Lavintus. Neapoli: excudebat Martinus de Ragusia, 1536.

————. *Questions diverses, et responces d'icelles, divisées en trois livres. A sçavoir, questions d'amour, questions naturelles, questions morales et politiques. Traduites de tuscan en françois.* Rouen: Chez P. Daré, 17th c.

Lange, Johannes (Langius; 1485–1565). *Medicinalium epistolarum miscellanea.* Basileae: apud I. Oporinum, 1544.

La Palud, Pierre de (Petrus Paludanus; d. 1342). *In quartum sententiarum.* Venetiis: impressum per B. Locatellum, mandato O. Scoti, 1493.

Lasserre, F. *La figure d'Éros dans la poésie grecque.* Lausanne: Impr. réunies, 1946.

Le Caron, Loys (Charondas; 1536–1617). *Questions divers et discours.* Paris: n.p., 1579.

L'Ecluse, Charles (Carolus Clusius; 1526–1609). *Atrebatis exoticorum liber decimus, sive simplicium medicamentorum ex nove orbe delatorum, quorum in medicina usus est, historia, Hispanico sermone tribus libris descripta à D Nicolae Monardo.* [Antverpiae]: ex officina Plantiniana, Raphelengii, 1605.

————. *Rariorum plantarum historia.* Antverpiae: ex officina Plantiniana, apud Joannem Moretum, n.d.

Le Long, Michel. *See* [Salerno].

Le Loyer, Pierre, Sieur de la Brosse (1550–1643). *Discours et histoires des spectres, visions et apparitions des esprits, anges, demons et ames, se monstrans visibles aux hommes, divisez en huict livres.* Paris: Chez Nicolas Buon, 1605.

Lemay, Helen Rodnite. "Human Sexuality in Twelfth- through Fifteenth-Century Scientific Writings." In *Sexual Practices and the Medieval Church.* Eds. Vern L. Bullough and James Brundage. Buffalo, N.Y.: Prometheus Books, 1982.

————. "William of Saliceto on Human Sexuaity." *Viator,* 12 (1981), pp. 165–81.

Lemnius, Levinus (1505–68). *Occulta naturae miracula, ac varia rerum documenta.* Antverpiae: apud Guilielmum Simonem, 1561.

————. *Occulta naturae miracula, ac varia rerum documenta probabili ratione atque artifici coniectura explicata.* Gandavi: ex officina Gisleni Manilii, 1572.

————. *The Secret Miracles of Nature; in four books.* London: J. Streater, 1658.

————. *The Touchstone of Complexions.* Trans. Thomas Newton. London: Thomas Marsh, 1576.

Leon Hebraeus. *See* Abravanel, Judah.

Leonidas of Alexandria (fl. 274 B.C.). In the *Greek Anthology,* vol. 3. Trans. W. R. Paton. Loeb Classics, 1948.

Le Roy, Louis (Ludovicus Regius; 1510–77). *Le Sympose de Platon, ou de l'amour et de beauté, traduit de grec en françois, avec trois livres de commentaires.* Paris: Sertenas, 1559.

Le Roy Ladurie, Emmanuel. *Histoire du Languedoc.* Paris: Presses Universitaires de France, 1962.

L'Estoile, Pierre de (1546–1611). *Journal pour le règne de Henri IV.* Ed. L. R. Lefèvre. 2 vols. Paris: Gallimard, 1948–58.

Letourneau, Dr. "De la maladie d'amour, ou mélancholie érotique." *L'Union Médicale,* 79 (2 Juillet, 1863). pp. 1–10.

Levi, Anthony. *French Moralists: the Theory of the Passions from 1585 to 1649.* Oxford: Clarendon Press, 1964.

Lewis, Walter H., and Memory P. F. Lewis. *Medical Botany.* New York: John Wiley & Sons, 1977.

Liébault, Jean (ca. 1535–96). *Trois livres appartenans aux infirmitez et maladies des femmes pris du latin de M. Jean Liebaut.* Lyon: par Jean Veyrat, 1598.

Livy (Titus Livius; 59 B.C.–A.D. 17). *[Histories].* Trans. B. O. Foster. Loeb Classics, 1963.

Lochner, Michael Frederich (1662–1720). *De nymphomania.* Altdorfii: typis Henrici Meyeri [1684].

Longinus, Dionysius (attributed to; 1st–2d cc.). *A Treatise Concerning Sublimity.* Ed. D. A. Russell. Oxford, Clarendon Press, 1967.

———. (attributed to). *On the Sublime.* Trans. G. M. A. Grube. New York: Bobbs-Merrill, 1957.

Lowes, John Livingston. "The Loveres Maladye of Hereos." *Modern Philology,* 11 (1914), pp. 491–546.

L. P., London Pharmacopoeia. See Pharmacopoeia Londinensis.

Lucian (Lucidnus Loukianos; ca. 115–ca. 200). *Complete Works.* Trans. Thomas Francklin. London, 1781.

———. *Dialogues of the Gods (Deorum dialogi).* Trans. M. D. MacLeod. 8 vols. Loeb Classics, 1961.

———. *Icaromenippus,* vol. 6. In *Lucian.* Trans. A. M. Harmon. 8 vols. Loeb Classics, 1962.

———. *Toxaris, or Friendship,* vol. 5. In *Lucian.* Trans. A. M. Harmon. 8 vols. Loeb Classics, 1962.

Luck, Georg. *Arcana Mundi: Magic and the Occult in the Greek and Roman Worlds.* Baltimore: Johns Hopkins University Press, 1985.

Lucretius (Titus Lucretius Carus; ca. 99–ca. 55 B.C.). *De rerum natura.* Trans. W. H. D. Rouse, Loeb Classics, 1966, 1975.

———. *On the Nature of Things (De rerum natura).* Ed. Cyril Bailey. Oxford: Clarendon Press, 1963.

Lyons, Bridget Gellert. *Voices of Melancholy: Studies in Literary Treatments of Melancholy in Renaissance England.* London: Routledge and Kegan Paul, 1971.

MacDonald, Michael. *Mystical Bedlam: Madness, Anxiety, and Healing in Sixteenth-Century England.* Cambridge: Cambridge University Press, 1981.

McIntosh, Christopher. *The Astrologers and Their Creed: An Historical Outline.* London: Hutchinson, 1969.

MacKinney, Loren Carey. *Early Medieval Medicine with Special Reference to France and Chartres.* Baltimore: Johns Hopkins University Press, 1937.

Macrobius Theodosius (fl. 400). *Commentary on Scipio's Dream.* Trans. William Harris Stahl. New York and London: Columbia University Press, 1952.

Maffei of Volterra, Raffaele (Volaterranus; 1451–1522). *Commentariorum urbanorum libri XXXVIII.* Venundantur Parrhasiis in via Jacobea ab Joanne Parvo et Jodoco Badio Ascensio, 1511.

Malleus maleficarum. See Kramer, Heinrich.

Manardo, Giovanni (1462–1536). *Epistolae medicinales diversorum authorum.* Lugduni: apud haeredes Jacobi Juntae, 1557.

Mandrou, Robert. *From Humanism to Science 1480–1700.* Trans. Brian Pierce.

Atlantic Highlands, N.J.: Humanities Press, 1979.

————. *Introduction à la France moderne 1500–1640.* Paris: Éditions Albin Michel, 1961.

————. *Magistrats et Sorciers en France au XVIIe siècle.* Paris: Librairie Plon, 1968.

Mantuanus. *See* Spagnuoli, Giovanni Battista.

Marcianus. *The Civil Code (Institutes).* Ed. S. P. Scott. 17 vols. Cincinnati: Central Trust, 1932.

Marcuse, Herbert. *Eros and Civilization: A Philosphical Inquiry into Freud.* Boston: Beacon Press, 1955.

Marguerite d'Angoulême, Queen of Navarre (1492–1549). *The Heptameron of Margaret, Queen of Navarre.* Trans. Walter K. Kelley. London: for the trade, n.d.

————. *Nouvelles.* Ed. Yves Le Hir. Paris: Presses Universitaires de France, 1967.

Marinelli, Giovanni (fl. 16th c.). *Le medicine partenenti alle infermità delle donne.* Venetia: apresso Giovanni Valgrisio, 1574.

Martial (Marcus Valerius Martialis; ca. 40–104). *Epigrams.* Trans. Walter C. A. Ker. 2 vols. Loeb Classics, 1961.

Martin, H.-J., "What Parisians Read in the Sixteenth Century." *French Humanism 1470–1600,* ed. Werner Gundersheimer, 131–45. London: Macmillan, 1969.

Massinger, Philip (1583–1640). *The Virgin Martyr.* [In *Selected Works*]. Ed. Arthur Symons. 2 vols. London: Vizetelly, 1889.

Masters, R. E. L. *Eros and Evil: The Sexual Psychopathology of Witchcraft.* New York: Matrix House, 1966.

Mattioli, Pietro Andrea. *See* Dioscorides.

Maximus of Tyre (Maximus Tyrius). *Dissertationes XLI graece.* Ed. Daniel Heinsius. Lugduni Batavorum: apud I. Patium, 1607.

————. *The Dissertations.* Trans. Thomas Taylor. 2 vols. London: C. Whittingham, 1804.

————. *Traitez de Maxime de Tyr autheur grec, qui sont quarante et un discours mis en françois* [by Guillebert]. Rouen: J. Osmont, 1617.

Medina, P. Miguel (1489–1578). *Christianae paraenesis, sive de recta in Deum fide libri septem.* Venetiis: ex officina J. Zileti, 1564.

Menander (ca. 342–292 B.C.). *The Principal Fragments.* Trans. Francis G. Allinson. Loeb Classics, 1964.

————. *Sententiae ex codicibus Byzantinis.* Ed. S. Jaekel. Leipzig: Teubner, 1964.

Mercado, Luis (Ludovicus Mercatus; 1520–1606). *De internorum morborum curatione libri IV.* In *Opera.* Francofurti: sumptibus haeredum D. Zachariae Palthenii, 1620.

————. *De morbis haereditariis.* In *Opera,* vol. 2. Francofurti: sumptibus haeredum D. Zachariae Palthenii, 1620.

————. *De mulierum affectionibus libri quatuor.* In *Opera,* vol. 3. Francofurti: sumptibus haeredum D. Zachariae Palthenii, 1620.

Mercuriale, Girolamo (1530–1606). *Commentarii eruditissimi in Hippocratis . . . prognostica, prorrhetica, de victus ratione, in morbis acutis, et epidemicas historias.* Francofurti: typis Joannis Saurii, 1602.

————. *De morbis muliebribus libri IV.* Venetiis: apud Felicem Valgrisium, 1587.

————. *De morbis muliebribus libri IV.* In *Gynaeciorum sive de mulierum affectibus commentarii.* Ed. Israel Spachius. Basileae: apud Conradum Waldkirch, 1596.

————. *Medicina practica . . . libri IV*. Francofurdi: in officina Joannis Schonwetteri, 1602.

————. *Variarum lectionum libri quatuor*. Venetiis: sumptibus Pauli et Antonii Meieti fratres librarii Patavini, 1571.

Meres, Francis (1565–1647). *Palladis Tamia*. London: P. Short for Cuthbert Burbie, 1598.

Mexía, Pedro (Pierre Messie). *Les diverse leçons*. Lyon: par Claude Michel, 1526.

————. *Les diverses leçons . . . contenans de variables histoires et autres choses mémorables*. Trans. Cl. Gruget. Paris: V. Sertenas, 1556.

Mizauld, Antoine (Mizaldus; d. 1578). *L'explication, usage, et practique de l'Epheme-ride celeste*. Paris: Chez Jacques Kerver, 1556.

Monardes, Nicholas of Seville (1493–1558). *Joyfull Newes out of the Newe Found Worlde* (*Historia medicinal de los coses que traen de nuestras Indias occidentales que sirven en medicina*). Trans. John Frampton. London, 1557; New York: AMS Press, 1967.

Montaigne, Michel de (1533–92). *Essais*. Ed. Maurice Rat. Paris: Garniers Frères, 1962.

————. *Essays*. Trans. John Florio. Ed. Desmond MacCarthy. 3 vols. London: J. M. Dent and Sons, 1928.

Montalto, Filoteo Elião de (Aelianus Montaltus; d. 1616). *Archipathologia, in qua internarum capitis affectionum essentia, causae, signa, praesagia et curatio . . . edisserunter*. Lutetiae: apud F. Jacquin, sumptibus Caldorianae societatis, 1614.

More, Thomas (1477–1535). *The Complete Works*. Ed. Clarence H. Miller et al. New Haven: Yale University Press, 1984.

Mornay, Philippe de (1549–1623). *The True Knowledge of Mans Owne Selfe*. Trans. Anthony Munday. London: printed by I. R. for William Leake, 1602.

Morris, Desmond. *Manwatching: A Field Guide to Human Behavior*. St. Albans: n.p., 1978.

Moschion (Mustio). *De morbis muliebribus liber, graece cum scholiis et emendationibus Conradi Gesneri*. Basileae: Th. Guarin, 1566.

Moschus (ca. 150 B.C.). In the *Greek Anthology*, vol. 3. Trans. W. R. Paton. 5 vols. Loeb Classics, 1948.

Muret, Marc-Antoine (Marcus Antonius Muretus; 1526–1585). *Opera omnia*. Ed. C.-H. Frotscher. Genève: Slatkine Reprints, 1971.

————. *Variarum lectionum libri XV*. Antverpiae: apud Christophorum Platinum, 1587.

Murphy, James. *Rhetoric in the Middle Ages: A History of Rhetorical Theory from St. Augustine to the Renaissance*. Berkeley: University of California Press, 1974.

Musaeus (4th-5th cc.). *The Loves of Hero and Leander*. Trans. Cedric Whitman. Loeb Classics, 1975.

Nardi, Bruno. "L'amore e i medici medievali." *Saggi e note di critica dantesca*. Milano-Napoli: Ricciardi, 1964: first published in *Studi in onore di Angelo Monteverdi*. Modena: S. T. E. M., 1959.

Nauclerus, Johannes. *See* Vergen, Johann.

Nelson, John Charles. *Renaissance Theory of Love: The Context of Giordano Bruno's "Eroici furori."* 1955; rpt. New York and London: Columbia University Press,

1963.

Nemesius of Emesa. *Of the Nature of Man* (*De natura hominis*). Trans. W. Telfer. *Cyril of Jerusalem and Nemesius of Emesa.* London: CCM Press, 1955.

Nicephorus Callistus Xanthopoulos of Constantinople (ca. 1256–ca. 1335). *L'histoire ecclesiastique.* Paris: Antoine le Blanc, 1587.

Neider (Nider), Johannes (d. 1438). *De maleficis et eorum deceptionibus.* In the *Malleus maleficarum ex plurimus auctoribus coacervatus.* Lugduni: apud P. Landry, 1615.

Nifo, Agostino (Niphus; ca. 1469–ca. 1546). *Medici libri duo, de Pulchro primus, de Amore secundus.* Lugduni: apud G. et M. Beringos fratres, 1549.

Nonnus of Panopolis (fl. 400). *Dyonisiaca.* Trans. W. H. D. Rouse. 3 vols. Loeb Classics, 1940.

Oppian of Cilicia (fl. 211–17). *Halieutica.* Trans. A. W. Mair. Loeb Classics, 1928.

Oribasius of Pergamon (326–403). *Synopsis.* In *Oeuvres.* Ed. U. C. Bussemaker and C. Daremberg. 7 vols. Paris: J. B. Baillière, 1851–76; Paris: Imprimerie National, 1873.

———. *Synopsis ad Eustathium.* Ed. I. Raeder. Leipzig: Teubner, 1926; rpt. Amsterdam: Adolf Hakkert, 1964.

Origen (185–254). *Contra Celsum.* Ed. H. Chadwick. Cambridge: Cambridge University Press, 1953.

Orléans, Louis d' (Dorléans, Ludovico; 1542–1629). *Novae cogitationes in libros Annalium C. Cornelii Taciti quae extant.* Parisiis: sumptibus T. Blasii, 1622.

Osler, Sir William, Edward Bensly and others. "Robert Burton and the *Anatomy of Melancholy.*" *Oxford Bibliographical Society Proceedings and Papers.* Ed. F. Madan. Oxford, 1927.

Otis, Brooks. *Ovid as an Epic Poet.* Cambridge: Cambridge University Press, 1966.

Otten, Charlotte F., ed. *A Lycanthropy Reader: Werewolves in Western Culture.* Syracuse: Syracuse University Press, 1986.

Ovid (Publius Ovidius Naso; 43 B.C.–A.D. 18). *Amores.* Trans. Grant Showerman. Loeb Classics, 1914.

———. *Amorum libri tres.* Ed. P. Brandt. Hildesheim: Georg Olms, 1963.

———. *The Art of Love, and Other Poems.* Trans. J. H. Mozley. Loeb Classics, 1962.

———. *Epistulae Heroidum.* Ed. Henricus Dörrie. Berlin: Walter de Gruyter, 1971.

———. *Heroides.* Ed. A. Palmer. Hildesheim: Georg Olms, 1967.

———. *The Metamorphoses.* Trans. Rolfe Humphries. Bloomington and London: Indiana University Press, 1967.

———. *Remedia amoris.* Ed. A. A. R. Henderson. Edinburgh: Edinburgh University Press, 1979.

———. *The Remedies of Love* (*Remedia amoris*). In *The Art of Love and Other Poems.* Trans. J. H. Mozley. Loeb Classics, 1962.

Pace, Giulio, interpreter (Julius Pacius de Berigo; 1550–1635). Aristotle. *Opera omnia quae extant, graece et latine.* Lutetiae Parisiorum, 1619.

Packard, Francis R. *Guy Patin and the Medical Profession in Paris in the XVIIth Century.* New York: 1924; rpt. New York: Augustus M. Kelley, Publishers, 1970.

Pacuvius, Marcus (ca. 220–ca. 130 B.C.). *Plays.* In *Remains of Old Latin*, vol. 2. Trans. E. H. Warmington. 4 vols. Loeb Classics, 1961.

Painter, William, trans. (ca. 1540–1594). *The Palace of Pleasure.* Ed. Joseph Jacobs. 3 vols. London: David Nutt, 1890; rpt. New York: Dover Publications, 1966.

Paludanus. *See* La Palud, Pierre de.

Paracelsus, Philippus Aureolus (Theophrastus Bombastus ab Hohenheim; 1493–1541). *De origine morborum invisibilium.* In *Opera omnia: medico-chemico-chirurgica, tribus voluminibus comprehensa.* Genevae: sumptibus I. Antonii et Samuelis De Tournes, 1658.

————. *Operum medico-chimicorum sive paradoxorum tomus genuinus sextus.* 4 vols. Francofurti: a collegio Musarum Palthenianarum, 1603–5.

Pardoux, Barthélemy (Bartholomaeus Perdulcis; 1545–1611). *De morbis animi liber.* Parisiis: L. Bollenger, 1639. Also in *Universa medicina.* Ed. Postrema. Lugduni: sumptibus Jacobi Carteron, 1649.

Paré, Ambroise (Pareus; 1510–90). "De la faculté et vertu de medicamens simples." In *Oeuvres complètes.* Ed. J.-F. Malgaigne. Paris: 1840–41; rpt. Genève: Slatkine Reprints, 1970.

————. *De monstres et prodiges.* In *Oeuvres complètes.* Ed. J.-F. Malgaigne. Genève: Slatkine Reprints, 1970.

————. *Oeuvres complètes.* Ed. J.-F. Malgaigne. Paris: 1840–41; rpt. Genève: Slatkine Reprints, 1970.

————. *On Monsters and Marvels.* Trans. Janis L. Pallister. Chicago: University of Chicago Press, 1982.

Parthenius of Nicea (fl. 50 B.C.). *Etymologicum genuinum.* In *The Love Romances of Parthenius and Other Fragments.* Ed. J. M. Edmonds. Loeb Classics, 1962.

Paul of Aegina (615–90). *Opera a Joanne Guinterio [Andernacus] conversa et illustrata commentariis.* Venetiis: apud F. Torrisanum, 1553. Greek original in vol. 9 of the *Corpus medicorum graecorum.* Ed. I. L. Heiberg. Leipzig: Teubner, 1921–24.

————. *The Seven Books.* Trans. Francis Adam. 3 vols. London: The Sydenham Society, 1844–47.

Pausanias (late 2d c.). *Description of Greece.* Trans. W. H. S. Jones. Loeb Classics, 1965.

Penot, Bernard (d. ca. 1617). *Tractatus varii, de vera praeparatione, et usu medicamentorum chymicorum.* Basileae: impensis Ludovico Regis, 1616.

Pereda, Pedro Pablo (Peredus; fl. 16th c.). *Michaelis Ioannis Paschalis methodum curandi scholia.* Lugduni: sumptibus Iacobi Cardon, 1630.

Pereira, Benito (ca. 1535–1610). *De magia, de observatione somniorum, et de divinatione astrologica libri tres.* Coloniae Agrippinae: apud Ioannem Gymnicum, 1598.

Perrier, François. "De l'érotomanie." *Le désir et la perversion.* Paris: Éditions du Seuil, 1967.

Petrarch, Francesco (1304–74). *Secretum.* In *Opere.* Ed. G. Ponte. Milano: Mursia, 1968.

————. *Trionfo d'Amore.* In *Opere.* Ed. G. Ponte. Milano: Mursia, 1968.

Petronius Arbiter, Gaius (d. 65). *Satyricon.* Trans. Michael Heseltine. Loeb Classics, 1939.

Petrus Apponensis. *See* D'Abano, Pietro.

Petrus de Palude, Patriarch of Jerusalem. *See* La Palud, Pierre de.

Pharmacopoeia Londinensis, 1618. Ed. George Urdang. Hollister Pharmaceutical Library Number Two. Madison: State Historical Society of Wisconsin, 1944.

Philodemus. In the *Greek Anthology*. Trans. W. R. Paton. Loeb Classics, 1948.

Philo of Alexandria (fl. 39). *Quod a deo mittantur somnia*. In *Les oeuvres de Philon D'Alexandrie*. Trans. Pierre Savinel. Paris: Éditions du Cerf, 1962.

Philostratus (2d–3d cc.). *Les Images* (*Eikones*). Trans. Blaise de Vigenère. Paris, 1614; rpt. New York: Garland Publishing, 1976.

―――. (attributed to). *Love Letters*. Ed. Allen Rogers and Francis H. Forbes. Loeb Classics, 1949.

Philostratus (III, known as the Athenian; 3d c.). *De la vie d'Appolonius Thyaneen en VIII livres*. Trans. Blaise de Vigenère. Paris: Chez la veufue Matthieu Guillemot, 1611.

―――. *In Honour of Appolonius of Tyana*. Trans. J. S. Phillimore. 2 vols. Oxford: Clarendon Press, 1912.

―――. *Life of Apollonius of Tyana*. Trans. F. C. Conybeare. 2 vols. Loeb Classics, 1960.

Phlegon of Tralles (fl. 2d c.). *De mirabilibus liber deest principium in Antigoni Corystii historiarum mirabilium collectanea*. Bound with Apollonius Dyscolus, *Historiae commentitiae liber*. Ed. Joannes Meursius. Lugduni Batavorum: apud Isaacum Elzevirium, 1620.

Piccolomini, Alessandro (1508–78). *Della institution morale*. Venetia: apresso Giordano Ziletti, 1569.

Piccolomini, Enea Silvio (Aeneas Sylvius; Pius II; 1405–64). *Historia Bohemica*. 1475; Basileae: Michael Furter, ca. 1489.

―――. *Le remède d'amour, translaté de latin en françoys par maistre Albin des Avenelles, avec les additions de Baptiste Mantuan*. Paris: 1556.

―――. *The Tale of Two Lovers* (*De duobus amantibus Eurialo et Lucrecia*). Trans. Flora Grierson. London: Constable, 1930.

―――. *Storia di due amanti e Rimedio d'amore*. Turin: U.T.E.T., 1973.

Pico della Mirandola, Giovanni (1463–94). *Disputationes adversus astrologiam*. Ed. Eugenio Garin. 3 vols. Firenze: Vallecchi Editore, 1946.

Pico della Mirandola, Giovanni Francesco (1470–1533). *De rerum praenotione libri novem*. Argentoraci: Joannes Knoblochus, 1507.

Pierius. *See* Valeriano Bolzani, Giovanni Pierio.

Pillorget, René. *La tige et le rameau: familles anglaise et française 16e-18e siècle*. Paris: Calmann-Lévy, 1979.

Pindar (522–ca. 442 B.C.). *The Odes*. Trans. Sir John Sandys. Loeb Classics, 1924; rpt. 1968.

Pineau, Severin (Pineus; d. 1619). *Opusculum physiologum et anatomicum*. Parisiis: ex typographia Stephanus Prenosteau, 1597.

Pius II, Pope. *See* Picclomini, Enea Sylvio.

Platina, Battista. *See* Secchi of Cremona, Bartolomeo.

Plato (c. 427–348 B.C.). *Cratylus*. Trans. H. N. Fowler. Loeb Classics, 1953.

―――. *Divini Platonis opera omnia Marsilio Ficino interprete*. Lugduni: apud Antonium Vincentium, 1557.

―――. *Eutyphro*. Trans. H. N. Fowler. Loeb Classics, 1966.

―――. *Laws*. Trans. R. G. Bury. Loeb Classics, 1971.

————. *Opera*. Ed. Joannes Burnet. Oxford: Clarendon Press, 1900–1907.

————. *Phaedrus*. Trans. Harold N. Fowler. Loeb Classics, 1953.

————. *Philebus*. Trans. Harold N. Fowler. Loeb Classics, 1962.

————. *Symposium*. Trans. W. R. M. Lamb. Loeb Classics, 1977.

————. *Theaetetus*. Trans. H. N. Fowler. Loeb Classics, 1961.

————. *Timaeus*. Trans. R. G. Bury. Loeb Classics, 1966.

Platter, Felix (1536–1614). *De mulierum partibus generationi dicatis accidentium*. In *Gynaelciorum sive de mulierum affectibus*. Ed. Israel Spachius. Basileae: per Conradum Waldkirch, 1586.

————. *Observationes et curationes aliquot affectuum partibus mulieris generationi dicitis accidentium*. In *Gynaeciorum sive de mulierum tum communibus*. Ed. Israel Spachius. Argentinae: sumptibus Lazari Zetneri, 1593.

————. *Observationum in hominis affectibus . . . libri tres*. Basileae: impensis Ludovici König, typis Conradi, 1614.

Plautus, Titus Maccus (ca. 254–184 B.C.). *The Comedy of Asses (Asinaria)*. In *Plautus*, vol. 1. Trans. Paul Nixon. 4 vols. London and New York: G. P. Putnam's Sons, 1916.

————. *Curculio*. In *Plautus*, vol. 2. Trans. Paul Nixon. 5 vols. Loeb Classics, 1963.

————. *Mercator*. In *Plautus*, vol. 3. Trans. Paul Nixon. 5 vols. Loeb Classics, 1963.

————. *Trinummus*. In *Plautus*, vol. 5. Trans. Paul Nixon. 5 vols. Loeb Classics, 1952.

Pliny the Elder (Gaius Plinius Secundus; 23–79). *Natural History*. Trans. H. Rackham, T. E. Page et al. Loeb Classics, 1961.

Plotinus (ca. 205–after 244). *Enneads*. Trans. Stephen MacKenna. London: Faber and Faber, 1969.

Plutarch (ca. 46–120). *Advice to Bride and Groom (Conjugalia praecepta)*. In *Moralia*, vol. 2. Trans. Frank Cole Babbitt. 15 vols. Loeb Classics, 1961.

————. *Beasts are Rational*. In *Moralia*, vol. 12. Trans. H. Cherniss and W. C. Helmbold. 15 vols. Loeb Classics, 1957.

————. *Bravery of Women*. In *Moralia*, vol. 3. Trans. Frank Cole Babbitt. 15 vols. Loeb Classics, 1961.

————. *De tuenda sanitate praecepta*. In *Moralia*, vol. 2. Trans. Frank Cole Babbitt. 15 vols. Loeb Classics, 1966.

————. *The Dialogue on Love*. In *Moralia*, vol. 9. Trans. W. C. Helmbold. 15 vols. Loeb Classics, 1969.

————. *Life of Alexander*. In *Lives*, vol. 7. Trans. Bernadotte Perrin. 11 vols. Loeb Classics, 1959.

————. *Life of Demetrius*. In *Lives*, vol. 9. Trans. Bernadotte Perrin. 11 vols. Loeb Classics, 1959.

————. *Life of Lucullus*. In *Lives*, vol. 3. Trans. Bernadotte Perrin. 11 vols. Loeb Classics, 1959.

————. *On Listening to Lectures (De recta ratione audendi)*. In *Moralia*, vol. 1. Trans. Frank Cole Babbitt. 15 vols. Loeb Classics, 1961.

————. *On Love*. In *Moralia*, vol. 13. Trans. E. L. Minar, F. H. Sandbach and W. C. Helmbold. 15 vols. Loeb Classics, 1961.

————. *Platonic Questions*. In *Moralia*, vol. 13. Trans. E. L. Minar, F. H. Sandbach and W. C. Helmbold. 15 vols. Loeb Classics, 1961.

———. *Progress in Virtue.* In *Moralia,* vol. 1. Trans. Frank Cole Babbitt. 15 vols. Loeb Classics, 1961.

———. *The Roman Questions.* In *Moralia,* vol. 4. Trans. Frank Cole Babbitt. 15 vols. Loeb Classics, 1962.

———. *Table-Talk.* In *Moralia,* vol. 8. Trans. Paul A. Clement. 15 vols. Loeb Classics, 1969.

———. *Vita Demitri.* Ed. K. Ziegler. Leipzig: Teubner, 1960.

Polemo, Antonius (Polemon; ca. 88–145). *Physiognomica.* In *Aristotle varia opuscula.* Francofurdi, 1587.

Pollux, Julius (fl. 180). *Onomasticum Graece et Latine.* Amstelaedami: ex officina Wetsteniana, 1706.

Polybius (brother-in-law of Hippocrates; fl. 5th c. B.C.). *The Sacred Disease.* In *Hippocrates,* vol. 2. Ed. W. H. S. Jones, Loeb Classics, 1962.

Pomponazzi, Pietro (1462–1525). *De naturalium effectuum admirandorum causis, sive de incantationibus liber.* In *Opera.* Basileae: ex officina Henricpetrina, 1567.

———. *Les causes des merveilles de la nature, ou les enchantements.* Trans. Henri Busson. Paris: Reider, 1930.

Porphyrius (233–ca. 301). *Life of Plotinus.* In Plotinus, *The Ethical Treatises.* Trans. Stephan MacKenna. London: P. L. Warner, 1917.

Postel, Guillaume (1510–81). *De la republique des Turcs: et là ou l'occasion s'offrera, des meurs et loys de tous muhamedistes.* Poitiers: de l'imprimerie Enguilbert de Marnes, n.d.

Pozzi, Mario. *Trattati d'amore del Cinquecento.* Roma-Bari: Laterza, 1975.

Pratis (Pratensis), Jason. *See* van der Velde, Jason.

Prieur, Claude (fl. 16th c.). *Dialogue de la lycanthropie ou transformation d'hommes en loups.* Louvain: Chez I. Maes & P. Zangre, 1596.

Proclus (ca. 411–85). *In Platonis theologiam libri sex.* Ed. Aemilium Portum et al. Frankfurt am Main: Minerva, 1960.

———. *Procli Hypotyposis astronomicarum positionum.* Ed. C. Manitius. Leipzig, 1909.

———. *Théologie platonicienne.* Ed. H. D. Saffrey and L. G. Westerink. Paris: Les Belles Lettres, 1968.

Propertius, Sextus (ca. 50–16 B.C.). *The Elegies of Propertius.* Trans. H. E. Butler. Loeb Classics, 1962.

Ptolemy (Claudius Ptolemaeus; fl. 2d c.). *Centiloquium, sive centum sententiae, Jo. Joviano Pontano interprete.* Basileae: per Joannem Hervagium, 1551.

———. *Tetrabiblos.* Trans. F. E. Robbins. Loeb Classics, 1956.

Publilius, Syrus (fl. 1st c. B.C.–1st c. A.D.). *Sententiae.* In *Minor Latin Poets.* Trans. Arnold M. Duff. Loeb Classics, 1934.

Quasten, J. *Patrology.* Westminster, Maryland: Newman Press, 1950-.

Quercetanus. *See* Du Chesne, Joseph.

Quintilian (Marcus Fabius Quintilianus; ca. 35–ca. 95). *Institutio oratoria.* Trans. H. E. Butler. Loeb Classics, 1966.

Rabelais, François (1483–1553). *Five Books of the Lives, Heroic Deeds and Sayings of Gargantua and his son Pantagruel.* Trans. Sir Thomas Urquhart of Cromarty and Peter Antony Motteux. 2 vols. London: Lawrence and Bullen, 1892.

_____ . *Le Tiers Livre,* Ed. Pierre Michel. Paris: Editions Gallimard, 1966.

Raemond (Rémond), Florimond de (ca. 1540–1602). *L'histoire de la naissance, progrez et decadence de l'heresie de ce siecle divisee en huit livres.* Paris: Chez la Vefue Guillaume de la Nore, 1610.

Rapine, Claude (Coelestinus; d. 1493). *Des choses merveilleuses en nature où est traicté des erreurs des sens, des puissances de l'âme, et des influences des cieux.* Trans. Jacques Girard. Lyon: Macé Bonhomme, 1557.

Rashdal, Hastings. *The Universities of Europe in the Middle Ages.* 2 vols. Oxford: Clarendon Press, 1895; new ed. Oxford: Clarendon Press, 1936.

Rather, L. J. *Mind and Body in Eighteenth Century Medicine: A Study Based on Jerome Gaub's "De regimine mentis."* Berkeley and Los Angeles: University of California Press. 1965.

Regius, Ludovicus. *See* Le Roy, Louis.

Remi, Nicolas (1530–1612). *Daemonolatreiae libri tres.* Lugduni: in officina Vincentii, 1596.

Renier, R. "Per la cronologia e la composizione del Libro de natura da Amore." *Giornale Storico della Letteratura Italiana,* 14 (1889), pp. 402–13.

Rhazes (Abū Bakr Muhammad ibn Zakarīyá al-Rāzī; ca. 841–926). *[Liber] Continens Rasis ordinatus et correctus per clarissimum artium et medicinae doctorem magistrum Hieronymum Surianum (Kitābu'l hawī fi't-tibb).* Venetiis: per Bon. Locatellum, 1505.

_____ . *Divisionum liber.* Basileae: in officina Henrichi Petri, 1594; rpt. Bruxelles, 1973.

_____ . *Liber divisionum (Taksimu-l-'ilal).* In *Opera.* Trans. Gerard of Cremona (1114–87). Lugduni: n.p., 1510.

_____ . *Liber ad Almansorem decem tractatus continens (Kitāb al-Mansuri).* In *Opera.* Trans. Gerard of Cremona. Lugduni: n.p., 1510.

Rhodoginus, Caelius. *See* Ricchieri, Ludovico Celio.

Ricchieri, Ludovico Celio (Rhodoginus; 1450–1520). *Lectionum antiquarum libri triginta.* Genevae: excudebat Philippus Albertus, 1620.

Riccio, Pieri (1465–1504). *De honesta disciplina.* Basileae: excudebat Henricus Petrus, 1532.

Riolan, Jean (1580–1657). *Ad libros Fernelii de abditis rerum causis.* Parisiis: apud H. Perier, in officina Plantiniana, 1598.

_____ . *Gigantologie, histoire de la grandeur des giants, où il est demonstré que, de toute ancienneté, les plus grands hommes et giants n'ont esté plus hauts que ceux de ce temps.* Paris: Adrian Perier, 1618.

Robbins, Rossell Hope. *The Encyclopedia of Witchcraft and Demonology.* New York: Crown Publishers, 1963.

Robertis, Domenico de. "La composizione del De natura de Amore e i canzonieri antichi maneggiati da M. Equicola." *Studi di Filologia Italiana,* 17 (1959), pp. 182–220.

Robertson, D. W. "The Concept of Courtly Love as an Impediment to the Understanding of Medieval Texts." *The Meaning of Courtly Love.* Ed. F. X. Newman. Albany: State University of New York Press, 1968.

Robinson, T. M. *Plato's Psychology.* Toronto: University of Toronto Press, 1970.

Rodrigues da Viega, Andreas (fl. 16th c.). *Exemplorum memorabilium.* Paris: Nicolas Nivelle, 1590.

Rodrigues da Viega, Tomás (1513–79). *Ars medica*. In *Opera omnia in Galeni libros edita, et commentariis in partes novem distincta*. Lugduni: apud Petrum Landry, 1593.

Rodriguez de Castello Branco, João (Amatus Lusitanus; 1511–68). *Curationum medicinalium centuriae duae*. Parisiis: apud Sebastianum Nivellium, 1554.

———. *Curationum medicinalium centuriae quatuor*. Venetiis: apud Balthesarem Constantinum, 1557.

———. *Curationum medicinalium centuriae septem*. Burdigalae: ex typographia Gilberii Vernoi, 1620.

Rohde, E. *Der Griechische Roman und seine Vorläufer*. Hildesheim: Georg Olms, 1960.

Rojas, Fernando de (ca. 1465–1541). *Celestina or the Tragi-comedy of Calisto and Melibea*. Trans. Phillis Hartnoll. London: J. M. Dent and Sons, 1959.

Rondelet, Guillaume (1507–66). *L'histoire entière des poissons, composée premierement en latin*. Lyon: par Mace Bonhome, 1558.

———. *Methodus curandorum omnium morborum corporis humani*. In *Opera omnia medica*. Genevae: apud Petrum et Jacobum Chouët, 1620.

———. *Methodus curandorum omnium morborum corporis humani, in tres libris distincta*. Francofurti: apud heredes Andreae Wecheli, 1592.

———. *Tractatus de fucis*, following the *Methodus curandorum omnium morborum corporis humani*. Francofurti: apud heredes Andreae Wecheli, 1592.

Ronsard, Pierre de (1524–85). *La Franciade*. In *Oeuvres complètes*, vol. 16. Ed. Paul Laumonier. Paris: Librairie Marcel Didier, 1952.

———. *Les ouevres*, text of 1587. Ed. Isadore Silver. Chicago: University of Chicago Press, 1967.

Rosarius, Albertus. *See* Alberico de Rosate.

Rosen, George. *Madness in Society: Chapters in the Historical Sociology of Mental Illness*. New York: Harper and Row, 1969.

Rougemont, Denis de. *The Myths of Love*. London: Faber and Faber, 1963.

Rueff, Jakob (Jacques le Roux; 1500–1558). *De conceptu et generatione hominis*. 1558; Francfort: ad Moenum, 1580.

———. *The Expert Midwife, or an Excellent and most necessary Treatise of the generation and birth of men*. London: by E. G. for S. E., sold by Thomas Alehorn, 1637.

Ruel, Jean (Ruellius; 1479–1539). *De nature stirpium libri tres*. Paris: ex officina Simonis Colinaei, 1536.

Rufus of Ephesus (fl. 98–117) Ed. Charles Daremberg and Emile Ruelle. Paris: J. B. Baillière and Sons, 1879; Amsterdam: Adolf Hakkert, 1963.

Ruland, Martin (Rulandus; 1532–1602). *Curationum empiricarum et historicarum centuria VII*. Basileae: Sebast. Henricpetri, 1595.

[Salerno] *Le Regime de Santé de l'eschole de Salerne*. Trans. Michel le Long. Paris, 1637. *See also* Arnald of Vallanova.

Santoro, Domenico. *Della vita e delle opere di Mario Equicola*. Chieti: Pei tipi di N. Jecco, 1906.

Sassonia, Ercole (Hercules of Saxonia, 1551–1607). *De melancholia tractatus perfectissimus*. Venetiis: apud Alexandrum Polum, 1620. Treatise included in *Opera practica*. Patavii: ex typographia Matthaei de Cardorinis, 1658.

Savonarola, Giovanni Michele (ca. 1384–ca. 1462). "De cerebri et capitis morbis," in *Practica Major* (*Practica de aegritudinibus a capite usque ad pedes*). Venetiis: apud Vincentium Valgrisium, 1560 (1479; Venetiis: apud Juntas, 1549).

Saxo Grammaticus (fl. 13th c.). *Danorum historiae libri XVI . . . des Erasmi Roterdami de Saxone censura.* Basileae: apud Jo. Bebëlium, 1534.

Schenck von Grafenberg, Johann Theodor (Schenckius; 1530–98). *Observationum medicarum rararum, novarum, admirabilium et monstrosarum.* Friburgi Brisgoiae: ex calcographia Martini Beckleri, 1599.

————. *Observationum medicarum rarum, novarum, admirabilium et monstrosarum, volumen tomis septem de toto homine institutum.* Francofurti: E. Paltheniana, sumptibus Jonae Rhodii, 1600.

Schreiber, Wilhelm Adolf (Scribonius; fl. 16th c.). *Rerum naturalium doctrina methodica.* Basileae: ex officina haeredum Petri Pernae, 1583.

Schumaker, Wayne. *The Occult Sciences in the Renaissance: A Study in Intellectual Patterns.* Berkeley: University of California Press, 1972.

Scot, Michael (1175–1234). *De secretis naturae opusculum.* In Albertus Magnus, *De secretis mulierum libellus.* Amstelodami: n.p., 1740.

Scribonius. *See* Schreiber, Wilhelm Adolf.

Scullard, H. H. *From the Gracchi to Nero.* London: Methuen, 1968.

Scultetus, Tobias (1563–1620). *Subsecirorum poëticorum tetras prima: in qua Suspiria: Phaleuci: Philotesia; Epigrammata.* Myrtilleti ad Nicrum: typis Abrahami Smesmanni, 1594.

Secchi of Cremona, Bartolomeo (Battista Platina; 1421–81). *Dialogos contra amores.* In *De falso et vero bono dialogi III.* Parisiis: M. Petrus Vidoveus, 1504.

————. *Dialogue contre les folles amours.* Trans. Thomas Sibelet. In *L'antéros ou contramour de Messire Baptiste Fulgose.* Paris: Chez Martin le Jeune, 1581.

Seneca, Lucius Annaeus (ca. 4 B.C.–A.D. 65). *Ad Lucilium epistulae morales.* Ed. L. D. Reynolds. Oxford: Clarendon Press, 1965.

————. *Hippolytus or Phaedra.* In *Tragedies*, vol. 1. Trans. Frank Justus Miller. 2 vols. Loeb Classics, 1967.

————. (attributed to). *Octavia.* Trans. Frank Justus Miller. Loeb Classics, 1968.

————. *On the Happy Life.* In *Moral Essays.* Trans. John W. Basore. Loeb Classics, 1951.

Sennert, Daniel (1572–1637). "De amore insano." In *Practicae medicinae liber primus-[sextus].* Wittebergae: impensis haeredum Doct. T. Mevii et E. Schuemacheri, 1652–62.

Serapion the elder (fl. 9th c.). *Serapionis medici arabis celeberrimi practica studiosis medicinae utilissima: quam postremo Andreas Alpagus . . . translatio nunc primum exit in lucem.* Venetiis: apud Juntas, 1550.

Servius Marius Honoratus (fl. 400). *In Vergilii carmina commentarii.* Ed. Thilo and Hagen. Leipzig: Teubner, 1881–84.

Shapiro, A. K. "Placebo effects in medicine, psychotherapy and psychoanalysis." *Handbook of Psychotherapy and Behavior Change.* Ed. A. E. Bergin and S. L. Garfield. New York: John Wiley, 1971.

Shapiro, Barbara J. *Probability and Certainty in Seventeenth Century England.* Princeton: Princeton University Press, 1983.

Shaw, J. E. *Guido Cavalcanti's Theory of Love, the Canzone d'Amore and Other Related Problems.* Toronto: Toronto University Press, 1949.

Siegel, Jerrold E. *Rhetoric and Philosophy in Renaissance Humanism.* Princeton:

Princeton University Press, 1968.

Siegel, Rudolph E. *Galen on Psychology, Psychopathology, and Functions and Diseases of the Nervous System.* Basel: S. Karger, 1973.

———. *Galen's System of medicine and physiology, an analysis of his doctrines on bloodflow, respiration, humours, and internal diseases.* Basel: S. Karger, 1968.

———. "Melancholy and Black Bile in Galen and Later Writers." *Bulletin of the Cleveland Medical Library,* 18 (1971), pp. 10–12.

Silvatico, Giovanni Battista (fl. 16th c.). *Controversiae medicae numero centum.* Francofurti: typis Wechelianis apud Claudium Marnium, et heredes Joannis Aubrii, 1601.

Simboli, Raphaël. *Disease-Spirits and Divine Cures among the Greeks and Romans.* Diss., Columbia University, 1921.

Simon, Jean Robert. *Robert Burton et "L'Antomie de la Mélancolie."* Paris: Didier, 1964.

Simonin, Michel. "*Aegritudo amoris* et *res literaria* à la Renaissance: Réflexions préliminaires." *La folie et le corps.* Ed. Jean Céard. Paris: Presses de l'école normale supérieure, 1985.

Singer, C. and D. Singer, "The Origin of the Medical School of Salerno." In *Essays on the History of Medicine.* Ed. Charles Singer and Henry E. Sigerist. Zürich: Landschlacht K. Hönn, 1924.

Singer, Irving. *The Nature of Love: Plato to Luther.* New York: Random House, 1966.

Sinibaldi, Giovanni Benedetto (1594–1658). *Geneanthropeiae sive de hominis generatione decateuchon.* Romae: ex typo Fran. Caballi, 1642.

Sirenius, Julius of Brescia. *De fato libri novem in quibus inter alia: de contigentia, de necessitate, de providentia divina, de praescentia divina, de prophetia, et de divinatione.* Venetiis: ex officina Jordani Zileti, 1563.

Sophocles (496–406 B.C.). *Trachiniae.* Trans. F. Storr. Loeb Classics, 1961.

Soranus of Ephesus (fl. 98–138). *Gynecology.* Trans. Owsei Temkin. Baltimore: Johns Hopkins University Press, 1956.

———. (attributed to). *Life of Hippocrates.* Ed. Ilberg in *Corpus medicorum graecorum,* vol. IV.

Sorbelli, A. *Storia dell'Università di Bologna.* Bologna: N. Zanchelli, 1944.

Spagnuoli, Giovanni Battista (Mantuanus; 1448–1516). *Opera omnia in quatuor tomos distincta, pluribus libris aucta.* Antverpiae: apud. J. Bellerum, 1576.

Spanneut, M. *Le Stoïcisme des Pères de l'Église.* Paris: l'Éditions du Seuil, 1957.

Speisshammer, Johann. *See* Cuspinianus.

Starobinski, Jean. *Histoire du traitement de la mélancolie des origines à 1900. Acta psychosomatica,* 4. Basle: J. R. Geigy, 1960.

———. "La mélancolie de l'anatomiste." *Tel Quel,* 10 (1962), pp. 21–29.

Statius, Publius Papinius (ca. 40–ca. 96). *Achilleid.* Trans. J. H. Mozley. 2 vols. Loeb Classics, 1961.

———. *Silvae.* Trans. J. H. Mozley. Loeb Classics, 1967.

Stechow, Wolfgang. "The Love of Antiochus with Faire Stratonica." *Art Bulletin,* 27 (1945), pp. 221–37.

Stephan of Athens. *Alphabetum empiricum, sive Dioscorides et Stephani Atheniensis philosophorum et medicorum, de remediis expertis liber, justa alphabeti ordinem digestus.* N.p., n.p., 1581.

Stesichorus (ca. 640–ca. 555 B.C.). In *Poetae melici graeci*. Ed. D. L. Page. Oxford: Clarendon Press, 1962.

Stobaeus, Joannes (fl. 500). *Anthologium*. Eds. Curtius Wachsmuth and Otto Hense. Berlin, 1884–1912; rpt. Berolini: apud Weidmannos, 1958.

Stone, Laurence, *The Family, Sex and Marriage in England, 1500–1800*. London: Weidenfeld and Nicolson, 1977.

Strabo (ca. 64 B.C.–A.D. 19). *Geography*. Trans. Horace Leonard Jones. Loeb Classics, 1944.

Struth, Joseph (Josephus Struthius; 1510–68). *Ars sphygmica; seu, pulsuum doctrina supra M. CC. an nos perdita, et desiderata, libris V*. Basileae: Impensis Ludovici Königs, 1602). Also Basileae: per Joannem Oporinum, [1555].

Sue, Eugène (1804–57). *Les Mystères de Paris*. 2 vols. Paris: Editions Jean-Jacques Pauvert, 1963.

Suetonius (Gaius Suetonius Tranquillus; ca. 70–160). *The Lives of the Caesars*. Trans. J. C. Rolfe. 2 vols. Loeb Classics, 1951.

Suidas. *Lexicon* (compiled late 10th c.). Ed. G. Bernhardy. Halle et Brunsvigae: sumptibus Schwetschkiorum, 1853.

Suydas. *Lexicon*. Ed. Ada Adler. Stuttgart: Teubner, 1961.

Sylvius, Aeneas. *See* Piccolomini, Enea Sylvio.

Sylvius, Jacobus. *See* Dubois, Jacques.

Syme, Ronald. *The Roman Revolution*. 1939; rpt. Oxford: Oxford University Press, 1960.

Tacitus, Publius Cornelius (ca. 55–ca. 117). *The Annals*. Trans. John Jackson. Loeb Classics, 1956.

Taxil, Jean (1504–80). *L'astrologie et physiognomie en leur splendeur*. Tournon: par R. Reynaud Libraire juré d'Arles, 1614.

Taylor, G. Rattray. *Sex in History*. New York: Vanguard Press, 1954.

Tellenbach, Hubertus. *Melancholy: History of the Problem, Endogeneity, Typology, Pathogenesis, Clinical Considerations*. Trans. Erling Eng. Pittsburgh: Duquesne University Press, 1980.

Terence (Publius Terentius Afer; 195–159 B.C.). *Andros*. In *Terence*, vol. 1. Trans. John Sargeaunt, 2 vols. Loeb Classics, 1912, 1964.

———. *The Eunuch*. In *Terence*, vol. 1. Trans. John Sargeaunt. 2 vols. Loeb Classics, 1912, 1964.

Tertullian (ca. 160–ca. 240). *Ad uxorem*. In *Opera*. Parisiis: apud Audoënum Parvum, 1566.

———. *Ad uxorem*. In *Treatises on Marriage and Remarriage*. Trans. William P. le Saint. Westminster, Md.: Newman Press, 1951.

———. *Apologeticus [adversus gentes]*. Trans. T. R. Glover. Cambridge, Mass.: Harvard University Press, 1960.

———. *De anima*. Ed. J. H. Waszink. Amsterdam: J. M. Meulenhoff, 1947.

———. *De spectaculis*. Trans. T. R. Glover, Loeb Classics, 1960.

———. *Liber de anima*. Vol. 2 of the *Patrologiae cursus completus, seria latina*. Ed. J. P. Migne. Paris: J. P. Migne, 1844–1902.

Themistius (fl. ca. 360). *In libros Aristotelis de anima paraphrasis*. Ed. Ricard Heinze. Berolini: G. Reimer, 1899.

———. *Orationes*. Ed. Wilhelm Dindorf. Hildesheim: Georg Olms Verlagsbuchhandlung, 1961.

Theocritis. (fl. ca. 270 B.C.). [*Works*]. Ed. A. S. F. Gow. 2 vols. Cambridge: At the University Press, 1950.

Theophrastus (ca. 371–ca. 287 B.C.). *De historia plantarum libri decem graece et latine . . . latinam Gazae versionem nova interpretatione . . . accesserunt Julii Caesaris Scaligeri in eosdem libros animadversiones.* Amstelodami: apud Henricum Laurentium, 1644.

————. *Opera qua supersunt.* Ed. Frederic Wimmer. Parisiis: Firmin-Didot et socii, 1931.

————. *Theophrasti Eresii Graece et Latine opera omnia.* Lugduni Batavorum: ex typographio Henrici ab Plaestens, 1613.

Theophrastus Bombastus ab Hohenheim. *See* Paracelsus.

Thomas Aquinas, St. (ca. 1225–74). *In Aristotelis stagiritae libros nonnullos commentaria.* In *Opera omnia.* Ed. Stanislaus Fretté. Paris: apud Ludovicum Vivès, 1872.

————. *Somme de la foi catholique contra les Gentils.* Trans. M. L'Abbé P.-F. Ecalle. Paris: Louis Vivès, 1856.

————. *Summa theologica.* In *Opera omnia.* Ed. Stanislaus Fretté. Paris: apud Ludovicum Vivès, 1871–1880.

Thomas à Viega. *See* Rodriguez da Viega, Tomás.

Thorndike, Lynn. *A History of Magic and Experimental Science.* New York: Columbia University Press, 1941.

Thucydides (ca. 460–ca. 400 B.C.). *The Peloponnesian War.* Trans. Charles Forster Smith. Loeb Classics, 1962.

Tibullus, Albius (ca. 60–19 B.C.). *The Elegies.* Ed. Kirby Flower Smith. Darmstadt: Wissenschaftliche Buchgesellschaft, 1964.

————. *Elegies.* Trans. Guy Lee. Cambridge: St. John's College, 1975.

Toffanin, G. "Petrarchismo e trattati d'amore." *Nuova Antologia,* March, 1928, pp. 30–51.

Tolet, Franciscus. *Instructio sacerdotum ac de septem peccatis mortalibus.* 2 vols. Lugduni: apud Horatium Cardon, 1604.

Trallianus. *See* Alexander of Tralles.

Tritheim. *See* Johann von Tritheim.

Trotula (Eros). *Curandorum aegritudinum muliebrium.* Lugduni: apud Sebastianum de Honoratis, 1558.

Ullmann, M. *Islamic Medicine.* Edinburgh: Edinburgh University Press, 1978.

Vairo, Leonardo, Bishop of Pozzuoli (d. 1603). *De fascino libri tres.* Venetiis: apud Aldum, 1589.

Valeriano Bolzani, Giovanni Pierio (Pierius; 1477–1558). *Les hieroglyphiques.* Trans. I. de Montlyart. Lyon: par Paul Frellon, 1615.

Valerius Maximus (fl. 14–37). *Factorum et dictorum memorabilium libri novem.* Ed. C. Kempf. Leipzig: Teubner, 1966.

Valesco de Taranta (Balescon de Tarente; fl. 1380–1418). *Epitome . . . morbis curandis in septem congesta libros.* Lugduni: apud Joan. Tornaesium, et Gulielmum Gazeium, 1560.

————. *Philonium pharmaceuticum et chirurgicum de medendis omnibus, tum internis, tum externis humani corporis affectibus.* Francofurti et Lipsiae: sumptibus Joannis Adami Kastneri, 1680.

Valleriola, François (1504–80). *Observationum medicinalium libri sex.* Lugduni:

apud Antonium Candidum, 1588.

Valles, Francisco (Valesius; 1524–92). *Controversiarum medicarum et philosophicarum libri X.* Hanoviae: typis Wechelianis apud Claudium Marnium, 1606.

———. *Controversiarum medicarum et philosophicarum . . . liber.* Compluti: excudebat Joannes Iñiguez à Lequerica, 1583.

———. *De iis quae scripta sunt physice in libris sacris.* Lugduni: apud Franciscum Le Fevre, 1588.

Valturio, Roberto (Robertus Valturius; 1405–75). *De re militari libris XII.* Paris: apud Christianum Wechelum, 1535.

———. (Robert Valtrin). *Les douze livres . . . touchant la discipline militaire.* Trans. Loys Meigret. Paris: Chez Charles Perier, 1555.

Van der Velde, Jason (Jason Pratensis; 1486–1558). *De cerebri morbis.* Basileae: per Henrichum Petri, 1549.

Vanini, Giulio Cesare (orig. Lucilio; 1585–1619). *Amphitheatrum aeternae providentiae divino-magicum, christiano-physicum, nec non astrologo catholicum, adversus veteres philosophos, atheos, epicureos, peripateticos, et stoicos.* Lugduni: apud viduam Antonii de Harsy, 1615.

———. *Oeuvres philosophiques.* Trans. X. Rousselot. Paris: C. Gosselin, 1842.

Varignana. *See* Guglielmo da Varignana.

Varinus Favorinus. *See* Guarino of Favora.

Varro, Marcus Terentius (82–ca. 36 B.C.). *In libro de lingua latina conjectanea Josephi Scaligeri.* In *Opera quae supersunt.* N.p., n.p., 1581.

———. *On the Latin Language.* Trans. Roland G. Kent. 3 vols. Loeb Classics, 1958.

Vega, Cristóbal de (ca. 1510–ca. 1573). *Liber de arte medendi.* In *Opera.* Lugduni: apud Gulielmum Rovillium, 1576.

Vegetius, Flavius (fl. 379–395). *De re militari libri quatuor.* Parisiis: apud Carolum Perier, 1553.

Veith, Ilza. *Hysteria: The History of a Disease.* Chicago: University of Chicago Press, 1965.

Velázquez, Andrés (fl. 16th c.). *Libro de la melancholía en el qual se trata de la naturaleza de esta enfermedad.* Seville: por Hernando Díaz, 1585.

Venette, Nicolas (1633–98). *Tableau de l'amour conjugal, ou histoire complete de la generation de l'homme.* Paris: Chez L. Duprat-Duverger, 1810; princeps 1687.

Verbeke, G. *L'évolution de la doctrine du pneuma du Stoïcism á S. Augustin. Étude philosophique.* Louvain: Academia Lovaniensis, 1945.

Vergen, Johann (Johannes Nauclerus; d. 1510). *Cronicon, tomus secundus.* Coloniae: apud haeredes Johannes Quentel et Gervuinum Calenium, 1564.

Vergil of Urbino, Polydore. *See* Virgilio, Polidoro.

Vergil (Publius Virgilius Maro; 70–19 B.C.). *Aeneid.* Trans. H. Rushton Fairclough. Loeb Classics, 1965.

———. *Eclogues.* Trans. H. Rushton Fairclough. Loeb Classics, 1965.

———. *Virgil's Works.* Ed. William C. McDermott. New York: 1960.

Verinus Favorinus. *See* Guarino of Favora.

Vesalius, Andreas (1514–64). *Opera omnia anatomica et chirurgica.* Eds. Hermann Boerhaave and Bernhard Siegfried Albini. Lugduni Batavorum: apud Joannem du Vivie, et Joan. et Herm. Verbeck, 1725.

Veyries, Jean de (fl. 1592–1609). *La genealogie de l'amour divisée en deux livres.*

Paris: Chez Abel l'Angelier, 1609.

Vial, S. C. "Equicola and the School of Lyons." *Comparative Literature* (1960), pp. 19–23.

————. "M. Equicola in the Opinion of his Contemporaries." *Italica*, 34 (1957), pp. 202–21.

Vianey, Joseph. *Le Pétrarquisme en France au XVIe siècle.* Montpellier: Coulet et fils, 1909.

Viarre, Simone. *La survie d'Ovide dans la littérature scientifique des XIIe et XIIIe siècles.* Poitiers: Centre d'études supérieures de civilisation médievale, 1966.

Vickers, Brian. "Analogy versus identity: the rejection of occult symbolism, 1580–1680." *Occult and Scientific Mentalities in the Renaissance.* Ed. Brian Vickers. Cambridge: Cambridge University Press, 1986.

Viega, Thomas à. *See* Rodriguez da Viega, Tomás.

Vigenère, Blaise de. *See* Philostratus.

Vigier, Françoise. "La folie amoureuse dans le roman pastoral Espagnol." *Visages de la folie (1500–1650).* Ed. Augustin Redondo and André Rochon. Paris: Publications de la Sorbonne, 1981.

Vigo, Giovanni di (fl. 1500). *La practique et cirurgie . . . nouvellement imprimee et racogneue diligentement sur le latin.* N.p., n.p., 1537.

Villanovanus, Arnaldus. *See* Arnald of Villanova.

Vincent, Jean-Didier. *Biologie des Passions.* Paris: Éditions Odile Jacob, Seuil, 1986.

Vincentino, Nicolao Leoniceno. *See* Hippocrates, *Aphorisms.*

Vincent of Beauvais (ca. 1190–ca. 1264). *Speculum doctrinale.* Graz: Akademische Druck-U. Verlagsanstalt, 1964–65.

————. *Speculum Quadruplex, naturale, doctrinale, morale, historiale.* Dauci: Baltazaris Belleri, 1624.

Vinge, Louise. *The Five Senses: Studies in a Literary Tradition.* Lund: University of Lund, 1975.

Virgilio, Polidoro (ca. 1470–ca. 1555). *Des inventeurs des choses, traduict de latin en françois, et de nouveau reveuz et corrigez.* Lyon: par Benoist Rigaud, 1576.

Vitruvius, Pollio (fl. 50–26 B.C.). *The Ten Books on Architecture.* Trans. M. H. Morgan. Cambridge, Mass.: Harvard University Press, 1914; rpt. New York: Dover Publications, 1960.

Volaterranus. *See* Maffei, Raffaele.

Wack, Mary Francis. "From Mental Faculties to Magical Philtres: The Entry of Magic into Academic Medical Writing on Lovesickness, 13th-17th Centuries." *Eros and Anteros: The Medical Traditions of Love in Renaissance Culture.* Ed. Donald Beecher and Massimo Ciavolella. Montreal: McGill-Queen's University Press, forthcoming.

————. "Memory and Love in Chaucer's *Troilus and Criseyde.*" Diss., Cornell University, 1982.

————. "Imagination, Medicine, and Rhetoric in Andreas Capellanus' 'De amore,'" *Robert Earl Kaske.* New York: Fordham University Press, 1986.

————. "New Medieval Medical Texts on *Amor Hereos.*" *Kongressakten zum Ersten Symposium des Mediävistenverbandes in Tübingen.* Ed. J. O. Fichte et al. Berlin: Walter de Gruyter, 1984.

————. "The Measure of Pleasure: Peter of Spain on Men, Women, and Lovesickness." *Viator*, 17 (1986), pp. 173–96.

Walker, D. P. *Spiritual and Demonic Magic from Ficino to Campanella*. London: Warburg Institute, 1958.

Walzer, R. "Aristotle, Galen, and Palladius on Love." In *Greek into Arabic*. Cambridge, Mass.: Harvard University Press, 1962.

Wear, Andrew. "Galen in the Renaissance." *Galen: Problems and Prospects*. Ed. Vivian Nutton. London: Wellcome Institute for the History of Medicine, 1981.

Webber, Joan. *The Eloquent "I": Style and Self in Seventeenth-Century Prose*. Madison: University of Wisconsin Press, 1968.

Wecker of Basel, Johann Jacob (1528–86). *Le grande thresor ou dispensaire et antidotaire*. Trans. Ian du Val. Genève: D'Estienne Gamonet, 1616.

————. *Les secrets et merveilles de nature, recueilles de divers autheurs, et divisez en XVII livres*. Lyon: Chez Louys Odin, 1652.

Wehrli, Fritz Robert, ed. *Die Schule des Aristoteles*. 10 vols. Basel: B. Schwabe, 1967.

Wheaton, Robert, and Tamara Hareven. *The Family and Sexuality in French History*. Philadelphia: University of Pennsylvania Press, 1980.

White, T. H. *The Bestiary: A Book of Beasts*. New York: G. P. Putnam's Sons, 1960.

Wickersheimer, Ernest. *Dictionnaire biographique des médecins en France au Moyen Age*. Paris: E. Droz, 1936.

————. *La médecine et les médcins en France a l'époque de la Renaissance*. Paris, 1905; rpt. Genève: Slatkine Reprints, 1970.

Wier, Johann (Wierus, Vier; 1515–88). *Cinq livres de l'imposture et tromperie des diables*. Trans. Jacques Grévin. Paris: n.p., 1567.

————. *De praestigiis daemonum et incantationibus ac veneficiis libri sex*. Basileae: ex officina Oporiniana, 1564.

————. *Histoires, disputes et discours des illusions et impostures des diables*. Paris: Chez Bonnet, 1579; Paris: aux Bureau de Progrès Médicale, 1885.

————. *Histoires, disputes, et discours, des illusions et impostures des diables, des magiciens infames, sorciers et empoisonneurs*. [Genevae]: pour Jacques Chouet, 1579.

————. *Histoires, disputes et discours . . . touchant le pouvoir des sorcières*. 2 vols. Paris: A. Delehaye, 1885.

————. *Medicarum observationum rararum liber I*. Basileae: per Joannem Oporinum, 1567.

William of Saliceto. *See* Guglielmo da Saliceto.

Winter, Johann (Andernacus; Johannes Guinterius; 1487–1574). *Anatomicorum institutionum libri IV*. Lugduni: Seb. Gryphius, 1541.

————. *De medicina veteri et nova tum cognoscenda, tum faciunda commentarii duo*. Basileae: ex officina Henricpetrina, 1571.

————. *Le régime de vivre et de prendre médecine que l'on doibt observer en tout temps et princallement en temps de peste*. Trans. Anthoine Pierre de Rieux. Poitiers: J. et E. de Marnef, 1544.

Wolfson, Harry Austryn. "The Internal Senses in Latin, Arabic and Hebrew Philosophic Texts." *Harvard Theological Review*, XXVII (1935), pp. 69–133.

Wright, Louis B. *Middle-Class Culture in Elizabethan England*. 1935; rpt. Ithaca, N.Y.: Cornell University Press, 1965.

Wright, Thomas (fl. 2d half 16th c.). *The Passions of the Mind in General.* Ed. William Webster Newbold. London, 1601; New York and London: Garland Publishing, 1986.

Wüstenfeld, Heinrich Ferdinand. *Die Übersetzungen Arabisher Werke in das Lateinische seit dem XI Jahrhundert.* Göttingen: Abhandlungen der Königlichen Gesellschaft der Wissenschaften zu Göttingen, 1877.

Xenophon (ca. 430–ca. 355 B.C.). *Symposium.* Trans. O. J. Todd. Loeb Classics, 1968.

Zilboorg, G., and G. Henry. *A History of Medical Psychology.* New York: Norton, 1941.

Zonta, Giuseppe. *Trattati d'amore del Cinquecento.* Bari: Laterza, 1912. Rpt. ed. Mario Pozzi. Roma-Bari: Laterza, 1975.

NAME INDEX

SUBJECT INDEX

A TREATISE ON LOVESICKNESS

was composed in 10 on 12 Palatino on a Printware 720 IQ Laser Printer
by Humanities Publishing Services, University of Toronto;
printed by sheet-fed offset on 50-pound, acid-free P&S Smooth Offset
and Smyth-sewn and bound over binder's boards in Hollison Roxite B
with dust jackets printed in one color
by Braun-Brumfield, Inc.;
and published by
SYRACUSE UNIVERSITY PRESS
SYRACUSE, NEW YORK 13244–5160